LOUISIANA MATRIMONIAL REGIMES

Cases & Materials

2014 EDITION

Andrea B. Carroll
Donna W. Lee Professor of Family Law
LSU Law Center

Elizabeth R. Carter
Judge Anthony J. Graphia & Jo Ann Graphia Associate Professor of Law
LSU Law Center

Louisiana Matrimonial Regimes: Cases & Materials

Carroll, Andrea B. & Carter, Elizabeth R.

Published by:

Vandeplas Publishing, LLC – July 2014

801 International Parkway, 5th Floor
Lake Mary, FL. 32746
USA

www.vandeplaspublishing.com

ISBN: 978-1-60042-207-2

ABOUT THE AUTHORS

Andrea Beauchamp Carroll is the Donna W. Lee Professor of Family Law at the Louisiana State University Paul M. Hebert Law Center. Before joining the LSU Law faculty, Professor Carroll clerked for The Honorable W. Eugene Davis of the United States Court of Appeals for the Fifth Circuit. She subsequently worked as an associate at the Dallas law firm of Baker Botts, L.L.P., handling appellate litigation. In 2003, Professor Carroll returned home to LSU Law, where she has been teaching and writing about family law, community property, and property for the last eleven years.

Professor Carroll is the author of more than a dozen books and articles in her field, and has recently been published in the Indiana, Tulane, Brooklyn, and Cardozo law reviews. Her Tulane article on civil law property was honored at the 2005 Stanford-Yale Junior Faculty Forum.

Professor Carroll is also active in law reform in Louisiana, as a Member of the Council of the Louisiana State Law Institute and the Institute's Persons, Children's Code, and Adult Guardianship Committees. She led the comprehensive revision of Louisiana's community property law in the area of reimbursement rights in 2009, the first substantial revision of Louisiana's community property rules since 1979. And she led a successful reform of Louisiana's child relocation rules in 2010. As Reporter of the Law Institute's Marriage and Persons Committee, Professor Carroll continues to work to improve the law related to marriage and the family.

Professor Elizabeth R. Carter is the Judge Anthony J. Graphia & Jo Ann Graphia Associate Professor of Law at the Louisiana State University Paul M. Herbert Law Center, where she teaches and writes in the areas of matrimonial regimes, estates, trusts, and taxation.

A graduate of Tulane University Law School and member of the Order of the Coif, Professor Carter graduated with the highest grade point average in the civil law curriculum and served as the research assistant to Professor A.N. Yiannopoulos. Her comment on Louisiana Civil Code article 466, published in Volume 80 of the Tulane Law Review, received the Dean Rufus C. Harris Award for the Best Writing on a Civil Law Subject. Professor Carter earned an LL.M. in Taxation from the University of Alabama. She also has degrees in biology and Spanish from the University of Memphis.

She serves on several Louisiana State Law Institute committees and maintains a private estate-planning practice. She has two dogs and a husband, in that order.

Louisiana Matrimonial Regimes

CHAPTER 1: INTRODUCTION

1.1 MATRIMONIAL REGIMES: DEFINITION AND COMPARATIVE PERSPECTIVES

A. Introduction

"A matrimonial regime is a system of principles and rules governing the ownership and management of the property of married persons as between themselves and toward third persons."[1] Two matrimonial regimes are prevalent in Western legal systems: the community property regime and the separate property regime. The community property regime is the default legal system in nine states in the United States[2] and is by far the most common regime internationally. Mexico, Quebec, and several Caribbean islands are community property jurisdictions. Nearly every[3] jurisdiction in Central and South America has a community property system. The same is true in continental Europe. The separate property regime, in contrast, is more common in those jurisdictions with a common law heritage. It is found in the remaining United States jurisdictions, Canada (with the exception of Quebec), the United Kingdom, Australia, and New Zealand.

In the modern era, it is sometimes difficult to discern the distinction between the community property systems and the separate property systems. When a marriage ends in divorce, the two systems can appear identical. However, meaningful distinctions remain in the ownership of property during the existence of the marriage and the ability of spouses to dispose of property at death. The community property system views marriage as an economic partnership between the spouses. Both spouses contribute labor and capital to the marriage and both share equally in its gains. Many community property systems, including those in the United States, adhere to a ganancial system of community property. Under this system, assets and gains during marriage resulting from either spouse's labor or industry are classified as community property. The spouses enjoy automatic, concurrent joint ownership of the community property. The property a spouse brings into the marriage and property a spouse receives by gift or inheritance is that spouse's separate property. Traditionally, spouses retained their separate property and one-half of the community property upon the termination of the marriage by

---

[1] LA. CIV. CODE art. 2325.

[2] Arizona, California, Idaho, Louisiana, Nevada, New Mexico, Texas, Washington, and Wisconsin.

[3] Belize and Guyana both have a common law heritage and, as a result, do not have community property regimes.

divorce. Similarly, each spouse had the authority to dispose of all of his separate property and one-half of the community property at death.

In contrast, separate property systems do not provide for the automatic sharing of property during marriage. Ownership of property is generally determined exclusively by title to that property. Historically, this system put women at a distinct disadvantage. Because women were less likely to acquire property in their own name during marriage, they were less likely to own any property during the marriage or upon its termination. At divorce the spouses retained those assets they owned, which, for women often meant they retained few assets. At death, each spouse was free to dispose of all assets titled in his name. Again this was a harsh result for many women. Women dying before their husbands did not have the ability to dispose of much property at death. Women who survived their husbands were not guaranteed an inheritance. In the modern era, however, most separate property systems recognized the inequity of this approach and enacted measures to ameliorate it.

B. Harriett Spiller Daggett, THE COMMUNITY PROPERTY SYSTEM OF LOUISIANA, 3-7, 229-237 (LSU 1945)

The Civil Law has ever been a most highly developed set of principles, more evolved as a concept of the rules by which human beings should be guided than any other body of laws. This is particularly true of the Community Property System. The Civil Law ideal of the marital relation, far kinder than the Common Law notion of a merged personality represented by the husband, has throughout the regulations for the community kept a more perfect balance between the rights of the spouses in their accumulations through the years. Furthermore, the strong framework which supports the community property edifice will permit of the minor adjustments necessary for perfect alignment with changing conditions.

The Common Law notion being fundamentally wrong and in accord with a more primitive state of society and designed for an age when the position of women entitled them to little education or recognition of any sort, cannot be readily adjusted to meet the social and economic changes of this era. When parts of the structure are torn away for replacements, the decayed condition of other timbers is only the more readily discernible. The Community Property System on the other hand being fundamentally sound needs only new decorations and a few modern additions to make it a perfect habitat for the husband and wife of today.

While the idea of community property as such did not originate in Rome, the strong impress of the Roman law is found in the working out of the details of the system as expressed in the Civil Law of Louisiana. The status of the Roman matron as she moved in the life of that great civilization at its height is well known and the comparison of her situation with that of the modern American wife is often made by historians, contrasting the two with the medieval wife for which the Common Law was written.

Apart from equity, without which a law should not exist, is the question of the effect of an outworn body of laws upon society. The problem of the adjustment of the sexes in this rapidly changing economic and social world is one of paramount importance. The divorce "evil" so called is often in the forum. In the delicately poised balance of the relationship between spouses, property laws play no small part. This has ever been true but is more important today than ever before due to the fact that this age has produced a legally and economically independent wife who will not brook the interference tolerated in fear by the dependent woman of yesterday.

The Supreme Court of the United States in the famous case of Adkins v. Children's Hospital of the District of Columbia held that the liberty of contract guaranteed to a woman by the Constitution could not be impaired by a Legislative body even in an effort to protect her by the passage of a minimum wage law. Justice Sutherland said:

> But the ancient inequality of the sexes, otherwise than physical, has continued with "diminishing intensity." In view of the great--not to say revolutionary--changes which have taken place in the contractual, political, and civil status of women, culminating in the Nineteenth Amendment, it is not unreasonable to say that these differences have now come almost, if not quite, the vanishing point.

When words like these are upon the tongue of a Justice of the Supreme Court in a case where all of the ancient and telling arguments involving the moral issue and whatnot were used, it is clear that laws made for wives who are chattels are doomed. It is a difficult if not impossible thing to wipe out an old body of law at one stroke or to formulate a body of living principles overnight, hence the necessity to cast about for a tried and proved foundation at least, upon which to erect a structure suited to present needs.

The Community Property System is the answer to the quest. This system has lived since the days of the rude tribes of Germany, when the wives who shared the fighting were thought to be worthy of a share in the spoils. This system governs the spouses in their property interests in a large percentage of the civilized countries of today. It is a system which, while not perfect, is readily adjustable and should furnish a most excellent guide to those states which are looking toward a more modern and more equitable method of adjusting property rights between the spouses.

Eight states of the Union have the community property system and of the eight types that of Louisiana seems most basically sound, most equitable in its variations, possibly because it is true parent stock and has been least weakened by the influence of the Common Law idea of marital rights.

There are minor changes which might be made to bring the structure more in accord with the present social and economic evolution and it is hoped that these will be made but fundamentally the Louisiana concept meets the needs of spouses whose ideal is cooperation and true partnership and yet provides for the individuals of the partnership and protects their rights.

The community system of Louisiana lived through the period when large classes of women were in what might be termed the parasitic stage with or without fault on their part. Note the following extract from an opinion written over one hundred years ago.

The doctrine of the community of acquets and gains, was unknown to the Roman Law; and, although now common, we believe to the greatest number of the European nations, its origin cannot be satisfactorily traced. The best opinion appears to be that it took its rise with Germans, among whom at a very early period of their history, the wife took, by positive law, the one-third of all the gains made during coverture. It is very probable that it was the real or presumed, care and industry of the wife, which first produced this legislation; and, in an early state of society, the facts most probably fully justify such a rule. But, in this case, as in many other instances, legislation survives long after the causes which occasioned it, have ceased to exist, and the non-existence of these causes will not authorize the courts of justice to refuse giving effect to the law. There are few, we believe, who think, at the present state of society, that the wife contributes equally with the husband to the acquisition of property. If such cases exist, they are exceptions to the general rule. And yet, in this state, neither idleness, wasteful habits, nor moral or physical incapacity, would deprive the wife of an equal share of the acquets and gains; for our code declares that every marriage in Louisiana, superinduces, a right partnership, or community, in all acquisitions. Such, also, was the rule in Spain.

Judge Porter's statements as to the origin are borne out as the authorities seem to be agreed that the community system must have had its origin in Germanic customary law. The customary or unwritten law of Northern France was incorporated into the Code Napoleon upon which the present Louisiana Civil Code was patterned. The community system, however, made its way to colonial Louisiana before the adoption of the first code in 1808 via the custom of Paris and the law of Spain. While the community system did not exist as such in Rome, the wife did come in for a child's share and it appears that in Egypt the community system actually operated. It is thought that it arose there as a natural development and indeed was a spontaneous thing answering practically the needs of the various peoples, whenever found, rather than an importation from any one country to another.

The Civil-Law Concept of the Wife's Position in the Family

The merger theory of husband and wife never obtained in the Civil law, and all of the relations were worked out on a basis of two individuals with obligations to each other and to third persons. This difference between the common law and the Civil law in regard to the marital relation is the key, perhaps, to the whole approach. The chattel theory of the wife, the basis for the property concept of marriage, has never obtained in the Civil law. Many of the Civil law provisions regarding marriage, the wife, and family, phrased at an early date, seem contemporaneous in spirit with discussions of today. For example, an article of the French code repeated verbatim in every Louisiana code provides that the husband and wife owe each other mutually "fidelity, support, and assistance"; and that idea of reciprocity runs throughout the provisions dealing with marriage and the rights of the parties.

It was expected that the woman would make proper contributions in order to maintain her place in tribal society and, hence, certain rights based on her accomplishments were fixed in the customary law. During the long period when the wife's contributions were, perhaps, in many if not in most cases more theoretical than real, these original laws were in the main retained and the juristic amplifications were also tinged with an individualistic quality. At the present time, when social and economic pressure and change are again forcing or permitting the wife, as the case may be, to become an individual, the Civil law's basic notions should simplify and energize the legal transition. Dr. Elina Guimares, in discussing the Portuguese law regarding illegitimate children under a codification of 1446, says: "In these times people had a frank, wholesome outlook towards life that strangely resembles our modern point of view." It is submitted that the individualistic concept of the wife's position in the Civil law has been for centuries superior as a matter of justice and practicality, and that it should be seriously considered as a tried pattern.

There seem now to be two definite notions as to the legal place the wife should take. One is that she should be entirely relieved of any property entanglements with her husband other than those that might arise out of contract as with any stranger. This idea is particularly noticeable in proposed legislation and litigation urging that the wife be permitted to keep her entire earnings as separate property. Another group believes that the husband and wife should form a unit of partnership in which the spouses stand upon an equal footing and in which ownership, management, and contributions should be joint. Both notions, of course, depart from the old idea of the personal and financial subordination of the wife to the husband. It would seem that each school of thought must of necessity allow certain mutual dependencies and should in all cases plan to protect the rights of third parties, including children, creditors and others. The Civil law provides plans answering the desires of both groups by offering the separate-property regime and the community regime, each of which stipulates the rights and duties of the spouses in their relations to each other and to third persons.

Under the separate-property plan, which is the legal plan under the German code and which may be contracted for in certain Civil law states before marriage and may occur in some cases after marriage, the wife may conduct her affairs as may any individual.

The Civil law of Louisiana has from the beginning given the wife full ownership of her separate estate. She could always administer it separately if she cared to, thus keeping the profits for herself. During the era when the husband's authorization was necessary for her appearance in court and the like, she could apply to the judge for the necessary authorization in case of the husband's unreasonableness. This was a helpful check on his arbitrariness and upon any feeling of complete power and superiority over the wife. Even under the community system, the legal regime in many states, her separate property and its accruals remain her own in fee and may be administered separately by her or her agent. This same, of course, is true of the husband. The wife was always permitted under the Civil law of France and Louisiana to will away her property without the authority of her husband, even the community share when there was a community.

When the legal regime (community) is stipulated against in Louisiana, third persons are protected and warned of their rights by the recordation of the marriage contract or of the judgment of separation of property.

Whenever the persons are living under the separate-property plan, the wife as well as the husband is responsible for her share of the expenses of maintaining the marital establishment and for support to the husband in time of need. Under the separate-property plan, of course, the earnings of the wife are her own.

The community plan of the Civil law makes the ideal of mutuality central. The very name of the system belies any notion of submergence of either individual. If the goal, as expressed by leading sociological, psychological, and legal thinkers on the subject, is to be one of a real partnership in an economic sense where contributions to the common good of the marital establishment are made, owned, and managed jointly by the spouses, legally as well as practically, this is at least two-thirds accomplished under the community-property system. The idea of mutual contribution to a joint fund had its inception in a custom of the Germanic tribes. The wife who fought at the side of her husband was entitled to her share of the spoils-an individualistic notion based on equality of effort. This idea has survived the vicissitudes of the romantic period and should be a sound basis upon which to build the new social and economic developments. The system obtains in eight states of the Union, as well as in those countries where the Civil law prevails, and has survived in most instances since its inception. Certainly under any system there will be parasites and drones, and no plan can be judged by their standards. The marriage partnership can always be dissolved if one's partner's contributions materially and otherwise become too inadequate. When women as a group were making their efforts in the home only, the community-property system gave them protection and a feeling of ownership. Now when contributions are more often made from the reward of efforts outside the home, the feeling of owning half should be a heartening one, and should lead to the effects hoped for by sociological and psychological scholars.

1.2 INDIVIDUAL COMMUNITY PROPERTY STATES

At present, there are nine community property states in the United States, namely:

(1) Arizona
(2) California
(3) Idaho
(4) Louisiana
(5) Nevada
(6) New Mexico
(7) Texas
(8) Washington
(9) Wisconsin

Puerto Rico is also a community property jurisdiction. These jurisdictions all boast a regime of community property as the default legal regime regulating property rights between spouses. At least two states, Alaska and Tennessee, allow spouses to "opt-in" to a community property system by transferring their assets to a community property trust.

Historical Differences Between the States

The history of statehood and adoption of the community property system in each of the community property states has both common threads and individual variations. With the exception of Wisconsin, the community property states generally trace their lineage to Spanish, and to a more limited extent, French, roots. Louisiana fought to retain the bulk of its civil law legal system wholesale. The other community property jurisdictions, in contrast, decided to integrate community property principles into their otherwise common law legal systems.

Louisiana. Louisiana has the oldest and historically purest form of community property in the United States. It is also recognized as the only state with the legal traditions of the civil law system, which nurtured the community property system. The present state of Louisiana bears only a slight resemblance to the vast territory that was named after Louis XIV of France. The shifting ownership of the mouth of the Mississippi River during the 17th and 18th centuries is a history in miniature of Spanish and French influence. When Napoleon terminated the alternating ownerships by selling the Louisiana Territory to the United States in 1803, the community property system was already been well established. The Custom of Paris prevailed in Louisiana until 1769; after that date the Spanish ganancial scheme of community property has been in effect. Of all the territory acquired in that vast purchase only the land south of the 33rd parallel (called by Congress the Territory of Orleans and now the State of Louisiana) retained the community property system. The balance of the states that were formed from this purchased land (like the territory of East and West Florida) did not continue the community property system.

Texas. As a colony, Texas followed Spanish and Mexican law—including community property laws—during the 1820's and early 1830's. When Texas gained its independence from Mexico in 1836, civil law initially remained the substantive law in force. However, the new Republic adopted the common law for its court system. The substantive law would soon change as well. Many of Texas' settlers were Anglo-American, were unfamiliar with the civil law system, did not speak Spanish, and had access to very few law books. In January of 1840, the Texas Congress officially adopted the common law system. Several areas of law, including the community property laws, withstood Texas' otherwise wholesale reception of common law. When it joined the union in 1845, Texas included a constitutional provision specifically protecting community property.

California. California was acquired by the United States in 1849 by the Treaty of Guadalupe Hidalgo, which officially terminated the Mexican-American war. The same treaty also ceded to the United States the territory now comprising the states of Utah, Arizona, Nevada, New Mexico, and parts of Colorado and Wyoming.

California, the first state to join the union following the Treaty of Guadalupe Hidalgo, served as the legal role model to other new states. After lengthy debates, California ultimately adopted common law while also retaining Spanish-Mexican community property law in its 1849 Constitution. The Treaty of Guadalupe Hidalgo contributed to the decision. The Treaty required the United States to respect certain existing private property rights of Mexican nationals within the ceded territory. Some legislators apparently believed that aspect of the Treaty required that the new government continue the Spanish-Mexican community property system. The United States quickly broke many of the promises it made in the Treaty and most Mexicans who fell under American rule as a result of the Treaty lost their land in a few years. Thus, some legislators favored retaining the community property system in order to show some sign of conciliation towards the Mexican nationals and to avoid further political instability.

The discovery of gold was also a factor in the adoption of the community property system in California. The community property system would provide women with some measure of protection among the wild speculation of the gold rush. Further, many of the men present at the constitutional debates came from back east and were aware that the common-law states were increasingly unhappy with their own matrimonial property laws and Texas' experience demonstrated that community property was a viable alternative. Finally, some legislators were aware that community property was offered women greater rights than existing common law and hoped that a system of community property would help attract more marriageable women to the frontier state. Since its first Constitution, California has maintained a system of community property by state constitutional provisions and many legislative tinkerings. It is unique in many of its decisions and trends, but serves as the experimental workshop for the western community property states.

Nevada. Like California, Nevada was part of the Utah Territory that was ceded to the United States as part of the Treaty of Guadalupe Hidalgo. Nevada, which had recognized community property prior to statehood, modeled many of its laws, including its community property laws, on California's laws. Since admission as a state in 1864, Nevada has had a state constitutional provision recognizing community property.

Washington & Idaho. Washington and Idaho, the next two community property states admitted to the Union (in 1889 and 1890 respectively), are somewhat unique. Both states were part of the Oregon Territory, which was originally inhabited by Native Americans and later subject to occupation by the United States and the British. Neither state had strong connection to French, Spanish, or Mexican traditions. The Oregon Territory—which comprised the present states of Oregon, Washington, and Idaho—were officially recognized by the United States in 1848. The territorial government adopted the common law wholesale, including its provisions with respect to marital property. Washington split from the Oregon Territory in 1853 and formed the Washington Territory. Idaho was added to the Washington Territory in two parts in 1853 and 1859; and then became its own territory in 1864. In 1867, the Idaho Territory departed from its common law past and adopted a community property system. The Washington Territory followed suit in 1869. Both states imported California's community property statutes virtually verbatim and have remained community property jurisdictions ever since.

Both Washington and Idaho present a bit of a legislative mystery. Few records have survived that explain what factors led to these states adopting a community property system despite having no meaningful connection with Spanish-Mexican culture. Scholars generally credit three factors as leading to the adoption of community property in these states. First, Washington and Idaho did share cultural and social ties with California—the first territory to attain statehood in the region. Both states adopted large portions of California law wholesale. Adopting California's matrimonial regimes laws in addition to its other substantive laws was probably a logical attempt for these states to align themselves with California. Indeed, many early settlers of Washington and

Idaho migrated from California. California housed the only major nearby publishing houses meaning that books pertaining to California law were more readily available than other legal texts. Second, some scholars have argued that community property was enacted in Washington and Idaho because it was better suited to a frontier environment than common law. On the one hand, it provided some measure of protection to a wife's separate property, a factor likely important during the days of wild speculation. On the other hand, it allowed married men to transfer real estate without the consent or signature of their wives—which was often required in common law jurisdictions. This allowed married men to engage in commerce without needing their wives to travel to remote and potentially dangerous locations. Finally, as in California, the adoption of community property by Washington and Idaho may have reflected an attempt by single men to lure more marriageable women to the frontier.

Whatever the reasons, it still remains curious that Idaho and Washington adopted the community property system while the neighboring areas of Oregon, Montana, and Wyoming, did not.

New Mexico and Arizona. New Mexico and Arizona were the last two western community property jurisdictions to join the union. Both attained statehood in 1912. New Mexico, consisting partly of land from the Republic of Texas and partly of land acquired by the Treaty of Guadalupe Hidalgo, included the present state of Arizona until 1863. New Mexico's borders between Texas and California were similar to Poland's borders between Germany and Russia—subject to change from time to time. Arizona was originally a part of New Mexico; at least since 1865, the community property system was recognized by the Arizona Territory. Historians may differ as to whether Mexican community property rules continued in an unbroken chain in these states, but it is clear that the community property system predated statehood in 1912 and has existed ever since.

Wisconsin. Wisconsin is the first, and to date the only, state to affirmatively elect to permanently become a community property jurisdiction after a lengthy common law history. Wisconsin attained statehood in 1848 and had a common law regime through 1985. Wisconsin, effective January 1, 1986, was the first state to enact any form of the Uniform Marital Property Act (UMPA). The UMPA was adopted by the National Conference of Commissioners of Uniform State Laws in an attempt to provide model marital property legislation that better reflected the evolving marital relationship. In particular, the UMPA enables both spouses to share in the assets and wealth that accumulate during marriage without regard to which spouse actually contributed any particular asset. The UMPA—and the Wisconsin Marital Property Act (the WMPA)—is similar to the more traditional community property systems in that it views marriage as an economic partnership between the spouses. Indeed, drafters of both the UMPA and the WMPA looked to the existing community property jurisdictions as part of the process of creating the new marital property laws. It does, however, have some significant differences.

1.3 CHANGING VIEWS OF MARRIAGE: THE PARTNERSHIP MODEL

A. Introduction

Marriage has evolved from a patriarchal model to a partnership and companionate model. The social evolution has necessitated legal evolution in both the community property states and the common law (separate property) states. This is particularly true with respect to the laws governing the division of assets upon divorce. The following materials consider various attempts to bring the laws regulating marital property into line with the social and economic realities of marriage.

B. Marjorie E. Kornhauser, Theory Versus Reality: *The Partnership Model of Marriage in Family and Income Tax Law*, 69 TEMP. L. REV. 1413 (1996)

Current legal theory in both family and tax law accepts the belief that a marriage is like a partnership. The formality and power of theory, however, can make us forget that despite their interactive nature, theory and reality differ. The partnership model of law blurs the distinction between aspiration and attainment; it elevates metaphor to reality. We may want our marriages to be partnerships; we may believe that they are partnerships, but in reality most marriages are not partnerships. At best a marriage is only like a partnership; it does not become one in all aspects. Theory emphasizes the similarities but ignores the differences, and we ignore those differences at our peril.

The dissonance between theory and reality does more than create psychic discomfort; it can create real physical hardship. As many commentators have noted, the switch in domestic law to the partnership model of marriage precipitated a slide into poverty for many divorcing women and their children. In the tax area the marital partnership is the premise behind the joint tax return which has created extra tax burdens or "marriage penalties" for many two-earner married couples.

The partnership model of marriage in both these legal areas ignores two crucial differences between theory and reality. First, the theory says that the partnership is an equal one, that both spouses contribute to and share in the benefits equally. The reality, more often than not, is that the spouses are unequal both in what they contribute to and receive from the marriage. Second, the partnership model assumes, as does most economic theory, a unity of interest between the marital partners which cannot exist in a reality constructed of individuals and a society that values their individuality.

***

I. Marriage as a Partnership

A. The Model

Marriage is a complex entity. It is both a personal state of being as well as a social, legal, political, and religious construct. The reality of an individual marriage differs--sometimes radically--from the ideal theory of the constructs. However, the relationship between the reality and the theory is an interactive one: each is shaped by and influences the other. As a result of this interplay, marriage--in both its real and ideal forms--is a dynamic concept; both forms change over time. In the United States, as in the western world generally, two of the most significant changes have been the movement from status to contract and from marriage as a social relationship to marriage as a vehicle for individual fulfillment.

At common law marriage was a status in which the husband and wife were "one person in law: that is, the very being or legal existence of the woman [was] suspended during the marriage, or at least [was] incorporated and consolidated into that of the husband: under whose wing, protection, and cover, she performs everything . . . ." The rights, duties, obligations, and requirements of marriage were set not by the individuals but by the state. Gradually, changes occurred in both the legal status of married women and in the social understanding of marriage. As to the former, women began to emerge as separate legal entities as they acquired rights to own property independently of their husbands. The role of marriage in society also changed as the family unit became less of a determinant of an individual's social and economic status. The trend of viewing marriage as a means to individual fulfillment--begun centuries earlier--greatly accelerated after the world wars. Thus, the decision whether to begin or end a marriage began to be viewed as a choice that should be determined more by the individuals involved than by state regulation. Fueled by the movement for women's equality, a new model for marriage emerged. Marriage changed from status to contract and the commercial partnership became the model.

Community property law in several states also articulates a partnership model of marriage by speaking of the "community" of marriage in which each spouse has an equal, vested interest in the property acquired during the marriage. Like the partnership "equality" rhetoric in the common law, the equality rhetoric expressed by community property laws fails to deliver in reality. This occurs in two ways: either the law itself does not provide equal treatment, or the actions and emotions of the spouses themselves cause practice to diverge from theory. Either way, the rhetoric of partnership and community which implies harmony and equality denies the existence of important inequalities and disunities.

One of the most important facts which mars the partnership metaphor in a community property marriage is that not all the property in the marriage is community property. Consequently, there is the problem of identifying what is community property and what is separate property. For example, states vary as to whether the increase in value accruing to separate property during the marriage is community or separate property. Perhaps, even more importantly, human capital--often the most important form of property in the marriage--is not identified as community property. Since the consequences of the label "community" or "separate" property matter so much, community property law may have the ironic consequence of heightening the adverse interests of the spouses, the homemaker wife arguing that the asset is community property and the husband that it is separate. Common law, in contrast, may foster a greater sense of community because joint ownership is voluntary; it occurs because of the mutual agreement of the parties, not by operation of a law--only partially understood--imposed upon the spouses.

Even when property is clearly community property under the law, each spouse does not always have equal access to the property. Sometimes this is the fault of the law itself since it does not always provide for equal participation by each spouse in the management and control of the property. Although older community property laws, which gave sole management to the husband, generally have been revised, complete joint management for all community property assets does not exist, even in theory. Even when the law does provide for joint management, reality often does otherwise. As shown in Part II below, frequently an earner spouse manages property and considers it his own. The lack of joint control can extend beyond control of physical property to control of the children. Even today, under Louisiana community property law the husband has ultimate say over how to raise the children. Equal access to property can be even more illusory after divorce than during the marriage. In Louisiana, for example, the division of community property occurs separately from the divorce decree. There are many women in Louisiana who can attest to the inability to acquire their share of community property assets years after the divorce.

The partnership model of marriage in both the common and civil (community property) law jurisdictions is an idealized version of the commercial partnership. In the business world a partnership is defined as a voluntary association of two people engaged in a joint enterprise for profit. The ideal partnership, codified in the default rules of the Uniform Partnership Act ("UPA") is one in which each partner is equal to the other in ownership and management rights. However, the law leaves room in theory and in practice for a wide variety of partnerships ranging from the idealized two-person partnership in which the partners share everything equally, to a large hierarchical partnership such as law and accounting firms (at least before they started switching to the limited liability company form) in which there are junior and senior partners and partners share various degrees of management, control, and profits.

The partnership model of marriage, in contrast, uses only the one idealized type: the simple, two-person equal partnership. It assumes that each partner contributes equally to the marriage, has equal say during the marriage, and on termination of the partnership (divorce) each gets an equal share (half) of the partnership assets. Because a partnership is a voluntary association, each spouse can terminate the marital partnership at will. Once termination occurs, the partnership model holds that there is a "clean break" between the ex-partners (spouses); they can begin new lives without continuing obligations to each other.

The emergence of the partnership model of marriage necessitated fundamental changes in family law. In particular, three notable changes occurred. First, the ability to terminate a marriage dramatically changed. The old "fault" regime presumed that marriages would last until one spouse died except for tightly regulated and enumerated conditions under which divorce could occur. The new no-fault divorce rules operate on reverse presumptions: A marriage's duration is only as long as both parties agree and may be terminated at will without meeting any state requirements regarding cause or fault.

The second change concerned rights in the marital assets at the time of divorce. Except for the few states with community property law, the old common law had held that ownership rights followed title. In other words, whoever had legal title to the asset during the marriage was entitled to keep that asset after the marriage. The partnership model of marriage weakened the hold of these title rules. Common law states have adopted equitable division laws which override mere title in order to achieve a fair property distribution upon divorce.

The final change involved alimony or the continuing of marital obligations beyond the marriage. The clean break concept contained in the partnership model of marriage meant that marital obligations should terminate at the breakup of the marriage so that each ex-spouse could start over fresh. As a consequence, the concept of alimony largely withered away except for short rehabilitative awards.

The partnership model of marriage is predominantly a theory about marriage rather than the family. It focuses on the relationship between the husband and wife and generally ignores the presence of children. In reality, the presence of children radically alters the marital relationship. This failure to consider children makes the partnership model incomplete and inaccurate whenever children are present. The model, however, does have an indirect influence on the treatment of children. To the extent that children are considered at all, the equality standard in the partnership model logically presumes equal participation in the raising of children--equality of time and money spent and control over child rearing decisions.

B. Critiques of the Model

The partnership model of marriage and the consequent changes in domestic law have proved to be disastrous for women and children, thrusting many into poverty when the marriage ends. Because most of the visible damage occurs at divorce, most of the critical attention has been focused on divorce and post-divorce issues. Criticisms of the partnership model run a wide gamut. Some accept the partnership model and argue that a more correct application of it would cure post-divorce problems. Others say that the equal partnership model would (or might) be appropriate if spouses actually were equal in marriage; because most marriages are not between equal partners, the equal partnership model is inevitably, and fatally, flawed. Still others reject the partnership model entirely as inappropriate for such an intimate relationship; the partnership model commoditizes private, non-market relations. By focusing on the contract aspect of marriage the model ignores the needs of women. Perhaps even more importantly, according to many critics, the model is fatally flawed because it focuses on the husband and wife to the exclusion of children. The important community, under this view, is not the married couple alone but the family which includes children.

Solutions as well as critiques vary. Some critics have argued that expanding the definition of property to include human capital would lead to adequate compensation to a spouse upon divorce. For example, a wife who had helped a husband through law school would have a property interest in his law degree. Consequently, during the property division at divorce she would be entitled to a share of his future earnings (reduced to present value). Courts, however, have been unwilling to accept this human capital argument for several reasons. First, some courts see it as unduly burdensome upon the husband. Such a buyout of the wife's investment in her spouse's degree could result in "involuntary servitude" for the husband since he would be unable to change to a more desirable but lesser paying job because of the need to buy out the spouse. Second, some courts view the value of the buyout as too speculative since the value of the law degree ultimately is based on how much and how hard the husband works--factors which are partially under the control of the "earner spouse" and partly independent of him (death, disability, etc.). Additionally, a buyout at present value means that later events (e.g., re-marriage) cannot affect the price.

Even if the idea of human capital is accepted, theorists differ as to how to measure it; should they use expectations, reliance, or restitution as the basis for measuring damages? One measure determines compensation on the basis of a spouse's contribution. Thus, a woman would receive compensation for money she earned during the marriage which was used to put a husband through school. Another measurement is forgone opportunities, as when a wife gives up her job as a tax attorney to take care of the children. Yet another possible measurement is the amount of future financial gains the spouse expected for her efforts, as when a doctor gives up her practice to take care of the children in the expectation that her husband will care for her and the children in the future.

Recently, many critics of current alimony and child support laws have argued for some type of income sharing after the divorce. The bases for this post-divorce sharing vary from Cynthia Starnes's partnership buyout theory to Joan Williams's theory of joint ownership of the husband's earnings.

***

C. American Law Institutes' Principles of Family Dissolution

[The American Law Institute has prepared Principles of the Law of Family Dissolution. Chapter 4 of the Project includes principles for division of property upon dissolution of marriage. The following, adopted in 1995, reflect the tremendous changes that have occurred in most states.]

CHAPTER 1
INTRODUCTORY DISCUSSION

I. The Background of Existing Law

a. Division of property. At one time there was a sharp division between most American states, which followed traditional common law principles in the allocation of property at divorce, and the eight states that followed community property principles. The common law treated property owned by the spouses during their marriage as the individual property of one of them unless, as to a particular piece of property, they had acted to create joint ownership. In the absence of such acts, ownership vested in the spouse who earned the money with which the property was purchased, and ownership remained so vested unless the spousal owner made a gift of it to the other spouse. At divorce each spouse was allocated his or her property. The result in most cases was to allocate the bulk of the property to the husband. Alimony was therefore often the only financial remedy available to meet claims the divorced wife might have on her own behalf, as contrasted with claims of child support she might make on behalf of her children.

Community property law begins with the contrary presumption: all earnings from spousal labor during the marriage are the property of the marital "community" in which each spouse has an undivided one-half interest. Property acquired with spousal earnings is therefore also owned equally by the spouses, regardless of whether purchased with funds earned by the husband, the wife, or both, unless the parties change the character of the property by agreement or gift. In California and two other community property states, all community property is divided at divorce into spousal shares equal in value, although not necessarily identical in kind. Alimony (renamed as "spousal support" or "maintenance" in most jurisdictions) may also be allowed.

This sharp dichotomy between common law and community property traditions no longer prevails in the United States. All the common law states now allow the divorce court to distribute spousal property between the divorcing parties on a basis other than common law principles of ownership, under a doctrine known generally as "equitable distribution." Five of the eight community property states also instruct their divorce courts to divide the community property between the spouses "equitably" (rather than "equally"). Equitable distribution is the dominant rule today, followed everywhere but in the three "equal division" community property states.

The consensus, however, is not so great as first appears. There are important differences between the common law and community property states in contexts other than dissolution of marriage. In community property states, the concept of joint ownership is applicable not only at dissolution but also at death and during the intact marriage. The common law states, in contrast, have generally retained their traditional separate ownership principles in all matters other than the system of equitable distribution they apply at divorce. More important for the purposes of this project, the widespread acceptance of equitable distribution at divorce masks differences among the states in the law's two most critical features: the property available to the divorce court to allocate on equitable grounds, and the presumptive allocation rule. Many equitable division states, for example, have statutory or judge made rules establishing a presumption that an equal division of the property is the most equitable result. But some states do not have such a presumption, and the strength of the presumption varies among the states that follow it. These differences in the allocation rule are sometimes related to differences in the definition of property available for allocation. For example, strong presumptions of equal division are more common among states that exclude from the allocable pool inherited property, or property owned by the spouses individually before their marriage, as compared to states that allow the divorce court to allocate all spousal property, however or whenever acquired. More generally, inclusive or open-ended rules defining the property available for allocation are associated with more discretionary and open-ended rules of allocation. A leading example at the other end of the spectrum is California. That state combines a required equal division in all cases with detailed and comprehensive rules distinguishing the divisible community property from each spouse's "separate property." The divorce court may not divide the latter but must instead assign it entirely to the individual spouse who owns it.

Looking behind these differences nonetheless reveals some common substantive themes. For example, even in those states that do not require or strongly presume equal division, property acquired with spousal labor is often divided equally at dissolution. At the same time, even in those states which in principle allow the court to allocate all property owned by the spouses, property inherited by one spouse during the marriage is treated differently from property acquired through spousal labor. Important distinctions among the states thus emerge primarily at the next level of detail: when is a case not "ordinary," so that an equal division presumption should not apply? When, if ever, should the court be allowed to divide property that one of the spouses inherited or owned before the marriage?

Generalization becomes more difficult at this finer level of detail for two reasons. First, the rules of many states leave so much to trial court discretion that statutes and reported decisions provide limited guidance to how the law actually operates in practice. Second, for reasons developed further below, there has been considerable effort in the past decade to persuade courts to include, within the rubric of property division, claims on post-marital earnings that could traditionally have been made only under the rubric of alimony. Some of these claims have been rejected by most courts, but others have been embraced in varying degrees. For example, nearly all courts have rejected attempts to treat degrees or professional licenses as property, while the treatment of professional goodwill has been considerably more varied. The significance of the resulting variations in marital property law cannot be understood without examining the bent of related alimony claims, which traditionally were the only basis for claims on post-marital earnings.

D. J. Thomas Oldham, *ALI Principles of Family Dissolution: Some Comments*, U. ILL. L. REV. 801-05 (1997)

II. The ALI Recommendations

The ALI recommendations that have been completed and tentatively approved to date deal with the economic consequences of divorce. The recommendations regarding property are, with a few exceptions, a restatement of the current majority views on this subject. This portion of the ALI recommendations therefore comprises a more conventional ALI restatement project. The recommendations regarding spousal support (compensatory payments), however, are much less of a restatement, and more of a model statute. Depending on one's fairness to the law of spousal support, a dangerous attempt to dramatically expand the economic consequences of marriage, or a policy that still does not adequately compensate women for their contributions during marriage.

A. Property Division

The ALI draft accepts the distinction between separate and marital property, one that has been accepted by a majority of states. Under the ALI draft, separate property is not to be divided at divorce, but marital property is divisible. Separate property is defined as it is in most states, to include premarital acquisitions, gifts and inheritances received by a spouse during marriage from third parties, and property exchanged for such property. As a general rule, separate property also includes acquisitions after the divorce action is filed, income received during marriage from separate property, and appreciation of separate property during marriage.

Some commentators have argued that a spouse's earning capacity at divorce should be considered divisible property, at least to the extent it increased during marriage. Others contend that, in many instances, increases in earning capacity of an adult are really merely returns on early human capital investment by the spouse. Like almost all states, the draft accepts the view that earning capacity is not divisible property at divorce. Similarly, occupational licenses and degrees are not considered divisible property. Professional goodwill can be marital property to the extent that the goodwill is separate from the spouse's earning capacity.

Other positions taken by the draft regarding the character of acquisitions during marriage largely are restatements of the current majority rule. For example, unvested or vested pension rights are marital property to the extent that they are earned during marriage. For things like personal injury recoveries or disability insurance payments, to the extent that the payment replaces wages that would have been earned during marriage before the divorce action was filed, or reimburses the marital estate for medical expenses paid, the benefit is marital property; recoveries for pain and suffering and lost post-divorce wages are the separate property of the injured spouse.

The marital estate presumptively is to be divided equally. An exception is created for those instances where a spouse is guilty of economic fault, such as making unreasonable unilateral gifts of marital property or intentionally or negligently destroying marital property. No other justification for unequal division is accepted. This is not the majority view. Although some community property states accept the rule suggested by the draft, most states now permit an "equitable" division of the marital estate, and this division does not have to be equal. In equitable distribution states, a number of discretionary factors are considered relevant when arriving at the division; commonly suggested factors include fault, need, and contribution. The reporters for the ALI draft include a lengthy discussion of why need and fault are considered inappropriate factors.

A number of factors militate toward the equal division principle. On one hand, current equitable distribution factors are so vague and contradictory that they may result in arbitrary and unpredictable awards, thereby discouraging settlement, increasing legal fees (for those parties with lawyers), and generating a perception of unfairness. A different concern may relate to judicial economy. Because most divorcing parties do not own much property (at least if one accepts the arguably narrow current definition of what constitutes property), it may not be worth a court's time to try to decide what a "fair" division might be. If the parties' home is the most valuable part of the marital estate and the parties have minor children, presumably an equal division rule would not bar the court from awarding as child support the right of the custodial parent to live in the home until the youngest child reaches majority. If one wanted to limit discretion in property division but not abolish it, one might consider the Nevada approach of requiring equal division unless "compelling reasons" justify an unequal division.

Aside from the general rule that marital property should be divided equally, the only other provision of the draft pertaining to property that reflects a minority view is the rule that separate property gradually becomes marital property, with this process beginning after a certain number of years of marriage. This rule is not currently accepted in any state. However, a minority of states do not distinguish between divisible and nondivisible property; others do distinguish between the two but permit the division of separate property to avoid hardship. Thus, a number of states do permit the division of what the draft would classify (at least initially) as separate property. The draft specifies clearer rules about under what circumstances separate property becomes divisible. This provision of the draft will be discussed in more detail below.

* * *

§ 4.03 Definition of Marital and Separate Property

(1) Property acquired during marriage is marital property, except as otherwise expressly provided in this Chapter.

(2) Inheritances, including bequests and devises, and gifts from third parties, are the separate property of the acquiring spouse even if acquired during marriage.

(3) Property received in exchange for separate property is separate property even if acquired during marriage.

(4) Property acquired during marriage but after the parties have entered into a written separation agreement and commenced living apart is the separate property of the acquiring spouse unless the agreement specifies otherwise.

(5) For the purpose of this section "during marriage" means after the commencement of marriage and before the filing of a petition for dissolution (if that petition ultimately results in a decree dissolving the marriage), unless there are facts, set forth in written findings of the trial court, establishing that use of another date is necessary to avoid a substantial injustice.

(6) Property acquired during a relationship between spouses that immediately preceded, and which was a domestic partner relationship as defined by § 6.03, is treated as if it were acquired during the marriage.

§ 4.04 Income from and Appreciation of Separate Property

(1) Both income during marriage from separate property, and the appreciation in value during marriage of separate property, are marital property to the extent the underlying asset is subsequently recharacterized as marital property, pursuant to § 4.12.

(2) Both income during marriage from separate property, and the appreciation in value during marriage of separate property, are marital property to the extent the income or appreciation is attributable to either spouse's labor during marriage, pursuant to § 4.05.

(3) Income from and appreciation of separate property are separate property if they are not marital property under Paragraph (1) or (2).

§ 4.05 Enhancement of Separate Property by Spousal Labor

(1) A portion of any increase in the value of separate property is marital property whenever either spouse has devoted substantial time during marriage to the property's management or preservation.

(2) The increase in value of separate property over the course of the marriage is measured by the difference between the market value of the property when acquired, or at the beginning of the marriage, if later, and the market value of the property when sold, or at the end of the marriage, if sooner.

(3) The portion of the increase in value that is marital property under Paragraph (1) is the difference between the actual amount by which the property has increased in value, and the amount by which capital of the same value would have increased over the same time period if invested in assets of relative safety requiring little management.

§ 4.06 Property Acquired in Exchange for Marital and Separate Property

(1) Property acquired during marriage in exchange for other property is presumed to be marital property.

(a) The presumption of Paragraph 1 is rebutted by evidence that the consideration for the acquired property included a spouse's separate property.

(b) If the presumption is rebutted, the acquired property consists of marital and separate property shares in proportion to the value of the marital and separate property for which it was exchanged.

(2) Property acquired on credit during marriage is presumed to be marital property.

(a) The presumption of Paragraph (2) is rebutted by evidence that a down payment, or any payments that reduce the loan's principal balance, were made from a spouse's separate property.

(b) If the presumption is rebutted as described in Paragraph (2)(a), the acquired property consists of marital and separate shares in proportion to the value of the marital and separate property that was applied to the down payment or to reduce the debt. Payments not shown to have been made from separate property are treated as having been made from marital property.

(c) The presumption of Paragraph (2) is rebutted by evidence that neither spouse has personal liability for the loan and that, under the terms of the loan instrument and governing law, the creditor's sole recourse for nonpayment is against one spouse's separate property.

(d) If the presumption is rebutted as described in Paragraph (2)(c), (i) the acquired property is the separate property of the spouse who owns the separate property that the creditor may reach, except that (ii) if either the down payment, or reductions in the principal balance of the loan, were made from marital property, the acquired property consists of marital and separate shares in proportion to the value of the marital and separate property that was applied to the debt or down payment. Any payments not shown to have been made from separate property are treated as having been made from marital property.

(3) Property acquired on credit before marriage is presumed to be the separate property of the acquiring spouse, except that the acquired property is marital property to the extent the principal balance of the loan is reduced with payments made from marital property.

(4) Any presumption under this section is also rebutted by evidence that the spouses shared an intention concerning the characterization of the property that is inconsistent with the presumption.

§ 4.07 Earning Capacity and Goodwill

(1) Spousal earning capacity, spousal skills, and earnings from post-dissolution spousal labor are not marital property

(2) Occupational licenses and educational degrees are not marital property.

(3) Business goodwill and professional goodwill earned during marriage are marital property to the extent they have value apart from the value of spousal earning capacity, spousal skills, or post-dissolution spousal labor.

(a) Evidence of an increment during marriage in the market value of business or professional goodwill establishes the existence of divisible marital property in that amount except to the extent that market value includes the value of post-dissolution spousal labor.

(b) Business or professional goodwill that is not marketable is nevertheless marital property to the extent a value can be established for it that does not include the value of spousal earning capacity, spousal skills or post-dissolution spousal labor.

§ 4.08 Deferred or Contingent Earnings and Wage Substitutes

(1) Property earned by labor performed during marriage is marital property whether received before, during, or after the marriage. Property earned by labor not performed during marriage is the separate property of the laboring spouse even if received during marriage.

(a) Vested pension rights are marital property to the extent they are earned during the marriage.

(b) Contingent returns on labor performed during marriage, including unvested pension rights, choses in action, and compensation contingent on post-marital events, are marital property to the extent they are earned during the marriage.

(2) Benefits received as compensation for a loss take their character from the asset they replace.

(a) Insurance proceeds and personal injury recoveries are marital property to the extent that entitlement to them arises form the loss of a marital asset, including income that the beneficiary-spouse would have earned during the marriage. The dissolution court may make a reasonable allocation of an undifferentiated award between its marital and separate property components.

(b) Disability pay and workers' compensation payments are marital property to the extent they replace income or benefits the recipient would have earned during the marriage but for the qualifying disability or injury.

(3) Where the value of the marital-property portion of a spouse's entitlement to future payments can be determined at dissolution, the court may include it in reckoning the worth of the marital property assigned to each spouse. Where the value of the future payments is not known at the time of dissolution, where their receipt is contingent on future events or not reasonably assured, or where for other reasons it is not equitable under the circumstances to include their value in the property assigned at the time of dissolution, the court may decline to do so, and either

(a) fix the spouses' respective shares in such future payments if and when received, or,

(b) if it is not possible to fix their share at the time of dissolution, reserve jurisdiction to make an appropriate order at the earliest practical date.

§ 4.15 Division of Marital Property Generally

(1) Except as provided in Paragraph (2) of this section, marital property and marital debts are divided at dissolution so that the spouses receive net shares equal in value, although not necessarily identical in kind.

(2) The spouses are allocated net shares of the marital property and debts that are unequal in value if, and only if,

(a) the court concludes, under § 5.11, § 5.12, or § 5.17, that it is equitable to compensate a spouse for a loss recognized in Chapter 5, in whole or in part, with an enhanced share of the marital property; or

(b) the court concludes under § 4.16 that one spouse is entitled to an enhanced share of the marital property because the other spouse previously made an improper disposition of some portion of it; or

(c) marital debts exceed marital assets, and it is just and equitable to assign the excess debt unequally, because of a significant disparity in the spouses' financial capacity, their participation in the decision to incur the debt, or their consumption of the goods or services that the debt was incurred to acquire.

§ 4.16 Financial Misconduct as Grounds for Unequal Division of Marital Property

(1) If one spouse, without the other spouse's consent, has made gifts of marital property to third parties that are substantial relative to the total value of the marital property at the time of the gift, the court should augment the other spouse's share of the remaining marital property by one-half of the value of such gifts. This paragraph applies only to gifts made after a date that is set by counting back, from the date on which the dissolution petition is served, a fixed period of time specified in a rule of statewide application.

(2) If marital property is lost, expended, or destroyed through the intentional misconduct of one spouse, the court should augment the other spouse's share of the remaining marital property by one-half the value of the lost or destroyed property. This paragraph applies only to misconduct after a date that is set by counting back, from the date on which the dissolution petition is served, a fixed period of time specified in a rule of statewide application.

(3) If marital property is lost or destroyed through the negligence of one spouse, the court should augment the other spouse's share of the remaining marital property by one-half the value of the lost or destroyed property. This paragraph applies only to negligence that took place after service of the dissolution petition.

(4) If one spouse is entitled to a remedy under Paragraph (1) or (2), or would have been entitled to a remedy had concealed or conveyed property

not been recovered, and if the court also finds that the concealment or conveyance either

(a) had the purpose of denying the first spouse his or her equitable share of the marital property at dissolution, or

(b) was undertaken with knowledge that such denial was its likely effect, the court should require the second spouse to compensate the first spouse for all reasonable costs, including professional fees, that were incurred to establish the improper concealment or conveyance. Such compensation may take the form of an enhanced share of the available marital property.

(5) Paragraphs 1, 2, and 3 may be applied to gifts, misconduct, or neglect that occurred prior to the date specified in the statewide rule required under those sections, if facts set forth in written findings of the trial court establish that their application to the earlier incidents is necessary to avoid a substantial injustice.

(6) If there is insufficient marital property for an adjustment in its allocation to achieve the compensation found appropriate under this section, the court may achieve an equivalent result by

(a) making an award to one spouse of some portion of the other's separate property, as allowed under § 4.17, or, if the available separate property is also inadequate for this purpose,

(b) requiring one spouse to make equitable reimbursement to the other in such installment payments as the court judges equitable in light of the financial capacity and other obligations of the spouse making reimbursement.

§ 4.17 Separate Property

(1) In every dissolution of marriage, all separate property should be assigned to its owner, except that when there is sufficient marital property to permit the reimbursement that would otherwise be required under § 4.16, the court may reassign the spouses' separate property in order to achieve the equivalent result.

(2) Separate property that is recharacterized as marital property under § 4.18 is allocated between the spouses under § 4.15 and not under this section.

§ 4.18 Recharacterization of Separate Property as Marital Property at the Dissolution of Long-Term Marriages

(1) In marriages that exceed a minimum duration specified in a uniform rule of statewide application, a portion of the separate property that

each spouse held at the time of their marriage should be recharacterized at dissolution as marital property.

(a) The percentage of separate property that is recharacterized as marital property under Paragraph (1) should be determined by the duration of the marriage, according to a formula specified in a rule of statewide application.

(b) The formula should specify a marital duration at which the full value of the separate property held by the spouses at the time of their marriage is recharacterized at dissolution as marital property.

(2) A portion of separate property acquired by each spouse during marriage should be recharacterized at dissolution as marital property if, at the time of dissolution, both the marital duration, and the time since the property's acquisition (the "holding period"), exceed the minimum length specified for each in a rule of statewide application.

(a) The percentage of separate property that is recharacterized as marital property under Paragraph (2) should be determined by a formula, specified in a rule of statewide application, that takes into account both the marital duration and the holding period of the property in question.

(b) The formula should specify a marital duration and holding period at which the full value of the property is recharacterized at dissolution as marital property.(3) For the purpose of this section, any appreciation in the value of separate property, or income from it, that would otherwise itself be separate property is treated as having been acquired at the same time as the underlying asset, and any asset acquired in exchange for separate property is treated as having been acquired as of the time its predecessor asset was acquired.

(3) A spouse should be able to avoid the application of this section to gifts or inheritances received during marriage by giving written notice of that intention to the other spouse within a time period following the property's receipt that is specified in a rule of statewide application.

(4) The provision of a will or deed of gift specifying that a bequest or gift is not subject to claims under this section should be given effect.

(5) This section should not apply to separate property if, as set forth in written findings of the trial court, preservation of the property's separate character is necessary to avoid substantial injustice.

E. Uniform Marital Property Act

[The Uniform Marital Property Act was approved by the national Conference of Commissioners on Uniform State Laws in 1983. The official commentary noted substantial movement towards more sharing of property by husbands and wives. It provides in part:]

Statistics are not the only evidence of dramatic change. State houses have reflected it. Beginning with California at the end of the 60's and promulgation of the Uniform Marriage and Divorce Act in the early 70's, no-fault divorce has swept the statute books. In 1983 Illinois and South Dakota stand alone in adhering to fault-based divorce, and efforts to change to no-fault continue in Illinois. "Equitable distribution" of property became the hand-maiden of no-fault divorce in the Uniform Marriage and Divorce Act and in most other reforms. Forty-one traditional common law jurisdictions now use some form of *property division* as a principal means of resolving economic dilemmas on dissolution. Adding the eight community property jurisdictions in which such a division is an inherent aspect of spousal property rights yields a total of 49. The one state missing on the property division roster is Mississippi. These property division developments address and typically adopt sharing concepts and bring many common law jurisdictions close to a deferred community property approach to divorce. Cheadle, *The Development of Sharing Principles in Common Law Marital Property States*, 28 UCLA L.REV. 1269 (1981); *see also Younger, op. cit., supra*.

The ferment of change has not been limited to dissolution. The Uniform Probate Code was promulgated in 1969. Fourteen states are now listed as Code states or as substantially conforming states. Article II of the Code contains the concept of an augmented estate. It borrows heavily from New York's 1966 version of the idea. It is an advance on traditional forced-share procedures, operating by the creation of a larger universe of property against which a spousal right of election is exercisable. It accomplishes this by penetrating the veil of title and other techniques which have developed to insulate assets from the reach of forced-share statutes. In the official comment to the Code the augmented estate provisions are described as preventing arrangements by the owner of wealth which would transmit property to others than a surviving spouse by means other than probate for the deliberate purpose of defeating the rights of a surviving spouse.

Thus the stage is set by substantial social and legislative change in the duration of marriages and in the economics of the termination of marriages by dissolution and death.

The Uniform Marital Property Act makes its appearance on that stage to offer a means of establishing present shared property rights of spouses *during* the marriage. This approach is bottomed on two propositions. The first is creation of an immediate sharing mode of ownership. The second proposition is that the sharing mode during marriage is an ownership right already in existence at the end of a marriage. Thus recognition and perfection of shared and vested ownership rights in marital property are in place at divorce or death. They do not have to come to fruition as a result of a court-ordained and possibly adversary "division" or by a statutorily-sanctioned "transfer."

Some of the root concepts can be traced to the sharing ideal which is at the center of the historical community property approach. The fundamental principle that ownership of all of the economic rewards from the personal effort of each spouse during marriage is shared by the spouses in vested, present, and equal interests is the heart of the community property system. It is also the heart of the Uniform Marital Property Act. Common law states have been moving closer and closer to the sharing concept in both divorce and probate legislation, and the Uniform Marital Property Act builds on the direction of that movement. Sharing is seen as a system of elemental fairness and justice so that those who share in the many and diverse forms of work involved in establishing and maintaining a marriage will have a protected share in the material acquisitions of that marriage. The Act creates and protects that share without forcing a spouse to await the completion of a gift from the other spouse or the garnering of proof of dollar-for-dollar contributions to the purchase price of assets acquired over the years of marriage. Under the Act, the sharing of property is recognized by creation of a present interest simultaneously with acquisition of property by effort during marriage. The interest is legally defined and enforceable. It permeates assets as they are acquired and continues to permeate them as they are invested and reinvested, as they are exchanged and transferred, and as they grow or diminish.

Such a law translates the emotional and perceived concept of "ours" into a verified legal reality. And while that parallels sharing under community property systems, the Act is more accurately characterized as a sui generis approach, and as one which utilizes equally useful ideas developed in common law jurisdictions, such as title based management and control. In addition, it is a response to the twenty-year-long challenge of the President's Commission on the Status of Women issued in 1963 to face the reality that each spouse makes a different but equally important contribution in marriage. Though drafted with an awareness of various community property statutes and cases, the Uniform Marital Property Act is not an image of any of them. It is a statute speaking to the realities and equities of marriages in America in the Eighties.

[The primary provisions of the UMPA are §§ 3, 4 & 5:]

§ 3. Variation by Marital Property Agreement

Except as provided in Sections 2, 8(e), 9(c) and 10(b), a marital property agreement may vary the effect of the [Act].

§ 4. Classification of Property of Spouses

(a) All property of spouses is marital property except that which is classified otherwise by the [Act].

(b) All property of spouses is presumed to be marital property.

(c) Each spouse has a present undivided one-half interest in marital property.

(d) Income earned or accrued by a spouse or attributable to property of a spouse during marriage and after the determination date is marital property.

(e) Marital property transferred to a trust remains marital property.

(f) Property owned by a spouse at a marriage after the determination date is individual property.

(g) Property acquired by a spouse during marriage and after the determination date is individual property if acquired:

(1) by gift or a disposition at death made by a third person to the spouse and not to both spouses;

(2) in exchange for or with the proceeds of other individual property of the spouse;

(3) from appreciation of the spouse's individual property except to the extent that the appreciation is classified as marital property under Section 14;

(4) by a decree, marital property agreement, written consent, or reclassification under Section 7(b) designating it as the individual property of the spouse;

(5) as a recovery for damage to property under Section 15, except as specifically provided otherwise in a decree, marital property agreement, or written consent; or

(6) as a recovery for personal injury except for the amount of that recovery attributable to expenses paid or otherwise satisfied from marital property.

(h) Except as provided otherwise in the [Act] the enactment of the [Act] does not alter the classification and ownership rights of property acquired before the determination date.

(i) Except as provided otherwise in the [Act] and to the extent it would affect the ownership rights of the spouse that existed in the property before the determination date, during marriage the interest of a spouse in property owned immediately before the determination date is treated as if it were individual property.

§ 5. Management and Control of Property of Spouses

(a) A spouse acting alone may manage and control:

(1) that spouse's property that is not marital property;

(2) except as provided in subsections (b) and (c), marital property held in that spouse's name alone or not held in the name of either spouse;

(3) a policy of insurance if that spouse is designated as the owner on the records of the issuer of it;

(4) the rights of an employee under an arrangement for deferred employment benefits that accrue as a result of that spouse's employment;

(5) a claim for relief vested in that spouse by other law; and

(6) marital property held in the names of both spouses in the alternative, including a manner of holding using the names of both spouses and the word "or".

(b) Spouses may manage and control marital property held in the names of both spouses other than in the alternative only if they act together.

(c) The right to manage and control marital property transferred to a trust is determined by the terms of the trust.

(d) The right to manage and control marital property does not determine the classification of property of the spouses and does not rebut the presumption of Section 4(b).

(e) The right to manage and control marital property permits gifts of that property only to the extent provided in Section 6.

(f) The right to manage and control any property of spouses acquired before the determination date is not affected by this [Act].

(g) A court may appoint a [conservator, guardian] to exercise a disabled spouse's right to manage and control marital property.

1.4 COMMUNITY PROPERTY JURISDICTIONS AND COMMON LAW (SEPARATE PROPERTY JURISDICTIONS): SIMILARITIES AND DISTINCTIONS

The community property jurisdictions and the common law (or separate property) jurisdictions have become more similar in recent decades. The economic partnership model of marriage, which has its roots in civil law, has gained traction in the modern era. As a result, the distribution of marital property at the death of a spouse or at divorce looks increasingly similar in common law jurisdictions and community property jurisdictions. The major remaining distinction between the two systems is that community property jurisdictions contemplate the automatic concurrent ownership of marital property by both spouses during marriage. This concurrent ownership is not automatic in the common law states.

Equal Division and Equitable Distribution Compared.

Two systems of asset division exist in the divorce context—both of which attempt to further the partnership model of marriage. Equal division simply continues the automatic sharing of marital assets by requiring that marital or community property be divided equally between the spouses. The system is predictable in that it leaves the judge with little, if any, discretion to alter the portion of marital assets to which each spouse is entitled. Its strict formulaic approach, however, can result in outcomes that seem unfair or inequitable in some circumstances. In contrast, the equitable distribution system affords the judge a good deal of discretion in dividing the marital assets between the spouses in light of a list of statutory factors. The equitable distribution system is certainly more flexible than the equal division system. It also allows the court to divide property unequally in lieu of alimony or spousal support. Vesting so much discretion in the judge, however, presents problems of its own.

Equal Division. Equal division has its roots in civil law. Under a system of equal division each spouse is entitled to one-half of the spouses' marital or community property. The judge is afforded little, if any, discretion in altering this formulaic division of assets. Equal division is consistent with community property rules providing for the automatic concurrent ownership of community property during marriage. Some community property states—notably Louisiana and California—continue to utilize the equal division approach at divorce. Under this system each spouse retains his or her separate property and is entitled to one-half of the community property. Louisiana Civil Code provides as follows:

> **Art. 2369.1. Application of co-ownership provisions**
>
> After termination of the community property regime, the provisions governing co-ownership apply to former community property, unless otherwise provided by law or by juridical act....
>
> **Art. 2369.2. Ownership interest**
>
> Each spouse owns an undivided one-half interest in former community property and its fruits and products.

Similarly, California Family Code §2550 provides that "in a proceeding for dissolution of marriage or for legal separation of the parties, the court shall, either in its judgment of dissolution of the marriage, in its judgment of legal separation of the parties, or at a later time if it expressly reserves jurisdiction to make such a property division, divide the community estate of the parties equally."

Equitable Distribution. Most American jurisdictions, including a number of the community property states, apply principles of equitable distribution in order to divide the property between divorcing spouses. Broadly, equitable distribution requires the court to divide the property owned by the spouses "equitably" between the spouses. Equitable, however, does not necessarily mean equal. Equitable distribution draws on partnership law as its theoretical basis. Upon the dissolution of a partnership, each partner is typically entitled to the portion of the partnership property that corresponds to his or her contribution to the partnership itself. Not all contributions are equal. In determining how to make a particular division of assets, courts in equitable distribution jurisdictions consider a list of statutory or jurisprudential factors that are fairly similar from state-to-state. The equitable distribution states vary, however, with respect to what property is available for division and with respect to the precise amount of discretion afforded to the judge. Some states only allow the court to divide the marital or community property between the spouses whereas other states allow the court to divide any property owned by either spouse regardless of the time or nature of its acquisition. States utilizing the former approach are referred to as "dual classification" states. States utilizing the latter approach are referred to as "all property jurisdictions."

Equitable Distribution with Dual Classification.

Arkansas is an example of an equitable distribution state that utilizes the dual classification approach. The applicable statute directs the judge to apportion marital property equitably according to a list of factors that are similar to those seen in other states. The statute then goes on to describe the distinction between marital and non-marital property—a division that has clearly been influenced by community property laws.

Arkansas Code §9-12-315. Property distribution

(a) At the time a divorce decree is entered:

(1)(A) All marital property shall be distributed one-half (½) to each party unless the court finds such a division to be inequitable. In that event the court shall make some other division that the court deems equitable taking into consideration:

(i) The length of the marriage;
(ii) Age, health, and station in life of the parties;
(iii) Occupation of the parties;
(iv) Amount and sources of income;
(v) Vocational skills;
(vi) Employability;
(vii) Estate, liabilities, and needs of each party and opportunity of each for further acquisition of capital assets and income;
(viii) Contribution of each party in acquisition, preservation, or appreciation of marital property, including services as a homemaker; and
(ix) The federal income tax consequences of the court's division of property.

(B) When property is divided pursuant to the foregoing considerations the court must state its basis and reasons for not dividing the marital property equally between the parties, and the basis and reasons should be recited in the order entered in the matter;

***

(b) For the purpose of this section, "marital property" means all property acquired by either spouse subsequent to the marriage except:

(1) Property acquired prior to marriage or by gift or by reason of the death of another, including, but not limited to, life insurance proceeds, payments made under a deferred compensation plan, or an individual retirement account, and property acquired by right of survivorship, by a trust distribution, by bequest or inheritance, or by a payable on death or a transfer on death arrangement;

(2) Property acquired in exchange for property acquired prior to the marriage or in exchange for property acquired by gift, bequest, devise, or descent;

(3) Property acquired by a spouse after a decree of divorce from bed and board;

(4) Property excluded by valid agreement of the parties;

(5) The increase in value of property acquired prior to marriage or by gift or by reason of the death of another, including, but not limited to, life insurance proceeds, payments made under a deferred compensation plan, or an individual retirement account, and property acquired by right of survivorship, by a trust distribution, by bequest or inheritance, or by a payable on death or a transfer on death arrangement, or in exchange therefor;

(6) Benefits received or to be received from a workers' compensation claim, personal injury claim, or social security claim when those benefits are for any degree of permanent disability or future medical expenses; and

(7) Income from property owned prior to the marriage or from property acquired by gift or by reason of the death of another, including, but not limited to, life insurance proceeds, payments made under a deferred compensation plan, or an individual retirement account, and property acquired by right of survivorship, by a trust distribution, by bequest or inheritance, or by a payable on death or a transfer on death arrangement, or in exchange therefor.

***

Arizona, a community property jurisdiction, has moved towards an equitable distribution approach at divorce. Arizona Revised Statute §25-318 provides, in part: "In a proceeding for dissolution of the marriage...the court shall assign each spouse's sole and separate property to such spouse. It shall also divide the community, joint tenancy and other property held in common equitably, though not necessarily in kind, without regard to marital misconduct." In addition to a handful of express statutory factors relating to actual financial contributions, concealment, and fraud, Arizona jurisprudence has developed a set of factors the court should consider in determining how to make an equitable division. The jurisprudential factors, including length or the marriage, age, income, needs, and health, are similar to the factors considered in other equitable distribution states.

Equitable Distribution with All Property Division.

A handful of equitable distribution states authorize the all property method of property division. Connecticut General Statute §46b-81, for example, allows the judge to "assign to either spouse all or part of the estate of the other spouse." In deciding how to divide assets between the spouses the statute instructs the court to consider a fairly typical set of factors:

> (c) In fixing the nature and value of the property, if any, to be assigned, the court, after considering all the evidence presented by each party, shall consider the length of the marriage, the causes for the annulment, dissolution of the marriage or legal separation, the age, health, station, occupation, amount and sources of income, earning capacity, vocational skills, education, employability, estate, liabilities and needs of each of the parties and the opportunity of each for future acquisition of capital assets and income. The court shall also consider the contribution of each of the parties in the acquisition, preservation or appreciation in value of their respective estates.

Washington, a community property jurisdiction, authorizes an all property method of equitable distribution at divorce.

WASH. REV. CODE §26.09.080. Disposition of property and liabilities--Factors

> In a proceeding for dissolution of the marriage or domestic partnership, legal separation, declaration of invalidity, or in a proceeding for disposition of property following dissolution of the marriage or the domestic partnership by a court which lacked personal jurisdiction over the absent spouse or absent domestic partner or lacked jurisdiction to dispose of the property, the court shall, without regard to misconduct, make such disposition of the property and the liabilities of the parties, either community or separate, as shall appear just and equitable after considering all relevant factors including, but not limited to:
>
> (1) The nature and extent of the community property;

(2) The nature and extent of the separate property;
(3) The duration of the marriage or domestic partnership; and
(4) The economic circumstances of each spouse or domestic partner at the time the division of property is to become effective, including the desirability of awarding the family home or the right to live therein for reasonable periods to a spouse or domestic partner with whom the children reside the majority of the time.

1.5 THE ROLE OF FEDERAL TAXATION IN THE HISTORY OF MATRIMONIAL PROPERTY

A. Introduction

The community property jurisdictions have had a profound effect on federal tax law and policy. As explained below, the joint nature of community property results in an automatic splitting of income by spouses in community property jurisdictions. This splitting resulted in a large tax savings for wealthy taxpayers in community property jurisdictions and prompted a number of states to briefly adopt community property systems of their own in an attempt to benefit from these savings. Congress ultimately enacted legislation allowing married taxpayers in all jurisdictions to file a joint income tax return. The joint income tax return treats married couples as a single economic unit regardless of applicable state law. As is also explained below, some tax savings are still available to couples—particularly wealthy couples—in community property jurisdictions. Consequently, at least two states, Tennessee and Alaska have enacted legislation allowing spouses to "opt-in" to a type of community property system.

B. Jennifer E. Sturiale, *The Passage of Community Property Laws, 1939-1947: Was "More than Money" Involved?*, 11 MICH. J. GENDER & L 213 (2005)

Introduction

In 1930, the Supreme Court decided two cases and reached seemingly contradictory results regarding the ability of a married couple to receive preferential tax treatment by one spouse diverting income to the other. The distinction between the two cases lay in the legal instrument that operated to divert that income. In the first case, Lucas v. Earl, a husband and wife entered into a contractual agreement that assigned half of the husband's income to his wife. In contrast, Poe v. Seaborn considered Washington state's community property statutes, which automatically diverted income from a husband to his wife. The Court held that where one spouse diverted income to the other by virtue of a private, contractual agreement, as in Earl, the couple was not entitled to file separate returns, each reporting only half of the household's total income. However, where one spouse diverted income to the other by operation of the state's community property regime, as in Seaborn, the couple was entitled to file separate returns with each spouse reporting only half of the income earned.

Significant tax consequences resulted from the ability of one spouse to divert income to the other. At the time Earl and Seaborn were decided, there was only one tax schedule used by all taxpayers, and husband and wife were treated as separate taxpayers. In addition, tax liability increased rapidly as income rose, imposing a heavy burden on the nation's taxpayers in the post-World-War-I and World-War-II era. For example, in 1944, a taxpayer was taxed at a marginal tax rate of fifty-nine percent on income between \$20,000 and \$22,000 and paid as much as ninety-four percent of his income in taxes for income over \$200,000. The ability to divert income from one spouse to another consequently allowed married couples to shift some of the household's income to a lower marginal tax rate. For example, if a husband earned \$22,000 in wages in 1944, the ability to divert his income to his wife for income tax purposes subjected both husband and wife to only a forty-one percent marginal tax rate, rather than the husband alone being subjected to the fifty-nine percent rate. This shifting of income would reduce the household's income taxes from \$9,040 to \$6,700, resulting in the addition of \$2,340 to a married couple's after-tax income.

In response to the disparate treatment of taxpayers that resulted from Earl and Seaborn, a flurry of states adopted community property statutes between 1939 and 1947—Michigan, Nebraska, Oklahoma, Oregon, and Pennsylvania. Eight states—Arizona, California, Idaho, Louisiana, Nevada, New Mexico, Texas, and Washington--already had community property laws in place. Before other states could similarly adopt community property statutes, Congress responded with the Revenue Act of 1948, which stated, in pertinent part, "[e]qualization is provided for the tax burdens of married couples in common-law and community property States." The Revenue Act achieved such equalization by allowing husbands and wives to file one return together—that is, a joint return—and calculating the tax liability on the joint income by determining the tax liability on half the income and multiplying that figure by two. In less than a year after the adoption of the Revenue Act of 1948, Michigan, Nebraska, Oklahoma, and Oregon repealed their community property statutes. Pennsylvania may have, as well, had the Pennsylvania Supreme Court not already found its state's community property laws unconstitutional.

These facts raise at least two interesting questions. First, was the adoption of community property regimes motivated by the beneficial tax treatment of married couples or was more than money involved? Second, what underlying facts and social conditions led such laws to be adopted with little fear of wives' newly created property rights?

***

II. Passage of Community Property Laws in The States

Earl and Seaborn made clear that the recently imposed federal income tax might be avoided by novel legal maneuvers. Married couples consequently engaged in various transactions in an effort to reduce the household's income tax liability. Some husbands gave gifts of income-producing property to their wives, while others established trusts for their wives or created partnerships "in which the wife was said to have invested time and energy in lieu of money." While married couples attempted to reduce their income tax liability through private action, state legislators attempted to reduce their constituents' federal income tax liability through state action by proposing and enacting community property laws.

A. Five States Take Action

In 1939, Oklahoma became the first of the common law states to enact laws creating a community property regime. Oklahoma's community property statute provided that the law only applied to those married couples that elected to come under the terms of the Act. In 1943, Oregon followed Oklahoma's lead and enacted its own community property statute, which similarly required that married couples elect to have the law treat their separate property as community property. The following year, however, in Commissioner of Internal Revenue v. Harmon, the Supreme Court held that Oklahoma's statute did not effectively create a community property system. Because Oklahoma's statute did not automatically transform married couples' property into community property, it did not create community property between a husband and a wife as an incident of matrimony. Thus, Oklahoma did not create a system "dictated by State policy," whereas the traditional community property system in states such as Washington, where the Seaborns lived, presumably reflected state policy and thus required deference by the Court. As the Court explained, "The most that can be said is that the present policy of Oklahoma is to permit spouses, by contract, to alter the status which they would otherwise have under the prevailing property system in the State." In other words, the statute provided for the same private ordering that the Court invalidated in Earl. Because Oregon's community property law also provided for private contracting similar to that struck down in Earl, Harmon effectively invalidated Oregon's community property law, as well.

This, however, did not discourage Oklahoma. During the next legislative session, in 1945, Oklahoma repealed the 1939 Act at issue in Harmon and enacted a new law that created community property between husband and wife as an incident to marriage, thus curing the 1939 Act's deficiencies. Oregon, however, lacked Oklahoma's confidence. It, too, promptly repealed its community property law during its 1945 legislative session, but Oregon waited until April 19, 1947, to enact a law that effected community property as an incident of marriage.

The legislators of Michigan, Nebraska, and Pennsylvania concurrently were considering enacting community property laws in their own states. In June of 1947, Nebraska enacted a community property statute; on July 1, 1947, Michigan enacted its own law; and just days later, on July 7, 1947, Pennsylvania approved a similar law.

B. Congress Takes Action

While the legislators of Oregon, Michigan, Nebraska, and Pennsylvania were considering community property laws in their states, Congress was relentlessly considering various tax reduction bills at the federal level. In January of 1947, the eightieth Congress introduced House Bill 1, which provided for a reduction in income tax rates. President Truman vetoed the bill, and supporters of the bill could not mobilize the two-thirds majority necessary to override the President's veto. Less than six months later, Congress attempted to pass House Bill 3950, a tax reduction bill that was almost identical to House Bill 1; the only difference was that it would take effect in January of 1948, rather than in January of 1947. Again, Truman vetoed the tax reduction measure, and again the veto was sustained. In 1948, Congress, during its second session, put forth a third attempt to enact a tax reduction bill, House Bill 4790, and for a third time, the President vetoed the bill. Determined to pass a tax reduction bill--and not discouraged by what seemed to be the bill's "ill-omened star"--the Congress mustered the two-thirds majority and overrode Truman's veto. An article in The New York Times reported, "Both houses overrode Mr. Truman's veto less than four hours after its receipt and with many votes to spare . . . . [T]he House overrode the veto without a word of debate, and the Senate followed suit after a brief discussion."

House Bill 4790, like its predecessors, reduced the "extremely high rates of the individual income tax." But it did more than merely reduce tax rates. It also introduced what is now known as the "married, filing jointly" tax return--married couples could elect to file a joint return, and, if they did, income tax liability would be calculated by determining the tax liability on half the income and multiplying the tax liability by two. The married filing jointly tax return effectively made community property law regimes inconsequential to a taxpayer's tax liability.

C. 4 Repealed, 1 Held Unconstitutional

In less than a year after the adoption of the Revenue Act of 1948, Michigan, Nebraska, Oklahoma, and Oregon repealed their community property statutes. Michigan led the way, repealing its community property law within just a few months of the enactment of the Revenue Act of 1948. The other states quickly followed, taking action during their next legislative sessions in 1949. The legislatures in Nebraska, Oklahoma, and Oregon introduced bills repealing the community property laws just days apart in January of 1949. Pennsylvania's Supreme Court had already declared Pennsylvania's statute unconstitutional in 1947. Not only did Michigan, Nebraska, Oklahoma, and Oregon take quick action to repeal their community property laws, but none of the five states seemed interested in enacting similar legislation.

***

C. Dan W. Holbrook, *Community Property Trusts*, 46 TENN. B. J. 26 (2010)

Ah, Alaska! Like its melting glaciers, its trust law, heated by an unabashed desire to promote Alaskan trust business, has largely dissolved into a lake of reform. Tennessee has fished this lake and brought home catch. Limited by the rule against perpetuities? Abolish it! Bothered by creditors reaching self-settled trusts? Shelter them! In these triumphs of trust economics, one might wonder whether state legislators have adequately weighed the long-term social costs and benefits of such radical innovations.

One Alaskan idea copied by Tennessee, however, is just unquestionably good news—Tennessee's Community Property Trust Act of 2010, the second such act in the nation after Alaska's. Effective July 1, 2010, Tennessee residents and nonresidents alike can elect to treat some or all of their assets as community property.

Income Tax Benefit

The primary advantage of electing community property status is that when the first spouse dies (other than in 2010), both spouses' interests in the community property, not just the decedent's interest, receive a step-up in basis for income tax purposes (up to fair market value) under Code section 1014(b)(6).

Example 1: H and W paid $1,000,000 for XYZ stock, titled as equal tenants in common. If H dies in 2011 and all the stock is worth $2,500,000, H's one-half interest gets a step-up in basis to $1,250,000, but W's basis in her half is still only $500,000. If W sells all the XYZ stock for $2,500,000, total basis is $1,750,000, so total gain is $750,000, which at a 20 percent capital gain rate causes $150,000 of income tax.

If, instead, H and W contribute their XYZ stock to a Community Property Trust, then when either spouse dies, all the stock gets a step-up in basis to fair market value, i.e., $2,500,000. The survivor can then sell all the stock without capital gain.

Gift and Estate Tax Benefits

There are two primary gift and estate tax advantages of electing community property status.

First, community property trusts make it easier for clients to "equalize" ownership of their assets, so that both spouses can be more likely to fully utilize their separate death tax exemptions. Since each spouse is treated as owning an undivided one-half of all community property, the effect of the death of one spouse is for the decedent's one-half interest to pass by will (presumably to create a credit shelter trust) and for the survivor's one-half interest to become his or her property outright.

Example 2: In 2011, both the federal estate tax exemption and Tennessee inheritance exemption are $1,000,000 per decedent. H and W have a combined net worth of $2,500,000. Each of them needs at least $1,000,000 in his or her separate name so that regardless of the order of death, the first to die will be able to fully utilize his or her exemption to fund a credit shelter trust. The usual solution is for the spouses to divide their assets, each having separate property of at least $1,000,000.

If, instead, H and W create a Tennessee Community Property Trust, then they need not keep track of how much is in each name. When one of them dies, one-half of all community property will automatically be part of the decedent's estate.

Second, because each spouse owns an undivided one-half interest in all community property, each half may be eligible for a discount in value for transfer tax purposes on account of being a fractional interest, especially if the community property is real property or a closely held business interest.

Example 3: H owns a business worth $1,000,000, W owns a lake house worth $1,000,000, and H and W own another $500,000 jointly, for a total net worth of $2,500,000. If both died in 2011, even if they both fully utilized their $1,000,000 federal and Tennessee death tax exemptions, the amount subject to tax at the second death is $500,000, and the combined Federal and Tennessee death tax is $210,000.

If, instead, H and W contribute all their assets to a Tennessee Community Property Trust, then when each spouse dies, his or her estate will consist of one-half of each asset in the Trust. If the one-half interest in the business is discounted by 25 percent, the discount on $500,000 would be $125,000. If the one-half interest in the lake property is discounted by 15 percent, the discount on $500,000 is $75,000. Accordingly, total discounts at each death are $200,000, or $400,000 combined for both estates. Effectively, they have reduced their net worth for death purposes from $2,500,000 to only $2,100,000. When the second spouse dies, the taxable estate is only $100,000, and the combined federal and Tennessee death tax is $41,000, a savings of $169,000.

Simplicity

The beauty of Tennessee's "opt-in" community property system is its simplicity. Whatever is in a married couple's Community Property Trust is community property, and whatever is not in the Trust is separate property.

By contrast, the laws of the various community property states are often complex and inconsistent. Examples are how to determine which assets are separate property, the treatment of income from separate property, the effect of commingling of separate and community property, or what happens when community funds are used to improve one spouse's separate property.

In designing a Tennessee Community Property Trust, spouses have wide latitude, and may agree between themselves on various rights and obligations, control, disposition upon death, divorce, or other contingencies, and whether the trust, or any specific provision of the trust, is revocable or irrevocable. Virtually the only statutory default that the spouses cannot alter is that at the death of the first spouse, each spouse owns one-half of each asset in the Trust and each retains control over his or her half.

Caveats

Since statutory defaults govern in the absence of the spouses' agreement in the trust instrument, each spouse should be diligent to review the language carefully. For example, in the event of a divorce, the default is not only that the trust is divided between the spouses, but each trust asset is split between them. This suggests that Community Property Trusts may, in many contexts, have the nature of post-marital agreements, with all the requirements and protections against overreaching those entail. Unlike other post-marital agreements, however, the statute does clarify that for this purpose there is no requirement of consideration.

Creditors of a spouse can reach that spouse's interest in a Tennessee Community Property Trust, and creditors of both spouses can reach both spouses' interests. In other words, there is little or no creditor protection, and spouses should be aware that other forms of ownership, such as tenancy by the entirety, may be more beneficial for that purpose.

Requirements

There are four simple requirements for creating a Tennessee Community Property Trust: (1) a declaration that it is such; (2) at least one "qualified trustee," meaning a Tennessee resident (which can be either or both spouses) or bank qualified in Tennessee; (3) signatures of both spouses; and (4) specific "warning" language in capital letters at the beginning of the trust instrument.

***

CHAPTER 2: WHAT IS "PROPERTY"?

2.1 PROPERTY SUBJECT TO THE MATRIMONIAL REGIME, GENERALLY

In classifying an asset the issue normally is whether it is community or separate and the focus is usually on the time of acquisition and the nature of the transaction by which the asset is acquired. A preliminary inquiry, however, is the determination of which assets will be subject to being shared at all. The Louisiana Civil Code does not address this issue in detail but has left its resolution to the courts. The Louisiana Civil Code provides as follows:

Art. 2325. Matrimonial regime

A matrimonial regime is a system of principles and rules governing the ownership and management of the property of married persons as between themselves and toward third persons.

REVISION COMMENTS—1979

(a) The definition of a matrimonial regime accords with civilian doctrine. See 8 Planiol et Ripert, Traité pratique de droit civil français No. 2 (2d ed. Boulanger 1957); 12 Toullier, Droit civil français 203 1833); 21 Laurent, Principes de droit civil français No. 3 (1876).

(b) In the Louisiana Civil Code of 1870, the word "property" is at times a translation of the word propriete and at times a translation of biens. See Yiannopoulos, Civil Law Property § 1 (2d ed. 1980). Following the terminology of the 1870 Code, the word "property" in this revision is at times used to mean things (see, e.g., Articles 2338, 2365 infra), and at times to mean patrimony (see e.g., Articles 2325, 2335, 2374-2376, infra).

Some things are so intimately a part of a spouse's body or personality that they are not subject to sharing, even though they may have a significant pecuniary value. Often, the attempt to implement this concept is referred to as deciding whether an asset is "property" or whether it is "patrimonial." The inquiry, however, goes beyond a definitional approach and considers a broad range of textual references, history and policy factors. Recent controversy has centered on college degrees, usually advanced or professional, and professional goodwill.

Aubry and Rau suggest that, except for rare cases, "the distinction between patrimonial and extrapatrimonial rights is in reality a distinction between rights which their subject may dispose of and those which he may not. The extrapatrimonial interests cannot be expressed in currency because there is no market offering a current price for them." Examples given by Aubry and Rau of extrapatrimonial rights include the rights resulting from marriage; rights derived from paternity and status as head of family; the right of one to his own body and name; and the intellectual right of an author to a work of art.

Government social welfare benefits and similar entitlements, which are personal and not heritable, are governed by their own regulations and should be considered essentially extrapatrimonial. Civil rights in general, such as the right to vote and the right to be free of deprivations of liberty without due process would fit the scheme as non-patrimonial.

More generally, one can acknowledge the necessity of there being a class of personal interests that are not meant to be shared. One can refer to these by various terms—personal rights, rights of personality, or extrapatrimonial—but the basic thrust is that they do not function traditionally like property and are to be treated as personal assets. This concept is important in a true community property state, which must comprehend of such assets being managed during the community and transmitted at termination by death, as well as which must be capable of being divided at termination by separation or divorce.

2.2 PROPERTY INTERESTS VS. MERE EXPECTANCIES AND CONTINGENT INTERESTS

A. Introduction

One area the courts have struggled with involves the distinction between a current property interest that ought to be subject to the community property regime, and mere expectancies that are too speculative to constitute property in the community property context. The following cases show the evolution of Louisiana's struggle in addressing these questions. As you read the cases consider whether the courts are attempting to fit equitable distribution ideas into Louisiana's equal division framework in order to achieve a result that seems more "fair" in the view of the court.

B. *Tatiana T. Dué v. Paul H. Dué*,

342 So.2d 161 (La. 1977)

TATE, Justice.

The issue before us is: Are a lawyer husband's contingent fee contracts pending as of the date of the dissolution of the marital community to be included in the accounting of the community assets as between the husband and his wife?

A wife here sues her former husband, an attorney, to set aside a community property settlement on the ground of fraud and lesion. She also prays that the court order an inventory of the assets of the former community, in order to partition it between the spouses.

Her discovery interrogatories included inquiries as to contingent fee contracts entered into by her husband in his law practice for a period during the marriage preceding the date of dissolution of the community.

The defendant husband objected to these interrogatories. He contends that contingent fee contracts which were not consummated when the community dissolved did not fall within the community of acquets and gains.

The trial court sustained the husband's contention. It concluded that such contracts do not form part of the community because no interest is vested in the attorney until the contract is completed by successful disposition of the case.

The court of appeal granted supervisory writs and reversed. 331 So.2d 858 (La.App. 3rd Cir. 1976). It reasoned that a contingent fee contract from the date of its execution creates a right to share in the eventual proceeds (albeit subject to successful conclusion of the litigation), and that this right constitutes a property right which falls into the community, although its value can be determined only when the proceeds are realized. When realized, the interest in the community is determined in the proportion that the value of the husband's services rendered at the date of the community's dissolution bears to the total services performed by the husband in earning the fee.

Because of the importance of the issue, we granted certiorari, 337 So.2d 518 (La. 1976), to review the husband's contention that a contingent fee contract cannot be included in the community because it creates no property right prior to completion of the attorney's work after the community's dissolution.

I.

In Louisiana, all property acquired by the labor and industry of the spouses during the marriage belongs to the community of acquets and gains existing between them. Civil Code Articles 2402, 2405, 2334. Included among the assets of the community, thus subject to inventory and spouses joint ownership at the community's dissolution, are obligations based upon the right to receive money to become due in the future, even though this right is contingent upon the happening of an event at a future time. Messersmith v. Messersmith, 229 La. 495, 86 So.2d 169 (1956). See also T. L. James & Co., Inc. v. Montgomery, 332 So.2d 834 (La. 1976).

The defendant husband contends, however, that this principle does not apply to an attorney's contingent fee contracts. He argues:

(1) A contingent fee contract, depending on an uncertain event (winning or compromising the litigation), is an aleatory contract, Articles 1776, 2982, which creates no obligation until the happening of the event;

(2) Even if the contingent fee contract is a conditional obligation creating contemporaneously a right to enforce it upon happening of the condition, Article 2041, the right so created is only of specific enforcement not to vest it retroactively to the contract's creation, Wampler v. Wampler, 239 La. 315, 118 So.2d 423 (1960);

(3) Further, however classified, the contingent fee contract has no ascertainable value prior to successful completion of the work; it therefore does not form part of his patrimony at any earlier time.

II.

We ultimately conclude that, whatever the theoretical nature of the right, a contingent fee contract creates in the husband a patrimonial asset, i. e. (in ordinary language) "property", which is acquired by him during the marriage, Article 2334, and which (to the extent that his labor and industry contribute during the marriage, Article 2402) is an asset of the community existing between his wife and himself at the time of its dissolution, Article 2405.

A contingent fee contract executed between a client and his attorney is legislatively recognized as creating in the attorney an enforceable right to share in the proceeds eventually recovered. La. R.S. 37:218. The obligation in his favor is, of course, subject to the suspensive condition that the outcome will be favorable, Articles 2021, 2043, and to the implied resolutory condition his interest may be divested if he does not perform the contractual services expected of him, Articles 2021, 2046.

Nevertheless, "The contract of which the condition forms a part is, like all others, complete by the assent of the parties * * *." Article 2028. As noted at Planiol, Civil Law Treatise, Volume 1, see. 319, p. 216 (LSLI translation, 1950): "The owner or creditor . . . is not therefore, properly speaking, either an owner or a creditor as long as the condition is still pending. The simple possibility of the realization of the condition, nevertheless, constitutes a chance which is already considered an asset or liability."

III.

The defendant's characterization of the contingent fee contract as aleatory, Articles 1776, 2982, or as involving a revocable mandate by the client for the attorney to render legal services for him, Articles 2985, 3028, does not convert the attorney's property interest in the contract into a non-asset.

(a) *Aleatory contract*:

The attorney's interest is "contingent" in the sense that he will be compensated for his efforts and will receive a benefit under the contract only in the uncertain event that a favorable judgment or settlement is arrived at. To this extent, the contract is an aleatory one, in which the rights and obligations of the parties depend on the happening of an uncertain event and there is a chance of either gain or loss. Articles 1776, 2982. See: 6 Litvinoff, La. Civil Law Treatise, Obligations, sections 105, 108 (1969); Planiol cited above, Volume 2, sections 954-956.

However, the distinction between contracts which are certain, on the one hand, and aleatory contracts, on the other, has no significance with regard to whether the contract creates an obligation which may be a property right. The code definitions "only . . . signify that a contract which is certain is exactly the opposite of an aleatory one, meaning that it gives rise to obligations which are pure and simple, neither of which is subject to a condition." 6 Litvinoff, previously cited, p. 193.

(b) *Revocable mandate*:

As with any other contract for the services of an attorney a contingent fee contract, as the decisions cited by the defendant show, involves a mandate or agency by which the client empowers the attorney to act for him. Article 2985 et seq. The contingent fee contract is thus subject to the rules of mandate, including revocation at the will of the client-principal (Article 3028; see, e. g., Foster, Hall, Barret & Smith v. Haley, 174 La. 1019, 142 So. 251 (1932)), and expiration on the death of the attorney-agent (Article 3027, see, e. g., Succession of Zatarain, 138 So.2d 163 (La.App. 1st Cir. 1962), certiorari denied).

Nevertheless, where the relationship is terminated at the will of the client, the attorney may recover at least the value of his services performed prior to termination. See, e. g.: Smith v. Westside Transit Lines, 313 So.2d 371 (La.App. 4th Cir. 1975), writ denied 318 So.2d 43, Guilbeau v. Firemen's Fund Ins. Co., 293 So.2d 216 (La.App. 3d Cir. 1974); Wright v. Fontana, 290 So.2d 449 (La.App. 2nd Cir. 1974).

Likewise, where the attorney-client relationship is terminated as a result of the attorney's death, his heirs may recover for the value of his services prior thereto. See, e. g.: Succession of Payne, 155 La. 177, 99 So. 2 (1923); Pittman Construction Co. v. Housing Authority of New Orleans, 183 So.2d 343 (La.App. 4th Cir. 1966), certiorari denied 249 La. 376, 186 So.2d 627 (1969); Annotation, Attorney's Death Prior to Final Adjudication or Settlement of Case, As Affecting Compensation Under Contingent Fee Contract, 33 A.L.R.3d 1375 (1970). See also Oil Purchasers, Inc. v. Kuehling, 334 So.2d 420 (La.1976).

Accordingly, we find no merit to the defendant's argument that, somehow by reason of technical characterization, no economic value should be attributed to an attorneys interest in a contingent fee contract until the successful prosecution of the claim entitles him to actual compensation for his services.

IV.

Our code articles refer to the community's ownership of the "produce of the reciprocal industry and labor of both husband and wife", Article 2402, and of the property "acquired by the husband and wife during marriage", Article 2334. At the dissolution of the community, "all effects which both husband and wife reciprocally possess, are presumed common effects or gains, unless it be satisfactorily proved which of such effects they brought in marriage, or which have been given them separately, or which they have respectively inherited." Article 2405.

The intent, we believe, is that all property (in the broad sense of the word) is to form part of the community, if acquired during the marriage (with the narrow and non-applicable exceptions noted). Property, in its broad sense, denotes all patrimonial rights. 2 Yiannopoulos, Louisiana Civil Law Treatise, Property, Section 1 (1967). The civil law concept of patrimony includes the total mass of existing or potential rights and liabilities attached to a person for the satisfaction of his economic needs. Yiannopoulos, above cited, Section 77; Creech v. Capital Mack, Inc., 287 So.2d 497 (La.1973). In general, "[p]atrimonial rights are those susceptible of pecuniary evaluation, and which, for this reason, may form part of a person's patrimony." Yiannopolous, Louisiana Civil Law System, Section 70, p. 243 (1971).

An attorney's rights under a contingent contract, whatever their nature, clearly have pecuniary value. We have noted above that the attorney himself, or his heirs, have enforceable rights that arise even before final completion of an attorney's services. The valuation of these interests in pending contracts have arisen, for example, in suits by former law partners for a division of the assets following dissolution of the partnership. Trice v. Simon, 233 So.2d 609 (La.App. 3d Cir. 1970).

We therefore hold that the attorney's interest in pending contingent fee contracts constitutes a patrimonial asset which, if the contract is acquired during the marriage, forms part of the community insofar as its value is based upon the attorney's services performed during the marriage.

V.

Because of the limited scope of the issues before us at this time, we do not find it necessary to determine just when a wife may obtain her share of the interest of the community in her husband's contingent fee contract attributable to his services during the marriage. With the case in its present posture, it is sufficient to hold that she is entitled to obtain information sought by her interrogatories as to the existence of such contracts acquired during the marriage and as to indicia of their value, whether at the time of dissolution of the community, or (if the husband's services were thereafter completed, on the contract) as of the date of the inventory sought.

It is sufficient now to note that she is entitled to this information and to inclusion of these assets in an inventory of the community's property, whether, as the court of appeal held, her right to share in the community's share of the proceeds does not accrue until the fee is collected, cf. Messersmith v. Messersmith, 229 La. 495, 86 So.2d 169, 174-75 (1956), or whether, as suggested in oral argument, she is entitled to a present accounting in the partition of the community from her husband for her share of the estimated value of the community interest at the date of its dissolution. Aside from not wishing at this time to pass in the abstract upon a theoretical issue is to which an evidentiary basis has not yet been presented, an additional reason we avoid doing so is that the issue may not actually arise, should the parties agree to amicable partition and settlement in accordance with the principles noted.

As to an ancillary point, we should note that the court of appeal correctly held that any contingent fee contracts which are the property of the defendant's law partnership cannot be considered as assets of the community. The partnership is a separate entity. However, the husband's interest in the partnership is, to the extent acquired during the marriage, a community asset the value of which should be included in the inventory. Dubuisson v. Moseley, 232 So.2d 870 (La.App. 3d Cir. 1970).

C. Note

Other community property jurisdictions have reached similar results and have held that contingency fee contracts pending at the time of divorce are community property and are subject to division at divorce. *See e.g. In re Garrett v. Garrett*, 683 P.2d 1166 (Ariz. 1983); *In re Kilbourne*, 232 Cal.App.3d 1518, 284 Cal.Rptr. 201 (1991); *Waters v. Waters*, 170 P.2d 494 (Cal. Ct. App. 1946); and *In re Estes*, 929 P. 2d 500 (Wash. Ct. App. 1997).

Separate property jurisdictions employing the dual classification method of equitable distribution have faced similar challenges. Several separate property states have refused to hold that contingency fee contracts are marital assets. In *Goldstein v. Goldstein*, 414 S.E. 2d 474 (Ga. 1992), the Georgia Supreme Court explained:

> We agree with husband that contingent fee agreements are not marital assets. Although we held in *Courtney v. Courtney,* 256 Ga. 97, 344 S.E.2d 421 (1986) that an unvested pension plan represents important contractual rights that may be considered in making an equitable division of property, we have not held that all unvested rights are subject to equitable division. *Courtney* involved an unvested pension plan that would vest during the normal course of the husband's employment over the next few years. We found that the pension was far less speculative in nature than the possibility of an inheritance. *Id.* at 98-99, 344 S.E.2d 421, comparing *Meeks v. Kirkland,* 228 Ga. 607, 187 S.E.2d 296 (1972). It was clear that the pension would vest two years after the divorce and would yield a certain benefit. In contrast, it is impossible to know in advance whether any specific contingent fee case will ultimately yield a fee-or, if it does, how much the fee will be. It is also nearly impossible to gauge how much work and expense will be required after the date of the divorce to become entitled to collect a contingent fee. These qualities of contingent fee agreements make them too remote, speculative and uncertain to be considered marital assets in making an equitable division of property. Accord, *In re Marriage of Zells,* 197 Ill.App.3d 232, 143 Ill.Dec. 354, 554 N.E.2d 289 (1990).

D. *Elizabeth D. Michel v. Melvin M. Michel*

484 So. 2d 829 (La. App. 1st Cir. 1986)

COLE, Judge.

This is a suit to partition community property.

The parties were married on February 4, 1956. A judgment of separation, based on mutual fault of the parties, was rendered on January 13, 1981. The plaintiff, Elizabeth Dubus Michel, filed a petition seeking a partition of community property. After trial, ending August 1, 1983, the parties entered into a written stipulation as to certain issues. The remaining issues were presented for the trial court's adjudication. Judgment was rendered on December 28, 1983, with comprehensive written reasons. The defendant, Melvin M. Michel filed this appeal and the plaintiff answered raising several additional questions for review.

***

II.

CLASSIFICATION OF THE PARTIES' INCOME AFTER THE TERMINATION OF THE COMMUNITY

1. The writings of Mrs. Michel.

The trial court ordered:

> "MELVIN MICHEL is granted a twenty-five percent (25%) interest in the value or revenues which have been or may be realized from all literary works of ELIZABETH DUBUS MICHEL partially completed prior to the date of filing of separation...."

except,

> "MELVIN MICHEL is granted a five percent (5%) interest in the value and receipts from the novel known as *The Cajuns*."

Mr. Michel assigned as error the trial court's grant of less than a 50% interest in all of Mrs. Michel's works. As a basis he contends the works were community property at dissolution and Mrs. Michel has not established the value of this community property was enhanced by necessary efforts on Mrs. Michel's behalf after dissolution. In opposition Mrs. Michel contends all the works were simply "in progress" and had no community property value. Therefore, she seeks a finding that all the literary works partially completed are her separate property. In the alternative, Mrs. Michel argues if the literary works are community property, even in part, she is entitled to a reimbursement "for any additional time and expense she spends in completing, changing or promoting any and all such works."

We find by analogy the rule stated by the court in Due v. Due, 342 So.2d 161 (La. 1977):

> "...that the attorney's interest in pending contingent fee contracts constitutes a patrimonial asset which, if the contract is acquired during the marriage, forms part of the community insofar as its value is based upon the attorney's services performed during the marriage."--at 165, 166.

is applicable to the partition of the literary works of Mrs. Michel. Therefore, a writer's literary works constitute a patrimonial asset which forms a part of the community insofar as its value is based upon the writer's services performed during the existence of the community.

Since a determination of the precise services performed during the existence of the community is a question of fact this court must defer to the trial court's finding unless manifest error has been committed. The trial court found:

> "Under LSA-Civil Code Article 2338 community property comprises property acquired during the existence of the legal regime through the effort, skill, or industry of either spouse. There is no question but that much of the research and preliminary work on all of Mrs. Michel's writings took place before the termination of the community in September of 1980. However, publishing contracts for her two novels 'Cajun' and 'Marguerite Tanner' were not entered into by her with the publishers until March 31, 1981, and June 1, 1981, respectively. Mrs. Michel testified that in connection with Cajun, she had merely prepared a preliminary outline for a novel entitled 'Happy Land' during the summer of 1980, and that it was not until well after the termination of the community did she prepare the manuscript of Cajun which was a completely rewritten version of Happy Land.
>
> It would be impossible for the court to delineate (sic) what portion of the work product of the authoress in each of these writings took place before or after the termination of the community. Suffice it to say that some of her work and effort which served as a foundation for the completed works took place during the community and should enure in part to the community's benefit. The court, in an effort to make a reasonable assessment of her work product prior to the termination of the community which may be attributable to these writings, determines that, with the exception of the novel 'Cajun', the community should share in fifty per cent of whatever value or revenues which have or may be realized from all of the disputed writings. Therefore, Melvin Michel's ownership of twenty-five per cent of all of these works except for 'Cajun' is recognized. It appears that Mrs. Michel's investment in time and research in the novel 'Happy Land', the forbearer of Cajun, prior to the dissolution of the community was minimal and the court fixes the community's share in this novel at ten per cent. Accordingly, Melvin Michel's ownership in the value and receipts from this novel is fixed at five per cent."

This court in Deliberto v. Deliberto, 400 So.2d 1096 (La. App. 1st Cir. 1981), while considering the proper allocations of value between work done during the community's existence and then after dissolution held:

> "In determining the amount of enhancement, any reasonable method may be used, even, in difficult cases, to the extent of averaging the conflicting and exaggerated estimates of witnesses." --at 1101.

Based on these criteria the judgment of the trial court as to this aspect of the partition is amply supported by the record and will not be disturbed.

2. The "Factor 1" commission of Mr. Michel.

The trial court provided the factual background as to this aspect of the partition as follows:

> "Mr. Michel received $18,472.00 as a commission on commissions received by agents of Jefferson Standard Life Insurance Company from the period of October 1, 1980 through the date of his termination with Jefferson Standard on May of 1981. This commission was received by virtue of an arrangement described as 'Factor 1 category' which was in effect in his contract with Jefferson Standard at the time of the dissolution of his marriage with Mrs. Michel. Under this 'Factor 1' arrangement, Mr. Michel received commissions from the efforts of those sales agents he had recruited and trained for the company."

Further, the trial court found:

> "Mr. Michel had no vested interest in these commissions of salesman he recruited, but as long as he worked for Jefferson Standard 'Factor 1' it was merely a method for computing his compensation as Regional Agency Manager for Jefferson Standard. The court is of the opinion that Mrs. Michel is not entitled to a claim against these earnings."

However, the record establishes Mr. Michel completed the recruiting and training of the sales agents prior to the dissolution of the community. In addition, his contract of employment with Jefferson Standard was effective during the existence of the community and the contracts of the sales agents were entered into during the existence of the community. Therefore, it is the opinion of this court the Factor 1 commission, pursuant to the rationale expounded in Due, are community property. To hold otherwise would be inconsistent with the view of this court Mrs. Michel's partially completed writings are community property. Merely, because Mr. Michel had to continue working as an insurance agent for Jefferson Standard to obtain the Factor 1 commissions does not defeat their community nature. Mrs. Michel never has to publish her writings, but if she does and is compensated for such publication then the percentage attributable to the community must be allocated. We find Mrs. Michel is entitled to one-half of the $18,472 in Factor 1 commissions received by Mr. Michel, or $9,236.

3. The commissions on policy renewals received by Mr. Michel after termination of the community but on policies sold prior to the community termination.

Mrs. Michel in her answer to this appeal raised as error the finding of the trial court that only a 50% community interest existed as to Mr. Michel's renewal commissions on policies sold prior to dissolution of the community but renewed after the dissolution.

In *Boyle v. Boyle,* 459 So.2d 735 (La.App. 4th Cir.1984), writ denied, 462 So.2d 651 (La.1985), the court affirmed a trial court finding that renewals attributable to the period after the separation are separate property of the agent spouse. However, for the following reasons expressed by the trial court in this instance, we consider the community to be entitled to a 50% interest in the renewal commissions.

The trial court detailed:

> "The parties have agreed that the amount at issue is $2,600.00. Of this amount, $1,135.00 was received by Melvin Michel after September 23, 1980 as first year commissions on policies issued by Jefferson Standard and written by Melvin Michel prior to September 23, 1980. The remaining $1,461.00 was received after September 23, 1980 as a result of renewal commissions. Sale of the above policies were prior to dissolution of the community. Elizabeth Michel makes a claim to one-half of the commissions on the policies sold prior to the dissolution of the community.
>
> There is very little question but that as to the first year commissions received in the amount of $1,135.00, Mrs. Michel should share in one-half of the commissions or $567.00 since the sale of the policies were effected prior to the dissolution of the community and the commissions were merely collected following the termination of the community. In this situation, there remained nothing more to be done. The certainty of collection of the commissions was assured. Such was not the case in connection with the renewals which were obtained following the termination of the community. While it is true that the spade work had been done when the original sale had been made, some service work had to be performed and in addition there was no certainty that the policies would be renewed. The collection of these renewals was of a speculative nature. The court believes that a fair apportionment in this latter case is that the community's interest in the renewal commissions is recognized at 50% and consequently, Mrs. Michel's interest is calculated at $365.00."

We find this view to be consistent with the rationales employed to partition Mrs. Michel's literary works and the Factor 1 commissions of Mr. Michel. Therefore, we find this assignment of error to be without merit.

* * *

E. Note

In *Williams v. Williams*, 590 So.2d 649 (La. App. 3d Cir.1991), the court held that an ex-wife was not entitled to a share of the husband's renewal premium commissions even though based on labor during the community. It suggested that the right was not a community asset, apparently on the basis that it was not a vested right. And even if vested, the court said the value could not be determined. The second circuit agreed with the *Michel* approach in *Futch v. Futch*, 643 So.2d 364 (La. App. 2d Cir. 1994). It held that renewal commissions received after the termination of the community, but based on policies written during its existence, were community property stating, "Although it may be impossible to perfectly divide renewal commissions..., we disagree with *Williams*, *supra*, and conclude that these renewal commissions are community property subject to partition." *Id.* at 367.

In *Keller v. Schilling*, 593 So.2d 926 (La. App. 4th Cir. 1992), the court did not decide whether a tomb purchased with community funds and which contained the remains of the wife's family members was a community or a separate asset. The court did hold, however, "that the trial court erroneously charged against her portion of the community" the value of the tomb. The court reasoned that a "used" rather than a "new" tomb had no value, relying on evidence that "there is no market for tombs other than new ones."

Goins v. Goins, 580 So.2d 477 (La. App. 4th Cir. 1991), held that a car leased by the husband during the community was not a community asset. The lower court had included the car's value, $20,000, in the list of community assets and the court of appeal reversed. On that issue, the result is unassailable. Less clear, however, is the court's analysis of the classification of the lease rights.

In *Goins*, the husband leased the car three months before termination of the community. It was a four year lease with a monthly rental of $437 and an option to purchase for $7,600 at the end of the term. A penalty was to be paid if the lease were canceled. The court stated that at the time of termination, "no equity had built up in the vehicle," that the defendant chose to keep the car for his own use, and became responsible for the monthly rental fee at that point. The court does not explain, though, why the husband alone had this choice. If the lease was a contract right subject to his management, he could make that choice during the existence of the community. But that fact does not answer the classification/ownership issue or the partition issue. The contract right was acquired during the community with community funds and was thus a community asset. It should have been valued at termination, and then allocated to one or the other spouses under 9:2801, with the other spouse being entitled to half that value. It may well be true, as the court seems to assume, that the lease had no value at that time, but it should have at least inquired as to the present value of the option to buy the Saab at that price at the termination of the lease.

F. *Vicki Coudrain Lanza v. Louis Lanza*

898 So.2d 280 (La. 2005)

VICTORY, Judge.

The issues presented in these two consolidated writ applications are (1) whether a State Farm Agency is community property subject to partition and, if not, (2) whether an ex-spouse is entitled to any portion of renewal commissions or "service compensation" received by the insurance agent spouse after termination of the community on insurance policies written during the community. After reviewing the record and the applicable law, we affirm the judgment of the court of appeal and hold that the State Farm Agency is not community property subject to partition, but that the ex-spouse is entitled to the portion of renewal commissions received after termination of the community to the extent that these commissions were the result of effort, skill, or industry of the insurance agent spouse during the community.

FACTS AND PROCEDURAL HISTORY

Louis Lanza and Vicki Lanza, now Vicki Coudrain, were married on August 1, 1975. On January 23, 1981, Mr. Lanza signed an Agent's Acceptance of Agreement to become a State Farm agent pursuant to the terms and conditions set out in a document entitled "State Farm Agent's Agreement." Mr. Lanza then began operation of the Lou Lanza State Farm Agency (the "Agency"). A Petition for Divorce was filed on September 11, 1997, and a Consent Judgment of Divorce was entered into on August 12, 1998, based on the parties having lived apart for the requisite time period. Mr. Lanza has remained a State Farm agent after the divorce. The parties were unable to reach an agreement as to the partition of community property, particularly as to whether the Agency managed by Mr. Lanza or any benefits derived therefrom are community property subject to partition.

After a three-day trial, the trial court first found the Agency was "a non-entity" and therefore, "not a 'thing' which is subject to partition." The trial court then rendered judgment in favor of Mr. Lanza on March 7, 2003, with the decree "that the State Farm agency, including any income earned by Mr. Lanza after the filing of the Petition for Divorce, is not property subject to partition, nor is it community property to which [Ms. Coudrain] holds an ownership interest." The court of appeal affirmed the portion of the judgment that held that the Agency was a non-entity and not a "thing" under the La. Civil Code subject to partition, but reversed the judgment with respect to whether "any income earned by Mr. Lanza after the filing of the Petition of Divorce" is property subject to partition or community property to which Ms. Coudrain holds an ownership interest, finding that Ms. Coudrain is entitled "to at least a portion of the renewal commissions from polices written during the existence of the community property regime." *Lanza v. Lanza,* 03- 1382 (La.App. 4 Cir. 4/28/04), 874 So.2d 890. The case was remanded to determine the extent to which the renewal commissions are the result of Mr. Lanza's effort, skill, or industry during the existence of the community property regime. We granted Ms. Coudrain's writ application which assigns as error that the appellate court erred in affirming the trial court's determinations that the Agency is a non-entity and not a "thing" under the La. Civil Code subject to partition and that the Agency was not community property in which Ms. Coudrain had an ownership interest. *Lanza v. Lanza,* 04- 1314 (La.10/8/04), 883 So.2d 1025. We granted and consolidated Mr. Lanza's writ application which assigns as error that the appellate court erred in overruling the trial court's determination that Ms. Coudrain was not entitled to any income earned by Mr. Lanza after the filing of the Petition for Divorce. *Lanza v. Lanza,* 04-1756 (La.10/8/04), 883 So.2d 1024.

DISCUSSION

Is the Agency community property subject to partition?

Ms. Coudrain asserts two theories to support her position that the Agency is community property subject to partition. First, she argues that the lower courts erred in finding that the Agency was a "non-entity" and not a "thing" subject to partition because the proper inquiry is whether the Agency is "property," which she argues is anything that meets the definition of the "patrimony" of Mr. Lanza. Second, she argues that the Agency is a "community enterprise" under La. C.C. art. 2369.3, in which she is entitled to share in the co-owned income generated thereby.

Before an asset can be classified as community or separate, it must first be identified as "property." *Hare v. Hodgins,* 586 So.2d 118, 122 (La.1991). Ms. Coudrain argues that "property" comprises not just "things" but is defined in the broadest sense of the word as follows:

> the word property is used broadly to denote rights forming part of a person's patrimony, and narrowly rights conferring on a person a direct and immediate authority for the use and enjoyment of a thing that is susceptible of appropriation.

> Thus, leases, contractual or delictual causes of action, interests in pension plans, the rights to pursue employment and to conduct a business, and uncopyrighted designs are property in the broad sense. All real rights, such as ownership, personal servitudes, predial servitudes, and mineral servitudes, are property in the narrow sense.

2 A.N. Yiannaopoulos, *Louisiana Civil Law Treatise, Property,* § 1 (1967). In *Due v. Due,* this Court adopted this broad definition of "property" in the community property context, concluding that "property, in its broad sense, denotes all patrimonial rights" and that "the civil law concept of patrimony includes the total mass of existing or potential rights and liabilities attached to a person for the satisfaction of his economic needs." 342 So.2d 161, 165 (La.1977) (citing Yiannopoulos, *supra*). However, as explained by Professors Spaht and Hargrave, while "it appears that the assets to be shared should be those that are considered patrimonial assets in a broad sense," the dividing line is unclear and "[i]t also appears impossible to determine that a right is or is not patrimonial for all purposes." Katherine S. Spaht and W. Lee Hargrave, *16 Louisiana Law Treatise,* § 2.3, pp. 26-27. As a pertinent example, they explain that while some cases have referred to "one's ability to work and enjoy the fruits of his labor" as a patrimonial right, that is only patrimonial from a substantive due process standpoint. *Id.* The ability to work and enjoy wages would not be patrimonial in the sense that it would be included as a community asset because "it is implicit in the Civil Code's scheme that only wages earned during the community are community property." *Id.,* § 2.3, p. 27. Thus, whether an asset is "patrimonial" under the broad definition is not determinative, and the "decision to be made for a particular asset will be one that has to be determined in light of basic policies and problems related to how the asset functions and how it was produced." *Id.* In addition, Professor Spaht notes that while anything capable of pecuniary evaluation may be a patrimonial right, in order to be community property, "it must also be classified as community by the legislation ..." *Id.,* § 2.8, p. 39, n. 4.

Perhaps the broadest view of a patrimonial right found to be community property was taken in *Due, supra,* where this Court held that a lawyer husband's contingency fee contract acquired during the community "creates in the husband a patrimonial asset, i.e., (in ordinary language) 'property,' ... and which (to the extent that his labor and industry contribute during the marriage ...) is an asset of the community," even though the attorney's right to collect this fee was conditional and uncertain. Consequently, the Court held that the ex-wife was entitled to obtain information regarding the existence and value of these contracts acquired during the marriage and to the inclusion of these contracts in an inventory of community property. However, we specifically did not reach the issue of whether her right to share in the community's share of the proceeds accrued when and if the fee was collected or whether she was entitled to a present accounting in the partition of the estimated value at the date of dissolution, which is, in effect, the issue before us today.

In addressing the distinct issues involved in this case, multiple factors emerge which mitigate against classifying the Agency as a community asset subject to partition. First and foremost, pursuant to the agency agreement confected between Mr. Lanza and State Farm, Mr. Lanza has no ownership interest in the Agency. Neither the State Farm Agent's Agreement nor any interest thereunder can be sold, assigned or pledged by the State Farm agent. In addition, no right in any sum due or to become due to a State Farm agent can be sold, assigned or pledged absent prior written consent of State Farm. The agent owns no "book of business" which would become his upon termination of the Agency. In the event of the death, retirement, and/or termination of an agent, neither the agent nor his heirs receive service compensation for anything other than work performed up until the death, retirement or termination of the agent. All information provided to an agent during the course and scope of his term as a State Farm agent are trade secrets wholly owned by State Farm and are the sole and exclusive property of State Farm. All monies collected by the agent, with the exception of service compensation received from State Farm, are the absolute property of State Farm. Once an agent's relationship with State Farm ends, all clients, income, and information related to those clients are the property of State Farm. In the event an agent dies, retires, or is terminated, the entirety of the policies previously serviced by him would be transferred to another agent. The new agent would receive the service compensation for servicing those policies. The State Farm Agent Agreement can be terminated at will by either State Farm or the agent. At such time, any and all right to receive service compensation from State Farm ceases based on work performed to that date. State Farm furnishes agents with manuals, forms, records and such other materials and supplies as State Farm deems advisable to provide and all such property remains the property of State Farm. Finally, State Farm retains the ultimate authority to prescribe all policy forms and provisions, to set the amount and determine premiums, fees and charges, to determine the rules governing the policies, and governing the adjustment of payment of losses.

Considering the above factors, we find Mr. Lanza's rights under the State Farm Agency Agreement do not constitute property rights in the community property law context. Thus, we reject Ms. Coudrain's argument that the trial court erred in finding that the Agency was a non-entity and not a "thing" subject to partition as the Agency does not meet even the broader definition of "patrimony."

Ms. Coudrain next argues that the Agency is a "community enterprise" under La. C.C. art. 2369.3, in which she is entitled to share in the co-owned income generated thereby. La. C.C. art. 2369.3 provides:

> A spouse has a duty to preserve and to manage prudently former community property under his control, including a former community enterprise, in a manner consistent with the mode of use of that property immediately prior to termination of

> the community regime. He is answerable for any damage caused by his fault, default, or neglect.
>
> A community enterprise is a business that is not a legal entity.

Ms. Coudrain contends that the Agency is a "business that is not a legal entity," and as such is a "community enterprise" under La. C.C. art. 2369.3. Ms. Coudrain reasons that the legislature would not have imposed "a duty to preserve and to manage prudently former community property under his control, including a former community enterprise ..." if community enterprises, i.e., businesses that are not legal entities, were not community property.

However, this Civil Code article's expansive definition of a community enterprise to include a business that is not a legal entity cannot be interpreted to circumvent the traditional definition of property under the Louisiana Civil Code. The community enterprise must still qualify as "property" under Louisiana's community property laws. We note that Ms. Coudrain does not make a claim for partition of the community enterprise good will, nor does she assert a claim for the Agency's office furnishings, fixtures, or equipment. She does not argue that the agency constituted a partnership or joint venture. Although Ms. Coudrain's expert valued the Louis Lanza Agency as a sole proprietorship, it is not a sole proprietorship, as Mr. Lanza's rights under the Agency Agreement are not commensurate with those of a sole proprietor. Instead, Ms. Coudrain argues that Mr. Lanza is an independent contractor for State Farm and that she is entitled to the stream of income produced. Indeed, the State Farm website clearly states that its agents are "independent contractor agents," which it defines as "self-employed, eligible for benefit coverage at the expense of the agent, and are paid commissions and service compensation from the products and services sold." While Mr. Lanza may be an independent contractor, based on the factors discussed above, his rights as an independent contractor do not constitute property for community property purposes.

Thus, we find that the lower courts were not manifestly erroneous in holding that the Agency is not community property subject to partition. In fact, to partition this agency as community property and thereby give Ms. Coudrain ownership rights in this agency would give Ms. Coudrain more rights in the Agency than Mr. Lanza can ever have. Ms. Coudrain's expert valued this "business" at $2,335,389.00 as of the trial date under a capitalization of earnings approach and at $2,795,063.00 using a discounted future earnings approach based on the Agency's stream of income. Ms. Coudrain seeks a judgment partitioning this asset, which would in effect require Mr. Lanza to pay her at least $1,000,000, representing half the value of the Agency. However, the inequity in this is clear, because if the Agency were permitted to be valued in a theoretical fashion and then partitioned, Ms. Coudrain would be paid in advance for an asset which does not belong to Mr. Lanza, and which cannot be realized by a sale or another method of liquidating value.

Are any portion of the renewal commissions or "service compensation" received by Mr. Lanza after termination of the community on insurance policies written during the marriage community property?

Ms. Coudrain argues that, if the Agency itself is not community property subject to partition, she is at least entitled to a portion of the income earned by Mr. Lanza after termination of the community under this Court's holding in *Ross v. Ross,* 02-2984 (La.10/21/03), 857 So.2d 384. She argues that *Ross* stands for the proposition that the policies are "things" capable of producing "fruits," i.e., the renewal commissions, and she and Mr. Lanza are co-owners of these fruits under La. C.C. arts. 2369.1 and 2369.2. Pursuant to these articles, Ms. Coudrain claims that the amount of labor expended by Mr. Lanza before and after termination of the community is irrelevant as they share equally these fruits. Mr. Lanza argues that the "service compensation" he received after termination of the community was based solely on post-community effort, skill and industry and is thus his separate property. Ms. Coudrain counters that even if the division of labor is germane to this issue, Mr. Lanza's argument that he expended no community labor to generate these renewal commissions is erroneous. In *Ross,* this Court recently addressed the rights of an ex-spouse of a State Farm insurance agent to renewal commissions or service compensation; however, in that case, the issue involved renewal commissions paid during the marriage on insurance policies sold prior to the marriage. *Ross v. Ross, supra.* The Court framed the issue before it as "whether the renewal commissions received by Mr. Ross during the community property regime on insurance policies written before the existence of the community are the result of labor, skill or industry, and are, thus, community property or whether, on the other hand, the renewal commissions are the 'civil fruit' of some asset acquired by Mr. Ross prior to the existence of the community, such that they are subject to his declaration of paraphernality." *Id.* at 387. Mr. Ross's ex-spouse argued that neither the insurance policies nor the State Farm Agency contract constituted "things" or "assets" in which Mr. Ross had an ownership interest and from which fruits may be derived.

After a lengthy discussion, *Ross* held that the insurance policies were "juridical acts" from which civil fruits (the renewal commissions) can be derived. Having found that the "insurance policies are 'things' from which civil fruits *may be derived,*" the Court set out to determine whether the renewal commissions "were in fact 'civil fruits' of Mr. Ross' separate property, and not the result of Mr. Ross' effort, skill, or industry during the existence of the community property regime," i.e., whether they were fruits or earnings. *Id.* at 392 (emphasis added). The Court noted that "if the renewal commissions are the result of Mr. Ross' effort, skill or industry during the existence of the community property regime, the renewal commissions, or at least a portion thereof, are community property ... in keeping with the basic notion that spouses should share equally 'the produce of reciprocal labor and industry of both husband and wife.' " *Id.*

In determining whether the commissions were fruits or earnings, the Court looked to several appellate cases that have considered whether renewal commissions paid after termination of the community on policies issued during the community were community property. In these cases, the First, Second, and Fourth Circuits have held that this revenue resulted from labor during and after the community, and was to be divided proportionately. *See Michel v. Michel,* 484 So.2d 829 (La.App. 1 Cir.1986) (affirming the trial court's one-half to one-half division of the revenues as an approximation of the proportionate division and holding that "[w]hile it is true that the spade work had been done when the original sale had been made, some service work had to be performed and in addition there was no certainty that the policies would be renewed"); *Futch v. Futch,* 26-149 (La.App. 2 Cir. 9/23/94), 643 So.2d 364 (holding that the renewal commissions are community property subject to partition and remanding case to determine the extent of work performed after termination on keeping the policies in force, placing the burden of proof on the husband to establish his entitlement to more than one-half of the renewal commissions); *Boyle v. Boyle,* 459 So.2d 735 (La.App. 4 Cir.1984), *writ denied,* 462 So.2d 651 (La.1985) (awarding wife one-half of the renewal commissions on policies written before termination of the community). In the only case to hold otherwise, the Third Circuit in *Williams v. Williams,* 590 So.2d 649 (La.App. 3 Cir.1991), held that renewal commissions, or "service commission," paid on State Farm policies issued during the marriage were not community property because even if the renewal premiums were attributed to work during and after the community, the value to the community was so speculative that it had no value at all. In *Ross,* we expressed our agreement with commentators who have opined that the "[e]quitable considerations as well as basic doctrinal principles support the *Michel-Boyle-Futch* approach, even if the division is approximate." 857 So.2d at 395 (citing *Matrimonial Regimes, Louisiana Civil Law Treatise,* § 3.4 at p. 58 (1997)). After holding that "[b]ecause the renewal commissions were received during the existence of the community, the burden was upon Mr. Ross to prove that they were not community property," the Court found that the "renewal commissions received by Mr. Ross during the existence of the community property regime were the result of Mr. Ross' effort, skill and industry exerted during the community regime." *Id.* Accordingly, the Court held that "Ms. Starks is entitled to share in the business income generated by Mr. Ross' work, industry and effort during the marriage." *Id.* at 397-398.

In this case, the court of appeal interpreted *Ross* as holding that renewal commissions were civil fruits, and that, therefore, Ms. Lanza was entitled to a portion thereof. 874 So.2d at 892. Specifically, the court of appeal held that "the *Ross* Court determined that the renewal of a pre-existing State Farm insurance policy constitutes a juridical act and, thus, a thing under La. Civ.Code art. 551 from which civil fruits may be derived and that 'if the renewal commissions are the result of the State Farm agent's effort, skill, or industry during the existence of the community property regime, the renewal commissions, or at least a portion thereof, are community property.'" *Id.* Further, after rejecting Mr. Lanza's argument that he received only service compensation, and thus salary from State Farm, and not renewal commissions, because *Ross* "reject[ed] the contention that renewal commissions could be deemed salary," the court held that "to the extent that the standard State Farm contract may be interpreted to circumvent basic concepts of Louisiana property law and the rights of spouses with regard to fruits under the Louisiana community property regime, it is against public policy and, therefore, unenforceable." *Id.* at 892-93.

Upon review, we affirm the judgment of the court of appeal, but for different reasons. In *Ross,* we did not hold that the insurance policies produced civil fruits, or that the renewal commissions were fruits. The holding in *Ross* left open the argument that these commissions are civil fruits, in whole or in part, of the contractual right acquired by the spouse-agent to the payment of these commission in accordance with the State Farm Agent's Agreement. *See* Spaht and Richard D. Moreno, *16 Louisiana Civil Law Treatise,* § 3.8, p. 22 (2004 Pocket Part). Further, while a determination of whether the commissions were fruits may have been relevant in *Ross* regarding the husband's declaration of paraphernality, it is not the determinative issue here, and it was not the determinative issue there, as *Ross* ultimately held that the renewal commissions were the product, in part, of the effort, skill, and industry of the husband exerted during the marriage, and were therefore community property. *See Ross, supra,* (Knoll, concurring and stating that the majority took an erroneous, and unnecessary circuitous, route to reach its result) *see also* Spaht and Moreno, *supra* at § 3.3, p. 13-14 (2004 Pocket Part) (characterizing the Court's discussion of whether the insurance policies are juridical acts from which civil fruits can be derived as "dicta" given the Court's ultimate holding that the renewal commissions were in fact the product, in part, of the labor, effort and skill or the husband exerted during the marriage).

We ultimately find that the legal issue in this case is a straightforward one, although the resulting factual issues resulting therefrom may not be. The Civil Code defines community property as follows:

> The community property comprises: property acquired during the existence of the legal regime through the effort, skill, or industry of either spouse; and all other property not classified by law as separate.

La. C.C. art. 2338. As explained in *Ross:*

> Wages are the premier community asset. It is wages paid in return for work done during the existence of the community that are included, regardless of when the payment is actually made. The "property acquired," in the language of Louisiana Civil Code Article 2338, is a right to payment at some point for the work done. If payment is made during the community for work done before its commencement, the money is separate. If the check is cut after termination, but is for work done during the community, the funds are community.

Ross, supra at 390 (citing Spaht and Hargrave, *supra,* § 3.3, p. 48). As stated above, in *Ross,* we held that renewal commissions paid pursuant to State Farm Agency contracts are community property, in whole or in part, depending on the extent they were earned as a result of the agent-spouse's effort, skill, or industry during the existence of the community property regime. As Justice Knoll explained in her concurrence in *Ross,* the issue before the court in *Ross* was the same issue that was before the courts in *Michel, Williams, and Futch,* [and consequently, this case], "i.e., whether renewal commissions are classified as community or separate when the initial policies were sold during one regime and the renewal commissions were earned in another." *Ross, supra* at 399-400 (Knoll, J., concurring) "The only difference is that in *Michel, Williams, and Futch,* [and this case], the policies were sold during the community and the renewal commissions were paid after its termination whereas, in [*Ross*], the situation is the complete opposite." *Ross, supra* at 400 (Knoll, J., concurring).

Indeed, we agree that the same principles that determined the outcome in *Ross* are determinative here. Pursuant to Article 2338, community property comprises "property acquired during the existence of the legal regime through the effort, skill, or industry of either spouse," and this includes the right to the payment of any compensation for work done during the community. Therefore, to the extent that Mr. Lanza has received compensation after the community regime for work performed during the community, this compensation is community property.

Regarding the applicable burden of proof, in *Ross,* this Court held that, because the renewal commissions were received during the existence of the community, the burden of proof was on the husband to prove that the commissions were not community. *Ross, supra* at 396. This is because property which comes into the possession of a spouse during the community regime is presumed to be community, regardless of the source. La. C.C. art. 2340; *Talbot v. Talbot,* 03-0814 (La.12/12/03), 864 So.2d 590, 597.

However, in this case, there is no presumption of community as to these renewal commissions because the income at issue did not come into Mr. Lanza's possession during the community regime. La. C.C. art. 2340. While Ms. Coudrain's argument that a portion of this income was for work done during the existence of the community and thus constitutes "property acquired" during the community under La. C.C. art. 2338, the presumption of community found in La. C.C. art. 2340 applies only to "[t]hings in the possession of a spouse during the existence of community of acquets and gains ..." Therefore, Ms. Coundrain will have the burden of proving, by a preponderance of the evidence, which portion Mr. Lanza's post-community income resulted from policies initially issued during the community, and of those policies, how much of the resulting service compensation was due to Mr. Lanza's effort, skill, or industry exerted during the community. We recognize that the trial court issued its judgment, after a trial on the merits, without the guidance of *Ross,* which was decided shortly thereafter. Therefore, in the interest of justice, on remand, the trial judge should receive and consider additional evidence relevant to whether any portion of Mr. Lanza's post-community income resulted from his effort, skill, and industry during the community.

CONCLUSION

In this case, because of the agency agreement confected between Mr. Lanza and State Farm, the Agency is not community property subject to partition because it does not constitute "property" under our community property laws. However, Ms. Coudrain is entitled to any portion of renewal commissions or "service compensation" received by Mr. Lanza after termination of the community on insurance policies written during the community that is due to Mr. Lanza's effort, skill, or industry during the community under La. C.C. art. 2338.

DECREE

For the reasons stated herein, the judgment of the court of appeal is affirmed and the matter is remanded to the trial court for further proceedings in accordance with this opinion.

AFFIRMED; REMANDED.

G. Questions

Consider whether the following claims or assets constitute property that is subject to the community property regime.

1. Accrued sick leave or vacation time. Would it matter whether the employee spouse had the right to receive money in lieu of using the vacation time or sick leave? *See e.g.* Arnold v. Arnold, 77 P.3d 285 (N.M. Ct. App. 2003); Preiss v. Preiss, 617 N.W. 2d 514 (Wis. 2000); and *In re* Lorenz, 146 Cal. App. 3d 464 (1985).

2. Benefits earned through a credit card program such as frequent flier miles, points, rewards, or cash back. *See e.g. In re* C.A.S. and D.P.S., 405 S.W. 3d 373 (Tex. App. 2013).

3. A membership to a gym, country club, or other organization. Would it matter whether or not the membership could be freely purchased by any member of the public? Would it matter whether the membership was provided by an employer as a fringe benefit?

2.3 CAREER ASSETS: PROFESSIONAL DEGREES AND LICENSES

A. Introduction

Career assets, such as professional degrees and licenses present an interesting problem. Nationally, most common law and community property jurisdictions agree that degrees and licenses are not property and, therefore, are not subject to division at divorce. Degrees and licenses lack many of the fundamental attributes of property under both a common law and civil law analysis. In one of the early cases examining the issue, the Colorado Supreme Court explained as follows:

> An educational degree, such as an M.B.A., is simply not encompassed even by the broad views of the concept of "property." It does not have an exchange value or any objective transferable value on an open market. It is personal to the holder. It terminates on death of the holder and is not inheritable. It cannot be assigned, sold, transferred, conveyed, or pledged. An advanced degree is a cumulative product of many years of previous education, combined with diligence and hard work. It may not be acquired by the mere expenditure of money. It is simply an intellectual achievement that may potentially assist in the future acquisition of property. In our view, it has none of the attributes of property in the usual sense of that term.[4]

However, many jurisdictions have also recognized that there is some inequity in this approach. In a later decision, the Colorado Supreme Court explained the inequity:

> We granted certiorari to reconsider our decision in *Graham v. Graham*, 194 Colo. 429, 574 P.2d 75 (1978), which held that an educational degree is not marital property. This reconsideration is based upon the recognition of the harsh and often unfair outcome in a dissolution proceeding where one spouse has postponed his or her own career and educational goals to support and contribute to the career and educational goals of the other spouse. The pursuit of advanced educational degrees and professional training often results in a deferral of earning capacity by the spouse who receives that educational degree or advanced training at the expense of the current standard of living of the couple. When a couple collectively works towards the attainment of an advanced educational degree or career goal, there is an expectation of a higher standard of living in the future. If a dissolution of the marriage occurs just as the graduate degree is attained, or the career goal achieved, or just subsequent to the attainment of the goal, the spouse that contributed to and

---

[4] *In re* Graham, 574 P.2d 75 (Colo. 1978) (*en banc*).

> supported the other spouse has his or her expectations of the higher standard of living frustrated, and as a result of the collective sacrifice and deferment of acquiring other possessions, is left in a position where there is little marital property to divide. The contributions to the other spouse's education or career goals are often made at the expense of the supporting spouse's own education or career goal. The supporting spouse is left without the resources to recover from the years of deferring the acquisition of property and security.[5]

Nationally, states have created several mechanisms for addressing this inequity. Courts in at least two states—New York[6] and Michigan[7]--have simply held that career assets are property and ought to be considered in dividing the marital assets. In the majority of jurisdictions, where career assets are not considered property, courts find other bases of relief. A number of equitable division jurisdictions have considered one spouse's contribution to the other spouse's education as a basis for making an unequal division of property at divorce. Where marital assets are inadequate to make such a division, some courts have used alimony or spousal support to compensate the injured spouse. Finally, some states have enacted specific statutes authorizing awards to the injured spouse. California and Louisiana—both equal division jurisdictions—have taken this approach. The California and Louisiana statutes are essentially statutory authorizations of equitable distribution in certain factual situations.

B. Louisiana Approach: Claim for Contributions to Education or Training

The Louisiana Civil Code articles allowing a claim for contributions to the education or training of a spouse follow.

Art. 121. Claim for contributions to education or training; authority of court

> In a proceeding for divorce or thereafter, the court may award a party a sum for his financial contributions made during the marriage to education or training of his spouse that increased the spouse's earning power, to the extent that the claimant did not benefit during the marriage from the increased earning power.
>
> The sum awarded may be in addition to a sum for support and to property received in the partition of community property.

REVISION COMMENTS--1990

(a) The articles of this Section are based on Civil Code Article 161 as enacted

[5] *In re* Olar, 747 P.2d 676 (Colo. 1987) (*en banc*).
[6] *See* O'Brien v. O'Brien, 489 N.E. 2d 712 (N.Y. 1985).
[7] Postema v. Postema, 471 N.W. 2d 912 (Mich. 1991).

by Act 780 of 1986.

(b) This Article restates the basic elements of the cause of action created by the 1986 act, including the discretionary character of the remedy. This cause of action is not based upon classification of an education or training as community property, nor is the claim subject to the same factors as spousal support.

(c) Under this Article the court is empowered to compensate a divorcing or former spouse for financial contributions made during the marriage to the education, training, or increased earning power of the other spouse. The court may do so by making a special monetary award, over and above those authorized by the preceding section of this Chapter, to the spouse who made the contributions. In making such an award the court should keep in mind that the relevant equitable considerations weigh most heavily in favor of the contributing spouse in cases where the timing of the divorce prevents him from realizing benefits from the contributions during the marriage. The usual situation that has prompted the making of awards of this kind in other states has involved a wife who supported her husband through professional school, only to be divorced by him shortly after his graduation. E.g., In re Marriage of Washburn, 677 P.2d 152 (Wash.1984); Lundberg v. Lundberg, 318 N.W.2d 918 (Wisc.1982). Usually the wife has had little opportunity to share in the husband's enhanced income, and ordinarily little or no community property has accumulated to be divided between them. Thus, the only way to compensate her is by means of a monetary award akin to support, but different from support in that it is not affected by the various factors that govern such an award. See Haugan v. Haugan, 343 N.W.2d 796 (Wisc.1984) (holding that trial court should have awarded wife compensation for her contributions to support of husband while he was in medical school). In particular, fault on the part of either spouse that contributed to the breakdown of the marriage is not relevant to a claim under this Article.

(d) “Financial contributions” include direct educational or training expenses paid by the claimant for the other spouse--such as tuition, books, and school fees. The term also includes financial contributions made to satisfy the living expenses of the supported spouse. For examples of how the figure that represents the supporting spouse's financial contributions can be calculated, see DeLaRosa v. DeLaRosa, 309 N.W.2d 755 (Minn.1981), and Reiss v. Reiss, 195 N.J.Super. 150, 478 A.2d 441 (Ch.Ct.1984).

(e) The limitation on awards under this Article expressed in the phrase “to the extent that the claimant did not benefit during the marriage ...” reflects the basic equitable consideration underlying this section. See comment (c) above. A spouse who contributed financially to the education or training of the other spouse in a marriage of significant duration may have already benefitted during the existence of the marriage by an improved standard of living or an accumulation of community property.

(f) This Article rejects the approach of treating the degree, trade, or license acquired by the supported spouse as marital property subject to distribution. The only Louisiana appellate court that has been presented with this issue has avoided it. Harmon v. Harmon, 486 So.2d 277 (La.App. 3d Cir.1986), writ denied, 489 So.2d 916 (La.1986) (holding that the question whether a wife had "a cause of action to partition a professional medical education" was moot because previously settled, indirectly, by agreement of the parties). Such claims have also not received widespread approval in other states. See Mahoney v. Mahoney, 182 N.J.Super. 598, 442 A.2d 1062 (N.J.Super.App.Div.1982). The second paragraph of this Article is intended to make clear that the contemplated award is not spousal support or a disposition of community property.

(g) Under the terms of this Article a spouse may assert a claim under this Section only after an action to dissolve his marriage has been filed. He may do so for three years after the resulting divorce judgment is signed. See Article 124, *infra.*

Art. 122. Nature of action

The claim for contributions made to the education or training of a spouse is strictly personal to each party.

REVISION COMMENTS--1990

(a) This Article is new. It was not included in former Civil Code Article 161, enacted by Act 780 of 1986. It clarifies the law.

(b) Under this Article and Civil Code Articles 1765 and 1766, the obligation recognized by this Section is neither transferable nor heritable prior to being reduced to judgment. Under this Article and Code of Civil Procedure Article 428, a pending action under this Section abates when either spouse dies.

Art. 123. Form of award; effect of remarriage or death

The sum awarded for contributions made to the education or training of a spouse may be a sum certain payable in installments.

The award shall not terminate upon the remarriage or death of either party.

REVISION COMMENTS--1990

(a) This Article is new. It was not included in former Civil Code Article 161 as enacted by Act 780 of 1986. It clarifies the law.

(b) This Article, drawing upon the spousal support example, makes available a special kind of money judgment that is likely to be used often in this context. This Section contemplates an award that will tend to be greater the earlier it is made in the defendant's career, because of the importance of the "realized benefit" factor discussed in comments (c) and (e) to Article 121, *supra*. Thus, a mechanism is needed whereby the award can be structured so as to shift some of its cost from the judgment debtor's early working years to his later, more productive ones. This Article provides that mechanism. Cf. R.S. 9:2801(3)(c).

(c) The periodic award made available by this Article is intended to be merely an alternative to the type of lump-sum money judgment normally awarded in other kinds of cases. A judgment under this Article is still a money judgment for a specified sum, not an open-ended award. Thus a judgment under this Article is similar to a spousal support award in only two ways: (1) It is payable periodically; and (2) it may be enforced by an action to make past-due installments executory under Code of Civil Procedure Article 3945 (rev. 1990). It is not, like a spousal support award, modifiable in light of changed circumstances, and under the second sentence of this Article it is not terminated by the death or remarriage of either party.

Art. 124. Prescription of spousal claim for contributions

The action for contributions made to the education or training of a spouse prescribes in three years from the date of the signing of the judgment of divorce or declaration of nullity of the marriage.

C. *Beverly D. Nugent Shewbridge v. Anthol William Shewbridge*

720 So. 2d 780 (La. App. 2d Cir. 1998)

GASKINS, Judge.

Anthol William Shewbridge, Jr., appeals from a trial court judgment awarding his former wife, Beverly D. Nugent Shewbridge, the sum of $15,314.30 for contributions she made to his education and training during their marriage. We amend the judgment and, as amended, affirm.

FACTS

The parties were married in December 1987. Prior to their marriage, Mr. Shewbridge was a student at Northwestern State University (NSU) studying in the area of aviation science. He was not employed. His father, Dr. Anthol Shewbridge, supported him providing money for education and living expenses. Once married, Mr. Shewbridge continued his studies at NSU, and Mrs. Shewbridge worked. Dr. Shewbridge continued to provide monthly financial support to his son. The financial support provided by Dr. Shewbridge ended in August 1992 after Mr. Shewbridge received his commercial pilot's license and moved with his wife to Harper's Ferry, West Virginia. The couple separated in 1993.

During their divorce proceedings, Mrs. Shewbridge asserted a claim under La. C.C. art. 121 for her contributions to her husband's education and training. At the hearing on this claim, Mrs. Shewbridge testified about her employment during the time her husband studied at NSU; she stated that at one point she worked two jobs. She testified that her work and Mr. Shewbridge's studies took away from their time together and their social life. Mrs. Shewbridge, who was working toward a nursing degree at the time of their marriage, explained that she and her husband reached an agreement whereby she would work while he attended school, and then when they moved to West Virginia he would support her while she enrolled in school to complete her nursing degree. She testified that she expected to benefit from this arrangement in the future when they would have a higher standard of living.

With regard to their financial situation during the marriage, Mrs. Shewbridge testified that they had difficulty making ends meet and that they lived "from paycheck to paycheck." She stated that she was only aware of $500 per month sent by Dr. Shewbridge to supplement their income and denied knowing about other amounts sent by Dr. Shewbridge. Her testimony indicated that payments for rent, groceries, tuition, and books came out of their joint account, that the money sent by Dr. Shewbridge was used on education expenses but that the amount was not sufficient, and that her income was used for all of her husband's living expenses. She also testified that the total cost of Mr. Shewbridge's education was $26,000 and that another $5,000 to $6,000 was spent to purchase tools needed for his training. She stated that the only income reported on their tax returns from 1988 to 1992 was her income. She further testified that Mr. Shewbridge did not work while attending NSU.

Mr. Shewbridge denied that any agreement existed whereby his wife agreed to put him through school. He further denied that she ever paid for his tuition or books, and he testified that she did not pay for all living expenses, such as rent and groceries. He stated that his father sent money for his education and living expenses both prior to and during the marriage. He also maintained that their financial circumstances were sufficiently comfortable to allow the couple to take weekend trips and purchase both a new car and antiques.

Mr. Shewbridge introduced several exhibits into evidence, including a financial compilation of the monies provided by his father and earned by Mrs. Shewbridge. He verified that all income reported on their tax returns for the years 1988 through 1992 was earned by his wife. However, he also testified that he worked thirty to forty hours per week for approximately thirty-two to thirty-six months earning five dollars per hour, paid in cash, as part of his educational program. However, none of this income was reported for tax purposes. With regard to the money provided by Dr. Shewbridge, he testified that his father never asked to be paid back and that his father supported his sister through school in the same way. Mr. Shewbridge further testified that his wife was aware of the money sent by his father on a monthly basis.

Dr. Shewbridge testified that he paid his son money for his education and living expenses while he was in school and that he did the same for his daughter. The payments began in 1985 and ended in August 1992. A copy of a log kept by Dr. Shewbridge of the money he paid to his son was introduced into evidence, along with copies of canceled checks. Dr. Shewbridge testified that he supported his son, as needed, both before and during the marriage. He stated that he gave the money to Mr. Shewbridge to do as he pleased with it and that he had never considered or asked to have the money paid back.

The trial court accepted the facts as recited in Mrs. Shewbridge's post-trial memorandum and ruled in her favor in accordance with the proposal in that memorandum. The proposed amount was determined using the formula set forth in *McConathy v. McConathy*, 25,542 (La.App.2d Cir.2/23/94), 632 So.2d 1200, writ denied, 94-0750 (La.5/6/94), 637 So.2d 1052. The amount of contributions attributed to Mrs. Shewbridge was $59,934; the amount of contributions attributed to her husband was $58,305; and the cost of education was set at $29,000. The amount granted by the trial court was $15,314.30. The trial court also awarded Mrs. Shewbridge legal interest from the date of judicial demand. From this judgment, Mr. Shewbridge appeals.

CONTRIBUTIONS TO SPOUSE'S EDUCATION OR TRAINING

Mr. Shewbridge generally complains of a lack of evidentiary support for the award. He asserts that there was no evidence--other than Mrs. Shewbridge's own self-serving testimony--of the amount of educational and living expenses she paid, of the sacrifices she made or the detriment she suffered in contributing to his education, and of her failure to realize any benefits from his education.

La. C.C. art. 121 provides:

In a proceeding for divorce or thereafter, the court may award a party a sum for his financial contributions made during the marriage to education or training of his spouse that increased the spouse's earning power, to the extent that the claimant did not benefit during the marriage from the increased earning power.

The sum awarded may be in addition to a sum for support and to property received in the partition of community property.

Comment (d) of Article 121 explains that "financial contributions" includes both direct educational or training expenses paid by the claimant, as well as living expenses. This award is discretionary. Factors that should be considered include: (1) the claimant's expectation of shared benefit when the contributions were made; (2) the degree of detriment suffered by the claimant in making the contributions; and (3) the magnitude of the benefit received by the other spouse. *Barrow v. Barrow*, 27,714 (La.App.2d Cir. 2/28/96), 669 So.2d 622, writs denied, 96-1057 and 96-1072 (La.6/21/96), 675 So.2d 1080.

In *McConathy v. McConathy, supra*, we adopted a formula from *DeLa Rosa v. DeLa Rosa*, 309 N.W.2d 755 (Minn.1981), for calculating an award under La. C.C. art. 121. Under this formula, an equitable award is determined as follows:

working spouse's financial contributions to joint living expenses and educational costs of student spouse

less

(working spouse's financial contributions plus student spouse's financial contributions less cost of education)

equals

equitable award to working spouse.

McConathy v. McConathy, 632 So.2d at 1205.

It is well settled that an appellate court may not set aside a trial court's factual findings in the absence of manifest error or unless the findings are clearly wrong. *Stobart v. State, through Department of Transportation and Development*, 617 So.2d 880 (La.1993). Even where an appellate court may feel that its own evaluations are more reasonable than those of the fact finder's, any reasonable determinations of fact should not be disturbed. *Arceneaux v. Domingue*, 365 So.2d 1330 (La.1978). This deference to the trial court's factual findings is based upon its opportunity to evaluate live witnesses and the distinction between the functions of the trial and appellate courts.

Stobart, supra. Where there are two permissible views of the evidence, the fact finder's choice cannot be manifestly erroneous or clearly wrong. *Rosell v. ESCO*, 549 So.2d 840 (La.1989).

Our review of the record reveals adequate support for the trial court's judgment. The testimony and evidence demonstrated that Mrs. Shewbridge worked during the marriage while her husband attended school. The income earned by Mrs. Shewbridge and at least some of the funds sent to Mr. Shewbridge by his father were placed into a joint account from which living expenses and some educational expenses were paid. It is clear that Mrs. Shewbridge provided support for Mr. Shewbridge while he attended school. While Mr. Shewbridge argues that the evidence does not show what expenses were paid by Mrs. Shewbridge, the evidence also does not show, contrary to his assertion, what particular expenses were paid by funds provided by Dr. Shewbridge. Furthermore, there is no indication in the record that the cash money allegedly made by Mr. Shewbridge was ever used for either educational or living expenses.

Mr. Shewbridge also asserts that there is no showing of any detriment or sacrifice suffered by Mrs. Shewbridge while contributing to his education. He points out that they purchased a car and antiques while married and took weekend trips. However, as previously noted, Mrs. Shewbridge explained in her testimony that most of the antiques were purchased after they moved to West Virginia and while they lived with Mr. Shewbridge's parents; also, most were purchased on layaway plans. She further clarified that the vehicle cost $8,000 and that she paid cash for it after working two jobs and receiving a tax refund. The record indicates that the couple's income during the period Mr. Shewbridge attended school was not substantial and that their income was provided by Mrs. Shewbridge. The fact that Mrs. Shewbridge worked and contributed to expenses while her husband attended school is sufficient to satisfy the requirement of La. C.C. art. 121 in this case.

Mr. Shewbridge also asserts that there is no showing of any benefit lost by Mrs. Shewbridge because his income in 1993, as reported in the financial compilation submitted into evidence, was only $14,338.65. This argument overlooks the purpose of La. C.C. art. 121 which is to compensate the working spouse for contributions which helped to increase the earning power of the other spouse when the working spouse will not benefit from the increased earning power during the marriage. The focus of this article is on increased earning power and not increased earnings. Mr. Shewbridge's earnings will likely rise and Mrs. Shewbridge will not benefit from the increase. Thus, she is entitled to compensation for the contributions she made which enabled him to increase his earning power during their marriage. We therefore find that Mrs. Shewbridge is entitled to a monetary award as provided in La. C.C. art. 121.

Our review of the record indicates that the calculation of the award, which was provided by Mrs. Shewbridge and adopted by the trial court, requires minor adjustment.

Mr. Shewbridge does not challenge the figure used for Mrs. Shewbridge's financial contributions. This amount--$59,934--is the total attributed to her in the financial compilation prepared by Mr. Shewbridge; by our calculations, it is derived by adding the income reported on the couple's tax returns. The amount of contributions attributed to Mr. Shewbridge was $58,305. This amount represents the money provided by Dr. Shewbridge; however, it is not apparent how this figure was computed. Mr. Shewbridge's financial compilation indicates in two different places that the amount of funds provided by Dr. Shewbridge during the marriage from 1988 through 1992 was $57,030. However, our calculations indicate that the sum was actually $57,330. We elect to use this amount--$57,330--in calculating the award rather than the amount apparently relied upon by the trial court.

The amount attributed to the cost of education was $29,000. This sum was apparently derived from Mrs. Shewbridge's testimony that she and her husband calculated the cost of his education at $26,000 and that he spent several thousand dollars on tools which were still in his possession. While Mr. Shewbridge argues that there is no evidence or documentation supporting Mrs. Shewbridge's testimony, he does not assert that the amount is incorrect nor did he offer an alternate amount at trial. We find $26,000 reasonable in light of the testimony and evidence in the record. With regard to the money paid for tools, we find that this amount should not be included in the educational expenses; the tools are an asset more appropriately addressed in the partition of community property. Consequently, only the $26,000 will be considered as the cost of education in calculating the award.

Calculating the award using $59,934 as Mrs. Shewbridge's contribution, $57,330 as Mr. Shewbridge's contribution, and $26,000 as the cost of education, we find that amount due to Mrs. Shewbridge for her contributions to her husband's education and training is $14,302.

AWARD OF INTEREST

Mr. Shewbridge also contends that the trial court erred in awarding interest from the date of judicial demand rather than from the date of judgment. We agree. In *McConathy v. McConathy, supra,* we characterized a claim for contributions to a spouse's education and training as an unliquidated debt which is due from the moment it is ascertainable by judgment. We determined that an award of legal interest was appropriate on such a claim and found that interest should be awarded from the date of judgment. We therefore amend the trial court's judgment to provide interest on the award from the date of judgment.

CONCLUSION

We amend the judgment of the trial court to award Mrs. Shewbridge $14,302 on her claim for contributions to Mr. Shewbridge's education and training. Interest on this award shall run from the date of the judgment. As amended, the judgment is affirmed. Costs are assessed against Mr. Shewbridge.

AMENDED AND, AS AMENDED, AFFIRMED.

D. *Loretta Credo Santistevan v. Alfredo Carlos Santistevan*

768 So. 2d 79 (La. App. 5 Cir. 2000)

DUFRESNE, Judge.

This is an appeal by Loretta Credo Santistevan, plaintiff-appellant, from a judgment dismissing her claim pursuant to La. Civ. Code Art. 121 for contributions made to her ex-husband Alfredo's education and training during the marriage. Because we find no abuse of discretion in the trial judge's determination that such an award is not warranted on the facts of this case, we affirm that judgment.

The following facts appear of record or were stipulated to by the parties. They were married in 1975, the community terminated on December 9, 1993, and a final judgment of divorce was signed on February 22, 1994. On December 31, 1986, Alfredo was in an automobile accident that disabled him from work during 1987 and 1988. In 1988, Alfredo settled the lawsuit arising out of that accident for $155,000. He began a construction company in 1988, but it was unsuccessful and he had no other income during 1988, 1989 and 1990. In 1990 he began classes at SUNO, and in December of 1992 received an associate degree in substance abuse counseling. It appears that he also attended SUNO during 1993, the last year of the marriage. In May of 1996, over two years after the divorce, he received his BS degree in substance abuse counseling. He is now a state certified substance abuse and compulsive gambling counselor and an internationally certified alcohol and drug abuse counselor.

The pertinent earnings records of the spouses are as follows:

	Alfredo	**Loretta**
1984	$15,266	$10,688
1985	$15,865	$17,075
1986	$7,312	$17,125
1987	$0	$15,742
1988	$0	$21,560
1989	($1,611)	$24,125
1990	$0	$25,332
1991	$6,453	$29,908
1992	$13,179	$29,248
1993	$10,999	$33,374

There are no earnings figures for Alfredo in 1994 and 1995, but since 1996, the year he received his bachelor's degree, his earnings have been a little over $25,000 per year.

Alfredo's tuition was paid by the Louisiana Department of Vocational Rehabilitation, but he also made student loans of $11,122 during the marriage. Loretta had student loans during this period of $5,355. The spouses assumed their own loans when the community property settlement was made.

On the above facts, the trial judge determined that no award for contributions made by the wife for the educational expenses of the husband was warranted. The wife now appeals that judgment.

The applicable law here is found in La. Civ. Code Art. 121, which provides that a court may award a party to a divorce a sum for that spouse's financial contributions made for the education or training of the other spouse. Because the article leaves to the trial judge the discretion to make or deny such an award, the standard of review in this court is whether he abused his discretion in making this determination, *see Barrow v. Barrow,* 27,714 (La. App. 2nd Cir.2/28/96), 669 So.2d 622, *writs denied,* 96-1057 and 96- 1072 (La.6/21/96), 675 So.2d 1080. The underlying facts upon which that decision is made, however, are subject to the manifest error standard, *Shewbridge v. Shewbridge,* 31,170 (La.App. 2nd Cir.10/28/98), 720 So.2d 780.

The above cases also set forth the same list of factors to be considered in making the ultimate determination of whether an award is to be made. These are: (1) the claimant's expectation of shared benefit when the contributions were made; (2) the degree of detriment suffered by the claimant in making the contributions; and (3) the magnitude of the benefit received by the other spouse.

In his reasons for judgment the trial judge stated his factual findings as they related to each of the above factors. He noted that Alfredo's tuition was paid by the state because of his disability and thus only his normal living expenses were paid for by the community. Implicit in the state's disability determination was the clear inference that Alfredo was not earning income not because he was in school, but rather because he was disabled from his prior occupation. He also noted that in addition to Loretta's salary, Alfredo's student loans (which he ultimately assumed) and the $155,000 settlement were also available for normal expenses. Loretta alleged that the settlement money was wasted on drugs and gambling, but the judge found that at least $50,000 of that amount was used for family expenses. He also found that as a result of his degree Alfredo was not earning appreciably more than he was prior to his accident.

The trial judge then looked to the three factors of the analysis. He acknowledged that because of Alfredo's drug and gambling problems, Loretta may well have had reasonable expectations of sharing in the benefits of her spouse's education. As to the degree of detriment suffered by Loretta because of contributions to the education of her spouse, he pointed out that Alfredo was not able to work during most of this period anyway, whether in school or not. He also pointed out that the student loans and at least $50,000 of the settlement money was available for expenses. He finally noted that Alfredo also babysat while Loretta was at work, thus avoiding childcare expenses. His ultimate conclusion was that Loretta had not suffered any significant financial detriment because Alfredo was attending school.

As to the third consideration, the trial judge found that Alfredo was not earning significantly more money after receiving his degree than he was before his accident. We further point out that when the community terminated, Alfredo had only earned a two-year associate degree, and not the bachelor's degree and certifications upon which his 1996 salary was predicated.

Considering the record in its entirety, we find neither manifest factual errors nor any abuse of discretion in the judgment of the trial judge. We therefore affirm that judgment.

AFFIRMED.

E. *Robert Charles Earle v. Mary Anne Hill Earle*

998 So. 2d 828 (La. App. 2d Cir. 2008)

PEATROSS, J.

Mary Anne Hill Earle ("Andy") appeals the trial court's judgment on issues incidental to her uncontested divorce from Robert Charles Earle ("Chuck"). In particular, she argues that the trial court erred in awarding Chuck overnight and out-of-state visitation with the two minor children of the marriage. She further argues that the trial court erred in the amount of child support and spousal support awarded and in failing to award any amount for her contribution to the education and training of Chuck. For the reasons set forth below, we affirm the custody arrangement ordered by the trial court and its denial of any claim for reimbursement for educational expenses, but amend the awards for child support and spousal support.

FACTS

After 19 years of marriage and an attempt at reconciliation, Chuck and Andy divorced. During the marriage, the parties had three children: Katelyn Ann Earle, a major at the time of trial, Robert Pierce Earle, who was sixteen years old at the time of trial, and John Abram Earle, who was two years old at the time of trial. Also, during the marriage, Chuck completed a Masters of Science degree in electrical engineering and he received his *juris doctorate* in 1998.

The youngest child, John Abram Earle, has a chronic medical condition diagnosed as reactive airway disease (RAD), an asthma-type disease. To treat this condition, he requires the use of a nebulizer, a portable device used to provide a breathing treatment, along with various medications. He has related episodes of respiratory distress that are life-threatening unless immediately recognized and treated.

Pursuant to its oral reasons, the trial court granted joint custody with Andy designated as the domiciliary parent. . . . After declining to find Andy at fault for the break up of the marriage, the trial court awarded her spousal support in the amount of $400 per month for 24 months and $250 per month for 36 months thereafter. The trial court declined to make an additional award for Andy's support of Chuck while he was in law school and his masters program.

DISCUSSION

* * *

Reimbursement for Contribution to Education

Andy seeks reimbursement under La. C.C. art. 121 for her contributions to Chuck's education, particularly through law school. Chuck graduated from law school in 1998.

We have recently addressed La. C.C. art. 121 in *Clemons v. Clemons*, 42,129 (La.App.2d Cir. 5/9/07), 960 So.2d 1068, *writ denied*, 07-1652 (La.10/26/07), 966 So.2d 583, and we will not be redundant here. In *Clemons*, we focused on whether a spouse had received sufficient benefit of the other spouse's education. If a contributing spouse has already benefited from the other spouse's education through an improved standard of living or an accumulation of community property, then no award under La. C.C. art. 121 is warranted. *Id.* Further, La. C.C. art. 121 awards are typically to address cases where the parties divorce shortly after the graduation of the supported spouse. *Id.*

In the case *sub judice*, Chuck filed for divorce six years after his graduation from law school. In that time, Andy received sufficient benefit from Chuck's education. We, therefore, deny Andy's request for an award under the provisions of La. C.C. art. 121.

* * *

AMENDED AND, AS AMENDED, AFFIRMED.

F. Note

Louisiana's approach to career assets has received a fair amount of criticism.[8] However, shifting demographics in the marriage arena have revealed a new inequity in Louisiana's law that is simply not addressed by Article 121. Couples are increasingly waiting to marry until after they have already completed their educations. As a result, spouses are entering marriage with not only their degrees, but also staggering student loan debts. When these debts are incurred before marriage Louisiana courts classify them as separate debts. To the extent that a spouse uses community funds during marriage to pay off the debt, he or she will owe reimbursement to the other spouse for one-half of the value of the funds used to pay off the debt. Article 121 is inapplicable to this situation and offers no relief. The issue is explored in more depth in Chapters 7 and 8.

2.4 INCREASE IN VALUE OF SEPARATE ASSETS

A. J. Thomas Oldham, *Separate Property Businesses That Increase in Value During Marriage*, 1990 WIS. L. REV. 585 (1990)

I. INTRODUCTION

The characterization of property as "separate" or "community" is significant in community property states. Each spouse has a fifty percent interest in community property when it is acquired. In contrast, separate property is owned solely by the owning spouse. Also, community property states permit either the equal or equitable division of community property at divorce; in most community property states separate property cannot be divided. At death, a spouse can devise all of the decedent's separate property and fifty percent of the community estate.

The distinction between separate and community property stems from a conception of marriage as an economic partnership. The partnership is perceived to encompass all property generated during marriage by the efforts of either spouse. Both spouses are awarded an equal interest in this property, regardless of which spouse's efforts were involved and regardless of title. Property owned before marriage is not considered part of this partnership; this remains the separate property of the owner.

A spouse sometimes marries after she has started a business. Under traditional community property theory, such a business started before marriage with "separate"

---

[8] *See e.g.* Meghan Doody Coleman, Comment *What is a Degree Worth: Inconsistencies and Inequities in Louisiana,* 53 LOY. L. REV. 905 (2007); and Caroline B. Blitzer, Note, *McConathy v. McConathy: A Diploma, A Divorce, and a Dilemma*, 55LA. L. REV. 973 (1995).

property consideration remains the separate property of that spouse. However, events after the wedding can complicate matters. For example, assume the business increases in value during the marriage. Before the community claim to this increase can be determined, more information must be obtained. If the increase in value stems from the "normal course of things," such as inflation or general industry conditions, there is no community claim. All of the business, including all increase in value, is separate property. This is consistent with the general principle that the community has no claim to the increase in value of separate property during marriage, as long as no community resources are expended upon the asset. If the increase in value stems at least in part from the efforts of one or both spouses, however, there can be a community claim to the increase. The "time, toil and talent" of each spouse during marriage is perceived to be a community asset. If a separate property asset increases in value because of a community investment of a spouse's efforts during marriage, a potential community claim arises. This claim only pertains to the increase in value during marriage (or possibly the value of the services contributed); the initial separate property investment at the time of the wedding remains separate property.

If community efforts are "invested" in a separate property business, a means must be found to determine the amount of the community claim. Different courts have suggested various approaches to this problem. For example, some courts have applied an "all or nothing" analysis. Pursuant to this approach, the chief contributing factor to the increase in value is determined. If the separate property capital was the chief factor, all of the increase is considered separate property. If the chief factor was the efforts of one or both spouses, the increase in value is deemed community property. This "all or nothing" analysis obviously lacks precision and is somewhat arbitrary and unfair. Most courts have attempted to create rules that permit an allocation of the increase between the spouse's separate property estate and the community. The different allocation rules that have been applied will be discussed in more detail below.

The two allocation approaches used by most courts today are the *Van Camp* and *Pereira* approaches. These two approaches derive from two California cases, *Van Camp v. Van Camp* and *Pereira v. Pereira.* Under *Van Camp,* the value of the services rendered during marriage is determined. This amount, less any compensation received, is the community claim. All other increase in the value of the business is separate property. In contrast, the *Pereira* approach provides a reasonable annual rate of return for the separate property capital invested in the business. The value of this capital, plus the annual rate of return addition, is the separate property claim. The community property claim is the amount, if any, by which the value of the business at dissolution exceeds the separate property claim.

B. Louisiana Approach

The Louisiana Civil Code addresses this inequity in the form of a reimbursement claim. Civil Code article 2368 requires the court to do an apportionment. Louisiana courts will apply the *Van Camp* approach, the *Pereira* approach, or some variation of those approaches depending on which is more appropriate in light of the particular facts.

Art. 2368. Increase of the value of separate property

> If the separate property of a spouse has increased in value as a result of the uncompensated common labor or industry of the spouses, the other spouse is entitled to be reimbursed from the spouse whose property has increased in value one-half of the increase attributed to the common labor.

C. *James W. Pellerin v. Cynthia Cerise, wife of James W. Pellerin*

550 So. 2d 1250 (La. App. 4 Cir. 1989)

BYRNES, Judge.

Mrs. Cynthia Cerise Pellerin appeals a judgment finding her ex-husband James Pellerin's controlling interests in Pellerin Laundry Machinery Sales Company (PLMSCO) to be his separate property in which their community had no claim for enhancement in value or for dividends. We affirm.

FACTS

On March 19, 1986, James Pellerin filed a petition seeking a divorce from Mrs. Pellerin, which was granted by final judgment of August 7, 1987. The legal regime of community property terminated as of March 19, 1986. As part of the divorce proceedings, Mr. Pellerin filed a petition for partition of community property and a trial on the partition was held on February 19 and 20 and April 21, 1987. In her sworn descriptive list of assets and liabilities, Mrs. Pellerin included:

> Acquisition and retention of controlling interests in Pellerin Laundry Machinery Sales Co., Inc. by James W. Pellerin during the existence of the community of acquets and gains.

On June 22, 1987, judgment was rendered in the partition proceedings, deleting from Mrs. Pellerin's descriptive list the above item which she claimed to be community property. Mrs. Pellerin appeals that judgment.

ISSUES

The issues presented on appeal are:

> (1) whether the wife is entitled to credit to the community for the increase in the husband's controlling interest in a family corporation which occurred during the marriage; and
>
> (2) whether the corporation unreasonably withheld dividends on the company's stock, which would have fallen into the community property during the marriage.

The record indicates that prior to his marriage of July 19, 1975, James Pellerin, his brother and his two sisters each acquired as donations from their father and grandfather, 25% of the common stock of PLMSCO, a business engaged in the purchase and sale of commercial laundry equipment. After James married, when the general manager of PLMSCO, Doug Brown, resigned, Norvin Pellerin asked his son James to manage the company instead of attending graduate business school at the Wharton School of the University of Pennsylvania. An arrangement was made wherein the PLMSCO sales manager, Jake Mathey, received stock representing 8% ownership interest, which reduced each child's interest to 23%. Thereafter, James Pellerin became president of PLMSCO in May, 1976. In 1977, the Board of Directors adopted a Plan of Recapitalization in which James' siblings exchanged their common stock for preferred stock, and James acquired controlling interest in the voting common stock of the corporation. His voting interest increased from 23% to 92%.

Mrs. Pellerin argues that James Pellerin acquired new property rights as a result of the recapitalization plan. The wife refers to the portion of the plan which provides:

> James W. Pellerin has been named, by the unanimous approval of the Board of Directors, to be the president and general manager of the Corporation and is active in the management of its daily operations. Although acting as the key executive of the Corporation, he presently does not own a controlling interest in the voting common stock of the Corporation. Jack W. Mathey (sic) is the vice-president of the Corporation and is active in its daily operations. The remaining stockholders have each indicated their present lack of professional knowledge and interest in directing and managing the affairs of the Corporation.

James W. Pellerin, as the key executive, spends considerable time managing and directing the daily operations of the Corporation and also has substantial management responsibilities. In view of the considerable time and effort which he provides in managing the Corporation, James W. Pellerin desires a controlling interest in the voting common stock of the Corporation. The remaining stockholders recognize the substantial benefits to the Corporation resulting from the exceptional services provided by James W. Pellerin in his capacity as president and general manager of the Corporation. Curtis A. Pellerin, Julie Pellerin Bukrey and Renee M. Pellerin, who have expressed their lack of interest in taking an active part in the management of the Corporation are unwilling to terminate their investment in order to give up control of the voting common stock. On the other hand, they realize that their investment in the Corporation can be best protected by having James W. Pellerin as the president and general manager, with control of the voting common stock to provide a greater financial incentive through an increased share in the future appreciation and growth of the Corporation and to allow greater efficiency and economy in the management of the Corporation's business. In addition, they desire the assurance of a substantial annual income from their continued investment in the Corporation. All the shareholders have expressed the opinion that the present capital structure could be detrimental to the future growth and welfare of the Corporation.

Mrs. Pellerin contends that this increased ownership interest is a form of compensation granted to James in return for making his services available and therefore is community property. Cynthia Pellerin claims that James Pellerin acquired "property" within the meaning of La. C.C. art. 2338, i.e., "property acquired during the existence of the legal regime through the effort, skill, or industry of either spouse ..." which is capable of being assigned a pecuniary or monetary value. Due v. Due, 342 So.2d 161 (La.1977). Mrs. Pellerin assigns a value of $2,000,000.00 as her one-half of the community asset based on her former husband's increased controlling interest in PLMSCO during the marriage.

James Pellerin maintains that he did not receive any additional shares of stock as a result of the recapitalization plan. He asserts that the controlling interest of stock ownership cannot exist separate and apart from the stock itself. On claiming no value could be assigned to his controlling interest in PLMSCO, James Pellerin notes that PLMSCO was totally dependent on the Pellerin Milnor Corporation (Milnor), which manufactures the products that PLMSCO sells. Therefore, his authority and control were restricted to managing the PLMSCO business. Increase in his ownership interest benefitted the Pellerin family, enabling him to have the power to run the company. Additionally, the other siblings could exchange their preferred stock for common stock if they became active in the business, making James' control temporary. James Pellerin asserts that he was more than reasonably compensated by his salary and bonus, which became part of the community regime.

Louisiana courts have recognized intangible rights resulting from a spouse's labor and industry as community assets. An attorney's contingent fee contracts are such "property" which can be assigned value and is an asset of the community. Even if dependant on a future event, value is based on the attorney's services rendered during the marriage. Due v. Due, supra.

In commercial business, goodwill is a property right which can exist as an asset in itself, which can be included in valuation of a business in a community property partition proceeding. Godwin v. Godwin, 533 So.2d 1009 (La.App. 1st Cir.1988), writ denied, 537 So.2d 1165 (La.1989). However, this court found that a husband's stock in the Steamship Pilots Association of which he was a member, was worth no more than the $100.00 he paid for the stock and would receive on his resignation or death. Although stock in the association represented the capability of future earnings, it was not a community asset to be partitioned but a factor to be considered in determination of permanent alimony. Taylor v. Taylor, 473 So.2d 867 (La.App. 4th Cir.1985), writ denied, 477 So.2d 1126 (La.1985).

The party claiming reimbursement for enhancement of value of separate property upon dissolution of the marriage has the burden of proving that the increase in value of the spouse's separate property is a result of uncompensated common labor and industry of the spouses. La.C.C. Art. 2368. Guarisco v. Guarisco, 526 So.2d 1126 (La.App. 1st Cir.1988), writ denied, 523 So.2d 1337 (La.1988). Although there was an increase in James Pellerin's controlling interest, it was not an asset by itself but was tied as an integral part of the position of president of PLMSCO. It served as an incentive for James to assume the position as head of the company because he had the control to manage the business, a necessary component of the office.

Article 2368 of the Louisiana Civil Code provides:

If the separate property of a spouse has increased in value as a result of the uncompensated common labor or industry of the spouses, the other spouse is entitled to be reimbursed from the spouse whose property has increased in value one-half of the increased attributed to the common labor.

In Guarisco, supra, the husband's stock bought prior to his marriage dramatically increased in value after he became president. That court found that the claimant spouse failed to show what the value of the husband's interest would have been had the community not provided uncompensated labor or industry. Nor did she establish that her former husband had not been adequately compensated. See also Beals v. Fontenot, 111 F.2d 956 (5th Cir.1940); Phillips v. Wagner, 470 So.2d 262 (La.App. 5th Cir.1985) writ denied, 474 So.2d 948 (La.1985).

This court is persuaded that the community was adequately compensated for James Pellerin's labor and industry by virtue of his salary and bonus. Henry Cooper, found to be an expert in finance, accounting and evaluation of closely held corporations, testified that a higher salary was paid to both James Pellerin and Jake Mathey than normal and a buyer could replace them with cheaper management. John McGrath, general manager of A.A. Harmon & Company, who originally drew up the plan of recapitalization noted that PLMSCO's management salary and incentive bonus arrangement provided compensation to the community. Daniel D. Lawrence, James Pellerin's expert witness in the field of executive compensation, concluded that James Pellerin was paid very well in relation to his peers, and any increase in controlling interest that James Pellerin acquired benefitted the community.

Cynthia Pellerin has failed to carry her burden of proof that Mr. Pellerin was not reasonably compensated or that there was any increase in the PLMSCO stock as a result of uncompensated labor.

Cynthia Pellerin also claims that PLMSCO unreasonably withheld dividends on the common stock which would have become community property during the marriage. Testimony of the expert witnesses indicates that PLMSCO's working capital ratios were high but that the company's auditor monitored the accumulated earnings taxes to be within IRS guidelines. Expert John McGrath pointed out that PLMSCO was in a 50% tax bracket. For each \$100.00 paid in dividends, \$50.00 would have to be paid in taxes. Mark Munson, qualified as an expert in the field of accounting and business valuation, testified that it was typical of small family corporations not to pay dividends on common shares. C.P.A. Wiley Lefdwich, referred to a double tax problem if dividends were issued. Norvin Pellerin asserted that dividends were never paid on common stock in any of the three family businesses, PLMSCO, Pellerin Milnor Corporation or Norvin Realty Company. Additional testimony reveals that the company retained liquid assets for exposure to at least two lawsuits. Mrs. Pellerin has failed to show that PLMSCO's refusal to pay dividends was capricious or retained to deprive the community.

D. Note

In *Mohr v. Mohr*, 374 So.2d 203 (La. App. 4th Cir. 1979), the husband owned separate stock in a closely held corporation fully controlled by him. The stock increased in value during the existence of the community. The wife claimed the increase was due to the husband's labor and industry. Evidence introduced established that during the community two substantial obligations owed by the corporation were satisfied. In a sales contract creating one of the obligations, the husband's salary was limited to \$20,000, and no dividends were paid on the stock. Recognizing that the \$20,000 contractual limit on the husband's salary was proper, the court nonetheless concluded that the salary did not represent "a fair return for the labors expended" by the husband. Therefore, the increase in value of the stock must be the result of the husband's labors "over and above that for which he (and thus the community) was compensated..." The court of appeal remanded the case with directions "to make a factual determination of the real value of Mohr's labors during that critical period -- notwithstanding the \$20,000 Talcott-imposed limitation." However, the court instructed the trial judge to compute the value of the husband's uncompensated labor. Then the trial judge was instructed to inventory it as a debt in favor of the community against the closely held corporation "in such a way as to accord credit for one-half of same to appellant, Mrs. Mohr."

E. *Brenda Bordelon v. Gregory P. Bordelon*

942 So. 2d 708 (La. App. 3d Cir. 2006)

THIBODEAUX, Chief Judge.

***

II.
FACTS AND PROCEDURAL HISTORY

At the time of the marriage in 1983, Gregory Bordelon owned a lot which was his separate property. The lot contained two buildings, a shop and a storage building, that are also Gregory's separate property.

In 1989, the couple built a house on the lot and subsequently lived in it with their children as the family residence. This home is the subject of the current dispute. During the construction of the home, Gregory, who was a carpenter, provided most of the labor in constructing the house, along with the couple's friends and family members who donated their time and assistance. Brenda cooked meals for the builders, organized and cleaned up the construction site, purchased materials and supplies, kept the financial records, paid the bills for the construction, and raised the children of the marriage. The house was built in approximately three months. Labor was performed in the days and evenings and on weekends. During this time, Gregory maintained his employment with Tomassi Construction. Brenda did not work outside the home at that time.

Most of the labor on the home was donated except for checks written to individuals for laying bricks and flooring and for finishing sheetrock, for a total of $2,940.50. Brenda wrote checks to cash and to Gregory, indicating some hourly work; she did not write checks to herself for hourly work. Notwithstanding the description on the checks as hourly work, the parties specifically stipulated that these checks were part of the $38,000.00 used to buy materials and goods to build the house. All of the construction costs were paid from community funds obtained from the proceeds of a community loan. The family lived in and maintained the home for eleven or twelve years after its construction.

At the time of the final divorce in September 2001 the parties entered into a partial settlement wherein the furniture was distributed, and each party accepted a vehicle and its attendant debt. The only asset in dispute is the house, and the only debt in dispute is the construction loan for the house.

The parties have stipulated that (1) the lot on which the house was built is Gregory's separate property; (2) the value of the materials to construct the house was $38,000.00; (3) the lot, two buildings, and the home constructed during the marriage are Gregory's separate property; and (4) a community loan was taken out by both parties in February 1989 for $41,440.00, from which the construction materials were purchased. The remainder of the loan was used to buy furnishings.

Brenda sought reimbursement for one-half of the $38,000.00 in community funds expended in the construction of the house under La. Civ. Code art. 2366, which is $19,000.00. Brenda, asserting that the house has a value of $115,000.00, also sought reimbursement under La. Civ. Code art. 2368 for one-half of the enhanced value of the property due to the construction of the house, which is $57,500.00. She seeks the total of $19,000.00 plus $57,500.00, or $76,500.00.

After the trial of this matter, the trial court rendered a judgment against Brenda, awarding her nothing. The court declined to address La. Civ. Code art. 2366 and specifically held that Brenda Bordelon was not entitled to one-half of the increased value of the property under La. Civ. Code art. 2368. It is from this judgment that Brenda appeals.

III.

LAW AND DISCUSSION

***

Reimbursements under La. Civ. Code art. 2368

Brenda contends that the trial court erred in failing to reimburse her one-half of the value of the improvement to Gregory's property resulting from the construction of the house, pursuant to La. Civ. Code art. 2368. We agree that an award should be made under Article 2368, but we do not agree with Brenda's calculations.

***

To prevail on a claim under Article 2368, the claimant spouse must prove: (1) that the improved property is separate; (2) that the property increased in value during the existence of the matrimonial regime; (3) that common or community labor of the spouses was expended on the separate property; and (4) that the common labor expended was uncompensated or undercompensated. If established, the burden shifts to the owner of the separate property to prove that some or all of the enhancement in value occurred because of factors other than the uncompensated or undercompensated community labor. The claimant spouse does not have to show that his or her labor was expended on separate property. It is enough to show that the labor of *either* spouse was so expended. *Salley v. Salley,* 95-0387 (La.10/16/95), 661 So.2d 437.

Moreover, once the claimant seeking reimbursement has established that the increase in the separate property of the other spouse is entirely or partially due to under- or uncompensated community labor of the other spouse, the claimant is entitled to one-half of the enhanced value of the separate property, even if that value *exceeds* the value of the uncompensated labor. *Krielow v. Krielow,* 93-2539 (La.4/11/94), 635 So.2d 180.

The rationale underlying Article 2368 is that:

> Because property acquired by the effort, skill or industry of a spouse is community, to the extent that a spouse's labor is producing some benefit, the community ought to share in the profit of that labor. Thus, in the case where a spouse's labor increases the value of a separate asset, the equitable solution is reimbursement for that effort by awarding the non-owner spouse one-half of the increase attributable to the common labor. La. C.C. art. 2368. If the labor is combined with separate capital or other separate property, equity would suggest a proportional division of the profits between the community and separate estates of the spouses. Katherine S. Spaht & W. Lee Hargrave, *Louisiana Civil Law Treatise, Matrimonial Regimes,* Vol. 16, § 3.8 & 3.49 (2d ed.1997).

McClanahan v. McClanahan, 03-1178 (La.App. 5 Cir. 2/23/04), 868 So.2d 844, 848, *writ denied,* 04-1175 (La.9/3/04), 882 So.2d 609.

With regard to the labors of the owner-spouse, it is further reasoned that "[a] spouse should not be permitted to deprive the community of a spouse's earnings that would be community property when that community labor enhances or increases the value of the laboring spouse's separately owned property." *Krielow,* 635 So.2d at 183.

In the present case, the parties stipulated that the property at issue is the separate property of Gregory. Therefore, the first criterion is met. Likewise, there is no dispute that the property increased in value during the marriage due to the construction of the home. Accordingly, the second criterion is met.

The third criterion that Brenda must prove is that the community labor of either spouse was expended on the separate property. The testimony at trial reflects that Gregory was an excellent carpenter and an all-around skilled builder and that he provided labor on the home in numerous capacities, including hanging the sheetrock. The record also contains testimony that he worked on the house every day for three months, often working alone and often until ten or twelve o'clock at night. The record also reflects that Brenda contributed her labor by purchasing supplies; maintaining the financial records; paying the construction bills; organizing, cleaning and sweeping the construction site; cooking meals for the helpers; and raising the children of the community during the construction. Clearly, both spouses contributed their labor in the construction of the home.

The final criterion that Brenda must prove under *Salley,* 661 So.2d 437, is that the common labor expended was uncompensated or undercompensated. Attrial, Gregory testified that he never received money and was not paid for the work he performed on the home. Likewise, there is no allegation or proof that Brenda was compensated for her labor on Gregory's separate property. There are checks written between April and July 1989 on the community construction account made payable to "cash" for hourly work in the total amount of \$3,000.00 and checks made to Gregory for hourly work in the total amount of \$3,743.00. Brenda testified that she wrote the checks on the construction account and deposited them to their joint personal account for the family to live on during the construction period. However, these checks came from the community loan and are part of the \$38,000.00 that the parties stipulated to as costs for construction materials. This \$38,000.00 has been covered in the previous section of this analysis as community *funds* used to enhance the separate property of Gregory.

As to labor belonging to the community, Gregory argues that he did not deprive the community of his paid labor during the building of the private home because he maintained regular employment with Tomassi Construction during that period. The record contains checks paid to Gregory by a homeowner for outside labor with Tomassi Construction during the same time period that he was working on his own property. At trial, he admitted that those checks did not reflect forty hours per week every week. In fact, there was only one check for \$315.00 in May of 1989. Mr. Tomassi testified that Gregory guaranteed him forty hours per week during that construction period in 1989 and indicated that Gregory maintained full-time employment with him. However, Mr. Tomassi did not have records from 1989 and testified that he destroyed his records after seven years due to the volume.

Hence, the record supports Brenda's contention that the house was built with community funds *and* with the labor of both spouses that was uncompensated to some degree. Accordingly, the final criterion in Brenda's burden of proof is met under *Salley,* 661 So.2d 437.

The burden shifted to Gregory to prove that some or all of the enhancement in value occurred because of factors other than the uncompensated or undercompensated community labor. As a threshold matter, it is simply untenable to imply that the large majority of the value of Gregory's property is not due to the construction of the house. The appraisal in the record values the land and small buildings at \$40,000.000 and the house constructed during the marriage at \$115,000.00. Gregory argues that there is absolutely no reimbursement due under Article 2368 because the enhanced value occurred due to other factors, not because of uncompensated community labor but because of the donated labor of friends and family and contractors paid for their work. The record does not support such a contention. Only six checks were written to contractors totaling $2,940.50 for cement floor finishing, bricklaying and sheetrock floating. The record further reveals that, while friends and family members of the couple assisted Gregory in the building of the home, Gregory did the majority of the actual construction work on the home. The only amount paid to contractors was $2,940.50.

Gregory further argues that the value of the labor on the house at the time that it was built was equal only to the cost of the materials, giving the house a total value of $76,000.00 in 1989, and that the more recent appraisal of $115,000.00 was due to a market phenomenon. However, Gregory overlooks the fact that the family lived in the house for eleven or twelve years after it was built, and it was the community labor of both spouses that maintained the home during that period. Moreover, we note that Brenda lived in the house and maintained it for another year after the marital regime ended. If left to sit dormant, a house will not maintain its value. If the house had been abandoned after completion in 1989 it would likely not be worth the materials used to build it. Nature has a way of reclaiming man's abandoned constructions. But for the continuing labor of the spouses, the house would have little value indeed. The photographs accompanying the appraisal depict a lovely brick-front home, which we find is the result mostly of the under-or uncompensated labor of both spouses.

In *Krielow,* 635 So.2d 180, Lynn Krielow established under La. Civ. Code art. 2368that Carl Krielow's undercompensated community labor for his separate corporation enhanced or increased his separately owned stock. The burden shifted to Carl, as the owner of the separate property, to prove that some or all of the enhancement occurred because of other factors. Carl failed to meet his burden of proof, and the court remanded the case to the trial court for a determination of the amount of reimbursement to Lynn Krielow. In that case, Carl worked solely for his own corporation, and he was paid in draws found to be relatively low. Once it was determined that he was undercompensated for his labor, the supreme court articulated that Lynn Krielow was entitled to one-half of the enhanced value of the corporate stock, even if that value exceeded the value of the uncompensated labor. The court stated that Article 2368 did not impose limitations on recovery and that the claimant is "entitled to recover the greater amount." *Krielow,* 635 So.2d at 185.

The value of assets are determined at the time of trial. La.R.S. 9:2801. The trial of this matter was held on June 17, 2005. The date on the appraisal is May 23, 2005. Accordingly, we find that the value of the improvement to Gregory's separate property due to the construction of the house is $115,000.00. Brenda is entitled to one-half of that amount *attributable to common or community labor* under La. Civ. Code art. 2368....

***

2.5 GOODWILL

A. Introduction

Goodwill presents another challenging issue for courts. All jurisdictions agree that a business or professional practice is property. For example, if a spouse becomes a partner in a law firm during marriage, then the spouse's partnership interest is likely to be classified as community property or marital property and is subject to division or consideration at divorce. The big question, however, is the value of that partnership interest. There is substantial disagreement among the states as to whether and to what extent goodwill should be included in determining the value of an asset at divorce.

Generally, there are two types of goodwill recognized by the courts: individual goodwill and enterprise goodwill.

> Factors affecting [enterprise] goodwill may include a business's location, its name recognition, its business reputation, or a variety of other factors depending on the business. Ultimately these factors must, in one way or another, contribute to the anticipated future profitability of the business. Enterprise goodwill is an asset of the business and accordingly is property that is divisible in a dissolution to the extent that it inheres in the business, independent of any single individual's personal efforts and will outlast any person's involvement in the business. *See Talty*, 166 Ill.2d 232, 209 Ill.Dec. 790, 652 N.E.2d at 334; 38 AM.JUR.2D *Goodwill* § 9 (1999). It is not necessarily marketable in the sense that there is a ready and easily priced market for it, but it is in general transferrable to others and has a value to others....
>
> In contrast, the goodwill that depends on the continued presence of a particular individual is a personal asset, and any value that attaches to a business as a result of this "personal goodwill" represents nothing more than the future earning capacity of the individual and is not divisible. *See Bressler v. Bressler,* 601 N.E.2d 392, 397 (Ind.Ct.App.1992) (future earnings are not marital property subject to division); *see also* Martin J. McMahon, Annotation, *Divorce and Separation: Goodwill in Medical or Dental Practice as Property Subject to Distribution on Dissolution of Marriage,* 76 A.L.R. 4TH 1025, 1044-48 (1990).

Jay Myoung Yoon v. Sunsook Yook, 711 N.E. 2d 1265 (Ind. 1999).

Today, most jurisdictions agree that enterprise goodwill should be included when valuing assets at divorce. The states are more divided, however, on the issue of individual (or professional) goodwill. Some states include both enterprise goodwill and individual goodwill when valuing assets at divorce. Most jurisdictions, however, refuse to include individual goodwill when valuing assets at divorce. Often, the decision comes down to whether goodwill of either type is considered an item of property. Individual goodwill, in particular, lacks many of the basic attributes of property.

B. Louisiana's Jurisprudential and Legislative Approach

Louisiana has wrestled with how to deal with goodwill in the divorce context. The first cases to consider the issue were initially faced with the question of whether goodwill constituted property. The courts resolved the question in the negative. However, the courts still faced the question of whether the value of goodwill should be considered when valuing a business in the divorce setting. As illustrated in *Depner* and *McGehee*, below, the courts essentially adopted the enterprise goodwill/individual goodwill distinction. Enterprise goodwill, in the view of the courts, was includable in valuing assets. Individual goodwill, in contrast, was essentially extrapatrimonial and should not be included in valuing assets. Louisiana courts, however, went a step further and essentially limited individual goodwill to members of the learned professions—doctors and lawyers. If the business in question was not a medical or law practice then the goodwill in question must be enterprise (or commercial) goodwill. This limitation soon proved problematic in *Ellington*, below. In *Ellington* the court included Mr. Ellington's individual goodwill when valuing his business because he was not a doctor or a lawyer. The goodwill was undoubtedly individual goodwill and probably would have been excludable if the prior courts had not unnecessarily limited individual goodwill to the learned professions.

In 2003, the Louisiana legislature enacted La. R.S. 9:2801.2 in response to the *Ellington* case. The statute was amended slightly the subsequent year. Both versions appear below. The statute clarifies the law to some extent but utterly fails to address the question of whether goodwill of either type should be considered when a spouse brings a claim relating to the increase in value of the *separate property* of the other spouse during the marriage.

2003 VERSION: R.S. 9:2801.2. Community property; valuation of goodwill

In a proceeding to partition the community, the court may include, in the valuation of a community commercial business, the goodwill of the business. Goodwill shall not be included in the valuation of a business when goodwill results solely from the identity, reputation, or qualifications of the owner or from his relationship with customers of the business.

2004 VERSION: R.S. 9:2801.2. Community property; valuation of goodwill

In a proceeding to partition the community, the court may include, in the valuation of any community-owned corporate, commercial, or professional business, the goodwill of the business. However, that portion of the goodwill attributable to any personal quality of the spouse awarded the business shall not be included in the valuation of a business.

C. *Stephen M. Depner v. Susan Benton Depner*

478 So.2d 532 (La. App. 1st Cir. 1985)

SAVOIE, Judge.

Stephen M. Depner (plaintiff) and Susan Benton Depner (defendant) were married on June 28, 1976. They were legally separated on August 2, 1979. Plaintiff brought suit to obtain a settlement of the community which had existed between them. Prior to trial, all issues were amiably resolved except the enhanced value of plaintiff's professional medical corporation.

Plaintiff, a medical doctor, incorporated his practice before he and defendant married. The corporation was his separate property. The parties were unable to place a value on the corporation as of the date of the dissolution of the community.

The law in effect at the time was La.C.C. art. 2408, which provided:

> When the separate property of either the husband or the wife has been increased or improved during the marriage, the other spouse, or his or her heirs, shall be entitled to the reward of one half of the value of the increase or ameliorations, if it be proven that the increase or ameliorations be the result of the common labor, expenses or industry; but there shall be no reward due, if it be proven that the increase is due only to the ordinary course of things, to the rise in the value of property, or to the chances of trade.

The trial court arrived at a figure of $33,047.04 as the value of the corporation. He refused to include in this valuation any sum for earning capacity or intangibles. Judgment was rendered accordingly in defendant's favor for $16,523.52. She has appealed. Plaintiff has answered the appeal, praying that the amount of the judgment be decreased. We find no error in the trial court's evaluation.

The main issue before us is whether the trial court erred when it failed to place any value on intangible assets, such as earning capacity or good will, of this corporation.

The court reasoned that defendant had no interest in and could not share the earnings of the corporation because under the provisions of La.R.S. 12:905(B) only a physician or medical corporation which owns stock in a medical corporation can participate in its earnings. Defendant argues she is not attempting to participate in the earnings of the corporation but that she is entitled to have its earning capability considered in valuing the corporation's worth.

We must first determine whether to classify the intangible assets such as goodwill and/or earning capacity as "property". The Louisiana Supreme Court has defined property as follows:

> The intent, we believe, is that all property (in the broad sense of the word) is to form part of the community, if acquired during the marriage (with the narrow and non-applicable exceptions noted). Property, in its broad sense, denotes all patrimonial rights. 2 Yiannopoulos, Louisiana Civil Law Treatise, Property, Section 1 (1967). The civil law concept of patrimony includes the total mass of existing or potential rights and liabilities attached to a person for the satisfaction of his economic needs. Yiannopoulos, above cited, Section 77; *Creech v. Capital Mack Inc.*, 287 So.2d 497 (La.1973). In general, "[p]atrimonial rights are those susceptible of pecuniary evaluation, and which, for this reason, may form part of a person's patrimony." Yiannopoulos, Louisiana Civil Law System, Section 70, p. 243 (1971). Due v. Due, 342 So.2d 161, 165 (La.1977). Whether professional good will is property is a res nova issue in Louisiana, but it has been considered in Law Review comments. See 43 La.L.REV. 119 (1982); 56 Tul.L.REV. p. 313 (1981).

In the present case, the community was dissolved as of August 2, 1979. Earnings of the plaintiff after that date became the separate property of the plaintiff. Therefore, earnings after the date of dissolution of the community cannot be considered as a factor in determining the corporation's value for the purpose of the community property partition.

The division of authority on the question of whether good will may exist in a profession dependent on the personal qualities of the professional himself has been stated in this manner; . . . It has frequently been held that good will does not adhere to a business or profession dependent solely on the personal ability, skill, integrity, or other personal characteristics of the owner. According to other decisions, however, good will may exist in a professional as well as a commercial business, and may be sold together with the estate, and, irrespective of whether there is technically a good will adherent to a business or profession dependent on personal qualities of the owner, contracts disposing thereof coupled with an agreement that the seller would not compete, if otherwise valid, are enforced. In any case, an involuntary sale cannot be made of a good will based on professional reputation." 38 C.J.S. Good Will § 3, pp. 952-953.

It is generally held that good will has no existence as property in and of itself, as a separate and distinct entity, but only as an incident of a continuing business having locality or name. 38 Am.Jur.2d Good Will § 3, p. 914 and cases therein cited. The rule has been otherwise stated that as good will must adhere to some principal property or right, the extinction of such right operates to extinguish the good will dependent upon it. 38 C.J.S. Good Will § 4, p. 953. The good will in which Mrs. Depner seeks to share is the professional competence, as perceived by his patients, with which her husband has practiced his art. Professional medical competence is personal to the physician and cannot be attributed to the corporation because it is a personal relationship between physician and patient, not between corporation and patient. Since good will must adhere to some principal property or right it is therefore dependent upon the property or right of either the corporation or the individual or both. In examining the good will in this case we find that it exists independent of the corporation. Absent the corporation it exists, absent the physician it does not exist. Therefore it is not an asset of the corporation. The corporation may profit from this relationship but it cannot share in it. The corporation cannot share in a personal relationship between physician and patient.

In any event it cannot be said that the accrued good will in the medical practice of Dr. Depner was an earned or vested property right at the time of the divorce or that it qualifies as property subject to division by decree of the court. It did not possess value or constitute an asset separate and apart from the person of Dr. Depner in his individual capacity to practice his profession. It would be extinguished in the event of his death or retirement or disablement as well in the event of the sale of his practice or the loss of his patients, whatever the cause.

The goodwill of the husband's medical practice may not be characterized as an earned or vested right or one which fixes any benefit in any sum at any future time. That it would have value in the future is no more than an expectancy, wholly dependant upon the continuation of existing circumstances. See Nail v. Nail, 486 S.W.2d 761 (Tex.1972).

Further support for the above conclusion is found in the very fact that the relationship between the individual medical practitioner and his patient is so personal as to have a statutory privilege protecting it.

Goodwill in Louisiana is defined as "the chance or probability that custom will be had at a certain place of business in consequence of the way that business has been conducted." *Vonderbank v. Schmidt*, 44 La.Ann. 264, 10 So. 616 (1892), as followed in *Ballero v. Heslin*, 128 So.2d 453 (La. App. 4th Cir.1961). In speaking of goodwill,

Am.Jur.2d. states "the narrowest definition is stated as the probability that old customers will resort to the old place." 38 Am.Jur.2d. Goodwill § 1, p. 912. That particular sentence is footnoted and the footnote makes reference to the aforementioned *Vonderbank v. Schmidt*. This narrow definition has been broadened in some cases. However, no case from Louisiana is cited as defining goodwill any broader than the way it is decided in *Vonderbank v. Schmidt*. 38 Am.Jur.2d Good Will § 4, p. 914 states as follows, "however, goodwill cannot be separated from the business in which it inheres, nor can it be disposed of independently from the business. It has no existence as property in and of itself, as a separate and distinct entity, but only as an incident of a continuing business having locality or name."

We note with interest the article in 43 La. Law Review page 119 et seq. which seems to indicate that goodwill is a community asset to be valued and divided upon termination of the community. We disagree. We agree with the Wisconsin Court of Appeals in *Holbrook v. Holbrook*, 103 Wis.2d 327, at 350-51, 309 N.W.2d 343 (Wis.Ct.App., 1981) in its rationale for the opposite view.

"We are not persuaded that the concept of professional goodwill as a divisible marital asset should be adopted in Wisconsin. We are not obligated nor inclined to follow the twisted and illogical path that other jurisdictions have made in dealing with this concept in the context of divorce.

The concept of professional goodwill evanesces when one attempts to distinguish it from future earning capacity. Although a professional business's good reputation, which is essentially what its goodwill consists of, is certainly a thing of value, we do not believe that it bestows on those who have an ownership interest in the business, an actual, separate property interest. The reputation of a law firm or some other professional business is valuable to its individual owners to the extent that it assures continued substantial earnings in the future. It cannot be separately sold or pledged by the individual owners. The goodwill or reputation of such a business accrues to the benefit of the owners only through increased salary.

Like an educational degree, a partner's theoretical share of a law firm's goodwill cannot be exchanged on an open market; it cannot be assigned, sold, transferred, conveyed or pledged. Although we recognize the factual distinction between a degree-holder and a partner or shareholder in a law firm, we think the similarities compel analogous treatment in a divorce setting. In both cases, the 'assets' involved is not salable and has computable value to the individual only to the extent that it promises increased future earnings.

There is a disturbing inequity in compelling a professional practitioner to pay a spouse a share of intangible assets at a judicially determined value that could not be realized by a sale or another method of liquidating value."

The above language was also quoted by Justice Herd of the Kansas Supreme Court in the case of Powell v. Powell, 648 P.2d 218. (Kan. 1982).

Justice Herd further stated:

> We are not persuaded a professional practice such as Dr. Powell's has a goodwill value. The practice is personal to the practitioner. When he or she dies or retires nothing remains. The professional's files and lists of clients are of no use to others. The very nature of a professional practice is that it is totally dependent upon the professional. We refuse to adopt the theory that goodwill in a professional practice is an asset subject to division in a divorce action.

Powell, supra.

Given Louisiana's narrow definition of good will and the total dependency of good will on the individual physician, we conclude that in the case of a sole medical practitioner like Dr. Depner, good will does not form a part of the corporate assets. For the above and foregoing reasons the judgment of the trial court is affirmed. Defendant, Susan Depner, is to pay all costs.

AFFIRMED.

SHORTESS, J., dissents and assigns reasons.

We are not dealing with an individual medical practice here but a professional medical corporation. The majority presumes that, absent Dr. Depner, no value can be assigned to the intangibles belonging to his wholly owned medical corporation. I cannot go that far because a corporation consists of intangible as well as tangible assets. Good will is an intangible asset and as such is a patrimonial right. Yiannopolous, Louisiana Civil Law System, § 70, p. 243 (1971). I would remand to determine the value of this corporation's good will.

D. Note

The fourth circuit followed *Depner* in *Pearce v. Pearce*, 482 So.2d 108 (La. App. 4th Cir. 1986), *writ denied*, 484 So.2d 140. The court of appeal for the Third Circuit expressed a similar view in *McCarron v. McCarron*, 498 So.2d 1139 (La. App. 3d Cir. 1986), *writ denied*, 501 So.2d 233 (1987) saying "we are convinced that the 'good will' of the plaintiff's medical practice in this case is not a community asset" susceptible of partition.

The court in *Taylor v. Taylor*, 473 So.2d 867 (La. App. 4th Cir. 1985), *writ denied*, 477 So.2d 1126 (1985), dealt with the value of a share of stock in a river pilot's association, the stock being a virtual prerequisite to being a river pilot. By the terms of the corporate charter, the stock cost $100 and was non transferable; it would revert to the corporation at death or resignation for a payment of $100.00. The wife argued her husband's stock should be valued to reflect goodwill or future income to be derived from membership in the corporation. The court reasoned that the stock was basically a "union card" and declined "to hold that Captain Taylor's individual interest in the Association has such value."

E. *William C. McGehee v. Rebecca Walker McGehee*

543 So. 2d 1126 (La. App. 1st Cir. 1989)

LANIER, Judge.

This is an action to partition community property. After a trial, the trial court rendered a judgment partitioning the community property which, among other things, allocated the community insurance agency to the husband and fixed a value for it of $225,000. The wife took this devolutive appeal asserting the community insurance agency should be valued at $413,673. The husband did not appeal or answer the appeal.

FACTS

Rebecca Walker McGehee and William C. McGehee were married in 1968. In 1983, they formed the Bill McGehee Insurance, Inc. corporation (Agency) and each received 150 shares of corporate stock. In 1985, the McGehees were legally separated on the grounds of mutual fault. Thereafter, Mr. McGehee filed this action to partition the community property. In 1986, the McGehees were divorced. In 1987, the partition action was tried and a judgment was rendered. The primary evidence concerning the value of the Agency was the testimony of Joseph R. Black, Elvis E. Thomas and Samuel Smith. Black was qualified as an expert certified public accountant. He kept the Agency's accounts since its beginning. Based on the Agency's December 31, 1986 balance sheet, Black fixed the "book value" of the Agency at $13,560. He defined "book value" in an accounting sense as the difference between assets and liabilities. He also fixed the "liquidation value" of the Agency at $100,000 less than "book value." He admitted he had never given a fair market value for a going business and could not give a value for a noncompetition agreement.

Smith was qualified as an expert certified public accountant. He was apparently retained by Mrs. McGehee to determine a value for the Agency. Smith brought Thomas into the case because Thomas had expertise in evaluating insurance agencies. Smith worked with Thomas to evaluate the Agency. Smith testified that the "book value" of the Agency corporation was different from the value of the Agency's "book of business", and these two values should be added together to obtain the total value of the asset. He observed that the Agency's financial records indicated that Mr. McGehee received $80,000 in salary from the Agency in 1986. (Mr. McGehee testified he received a salary of $6,000 per month from the Agency.)

Thomas was qualified as an expert in insurance agency analysis and evaluation. He had extensive experience in this field. Thomas testified that the profitability of an insurance agency for tax purposes is a concept different from its sale value as a business. Often an insurance agency's "book of business" is sold, and the corporation which owned and sold the "book of business" is not part of the sale because the buyer does not want to acquire unknown liabilities in the seller's corporation. In such a situation, the seller will give the buyer a noncompetition agreement to protect the value of the "book of business" sold. If a noncompetition agreement was not given, the seller could sell the "book of business" and reopen around the corner and take the "book of business" away. However, in a divorce case, a noncompetition agreement is not that important if the spouse who is operating the business acquires its sole ownership (as does Mr. McGehee in the partition herein). A noncompetition agreement would be meaningful if Mrs. McGehee would give one to Mr. McGehee, or if Mr. McGehee would agree to give a noncompetition agreement to a third party purchaser of the "book of business" if Mr. McGehee decided to sell the "book of business" in the future. Thomas only knew of three or four agencies sold without noncompetition agreements.

Thomas testified that an insurance agency's "book of business" is evaluated by determining the amount of insurance commissions and applying a multiplier that ranged from 1.4 to 1.7. The amount of the multiplier to be used depended on various factors concerning the Agency. Thomas felt a multiplier of 1.5 was proper for the Agency herein. He examined the Agency's balance sheets and determined that the Agency received $275,782 in insurance commissions in 1985 and $240,859 in 1986. After applying the multiplier, Thomas determined the Agency's "book of business" was worth $413,673 at the end of 1985 and $361,298 at the end of 1986. These valuations were based on the assumption that the Agency would be sold with a noncompetition agreement, but no value was assigned to a noncompetition agreement. Thomas was of the opinion that the 1985 evaluation was the most accurate because all financial data was available for that year and that was the year in which the parties separated, whereas, the 1986 evaluation was based on only ten months of financial data that had to be annualized.

The trial court fixed the "value" of the Agency at $225,000 with the following rationale:

Testimony regarding the insurance agency provided valuation estimates ranging from a negative book value of $86,500.00, to a sales value between $361,298.00 and $413,000.00, if the business is sold at this time. This latter figure includes the consideration that Mr. McGehee would be required to sign a "non-competitive clause" to be in effect for a period of five (5) years, and which would in effect prevent Mr. McGehee from engaging in the general insurance business in this immediate area. The court finds that this is not a viable alternative, in that this involuntary "non-competitive clause" would violate Mr. McGehee's constitutional rights.

Mrs. McGehee argues that the valuation of the business should include an additional value for the "good will" of the business. Louisiana case law states that good will is not to be treated as a community asset, nor does it form a part of the corporate assets in the case of a sole practitioner such as an attorney or physician. *Depner v. Depner*, 478 So2d [sic] 108 (La.App. 4th Cir.1986). Although the Court recognizes the basis of this decision, it is also cognizant of the realization that an insurance agency operates in a different manner than professions such as attorneys or physicians. An insurance agency could maintain some degree of perpetual operation regardless of the presence of the insurance agent himself, whereas no ongoing good will exists absent the participation of a sole professional, such as an attorney or physician. The Court concluded that the agency is worth considerably more than the book value testified to by CPA Joe Black, but less than the value estimated by Mr. Thomas. Although the agency could operate without the efforts of Mr. McGehee, its value would be substantially diminished in the event Mr. McGehee became an active competitor of the agency. Since the Court will not order Mr. McGehee to execute a "no compete" agreement, the value of the business as determined by Thomas must be substantially reduced to take this into consideration. Accordingly, the Court finds the agency to have a value of $225,000.00.

VALUE OF THE AGENCY
(Assignments of Error Numbers 1 and 2)

Mrs. McGehee contends the trial court erred in fixing the value of the Agency "when it discounted the value of the corporation for purposes of community property partition when it took into consideration the effect of a 'non-compete' clause" and by not accepting one of the valuations fixed by Thomas.

The evidence does not indicate any intention by Mr. McGehee to sell the Agency at anytime in the future. The evidence does not reflect that Mrs. McGehee had any intent to compete with the Agency in the past or in the future. In this factual posture, the observation by Thomas that a noncompetition agreement is not an important factor for purposes of partition in a divorce case is correct. The trial court judge fell into error when he considered the noncompetition agreement to be a significant factor and reduced the value of the Agency because Mr. McGehee could not legally be required to give one. The trial court judge committed further error by substituting his own opinion for the "book of business" value of the Agency if no noncompetition clause were given. There is no evidence of record to support the $225,000 award for the "book of business" value. None of the experts assigned any value for a noncompetition clause. The opinion of the court cannot supersede the opinion of an expert in this factual posture. The court can only accept or reject the opinion of the expert.

When community property is partitioned, the court shall value its assets as of the time of trial. La.R.S. 9:2801; *Queenan v. Queenan*, 492 So.2d 902 (La.App. 3rd Cir.), *writ denied*, 496 So.2d 1045 (La.1986); *Cheramie v. Bone*, 444 So.2d 200 (La.App. 1st Cir.1983). Thus, the 1986 valuation of the "book of business" given by Thomas should be utilized instead of the 1985 evaluation. After carefully reviewing Thomas' testimony, we find his opinion well grounded from the standpoint of good reason and accept it. The value of the Agency's "book of business" is fixed at $361,298 for purposes of this partition.

Because we are raising the partition value of the Agency from $225,000 to $361,298, the allocation of assets and liabilities in the judgment of partition will have to be altered. Accordingly, the judgment of partition is reversed, and this action is remanded to the trial court to accomplish this.

F. *Noble Edward Ellington, Jr. v. Peggy Marie McDowell Ellington*

844. So. 2d 1160 (La. App. 2d Cir. 2003)

BROWN, Chief Judge

In this community property dispute, both parties have appealed, assigning as error, *inter alia,* the trial court's valuation of a community corporation. For the reasons set forth below, we affirm.

Factual and Procedural Background

Peggy McDowell Ellington and Noble Ellington, Jr., were married in 1964 and divorced by judgment dated May 11, 1998. During most of their 35-year marriage, they worked together in the family business, Noble Ellington Cotton Company, Inc. ("NECC"). Noble primarily handled negotiating deals with suppliers and customers, while Peggy ran the office, kept the books and did the paperwork associated with the business. The parties' sons, Ryan and Noble III, were hired by their parents, Ryan in 1992 and Noble III in 1995, and continue to work in the family business.

The business of NECC is buying and selling cotton. NECC buys from farmers, cotton gins and other producers and sells to textile mills and shippers. The gross profit of the company comes from the margin made from this activity. NECC made a profit every year from 1979 through 1998. By 1996, the Ellingtons had made more than two million dollars in the cotton business. With profits, the parties purchased office buildings, farms and apartment complexes.

The parties separated in 1996 and were divorced in May 1998. The instant action is an ancillary proceeding, brought by Peggy Ellington Traylor to partition the community property. Shortly before trial, a considerable part of the community was partitioned by agreement, which, by consent of the parties, was incorporated into a partial judgment of partition dated January 2, 2002.

The trial court was left with two primary issues to address: (1) the value of NECC, a community corporation; and (2) whether Noble caused or permitted the diversion of NECC assets, thereby reducing the corporation's earnings and value to the prejudice of Peggy and, if so, the extent of this diversion.

Both parties had expert witnesses who prepared valuation reports and testified regarding their opinions as to the value of NECC. Peggy's expert was Zoe Meeks, a C.P.A. with experience in agricultural business and familiarity with the cotton buying business. Ms. Meeks' method of valuation was the capitalization of earnings method. According to Ms. Meeks, as of March 31, 2000, the fair market value of NECC was $668,000 and the community interest of each of the parties (and therefore the equalizing payment due to Peggy was $334,000). This valuation method includes a substantial intangible asset value which she referred to as goodwill. Noble's expert was Carlton Clark, a certified valuation expert. Mr. Clark used a net asset method of valuing the business because he felt that an earnings or income approach, which included goodwill, was inappropriate. According to Mr. Clark, as of December 10, 2001, NECC's liabilities exceeded assets by $54,968; therefore, the company had zero value.

The trial court did not accept totally the methodology of either Ms. Meeks or Mr. Clark, but instead calculated a value using some of the conclusions of each expert.

* * *

The second issue before the trial court was Peggy's claim that Noble intentionally diverted community assets out of NECC, causing lost earnings and a diminution in the value of the corporation. The court accepted Noble's explanations for the losses incurred by NECC and rejected Peggy's claim for reimbursement/ damages. Both parties have appealed.

Discussion

Valuation of NECC

Former spouses continue to be co-owners of the former community property even after the termination of the community and until it has been finally partitioned. La. C.C. arts. 2369, 2369.1; *Robinson v. Robinson,* 99-3097 (La. 01/17/01), 778 So.2d 1105. In allocating the community assets and liabilities, the court may divide a particular asset or liability equally or unequally or may allocate it in its entirety to one of the spouses. The court must consider the nature and source of the asset or liability, the economic condition of each spouse and any other circumstance the court deems relevant. La. R.S. 9:2801 A(4)(c); *Robinson, supra.*

The court is required to divide the community assets and liabilities so that each spouse receives property of an equal net value. La. R.S. 9:2801 A(4)(b); *Robinson, supra.* In order to avoid an unequal net distribution of assets and liabilities, the court may order the payment of an equalizing sum of money. La. R.S. 9:2801 A(4)(d); *Robinson, supra.*

La.R.S. 9:2801 A(4)(a) provides that the court shall value the assets at the time of trial on the merits, determine the liabilities, and adjudicate the claims of the parties. *Id.* When the parties, however, do not submit evidence of the current value of community assets, the trial court does not err in making its valuations based upon the evidence presented by the parties. See *Barrow v. Barrow,* 27,714 (La. App.2d Cir. 02/28/96), 669 So.2d 622, *writs denied,* 96-1057, 96-1072 (La. 06/21/96), 675 So.2d 1080; *Roberts v. Roberts,* 542 So.2d 517 (La. App. 5th Cir. 1989), *writ denied,* 547 So.2d 1317 (La. 1989). As the Fifth Circuit observed in *Roberts, supra* the trial court is not required to value assets as of the date of trial when the parties do not submit current appraisals or valuations. See also *Bridges v. Bridges,* 96-1191 (La. App. 3d Cir.03/12/97), 692 So.2d 1186; *Monje v. Monje,* 94-622 (La. App. 5th Cir. 12/28/94), 648 So.2d 1086.

The trial court has broad discretion in partitioning community property. As noted by the Third Circuit in *Razzaghe-Ashrafi v. Razzaghe-Ashrafi,* 558 So.2d 1368, 1371 (La. App. 3d Cir. 1990):

> The purpose of [La. R.S. 9:2801(4)(a)] is to provide an occasion for the court to get a handle on the situation. It does not mean that the court is frozen by any statutory time level or particular valuation at any particular time or for any particular purpose, but simply to place values on the assets for the purpose of accounting, allocation and adjudication in accordance with the further provisions of La. R.S. 9:2801(4)(b, c, d and e).

In light of the discretion granted to the trial court by La. R.S. 9:2801, the court is not required to accept at face value a party's valuation of assets, debts or claims against the community. *Gay v. Gay,* 31,974 (La. App.2d Cir. 06/16/99), 741 So.2d 149; *Kaplan v. Kaplan,* 522 So.2d 1344 (La. App. 2d Cir. 1988); *Alford v. Alford,* 94-1464 (La. App. 3d Cir. 04/05/95), 653 So.2d 133. If the trial court's valuations are reasonably supported by the record and do not constitute an abuse of discretion, its determinations should be affirmed. *Alford, supra.* As noted by the court in Starr v. Starr, 557 So.2d 1026 (La. App. 4th Cir. 1990), the law provides no mathematical formula for determining the value of community assets.

If the community asset to be valued is an interest in a partnership or corporation, the court must be careful to value the interest, not just the assets of the business entity. *Moody v. Moody,* 622 So.2d 1381 (La. App. 1st Cir. 1993), *writ denied,* 629 So.2d 1168 (La. 1993); *Borrello v. Borrello,* 614 So.2d 91 (La. App. 4th Cir. 1992); *Mexic v. Mexic,* 577 So.2d 1046 (La. App. 4th Cir. 1991). The trial court's determination of the value of a community business is a factual one which will not be disturbed absent manifest error. *Monje, supra; Moody, supra.* Furthermore, the trial court's choice of one expert's method of valuation over that of another will not be overturned unless it is manifestly erroneous. *Preis v. Preis,* 94-442 (La. App. 3d Cir. 11/02/94), 649 So.2d 593, *writs denied,* 94-2939, 94-2942 (La. 01/27/95), 649 So.2d 392; *Guillaume v. Guillaume,* 603 So.2d 235 (La. App. 4th Cir. 1992); *Stewart v. Stewart,* 585 So.2d 1250 (La. App. 4th Cir. 1991), *writs denied,* 590 So.2d 594, 597 (La. 1992).

Both parties urge on appeal that the trial court erred in not accepting their respective expert's opinion regarding the value of NECC.

* * *

In his written reasons for judgment, the trial court gave detailed support for each of his factual findings regarding the value he assigned to the community corporation. We will examine each one of these determinations in light of the record in its entirety to address the various valuation issues raised by the parties. In this process, given that each of the trial court's conclusions is based upon expert opinion, we will address each party's assignment of error regarding the calculations, conclusions and methodology of the other spouse's valuation expert.

Determination of "Fair Market Value" and Allocation of NECC to Noble Ellington

Noble complains that the trial court erred in first allocating the community corporation to him, then valuing the business. The following is excerpted from the trial court's written reasons:

Both [parties'] expert witnesses acknowledged that their duty was to determine, or estimate, the fair market value of NECC. Meeks' report on page one defines fair market value as "the value, expressed in cash or its equivalent, at which property would change hands between a willing buyer and a willing seller when the former is not under any compulsion to buy and the latter is not under any compulsion to sell, both parties having reasonable knowledge of relevant facts." Clark cites the definition from Treasury Regulations Par. 25.2512-1 which is essentially the same.

It is immediately evident that a community partition is not the "willing buyer and willing seller" situation contemplated by the above definition in the situation where one spouse is to acquire the other spouse's interest. In testimony, Meeks acknowledged that "when you do valuations you have to consider the purpose for which the valuation is to be used and normally in a divorce situation when you're settling property its very rare to have a willing seller." She also testified that as to the valuation done in this case "this is for property settlement purposes, you don't have to have a willing buyer or a willing seller." When you consider that explanation, it renders the recited definition of fair market value useless. Perhaps more accurate than "the purpose for which the valuation is used" would be the estimation of the different values when the business is acquired by different persons. On cross examination, Meeks readily admitted that her opinion as to value was based upon present management remaining the same ...

In response to questions by the court, she specifically admitted that her estimated value would be different if the company was acquired by anyone other than Noble Ellington. There was no predetermination that the business would be allocated to Noble Ellington and there was no basis for her to proceed on that assumption. Nevertheless, that is what she did. Although her valuation is limited to that one situation and would be of no value for any other allocation of the business, it will nevertheless be used to a limited extent because of the court's decision that the company should be so allocated to Noble Ellington.

Following the lead in his expert's testimony that NECC was worthless, Noble Ellington's "solution" is for the court to allocate the business to Peggy Traylor "at zero" meaning she would acquire all of the assets, assume all liabilities and pay no equalizing payment. Such a solution would be unjust. In the first place, Peggy Traylor is clearly not capable of operating the business. Without demeaning the work she performed during her many years in the company, the testimony makes it very clear that her duties were essentially clerical. She neither bought nor sold cotton, nor did she make business decisions. Secondly, considering the family bitterness preceding the trial and which presumably still prevails, it is virtually certain that if she acquired the business, none of the present management would remain. It is almost too obvious to merit mention that Noble, Ryan, Noble III and Denise Ellington could, without any legal impediments, immediately open a new business with a very similar name and

> retain all of the customer base which has been developed through the years. Even if Peggy Traylor were capable of operating the business as claimed in Noble Ellington's memorandum, or even if she could hire an experienced cotton buyer, she would almost certainly have no customers. Even Noble Ellington's expert witness recognized that 92% of the customer base was attributable to Noble and Ryan Ellington and none was attributed to Peggy Traylor. Counsel for Ellington claim[s] that it would be unfair to allocate the company to Noble Ellington at a value disproportionate to the value of the same company if allocated to Peggy Traylor. That would be a valid statement if the property at issue was a house, or a car, or a piece of farmland. However, it loses its validity in partitioning NECC. The court is not aware of either statutory or jurisprudential law prohibiting courts from recognizing that a community business can have different values depending upon which spouse acquires it.
>
> The business which has made both Noble Ellington and Peggy Traylor wealthy while at the same time enjoying a comfortable life style is, in this court's opinion, capable of generating handsome incomes for the four members of the family who are presently operating the business. For the court to find that the company has no value in the hands of Noble Ellington based upon financial records showing a negative net worth based on tangible assets only, would be error and a clear abuse of the court's discretion in partitioning the community.

We agree. As noted by the supreme court in *Robinson, supra,* in allocating community assets and liabilities pursuant to La. R.S. 9:2801, the trial court has the discretion to divide an asset such as a community owned corporation equally or unequally or to allocate it in its entirety to one of the spouses. In doing so, the court has to consider the nature and source of the asset, the economic condition of each spouse and ***any other circumstance the court thinks is relevant.*** (Emphasis added). In the instant case, the trial court determined that the value it placed on NECC was dependent upon which spouse would receive the business. The record, particularly the testimony of the parties and their sons, as well as their respective expert witnesses, supports this conclusion. This assignment of error is without merit.

Use of Capitalization of Earnings Method Based upon an Average of Ten Years' Corporate Earnings

The trial court rejected the valuation method of Noble's expert, Carlton Clark, because it did not include a value for goodwill and instead used the capitalization of earnings method espoused by Peggy's expert, Zoe Meeks, into which an amount for goodwill was factored. In support of its choice of methodology, the court noted the following:

Noble Ellington is the heart of the business. That is one of the difficulties in attempting to use the ordinary meaning of goodwill in a community partition. Perhaps the answer is that NECC has an intangible value which should be recognized but simply does not fit the usual definition of goodwill. Clark, who testified on behalf of Noble Ellington, said that there was no goodwill but later said that the goodwill is personal and non-transferable without the efforts of Noble Ellington. Whether the designation is goodwill or simply intangible asset or some other term should not be important. What is important is what it does to the value of the business, irrespective of its designation.... In this court's opinion, there is something which makes NECC a successful business. For lack of a better term, it appears to the court that the item being dealt with is the customer base which the company has built through the years beginning in 1979. There is no magic in the term "customer base" other than it may be free of the restrictive definitions of goodwill. In his testimony, Clark, while denying the existence of goodwill, used the term customer base, estimating that 55% of the customer base of the company is attributable to Noble Ellington and 37% is attributable to Ryan Ellington.

The court has reviewed the Louisiana case law relating to goodwill, particularly with reference to community businesses which were partitioned by the courts. It is essential to distinguish the cases which decided that goodwill could not even be considered because of the nature of the business from the cases in which the courts have determined that, although goodwill may be an issue, the evidence did not establish a separate value based on goodwill. As this court understands the case law, the only businesses which have thus far been excluded from the consideration of goodwill because of the nature of the services provided are medical, legal and engineering practices. Based upon the testimony of Clark and the argument in memorandum, apparently Noble Ellington contends that his cotton buying business should also be excluded from having a goodwill value on the same basis as physicians, attorneys and engineers.

Godwin v. Godwin [533 So.2d 1009 (La. App. 1st Cir.1988), *writ denied,* 537 So.2d 1165 (La. 1989)], had facts similar to the present case. The community owned a carpet, drapery and wallpaper installation business. The husband did most of the work himself but sometimes used contract labor. The wife sometimes assisted in the business by answering the telephone and maintaining the books. The business had very limited tangible assets but the wife claimed the business was worth $300,000 based on goodwill. As in this case, the husband claimed that the business had no value. He asserted that goodwill should not be used in determining value because of the nature of the service he rendered, citing cases in which the husbands had medical practices. The court [in *Godwin*] distinguished the facts from the "one man 'professional' corporations" and referred to the business ... as a "commercial business." The trial court accepted an expert's valuation of $64,000 based upon the business' goodwill and that valuation was affirmed on appeal. By way of comparison,

> there is no doubt that the husband was a "professional" carpet installer and wallpaper hanger but his relationship with his customers was clearly different from the relationship of a physician to a patient or an attorney to a client.
>
> ... [T]his court finds that NECC can and does have an intangible asset value and whether that intangible value is termed goodwill, customer base or something else is not important. What is important, and also much more difficult, is using that intangible value in determining the total value of the business.

Having reviewed extensively the jurisprudence regarding goodwill and the propriety of its inclusion in the value of a community corporation such as NECC, we agree with the trial court that valuation of the Ellingtons' business should include consideration of an intangible value predominantly attributable to NECC's customer base.

Therefore, we will continue our analysis into the trial court's choice of valuation methodology. Clearly, having determined that goodwill would be a factor, the trial court could not accept the net asset valuation method espoused by Mr. Clark, which did not include a value for goodwill. The trial court concluded as follows:

> The court finds that the income or earnings approach is the most reasonable in the present factual setting but not in the manner applied by Meeks. Although she had compiled the financial information of the company over a period of nine years, she chose to simply choose one year (2000) upon which to determine "Normalized Net Income." That figure is $153,752 after provision for income taxes. That was the amount used as the "Benefit Stream" in the formula leading to a value of $682,342. She next did what she termed an "Excess Earnings Calculation" which resulted in a value of $653,509. By averaging the Normalized Net Income amount and the Excess Earnings Calculation, she arrived at a rounded value of $668,000.
>
> By comparison, Clark did an earnings calculation based upon the last six years of the company's operation and arrived at an annual adjusted pre-tax earnings figure of $18,427. However, he decided against an earnings approach and concluded that a net asset value method was necessary, presumably because the earnings figure would include goodwill which he felt should be excluded. Accordingly, he did not calculate a value of the business based upon his earnings calculations. Although he chose not to use the income approach, Clark testified that if an income approach is used, a single year, which was used by Meeks, is not an accurate basis to determine the company's value and that a number of years can better reflect the expected "benefits stream." The court accepts Clark's opinion on that issue and finds that Meeks' choice of using earnings only in the most recent year to determine a "benefits stream" is not the most accurate method available.

Having reviewed the testimony and reports of the two experts, we agree with the trial court's conclusion to use the income approach, but with an average from a number of years as opposed to a single year's income. As noted by Noble, Ms. Meeks' valuation did not include up-to-date figures which were available to her; the trial court's reluctance to base a corporate value upon a single year's income, that year not even reflecting the most recent activity, is understandable. Therefore, we will not disturb steps one through six of the trial court's calculation.

Regarding adjustments, the trial court determined that Ms. Meeks' adjustments to income were more appropriate than those of Mr. Clark. Again, this is reasonable and is supported by the record, given that the trial court chose an income methodology over a net asset approach. We likewise find no error in the fact that the trial court factored into its valuation Mr. Clark's determination that NECC had a negative net worth of $55,000.

* * *

Conclusion

For the reasons set forth above, the trial court's judgment is AFFIRMED.

Costs of this appeal are to be divided equally between the parties.

AFFIRMED.

G. *Marsha Jo Stratham v. Harry Rufus Stratham*

986 So. 2d 894 (La. App. 2d Cir. 2008)

GASKINS, J.

In this community property partition, the wife appeals from a judgment classifying property and assessing value. In particular, she objects to the trial court's classification of a diamond ring she received as community property. Additionally, she complains of the trial court's classification of post-termination distributions to the husband from the community business as his separate property, and the court's assessment of a value of $34,000 to the community business. We affirm the trial court judgment.

FACTS

The parties, Marsha Jo "Jody" Statham and Harry Rufus "Butch" Statham were married in 1970. They divorced in 2005. The community terminated on February 16, 2005, the date of the filing of the divorce petition.

***

A bench trial on the community property partition was held on July 27, 2007. Six witnesses testified. In addition to the parties, Jody **2* presented the testimony of Richard W. Guillot, a business valuation expert, and Gary L. Booth, a certified public accountant (CPA) who performed work for Butch's insurance brokerage company, P & S Benefits Consultants, Inc. (P & S). Butch presented the testimony of Albert Carlton Clark, III, a business valuation expert, and Troy Pardue, an insurance agent who was Butch's business partner for 11 years.

According to Mr. Guillot's analysis, the fair market value of P & S as of February 2005 was $310,766. When he compiled his report in June 2006, he based his opinions on fair market value, a willing buyer and a willing seller. However, Mr. Clark-who was hired two months before trial-estimated the value at $34,000 for purposes of the community property partition. In reaching this figure, he estimated that P & S had a total value of $220,008, but a total goodwill value of $207,094. He then assessed 90 percent of the total goodwill value of the company to personal goodwill, as opposed to enterprise goodwill.

***

As to the value assessment of P & S, the court found the testimony of Mr. Clark more convincing than that of Mr. Guillot. Specifically, it concluded that the basis of Mr. Clark's opinion was more valid since Mr. Guillot's report used 2005 data and failed to assess goodwill. Thus, the court assigned a value of $34,000 to the company. On the issue of post-termination distributions from P & S to Butch, the court found that this income resulted from effort, skill and industry exercised by Butch after the **4* termination of the community; thus, it was classified as his separate property.

On October 22, 2007, the trial court signed a judgment in conformity with its ruling.

Jody appealed.

***

VALUATION OF COMPANY

As to the valuation of P & S, Jody contends that the trial court erred in concluding that Mr. Clark's opinion was more valid because it used more recent financial information; according to Jody, the evidence shows that P & S's cash flow has remained consistent through 2007. She claims that the 90 percent figure used for personal goodwill by Mr. Clark cannot be sustained and it ignores the fact that much of the company's stability came from selling policies from major companies like Blue Cross/Blue Shield.

Butch argues that his expert, Mr. Clark, properly applied La. R.S. 9:2801.2 which provides for the exclusion of "goodwill attributable to any personal quality of the spouse awarded the business" from the business' valuation. On the other hand, he asserts that Jody's expert failed to apply the statute in his analysis. Butch also maintains that the testimony of his former business partner, Mr. Pardue, corroborated his own testimony about the nature of the business and his personal relationship with his clients.

***

Where one spouse holds a professional degree or license and the goodwill results solely from that professional's personal relationship with clients, that goodwill is not included in the community. *Clemons v. Clemons,* 42,129 (La.App. 2d Cir.5/9/07), 960 So.2d 1068, *writ denied,* 2007-1652 (La.10/26/07), 966 So.2d 583.

The rule that questions of credibility are for the trier of fact applies to the evaluation of expert testimony, unless the stated reasons of the expert are patently unsound. Credibility determinations, including the evaluation of and resolution of conflicts in expert testimony, are factual issues to be resolved by the trier of fact, which should not be disturbed on appeal in the absence of manifest error. *Hanks v. Entergy Corporation,* 2006-477 (La.12/18/06), 944 So.2d 564.

The two experts used similar methodologies to value P & S. However, they differed substantially on the methods used to determine goodwill. To make this assessment, Mr. Clark began with his fair market calculation of $220,008 and subtracted $12,914 for business assets (like accounts receivable, furniture, and fixtures). Mr. Clark found the remaining value of $207,094 was goodwill. In determining the percentage of goodwill attributable to personal goodwill and to enterprise goodwill, Mr. Clark considered Butch's personality, his relationship with his customers, the amount of his business coming from referrals, the loyalty of his customers who would follow him regardless of his company name, and the good service Butch provides to his customers. Mr. Clark assigned little value to the product because other insurance agents sell the same group health lines. Pursuant to La. R.S. 9:2801.2, for purposes of the community property partition, Mr. Clark concluded that 90 percent of the value was attributable to Butch's personal attributes and only 10 percent to the enterprise or business itself. Thus, he found that the company's value, for partition purposes, was $34,000.

Mr. Guillot testified that Mr. Clark's assignment of 90 percent to personal goodwill was unreasonable and that any methodology to assign personal goodwill was, at best, subjective. His analysis does not appear to assess goodwill under La. R.S. 9:2801.2. Instead, to compensate for goodwill, he merely increased the salary for Butch in the analysis by which he determined the value of P & S.

Our review of the testimony of the experts reveals that the trial court made a credibility determination in favor of Butch's expert, Mr. Clark. As we do not find any indication that Mr. Clark's reasons are "patently unsound," we are obliged to defer to the trier of fact. The trial court's ***9* findings on this issue are not manifestly erroneous or clearly wrong. Therefore, the trial court did not err in accepting Mr. Clark's valuation of the company.

***

CHAPTER 3: THE PRESUMPTION OF COMMUNITY

3.1 PRESUMPTION FORMULATIONS

A. Generally

All of the community property jurisdictions have a presumption in favor of community property. These presumptions have are significant from an evidentiary standpoint. The Louisiana Code of Evidence explains as follows:

Art. 302. Definitions

The following definitions apply under this Chapter:

(1) The "burden of persuasion" is the burden of a party to establish a requisite degree of belief in the mind of the trier of fact as to the existence or nonexistence of a fact. Depending on the circumstances, the degree of belief may be by a preponderance of the evidence, by clear and convincing evidence, or as otherwise required by law.

(2) A "predicate fact" is a fact or group of facts which must be established for a party to be entitled to the benefits of a presumption.

(3) A "presumption" is an inference created by legislation that the trier of fact must draw if it finds the existence of the predicate fact unless the trier of fact is persuaded by evidence of the nonexistence of the fact to be inferred. As used herein, it does not include a particular usage of the term "presumption" where the content, context, or history of the statute indicates an intention merely to authorize but not to require the trier of fact to draw an inference.

(4) An "inference" is a conclusion that an evidentiary fact exists based on the establishment of a predicate fact.

The community property jurisdictions employ at least three different community property presumptions: the possession formula, the acquisition formula, and the unlimited formula. The element that varies between the formulations is the predicate fact. Common law jurisdictions employing a dual classification approach to equitable distribution have similar presumptions and formulations. The evidence required to overcome the community presumption will also vary among the states and may vary depending on the factual circumstances at hand. The formula used by a state as well as the evidence required to overcome the presumption can be viewed as reflecting the strength of the public policy favoring community property in that particular jurisdiction.

Possession Formula. The predicate fact in the possession formula is simply that either spouse possessed the property during the marriage. If a spouse possessed property during the marriage then the property is presumed to be community property. Texas utilizes a possession formula and requires clear and convincing evidence to rebut the presumption.

Tex. Fam. Code § 3.003. Presumption of Community Property

(a) Property possessed by either spouse during or on dissolution of marriage is presumed to be community property.

(b) The degree of proof necessary to establish that property is separate property is clear and convincing evidence.

Acquisition Formula. The predicate fact in the acquisition formula is that property was acquired during the marriage by either spouse. The formula is less supportive of community property because it is more limited in its application than the possession formula. The possession formula applies to all property regardless of its time of acquisition. Property acquired before marriage is presumed community property under the possession formula provided that the spouse possessed the property during marriage. The acquisition formula, in contrast, requires that the property be acquired during the marriage in order for the community property presumption to apply. New Mexico uses an acquisition formula. Specifically, New Mexico Statute §40-3-12 provides, in part, that "[p]roperty acquired during marriage by either husband or wife, or both, is presumed to be community property." In New Mexico, the presumption may be overcome by a preponderance of the evidence.[9]

The acquisition formula can be problematic where there is no credible evidence regarding the date of the acquisition of the asset. California, which also uses the acquisition formula, solves this problem by imposing a second presumption in the case of long marriages. If there is no evidence with respect to the date of acquisition, and the couple has been married for a long time, then the court is allowed to presume that the asset was acquired during marriage.

Unlimited Formula. The unlimited formula is the most generous of the three formulations. The predicate fact under this formula is merely that either spouse has

[9] *See e.g.* Nichols v. Nichols, 648 P. 2d 780 (N.M. 1982).

property. The timing of the possession or acquisition of the property is not relevant. Wisconsin Statute §766.31(2) is an example of this type of formula. It provides that "[a]ll property of the spouses is presumed to be marital property."

B. Louisiana Approach

The Louisiana Civil Code uses a possession formula, as follows:

Art. 2340. Presumption of community

Things in the possession of a spouse during the existence of a regime of community of acquets and gains are presumed to be community, but either spouse may prove that they are separate property.

Civil Code article 2340 is a departure from Louisiana's former approach.

3.2 PRIOR LOUISIANA LAW AND RETROACTIVITY OF CURRENT LAW

A. Introduction

A dramatic change from the prior law is masked by the simple phrase in La. Civ. Code art. 2340 that "either spouse may prove that they are separate property." As Comment (b) states, "This provision suppresses the requirement of a double declaration established by Louisiana jurisprudence." Under the double declaration rule, a jurisprudential innovation based on doubtful authority, a husband (but not a wife) was precluded from proving that an immovable was his separate property if the act of acquisition did not contain a declaration that (1) the asset was acquired with separate funds and (2) that he intended it to be his separate property. The rule was being whittled away in recent cases, and its constitutionality was also questioned as a denial of equal protection.

Before 1980, a wife could overcome the presumption of community without a double declaration, but the cases required proof (1) of the use of separate funds; (2) that the wife administered those funds; (3) that the funds were invested by her and (4) in case of credit purchases, of the ability to accumulate separate funds in the future to pay the price. Under the new provisions, those requirements should also be suppressed. Gone from the law for some time has been the doctrine of the husband administering the wife's separate property. The fourth requirement concerning credit purchases was eliminated by the supreme court in *Curtis v. Curtis* (discussed *infra*, Chapter 4). The court observed that although this restriction "may have been justified in previous years when most women stayed home and did not have separate incomes" it was no longer supportable because "an ever increasing number of women" are "entering the work force." With the increased possibility for matrimonial agreements changing the regime during marriage, as well as partitions and donations, it is simple for the wife to generate a separate estate. Continuing the old rule would also raise equal protection problems because of the discrimination against the wife.

The result, both as to the husband and the wife, is that the encrustations of the jurisprudence that had hardened into rules the means of proving the separate nature of the property are gone. More flexiblity is available now, and any means of proof may be used to establish that the asset is not community.

See SPAHT & HARGRAVE, LOUISIANA MATRIMONIAL REGIMES, Chapter 4 (West 1996).

B. *Brenda Marie Brignac Tullier v. Benjamin J. Tullier, Jr.*

464 So.2d 278 (La. 1985)

BLANCHE, Justice.

This suit involves the partition of a community property regime. Plaintiff, Brenda Marie Tullier and defendant, Benjamin J. Tullier, Jr. were divorced on February 7, 1980. After their divorce, plaintiff filed suit to partition the community which existed during their marriage and claimed that three tracts of immovable property acquired by her husband during their marriage were community property. The trial court found that these tracts of land were community property. The Court of Appeal reversed the trial court holding that the land was the separate property of Benjamin Tullier, Jr. 450 So.2d 1016. Because this lawsuit involves important issues of community property law which this Court has not addressed, we granted writs.

The property in question was acquired by defendant from his mother, Pearl Tullier. Pearl Tullier had purchased the three lots during a period from February 21, 1951 to December 9, 1959 for a total price of $16,800.00 and these lots were her separate property. When Pearl Tullier's husband died in 1966, these tracts were included in the Succession of Benjamin J. Tullier, Sr. as a result of opposition to the succession. The heirs of Benjamin Tullier, Sr. eventually compromised their differences concerning the succession and in order to facilitate the compromise agreement, defendant agreed to pay the succession $15,000.00 in cash. These funds came from the redemption of Series E Savings Bonds held in co-ownership with his mother and which were acknowledged by her to be solely the property of her son. Although defendant signed the compromise agreement, he did not receive any consideration from the agreement in exchange for his bonds and by the terms of the compromise agreement received nothing from the succession of his father. After the succession was closed Pearl Tullier transferred the property in question by executing three "cash sales" to defendant for a total price of $14,899.00, which was approximately the value of the savings bonds. Although the deeds were entitled "cash sales", no money actually was transferred. Likewise, these "cash sales" lacked a double declaration that the property was acquired with funds belonging to defendant separately and that it was being acquired for his individual estate.

At issue in this lawsuit is the retroactive application of Louisiana Civil Code Article 2340 and the continued validity of the double declaration rule. This precise issue was recently considered in Wood v. Wood, 424 So.2d 1143 (La. App. 1st Cir. 1982) and for the most part, we adopt the reasoning set forth in that opinion to find a retroactive application of the codal article.

The jurisprudence interpreting now repealed Louisiana Civil Code Articles 2334 and 2402 had established that as to movable property conveyed to the husband for a cash consideration during the marriage, there is a presumption which may not be rebutted that the property is community property unless there is contained in the act of acquisition a double declaration that the property was acquired with funds belonging to the husband separately and that it was being acquired for his individual estate. Wood v. Wood, *supra*; Phillips v. Nereaux, 357 So.2d 813 (La. App. 1st Cir. 1978); Thomas v. Thomas, 27 So.2d 758 (La. App. Orl. 1946). While there has been much discussion as to the original purpose of the double declaration rule and as to whether it ever accomplished its desired result, the rule was nonetheless applied by the courts of this state until the enactment of Civil Code Article 2340 which legislatively eliminated the double declaration rule. Therefore, although we agree it is questionable whether the double declaration rule ever accomplished its desired goal, its relative success or failure is immaterial to our determination that Article 2340 may be applied retroactively.

Louisiana Civil Code Article 2340 provides:

> Things in the possession of a spouse during the existence of a regime of community of acquets and gains are presumed to be community, but either spouse may prove that they are separate property.

Comment (b) states that this provision was intended to suppress the requirement of a double declaration which was established by Louisiana jurisprudence. Therefore, as of January 1, 1980, which was the effective date of Article 2340, the double declaration is no longer required. However, as in the present case, numerous transactions among married persons involving immovable community property took place prior to January 1, 1980 thereby bringing into focus the question of whether Article 2340 should be applied retroactively. If Article 2340 is not applied retroactively, the property in question will be conclusively presumed to be community property. However, if Article 2340 is given retroactive application, the husband will be allowed to introduce evidence as to the separate nature of the property.

There were two separate revisions to the Code articles dealing with Matrimonial Regimes. Title VI of Book III of the Revised Civil Code entitled "Matrimonial Regimes" was initially repealed by Acts 1978, No. 627, § 6. This Act added La.R.S. 9:2831 through La.R.S. 9:2856 to the Revised Statutes. La.R.S. 9:2838 contained a paragraph with language almost identical to that recited above in Article 2340, eliminating the double declaration requirement. Wood v. Wood, supra.

Section Nine of Act 627 of 1978 provided that statutes therein enacted would take effect January 1, 1980, and would apply to the property and obligations of all spouses, regardless of when the spouses were married or the property acquired. However Section Nine also provided that the new provisions concerning the legal regime could not be construed so as to change the characterization as separate or community of assets acquired prior to the effective date by a spouse who relied on the law in force at the time of the transaction. Thus under the first revision the provisions of the new legal regime could not apply retroactively to change the classification of property as separate or community. Wood v. Wood, supra.

The following year, Acts 1979, No. 709 repealed Acts 1978, No. 627 in its entirety and enacted a new Title VI of Book III of the Revised Civil Code, again entitled "Matrimonial Regimes" including Article 2340 as stated above. Section Thirteen of Act 709 also provided January 1, 1980 as the effective date of the new matrimonial regimes code articles. However, unlike Section Nine of Acts 1978, No. 627, no provision was made for the retroactivity of the new laws. Thus, the second revision did not preclude a retroactive application of the elimination of the double declaration requirement, as was formerly the case with the 1978 legislation. Wood v. Wood, supra.

Conclusive presumptions have been considered to be rules of substantive law rather than rules of evidence. 31 A C.J.S., Verbo "Evidence," § 115; C. Samuel, The Retroactivity Provisions of Louisiana's Equal Management Law: Interpretation and Constitutionality. 39 La.L. Rev. 347 at 400 (1979). Since the double declaration rule has been interpreted to be a conclusive presumption, it is argued by plaintiff and others that the double declaration rule is a rule of substantive law. Louisiana has several other conclusive presumptions including the presumption of survival when more than one person perishes in the same event, not allowing evidence of the absence or failure of consideration for a note against a holder in due course and the conclusiveness of res judicata. S. Dwyer, *Presumptions and Burden of Proof* 21 Loy.L.REV. 377 (1975). However, as distinguished from the double declaration rule which was purely of a judicial origin, these conclusive presumptions were enactments of the Louisiana legislature. In Louisiana, the law is the solemn expression of legislative will.

La.Civ.Code art. 1. The judicial branch of government merely interprets such expressions of legislative will. The decisions of our state courts do not create or eliminate substantive rights as this is the proper function of the legislature. Wood v. Wood, supra. Lee v. Peerless Insurance Company, 248 La. 982, 183 So.2d 328 (1966); Carpenter v. Metropolitan Life Insurance Company, 182 La. 813, 162 So. 630 (1935); State v. Murtes, 232 La. 486, 94 So.2d 446 (1957); State v. Vallery, 212 La. 1095, 34 So.2d 329 (1948); Pfister v. St. Bernard Cypress Company, 155 La. 575, 99 So. 454 (1924). Therefore, the jurisprudentially created double declaration rule did not and could not have created any substantive right of ownership in property.

As a general rule in Louisiana, a law can proscribe only for the future. La. Civ.Code art. 8. However, laws which are not substantive but which are merely procedural or remedial will be given retroactive effect in the absence of language to the contrary. Ardoin v. Hartford Accident & Indemnity Company, 360 So.2d 1331 (La.1978); General Motors Acceptance Corporation v. Anzelmo, 222 La. 1019, 64 So.2d 417 (1953). Likewise, a law cannot be applied retroactively which will impair obligations of contracts or divest or impair vested rights. Long v. Northeast Soil Conservation District of Louisiana, 226 La. 824, 77 So.2d 408 (1955); Brown Indemnity Insurance Company of North American, 108 So.2d 812 (La.App. 2nd Cir. 1959).

Civil Code Article 2340 establishes a presumption in favor of the community which can be rebutted by either spouse. Since this presumption is rebuttable, the article is procedural in nature and can be applied retroactively. Ardoin v. Hartford Accident & Indemnity Company, supra Wood v. Wood, supra. Since we have already concluded that the double declaration rule did not establish substantive rights, the retroactive application of Article 2340 will not divest the wife or any vested rights. Therefore, there is no bar to the retroactive application of Article 2340.

While we have concluded that there is no bar to the retroactive application of Article 2340, it has been suggested that there is no need to apply Article 2340 retroactively and that to do so would be unfair to the wife. Note, "Retroactivity of the Repeal of the Double Declaration Rule: Wood v. Wood", 44 La.L.REV. 823 (1984). The intent of Article 2340 was to terminate the double declaration rule and to allow either spouse to prove the separate nature of property acquired during the community. Since the legislature has concluded that the better policy would permit a spouse to prove in court the true nature of property rather than to rely on the conclusive presumption fashioned by the Court, the logical application of the rule would subject all property to its rule regardless of when acquired. Neither is there any unfairness to the wife in giving retroactive affect to Article 2340. Under the double declaration rule, property that may have been truly the separate property of the husband was arbitrarily presumed to he property of the community absent the double declaration. Under Article 2340, the husband would have the opportunity to prove the separate nature of this property. While a retroactive application of Article 2340 will prevent the wife from placing property in the community that but for the double declaration rule would be classified as separate, the wife will not be deprived of any property which is in truth and fact community property. There is therefore ample reason to apply Article 2340 retroactively.

Having concluded that Article 2340 should be applied retroactively, we must determine whether defendant has proved the separate nature of the property in question. Under Article 2340, the property is presumed to be community. The party asserting the separate nature of the property acquired during the marriage has the burden of overcoming a strong presumption in favor of the community. Curtis v. Curtis, 403 So.2d 56 (La. 1981). Defendant was the owner of bonds which had been set aside for him by his father and which were his separate property. These bonds were transferred to defendant's mother in order to compromise adverse succession claims. In return, Pearl Tullier transferred by "cash sale" the three tracts of land in question to defendant. At the time of these "cash sales" no money was transferred. It is arguable whether this was a true cash sale or whether this was a donation. If this was in fact a cash sale, the funds used by defendant to purchase the land were his separate property. Likewise, if this was a donation by Pearl Tullier to her son, then the land would also be the separate property of defendant. La. Civil Code art. 2341. McElwee v. McElwee, 255 So.2d 883 (La. App. 2d Cir. 1971). In either case, we conclude that defendant has proved the property to be his separate property under Louisiana Civil Code Article 2341.

DECREE

AFFIRMED.

3.3 STRENGTH OF THE COMMUNITY PRESUMPTION

A. *Byron Ellis Talbot v. Bernice Ellen Harang Talbot*

864 So.2d 590 (La. 2003)

KNOLL, Justice.

This writ concerns issues in a community property partition, the most important being the burden of proof necessary to overcome the presumption of community contained in La. Civ. Code article 2340. The parties in this matter were married in 1974 and subsequently divorced in 1997. In March 2000, the district court rendered a final judgment valuing and allocating the assets of the former community. The First Circuit Court of Appeal reversed several of the district court's findings, holding that the defendant failed to carry her burden of proof in establishing the Hibernia Bank and Bank One stocks and two certificates of deposit in her possession during the marriage were her separate property. The First Circuit also reversed the district court's ruling awarding the defendant ownership of the Great Southern Life Insurance Policy, which insured the plaintiff's life, and awarded the defendant a share in the cash surrender value of the policy.

We granted this writ to consider the burden of proof necessary to overcome the presumption of community and to further examine the allocation of ownership of a life insurance policy which insures the life of an ex-spouse. *Talbot v. Talbot* 03-C-0814 (La. 6/20/03), 8947 So. 2d 1247. For the following reasons we find the proper burden of proof in overcoming the presumption of community contained in La. Civ. Code article 2340 is a preponderance of the evidence. Thus, we reverse in part the court of appeal's determination that the defendant failed to carry her burden in establishing the separate nature of her Hibernia and Bank One bank stocks. In all other respects the court of appeal's decision is affirmed.

FACTS AND PROCEDURAL HISTORY

On September 27, 1974, Byron Talbot ("Mr. Talbot") and Bernice Harang ("Mrs. Talbot") were married, and three children were born of their marriage. During their marriage, the parties amassed an estate consisting of extensive amounts of property and ownership of various businesses. On March 20, 1997, Mr. Talbot filed a petition for divorce, joint custody, partition of the community property, court costs, and attorney's fees. Mrs. Talbot answered the petition and filed for divorce in reconvention. On August 22, 1997, the district court rendered a judgment of divorce and terminated the community regime retroactively to the date Mr. Talbot filed his petition for divorce.

The parties filed several preliminary detailed descriptive lists, and finally on October 27, 1998, the parties filed a joint detailed descriptive list. The district court held a trial on the merits on October 26, 27, 28, and 29, and November 4, 5, 6, and 10 in 1998. During the trial, Mrs. Talbot and her two siblings, Mr. Ben Harang ("Mr. Harang") and Mrs. Sally Harang Naquin ("Mrs. Naquin"), testified as to the source of Mrs. Talbot's interest in the Hibernia and Bank One bank stocks and the funds, which comprise the two Hibernia CDs numbered 11140 and 11141 ("CDs"), respectively.

At the trial, all three siblings testified that they had received shares of stock in Citizens Bank and Trust Company from their grandfather, Harvey Peltier. Although Mr. Harang could not testify conclusively as to whether the stocks presently in Mrs. Talbot's possession were the stocks received from their grandfather, both Mrs. Talbot and Mrs. Naquin adamantly asserted that Mrs. Talbot inherited shares of stock in Citizens Bank and Trust Company from their grandfather when she was a young girl years before she was married. After a series of buyouts and mergers, the shares of Hibernia stock in question were a direct byproduct of those shares of Citizens Bank and Trust Company stock and the shares of Bank One stock were a direct byproduct of the

Raceland Bank and Trust Company stock. We note with significance that Mr. Talbot testified he was not aware that he and his wife ever bought Argent or Bank One stock during their marriage.

As to the funds comprising the CDs at issue, Mrs. Talbot explained that she received from a grandfather a 1/25 interest in Bay Drilling, a limited liability company. She received from her father an interest in two other limited liability companies, Tex-Emma and Cameco. Her interests in these three companies were subsequently sold, and she placed the money she received from these sales in CDs, which she believed continuously "rolled over" and presently exist as the CDs at issue.

At the close of this eight-day trial, the district court appointed experts to conduct appraisals of the community's immovable property and businesses from which the experts were to provide the court with reports of their evaluations for its consideration. On March 30, 2000, the district court signed a final judgment valuing and allocating assets of the former community. In its judgment, the district court found:

> That the certificates of deposit numbers 11140 and 11141 at Hibernia Bank are Bernice H. Talbot's separate property. This Court finds that Mrs. Talbot testified that she received these funds from her grandfather and received stock from her grandfather. Her separate property was sold and placed in certificates of deposit, that the fruits from the certificates of deposit were expended on community expenses, and that in fact, the certificates of deposit are less than the total amount she received from her grandfather. Accordingly, this Court found clear and convincing evidence that these certificates of deposit are Bernice H. Talbot's separate property. The only evidence that the Court had before it is that they are her separate property. The testimony of Mrs. Talbot stated that they were her separate property, and the testimony of her sister that she received similar amounts and the other grandchildren received the same amount was refuted.

The district court also held "that the Argent Bank stock and the Bank On stock are Bernice H. Talbot's separate property" and transferred the ownership of the Great Southern Life policy number 1822260 to Mrs. Talbot at a value of $48,485.

On appeal to the First Circuit, the parties asserted fourteen assignments of error. Applying the clear and convincing standard of proof, the First Circuit held that "the record demonstrates that [Mrs. Talbot] failed to establish the separate nature of the CDs, to prove the CDs were purchased with her separate funds, and to furnish evidence that the CDs had been 'rolled over' from term to term." Accordingly, the court of appeal found that Mrs. Talbot failed to sustain her burden of overcoming the presumption that the funds contained in the CDs were community. Applying the "best evidence" rule and the clear and convincing standard of proof, the First Circuit also found that the district court erred in accepting parol evidence to sustain Mrs. Talbot's burden of proof that the Bank One stock certificates P178497 and 1252643 were her separate property. On rehearing, the First Circuit amended its ruling on the bank stocks to include the Citizens Bank and Trust Company, and Argent Bank stock, designating all the bank stocks as community property.

In addition, on original hearing, the First Circuit reversed the district court's allocation of ownership of the Great Southern Life insurance policy number 1822260, which insured Mr. Talbot's life, to Mrs. Talbot, finding that the community asset in question in this case was the cash surrender value of the policy, and not the ownership of the policy, and awarded Mrs. Talbot a share in the cash surrender value of the policy.

LAW AND ANALYSIS

Although marriage is designated a civil contract under La. Civ. Code article 86, "it is more than a contract." *Holliday v. Holliday*, 358 So.2d 618, 619 (La. 1978). "The law prescribes the manner of contracting and celebrating marriages, the legal effects and consequences of marriage, and the manner in which marriages may be dissolved." *Id.* Accordingly, "marriage is a relationship established according to law and it is the policy of the state to maintain it." *Id.* In the public interest, the state has deemed that "the legal regime of community of acquets and gains applies to spouses domiciled in this state." La. Civ. Code art. 2334 (2003).

In *Succession of Lyons*, 425 So.2d 1161, 1165 (La. 1984), this Court stated that "persons attempting to overcome the presumption of community property status ... must ... satisfy this intermediate level of proof." referring to the clear and convincing standard. *Lyons*, 452 So.2d at 1165. However, in making this statement, the court reproduced article 2340 and cited two cases: *R.D.M. Corp. v. Patterson*, 255 La. 301, 230 Sao.2d 820 (1970) and *Succession of Hemenway*, 228 La. 572, 83 So.2d 377 (1955). Both cases relied upon by the Court predated the 1979 revision of Book III, Title IV of the Civil Code.

In *Tullier v. Tullier*, 464 So.2d 278 (La. 1985), this Court upheld the retroactive application of La. Civ. Code art. 2340 without comment as to the presumption and the burden of proof necessary to rebut the presumption of community under the new codal provisions. *Tullier*, 464 So.2d at 282. The *Tullier* court merely described the presumption as "a strong presumption in favor of the community." *Id.* at 283.

Repeatedly, the lower courts have relied upon pre-vision case law in applying the clear and convincing standard of proof, but the leading authorities in this area of law are critical of this practice and advocate the application of the lower preponderance of the evidence standard. *See* Katherine S. Spaht & W. Lee Hargrave, 16 *Louisiana Civil Law Treatise, Matrimonial Regimes* § 4.8, at 207-08 (2nd ed. 1997).

This court has yet to examine whether it is necessary to rebut the presumption of community in article 2340 as to "things in the possession of a spouse during the existence of a regime of community" by the heightened burden of clear and convincing proof. With the 1979 revisions of the community property laws doing away with the necessity for strict proof of paraphernality and the double declaration rule, the burden of proof necessary to rebut the community presumption os squarely before us in this case.

Presumption of Community

Louisiana Civil Code Article 2340 provides:

> Things in the possession of a spouse during the existence of a regime of community of acquets and gains are presumed to be community, but either spouse may prove that they are separate property.

La. Civ. Code art. 2340 (2003) Enacted by 1979 La. Acts 709, article 2340 broadened the reach of the community presumption previously contained in La. Civ. Code article 2405 to apply to all property possessed by either spouse during the community regime. *See Matrimonial Regimes: The Work of the Louisiana Legislature for the 1978 Regular Session: Private Law*, 39 La. L.Rev. 129, 141 (1978-1979). Obviously favoring the community, this article strengthens the regime through its broader language.

Presently, the presumption applies to all property possessed by either spouse during the community regime, regardless of the time of acquisition. *Matrimonial Regimes, supra*, at 142. This includes "even separate property acquired before the establishment of the regime, and if the character of any property is contested, the spouse claiming separate ownership of the property will have the burden of proving its separate character." *Id.* at 142.

Clearly, the revised community presumption has the potential for unfairness, especially in situations where prior to entering the community regime one spouse acquires property either through donations or independent purchases. Under the new regime, that property is presumed community, and the donee or purchaser spouse has to prove the separate nature of the property he or she brought into the community. La. Civ. Code article 2340 subjects property, which is clearly separate property at the time of its acquisition and prior to marriage, to a community classification potentially effecting a legal change in the nature of the property upon marriage.

Moreover, as evident in this case, the legal presumption creates the possibility and the potentiality that a spouse will be called upon to establish the source or origin of property that may have been acquired years before the marriage and potentially decades before the termination of the community regime. Because this expanded community presumption does have this potential for unfairness, the presumption was made clearly rebuttable. *Matrimonial Regimes, supra,* at 142.

Burden of Proof

"A 'presumption' is an inference created by the legislature that the trier of fact must draw if it finds the existence of the predicate fact unless the trier of fact is persuaded by evidence of the nonexistence of the fact to be inferred." La. Code Evid. Art. 302(3) (2003). Article 302(1) of the Louisiana Code of Evidence provides that "the 'burden of persuasion' is the burden of a party to establish a requisite degree of belief in the mind of the trier of fact as to the existence or nonexistence of a fact." La.Code Evid. Art. 302(1) (2003). "Depending on the circumstances, the degree of belief may be by a preponderance of the evidence, by clear and convincing evidence, or as otherwise required by law." *Id.* Article 2340, however, does not provide the level of proof or persuasion necessary to overcome the presumption of community.

In civil cases, a party who has the burden of proof must prove the fact in issue by a preponderance of the evidence, and not by some artificially created greater standard. *Lasha v. Olin Corp.*, 625 So.2d 1002, 1005 (La. 1993); *Jordan v. Travelers Ins. Co.*, 257 La. 995, 245 So.2d 151, 155 (1971); *McCormick on Evidence* § 339, at 421 (5th ed. 1999). Only in exceptional controversies is the clear and convincing standard applied in civil cases "where there is thought to be special danger of deception, or where the court considers that the particular type of claim should be disfavored on policy." *McCormick, supra*, at 421; *Succession of Lyons*, 452 So.2d at 1165. The clear and convincing standard requires a party to prove the existence of a contested fact is highly probably, or much more probable than its non-existence. *McCormick, supra*, at 421; *Succession of Lyons*, 452 So.2d at 1165.

Through the years, however, the lower courts have repeated the formula of *Prince v. Hopson*, 230 La. 575, 89 So.2d 128 (1956), requiring a spouse to prove the separate nature of his or her property by a "strict, clear, positive and legally certain" standard, or stated more traditionally, the clear and convincing standard. *See, Succession of Broussard*, 306 So.2d 399, 403 (La. App. 3d Cir. 1975) (setting forth the clear and convincing standard). *See e.g., Knighten v. Knighten*, 00-1662 (La. App. 1st Cir. 9/28/01), 809 So.2d 324, 331, *writ denied*, 01-2846 (La. 1/14/02), 805 So.2d 207; *Barrow v. Barrow*, 27,714 (La. App. 2nd Cir. 2/28/96), 669 So.2d 622, 624, *writ denied*, 96-1057, 96-1072 (La. 6/21/96), 675 So.2d 1080; *Hinckley v. Hinckley*, 583 So.2d 125, 127 (La. App. 4th Cir. 1991), *writ denied*, 590 So.2d 64 (La. 1991); *Morris v. Morris*, 96-788 (La. App. 3rd Cir. 12/26/96), 685 So.2d 673, 674, *writ denied*, 97-0237 (La. 3/14/97), 609 So.2d 40; *Succession of Lyons*, 452 So.2d 1161, 1165 (La. 1984). All the cases that purport to impose this intermediate standard of proof rely on a standard that reverts to a time when the courts required strict proof of paraphernality and when the double declaration rule was in effect. Spaht & Hargrave, *supra*, at 209.

Under the strict proof of paraphernality doctrine, a wife could only overcome the presumption of community by satisfying a triple burden of proof showing "(1) that the funds constitution the price paid for the property were paraphernal funds, (2) that they were administered by her, and (3) that they were invested by her." *Prince*, 89 So.2d at 130-31. In *Curtis v. Curtis*, this Court abandoned these strict elements of proof in a case involving a wife's credit sale. *Curtis*, 403 So.2d 56, 58 (La.1981); *see also,* K. Spaht, *Developments in the Law, 1980-198 Matrimonial Regimes*, 42 La. L.Rev. 347, 363-73 (1982); Spaht & Hargrave, *supra*, at 208, n. 3.

The double declaration rule provided that when a husband acquired property during the existence of the community regime, a presumption of community existed, which could not be rebutted unless in the act of acquisition, there was "a double declaration that the property was acquired with funds belonging to the husband separately and that it was being acquired for his individual estate." *Tullier*, 464 So.2d at 281; *see also, Wood v. Wood*, 424 So.2d 11443 (La. App. 1st Cir. 1982). Through the enactment of article 2340, the Legislature abolished the double declaration rule. La. Civ.Code art. 2340, cmt. (B); *Tullier*, 464 So.2d at 281. This abolition "reflects a policy of greater flexibility." Spaht & Hargrave, *supra*, at 209.

An examination of the history of the "strict, clear, positive and legally certain" or the clear and convincing standard of proof reveals that this higher standard apparently evolved in conjunction with the rules requiring strict proof of paraphernality and the double declaration rule, which created a conclusive presumption of community if the husband could not establish evidence of the existence of a double declaration in the act of acquisition. *See Tullier*, 464 So.2d at 281; Spaht & Hargrave, *supra*, at 208-09. With the abolition of the double declaration rule, the Legislature sought to allow for more flexibility in the community presumption and the level of persuasion necessary to rebut that presumption.

With the 1979 revisions of the community property regime, we find it difficult now to discern the basic policies which necessitate a higher than normal level of proof. We quote with approval, the comments of Spaht and Hargrave, leading authorities in this area of the law:

> A suggestion in passing that it involves "the sanctity of the family" may be proper in evaluating the presumption that the husband of the mother is the father of the child, but that does not directly extend to the classification of property as community or separate. Basic fairness does not seem to require the high level, for the law allows the spouses enter into a separate regime in which no community property exists. Judicial efficiency would not seem to demand the higher burden.

> Perhaps there does exist a basic policy in favor of the community classification to promote sharing, but it would seem that the presumption itself satisfied that policy. Also, the simple preponderance of the evidence standard applied regularly in civil cases is the norm unless something higher is called for, and no statute calls for a higher level of proof here.

Spaht & Hargrave, *supra*, at 209-10.

Given the broadened community presumption of the revision, imposing the prior burden of proof by clear and convincing evidence will render near impossible the ability of some spouses to prove the separate nature of property acquired, as in this case, years before the establishment of the regime and decades before its termination. During that broad expanse of time, records are lost, destroyed, and possibly even stolen, and to satisfy this burden of proof, a spouse will potentially need to keep evidence of every donation and gift received and purchase and transfer made dating back years before marriage, even as in this case into childhood. This is an impractical and unwieldy burden, which the Legislature and the Law Institute did not intend through their revision of the community presumption. *See* Spaht & Hargrave, *supra; Matrimonial Regimes, supra.*

As a matter of public policy and in the interest of fairness, we find that the community presumption contained in article 2340 is rebuttable by either spouse upon a showing by a preponderance of the evidence the separate nature of property brought into the community.

* * *

DECREE

For the foregoing reasons, we reverse the court of appeal's judgment on the community nature of the Hibernia and Bank One bank stocks and reinstate the district court's judgment. On all other issues, the court of appeal is affirmed.

REVERSED IN PART OTHERWISE AFFIRMED.

TRAYLOR and HIGHTOWER, JJ., concur in part and dissent in part and assign reasons.

JOHNSON, J., concurs inp art and dissents in part for reaasons assigned by TRAYLOR, J.

TRAYLOR, J., dissenting in part, concurring in part.

I respectfully dissent in part and concur in part. I disagree with the majority decision to lower the burden of proof necessary to overcome the La. Civ. Code art. 2340 presumption of community property. Although the majority relies extensively on pre-revision jurisprudence as a basis for changing the burden of proof, I am unpersuaded by this argument. By the time the 1979 revisions were passed, the law regarding the burden of proof necessary to overcome the presumption of community property was well-established. *See, Prince v. Hopson*, 230 La. 575, 89 So.2d 128 (1956); *Succession of Smith*, 247 La. 921 (175 So.2d 269 (1965); *Succession of Lyons*, 452 So.2d 1161 (La. 1984). The legislature was certainly aware of this law and could have statutorily changed the burden of proof necessary for a rebuttal, yet id did not address the situation.

In addition, I am unconvinced that the repeal of the double declaration and strict proof of parphernality requirements serve as evidence of the legislature's intent to lower the burden of proof. With regard to the double declaration rule, the legislature simply repealed a law which, by this court's acknowledgment, was arbitrary and offered little insight into the determination of whether immovable property was in fact separate property. The "greater flexibility" provided by the repeal of the double declaration rule did not change the burden of proof, but rather allowed for alternative avenues to prove that immovable property is separate under the clear and convincing standard. Likewise, the strict proof of paraphernality requirement was eliminated as a recognition that rules which may have produced a just result under the head-and-master community regime do not necessarily do so when conditions change. *Curtis v. Curtis*, 403 So.2d 56, 58 (La. 1981). It does not follow that at the legislature's repeal of certain types of proof which provided arbitrary results requires a lower burden of proof.

Furthermore, strong policy considerations support the use of the clear and convincing standard. The clear and convincing standard is usually employed "where there is thought to be special danger of deception, or where the court considers that the particular type of claim should be disfavored on public policy grounds." *Lyons*, 452 So.2d at 1165 (quoting *McCormick on Evidence,* § 340(b), p. 708 (2nd ed. 1972)). The rebuttable presumption of community property falls under an exceptional controversy which requires the "strict, clear, positive and legally certain" or the clear and convincing standard. The ease with which the parties may claim lost documents combined with the emotionally charged, intensely personal nature of these proceedings give ample opportunity for deception.

Applying the clear and convincing standard to the case sub judice, Mrs. Talbot has failed to prove the bank stocks are her separate property. The "clear and convincing" standard is a heavier burden of proof than the usual civil case standard of "preponderance of the evidence" but is less burdensome than the "beyond a reasonable doubt" standard of a criminal prosecution. *Lyons*, 452 So.2d at 1165; *Chatelain v. State, Department of Transportation and Development*, 586 So.2d 1373, 1378 (La. 1991). Although I acknowledge that transfer or donation of stocks are not subject to the Civil

Code's strict form requirements in accordance with *Primeaux v. Libersat*, 322 So.2d 147, 151 (La.1975), no evidence reveals that Mrs. Talbot received the stocks in the form provided for donation of stocks. Moreover, I do not believe that Mrs. Talbot's failure to keep records of this event excuses here from producing evidence on this issue. Her possession of the stock, standing alone, does not prove that the stock was in fact transferred to her as the result of an inheritance. Mrs. Talbot could have furnished the trial court with a judgment of possession from her grandfather's estate, which would have established a date of acquisition. Instead, she provided the circumstantial testimony of her brother and sister, which under La. R.S. 12:603 would not serve as evidence for a corporation to transfer stock from the record owner to an heir. Moreover, Mrs. Talbot failed to prove the date of acquisition of stock through her sister's testimony that Citizen's Bank and Trust Company had merged with other banks. I find it incredible that Mrs. Talbot could not produce bank records regarding the various mergers and therefore trace her stock to the date of acquisition.

Accordingly, I respectfully concur in the majority's ultimate decision concerning the life insurance policy and the classification of the certificates of deposit as community property. With regard to the lowering of the standard of proof, however, I respectfully dissent and would maintain the clear and convincing standard for both commingled and non-commingled property. Accordingly, I would find the bank stocks are community property.

HIGHTOWER, J. ad hoc, concurring in part and dissenting in part.

I likewise concur in the rationale of the opinion concerning the life insurance policy and the majority's concluding classification of the CDs. In reference to the lowering of the standard of proof, however, I respectfully dissent and would essentially join with Justice Traylor to affirm the court of appeal's designation of the bank stock as community property.

3.4 LIMITS OF THE SCOPE AND APPLICABILITY OF THE COMMUNITY PRESUMPTION

A. Estoppel

Paragraph A of Louisiana Civil Code article 2342 establishes a limited estoppel rule that prevents a spouse from relying on the community property presumption in some instances. Specifically, the Article provides:

> A. A declaration in an act of acquisition that things are acquired with separate funds as the separate property of a spouse may be controverted by the

> other spouse unless he concurred in the act. It may also be controverted by the forced heirs and the creditors of the spouses, despite the concurrence by the other spouse.

The operation of this rule is examined in more detail in Chapter 5.

B. Actual Knowledge: *Ford Motor Credit Company v. Albert Corbello*

482 So.2d 203 (La. App. 3d Cir. 1986)

STOKER, J.

This suit arises out of the allegedly illegal seizure of Eula Corbello's car to satisfy a judgment rendered against her husband.

Albert Corbello executed a promissory note for $10,902.24 on October 21, 1983, secured by a mortgage on a 1983 Mercury Marquis. The note was assigned to Ford Motor Credit Company (Ford). When Corbello failed to make two payments, Ford accelerated the balance due. The car was seized and sold, but a debt of $6,543.01 remained. Ford obtained a valid default judgment on the deficiency. Ford attempted to execute the judgment by seizing a 1979 Chevrolet registered in Eula Corbello's name, but it was met with the Corbellos' claim that the car was the separate property of Mrs. Corbello. A temporary restraining order was granted, halting the sale of the car, but the Corbellos filed no security. Trial was held on three dates to determine whether a permanent injunction should be issued.

At trial, the judge found that the Chevrolet was Mrs. Corbello's separate property, as it was purchased with funds received from the sale of a home she had owned with her former husband, now deceased. The court labeled the seizure illegal and wrongful, and awarded $52.95 in special damages, $1,100 in general damages and $3,200 in attorney's fees to Mrs. Corbello.

Ford appeals, assigning as error (1) the trial court's conclusion that the seizure of Mrs. Corbello's car was illegal and wrongful, (2) the damage award to Mrs. Corbello, and (3) the failure of the court to award damages to Ford for the wrongful issuance of a temporary restraining order without security.

The trial court concluded that the Chevrolet was the separate property of Mrs. Corbello. We find no manifest error in this conclusion. The undisputed testimony showed that Mrs. Corbello owned a house before her marriage to Mr. Corbello, that she sold the house for $10,000 on February 7, 1984, that she opened a new bank account on that day, that the proceeds of the sale of the house were deposited in it, and that those proceeds were used to buy a Chevrolet in her name on the same day.

Under LSA-C.C. art. 2345, a community obligation may be satisfied during the community from community property and from the separate property of the spouse who incurred the obligation. Mr. Corbello was the only obligor on the promissory note. Mrs. Corbello's separate property could not be seized to satisfy the debt.

Ford alleges that the seizure of the second car was not illegal or wrongful. The company claims that it could rely on LSA-C.C. art. 2340, which states that things in the possession of a spouse are presumed to be community property. Even if Ford initially was entitled to such a presumption, the trial judge had evidence before him which showed that Ford's attorney had notice before the seizure that the car was Mrs. Corbello's separate property. We find no error in the judge's finding of fact that Ford's attorney knew of Mrs. Corbello's claim. Therefore, we agree with his conclusion that the seizure was wrongful.

There is no indication in this case that plaintiff's attorney was in bad faith or acted from improper motives; his view of the law, although honestly held, was erroneous. Acting on this error of law, the attorney provoked a seizure which is considered wrongful in a context of facts such as are presented here. Moreover, proof of malice or bad faith is not a prerequisite for recovery of damages for wrongful seizure in cases of this nature. Escat v. National Bank of Commerce in N.O., 284 So.2d 832 (La. App. 4th Cir. 1973).

Damages may be awarded in the case of a wrongful seizure pursuant to a writ of fieri facias. In addition to actual damages, the award may include general damages for deprivation of use, humiliation and mental anxiety. Peterson v. Olinde Hardware & Supply Co., 356 So.2d 92 (La. App. 1st Cir. 1978), *writ denied*, 357 So.2d 1169 (La. 1978). We find no error in the trial court's award of $52.95 for special damages, or in the provision of $1,100 for general damages. However, we can find no basis for the $3,200 awarded for attorney's fees. LSA-C.C.P. art. 2298 provides for attorney's fees when a judgment debtor or a third party claims ownership of property wrongfully seized under one of the circumstances enumerated in the article. Mrs. Corbello's situation does not fit within this article, and she concedes that she does not rely on its provisions

CHAPTER 4: CLASSIFICATION OF ASSETS

4.1 INTRODUCTION

The classification of property as either community or separate is of obvious importance. All of the community property jurisdictions adhere to the Spanish gananical system of community of acquets and gains. Under the gananical system the spouses retain all of the property they owned prior to marriage as their separate property. Only property acquired or gained during marriage is susceptible of community ownership. Similarly, gifts and inheritances a spouse receives during marriage remain that spouse's separate property—furthering a policy aimed at keeping family property within the family. There are, however, some significant distinctions between the various community property jurisdictions with respect to classification of assets. In particular, the community property jurisdictions differ considerably in the treatment of earnings from separate property.

A. William A. Reppy, Jr., *Major Events in the Evolution of American Community Property Law and Their Import to Equitable Distribution States*, 23 FAM. L. Q. 163 (1989)

***

II. Classification of Rents and Profits of Separate Property

The basic question whether rents and profits of nonmarital property are marital is statutorily answered in some equitable distribution statutes, usually by a provision that they are nonmarital. Some states have reached this result by construing legislation that does not directly address the issue. Problems will arise as how to implement the rule in those states where rents and profits are nonmarital. It may be of interest to such states, aware that an apparently analogous treatment of rents and profits is part of the law of California, Arizona, New Mexico, Washington, and Nevada, that their major departure from historic community property law apparently stemmed from a concern as to how community property classification would affect wives during marriage, particularly in the area of management and control. In Spain several hundred years ago, the rule classifying fruits, rents, and profits of separate property as community was essential if there was to be any substantial community wealth and avoided apportionment problems. Land was almost the only capital asset producing income, primarily by farming and renting out. The propertied nobility for whose families the marital property law was structured were themselves unlikely to work on the land but had servants or serfs who did this and who were paid or maintained out of gains arising from use of the land (which was, as noted, usually the husband's separate property). Old Spain's classification of rents and profits enabled a substantial community estate to be amassed for the typical propertied family and avoided the difficult apportionment problems well-known to students of American community property intimate with the *Pereira* and *Van Camp* apportionment formulae necessary where, as so often happens, a spouse's labor on separately owned capital is part of the reason rents or profits are generated. The present "American" rule, now in effect in the majority of this country's community property jurisdictions, classifies rents and profits from separately owned land also as separate property. All profits from the typical family estate would be separate unless some small fraction were apportioned out, attributed to the landowner spouse's modest activities as overseer, and classified as community property.

The Civil Law rule itself causes commingling and uncommingling problems avoided under the American rule when separate money is invested in a securities account, with gains reinvested, or deposited in an interest-earning bank account. As far as I know, none of the Spanish treatises on marital property law address such problems. Apparently corporate stock was unknown when the Civil Law rule for classification of rents and profits was created. Interest-earning bank accounts may have been unknown, or at least were then rare.

It is rather clear, however, that avoidance of commingling problems had nothing to do with the California Supreme Court's rejection of the Civil Law rule for the American rule in *George v. Ransom,* decided in 1860, a time by which money had perhaps become about as important a resource as land for generating profits. (At least by 1860 a court could observe that the Civil Law rule for profits from separate capital was going to result in automatic commingling in several kinds of investment accounts where earnings were retained.) It was, instead, a perceived unfairness in the early management and control law of California that spawned *George.*

The initial California constitution (adopted in 1849) attempted to cast some protection on married women that the legislature could not withdraw by providing that property owned by a wife before marriage and acquired during marriage by gift, by will, and by inheritance "shall be her separate property" and that laws should "be passed more clearly defining the rights of the wife in relation as well to her separate property as that held in common with her husband." It is rather clear from the debates that the constitutional convention intended to retain for California at least those aspects of Mexican marital property law that were favorable to married women and that treated the wife with respect to property better than wives fared under the coverture doctrine of English common law.

What the California legislature promptly did in 1850 was codify, with a limited exception added in 1853 for wives, the Civil Law rule that rents and profits of separate property of either spouse are community. It also made the husband the sole manager of all community assets, stating he could do with them anything he could do with his own separate property, seemingly implying that he could give away community assets. The husband was also given management power over the wife's separate property, although he could not alienate it or encumber it without her consent.

In 1860, the California Supreme Court held the statute classifying rents and profits of a wife's separate property as community violative of the constitutional provision recognizing a wife's right to own separate property. The statutory management provision giving unlimited control to the husband divested the wife of all beneficial use, leaving her with the "barren right to hold." This was an "anomaly" the state constitution could not have contemplated; hence, the husband's creditor in the case could not reach the property at issue, which all assumed had to be the wife's separate property by force of the opinion. Legislation followed making rents of the husband's separate capital his separate property as well, and California had created the phenomenon of a marital union without community property for couples who do not work but live off the revenues of inherited property or capital brought to the marriage that is managed by a person paid out of the profits he or she generates. Washington, Nevada, Arizona, and New Mexico soon legislatively copied California's answer to the problem of classifying rents and profits from separate capital, and these states struck out on a quite different path toward development of basic principles of community property law from that followed generally in the states adhering to the Spanish rule.

***

B. Louisiana Approach, Generally

Louisiana Civil Code Article 2341 specifies the assets that are a spouse's separate property--acquisitions before establishment of a community regime; reinvestment of separate property; donations to one spouse individually and inherited property; most damage awards; and partitioned community assets. Article 2339 also allows a spouse to elect to make the fruits of separate assets separate. These provisions, coupled with the residual clause of Article 2338 (all property not classified as separate is community) would be sufficient to cover this area of the law. However, presumably for the sake of continuity with prior law and for didactic reasons, the drafters also included in Article 2338 a listing of community assets--property acquired through the effort, skill or industry of either spouse; things acquired with separate and community assets; joint donations; fruits of community assets; and some damage awards.

Special problem areas are also covered: fruits of separate property, interspousal transfers, damage awards. The presumption of community is established in Article 2340 and an estoppel provided for in Article 2342. *See also* the unique provisions for recognition of "mixed title" to property in Article 2341.1.

This scheme is a relatively simple one that has not changed substantially in modern times. The 1980 revision dealt primarily with establishing equal management and made few changes in the classification of assets. The modern innovations in the area, especially pro-rata classification of pensions and other incorporeal assets as partly community and partly separate, have come from court development.

4.2 REAL SUBROGATION

The principle of real subrogation underlies the application of many of the classification rules examined in this chapter. The following cases are aimed at introducing this concept.

A. *Donna Wesley Albert v. Harry John Albert, Jr.*

625 So. 2d 765 (La. App. 1st Cir. 1993)

LOTTINGER, Chief Judge.

Plaintiff, Donna Wesley Albert, filed a petition for partition of community property against her former husband, Harry J. Albert, Jr. Mrs. Albert seeks to have certain immovable property known as the University Park Apartments Complex classified as community property.

FACTS

In 1949, Harry Albert, Sr., father of the defendant, formed University Park Apartments, Inc. Subsequent to the incorporation, the University Park Apartments were sold to the corporation by Harry Albert, Sr. In 1982, through a donation inter vivos, Harry Albert, Jr. became the sole owner of the 1000 shares of stock in University Park Apartments, Inc.

The corporation sold the apartment complex to Mr. and Mrs. Frank Clark and Mr. and Mrs. Robert MacDonell on October 31, 1984. The sale price of $450,000 was represented by $60,000 in cash with the balance evidenced by a promissory note payable to University Park Apartments, Inc. Thereafter, the Clarks sold their interest in the complex to the MacDonells.

On December 19, 1984, Harry Albert and Donna Wesley Albert were married. Mrs. Albert owned no interest in the apartment complex or the corporation. The corporation was dissolved on September 18, 1985.

On May 1, 1987, in consideration for the cancellation of the $390,000 note, the MacDonells transferred their interest in the complex to Mr. Albert by a dation en paiement. Mrs. Albert's signature appears on the dation and a collateral mortgage issued contemporaneously with the dation. Both of these documents contain a statement of paraphernality.

The trial judge classified the apartment complex as community property.

***

DATE OF CORPORATE DISSOLUTION AND REAL SUBROGATION

The trial court agreed with Mrs. Albert's contention that the dissolution of the corporation occurred on June 10, 1987, two years after the dation. However, a close review of the documentary evidence from the Secretary of State's Office (Albert Exhibit 1 and Donna Albert Exhibit 5), reveals that the corporate dissolution occurred on September 18, 1985.

A certificate submitted by Mr. Albert and signed by Jim Brown, Secretary of State, on October 5, 1987, reflects that the corporation was dissolved on September 18, 1985. Mr. Albert also submitted a Certificate of the Liquidator signed by Jim Brown on June 10, 1987, which states that "on September 18, 1985, the date the dissolution became effective, has been filed in this Office in compliance with R.S.1950, 12:148, and recorded in Record of Charters Book 342, and the corporation stands dissolved."

Although Mrs. Albert submitted a certificate reflecting a dissolution date of June 10, 1987, this date merely reflects the filing date of the aforementioned Certificate of the Liquidator. The trial court was manifestly erroneous and clearly wrong in finding that the corporate dissolution occurred on June 10, 1987, rather than September 18, 1985.

The trial court also found that the classification of the property was affected by the transfer of the apartment complex to Mr. Albert individually rather than to the corporation. However, because the corporation no longer existed at the time of the dation it was necessary to place the apartment complex in Mr. Albert's name.

The classification of the property before and after the dation is governed by the following legal principles. La.Civ.Code art. 2341 identifies the separate property of a spouse as follows:

> The separate property of a spouse is his exclusively. It comprises: property acquired by a spouse prior to the establishment of a community property regime; property acquired by a spouse with separate things or with separate and community things when the value of the community things is inconsequential in comparison with the value of the separate things used; property acquired by a spouse by inheritance or donation to him individually; damages awarded to a spouse in an action for breach of contract against the other spouse or for the loss sustained as a result of fraud or bad faith in the management of community property by the other spouse; damages or other indemnity awarded to a spouse in connection with the management of his separate property; and things acquired by a spouse as a result of a voluntary partition of the community during the existence of a community property regime.

Comment (c) to this article provides that the principle of real subrogation is applicable to both separate and community property. Thus, when a thing forming a part of the separate property of a spouse is converted into another thing, the mass of the separate property is not diminished. The new thing takes the place of the old: "*Subrogatum capit naturam subrogati.*" *Newson v. Adams*, 3 La. 231, 233 (1882); Yiannopoulos, Civil Law Property § 79 (1966).

Mr. Albert became the sole shareholder of University Park Apartments, Inc. through a donation inter vivos. Under La.Civ.Code art. 2341 this property was his separate property because it was "acquired by a spouse prior to the establishment of a community property regime" and because it was "acquired by a spouse by inheritance or donation to him individually."

According to comment (c), when Mr. Albert sold the complex, the cash and the promissory note took the place of the apartment complex as his separate property. See *Succession of Davis*, 496 So.2d 549, 552 (La.App. 1st Cir.1986). The dissolution of the corporation and the subsequent transfer to Mr. Albert individually did not affect the separate nature of the property. The note held by Mr. Albert represented his separate property interest in the dissolved corporation. The subsequent cancellation of the note in exchange for the apartment complex was a real subrogation of his separate property interests.

CONCLUSION

Mrs. Albert has failed to establish that her signature on the dation or the collateral mortgage was obtained in error. Thus, she is estopped to deny the separate nature of the property at issue. Furthermore, the property remains the separate property of Mr. Albert through the principle of real subrogation. Therefore, we find that the trial court was manifestly in error and clearly wrong in classifying the apartment complex as community property.

For these reasons the judgment of the trial court is reversed. Costs of this appeal are to be borne by appellee, Donna Wesley Albert.

REVERSED AND RENDERED.

B. *Lynn Marie Sorola Curtis v. Lawrence N. Curtis*

969 So. 2d 1277 (La. App. 3d Cir. 2007)

GREMILLION, Judge.

The plaintiff, Lynn Marie Sorola Curtis (Sorola), appeals the trial court's judgment in favor of the defendant, Laurence Curtis (Curtis), finding that he was involved in a joint venture and that Lawrence N. Curtis, Ltd. (Curtis Ltd.), owned interest in certain cases which were exchanged for stock in Curtis & Lambert, APLC (Curtis and Lambert). For the following reasons, we affirm.

FACTUAL AND PROCEDURAL BACKGROUND

Sorola and Curtis, an attorney, married in 1987 and divorced May 1, 1998. Sorola filed a petition for partition of community property in October 1998. In September 2000, she filed an amendment to the petition for partition of community property. In October 2000, the trial court rendered a judgment ordering mediation. In December 2002, Sorola filed a motion and traversal as to why certain investments accounts should not be classified as community assets and for valuation of said accounts for partition purposes. In March 2003, Sorola and Curtis were able to agree to a partial community property partition of all of the community movables. In June 2003, Curtis filed a memorandum regarding Sorola's motion to traverse admitting that certain investment accounts were community property, but denying that any community property existed in his law firm. He further filed a second supplemental and amended sworn detailed descriptive list. Sorola, thereafter, filed a traversal pertaining to the second detailed descriptive list. Following a two day trial in May 2004, the trial court found that all stock issued to Curtis in the Curtis and Lambert Corporation, "formerly known as Curtis, Robideaux and Lambert, APLC and formerly known as Curtis Tilley & Robideaux APLC," was his separate property. Sorola now appeals.

ISSUES

Sorola assigns as error:

1. The trial court's finding that there was a joint venture between Curtis, Ltd. and J. Minos Simon, Ltd. and/or J. Minos Simon, individually.

2. The trial court's finding that Curtis, Ltd. owned interest in certain cases (files) which were exchanged for stock in Lambert.

LAW

The trial court's determination of what is community property as opposed to what is separate property is a finding of fact. *Young v. Young*, 06-77 (La.App. 3 Cir. 5/31/06), 931 So.2d 541. Factual findings of the trial court will not be disturbed in the absence of manifest error. *Stobart v. State through DOTD*, 617 So.2d 880 (La.1993). If a reasonable basis exists in the record for the trial court's finding, no error has occurred. *Id.*

Things in the possession of a spouse during the existence of a community regime are presumed to be community; however, that presumption can be rebutted by proof that the thing is separate property. La.Civ.Code art. 2340. In this case, the burden rests with Curtis to prove that the stock was his separate property. Pursuant to La.Civ.Code art. 2338, community property includes:

> [P]roperty acquired during the existence of the legal regime through the effort, skill, or industry of either spouse; property acquired with community things or with community and separate things, unless classified as separate property under Article 2341; property donated to the spouses jointly; natural and civil fruits of community property; damages awarded for loss or injury to a thing belonging to the community; and all other property not classified by law as separate property.

Louisiana Civil Code article 2341, defines separate property in part as:

> [P]roperty acquired by a spouse prior to the establishment of a community property regime; property acquired by a spouse with separate things or with separate and community things when the value of the community things is inconsequential in comparison with the value of the separate things used[.]

Curtis acquired the stock in question in February 1991. Thus, as it was during the existence of the community of acquets and gains, it is presumed to be community property. Curtis bears the burden of proving that the stock was his separate property. The trial court found that he met that burden. In the trial court's extensive oral reasons for judgment it stated:

> The Court is being asked to determine whether the stock issued to Lawrence N. Curtis individually by Curtis and Lambert, A Professional Law Corporation, belonged to Mr. Curtis' separate estate or to the community of acquets and gains formerly existing between him and Lynn Marie Sorola.

In 1982, Mr. Curtis and Mr. Simon entered into discussions concerning forming some kind of relationship to handle legal matters for mutual clients.

Mr. Curtis and Mr. Simon met personally on at least two occasions to discuss this relationship. Mr. Curtis had two goals in mind. He did not want to become an employee of Mr. Simon. And he wanted to practice in the same building complex where Mr. Simon practiced. Mr. Curtis consulted Mr. John Wright who suggested he form Lawrence N. Curtis, Ltd., A Professional Law Corporation.

The arrangement worked out between Mr. Simon and Mr. Curtis was that Mr. Curtis would arrange to have clients of [his former employer's corporation] discharge their corporation as their attorney, and the clients would sign new contracts with J. Minos Simon, Ltd. On those cases and every new case brought in by either attorney, there would be a fee split of two-thirds to Simon and one-third to Curtis.... All new case contracts would also be between the clients and J. Minos Simon, Ltd., as well. As part of this arrangement, Simon would pay the expenses of the case, as well as the library, overhead, and office salaries.

....

The arrangement was struck and Mr. Curtis moved his law office into the building complex where Mr. Simon practiced and which was owned by a company Simon owned. Lawrence N. Curtis, Ltd., a Professional Law Corporation, was formed a week or two after on June 14, 1982.

The Court notes that the arrangement reached between Mr. Simon and Mr. Curtis was completely verbal and no written documents exist as to this transaction. The Court finds this arrangement to be a joint venture where the participants each acquired an interest in cases and shared in profits and losses according to a fixed formula.

....

The Court, therefore, finds that Lawrence N. Curtis, Ltd., A Professional Law Corporation, was engaged in a joint venture with J. Minos Simon, Ltd., and later with J. Minos Simon individually. Also Lawrence N. Curtis., Ltd., had an ownership interest in the cases represented by contracts signed between clients and J. Minos Simon, Ltd., and later between the clients and J. Minos Simon individually. This was true from the date of incorporation, as well as during the marriage between Mr. Curtis and Ms. Sorola.

When Curtis, Tilly & Robideaux, A Professional Law Corporation, was formed, the court finds that Lawrence N. Curtis, Ltd., transferred its interest in

> the existing cases to Mr. Curtis individually. Mr. Curtis then transferred these cases to the new corporation in exchange for his share of stock by having the clients who had contracts with Simon execute new [contracts] with Curtis, Tilly & Robideaux, A Professional Law Corporation.

....

> The question is whether the distribution of these cases from the corporation [Curtis, Ltd.] to Mr. Curtis is a civil fruit or a distribution of an equity interest which is subject to the theory of real subrogation.

....

> The court does not find that the distribution of the ownership in the cases from Lawrence N. Curtis, Ltd., to Lawrence Curtis, individually, was the distribution of a civil fruit. Instead, it caused a diminution in the substance of the corporation [Curtis, Ltd.]. As such, the corporation's interests in the legal cases belonged to Mr. Curtis' separate estate.

***

REAL SUBROGATION

Finally, the trial court found that via real subrogation, Curtis' stock in Lambert remained his separate property. We agree.

> The principle of real subrogation has long been applied to allow a spouse with separate assets to manage and replace those assets as a patrimonial mass independent of the community.

....

> Partnership interests owned by a person before marriage remain separate property. If that equity position is replaced with a similar equity interest in a succeeding partnership or corporation, real subrogation occurs and the new interest remains a separate asset.

Katherine S. Spaht & W. Lee Hargrave, LOUISIANA CIVIL LAW TREATISE: MATRIMONIAL REGIMES, § 3.47 (2d ed.1997) (citations omitted).

The trial court found that Curtis' equity interest in Curtis, Ltd. was replaced with a similar equity interest in Curtis and Lambert when he exchanged the case files that were distributed to him from Curtis, Ltd. for stock in Curtis and Lambert. The original equity position (case files) was replaced with a similar equity portion in the new corporation; accordingly real subrogation occurred and the new interest (stock) remained Curtis' separate asset. Therefore, we find no manifest error in that finding. Accordingly, this assignment of error is without merit.

CONCLUSION

The judgment of the trial court in favor of the defendant, Lawrence N. Curtis, is affirmed. All costs of this appeal are assessed against the plaintiff, Lynn Marie Sorola Curtis.

AFFIRMED.

4.3 PROPERTY ACQUIRED THROUGH EFFORT, SKILL OR INDUSTRY; EARNINGS

Louisiana Civil Code article 2338 provides that property acquired through "through the effort, skill, or industry of either spouse" during the existence of the community property regime is community property. These so-called earnings are the quintessential community property under a gananical system. All of the community property jurisdictions recognize earnings as community property. Some earnings are easy to identify. For example, a spouse's weekly paycheck is compensation for his labor and is quite clearly community property. Challenges arise, however, when there is a lag-time between the labor itself and the earnings resulting from that labor. A spouse might receive a payment after the termination of the community property regime that is attributable to labor performed during the existence of the community property regime. Challenges also arise when it is difficult to ascertain whether the acquisition of property is the result of a spouse's labor or is a return on capital. Finally, in some cases a spouse acquires property through labor so minimal the receipt is more like a windfall. The following cases consider these issues.

A. *Stephen A. Hansel v. Sarah Holyfield*

779 So.2d 939 (La. App. 4th Cir. 2000)

MCKAY, Judge.

Stephen Arthur Hansel and Sarah Holyfield Hansel were married in Florida on November 16, 1985. At the time of the marriage, both Mr. And Mrs. Hansel were employed by Barnett Bank in Jacksonville, Florida. Mrs. Hansel left her employment with Barnett the year following the marriage in order to stay home and help raise Mr. Hansel's children from a previous marriage.

In January 1992, Barnett terminated Mr. Hansel's employment. Shortly thereafter, Mr. Hansel went through the interview process with Hibernia Bank in New Orleans and was subsequently hired. On March 25, 1992, Mr. Hansel moved to New Orleans and on March 26, 1992, he began his employment as Hibernia's president and chief executive officer. Mrs. Hansel did not move to New Orleans until the summer of 1992 so that one of Mr. Hansel's children from his prior marriage could finish school in Jacksonville. Upon Mrs. Hansel's move to New Orleans, the couple purchased a residence at 1907 Palmer Avenue.

In November 1996, Mr. Hansel decided that he wanted to leave the marriage and he moved out of the Palmer Avenue residence. On November 7, 1996, Mr. Hansel filed for divorce which the trial court granted in June 1997. Later, Mrs. Hansel filed a petition to partition the community property. During the Hansel's eleven year marriage, they amassed a considerable amount of property; this included stock in and stock options for both Barnett and Hibernia banks as well as the family home at 1907 Palmer Avenue. The partition trial took place over nine days from April 13, 1998 to May 11, 1998. On June 16, 1998, the matter was submitted on post-trial memoranda by counsel for the parties. The trial court rendered its judgment along with incorporated reasons for judgment on January 25, 1999. The trial court found that the legal regime of acquets and gains between the Hansels existed from March 25, 1992 until its termination on November 7, 1996. The trial court further found that the Hansels' community was worth $31,758,051. The trial court allocated community assets worth $25,673,272 to Mr. Hansel and allocated community assets worth $5,135,856 to Mrs. Hansel. The trial court then offset each party's claims for reimbursement, determining that Mr. Hansel was due $909,672 and found that an equalizing payment of $9,359,036 was due Mrs. Hansel. Mr. Hansel appeals this judgment and raises eleven assignments of error. Mrs. Hansel answered the appeal and raises thirteen assignments of error.

APPELLANT'S ASSIGNMENT OF ERROR No. 3

The trial court refused to consider the income taxes which must be paid when the Hibernia stock options are exercised. Mr. Hansel contends that it is inequitable to value the stock without taking into account the tax liability. We agree.

At some point, Mr. Hansel will have to exercise each stock option grant or he will lose the right to do so. When Mr. Hansel exercises a stock option grant, any amount over the exercise price which Mr. Hansel receives for the stock will be recognized as ordinary income for tax purposes. As ordinary income the money which Mr. Hansel receives is subject to state and federal income taxes. The trial court disallowed tax consequences not because it found the exercise of the options or the imposition of the taxes to be speculative, but rather because it found the amount of taxes to be speculative. However, at trial Mr. Hansel submitted evidence that he is subject to the maximum applicable tax rate (39.5% in federal tax and 6% in state taxes). Although it is possible that Mr. Hansel may be taxed at a lower rate, the rate of taxation is no more speculative than the value of the stock options themselves. Recognizing the speculative value of a stock option but refusing to recognize the speculative rate of taxation on the value of those options is simply inequitable. Accordingly, the trial court erred in failing to consider the income taxes which must be paid when the Hibernia stock options are exercised. We look to the date of trial to determine what the tax liability would have been had all the options been exercised at that time and give Mr. Hansel the appropriate tax credit.

APPELLANT'S ASSIGNMENT OF ERROR No. 5

With regard to the Hibernia stock options that had not vested before the termination of the community, Mr. Hansel argued that these options should be deemed to be his separate property or at least pro-rated while Mrs. Hansel argued that they should be treated as community property. Therefore, the appropriate inquiry is whether the Hibernia stock options were property rights either acquired by Mr. Hansel during the community or acquired by him as a result of his effort, skill and industry during the community. The trial court found that the stock options granted to Mr. Hansel served a dual purpose of rewarding him for past service and as an incentive for future performance. Based on this, the trial court ruled that the options should be pro-rated based on the amount of time between the grant date and the vesting date that took place during the community. This is in accordance with the principle that the determinative factor is whether work performed during the existence of the community was taken into consideration in granting the option. *Goodwyne v. Goodwyne*, 94-0079 (La. App. 4th Cir. 6/30/94) 639 So.2d 1210, writ denied, 94-2035 (La. 11/4/94) 645 So.2d 211. Accordingly, we find no error in the trial court's pro-rating the stock options.

APPELLANT'S ASSIGNMENT OF ERROR No. 8

Mr. Hansel contends the trial court erred in valuing and allocating 71,640 Hibernia incentive stock options. Mrs. Hansel does not dispute that there had already been a partial partition of the 71,640 Hibernia incentive stock options prior to judgment being rendered. Therefore, these options which the trial court valued at $1,182,060, should not have been included in the judgment. Accordingly, $591,030 should be deducted from the equalizing payment to Mrs. Hansel.

APPELLANT'S ASSIGNMENT OF ERROR No. 9

Mr. Hansel contends the trial court erred when it valued 25,672 unvested stock options because it omitted the strike price when it calculated the value of these options. Mrs. Hansel concedes that this is true. Both parties agree that the total strike price of these options was $216,069.25. Therefore, one-half of this amount, i.e. $108,034.62, should be deducted from the equalizing payment to Mrs. Hansel.

APPELLEE'S ASSIGNMENT OF ERROR No. 1

Mrs. Hansel contends that the trial court erred in finding a portion of the Barnett Bank stock to be Mr. Hansel's separate property. At trial, Mrs. Hansel argued that all shares acquired through the exercise of Mr. Hansel's separately owned options were community property because community funds were used in paying the strike prices when the options were exercised. Mr. Hansel argued that all Barnett Bank stock acquired through the exercise of options that vested before his marriage to Mrs. Hansel were his separate property. Alternatively, Mr. Hansel argued that the options should be classified as separate or community property based on a time line approach utilizing each option's date of grant and the date that the option vested.

The trial court accepted Mr. Hansel's alternative position and classified some of the options as community property while others were classified as separate property. On the basis of this allocation, 29,054 shares were found to be community property, 27,762 shares were found to be Mr. Hansel's separate property, and 522 shares were Mrs. Hansel's separate property (she had acquired these shares before her marriage to Mr. Hansel). It was the trial court's opinion that Mr. Hansel established, contrary to the testimony of Mrs. Hansel, that only he had signed and was obligated on any note secured for the purposes of acquiring this stock. Consequently, the trial court found that a portion of the stock which resulted from Mr. Hansel's separate Barnett stock options was his separate property, as they were exercised by his separate obligation. The trial court evidently found Mr. Hansel's testimony and evidence more persuasive than that of Mrs. Hansel. This is a finding of fact and an issue of pure credibility. In reviewing the factual findings of a trial court, an appellate court is limited to a determination of manifest error. *Hill v. Morehouse Parish Police Jury*, 95-1100 (La. 1/16/96), 666 So.2d 612, 614; *Ferrell v. Fireman's Fund Ins. Co.*, 94-1252 (La. 2/20/95), 650 So.2d 742, 745, *Stobart v. State through Dept. of Transp. and Development*, 617 So.2d 880 (La. 1993); *Arceneaux v. Domingue*, 365 So.2d 1330 (La. 1978). Based on our review of the record, we cannot say that the trial court's finding was manifestly erroneous.

APPELLEE'S ASSIGNMENT OF ERROR No. 4

Mrs. Hansel next contends that the trial court erred in not finding that all of the Hibernia stock options granted during the community were community property regardless of the vesting date of the options. The trial court found the options to be part community and part separate and pro-rated the options based on the vesting date where the vesting date was after termination of the community. The trial court also found that there was a dual purpose in awarding the options, that is to reward Mr. Hansel for past performance as well as to serve as an incentive for him to perform well in the future.

It indisputable that the Hibernia stock options were derived from Mr. Hansel's employment with Hibernia. The issue is what part derives from community, and what part from separate, efforts, skill and industry. To the extent that a right derives from the spouse's employment during the existence of the marriage, it is a community asset subject to division upon dissolution of the marriage. La. C.C. art. 2338; *Sims v. Sims*, 358 So.2d 919 (La. 1978); *T. L. James & Co., Inc. v. Montgomery*, 332 So.2d 834 (La. 1976). The key words here are **to the extent**. In the instant case the trial court found that the options were partly earned during the existence of the community and partly earned after its termination. The Supreme Court has held that if part of an employee's pension right was earned before or after the existence of the community, that part of the pension right must be classified as the employee's separate property (or as property of a different marital regime) and separated from the community property interest to be divided. La. R.S. 9:2801 (1991); *T. L. James & Co., Inc. v. Montgomery, supra.*; *Hare v. Hodgins*, 586 So.2d 118 (La. 1991). This same principle should apply to stock options which were granted during the community but which vested at some point in time after the community's termination. Therefore, there was nothing manifestly erroneous or clearly wrong in the trial court's prorating the stock options based on the vesting date.

APPELLEE'S ASSIGNMENT OF ERROR No. 6

Mrs. Hansel also contends that the trial court erred in classifying the 1997 Hibernia stock option grant as Mr. Hansel's separate property. The trial court did this because both the grant date and the vesting date occurred after the community terminated. The trial court reasoned that the asset did not even exist until after the community terminated and therefore there was no way that the 1997 grant could be deemed to be community property. We cannot say that this finding was clearly wrong or manifestly erroneous.

AFFIRMED IN PART; REVERSED AND RENDERED IN PART

B. Note

An alternative to valuing the options would have been simpler--to divide them in kind between the former spouses. Another advantage of that approach would be to have the spouses share equally in the risk of fluctuation of the value of the options as the underlying stock price fluctuates. Mr. Hansel, however, demanded that all the options be awarded to him, with an equalizing payment made to his ex-wife. The lower court granted his request because it agreed that ownership and control of the options affected his ability to do his job as bank president, giving him more credibility with shareholders and board members. The disadvantage of that approach became apparent when the price of Hibernia stock decreased and Mr. Hansel sought a new trial to revalue the options. The trial court refused to reopen the issue, relying on La. R.S. 9:2801(4) which directs the trial court to value community property on the date of the trial on the merits. The court of appeal affirmed.

Another complexity that results in valuing such options is the potential tax liability incurred upon their exercise. The options at issue were of the type that would produce ordinary income rather than capital gains--the difference between the strike price and the price of the stock at the time. The lower court determined that the amount of this tax liability was speculative and did not discount the value of the options uncertain. The court of appeal reversed on that point and gave Mr. Hansel credit for the potential tax liability.

C. *Sandra Smith Kees v. Thomas Hickman Kees*

509 So.2d 189 (La. App. 1st Cir. 1987)

GROVER L. COVINGTON, Chief Judge.

Plaintiff appeals the judgment of the trial court which denied her motion to traverse the detailed descriptive list filed by the defendant in this proceeding to partition the community property of the parties. The parties were divorced on June 9, 1975; however, these proceedings were not instituted until May 17, 1985. The only two items of alleged community property on plaintiff's detailed descriptive list were the defendant's retirement fund with Ethyl Corporation, his former employer, and the severance pay which defendant received from Ethyl when he was "laid off" on May 31, 1985. The defendant also sought to traverse plaintiff's detailed descriptive list, denying that the items listed by plaintiff were community property. The trial judge ruled that defendant's severance pay was his separate property, and this appeal followed. For the reasons hereinafter discussed, we affirm the judgment of the trial court.

Our consideration of the nature of the severance pay involved here begins with the provision in the labor union contract governing severance pay from Ethyl Corporation, which was stipulated into evidence by both parties. It reads, in pertinent part, as follows:

> Severance Pay Allowance
>
> The following are provisions applicable to a severance allowance for an employee permanently terminated by the COMPANY on account of excess manpower, beyond that required for anticipated production requirements. A permanent termination must be by reason of a technological change, permanent manpower assignment or reassignment, permanent consolidation or rearrangement of job duties and content, or production changes of any kind. A severance allowance will not be granted for layoffs due to strike, lockout, fire, or other casualties, national emergency, act of God or of the public enemy, any other cause beyond reasonable control of the COMPANY, employee's failure to meet physical or other qualifications, voluntary

resignation, retirement, or any similar causes, the foregoing enumeration being illustrations and not limitations.

A. Eligibility

An employee will be selected for permanent termination in accordance with the layoff procedure as set forth in the then current Collective Bargaining Agreement between the COMPANY and the UNION. Each employee so selected who has completed at least one (1) year of service with the COMPANY will be eligible for a severance allowance.

B. Severance Pay Allowance

An employee who is eligible to receive a severance allowance will receive a severance allowance in an amount equal to one (1) week's pay for each completed year of COMPANY service; and for fractional years of COMPANY service beyond one (1) completed year of COMPANY service, one-twelfth (1/12) of one (1) week's pay for each completed month of COMPANY service; provided that the maximum severance allowance will not exceed an amount equal to twenty-five (25) weeks' pay. COMPANY service will be calculated in accordance with the COMPANY'S service rules. An employee's week's pay will be computed at the highest permanent base rate of pay for his regularly scheduled work during the six-month (6-month) period immediately preceding his date of termination, plus merit pay if applicable. This severance allowance will be paid in a lump sum at time of termination. The check covering the severance allowance will be reduced by deduction required or permitted by law.

Thus, the conditions precedent to receiving severance pay are: (1) permanent termination; (2) initiated by the company, not the employee; (3) based on an excess of manpower, rather than other causes for termination; (4) not coincident with a voluntary resignation or retirement. The lump sum payment is referred to as an "allowance," rather than "benefits." Finally, the pay is subject to standard payroll deductions, such as F.I.C.A.

Appellant argues that this severance pay must be analogized to retirement benefits, in that it represents property attributable to employment during the existence of the community, "the produce of the reciprocal industry and labor" of the earning spouse. She claims that the fundamental reason for severance pay is it was a contractual right which Ethyl bound itself to pay that vested after one year of employment by the appellant. The thrust of her argument seems to be that since appellee did not expend any labor, skill, or industry after his termination, the severance pay cannot be separate funds in the sense that salary earned at that time would be.

Appellee contends that it is improper to make such an analogy, as there are crucial differences between severance pay and retirement benefits. He argues that the rationale under which retirement or pension benefits are considered community in our jurisprudence is that certain contributions are made or accrue to some certain plan or fund periodically. If these periodic contributions or accruals occur during the existence of the community, they must be considered to be in the nature of additional remuneration to the employee. Thus, they are community assets to the extent attributable to employment during the existence of the community. Severance pay, on the other hand, involves no periodic payments or accruals. It is a lump sum benefit paid to an employee, if he is forced to leave his employment, in lieu of further wages. Thus, appellee argues, one must look to the nature of the wages the employee would have received at the time of severance had he not been severed from employment. If the wages would have been separate property, then the severance pay must be considered separate. We agree.

Article 2338 of our Civil Code, which was in effect at the time appellee received the severance pay in question, provides in pertinent part that "[t]he community property comprises: property acquired during the existence of the legal regime through the effort, skill, or industry of either spouse...." [Emphasis added.] There is no question that the severance pay was received after the legal regime between the parties had been terminated, as more than ten years had elapsed between the two events. Our focus is on whether the right to the severance pay was acquired during the existence of the community. We think not.

The cases cited by appellant, Sims v. Sims, 358 So.2d 919 (La.1978) and others, are not persuasive. Those cases all dealt with retirement funds and pension plans which involved periodic, fixed contributions or credits into certain accounts destined to be received by employees upon the happening of a certain event. Such is not the situation with severance pay, which is not accumulated in a certain fund or account, is not based on periodic credits or accruals, and does not vest with the employee. The one-year employment requirement in this instance does not vest the employee with the certain contractual right of severance pay at the end of his employment; it merely establishes him as eligible to receive severance pay if all the other requirements for entitlement to severance pay are met. Thus, it is not connected with a certain future event, but merely a possibility--involuntary termination by the company because of excess manpower. It is significant that under the terms of the contract, an employee might never receive severance pay. Therefore, severance pay cannot be considered to be acquired until such time as the employee may be involuntarily terminated, if ever.

We find the method of calculating severance pay by Ethyl--measuring the years of service of the employee--to be irrelevant to determining the nature of the payment, as this method is an arbitrary one. Ethyl could just as easily have decided payment was to be based on the job classification of the employee, or some other factor. Thus, any undue emphasis on the formula used is inappropriate.

Finally, we note that the contract itself distinguishes severance pay from retirement benefits by specifying that the employee is not eligible for the severance allowance at retirement. Such a provision lends credence to the contention by appellee that the severance payment is in lieu of future wages and is not to be considered additional remuneration for past services. For these reasons, we hold that the severance pay received by appellee more than ten years after the termination of the community of acquets and gains between him and appellant is his separate property, and the trial court was correct in so treating it on the parties' motion to traverse each other's detailed descriptive lists. All costs of this appeal are assessed to plaintiff-appellant.

D. Note

The property acquired need not necessarily be money. In *Humble Oil & Ref. Co. v. Lewis*, 159 So.2d 132 (La. 1964), an oil operator "employed the service of Lewis, an oil and gas lease broker, to acquire a seventy-five per cent working interest in approximately 203 acres . . . and as consideration of such services Lewis was to receive a three per cent overriding royalty." The court held that the royalties received were community property.

In *Terry v. Terry*, 565 So.2d 997 (La. App. 1st Cir. 1990), the husband argued that an overriding mineral royalty transferred to him during marriage was actually to compensate him for consulting services related to the mineral leases involved, some of which were to be performed after the termination of the community. He thus urged that royalty payments made to him after termination were separate. Testimony in his favor included the execution, at about the same time he acquired the royalties, of a consulting agreement whereby he agreed to provide services at no charge. (It does not appear from the opinion what, if any, services were performed before the royalties were transferred.) Also, when the underlying royalties were transferred to a new owner, he executed a consulting agreement at no fee with the transferee. On the other hand, the obligation to provide consulting services would terminate upon his death or bad health, but the overriding royalties would continue. None of the contracts clearly provided that the royalties were in return for future consulting services.

Relying on the presumption of community and giving deference to the lower court, the court of appeal held that the husband had failed to prove that the royalty assignments were in compensation for future wages. The royalty right was thus considered a community asset.

In a case, however, in which such royalties could be proved to be compensation for services over a period of time, apportionment would seem to be the appropriate remedy.

The problem would be determining how much of the services were in the past and how much in the future. When future services would be "as needed" for consulting, presumably the guide for apportionment would be the customs of the oil and gas industry with respect to such compensation. Under those customs, it may well be that a large part of the effort would be related to initial acquisition and geologic work, and that the future consulting may well be minimal. See e.g., *Audubon Exploration v. Linder Oil Co.*, 573 So.2d 1180 (La. App. 5th Cir. 1991) (Geologists presented a "prospect" to an oil company, "a geological interpretation of data which delineates or pinpoints a previously undrilled accumulation of oil and gas which might be exploited" in anticipation of being compensated in part with a mineral royalty.)

In *Callender v. Callender*, 625 So.2d 257 (La. App. 5th Cir. 1993), the wife's wages for work during the community were community property, including the last paycheck before termination. A $1,000 certificate of deposit purchased with those funds was also a community asset. This was so even though the husband's last paychecks were apparently spent and not used to purchase any assets.

In *Stewart v. Stewart*, 585 So.2d 1250 (La. App. 4th Cir. 1991), *writ denied,* 590 So.2d 594 (La. 1992), more than 200 pieces of art done by the wife during marriage were community property.

Calling the funds bonuses does not make them any the less the produce of the effort, skill or industry of spouse. *McMichael v. McMichael*, 205 So.2d 433 (La. 1967).

Burford v. Burford, 541 So.2d 341 (La. App. 2d Cir. 1989), involved government subsidies paid to dairy farmers who agreed to cease operations. The husband had been primarily responsible for the dairy farming operation, and the trial court apparently reasoned that the payments would be compensating him part for not working in the future. It then classified such payments as his separate property since he would no longer be married at the time. The court of appeal, however, determined that such a classification was unnecessary and ruled that the matter was governed by contract. That contract between the spouses and the U.S. government by its terms provided that each spouse would received 50% of the subsidy.

E. *Bernadine Sept Noil v. Larry William Noil*

699 So. 2d 1134 (La. App. 1st Cir. 1997)

LOTTINGER, Chief Judge.

The issue presented in this dispute is whether a home purchased in the names of both spouses during the existence of the marital community with prize money awarded to a spouse individually should be classified as a community asset. From a judgment declaring the home to be the separate property of the plaintiff, defendant now appeals.

FACTS

On September 12, 1994, Bernadine Sept Noil (hereafter, "Ms. Noil"), was granted an uncontested divorce from her husband, Larry William Noil (hereafter, "Mr. Noil"). Through a petition filed on January 4, 1995, Ms. Noil sought to partition the remaining assets of the former community. A detailed descriptive list filed together therewith listed the family home as the separate property of Ms. Noil. In his subsequent answer, Mr. Noil disputed his ex-wife's classification of the home as separate property.

At the trial of this matter, the trial court was presented with issues relating to the classification of the family home, as well as a claim for reimbursement by Mr. Noil based upon his payment of a community debt. The trial court took the matter under advisement, and without written or oral reasons, later ruled in favor of Ms. Noil on both issues. Mr. Noil now appeals from the trial court's determination that the family residence is the separate property of Ms. Noil.

ASSIGNMENT OF ERROR

The sole issue presented for our review is whether the trial court erred in its determination that the family home was the separate property of Ms. Noil.

APPLICABLE LAW

Under Louisiana law, property is characterized as either community or separate. La. Civ.Code art. 2335. Property acquired during the existence of the community is presumed to be community, but either spouse may rebut the presumption and prove the separate nature of said property. La. Civ.Code art. 2340. The classification of property as separate or community is fixed at the time of its acquisition. *Smith v. Smith*, 95-0913 (La.App. 1st Cir. 12/20/96), 685 So.2d 649.

Pursuant to La. Civ.Code art. 2338, community property is comprised of:

> property acquired during the existence of the legal regime through the effort, skill, or industry of either spouse; property acquired with community things or with community and separate things, unless classified as separate property under Article 2341; property donated to the spouses jointly; natural and civil fruits of community property; damages awarded for loss or injury to a thing belonging to the community; and all other property not classified by law as separate property.

Conversely, La. Civ.Code art. 2341 provides, in pertinent part, that a person's separate estate is comprised of:

> property acquired by a spouse prior to the establishment of a community property regime; property acquired by a spouse with separate things or with separate and community things when the value of the community things is inconsequential in comparison with the value of the separate things used; property acquired by a spouse by inheritance or donation to him individually; damages awarded to a spouse in an action for breach of contract against the other spouse or for the loss sustained as a result of fraud or bad faith in the management of community property by the other spouse; damages or other indemnity awarded to a spouse in connection with the management of his separate property; and things acquired by a spouse as a result of a voluntary partition of the community during the existence of a community property regime.

DISCUSSION

At trial, Ms. Noil testified that the residence in question was purchased in January of 1991 during which time she was married to Mr. Noil. Ms. Noil urged that while the sale documents reflect the names of both she and Mr. Noil, the home should, nevertheless, be considered her separate property inasmuch as it was acquired with a portion of the prize money awarded to her as the winner of a sweepstakes.

According to the testimony of Ms. Noil, she entered a sweepstakes contest in November of 1990, by filling out and sending in a "word search puzzle" which appeared in the Baton Rouge Sunday Advocate newspaper. She was later notified that she had won and was awarded a check in the amount of $25,000.00.2 Upon receipt of the prize money, Ms. Noil testified that she deposited the check into the joint checking account she held with Mr. Noil. Thereafter, Ms. Noil stated that she purchased the house in question for the sum of $5,000.00. Ms. Noil claimed that because she was married, the act of sale reflected her husband's name in addition to her own.

Due to the small size of the house, Ms. Noil testified that she and her husband used "a lot of the sweepstakes money to add on to the house." In order to complete the remodeling job, she and her husband borrowed an additional $6,712.73 from People's Bank and pledged the house as security. Ms. Noil testified that when her husband left in June of 1994, she continued, with some assistance from him, to pay the household bills, a car note, and the mortgage on the house of $155.91 a month. Ms. Noil subsequently paid off the $2,545.87 balance owed on the mortgage with her portion of the proceeds from her husband's retirement and worker's compensation settlement.

Generally, the party asserting the separate nature of property acquired during marriage has the burden of overcoming the presumption of community established in La. Civ.Code art. 2340. *Albert v. Albert*, 625 So.2d 765 (La.App. 1st Cir.1993). In the instant case, Ms. Noil contends that the house should be considered her separate property inasmuch as funds derived from her sweepstakes prize money were used to purchase and remodel the home. It is undisputed that the parties were married at the time the house was purchased, and based upon the testimony of Ms. Noil, the names of both parties appear on the act of sale.

Professors Katherine Spaht and Lee Hargrave point out however, in their work, *Matrimonial Regimes*, 16 Louisiana Civil Law Treatise, § 3.41 (1989), that "[c]lassification of an asset as separate or community, whether the asset is movable or immovable, is not determined by the name on documents of title. Classification depends on the time of acquisition, the character of the transaction, and the source of funds." (Footnotes omitted). A copy of the act of sale was not introduced or filed into the record; however, it seems abundantly clear that the sale did not contain a declaration by Mr. Noil acknowledging that the house was the separate property of Ms. Noil. For this reason, we must look to the source of the funds used for the acquisition of the home in order to determine its classification as a separate or community asset.

It is undisputed that the source of the funds used to acquire and remodel the home came from Ms. Noil's sweepstakes prize money; however, the classification of a spouse's lottery or sweepstakes winnings appears to be a res nova issue in Louisiana. It is clear that Ms. Noil entered the sweepstakes on her own initiative during her marriage, and that the prize money was subsequently awarded to her during marriage. Ms. Noil's winnings were awarded as a result of her own skill and effort in correctly finding the hidden words, and thereafter mailing her entry for submission into the sweepstakes. Inasmuch as the legislature has not specifically amended La. Civ.Code art. 2341 to provide that winnings of this nature are the separate property of the spouse to whom they are awarded, they must be classified as community property.

The judgment of the trial court is accordingly reversed to the extent it classifies the family home as the separate property of the plaintiff, Bernadine Sept Noil.

CONCLUSION

For the reasons set forth above, the judgment of the trial court is reversed insofar as it classifies the family home as the separate property of plaintiff, Bernadine Sept Noil, and the same is declared community property.

This matter is remanded to determine any amount which Ms. Noil may be entitled to in paying off the loan on the family home. All costs associated with this appeal shall be shared equally by the parties.

REVERSED AND RENDERED IN PART AND REMANDED.

F. Note

Lotteries, sweepstakes, and similar prizes have resulted in some interesting litigation in the community property jurisdictions. Most states hold winnings to be community property, even where minimal effort is involved. In *Lynch v. Lynch*, 791 P. 2d 653 (Ariz. App. Ct. 1990), the husband and wife had been living apart for some time when the husband and his girlfriend won the Arizona State Lottery. Mrs. Lynch filed for divorce and an uncontested default hearing was held on February 10, 1987. Ordinarily, the judgment of divorce would have been issued that day or a few days later. However, the court vacated the hearing on February 19, 1987 because the Mr. Lynch did not receive a timely notice of the hearing. The error was Mrs. Lynch's attorney's fault—and in this case that error inured to her benefit. Mr. Lynch and his girlfriend won a $2.2 million jackpot on February 21, 1987. Mrs. Lynch then sought half of his winnings claiming they were community property. She was successful. In classifying the winnings as community, the court explained:

> No legal separation decree was entered in this case, and the parties' marriage had not ended when husband won the lottery. Husband's lottery share was not "acquired by gift, devise or descent"; thus, it qualifies as a marital community asset pursuant to A.R.S. § 25–211.

Seizer v. Sessions, 940 P.2d 261 (Wash. 1997) (*en banc*), also involved the Arizona State Lottery. Elmer Sessions won the Arizona State Lottery. When he died two years later, two women claimed to be married to him: one a resident of Washington, the other a resident of Texas. The court was asked to decide whether Washington or Texas law applied. The distinction mattered for several reasons. Under Washington law, when spouses live separate and apart because their marriage is defunct, all earnings are the acquiring spouse's separate property. Texas had no comparable rule. However, Texas does recognize the putative spouse doctrine, which would have afforded relief to the second wife. Ultimately, the court decided Washington law applied and remanded for further determinations of fact.

Spouses in California who intentionally try to conceal their lottery winnings during the divorce process face a harsh penalty. In the case of *In re Rossi*, 90 Cal. App. 4th 34 (2001), Mrs. Rossi and a group of co-workers formed a lottery pool—each contributed $5 per week. In 1996, Mrs. Rossi's group won the California State Lottery. Mrs. Rossi, whose share of the jackpot was around $1.3 million, intentionally hid her winnings from her husband and filed for divorce shortly thereafter. She never disclosed the existence of the lottery winnings during the divorce proceeding or the partition of their community assets. When Mr. Rossi later discovered his ex-wife's deception he sought to be awarded the entirety of the winnings under a California statutory regime that essentially requires a spouse to disclose all pertinent financial information to the other spouse. Where a spouse fraudulently breaches that fiduciary duty, California Family Code §1101 gives an award to the aggrieved spouse "of 100 percent, or an amount equal to 100 percent, of any asset undisclosed or transferred in breach of the fiduciary duty." Mrs. Rossi was required to hand over all of her lottery winnings to her ex-husband.

G. Questions

1. Bonuses and similar large payments can present challenging timing questions. See *Preis v. Preis*, 649 So. 2d 593 (La. App. 3 Cir. 1994) and *Pelafigue v. Sudduth*, 820 So. 2d 583 (La. App. 3 Cir. 2002). In answering the following questions, consider whether the presumption in favor of community property would apply and what other factors might affect the classification of the payment.

   a. W is an attorney. Each December she receives a large bonus from her firm. W receives the bonus while she is married to H. Is the bonus separate or community?

   b. What if H and W divorce just days before W receives the bonus? How should the bonus be treated in that case?

   c. What if H and W got married the day before W received her bonus? How should the bonus be treated in that case?

2. Works in progress at the dissolution of a marriage also present challenging questions. In some cases, an apportionment may be most equitable. *See Michel v. Michel*, 484 So. 2d 829 (La. App. 1st Cir. 1986). Consider the following:

   a. W is an artist and an author. When she marries H she has one book halfway completed and several paintings in progress. W completes both the book and the paintings during marriage. W also produces more books and paintings, some of which are only partially completed when H and W divorce. How should the paintings and books be treated at divorce?

3. H is a carpenter who does a lot of business on trade. During his marriage to W, H does some carpentry work for his friend for free. It is a very specialized

job and H does not have the tools he needs to do the job. So, H's friend gives H the tools. How should the tools be treated at divorce?

4.4 FRUITS AND REVENUES OF SEPARATE AND COMMUNITY PROPERTY

A. Introduction

Like all other community property jurisdictions, Louisiana Civil Code article 2338 provides that the natural and civil fruits of community property are likewise community property. As discussed in the introductory materials, Louisiana is in the minority with respect to its treatment of the natural and civil fruits of separate property. Louisiana, Idaho, Wisconsin, and Texas all adhere to the Spanish Rule, which classifies the fruits and revenues of separate property as community property. The remaining community property jurisdictions, following California's lead, adopted the American Rule, which classifies the fruits and revenues of separate property as separate property.

All four of the Spanish Rule states, however, allow the spouses to opt-in to the American Rule approach in certain circumstances. Whether the spouses must both agree to this treatment, however, varies among the Spanish Rule states. Idaho, for example, requires an agreement in some circumstances. Idaho Code §32-906(1) provides, in part, as follows:

> ...The income, including the rents, issues and profits, of all property, separate or community, is community property unless the conveyance by which it is acquired provides or both spouses, by written agreement specifically so providing, declare that all or specifically designated property and the income, including the rents, issues and profits, from all or the specifically designated property shall be the separate property of one of the spouses or the income, including the rents, issues and profits, from all or specifically designated separate property be the separate property of the spouse to whom the property belongs...

For years, Louisiana allowed a spouse to unilaterally execute a declaration—often called a declaration of paraphernality—opting in to the American Rule with respect to his or her own separate property without even providing notice to the other spouse. In 2008, Louisiana Civil Code article 2339 was amended to require that a spouse provide the other spouse with some sort of notice. The article continues to fall short of requiring an actual agreement between the spouses.

<u>Prior Version</u>: La. Civ. Code art. 2339. Fruits and revenues of separate property

The natural and civil fruits of the separate property of a spouse, minerals produced from or attributable to a separate asset, and bonuses, delay rentals, royalties, and shut-in payments arising from mineral leases are community property. Nevertheless, a spouse may reserve them as his separate property by a declaration made in an authentic act or in an act under private signature duly acknowledged.

As to the fruits and revenues of immovables, the declaration is effective when filed for registry in the conveyance records of the parish in which the immovable property is located. As to fruits of movables, the declaration is effective when filed for registry in the conveyance records of the parish in which the declarant is domiciled.

<u>Current Version</u>: La. Civ. Code art. 2339. Fruits and revenues of separate property

The natural and civil fruits of the separate property of a spouse, minerals produced from or attributable to a separate asset, and bonuses, delay rentals, royalties, and shut-in payments arising from mineral leases are community property. Nevertheless, a spouse may reserve them as his separate property as provided in this Article.

A spouse may reserve them as his separate property by a declaration made in an authentic act or in an act under private signature duly acknowledged. A copy of the declaration shall be provided to the other spouse prior to filing of the declaration.

As to the fruits and revenues of immovables, the declaration is effective when a copy is provided to the other spouse and the declaration is filed for registry in the conveyance records of the parish in which the immovable property is located. As to fruits of movables, the declaration is effective when a copy is provided to the other spouse and the declaration is filed for registry in the conveyance records of the parish in which the declarant is domiciled.

Even when a spouse properly executes and files a declaration of paraphernality, controversy can still arise. In a number of cases the issue is whether the property in question is properly classified as the fruit of separate property or whether it represents earnings from the effort, skill or industry of a spouse. In many of these cases the court will look to see whether property was acquired by a passive investment or an active investment.

B. *Audrey Paxton v. Hugh T. Bramlette*

228 So. 2d 161 (La. App. 3d Cir. 1969)

CULPEPPER, Judge.

The general facts show that the plaintiff, Audrey Paxton, was first married to J. W. Low, who died in 1953. Of this marriage one child was born, Mrs. Billie Low McRight.

Considerable property was accumulated during the marriage of Audrey Paxton and J. W. Low. A financial statement dated January 1, 1957 (approximately 8 months before the marriage of Audrey Paxton and Hugh T. Bramlette) shows gross assets of $616,913, liabilities of $111,265, or a net value of $505,647. Of this amount, Audrey Paxton owned a 5/6 interest and Mrs. McRight a 1/6 interest. These assets consist principally of stock in J. W. Low, Inc., a variety store chain founded by plaintiff's first husband, and certain commercial rental properties located in the city of Opelousas.

Audrey Paxton married Hugh T. Bramlette on August 2, 1957.

The initial issue is whether the salaries received by Mrs. Bramlette during the marriage were separate or community property. We will first state the applicable law. The wife's earnings from her own labor and industry, while living in community with her husband are community property, LSA-CCP Article 2334, Houghton v. Hall, 177 La. 237, 148 So. 37 (1933); Fazzio v. Krieger, 226 La. 511, 76 So.2d 713 (1964). LSA-CC Article 2386, as amended in 1944, reads as follows:

> 'The fruits of the paraphernal property of the wife, wherever the property be located and however administered, whether natural, civil, including interest, dividends and rents, or from the result of labor, fall into the conjugal partnership, if there exists a community of acquets and gains; unless the wife, by written instrument, shall declare that she reserves all of such fruits for her own separate use and benefit and her intention to administer such property separately and alone. The said instrument shall be executed before a Notary Public and two witnesses and duly recorded in the Conveyance Records of the Parish where the community is domiciled.
>
> 'If there is no community of gains, each party enjoys, as he chooses, that which comes to his hand; but the fruits and revenues which are existing at the dissolution of the marriage, belong to the owner of the things which produce them.'

Succession of Lagan, 221 La. 437, 59 So.2d 446 (1952) and *Abraham v. Abraham*, 230 La. 78, 87 So.2d 735 (1956) make it clear that the 1944 amendment to LSA-CC Article 2386 does not change the law as to earnings produced by the industry and labor of the wife. These are community assets regardless of whether she files the written instrument provided for under Article 2386. The Law Review Articles found in 25 La.Rev. 95 at pg. 104 and 34 Tul.Law Rev. 3 discuss the problem of what income represents 'fruits', which become the wife's separate property, and what income represents 'earnings' which fall into the community, under LSA-CC Article 2386, after the affidavit is filed. The authors suggest the courts should use the ratio of labor to capital as a criterion for classifying the income as fruits or earnings. 'Thus if the revenue received was the result of substantial capital investment with relatively little labor, it would be a fruit governed by Article 2386; but if the revenue represents the return on substantial labor with relatively little capital investment, it would be earnings governed by Article 2334.' 25 La.Law Rev. at pg. 104.

On June 28, 1963, Mrs. Bramlette filed a written instrument, pursuant to Article 2386 quoted above, declaring her intention to administer her paraphernal property for her separate benefit. There is no question that the salaries received by Mrs. Bramlette from the date of the marriage, August 2, 1957, until the date she filed the affidavit for separate administration, June 28, 1963, are community property. At $1,000 per month, she received salaries totaling $70,000 from J. W. Low, Inc. during this period. Clearly, this $70,000 was community property.

At the time of the marriage, Mrs. Bramlette's real estate interests were not incorporated. She simply received the rents which were fruits of her paraphernal property. These totaled at least $1,800 per year. On June 1, 1959, A. & J. Realty, Inc. was organized and the realty transferred to it. Thereafter Mrs. Bramlette received the annual salary of $1,800 from the corporation. This means that from the realty business she received about $10,000 in rent and salary by June 28, 1963 also is community. Hence a total of $80,000 in community funds was received by Mrs. Bramlette from these sources before she filed the affidavit.

Furthermore, there can be little question that the salary received by Mrs. Bramlette from A. & J. Realty, Inc. after she filed the affidavit in 1963 is community property. The evidence shows that Mrs. Bramlette personally performed most of the managerial duties in the operation of A. & J. Realty, Inc. She maintained a desk in the building which the realty company owned and which housed A. J. Low, Inc. She collected all of the rents, deposited them in the bank, handled all of the maintenance and repairs of the various buildings owned by A. & J. Realty, Inc. and generally had the full responsibility for this corporation's management. Hence, it is clear that the salary of about $8,000 received by Mrs. Bramlette from A. & J. Realty, Inc. from the date she filed the affidavit, June 28, 1963, until the date of the judgment of the separation, December 1, 1967, is also community property. Adding this to the $80,000, which we have already found above is community, makes a total of $88,000 in community funds which were commingled in the two bank accounts in question.

There may be some question as to the salary received by Mrs. Bramlette from A. J. Low, Inc. after she filed the affidavit in 1963. She owned 82% of the stock in this corporation but received no dividends. She received a salary of $12,000 per year but says she performed little labor for the corporation. According to Mrs. Bramlette's testimony, she had a desk in the building which housed the corporate offices but had no specific duties. The company was managed by Mr. Leon Huckaby, who owns 8% of the stock. She says she usually went to the office after lunch, at about 1:00 p.m., and remained until about 4:00 p.m., after which she customarily visited friends until she returned to the family home at the farm. Furthermore, she testified that two or three times a year she visited the other stores in the chain (as we understand the record there were three stores other than that in Opelousas) but that each store had a manager.

Mr. Bramlette's testimony is different. He says Mrs. Bramlette usually went to her office about 10:00 a.m. and remained until 5:00 p.m. and occasionally until 7:00 p.m. It was Mr. Bramlette's understanding that no important business decisions were made without Mrs. Low's approval. This seems logical, since she owned 82 per cent of the stock.

Ultimately, it is our conclusion that Mrs. Bramlette performed substantial services to the corporation and that the $12,000 paid to her annually constituted earnings derived from her labor and industry. It is noteworthy that she reported these sums on her Federal Income Tax Returns as salary. We think it was salary in the true sense of the word and not merely an amount paid in lieu of dividends on her corporate stock.

The salary earned by Mrs. Bramlette from A. J. Low, Inc. for the period from June 28, 1963 to the date of the judgment of separation, December 1, 1967, was approximately $54,000. This amount added to the $88,000 previously found to be community property makes a total of $142,000 of community money which was commingled indiscriminately in the two bank accounts in question during the ten years of the marriage.

In addition, the record shows Mrs. Bramlette received substantial sums of interest on mortgages she and her daughter held on the property of A. &` J. Realty, Inc. Also, interest on loans she made from her personal funds to the various stores. All of this interest which she received before she filed the affidavit in 1963 is community property, LSA-CC Article 2386.

C. Note

Kyson v. Kyson, 596 So.2d 1308 (La. App. 2d Cir., Aug. 21, 1991), *writ denied*, 599 So. 2d 314 initially determined that rents from the husband's separate property were part separate and part community because the husband "handled and managed the property which included responsibilities of finding tenants, collecting the rent, and making repairs and improvements on the property." The court concluded, "the rental payments were the result of a substantial amount of time spent by Mr. Kyson on managing the rental properties." It remanded for proration on the rental income based on the portion that was return of capital and the portion that was the product of effort, skill or industry.

On rehearing (Mar. 10, 1992) the court re-evaluated the facts, determined that the husband's contributions as a rental manager had not been proven to be substantial, and classified all the rental income as his separate property. The court stated, "Mr. Kyson's personal management efforts toward these four properties during the marriage cannot be viewed on this record as so extraordinary as to result in his abdication of the rentals he expressly reserved unto himself.

Whatley v. Whatley, 439 So.2d 444 (La. App. 2d Cir. 1983), held that lease proceeds from a mineral lease of separate property were community. Involved was a short marriage in which older spouses separated after 8 months of living together. At issue was $31,928 for a 5-year paid up mineral lease of the husband's separate property. The draft was issued October 30 and paid on December 15, one day before the termination of the community. The court did not apportion the lease payments in an opinion that does not refer to Louisiana Civil Code Article 556, the most directly applicable text. The court held that all the money was property acquired during the existence of the community and was to be partitioned equally. It hardly appears that there are any policy reasons for favoring the wife in this manner in such a short-lived marriage involving money she had little to do with producing. The court recognized the result was inequitable but said it "must yield to the positive expression of law contained in LSA-C.C. Art. 2339." It then cited the rule that "Property is either separate or community, not mixed" and found no authority for proration as exists for tort awards and pension plans. However, Article 556 would seem to be more than adequate authority for apportionment in such a case. Though it is arguable that Article 556 by its terms applies only to usufruct, the general view has long been that the community's interest in the separate assets of the spouses is like a usufruct, and the notion of fruits developed in the code provisions on usufruct have carried over in other respects to community rules. Furthermore, the trend in the cases and in the legislation has been to weaken the rule against mixed titles, especially in cases as this one in which no obstacle to simple management of the asset arises.

A number of cases held that revenues from timber operations on separate property were not fruits and thus were separate property. *Kennedy v. Kennedy*, 699 So.2d 351 (La. 1996); *E.g. Succ. of Rugg*, 339 So.2d 519 (La. App. 4th Cir. 1977). *Succession of Doll v. Doll*, 593 So.2d 1239 (La. 1992), furnished an opportunity for the Supreme Court to clarify the developing rule that some proceeds from timber operations are fruits. Traditionally, revenues from the sale of timber were classified as products or capital assets on account of their slow growth and high value. However, cases and the comments to Louisiana Civil Code article 551 suggested that "trees in a tree farm or in a regularly exploited forest may be regarded as fruits, because they are produced according to the destination of the property and without diminution of its substance." Indeed, Louisiana Civil Code article 562 particularized that rule to usufructs: "The proceeds of timber operations that are derived from proper management of timberlands belong to the usufructuary."

The Supreme Court followed these suggestions and looked to whether the funds received were compensation for seriously depleting the substance of the property. In *Doll*, the donee of the land obtained naturally seeded forest and timberland. She hired a forestry consultant and, following his recommendations, engaged in selective thinning and planting of new pine seedlings in the bulk of the open acreage. Revenues of $73,000 from sales of timber were received, but she rejected a bid of $103,000 to clear cut the remaining timber, "evidencing an intention to manage the property to provide sustained income." Justice Cole, writing for the court, noted the criteria for the kinds of tree farming operations that would result in fruits:

> From the foregoing we determine designation as a "tree farm" is premised upon the existence of management techniques aimed at securing continuous production of timber, a conclusion which comports with the principle of article 551 and comment be thereto. It is clear a tree farm cannot be defined by reference to its character at the time of the growth, but rather by the land's ability, through proper management techniques such as selective thinnings and plantings, to provide sustained yields. The timber sales at issue here were nothing more than selective thinnings intended to spur a fruitful and continuous yield over a prolonged stretch of time.

D. *Susan Diane Starks Ross v. Billy Wayne Ross*

857 So. 2d 384 (La. 2003)

JOHNSON, Justice.

We are called upon to determine whether renewal commissions received by the ex-husband during the marriage on insurance policies issued prior to the marriage were the ex-husband's separate property subject to his declaration of paraphernality. The trial court and court of appeal found that the renewal commissions were separate property.

We granted the ex-wife's writ of certiorari to determine the correctness of the lower courts' rulings. For the reasons that follow, we conclude that effort, skill, and industry were exerted to obtain the renewals, and we reverse the lower courts' rulings.

FACTS AND PROCEDURAL HISTORY

Mr. Billy Wayne Ross (Mr. Ross) and Ms. Susan Diane Starks Ross (Ms. Starks) were married on May 29, 1992. Mr. Ross has been an independent insurance agent with State Farm since 1963 and operates the Billy Ross Agency in Baton Rouge, Louisiana. Shortly after their marriage, Mr. Ross filed a declaration of paraphernality on July 10, 1992, wherein he declared:

> that in accordance with the provisions of Article 2339 of the Civil Code of Louisiana, as amended by Act 709 of 1979, he reserves all fruits of his paraphernal and separate property, wherever located and however administered, whether such fruits be natural and civil, including interest, dividends and rents, bonuses, royalties, delay rentals and shut-in payments arising from mineral leases on separate property, or from the result of labor, or otherwise, for his own separate use and benefit and that it is his intention to administer such property separately and alone.

In the declaration, Mr. Ross acknowledged that a regime of acquets and gains otherwise existed between him and his wife.

Ms. Starks filed for divorce on November 18, 1996 and a judgment of divorce was rendered on June 11, 1997. Ms. Starks subsequently filed a petition to partition community property on November 6, 1997 in which she asserted that Mr. Ross had used community funds to satisfy his separate debts. In his answer, Mr. Ross claimed that the income in question, which he received from his insurance business, was his separate property subject to the declaration of paraphernality.

The trial court held a hearing on the single issue of whether the income derived from Mr. Ross' separate property and thus subject to the declaration of paraphernality. Following the hearing, the trial court rendered judgment, finding that any and all renewal commissions for policies originally issued before the date of marriage and received by Mr. Ross prior to or during the marriage are classified as his separate, paraphernal property. The court also found that Ms. Starks bore the burden of proving any entitlement to a pro rata share of renewals received by Mr. Ross between the date of the marriage and the filing of the declaration of paraphernality. The court further concluded that any income generated from new policies issued during the marital regime, as well as any renewal commissions derived therefrom are deemed to be community property.

In extensive written reasons for judgment, the trial court relied on jurisprudence that has held that renewal commissions received after the termination of the community as a result of the sale of insurance policies during the existence of the community are community property. *Futch v. Futch,* 26-49 (La. App. 2nd Cir. 9/23/94), 643 So. 2d 364; *Michel v. Michel*, 484 So.2d 829 (La. App. 1st Cir. 1986); *Boyle v. Boyle*, 459 So.2d 735 (La. App. 4th Cir. 1984). The court then reasoned that income generated from policies issued prior to the establishment of the community were Mr. Ross' separate property. Based on Mr. Ross' declaration of paraphernality, the trial court held that the renewal commissions generated from those policies issued prior to the establishment of the matrimonial regime were also Mr. Ross' separate property. The court further found that the effort, skill and industry which ultimately produced the renewals was performed by Mr. Ross prior to the marriage which rendered them to be his separate property. Addressing Ms. Starks' argument that no "thing" exists from which fruits may be produced, the trial court concluded that the "thing" or "asset" from which civil fruits derived were the actual policies of insurance written by Mr. Ross.

The court of appeal affirmed the trial court's ruling in a 2-1 decision. The majority concluded that "Mr. Ross received renewal commissions based on his contract with State Farm and renewals of pre-existing insurance polices, and since both the contract and the insurance policies are juridical acts, we find no error in the trial court's determination that the policies are things or assets from which civil fruits may be derived." *Ross v. Ross*, 01-2691 (La. App. 1st Cir. 11/8/02), 835 So. 2d 817, 820.

The court of appeal disagreed with Ms. Starks' contention that the renewal commissions should be deemed Mr. Ross' salary because the majority, if not all of his income, is attributable to the renewal commissions. The court cited *Kyson v. Kyson,* 596 So.2d 1308 (La. App. 2nd Cir. 1991) (on re'g), *writ denied*, 599 So.2d 314 (La. 1992); *Gautreau v. Gautreau*, 96-1548, 697 So.2d 1339 (La. App. 3rd Cir. 6/18/97); and *Paxton v. Bramlette*, 228 So. 2d 161 (La. App. 3rd Cir. 1969), *writ denied*, 255 La. 241, 230 So.2d 92 (La. 1970) for the proposition that in order to disprove that the renewal commissions received by Mr. Ross were not civil fruits, it was necessary for Ms. Starks to prove that substantial labor was exerted by Mr. Ross to obtain the renewal commissions during the existence of the community property regime.

The court of appeal further found that:

> [h]ad the trial court found that Mr. Ross had expended any significant effort skill or industry in effecting the renewal of policies pre-existing the community property regime, then the commissions would constitute community property and be subject to a claim of partition, to the extent or percentage community labor or "effort skill and industry was attributable to the renewal so effected."

Ross v. Ross, 835 So.2d at 821.

The appellate court further found that "[a]lthough Mr. Ross may have listed the renewal commissions as income on his tax statements and such income comprised a disproportionate share of his total income, the evidence shows that Mr. Ross received this income as a result of little or no effort, skill or industry exerted on his part during the community." *Id* at 821.

Judge Pettigrew dissented, stating:

> Mr. Ross had no ownership interest in the insurance policies that renewed during the existence of the community of acquets and gains between him and his former wife. In my humble opinion, the commissions earned on those renewal premiums fit no description of separate property or asset that produces natural or civil fruits as utilized in La. Civ. Code art. 2339.
>
> * * *
>
> Premiums earned during the community of acquets and gains on renewal policies are nothing more than wages or compensation earned during the community acquets and gains and are therefore community property.

DISCUSSION

Civil Fruits

The only issue before this court is whether the renewal commissions received by Mr. Ross during the community property regime on insurance policies written before the existence of the community are the result of labor, skill or industry, and are, thus, community property or whether, on the other hand, the renewal commissions are the "civil fruit" of some asset acquired by Mr. Ross prior to the existence of the community, such that they are subject to his declaration of paraphernality. We are called upon to determine, in other words, whether the renewal policies are "property" from which Mr. Ross may derive such civil fruits.

We begin our discussion with a historical background of the concept of "fruits" in Louisiana as well as the rights of spouses with regard to fruits under the Louisiana community property regime.

Professor A.N. Yiannopoulos in his discussion of the notion of fruits and products in Louisiana and comparative law describes the basic principle of fruits and products as follows:

> Certain things are capable of producing other things, namely, corporeal objects or incorporeal economic advantages. In Louisiana and in France, the things that are produced by another thing without diminution of its substance are termed fruits. The fruit-producing thing is often termed a *principal* thing. Things produced by another thing whose substance is thereby diminished are termed *products*. (Emphasis by author)

Yiannopoulos, *Property* § 37, Louisiana Civil Law Treatise (4th ed. 2001).

In a comparison with Roman law, Yiannopoulos notes that under classical Roman law, fruits were, generally, the products derived from a thing regardless of diminution of its economic value. Yiannopoulos, *supra*, at § 38. Distinction was made between natural and civil fruits. Ordinarily, natural fruits were corporeal objects while civil fruits were values resulting from the ownership of a thing or from the conduct of business. *Id.* Also under Roman law, fruits followed the juridical situation of the principal thing in all cases. The owner of a thing ordinarily acquired its fruits. It was only exceptional cases that other persons- a lessee, for instance, or usufructuary, or a bona fide possessor, acquired them. *Id.*

In discussing the French Code, Professor Yiannopoulos notes:

> The French Civil Code does not define the generic term fruits. The definition accepted by courts and writers is that fruits are things that are produced periodically from a principal thing without diminution of its substance. (Citations omitted). Things produced by, or derived from, another thing whose substance is thereby diminished are not fruits but products (produits). Once separated from the principal thing, products are not reproduced.

According to Yiannopoulos, the significance of the distinction between fruits and products is that it provides the standard for the apportionment of economic advantages between the owner of a thing and other persons entitled to its fruits. "The owner is entitled to all products, whereas persons entitled to fruits only receive revenues produced by a thing periodically without diminution of its substance." Yiannopoulos at § 39. He further explains that under French law ordinarily, fruits as well as products, follow the juridical situation of the principal thing. The owner of the principal thing acquires, upon separation, the ownership of fruits and products as individual things. However, "[i]n certain circumstances, principal things and fruits are disassociated; their juridical situation is not the same. *In these circumstances, fruits do not follow the ownership of the principal thing,* though products still do. Thus, when a usufruct is established, the fruits belong to the usufructuary, but products ordinarily belong to the naked owner." *Id.* (Emphasis added).

In interpreting the corresponding provisions of the Louisiana Civil Code of 1870 in this area, Yiannopoulos notes that Louisiana frequently followed French doctrine and jurisprudence. The terminological distinction between "fruits" and "products," however, was not at first accepted. As a result, a different conceptual apparatus had to be employed for the apportionment of economic advantages between the owner of a thing and other persons entitled to "fruits" such as usufructuaries, possessors in good faith, or as spouses living under the regime of community property. However, Article 551 of the Louisiana Civil Code established a unitary notion of fruits for all purposes, and following the French doctrine, the 1979 legislation has adopted the distinction between "fruits" and "products."

The Louisiana Code of 1870 established three categories of fruits, namely, natural fruits, fruits of industry, and civil fruits. La. C.C. art. 545 (1870). Fruits of industry differed from natural fruits in that they were the result of effort and industry, whereas natural fruits were the spontaneous product of the earth or of animals. Since the rules governing natural fruits and fruits of industry have always been the same, the two categories were combined in the 1976 codal revision into one. See, La. C.C. art. 551 (Acts 1967, No. 103, § 1, eff. Jan. 1-1977). *Louisiana Civil Law Treatise*; Property; Yiannopoulos.

Prior to the effective date of article 551, the jurisprudence, as well as doctrinal materials, indicated "fruits" was construed according to the context in which the issue of classification arose. *Succession of Doll*, 593 So.2d 1239, 1244, 1245 (La. 1992). Citing *Gueno v. Medlenka*, 238 La. 1081, 117 So.2d 817 (1960) (usufruct); *Milling v. Collector of Revenue*, 220 L. 773, 57 So.2d 679 (1952) (taxation); *Harang v. Bowie Lumber Co.,*, 145 La. 96, 81 So. 769 (1919) (good faith possession); *Elder v. Ellerbe*, 135 La. 990, 66 So. 337 (1914) (good faith possession). Finally, a unitary notion of fruits ensued with the enactment of article 551.

As it relates to the mode of acquisition of fruits, Yiannopoulos states:

> According to civilian conceptions, nonsepar[a]ted fruits from a part of the fruit-producing thing and belong to the owner of that thing by right of assession. Upon separation, natural fruits become individual things, and question arises as to how the ownership of these things are acquired. Owners, good faith possessors, and persons having real rights in fruit-producing things acquire ownership of natural fruits upon separation, without the need of any act on their part. Persons having real rights acquire ownershjp of natural fruits by virtue of an act of collection, namely by the taking of possession. *The mode of acquisition of civil fruits involves distinct problems. According to traditional civilian ideas, maintained in modern codes, civil fruits accrue by virtue of an obligation; hence one entitled to civil fruits rather than "ownership" thereof. Accordingly, the mode of acquisition of civil*

> *fruits is ordinarily a matter governed by the agreement of the parties and the law of obligations.* (Emphasis added).

Yiannopoulos, *supra*, § 41.

With regard to the classification of property among married persons, the legal principles are found the Louisiana Civil Code. La. C.C. art. 2338 provides:

> The community property comprises: property acquired during the existence of the legal regime through the effort, skill, or industry of either spouse; property acquired with community things or with community separate things, unless classified as separate under Article 2341; property donated to the spouses jointly; natural and civil fruits of community property; damages awarded for loss or injury to a thing belonging to the community; and all other property not classified by law as separate property.

As was explained in 16 Spaht and L. W. Hargrave, Louisiana Civil Law Treatise, *Matrimonial Regimes* § 3.3 at 48 (1997):

> Wages are the premier community asset. It is wages paid in return for work done during the existence of the community that are included, regardless of when the payment is actually made. The "property acquired," in the language of Louisiana Civil Code Article 2338, is a right to payment at some point for the work done. If payment is made during the community for work done before its commencement, the money is separate. If the check is cut after termination, but is for work during the community, the funds are community.

Property acquired by a spouse prior to the establishment of the community property regime is separate property. La. C.C. art. 2341. However, the natural and civil fruits of separate property produced during the existence of the community property regime are community unless a spouse reserves them as his separate property in a declaration made by authentic act or an act under private signature duly acknowledged. La. C.C. art. 2339.

The Code also provides that things in the possession of a spouse during the existence of a regime of acquets and gains are presumed to be community. La. C.C. art. 2340.; However, either spouse may rebut this presumption. La. C.C. art. 2340. The spouse seeking to rebut the presumption bears the burden of proving that the property is separate in nature. *Knighten v. Knighten*, 00-1662 (La. App. 1st Cir. 9/28/01), 809 So.2d 324, *writ denied*, 01-2846 (La. 1/4/02), 805 So.2d 207.

The current definition of fruits is found in La. C.C. art. 551, which provides:

Fruits are things that are produced by or derived from another thing without diminution of its substance.

There are two kinds of fruits; natural and civil fruits.

Natural fruits are products of the earth or of animal.

Civil fruits are revenues derived from a thing by operation of law or by reason of juridical act, such as rentals, interest, and certain corporate distributions.

Is there a fruit producing "thing" or "asset?"

With this background, we will now address Ms. Stack's first argument that the lower courts erred in finding that the insurance policies between State Farm and the individual policy holders constitutes "things" or assets from which fruits may be produced.

Ms. Starks argues that neither the insurance policies written by Mr. Ross prior to the marriage nor his agency contract with State Farm Insurance Company (the agency contract) constitute "things" or "assets" in which Mr. Ross had an ownership interest and from which fruits may be derived. Without any ownership interest, Ms. Starks argues, the agency contract is no different in function than a medical license, a law license, or an exclusive franchise agreement. She maintains that like these examples, the agency contract has no inherent value, cannot be inherited by children or transferred for value to a third person, and returns nothing on the "investment" require to acquire it.

Ms. Starks further maintains that the individual insurance policies sold to the customers prior to the marriage did not create "property" because Mr. Ross had no legal interest in those policies. Only the policyholders or State Farm could enforce, cancel, renew, modify, or avail themselves of the provisions of those policies. Mr. Ross could not transfer or assign the policies themselves, and his ability to collect premiums from the renewal of the policies is conditioned upon his possession of a valid Louisiana insurance license, the continuation of the State Farm Agency Contract, the decision of the policyholder to renew the policy, and the payment of the premiums. Thus, according to Ms. Starks, the renewal commissions could not have been classified as fruits.

Mr. Ross counters that the lower courts correctly determined that the insurance policies entered into between the policyholders and State Farm were "things" in themselves. He argues that although the policies themselves did not create property rights per se, they were things themselves which produced revenue by juridical act (the State Farm Agency contract with Mr. Ross). Mr. Ross contends that the renewals flowing from the things in question (the insurance policies) produced civil fruits (renewal commissions). As the policies were sold prior to the marriage, Mr. Ross argues that the lower courts correctly concluded that the civil fruits inured to his separate estate and could be reserved under article 2339.

After careful review of the law, we must agree with the court of appeal's finding that the individual policies of insurance are "juridical acts" from which civil fruits may be derived. As stated, the definition of "civil fruits" contained in La. C.C. art 551 is "revenues derived from a thing by operation of law or *by reason of juridical act.*" (Emphasis added). Examples given of civil fruits include rent, interest and some corporate distributions. To qualify as a "fruit," a thing must first be "produced by or derived from" another thing. La. C.C. art. 551. Thus, the example of "civil fruits" provided in the code must necessarily be derived from a "thing" or "asset," i.e. rental property, money, or some corporate investment.

We reject Ms. Starks' argument that not only must there be a "thing," there must be an ownership interest in the thing in order to claim ownership of the civil fruits. There is no dispute that Mr. Ross has no ownership interest in the insurance policies per se as he has no direct, immediate or exclusive authority over these contracts. Further, he cannot transfer, enjoy, or dispose of these contracts.

However, the record indicates that Mr. Ross received commissions based on his agency contract with State Farm coupled with the securing of the individual insurance policies. By virtue of these juridical acts, Mr. Ross gained "the right" to collect or a "claim" to the insurance commissions on these policies. As long as these same policies of insurance are renewed, Mr. Ross has the same "right" or "claim" to the commissions. Thus, under the definition of civil fruits contained in La. C.C. art 551, Mr. Ross received revenue (renewal commission) by reason of juridical acts (the insurance policies). As explained above fruits do not always follow the ownership of the principal thing, as is the case with products. As stated by Yiannopoulos, the mode of acquisition of civil fruits is ordinarily a matter governed by the agreement of the parties and the law of obligations.

Fruits or Earnings?

Having decided that the insurance policies are "things" from which civil fruits may be derived, we must now determine whether the lower courts erred in finding that the renewal commissions were in fact "civil fruits" of Mr. Ross' separate property, and not the result of Mr. Ross' effort, skill or industry during the existence of the community property regime. As evidenced in the instant case, our courts have experienced some difficulty in determining whether a spouse's property should be classified as earnings or fruits.

Spaht and Hargrave explained:

> From the earliest times, the most important legislative policy underpinning the Louisiana community property regime has been that spouses share equally "the produce of the reciprocal labor and industry" of both "husband and wife." No matter how married couples organize their lives - one earning income, the other managing the home; both working for wages; neither earning wages and both producing things; or whatever–the basic rule is that they share equally in whatever each produces and accumulates. Historically, this policy protected the wife who was not a wage earner by giving her a share in the husband's accumulations of income. In more modern times, the policy fosters equality as the household with two working spouses becomes more common.

Spaht and Hargrave, Louisiana Civ. Law Treatise, *Matrimonial Regimes*, § 3.2 at p. 47 (1997).

In the instant case, if the renewal commissions are the result of Mr. Ross' effort, skill or industry during the existence of the community property regime, the renewal commissions, or at least a portion thereof, are community property. This is in keeping with the basic notion that spouses should share equally "the produce of the reciprocal labor and industry of both husband and wife." Spaht and Hargrave, *Matrimonial Regimes*, *supra,* § 3.2 at p. 47.

Spaht and Hargrave also discussed the issue of "fruits vs. earnings" in their treatise:

> Fruits may be separate property if the appropriate declaration is filed; otherwise, they are community. [footnote omitted]. Property acquired by the effort, skill or industry of a spouse is community, and there is no mechanism provided for making it separate. [footnote omitted]. In the simplest case, production of the fruits would not involve labor or industry of a spouse–the typical passive investment. However, it is quite common for many investments to combine one spouse's separate capital or property with community labor to produce fruits.

Spaht and Hargrave, *supra*, § 3.8 at p. 64. The authors then suggest that:

> [t]o the extent that labor is producing some benefit, the community ought to share in the profit of that labor. If it is combined with separate capital or other separate property, equity would suggest a proportional division of the profits between the community and separate estates of the spouses. If such a pro rata division is not adopted, it would allow a spouse with separate property to act in bad faith and deprive the community of the revenues by putting all one's efforts into production of fruits from the separate asset.

Id.

Other authors and commentators have suggested the equitable solution of a pro rata division of the property when labor is combined with capital investment to produce fruits. Our courts have also adopted this notion.

On original hearing in *Kyson v. Kyson*, *supra*, the second circuit court of appeal found that while money received by the husband, Mr. Kyson, qualified as rental revenue, the rental payments were the result of a substantial amount of time spent by Mr. Kyson on managing the rental property. The court stated:

> [E]ven if Mr. Kyson had not participated in the rental management he would have received some rentals as passive investment. We find this to be a case in which "separate capital is combined with community labor to produce fruits. Thus, a determination must be made as to the amount of labor attributed to the investment. An appropriate analysis is to examine the relative contributions of labor and capital to the funds involved and a proration of the funds according to these contributions."

Because the court was unable to determine from the record before it the value of Mr. Kyson's labor in order that the required proration of funds could be made, the court remanded the matter to the trial court for this determination. On rehearing, the court in *Kyson*, noting that the trial court made no factual finding in this regard, concluded that it was unable to discern from the record sufficient quantification of Mr. Kyson's time and labor associated with the disputed rental income from which it could draw any meaningful conclusion. The court, therefore, reversed its original decision on the basis that the facts did not support its initial conclusion. Although reversed on other grounds, the case remains as authority for prorating income that results both from a spouse's labor and from a return on a separate property investment.

In an earlier case, *Paxton v. Bramlette*, *supra*, the court was faced with a dispute over whether corporate distributions to the wife were community salary or separate dividends. The court concluded that the funds were community earnings since it found the wife contributed "substantial services" to two corporations in which she had controlling interests. The wife owned real estate and received rents from those properties that the court characterized as "fruits of her parphernal property." She later transferred the properties to a newly formed realty corporation. She was paid a salary by the corporation before and after she filed an affidavit reserving the fruits of her separate property. The court, finding that the wife performed most of the managerial duties in operating the corporation, including collecting rents, depositing them, and handling maintenance and repairs, held that the payments after the filing were community and were not fruits of separate property. The wife also owned as separate property 82% of the stock in a corporation that operated furniture stores. She went to the store daily and participated in important decisions, none of which were made without her approval. The court quoted approvingly from law review writers suggesting that the basic analysis in such a case is to examine the relative contributions of labor and capital to the funds involved; if the revenue was the result of substantial capital, it would be a fruit; if it represented substantial labor with little capital, it would be earnings. The court then concluded that her labor was substantial and thus the payments were community earnings.

The court in *Gautreau v. Gautreau, supra,* also followed this approach and found that to the extent the income derived by the wife from her separate property was paid to her because of her "effort, skill or industry" and was not simply passive income accruing as the result of corporate distributions or the increase in value of the corporation distributions or the increase in value of the corporation, the income was community property. *Gautreau*, 96-1548 at 12, 13, 697 So.2d at 1349.

Although the issue is res nova in this Court, the difficulty in determining whether revenue is earnings or fruit has been considered in the context of renewal commissions by our colleagues on the courts of appeal. In *Michel v. Michel, supra*, the husband received commissions on life insurance policies he sold as well as "Factor 1" commissions based on the performance of salesmen he recruited and trained. The husband's work in recruiting and training the sales staff was performed during the existence of the community, however, the sales by the latter and the payments to him came after termination of the community. The first circuit court of appeal held that the wife was entitled to share in her husband's insurance sales commissions on the policy renewals received by her husband after termination, since all of the sums involved related to community effort. The court stated, "while it is true that the spade work had been done when the original sale had been made, some service work had to be performed and in addition there was no certainty that the policies would be renewed." *Michel*, 484 So.2d at 835. Since the revenue resulted from labor during and after the community, it was to be divided proportionally. Although the court admitted that the amount attributed to post-community work was "speculative," the court of appeal affirmed the trial court's approximation of this interest in giving one-half to the husband's separate estate and one-half to the community.

A different approach was undertaken by the third circuit in *Williams v. Williams,* 590 So.2d 649 (La. App. 3rd Cir. 1991). In that case, the court concluded that an ex-husband's renewal commissions attributed to insurance policies sold during the community but paid after termination were not be shared with his ex-wife. The court suggested that even if the renewal premiums were attributed to work during and after the community, the value to the community was speculative in nature. Thus, it found that the wife's interest was so speculative that it had no value at all.

The court in *Futch v. Futch*, 26-149 (La. App. 2nd Cir. 9/23/94), 643 So.2d 364, expressly disagreed with the holding in *Williams* and followed the rationale in *Michel*, *supra*. The court in *Futch* stated, "although it may be impossible to perfectly divide renewal commissions generated by insurance policies written during the marriage, we disagree with *Williams, supra*, and conclude that these renewal commissions are community property subject to partition." *Futch*, 643 So.2d at 367. The court further found that "[e]quity requires a division in which Mr. Futch's separate labor and costs to keep the policies in effect are considered in determining the community's share." *Id.* At 369. Finding the record lacked evidence needed to make this determination, the court remanded the matter to the trial court for the taking of such evidence. The court of appeal further found that the burden would be on the husband "to establish his entitlement to more than one-half of the renewal commissions. For many of the policies, no significant servicing may be required; however, for the policies that generate renewal commissions based on Mr. Futch's post-termination efforts or achievement, he, not the former community, is entitled to the fruits of this enhancement." *Id.*

Spaht and Hargrave have opined that the "[e]quitable considerations as well as basic doctrinal principles support the *Michel-Boyle-Futch* approach, even if the division is approximate." Matrimonial Regimes, *Louisiana Civil Law Treatise*, § 3.4 at 58 (1997).

In the case sub judice, Ms. Starks argues that this case does not involve the "return" on some separate property asset, but rather the income at issue is entirely due to the sales efforts of Mr. Ross. She maintains that the renewal commissions were not "passive income," but were the result of labor expended during the existence of the community.

Ms. Sparks argues that under the test enunciated in *Paxton, supra*, and *Gautreau, supra*, it is clear that the revenues at issue are community property because Mr. Ross had minimum "capital investment" in his insurance agency, but contributed substantial labor, which produced income during the community regime. She maintains that it was Mr. Ross' sales efforts, his personality, his knowledge of his customers and their insurance needs, and his ability to preserve the right to sell insurance policies by meeting his contractual and legal requirements to do so that created the revenues at issue. Thus, she argues, the only significant investment in the insurance agency was Mr. Ross himself. In other words, the investment was human labor and not economic capital. Ms. Starks further contends that all of the reported decisions by Louisiana courts which have considered renewal commissions acknowledge the rule that some effort is expended by insurance agents to generate renewal commissions.

To the contrary, Mr. Ross argues that the record shows that he did not expend effort, skill or industry during the marriage as it relates to receiving renewals from policies sold some 30 years prior. He contends that he expended no labor during the marriage which was in any way attributable to renewals received during the marital regime. Mr. Ross further maintains that the "balancing test" required in determining the proper characterization of renewal assets was undertaken by the trial court in this matter, which correctly resulted in the court's judgment that Mr. Ross expended little or no effort during the marriage for purposes of receiving these renewals.

We first note, as did the court of appeal, that a trial court's findings regarding the nature of the property as community or separate is a factual determination subject to manifest error review. *Biondo v. Biondo*, 99-0890, pp. 4-5 (La. App. 1st Cir. 7/31/00), 769 So.2d 94, 99. The trial court in this case did in fact make a factual determination as to the classification of the renewal premiums in this case. The court noted that with the exception of the *Williams* case, *supra*, Louisiana jurisprudence has held that renewal commissions received after the termination of the community as a result of the sale of policies (effort, skill or industry) during the existence of the community are community. The trial court then reasoned that it follows that the sale of insurance policies (effort, skill or industry) before the existence of the community were separate property.

In determining whether any effort, skill or industry was expended during the community, the trial court reviewed the trial testimony of Mr. Ross in this regard. The court noted Mr. Ross' testimony that:

> "[w]hen he began his business, 'Billy Ross Insurance Agency,' he called people all day everyday; occasionally went door-to-door; and attempted to 'gain a listening ear' in an effort to generate business. However, by 1992, when married Mrs. Ross, his business had grown to the level that he was no longer required to 'prospect.'" He stated that the nature of effort, labor, skill and industry put into the business since 1992 consists of training employees and evaluating office products. He stated that during the marriage he went to the office three to five days a week for approximately three to eight hours each day. He testified that it has been years since he personally has completed a new application for insurance. However, he has employees who may have done so.
>
> Mr. Ross testified that the majority of the money generated by his business is from renewals of policies written prior to the marriage. He further stated that he cannot think of a single thing he did to induce people to renew their policies, nor does he know what he can do to induce people to renew them.
>
> Trial court judgment, p. 3.

The trial court went on to conclude that the effort, skill and industry which ultimately produced the renewals received during the existence of the community were performed prior to the marriage which renders them to be separate property. However, the court did recognize that "despite Mr. Ross' denial that he put forth any effort to generate renewals that were received during the marriage, some servicing may have been required." Thus, the trial court found Ms. Starks would bear the burden at trial to quantify Mr. Ross' efforts, during the minute time frame between the date of marriage and the filing of the declaration, to prove the amount of effort Mr. Ross put forth toward the renewals.

The court of appeal affirmed the trial court's conclusion, finding that "in order to disprove that the renewal commissions received by Mr. Ross were not civil fruits, it was necessary to prove that substantial labor was exerted by Mr. Ross to obtain the renewal commissions during the existence of the community property regime." *Ross*, 835 So.2d at 821. The court of appeal concluded, based on its own review of the record, that the evidence supports the trial court's determination that Mr. Ross had not expended any significant effort, skill or industry in effecting the renewal of policies pre-existing the community during the existence of the community property regime.

We find that the lower courts erred in assigning the burden of proof and in finding that little or no effort was exerted to generate the renewal commissions. The evidence in the record is to the contrary. Because the renewal commissions were received during the existence of the community, the burden was upon Mr. Ross to prove that they were not community property. *Knighten v. Knighten, supra.* Despite Mr. Ross' assertions that no effort was required to service customers and maintain his book of business, his deposition testimony reveals that he indeed exerted substantial effort, skill and industry t to insure the maintenance of his existing business and to satisfy existing policyholders. According to Mr. Ross, he spent three to five days per week, and an average of five to ten hours per day working at his insurance agency. The parties agree that Mr. Ross certainly did not spend this time generating new business. In fact, new business constituted only 6-7% of the business income. The majority of income from the Billy Ross Insurance Agency came from renewal of policies.

Despite Mr. Ross' assertion that he did nothing, and could do nothing, to produce the renewals, the record reveals that he did in fact provide substantial services to existing policyholders. In his deposition, Mr. Ross testified that he entertained existing policyholders by way of receiving and returning phone calls; answering questions regarding, among other things, accident reports, claims, and general insurance matters. He sent Christmas cards and birthday cards. Further, the business records show that money was allocated to advertising, newsletters, postage and entertaining clients. Mr. Ross maximized his income by servicing and entertaining existing policyholders. We can only conclude that had the customers received no services, "shmoozing," if you will, the agency income would have dropped significantly.

In his testimony, Mr. Ross describes his work as office management and training employees. The fact that Mr. Ross' role at some point changed from direct sales to a supervisory role, does not change this court's decision. The employees were mandataries or agents, acting on behalf of the agency servicing old clients and prospecting for new clients. Any servicing by employees equates to servicing by Mr. Ross himself. Mr. Ross' employees were hired and trained by the Billy Ross Agency and were compensated by the agency, not State Farm.

State Farm even recognizes that its agents perform "service" on existing accounts. In addition to other forms of compensation, the company pays its agents "service compensation." The term is defined in the State Farm Agent's Agreements as follows:

> SERVICE COMPENSATION. For services rendered by you in any month while this Agreement is in force, in assisting policyholders, cooperating with adjusters in reporting and handling claims, and cooperating with and promoting the interests of the Company, you shall be paid for such month and amount equal to ...

We find it is inconceivable that Mr. Ross would spend such a significant amount of time "working" at his office, producing substantial income mostly attributable to renewal commissions, and then assert that he did not exert any effort, skill or industry toward producing the renewal commissions. Mr. Ross's assertions in this regard are simply unconvincing.

Based on the above, we must conclude that the renewal commissions received by Mr. Ross during the existence of the community property regime were the result of Mr. Ross' effort, skill and industry exerted during the community regime. Our holding is consistent with the well settled law with regard to w hat constitutes community property in our state and is in accord with the notion that to the extent that labor is producing some benefit, the community ought to share in the profit of that labor. Accordingly, we find that the lower courts' decisions to the contrary are manifestly erroneous, as they are not supported by the evidence. Ms. Starks is entitled to share in the business income generated by Mr. Ross' work, industry and effort during the marriage.

CONCLUSION

Accordingly, we reverse the lower court's findings that Mr. Ross did not exert effort, skill or industry during the existence of the community property regime to produce the renewal commissions he received during the regime. We also reverse the lower courts' decision in so far as it places the burden of proof on Ms. Starks to prove her entitlement to a share of renewal commissions during the marriage.

REVERSED.

KNOLL, Justice, concurring.

I concur with the majority's result that the renewal commissions Mr. Ross received during the existence of the community were the result of his effort, skill and industry exerted during the community regime. In my view the majority errs, however, in its analysis that these commissions are civil fruits that are subject to the community regime due to the effort expended by Mr. Ross during the regime, because these commissions are not civil fruits.

I disagree from the majority's holding that the individual insurance policies are juridical acts from which civil fruits may be derived. This is not a matter where Mr. Ross's effort, skill and industry were combined with *capital investment.* The renewal premiums were not the result of Mr. Ross's separate capital investment or separate property. The renewal premiums, as the majority concludes, were the result of Mr. Ross's effort, skill and industry. "Property acquired by the effort, skill or industry of a spouse is community, and there is no mechanism provided for making it separate." Katherine Spaht & W. Lee Hargrave, *Louisiana Civil Law Treatise--Matrimonial Regimes* § 3.8, p. 64 (2d ed.1997).

As the majority correctly notes, the treatise suggests that:

If [labor] is combined with *separate capital* or other *separate property,* equity would suggest a proportional division of the profits between the community and separate estates of the spouses. If such a pro rata division is not adopted, it would allow a spouse with *separate property* to act in bad faith and deprive the community of the revenues by putting all one's efforts into production of fruits from the *separate asset.*
Id. (Emphasis added.)

Mr. Ross's effort and industry were not combined with separate capital or separate property to generate the renewal commissions. In my view, renewal commissions are not civil fruits from an asset; the insurance policies were not Mr. Ross's asset or property.

Certainly the policies are juridical acts and "things;" conceivably they are even assets of the policyholders. The majority's analysis is flawed, however, in finding that because insurance policies are juridical acts and things, civil fruits necessarily flow from them.

"The right of ownership, which according to traditional civilian analysis includes the elements of usus, fructus and abusus, may lawfully be dismembered in a variety of ways either by the intention of the owner or by operation of law." Exposé des Motifs, Title III: Personal Servitudes, La. Civ.Code Ann. (West 1980). Because fruits are a right of ownership, the majority errs in rejecting Ms. Starks's argument that there must be ownership interest in the thing in order to claim ownership of the fruits. Although acquisition of the fruits may be dismembered by a personal servitude, thereby precluding the owner of the thing from claiming ownership of the fruits, it is elemental that if the rights of ownership have not been dismembered, the rights, including the fruits, remain with the owner of the thing. Fruits are a right of ownership; "[i]n the absence of rights of other persons, the owner of a thing acquires the ownership of its natural and civil fruits." La. Civ.Code art. 483.

The majority's analysis that "... under the definition of civil fruits contained in La. C.C. art. 551, Mr. Ross received revenue (renewal commission) by reason of juridical acts (the insurance policies.)" fails to account for the ownership element of the "fruit producing thing" and fails to address the acquisition of the (misnamed) fruits. The insurance policies are contracts between the policyholders and State Farm. The agency contract between Mr. Ross and State Farm was the mechanism that provided for the payment of commissions to Mr. Ross for the renewal of insurance policies sold by him. These commissions are compensation paid to Mr. Ross per the terms of the contract between him and State Farm. Article 551's reference to juridical acts concerns acts that create the civil fruits such as rent, interest and dividends. The code article is not authority that any juridical act that gives rise to payment transforms that payment into a civil fruit. The majority's conclusion that these commissions are civil fruits (a right of ownership) does violence to the civilian concept of ownership.

The majority cites to various appellate court decisions declaring that the courts of appeal have addressed the issue of whether renewal commissions are earnings or fruit. *Ross, op.* at 394. The majority errs in finding that those courts addressed this issue. In each of those cases, the court was deciding whether the effort, skill and industry were performed during the community regime so that the resulting commissions would be classified as community property. *Michel v. Michel,* 484 So.2d 829, 835 (La.App. 1 Cir.1986)(Wife was entitled to share in renewal commissions received by husband after termination of the community where policies were sold during the community; because the money was the product of labor during and after the community it was to be divided proportionately); *Williams v. Williams,* 590 So.2d 649, 653 (La.App. 3 Cir.1991)(Service work performed after termination of the community contributed in great measure to policy renewals making service work performed during the marriage less important vis-a-vis renewals); *Futch v. Futch,* 26-149 (La.App. 2 Cir. 9/23/94), 643 So.2d 364, 369 (The husband is entitled to deduct from the renewal commissions an amount representative of his post-termination efforts in producing these commissions; he is entitled to the commissions generated by his post-termination efforts and apportionment between the community's and his separate interest should be made accordingly). In none of these cases was the issue ever raised that the commissions were civil fruits. The issue in the matter before us is the same issue that was before the appellate courts in *Michel, Williams*, and *Futch, i.e.,* whether renewal commissions are classified as community or separate when the initial policies were sold during one regime and the renewal commissions were earned in another. The only difference is that in *Michel, Williams* and *Futch,* the policies were sold during the community and the renewal commissions were paid after its termination, whereas, in the matter presently before us, the situation is the complete opposite.

The majority takes an unnecessary circuitous route to reach its result. The issue was simply whether any effort was expended by Mr. Ross during the regime that resulted in commissions earned by him from policies sold before the establishment of the community. Mr. Ross exerted substantial effort, skill and industry to ensure the maintenance of his existing business and to satisfy existing policyholders. Because of his efforts, he continued to receive renewal commissions. These renewal commissions were reported as income on his income tax statements and comprised a significant portion of his total income. Property acquired during the existence of the legal regime through the spouse's effort, skill or industry is community property. *See* La. Civ.Code art. 2338. All forms of payments in return for one's labor, whatever they may be called, are included. Spaht, § 3.3, p. 48. Commissions representing a percentage of sales or premiums would also be included. *Id.*

Because, as the majority correctly concludes, Mr. Ross expended significant effort, skill and industry in effecting the renewal of policies pre-existing the community during the existence of the community property regime, these renewal commissions constitute compensation paid in return for work done during the community property regime. Therefore the commissions constitute community property and are subject to Ms. Starks's claim for partition, to the extent or percentage community labor was attributable to the renewals so effected. I find the majority has erred in classifying the renewal commission as civil fruits.

For these reasons, I do not agree with the majority's analysis. I concur only with the majority's result which found the trial court was manifestly erroneous in its determination that the commissions were Mr. Ross's separate property, and the determination that the renewal commissions were the result of Mr. Ross's effort, skill and industry exerted during the community regime.

E. *Glynn W. Reynolds v. Margaret Susan Romero Reynolds*

388 So. 2d 1135 (La. 1980)

SUMMERS, Chief Justice.

Minnie Smith, widow of W. H. Sledge, executed her last will and testament on January 8, 1957. Her will created a spendthrift trust in which she bequeathed her farm consisting of 640 acres in Vermilion Parish, together with its improvements, to C. H. Brookshire as trustee. The will stipulated the trustee was to hold the property in trust for her grandchildren who survived her and until her youngest grandchild attained the age of twenty-one. The trustee was directed to hold, process, manage and control the trust estate with full power to alienate and encumber the trust estate.

Thereafter, while the property was still held in trust, one of the grandchildren Margaret Susan Romero married Glynn W. Reynolds on July 9, 1966. During the existence of the marriage the wife received as distributed trust income the sum of $11,913.85. These funds were deposited in a checking account in the Kaplan State Bank under her exclusive control. At trial the parties stipulated that from this account the wife expended the sum of $9,660.26 on items of clothing for herself and the children and for household expenses. On February 6, 1970 Margaret and Glynn were judicially separated. Upon dissolution of the community a balance of $555.18 remained of this distributed trust income. And on February 6, 1970 when the community was dissolved there existed the sum of $11,434.80 in the account of the trustee representing undistributed earnings of the trust estate in which Margaret owned an interest.

The wife did not execute and record an affidavit of paraphernality pursuant to Article 2386 of the Civil Code which provides:

> "The fruits of the paraphernal property of the wife, wherever the property be located and however administered whether natural, civil, including interest, dividends and rents, or from the result of labor, fall into the conjugal partnership, if there exists a community of acquets and gains; unless the wife, by written instrument, shall declare that she reserves all of such fruits for her own separate use and benefit and her intention to administer such property separately and alone. The said instrument shall be executed before a Notary Public and two witnesses and duly recorded in the Conveyance Records of the Parish where the community is domiciled.
>
> "If there is no community of gains, each party enjoys, as he chooses, that which comes to his hand; but the fruits and revenues which are existing at the dissolution of the marriage, belong to the owner of the things which produce them.

On July 5, 1971 the trust was terminated and the share of the trust property to which she was entitled was transferred by the trustee to Margaret Susan Romero. On August 21, 1972 the parties were divorced.

An agreement was entered into between the husband and wife on December 6, 1977 in which they settled the bulk of the community property. The only property, the status of which remained in dispute, was the $555.18 distributed to the wife by the trustee and the $11,434.80 in the account of the trustee representing undistributed earnings of the trust estate.

The wife contends that the distributed trust income and her proportionate share of the undistributed trust income constitutes her separate property. She asserts also that she is entitled to restitution of the $9,660.26 expended from those separate funds for the benefit of the community. It is the husband's position that the distributed and undistributed income constitute "fruits" of the paraphernal property of his former wife, which, because she did not execute and record the affidavit of paraphernality required by Article 2386 of the Civil Code, formed part of the community of acquets and gains which existed between them. Therefore, the husband contends that the wife's demand for restitution of the $9,660.26 should be rejected. He should be awarded, he asserts, judgment against his former wife for half of the distributed trust income on deposit at the time of the dissolution of the community, the sum of $277.59; and half of his former wife's proportionate share of the undistributed income amounting to $1,429.25 which he contended is also part of the community which existed between them.

ON REHEARING

WATSON, Justice.

This is a dispute between two former spouses over income from a trust. This court originally held that the trustee owned the corpus of the trust; that the wife's beneficial interest did not have the indicia of ownership; therefore, that the income from the trust was not a fruit of the wife's separate property and did not fall into the community; that both the distributed and undistributed trust income was the wife's separate property; and that the wife was not entitled to reimbursement of the funds expended from the distributed trust income because there was no enhancement of the community.

A rehearing was granted to reconsider the status of the trust income and the wife's right to reimbursement.

The beneficiary wife is Margaret Susan Romero Reynolds. The trust was established in the will of her grandmother, Minnie Smith Sledge. A farm was placed in trust for the benefit of Ms. Sledge's grandchildren, present and future. Ownership of the property was transferred to the trustee, who had authority to sell or otherwise dispose of the property as he saw fit. The time and amount of disbursements to the beneficiaries for their support were at his discretion.

The beneficial interest of Ms. Reynolds in the trust is clearly less than full ownership. LSA-C.C. art. 477 and former art. 489. Title to the property vested in the trustee. LSA-R.S. 9:1731. The undistributed income from the trust was under the control and dominion of the trustee. It accrued to the trustee during the term of the trust, as a civil fruit unseparated from the corpus of the trust. LSA-C.C. art. 489 and former art. 499. Ms. Reynolds had no right to this money until the trustee decided to distribute it. The undistributed income did not fall into the community.

Although Margaret Susan Romero Reynolds did not own the corpus of the trust, her paraphernal estate included a beneficial interest, an incorporeal right. LSA-C.C. art. 461 and former art. 460. The distributed revenues from that incorporeal right were civil fruits. LSA-C.C. art. 551 and former art. 545. See the definitive discussion by Professor A. N. Yiannopoulos, 2 La.Civ.Law Treat.2d, § 25 and § 26. Once distributed, the wife had full ownership of this income. These fruits of the wife's paraphernal property fell into the community because no instrument was filed to reserve them for the wife. LSA-C.C. art. 2386 and the successor article, LSA-C.C. art. 2339.

Since the wife kept the distributed fruits under her control in a separate checking account, they were not delivered to the community for its use. She has no right to restitution of the income from the trust which she spent during the marriage. The funds were expended prior to the effective date of the new Matrimonial Regimes legislation, January 1, 1980, and the matter is governed by former Civil Code articles, 2388, 2390, and 2391. Slater v. Culpepper, 233 La. 1071, 99 So.2d 348 (1957). The test is not enhancement or benefit to the community. Under the prior law, only the husband, who manages the community assets, is required to show an enhancement of the community to obtain restitution of his separate funds. The wife must only show delivery to the community for its use. The wife did not meet that burden here, and her claim must be denied.

Therefore, the original opinion correctly held that: (1) the undistributed trust income of $11,434.80 did not fall into the community; and (2) the wife had no right to reimbursement of the funds she expended. However, the opinion erred in holding that the balance of the distributed income was not a civil fruit of the wife's paraphernal property. The $555.18 balance the distributed trust income is a community asset.

Therefore, the original opinion is amended as to the trust income distributed during the existence of the community, to declare the sum of $555.18 to be a community asset.

F. Note

In *Bergeron v. Bergeron*, 693 So. 2d 199 (La. App. 3d Cir. 1997), the court carefully traced and then tracked separate property which had been combined with community property in the form of interest in an annuity account.

G. *Susan Marie Gisleson v. Stephen Russell Deputy*

122 So. 3d 1089 (La. App. 4 Cir. 2013)

MAX N. TOBIAS, JR., Judge.

The defendant/appellant, Steven Russell Deputy, M.D., appeals from a judgment that settled the remaining issues in this divorce case between Dr. Deputy and his former wife, Susan Marie Gisleson. For the reasons that follow, we affirm the judgment.

Ms. Gisleson and Dr. Deputy met in San Francisco, California while he was in medical school and Ms. Gisleson was an undergraduate. They subsequently married in June 1992 in San Francisco. Before the marriage, Dr. Deputy had borrowed money (student loans) to attend school. The loans were repaid during the marriage. After he completed his residency, he, his wife, and their infant son moved to New Orleans where they remained married for 19 years.

In 2009, Dr. Deputy was diagnosed with cancer. He was given chemotherapy and underwent a bone marrow transplant in April 2010. When he returned from his treatment in California, Ms. Gisleson told him she wanted to separate. She moved out of the home on 1 July 2010. The parties attended counseling for a few months without success. Thereafter, Ms. Gisleson informed Dr. Deputy that she was not returning to the marriage.

After living separate and apart for one year, Ms. Gisleson filed for divorce pursuant to La. C.C. art. 103 and sought permanent spousal support, a division of the community of acquets and gains, and reimbursement for the value of Dr. Deputy's student loans that were paid off during the marriage.

***

Next, Dr. Deputy asserts that the trial court erred in failing to find that the interest paid on his student loans was a community obligation for which no reimbursement was due. In making this argument, Dr. Deputy cites, *inter alia,* La. C.C. art. 2339 and *Gill vl Gill*, 39,406 (La. App. 2 Cir. 3/09/05), 895 So. 2d 807.

Article 2339 states in pertinent part:

> The natural and civil fruits of the separate property of a spouse, minerals produced from or attributable to a separate asset, and bonuses, delay rentals, royalties, and shut-in payments arising from mineral leases are community property. Nevertheless, a spouse may reserve them as his separate property as provided in this Article.

Dr. Deputy contends that the interest is the cost of the civil fruit that was his increased earning power. While this is an interesting argument, it is unsupported in the law or jurisprudence.

"Fruits" are defined in La. C.C. art. 551 as "things that are produced by or derived from another thing without diminution of its substance." Civil fruits "are revenues derived from a thing by operation of law or by reason of a juridical act,...." Thus, pursuant to the Civil Code, Dr. Deputy's increased earning power as the result of his medical education is not a "fruit."

In *Gill, supra,* the court stated:

> Nevertheless, interest on a separate debt is chargeable to the community where the debt is part of the price of (or secured by mortgage on) **separate property which itself produces revenue.** *Hurta v. Hurta*, 260 So.2d 324 (La. App. 4th Cir. 1972). Wages are the premier community asset acquired through the effort, skill or industry of either spouse. *Ross v. Ross*, 02-2984 (La. 10/21/03, 857 So.2d 384, 390[,] *quoting* K. Spaht and W. Hargrave, *Matrimonial Regimes,* § 3.3 in 16 *Louisiana Civil Law Treatise* (2d Ed.1997); La. C.C. art. 2338.
>
> A recent ruling applying Article 2364 addressed mortgage payments during the marriage made for separate debt on a spouse's separate property which neither generated rent nor was used to benefit the community as the family home. *Munson v. Munson,* 00–348 (La.App. 3d Cir. 10/4/00), 772 So.2d 141, 145–146. The trial court awarded the reimbursement under Article 2364 for one-half of the total mortgage payment, including principal and interest.

Id at pp. 16-17, 895 So.2d at 817. The cases cited by Dr. Deputy all involve separate immovable property purchased by one spouse before the marriage with community funds used to satisfy the mortgage and interest payments. We find no case that extends this codal article to obligations, such as student loans, borrowed by a spouse before the establishment of the community property regime. We decline to do so. This assignment of error is also without merit.

***

Based on the foregoing, we affirm the judgment of the trial court.
AFFIRMED.

H. Questions

Unless otherwise stated, assume that neither spouse has executed a declaration of paraphernality.

1. H owns a savings account. Prior to his marriage to W, H has $100,000 in the account. During his marriage to W, H receives $5,000 in interest from the savings account. Is the interest community or separate? Why?

2. Suppose H uses his $100,000 of separate property in the savings account to buy an annuity during his marriage to W. The annuity earns $5,000 in interest during H and W's marriage. Is the annuity separate or community? Why? Is the interest separate or community? Why?

3. W owns 100 shares of stock in Corporation as her separate property. Each quarter, Corporation declares a cash dividend and distributes it to its

shareholders. Are the cash dividends received during W's marriage to H community or separate? Why?

4. Assume the same facts as number 3, except that Corporation is a closely held Corporation. During her marriage to H, W performs substantial managerial functions in connection with Corporation which result in increased earnings and, thus, increased dividends. W validly executed and filed a declaration of paraphernality. Are the cash dividends received by W community or separate? Why?

5. Assume H owns 100 shares of stock in Corporation as his separate property. During H's marriage to W, the Corporation's stock splits. H receives an additional 100 shares of stock as a result of the split. Are the new 100 shares of stock community or separate? Why?

6. Prior to his marriage, H inherited a lot of money from his parents and no longer has to work. H has invested much of his money in stocks. H validly executes and files a declaration of paraphernality. During his marriage to W some of his stocks split, he receives dividends on some, and he receives stock dividends on some. Further, the total value of H's investments increases in value during marriage because he spends a significant amount of time studying the market and making trades. H has a home office and a computer he uses for these activities. H spends several hours a day managing his money. Are the various dividends, splits, and increases in total value community or separate? Why? What rights might W have?

4.5 INHERITANCES AND DONATIONS FROM THIRD PARTIES

A. Introduction

Louisiana, like other community property jurisdictions, classifies a donation or an inheritance received by a spouse as his or her separate property. The same result is usually seen in common law jurisdictions. This approach furthers a historical preference for keeping inherited property within familial bloodlines. The approach also attempts to maintain the expectations of donors. As one court explained:

> Looking to other jurisdictions for guidance shows that a substantial majority of states deem inherited property to be the separate non-marital property of the inheriting spouse. Hussey v. Hussey, 280 S.C. 418, 312 S.E.2d 267, 270 (1984). By

statute, twenty-one states and the District of Columbia either define inherited property as separate property or exclude it from the definition of marital property. See L. Golden, Equitable Distribution of Property § 5.20, at 113–14 (1983). Accord, Uniform Marital Property Act § 4, reprinted in 9A U.L.A. 29 (Supp.1986). Other jurisdictions have reached the same result by judicial decision. See Bailey v. Bailey, 250 Ga. 15, 295 S.E.2d 304, 305 (1982); Van Newkirk v. Van Newkirk, 212 Neb. 730, 325 N.W.2d 832, 834 (1982); Anderson v. Anderson, 282 S.C. 162, 318 S.E.2d 566, 567 (1984); Hussey, 312 S.E.2d at 270. See generally, Golden, supra § 5.20, at 113–14; 1 J. McCahey, Valuation and Distribution of Marital Property § 18.05[4], at 18–72 to 18–75 (1986).

The policy considerations underlying this view have been stated as follows:

> The philosophy underlying equitable distribution is that marriage is a partnership and both spouses contribute, either directly or indirectly to the acquisition of property obtained during the marriage. If property is acquired without the joint efforts of the parties such property arguably should not be subject to division. For this reason, and because most inheritances are from family members and may have strong sentimental value, many states ... categorize inherited property as separate property.

Golden, supra, § 5.19, at 113 (footnote omitted). Other rationales variously identified include (a) tradition; (b) a belief that property which does not come into the marriage through the spouses' mutual efforts owes nothing to the marriage and is not intended to be shared; (c) the recognition that marital property is or should be only that property which arises from or to some extent is augmented by the efforts of the marital parties; and (d) the fact that inclusion of inherited property in the marital estate removes it from the natural line of succession, thus thwarting the intent of the person who acquired the property and passed it on to the inheriting spouse. See Bailey, 295 S.E.2d at 305; Hussey, 312 S.E.2d at 270.

Julson v. Julsen, 741 P. 2d 642 (Alaska 1987).

It is not uncommon, of course, for someone to make a gift to the spouses jointly. In the case of a joint gift or bequest the Louisiana Civil Code requires a different classification. Article 2338 provides that "property donated to the spouses jointly" is community property. When the donation is made in the form of a testament or is accompanied by some other formality there is usually no question whether the property was intended for one spouse individually or was intended for both spouses. Most inter vivos donations, however, are manual donations. Louisiana Civil Code article 1543 specifically allows the inter vivos donation or a corporeal movable without the necessity of an authentic act or other formality. Rather, "[t]he donation inter vivos of a corporeal movable may [] be made by delivery of the thing to the donee without other formality."

As the following cases demonstrate, it is necessary first to prove an intent by the donor to give and the donee bears the burden of proving the alleged donation. *See Succession of Broussard*, 306 So.2d 399 (La. App. 3d Cir. 1975) (wife alleged deceased husband gave her the earnings each month from her beauty shop operations). If the donee can successfully prove an intent to donate and actual possession of the corporeal movable property simultaneously, then it may be necessary to establish to whom the donor intended the gift to be given. If the donor intended the donee to be one spouse alone, then the property donated is separate property of the donee. LA. CIV. CODE art. 2341. However, if the donor intended that the donation be to the spouses jointly, the property donated is community property. LA. CIV. CODE art. 2338. Of course, the property cannot be community property even if donated to both spouses unless a community property regime exists at the time of the donation.

When reading the cases that follow, consider what sort of evidence is most persuasive in establishing that one spouse alone was the intended donee.

B. *Willard Hamilton v. Suzanne Hamilton*

381 So. 2d 517 (La. App. 1st Cir. 1979)

ELLIS, Judge.

This is a suit for partition of certain property held in common by Willard Hamilton and Suzanne Hamilton, who were married in 1973, legally separated in 1977, and subsequently divorced. At issue is the status of certain items which were shower gifts, received prior to the marriage.

Mrs. Hamilton claims them to be her separate property, because they were given to her as manual donations at a miscellaneous shower given for her prior to the marriage. Mr. Hamilton claims that the gifts were made to both of the parties in contemplation of the marriage. There is no evidence in the record as to whether the donors intended the gifts to be for Mr. Hamilton, Mrs. Hamilton or both of them.

The items in question include eight dinner plates, one salad plate, one bread and butter plate, three cups and saucers and a vegetable bowl; two ice tea glasses and two water glasses; some monogrammed glasses; two silver trays; a ceramic soap dish, a cake and pie saver, a candle holder, wooden salt and pepper shakers, a coffee percolator and some towels. The trial judge was of the opinion that these items were "obviously for the use of plaintiff and defendant jointly", and concluded that the parties owned them in common. Article 1539 of the Civil Code provides: "The manual gift, that is, the giving of corporeal movable effects, accompanied by a real delivery, is not subject to any formality."

The validity of the manual donation is dependent on the intention of the donor to give and the delivery of the thing to the donee. The intention of the donor controls the identity of the donee or donees. The delivery may be made to the donee, or to one of them, if there be more than one, or even through a third party. See Aubry *et Rau, Droit Civil Francais, Civil Law Translations*, v. 3, § 659; Planiol, *Traité Elémentaire de Droit Civil*, v. 3, part 2, § 2538 et seq. (Louisiana State Law Institute Translation); Faison v. Patout, 212 La. 37, 31 So.2d 416 (1947).

Although the gifts in this case were made at a shower given for the bride, Mrs. Hamilton, before the wedding, we find that the intent of the donors is the fact controlling the present ownership of the gifts. We agree with the trial judge that, absent any proof as to the intent of the donors, it must be presumed that gifts of the nature here involved, which would appear to be for use by both parties, are therefore jointly owned by them.

The judgment appealed from is therefore affirmed, at the cost of defendant, Mrs. Hamilton.

AFFIRMED.

C. *Bert Fowler Allbritton v. Linda Tannehill Allbritton*

561 So. 2d 125 (La. App. 3d Cir. 1990)

KING, Judge.

FACTS

Plaintiff claims that the moveable property listed below consists of gifts, given by defendant's grandmother, Mrs. G. M. Tannehill, and defendant's father, Mr. C. F. Tannehill, to the community. Defendant claims that this property consists of gifts to her only, and therefore, is her separate property. The moveable property is described and valued as follows: [Furnishings worth more than $7,000 and checks for more than $60,000 were at issue.]

LAW

There is no dispute that the gifts made by Mrs. G. M. Tannehill and Mr. G. F. Tannehill to the defendant were valid donations. The only issue with respect to these gifts is whether the donors intended their respective donations to be gifts to the community or to the defendant only. Under Louisiana law, the intention of the donor controls the identity of the donee or donees. Hamilton v. Hamilton, 381 So.2d 517 (La. App. 1 Cir. 1979).

Gifts from Mrs. G. M. Tannehill.

At trial there was little evidence presented as to the intent of Mrs. G. M. Tannehill, defendant's grandmother as to the gifts of cash. Plaintiff testified that the gifts were for both him and his wife and that Mrs. G. M. Tannehill liked him. Defendant testified the gifts were strictly to her from her grandmother for her benefit. Since Mrs. G. M. Tannehill had passed away before the trial, there is no other evidence as to the intent of Mrs. G. M. Tannehill with regard to the cash gifts or with regard to the two recliners, sofa, five brass lamps, or dining table and chairs. As to the silver flatware, the evidence shows that a set of silver flatware was given to both the plaintiff and the defendant at a wedding shower, and that the flatware given at the wedding shower was admitted by defendant to be community property. The additional pieces of flatware, according to defendant, were to finish out the set.

The burden of overcoming the presumption of community property set out in La. C.C. Art. 2340 rests upon the party who asserts that the property is separate. To meet this burden, the proof must be clear, positive and of a legally certain nature that the property was separate instead of community. Allen v. Allen, 539 So.2d 820 (La. App. 3 Cir. 1989), *writ den.*, 541 So.2d 840 (La. 1989); Succession of McVay v. McVay, 476 So.2d 1070 (La. App. 3 Cir. 1985). Under this standard, it is clear that defendant has not carried her burden of proving that the non-cash gifts from Mrs. G. M. Tannehill were her separate property. There could be no testimony from Mrs. G. M. Tannehill, since she was deceased, and defendant offered no other proof, other than her self-serving testimony, that these non-cash gifts were her separate property. Therefore, since the property was in the possession of both parties during the existence of the community of acquets and gains, it is presumed to be community property. La. C.C. Art. 2340.

Mrs. G. M. Tannehill also made three cash gifts. The first of these was a check in the amount of $10,430.00 made payable to Troy & Nichols to pay off a mortgage note on a house which was the community property of plaintiff and defendant. There is no other evidence, except for the self-serving testimony of both plaintiff and defendant, of the intention of Mrs. G. M. Tannehill with regard to this gift. Therefore, defendant has not met her burden of proof. This gift, like the non-cash gifts discussed above, was used to benefit the community and was received during the existence of the community. Therefore, we find that this cash gift was community property. La. C.C. Art. 2340; See also Hamilton v. Hamilton, supra, where in the absence of proof of intent, the nature of the property is relevant in deciding whether property is separate or community.

The other two cash gifts given by Mrs. G. M. Tannehill were for improvements to the house owned in community by plaintiff and defendant, and to buy land, also owned in community, by plaintiff and defendant. The gifts were respectively in the amounts of $11,481.57 and $2,000.00. Mrs. G. M. Tannehill wrote the checks for these amounts, made payable only to defendant. Defendant deposited these checks into a joint checking account held by her and plaintiff. Defendant then used the money to pay community creditors. These funds are traceable and are not community simply because they were deposited in a joint account. See, Curtis v. Curtis, 403 So.2d 56 (La. 1981). However, we find that the trial court clearly erred in finding these two gifts to be defendant's separate property. The fact that these checks were made payable to defendant is not of itself enough, when the gift was given for the purpose of paying a community debt, to overcome the presumption of community when the donor, Mrs. G. M. Tannehill, did not testify as to her intent.

For these reasons, we find that the trial judge was manifestly erroneous and clearly wrong in classifying these gifts from Mrs. G. M. Tannehill as separate property of the defendant and in allowing her reimbursement from the community for these funds.

Gifts from Mr. G. F. Tannehill.

Defendant testified that the microwave oven and the washer were bought with cash she received as a Christmas gift from her father. Plaintiff stated that he did not know where defendant obtained the money to buy the microwave and washer. Plaintiff did not contradict defendant's assertion, nor claim that the appliances were bought with community funds. Mr. G. F. Tannehill testified he intended the cash as a personal gift to his daughter. Under these circumstances, we find that plaintiff has carried her burden of proving that the microwave and washer are her separate property.

Mr. G. F. Tannehill also wrote a check in the amount of $36,000.97 made payable to the Federal Land Bank. This check paid off the mortgage on a second house which was the community property of plaintiff and defendant. The last gift was a check from Mr. G. F. Tannehill in the amount of $2,000.00 made payable to defendant. This money was to be used and was in fact used as a down payment on a piece of land purchased by plaintiff and defendant as community property. This check was deposited by defendant in the joint checking account she held with plaintiff. Defendant then wrote another check drawn on the account to make payment for the community.

Mr. G. F. Tannehill testified that he intended these two gifts to be only for defendant's benefit, though he knew that in reality plaintiff would benefit as well. Mr. G. F. Tannehill also testified that he and plaintiff treated each other politely but that plaintiff had not married his daughter with his blessing. Plaintiff agreed with this assessment of Mr. G. F. Tannehill's relationship with him. Defendant also testified that these gifts from her father were intended to be her separate property. Taking into account this evidence, and the fact that one check was made out exclusively to defendant, we find that the trial court did not clearly err in concluding that these two gifts were the separate property of defendant. The trier of fact, who has the unique advantage of hearing and viewing evidence when given, is not to be reversed on an evaluation of credibility which furnishes a basis for the trial court's finding of fact unless that finding is manifestly erroneous. Patin v. Patin, 462 So.2d 1356 (La. App. 3 Cir. 1985), *writ den.*, 466 So.2d 470 (La. 1985), citing Arceneaux v. Domingue, 365 So.2d 1330 (La. 1978).

For these reasons, we find that the trial judge was correct in finding the microwave oven and washer were defendant's separate property and that the gifts by Mr. G. F. Tannehill to defendant in the amounts of $ 36,000.97 and $ 2,000.00 were defendant's separate property and, even though used for the benefit of the community by defendant, that she was entitled to reimbursement of these sums by the community.

KNOLL, Judge, concurring in part and dissenting in part.

I agree with the majority that the donations by the wife's father were gifts only to the wife and not to the community.

For reasons which follow, I respectfully disagree with the majority reversing the trial court on a factual determination that the grandmother's gifts were the separate property of the wife....

This case was complicated by the fact that the wife's grandmother was deceased at the time of trial and was thus unable to testify about her donative intent. However, I disagree with the majority's determination that the wife failed to prove that the grandmother intended to donate to the wife only. In making this determination, the majority finds that the only evidence on this issue was the wife's self-serving testimony. The fact that the wife's testimony was self-serving is an insufficient ground to disregard her testimony. Rather, it is a factor which the trial court weighs in its evaluation of the testimony. Lambert v. Heirs of Adams, 325 So.2d 331 (La. App. 3rd Cir. 1975), *writ denied*, 329 So.2d 458 (La. 1976). When the donor is deceased, the intentions of the donor can be inferred from the relation of the parties and from all the facts and circumstances of the case. Succession of Zacharie, 119 La. 150, 43 So. 988, 990 (La. 1907).

With regard to the grandmother's checks, the record shows:

> (1)the grandmother never gave cash or checks to the husband anytime during the marriage;
>
> (2)the grandmother physically gave the wife the $10,430 check made payable to Troy & Nichols and the wife delivered it to Troy & Nichols where she paid off the mortgage;
>
> (3)the husband testified that he did not recall the grandmother telling him she would pay the Troy & Nichols indebtedness;

(4)all the checks were negotiable instruments under LSA-R.S. 10:3-104 and were valid donations to the wife as to the "form" designated in LSA-R.S. 10:3-201(4).

Taking into consideration the aforementioned corroborative evidence, it is apparent that the trial judge believed the wife's testimony regarding the grandmother's intent. This was a factual determination which should not be disturbed absent manifest error. Succession of Walker, 533 So.2d 70 (La. App. 3rd Cir. 1988), *writ denied*, 536 So.2d 1254 (La. 1989). I find the totality of the evidence strong and convincing evidence of the grandmother's intent to donate to her granddaughter only. On the other hand, I find the husband's evidence weak he relies only upon the use of the money to benefit the community in proving donative intent.

The majority relies upon Allen v. Allen, 539 So.2d 820 (La. App. 3rd Cir. 1989), *writ denied*, 541 So.2d 840 (La. 1989), in classifying the gifts from the grandmother as community property because of a failure to prove donative intent. Allen is clearly distinguishable. As pointed out by Judge Guidry's concurring opinion at page 823: ". . . I believe it to be significant that William Grinnell did not testify and his failure to testify is left unexplained." William Grinnell was not dead as the donor is in the present case. Since the grandmother could not testify because she was dead, the majority looks only to how the gifts and money to the granddaughter were used to prove donative intent. In my view, when the donor is dead and there is other evidence to prove donative intent, use of how the gifts were used is not controlling.

In reaching this conclusion, I find support from Justice Lemmon's realistic observation in Campo v. Campo, 376 So.2d 519, 521 n. 1 (La. App. 4th Cir. 1979), *writ denied*, 378 So.2d 1390 (La. 1980). In *Campo*, the father gave his son $25,000 to build a shrimp boat in his backyard; at the termination of marriage, the wife urged that she had a community interest in the boat. Although in *Campo* the father testified about his intent to donate only to the son, not the son's wife, and the boat was found to be his separate property, Justice Lemmon stated, "even in the absence of positive testimony of the donor, one could presume a preference for the donor's son when cash is donated by manual delivery to the son without an express intention to donate to both spouses." I find this practical approach especially applicable to the case sub judice. In none of the instances in the present case did the grandmother even present the check to the husband; all actions were either from her to her granddaughter or by her directly to a third-party. Moreover, the grandmother never made the husband a co-payee on any of the checks. Therefore, I find the lack of manual delivery to the husband together with the lack of express intention to donate to both spouses further evidence indicative of the grandmother's intent only to donate to the wife. See also Spaht & Hargrave, Matrimonial Regimes, at 64 (1989).

I now turn to the issue concerning the various furnishings given by the grandmother. As stated above, the focus is primarily on the donor's intent. In the case sub judice, this subjective inquiry is made more difficult because of the death of the grandmother-donor. In reversing the trial court on this aspect of the case, the majority focuses solely on the question of how the items were used.

The jurisprudence has developed a rule that in the absence of evidence of intent, the nature of the property is relevant in deciding whether the property is separate or community. Swilley v. Swilley, 489 So.2d 456 (La. App. 3rd Cir. 1986) (no manifest error in the trial court's determination that unspecified furniture and a microwave oven were community property); Campo v. Dupre, 470 So.2d 234 (La. App. 4th Cir. 1985) (a stove and freezer used by both parties were community property); Hamilton v. Hamilton, 381 So.2d 517 (La. App. 1st Cir. 1979) (plates, cups, saucers, glasses, trays, etc.--gifts of relatively small value - given at a wedding shower were community property).

The jurisprudence is clear that use is referred to only in the absence of evidence of intent. As stated hereinabove, when a donor is deceased, donative intent can be inferred from all the facts and circumstances of the case. Succession of Zacharie, supra.

In the case sub judice, evidence shows that all the furnishings were purchased on shopping trips made by the grandmother and wife; in none did the husband accompany them. Moreover, the husband testified that the grandmother never discussed the purchases with him, and never told him that she wanted to give these items to him also. A close reading of the husband's testimony fails to disclose any testimony which would preponderate that the grandmother had donative intent regarding him; his testimony was at times non-responsive, equivocal, and sprinkled with lapses of memory.

Considering the wife's testimony with the circumstances surrounding the gifts and the failure of the husband to establish the grandmother's donative intent regarding him, I cannot say that the trial court was manifestly erroneous in its determination that these furnishings were the wife's separate property. Therefore, I would affirm the trial court's determination that these furnishings were the wife's separate property.

D. Note

In *Campo v. Campo*, 376 So.2d 519 (La. App. 4th Cir. 1979), the issue was whether a shrimp boat constructed by the husband was community or separate property. After having worked long hours for his father in the bait business for 12 years, Mr. Campo desired to purchase a shrimp boat and go into business for himself. Mr. and Mrs. Campo discussed obtaining a loan from her parents, but when Mr. Campo approached his father, the latter offered to donate the necessary money to build the boat.

During the period of construction Mr. Campo's father handed him in cash a total of almost $25,000.00. Mrs. Campo did some painting and made the curtains, and they bought some small items on a community charge account.

There were no documents executed at the time of the donation. At the trial (after the divorce) Mr. Campo's father testified that he donated the money to his son and not to his daughter-in-law. Mr. Campo also testified (without contradiction) that his father and his wife never got along well and that he and his wife were having serious marital problems at the time of the donation.

Here, the donor himself testified positively that he made the donation to his son particularly. Such an intent cannot be said to be so highly improbable that it must be disregarded by the trier of fact in a credibility determination. Moreover, the facts of serious marital problems between the spouses and of a poor relationship between Mrs. Campo and her father-in-law provide other corroborating circumstances supporting the donor's testimony.

E. *Patricia Thompson Noel v. Rickey Martin Noel, Sr.*

884 So. 2d 615 (La. App. 4 Cir. 2004)

JOAN BERNARD ARMSTRONG, Chief Judge.

The plaintiff, Patricia Thompson Noel (hereinafter "Patricia"), divorced wife of the defendant, Rickey Martin Noel, Sr. (hereinafter "Rickey"), appeals from the judgment of the trial court holding that Rickey's interest in the Noel Family Partnership is his separate property and does not form a part of the community of acquets and gains formerly existing between the couple and arising out of their seven-year marriage. The remaining community assets were apportioned by joint stipulation of the parties. We affirm.

The parties stipulated that the Noel Family Partnership ("NFP") was created in 1992; that Rickey is a member of NFP; that Rickey's mother, Ida Noel (hereinafter "Mrs. Noel, Sr.") did not execute a written Act of Donation of an NFP interest to Rickey; that Mrs. Noel, Sr. did not file a gift tax return for the taxable year 1992; that the petition for divorce was filed on April 6, 1998, terminating the community property regime between Patricia and Rickey; that the amount due to Rickey as his partnership share in NFP for the period 1998 through 2011 is $614,250, pre-tax; and that the reports of Patricia's [FN1] and Rickey's Certified Public Accountants would be accepted by affidavit. NFP stipulated that it would not distribute the proceeds for the year 2003 that are due to Mr. Noel as a member of NFP but will hold those funds in escrow pending resolution of this litigation.

Notary Public Kristen Shapiro testified that she met Ida and John Noel, Sr. (hereinafter, "Mr. Noel, Sr.") in the summer of 1992. The senior Noels told Ms. Shapiro that they had purchased a winning lottery ticket and asked Ms. Shapiro to draft a partnership agreement to deal with their $7,000,000 lottery winnings. Ms. Shapiro advised them to consult a Certified Public Accountant. Without objection from any of the parties, the trial judge asked for clarification from Ms. Shapiro:

> THE COURT:
> Was it clear to you that when Mrs. Ida had come to see you that she had won the ticket?
> THE WITNESS:
> Yes.
> THE COURT:
> Did she win the ticket with her husband?
> THE WITNESS:
> Yes. She and her husband.
> THE COURT:
> They were the ones who purchased the ticket?
> THE WITNESS:
> Correct. In fact, she said her husband would go down and buy lottery tickets periodically and this one was a winner.

Patricia testified that between 1992 and the termination of their community in 1998, she and Rickey received proceeds from the lottery winnings with which they paid their house note, paid for their children's private schooling, purchased Cadillacs, jewelry, furniture and "everything we needed." She identified the NFP Agreement, an authentic act executed before Ms. Shapiro on July 6, 1992. The preamble to the NFP agreement states that it is "entered into by and between the following individuals" and then names those individuals as John and Ida Noel and their children Elinus P. Noel, Peggy A. Daigle, Jill Lewis, John W. Noel, Jr., Rickey, and Lisa M. Noel, all of whom signed as parties principal to the agreement. Patricia was not named in the agreement and signed only in the capacity of witness.

According to the document, the purpose of the NFP is to collect and distribute all proceeds received from the Louisiana Lottery Commission. All income, gain, loss, deduction, credit and cash distributions are to be allocated equally among the partners in the percentage of 12.5% to each. Mrs. Noel, Sr. was designated as Managing Partner, responsible for collecting and distributing all proceeds, and filing all necessary forms and tax returns. Ms. Lewis was named successor Managing Partner. The agreement contains no recital that the assets of the partnership shall be the separate property of the partners.

Patricia admitted on cross-examination that she was not a partner in NFP and did not supply any skill to or work for NFP.

Mrs. Noel, Sr. testified that she is the mother of Rickey and of five other children. On July 4, 1992, she and her husband won the lottery with a ticket she had filled out and for which she paid. The lottery proceeds were seven million dollars. She testified that when she discovered that she and her husband had won the lottery, they decided to donate a share of it to their children. She did not intend for the spouses of her three, or possibly four, married children to participate in the lottery proceeds. She did not expect anything from Rickey in return for the money.

Patricia, along with a daughter's husband and another friend, accompanied Mr. and Mrs. Noel, Sr. and their children to Baton Rouge to confect the partnership agreement. This was done two days after Mrs. Noel, Sr. won the lottery. Mrs. Noel, Sr. testified that she told Ms. Shapiro that she and her husband had just won the lottery and wanted to donate a share of the money to their six children. She and Mr. Noel, Sr. paid Ms. Shapiro for having drawn up and notarized the Partnership Agreement. Neither Patricia nor Rickey contributed anything to the cost of confecting the NFP document.

The lottery paid the proceeds to the Partnership, and each month, Mrs. Noel, Sr. receives a check from the lottery office and distributes the proceeds to the NFP members. She testified that Rickey does not do anything in furtherance of NFP. She testified that she and her husband had not discussed forming a partnership before they won the lottery.

On cross-examination, Mrs. Noel, Sr. testified that she could not remember if she had told the Louisiana Lottery that she and Mr. Noel, Sr. were the owners of the lottery proceeds, or whether she told the federal government that she and Mr. Noel, Sr. owned the proceeds, or whether she and Mr. Noel, Sr. paid the tax liability related to the lottery proceeds other than for their respective shares of NFP. On re-direct examination, Mrs. Noel, Sr. testified that the purpose of the partnership was to avoid paying tax and to protect the children's interest in the proceeds in the event of her and her husband's deaths.

Rickey testified that he did not contribute effort or skill in the creation of NFP or in the purchase of the winning lottery ticket. He corroborated his mother's testimony that he was not expected to do anything in return for his share of the lottery proceeds. Rickey identified his signature on the Partnership Agreement, but denied that he was able to read or write, a disability of which his parents and siblings were aware, and testified that his formal education ended at the seventh grade. He could not recall whether he executed other documents at the time he signed the Partnership Agreement.

Rickey testified that Patricia managed their family's finances for approximately two years, and denied that the lottery proceeds were spent for the benefit of his family, contending that Patricia spent the money for the benefit of her mother and sisters, paying their house notes and their children's tuition, and lending them money over his objection. His parents paid his children's tuition from their share of the lottery proceeds. He did not know if he had any of the lottery proceeds paid since the termination of the community, and referred that question to his mother. Since then, he has supported himself on odd landscaping jobs and the lottery proceeds.

The parties stipulated that Mr. Noel, Sr. would testify that he purchased the winning lottery ticket, and he and his children would testify that when he and Mrs. Noel won the lottery, NFP was formed and the lottery proceeds were placed into NFP with the intention that the proceeds be donated to John and Ida Noel's children.

K. Justin Gibson, a Certified Public Accountant, testified by affidavit in accordance with the parties' pre-trial stipulation. Mr. Gibson said that he has been the tax preparer for NFP since 1995, and his file contains NFP's Partnership Tax Returns from 1992 through 2001. According to Mr. Gibson, NFP was formed on July 6, 1992 for the purpose of receiving Louisiana lottery proceeds for Mrs. Noel, Sr. NFP receives an annual installment in the amount of $351,000 from the Louisiana Lottery Corporation, and declares "lotto proceeds" as its principal business activity and principal service. It has never engaged in investment or business activities and acts solely as a pass-through entity for Federal and State Income Tax purposes. It has not distributed proceeds to Rickey since 1998. The present value of the future stream of revenue payments to NFP and, through NFP to each of its partners, is $444,187.04.

The trial court made only one explicit finding of fact in its judgment, that the lottery proceeds were not acquired through Rickey's effort, skill or industry, but through the effort, skill and industry of Ida and John Noel. This finding is to be reviewed under the manifest error standard. *Hill v. Morehouse Parish Police Jury,* 95-1100, p. 4 (La. 1/16/96), 666 So.2d 612, 614. Implicit in this finding were several subsidiary findings either necessary to reaching the aforementioned explicitly stated finding or necessarily resulting from that finding. These implicit findings are also subject to the manifest error standard of review. *Delaney v. Humana Hosp.,* 01-0389, p. 8 (La.App. 4 Cir. 10/16/02), 830 So.2d 1072, 1078; *Ruby v. Jaeger,* 99-1235, p. 4 (La.App. 4 Cir. 3/22/00), 759 So.2d 905, 907.

The record contains no evidence that Rickey suggested the winning numbers to his parents or participated in the purchase of the tickets. Furthermore, there is no evidence that Rickey, who was illiterate according to his mother's uncontradicted testimony and unable even to prepare a check, has participated in the management of NFP. Therefore, we accept for the purposes of this appeal the finding that the lottery proceeds were not acquired through Rickey's effort, skill or industry and that they were instead acquired by his parents. Implicit in this finding is the further finding that any interest Rickey acquired, he necessarily acquired from his parents and any such acquisition by him was "purely gratuitous" as that term is employed in the donation articles, La. C.C. art. 1467, et seq.

The trial court's legal conclusions, that Mr. and Mrs. Noel, Sr. donated the proceeds to Rickey via the NFP and that Rickey's interest in NFP is his separate property are reviewed on appeal *de novo.*

There is no evidence of record that Rickey contributed efforts or resources to the NFP or to the purchase of the winning ticket. To the contrary, the evidence is uncontroverted that he contributed nothing to the partnership or to purchase of the lottery ticket.

La. C.C. art. 2338 provides that:

> The community property comprises: property acquired during the existence of the legal regime through the effort, skill, or industry of either spouse; property acquired with community things or with community and separate things, unless classified as separate property under Article 2341; property donated to the spouses jointly; natural and civil fruits of community property; damages awarded for loss or injury to a thing belonging to the community; and all other property not classified by law as separate property.

La.C.C. art. 2341 defines separate property in pertinent part as follows:

> The separate property of a spouse is his exclusively. It comprises: property acquired by a spouse prior to the establishment of a community property regime; property acquired by a spouse with separate things or with separate and community things when the value of the community things is inconsequential in comparison with the value of the separate things used; **property acquired by a spouse by inheritance or donation to him individually....** [Emphasis added.]

Rickey argues that the effect of these codal provisions is to make his partnership payments separate, since they were not earned through his effort, skill or industry, but were instead acquired by his parents and transferred to him gratuitously.

La. C.C. art. 2339 provides that the natural and civil fruits of the separate property of a spouse, are community property. While La. C.C. art. 2339 allows a spouse to reserve such civil fruits as separate property by a declaration made in an authentic act or in an act under private signature duly acknowledged, such was not done in the instant case. *Id.* La. C.C. art. 2340 establishes a rebuttable presumption, upon which Patricia relies, that everything of value in the possession of a spouse during the existence of the regime of community is community property. However, the Supreme Court recently held in *Talbot v. Talbot,* 03-0814, p. 6 (La. 12/12/03), 864 So.2d 590, 600, that the Article 2340 presumption of community is rebuttable upon a mere preponderance of the evidence, rejecting all prior jurisprudence requiring a stricter standard of proof.

Whatever interest Rickey may be said to have acquired in the NFP and/or the proceeds of the lottery was acquired gratuitously, which is implicit in the trial court's finding that it was not acquired through his effort, skill or industry. La. C.C. art. 1523 refers to three kinds of donations:

> There are three kinds of donations *inter vivos:*
>
> The donation purely gratuitous, or that which is made without condition and merely from liberality;
>
> The onerous donation, or that which is burdened with charges imposed on the donee;
>
> The remunerative donation, or that the object of which is to recompense for services rendered.

Clearly, whatever interest Rickey acquired in the NFP and/or the lottery proceeds was acquired "purely gratuitously." Patricia does not contend that any charges were imposed upon him such that the transfer would be characterized as an onerous donation under La. C.C. art. 1524.

Likewise, Patricia does not contend that any interest acquired by Rickey in the NFP and/or the lottery proceeds was acquired by him as recompense for any services rendered by him such that the transfer might be characterized as a remunerative donation under La. C.C. art. 1525.

The essence of one of Patricia's arguments is that the lottery ticket and the right to receive the proceeds therefrom are among those "incorporeal things, such as rents, credits, rights or actions," described in La. C.C. art. 1536. La. C.C. art. 1536 requires any donation of incorporeal things, such as the donation to Rickey of an interest in the lottery ticket or the right to the lottery proceeds to be in the form of a notarial act "under the penalty of nullity." There is no document in this case expressly styled, "Act of Donation." However, if the donation to Rickey is a nullity it does not result in effectively transferring a one-half interest therein to Patricia as community property. If the transfer to Rickey is a nullity it merely means that his parents were never divested of his share of the lottery proceeds. Accordingly, we are compelled to find that Patricia has no right of action to assert the invalidity as to form of the donation. That is an action that could only be brought by Rickey's parents, heirs or creditors, depending on the circumstances.

For the same reason, we are compelled to note that it avails Patricia nothing to assert the impropriety of the assignment of the right to the lottery proceeds to Rickey or to the NFP under La. R.S. 47:9025B(1) as the ineffectiveness of any such assignment could mean only that the interest in the lottery proceeds claimed by Patricia is still vested in Rickey's parents.

As a result of our foregoing analysis of Patricia's contention concerning the questions of donation and assignment we have exercised our authority under La. C.C.P. art. 927B to notice on our own motion that Patricia has no right of action to assert the nullity of any donation made to Rickey by his parents and no right of action to assert the nullity of any assignment of lottery proceeds to Rickey and/or the NFP as Patricia can gain nothing from the success of such assertions. Therefore, we need not address the status of either the donation or the assignment. All that we are in a position to do is to find that if Rickey has any interest in the lottery proceeds and/or NFP, then he acquired such interest from his parents gratuitously, and as such the interest would be his separate property under La. C.C. art. 2341.

Patricia also contends in her original brief, in the alternative, that Rickey failed to prove that she was not also a donee of the lottery proceeds:

> [E]ven if there were competent evidence of a donation, sufficient evidence was not presented to show the donation was intended to be *only* to Rickey....

Mrs. Noel, Sr. testified that it was her intention to make a donation to her children and this was supported by the stipulation that John and Rickey's siblings would give the same testimony if called upon to do so. This is corroborated by the fact that Patricia admitted to being present when the NFP document was executed, but she was not named therein. We infer that Patricia seeks to extend the presumption of community to a presumption of donative intent to her, but there is no such presumption to support her position. There is much competent evidence in the record indicating that there was no intention of donating anything to Patricia and none to the contrary other than Patricia's own testimony. When asked on cross-examination why she was not included as a partner in spite of the fact that she was present when the document was executed, she testified:

> Because his mother said it was for her and the kids. They had eight children and they went to an attorney in Baton Rouge and put the mother, the father and the eight children which the mother also included all the married spouses for their families too.

The trial court made the implicit finding that there was no donation to Patricia when it found the property to be Rickey's separate property. The identity of the donee or donees is controlled or determined by the intention of the donor. *Purcell v. Purcell,* 29,663, p. 7 (La.App. 2 Cir. 6/23/97), 697 So.2d 728, 733. Resolution of this issue is a factual determination to be made by the trial court. *Id.,* p. 8. Such a resolution will not be disturbed on appeal unless clearly wrong, i.e., manifestly erroneous. *Id.* As is shown by our analysis of the evidence on this issue derived from our review of the entire record, there is more than ample evidence to support the trial court's implicit finding based on a manifest error standard of review or even based on a *de novo* standard of review.

Patricia's final contention is that even if Rickey's interest in the NFP had been acquired by him by donation as his separate property, his share of the annual lottery payments accruing after termination of the community constitutes fruits belonging to the community under La. C.C. art. 2339. Patricia's position as expressed in her original brief is that because Rickey's "*right* to receive his share of the lottery annual payments from the partnership became exigible at the moment the lottery prize was claimed, *all* of the payments, including those that may come due *after* termination of the community, constitute fruits and revenues under La. Civ.Code art. 2339." We are compelled to disagree because if we follow this reasoning to its conclusion it means that all of the future payments are conflated into a single immediate present right which then must be viewed as the asset itself rather than the community fruits of the asset. We can find no authority in support of this contention.

Accordingly, we find no manifest error in either the express factual findings of the trial court that the lottery proceeds were not acquired through any effort, skill or industry of Rickey's, but were acquired through the effort, skill and industry of his parents. We find no error in the implicit conclusion that whatever interest Rickey may have acquired, he acquired gratuitously. We further find no error in the trial court's conclusion that whatever interest Rickey had was his separate property and that Patricia has no community interest in the lottery proceeds and/or NFP.

For the foregoing reasons the judgment of the trial court is affirmed.

AFFIRMED.

F. Questions

1. H and W are married. H has a son from a previous marriage, S. S dies leaving a will giving all of his property to a friend. H would have been S's sole heir in intestacy—that is, if there was no will. H challenges the validity of the will. The court holds the will is invalid and H is awarded S's estate. Is the estate community or separate? Why?

2. Same facts as above, except that while the case challenging the will is pending, H and S's friend reach a settlement agreement pursuant to which H agrees to dismiss the suit and S's friend agrees to give ½ of S's estate to H. Is the portion of the estate H receives by virtue of the settlement agreement community or separate? See e.g. *Estate of Clark* 271 P. 542 (Ca. 1928); *Forest Oil Corp. v. Wood*, 240 So.2d 401 (La. Ct. App. 3d Cir. 1970); *Succession of Land*, 212 La. 103, 31 So.2d 609 (La. 1947).

3. H and W are married. Each year W's employer gives her the option of cash or stock in Apple at Christmas. W always picks stock. The stock certificates are accompanied by a letter stating that the shares of stock are a gift. Are the shares of stock community or separate? See e.g. *Holby v. Holby*, 638 P. 2d 1359 (Ariz. 1981); *Downer v. Bramet*, 152 Cal. App. 3d 837 (1984); *Succession of Ratcliff*, 24 So. 2d. 456 (La. 1945)

4.6 DONATIONS BETWEEN SPOUSES

A. Introduction

Donations between spouses are subject to a different set of classification rules. These rules affect both the classification of the property donated as well as the classification of the natural and civil fruits of the donated property.

La. Civ. Code art. 2343. Donation by spouse of interest in community

> The donation by a spouse to the other spouse of his undivided interest in a thing forming part of the community transforms that interest into separate property of the donee. Unless otherwise provided in the act of donation, an equal interest of the donee is also transformed into separate property and the natural and civil fruits of the thing, and minerals produced from or attributed to the property given as well as bonuses, delay rentals, royalties, and shut-in payments arising from mineral leases, form part of the donee's separate property.

La. Civ. Code art. 2343.1. Transfer of separate property to the community

> The transfer by a spouse to the other spouse of a thing forming part of his separate property, with the stipulation that it shall be part of the community, transforms the thing into community property. As to both movables and immovables, a transfer by onerous title must be made in writing and a transfer by gratuitous title must be made by authentic act.

B. *Charlotte Chambers v. William Chambers*

488 So. 2d 393 (La. App. 3d Cir. 1986)

YELVERTON, Judge.

The sole issue raised by this appeal is whether the trial court erred in determining that a 1981 Toyota was the separate property of the husband, thereby refusing to consider the vehicle as a former asset of the community. The issue arises from the following circumstances.

Charlotte Chambers filed a petition for separation on November 3, 1981, and a judgment of separation was thereafter rendered on December 2, 1983. On May 3, 1984, Charlotte donated by authentic act all of her rights and interests in the Toyota to her husband. On June 5, 1984, she filed a petition for divorce and also sought a partition of property formerly belonging to the community. The detailed descriptive list included the Toyota as community property. On November 26, 1984, a judgment of divorce was granted. Subsequently the parties entered into a voluntary partition of the community property and agreed to submit the question of whether Mrs. Chambers was entitled to any reimbursement to the trial court. In finding Mrs. Chambers was not entitled to any reimbursement and in finding the Toyota the separate property of Mr. Chambers the trial court stated:

> "The record indicates (defendant's exhibit A) that on May 3, 1984, Ms. Chambers donated by authentic act all of her interest in a 1981 Toyota, a community asset, to Mr. Chambers. The character of this asset after the donation is governed by LSA Civil Code Art. 2343. It provides:
>
>> 'The donation by a spouse to the other spouse of his undivided interest in a thing forming part of the community transforms that interest into separate property of the donee. Unless otherwise provided in the act of donation, an equal interest of the donee is also transformed into separate property ...'
>
> Because of this, the Court finds that the Toyota, as of the date of the

> donation, became, in its entirety, the separate asset of Mr. Chambers. As such the Court will not consider it as an asset of the community held by Mr. Chambers.
>
> "Considering the foregoing, and after further consideration of each party's descriptive list and brief, the Court finds that no reimbursement is due the plaintiff. Although the record shows that some of the debts which Ms. Chambers paid were community debts, the plaintiff has failed to show by a preponderance of the evidence that when all calculations are made, she is due any reimbursement from her former husband. Therefore, it is ordered that the voluntary partition of the community is finalized and that there are no further sums owing between the parties."

Appellant argues that the trial court erred in applying C.C. art. 2343 to a donation subsequent to the termination of the community of acquets and gains, and that the Toyota should have been found to be property formerly belonging to the community.

Under C.C. art. 2356 the "legal regime of community property terminates ... by ... separation from bed and board ..." Once the community of acquets and gains is terminated the former spouses become co-owners in indivision of those assets formerly belonging to the community. *Lococo v. Lococo*, 462 So.2d 893(La.App. 4th Cir. 1984), writ denied 462 So.2d 889 (La.1985). Either party then has an absolute right to demand a partition of the property formerly belonging to the community. *Id.*

In the present case we agree with appellant that C.C. art. 2343 has application only to donations made prior to the termination of the community. The statute clearly applies to property "forming part of the community." In the present case the community of acquets and gains had been terminated by the judgment of separation, and the donation was of property *formerly* belonging to the community.

At the time of the judgment of separation the Toyota was community property. Therefore, the Toyota vehicle should have been included in the partition. The parties stipulated that its value was $5,000. At the termination of the community each spouse became an owner in indivision of the vehicle. However, the trial judge found and we agree that after the termination of the community Mrs. Chambers donated her interest in the car to Mr. Chambers. The act of donation did not provide that Mrs. Chambers was to receive credit in the partition proceedings for this donation.

Since Mrs. Chambers had a one-half interest in the vehicle and disposed of it by act of donation, each party received an equal interest in the vehicle for partition purposes. Therefore, each spouse received property of equal net value in the partition, and the trial judge was correct in finding that plaintiff was not entitled to any reimbursement for the Toyota.

For these reasons the judgment is affirmed at appellant's costs.

AFFIRMED.

C. *Nathaniel Goines, Jr. v. Dianne B. Goines*

989 So. 2d 794 (La. App. Ct. 5 Cir. 2008)

CLARENCE E. McMANUS, Judge.

STATEMENT OF THE CASE

Diane and Nathaniel Goines were married on June 20, 1986. The parties filed a Petition for Divorce and Related Matters seeking a divorce and to partition the community property. At the time of separation, the parties lived in a home located at 2232 Country Club Drive in Laplace, Louisiana. The home was purchased by Nathaniel Goines ("Nathaniel") on August 31, 1985, prior to the marriage, and the parties had resided in the home throughout their marriage.

It is the classification of this home as either community property or the separate property of Nathaniel, that is at issue in this appeal.

Nathaniel filed a Community Property List of Assets and Expenses on November 5, 2003 listing the home as community property. A hearing was also held on that day and the trial court ordered the parties to file sworn detailed descriptive lists no later than December 15, 2003. The trial court also ordered that the Traversal of the community property lists would be held on January 15, 2004. On November 14, 2003, Nathaniel filed a Petition for Temporary Restraining Order and Injunction Against Alienation or Encumbrance of Community Property.

Then on December 15, 2003, Dianne Goinnes ("Dianne") filed a Sworn Detailed Descriptive List of Community Property, which also listed the home as community property. Nathaniel filed another Community Property List of Assets & Expenses on December 15, 2003, and again listed the home as community property.

Thereafter, on September 9, 2004, Nathaniel filed a Motion for Rule to Show Cause Why the Former Family Home Should Not Be Declared the Sole Property of Nathaniel Goines, Jr. and Placed in His Name Only. In this motion, Nathaniel argued the house should be placed solely in his name because Dianne had incurred debts which encumbered the home and had signed over her interest in the home to creditors.

Nathaniel made no argument in this motion that the home was his separate property and not part of the community.

Nathaniel filed another Detailed Descriptive List on November 6, 2006 and again listed the home as community property. On April 30, 2007, Nathaniel filed a Motion to Traverse Descriptive List and for the first time asserted that the home was his separate property.

A hearing was held on May 17, 2007 to partition the community property and decide the status of the home. At that hearing, Diane presented evidence that on March 30, 1988, after the parties were married, they refinanced the home and both signed an Affidavit designating and recognizing the property as community property for the purpose of refinancing. Diane argued that by this Affidavit, Nathaniel had donated the home to the community.

The trial court issued a Judgment May 31, 2007 finding the home to be the separate property of Nathaniel. The trial court found that, while the affidavit designated the property as community property for the purpose of refinancing and was in authentic form, the language of the affidavit does not express Nathaniel's wish to donate or convey his one-half interest in the property to Diane, as required by La. C.C. art. 1747. Therefore, the trial court found Nathaniel had not transferred his separate property to the community property regime.

Diane now appeals this Judgment arguing the trial court erred because Nathaniel had judicially admitted the house was community property and the affidavit successfully transferred the property to the community. For the reasons which follow, we reverse the trial court's judgment and find the home to be community property of Nathaniel and Dianne Goines.

DISCUSSION

La. C.C. art. 2341 provides that the separate property of a spouse includes property acquired by the spouse prior to the establishment of a community property regime. According to La. C.C. art. 2341.1, a spouse's undivided interest in property classified as separate property remains his separate property regardless of who manages, uses or enjoys. A spouse may transfer separate property to the community. La. C.C. art. 2343.1. The transfer by gratuitous title, or a donation, must be made by authentic act. *Id.* La. C.C. art. 1747 provides that an interspousal donation shall be made by a single instrument in authentic form and must expressly state that the donor makes the donation in consideration of his present marriage. It shall be signed by the donor and donee at the same time and place.

The house at 2232 Country Club Drive in Laplace was purchased by Nathaniel prior the marriage. However, the Affidavit executed by Nathaniel and Dianne, for the purpose of refinancing the home, states the home is the community property of the parties. We note that the Affidavit executed by the parties only stated that the parties were recognizing and designating the property as community property for the purpose of refinancing. However, we find this affidavit, as well as the actions of Nathaniel, clearly indicate his intent for the home to be designated as community property.

Additionally, we find the filings of Nathaniel to be judicial admissions that the home is community property. LSA-C.C. art. 1853 provides that "[a] judicial confession is a declaration made by a party in a judicial proceeding. That confession constitutes a full proof against the party who made it. A judicial confession is indivisible and it may be revoked only on the ground of error of fact."

A declaration that expressly acknowledges an adverse fact and is made by a party in a judicial proceeding is a judicial confession that constitutes full proof against the party who made it. *Tucker v. St. Tammany Parish School Bd.*, 03-2401 (La.App. 1 Cir. 9/17/04), 888 So.2d 235, 237, citing, *Perry v. Perry & Sons Vault & Grave Service*, 03-1519 (La.App. 3 Cir. 5/12/04), 872 So.2d 611, 614. A judicial confession is indivisible and may be revoked only on the ground of error fact. Id. An admission in a pleading falls within the scope of a judicial confession and is full proof against the party making it. *Monfore v. Self*, 99-459 (La.App. 3 Cir. 12/8/99), 755 So.2d 907, 909, citing, *Smith v. Board of Trustees*, 398 So.2d 1045 (La.1981). A judicial confession must be explicit and not merely implied. *Monfore*, *supra*, citing, *Hoffman v. Hoffman*, 430 So.2d 149 (La.App. 2 Cir.1983).

Both parties submitted detailed descriptive lists, which indicated what they considered to be the community assets and debts. These lists also provided any items the parties considered to be their own separate property or separate debts.

These detailed descriptive lists filed by both parties constitute pleadings and, therefore, any admission or statement made in the documents, falls within the scope of a judicial confession. Statements made by Nathaniel in the detailed descriptive lists and motions he filed explicitly stated the home was community property and was his separate property that he had donated to the community.

On November 5, 2003, Nathaniel listed the home as community property in his Community Property List of Assets and Expenses and even listed his donation of the family home as a donation of his separate property to the community. In his November 14, 2003 Petition for Temporary Restraining Order and Injunction he again referred to the home as community property and stated "[t]he parties own property that is part of the former community of acquets and gains, consisting principally of the residence located at 2322 Country Club Dr., Laplace, Louisiana." Nathaniel's Community Property List of Assets and Expenses filed December 15, 2003 also listed the home as a community asset. That document designates other assets as separate property and again specifically lists "Donation of the Family Home" as his separate property donated to the community. Finally, Nathaniel's Detailed Descriptive List filed on November 6, 2006, listed the home as community property and again listed the home as his separate property that had been donated to the community and he was seeking a reimbursement for this donation.

Nathaniel did not assert that the home was his separate property, and that he had not donated the property to the community, until his Motion to Traverse Descriptive List filed on April 30, 2007.

Based on the above, we find Nathaniel's statements in his lists and motions to be judicial confessions that the home located at 2322 Country Club Drive in Laplace, LA was community property. We also find that Nathaniel has not proven any error of fact on which to revoke the judicial confession. Additionally, we note the affidavit executed by Nathaniel and Dianne, which recognized the home as community property, further demonstrates Nathaniel's intent that the home be considered community property.

Accordingly, we find the statements made by Nathaniel in the pleadings filed to be judicial confessions, which explicitly state that the home is community property. Thus, we reverse the judgment of the trial court and find the home located at 2322 Country Club Drive in Laplace, Louisiana to be the community property of Nathaniel and Dianne Goines.

REVERSED.

D. *Succession of William Edward Faget*

53 So. 3d 414 (La. 2011)

CLARK, Justice.

We granted this writ application to determine whether the court of appeal erred in reversing a trial court judgment which declared the decedent's wife a one-half owner of the family home and its furnishings. Because we find the agreement at issue was enforceable without judicial approval for purposes of La.Civ.Code art. 2329, and the existence of a community property regime is not a prerequisite to the applicability of La.Civ.Code art. 2343.1, we reverse the judgment of the court of appeal and reinstate the trial court judgment.

FACTS AND PROCEDURAL HISTORY

Dr. William E. Faget ("William") married Audrey Menard ("Audrey") on December 22, 1977. This union was each party's second marriage, and both had children from their previous marriages. On December 15, 1977, prior to William and Audrey's marriage, they entered into a matrimonial agreement establishing a contractual matrimonial regime.

In November 1992, William suffered a stroke and was admitted into the intensive care unit at St. Tammany Parish Hospital. On November 30, 1992, while in the hospital, William and Audrey executed a contract, the "Residence Agreement." The document, made by authentic act, purported to make the family home and its furnishings community property. The Residence Agreement provided, in pertinent part:

> It has been the intention and wish of each appearer that though separate in property per [m]arriage [c]ontract dated December 15, 1977, the residence be treated as community, and that in the event of the death of either party, that individual 50% interest in the residence and all furnishings is to be inherited by that individual's children.

William and Audrey remained married and resided together until his death on May 12, 2003. The Residence Agreement was filed into the public records after his death on September 5, 2003.

In July 2003, William's three children from his first marriage filed a petition to open the succession and appointed Pier Marie Faget Jenkins ("Pier") as independent administratrix. Pier, as the independent administratrix, filed a petition for a revendicatory action against Audrey, seeking to have the succession declared full owner of the residence and furnishings. Additionally, the succession sought an order to compel Audrey to account for and deliver the property. On April 22, 2005, the revendicatory action and the succession proceeding were consolidated.

Thereafter, Audrey filed a partial motion for summary judgment asking that the Residence Agreement be declared enforceable and that a judgment recognize her as a one-half owner of the property at issue. The Faget children filed a cross-motion for summary judgment, asserting the Residence Agreement was invalid on three grounds: (1) William lacked capacity to enter into the agreement; (2) there was no court approval to modify the regime; and (3) the language of the agreement was precatory. On April 5, 2006, the cross-motions for summary judgment were argued to the trial court.

First, the trial court found William was lucid at the time the Residence Agreement was signed in light of William's attorney's testimony that the attorney spoke to William before the document was executed and was satisfied William did not lack capacity. Moreover, no one could testify William was not lucid at the time the Residence Agreement was signed. The hospital nurse's notes for the relevant time show William requested his lawyer in order to sign papers. The two witnesses to the Residence Agreement also testified that, though they did not recall signing the document, the signatures were indeed their own and they would not have signed without first seeing William sign.

Next, the trial court found the Residence Agreement did not require judicial approval, reasoning that under La.Civ.Code art. 2329 a single separate asset can be made community just as an entire separate estate can be made community without the requirement of judicial approval.

Lastly, the trial court found no merit to the argument that the language expressed an intent to do something at a later date. Accordingly, the trial court granted Audrey's motion for partial summary judgment, denied the Faget children's motion for summary judgment, and declared Audrey to be a one-half owner of the family residence and its furnishings. Additionally, the judgment recognized that Audrey was entitled to a life-time usufruct over the remaining one-half of the relevant property and declared the Faget children the naked owners thereof, subject to Audrey's usufruct. The Faget children appealed.

The court of appeal reversed the trial court and remanded. The court of appeal found the Residence Agreement constituted a matrimonial agreement that modified a matrimonial regime (making a contractual regime partly legal and partly contractual) and, thus, required court approval prior to its execution pursuant to La.Civ.Code art. 2329. The court of appeal found, without court approval, the Residence Agreement was unenforceable. Additionally, it reasoned the Residence Agreement could not act as a donation under La.Civ.Code art. 2343.1 because there was no existing legal regime. The court of appeal reached this conclusion by finding the legislature chose to use "the community" as opposed to "a community." Audrey filed a writ application with this court.

We granted certiorari to determine whether a single asset modifies a regime so as to trigger the need for court approval under La.Civ.Code art. 2329 and, alternatively, to determine whether a community regime must exist in order for a separate asset to be transformed into community property pursuant to La.Civ.Code art. 2343.1.

APPLICABLE LAW

Summary judgments are reviewed de novo on appeal, with the reviewing court using the same criteria that govern the trial court's determination of whether summary judgment is appropriate; whether there is any genuine issue of material fact, and whether the movant is entitled to judgment as a matter of law. *Louisiana Safety Ass'n of Timbermen Self–Insurers Fund v. Louisiana Ins. Guar. Ass'n*, 2009–0023, p. 5 (La.6/26/09), 17 So.3d 350, 353. A court must grant a motion for summary judgment "if the pleadings, depositions, answers to interrogatories, and admissions on file, together with the affidavits, if any, show that there is no genuine issue as to material fact, and that mover is entitled to judgment as a matter of law." La.Code Civ. P. art. 966(B); *Costello v. Hardy*, 2003–1146, p. 8 (La.1/21/04), 864 So.2d 129, 137.

DISCUSSION

From the outset we note two issues are before us: (1) the validity of the Residence Agreement, which attempts to transfer a separate asset into community property without court approval; and (2) William's capacity to enter into the Residence Agreement. Audrey's counsel argues the latter is not before this court insofar as the Faget children did not file a writ application or specifically assign this issue as error in their opposition brief. However, under La.Code Civ.P. art. 2133, the argument is properly before us because the Faget children asserted an argument in support of the court of appeal judgment without seeking to attack or modify the judgment.

[The court holds that the heirs are estopped from challenging the donation. Eds.]

***

Next, we address the validity of the Residence Agreement in the absence of court approval. La.Civ.Code art. 2325 defines a matrimonial regime as "a system of principals and rules governing the ownership and management of the property of married persons as between themselves and toward third persons." There are three types of matrimonial regimes: (1) legal; (2) contractual; and (3) partly legal and partly contractual. La.Civ.Code art. 2326. The legal regime is the community of acquets and gains. La.Civ.Code art. 2327. The contractual regime is contemplated in La.Civ.Code art. 2328, which provides, in pertinent part: "[a] matrimonial agreement is a contract establishing a regime of separation of property or modifying or terminating the legal regime." Logically, the partly legal and partly contractual regime is one regime that governs both community and separate assets. As cited earlier, La.Civ.Code art. 2329 allows spouses to "enter into a matrimonial agreement that modifies or terminates a matrimonial regime during marriage only upon joint petition and a finding by the court that this serves their best interests and that they understand the governing principles and rules."

The Faget children aver the Residence Agreement was a matrimonial agreement that modified the existing contractual regime, making part of the estate separate and part of the estate community. As such, the original regime was modified from a contractual regime to a partly contractual and partly legal regime, which required court approval.

Audrey, on the other hand, contends the agreement is not a matrimonial agreement that modified a matrimonial regime. She asserts there is a distinction between matrimonial agreements and interspousal contracts. The former concerns the classification and management of future acquisitions while the latter involves existing assets. The Residence Agreement relates only to one existing asset (the house/furnishings) and does not affect the contractual regime of separate property in any other respect. As such, judicial approval was not required.

We agree with Audrey. We find the legal effect of the Residence Agreement pertained only to a single asset and amounted to a single transaction. The agreement does not purport to and will not govern future acquisitions. Thus, the Residence Agreement is not a matrimonial agreement that modified William and Audrey's contractual regime. Importantly, the first sentence of La.Civ.Code art. 2329 permits spouses to enter into matrimonial agreements before or during marriage as to all matters that are not prohibited by public policy. The second sentence of the second paragraph of La.Civ.Code art. 2329 additionally allows spouses to "subject themselves to the legal regime by a matrimonial agreement at any time without court approval." These two sentences, read together, indicate the legislative favoring of legal regimes. To hold that spouses can subject the entirety of their estate to the legal regime without court approval but they must obtain court approval to subject a specific asset to the legal regime is nonsensical. The larger category subsumes the smaller category; accordingly, we find there existed no legal need to obtain judicial approval. Thus, the Residence Agreement is enforceable pursuant to La.Civ.Code art. 2329.

Alternatively, we find, as also argued by Audrey, that La.Civ.Code art. 2343.1 applies. La.Civ.Code art. 2343.1 provides, "the transfer by a spouse to the other spouse of a thing forming part of his separate property, with the stipulation that it shall be part of the community, transforms the thing into community property." When determining the meaning and application of a statute, we must observe the rules of statutory interpretation.

"[T]he paramount consideration in statutory construction is ascertainment of the legislative intent and the reason or reasons which prompted the legislature to enact the law." *M.J. Farms, Ltd. v. Exxon Mobil Corp.*, 2007–2371, p. 13 (La.7/1/08), 998 So.2d 16, 27, citing *State v. Johnson*, 2003–2993, p. 12 (La.10/19/04), 884 So.2d 568, 575. It is well established that "[t]he starting point for the interpretation of any statute is the language of the statute itself." *Dejoie v. Medley*, 2008–2223 (La.5/5/09), 9 So.3d 826, 829. When a statute is clear and unambiguous and its application does not lead to absurd consequences, the provision is applied as written with no further interpretation made in search of the legislature's intent. *Id.*; La. Civ.Code art. 9; La. R.S. 1:4. In the event the language of a statute is susceptible of different meanings, the interpretation must best conform to the purpose of the law. La. Civ.Code art. 10. When analyzing legislative history, it is presumed the legislature's actions in crafting a law were knowing and intentional. *M.J. Farms, Ltd.*, 2007–2371 at pp. 13–14, 998 So.2d at 27. More particularly, this court must assume the legislature was aware of existing laws on the same subject, as well as established principles of statutory construction and the effect of their legislative acts. Id.

The court of appeal inserted into La.Civ.Code art. 2343.1 a requirement that the community regime must pre-exist the agreement to transfer separate property to the community. We find a plain reading of the statute does not contain such a requirement. The Residence Agreement, executed by authentic act, fully satisfies the elements of La.Civ.Code art. 2343.1 and makes the property at issue community inasmuch as William transferred to Audrey the residence/furnishings, which formed part of his separate property, with the stipulation that it be considered community property. This application does not lead to absurd results; rather, a wife who was still married to her husband at the time of their death is allowed to continue her life in their family home and enjoy a one-half interest in it. The fact that all their other assets were separate in nature does not render the article inapplicable.

While we find the statute to be clear and unambiguous and acknowledge the inquiry ceases there, consideration of the legislative history further supports our holding. La.Civ.Code art. 2343.1 was enacted by 1981 La.Acts, No. 921, § 2, which also added the second paragraph to La.Civ.Code art. 2336. This added paragraph of La.Civ.Code art. 2336 provides:

During the existence of the community property regime, the spouses may, without court approval, voluntarily partition the community property in whole or in part. In such a case, the things that each spouse acquires are separate property. The partition is effective toward third persons when filed for registry in the manner provided by Article 2332.

The legislature's act of allowing spouses to contractually transform their community property into separate property via La.Civ.Code art. 2336, and their separate property into community property via La.Civ.Code art. 2343.1, evidences an intent to allow spouses to voluntarily classify individual assets as they so desire. La.Civ.Code art. 2336 specifically contemplates a situation where all property is community in nature (such that a contractual regime was not in existence) and allows spouses to partition that community property, transforming it to separate property. This statutory provision does not require the contractual regime to pre-exist an agreement to transfer. Similarly, La.Civ.Code art. 2343.1, enacted by the same legislative act, does not require the legal regime to pre-exist an agreement to transfer.

Also, notably, the partition described in La.Civ.Code art. 2336 permits spouses to transform community property into separate property, either "in whole or in part" and does not require judicial approval for doing so. This article further supports our holding stated above regarding La.Civ.Code art. 2329 that an agreement as to specific assets does not change the matrimonial regime, necessitating court approval. The legal regime is the default regime and is favored by the legislature. Thus, it is illogical to interpret La.Civ.Code art. 2329 as requiring judicial approval for a non-favored regime to incorporate assets subject to the rules of the favored regime, when La.Civ.Code art.

2336 allows a favored regime to incorporate assets subject to the rules of the non-favored regime, without the requirement of court approval.

Accordingly, we conclude the Residence Agreement is enforceable inasmuch as we find it did not operate as a matrimonial agreement that modified or terminated a matrimonial regime, requiring judicial approval. Additionally, we conclude La.Civ.Code art. 2343.1 is applicable and does not require the existence of a community regime in order for a valid transfer of separate property to the community to have legal effect.

DECREE

For the reasons stated herein, the judgment of the court of appeal is reversed and the trial court judgment is reinstated.

REVERSED; TRIAL COURT JUDGMENT REINSTATED.

4.7 DAMAGE AWARDS

A. Introduction

The Louisiana Civil Code reflects real subrogation principles in classifying damage awards. Article 2338 provides that sums of money awarded to compensate for damage to community property are classified as community. Similarly, Article 2341 provides that sums of money awarded to compensate for damage to separate property are classified as separate. Proceeds of property damage insurance are treated in the same way. Article 2341 also expressly provides that damages awarded to one spouse because of the other spouse's breach of contract, fraud or bad faith management are separate property. The rule governing the classification of personal injury awards is slightly more complicated:

> **Art. 2344. Offenses and quasi-offenses; damages as community or separate property**
>
> Damages due to personal injuries sustained during the existence of the community by a spouse are separate property.
>
> Nevertheless, the portion of the damages attributable to expenses incurred by the community as a result of the injury, or in compensation of the loss of community earnings, is community property. If the community regime is terminated otherwise than by the death of the injured spouse, the portion of the damages attributable to the loss of earnings that would have accrued after

termination of the community property regime is the separate property of the injured spouse.

REVISION COMMENTS--1979

(a) The notion of personal injury includes injuries to the personality of a spouse and workman's compensation benefits.

(b) Under this provision, the classification of damages as separate or community property no longer depends on the sex of a spouse. An award of damages may be partly community and partly separate property of the injured spouse. Apportionment of the award between the community and the separate property of the injured spouse is required when the community terminates otherwise than by the death of the injured spouse. The noninjured spouse does not, ordinarily, have an interest in the portion of the award designed to compensate the injured spouse for loss of earnings that would have accrued after the termination of the community property regime. This segment of the award, which would fall into the community during the existence of a community property regime, upon termination of the regime is classified as the separate property of the injured spouse. When the regime terminates by the death of the injured spouse, the portion of the award designed to compensate the injured spouse for loss of earnings continues to be classified as community property in the interest of the surviving spouse.

Louisiana's approach to the classification of personal injury awards is similar to the approach taken in most other community property jurisdictions.[10] In most community property jurisdictions, real subrogation principles require that awards be classified by reference to the funds or damage for which they are intended to compensate. Any portion of an award intended to compensate for the pain and suffering incurred by a spouse is that spouse's separate property because it is essentially compensating for an extrapatrimonial loss. Awards for lost wages are classified as either community or separate depending the period of time in which the loss of wages occurred. Any portion of an award for lost wages that is intended to compensate for wages lost during the existence of the community property regime is community property. Any portion of an award for lost future wages—wages that would have been earned after the termination of the marriage—are generally classified as separate property. Louisiana Civil Code article 2344 adds an additional consideration at this point—the cause of the dissolution of the marriage. If the marriage ends because of divorce or the death of the non-injured spouse, then the wages are the separate property of the injured spouse. If the marriage ended due to the death of the injured spouse, then the wages are community property.

---

[10] California appears to be the only exception to this rule. California treats personal injury awards as community property. CAL. FAM. CODE §780.

B. *Sandra Touchet Young v. Phillip Mark Young*

549 So. 2d 437 (La. App. 3d Cir. 1989)

KNOLL, Judge.

The issue before us is whether the proceeds from three separate personal injury settlements to the husband, Phillip Mark Young, were his separate property. Phillip had three accidents. The first accident occurred four months before Phillip married Sandra Touchet Young. The other two accidents occurred during the marriage.

The trial court ruled that: (1) at least 50% of the March 18, 1980, settlement (first accident) was attributed to loss of community earnings; (2) Phillip indiscriminately commingled the balance of the settlement, therefore, he was not due reimbursement; and, (3) the McSween lot was community property. From this judgment Phillip appeals.

PROCEEDS FROM PREMARITAL INJURY

Phillip contends the trial court erred in finding that at least 50% of the March 18, 1980, personal injury settlement is attributable to loss of community earnings and thus, community property. We agree.

There is no dispute that Phillip's first accident occurred four months before his marriage to Sandra. It is well settled that where an injury has occurred for which the injured party has a cause of action, such cause of action is a vested property right. *Pillow v. Board of Com'rs*, 425 So.2d 1267 (La. App. 2nd Cir. 1982), *writ granted*, 427 So.2d 1200 (La. 1983), *writ recalled and denied*, 445 So.2d 1225 (La. 1984).

Article 2344 of our Civil Code provides when damages are considered part of the community:

> "Damages due to personal injuries sustained during the existence of the community by a spouse are separate property.
>
> Nevertheless, the portion of the damages attributable to expenses incurred by the community as a result of the injury, or in compensation of the loss of city earnings, is city property. If the city regime is terminated otherwise than by the death of the injured spouse, the portion of the damages attributable to the loss of earnings that would have accrued after termination of the city property regime is the separate property of the injured spouse." (Emphasis added.)

Article 2344 is not applicable to damages incurred before marriage, but paid during the existence of the community.

In Broussard v. Broussard, 340 So.2d 1309 (La. 1976), a case very similar to the present one, our Supreme Court held that a husband's recovery, during marriage, of personal injury damages, which resulted from a premarital accident, was the husband's separate property, though a portion of the funds recovered included compensation for loss of future earnings. The court reasoned: "None of Broussard's personal injury settlement money can be said to constitute 'the produce of the reciprocal industry and labor of both husband and wife,' La.C.C. art. 2402, because at the time of the accident Mrs. Broussard had contributed nothing to the non-existent community and had no influence upon her future husband's projected earning capacity."

In the present case, Phillip was injured in a work-related accident on December 28, 1977, four months prior to marrying Sandra. An action for damages resulting from offenses and quasi-offenses suffered by a single man is clearly his separate property. The enforcement or settlement of a cause of action does not change its character as separate or community. None of Phillip's personal injury settlement can be said to constitute "the produce of the reciprocal industry and labor of both husband and wife," because at the time of the accident, Sandra contributed nothing to the non-existent community and had no influence upon her future husband's projected earning capacity.

C. *Kevin E. Ellithorp v. Lisa S. Ellithorp*

509 So. 2d 178 (La. App. 1st Cir. 1987)

COVINGTON, J.

Lisa A. Ellithorp, the former wife of Kevin E. Ellithorp, devolutively appealed the district court's judgment in Kevin's suit to partition the assets of the community of acquets and gains which formerly existed between them. The primary bone of contention which this case presents is how the proceeds of a personal injury settlement which Kevin received during the existence of the community for injuries sustained during that regime should be divided between the former spouses. The controversy has its genesis in Kevin's having deposited the net settlement proceeds into an existing community checking account which will be discussed in greater detail in this opinion.

Kevin filed suit for personal injuries sustained in a vehicular collision on December 29, 1981. The trial of that suit began on February 13, 1984 and after almost a day of trial the case was settled and the terms of the settlement were read into the record. La. C.C. art. 3071. The transcription of the terms of settlement, as well as Kevin and Lisa's acquiescence in it, as elicited by the trial judge's questions and their answers, is Kevin's

Exhibit No. 2 in this partition suit. The settlement was for $360,000.00. Of that sum $358,000.00 was Kevin's; $100,000.00 was attributable to his pain and suffering and $258,000.00 represented loss of income, both past and future, from the date of injury through work life expectancy. Lisa received $1,000.00 for loss of consortium and the minor child received the same amount.

The record of the instant case reveals that the tortfeasor's insurer paid medical bills on behalf of Kevin in the approximate amount of $52,000.00 and "salary continuation" payments totaling $19,959.80 between January 2, 1982 and January 24, 1983. Additionally, the record shows that Kevin earned about $3,000.00 during the latter part of 1983 and the early part of 1984 for work performed for a pest control exterminating business. Neither the medical expenses nor the "salary continuation" was deducted from the $358,000.00 settlement.

Kevin's attorneys issued to Kevin their check for $248,057.24 on April 4, 1984, after deducting the attorney's fees and litigation expenses totaling $109,942.76. The settlement check was deposited into an existing community checking account which had a balance of $493.49 for the period ending March 19, 1984, the previous balance date for that account. Kevin issued three checks on that account, totaling $10,822.80, on April 6, 1984 to pay community debts at a bank and a finance company. On April 9, 1984, Kevin issued twelve checks on that community account, totaling $202,000.00 to purchase single premium annuities and a single premium life insurance policy. On April 10, 1984 Kevin issued a check on the community account to South Louisiana Bank for a $13,000.00 certificate of deposit and a check for $18,000.00 made payable to the order of "cash," which he used to open a checking account, designated "Mr. or Mrs. Kevin E. Ellithorp," to be used for the purpose of paying himself $1,500.00 per month for the next twelve months.

Kevin "cashed in" enough of the single premium annuities to produce a cash payment of $28,935.00 necessary when the Ellithorps bought a residence on June 21, 1984, in which transaction they assumed the vendors' mortgage balance of $27,530.05.

Checks were issued by Kevin on the community account, replenished by his depositing $1,500.00 checks written periodically on the account he opened with the $18,000.00 deposited on April 10, 1984. He expended $4,500.00 of the funds from that latter account to purchase a motorcycle. Some checks were issued by Lisa on the community account, but with few exceptions, the checks were for small amounts written to grocers, utility suppliers and the like.

DISTRICT COURT

The trial court assigned oral reasons for apportioning the personal injury settlement, stating that West v. Ortego, 325 So.2d 242 (La. 1975), Placide v. Placide, 408 So.2d

330 (La.App. 3d Cir.1981), La. R.S. 9:2801, "and the evidence produced" at the trial "served as a rational basis" for apportioning it. Because the trial court's method is instructive, we quote it as follows:

> [I] first determined the appropriate percentage of general damages, that is, for the physical injury, pain and suffering to the total recovery. In this case, the plaintiff, herein, Mr. Ellithorp, recovered $358,000 of which $100,000 was in general damages. That proportion is 27.93 %. I likewise apportioned the special damages, that is, for loss of past and future income to the total recovery, the total recovery again being $358,000, special damages totaling $258,000 yielding a percentage of 72.07 %. I further apportioned the attorneys fees and expenses to the general damages. The attorneys fees and expenses totaled $109,942.76 and taking 27.93 % of that sum, yields a total of $30,707.01 which is the apportionment of the attorneys fees and expenses to the general damages. I likewise apportioned the same attorneys fees and expenses to the special damages, that is, $109,972.76 and taking 72.07 % of that yields attorneys fees for special damages of $ 79,235.75. To determine the net general damages received I took the $100,000, which was the general damage award, and reduced that by the amount of the attorneys fees apportioned to the net general damages which was $30,707.01 yielding general damages of $69,292.99 of all which is separate in accordance with Civil Code Article 2344. I likewise determined net special damages received by taking the $258,000 that was the net -- which was the gross special damages and reduced it by its proportionate sum of the attorneys fees and expenses of $79,235.75 which made the net special damages equal $178,764.25. This sum would be community property except for the fact that the community was terminated shortly after receiving these funds so, in fact, a portion of this ended up being community and a portion of it ended up being separate funds all in accordance with Civil Code Article 2344.
>
> The Court had to again apportion this $178,762.25 between separate and community funds. In order to do this the Court computed that sum which was attributable to the gross loss of past income to the date of settlement. In order to do that we considered what Mr. Ellithorp's wages would have been from Otis Engineering Company through the date of settlement which would have been $68,000 and that is using the $32,000 of annual income that Mr. Ellithorp was earning at the time. I reduced that sum by the amount of the salary continuation checks that Sweco was paying Mr. Ellithorp during this period of time which sum amounted to $19,959.80 reducing that $68,000 gross income settlement figure to $48,040.20. I further reduced that sum by the $3,000 which he earned while working for Terminix reducing the sum to $45,040.20. I thereafter computed the expense and attorneys fees attributable to this gross loss past of income. And that is I took the total settlement figure of $358,000 and apportioned that sum to the $45,040.20 which gave me a percentage of 12.58106 %. Then I took that percentage and allocated the total

attorneys fees and expenses of $109,942.76 of that sum which is $13,831.96. I reduced the gross salary loss of $45,040.20 by this allocation of attorneys fees and expenses of $13,831.46 which gave me a net loss of past income to date of settlement of $31,208.24, all of this sum being community property.

To determine the future loss of income applicable for the period of time from the date of settlement to the date of separation I again had to determine what funds were available which was the $258,000 in special damages less the $45,040.20 attributable to the income from the date of injury until the date of settlement and apportioned that over the balance -- reduced it rather. What I did was I reduced the $258,000 by that sum and proportioned the balance of that net special damage over the work life expectancy of Mr. Ellithorp which was forty-three years. I then derived an amortization schedule of 8 % to determine what monthly income would be derived from that net special damages after reducing it by the gross salary loss. That sum is $1,470.00. I then multiplied that $1,470 by the six months in between the settlement date and the termination of the community yielding $8,820. I then reduced the $8,820 by the apportion of attorney fees and expenses that related to the special damage award of $258,000. That apportionate expense is 3.42 %. The attorneys fees attributable to the special damages was $79,235.75 and I took 3.42 % of that which is $2,708.75 which means that monthly income for that six month (sic) is reduced by the sum of $2,708.75 yielding $6,111.24 which is also community property. If you add the gross -- you reduced the gross special damages of $258,000 by the amount of the attorneys fees $79,235.75, further reduce it by past loss of income of $31,208.24, and further reduce it by the future loss (sic) income of $6,111.25 you net out $141,444.76 which will also become his separate property.

In recap of the settlement funds the Court has determined that the net general damages of $69,292.99 as well as the special future damages which he received at $141,444.76 is Mr. Ellithorp's separate funds which total $210,737.75. The community consists of past lost wages of $31,208.24 and the future lost wages of $6,111.25 or a total of $37,319.49. If you add a separate figure of $210,737.75 to the community property of $37,319.49 plus the total attorneys fees and expenses of $109,942.76 you end up with a total settlement figure which Mr. Ellithorp received of $358,000.

The trial court declared that the motorcycle, residence, and single premium annuities "were paid for with separate funds of the plaintiff and therefore his separate property," relying on the rationale of Succession of Sonnier, 208 So.2d 562 (La.App. 3d Cir.1968) Succession of Russo, 246 So.2d 26 (La.App. 4th Cir.1971), writ refused, 258 La. 760, 247 So.2d 861 (La. 1971). The court awarded the First National Bank of Houma certificate of deposit for $17,000.00 to Lisa and the South Louisiana Bank certificate of deposit for $13,000.00 to Kevin, subject to the pledge of both certificates in favor of South Louisiana Bank which held them as collateral for a loan made to one of Lisa's relatives. The court declared specified items of movable property to be either Kevin's or Lisa's, utilizing the numbers and values stated on Kevin's detailed descriptive list.

The characterization of funds as either community or separate, including the personal injury settlement proceeds which were deposited into the pre-existing community checking account and which quickly passed through it, was addressed by the trial court's taking into account the numerous bank statements and canceled checks, as well as Kevin's lengthy request for admissions relating to deposits and expenditures. The court observed that the requests for admissions were not answered by Lisa and are deemed admitted, citing La. C.C.P. art. 1467.

The court found a beginning balance of $493.49 in the community account before the personal injury settlement check was deposited. He added deposits made to that account and subtracted community withdrawals and concluded Kevin obtained "a net figure of approximately $10,000 of community funds."

ASSIGNMENTS OF ERROR

Lisa's lone assignment of error addresses the trial court's finding that the personal injury settlement proceeds of $248.057.24 which were deposited into the community checking account was Kevin's separate property.

ISSUE

Appellant states the issue to be whether the proceeds "deposited to a community account and used indiscriminately by the parties, became community."

Appellee timely answered appellant's devolutive appeal but did not brief the alleged errors complained of in the answer to the appeal and for that reason, those assignments are deemed abandoned.

DISCUSSION

Lisa filed for separation on August 17, 1984 and a judgment of separation was rendered in that proceeding. Thus, the community was terminated on August 17, 1984.

Damages for personal injuries constitute separate property of the injured spouse. La. C.C. art. 2344. Damages to compensate for diminished earning capacity, also known as future loss of earnings, constitute the injured spouse's separate property to the extent the "future loss" is deemed to be attributable to a time after termination of the community property regime.

In determining what part of the net loss of earnings proceeds was attributable to the community regime, the trial court determined the amount Kevin would have earned, at the stipulated rate of $32,000.00 per annum from December 29, 1981 to February 13, 1984, and subtracted therefrom the "salary continuation" payments totaling $19,959.80 and earned salary of $3,000.00, and determined that $31,208.24 of the net future loss of wages ($178,764.25) for the period beginning December 29, 1981 and ending February 13, 1984, was community property. The court further determined that the net "future loss of income" for the period commencing February 13, 1984, the date of the settlement, and ending August 17, 1984, when Lisa filed for separation, totaled $6,111.24 and was also community property.

Thus, the trial court held that the net settlement proceeds owned by Kevin separately consisted of post-community future loss of income amounting to $141,444.76 and net general damages amounting to $69,292.99, and that property purchased with those funds retained its separate character.

Our review of the record as a whole fails to reveal that the trial court was manifestly erroneous in holding the funds received in the settlement consisted of both Kevin's separate property and Kevin and Lisa's community property by uncommingling the settlement funds from the exceedingly sparse community funds in the community checking account. In the absence of manifest error on the part of the trial court, we must affirm. Arceneaux v. Domingue, 365 So.2d 1330 (La. 1978). In the instant case the record overwhelmingly supports the trial court's findings of fact and conclusions of law.

Accordingly, appellant's assignment of error is without merit. The judgment of the trial court is affirmed at appellant's cost.

AFFIRMED.

D. Note

Two approaches for apportioning the lost wages were suggested in *Thomas v. Thomas*, 539 So.2d 1242 (La. App. 4th Cir. 1989), but both of them yielded the same amounts to the former wife. The husband was injured working for Gulf Engineering while performing contract work for Shell Oil Co. It was determined that the amount of lost wages from the time of injury to the termination of the community was $40,639.83. That figure, presumably, was based on the husband's wage scale at the time of the injury. During that period, the husband was paid worker compensation benefits of $21,824 ($248 per week). Ultimately, his third party claim against Shell was settled for $185,000, yielding him $105,400 after attorney fees and expenses that amounted to 43% of the award. An attempt was made to determine the part of the $185,000 figure attributable to lost wages through the testimony of the attorney who negotiated the settlement for the husband. The court refused to employ that procedure, "finding it too speculative." Instead it relied on the amount the husband would have earned during the period, based on his current level of salary.

In the simple case of $40,639.83 of lost wages that would be obtained in a damage award, the amount of community funds obtained would be that sum less the attorney fees–here 43% or $17,475.13. That would leave $23,164.70 or $11,582.35 to each spouse.

In *Thomas*, however, $21,824 in worker compensation payments had already been paid, not subject apparently, to any deduction for attorney fees and expenses. The court then determined that the remainder of the lost wage claim, $18,815.83, would be the amount of the settlement attributable to compensation for lost wages. Of that amount, 43% would be deducted for attorney fees ($8,090.81) leaving $10,725.02 to the spouses. Adding to this community part of the settlement the compensation payments already made would produce a total of $32,549.02. Dividing that in half gave $16,274.50 to each spouse. Because the compensation payments were not reduced by attorney fees, each spouse got $4,692.15 more than would have been the case in a simple claim against a third party for the lost wages. In effect, the spouses split equally the windfall resulting from not paying attorney fees for the compensation payments.

Thomas resulted as it did in part because in the settlement negotiations, the compensation insurer waived its right to reimbursement from the plaintiff for compensation benefits paid to the injured worker. If that claim had been made in a case like *Thomas*, the $185,000 award would have been reduced by $21,824. In that case, presumably, all of the award attributable to lost wages would have been reduced by the 43% attorney fee and the parties would have obtained less on the bottom line. On the other hand, if the fee was determined otherwise, the outcome would be the same as in *Thomas*.

The majority in *Thomas* appeared to disagree with the First Circuit approach in *Ellithorp v. Ellithorp* "insofar as it can be interpreted to allow worker's compensation benefits received as damages in compensation of the loss of community earnings to either (1) be deducted from the total of lost community earnings to reduce that loss, as the Ellithorp court did with the salary continuation payments, or (2) be deducted from the portion of damages received from a personal injury suit in compensation of the loss of community earnings." Judge Ciaccio, concurring in the judgment, found no reason to disagree with *Ellithorp*, but his calculation produced the same ultimate award to the wife, $5,362.51 from the settlement. The apparent conflict is explained by the fact that both the majority and the concurring opinion took as a starting point the same amount of lost wages ($40,639.83). In compensation for that loss, payment was made from two funds, the compensation paid and part of the settlement award, and there was no double recovery. And both deducted from the share of the settlement the attorney fee attributable to that award. The ultimate result would seem to be consistent with

Ellithorp, for both approaches reduce the part of the settlement with what was paid in wages during the period of lack of employment.

The approach of the Third Circuit Court of Appeal in *Placide v. Placide*, 408 So.2d 330 (La. App. 3d Cir. 1981), is perhaps indicative of the general equitable approach to be used in these cases. Applying pre-1980 law, the court considered an award of general damages for pain and suffering resulting from surgery and also from the loss of sexual ability for the rest of the plaintiff's life. Two years after the injury, the plaintiff and his wife were separated and the community was terminated. The court "on an equitable basis" simply designated the round figure of $20,000 as suffered during the two years of the existence of the community and designated the remainder of the pain and suffering award, $187,713.71, as separate property. [Under the revised law, the entire award for pain and suffering would be separate, but any lost wages would be apportioned.]

Even the rough justice of *Placide* seems concrete when compared with the necessity of dealing with a lump sum compromise or a lump sum award that does not designate the various elements of damages. Civil Code Article 2344 speaks only in general terms to the "portion of the damages attributable to the loss of earnings that would have accrued after termination of the community." Another level of assumptions enters the picture, assumptions as to how much of the total was for loss of earnings and how much for pain and suffering. Here again, the flexibility is apparent, and the necessity of rough, equitable concerns is unavoidable. To the extent that a spouse about to receive such an award manipulates its designation to the detriment of the other spouse, Civil Code Article 2354 could be invoked to the extent the loss is caused by "fraud or bad faith in the management of the community property."

E. *Raymond R. Egan v. Jeanette Huck Egan*

729 So. 2d 1143 (La. App. 4th Cir. 1999)

MCKAY, Judge.

This appeal arises out of a lower court's ruling that federal worker's compensation benefits paid after divorce and dissolution of the community are community property. We reverse.

FACTS AND PROCEDURAL HISTORY

Appellant, Raymond r. Egan, worked as a drug enforcement agent with the United States Drug Enforcement Agency throughout his marriage to Jeanette Huck Egan. In August 1982, Mr. Egan suffered a disabling injury while in the course and scope of his employment. Mr. Egan filed an accident report and made a claim for worker's compensation benefits through the Department of Labor Office of Worker's Compensation Programs (OWCP). Mr. Egan also filed a claim with the Office of Personnel Management (OPM) for civil service disability retirement benefits. Both of these agencies approved Mr. Egan's claims for benefits. However, Mr. Egan was informed by OWCP that he must elect between benefits from OWCP or benefits from OPM because benefits could not be received concurrently. Mr. Egan elected to receive worker's compensation benefits from OWCP and has received such benefits since November 23, 1983.

On October 15, 1984, the parties entered into a Community Property Partition Agreement in which Mrs. Egan specifically reserved "her rights to claim benefits under any government retirement plan in the name of Raymond R. Egan." On June 4, 1985, Mr. Egan filed a petition for divorce and judgment of divorce was entered on July 17, 1985.

On September 25, 1995, Mrs. Egan filed a Motion for Qualified Domestic Relations Order to establish her rights to receive a portion of Mr. Egan's retirement and any disability retirement benefits which may be due him from OPM. On March 22, 1996, the parties entered into a consent judgment which recognized Mrs. Egan's one-half interest in any retirement or disability retirement benefits that Mr. Egan may be entitled to in the future. Mrs. Egan then filed a pleading entitled "MOTION FOR SUPPLEMENTAL ORDER REGARDING DISABILITY PENSION" by which she sought to have the worker's compensation benefits received by Mr. Egan after the dissolution of the community to be declared community property. In response, Mr. Egan filed Exceptions of No Cause of Action and Res Judicata. These exceptions were denied by the trial court. Mr. Egan then filed a writ of review with this Court, which was subsequently denied as was his Application for Writ of Certiorari and/or Review with the Louisiana Supreme Court. A hearing on Mrs. Egan's motion was held on October29, 1997. The trial court granted Mrs. Egan's motion on January 28, 1998. In its written reasons for judgment, the trial court concluded that Mr. Egan's election to receive worker's compensation benefits during the marriage automatically converts the worker's compensation benefits form a separate property classification to a community property classification. Accordingly, the trial court found that Mrs. Egan was entitled to one-half of all past and future worker's compensation benefits.

On February 27, 1998, Mr. Egan filed a writ application with this Court. On April 9, 1998, this Court ordered that the writ application be converted to an appeal. Accordingly, Mr. Egan filed this appeal.

DISCUSSION

The issue before this Court is whether worker's compensation benefits received after the dissolution of the community constitute community property when during the marriage an injured spouse makes an election to receive them rather than benefits from a retirement/disability fund which would be community property.

In its written reasons for judgment, the trial court found that Raymond Egan's election to receive worker's compensation benefits rather than disability retirement benefits defeated the community interest of Mrs. Egan. In reaching its decision, the trial court relied upon the 1991 Second Circuit case of *Johnson v. Johnson*, 582 So.2d 926 (La. App. 2nd Cir. 1991). The trial court reasoned that the worker's compensation benefits received by Mr. Egan were analogous to the disability benefits addressed in *Johnson* and therefore, Mrs. Egan was entitled to a one-half interest in such benefits.

The trial court's reasoning is flawed. What the trial court fails to appreciate is that the disability benefits in *Johnson* and the worker's compensation benefits in the instant case are fundamentally different. In *Johnson*, the injured employee's right to receive disability benefits was based upon his contributions to the disability fund, which were made from community funds, and were calculated based on the number of years of service which occurred during the existence of the community. By contrast, the worker's compensation benefits in the instant case did not flow from a community endeavor. Mr. Egan received worker's compensation benefits because he was on the job when he was injured.

In their briefs, both appellant and appellee allude to cases that deal with disability insurance policies. However, the worker's compensation benefits Mr. Egan is receiving flow from a statutory creation. The purpose of worker's compensation is to compensate the injured worker not only for lost wages, but also for reduced or lost earning capacity. *Thibodeaux v. Stamm-Scheele, Inc.*, 97-1461 (La. App. 3rd Cir. 04/15/98), 711 So.2d 426, writ denied, 98-1285 (La. 06/26/98), 719 So. 2d 1061. This is true not only under the Louisiana Act but also under the federal program which covered Mr. Egan. Consequently under a community property analysis, worker's compensation benefits are akin to salary. Therefore, just as a former spouse's post-dissolution salary would be his separate property, worker's compensation benefits he receives after the dissolution of the community are also his separate property.

Our finding that Mr. Egan's worker's compensation benefits are his separate property is additionally supported by analogy to damages due to personal injuries. According to La. C.C. art. 2344:

> Damages due to personal injuries sustained during the existence of the community by a spouse are separate property. Nevertheless, the portion of the

> damages attributable to expenses incurred by the community as a result of the injury, or in compensation of the loss of community earnings, is community property. If the community regime is terminated otherwise than by the death of the injured spouse, the portion of the damages attributable to the loss of earnings that would have accrued after termination of the community property regime is the separate property of the injured spouse.

Therefore, under this analysis, Mr. Egan's worker's compensation benefits are also his separate property.

Mrs. Egan's argument that her former husband's election to receive worker's compensation benefits rather than disability retirement benefits somehow defeats her community interest in his pension is without merit. At the time Mr. Egan elected to receive worker's compensation in lieu of disability, he was still married to Mrs. Egan. He made the decision to receive these benefits because they paid more than disability benefits. His election to receive these benefits has in no way diminished his interest in the pension he may one day be entitled to. Mr. Egan may one day return to work with the federal government and become fully vested in his retirement. However, to allow his former wife to force him to now either elect to receive disability or have his worker's compensation benefits declared community property is wrong. It is but for his injury that he is even eligible to receive disability from OPM. If he had never been injured and had merely quit his job his former wife would be entitled to nothing. To award her half of the worker's compensation benefits he receives because his injury keeps him from working makes no sense.

CONCLUSION

We find that the trial court was manifestly erroneous as a matter of law when it ruled that the worker's compensation benefits received by Mr. Egan, after the dissolution of the community, were community property. Accordingly the judgment of the trial court is reversed.

REVERSED.

F. *Patricia A. Morris v. Caszell Morris*

685 So. 2d 673 (La. App. 3d Cir. 1997)

SAUNDERS, Judge.

On June 14, 1995, Patricia Morris filed for a partition of the community property formerly owned by herself and her ex-husband, Caszell Morris. The trial judge decided, *inter alia,* that a $40,000.00 settlement received by Mr. Morris for damages constituted community property, one-half of which belonged to plaintiff/appellee, Patricia Morris. The trial judge also concluded that a separate settlement received by Mrs. Morris in the amount of $35,000.00 for compensatory damages was in fact her separate property. From this judgment, defendant/appellant appeals these conclusions, which we affirm.

CLASSIFICATION OF PUNITIVE DAMAGES

La.Civ.Code art. 2340 provides the following: "Things in the possession of a spouse during the existence of a regime of community of acquets and gains are presumed to be community, but either spouse may prove that they are separate." The burden of overcoming the community presumption falls upon the party who asserts that the disputed property is separate. To meet the burden, the party is generally required to present proof that is clear, positive and legally certain that the property was separate and not community. *Hebert v. Hebert,* 94-864 (La.App. 3 Cir. 2/15/95); 650 So.2d 436.

Our first question is whether a punitive damages award constitutes separate or community property. This issue is apparently *res nova* in Louisiana. The defendant, Mr. Morris, contends that the trial judge erred in finding that his punitive damage award constituted community property. Initially, he argues that by its very nature the punitive damages awarded him constitutes his separate property under the same rationale and authority that would govern a compensable damages award arising from a delictual obligation. Alternatively, he contends that they are his separate property because the funds received in settlement for his tort action were received after dissolution of the couple's marital community.

In support of his arguments, appellant relies on the case of *West v. Ortego,* 325 So.2d 242 (La.1975). *West* provided an equitable formula for classifying and distributing funds received after dissolution of the community, in settlement of a predissolution accident-related cause of action.

> The case of *West v. Ortego,* supra, dictates that we resort to equity to apportion monies acquired after dissolution of the community for damages awarded in compensation for an accident which occurred before the dissolution of the community when the award covers both pre-dissolution and post dissolution losses.

Placide v. Placide, 408 So.2d 330, 333 (La.App. 3 Cir.1981).

In *Placide v. Placide,* 408 So.2d 330 (La.App. 3 Cir.1981), we allocated to the community that portion of a husband's *compensatory* damages associated with his partial loss of sexual function which affected the community, i.e., that portion of the award allocated for his losses coinciding with his marriage, but characterized as the husband's separate property those damages to which the community had no claim. On essentially the same basis, the Supreme Court in *West* apportioned a husband's workers' compensation benefits along the lines of the marital divide:

> While a husband and wife are living together and the community is still in existence, it is reasonable to designate these damages as community property. However, when the community has been terminated, it is both unreasonable and inequitable to deprive the husband of funds which are to sustain him into the future, or compensate him for future pain, suffering and disability merely because the law has required assertion of all such damages as part of a single claim.

West v. Ortego, 325 So.2d at 246.

The reasoning of *West* and *Placide* have since been incorporated (or, at least, not repudiated) by the legislature in Civil Code art. 2344, which apportions *compensatory* damages as follows:

> Damages due to personal injuries sustained during the existence of the community by a spouse are separate property.
>
> Nevertheless, the portion of the damages attributable to expenses incurred by the community as a result of the injury, or in compensation of the loss of community earnings, is community property. If the community regime is terminated otherwise than by the death of the injured spouse, the portion of the damages attributable to the loss of earnings that would have accrued after termination of the community property regime is the separate property of the injured spouse.

However, we conclude that the authority cited by Mr. Morris does not control, for here we are not concerned with *compensatory* damages for which the *West* and *Placide* rationale is applied, but with *punitive* or *exemplary* damages received.

Additionally, we conclude that Louisiana Civil Code article 2344 is not applicable here for the simple reason that the damages Mr. Morris received were not compensatory damages due to his personal injuries, but rather constituted society's sanctions against a tortfeasor's inexcusable conduct. As the Louisiana Supreme Court has had occasion to observe:

> [T]he purpose of Article 2315.3 is threefold: (1) to penalize and punish defendants for engaging in wanton or reckless disregard for public safety in the storage, handling, or transportation of hazardous or toxic substances that causes injury to others; (2) to deter the tortfeasors and others who might follow their example from exposing the public to dangers of that kind in the future; and (3) to provide victims injured by such conduct with the incentive to act as the prosecutors of penal laws against such wrongdoers. Article 2315.3 is not designed to repair the injuries of tort victims.

Billiot v. B.P. Oil Co., 645 So.2d at 612.

This distinction is significant, for while damages due to personal injuries generally constitute the separate property of the spouse, La.Civ.Code art 2344, "punitive damages are sums awarded apart from any compensatory or nominal damages...." *Billiot v. B.P. Oil,* 93-1118 (La.1994); 645 So.2d 604, 612.

Rather, we conclude that the answer may be found elsewhere, in La.Civ.Code art. 2338, most commonly referred to as the "omnibus clause," which clearly states that "community property comprises: all other property not classified by law as separate property." Accordingly, Mr. Morris, in order to overcome the presumption set forth in La.Civ.Code art 2340 and encompass the receipt of punitive damages as his separate property, would have to fit the property at issue into one of the following articles classifying property as separate in nature: La.Civ.Code art. 2341, La.Civ.Code art. 2341.1, La.Civ.Code art. 2342, La.Civ.Code art. 2343, or La.Civ.Code art. 2344.

Inasmuch as none of these articles can be said to classify punitive damages as separate property, we affirm the trial judge's finding that the punitive damages settlement received by Mr. Morris constituted community property to which Mrs. Morris is entitled to her one-half interest.

CLASSIFICATION OF DAMAGES

Next, Mr. Morris contends that he is entitled to a share of the $35,000.00 proceeds of an automobile accident Mrs. Morris received from Allstate Insurance Company. Specifically, he urges that the funds should have been apportioned on a pre-dissolution and post dissolution basis.

Clearly, La.Civ.Code art. 2344 speaks to the issue presented:

> As stated above, damages, due to personal injuries sustained during the existence of a community by a spouse are separate property of that spouse. While the portion of damages attributable to loss of earnings that would have accrued after termination of the community are the separate property of the injured spouse, the portion of the damage award attributable to expenses incurred by the community as a result of the injury, or in compensation of the loss of community earnings, is community property. LSA-C.C. art. 2344.

Fountain v. Fountain, 93-2176 (La.App. 1 Cir. 10/7/94); 644 So.2d 733, 741.

Thus, there is no question that an award of damages can be classified as both community and separate property. However, without sufficient evidence to permit an equitable apportionment of the damages, *i.e.,* proof that a portion of the damage award is attributable to expenses incurred by the community (medical expenses), or the payment was for loss of community earnings, the court is unable to adequately do so. See *Fountain v. Fountain,* CA 93-2176 (La.App. 1 Cir. 10/7/94); 644 So.2d 733.

As recognized by the trial judge, only two documents were presented at trial which spoke to the nature of the damages compensated by Allstate Insurance Company. The first was a "Receipt and Release," in which Mrs. Morris agreed to discharge:

> "Allstate Insurance Company from all medical expenses and pecuniary losses, liability, penalties and attorney's fees and any and all claims of compensatory and exemplary damages, past, present and future arising out of or in any connected with the asserted property damage and/or bodily injuries and/or aggravation of bodily injuries and/or medical injuries, sustained by appearer as a result thereof ..."

The second document filed, with the trial memorandum presented by Mrs. Morris' attorney, included Mrs. Morris' income records for 1990 and 1991.

After considering all of the evidence, the trial judge held in Mrs. Morris' favor, noting that "while the testimony of Mrs. Morris is self serving and obviously designed to produce the best result for the witness, it is corroborated and essentially uncontradicted and is the only evidence the court has as to the nature of the funds received from that lawsuit."

Our review of the record leads us to agree with the trial court's finding that Mrs. Morris was successful in overcoming the presumption set forth in La.Civ.Code art. 2340 to establish that the funds she received from Allstate in fact constituted her separate property.

DECREE

For the foregoing reasons, the judgment of the trial court is affirmed, with costs assessed to the defendant/appellant, Mr. Caszell Morris.

AFFIRMED.

G. Note

Punitive damage awards are relatively uncommon in Louisiana. Yet, few cases exist in the other community property jurisdictions that consider the classification of punitive damage awards. The few cases that do exist suggest that classification may be more complex than the *Morris* court indicated.

In *Harrell v. Hochderffer*, 345 S.W. 3d 652 (Tex. App. Ct. 2011), the court indicated that the nature of the underlying action is relevant to classifying punitive damages:

> The petition filed in the personal-injury lawsuit also sought exemplary damages. Harrell and Temesgen cite *Rosenbaum v. Texas Building & Mortgage Co.*, 140 Tex. 325, 167 S.W.2d 506, 508 (1943), for the proposition that a recovery for exemplary damages is characterized as community property. In *Rosenbaum*, the supreme court noted that where one spouse sought exemplary damages in a suit for fraud, rescission of a contract, and cancellation of a note, "such damages, if recovered, would have belonged to the community." *Id.* This statement is not only dicta, but was made in the context of a contract dispute, rather than a claim for personal injuries. A recovery for personal injuries, such as the one at issue here, is expressly characterized as separate property under the family code, with a statutory exception for any recovery for loss of earning capacity during the marriage. See Tex. Fam.Code Ann. § 3.001(3). The only additional exceptions acknowledged by Texas courts are funds recovered for "medical expenses incurred during marriage, and ... other expenses associated with injury to the community estate." *Licata*, 11 S.W.3d at 273. Unlike lost earning capacity and medical expenses, however, exemplary damages do not represent income to which the community is entitled or an expense for which the community is liable. An exemplary damages recovery is merely "a private windfall," levied for the public purpose of punishment and deterrence, and is not associated with an injury to the community estate. *See Transportation Ins. Co. v. Moriel*, 879 S.W.2d 10, 17 (Tex.1994). Because an exemplary-damages award does not fall under any exception to the general rule that the recovery for personal injuries is separate property, such damages must be characterized as separate property under family code section 3.001(3). *See* Tex. Fam.Code Ann. § 3.001(3). Thus, assuming without deciding that any of the settlement proceeds received by Rudie were meant to represent exemplary damages, such proceeds would have been characterized as his separate property. Likewise, any settlement proceeds received by Jessie Mae as exemplary damages in connection with her loss of consortium claim would have been characterized as her separate property.

A handful of cases from other community property jurisdictions have considered the proper classification of federal qui tam actions. *See Estate of Duxbury*, 304 P. 3d 480 (Wash. App. Ct. 2013) and *D.B. v. K.B.*, 176 S.W. 3d 343 (Tex. App. Ct. 2004). *In re Biddle*, 52 Cal. App. 4th 396 (1997), explained as follows:

> With antecedents older than the Republic, the qui tam action is a type of private attorney general lawsuit; it allows an individual to sue to enforce a public statutory right and to retain a portion of any monies recovered thereby…

While employed by the United States Government as a contract administrator at Stanford University, Paul Biddle became aware of what he believed were questionable billing practices by Stanford that could amount to many millions of dollars. In 1991, he filed a qui tam complaint in federal district court on behalf of the United States. (United States ex rel. Biddle v. Leland Stanford Jr. University Board of Trustees (N.D.Cal. Sept. 9, 1991) [Dock. No. 91–CV–20618].) Three years later, the Biddles' marriage of 21 years was dissolved. The qui tam action, which the United States had declined to take over, was still at the pleading stage when the trial court had to decide whether any derivative recovery Mr. Biddle might obtain for his efforts would constitute community property.

"Except as otherwise provided by statute, all property, real or personal, wherever situated, acquired by a married person during the marriage ... is community property." (Fam.Code, § 760.) Causes of action are ordinarily deemed a form of property. (See 4 Witkin, Summary of Cal. Law (9th ed. 1987) Personal Property, § 3, p. 10.) Beyond these generalities, the parties cannot agree.

Mr. Biddle argues that property is statutorily defined in this state as something which can be owned (Civ.Code, § 654). No individual can "own" a qui tam cause of action because it belongs to the United States. Therefore in his view he has no property interest in the cause of action that would qualify it for division as community property. The former Mrs. Biddle counters that a qui tam cause of action may not be "owned" by her ex-spouse but it nevertheless amounts to a contingent right to future income, of the sort that California law treats as community property. (*See In re Marriage of Brown* (1976) 15 Cal.3d 838, 844–847, 126 Cal.Rptr. 633, 544 P.2d 561.) We agree with Mrs. Biddle—the dispositive focus is on what the qui tam action may produce, not whether Mr. Biddle will have the power to control the litigation.

It is true that a qui tam plaintiff does not "own" the cause of action in the conventional sense of that word. The right the qui tam plaintiff seeks to vindicate belongs to the United States Government; even if it takes no active part in that effort, the United States Government is always the real party in interest. (E.g., *U.S. ex rel. Kreindler v. United Technologies* (2d Cir.1993) 985 F.2d 1148, 1154; *United States v. Baker–Lockwood Mfg. Co.* (8th Cir.1943) 138 F.2d 48, 51.) It is the United States Government which can, if it is conducting the prosecution, settle or dismiss the case notwithstanding any objections the qui tam plaintiff may have. (31 U.S.C. § 3730(c)(2)(A)–(c)(2)(B).) If the government declines to take over the case, it may nevertheless intervene at virtually any point in the litigation. (*See U.S. v. Texas Instruments Corp.* (9th

Cir.1994) 25 F.3d 725, 727 [govt. allowed to intervene on appeal to challenge settlement by qui tam plaintiff].) But if the government does decline to prosecute the case, "[t]he qui tam plaintiff is the only person 'charged with responsibility to act in the circumstances.' " (*U.S. ex rel. Hyatt v. Northrop Corp.* (9th Cir.1996) 91 F.3d 1211, 1217.) If the government allows the qui tam plaintiff to prosecute, the plaintiff becomes the de facto assignee of the government's cause of action pursuant to a statutory "enforceable unilateral contract." (*See U.S. ex rel. Kelly v. Boeing Co.* (9th Cir.1993) 9 F.3d 743, 748 and decisions cited.) The qui tam plaintiff in a successful case is ensured of a monetary return (in the form of "proceeds," attorneys' fees and expenses) regardless of whether the case was conducted by the government or the plaintiff unless the plaintiff is convicted in connection with the commission of the underlying fraud. (31 U.S.C. § 3730(d).)

The cause of action may not be "property" in the strict sense that it can be owned without restriction by a qui tam plaintiff, but the money generated by the cause of action which ends up in the plaintiff's hands clearly is property. The realization of that is dependent upon at least two contingencies—a judicial action must be initiated by the qui tam plaintiff, and the defendant must part with the money after trial or settlement. If these contingencies are satisfied, the plaintiff's entitlement to a cash recovery is, to all intents and purposes, established. This situation is indistinguishable from that of a married producer who starts work on a movie and, after separating from her husband, completes the movie which becomes a smash hit; the contingency of success results in a divisible community asset. (*See In re Marriage of Zaentz* (1990) 218 Cal.App.3d 154, 164, 267 Cal.Rptr. 31; *see also In re Marriage of Kilbourne* (1991) 232 Cal.App.3d 1518, 1524, fn. 5, 284 Cal.Rptr. 201 [listing contingent future interests held to be community property].)

It is undisputed that Mr. Biddle was married when he discovered and investigated the billing practices that are the subject of the qui tam action. It is also undisputed that the qui tam action had been filed prior to the Biddles' separation. The action thus amounts to a contingent future interest and divisible community property. (*In re Marriage of Brown, supra*, 15 Cal.3d 838, 846–847, 126 Cal.Rptr. 633, 544 P.2d 561.) The specifics of the division are for the trial court's discretion. (See Fam.Code, § 2550; In re Marriage of Gillmore (1981) 29 Cal.3d 418, 423, 174 Cal.Rptr. 493, 629 P.2d 1.)

H. Questions

1. During H's marriage to W, H is sexually harassed at work. H sues his boss for intentional infliction of emotional distress. H also develops an ulcer as a result of the stress from the sexual harassment. H has to go see a doctor for

treatment—which costs $10,000. H pays the bill with community funds. H's boss settles with him for $50,000. Classify the $50,000.

2. H and W are married. W is carjacked and her vehicle—which is community property—is damaged. W suffers physical and emotional injuries as a result of the events. The assailant is identified and W sues for the damage caused to the car, the physical injuries, and the emotional trauma. W recovers on all her claims. How will the damages be classified?

a. How would your answer change if the car was W's separate property?

b. What if the car was H's separate property?

3. La. Civ. Code art. 2315.4 allows for the award of exemplary damages when an intoxicated person operating a vehicle causes damages. H and W are hit by a drunk driver. They both sue the driver for personal injuries, lost wages, property damage to the car—a community asset—and each spouse is also awarded punitive damages. How are these awards classified?

4.8 ACQUISITIONS WITH SEPARATE AND COMMUNITY PROPERTY AND ASSETS ACQUIRED OVER TIME

A. William A. Reppy, Jr., *Acquisitions With a Mix of Community and Separate Funds: Displacing California's Presumption of Gift by Recognizing Shared Ownership or a Right of Reimbursement*, 31 IDAHO L. REV. 965 (1995)

***

II. SPANISH-MEXICAN BACKGROUND -- FAR FEWER RULES AND WIDESPREAD USE OF INCEPTION OF TITLE

Under the Civil Law of Spain and Mexico, an acquisition was either entirely separate property or entirely community, never a cotenancy comprised of shares owned by both the community estate and a separate estate (or by the community and two separate estates, the husband's and the wife's). If prior to marriage, a man or woman initiated acquisition of title, as by entering into a contract for purchase, his or her unmarried status at that time impressed upon the property to be acquired a separate classification. That after his marriage, the husband (then sole manager of the community) used community funds to make some (or even all) payments on the acquisition did not create a community interest in the property. Nor did the fact that the deed was delivered and title passed during marriage. Despite favoring community ownership, Spanish-Mexican law had an even stronger preference for unified ownership as expressed in the "inception of title" doctrine. In most families the most significant separate property asset was the family home and surrounding lands, which the law sought to have pass generation by generation to the eldest son, always remaining in the blood line. If the family home were even partly community rather than Husband's separate property, half the community share would be owned at Husband's death by the widow, who might remarry and give birth to a child not related to the deceased husband who might in turn inherit a fractional ownership in the "family" estate. For similar policy reasons, and also because of the Civil Law's acceptance of the fixtures doctrine, use of community funds to build structures on or otherwise improve separately owned land did not give the community an interest in the property.

If during marriage, a husband -- it would not be the wife as she could not under Civil Law manage community funds -- took some community cash and some cash separately owned by him and purchased property, it was community because of his status as a member of the marital community at that time. If Husband used his separate funds to build a structure on community land, the preference for unified ownership coupled with fixtures doctrine theory denied the separate estate an interest in the land. The same application of the fixtures doctrine was made in the converse situation where community funds were used to improve separate land.

In none of the situations above did Spanish or Mexican law recognize a presumption of gift. Instead the estate paying a share of the purchase price for, or paying for the structure built on, land owned by the other estate obtained a right to be reimbursed, assertable at the end of the community (which meant, since divorce was virtually unknown, at the death of one of the spouses). The logic of the community of acquets and gains (established in lieu of a universal community) was that the separate estates of both spouses contributed the assets brought to the marriage all potential for growth. If one million realos was the value of the separate estate brought to marriage, when death ended the community one million realos would properly be returned to the separate property owner in specie or via a claim for reimbursement. On this theory if a spouse brought money to the marriage or inherited money during the marriage, assets bought with such funds were community property, with the separate estate obtaining a right of reimbursement.

Nevertheless, and apparently in order to keep the family home within the bloodline (usually of the husband-father), a limited amount of tracing of separate assets was permitted. If land owned before marriage or inherited (or received by gift) during marriage were traded for another property, the newly acquired parcel would also be separate. Some Spanish jurisconsults -- but not all -- expanded this concept of tracing, taking the position that if a separately owned rancho were sold and the proceeds promptly reinvested in another parcel of land, separate identity was not lost if the deed expressed an intent for separate ownership.

At Civil Law all of the rents and profits accrued during marriage from separate property were community. Hence when a spouse's separate estate was entitled to reimbursement for a cash contribution towards the purchase of community property or for having paid for a structure built on community realty, it was logical to return to the separate estate no more than the amount expended. To have reimbursed with interest would have treated the separate estate as making an investment for gain, which was inconsistent with the basic theory of a community regime. When it was the community that was reimbursed, interest was also not granted. Almost always the community had already benefited from its contribution that paid for part of or added an improvement to property separately owned by one of the spouses, either because the land generated community profits or because it was occupied by the community as the family home. It was theoretically possible that community funds were used to pay for unimproved land -- acquired under a pre-marriage contract for purchase -- that was unsuitable for farming or grazing and which was bought on speculation to hold for resale. If the spouse separately owning this parcel was not in the business of buying and selling land, the capital gain on sale would be separate property, and the community would be treated unfairly when it was ultimately reimbursed without interest for the funds it had advanced. Apparently the jurisconsults expounding on problems raised by a community property regime never had heard of such a situation (buying land that could not even be rented out pending resale) or had never thought about it, for none of them discusses the problem of denying interest on the community reimbursement claim in this posture.

The above summary of Civil Law suggests that inflation apparently was not much of a problem in Spain and Mexico. Obviously, however, when land owned before marriage or inherited during it was held for many years and then sold, the sales price could be higher than the value of the land at the time of marriage or the time of succession or gift, due to fluctuation in land values caused by economic factors such as the prices being earned by crops suitably grown on the land, prices for minerals thought to be extractable from the land, etc. Apparently drawing from the notion that a spouse's simply holding on to separately owned land could result in the separate estate's enjoying a "natural" increase -- so that at the end of marriage the value of the separate estate was not, as posited above, always the same as that brought to the marriage -- some jurisconsults took the position that in the case of a physical improvement (such as building a structure) to community land paid for with separate funds, the proper measure of reimbursement was not the amount spent but value added, measured at the date the community ended. These authorities were consistent in stating that, since this approach gave the separate estate a chance to share in the gain resulting from the improvement, that estate also risked sharing in the loss, when the value added was less than the amount spent. Since many such improvements were structures that would deteriorate over time, the chance that reimbursement under this approach would result in a loss probably was greater than the possibility of receiving more than the amount spent.

If use of separate funds to build a structure on community land entitled the separate estate to participate in subsequent gain (or share in any subsequent loss as the value of the improvement fell), the community that contributed its funds to pay for a structure on separate land could likewise share in the gain or loss attributed to that expenditure. That the community, while sharing in such a gain, was at the same time enjoying use of the structure or the profits from renting it out would not have barred the claim to share in any "natural increase," since that kind of capital gain was viewed as something different from a fruit, rent or profit derived from the capital.

One who took the view that the marital estate paying for a structure on land owned by the other estate would participate in gain or loss could readily extend this notion so that the payment of an installment on the contract price by the community after a separate inception of title would create a right to share in natural increase proportionally. However, so far as I am aware, none of the Spanish or Mexican treatises discusses this problem specifically. The concept of buying-in to title was not part of Civil Law.

The preceding points about the Spanish-Mexican law are pertinent to the examination in this Article of the far more complicated responses of California to these mixed-funds problems. The preference for a unified title (i.e., all community or all separate) resulted in simplified management and easier resolution of problems concerning creditors' rights. Because a community-separate cotenancy was never created, one spouse alone was always able to sell or otherwise deal with the property. Likewise there would be no small, fractional interest reachable by the creditor of one spouse who could not levy on the major portion of the title. (Had Spain and Mexico employed California's rule that rents and profits from separate property are also separate, there would have been an additional simplification: the profits derived from a capital asset could never have been a mixture of separate and community property.)

Not only was a "buy-in" to title a complication the Civil Law never dealt with, but problems arising out of a presumption of gift were avoided. Moreover, with one possible exception, the Civil Law equated making a contribution to the purchase price with paying for a physical improvement. In all instances the remedy was reimbursement. No situation was encountered in which it would have been logical to award reimbursement with interest. The only tension was whether to keep the reimbursement remedy simple by always reimbursing just for the amount spent -- either in the form of a purchase-price payment or a contribution for a physical improvement -- or to reimburse based on value added. Many jurisconsults were, in the case of the physical improvement, willing to depart from the simple rule by measuring reimbursement based on value added --

measured at the time of reimbursement, which could be more or less than amount spent. Apparently the rule that rents and profits from separate property were community eliminated a need for the Spanish jurisconsults to deal with offsetting a community reimbursement claim in whole or in part due to use value to the community that had made a payment to acquire separate property or had paid for a structure on separate property. That is, if the property were occupied rather than rented out, the community owed no fair rental value because the occupance had simply cancelled out community rental income rather than depriving the separate estate of a chance to make profit (as would be the case in California).

***

B. Louisiana Approach

In many respects, Louisiana has continued the traditional Spanish approach. Louisiana courts, in the Spanish tradition, have been hesitant to allow mixed title to assets. In most instances, the asset must be classified as either community property or separate property. Cases allowing for a pro-rata apportionment, however, do exist. Two considerations affect the classification of the asset as community or separate: (1) timing of the acquisition; and (2) the source of the funds of the acquisition.

Timing of the Acquisition. The timing of an acquisition is critical because assets acquired before marriage are separate property and assets acquired during marriage are presumptively community property. Where assets are acquired over time, however, the timing of the acquisition can be difficult to discern. Following the Spanish tradition, Louisiana utilizes two distinct doctrines to determine the timing of an acquisition. The first, the inception of title (or time of vesting) doctrine, holds that the status of property is determine at the moment the spouse first acquires an ownership interest in the property. Under this approach, if title to the property passes to the spouse before marriage it is his or her separate property even though some, or all, of the purchase price might be paid during the existence of the community property regime. This approach is typically applied to the classification of immovables. The second approach, the inception of right doctrine, is more commonly applied in the case of movable property. This inception of right doctrine looks to the beginning of the transaction to determine when a spouse first acquired an enforceable right or interest. This approach is evident in a number of the cases previously examined. For example, in *Dué v. Dué*, 342 So.2d 161 (La. 1977), the court held that the wife had an interest in her attorney-husband's contingency fee contracts entered into during marriage even though the contracts would not be complete until some time after the dissolution of the marriage.

If the timing of the acquisition indicates that the asset is community property, then the source of the funds used to acquire the asset determines its classification. Real subrogation principles dictate that property acquired with separate funds is separate property and property acquired with community funds is community property. Where property is acquired with both community and separate funds, however, the situation is more complicated. Louisiana law, in the Spanish tradition, typically requires the asset to be classified as entirely community or entirely separate and relegates the aggrieved spouse to a reimbursement claim. Louisiana Civil Code article 2341, for example, classifies as separate property any "property acquired by a spouse with separate things or with separate and community things when the value of the community things is inconsequential in comparison with the value of the separate things used." Louisiana Civil Code article 2338 similarly provides that community property includes "property acquired with community things or with community and separate things, unless classified as separate property under Article 2341." If property that acquired with a mix of community and separate funds is classified as one spouse's separate property pursuant to Article 2341, then Article 2366 provides that the other spouse is "entitled to reimbursement for one-half of the amount or value that the community had at the time it was used." Similarly, if property that is acquired with a mix of separate and community property is classified as community property pursuant to Article 2338, then Article 2367 provides that the spouse who contributed his or her separate property "is entitled to reimbursement for one-half of the amount or value that the property had at the time it was used."

When an asset is acquired during marriage with a mix of community and separate funds, classification of the asset as community or separate hinges on whether the value of the community contribution is inconsequential in comparison to the value of the separate contribution. The Louisiana Civil Code is silent with respect to how we should determine whether a contribution is consequential or inconsequential. This decision has been left open to the courts and is considered in the following cases. The cases also consider the issue of commingling and tracing—important evidentiary issues in many of these cases.

C. *Lottie Newcomb Lambert v. Vernon E. Lambert*

480 So. 2d 784 (La. App. 3d Cir. 1985)

YELVERTON, Judge

Vernon next contests the finding that the computer camera was community property. The $9,000 camera was purchased with $6,000 from Lottie Lambert's separate estate and $3,000 from the community. Property acquired with separate and community things is separate property when the value of the community thing used is inconsequential as compared to the value of the separate things used. C.C. art. 2341. We do not believe that $3,000 is inconsequential when compared to $6,000; therefore, the camera is not the separate property of Mrs. Lambert. It was correctly found to be a community asset. C.C. art. 2338

D. Note

In *Reeves v. Reeves*, 607 So.2d 626 (La. App. 2d Cir. 1992), *writ denied*, 608 So.2d 1010, the husband, to partition inherited property, used $7,030 in community funds to pay the "boot" and thereby obtained an interest in a plantation, an interest apparently worth $38,340. That valuation was based on testimony that "solely for the purposes of the partition among family members, the value assigned to the property by appellee and his mother was $50.58 per acre." The lower court found that this community contribution of 18% of the total value was inconsequential and classified the property as the husband's separate property. With little discussion, the court of appeal affirmed the lower court determination.

E. *Brian Keith Gautreau v. Elizabeth S. Gautreau*

697 So. 2d 1339 (La. App. 3d Cir. 1997)

WOODARD, Judge.

Defendant in a divorce action including community property and child custody issues appeals the determinations of the trial court granting plaintiff sole custody of the minor children and various community property rulings. We affirm in part, reverse in part and remand.

FACTS

Brian K. Gautreau and Elizabeth Gautreau were married on February 13, 1982, and made their matrimonial domicile in Lafayette Parish, Louisiana. Three children were born of the marriage: Shannon Nicole Gautreau on March 26, 1985; Shelly Renee Gautreau on April 19, 1986; and Mary Elizabeth Gautreau on February 23, 1990. The parties physically separated, and Mr. Gautreau filed for divorce on May 27, 1993. This case concerns the community property determinations of the trial court as well as custody of the Gautreau's minor children.

***

208 RUTHWOOD DRIVE PROPERTY

In her eighth assignment, Ms. Gautreau asserts that the trial court erred in holding that the property and domicile located at 208 Ruthwood Drive, Lafayette, Louisiana, was community property. Ruthwood was purchased with funds derived from the sale of

407 Courtney, thus, we must analyze the makeup of the Courtney property to address this assignment.

On August 10, 1989, Ms. Gautreau purchased the property at 407 Courtney for $8,000.00, by a cash sale and in her name. Mr. Gautreau acknowledged that it was being purchased by her as her separate property.

Generally, property is classified as either community or separate. As the supreme court stated in *Curtis v. Curtis*, 403 So.2d 56, 57–59 (La.1981):

> While other community property states may categorize property paid for in part with separate funds and in part with community funds as mixed, Louisiana does not do so. Under our law property is characterized as either community or separate. The Civil Code articles applicable to this case (as they existed before revision by La. Acts 1978, No. 627 and La. Acts 1979, No. 317) created a strong presumption that all property acquired during the existence of a marriage fell into the community of acquets and gains. C.C. 2402.
>
> However, this presumption was rebuttable. A married person could acquire separate property during marriage by inheritance, by donation, or by acquisition with separate funds. C.C. 2334. The jurisprudence established that the burden of overcoming the presumption in favor of the community rested on the party asserting the separate nature of the property. The husband who took title in his name was required to declare in the act of sale that he was purchasing with his separate funds for his separate estate; if he failed to make such a declaration, title was presumed to be in the community, and he was barred from presenting evidence to rebut the presumption.

....

> This court has held on several occasions that a husband who declares in a deed that his wife is buying property for her separate estate with her separate funds cannot later dispute the separate nature of the property, even if it was bought on credit. These cases, among others, also establish that property declared to be separate at acquisition does not change character if a subsequent credit payment is made with community funds. Proof that the community contributed to the purchase of separate property would only create a debt on the part of the wife's separate estate to the community for the amount of community funds used. It would not convert the property or any portion of it to community property. Only when community and separate funds are mingled in the initial acquisition may the property be regarded as community. We have stated in cases involving bank accounts that the mere mixing of separate funds and community funds in the same account does not of itself convert an entire account into community property; only when separate funds are commingled with

> community funds indiscriminately so that the separate funds cannot be identified or differentiated from the community funds are all the funds characterized as community funds.

(Citations and footnote omitted). Footnote four in *Curtis* recognized that under La.Civ.Code arts. 2338 and 2341, that "property purchased with both separate and community funds would appear to be community property, unless the amount of community funds used is inconsequential in comparison with the amount of separate funds used." *Id.* at 59 n. 4.

La.Civ.Code art. 2341 defines separate property and provides that:

> The separate property of a spouse is his exclusively. It comprises: property acquired by a spouse prior to the establishment of a community property regime; property acquired by a spouse with separate things or with separate and community things when the value of the community things is inconsequential in comparison with the value of the separate things used; property acquired by a spouse by inheritance or donation to him individually; damages awarded to a spouse in an action for breach of contract against the other spouse or for the loss sustained as a result of fraud or bad faith in the management of community property by the other spouse; damages or other indemnity awarded to a spouse in connection with the management of his separate property; and things acquired by a spouse as a result of a voluntary partition of the community during the existence of a community property regime.

Both parties acknowledged that the property at 407 Courtney was purchased with Ms. Gautreau's separate funds. Thus, on August 10, 1989, it was her separate property. Furthermore, due to his acknowledgment that the property was purchased with Ms. Gautreau's separate funds, Mr. Gautreau is estopped from asserting that, on August 10, 1989, 407 Courtney was not Ms. Gautreau's separate property.

The testimony established that, subsequent to August 10, 1989, the property rose in value due to substantial improvements made by the Gautreaus and others. La.Civ.Code. art. 2368 states that:

> If the separate property of a spouse has increased in value as a result of the uncompensated common labor or industry of the spouses, the other spouse is entitled to be reimbursed from the spouse whose property has increased in value one-half of the increase attributed to the common labor.

Thus, based on Article 2368, had the community terminated while Ms. Gautreau still owned 407 Courtney, Mr. Gautreau would be entitled, upon termination, to reimbursement for one-half of the increase in value attributable to the common labor.

However, the community did not terminate during the time period that Ms. Gautreau owned 407 Courtney. On October 16, 1990, it was sold for $37,000.00. The proceeds of the sale, after expenses, totaled $33,314.69 and were deposited into a joint checking account the Gautreaus had at Shearson/Lehman.

As the supreme court stated in *Curtis*, separate property does not change classification based solely on commingling with community property. In *Succession of Davis*, 496 So.2d 549, 552, (La.App. 1 Cir.1986), the court held that:

> Comment (c) to this provision [art. 2341] states that the principle of real subrogation is applicable to both separate and community property. Thus, when a thing forming part of the separate property of a spouse is converted into another thing, the mass of the separate property is not diminished. The new thing takes the place of the old: "*Subrogatum capit naturam subrogati.*"

(Citations omitted). Thus, property is properly regarded as community "only when the community and separate funds are mingled in the initial acquisition," or "when separate funds are commingled with community funds indiscriminately so that the separate funds cannot be identified or differentiated from the community funds." *Curtis*, 403 So.2d at 59. Therefore, when 407 Courtney was sold, and Ms. Gautreau combined her separate funds from the sale with the couple's community funds from their common labor into their joint Shearson/Lehman account, each retained its prior classification as either separate or community.

On April 24, 1991, Ms. Gautreau transferred the $29,098.49 from the joint Shearson/Lehman account to her separate account. As cited earlier, La.Civ.Code art. 2341 states that, among other things, separate property comprises "property acquired by a spouse with separate things or with separate and community things when the value of the community things is inconsequential in comparison with the value of the separate things used." (Emphasis added). Further, comment (b) states that "the value of the community things at the time of acquisition should be used for determining whether it is "inconsequential" in comparison with the value of the separate things used." For example, this court, in *Lambert v. Lambert*, 480 So.2d 784, (La.App. 3 Cir.1985), found that $3,000.00 of community funds used to purchase a digital camera was not inconsequential when compared to the $6,000.00 in separate funds used. As such, the camera was properly classified as community property.

On April 24, 1991, the commingled funds, derived from the sale of 407 Courtney and transferred to Ms. Gautreau's separate account, were withdrawn and used to purchase the "Ruthwood lot." The Ruthwood lot was purchased in the names of Mr. & Ms. Gautreau and no declaration of paraphernality was contained in the act of sale. The trial court correctly held that the funds used to purchase the Ruthwood lot were commingled separate and community funds; again, based on the principle that separate property, under La.Civ.Code art. 2341, comprises "property acquired by a spouse ... with separate and community things when the value of the community things is inconsequential in comparison with the value of the separate things used." The trial court found that, after expenses, when the separate and community funds realized from the sale of 407 Courtney were used to purchase the Ruthwood lot, 77% of the funds used were community funds. Based on Lambert, this is not an "inconsequential" amount. Therefore, the trial court did not err, and this assignment is without merit.

PROPERTY AT 406 COURTNEY DRIVE

In her ninth assignment, Ms. Gautreau asserts that the trial court erred in classifying the property and home located at 406 Courtney Drive, Duson, Louisiana as community property. Specifically, she argues that her mother, Gwen Spillers, provided $10,000.00 dollars of the down payment on the property, and, as such, those funds were her separate property since they comprised a donation to her. Ms. Spillers testified that the $10,000.00 was a loan and, if it were a gift, that it was a gift to Ms. Gautreau alone, and not to Mr. Gautreau. However, Mr. Gautreau testified that the money was a gift to him and Ms. Gautreau, because Ms. Spillers could give that exact amount away, $10,000.00, tax free.

In domestic relations cases, a trial judge's determinations of fact are entitled to great weight on appeal and will not be disturbed unless manifest error is shown. *Morris v. Morris*, 336 So.2d 254 (La.App. 1 Cir.1976). Where there is conflict in testimony, reasonable evaluations of credibility and reasonable inferences of fact should not be disturbed upon review. *Canter v. Koehring Company*, 283 So.2d 716 (La.1973). After reviewing the record, we find no manifest error in the trial court's determination. While the testimony was conflicting, Mr. Gautreau's testimony was not unbelievable, and the court had ample reason to find that the money was a gift to him and his wife.

Because we find no error in the trial court's finding of fact on this matter, we need only apply the same reasoning used in assignment of error number eight. As a gift to him and his wife, the $10,000.00 is classified as community property, and things acquired with both community and separate funds are community unless the value of the community thing used is inconsequential when compared with the value of the separate thing. The trial court determined that the initial down payment on the house was made with 63% separate funds, and 37% community funds. We agree with the trial court that 37% of the funds used is not an inconsequential amount. Therefore, we find that the trial court did not err in determining that 406 Courtney was community property.

OWNERSHIP OF PICKUP TRUCK

In her tenth assignment, Ms. Gautreau asserts that the trial court erred in classifying the 1990 red Chevrolet pickup truck as community property. Specifically, she asserts that the $3,000.00 down payment, as well as several other payments on the vehicle came from her separate checking account. The trial court held, and the evidence showed, that: (1) both party's names appeared on the title to the vehicle, (2) all of the payments on the truck, except three, were made with community funds, and (3) that the separate account, from which Ms. Gautreau claims payments were made, actually contained the income she received from Strataform, Inc., rendering these sums community funds due to commingling.

While the down payment on the pickup truck was arguably made with separate funds, both Mr. and Ms. Gautreau's names appear on the title, the truck was used for the benefit of the community, and no decree of paraphernality was introduced. The trial court also noted that Ms. Gautreau listed the truck as community property.

The trial court held that the truck was acquired with both community and separate funds since the payments after the down payment were made with community funds. Accordingly, it held that the truck was a community asset acquired with both separate and community funds. The trial court then applied the Lambert analysis and La.Civ.Code art. 2338 in holding that the community funds used to acquire the vehicle were not inconsequential in relation to the separate funds used. Therefore, it properly concluded that the truck was a community asset.

While the court correctly determined the truck to be a community asset, Ms. Gautreau's separate money was used as the down payment. La.Civ.Code art. 2365 states, in pertinent part:

> If separate property of a spouse has been used to satisfy a community obligation, that spouse, upon termination of the community property regime, is entitled to reimbursement for one-half of the amount or value that the property had at the time it was used.

The trial court properly applied this article and ordered Ms. Gautreau to be reimbursed for payments made by her on the truck.

Based on the analysis of assignment of error number eight, we find no merit in this assignment and affirm the judgment of the trial court.

***

F. *Mary Ann Nini McMorris v. Tommie Edward McmMorris, Sr.*

654 So. 2d 742 (La. App. 1st Cir. 1995)

REDMANN, Judge Pro Tem.

***

Damages from pre-marital personal injury.

A cause of action for damages due to personal injuries sustained prior to marriage is "property acquired by a spouse prior to the establishment of a community property regime," C.C. art. 2341, and therefore is separate property. It is not converted into community when settled by payment during marriage (not even in part, as by prorating for future lost earnings). *Broussard v. Broussard*, 340 So.2d 1309 (La.1976); *Young v. Young*, 549 So.2d 437 (La.App. 3d Cir.1989).

The ex-husband also argues that the checks having been payable to both spouses shows that part of the settlement was for his loss of consortium (his automobile damage was separately paid). But the ex-husband had no right of action for loss of consortium. Although he then lived with the victim and thus may have suffered a loss of consortium, he was her fiancé and not her husband at the time of the injury. C.C. art. 2315 allows consortium-loss damages only to "persons who would have had a cause of action for wrongful death of an injured person," and C.C. art. 2315.2 limits wrongful death actions to sue on that cause of action exclusively to spouse and children, then parents, and then siblings. *Leckelt v. Eunice Superette, Inc.*, 555 So.2d 11 (La.App. 3d Cir.1989), writ denied 559 So.2d 141 (La.1990).

Contract payments during community for pre-marital disability

The ex-wife's monthly payments for her pre-marital disability became due before her marriage, under the terms of her pre-marital employment contract. Her right to those contractual payments was property, and was acquired by her when she became disabled by injury before her marriage, and was therefore her separate property (like her right to the tort damages). C.C. art. 2341.

The ex-husband contends that, on similar facts, *Johnson v. Johnson*, 532 So.2d 503 (La.App. 1st Cir.1988) (cited by the trial judge), concluded that disability benefits were community. We do not agree that the facts are similar, except that in both cases the disability benefits came from employment. The distinction is that the employment and all disability entitlements came after the marriage in Johnson, while here they came before the marriage.

Thus Mrs. McMorris's $39,684.93 total of monthly disability payments, as well as her $55,000 settlement (and by stipulation her $1,184.82 vacation pay), were her separate property.

A large part of the $55,000 is traceable, but the funds were not segregated, and the doctrine of commingling, as affected by the 1979 revision of the marital regimes law, is therefore addressed.

Commingling

Under the 1979 marital regimes law, with the husband no longer the exclusive manager of the community, there is little reason for differing treatments of the two spouses' separate funds.

C.C. art. 2341 makes separate (among other things) any property acquired before marriage, or "acquired by a spouse with separate things or with separate and community things when the value of the community things is inconsequential in comparison with the value of the separate things used." Perhaps most important to accounting at dissolution, art. 2367 provides that separate property "used for the acquisition, use, improvement, or benefit of community property" is reimbursable as to half by the other spouse, although only to the extent of the other's half of the community net of community debts.

Katherine S. Spaht and W. Lee Hargrave, Matrimonial Regimes (16 La. Civil Law Treatise), s 3.40, at 117-18 (1989) (hereafter, Spaht and Hargrave), analyze commingling, and its possible loss of effect on net result, under today's law: A necessary implication of the text of Civil Code Article 2341 is that only a new thing acquired with other property or funds becomes community. Combinations of separate and community fungible items do not produce a new thing. [Citing La. Civ.Code arts. 507-516; Aubry & Rau, Droit Civil Francais, Vol. II (7th ed. updated) in J. Mayda, 2 Civil Law Translations 265- 266 (1966).] In such a case, the mixture may be presumed community, but if proof is made of the separate contribution, the separate estate of one spouse will remain owner of those things. [Citing *Succession of Sonnier*, 208 So.2d 562 (La.App. 3d Cir.1968), *inter alia.*] .... It is arguable that separate and community funds put into one bank account do not produce a new thing; money is the ultimate fungible item. In such an analysis, the funds in the account are presumed community, but if it can be proved that separate funds were deposited and not withdrawn, those funds would remain separate. On the other hand, it might be argued that a new thing, an account, is produced and is all community. Even so, if it can be proved that separate funds were contributed, the separate estate of that spouse is entitled to reimbursement for the use of those separate funds. [C.C. art. 2367.] The sum involved would be the same under either analysis. Under the first analysis, the spouse whose separate funds were deposited still owns them. In the second case, that spouse has a personal claim against the other

[sic] for that amount. In most cases, this would make no difference between the parties....

Since the 1979 enactment of art. 2341, mixing of funds in the same account need not extinguish the separate character of either the husband's or the wife's separate funds; only indiscriminate commingling, so that one cannot identify or differentiate among the funds, results in the account being deemed community. *Curtis v. Curtis*, 403 So.2d 56 (La.1981). See also *Kyson v. Kyson*, 596 So.2d 1308 (La.App. 2d Cir.1991), *writ denied* 599 So.2d 314 (1992), holding commingling did not convert separate funds into community.

Moreover, when a joint account is deemed community because of indiscriminate commingling, it is not inescapable that a spouse loses entitlement to recoup the value of funds invested into community assets or payment of community debts. See *Young v. Young*, 549 So.2d at 441, n. 8.

Tracing the separate funds

It seems reasonable that under art. 2341, and as pointed out by *Curtis v. Curtis* and by Spaht and Hargrave, separate and community funds could remain identifiable as such if left untouched in the same account; and, if the trial judge deems all the evidence properly supportive of such an inference, he might reasonably infer and conclude that the remaining balance in the joint account represents, in whole or part, a remainder of the ex-wife's monthly deposits of separate disability payments. Ultimately, this is a question for the careful analysis and disposition of the trial judge. Thus, where art. 2340's presumption of community is arguably questioned by the showing of a large initial deposit and then significant monthly deposits of the ex-wife's separate funds, there is room for the trial judge by careful analysis and application of the Code articles to reach appropriate fact-dependent results, notwithstanding numerous withdrawals and deposits over the course of the brief marriage.

Tracing: some notes on debts

The trial judge was also clearly wrong in not recognizing the ex-wife's separate property contributions to the acquisition of the community home. She contributed a motor home (the separateness of which seems to be undisputed, bought for $4,000 at the time she received the $55,000 settlement), which was accepted as worth $6,500 towards the price of the home (increasing the community's value by that amount, and the ex-husband's half by half that amount, for which she is entitled to reimbursement from him under C.C. art. 2367). Additionally, her funds provided the bulk, and the community an "inconsequential" part, C.C. art. 2341, if any, of the two $13,250 certificates of deposit cashed for $28,546.58, of which $20,470 was the "down payment" on the community home purchase. The certificates were bought four months after she expended the $35,861.30 just noted, out of her $55,000 settlement, leaving $19,138.70. She had previously deposited her $1,184.82 vacation pay plus the payoff of her pension plan (when she resigned from the employment she was disabled to continue). From July 1988 to January 1989 (the certificates were bought in December 1988), she deposited $7,018.77 of disability payments. Her funds were adequate to have provided the bulk if not all of the certificates' $26,500 cost as she testified. She was not disbelieved by the trier of fact, whose error was one of law only. She is entitled to recover half of the total of $26,970 from the ex-husband under art. 2367 (and will recoup the other half by the presumed increase in value of the community).

The ex-wife is not entitled to have this court, by specifying an amount, convert the trial court's empty judgment into an effective, executable judgment.

On the other hand, the ex-husband may not be entitled to recover from the ex- wife a full half of the $1,882.90 insurance, $11,664.41 maintenance costs, and $346.84 taxes on that home. C.C. art. 806 gives, to a co-owner who incurs necessary expenses, maintenance and repairs, reimbursement from the other co- owners in proportion to their shares. Art. 806 adds, however, that if the co- owner "had the enjoyment of the thing held in indivision, his reimbursement shall be reduced in proportion to the value of the enjoyment." This, too, is a question for the trial judge.

***

G. *Angelo John Longo v. Ruth Damont Longo*

474 So. 2d 500 (La. App. 4 Cir. 1985)

WILLIAMS, Judge.

Angelo John Longo and Ruth Damonte Longo were divorced on May 11, 1983. After the divorce the parties were unable to amicably settle their claims regarding certain property, and Mrs. Longo filed a partition suit to remedy the matter. The case was heard, and the trial court rendered judgment on June 28, 1984, determining the status of certain property in question as well as determining an amount due as repayment for community funds expended on Angelo Longo's separate property. Ruth Longo appealed the judgment of the trial court and Angelo Longo answered the appeal. We have reviewed the record and affirm the judgment of the trial court as modified.

Angelo and Ruth Longo began their relationship in open concubinage. In 1964, they moved into a house at 4911 Warren Drive, New Orleans, which was owned by Mr. Longo's brother. At the time of their cohabitation, Angelo Longo was married to another woman.

On December 31, 1965, following a divorce from his first wife, Mr. Longo bought the house on Warren Drive by assuming a mortgage balance of approximately $15,000.00 and relinquishing his interest in a restaurant-grill business which the two brothers operated. The share in the grill was valued at $3,000.00. On December 7, 1971, the Longos were married. The couple physically separated in March of 1980. Neither party filed for a legal separation. On January 10, 1983, a petition for divorce was filed and a judgment granting divorce was rendered and signed on May 11, 1983.

During the period of concubinage and following the marriage, the Longos participated in various business ventures. From the time they began living together they pooled their money and paid their living expenses. Testimony at trial indicated that the mortgage payments on the Warren Drive home were made out of these pooled funds. Additionally, after the physical separation but prior to the petition for divorce, certain repairs and renovations were made to the house by order of Ruth Longo.

The house on Warren Drive was acquired by Mr. Longo while he was unmarried and is, therefore, his separate property.

H. Questions

1. Prior to marriage H enters into a bond for deed contract to acquire immovable property pursuant to La. Rev. Stat. §9:2941 which provides "*A bond for deed is a contract to sell real property, in which the purchase price is to be paid by the buyer to the seller in installments and in which the seller after payment of a stipulated sum agrees to deliver title to the buyer.*" H makes many of the scheduled payments before marriage but some of them are made after marriage. The title is delivered during marriage. Is the property community or separate? Why? *See Kendall v. Kendall*, 140 So. 6 (La. 1932); *Cosey v. Cosey*, 376 So. 2d 486 (La. 1979).

2. Assume the same facts as (1), except that H enters the bond for deed contract during marriage, but title is not delivered until after marriage. Is the property community or separate? Why?

3. Prior to marriage, H strikes a deal with his brother to buy his brother's car whereby H will make monthly payments to his brother for the car and once the full price is paid brother will deliver the title to the car to H. Some payments are made before H marries W, some after. Title is delivered during marriage. Assume the contract is to be governed by the law of a common law state where such a contract would be valid. Is the car community or separate? Why? *See Succession of Dunham*, 408 So. 2d 888 (La. 1981)

4. H and his brother possess immovable property for 10 years. H then gets married to W and continues his possession of the property for another 20 years. Brother also continues possessing his possession of the property for another 20 years. At the completion of that 20 years, H and his brother have acquired ownership of the property by 30 year acquisitive prescription. They are each co-owners of an undivided ½ interest in the property. Is H's interest community or separate? *See e.g. Crouch v. Richardson*, 158 La. 822 (1925).

5. Assume the same facts as (4). After the brothers successfully acquire ownership of the property by acquisitive prescription, H's brother dies leaving his interest in the property to H. Describe the ownership of the entirety of the property.

4.9 ACQUISITION OF UNDIVIDED INTERESTS IN PROPERTY

Louisiana Civil Code article 2341.1 specifically allows spouses to have mixed title to an asset in limited circumstances:

Art. 2341.1. Acquisition of undivided interests; separate and community property

A. A spouse's undivided interest in property otherwise classified as separate property under Article 2341 remains his separate property regardless of the acquisition of other undivided interests in the property during the existence of the legal regime, the source of improvements thereto, or by whom the property was managed, used, or enjoyed.

B. In property in which an undivided interest is held as community property and an undivided interest is held as separate property, each spouse owns a present undivided one-half interest in that portion of the undivided interest which is community and a spouse owns a present undivided interest in that portion of the undivided interest which is separate.

Act 329 of 1991, which added Article 2341.1 to the Civil Code, was adopted to change the outcome of cases like *Martinez v. Martinez*, 556 So.2d 668 (La. App. 4th Cir. 1990), but the statute also has a broader impact. It imposes heretofore disfavored "split titles" to immovable property in which an undivided part of the thing is classified as separate property and the remaining part is community.

In *Martinez*, the husband inherited a 1/3 interest in his parents' home and later purchased the 2/3 interest of his siblings for $60,000, using community funds. The lower court determined that the house was 1/3 separate and 2/3 community, allocated it to the husband, and then ordered him to reimburse the wife for community funds expended on the house. Under the authority of Curtis v. Curtis, the fourth circuit court of appeal held that such pro rata division of immovables between the community and separate estate was not authorized. It concluded that the house was acquired in part with separate property (the 1/3 inherited interest) and in part with community property ($60,000 in community funds). Under Civil Code Articles 2338 and 2341, the house was thus a community asset because the contribution of community funds was not inconsequential.

More significantly, the court of appeal used the discretion granted by La. R.S. 9:2801 to allocate this community asset to the wife. The family home of the husband thus became the separate property of the former wife. The court supported its conclusion with testimony by the husband that the wife "butchered" the house with her redecoration and that she had "destroyed what he remembered as his family home." Critics of the result suggested: "In the more usual case, however, one would expect that a court would allocate a family home to the spouse from whose family it descends in light of the reference in 9:2801(c) that the court ... "shall consider the nature and source of the asset" in making the allocation.

Legislation to overturn the *Martinez* result could have simply strengthened that quoted language in 9:2801 to make the court allocate the house to the husband in such a case. Act 329, however, goes beyond that. It establishes a split title to the property and requires a pro rata classification of the asset as part separate and part community.

The amendments to the Civil Code, however, change the direction of the policy trend. To the extent the text of Art. 2335 supported a prohibition against mixed titles (Property of married persons is either community or separate.), Act 329 revises the article to indicate the rule applies "except as provided in Article 2341.1"; the latter provision then goes on to adopt a split title theory. The requirement of split titles in some instances will no doubt support courts finding that such pro rata division of assets will be proper in other contexts.

Louisiana Civil Code Art. 2341.1 states that a spouse's "undivided interest in property otherwise classified as separate" remains such "regardless of the acquisition of other undivided interests in the property" during the legal regime. In a *Martinez* situation, the husband's inherited interest would remain his separate property. The other 2/3 interest bought from the siblings during the community with community funds would be community property.

On Partition

The unique provisions of La. R.S. 9:2801 govern partitions of community property. The husband's separate 1/3 ownership of the house, in a *Martinez* situation, would not be part of the 9:2801 partition at all. The judge could allocate the community asset (the 2/3 interest) to the husband, to the wife, or divide it between them. The judge could not affect the separate property, however. If a partition by licitation were the solution, the judge in the 9:2801 proceeding could order sale of only the 2/3 community interest. Of course, in the normal situation, the judge should allocate the community 2/3 to the spouse owning the separate 1/3 interest and offset that award with other community assets to the other spouse. At least that is the preferable solution if there are sufficient other assets. In a Martinez situation, the family home would thus remain in the husband's family, with his having to provide other community assets to provide an equal division of the value.

Other Effects

Classification of assets as partly separate and partly community produces other effects that may be a trap for the unwary.

If the husband died intestate with children in a *Martinez* case, his 1/3 interest would devolve as separate property, to be inherited by his children in full ownership. His 1/3 interest in the house that was part of the community would devolve as community property. The children's 1/3 interest would be automatically subject to the legal usufruct of the surviving spouse. In addition, the wife would come into full ownership of the remaining 1/3 interest that was part of the community. In such a case, Civil Code Art. 543 does not preclude a partition of the property free of usufruct; the children could cause a sale of the home. This result is contrary to the usual policy, with respect to community property, of keeping the family home available to the surviving spouse until death or remarriage.

Under Civil Code 2345, creditors of the wife could reach 2/3 of the property, but not the 1/3 that was the husband's separate property. Creditors of the husband could reach all of the property.

If the thing involved is an immovable, the husband could not sell the community 2/3 interest without the wife's consent. But, nothing prohibits him from selling his 1/3 undivided separate interest to a third person.

Breadth of the Provision?

Though the article was adopted in response to *Martinez*, it is not limited to immovables or to family homes. It covers any property. It is not limited to inherited property, but covers "any undivided interest in property otherwise classified as separate property under Article 2341."

The text indicates that the separate undivided interest "remains his separate property" regardless of the acquisition of other undivided interests. A time relationship is suggested by this language. If an undivided part is separate, it remains so, even though at a later time, a community undivided part is acquired. On the other hand, if the separate and community funds are used contemporaneously, the usual rule of commingling would apply. In such a case, the literal text of 2338 and 2341 applies and the asset is community so long as the community funds were not inconsequential.

But what if the community undivided interest is bought first, and then separate funds of a spouse are used to acquire the remaining undivided interest. Art. 2341.1 by its terms would not seem to apply. In terms of existing doctrine, one could argue this would be the use of separate funds to improve or acquire a community asset, and the husband would be relegated to a monetary claim for reimbursement. Or, as in Martinez, one could argue the asset was obtained with both separate and community funds at different times, resulting in classification of the whole thing as community. However, policy reasons to support different results based on whether the separate or the community interest were acquired first seem difficult to fathom. Perhaps such concerns could be further impetus to classify the thing acquired to be pro rata owned as separate property of one spouse in part and a community asset of both for the remaining part.

4.10 ASSETS ACQUIRED OVER TIME: LIFE & DISABILITY INSURANCE

A. Introduction

In Louisiana, separate rules apply to the classification of a life insurance policy and the classification of the proceeds of the policy. Classification of the policy generally follows the rules governing classification of community and separate property. A policy acquired before marriage or during marriage, but with separate funds, is a spouse's separate property. A policy acquired during marriage with community funds or as an employee benefit is community property. The proceeds, however, are treated *sui generis*, as is more fully explained below.

B. LOUISIANA CIVIL LAW TREATISE: MATRIMONIAL REGIMES

Andrea Carroll, Richard D. Moreno

§3.36. Life Insurance

Louisiana courts have historically treated life insurance as a unique contract governed by its own rules rather than by the Civil Code rules on donations. Subsequent statutes have confirmed that basic policy decision. As a result, policy proceeds paid upon the insured's death go to the beneficiary of the policy without regard to community property concerns. Thus, because the primary benefit of the policy is the proceeds payable upon insured's death which are paid to the beneficiary outside the rules of community property, it often occurs that such contracts are not important community assets. This is particularly true in case of a term life insurance policy which has no cash value, except where the insured spouse has become uninsurable. As discussed below, in that latter case, even a term policy may be a significant consideration in a community property partition.

Although the adoption of a unique scheme for life insurance proceeds might be seen as harmful to the community property system, the scheme also frees the proceeds from the claims of forced heirs and, thus, can benefit a surviving spouse beneficiary. Life insurance is often purchased to benefit a surviving spouse as beneficiary, who obtains the liquid proceeds as full owner not subject to the claims of the forced heirs.

Nothing in the Civil Code prohibits a spouse in community from entering into a life insurance contract without the consent of the other. Payment of premiums is an alienation of corporeal movables, which one spouse acting alone may do under the authority of Civil Code Article 2346.5 Under the rules of privity of contract, during the regime, the contracting spouse is the sole manager of the contractual rights that are provided under the policy. If a spouse uses community funds to pay for life insurance payable to a person other than the spouse, there may be a limited basis for a claim against that spouse's succession for fraud or bad faith in the management of community assets. Such a claim, however, would not reach the insurance proceeds in the hands of the beneficiary.

Community property law issues more often concern the economic benefits available under the policy before the death of the insured, including loan value, cash surrender value, changes of beneficiary and transfer of ownership of the policy. As life insurance also becomes a more common investment medium, with variable life benefits and combination life insurance and annuity plans, these issues become more complex. Here, the rights which attach to ownership of a policy can be classified as separate or community, and the value of those rights become important in the case of termination of the community by divorce.

In the absence of special rules for life insurance policies, the jurisprudence applied the general rules, classifying the policy contract upon its acquisition. If acquired before marriage, the policy is separate property and if acquired during the existence of a community regime with community funds, it is community. Even if most of the funds used to pay the premiums on a separate policy are community, the policy itself remains a separate asset.

However, though it has not been raised in the cases, on general principles it would seem that a policy acquired during the existence of the community with separate funds should be classified as separate. To meet the requirements of Civil Code Article 2338, the thing must not only be acquired during the community, but must be acquired with community funds. But even if the policy itself is community, the principle of privity intervenes and provides that the contracting spouse is the sole manager of the policy rights during the community. Absent an assignment of such rights, or an injunction, that spouse alone can surrender the policy or change the beneficiary or exercise whatever other rights are attached to policy ownership.

The fact that a spouse is the insured or the beneficiary is irrelevant to the question of ownership of the policy, and if the policy is owned by someone else, it is not an asset of either spouse and does not form a part of the community between them. In *Doland v. Doland*, the court concluded that the husband's father contracted for the policy, paid the premiums and was, thus, the owner of the policy. The policy was not an asset to be divided at divorce even though the husband was the insured and the wife was the beneficiary. The court also found the father had not intended to donate the policy to the couple.

By application of the doctrine of real subrogation, if the beneficiary of a separate property policy is the estate of the insured, the proceeds become separate property of the deceased, and if a community policy is payable to one's estate, the proceeds are treated as community property subject to being divided with the surviving spouse.

Upon termination of a community by divorce, a community property insurance policy is a co-owned asset subject to partition by the co-owners. Because of the privity principle, the policy should be allocated to the owner of the policy with the other spouse obtaining property of an equal value. Perhaps the ex-spouses could be required to remain as co-owners in some cases, but that solution has potential for misuse since only the contracting spouse would be able to manage the policy.

In a typical whole life policy, the value would normally be the cash surrender value at the time of the partition. In a typical term life insurance policy, there is no cash surrender value and no loan value, so arguably there is nothing to divide. However, the cases have not yet faced the question that arises when there may be value other than cash surrender value. If a term policy is guaranteed renewable, and the insured is no longer insurable because of disease or age, that existing policy may be quite valuable. Though the market value of such may be difficult to determine, it still is a situation where one spouse will have an asset that undoubtedly has some value, and some effort to estimate that value would have to be made.

If community funds are used to pay the premiums for a separate policy and a divorce occurs, the non-owner spouse would have a reimbursement claim against the owner spouse. Under pre-1980 law, the measure of reimbursement was half the community funds so used, up to the increased value of the separate asset attributable to those funds. This has traditionally been half of the increase in the cash surrender value of the policy during the marriage as expressed in *Connell v. Connell*. It also follows that if there is no increase in the cash surrender value (or other value), no reimbursement is due. That changed in 1980.

The 1980 Revision complicated the problem of the amount of reimbursement. Article 2366 provides reimbursement for community property used for the "acquisition, use, improvement, or benefit of the separate property of a spouse" and provides that the level of reimbursement is "one-half the amount or value that the community property had at the time it was used." Reimbursement is no longer limited to the increase in value of the separate asset. Reimbursement is due if the community property was used as Article 2366 specifies. It is arguable that even if the community funds were used merely to continue a separate term policy, reimbursement is due. In a typical case, a husband acquires the policy before marriage, pays most of the premiums with community funds, and designates his wife as beneficiary of the policy. At termination upon death, under this view, his separate estate still owes her one-half the community funds paid as premiums even though she obtains the proceeds of the policy.

The basic question is whether use of community funds to pay premiums on an existing separate policy is "for the acquisition, use, improvement, or benefit of the separate property of a spouse." It would seem that acquisition had already occurred and does not apply. It would seem that the separate property does not "use" the community funds. "Improvement" is a term more often confined to buildings on land. "Benefit" may fit here, however. Payments keep the policy in force, and, thus, benefit the separate estate which has control over the policy and determines who will get the proceeds. However, it is the "separate property" that must be benefited to invoke the reimbursement; benefiting the "separate estate" may not be enough. It would seem that this word choice means that something more than an abstract overall benefit to the separate patrimony is needed; benefit to an asset called "property" is required.

Nevertheless, the funds which keep the policy in force may also "benefit" that separate asset. But, if the insured is one spouse and the other spouse is the beneficiary, the funds would seem to be spent in the interest of the spouses or in the interest of the other spouse. No doubt, this is use of community funds to benefit the community, also.

It may well be that this analysis, though convoluted, will produce the same result as under the old law. To the extent the community funds add to the cash value of a whole life policy, there has been a "benefit" to the separate property which should be compensated. That "benefit" is the increase in the cash value. To the extent that the funds buy protection, it is the use of community funds to benefit the community, so there is no compensation for the use of that part of the premiums paid.

In *White v. Broussard*, the third circuit departed from the Connell view and reasoned that the revised Article 2366 changed the measure of reimbursement. There, community funds were used to pay some premiums for the wife's separate insurance policy issued on her father's life. The court held the husband was entitled to reimbursement for one-half of the premiums paid, without regard to the cash value increase in the policy. The court stated: "However, article 2366 is clear and unambiguous in establishing the calculation of reimbursement by the amount or value of the community property had [sic] at the time it was used to benefit the separate property. C.C. art. 9. The effect of article 2366 is to legislatively overrule Connell."

Cases involving murder of a beneficiary by the insured demonstrate the unfairness that can arise from strict application of insurance rules to determine the payee on death of the beneficiary. In Jackson Nat'l Life Ins. Co. v. Kennedy-Fagan, the executrix of the estate of her mother who was murdered by her stepfather in a murder-suicide in which the wife predeceased the husband. The executrix urged that her mother's beneficial share of the proceeds from a life insurance policy on her stepfather should not be awarded pro-rata among the surviving beneficiaries who were the children of the stepfather. Acknowledging that the life insurance policy itself may have been community property, the court held that "[t]here is no general concept of hereditary guilt in [Louisiana] law" that would deprive the murdering stepfather's beneficiaries from their rights under the policy. The court also suggested in dicta that the mother's succession might have a claim against her stepfather's succession for reimbursement for premiums paid with community funds, a right which exists only if community funds are used to pay premiums on a policy which is the separate property of the other spouse. See C.C. art. 2366.

In *Graves v. Garden State Life Ins. Co.,* the first circuit held where the wife who was sole beneficiary of an insurance policy on her husband was murdered by her husband who then committed suicide, the proceeds of the insurance policy devolved to the estate of the husband. As it had in the related Jackson Nat'l Life Ins. Co. case, the court acknowledged that the life insurance policy itself may have been community property, but, the insurance proceeds pass by virtue of the contract provisions. The beneficiary receives those funds with no obligation to compensate the spouse of the insured or the owner of the policy, regardless of the source of funds used to pay the policy premiums.

To the extent that National Service Life Insurance, Railroad Retirement Act, Uniformed Services Former Spouses' Protection Act, Veteran's Pensions, Servicemember's Group Insurance Act, Foreign Service Act of 1980 and, most recently, the Federal Employee's Group Insurance Act. or other federal insurance schemes are inconsistent with state law, federal preemption will apply. However, because federal provisions provide for paying policy proceeds to the named beneficiary, there would seem to be little inconsistency with the state law.

Disability insurance may be added to a life insurance policy, a health insurance policy or may be a separate policy. The key to characterization is that the benefits are payable to compensate a named insured for loss of income in the event of disability. The proceeds are paid to the insured, and real subrogation seems to be the applicable principle. If the payments substitute for income that would be community property during marriage, they are community. If they substitute for income that would be received after divorce, they are separate property.

C. *James George Kambur v. Gloria Failla Kambur*

652 So. 2d 99 (La. App. 5 Cir. 1995)

GOTHARD, Judge.

This is an appeal of a trial court judgment partitioning assets of a former community of acquets and gains. For the following reasons, we affirm.

FACTS

On June 22, 1969, plaintiff/appellee, Gloria Failla Kambur, and defendant/appellant, James George Kambur were married. One child, who has now reached the age of majority, was born of this marriage. On February 20, 1991, Ms. Kambur filed a petition for divorce and a petition for partition of the community property. Several consent judgments relative to the divorce and partition ensued. Finally, on January 5, 1993, the parties entered into a "Consent Judgment of Partition," wherein virtually all of the assets of the former community were partitioned between the parties. The judgment provided in part that "with respect to the life insurance policies, annuities and IRA accounts, owned by the community of acquets and gains existing between James G. Kambur and Gloria F. Kambur, the parties shall mutually agree to divide them under a separate agreement or by judicial partition if the parties are unable to agree."

Thereafter, on October 22, 1993, Mr. Kambur filed a rule to partition the life insurance policies, annuities and IRA accounts. Each side submitted proposals to the trial court on how to distribute the assets. On June 24, 1994, the trial court rendered judgment, ordering that the assets be partitioned in accordance with Ms. Kambur's proposal. Mr. Kambur thereafter brought this suspensive appeal, arguing as his assignments of error: the trial court committed error by holding that the laws of community property do not apply in this matter; the trial court abused its discretion and erred when it divided the life insurance policies, annuities, and IRA accounts strictly according to record ownership of the assets at issue and not according to the criteria established in LSA-R.S. 9:2801; and, assuming arguendo that the trial court's allocation of the insurance policies, annuities, and IRA accounts pursuant to Catalano v. United States1 is proper, the trial court erred in not allocating the Connecticut Mutual Company policy no. 2007142561 to Mr. Kambur. Ms. Kambur answered the appeal, seeking damages pursuant to La.C.C.P. art. 2164 for a frivolous appeal.

ANALYSIS

It is well settled that a trial court has broad discretion in adjudicating issues raised by divorce and partition of the community regime. *Dilley v. Dilley*, 561 So.2d 799 (La.App. 2 Cir.1990); *Queenan v. Queenan,* 492 So.2d 902 (La.App. 3 Cir.1986), writ denied, 496 So.2d 1045 (La.1986); *Feazel v. Feazel*, 471 So.2d 851 (La.App. 2 Cir.1985). LSA-R.S. 9:2801 provides the procedure for judicial partitions of community property and settlement of claims after dissolution of the marriage. The trial judge is afforded a great deal of latitude in arriving at an equitable distribution of the assets between the spouses. *Kaplan v. Kaplan*, 522 So.2d 1344 (La.App. 2 Cir.1988); *Hall v. Hall*, 460 So.2d 1053 (La.App. 2 Cir.1984).

***

In allocating assets and liabilities, the court may divide a particular asset or liability equally or unequally or may allocate it in its entirety to one of the spouses. The court shall consider the nature and source of the asset or liability, the economic condition of each spouse, and any other circumstances that the court deems relevant. As between the spouses, the allocation of a liability to a spouse obligates that spouse to extinguish that liability. The allocation in no way affects the rights of creditors.

In the event that the allocation of assets and liabilities results in an unequal net distribution, the court shall order the payment of an equalizing sum of money, either cash or deferred, secured or unsecured, upon such terms and conditions as the court shall direct. The court may order the execution of notes, mortgages, or other documents as it deems necessary, or may impose a mortgage or lien on either community or separate property, movable or immovable, as security.

In allocating the community assets and liabilities, the trial court has the discretion to divide a particular asset or liability equally or unequally or to allocate it in its entirety to one of the spouses. The court must consider the nature and source of the asset or liability, the economic condition of each spouse, and any other circumstances that the court deems relevant. LSA-R.S. 9:2801(4)(c); *Hare v. Hodgins*, 586 So.2d 118, 122-23 (La.1991); *Reeves v. Reeves*, 607 So.2d 626, 633 (La.App. 2 Cir.1992), *writ denied*, 608 So.2d 1010 (La.1992).

The court is required to divide the community of assets and liabilities so that each spouse receives property of an equal net value. LSA-R.S. 9:2801(4)(b). In order to avoid an unequal net distribution of assets and liabilities, the court may order the payment of an equalizing sum of money, either cash or deferred, secured or unsecured, upon specified terms and conditions; and the court may order the execution of notes, mortgages, or other documents as it deems necessary, or may impose a mortgage or lien on either community or separate property as security. LSA-R.S. 9:2801(4)(c); *Hare*, supra.

In the matter before us, Mr. Kambur argues in his first two assignments of error that the trial court held that the laws of community property do not apply and the trial court did not follow the criteria established in LSA-R.S. 9:2801(4). We disagree. After a thorough review of the record and jurisprudence, we find that the trial court applied the applicable community property statute, LSA-R.S. 9:2801(4), in reaching the June 24, 1994 judgment of partition.

Appellant argues that the trial court erred by holding that, pursuant to *Catalano*, supra, life insurance policies are *sui generis*, and are not subject to the laws of community property. While life insurance is generally considered sui generis in Louisiana, it is the proceeds of the life insurance policy, not the policy itself, which are not subject to claims of the community.

It is well settled in Louisiana that life insurance *proceeds*, if payable to a named beneficiary other than the estate of the insured, are not considered to be a part of the estate of the insured. The insurance *proceeds* do not come into existence during the life of the insured, never belong to him, and are passed by virtue of the contractual agreement between the insured and the insurer to the named beneficiary. Life insurance proceeds are not subject to the Civil Code Articles relating to donations inter vivos or mortis causa, nor are they subject to community claims or the laws regarding forced heirship. (emphasis ours) *American Health & Life Ins. Co. v. Binford*, 511 So.2d 1250, 1253 (La.App. 2 Cir.1987), citing *T.L. James and Company, Inc. v. Montgomery*, 332 So.2d 834 (La.1976).

There is a clear distinction between the ownership of a policy of life insurance and the right to receive the proceeds of a life insurance policy after the death of the insured. The issue of life insurance proceeds is not before us today. The record reveals that the life insurance policies, annuities and IRAs in question were community property. As appellant properly points out in brief, and as noted above, the parties stipulated that these assets were community property in their January 5, 1993 Consent Judgment of Partition. Further, La.C.C. Art. 2338 provides in pertinent part that community property consists of "... property acquired during the existence of the legal regime through the effort, skill, or industry of either spouse ..." The assets in question were acquired during the existence of the legal regime and are presumed to be community property. La.C.C. Art. 2340.3

Although the trial court made reference to the *Catalano* decision in its reasons for judgment, we find that the trial court properly applied R.S. 9:2801(4), not *Catalano*, in rendering judgment. Further, appellate review lies only from the trial court's judgment, not the reasons therefor. Regardless of what may have been a trial court's reasons for rendering judgment, if the judgment is correct it should be affirmed. Fowler v. St. Charles Hospital, 630 So.2d 293, 295 (La.App. 5 Cir.1993), writ denied, 634 So.2d 860 (La.1994) (citations omitted).

The record reveals that the trial court, using Ms. Kambur's proposal, divided the various life insurance policies, annuities and IRAs based essentially on who was the named beneficiary of the asset. This division resulted in Mr. Kambur retaining a total of $331,474.25 in policy value ($295,393.14 of insurance coverage on his own life), with a cash value of $105,910.93. Ms. Kambur retained a total of $340,528.95 in policy value ($325,000.00 of insurance coverage on Mr. Kambur's life), with a cash value of $77,679.80. The parties remained co-owners of two other life insurance policies in which their daughter is the named beneficiary. A final life insurance policy (the Connecticut Mutual Company policy no. 2007142561), insuring Ms. Kambur's life and in which Mr. Kambur is the named beneficiary, with a cash value of $22,643.00, was ordered to be cashed-in and divided equally between the parties.

In order to equalize the net distribution of assets, Mr. Kambur was ordered to pay off a $37,059.09 loan on a life insurance policy retained by Ms. Kambur and Ms. Kambur was ordered to pay an equalizing sum of $2,396.00 to Mr. Kambur-which resulted in each spouse receiving property (cash value of the policies) of an equal net value.

In reaching its judgment, the trial court felt Ms. Kambur's proposal was more equitable than Mr. Kambur's. On appeal, Mr. Kambur argues that the trial court was manifestly erroneous in choosing Ms. Kambur's proposal over his own. The crux of his argument centers around Ms. Kambur retaining more insurance coverage on Mr. Kambur's life than Mr. Kambur retains. While there is some disparity in the amount of coverage retained by each party, the coverage is comparable. More importantly, the net cash value of the assets (the focus of R.S. 9:2801(4)) granted to each party is equal.

We are also cognizant of the fact that Mr. and Ms. Kambur were married for more than twenty years and that during their marriage Mr. Kambur obtained several life insurance policies on his life for the benefit of Ms. Kambur. Further, out of the eleven insurance policies subject to partition in the record before us, only one, the Connecticut Mutual policy (which was ordered to be cashed-in and divided equally between the parties), insures the life of Ms. Kambur.

Because the above-mentioned requirements of R.S. 9:2801(4) were followed by the trial court, the net cash value of the assets was equally divided between the parties, and the amount of insurance coverage each party receives is comparable, we cannot say that the trial court abused its discretion in choosing Ms. Kambur's proposal over Mr. Kambur's. Appellant's first two assignments of error are therefore without merit.

Appellant's argument in his final assignment of error, that the trial court should have awarded the Connecticut Mutual policy to Mr. Kambur, is misplaced. Appellant argues that the trial court relied on the Catalano decision in reaching its judgment, and that pursuant to the rationale in *Catalano*, Mr. Kambur is entitled to the Connecticut Mutual policy. We disagree.

As stated above, we find that the trial court properly applied LSA-R.S. 9:2801(4), not Catalano, in reaching its June 24, 1994 judgment of partition. R.S. 9:2801(4)(c) grants the trial court the discretion to order that the Connecticut Mutual policy be cashed-in and divided equally between the parties, which the trial court did in its judgment of partition. Furthermore, because *Catalano* is clearly distinguishable from the instant matter (see footnote 4, supra), the rationale in *Catalano* is not applicable to the situation before us today.

FRIVOLOUS APPEAL

Ms. Kambur answered Mr. Kambur's appeal, seeking damages and contending that the appeal is frivolous. Ms. Kambur is also seeking additional attorney's fees for defending against appellant's appeal.

La.C.C.P. art. 2164 provides for the imposition of damages for frivolous appeals. This provision is penal in nature and must be strictly construed. Damages will not be awarded unless it appears that the appeal was taken solely for the purpose of delay, serious legal questions are not raised, or that the appealing counsel does not seriously believe in the position he advocates. Even when the contentions on appeal are found to lack merit, but raise legitimate issues, damages for frivolous appeals are not allowed. *Barnes v. L.M. Massey, Inc.*, 612 So.2d 120 (La.App. 1 Cir.1992), *writ denied*, 614 So.2d 81 (La.1993); *Champagne v. Hartford Casualty Insurance Group*, 607 So.2d 752 (La.App. 1 Cir.1992).

In this case, we do not find that the appeal was taken solely for the purpose of delay. While we find that the contentions on appeal lack merit, legitimate issues were raised. Therefore, appellee's claim for damages for frivolous appeal is denied.

For the foregoing reasons, the judgment of the trial court is hereby affirmed. Costs of this appeal are taxed against appellant.

AFFIRMED.

CANNELLA, Judge, dissents.

I respectfully disagree with the majority opinion affirming the trial court judgment in this community property partition action. In my view the trial court erred in awarding the ownership of life insurance policies to someone who has no insurable interest in the insured's life and in valuing the life insurance policies solely on the cash surrender value of the policies.

We were called upon, in this case, to consider the question of whether the trial judge erred in this partial community property partition by awarding life insurance policies on the ex-husband's life to his ex-wife and ordering that policies on the ex-wife's life be sold and the proceeds divided. In my view the trial court judgment was manifestly erroneous and should be reversed.

I agree with the majority in the general statement of facts and law in this case. The insurance policies at issue here were purchased during the community and are community property regardless of the named owner on the policies. Ownership rights in a life insurance policy and how insurance proceeds are disbursed present different considerations and legal effects. We are here only concerned with the ownership of the policies.

However, in my view the majority errs in limiting its analysis of the issue, which spouse should be awarded ownership of which policies, by simply looking at the cash surrender values of the policies without regard to who's life is insured or other aspects of the policies that might effect the values of the policies.

In properly considering the question of which spouse should be awarded ownership of life insurance policies, the court errs by not considering who's life is being insured. La. R.S. 22:613 requires that one have an "insurable interest" in a person before one "procures" life insurance on that person. The public policy behind this mandate is to protect the safety of the public by preventing anyone from acquiring a greater interest in another person's death than in his continued life. *Rubenstein v. Mutual Life Ins. Co.*, 584 F.Supp. 272 (D.C.1984). Public policy dictates that one should not be allowed to gamble on the death of another. In this case, involving divorced persons, where the ex-husband has not been ordered to pay alimony, the ex-wife has no insurable interest in her ex-husband and only gains a monetary advantage by his death. In my view public policy, if not the clear intent of the statutory provision, leads to the conclusion that the trial court erred in condoning this death gamble by awarding life insurance policies on the ex-husband's life to his ex-wife with no insurable interest, rather than simply awarding her the policies on her own life.

Furthermore, in my view, the majority fails to recognize the trial court error of valuing the policies solely by the cash surrender values. There are other factors, like the insurability of the insured, to be considered in valuing a life insurance policy other than simply the cash surrender value of the policy. As argued in this case, the ex-husband/insured is now ill and uninsurable. Under such circumstances, the life insurance policies on his life are irreplaceable and, accordingly, increase the value of the policy far beyond simply their cash surrender value. Catherine Spaht, Lee Hargrave, Matrimonial Regimes Treatise, § 3.26, at 85 (ed. 19). Therefore, the majority errs in affirming the division of the life insurance policies, made on a valuation based solely on the cash surrender values of the policies.

Accordingly, I dissent from the majority opinion, being of the view that the trial court judgment was manifestly erroneous and should be reversed.

D. *Succession of Allen Sneed Jackson*

402 So. 2d 753 (La. App. 4 Cir. 1981)

BOUTALL, Judge.

This appeal arises from a judgment of the trial court which disposed of the proceeds of several life insurance policies and an annuity policy to various parties. The disposition of these items forms the bases of the appeal.

On November 21, 1970, Allen Sneed Jackson married his second wife, Dorothy Gray Jackson. During this marriage Mr. Jackson acquired several life insurance policies and one annuity policy which are described in pertinent part as follows:

a) Boston Mutual Life Insurance Co. (hereinafter referred to as Boston Mutual) group term life insurance policy in the amount of $35,000;

b) John Hancock Mutual Life Insurance Co. (hereinafter referred to as John Hancock) group term life insurance policy in the amount of $25,000;

c) Commercial Union Life Insurance Co. (hereinafter referred to as Commercial Union) annuity contract in the amount of $9,284.35.

On November 23, 1976, Mr. Jackson filed a suit for a separation from bed and board which was granted on October 20, 1977, thereby terminating the community retroactive to the date of filing of the suit. During the course of these proceedings the trial court issued a preliminary injunction against both of the Jacksons ordering them not to dispose of the community property acquired by them. At the time of the judgment of separation, Dorothy Jackson was the named beneficiary on the three policies described above. On February 10, 1979, Allen Jackson obtained a Haitian divorce against Dorothy Jackson and on February 12, 1979, he married Elaine Mead Jackson. Mr. Jackson changed the beneficiary on the three policies above to Elaine Jackson. Thereafter, on September 25, 1979, Mr. Jackson died, at which time Elaine Jackson continued to be the named beneficiary.

On October 9, 1979 Dorothy Jackson filed a petition for a preliminary injunction seeking to restrain the insurance companies from disposing of the proceeds of the insurance policies enumerated above. Her request for a preliminary injunction was granted by the trial court but was later dissolved on grounds that it was improperly issued. Subsequently, the proceeds of the three policies were deposited into the registry of the trial court by the respective insurance companies via concursus proceedings for disbursement by the court to the proper parties. Those parties filing a claim to the proceeds include both Dorothy and Elaine Jackson and the children of the first marriage of the decedent.

The trial court awarded the proceeds of the two life insurance policies in favor of Elaine Jackson. Dorothy Jackson was awarded one half of the proceeds of the annuity policy which accrued during her marriage to the decedent, which amounted to $2724.55, and the remaining funds totalling over $6559.80 were awarded to the estate of the decedent. From this judgment both Dorothy and Elaine Jackson have appealed devolutively. The executor of the estate of Mr. Jackson answered the appeal seeking damages for frivolous appeal from Dorothy Jackson and seeking affirmation of the judgment of the trial court. Elaine Jackson answered the appeal filed by Dorothy Jackson seeking reversal of the trial court's judgment regarding distribution of the proceeds of the annuity policy, together with damages and costs of trial from Dorothy Jackson, and damages for frivolous appeal.

On appeal the issues before us are as follows: 1) whether the community formerly existing between Dorothy and Allen Jackson has ownership of both the term life insurance policies acquired during the existence of the community as well as the proceeds of these policies; 2) whether the community formerly existing between Dorothy and Allen Jackson is entitled to restitution for the community funds used to pay the premiums on the two term life policies acquired during the existence of the community....

***

We are aided in our resolution of these issues by the detailed and well-reasoned opinion of the trial judge with which we agree in the main.

I

Regarding the first issue before us, the jurisprudence draws a clear distinction between ownership of a life insurance policy as opposed to the ownership of the proceeds of such a policy. The ownership of a policy of life insurance, whether it is separate or community property, is determined by the marital status of the owner at the time the policy is issued. Equally well known is the rule that death benefits or proceeds of a life insurance policy with a named beneficiary other than the estate of the insured owner, do not form part of the owner's estate either separate or community, but belong to the validly designated beneficiary. Consistent with these two different forms of ownership there are different benefits. The policy owner is entitled to the lifetime benefits payable under the insurance policy, that is, those exercisable by the owner pursuant to policy terms and provisions, during the lifetime of the owner. These benefits include: the right to cash surrender value, receive dividends, assign or pledge policy proceeds, borrow against the policy, name and change of beneficiary, and execute conversion rights. On the contrary, the owner of the death benefits or proceeds is entitled exclusively to the proceeds when the policy accrues at death. Another point to consider here is that the existence of the lifetime benefits for the policy owner differs when there is a term policy or a whole life policy. In the case of the term policy the lifetime benefits are limited, whereas, the entire package of benefits is generally available for the whole life policy. No distinction as to the existence of benefits is made for the owner of the death benefits or proceeds as the proceeds for either a whole life or a term life policy are payable when the policy accrues. *Berry v. Metropolitan Life Insurance Company*, 327 So.2d 521, 523 (La.App. 1st Cir. 1976); *T. L. James and Co., Inc. v. Montgomery*, 332 So.2d 834 (La.1975).

In the matter before us both of the term life insurance policies namely the Boston Life Policy and the John Hancock Life Policy, were acquired during the existence of the community between Dorothy and Allen Jackson. Therefore, ownership of these policies belongs to the community existing between them. As such the community was entitled to all of the lifetime benefits attributable to a term life policy which, upon accrual of the policy as has occurred here with the death of Allen Jackson, amounts to nothing. Regarding the proceeds of the two term life policies, Elaine Jackson was the named beneficiary at the time when the policies accrued upon the death of Allen Jackson. Therefore, she is the exclusive owner of these proceeds and is entitled to them. The claim made by Dorothy Jackson to these proceeds is denied.

II

With respect to the issue of restitution of community funds used for the payment of premiums on life insurance policies the jurisprudence draws a distinction between policies acquired prior to the existence of the marriage and those acquired during the marriage. For the former type they are the separate property of the spouse acquiring them and the community is entitled to restitution only when the cash value of the policy has increased during the community's existence and then only for one-half the extent of the increase in value. For those policies acquired during marriage they are community property and the community is entitled to reimbursement according to the value that the policy had at the time of the dissolution of the community. In this case the term insurance policies never had a cash surrender value. Therefore, no accounting is due to the community for premiums paid. *Connell v. Connell*, 331 So.2d 4 (La.1976); *T. L. James & Co., Inc. v. Montgomery*, 332 So.2d 834 (La.1975).

***

E. *Succession of Patricia Goudeau*

480 So. 2d 806 (La. App. 3d Cir. 1985)

KING, Judge.

This appeal presents the issue of whether or not the trial court was correct in its determination of the status of assets and liabilities of this succession.

Willie J. Goudeau and his second wife, Patricia Ducote Goudeau (hereinafter referred to as the decedents), were killed in an airplane crash in Kenner, Louisiana on July 9, 1982. On October 6, 1983, Rhonda Ducote Gaspard, individually, and as Administratrix of the Succession of Patricia Ducote Goudeau, Floyd J. Ducote, Mae Desselle Ducote and Cynthia Ann Ducote, all heirs of Patricia Ducote Goudeau (hereinafter referred to as the Ducotes), plaintiffs-in-rule, filed a Rule to Show Cause against Darlene Goudeau Bordelon, individually, and as Administratrix of the Succession of Willie J. Goudeau, Kathleen Goudeau Mayeaux and Gwendolyn Marie Goudeau, all daughters of Willie J. Goudeau by a previous marriage (hereinafter referred to as the Goudeaus), defendants-in-rule. After the Ducotes filed an amended Rule to Show Cause, the Goudeaus filed an Answer and a Rule in Reconvention. The Ducotes then filed an Answer to the Rule in Reconvention.

Both rules, which presented various disputed issues between the estate of Willie J. Goudeau and Patricia Ducote Goudeau, were tried on May 2, 1984, and after the hearing the trial court rendered a judgment which was read and signed on June 27, 1984. The Ducotes were granted a suspensive appeal on July 6, 1984. On appeal the Ducotes urge the following assignments of error:

...

(4) The trial court erred in holding that the Goudeaus were entitled to recover from the Estate of Patricia Ducote Goudeau the sum of one-half (½) of One Thousand Sixteen and 80/100 ($1,016.80) Dollars, or the sum of Five Hundred Eight and 40/100 $508.40) Dollars, being the proceeds paid to her estate by Commonwealth Life Insurance Company from an insurance policy on the life of Patricia Ducote Goudeau.

***

ASSIGNMENT OF ERROR NUMBER 4

In their fourth assignment of error, the Ducotes contend that the trial court erred in holding that the Goudeaus were entitled to recover $508.40 (one-half of $1,016.80) from the Estate of Patricia Ducote Goudeau, which represented proceeds paid by Commonwealth Life Insurance Company under a life insurance policy on the life of Patricia Ducote Goudeau.

Patricia Ducote Goudeau obtained the policy in question on October 1, 1970, prior to marrying Willie J. Goudeau. She changed the named beneficiary to Willie J. Goudeau on November 20, 1973, after marrying him. Patricia was fifteen years younger than Willie J. Goudeau. They were both killed on July 9, 1982 in an air crash in Kenner, Louisiana.

***

In this instance, there is no ascertainable evidence that one spouse survived the other. Therefore, the presumptions of LSA-C.C. Art. 939 are applicable and Patricia Ducote Goudeau is presumed to have survived Willie J. Goudeau. Thus, Willie J. Goudeau's heirs are not entitled to recover on this policy from the Succession of Patricia Ducote Goudeau.

In addition, LSA-R.S. 22:645 provides:

> "Where the individual insured and the beneficiary designated in a life insurance policy or policy insuring against accidental death have died and there is not sufficient evidence that they have died otherwise than simultaneously, the proceeds of the policy shall be distributed as if the insured had survived the beneficiary, unless otherwise expressly provided in the policy."

For these reasons, the proceeds of this policy owned by Patricia Ducote Goudeau are to be distributed to the Succession of Patricia Ducote Goudeau, who was the insured.

The Goudeaus argue that if a policy of life insurance is acquired during the marriage, its ownership is community, relying on *Succession of Jackson*, 402 So.2d 753 (La.App. 4th Cir.1981). However, the Goudeaus are in error in their reliance on this case, because here, the insurance policy in question was not acquired by Patricia Ducote Goudeau during her marriage to Willie J. Goudeau, but prior to her marriage. In *Succession of Jackson*, supra, the insurance policies were actually acquired during the marriage. Though premiums may have actually been paid during the marriage of decedents, the insurance policy would still be the separate property of Patricia Ducote Goudeau, with the community being entitled only to reimbursement for premiums paid with community funds. *Succession of Jackson*, supra. However, no evidence was presented regarding the use or amount of community funds which might have been used for payment of the premiums on this policy.

For these reasons, we find that the trial court was manifestly in error in determining this insurance policy to be community property and in awarding one-half (½) of the proceeds of the policy to the Goudeaus. We, therefore, reverse the trial court's judgment, and hold that all of the proceeds from the life insurance policy on the life of Patricia Ducote Goudeau belong solely to her estate, which is entitled to the entire proceeds in the amount of $1,016.80.

***

F. *Susan McKneely Fowler v. Claude Ed Fowler*

862 So.2d 181 (La. 2003)

TRAYLOR, Justice.

In the instant case, we granted certiorari to determine whether the proceeds of a life insurance policy paid during the matrimonial regime of acquets and gains are the separate or community property of the beneficiary spouse. We conclude that life insurance proceeds are sui generis and not governed by codal principles which govern community property. We thus overrule *Thigpen v. Thigpen*, 231 La. 206, 91 So.2d 12 (1956) and hold that life insurance proceeds received by a spouse during the existence of a matrimonial regime of acquets and gains are separate property.

FACTS AND PROCEDURAL HISTORY

Charles Ed Fowler and Susan McKneely Fowler were married on June 5, 1965. Their son, Claude E. Fowler, Jr, was born February 22, 1969. During the Fowler's marriage, the Mutual Life Insurance Company of New York issued three whole life insurance policies on Claude Fowler, Jr., totaling $500,000. The first policy, issued when Claude, Jr. Was seventeen years old with a face amount of $100,000, was acquired on January 16, 1986; the second policy was issued on September 17, 1987 (1987 policy), with a face amount of $100,000; and the third policy was issued on February 3, 1988 (1988) policy), with a face amount of $300,000. In all three policies, Susan M. Fowler was designated as first beneficiary and Claude Ed Fowler was designated as second beneficiary. Although Susan Fowler retained all rights of ownership arising out of the three whole life policies, the last two policies reverted the right to designate a beneficiary to her son, Claude, Jr., upon his twenty-first birthday.

Claude Fowler, Jr. died in an automobile accident in March 1990, at the age of twenty-one, having never exercised the right to change the beneficiary on the 1987 and 1988 policies. Accordingly, the proceeds of all three policies were paid to Susan M. Fowler. Mrs. Fowler initially deposited the funds in a Prudential Annuity account in the name of Susan M. Fowler and, subsequently, in a Merrill Lynch account in the name of Susan M. Fowler.

In 1999, eight years after receiving the insurance proceeds, Susan Fowler filed a petition for divorce. A judgment of divorce was rendered on April 5, 1999, and Susan Fowler subsequently filed a community property partition suit on June 1, 1999. Although all claims arising out of the dissolution of the community were resolved by a written stipulation, the Fowlers reserved for a decision by the court the sole issue of whether $450,000 of the life insurance proceeds are the community or separate property of Mrs. Fowler.

After a partition hearing, the trial court declared the proceeds of the life insurance policies to be the separate property of Susan M. Fowler. On review, the Court of Appeal, First Circuit, affirmed. *Fowler v. Fowler,* 02-0222 (La. App. 1st Cir. 12/31/02), 834 So.2d 659. Mr. Fowler sought writs of cerrtiorari with this court, which we subsequently granted. *Fowler v. Fowler*, 03-0590 (La. 5/2/03), 842 So.2d 1089.

DISCUSSION

The only issue this court must decide is whether life insurance proceeds are governed by the principles of community property. Mrs. Fowler argues that life insurance is sui generis, as established by a long line of jurisprudence which repudiates the *Thigpen* holding. We agree and find that life insurance proceeds are sui generis in this state, and thus subject to separate rules. Therefore, we overrule this court's decision in *Thigpen v. Thigpen*, 231 La. 206, 91 20.2d 12 (1956), and extend to the instant situation the rationale of the long line of jurisprudence which treats life insurance proceeds as sui generis.

A life insurance policy is a legal contract between the policy owner and the insurance company, Dennis C. Cuneo, Life Insurance As An Estate Planning Tool, 23 LOY.L.REV. 59, 59 (1977). Life Insurance contracts originate from common law countries; the French Civil Code in fact viewed life insurance as a form of gambling. Cuneo, at 69; Eugene A. Nabors, Civil Law Influences Upon the Law of Insurance in Louisiana, 6 TUL.L.REV. 369, 369 (1932). Consequently, the community property provisions of the Louisiana Civil Code were not drafted with insurance in mind; the legislature in the Louisiana Code of 1808 provided that insurance is "foreign to this code." Nabors, at 369-372. As a result, the legislature's failure to account for life insurance has resulted in irreconcilable principles between the rights of life insurance proceeds beneficiaries and traditional civilian principles. Louisiana jurisprudence has responded to this conundrum by traditionally finding that life insurance is sui generis and therefore not subject to many traditional civilian principles. Thus, the protection afforded to life insurance proceeds, although now adopted and codified in the Insurance Code, are the outgrowth of judicial precedent and not legislation. *Mary Ticker v. Metropolitan Life Ins. Co.*, 11 Orleans App. 55 (1914); *Sizeler v. Sizeler*, 170 La. 128, 127 So. 388 (1930).

As a result of the Civil Code's failure to address this problem, life insurance proceeds enjoy a status not accorded to other property in Louisiana. This court has repeatedly refused to extend the civilian principles enunciated by the Civil Code to the realm of life insurance proceeds. Thus, insurance proceeds are protected from the heirs and legatees of the insured, *Nulsen v. Herndon*, 176 La. 1097, 147 So. 359 (1933), *Succession of Erwin*, 169 La. 877, 126 So. 223 (1930); creditors of the insured, *Succession of Porter*, 4 Pelt. 200 (La. 1 921).; claims for collation, *Sherwood v. New York Life Ins. Co.*, 166 La. 829, 118 So. 35 (1928); actions for reduction; *Sizeler v. Sizeler*, 170 La. 128, 127 So. 388 (1930); and form of donations inter vivos, La.Rev.Stat. Ann. § 22:1521.

It has long been settled authority that the disposition of life insurance proceeds are sui generis and subject to separate rules which may or may not coincide with the rules of the Civil Code generally applicable to community property. The jurisprudence has traditionally based this protection on the contractual nature of insurance. In *Mary Ticker v. Metropolitan Life Ins. Co.*, 11 Orleans App. 55 (1913), a husband took out a life insurance policy during marriage, and subsequently changed the primary beneficiary from his wife to his mother. After his death, the decedent's wife and minor son attempted to claim the proceeds, which comprised the entirety of the estate. On rehearing, the *Ticker* court held that the decedent's change in beneficiary was effective based on the form provided by the policy. *Id.* At 59-60. Noting that the change in beneficiary was correct in form, the court awarded the proceeds to the mother over the claims of the decedent's widow and son. *Id.* The *Ticker* court justified the result on the contractual nature of the insurance contract, stating:

> For the contract, being lawful, must be given its effect according to the intention of the parties thereto; and we cannot for the purpose of defeating that intention apply to the contract provisions of law governing contracts of a different nature.
>
> As we appreciate the jurisprudence of this State, a life insurance policy is a contract, sui generis, governed by rules peculiar to itself, the outgrowth of judicial precedent, and not of legislation. *Id.* at 60.

Likewise, in *Sizeler v. Sizeler*, 170 La. 128, 127 So. 388 (1930), this court refused to recognize the collation claims of a forced heir to receive proceeds vis-a-vis a beneficiary wife based on contractual provisions in the insurance policy. Following the rationale of *Mary Ticker,* the *Sizeler* court found that life insurance proceeds inure to the beneficiary directly, by the sole terms of the policy itself, and are not subject to the laws of donation mortis causa or donation inter vivos, stating:

> As the proceeds of life insurance policies form no part of the estate of the deceased, and inure to the beneficiary directly and by the sole terms of the policy itself, the right of defendant to the avails of the policies in this case does not arise from legal coverture, nor from the civil effects of marriage contracted in good faith, but solely from the terms of the policies in which she has been named the beneficiary by the decedent.

Id. at 389. Accordingly, the *Sizeler* court refused to draw distinction between the classes of beneficiaries named in life insurance policies. *Id.* at 389-390.

More recently, this court addressed life insurance proceeds in *T.L. James & Co. V. Montgomery*, 332 So.2d 834 (La. 1975) and *Standard Life Ins. Co. v. Franks*, 278 So.2d 112 (La. 1973). *T.L. James* held that a son, as beneficiary of a life insurance policy, was entitled to life insurance proceeds above the claims of the decedent's widow and heirs. *Id.* at 847-848. This court specifically rejected the widow's argument that allowing a husband to separate life insurance proceeds from the estate circumvents the laws relating to forced heirship and community property. *Id.* Commenting on the nature of life insurance, the court stated:

> It is well-settled in Louisiana that the proceeds of life insurance, if payable to a named beneficiary other than the estate of the insured, are not considered to be a part of the estate of the insured. They do not come into existence during his life, never belong to him, and pass by virtue of the contractual agreement between the insured and the insurer to the beneficiary. Life insurance proceeds are not subject to Civil Code articles relating to donation inter vivos or mortis causa, nor are they subject to community claims or the laws regarding forced heirship. (Citations omitted).

Id. at 847.

Finally, this court in *Standard Life Insurance* upheld an ex-wife's claim as beneficiary of a life insurance policy. In rejecting the argument that a catch-all phrase which conveyed to her husband all community assets not specifically described in the community settlement agreement, the court stated:

> The death benefits of the life insurance policy were never community property, for there was a named beneficiary other than the estate of the insured. Death benefits payable to one other than the estate are not part of the community of acquets and gains, and they were not made here part of that community through the settlement agreement. We need only examine the contract of insurance, therefore, to determine to whom are due the funds on deposit. The contract of insurance contained a provision for the change of beneficiary. The deceased did not exercise the right to change the beneficiary. We need not inquire into whether he desired to changed the beneficiary, for we are bound by the unambiguous contract which names the beneficiary. *Standard*, 278 So.2d at 114.

Mary Ticker, Sizeler, T.L. James, and *Standard*, clearly stand for the proposition that the disbursement to the beneficiary of life insurance proceeds are governed by the contractual provisions, and that Civil Code provisions are inapplicable. Although these cases are factually dissimilar from the instant case because they involve the devolution of an estate rather than the dissolution of community property, we believe the principles are the same. Thus, the rules of contract provide the primary basis for the protection traditionally afforded to life insurance proceeds in Louisiana.

Based on the foregoing cases, the principle that life insurance proceeds are sui generis has led Louisiana courts for decades to look to the provisions of the policies themselves and any pertinent portions of the Insurance Code to resolve disputes concerning such policies.

Applying these precepts to the instant case, the language in all three policies inure solely to Mrs. Fowler's benefit; Mr. Fowler is clearly named as a second beneficiary to receive proceeds only if Mrs. Fowler predeceased the insured. Although Mr. Fowler argues that the proceeds were not in dispute during the existence of the community and therefore the insurance company was not required to pay the proceeds to anyone other than the name d beneficiary, we refuse to require Mrs. Fowler, as sole beneficiary, to split ownership of the proceeds upon termination of the community. Such a finding would derogate from the contractual provisions designating her right as sole beneficiary.

Moreover, the *Thigpen* court's reliance on those cases where the insured named his estate as beneficiary was erroneous. We find that the case sub judice is also distinguishable from that line of cases where the insured names his estate as beneficiary. *See Berry v. Franklin State Bank & Trust Co.,* 186 La. 623, 173 So. 126 (1937); *Messersmith v. Messersmith*, 229 La. 495, 86 So.2d 169 (1956).

Thigpen v. Thigpen, 231 La. 206, 901 So.2d 12 (1956), involved a similar fact situation as the instant case. The *Thigpen* husband, as the named beneficiary, received life insurance proceeds on the life of his son during the community regime. Upon divorce, Mrs. Thigpen claimed one-half of the proceeds as community property. With little analysis, the *Thigpen* court adopted the principles applied to the situation where life insurance is taken out in favor of the insured's estate. *Id.* at 21. However, the cases in which life insurance is taken out in favor of the insured's estate involve significant distinctions from the situation where life insurance is taken out in favor of an individual. The application of codal principles to proceeds in cases where the insured's estate is named as beneficiary does not interfere with the contractual right of the beneficiary to receive proceeds. When the insured names his estate, the proceeds must devolve accordingly and may not stay in the estate indefinitely. The estate is not a person and cannot keep the proceeds, nor does the insurance contract provide the manner in which the executor or estate should distribute such funds. Thus, it is consistent with the contractual intent to apply codal principles of community property and succession law to the estate of the insured. In the instant case, however, the beneficiary is a named individual. Thus, the right to ownership of the proceeds should devolve in accordance with the contract provisions which are clear and unambiguous.

CONCLUSION

We therefore hold that the right to life insurance proceeds are sui generis and not governed by the codal principles. Accordingly, life insurance proceeds go to the named beneficiary in accordance with the provisions of the life insurance contract, without regard to community claims and, as such, are the separate property of the named beneficiary spouse.

DECREE

For the reasons assigned, the judgments of the lower courts are affirmed.

AFFIRMED.

G. *Succession of Julius Arabie*

57 So. 3d 573 (La. App. 3d Cir. 2011)

Doris Arabie appeals the decision of the trial court ruling that benefits from an AFLAC cancer policy held by her late husband, Julius Arabie, were his separate property.

For the following reasons, we affirm the decision of the trial court.

On March 1, 1986, during his first marriage, Mr. Arabie purchased an AFLAC cancer indemnity policy. After becoming a widower in 1995, Mr. Arabie was diagnosed with prostate cancer in 1996 and collected benefits under the policy. Mr. Arabie married Doris in 1999. At the time he married Doris, Mr. Arabie's cancer was in remission.

In September 2008, Mr. Arabie was again diagnosed with cancer. He again received benefits from the AFLAC policy totaling roughly $40,000.00, which were deposited into a joint checking account owned by Mr. and Mrs. Arabie. On May 12, 2009, Mr. Arabie died from the disease. Mr. Arabie died testate, and in accordance with his will, his son, Mark, was appointed executor of his succession. Also according to his will, any money in the joint account was to remain the property of Mrs. Arabie. At the time of his death, $65,776.81 was owed Mr. Arabie under the policy. In accordance with policy language, proceeds were paid to his estate in that amount. Mark Arabie filed a petition for declaratory judgment, seeking to establish that the 1986 AFLAC cancer policy and the $65,776.81 in benefits paid to his father's estate were his father's separate property. Mrs. Arabie reconvened, seeking to recover what she claimed was her half of the remaining benefits arising from the AFLAC policy, which she claimed was a community asset.

The trial court ruled that the policy and remaining benefits were Mr. Arabie's separate property, but that Mrs. Arabie was entitled to recover $1,480.00 from the estate, equal to one half of community proceeds used to pay the premiums for the policy. From that decision, Mrs. Arabie appeals.

On appeal, Mrs. Arabie asserts as her sole assignment of error that the trial court erred in failing to designate all the AFLAC cancer policy benefits as community property of the spouses.

It is well-settled that "a trial court's findings regarding the nature of the property as community or separate is a factual determination subject to manifest error review." *Ross v. Ross*, 02–2984, p. 18 (La.10/21/03), 857 So.2d 384, 395. "All things, corporeal or incorporeal, that the law does not consider as immovables, are movables." La.Civ.Code art. 475. "Rights, obligations, and actions that apply to a movable thing are incorporeal movables." La.Civ.Code art. 473. The AFLAC cancer policy was thus incorporeal movable property belonging to Mr. Arabie. *See Messersmith v. Messersmith*, 229 La. 495, 86 So.2d 169 (1956).

Louisiana Civil Code Article 2338 (emphasis ours) states: "[t]he community property comprises: property acquired during the existence of the legal regime through the effort, skill, or industry of either spouse...." "Things in the possession of a spouse during the existence of a regime of community of acquets and gains are presumed to be community, but either spouse may prove that they are separate property." La.Civ.Code art. 2340. A spouse may rebut the presumption of community by showing he acquired the property "with separate things or with separate and community things when the value of the community things is inconsequential in comparison with the value of the separate things used...." La. Civ.Code art. 2341. More succinctly, the classification of property as separate or community is fixed at the time of its acquisition. *Robinson v. Robinson*, 99–3097 (La.1/17/01), 778 So.2d 1105.

The policy in question was purchased in March 1986, some thirteen years before Mr. Arabie married Doris. The policy named Mr. Arabie as its sole owner and insured. Benefits of the policy were payable to Mr. Arabie alone. The final, disputed payment was paid to Mr. Arabie's estate, as the policy provided. While community funds were used to pay some of the premiums, the amount paid by the community was far less than the amount paid by Mr. Arabie separately, and Mrs. Arabie was compensated by the trial court for the amount paid by the community. Because the policy was acquired long before the existence of community regime, it is obvious that the policy itself was the separate property of Mr. Arabie.

However, because the cancer that was the condition triggering AFLAC's obligations under the policy occurred during the marriage, Mrs. Arabie claims that the benefits arising from the policy themselves are community property. We disagree. Although the condition giving rise to the currently disputed benefits arose during the community, the right to recover those benefits arose from the insurance contract which was clearly the separate property of Mr. Arabie. Simply put, Mr. Arabie acquired his right to recover under that policy in 1986. Likewise, AFLAC's obligation to pay him in the event he developed cancer also arose in 1986, regardless of when the triggering event occurred. Because the benefits stem solely from his separate property, they also remain the separate property of Mr. Arabie, regardless of when the events triggering the benefits occurred.

Finally, Mrs. Arabie seeks to compare the benefits payable under the policy to those of a disability insurance policy. However, we agree with the trial court that the policy was not written nor intended to replace wages that would have been community property. The benefits of the policy were to compensate Mr. Arabie, and him alone, for damages arising from a specific disease causing injury to his body. Nowhere in the listed policy benefits is there any indication that lost wages were recoverable under the policy. Further, Mr. Arabie's ability to work had no bearing whatsoever on his ability to recover benefits under the policy, as benefits hinged on a cancer diagnosis alone. We do not find the comparison to disability insurance compelling; thus, any jurisprudence on disability policies is distinguishable from and irrelevant to the case at hand.

Based on the record before this court, we can find no manifest error in the decision of the trial court that an insurance policy purchased thirteen years before the commencement of a community regime, and the benefits arising therefrom, were the separate property of its owner. Accordingly, we must affirm the decision of the trial court.

The decision of the trial court is hereby affirmed. Costs of this appeal are assessed against Doris Arabie.

AFFIRMED.

H. Other Community Property Jurisdictions

Louisiana's treatment of proceeds is fairly unique. In community property most jurisdictions give more weight to the classification of the funds used to pay the policy premiums. Generally, the classification of the funds used to pay the policy premiums determines the classification of the proceeds. Where a mix of community and separate funds is used to pay the premiums, some courts allow an apportionment "under which ownership of an insurance policy or its proceeds is separate or community property in proportion to the premiums paid by the separate or community property." *Aetna Life Ins. Co. v. Wadsworth*, 689 P. 2d 46, 49 (Wash. 1984) (*en banc*).

In the case of term life insurance policies, a number of community property jurisdictions have adopted the so-called "risk-payment" theory. In *Banner Life Insurance Company v. Mark Wallace Dixson Irrevocable Trust,* 206 P. 3d 481 (Idaho 2009), Idaho explained the issue as follows:

> The classification of life insurance policies as separate or community property is somewhat more complicated. Generally, life insurance policies insuring the life of a spouse are regarded as community property when they are acquired during the marriage and the premiums are paid with community funds. *Travelers Ins. Co. v. Johnson*, 97 Idaho 336, 340, 544 P.2d 294, 298 (1975); *Anderson v. Idaho Mut. Benefit Ass'n*, 77 Idaho 373, 377, 292 P.2d 760, 762 (1956). The rule as applied to term life insurance policies, however, requires slight modification to account for the unique nature of such policies. *See Aetna Life Ins. Co. v. Wadsworth*, 102 Wash.2d 652, 689 P.2d 46, 49–50 (1984).
>
> Unlike whole life insurances policies, term life insurance policies only protect against the risk of the insured's death for a fixed period of time. *Id.* at 49. They do not acquire any cash surrender or loan value nor do they accumulate interest. *See*, *Guy*, 98 Idaho at 207, 560 P.2d at 878. If the insured does not die during the covered term, the policy loses all of its value. *Johnson*, 97 Idaho at

340, 544 P.2d at 298; see also *United Investors Life Ins. Co. v. Severson*, 143 Idaho 628, 632, 151 P.3d 824, 828 (2007). Under such circumstances "[t]he insured has had the benefit of protection for the [term] and it has been 'used up.' He must pay another premium to enjoy further protection." *Guy*, 98 Idaho at 207, 560 P.2d at 878 (quoting Comment, *Community and Separate Property Interests in Life Insurance Proceeds: A Fresh Look*, 51 WASH. L.REV.. 351, 353 (1976)). This is true regardless of the "length of time the insured has had the policy and the number of premiums previously paid." *Id.*; see also *Wadsworth*, 689 P.2d at 49. Essentially, term life insurance policies are "a series of unilateral contracts, each beginning with the payment of a premium for a specified period ... and terminat[ing] at the expiration of that ... period." *Guy*, 98 Idaho at 207, 560 P.2d at 878.

In light of the unique nature of term life insurance policies, several community property states have adopted the risk payment theory to guide the classification of such policies. See, e.g., *Estate of Logan*, 191 Cal.App.3d 319, 325–26, 236 Cal.Rptr. 368 (1987); *In re Estate of Schleis*, 97 N.M. 561, 642 P.2d 164, 164 (1982); *Wadsworth*, 689 P.2d at 50; see also *Guy*, 98 Idaho at 208, 560 P.2d at 879. "The risk payment theory is a functional approach which takes into account the manner in which values accrue under various types of policies." *Wadsworth*, 689 P.2d at 49. Under the theory, the character of life insurance policy proceeds is determined by the source of the funds used to pay the risk portion of the policy, which for a term life insurance policy is the last policy premium. Id. at 49–50. In other words, term life insurance policy proceeds are only regarded as community property when the last premium payment was made with community funds.

Although we have not specifically held that the risk payment theory governs the classification of term life insurance policy proceeds, the theory is in accord with Idaho case law. *See Guy*, 98 Idaho at 207–08, 560 P.2d at 878–79 (relying on the risk payment theory in classifying a group term disability policy as a series of unilateral contracts, the proceeds of which could not be characterized based solely on the source of the initial premium payment); *Johnson*, 97 Idaho at 340, 544 P.2d at 298 (holding that proceeds from a term life insurance policy became vested in the surviving spouse upon the insured's death because the premiums were paid with community assets); *Noyes v. Noyes*, 106 Idaho 352, 356, 679 P.2d 152, 156 (Ct.App.1984) (holding that the community did not have an interest in proceeds from a term life insurance policy because the insured did not die during a "policy period covered by any prepayment of premiums from community funds"). Additionally, the theory is beneficial in that it accounts for the interest the community actually acquires when it makes premium payments on a term life insurance policy. *See Guy*, 98 Idaho at 207, 560 P.2d at 878 ("The risk payment doctrine correctly treats term insurance as a series of unilateral contracts, rather than as one bilateral contract." (quoting Comment, *Community and Separate Property Interests in Life Insurance Proceeds*: A Fresh Look, 51 WASH. L.REV.. 351, 374 (1976))). Upon the expiration of the term paid with community assets, the community interest in the policy lapses. Only if the community pays for an additional term will it retain its interest in the policy.

I. Uniform Marital Property Act

Section 12. Classification of Life Insurance Policies and Proceeds.

(a) In this section:

(1) "Owner" means a person appearing on the records of the policy issuer as the person having the ownership interest or, if no person other than the insured appears on those records as a person having that interest, it means the insured.

(2) "Ownership interest" means the rights of an owner under a policy.

(3) "Policy" means an insurance policy insuring the life of a spouse and providing for payment of death benefits at the spouse's death.

(4) "Proceeds" means the death benefit from a policy and all other economic benefits from it, whether they accrue or the death benefit from a policy and all other economic benefits from it, whether they accrue or become payable as a result of the death of an insured person or upon the occurrence or nonoccurrence of another event.

(b) If a policy issuer makes payments or takes actions in accordance with the policy and the issuer's records, the issuer is not liable because of those payments or actions unless, at the time of the payments or actions, it had actual knowledge of inconsistent provisions of a decree or marital property agreement or of an adverse claim by a spouse, former spouse, surviving spouse, or persons claiming under a deceased spouse's disposition at death.

(c) Except as provided in subsections (d), (e), and (f):

(1) The ownership interest and proceeds of a policy issued after the determination date which designates the insured as the owner are marital property without regard to the classification of property used to pay premiums on the policy.

(2) The ownership interest and proceeds of a policy issued before the determination date which designates the insured as the owner are mixed

property if a premium on the policy is paid from marital property after the determination date without regard to the classification of property used to premiums on that policy after the initial payment of a premium on it from marital property. The marital property component of the ownership interest and proceeds is the part resulting from multiplying the entire ownership interest and proceeds by a fraction of which the numerator is the period during marriage that the policy was in effect after the date on which a premium was paid from marital property and the denominator is the entire period the policy was in effect.

(3) The ownership interest and proceeds of a policy issued during marriage which designates the spouse of the insured as the owner are individual property of its owner without regard to the classification of property used to pay premiums on the policy.

(4) The ownership interest and proceeds of a policy that designates a person other than either of the spouses as the owners are not affected by this [Act] if no premium on the policy is paid from marital property after the determination date. If a premium on the policy is paid from marital property after the determination date, the ownership interest and proceeds of the policy are in part property of the designated owner of the policy and in part marital property of the spouses without regard to the classification of property used to pay premiums on that policy after the initial payment of a premium on it from marital property. The marital property component of the ownership interest and proceeds is the part resulting from multiplying the entire ownership interest and proceeds by a fraction of which the numerator is the period during marriage that the policy was in effect after the date on which a premium was paid from marital property and the denominator is the entire period the policy was in effect.

(5) Written consent by a spouse to the designation of another person as the beneficiary of the proceeds of a policy is effective to relinquish that spouse's interest in the ownership interest and proceeds of the policy without regard to the classification of property used by a spouse or another to pay premiums on that policy. A designation by either spouse of a parent or child of either of the spouses as the beneficiary of the proceeds of a policy is presumed to have been made with the consent of the other spouse.

(6) Unless the spouses provide otherwise in a marital property agreement, designation of a trust as the beneficiary of the proceeds of a policy with a marital property component does not reclassify that component.

(d) This section does not affect a creditor's interest in the ownership interest or proceeds of a policy assigned or made payable to the creditor as security.

(e) The interest of a person as owner or beneficiary of a policy acquired under a decree or property settlement agreement incident to a prior marriage or parenthood is not marital property without regard to the classification of property used to pay premiums on that policy.

(f) This section does not affect the ownership interest or proceeds of a policy if neither spouse is designated as an owner in the policy or the records of the policy issuer and no marital property is used to pay a premium on the policy.

J. Questions

1. H's employer provides him with a life insurance policy. H marries W after the policy is instated and he names W as the beneficiary of the policy. Is the policy community or separate?

2. W purchases a $1,000,000 term life insurance policy during her marriage to H and pays all premiums with community funds. At divorce, the court finds that the policy is a community asset and assigns it to W. H and W have no other community assets. Will W have to make an equalizing payment to W to account for the policy being awarded to her? If so, how much will the payment be for?

3. Would your answer to (2) be different if, at the time of divorce, W had a chronic and likely terminal illness, which made it unlikely she could procure a new policy of insurance?

4. H purchases a whole life policy prior to his marriage to W. Five years after purchasing the policy, H marries W. H and W divorce 5 years after their marriage. At the date of divorce H has paid $100,000 in premiums on the policy. Of that, $40,000 was paid prior to marriage and $60,000 was paid during marriage using community funds. At the date of marriage the policy had a cash surrender value of $2,000,000.00. At the date of divorce the policy has a cash surrender value of $10,000,000.00. How will the policy be characterized under Louisiana law? What rights does W have? How are W's rights, if any, valued?

4.11 ASSETS ACQUIRED OVER TIME: RETIREMENT PLANS (NOT SUBJECT TO FEDERAL PREEMPTION OR OTHER SPECIAL LEGISLATION)

A. Introduction

Pensions and retirement plans often represent a form of deferred compensation—compensation that is earned at an earlier date but is not paid to the employee until a later time. Retirement and pension plans are typically governed by an assortment of state and federal laws, which will sometimes trump state community property laws. These issues will be considered in more detail a subsequent section of the text.

Broadly speaking there are two types of retirement plans: the defined benefit plan and the defined contribution plan. In a defined benefit plan the employee earns the right to specified benefits after a certain amount of time on the job. These plans typically promise a specified monthly benefit when the employee retires. Neither the employer nor the employee actually makes a specified contribution to the plan and there is often no account maintained in the employee's name. These plans rely on the assumption that the employer will be able to pay the promised benefits in the future—an assumption that is not always correct. The popularity of defined benefit plans peaked in the mid-1980's and they have been on the decline ever since. Many state, local, and federal government employees are still offered defined benefit plans but they are increasingly rare in the private sector.

The second type of plan, the defined contribution plan, has gained popularity in recent years. In a defined contribution plan an account is kept for each employee participating in the plan and periodic contributions are made by the employee, the employer, or both, to the account. If the employee changes jobs he can usually take his account with him. At retirement, the employee is entitled to the funds in the account, plus or minus any investment gains or losses. In many defined contribution plans the employee can manage the investment of the contributed funds himself and can even withdraw them at an earlier date if needed. The availability of the funds does not depend on the continued existence or solvency of the employer. Many defined contribution plans receive special income tax treatment and, consequently, are often referred to by reference to that tax treatment.

The 401(k) Plan is probably the best-known defined contribution plan. A 401(k) plan is simply an employer created plan administered in accordance with Section 401(k) of the Internal Revenue Code. These plans allow employees to reduce their tax liability during their working years and defer payment of taxes until retirement—a time at which their annual income and resulting tax liability will presumably be lower. In essence, the employee designates a certain portion of each paycheck to be added to his 401(k) plan account and, by doing so, reduces his taxable income for the year. The employee's contributions to his 401(k) plan are invested in the manner he designates. Investment earnings are not subject to immediate taxation either. Rather, when the employee retires and begins making withdrawals from the plan the withdrawals will be subject to ordinary income tax. Employers offering 401(k) plans may make matching or non-elective contributions to the plan on behalf of the eligible employees and may add a profit sharing feature to the plan.

The IRA ("Individual Retirement Arrangement") is probably the second best known defined contribution plan. Traditional IRA's operate similarly to 401(k) plans. The major difference between the two is that an IRA is not typically an employer provided plan. Thus, IRA's are popular among the self-employed and small businesses. The Roth IRA is another variation. Its distinguishing factor is its tax treatment—which is basically the opposite of a 401(k) plan or traditional IRA. Contributions to a Roth IRA do not lower the owner's current income tax. Distributions from a Roth IRA at retirement, however, are not subject to income tax. For this reason, contributions to Roth IRA's are recommended in the early years of a person's career when he expects his current income tax liability to be comparatively lower than it will be at retirement.

There are many other types of defined contribution plans. An ESOP (Employee Stock Ownership Plan) is a form of defined contribution plan in which the investments are primarily in employer stock. A 403(b) plan is a defined contribution plan that is similar to a 401(k) plan but that is only available to certain employees of schools, non-profit organizations, and similar entities. A SEP (Simplified Employee Pension Plan) is a plan that allows employers to make contributions on a tax-favored basis to IRA's set up for its employees.

One issue illustrated in the cases that follow is the treatment of deferred compensation at death or divorce. Unlike other assets, the courts have readily allowed a pro-rata apportionment of funds attributable to these plans. Two types of apportionment are used: time apportionment and money apportionment. The proper type of apportionment often turns on the type of plan being divided. A time apportionment is often better suited for dividing a defined benefit plan like that in *Sims*. A money apportionment may be more appropriate for dividing a defined contribution plan.

At divorce, the court has several options for implementing the division of the retirement plan. Under the retained jurisdiction approach the court waits to do the actual mathematical division until the employee spouse begins to draw a pension or collect other retirement benefits. Alternatively, the court may go ahead and award a lump sum to the non-employee spouse. After determining the present value of the pension—

usually with the help of an actuary—the court orders the employee spouse to pay the non-employee spouse a lump sum award. Finally, the court may divide the retirement plan into two separate plans, one for each spouse. This approach, called the separate annuities approach, requires the court to apportion ownership of the retirement plan as of the date of divorce and then order the retirement plan administrator to divide the existing funds into two separate retirement accounts or annuities, one for each spouse.

B. *Winston H. Sims v. Marcella McGinnis Sims*

358 So. 2d 919 (La. 1978)

TATE, Justice.

The issue before us concerns the determination of a divorced wife's interest in her former husband's pension rights, insofar as they are attributable to his employment during the existence of the community.

The issue arises in the context of a suit to partition the community's assets following its dissolution as the result of a divorce. The trial court held that the wife's interest in the husband's pension rights was limited to one-half its cash withdrawal value at the date of dissolution of the community ($14,446.95), and the court of appeal affirmed. 349 So.2d 974 (La.App. 1st Cir. 1977).

We granted certiorari, 351 So.2d 175 (La. 1977), because we believed the wife's contention to be meritorious that, instead, she was entitled to have recognized her interest in the pension funds or rights, when they become actually payable to or for the husband, in the proportion that they are attributable to the husband's employment during the community.

Facts

Mr. and Mrs. Sims were married on May 30, 1946. They were divorced on November 19, 1975, nearly thirty years later. The husband has been employed by the federal government since June 18, 1956 as an air traffic controller.

During the existence of the community, he had acquired certain federal pension rights as a result of his employment. 5 U.S.C. 8331 et seq. The parties agree that the retirement plan, or at least the funds contributed by the husband to it, are a community asset.

The federal retirement plan is contributory -- the employee and the government each deposit 7% of the employee's basic pay into the United States Treasury. 5 U.S.C.

§ 8334(a)(1),(2). The annuity, however is not tied to the amount of those contributions, but is made according to a schedule provided by statute. 5 U.S.C. § 8339.

The plan includes several alternative rights acquired by contributions to the plan. At least two annuity rights are here pertinent:

An annuity based upon a percentage of average pay during federal employment: (1) is payable to an employee with at least five years' creditable service, which will become payable when the employee reaches 62 years of age 5 U.S.C. § 8333, 8338; or (2) is payable to an air controller who is voluntarily or involuntarily separated from the service after the employee becomes 50 years of age and has completed 20 years of service in that capacity, 5 U.S.C. 8336(e) (1972).

An employee, upon separation from the federal service, may also obtain the refund of contributions made by him (not including the matching employer contributions) in lieu of any annuity right. 5 U.S.C. § 8342(a).

At the time the community was dissolved by divorce in 1975, the husband had 19 years and 5 months of creditable service. He did not become 50 years of age until September 23, 1976, about ten months later. He thus did not become eligible to retire and receive *immediate* retirement benefits until that latter date.

On the date the community was dissolved, *if* the husband had then separated from the federal service, his retirement annuity would not commence until he was 62 years of age; or, upon such separation he could have received the return of the $14,446.95 contributions made by him from community funds. (For later reference, illustrative computations of annuities payable are included in Appendix A of this opinion.)

The community's interest in the pension plan or in payments made to or for the husband or as a result of his employment or contributions to such plan during the community

The trial and intermediate courts held that the wife's interest in the pension plan was limited to the return of one-half of the community funds contributed to it, *as if* the husband had resigned his job and had elected this option on the date the community was dissolved.

This reasoning and result is erroneous on several accounts: (1) *in fact*, the husband did not elect this option but, instead, continued his employment; and (2) if this method of fictitious valuation had been appropriate, it overlooks that the contributions which established the pension rights, under the actual circumstance of *continued* employment, included not only the employee's contributions but also the matching contributions by employer, which we have previously held represent an asset acquired by community earning and efforts, T. L. James & Co., Inc. v. Montgomery, 332 So.2d 834 (La.1976).

More essentially, however, this reasoning and result overlook the fundamental nature of the community asset acquired in a retirement plan through employment of either spouse during the existence of the community. The community interest stems not only from contributions made by community funds, but also by reason of any right to receive proceeds attributable to such employment during the community (i.e., as an asset "acquire[d] during the marriage," Civil Code Article 2402), whether based on the community's contributions or not. T. L. James & Co., Inc. v. Montgomery, cited above.

As stated in T. L. James & Co., 332 So.2d 851: "When acquired during the existence of a marriage, the right-to-share [in a retirement plan] is a community asset which, at the dissolution of the community, must be so classified--even though at the time acquired or at the time of dissolution of a community, the right has no marketable or redeemable cash value, and even though the contractual right to receive money or other benefits is due in the future and is contingent upon the happening of an event at an uncertain time." See also Messersmith v. Messersmith, 229 La. 495, 86 So.2d 169 (1966).

A spouse's right to receive an annuity, lump-sum benefit, or other benefits payable by a retirement plan is, to the extent attributable to his employment during the community, therefore an asset of the community. Further, the community interest is not limited to the refund of community funds paid, usually (as here) greatly less in monetary value than the pension rights acquired as a result of the employment of one spouse of the community.

Accordingly, except in an isolated decision to be noted below, our courts have uniformly held that, at the dissolution of the community, the non-employed spouse is entitled to judgment recognizing that spouse's interest in proceeds from a retirement annuity, or profit-sharing plan or contract, if and when they become payable, with the spouse's interest to be recognized as one-half of any payments to be made, insofar as they are attributable to the other spouse's contributions or employment during the existence of the community.

See: T. L. James & Co., Inc. v. Montgomery, 332 So.2d 834 (La.1976); Messersmith v. Messersmith, 229 La. 495, 86 So.2d 169 (1956); Moon v. Moon, 345 So.2d 168 (La. App.3d Cir. 1977), *certiorari denied*, 347 So.2d 250 (La.1977); Swope v. Mitchell, 324 So.2d 461 (La.App.3d Cir. 1975); Lynch v. Lawrence, 293 So.2d 598 (La.App.4th Cir. 1974), *certiorari denied*, 295 So.2d 809 (La.1974); Laffitte v. Laffitte, 253 So.2d 120 (La.App.2d Cir. 1971). Cf. Berry v. Equitable Life Assurance Society of U.S., 316 So.2d 399 (La.App.1st Cir. 1975). See also LeVan, Allocating Deferred

Compensation in Louisiana, 38 La.L.Rev. 35 (1977); Hughes, Community-Property Aspects of Profit-Sharing and Pension Plans in Texas, 44 Tex. L. Rev. 860 (1966).

Not in accord with the above decisions is Langlinais v. David, 289 So.2d 343 (La. App. 3d Cir. 1974), followed by the intermediate court in the present case. There, the intermediate court rejected the wife's claim to a share of the retirement benefits, since the husband had not retired at the date of the community's dissolution; it awarded her only one-half the value of the husband's account in the retirement fund. The result and reasoning are inconsistent with T. L. James & Co. and the other decisions cited, and the decision is overruled insofar as inconsistent with them and with the present opinion.

As in T. L. James & Co., Messersmith, and the other decisions cited, our decree will recognize the wife's proportionate interest in the retirement annuities, if and when they become payable, without attempting to fix a present monetary value for this interest, since it has none. (Unless the employment actually terminated following dissolution of the present community, for instance, the cash withdrawal value of the contributions is a fictitious value not proportionate to the actual retirement rights retained by the still-employed husband. See footnote 4 below.)

Due to the nature of the interest acquired by the community, as these decisions likewise recognize, it is not merchantable or susceptible to partition by licitation. The recognition of the respective interests of the spouses in this non-merchantable asset acquired during the community is analogous to a partition or division in kind. Of course, the parties between themselves can agree upon a valuation for purposes of conventional partition. See Due v. Due, 342 So.2d 161, 166 (La.1977).

The wife's proportionate interest in any retirement plan proceeds, if and when payable to or for the husbands account.

At the time of the dissolution of the community, as well as of the present date (at which, we are informed by the briefs, the husband is still employed as an air traffic controller), the community interest in the retirement plan has no immediate redeemable cash value. Until the employee is separated from the service, dies, retires, or becomes disabled, no value can be fixed upon his right to receive an annuity or upon lump-sum payments or other benefits to be paid on his account.

Nevertheless, under the decisions cited, the wife is entitled to a declaration at this time of the interest attributable to the community of any such payments, if and when they become due in the future. The interest attributable to (acquired by) the community in such payments, when they become due, is the proportionate part of them which results from a spouse's employment or contributions during the existence of the community. When the community is dissolved, the non-employed spouse is entitled to have recognized his or her one-half interest in this community asset, i.e., the right to receive payments from employee benefit plans, to the extent (proportion) that these payments result from the employment or contributions during the community. T. L. James & Co. v. Montgomery, 332 So.2d 834 (La.1976) and decisions therein cited.

In the present plan, the federal employee's annuity is determined by multiplying his average pay, as determined by the statute, by from 1 ½ to 2 per cent, depending upon his years of service. 5 U.S.C. § 8339(a). The amount of the annuity to which the employee will eventually be entitled, if he retires, cannot yet be fixed; the employee has not yet retired, and it is the date of his retirement (or separation or death) which fixes the employer's obligation.

The contractual arrangements between the employer and the employee, by which benefits are not payable until such determinative date, is not altered by the dissolution of the community prior thereto. The community's dissolution before such date does not substitute for the employee's retirement (or separation or death) as the event which fixes the employer's liability and which causes payments to become due. When they *do* become due, however, so as then to have a determinate value, the non-employed spouse is entitled to receive the proportion of them recognized by this judgment as attributable to the other spouse's employment during the existence of the community.

In the present case, the husband's creditable service during the existence of the community was 19 years, 5 months. The defendant wife has a one-half interest in compensation to the plaintiff husband which is attributable to that period. The proper ratio can be expressed in this way:

$$\frac{\text{Portion of pension attributable to creditable service during existence of community (19 years, 5 months)}}{\text{Pension attributable to total creditable service (still not determined)}} \times 1/2 \times \text{annuity (or lump sum payment)}$$

This computation determines the wife's interest in each installment ultimately paid by the government to the husband or his designee.

(As has been stated, the ultimate amount of the annuity payable to the husband cannot be determined until the date of his retirement or separation from the service. We have, however, attached as Appendix A to this opinion an illustration of the application of the above formula to retirement benefits to which the husband would be entitled if he had retired on March 18, 1978.)

Decree

For the foregoing reasons, we reverse the judgments of the previous courts. It is ordered, adjudged, and decreed that there be judgment in favor of the defendant, Mrs. Marcella McGinnis Sims, and against the plaintiff, Winston H. Sims, recognizing and declaring her interest in any annuities, lump-sum payments, or other benefits from the Civil Service Retirement and Disability Fund, 5 U.S.C. § 8331 et seq., to or for her husband, Winston H. Sims, as a result of his federal employment for the 19 years and 5 months he was so employed during the community formerly existing between the plaintiff and the defendant.

All costs of this court and of appellate review are assessed against the husband-appellee; all other costs, as imposed by the district court.

REVERSED AND RENDERED.

SUMMERS, J., concurs in the result.

DIXON, J., dissents. A right need not be marketable to have value. If the value of the right is ascertainable, the wife is entitled to ½ that value on dissolution of the community. If it is not ascertainable, she is entitled to naught.

Appendix A

In illustration of the application of the formula, we compute the community's (and the wife's) interest in any pension payable to the husband, if he had retired on March 18, 1978 (i. e., after 21 years and 9 months of service as federal air controller, during 19 years and 5 months of which he was married to the defendant and living in community with her). The figures below are set forth merely by way of illustration. No claim is made to exact mathematical accuracy or to the necessary correctness of the husband's average pay ($19,599.30) roughly calculated as the basis for the pension annuity.

As presently enacted, 5 U.S.C. § 8339(a) apparently provides that Mr. Sims' annuity will be calculated on the basis of 1 1/2 per cent for his first five years, 1 3/4 per cent for his next five years, and 2 per cent for each additional year.

If he were to retire March 18, 1978, the calculation would be as follows:

1 1/2% X average pay ($19,599.30) X 5	=	$1,469.95 plus
1 3/4% X $19,599.30 X 5	=	$1,714.94 plus
2% X $19,599.30 X 11.75	=	$4,605.88
(11 years, 9 mos.)	=	
TOTAL ANNUITY:		$7,790.77

Of this amount the following is attributable to his employment during the community:

1 1/2% X average pay X 5	=	$1,469.95 plus
1 34% X average pay X 5	=	$1,714.94 plus
2% X average pay X 9.42	=	$3,692.45
(9 years, 5 mos.)	=	

PORTION OF ANNUITY ATTRIBUTABLE TO EMPLOYMENT DURING THE COMMUNITY:

$6,877.34

The wife's share of the community attributable to her one-half interest in the community is therefore calculated as follows:

$$\frac{\$6,877.34}{\$7,790.77} \text{ X } 1/2 \text{ X } \$7,790.77 = \$3,438.67$$

(It is to be noted that, if the husband had retired on the date the community was dissolved, he was entitled to elect to receive a deferred annuity commencing at age 62, 5 U.S.C. § 8333, 8338, instead of withdrawing his contributions, 5 U.S.C. § 8342(a). Had he done so, under the above computations his pension would have been $6,877.34 annually, based upon his 19 years and 5 months of employment, from age 62 for the remainder of his life, together with certain survivor's benefits, instead of the refund of $14,446.95 of contributions.)

C. Subsequent History

Sims demonstrates how the court's formula also provides an equal sharing of the risks involved in the contingent right that the pension represents. After the 1975 divorce, Sims remarried in 1977 and then died in 1981 while still employed by the United States government as an air traffic controller. He had collected no retirement benefits, and upon his death his right to retirement benefits ceased to exist. The first wife obtained no proceeds from the retirement rights; she had an interest in a contingent right, and the death of the employee terminated that right, and her interest. *Succession of Sims*, 464 So.2d 991 (La. App. 1st Cir. 1985).

D. Note

The 1992 supreme court decision in *Frazier v. Harper*, 600 So.2d 59 (La. 1992), continues the trend recognizing pension benefits as an important element of the community's shared assets. In *Frazier*, the ex-husband's employee pension rights remained co-owned by him and his former wife. That plan was then replaced by the employer with a new (ERISA qualified) plan. The court of appeal concluded that the co-owned asset ceased to exist, with both spouses losing their interest in that lost asset. It concluded further that the wife had no interest in the new plan formed after their divorce since she was not married to the employee at that time. This conclusion was reached even though the new plan gave the husband credit for the years of employment during his earlier marriage.

A unanimous supreme court reversed and held the wife had an interest in the new plan. The court reasoned that the old pension rights were converted into new ones and that the wife acquired an undivided interest in the new plan under a novation theory. The former spouses were co-owners of the pension rights and both of them, under the court's approach to the law of novation, would normally have to consent to the novation for it to be effective. The wife's consent was not clear from the record, but the court concluded that if the change in the plan was not actually within the husband's authority to act alone, the wife ratified the transaction "by commencing and prosecuting this lawsuit" and could benefit from the novation.

The equities of the decision are apparent, although the reliance on a ratification theory is problematical. Ratification occurs when a person consents to an obligation incurred on his behalf by another. It is not at all clear that the husband was acting on his co-owner's behalf, and in future cases the covered employee could prevent the ratification theory from being used by clearly contracting only on his own authority and not on the other's behalf.

The court did offer additional reasons for its conclusion, citing Aubry and Rau to support a "de facto agency" concept and the Louisiana Civil Code negotiorum gestio concept. The latter two theories are preferable because they do not depend on the consent of both parties to produce the result.

A more direct analysis, however, is available to support the court's basic real subrogation approach. Indeed, part of the problem in this area of the law is that of conceptualizing it in terms of co-ownership. Co-ownership rules were developed in light of and apply clearly to things, but not to rights such as the claim against a pension fund administrator. Under normal rules, things are substituted for other things under real subrogation concepts, and rights are replaced by other rights under novation concepts. However, the Louisiana Civil Code has adopted the notion of ownership of incorporeals and governs what it calls their co-ownership. Fortunately, however, in doing this, the code provides some flexibility, which justifies the decision in the case.

The key article is Louisiana Civil Code article 818, which applies the laws governing co-ownership to rights only "to the extent compatible with the nature of those rights," allowing some deviation from the strict laws of co-ownership that are designed to govern things. When the rights involved are claims to performance by third persons under a contract, protection of the third person's interests from conflicting demands of co-owners would require that only the party in privity be able to manage or alienate the contractual right. Under this analysis, the consent of the ex-wife in Frazier was unnecessary. The husband could exchange the pension plan for another acting on his own authority, and real subrogation would occur to make the new right co-owned according the community and separate interests in the old plan.

This approach is not inconsistent with the novation concept, which is in effect real subrogation under another name. Louisiana Civil Code Article 1879 does not require that a novation be contractual. Comment (a) to Article 1879 states, "It changes the law only insofar as it does not define novation as a contract. Indeed, novation is not in itself a transaction but the legal effect of certain acts. Novation may even result by operation of law." In other words, by operation of law, real subrogation of the co-owned right occurs. Or putting it another way, a novation occurs with the new obligation replacing the old one. In any event, the replacement occurs by the consent of the parties in privity and the consent of the other party is not necessary.

In terms of basic policies, this result accommodates the interests of the ex-spouses and of the third party. The approach would seem to be necessary here when only one of the co-owners has management rights with respect to the co-owned intangible asset. It is analogous to the situation during the community regime when only one spouse has management rights to a community asset that is a claim against a third person.

E. *Louisiana State Employees' Retirement System (LASERS) v. McWilliams*

996 So. 2d 1036 (La. 2006)

ON REHEARING

VICTORY, J

We granted a rehearing application in this concursus proceeding to reconsider our opinion on original hearing overruling *Johnson v. Wetherspoon,* 96-0744 (La.5/20/97), 694 So.2d 203, and holding that a former spouse is not entitled to her community property interest in survivor benefits payable by a retirement plan owned by the former community. After considering the record and the applicable law, we now hold that the former spouse is entitled to her share of the survivor benefits payable under the retirement plan and that the retirement plan should have been ordered to pay these benefits directly to her as directed by judgments dated December 15, 1989 and August 24, 1998, which partitioned the former community. Accordingly, we vacate our decision on original hearing in its entirety, reverse the decision of the court of appeal, and remand this case to the trial court.

FACTS AND PROCEDURAL HISTORY

On April 26, 1969, Joel McWilliams and Dianne McWilliams were married in Louisiana. On January 10, 1972, Joel began working as an engineer for the State of Louisiana, Department of Transportation and Development, and became enrolled in the Louisiana State Employees Retirement System ("LASERS"). Joel and Dianne had two children, Jodee, born August 24, 1973, and Joelle, born November 10, 1981. After 18 years of marriage, the community property regime between Joel and Dianne terminated on June 15, 1987, and they were divorced on October 12, 1987. On December 15, 1989, a judgment was signed by the 21st Judicial District Court, Parish of Tangipahoa, which stated in pertinent part, as follows:

> Dianne McWilliams' interest in Joel McWilliams' Louisiana State Employee Retirement System plan is hereby recognized and shall be calculated as follows when and if he retires, terminates employment, or *dies:* (emphasis added)

$$\frac{\text{Portion of retirement/pension attributable to creditable service } \textit{during existence of community}}{\text{Pension/retirement attributable to total creditable service}} \text{ x 50\% x annuity (or lump sum payment)}$$

Dianne McWilliams' portion shall be paid directly to her from the retirement agency.

On August 24, 1998, the judgment was amended by the 21st Judicial District Court to specify the numerator for the above formula as follows:

> Dianne McWilliams' interest in Joel McWilliams' Louisiana State Employee Retirement System plan is hereby recognized and shall be calculated as follows when and if he retires, terminates employment, or *dies:* (emphasis added)

Portion of retirement/pension attributable to creditable service from 04/26/69-06/15/87 *(217 months, 20 days)*	
Pension/retirement attributable to total creditable service (undetermined)	x 50% x annuity (or lump sum payment = Dianne McWilliams' portion

Dianne McWilliams' portion shall be paid directly to her from the retirement agency.

* * *

On May 15, 1993, Joel married Jane McMahon and after approximately 10 years of marriage, Joel died on May 24, 2003 while still employed by the State of Louisiana. Following Joel's death, three individuals filed applications for survivor benefits with LASERS: (1) Jane (also naming Joelle as a child of the deceased member and a full time student at Southeastern Louisiana University); (2) Joelle; and (3) Dianne (also naming Joelle as a child of the deceased). Believing Dianne was entitled to her share of survivor benefits, both by virtue of the community property judgments and the jurisprudence recognizing a former spouse's rights to such assets, LASERS invoked a concursus proceeding pursuant to La. C.C.P. art. 4651 to determine who was entitled to the benefits. At the hearing, the parties stipulated that Dianne's interest in the retirement plan would be 24.60%, that the monthly payments would be $1,144.92 per month, and that the community contributions during the community years to the LASERS plan totaled $25,963.62. Using these stipulations, LASERS either retained the disputed portion of the benefits, $1,144.92 per month, or placed the disputed portion in the registry of the court as required by La. C.C.P. art. 4658 in order to be relieved of liability, and then began distributing the remainder of the survivor benefits to Jane and Joelle in accordance with the percentages set forth in the LASERS Member Handbook and La. R.S. 11:471.

The district court found that "the funds to be deposited to the registry of this Court by LASERS are survivor benefits rather than retirement benefits," and that the formula set forth in *Sims v. Sims,* 358 So.2d 919 (La.1978) did not apply to survivor benefits. Instead, the district court held that survivor benefits were governed solely by La. R.S. 11:471 pursuant to which only Jane and Joelle were entitled to the benefits.

Dianne appealed this judgment, arguing that the trial court erred in distinguishing survivor benefits from retirement benefits, and in refusing to give effect to the judgments of the 21st Judicial District Court recognizing Dianne's interest in the LASERS plan when Joel died. In the alternative, Dianne asserted that the trial court erred in refusing to award Dianne one-half of the community contributions made during her marriage to Joel. The court of appeal found that because La. R.S. 11:471, setting forth the provisions relating to the distribution of survivor benefits under LASERS, did not list the former spouse among the categories of individuals entitled to receive survivor benefits, Dianne was precluded from receiving her share of the survivor benefits. *Louisiana State Employees' Retirement Systems (Lasers) v. McWilliams,* 05-0938 (La.App. 1 Cir.6/9/06), 938 So.2d 782. The court of appeal also relied on its prior decision in *Bonfanti v. Percy,* 95-1189 (La.App. 1 Cir. 4/6/96), 672 So.2d 415, to find that the intent behind survivor benefits is to ensure that family members are not left destitute upon the death of a member. *Id.* at 785. However, in apparent attempt to fashion an equitable remedy, the court found that Dianne was entitled to recoup from LASERS an amount of money equal to 50% of the amount stipulated by the parties to be the total amount of accumulated contributions attributable to the community, $25,963.62. *Id.* at 786. Thus, the court of appeal ordered LASERS to pay the lump-sum refund of 50% of that amount, $12,981.81, to Dianne's widower and representative of her estate, Richard Sanders. *Id.* We granted writ applications filed by LASERS and Mr. Sanders. *Louisiana State Employees' Retirement Systems (Lasers) v. McWilliams,* 06-2191, 06-2204 (La.2/2/07), 948 So.2d 183.

DISCUSSION

LASERS is a comprehensive qualified defined benefit pension and retirement plan under Section 401(a) of the Internal Revenue code, and its provisions and regulations are outlined in La. R.S. 11:401, *et seq.* The statute provides that each person who becomes an employee in the state service, except those specifically excluded, shall become a member of the system as a condition of employment. La. R.S. 11:411(1). Under LASERS, any member hired on or before June 30, 2006, shall be eligible for retirement if he has thirty years or more of service at any age, twenty-five years or more of service at age fifty-five or thereafter, or ten years or more of service at age sixty or thereafter. La. R.S. 11:441(A)(1)(a)-(c).

LASERS retirement benefits are computed as follows: "[a] member who retires effective on or after July 1, 1973, shall receive a maximum retirement allowance equal to two and one-half percent of average compensation, as determined under R.S. 11:231, for every year of creditable service, plus three hundred dollars." La. R.S. 11:444(A). The member will receive this retirement benefit throughout his lifetime, unless he elects some other option pursuant to La. R.S. 11:446, whereby he receives a reduced retirement benefit and benefits are paid to another person he nominates upon his death. A former spouse of a LASERS member may be the person "nominated" to receive this "survivor annuity" following the member's death. La. R.S. 11:446. LASERS also provides for optional enrollment in a Deferred Retirement Option Plan, in lieu of terminating employment and accepting a retirement allowance. La. R.S. 11:447-451.4.

If a member dies before he retires, no retirement benefits are payable under La. R.S. 11:441-454. Instead, LASERS sets forth a provision for the distribution of survivor benefits which are payable when a member dies before he retires, and directs LASERS to pay a certain amount of money to the member's surviving spouse, and any surviving minor children or surviving handicapped or mentally disabled children, which become payable upon application therefor and become effective as of the day following the death of the member. La. R.S. 11:471; *see supra* note 6, page 1039. La. R.S. 11:471(D) provides the amounts to be paid by LASERS to these beneficiaries is dependent on whether there is a surviving spouse and/or surviving minor or handicapped or mentally disabled children. If no survivor benefits are payable, LASERS must pay to the estate or named beneficiary, which can be a former spouse, a lump-sum refund of accumulated contributions. La. R.S. 11:476. Further, if total monthly benefits paid are not equal to the accumulated contributions of the member, LASERS must pay a lump-sum refund equal to the difference between the two to the beneficiaries or the estate of the beneficiary. La. R.S. 11:475.

The issue presented in this case is whether the exclusion of the "former spouse" from the list of persons to whom survivor benefits are to be distributed under La. R.S. 11:471 operates to deprive a former spouse of her community property interest in these benefits which have been previously recognized by this Court as community property and which have been awarded to her in a valid community property judgment. For the reasons that follow, we hold that La. R.S. 11:471 does not operate to deprive her of her community property rights to these benefits.

"Since colonial days, Louisiana has been a community property state, whose basic policy has always been that the spouses share equally the acquets and gains of either spouse during marriage." Kenneth Rigby, *Matrimonial Regimes: Recent Developments*, 59 La. L.Rev. 465, 467 (Winter, 1999). This Court has consistently and faithfully adhered to this cardinal community property principle:

There is nothing more fundamental in our law than the rule of property which declares that this community is a partnership in which the husband and wife own equal shares, their title thereto vesting at the very instant such property is acquired. (Citations omitted).

We have repeatedly adhered to the doctrine that the half ownership of the wife in the community effects, its status not resting upon the mere gratuity of the husband, is entitled to a dignity equal to that of the husband's; and upon its dissolution and liquidation the wife is entitled to secure the delivery of this one-half right and ownership into her own exclusive management and control; and the courts have no discretion or power whatever to award her less.

Messersmith v. Messersmith, 229 La. 495, 86 So.2d 169, 173 (1956).

Our basic policy is reflected in Louisiana Civil Code Article 2338, which defines and classifies community property as follows:

The community property comprises: property acquired during the existence of the legal regime through the effort, skill, or industry of either spouse; property acquired with community things or with community and separate things, unless classified as separate property under Article 2341; property donated to the spouses jointly; natural and civil fruits of community property; damages awarded for loss or injury to a thing belonging to the community; and all other property not classified by law as separate property.

Accordingly, a long line of cases dating back to 1975 has held that, pursuant to La. C.C. art. 2338, the right to share in a retirement plan is a community asset, co-owned by the spouses, and subject to division upon dissolution of the marriage. *T.L. James & Co., Inc. v. Montgomery,* 332 So.2d 834 (La.1975); *Sims, supra; Frazier v. Harper,* 600 So.2d 59, 62-63 (La.1992); *Johnson v. Wetherspoon, supra; Bailey v. Bailey,* 97-1178 (La.2/6/98), 708 So.2d 354. As we explicitly stated in *Sims*, "[a] spouse's right to receive *an annuity, lump-sum benefit, or other benefits payable by a retirement plan* is, to the extent attributable to his employment during the community, therefore an asset of the community." 358 So.2d at 922 (emphasis added). We summarized the basis behind our community property law principles surrounding retirement benefits in *Frazier* as follows:

(1) an employee's contractual pension right is not a gratuity, but a property interest owned by him; (2) to the extent that the right derives from the spouse's employment during the existence of the marriage, it is a community asset subject to division upon dissolution of the marriage; (3) the right to share in a retirement plan is a community asset which, at the dissolution of the community, must be so classified-even though at the time acquired or at the time of dissolution of a community, the right has no

marketable or redeemable cash value, and even though the contractual right to receive money or other benefits is due in the future and is contingent upon the happening of an event at an uncertain time. *Frazier, supra* at 62-63 (citing *Sims, supra* at 921-22 and *T.L. James, supra*).

Specifically regarding survivor benefits, *T.L. James,* and *Wetherspoon* each held that survivor benefits were community property under La. C.C. art. 2338. *T.L. James* was a concursus proceeding brought by a private profit sharing and retirement plan to resolve a dispute regarding survivor benefits. There, this Court held that benefits payable under a retirement plan are earned income and not a gratuity, and are therefore community property. Accordingly, *T.L. James* held that the employee spouse could not contractually name a beneficiary to the survivor benefits to the prejudice of forced heirs or the community ownership of spouses, both present and former, of the wage earner, because rights of "spouses in community acquisitions are fundamental concepts of our legal system." 332 So.2d at 853 (on rehearing). In *Wetherspoon,* recognizing this Court's previous decisions that declined to distinguish between retirement and survivor benefits and that held that "any benefit payable by a retirement plan, to the extent attributable to the community, is an asset of the community," we likewise held that survivor benefits were clearly a "benefit payable by a retirement plan". 694 So.2d at 207. Harmonizing the provisions of the Teacher's Retirement System of Louisiana ("TRSLA") statute and our community property laws, we held that survivor benefits payable by TRSLA were an asset the community, regardless of the fact that TRSLA, like LASERS, lists only the surviving spouse and surviving minor and handicapped children as survivor benefit beneficiaries. *Id.* at 211. Thus, *T.L. James* and *Wetherspoon* involved contracts or statutes which distributed a community asset to certain beneficiaries to the exclusion of the owner of the community asset, i.e., the former spouse in the case of *Wetherspoon,* and the current and former spouses in the case of *T.L. James.* In each case, this Court held that these contracts and statutes could not operate to deprive the owner of his or her property in violation of La. C.C. art. 2338, which classifies those benefits as community property. Courts of appeal have followed *T.L. James, Sims*, and *Wetherspoon* and have likewise held that survivor benefits are community property under La. C.C. art. 2338 to the extent attributable to the community to be distributed to the former spouse upon the death of the member. *See e.g., Smith v. Smith,* 36910 (La.App. 2 Cir. 3/14/03), 839 So.2d 1255; *Vicknair v. Firefighters' Pension and Relief Fund of New Orleans, et al.,* 05-0467 (La.App. 4 Cir. 6/15/05), 907 So.2d 787,*writ denied,* 05-2327 (La.5/26/06), 929 So.2d 1233; *Succession of Silbernagel,* 96-2755 (La.App. 1 Cir. 2/20/98)), 708 So.2d 485; *see also Herrington v. Skinner,* 93-1556 (La.App. 3 Cir. 6/1/94), 640 So.2d 748; *Kennard v. Kennard,* 99-445 (La.App. 3 Cir. 10/06/99), 747 So.2d 628,*writ denied,* 99-3550 (La.2/25/00), 755 So.2d 252; *Ordoyne v. Ordoyne,* 94-1766 (La.App. 1 Cir. 4/7/95), 653 So.2d 839,*writ denied,* 95-1170 (La.6/23/95), 656 So.2d 1018 (all holding that the former spouse's relinquishment in community property settlement of interest in retirement plan also constituted relinquishment of rights to survivor benefits). In fact, only one case and the one relied upon by the court of appeal in this case, *Bonfanti v. Percy,* 95-1189 (La.App. 1 Cir. 4/6/96), 672 So.2d 415, has distinguished survivor benefits from retirement benefits in a public plan and held that survivor benefits are not community property.

Relying on our long-standing community property doctrine and jurisprudence, attorneys, governmental agencies administering public pension plans, and the public have conducted their affairs in the belief that every benefit of a retirement plan, including survivor benefits, acquired in whole or in part with community effort, is community property co-owned by the spouses and to be shared equally. Accordingly, judges have issued judgments and divorcing spouses have entered into settlements whereby benefits in an employee-spouse's retirement plan are partitioned and valued under the *Sims* formula, or some other manner, to be paid to the former spouse when the employee-spouse retires, terminates employment, or dies. Recognizing this, La. R.S. 11:291, applicable to LASERS and all other state and statewide plans and entitled "Community Property Interest," provides:

> (B) *Notwithstanding any other provision of law to the contrary, any benefit* or a return of employee contributions *shall be subject* to a *court order issued by a court upon or after termination of a community property regime,* which order *recognizes the community interest of a spouse or former spouse* of a member or retiree of the retirement system *and provides that a benefit or a return of employee contributions be divided by the retirement system with the spouse or former spouse,* but only after a certified copy of such order has been received by the retirement system and has been determined by the retirement system to be in compliance with applicable laws, rules, and regulations governing the retirement system. (Emphasis added.)

La. R.S. 11:291(B). As can be seen, this statute applies "notwithstanding any other provision of law to the contrary," i.e. La. R.S. 11:471's designation of only the surviving spouse, and surviving minor and handicapped children as statutory beneficiaries. Further, it applies broadly to "any benefit" payable by LASERS, not just retirement benefits. La. R.S. 11:291 recognizes the common circumstance where a former spouse has a community property judgment recognizing her rights to benefits, whether they be retirement or survivor benefits, and mandates that LASERS pay these benefits directly to her, if the court order is certified and LASERS determines that it is in compliance with certain administrative requirements. Accordingly, LASERS statutes, policy, and practice recognize that survivor benefits are payable to more than one person when a community property judgment is in effect which recognizes a former spouse's rights to such benefits. This practice is so common that LASERS provides "sample court orders" which contain a paragraph allowing the parties to specifically agree to the division of survivor benefits. Likewise, in the LASERS' *Membership Handbook,* in the section entitled "***Survivors' benefits,***" there is a provision entitled "**Benefits payable to more than one person**" which states: "Whenever benefits are payable to more than one person due to divorce, or remarriage, the benefit will be split and issued under each recipient's Social Security number. Under La. R.S. 11:291(B), LASERS' actuarial soundness is not affected because it is simply dividing the benefit payable to the statutory beneficiaries with the former spouse. La. R.S. 11:291(B) never requires it to pay more.

Accordingly, in this case, a very specific community property judgment was entered which recognized Diane's interest in the LASERS plan in accordance with the *Sims* formula. The language and intent of the judgments are clear and unambiguous regarding the words "plan" and "dies," recognizing Dianne's interest in the LASERS plan, not just retirement benefits under the plan, to be calculated and paid by LASERS when and if Joel dies, not just if he retires. Pursuant to La. R.S. 11:291(B), any benefits payable to the surviving spouse and minor child "shall be subject to [this] court order" and LASERS is required to pay the former spouse her share of the benefits as provided by that court order. Because the surviving spouse in this case married a member who had a former spouse entitled by a community property judgment to receive a *Sims* portion of survivor benefits directly from LASERS, the surviving spouse and minor child's benefit must be split with her according to the terms of that judgment. In this case, Dianne should have been awarded the disputed portion of the survivor benefits according to the amount stipulated to by the parties, $1,144.94 per month, payable for 24 months. The lower courts erred in failing to recognize Dianne's estate's ownership interest in these survivor benefits and in failing to award them to her estate.

Lastly, in an attempt to fashion an equitable remedy after denying Dianne her community property rights in the survivor benefits, the court of appeal ordered LASERS to pay Dianne 50% of the accumulated contributions attributable to the community. This was error. Not only should the court of appeal have found that Dianne was entitled to her share of the survivor benefits, pursuant to La. R.S. 11:475, LASERS may be required to refund accumulated contributions only when "all eligible monthly benefits have ceased." Nothing in the statutes governing LASERS allows the refund of accumulated contributions at the same time LASERS is required to pay survivor benefits, which it is in this case.

CONCLUSION

Louisiana is a community property state. "From the earliest times, the most important legislative policy underpinning the Louisiana community property regime has been that spouses share equally 'the produce of the reciprocal labor and industry' or both 'husband and wife.' " *Ross v. Ross,* 02-2984 (La.10/21/03), 857 So.2d 384, 392 (citing 16 Spaht & Hargrave, Louisiana Civil Law Treatise: *Matrimonial Regimes,* § 3.2 at p. 47 (1997)). This bedrock principle of community property law is found in La. C.C. art. 2338, which classifies "property acquired during the existence of the legal regime through the effort, skill, or industry of either spouse" as community property. For 33 years, this Court has consistently held that, pursuant to La. C.C. art. 2338, a spouse's right to receive an annuity, lump-sum benefit or other benefit payable by a retirement plan is, to the extent attributable to the community, a community asset. *T.L. James, supra; Sims, supra; Hare v. Hogkins, supra; Frazier v. Harper, supra; Johnson v. Wetherspoon, supra; Bailey v. Bailey, supra.* As a survivor benefit is clearly an "other benefit payable by a retirement plan," it is classified as community property pursuant to La. C.C. art. 2338 and the spouses are co-owners of that benefit. The fact that La. R.S. 11:471, a distribution statute, does not list the former spouse as a mandatory beneficiary of a survivor benefit does not change the classification of that benefit from community property to separate property, and cannot legally serve to deprive the former spouse of her ownership rights to those benefits. While it is laudable for the legislature to provide some benefit for spouses and minor and handicapped children who have lost spouses and fathers while they were employed by the state, this simply cannot be done with a former spouse's property.

In this case, the former spouse has a community property judgment instructing LASERS to pay her judicially recognized share of these survivor benefits directly to her. La. R.S. 11:291(B) applies "notwithstanding" La. R.S. 11:471's designation of only the surviving spouse, and surviving minor and handicapped children as statutory beneficiaries, and provides that "any benefit ... shall be subject to a court order issued by a court upon or after termination of a community property regime ... which recognizes the community interest of ... a former spouse ... and provides that a benefit ... be divided by the retirement system with ... the former spouse." The community property judgment granted to Dianne an ownership interest in Joel's LASERS plan, calculated according to the *Sims* formula, and directed LASERS to pay these benefits directly to her in the event Joel died. La. R.S. 11:291(B) mandates that LASERS pay Dianne these benefits under these circumstances and LASERS attempted to do so. LASERS then filed a concursus proceeding and began paying the benefits to Jane and Joelle after deducting the portion claimed by Dianne. The lower courts erred in failing to recognize Dianne's ownership interest in these survivor benefits, in holding that La. R.S. 11:471's exclusion of former spouses from the list of mandatory statutory beneficiaries deprived her of her community property, and in failing to apply La. R.S. 11:291(B), which clearly directs LASERS to pay a former spouse these survivor benefits when ordered by a community property judgment which meets that statute's requirements. Thus, the trial court's judgment ordering that Jane and Joelle were entitled to "the funds to be deposited to the registry of this Court" pursuant to La. R.S. 11:471 was error. Dianne's estate is entitled to these benefits according to the *Sims* formula as provided by the community property judgments and in the amount stipulated to by the parties, $1,144.94 per month, for a period of 24 months. Finally, the court of appeal erred in ordering LASERS to pay 50% of the amount stipulated by the parties to be the accumulated contributions attributable to the community in a lump-sum refund to Dianne's estate.

DECREE

For the reasons stated herein, our opinion on original hearing is vacated in its entirety, and the judgment of the court of appeal is reversed. The case is remanded to the trial court for further proceedings consistent with this opinion.

REVERSED AND REMANDED.

CALOGERO, C.J., and KIMBALL and TRAYLOR, JJ., dissent and assign reasons.

WEIMER, J., additionally concurs and assigns reasons.

CALOGERO, Chief Justice, Dissenting and Assigning Written Reasons.

Because I believe that we reached the correct result when we found on original hearing in this case that the LASERS survivor benefits at issue do not constitute community property, I respectfully dissent from the majority's decision on rehearing. Although the former spouse in this case has a community property interest in the deceased member's LASERS pension plan, valid methods for protecting that interest exist that would not violate the express statutory provisions that govern distribution of LASERS survivor benefits. Moreover, in its zeal to protect the community property interest of the former spouse in this case, the majority ignores the express statutory rights of the qualified survivors, which are severely prejudiced by the majority's holding.

Although rarely mentioned by lawyers or judges, most legal arguments and conclusions are based on a form of deductive logic that depends on a conditional syllogism. A conditional syllogism consists of a three-part argument that begins with a major premise that is stated as an if-then proposition. This major premise is typically a statement of the principle of law that controls the case. The second part of the deductive argument is a minor premise that, in a legal context, typically applies the legal principle stated in the major premise to the specific facts of the case. What follows is the conclusion. To be valid, a conditional syllogism must consist of these three propositions. By its nature, the conclusion in a valid conditional syllogism necessarily follows from the premises, such that if the premises are true, the conclusion must be true. However, if either or both premises are false, the conclusion is likewise false. In fact, because a major premise includes both an "if" clause and a "then" clause, if either of those clauses is false, the conclusion is false.

A simple example will illustrate. In Louisiana, virtually every finding of tort liability flows from the following conditional syllogism:

Major premise: If the defendant's negligent act caused the plaintiff's damages, then the defendant is liable for the plaintiff's damages.

Minor premise: The defendant's negligent act caused the plaintiff's damages.

Conclusion: Therefore, the defendant is liable for the plaintiff's damages.

The major premise in the above syllogism is true because it is based on a principle of Louisiana law found in La. Civ.Code art. 2315(A). In the typical tort case, the argument revolves around the minor premise.

The majority's conclusion that the former spouse in this case is entitled to receive survivor benefits flows largely from the following conditional syllogism:

Major premise: If retirement benefits paid by LASERS are community property, then survivor benefits paid by LASERS are community property.

Minor premise: Retirement benefits paid by LASERS are community property.

Conclusion: Therefore, survivor benefits paid by LASERS are community property.

As I will show, because the majority's major premise set forth above, and specifically the "then" clause, is false, the majority's conclusion is false.

At the outset, I want to be clear that the "if" clause of the majority's major premise is true. As the majority states, this court has, since its seminal decisions in *T.L. James & Co., Inc. v. Montgomery,* 332 So.2d 834 (La.1975), and *Sims v. Sims,* 358 So.2d 919 (La.1978), consistently held that retirement benefits being paid to a retiree by a private or a public pension plan are community property. I signed *T.L. James* and *Sims,* and have, since the late 1970's, signed every decision released by this court that has properly applied the principles derived from those decisions. There is no question that retirement benefits being paid by LASERS are community property that is co-owned by spouses and subject to division upon termination of the community. Thus, a former spouse is entitled to receive a so-called *Sims* portion of retirement benefits due his or her former spouse. This is true despite the fact the former spouse is not listed as a qualified recipient of retirement benefits in the statutes governing distribution of retirement benefits. Significantly, in this case, LASERS never paid any retirement benefits to Mr. McWilliams that would have been subject to Ms. Sanders' *Sims* portion, because Mr. McWilliams never retired. Instead, he died while he was still employed by the State DOTD, thus triggering LASERS's obligation to pay survivor benefits.

Where the majority errs is in its formulation of the "then" clause in its major premise. It is simply not true that the survivor benefits being paid by LASERS that are at issue in this case are necessarily community property simply because retirement benefits that might have been paid by LASERS would have been community property, had Mr. McWilliams retired before he died. Although some similarities exist between LASERS retirement benefits and LASERS survivor benefits, primarily because they are both benefits paid by LASERS, determination of whether the LASERS survivor benefits are community property should not be based on a finding that the two types of benefits are similar in some ways, especially because the two types of benefits are also significantly different in a number of ways. Determination of whether the LASERS survivor benefits are community property should instead be based on the same criteria used to determine whether any contested item is community property-i.e., an examination of the legal principles governing classification of community property. Thus, the majority should have begun its analysis with the following major premise: "If LASERS survivor benefits do not qualify as 'community property' under the language of the applicable codal articles as interpreted by the jurisprudence, then LASERS survivor benefits are not community property." Both the "if" clause and the "then" clause in that major premise are true because they are based on basic principles of Louisiana law. As shown by the discussion below, LASERS survivor benefits simply do not qualify as community property under the applicable codal articles as interpreted by the jurisprudence.

The Louisiana legislature originally adopted statutes governing survivor benefits under Louisiana public pension plans, like LASERS, by 1956 La. Acts, No. 21, for the stated purpose of providing "benefits to the surviving widow or dependent widower or children of any deceased." Pursuant to the statutes governing LASERS pension plans, when a LASERS member dies before he has retired, LASERS is not obligated to pay "retirement benefits." Instead, LASERS has an obligation to do one of two things upon the death of an employed member who has met certain qualifications. Perhaps in the majority of cases, LASERS pays statutorily defined survivor benefits to specified groups of qualified survivors pursuant to rules set forth in La.Rev.Stat. 11:471 through 482. Alternatively, if, upon the death of an employed LASERS member, there are no qualified survivors under La.Rev.Stat. 11:471, LASERS is obligated, pursuant to La.Rev.Stat. 11:475, to pay a lump-sum refund of "the total accumulated contributions of the member, to the beneficiaries or the estate of the beneficiaries...."

In Louisiana, "[p]roperty of married persons is either community or separate." La. Civ.Code art. 2335. It follows from that statement that a contested item cannot be classified as community property unless it is the "property" of a "married person." Thus, an asset cannot be classified as community or separate until it has first been identified as "property." *Robinson v. Robinson,* 99-3097, p. 7, (La.1/17/01), 778 So.2d 1105, 1114 (citing K. Spaht & L. Hargrave, *Matrimonial Regimes,* 16 Civil Law Treatise § 2.1 (1989 & Supp.1991)). By definition, survivor benefits cannot be considered "property" at any time during the existence of a community regime because under the governing codal articles LASERS's obligation to pay survivor benefits is triggered by the death of the LASERS member, at which time the community terminates. La. Civ.Code art. 2356. Further, LASERS survivor benefits do not belong to "married persons" because the only qualified recipients of survivor benefits are surviving spouses (i.e., widows and widowers) and minor or handicapped children. La.Rev.Stat. 11:471. La. Civ.Code art. 2340 provides that "[t]hings in the possession of a spouse during the existence of a regime of community of acquets and gains are presumed to be community" Certainly, survivor benefits cannot be said to ever be "in the possession of a spouse" during the existence of a community regime.

Moreover, LASERS survivor benefits do not fall under any of the five categories of community property set forth in La. Civ.Code art. 2338. The majority quotes La. Civ.Code art. 2338, but does not explain how LASERS survivor benefits fall within any of the categories of community property identified there. I submit that they do not fit into any of the categories set forth. First, survivor benefits are not "property acquired during the existence of the legal regime through the effort, skill, or industry of either spouse" because survivor benefits cannot be said to have been "acquired" during the existence of the community's legal regime. Even if the member is married at the time of his death, the community is terminated when the member dies such that it no longer exists to "acquire" the survivor benefits. Further, the LASERS member never has a right to receive survivor benefits, so they cannot be considered property that the member must share with his former or current spouse.

For the same reason, survivor benefits cannot be considered "property acquired with community things or with community or separate things, unless classified as separate property under Article 2341," the second definition of community property set forth in La. Civ.Code art. 2338. This is true because, as I have shown, survivor benefits are not "acquired" during the existence of the community regime. Likewise, survivor benefits are not "property donated to the spouses jointly" (the third definition of community property) because they are not "donated" and because they do not become due until the member spouse has died, at which time the spouses cannot receive anything "jointly." Neither do LASERS survivor benefits fall into the third, fourth, or fifth categories of community property because are not "natural [or] civil fruits of community property,""damages awarded for loss or injury to a thing belonging to the community," or any type of "other property not classified by law as separate property." As I have said, they are not "property" at all until after termination of the community. Since they do not fall into any of the categories of community property identified by La. Civ.Code art. 235, LASERS survivor benefits are not community property. The entire three-part syllogism from which that conclusion flows is as follows;

Major premise: If LASERS survivor benefits do not qualify as "community property" under the language of the applicable codal articles as interpreted by the jurisprudence, then the survivor benefits are not community property.

Minor premise: The LASERS survivor benefits do not qualify as community property under the language of the applicable codal articles as interpreted by the jurisprudence.

Conclusion: Therefore, the LASERS survivor benefits are not community property.

The majority describes the issue presented by this case, in pertinent part, as "whether the exclusion of the 'former spouse' from the list of persons to whom survivor benefits are to be distributed under La. R.S. 11:471 operates to deprive a former spouse of her community property interest in those benefits...." As the majority correctly notes, former spouses are omitted from the list of qualified, defined survivors. The majority correctly finds that the omission of former spouses from the list of qualified survivors could not, in and of itself, defeat a former spouse's community property right to receive a *Sims* portion of survivor benefits, if it existed, any more than the omission of former spouses from the persons qualified to receive retirement benefits prevents a former spouse from receiving a *Sims* portion of those benefits. Such a result would indeed violate Louisiana's overarching community property laws. Rather, the reason former spouses are entitled to receive a portion of retirement benefits, but not survivor benefits, is the fact that retirement benefits qualify as community property under the applicable codal articles as interpreted by the jurisprudence, while survivor benefits do not. As this court has held, retirement benefits are property acquired by the member spouse during the existence of the community that therefore fall into the first category of community property set forth in La. Civ.Code art. 2335. Thus, the statutory provisions governing distribution of retirement benefits are indeed subject to the requirement that a former spouse is entitled to his or her *Sims* portion of retirement benefits under the basic principles governing division of community property.

On the other hand, because survivor benefits do not qualify as community property under the applicable codal articles as interpreted by the jurisprudence, the statutes governing the distribution of retirement benefits are not subject to the requirement that a former spouse is entitled to receive a portion of survivor benefits. In other words, because LASERS survivor benefits are not community property, the general provisions governing distribution of survivor benefits control without regard for community property concerns. That being the case, a former spouse is not entitled to receive any portion of survivor benefits because former spouses are not qualified recipients of survivor benefits.

I must also comment on a couple of other points made in the majority opinion. As support for its conclusion that LASERS survivor benefits are community property, the majority quotes the following statement from *Sims:* "A spouse's right to receive an annuity, lump-sum benefit, or other benefits payable by a retirement plan is, to the extent attributable to his employment during the community, therefore an asset of the community." 358 So.2d at 922. The majority emphasizes the language referring to "other benefits payable by a retirement plan" in support of its conclusion, finding essentially that *Sims* stands for the proposition that any benefit paid by a retirement plan, such as LASERS, is automatically classified as community property, apparently regardless of whether it fits within any of the recognized categories of community property set forth in La. Civ.Code art. 2335. However, the majority's conclusion ignores another important predicate for finding that a particular benefit is community property expressly recognized in that quote from *Sims.* According to *Sims,* "other benefits" are community property only if a "spouse" has a right to receive that other benefit. In the case of LASERS survivor benefits, no "spouse" has a right to receive the benefits because it is the death of the employed LASERS member that triggers LASERS's obligation to pay survivor benefits.

The majority also states that this court's *T.L. James* decision "held that survivor benefits were community property" under La. Civ.Code art. 2338. Indeed, this court did find in *T.L. James* that the "benefits" that the retirement plan was required to pay following the death of the employee were community property. However, the term "survivor benefits" does not appear in *T.L. James.* More significantly, *T.L. James* involved a private retirement plan, subject to specific contractual provisions, and the court was simply applying community property principles to the contract in that case. This case involves a *public* retirement plan, subject to statutory provisions. Further, *T.L. James* is most assuredly not based on an analysis of current La. Civ.Code art. 2338. The case does cite the community property articles and principles applicable at the time the case was decided, but does not stand for the proposition that LASERS survivor benefits at issue here are necessarily community property.

That having been said, I hasten to point out that the very first case ever decided by this court that held that *statutory* survivor benefits distributed by a *public* retirement plan qualify as community property was *Johnson v. Wetherspoon,* 96-0744 (La.5/20/97), 694 So.2d 203, to which I dissented. In fact, in a follow-up proceeding to our *Sims* decision, the former spouse for whose benefit the *Sims* formula was derived was in fact denied the right to receive statutory survivor benefits distributed by a public retirement plan. *See In re Succession of Sims,* 464 So.2d 991 (La.App. 1 Cir.), *writs denied,* 467 So.2d 532, 541 (La.1985).

In addition to its improper reliance on previous decisions, most of which are in fact readily distinguishable from this case, the majority also relies heavily on La.Rev.Stat. 11:291 to support its conclusion that the former spouse in this case is entitled to receive a portion of the survivor benefits. The language of that provision is indeed broad, but it is not so broad that it can bear the weight of the rule that the majority would derive from it. Yes, La.Rev.Stat. 11:291 does provide generally that "any benefit.. shall be subject to a court order" that recognizes a former spouse's community interest in a retirement plan. However, the statute was designed only to facilitate the division of property that qualifies as community property, and CANNOT logically be interpreted to require the division of a benefit that does not fall into any of the categories of community property set forth in La. Civ.Code art. 2338. This court should not apply the law mechanically, but should look to the purpose of the provision. Because LASERS survivor benefits are not community property, they are *not* subject to a community property claim by a former spouse. La.Rev.Stat. 11:291 cannot be read to create a claim where none exists.

Further, the majority completely ignores the fact that, under its decision, the former spouse in this case receives a benefit because of the existence of a surviving spouse and/or surviving minor or handicapped child. If there were no qualified survivors in this case, there would be no survivor benefits and no opportunity for the former spouse to receive a portion of those benefits. Had Mr. McWilliams died without a surviving wife or a surviving minor or handicapped child, the Ms. Sanders claims would have been limited to half of the accumulated contributions to LASERS that are "attributable to the community." I see no logical or legal reason that Ms. Sanders should be entitled to receive additional monies because of the existence of the surviving spouse and child. Her only entitlement at law is to receive half of the accumulated contributions attributable to her community. I would therefore afford Ms. Sanders a right of action for that amount against Mr. McWilliams' estate.

Finally, I would point out what I believe is, in some ways, the most egregious result of the majority decision herein. Under the majority's interpretation, the former spouse in this case is entitled to receive not only a portion of the survivor benefits due to the surviving spouse, but also a portion of the benefits due to the surviving minor child. Even if the majority were correct that the surviving spouse's entitlement to survivor benefits is somehow a community asset (which it is not), I can conceive of no provision of statutory or jurisprudential law that could be manipulated to support a finding that the surviving minor child's right to survivors' benefit is an asset of a community that terminated long before survivor benefits became due to anyone. The absurdity of allowing this former spouse to recoup almost 25 percent of the benefits due the surviving minor child perhaps demonstrates better than anything else the flaw in the majority decision.

Further, the impact of this decision is relatively minor in this case, where the "minor" child was in reality a "major" who was only entitled to receive benefits for a short period of time (between her 18th and 23rd birthdays) because she was a student. However, under the rule established by the majority in this case, the former spouse would receive a Sims portion of the LASERS survivor benefits due the minor child even if that child was only six months old and was totally dependent on those benefits. As I have stated, survivor benefits were adopted by the 1956 Louisiana Legislature for the stated purpose of providing "benefits to the surviving widow or dependent widower or children of any deceased." The majority's decision errs by granting a right to a portion of the benefits designed to provide for dependent widows and children of deceased workers, despite the fact those benefits do not qualify as community property under the applicable codal articles as interpreted by the jurisprudence. The present majority's resolution of the case is not only legally wrong, but is contrary to what the Legislature has commanded. Further, the result is unfair.

KIMBALL, J., dissents.

I dissent from the majority's opinion on rehearing for the reasons expressed in Justice Traylor's dissent. I would add, however, that although survivors' benefits are not community property, the former spouse does possess a judgment recognizing a community interest in her former husband's retirement plan. In my view, the former spouse can seek to recover the unrealized value of her community property interest, which includes contributions to the retirement plan made during the former community, from her former husband's estate.

TRAYLOR, Justice, dissenting.

I dissent because I have a fundamental difference of opinion as to the characterization of the LASERS survivor benefit at issue. To the extent that the opinion on rehearing finds this particular LASERS survivor benefit to be community property of the LASERS employee, I dissent. LASERS pays, as a perquisite of employment, a determinate amount to statutory survivors. This emolument arises only ***after*** the death of the employee. Thus, a LASERS survivor benefit can never be the property of the employee, to whom it can never belong, and is certainly not property belonging to a community which ceased to exist for several years prior to the death of the employee. The only persons entitled to LASERS survivor benefits are identified by statute, La. R.S. 11:471, and are a surviving spouse, a surviving minor child, and a surviving handicapped child.

Until Joel McWilliams died, no one, not even Joel McWilliams, had a vested right in a LASERS survivor benefit. As this court has previously stated in opinions authored by Chief Justice Calogero and Justice Victory, the author of the instant majority opinion on rehearing:

A vested right is defined as that case when "the right to enjoyment, present or prospective, has become the property of some particular person or persons as a present interest. The right must be absolute, complete and unconditional, independent of a contingency, and a mere expectancy of future benefit [or a contingent interest in property]... does not constitute a vested right."

Sawicki v. K/S Stavanger Prince, 2001-0528 p. 10 (La.12/7/01), 802 So.2d 598, 604, *citing Tennant v. Russell,* 214 La. 1046, 39 So.2d 726 (1949) [quoting 16 C.J.S., Constitutional Law, § 215, p. 624; *see also Smith v. Bd. of Trustees of Emp. Retirement,* 2002-2161 p. 9 (La.6/27/03), 851 So.2d 1100, 1106.

No one had the right to enjoyment of the survivor benefit until ***after*** Joel McWilliams died and the survivor benefit became the property of the particular persons defined by statute. Being a benefit of a retirement program, the survivor benefit, prior to its vesting in statutorily-defined survivors, could have been eliminated entirely by the retirement program. As this court found in *Smith,* when discussing changes to reemployment benefits for retirees:

Prior to the achievement of eligibility, courts have deemed the right to be inchoate and the details of a contributory retirement system ... could be modified to the prejudice of the employee.

Id., 2002-2161 p. 11, 851 So.2d at 1107. Similarly, the statutorily-defined survivors did not achieve "eligibility" or entitlement to the survivor benefit until ***after*** Joel McWilliams died. Until that circumstance occurred, the statutorily-defined survivors' right to the benefit was inchoate and the legislature could have changed the requirements of eligibility.

Simply put, the benefit offered by the retirement system did not become property of any kind until the day ***after*** the death of the employee -until that time it was a "mere expectancy." The property did not belong to the employee, nor can it be properly characterized as community property. Although this court has recognized as community property the right of a spouse to receive money to become due in the future, even if the right is contingent, based on the effort of a spouse during the community, *i.e. Due v. Due,* 342 So.2d 161 (La.1977), the survivor benefits at issue here are easily distinguishable. As found in *Due,* and other cases, the important difference is that **the former spouse has the right to receive the money contingently due in the future.** Here, Joel McWilliams was not ever entitled to receive the survivor benefit. The survivor benefit was not money due to him and it was not money that was otherwise heritable from him.

Consequently, while the opinion on rehearing holds that La. R.S. 11:471 "does not operate to deprive [Dianne Sanders] of her community property rights to these [survivor] benefits," I do not believe that the survivor benefits constitute community property in the first place. Thus, the former spouse of decedent Joel McWilliams is not entitled to the survivor benefit because La. R.S. 11:471 does not name former spouses as LASERS survivor benefit beneficiaries. Moreover, because I believe that there is a distinction between retirement and survivor benefits in this case, I would overrule

Johnson v. Wetherspoon, 1996-0744 (La.5/20/97), 694 So.2d 203, as did the original opinion in this case.

Finally, I disagree with the portion of the opinion on rehearing which finds that the community property partition judgment gives someone greater rights than he or she would have under the law.

For the foregoing reasons, I respectfully dissent from the opinion on rehearing.

WEIMER, J., concurring.

My initial consideration of this case focused on the language of LSA-R.S. 11:471, and was ultimately directed by reading that statute and concluding that pursuant to its language, a former spouse does not meet the definition of a surviving spouse; thus, survivor's benefits are not subject to community property division. I am now convinced that I did not sufficiently consider other laws that touch upon the same subject matter, as directed by LSA-C.C. art. 13. ("Laws on the same subject matter must be interpreted in reference to each other.") Specifically, I did not sufficiently weigh the interplay between LSA-R.S. 11:471 and the civil code articles that define community property and its ownership (LSA-C.C. arts. 2335, 2336, and 2338), as well as the provisions of LSA-R.S. 11:291, which is entitled "Community property interest" and is found in the same title of the revised statutes as the LASERS provisions.

When these provisions are considered together, and harmonized, the inevitable conclusion to be drawn is that the LASERS provisions, LSA-R.S. 11:401 *et seq.,* do not purport to *classify* any type of benefit as community property or separate property, but simply provide rules for the *distribution* of the benefits of the *member* upon his or her death or retirement. Louisiana Revised Statutes 11:471 is a distribution statute; it allocates, or distributes, that which has been classified by provisions of the Civil Code (LSA-C.C. arts. 2335, 2336, and 2338) as community property. Louisiana Revised Statutes 11:471 does not change the classification of the property itself, unless we are to presume that with LSA-R.S. 11:471, the legislature intended to supplant community property laws and to give to a third party property owned by a former spouse. There is no support for such a presumption in the language of LSA-R.S. 11:471, which clearly speaks to the distribution of the *member's* interest, mentioning nothing whatsoever about the interest of any non-member, such as a former spouse.

Further, LSA-R.S. 11:291 appears in the section of the revised statutes that addresses public retirement systems generally, under the subpart entitled "Applicability of Certain Court Orders"; LSA-R.S. 11:291 is, at a minimum, a recognition that state retirement plans pay directly to certain persons when ordered to do so by a judgment. The language of the provision, applying as it does to "any benefit" recognized as belonging to the former spouse, is broad enough to include LASERS survivors' benefits.

Louisiana Revised Statutes 11:291 is the mechanism provided for disbursement of benefits recognized by community property law to the former spouse. This disbursement statute appears in Title 11, along with LSA-R.S. 11:471, and recognizes a former spouse's interest "[n]otwithstanding any other provision of law to the contrary."

This court's decision in *Johnson v. Wetherspoon,* 96-0744 (La.5/20/97), 694 So.2d 203, flows from the decisions in *Sims v. Sims,* 358 So.2d 919 (La.1978), and *T.L. James & Co., Inc. v. Montgomery,* 332 So.2d 834 (La.1975), to form an unbroken line of jurisprudence which the legislature has not attempted to alter statutorily. In light of the well-settled rule of statutory interpretation that those who enact statutory provisions are presumed to act deliberately and with full knowledge of existing laws on the same subject, with awareness of court cases and well-established rules of statutory construction, and with knowledge of the effect of their acts and a purpose in view, the lack of legislative response is revealing. *State, Department of Public Safety and Corrections, Office of State Police, Riverboat Gaming Division v. Louisiana Riverboat Gaming Commission and Horseshoe Entertainment,* 94-1872, 94-1914, p. 17 n. 10 (La.5/22/95), 655 So.2d 292, 301 n. 10. As the court noted in *Borel v. Young,* 07-0419, p. 21 (La.11/27/07), 989 So.2d 42, 65 (on reh'g), once this court has ruled on an issue, we should be extremely reluctant to change our position, as both the legislature and society in general should be able to rely on the finality of our pronouncements. In our civil law jurisdiction, we must always seek a statutory basis for our decisions. In this case such a statutory basis exists, and can be found when the provisions of LSA-R.S. 11:471 are read in conjunction with the civil code articles on the definition and ownership of community property and with LSA-R.S. 11:291. Pursuant to such a reading, it becomes clear that LSA-R.S. 11:471 is a distribution statute, not a classification provision. The provision speaks to distribution of the member's interest; the non-member's interest is not affected. This interpretation of the statute has been applied by the courts and LASERS in the past and has become the expectation and the custom which should not be disturbed in the absence of action by the legislature.

F. *Sherrie Jean Eddlemon Bailey v. James Marvin Bailey*

708 So. 2d 354 (La. 1998)

LEMMON, Justice.

This is an action to partition community property. The asset at issue at this stage of the proceeding is a retirement account in the name of James Bailey, an employee of the State of Louisiana and a member of the Louisiana State Employees Retirement System (LASERS). The funds in the account were credited by LASERS over a maximum period of three years as part of a deferred retirement plan in accordance with

La.Rev.Stat. 11:447-451, the Deferred Retirement Option Plan (DROP) for eligible members of LASERS which allowed payment of earned retirement benefits into a DROP account based on fictitious retirement while the employee continued to work.

At the beginning of, and during part but not all of, the three-year period that LASERS credited funds into the account, Bailey was married to Sherrie Eddlemon Bailey. The principal issue in this court is whether the spouse of a state employee in LASERS' DROP program is entitled to any portion of the DROP account that is attributable to funds credited by LASERS after the termination of the community.

FACTS

In July 1977, James Bailey married Sherrie Bailey. Mr. Bailey had been a member of LASERS since 1963. In October 1993, Mr. Bailey opted to participate in LASERS' DROP program, and LASERS credited funds monthly into his DROP account, as described hereinafter, for a period of three years. In the meantime, James and Sherrie Bailey divorced, and the community of acquets and gains formerly existing between the parties was terminated retroactive to January 28, 1994.

At the partition trial, the parties stipulated that Mrs. Bailey was entitled, as of the date Mr. Bailey entered the DROP program, to one-half of 53.65 percent of Mr. Bailey's regular retirement benefits under the formula set forth in Sims v. Sims, 358 So.2d 919 (La.1978), as the non-employee spouse's share of the pension rights attributable to the employee spouse's employment during the existence of the community.

The trial court rendered a judgment partitioning the community property. As to Mr. Bailey's DROP account, the judgment divided the account into two components: (1) that portion attributable to funds credited by LASERS to the account between the date Mr. Bailey entered the DROP program and January 28, 1994, the date the community was terminated; and (2) that portion attributable to funds credited by LASERS to the account after the termination of the community. The judge classified the first portion as community property and awarded Mrs. Bailey one-half of 53.65 percent of that amount. The judge further classified the second portion as Mr. Bailey's separate property.

In an unpublished opinion, the court of appeal affirmed. The court noted that while an employee's entitlement to optional participation in the DROP program is contingent upon past years of service, the program "contemplates that an employee continue working for three years." Slip opinion p. 4. Hence the court concluded that the trial court correctly characterized the disputed portion of Mr. Bailey's DROP account as "earned" after the termination of the community and therefore his separate property.

The dissenting judge reasoned that since an employee's right to participate in the DROP program is based entirely on past participation in the retirement system, the majority improperly focused on the employee's employment while in the DROP program. For purposes of the DROP program, the dissenting judge observed, the employee became a retiree and was entitled to receive retirement benefits at the time he entered the DROP program, and not when he completed the three years in the program. Thus the DROP account was an asset attributable to the employee's employment before the termination of the community, although a portion of the funds were credited to the account after the termination.

On Mrs. Bailey's application, we granted certiorari primarily to consider the res nova question of whether an employee spouse's DROP account, to the extent attributable to funds credited by LASERS after the termination of the community, constitutes the separate property of the employee spouse, or is apportionable between community property and separate property in accordance with the Sims formula. 97-1178 (La.6/30/97); 696 So.2d 996.

DEFERRED RETIREMENT OPTION PLAN

The DROP program is described by LASERS in its publication to members as follows:

> DROP is an optional method of retiring from the Louisiana State Employees' Retirement System (LASERS).... When an employee enters DROP, his status in LASERS changes from active member to retiree, even though he continues working at his regular job. The employee can participate in DROP for up to three years. During his DROP participation, he accumulates money in an individual account based on what he would have received as a monthly retirement benefit. He also continues to earn his regular salary. He can withdraw the money from his DROP account after he ends state employment-either as a lump sum or a series of payments spread out over time.

La.Rev.Stat. 11:447-451 authorize a state employee who is eligible for retirement to participate in the deferred retirement option plan, "[i]n lieu of terminating employment and accepting a retirement allowance." La.Rev.Stat. 11:447 A. Under DROP, an eligible state employee may enroll in the plan and is thereafter "considered by the system to be in a retired status" for the period he or she participates in the program. La.Rev.Stat. 11:448 A. Although the employee continues to work, payments are credited monthly into the employee's DROP account in the amount of the retirement benefits that the employee was eligible to receive if he or she had retired. La.Rev.Stat. 11:448 C. The base amount of the employee's eventual monthly retirement benefits is fixed as of the time he or she enters the DROP program. La.Rev.Stat. 11:448 B. The employee does not receive the funds credited into the account until he or she actually retires, La.Rev.Stat. 11:450 A, but neither does the employee receive any service credit in the calculation of the eventual monthly retirement benefits for the years that the employee continues to work while in the DROP program. La.Rev.Stat. 11:448 B.

As far as LASERS is concerned, the employee is retired and is credited in the DROP account with the amount of retirement benefits that would be due; as far as the employer is concerned, the employee continues to work and receives the salary for work performed; and as far as the employee is concerned, he or she receives the salary for the work performed and receives credit in the DROP account (which is not available to the employee until sometime in the future) for the retirement benefits that would have been paid had he or she retired, but is ineligible during the DROP period for accruing additional credits toward the calculation of either the base retirement benefits or the possible supplemental benefits earnable upon employment after the DROP period ends.

After the period of participation in the DROP program, the employee, if he or she elects to remain in service, begins accruing additional service credit in the calculation of his or her eventual monthly retirement benefits, but such additional credit is in the nature of a supplemental pension, in addition to the base benefits that were fixed at the time the employee entered the DROP program. La.Rev.Stat. 11:450 D.

PARTIES' POSITION

Neither party disputes that the portion of the DROP account attributable to funds credited by LASERS to the account before the termination of the community is apportionable in accordance with the Sims formula. The parties differ as to the portion of the DROP account attributable to funds credited by LASERS to the account after the termination. Mr. Bailey contends that since the funds were credited by LASERS only if he continued to work, such credits are a form of incentive earnings and are thus his separate property. Mrs. Bailey, on the other hand, contends that the entirety of the DROP account is a retirement benefit attributable to her former husband's employment prior to or during the existence of the community and that she is entitled to her Sims formula percentage of the entirety of the DROP account.

COMMUNITY PROPERTY STATUS OF DROP ACCOUNT

The employment and retirement contributions that gave rise to Mr. Bailey's right to have funds credited to the DROP account occurred prior to and during the existence of the community, and not after the termination. It follows then that the right to receive the funds in the DROP account, at least the portion attributable to Mr. Bailey's labor and efforts and retirement contributions during the existence of the community prior to entering the DROP program, constitutes a community asset.

This court addressed the interplay between ordinary retirement plans and community property rights in two seminal cases: T.L. James & Co. v. Montgomery, 332 So.2d 834 (La.1975), and Sims v. Sims, 358 So.2d 919 (La.1978).

In T.L. James, we recognized that deferred compensation earned during the existence of the community accrues to the benefit of both spouses. In Sims, we articulated the following principle:

> [A]t the dissolution of the community, the non-employed spouse is entitled to judgment recognizing that spouse's interest in proceeds from a retirement annuity ... when they become payable with the spouse's interest to be recognized as one-half of any payments to be made, insofar as they are attributable to the other spouse's contributions or employment during the existence of the community.

Id. at 922 (collecting cases). We noted that the community interest in the retirement benefits "stems not only from contributions made by community funds, but also by reason of any right to receive proceeds attributable to such employment during the community (i.e., as an asset 'acquire[d] during the marriage,' Civil Code Article 2402)," (now La. Civ.Code art. 2338). Id. at 921. We held that although the benefits would not become due until sometime in the future, the non-employee spouse was entitled, at the time of the dissolution of the community, "to have recognized his or her one-half interest in this community asset, i.e., the right to receive payments from employee benefit plans, to the extent (proportion) that these payments result from the employment or contributions during the community." *Id.* at 923.

Still further, we enunciated in Sims the following formula for calculating the non-employee spouse's interest (in cases in which the employee spouse has not yet retired):

$$\frac{\text{Portion of pension attributable to creditable service during existence of community}}{\text{Pension attributable to total creditable service (yet to be determined)}} \times \text{annuity (or lump sum)} \times \frac{1}{2}$$

Application of the Sims formula to a DROP account is complicated by the fact that the employee spouse's base retirement benefits are fixed as of the date of entry into DROP and by the fact that the retirement is a fictitious retirement. The fixing of ordinary retirement benefits is deferred until the employee spouse retires and is then divided according to the formula set forth in Sims. In the DROP situation, the employee spouse's election to enter the DROP program operates, as of the date of that election, to fix the base amount of the employee's eventual monthly retirement benefits, and this amount is credited to the DROP account monthly as retirement benefits, although the actual receipt of the funds in that account is deferred until the employee actually retires.

In the case of ordinary retirement benefits, the non-employee spouse's right to share is calculated under the Sims formula as of the date the community terminates, but the exact percentage cannot be fixed until the employee spouse actually retires. In the DROP context, however, the Sims formula must be applied as of the date of the employee spouses's entry into the DROP program, because that is the date the base amount of the eventual monthly retirement benefits is fixed, and the employee spouse earns no further credit toward these retirement benefits while in the DROP program. Significantly, the trial court applied the Sims formula as of the date Mr. Bailey entered DROP, albeit without discussion. Thus the trial court implicitly recognized that Mrs. Bailey's right to share in Mr. Bailey's eventual monthly retirement benefits was fixed as of that date, but then proceeded to treat Mrs. Bailey's right to share in the DROP account as if the funds in that account were attributable to Mr. Bailey's employment after he entered the DROP program. This is where the trial court erred.

If Mr. Bailey had actually retired on the date he entered the DROP program, Mrs. Bailey clearly would have had the right to share, in the stipulated percentage, in the retirement benefits he would have received. The fact that the same amount of monthly retirement benefits was credited to a deferred-receipt account under a fictitious retirement for a specific temporary period should not change that result.

The amount of the base retirement benefits that Mr. Bailey will receive upon actual retirement was fixed as of the date he entered the DROP program. Mrs. Bailey is entitled to her Sims formula percentage of that fixed amount. When Mr. Bailey reentered LASERS upon completion of the DROP program, he began accruing supplemental retirement credits to be added to his base retirement benefits in the eventual calculation of his total monthly benefits when he retires. Mrs. Bailey, of course, is not entitled to any portion of the supplemental benefits he will receive upon retirement, because these benefits are attributable to Mr. Bailey's employment after the termination of the community. But just as Mrs. Bailey is entitled to her Sims formula percentage of Mr. Bailey's base benefits he will receive upon retirement, she also is entitled to the same percentage of his DROP account, inasmuch as both the base retirement benefits and the funds in the DROP account are attributable to Mr. Bailey's employment and retirement contributions prior to the termination of the community.

The statutory provisions governing the DROP program refer repeatedly to the DROP benefits as "retirement benefits" and fix such benefits as of the date of entry into DROP. Moreover, the statutes expressly provide that if an employee elects to remain in state employment after the DROP period, any future retirement credits earned are in the nature of a supplemental pension. La.Rev.Stat. 11:450 D. The latter treatment fully supports our holding that the date of entry into DROP fixes a non-employee spouse's interest in the entirety of the retirement benefits, both the DROP benefits and the regular retirement benefits. Thus we glean no legislative intent to alter a non-employee spouse's right to such retirement benefits by virtue of the employee spouse's opting to participate in the DROP program. We hold that the entirety of Mr. Bailey's DROP account is apportionable between community property and the employee spouse's separate property, in accordance with the Sims formula--i.e., 53.65 percent to the community.

Accordingly, that portion of the judgments of the lower courts declaring the funds credited to the DROP account between the date of the termination of the community and the date of the completion of the DROP program to be Mr. Bailey's separate property is set aside. Judgment is rendered declaring these funds to be community property to the extent of 53.65 percent.

G. *Audrey Coogan Hodgins Hare v. Norman F. Hodgins*

586 So. 2d 118 (La. 1991)

DENNIS, Justice.

We granted certiorari to decide whether the court of appeal correctly partitioned a divorced couple's community property interest in the employee spouse's defined benefits pension after it matured in 1988. The trial court divided the community interest by awarding the non-employee spouse a fixed percentage of the pensioner's retirement payments. The court of appeal amended, restoring full pension payments to the retiree spouse, and relegating the non-employee spouse to a lump sum representing her share of the unmatured pension as of the date in 1975 when the community was terminated. Hare v. Hodgins, 567 So.2d 670 (La. App. 5th Cir. 1990). We vacate the partition decree and remand for further proceedings by the trial court consistent with this opinion.

The appeals court erred in basing its distribution to the non-employee spouse upon a valuation of the pension right as of the termination of the community in 1975. Procedurally, a court partitioning community property is required to value the assets as of the time of trial on the merits. La. R.S. 9:2801(4)(a). Moreover, and perhaps more important, the appellate decision is in conflict with substantive law in several respects. The termination of the community does not have the effect of freezing the value of each spouse's undivided interest in the community assets. Each spouse continues to be a co-owner of the assets until they are partitioned and, as such, is entitled to benefit from any appreciation in their value. In the present case, because the pension right ascribable to the community was not partitioned prior to its maturity in 1988, each spouse is entitled to a distribution based on the actual value of the fully matured pension. Consequently, it is incorrect to base the 1988 partition on the much lower valuation as of 1975 when the pension right was subject to contingencies that might have prevented its maturity.

On the other hand, the trial court did not err or abuse its discretion by choosing a fixed percentage approach to partition the community interest in the pension right, but its application of that method, without any adjustment, may have overstated the part of the pension attributable to the community. If substantial post-community increases in the pension benefits were due to the employee spouse's individual meritorious efforts or achievement, and not related to prior contributions ascribable to the community, the percentage of the pension asset recognized as community property should be decreased accordingly.

Audrey brought the action in the present case to partition the community interest in the pension benefits on March 23, 1988. The trial court overruled exceptions of prescription and res judicata filed by Norman. On the merits, the trial court followed a fixed percentage method and awarded Audrey a certain fraction of all Norman's past and future retirement payments. The fixed percentage awarded Audrey was based on the community or marital fraction rule under which the community's percentage of the pension benefits is assumed to be the same as that percentage of the employee spouse's creditable employment which occurred during the existence of the community.

Norman appealed. The court of appeal affirmed the procedural rulings, reversed the partition decree and substituted its own partition judgment awarding the pension to Norman and granting Audrey a lump sum based on the "Termination of Employment" provisions of the retirement plan. Under the plan, if Norman had chosen to terminate his employment at the time of the termination of the community in 1975, he would have been entitled to "a paid-up Deferred Annuity Contract payable at age 65." The court accepted the calculation of the value of such an annuity in 1975 by Norman's actuary witness and awarded Audrey one-half of that amount, $15,219, with legal interest from 1975 until paid. Hare v. Hodgins, 567 So.2d 670 (La. App. 5th Cir. 1990).

We granted the applications of the parties for writs. Hare v. Hodgins, 571 So.2d 638 (La. 1990). After considering the arguments and briefs, we conclude that the court of appeal correctly reviewed and disposed of the prescription and res judicata issues. Accordingly, the court of appeal's judgment will be affirmed to this extent for the reasons assigned in its opinion. Therefore, in this review we will deal only with the question of whether the classification, valuation and distribution of the couple's interests in the pension complied with law and equity.

2. Valuating and Dividing The Pension Right

In determining the value of each community asset, including the community interest in the pension right, the court must valuate the asset as of the date of the partition trial on the merits. La. R.S. 9:2801(4)(a); Spaht & Hargrave, supra, at 346. The former spouses continue to be co-owners of the community property even after the termination of the community and until it has been finally partitioned. See La. Civ. Code arts. 2369, 2369.1; La. Civ. Code art. 2369 comment (c); Spaht & Hargrave, supra, § 7.19. Consequently, when the court partitions a community property interest in a pension right by granting a former spouse cash or other property in lieu of an actual percentage of the pension payments, the court is required to valuate the community's interest in the pension right and the spouse's portion thereof as of the time of the partition trial on the merits.

3.Comparable Equitable Principles

Although there are important differences between the doctrines of community property and equitable distribution, and between the rules of individual jurisdictions, the problems of valuating and dividing community or marital pension rights in other fora are sufficiently analogous to our own to make the reasoning of their courts and commentators considerable and useful. See Niroo v. Niroo, 313 Md. 226, 545 A.2d 35, 40 n.3 (1988); Rodgers v. Rodgers, 98 A.D.2d 386, 470 N.Y.S.2d 401 (1980); See *e.g.*, Weisfeld v. Weisfeld, 513 So.2d 1278, 1280 n.1 (Fla. Dist. Ct. App. 1987), aff'd, 545 So.2d 1341 (Fla. 1989); See also, 3 Family Law and Practice § 38A.08 (A. Rutkin, ed. 1990); Goldberg, Valuation of Divorce Assets § 9.1 (1984 & Supp. 1987); L. Golden, Equitable Distribution of Property §§ 1.01-1.12 (1983 & Supp. 1990).

In general, the valuation and division of pension rights is a matter for the trial court's discretion, but usually calls upon the court to evaluate various alternatives developed and approved by the appellate opinions and scholarly commentary. There is a wealth of legal literature regarding the basic methods of dividing the pension in community property and equitable distribution jurisdictions, as well as variations and alternatives to them. See appendix. Two of the principal methods of apportioning the pension benefits are the "present value" and the "fixed percentage" methods. *Id.*

A trial court can attempt to calculate the "present value" of pension benefits projected for the employee spouse's future retirement years. Under this approach, the benefits payable must be adjusted and discounted for contingencies such as mortality, interest, probability of vesting, probability of continued employment and retirement life expectancy. [Citations omitted.]

An alternative method is to determine a "fixed percentage" for the non-employee spouse of any future payments the employee spouse receives under the plan, payable as, if and when paid to the pensioner. Under this approach, it is not necessary to determine the value of the pension fund. Instead, as a general rule, the percentage is based on a fraction arrived at by dividing the length of time worked under the plan during marriage by the total length of time worked toward earning the pension. [Citations omitted.]

In using the present value method, the court calculates the present cash value of the community or marital property benefits and awards to the non-employee spouse his or her rightful share in a lump sum or in the form of equivalent property. With the fixed percentage method the formula for the division is determined at the time of the decree but the court may reserve jurisdiction and delay actual division until the pension payments are received. [Citations omitted.]

Many courts maintain that the present value method is to be preferred if the pension rights can be valued accurately and if the marital estate includes sufficient equivalent property to satisfy the claim of the non-employee spouse without undue hardship to the employee spouse. Fondi v. Fondi, *supra*; Gemma v. Gemma, *supra*; Johnson v. Johnson, *supra*; Shill v. Shill, 100 Idaho 433, 599 P.2d 1004 (1979); Kikkert v. Kikkert, *supra*; Damiano v. Damiano, 94 A.D.2d 132, 463 N.Y.S.2d 477 (1983); 3 Family Law and Practice, supra, § 37.07[4][b]. On the other hand, the fixed percentage method is called for when the calculation of the present value of benefits will be too speculative. [Citations omitted.]

4. Dividing the Pension in the Present Case

In the present case, the trial court was confronted with the problem of dividing the community portion of an employee spouse's fully matured defined benefits pension. This task was complicated by the fact that the pension had been overlooked and omitted from a previous partition of community assets. The community was terminated in 1975 by judgment of separation of bed and board retroactive to the date on which the petition for same was filed. La. Civil Code art. 159. But because of the omission, the former spouses continued to be owners in indivision of the community pension asset. The present partition action was brought in 1988 after the former husband retired and began to draw matured pension benefits.

The trial court in effect classified and divided the pension by using a fixed percentage method, considering itself bound to award the wife one half of a fixed fraction of all past and future retirement payments according to the formula set forth in *Sims v. Sims*, 358 So.2d 919 (La. 1978). Under that formula the community portion of the pension right is deemed to be the same fraction that results when the length of the employee spouse's creditable employment during the community is divided by the length of his total creditable employment. We see no abuse of discretion or reversible error in the trial court's use of a fixed percentage approach, although, as we will explain, some adjustment of the formula may be necessary in order to prevent inequity in the present case.

The trial court correctly rejected the husband's proposed method of division, under which the court would have been required to award him the entire pension and grant the wife a lump sum of $15,219 plus legal interest from the date of the termination of the community in lieu of her interest in retirement payments. According to the husband's actuary witness, this amount was equivalent to one-half the paid-up deferred annuity contract payable at age 65 that the husband could have obtained had he terminated employment on the date of the termination of the community in 1975. If the husband had left employment then, he would have been entitled to a deferred pension of $952 per month payable in the future when he became 65 years old. According to the actuary, the $952 per month pension payable at age 65 would have had a lump sum equivalent of $30,438 in 1975, if the husband had terminated employment and if the company had chosen to pay a lump sum.

The husband's proposal, which was later adopted by the court of appeal, was legally incorrect and inequitable. The wife owns a present undivided one-half interest in the pension right insofar as it is ascribable to the community. The pension right fully matured in 1988 prior to the commencement or trial of this partition suit. To relegate the wife to a one-half interest in the value that the pension may have had in 1975 long before its maturity would fail to recognize her legal status as the co-owner of an interest in the present fully matured pension. La. Civ. Code arts. 2336, 2369, 2369.1; 2369.1 comment (c). The husband's proposal also conflicts with the procedural requirement that in the partition of community property the court shall value the assets "as of the time of trial on the merits." La. R.S. 9:2801(4)(a).

Moreover, the effects of the husband's proposal would be profoundly inequitable. If the wife's interest in the pension were valuated as of 1975, instead of after its maturity and at the time of the partition trial, she would be deprived of the substantial appreciation in value of her interest that occurred after 1975. As of that date the pension right was not fully developed and was subject to several contingencies that might have prevented its maturation, e.g., the employee spouse's mortality and termination of his employment. Consequently, the value of the unmatured pension right in 1975, which reflected a heavy discount because of these contingencies, was significantly less than the value of the pension right in 1988, which had survived all contingencies to become fully matured. Thus, the husband's proposal would have deprived the wife of the equal share of the pension ascribable to the community to which she was due, and, by the same token, would have created a windfall for the husband by allowing him to retain the fully matured pension right attributable to the community while paying the wife substantially less than one-half of its actual matured value.

For all these reasons, the trial court concluded that the fixed percentage method was preferable to the husband's inequitable and legally incorrect approach. In the absence of an acceptable alternate proposal with supporting evidence, we find no abuse or error in the trial court's selection of the fixed percentage method as a basic approach to partition.

We disagree, however, with the trial court's conclusion that a partitioning court is bound to use the fixed percentage method in every case analogous to Sims. In Sims this court required the trial court to apply a fixed percentage formula to determine the wife's interest in any retirement payments if and when they became due in the future. In doing so, however, we did not say that the fixed percentage method is the only technique that may be applied to divide pension benefits.

The Sims court added, perhaps unnecessarily, that

> [T]he community interest in the retirement plan has no immediate redeemable cash value. Until the employee is separated from the service, dies, retires or becomes disabled, no value can be fixed upon his right to receive an annuity or upon lump-sum payments or other benefits to be paid on his account.

Sims v. Sims, *supra* at 923.

In retrospect, the statement was unfortunate. If it was intended to signify that the employer could not be required to pay benefits until due under its contractual obligation, the statement was correct but ambiguous. But if it was meant to indicate that a pension right could not be valuated for purposes of voluntary or judicial partition prior to maturity the statement must be acknowledged as error.

Neither the Civil Code nor La. R.S. 9:2801 contains anything that requires courts to follow the fixed percentage method to the exclusion of others. In fact, La. R.S. 9:2801, which was enacted subsequent to Sims affords the partitioning tribunal a great deal of flexibility and clearly implies that the goals of equality and equity require that no one method should be used to the exclusion of other apportionment techniques. Moreover, our study of legal developments both here and in other jurisdictions convinces us that because of the great variations in pension plans and communal situations no one method can accomplish justice in every case. It is essential, therefore, that courts be able to take advantage of reasonable alternatives and adjustments in order to accomplish an equal distribution in an equitable manner in all situations. McDermott v. McDermott, 150 Vt. 258, 552 A.2d 786 (1988); In re Marriage of Rogers, 45 Ore. App. 885, 890, 609 P.2d 877, 882, mod. 47 Ore. App. 963, 615 P.2d 412, mod. 50 Ore. App. 511, 623 P.2d 1108 (1988); Gregory, The Law of Equitable Distribution § 5.05[1], supra; see generally, Thiede, The Community Property Interest of the Non-Employee Spouse in Private Employee Retirement Benefits 9 U.S.F.L.Rev. 635 (1975); Comment, Retirement Equity Inaction: Division of Pension Benefits upon Divorce in Louisiana, 48 La. L. Rev. 675 (1988); Comment, Distribution of Pension Benefits in Marital Dissolutions: Determining the Time and Valuation of the Community Interest, 24 Santa Clara L. Rev. 999 (1984) [hereinafter "Distribution of Pensions"].

For the foregoing reasons, the judgment of the court of appeal is reversed and vacated to the extent that it partitioned the community pension right. To the extent that the court of appeal judgment affirmed the trial court's decision to overrule the exceptions of res judicata and prescription, however, it is affirmed. The case is remanded to the trial court with a direction to render a new partition judgment after conducting further proceedings to determine whether the community fraction rule underlying the fixed percentage method applied herein should be modified to reflect that some of the post-community increases in earnings by the employee spouse should be attributed solely to his personal effort or skill and not related to the prior community earnings.

COURT OF APPEAL JUDGMENT AFFIRMED IN PART, REVERSED IN PART; CASE REMANDED TO TRIAL COURT TO CONDUCT FURTHER PROCEEDINGS TO DETERMINE WHETHER THE METHOD OF DIVIDING COMMUNITY PROPERTY SHOULD BE MODIFIED AND TO RENDER JUDGMENT ACCORDINGLY.

H. *Lisa A. Legaux-Barrow v. Clarence Barrow, Js.*

8 So. 3d 87 (La. App. 5th Cir. 2009)

MARION F. EDWARDS, Judge.

This is an appeal from a trial court judgment partitioning community property pursuant to a divorce. For reasons that follow, we affirm.

The parties were divorced by judgment dated May 23, 2006. In the course of these divorce proceedings, the husband, Clarence Barrow, Jr. ("Mr. Barrow"), filed a motion to partition community property. Each party filed a sworn descriptive list itemizing the assets and liabilities of the community, and a traversal hearing was held by the trial court. After the hearing, the trial court rendered judgment dividing the assets and liabilities of the community between the parties and ordered Mr. Barrow to pay an equalizing payment to his wife, Lisa A. Legaux-Barrow ("Mrs. Barrow"), in the amount of $3,433.

The judgment allocated the family home and much of the furnishings to Mrs. Barrow. She also received her retirement fund of $11,039, savings bonds valued at $1,200, and a 1997 Toyota Camry valued at $1,500. Additionally, the responsibility for the mortgage on the family home ($136,000) was allotted to Mrs. Barrow.

Mr. Barrow received a 2003 Dodge Ram Truck ($22,500), a Harley-Davidson Motorcycle ($14,600), his pension valued at $68,800, some household items, and cash in the amount of $14,000 for proceeds from a prior sale of a motorcycle, and $6,397 in hurricane insurance proceeds.

The trial court allocated responsibility for the credit card bills ($3,783) and the note on the dodge Ram ($12,000) to Mr. Barrow.

The net amount allocated to Mrs. Barrow was $92,156, and the net to Mr. Barrow was $111,664, leaving an equalizing payment of $3,433 due to Mrs. Barrow.

Mr. Barrow appeals from that judgment and presents only one issue for our review. He argues that the trial court erred in applying the Hare present value methodology, rather than the Sims fixed-percentage formula to his pension. At the trial on the matter, Mr. Barrow requested the trial court to use the Sims formula.

When the Louisiana Supreme Court handed down the decision in Sims, the Louisiana statutory scheme for partitioning community property did not allow a judicial partition of unmatured pension benefits. Since that time several changes in Federal and State law, including the enactment of LSA-R.S. 9:2801 were recognized by the Louisiana Supreme Court in its decision in Hare. The Hare Court found that:

> Neither the Civil Code nor La.R.S. 9:2801 contains anything that requires courts to follow the fixed percentage method to the exclusion of others. In fact, La.R.S. 9:2801, which was enacted subsequent to Sims affords the partitioning tribunal a great deal of flexibility and clearly implies that the goals of equality and equity require that no one method should be used to the exclusion of other apportionment techniques. Moreover, our study of legal developments both here and in other jurisdictions convinces us that because of the great variations in pension plans and communal situations no one method can accomplish justice in every case. It is essential, therefore, that courts be able to take advantage of reasonable alternatives and adjustments in order to accomplish an equal distribution in an equitable manner in all situations. (Citations omitted.)

It is clear from the written Reasons for Judgment that the trial court considered Mr. Barrow's request but found it inappropriate in this matter.

In its Reasons for Judgment, the trial court stated:

> Mr. Barrow has urged this court to allocate only the tangible assets and apply the Sims formula to the distribution of the pension funds. To do so would require Mrs. Barrow to pay a large sum of money as an equalizing payment to Mr. Barrow, and Mrs. Barrow cannot afford to make such payment due to her assumption of the mortgage on the family home. Allocation of the parties' pension funds in their entirety to the respective owners results in a more feasible, less burdensome, distribution and is permitted by La. R.S. 9:2801 A(4)(c)[.]

Thus, the trial court relied on LSA-R.S. 9:2801(A)(4)(c) in allocating pension funds in their entirety to the respective owners, rather that applying the Sims formula to this matter. This is clearly permitted by the statute and the jurisprudence.

It is well-settled that a trial court has broad discretion in adjudicating issues raised by divorce and partition of the community. The trial judge is afforded a great deal of latitude in arriving at an equitable distribution of the assets between the spouses. In deciding to whom an asset or liability shall be allocated, the court shall consider the nature and source of the asset or liability, the economic condition of each spouse, and any other circumstances the court deems relevant. The trial court's allocation or assigning of assets and liabilities in the partition of community property is reviewed under the abuse of discretion standard.

In support of his argument that this Court should use the Sims fixed-formula method, Mr. Barrow cites Blanchard v. Blanchard. We find the facts of Blanchard to be distinguishable from the matter before us and; therefore, not controlling. In Blanchard the community property consisted of only two assets subject to division, the home valued at $44,000 and the wife's pension fund with a present value of $50,267. In that case we ruled that the vast differences in nature and character between the two assets required the use of the Sims formula.

In the instant case there are many other assets of the community that were divided by the trial court, including two pensions. Further, in this matter, unlike in Blanchard, the home is not mortgage-free. While it is true the community home has a value of $200,000, it is encumbered by a mortgage in the amount of $136,000, leaving a net value of 64,000. Mr. Barrow's pension fund has a current value of $68,800. But, these are not the only two assets at issue in the division of property. Unlike Blanchard, the Barrows each have a pension and several other assets including vehicles, household goods, and cash. In addition to his pension, Mr. Barrow also received two vehicles, hurricane proceeds and cash from the sale of motorcycle, while Ms. Barrow received most of the household effects.

In the matter before us, the trial court gave valid reasons for the decision. The court allocated to each party their own pension. Accordingly, Mr. Barrow received his pension, currently valued at $68,800, and Mrs. Barrow received hers, currently valued at $11,039. Ms. Barrow did receive the house, but she also assumed the mortgage. Other assets were divided up by the trial court as discussed herein.

Considering those allocations and the allocations as a whole, we can find no abuse of discretion in the trial court's decision.

Accordingly, we affirm the judgment.

AFFIRMED.

GUIDRY, J., concurs.
JASMINE, J., dissents.
JASMINE, J., dissents.

I respectfully dissent from the majority's opinion. While the purpose of LSA-9:2801 is to effect an equitable distribution of community assets and liabilities, and recognizing that the trial judge has vast discretion in carrying out this duty, I find that the trial court abused that discretion in awarding the former community home to Mrs. Barrow and his pension to Mr. Barrow. Given the vastly different character of the assets, I find that the partition is not equitable.

Given the difference in the character of the assets (the home and the pension) and the length of time before the pension matures and is payable, I find that the trial court should have partitioned the pension using the "fixed percentage" method as approved by the court in *Blanchard v. Blanchard,* 97-2305 La. 1/20/99, 731 So.2d 175.

I further find that the trial court abused its discretion when it appeared to consider only the burden upon Mrs. Barrow of finding cash to purchase Mr. Barrow's portion of the community home, if it were partitioned, and not considering the burden to Mr. Barrow of receiving an asset, his pension, that has no present value, of which the contingencies have not yet been met, and is years away from maturing. I find that an equitable distribution of the community assets could be realized by dividing both pensions by the fixed percentage method, and partitioning the former community home. The remainder of the community assets could be equitably partitioned and/or awarded in such a way as to enable Mrs. Barrow to purchase Mr. Barrow's portion of the community home. This way, both parties immediately share in the value of largest tangible asset of the community, the home, while both share the risks of the unmatured pensions.

I. Uniform Marital Property Act

Section 13. Classification of Deferred Employment Benefits.

(a) A deferred employment benefit attributable to employment of a spouse occurring after the determination date is marital property.

(b) A deferred employment benefit attributable to employment of a spouse occurring during marriage and partly before and partly after the determination date is mixed property. The marital property component of that mixed property is the part resulting from multiplying the entire benefit by a fraction of which the numerator is the period of employment giving rise to the benefit that occurred after the determination date and during marriage and the denominator is the total period of the employment. Unless provided otherwise in a decree, marital property agreement, or written consent, valuation of a deferred employment benefit that is mixed property shall be made as of the death of a spouse or a dissolution.

(c) Ownership or disposition provisions of a deferred employment benefit which conflict with subsections (a) and (b) are ineffective between spouses, former spouses, or between a surviving spouse and a person claiming under a deceased spouse's disposition at death.

(d) If an administrator of an arrangement for deferred employment benefits makes payments or takes action in accordance with the arrangement and the administrator's records, the administrator is not liable because of those payments or actions unless, at the time of the payments or actions, it had actual knowledge of inconsistent provisions of a decree or marital property agreement or of an adverse claim by a spouse, former spouse, surviving spouse, or a person claiming under a deceased spouse's disposition at death.

4.12 ASSETS ACQUIRED OVER TIME: RETIREMENT PLANS AND PENSIONS SUBJECT TO FEDERAL PREEMPTION OR OTHER SPECIAL LEGISLATION

A. Introduction

The Employee Retirement Income Security Act of 1974 (ERISA) is a federal law applicable to most pension, retirement, and health plans established by private (non-governmental) employers. As initially enacted, ERISA imposed various disclosure, reporting, and fiduciary responsibilities on those who manage and control retirement plan assets. ERISA touches on many areas of law. When ERISA conflicts with applicable state law, which it often does, questions of federal preemption arise. During its 1996-1997 term alone, the U.S. Supreme Court decided three ERISA preemption cases—including *Boggs v. Boggs*, 520 U.S. 833 (1997). In the community property context, ERISA presented conflicts in the division of pension and retirement benefits at divorce and at death. The Retirement Equity Act of 1984 (REA), one of many amendments to ERISA, specifically addressed the issue of division at divorce.

> This major piece of pension legislation amends the Employee Retirement Income Security Act (ERISA) and the Internal Revenue Code (IRC) primarily in response to public concerns that working women are not receiving their fair share of private pension benefits.

> ....Confusion also existed over whether ERISA preempted State divorce laws, thereby preventing pension plans from complying with domestic relations court orders allocating to a spouse a portion of the worker's pension as part of a property settlement.

48 SOC. SEC. BULL. NO. 5, p. 38 (1985). The REA clarified the treatment of pension and retirement plans at divorce and specifically allowed them to be divided in accordance with state law provided that a specific procedural mechanism—the QDRO—was followed:

> Under ERISA, benefits paid by qualified retirement plans are subject to prohibitions against assignment or alienation. These rules precluding the transferring of plan benefits are often referred to as spendthrift provisions. ERISA also contains express provisions superseding or preempting State laws regarding pension plans. As a result, a pension plan that does not include the required spendthrift provisions is not qualified under the IRC, and State laws permitting an assignment or transfer of benefits are generally preempted by ERISA.
>
> Recently, courts have disagreed over whether ERISA's preemption and spendthrift provisions were intended to prevent the application of State domestic relations laws permitting the division of vested pension benefits for the purpose of meeting family support obligations (for example, alimony, separate maintenance, and child support obligations). Before REA was enacted, the Internal Revenue Service (IRS) had ruled that the spendthrift provisions were not violated when a plan trustee complied with a court order requiring the distribution of benefits of a participant in pay status to the participant's spouse or children to meet the participant's alimony or child support obligation. The IRS had taken no position when the participant's benefits were not in pay status.
>
> The new legislation clarifies ERISA's spendthrift provisions by providing new rules for the treatment of certain domestic relations orders. In addition, REA creates an exception to the ERISA preemption provision with respect to these orders.
>
> REA provides that distributions ordered under a "qualified domestic relation order" will not be subject to the spendthrift provisions of ERISA and that the plan must pay for them. A domestic relations order is any judgment, decree, or order (including the approval of property settlement agreements) that relates to child support, alimony payments, or marital property rights of a spouse or child of the participant made pursuant to State domestic relations law.

To be qualified, the order must list the amount or percentage of benefits payable to the spouse and/or child payee, or the manner in which this amount is to be determined, and the number of payments or the period for which the payments are required. The order will not be a qualified order if it requires the plan to provide any type of payment or form of benefit or option not otherwise provided under the plan, requires the plan to increase benefits, or requires payment to someone when such payments are already required to be paid to some- one else under a previously existing qualified domestic relations order.

The order may require payments to begin to a spouse or dependent only after the date on which the participant attains the earliest retirement age. The value of the payee's benefits need not take into account the value of any employer subsidy for early retirement.

The plan administrator must establish reasonable procedures in writing for determining the qualified status of domestic-relations orders and for administering payments under these orders. The participant and those individuals entitled to benefits must be promptly notified of receipt of the order and the plan's procedures for dealing with it. While the determination is being made as to whether the order is qualified, the plan administrator must segregate, either in a separate account in the plan or in an escrow account, the amounts that would be payable if the order is truly payable.

48 SOC. SEC. BULL. NO. 5, p. 43 (1985). In other words, at divorce, an ERISA governed plan should be divided in accordance with state law. In order to implement the state law, the court must issue (typically at the request of the non-employee spouse) an order dividing the asset. The order must meet the requirements of a QDRO and should be sent to the plan administrator. The requirements of the QDRO, which are found in Section 414(p) of the Internal Revenue Code, are not particularly onerous:

(p) Qualified domestic relations order defined: For purposes of this subsection and section 401 (a)(13)—

(1) **In general**

(A) **Qualified domestic relations order.** The term "qualified domestic relations order" means a domestic relations order—

(i) which creates or recognizes the existence of an alternate payee's right to, or assigns to an alternate payee the right to, receive all or a portion of the benefits payable with respect to a participant under a plan, and

(ii) with respect to which the requirements of paragraphs (2) and (3) are met.

(B) **Domestic relations order**. The term "domestic relations order" means any judgment, decree, or order (including approval of a property settlement agreement) which—

(i) relates to the provision of child support, alimony payments, or marital property rights to a spouse, former spouse, child, or other dependent of a participant, and

(ii) is made pursuant to a State domestic relations law (including a community property law).

(2) **Order must clearly specify certain facts**. A domestic relations order meets the requirements of this paragraph only if such order clearly specifies—

(A) the name and the last known mailing address (if any) of the participant and the name and mailing address of each alternate payee covered by the order,

(B) the amount or percentage of the participant's benefits to be paid by the plan to each such alternate payee, or the manner in which such amount or percentage is to be determined,

(C) the number of payments or period to which such order applies, and

(D) each plan to which such order applies.

. . .

As explained in the *Boggs* decision, however, the treatment of pensions and retirement plans at death is not necessarily consistent with applicable state law.

B. *Sandra Jean Dale Boggs v. Thomas F. Boggs, Harry M. Boggs and David B. Boggs*

520 U.S. 833 (1997)

Justice KENNEDY delivered the opinion of the Court.

We consider whether the Employee Retirement Income Security Act of 1974 (ERISA), 88 Stat. 832, as amended, 29 U.S.C. § 1001 et seq., pre-empts a state law allowing a nonparticipant spouse to transfer by testamentary instrument an interest in undistributed pension plan benefits. Given the pervasive significance of pension plans in the national economy, the congressional mandate for their uniform and comprehensive regulation, and the fundamental importance of community property law in defining the marital partnership in a number of States, the question is of undoubted importance. We hold that ERISA pre-empts the state law.

I

Isaac Boggs worked for South Central Bell from 1949 until his retirement in 1985. Isaac and Dorothy, his first wife, were married when he began working for the company, and they remained husband and wife until Dorothy's death in 1979. They had three sons. Within a year of Dorothy's death, Isaac married Sandra, and they remained married until his death in 1989.

Upon retirement, Isaac received various benefits from his employer's retirement plans. One was a lump-sum distribution from the Bell System Savings Plan for Salaried Employees (Savings Plan) of $151,628.94, which he rolled over into an Individual Retirement Account (IRA). He made no withdrawals and the account was worth $180,778.05 when he died. He also received 96 shares of AT & T stock from the Bell South Employee Stock Ownership Plan (ESOP). In addition, Isaac enjoyed a monthly annuity payment during his retirement of $1,777.67 from the Bell South Service Retirement Program.

The instant dispute over ownership of the benefits is between Sandra (the surviving wife) and the sons of the first marriage. The sons' claim to a portion of the benefits is based on Dorothy's will. Dorothy bequeathed to Isaac one-third of her estate, and a lifetime usufruct in the remaining two-thirds. A lifetime usufruct is the rough equivalent of a common-law life estate. See La. Civ.Code Ann., Art. 535 (West 1980). She bequeathed to her sons the naked ownership in the remaining two-thirds, subject to Isaac's usufruct. All agree that, absent pre-emption, Louisiana law controls and that under it Dorothy's will would dispose of her community property interest in Isaac's undistributed pension plan benefits. A Louisiana state court, in a 1980 order entitled “Judgment of Possession,” ascribed to Dorothy's estate a community property interest in Isaac's Savings Plan account valued at the time at $21,194.29.

Sandra contests the validity of Dorothy's 1980 testamentary transfer, basing her claim to those benefits on her interest under Isaac's will and 29 U.S.C. § 1055. Isaac bequeathed to Sandra outright certain real property including the family home. His will also gave Sandra a lifetime usufruct in the remainder of his estate, with the naked ownership interest being held by the sons. Sandra argues that the sons' competing claim, since it is based on Dorothy's 1980 purported testamentary transfer of her community property interest in undistributed pension plan benefits, is pre-empted by ERISA. The Bell South Service Retirement Program monthly annuity is now paid to Sandra as the surviving spouse.

After Isaac's death, two of the sons filed an action in state court requesting the appointment of an expert to compute the percentage of the retirement benefits they would be entitled to as a result of Dorothy's attempted testamentary transfer. They further sought a judgment awarding them a portion of: the IRA; the ESOP shares of AT

& T stock; the monthly annuity payments received by Isaac during his retirement; and Sandra's survivor annuity payments, both received and payable.

In response, Sandra Boggs filed a complaint in the United States District Court for the Eastern District of Louisiana, seeking a declaratory judgment that ERISA pre-empts the application of Louisiana's community property and succession laws to the extent they recognize the sons' claim to an interest in the disputed retirement benefits. The District Court granted summary judgment against Sandra Boggs. 849 F.Supp. 462 (1994). It found that, under Louisiana community property law, Dorothy had an ownership interest in her husband's pension plan benefits built up during their marriage. The creation of this interest, the court explained, does not violate 29 U.S.C. § 1056(d)(1), which prohibits pension plan benefits from being "assigned" or "alienated," since Congress did not intend to alter traditional familial and support obligations. In the court's view, there was no assignment or alienation because Dorothy's rights in the benefits were acquired by operation of community property law and not by transfer from Isaac. Turning to Dorothy's testamentary transfer, the court found it effective because "[ERISA] does not display any particular interest in preserving maximum benefits to any particular beneficiary." 849 F.Supp., at 465.

A divided panel of the Fifth Circuit affirmed. 82 F.3d 90 (1996). The court stressed that Louisiana law affects only what a plan participant may do with his or her benefits after they are received and not the relationship between the pension plan administrator and the plan beneficiary. *Id.*, at 96. For the reasons given by the District Court, it found ERISA's pension plan anti-alienation provision, § 1056(d)(1), inapplicable to Louisiana's creation of Dorothy Boggs' community property interest in the pension plan benefits. It concluded that the transfer of the interest from Dorothy to her sons was not a prohibited assignment or alienation, as this transfer was "two steps removed from the disbursement of benefits." *Id.*, at 97.

Six members of the Court of Appeals dissented from the failure to grant rehearing en banc. 89 F.3d 1169 (1996). In their view, a testamentary transfer of an interest in undistributed retirement benefits frustrates ERISA's goals of securing national uniformity in pension plan administration and of ensuring that retirees, and their dependents, are the actual recipients of retirement income. They believed that Congress' creation of the qualified domestic relations order (QDRO) mechanism in § 1056(d)(3), whose requirements were not met by the 1980 judgment of possession, further supported their position. (A QDRO is a limited exception to the pension plan anti-alienation provision and allows courts to recognize a nonparticipant spouse's community property interest in pension plans under specific circumstances.)

The reasoning and holding of the Fifth Circuit's decision is in substantial conflict with the decision of the Court of Appeals for the Ninth Circuit in *Ablamis v. Roper*, 937 F.2d 1450 (1991), which held that ERISA pre-empts a testamentary transfer by a nonparticipant spouse of her community property interest in undistributed pension plan benefits. The division between the Circuits is significant, for the Fifth Circuit has jurisdiction over the community property States of Louisiana and Texas, while the Ninth Circuit includes the community property States of Arizona, California, Idaho, Nevada, and Washington. Having granted certiorari to resolve the issue, 519 U.S. 957, 117 S.Ct. 379, 136 L.Ed.2d 297 (1996), we now reverse.

II

ERISA pre-emption questions are recurrent, two other cases on the subject having come before the Court in the current Term alone, see *Cal. Div. of Labor Standards Enforcement v. Dillingham Constr., N.A., Inc.*, 519 U.S. 316, 117 S.Ct. 832, 136 L.Ed.2d 791 (1997); *De Buono v. NYSA–ILA Medical and Clinical Services Fund*, 520 U.S. 806, 117 S.Ct. 1747, 138 L.Ed.2d 21 (1997). In large part the number of ERISA pre-emption cases reflects the comprehensive nature of the statute, the centrality of pension and welfare plans in the national economy, and their importance to the financial security of the Nation's work force. ERISA is designed to ensure the proper administration of pension and welfare plans, both during the years of the employee's active service and in his or her retirement years.

This case lies at the intersection of ERISA pension law and state community property law. None can dispute the central role community property laws play in the nine community property States. It is more than a property regime. It is a commitment to the equality of husband and wife and reflects the real partnership inherent in the marital relationship. State community property laws, many of ancient lineage, "must have continued to exist through such lengths of time because of their manifold excellences and are not lightly to be abrogated or tossed aside." 1 W. de Funiak, Principles of Community Property 11 (1943). The community property regime in Louisiana dates from 1808 when the territorial legislature of Orleans drafted a civil code which adopted Spanish principles of community property. *Id.*, at 85–89. Louisiana's community property laws, and the community property regimes enacted in other States, implement policies and values lying within the traditional domain of the States. These considerations inform our pre-emption analysis. See *Hisquierdo v. Hisquierdo*, 439 U.S. 572, 581, 99 S.Ct. 802, 808, 59 L.Ed.2d 1 (1979).

The nine community property States have some 80 million residents, with perhaps $1 trillion in retirement plans. See Brief for Estate Planning, Trust and Probate Law Section of the State Bar of California as Amicus Curiae 1. This case involves a community property claim, but our ruling will affect as well the right to make claims or assert interests based on the law of any State, whether or not it recognizes community property. Our ruling must be consistent with the congressional scheme to assure the security of plan participants and their families in every State. In enacting ERISA,

Congress noted the importance of pension plans in its findings and declaration of policy, explaining:

> "[T]he growth in size, scope, and numbers of employee benefit plans in recent years has been rapid and substantial; ... the continued well-being and security of millions of employees and their dependents are directly affected by these plans; ... they are affected with a national public interest [and] they have become an important factor affecting the stability of employment and the successful development of industrial relations...." 29 U.S.C. § 1001(a).

ERISA is an intricate, comprehensive statute. Its federal regulatory scheme governs employee benefit plans, which include both pension and welfare plans. All employee benefit plans must conform to various reporting, disclosure, and fiduciary requirements, see §§ 1021–1031, 1101–1114, while pension plans must also comply with participation, vesting, and funding requirements, see §§ 1051–1086. The surviving spouse annuity and QDRO provisions, central to the dispute here, are part of the statute's mandatory participation and vesting requirements. These provisions provide detailed protections to spouses of plan participants which, in some cases, exceed what their rights would be were community property law the sole measure.

ERISA's express pre-emption clause states that the Act "shall supersede any and all State laws insofar as they may now or hereafter relate to any employee benefit plan ...." § 1144(a). We can begin, and in this case end, the analysis by simply asking if state law conflicts with the provisions of ERISA or operates to frustrate its objects. We hold that there is a conflict, which suffices to resolve the case. We need not inquire whether the statutory phrase "relate to" provides further and additional support for the pre-emption claim. Nor need we consider the applicability of field pre-emption, see *Fidelity Fed. Sav. & Loan Assn. v. De la Cuesta*, 458 U.S. 141, 153, 102 S.Ct. 3014, 3022, 73 L.Ed.2d 664 (1982).

We first address the survivor's annuity and then turn to the other pension benefits.

III

Sandra Boggs, as we have observed, asserts that federal law pre-empts and supersedes state law and requires the surviving spouse annuity to be paid to her as the sole beneficiary. We agree.

The annuity at issue is a qualified joint and survivor annuity mandated by ERISA. Section 1055(a) provides:

"Each pension plan to which this section applies shall provide that—

> "(1) in the case of a vested participant who does not die before the annuity starting date, the accrued benefit payable to such participant shall be provided in the form of a qualified joint and survivor annuity."

ERISA requires that every qualified joint and survivor annuity include an annuity payable to a nonparticipant surviving spouse. The survivor's annuity may not be less than 50% of the amount of the annuity which is payable during the joint lives of the participant and spouse. § 1055(d)(1). Provision of the survivor's annuity may not be waived by the participant, absent certain limited circumstances, unless the spouse consents in writing to the designation of another beneficiary, which designation also cannot be changed without further spousal consent, witnessed by a plan representative or notary public. § 1055(c)(2). Sandra Boggs, as the surviving spouse, is entitled to a survivor's annuity under these provisions. She has not waived her right to the survivor's annuity, let alone consented to having the sons designated as the beneficiaries.

Respondents say their state-law claims are consistent with these provisions. Their claims, they argue, affect only the disposition of plan proceeds after they have been disbursed by the Bell South Service Retirement Program, and thus nothing is required of the plan. ERISA's concern for securing national uniformity in the administration of employee benefit plans, in their view, is not implicated. They argue Sandra's community property obligations, after she receives the survivor annuity payments, "fai[l] to implicate the regulatory concerns of ERISA." *Fort Halifax Packing Co. v. Coyne*, 482 U.S. 1, 15, 107 S.Ct. 2211, 2219, 96 L.Ed.2d 1 (1987).

We disagree. The statutory object of the qualified joint and survivor annuity provisions, along with the rest of § 1055, is to ensure a stream of income to surviving spouses. Section 1055 mandates a survivor's annuity not only where a participant dies after the annuity starting date but also guarantees one if the participant dies before then. See §§ 1055(a)(2), (e). These provisions, enacted as part of the Retirement Equity Act of 1984 (REA), Pub.L. 98–397, 98 Stat. 1426, enlarged ERISA's protection of surviving spouses in significant respects. Before REA, ERISA only required that pension plans, if they provided for the payment of benefits in the form of an annuity, offer a qualified joint and survivor annuity as an option entirely within a participant's discretion. 29 U.S.C. §§ 1055(a), (e) (1982 ed.). REA modified ERISA to permit participants to designate a beneficiary for the survivor's annuity, other than the nonparticipant spouse, only when the spouse agrees. § 1055(c)(2). Congress' concern for surviving spouses is also evident from the expansive coverage of § 1055, as amended by REA. Section 1055's requirements, as a general matter, apply to all "individual account plans" and "defined benefit plans." § 1055(b)(1). The terms are defined, for § 1055 purposes, so that all pension plans fall within those two categories. See § 1002(35). While some individual account plans escape § 1055's surviving spouse annuity requirements under certain conditions, Congress still protects the interests of the surviving spouse by requiring those plans to pay the spouse the nonforfeitable accrued benefits, reduced by certain security interests, in a lump-sum payment. § 1055(b)(1)(C).

ERISA's solicitude for the economic security of surviving spouses would be undermined by allowing a predeceasing spouse's heirs and legatees to have a community property interest in the survivor's annuity. Even a plan participant cannot defeat a nonparticipant surviving spouse's statutory entitlement to an annuity. It would be odd, to say the least, if Congress permitted a predeceasing nonparticipant spouse to do so. Nothing in the language of ERISA supports concluding that Congress made such an inexplicable decision. Testamentary transfers could reduce a surviving spouse's guaranteed annuity below the minimum set by ERISA (defined as 50% of the annuity payable during the joint lives of the participant and spouse). In this case, Sandra's annuity would be reduced by approximately 20%, according to the calculations contained in the sons' state-court filings. There is no reason why testamentary transfers could not reduce a survivor's annuity by an even greater amount. Perhaps even more troubling, the recipient of the testamentary transfer need not be a family member. For instance, a surviving spouse's § 1055 annuity might be substantially reduced so that funds could be diverted to support an unrelated stranger.

In the face of this direct clash between state law and the provisions and objectives of ERISA, the state law cannot stand. Conventional conflict pre-emption principles require pre-emption "where compliance with both federal and state regulations is a physical impossibility, ... or where state law stands as an obstacle to the accomplishment and execution of the full purposes and objectives of Congress." *Gade v. National Solid Wastes Management Assn.*, 505 U.S. 88, 98, 112 S.Ct. 2374, 2383, 120 L.Ed.2d 73 (1992) (internal quotation marks and citation omitted). It would undermine the purpose of ERISA's mandated survivor's annuity to allow Dorothy, the predeceasing spouse, by her testamentary transfer to defeat in part Sandra's entitlement to the annuity § 1055 guarantees her as the surviving spouse. This cannot be. States are not free to change ERISA's structure and balance.

Louisiana law, to the extent it provides the sons with a right to a portion of Sandra Boggs' § 1055 survivor's annuity, is pre-empted.

IV

Beyond seeking a portion of the survivor's annuity, respondents claim a percentage of: the monthly annuity payments made to Isaac Boggs during his retirement; the IRA; and the ESOP shares of AT & T stock. As before, the claim is based on Dorothy Boggs' attempted testamentary transfer to the sons of her community property interest in Isaac's undistributed pension plan benefits. Respondents argue further—and somewhat inconsistently—that their claim again concerns only what a plan participant or beneficiary may do once plan funds are distributed, without imposing any obligations on the plan itself. Both parties agree that the ERISA benefits at issue here were paid after Dorothy's death, and thus this case does not present the question whether ERISA would permit a nonparticipant spouse to obtain a devisable community property interest in benefits paid out during the existence of the community between the participant and that spouse.

A brief overview of ERISA's design is necessary to put respondents' contentions in the proper context. The principal object of the statute is to protect plan participants and beneficiaries. See *Shaw v. Delta Air Lines, Inc.,* 463 U.S. 85, 90, 103 S.Ct. 2890, 2896, 77 L.Ed.2d 490 (1983) ("ERISA is a comprehensive statute designed to promote the interests of employees and their beneficiaries in employee benefit plans"). Section 1001(b) states that the policy of ERISA is "to protect ... the interests of participants in employee benefit plans and their beneficiaries." Section 1001(c) explains that ERISA contains certain safeguards and protections which help guarantee the "equitable character and the soundness of [private pension] plans" in order to protect "the interests of participants in private pension plans and their beneficiaries." The general policy is implemented by ERISA's specific provisions. Apart from a few enumerated exceptions, a plan fiduciary must "discharge his duties with respect to a plan solely in the interest of the participants and beneficiaries." § 1104(a)(1). The assets of a plan, again with certain exceptions, are "held for the exclusive purposes of providing benefits to participants in the plan and their beneficiaries and defraying reasonable expenses of administering the plan." § 1103(c)(1). The Secretary of Labor has authority to create exemptions to ERISA's prohibition on certain plan holdings, acquisitions, and transactions, but only if doing so is in the interests of the plan's "participants and beneficiaries." § 1108(a)(2). Persons with an interest in a pension plan may bring a civil suit under ERISA's enforcement provisions only if they are either a participant or beneficiary. Section 1132(a)(1)(B), for instance, provides that a civil action may be brought "by a participant or beneficiary ... to recover benefits due to him under the terms of his plan, to enforce his rights under the terms of the plan, or to clarify his rights to future benefits under the terms of the plan."

ERISA confers beneficiary status on a nonparticipant spouse or dependent in only narrow circumstances delineated by its provisions. For example, as we have discussed, § 1055(a) requires provision of a surviving spouse annuity in covered pension plans, and, as a consequence, the spouse is a beneficiary to this extent. Section 1056's QDRO provisions likewise recognize certain pension plan community property interests of nonparticipant spouses and dependents. A QDRO is a type of domestic relations order that creates or recognizes an alternate payee's right to, or assigns to an alternate payee the right to, a portion of the benefits payable with respect to a participant under a plan. § 1056(d)(3)(B)(i). A domestic relations order, in turn, is any judgment, decree, or order that concerns "the provision of child support, alimony payments, or marital property rights to a spouse, former spouse, child, or other dependent of a participant" and is "made pursuant to a State domestic relations law (including a community property law)." § 1056(d)(3)(B)(ii). A domestic relations order must meet certain requirements to qualify as a QDRO. See §§ 1056(d)(3)(C)-(E). QDRO's, unlike domestic relations orders in general, are exempt from both the pension plan anti-alienation provision, § 1056(d)(3)(A), and ERISA's general pre-emption clause, § 1144(b)(7). In creating the QDRO mechanism Congress was careful to provide that the alternate payee, the "spouse, former spouse, child, or other dependent of a participant," is to be considered a plan beneficiary. §§ 1056(d)(3)(K), (J). These provisions are essential to one of REA's central purposes, which is to give enhanced protection to the spouse and dependent children in the event of divorce or separation, and in the event of death the surviving spouse. Apart from these detailed provisions, ERISA does not confer beneficiary status on nonparticipants by reason of their marital or dependent status.

Even outside the pension plan context and its anti-alienation restriction, Congress deemed it necessary to enact detailed provisions in order to protect a dependent's interest in a welfare benefit plan. Through a § 1169 "qualified medical child support order" a child's interest in his or her parent's group health care plan can be enforced. A "medical child support order" is defined as any judgment, decree, or order that concerns the provision of child support "made pursuant to a State domestic relations law (including a community property law) and relates to benefits under such plan." § 1169(a)(2)(B)(i). As with a QDRO, a "medical child support order" must satisfy certain criteria in order to qualify. See §§ 1169(a)(3)-(4). In accordance with ERISA's care in conforming entitlements to benefits with participant or beneficiary status, the statute treats a child subject to such a qualifying order as a participant for ERISA's reporting and disclosure requirements and as a beneficiary for other purposes. § 1169(a)(7).

The surviving spouse annuity and QDRO provisions, which acknowledge and protect specific pension plan community property interests, give rise to the strong implication that other community property claims are not consistent with the statutory scheme. ERISA's silence with respect to the right of a nonparticipant spouse to control pension plan benefits by testamentary transfer provides powerful support for the conclusion that the right does not exist. Cf. *Massachusetts Mut. Life Ins. Co. v. Russell*, 473 U.S. 134, 147–148, 105 S.Ct. 3085, 3092–3093, 87 L.Ed.2d 96 (1985). It should cause little surprise that Congress chose to protect the community property interests of separated and divorced spouses and their children, a traditional subject of domestic relations law, but not to accommodate testamentary transfers of pension plan benefits. As a general matter, "[t]he whole subject of the domestic relations of husband and wife, parent and child, belongs to the laws of the States and not to the laws of the United States." *In re Burrus*, 136 U.S. 586, 593–594, 10 S.Ct. 850, 853, 34 L.Ed. 500 (1890). Support obligations, in particular, are "deeply rooted moral responsibilities" that Congress is unlikely to have intended to intrude upon. See *Rose v. Rose*, 481 U.S. 619, 632, 107 S.Ct. 2029, 2037, 95 L.Ed.2d 599 (1987); see also id., at 636–640, 107 S.Ct., at 2039–2041 (O'CONNOR, J., concurring). In accord with these principles, Congress ensured that state domestic relations orders, as long as they meet certain statutory requirements, are not pre-empted.

We conclude the sons have no claim under ERISA to a share of the retirement benefits. To begin with, the sons are neither participants nor beneficiaries. A "participant" is defined as an "employee or former employee of an employer, or any member or former member of an employee organization, who is or may become eligible to receive a benefit." § 1002(7). A "beneficiary" is a "person designated by a participant, or by the terms of an employee benefit plan, who is or may become entitled to a benefit thereunder." § 1002(8). Respondents' claims are based on Dorothy Boggs' attempted testamentary transfer, not on a designation by Isaac Boggs or under the terms of the retirement plans. They do not even attempt to argue that they are beneficiaries by virtue of the judgment of possession qualifying as a QDRO.

An amicus, the Estate Planning, Trust and Probate Law Section of the State Bar of California, in support of respondents' position, points to pre-REA case law holding that ERISA does not pre-empt spousal community property interests in pension benefits, regardless of who is the plan participant or beneficiary. As did the District Court below, the amicus relies in particular upon *In re Marriage of Campa*, 89 Cal.App.3d 113, 152 Cal.Rptr. 362 (1979), in which the California Court of Appeal for the First District held that ERISA does not bar California courts from joining pension funds in marriage dissolution proceedings and ordering the pension plan to divide pension payments between the employee and his or her former nonparticipant spouse. We dismissed the pension plan's appeal for want of a substantial federal question, 444 U.S. 1028, 100 S.Ct. 696, 62 L.Ed.2d 664 (1980), and, although not entitled to full precedential weight, see *Edelman v. Jordan*, 415 U.S. 651, 670–671, 94 S.Ct. 1347, 1359–1360, 39 L.Ed.2d 662 (1974), that disposition constitutes a decision on the merits, see *Hicks v. Miranda*, 422 U.S. 332, 344, 95 S.Ct. 2281, 2289, 45 L.Ed.2d 223 (1975). The state court in *Marriage of Campa* was not alone in refusing to find ERISA pre-emption in the divorce context. See, e.g., *Stone v. Stone*, 450 F.Supp. 919 (N.D.Cal.1978), aff'd, 632 F.2d 740 (C.A.9 1980), cert. denied, 453 U.S. 922, 101 S.Ct. 3158, 69 L.Ed.2d 1004 (1981); *Savings and Profit Sharing Fund of Sears Employees v. Gago*, 717 F.2d 1038 (C.A.7 1983); *Eichelberger v. Eichelberger*, 584 F.Supp. 899 (S.D.Tex.1984). This judicial consensus, amicus argues, was codified by the QDRO provisions which were contained in the 1984 REA amendments. The amicus contends that since REA, or the pre-REA case law which it allegedly adopted, did not consider the community property rights of a nonparticipant spouse in the testamentary context, it should not be construed to pre-empt state law governing this different subject.

We disagree with this reasoning. It is true that the subject of testamentary transfers is somewhat removed from domestic relations law. The QDRO provisions address the rights of divorced and separated spouses, and their dependent children, which are the traditional concern of domestic relations law. The pre-REA federal common-law extension of § 1002(8)'s definition of "beneficiary" by courts in the context of marital dissolution was in part based on an appreciation of the fact that domestic relations law is primarily an area of state concern, see *Marriage of Campa*, supra, at 124, 152

Cal.Rptr., at 367–368, and the basic principle that a beneficiary's interest in a spendthrift trust, despite otherwise applicable protections, can be reached in the context of divorce and separation. See E. Griswold, Spendthrift Trusts 389–391 (2d ed.1947) (summarizing state case law); Restatement (Second) of Trusts § 157 (1959). The state court in *Marriage of Campa* took its implicit determination that the nonparticipant spouse was a beneficiary to its logical conclusion, forcing the pension plan to join the marital dissolution proceedings as a party and compelling it to pay the spouse her share of the pension benefits. Whether or not this extension of the definition of "beneficiary" was consistent with the statute then in force, these authorities are not applicable in light of the REA amendments. The QDRO and the surviving spouse annuity provisions define the scope of a nonparticipant spouse's community property interests in pension plans consistent with ERISA.

Respondents and their amicus in effect ask us to ignore § 1002(8)'s definition of "beneficiary" and, through case law, create a new class of persons for whom plan assets are to be held and administered. The statute is not amenable to this sweeping extratextual extension. It is unpersuasive to suggest that third parties could assert their claims without being counted as "beneficiaries." A plan fiduciary's responsibilities run only to participants and beneficiaries. § 1104(a)(1). Assets of a plan are held for the exclusive purposes of providing benefits to participants and beneficiaries and defraying reasonable expenses of administration. § 1103(c)(1). Reading ERISA to permit nonbeneficiary interests, even if not enforced against the plan, would result in troubling anomalies. Either pension plans would be run for the benefit of only a subset of those who have a stake in the plan or state law would have to move in to fill the apparent gaps between plan administration responsibilities and ownership rights, resulting in a complex set of requirements varying from State to State. Neither result accords with the statutory scheme.

The conclusion that Congress intended to pre-empt respondents' nonbeneficiary, nonparticipant interests in the retirement plans is given specific and powerful reinforcement by the pension plan anti-alienation provision. Section 1056(d)(1) provides that "[e]ach pension plan shall provide that benefits provided under the plan may not be assigned or alienated." Statutory anti-alienation provisions are potent mechanisms to prevent the dissipation of funds. In *Hisquierdo* we interpreted an anti-alienation provision to bar a divorced spouse's interest in her husband's retirement benefits. See 439 U.S., at 583–590, 99 S.Ct., at 809–813. ERISA's pension plan anti-alienation provision is mandatory and contains only two explicit exceptions, see §§ 1056(d)(2), (d)(3)(A), which are not subject to judicial expansion. See *Guidry v. Sheet Metal Workers Nat. Pension Fund*, 493 U.S. 365, 376, 110 S.Ct. 680, 687, 107 L.Ed.2d 782 (1990). The anti-alienation provision can "be seen to bespeak a pension law protective policy of special intensity: Retirement funds shall remain inviolate until retirement." J. Langbein & B. Wolk, Pension and Employee Benefit Law 547 (2d ed.1995).

Dorothy's 1980 testamentary transfer, which is the source of respondents' claimed ownership interest, is a prohibited "assignment or alienation." An "assignment or alienation" has been defined by regulation, with certain exceptions not at issue here, as "[a]ny direct or indirect arrangement whereby a party acquires from a participant or beneficiary" an interest enforceable against a plan to "all or any part of a plan benefit payment which is, or may become, payable to the participant or beneficiary." 26 CFR § 1.401(a)–13(c)(1)(ii) (1997). Those requirements are met. Under Louisiana law community property interests are enforceable against a plan. See *Eskine v. Eskine*, 518 So.2d 505, 508 (La.1988). If respondents' claims were allowed to succeed they would have acquired, as of 1980, an interest in Isaac's pension plan at the expense of plan participants and beneficiaries.

As was true with survivors' annuities, it would be inimical to ERISA's purposes to permit testamentary recipients to acquire a competing interest in undistributed pension benefits, which are intended to provide a stream of income to participants and their beneficiaries. See *Guidry*, supra, at 376, 110 S.Ct., at 687 ("[The anti-alienation provision] reflects a considered congressional policy choice, a decision to safeguard a stream of income for pensioners ... and their dependents ..."). Pension benefits support participants and beneficiaries in their retirement years, and ERISA's pension plan safeguards are designed to further this end. See § 1001(c). Besides the anti-alienation provision, Congress has enacted other protective measures to guarantee that retirement funds are there when a plan's participants and beneficiaries expect them. There are, for instance, minimum funding standards for pension plans and a pension plan termination insurance program which guarantees benefits in the event a plan is terminated before being fully funded. See §§ 1082, 1301–1461. Under respondents' approach, retirees could find their retirement benefits reduced by substantial sums because they have been diverted to testamentary recipients. Retirement benefits and the income stream provided for by ERISA-regulated plans would be disrupted in the name of protecting a nonparticipant spouses' successors over plan participants and beneficiaries. Respondents' logic would even permit a spouse to transfer an interest in a pension plan to creditors, a result incompatible with a spendthrift provision such as § 1056(d)(1).

Community property laws have, in the past, been pre-empted in order to ensure the implementation of a federal statutory scheme. See, e.g., *McCune v. Essig*, 199 U.S. 382, 26 S.Ct. 78, 50 L.Ed. 237 (1905); *Wissner v. Wissner*, 338 U.S. 655, 70 S.Ct. 398, 94 L.Ed. 424 (1950); *Free v. Bland*, 369 U.S. 663, 82 S.Ct. 1089, 8 L.Ed.2d 180 (1962); *Hisquierdo v. Hisquierdo*, 439 U.S. 572, 99 S.Ct. 802, 59 L.Ed.2d 1 (1979); *McCarty v. McCarty*, 453 U.S. 210, 101 S.Ct. 2728, 69 L.Ed.2d 589 (1981); *Mansell v. Mansell*, 490 U.S. 581, 109 S.Ct. 2023, 104 L.Ed.2d 675 (1989); cf. *Ridgway v. Ridgway*, 454 U.S. 46, 102 S.Ct. 49, 70 L.Ed.2d 39 (1981). *Free v. Bland*, supra, is of particular relevance here. A husband had purchased United States savings bonds with community funds in the name of both spouses. Under Treasury regulations then in effect, when a co-owner of the bonds died, the surviving co-owner received the entire interest in the bonds. After the wife died, her son—the principal beneficiary of her will—demanded either one-half of the bonds or reimbursement for loss of the community property interest. The Court held that the regulations pre-empted the community property claim, explaining:

> "One of the inducements selected by the Treasury is the survivorship provision, a convenient method of avoiding complicated probate proceedings. Notwithstanding this provision, the State awarded full title to the co-owner but required him to account for half of the value of the bonds to the decedent's estate. Viewed realistically, the State has rendered the award of title meaningless."

Id., at 669, 82 S.Ct., at 1093.

The same reasoning applies here. If state law is not pre-empted, the diversion of retirement benefits will occur regardless of whether the interest in the pension plan is enforced against the plan or the recipient of the pension benefit. The obligation to provide an accounting, moreover, as with the probate proceedings referred to in *Free*, is itself a burden of significant proportions. Under respondents' view, a pension plan participant could be forced to make an accounting of a deceased spouse's community property interest years after the date of death. If the couple had lived in several States, the accounting could entail complex, expensive, and time-consuming litigation. Congress could not have intended that pension benefits from pension plans would be given to accountants and attorneys for this purpose.

Respondents contend it is anomalous and unfair that a divorced spouse, as a result of a QDRO, will have more control over a portion of his or her spouse's pension benefits than a predeceasing spouse. Congress thought otherwise. The QDRO provisions, as well as the surviving spouse annuity provisions, reinforce the conclusion that ERISA is concerned with providing for the living. The QDRO provisions protect those persons who, often as a result of divorce, might not receive the benefits they otherwise would have had available during their retirement as a means of income. In the case of a predeceased spouse, this concern is not implicated. The fairness of the distinction might be debated, but Congress has decided to favor the living over the dead and we must respect its policy.

The axis around which ERISA's protections revolve is the concepts of participant and beneficiary. When Congress has chosen to depart from this framework, it has done so in a careful and limited manner. Respondents' claims, if allowed to succeed, would depart from this framework, upsetting the deliberate balance central to ERISA. It does not matter that respondents have sought to enforce their rights only after the retirement benefits have been distributed since their asserted rights are based on the theory that they had an interest in the undistributed pension plan benefits. Their state-law claims are pre-empted.

The judgment of the Fifth Circuit is
Reversed.

Subsequent Developments

SB 1616 (2003) proposing an amendment to ERISA suggested by Professors Samual and Spaht was introduced in Congress by Senator Mary Landrieu. *See* Cynthia A. Samuel and Katherine S. Spaht, *Fixing What's Broke: Amending ERISA to Allow Community Property to Apply upon the Death of a Participant's Spouse*, 35 Fam. L. Q. 425, 449-50 (2001) in which the authors urge the adoption of the following amendment to ERISA:

"(9)(A) Subsection (a) [preemption provision] shall not apply to any spousal probate order as defined herein.

(B) A spousal probate order is an order (i) that is rendered in the estate of the spouse of a participant in a pension plan, (ii) that disposes of the portion of the participant's accrued benefit in the pension plan that the participant's spouse owned under the community property law, and (iii) that is not enforceable against the participant during his or her lifetime or directly against the qualified joint and survivor annuity or qualified pre-retirement survivor annuity of the surviving spouse of the participant.

(C) This paragraph shall not be construed to allow a claim under a spousal probate order for a benefit directly from the pension plan."

C. *Judith Romano, wife of Dean W. Halverson v. Dean W. Halverson*

589 So. 2d 1153 (La. App. 5th Cir. 1991)

FINK, Judge Pro Tem.

This appeal arises from a dispute between Dean W. Halverson and Judith Romano Peck (formerly Mrs. Halverson) over the division of Dean Halverson's pension plan benefits in the community property partition following their divorce. Mr. Halverson has appealed from a judgment of November 27, 1990, in favor of Mrs. Peck. We affirm, for the reasons that follow.

At issue are, first, whether the trial court erred in calculating the amount of the pension plan benefits to which Mrs. Peck is entitled; second, whether the court erred in ruling that Mrs. Peck is entitled to begin receiving her interest in the pension plan immediately; third, whether the court erred in refusing to order that Mr. Halverson's separate estate is entitled to full reimbursement for his monthly payments on the family home after the parties ended their community regime.

Mr. Halverson has been employed as a pilot for Delta Airlines since March 4, 1964. He and Mrs. Peck were married on October 28, 1967, and a community property regime existed between the parties until their divorce on November 13, 1979. During his employment with Delta, Mr. Halverson has been a participant in the Delta Pilots' Retirement Plan.

ASSIGNMENT OF ERROR NUMBER TWO

Mr. Halverson's second contention is that the trial court erred in ruling that Mrs. Peck is entitled to remove her interest in his pension plan immediately.

In Sims v. Sims, *supra*, the court ruled that the wife could not be forced to have her interest in her husband's pension rights valued at one-half its cash withdrawal value at the date the community was dissolved. Rather, the court concluded, when a former spouse-in-community's pension benefits become due, so as then to have a determinative value, the non-employed spouse is entitled to receive the proportion of the benefits attributable to the other spouse's employment during the existence of the community. The court stated its decree would recognize the wife's proportionate interest in the retirement annuities, "if and when they become payable," without attempting to fix a present monetary value for the interest because it would have none until the husband actually retired or terminated his employment. 358 So.2d at 922-923.

Based on the "if and when they become payable" phrase used by the Sims court, Mr. Halverson contends Mrs. Peck cannot receive her share of his pension benefits until he actually begins drawing his pension. He contends the amount of the benefits will not be fixed and determinable until he has retired.

Mrs. Peck, however, asserts that an amount can be fixed because Mr. Halverson has served three consecutive years of his last ten years of employment. Thus, his minimum Final Average Earnings can be calculated based on those three years, so that her share of pension benefits can be calculated at their present value as if they were now payable to Mr. Halverson. She is willing to waive her right to prospective higher benefits in order to receive immediate disbursement of the funds due her.

For assistance in understanding the pension plan and in determining how the Sims formula should be applied, the trial court appointed its own expert, Professor Dian Arruebarrena of Loyola School of Law. She testified as follows:

> In the *Sims* case the court concluded that to assure fairness in valuing pension benefits pursuant to a community property partition, the parties must wait until the

employed spouse actually retires. Professor Arruebarrena felt, however, that the Halverson case should be considered an exception to the *Sims* rule because the factors involved will allow Mrs. Peck to receive her share of the pension immediately without prejudice to Mr. Halverson's interests. Arruebarrena explained the factors she considered:

First, under the Delta Pilots' Retirement Plan as applied to Mr. Halverson, the Sims formula is fixed; the denominator of the formula must be 25, because that is the greatest number of years of service creditable under the Plan. Upon achieving 25 years of service, Mr. Halverson became entitled to 60% of his Final-Average Earnings upon retirement. No matter how many more years he works that percentage figure will not increase, although the actual dollar amount of his pension will increase if his earnings increase. Waiting until he retires will not dilute Mrs. Peck's proportionate share, earned during their 12.055 years of marriage.

Second, because Mr. Halverson is 53, not only is he within his last ten years of employment prior to retirement, but also an average earnings figure can be computed for the last three years that would be the minimum for his Final-Average Earnings under the Plan's provisions. (Because his Final-Average Earnings are computed from his *highest* 36 months of earnings, even if his income decreases between the time of trial and the time he retires his Final-Average Earnings could be calculated based on the three years prior to trial.)

Third, Mr. Halverson has attained the earliest possible retirement age and thus is entitled to retire.

Fourth, under the Retirement Equity Act of 1984 (Pub. L. 98-397, 98 Stat. 1426), a non-employed spouse can receive her share of the pension directly from the pension administrator prior to the employed spouse's retirement if state law permits such an arrangement.

Fifth, distribution of Mrs. Peck's share at its present value is not unfair to Mrs. Peck if she is willing to waive her right to future increases in order to receive the benefits immediately.

Finally, the court can structure a Qualified Domestic Relations Order (required by the Employee Retirement Income Security Act, Pub. L. 93-406, 88 Stat. 829, to partition pension benefits) so that the amount Mrs. Peck receives is no greater than the amount she might receive if she were required to wait until Mr. Halverson retires. This could be done by assessing against her share the early retirement penalty of 3% per year for every year prior to Mr. Halverson's reaching age 60 that she begins drawing her share of the benefits.

Professor Arruebarrena mentioned, in addition, that if Mrs. Peck is required to wait for her share until Mr. Halverson retires and if he dies prior to retirement, Mrs. Peck will receive nothing; her right to her share of his pension will lapse upon his death.

Based on these factors, Professor Arruebarrena stated, she felt this case is a "likely candidate to be an exception to Sims." The trial court agreed with her, hence the ruling of which the appellant complains.

In Hare v. Hodgins, No. 90-C-2405 c/w 90-C-2445 (La. S.Ct. September 9, 1991), rendered the day before this case was submitted to us for decision, our Supreme Court cautioned lower courts against a too-literal application of the Sims court's statement that no value can be fixed upon an employee's pension right until the employee is separated from the service, dies, retires or becomes disabled. . . .

Considering these factors, we conclude the trial court was correct in ruling that Mrs. Peck is entitled to begin drawing her share of the pension immediately. This conclusion does not violate the rule enunciated in the Sims case, because the purpose of that rule was to insure fairness to both spouses. The decision here also insures fairness to both spouses, in view of Mrs. Peck's willingness to accept a lesser pension than she would receive if she waited until Mr. Halverson retires, and because payment of her share now, in the manner explained by Arruebarrena, will not lessen Mr. Halverson's share.

D. Social Security Benefits

Rights in social security benefits are subject to federal preemption. Following the *Boggs* decision, the Louisiana legislature enacted the following legislation:

La. Rev. Stat. § 2801.1. Community property; allocation and assignment of ownership

When federal law or the provisions of a statutory pension or retirement plan, state or federal, preempt or preclude community classification of property that would have been classified as community property under the principles of the Civil Code, the spouse of the person entitled to such property shall be allocated or assigned the ownership of community property equal in value to such property prior to the division of the rest of the community property. Nevertheless, if such property consists of a spouse's right to receive social security benefits or the benefits themselves, then the court in its discretion may allocate or assign other community property equal in value to the other spouse.

Serious questions remain regarding the constitutionality of this statute. *See* Andrea Carroll & Richard D. Moreno, 16 LOUISIANA CIVIL LAW TREATISE: MATRIMONIAL REGIMES §3:46 (3d ed.)

E. *Sheila Gail Comeaux v. Douglas Julien Comeaux*

7 So. 3d 110 (La. App. 3d 2009)

PETERS, J.

Douglas Julien Comeaux appeals a portion of the trial court judgment partitioning the community of acquets and gains previously existing between himself and his former wife, Sheila Gail Romero Comeaux, wherein he was ordered to pay her an equalizing payment of $35,965.87. For the following reasons, we amend the trial court judgment and affirm as amended.

DISCUSSION OF THE RECORD

Sheila Gail Romero Comeaux (Sheila) and Douglas Julien Comeaux (Douglas) were married on December 7, 1996, and physically separated in September of 2005. In her October 12, 2005 petition for a divorce under La.Civ.Code art. 102, Sheila sought, among other relief, a judicial partition of the community of acquets and gains previously existing between her and her husband. The matter went to trial on the partition issue on March 14, 2007.

Prior to trial, the parties had agreed upon the classification and value of most of their assets. Thus, the primary issue facing the trial court was the status of the social security benefits Douglas had earned during the marriage. After completion of the evidence phase of the trial, the trial court informed the litigants that it would appoint an appraiser to assess the value of the property still in dispute, allowed the attorneys to address the social security issue through briefs to the court, and took the remaining matters under advisement. After receiving the report of the court-appointed appraiser as well as the briefs of the attorneys, the trial court issued written reasons for judgment on June 2, 2008.

In its written reasons for judgment, the trial court recognized that the value of the social security benefits Douglas earned during the marriage is not community property, noting that "the Supremacy Clause of the United States Constitution preempts classification of social security benefits under the Louisiana community property laws." However, the trial court also noted the discretion afforded it by La.R.S. 9:2801.1 to award a spouse community property equal in value to social security benefits that cannot be considered as community property.

On the same day it released its reasons for judgment, the trial court executed a judgment wherein it assigned the various community assets and liabilities to each party. The judgment first noted that the social security benefits Douglas earned during the marriage had a value of $42,586.00 and expressed the trial court's intention to use its discretion, afforded by La.R.S. 9:2801.1, "to equalize an unequal net distribution," stating that it would do so by awarding Sheila the couple's home. Next, the judgment awarded Sheila community assets totaling $97,595.00,4 and awarded Douglas community assets totaling $35,709.73. It then assigned $91,529.21 in community debts to Sheila5 and $31,171.32 in community debts to Douglas, leaving Sheila with a net community property recovery of $6,065.79 and Douglas with a net community property recovery of $4,538.41. The judgment also recognized that Sheila was entitled to reimbursement for one-half of the $21,224.48 she had paid on community obligations, or $10,612.24. The trial court judgment awarded Sheila an equalizing payment of $35,965.87 to balance the assets and liabilities allotted to both after taking into consideration Douglas' social security benefits, as allowed by La.R.S. 9:2801.1.

Douglas has appealed this judgment, and his nine assignments of error on appeal can be condensed into four issues:

> 1) Did the trial court err in awarding Sheila community property equal in value to the social security benefits earned by Douglas during the marriage;
>
> 2) Did the trial court err in valuing the social security benefits Douglas earned during the marriage at $42,586.00;
>
> 3) Did the trial court err in stating that the total value of the guns awarded to Douglas was $1,145.00; and
>
> 4) Did the trial court err in ordering Douglas to pay Sheila an equalizing payment of $35,965.87?

OPINION

Award of community property equal in value to social security benefits

The determination whether a former spouse's social security benefits are community property is preempted by federal law. U.S. Const. art. VI, cl. 2; 42 U.S.C. § 407 (2002); and Young v. Young, 06–77 (La.App. 3 Cir. 5/31/06), 931 So.2d 541. Under federal law, Douglas' social security benefits are his separate property because Sheila and Douglas were married fewer than ten years before they divorced. 20 C.F.R. § 404.331(a)(2). However, La.R.S. 9:2801.1 provides:

> When federal law or the provisions of a statutory pension or retirement plan, state or federal, preempt or preclude community classification of property that would have been classified as community property under the principles of the Civil Code, the spouse of the person entitled to such property shall be allocated or assigned the ownership of community property equal in value to such property prior to the division of the rest of the community property. Nevertheless, if such property consists of a spouse's right to receive social security benefits or the benefits themselves, then the court in its discretion may allocate or assign other community property equal in value to the other spouse.

(Emphasis added.) Thus, under La.R.S. 9:2801.1, a trial court has the discretion to assign a spouse community property equal to the amount the other spouse will receive in social security benefits.

Louisiana Revised Statutes 9:2801.1 was not enacted until 2001, and only became effective August 15, 2001. Douglas argues that the statute cannot be applied retroactively to a marriage that began in December of 1996. When a trial court interprets and applies state statutes, the appellate court reviews that statutory interpretation under the de novo standard of review. *Ducote v. City of Alexandria*, 95–1269 (La.App. 3 Cir. 7/17/96), 677 So.2d 1118.

This is the first time that a court has been faced with the question whether La.R.S. 9:2801.1 applies to social security benefits that were earned prior to the statute's effective date. Louisiana Civil Code Article 6 provides that "[i]n the absence of contrary legislative expression, substantive laws apply prospectively only. Procedural and interpretative laws apply both prospectively and retroactively, unless there is a legislative expression to the contrary," and La.R.S. 1:2 states that "[n]o Section of the Revised Statutes is retroactive unless it is expressly so stated."

Our supreme court has recognized that "[d]etermining whether a statute operates retroactively can be difficult when the statute must be applied to a case in which some operative facts pre-date the law while others occurred after the law's effective date," stating that "[i]t is imperative to understand that a law may permissibly change the future consequences of an act and even the consequences of acts committed prior to the law's enactment without operating retroactively." *Walls v. Am. Optical Corp.*, 98–455, p. 4 (La.9/8/99), 740 So.2d 1262, 1266 (citing 1 M. Planiol, Treatise on the Civil Law, Sec. 243 (La.St.L.Inst.Trans.1959)). The supreme court adopted Planiol's rule for determining the two situations in which a law operates retroactively: "[A] law is retroactive when it goes back to the past either to evaluate the conditions of the legality of an act, or to modify or suppress the effects of a right already acquired. Outside of those conditions, there is no retroactivity." *Id.* at 1267 (citations omitted).

Employing Planiol's formula in this case, we find that La.R.S. 9:2801.1 neither evaluates the conditions of the legality of a past act, nor modifies or suppresses the effects of a right already acquired. Nothing in the statute attempts to disturb, modify, or suppress any of Douglas' acquired or vested rights in his social security benefits, nor does it attempt to change Douglas' right to the social security benefits he earned during the marriage. Instead, it allows the trial court to allocate additional community property to Sheila in light of the fact that those social security benefits are Douglas' separate property. Douglas did not have a vested right in how their community property would be divided prior to October 12, 2005, when Sheila filed her petition. That being the case, the trial court did not abuse its discretion in applying the balancing provisions of La.R.S. 9:2801.1. We find no merit in this assignment of error.

Value of social security benefits

Douglas also contends that the trial court erred by accepting the valuation of his social security benefits set out in the report prepared by True North Assets Management. We find no merit in this argument. At trial, Sheila's counsel submitted this report as a joint offering. The report states that the marital amount of Douglas' social security benefits is $42,586.00. Douglas' counsel did not object to the amount, but stated that he wanted to "retain and reserve my rights to submit to the Court the issue over the 10–year requirement that a party has to be married before the Social Security law in Louisiana is applicable," and that "I'm agreeing to the report being offered as an exhibit. I'm reserving my rights to brief it, Judge." At trial, Douglas offered no evidence to contradict this valuation of his social security benefits.

We may not reverse the trial court's valuation of property absent an abuse of discretion. *Alford v. Alford*, 94–1464 (La.App. 3 Cir. 4/5/95), 653 So.2d 133. Where the trial court relied on the only evidence presented at trial, we find no abuse of the trial court's discretion in setting the value of the social security benefits earned during the marriage at $42,586.00.

Value of the pistols, rifles, and shotguns

In its judgment, the trial court set the value of nine guns at $1,145.00 and assigned the guns to Douglas. On appeal, Douglas contends that this was an error, that Mr. Peterson actually assigned a value of $695.00 to the guns he appraised. The appellate record does not contain a copy of Mr. Peterson's appraisal; Douglas filed a motion to correct the record, seeking to supplement the record with a March 28, 2007 letter listing the values that Mr. Peterson set on the disputed property. Sheila, in brief, agrees that the guns were actually valued at $695.00. That being the case, we find that Douglas' motion to correct the record is moot and reduce the total of the community assets awarded to Douglas by the difference between $1,145.00 and $695.00, to a total of $35,259.73.

Equalizing payment

On appeal, Douglas questions the amount of the $35,965.87 equalizing payment; in her brief to this court, Sheila agrees that the trial court erred in awarding that amount. We also agree that the trial court erred.

Unfortunately, neither the reasons for judgment nor the judgment itself explains how the trial court reached the $35,965.87 total. Douglas offers us no alternative figure, but Sheila asserts that the total amount due to her is $19,627.99. According to Sheila, that amount is the sum of $9,015.72 (the amount necessary to balance the distribution of the community assets) and $10,612.24 (the amount due to her for payment of community debts). She reached the first amount by accepting the trial court's statement that it intended to balance the social security benefits by the net value of the family home.8 She then removed that figure from the balancing equation and balanced the then-remaining assets and liabilities. We accept her calculations and amend the trial court judgment to provide that the equalizing payment necessary to balance the community of acquets and gains and to reimburse Sheila for payments she made for the community is $19,627.99.

DISPOSITION

For the foregoing reasons, we amend the trial court judgment to set the value of the guns allotted to Douglas Julien Comeaux at $695.00 instead of $1,145.00 and amend the judgment to set the equalizing payment at $19,627.99 instead of $35,965.87. Because the only relief granted Douglas Julien Comeaux on appeal was stipulated to by Sheila Gail Romero Comeaux, we assess all costs of this appeal to Douglas Julien Comeaux.

AFIRMED AS AMENDED

F. Individual Retirement Accounts

Individual Retirement Accounts are not subject to ERISA preemption. Ownership of an IRA is, generally, governed by state law. In Louisiana, the combination of state community property laws and special legislation results in outcomes that are somewhat similar to ERISA governed plans. Several issues, however, remain unresolved.

At divorce, state community property laws apply to the classification of the IRA. If an IRA is community property it could be allocated entirely to the owner-spouse with an equalizing payment or other property allocated to the other spouse. Alternatively, the

IRA could be divided between the two spouses. Such division, however, can result in unfavorable income tax consequences if the requirements of Sections 71(b)(2) and 408(d)(6) are not followed.

Special legislation governs the rights to the IRA upon the death of the owner-spouse:

La. Rev. Stat. § 2449. Individual retirement accounts; payment of benefits

A. Any benefits payable by reason of death from an individual retirement account established in accordance with the provisions of 26 U.S.C. 408, as amended, shall be paid as provided in the individual retirement account agreement to the designated beneficiary of the account. Such payment shall be a valid and sufficient release and discharge of the account holder for the payment or delivery so made and shall relieve the trustee, custodian, insurance company or other account fiduciary from all adverse claims thereto by a person claiming as a surviving or former spouse or a successor to such a spouse.

B. The provisions of this Section shall apply even when the decedent designates a beneficiary by last will and testament.

C. Repealed by Acts 2010, No. 175, § 6.

The impact of this statute is considered in *Succession of Egan*, below.

Special legislation also affords some protection to the owner-spouse who has begun receiving distributions from a community IRA at the time of the death of the other spouse:

La. Rev. Stat. § 9:1426. Retirement plan; usufruct of surviving spouse

A. (1) If a recurring payment is being made from a public or private pension or retirement plan, an annuity policy or plan, an individual retirement account, a Keogh plan, a simplified employee plan, or any other similar retirement plan, to one partner or to both partners of a marriage, and the payment constitutes community property, and one spouse dies, the surviving spouse shall enjoy a legal usufruct over any portion of the continuing recurring payment which was the deceased spouse's share of their community property, provided the source of the benefit is due to payments made by or on behalf of the survivor.

(2) This usufruct shall exist despite any provision to the contrary contained in a testament of the deceased spouse.

B. The usufruct granted by this Section shall be treated as a legal usufruct and is not an impingement upon the legitime and a naked owner shall not have a right to demand security.

The impact of this statute is also considered in *Succession of Lambert*, below.

The proper distribution of the IRA funds where the non-owner spouse is the first to die is less clear.

G. *Succession of Earl Ernest Egan, Jr.*

543 So. 2d 940 (La. App. 5th Cir. 1989)

WICKER, Judge.

Ilsa Tatum Egan, a surviving spouse, appeals a judgment ordering certain reimbursement to Donna Egan Pechon, Dawn M. Egan, and Earl E. Egan, III, the children and forced heirs of the decedent, Earl Ernest Egan, Jr. We reverse.

Ilsa and Earl married on October 22, 1980. It was Earl's second marriage, and he had children from his first marriage. Earl executed a will in notarial form on June 24, 1986, and died on December 1, 1986. Ilsa, his widow, probated Earl's will on May 18, 1987; and on May 21, 1987, Earl's children filed a petition for injunctive relief and rules to annul probate, appoint a succession representative, traverse the detailed descriptive list, take inventory, and vacate the marital residence.

Among the assets of the succession were several individual retirement accounts, some of which Earl had begun prior to his marriage to Ilsa. Contributions were made from community funds following the marriage. Earl had designated Ilsa as the sole beneficiary of these I.R.A.'s. The trial judge ruled that the beneficiary designation did not transfer Earl's community or separate interest in these I.R.A.'s to Ilsa. Ilsa applied for writs on this ruling; but a panel of this court refused writs, finding that judgment an interlocutory one and further finding that Ilsa had not shown irreparable injury. # 88–C–255.

A judgment on the merits awarded the I.R.A.'s to Ilsa but also ordered

> that the Decedent's forced heirs, Donna Egan Pechon, Dawn M. Egan and Earl E. Egan, III, inheriting through the Decedent's estate, are entitled to reimbursement for the Decedent's community and separate property interest in and to the Decedent's Individual Retirement Accounts from the designated

> beneficiary, Ilsa Tatum Egan, amounting to Seven Thousand Seven Hundred Forty–Seven and No/100 ($7,747.00) Dollars, cash.

The judgment also annulled the probate of Earl's testament, finding the testament invalid as to form as required by La.R.S. 9:2442.

Ilsa appeals only that ruling by the trial judge which dealt with the beneficiary designations on the I.R.A.'s:

> [T]he beneficiary designations on the individual retirement accounts of the Decedent, Earl Ernest Egan, Jr., designating his surviving spouse, Ilsa Tatum Egan as beneficiary, do not transfer, under Louisiana law, the Decedent's separate or community property interest in and to said IRAs. This situation is distinguished from the Supreme Court Case of *T.L. James & Company, Inc. v. Montgomery*, 332 So.2d 834 (La.1976), in that said case delt [sic] with an employer's pension plan, the same being subject to strict guidelines, as opposed to individual retirement accounts (emphasis by the trial judge).

Individual retirement accounts were created by Pub.L. 93–406, Title II, Section 2002(b) on September 2, 1974. (The law has been amended in 1976, 1978, twice in 1980, in 1981, 1982, 1983, 1984 and 1986.) The provisions are found in the Internal Revenue Code, 26 U.S.C. Section 408:

> (a) Individual retirement account.—For purposes of this section, the term "individual retirement account" means a trust created or organized in the United States for the exclusive benefit of an individual or his beneficiaries (emphasis added), ...

....

> (d)(3)(C)(ii) Inherited individual retirement account or annuity.—An individual retirement account or individual retirement annuity shall be treated as inherited if—
>
> > (I) the individual for whose benefit the account or annuity is maintained acquired such account by reason of a death of another individual, and
> >
> > (II) such individual was not the surviving spouse of such other individual.

....

> (g) Community property laws.—This section shall be applied without regard to any community property laws.

....

We have found no federal cases dealing specifically with the issues presented here: whether a beneficiary designation transfers a decedent's separate and/or community interest in his I.R.A.; and whether his beneficiary is required to reimburse the decedent's separate and community estates, to the benefit of his surviving major children, for the contributions made to those I.R.A.'s. The three above-cited provisions, however, would seem to bear on the issue:

(1) the I.R.A. is for the exclusive benefit of the individual or his beneficiaries;
(2) a surviving spouse is not considered to have inherited the I.R.A.; and
(3) our community property laws do not apply to I.R.A.'s.

Specific provisions dealing with payment of benefits are found in Louisiana's legislation.

Section 2449. Individual retirement accounts; payment of benefits

> A. Any benefits payable by reason of death from an individual retirement account established in accordance with the provisions of 26 U.S.C. 408, as amended, shall be paid as provided in the individual retirement account agreement to the designated beneficiary of the account. Such payment shall be a valid and sufficient release and discharge of the account holder for the payment or delivery so made and shall relieve the trustee, custodian, insurance company or other account fiduciary from all adverse claims thereto by a person claiming as a surviving or former spouse or a successor to such a spouse.
>
> B. No account holder paying a beneficiary in accordance with this Section shall be liable to the estate or any heir of the decedent nor shall the account holder be liable for any estate, inheritance, or succession taxes which may be due the state.
>
> C. The provisions of this Section shall apply notwithstanding the fact the decedent designates a beneficiary by last will and testament.

R.S. 9:2449 (emphasis added). See also R.S. 6:766(5)(a-c) which is substantially the same.

Section 33. Pension, annuity, and gratuity payment by employers

> The following shall be exempt from all liability for any debt except alimony and child support:
>
> (1) All pensions, all proceeds of and payments under annuity policies or plans, all individual retirement accounts, all Keogh plans, all simplified employee pension plans, and all other plans qualified under Sections 401 or 408

> of the Internal Revenue Code. However, an individual retirement account, Keogh plan, simplified employee pension plan, or other qualified plan is only exempt to the extent that contributions thereto were exempt from federal income taxation at the time of contribution, plus interest or dividends that have accrued thereon. No contribution shall be exempt if made less than one calendar year from the date of filing for bankruptcy, whether voluntary or involuntarily, or less than one calendar year from the date writs of seizure are filed against such account or plan.

R.S. 20:33.

We can also look at those provisions of community property, succession, and retirement law which might arguably apply. La.R.S. 23, Labor and Worker's Compensation, provides:

Section 651. Definitions

> (1) "Plan" shall mean any arrangement, agreement, contract, plan, system or trust whereby a participant acquires an enforceable right to retirement income or other compensation where payment is deferred until the termination of employment or thereafter, regardless of the method of calculating the amount of plan benefits or the mode of their distribution. Included in this definition are plans which provide pension, retirement, disability or death benefits and deferred compensation by employment, agency, trade union, stock bonus, stock ownership, stock option and profit sharing plans. The term plan shall also include employee pension benefit plans as defined by Section 3(2) of the Employee Retirement Income Security Act of 1974, Public Law 93–406, 88 Stat. 829.
>
> (2) "Benefit" shall mean anything of value payable or distributable to a participant, his spouse, a beneficiary, to a participant's estate or to any other person pursuant to the terms of the plan.
>
> (3) "Beneficiary" shall mean any person, including the participant, entitled to receive benefits under a plan.
>
> (4) "Participant" shall mean an employee or other person entitled to participate and participating or formerly participating in a plan.
>
> (5) "Designation form" shall mean any document by which a plan permits a participant to name a beneficiary to receive plan benefits.

Section 652. Designation form

(1) Any designation form permitted by a plan shall be valid for the purpose of naming a beneficiary, or selecting the mode of payment of plan benefits, or both.

(2) A designation form need not be in testamentary form, nor authentic form, nor in any form other than that permitted or required by the plan.

(3) As is provided by R.S. 23:638, benefits may be paid in reliance on a properly executed designation form until the payor receives notice of an adverse claim.

(4) The designation form shall remain in effect until revoked, terminated, amended or modified as provided by the plan. Unless otherwise specifically provided by the plan, a designation form is not deemed revoked, invalidated or otherwise affected by any act or occurrence which would have the effect of revoking, invalidating or otherwise affecting a will.

The Civil Code provides:

The community property comprises: property acquired during the existence of the legal regime through the effort, skill, or industry of either spouse; property acquired with community things or with community and separate things, unless classified as separate property under Article 2341; property donated to the spouses jointly; natural and civil fruits of community property; damages awarded for loss or injury to a thing belonging to the community; and all other property not classified by law as separate property.

La.C.C. art. 2338.

The separate property of a spouse is his exclusively. It comprises: property acquired by a spouse prior to the establishment of a community property regime; property acquired by a spouse with separate things or with separate and community things when the value of the community things is inconsequential in comparison with the value of the separate things used;

. . . . .

La.C.C. art. 2341.

In the absence of valid testamentary disposition, the undisposed property of the deceased devolves by operation of law in favor of his descendants, ascendants, and collaterals, by blood or by adoption, and in favor of his spouse not judicially separated from him, in the order provided in and according to the following articles.

La.C.C. art. 880.

> If the deceased spouse is survived by descendants, and shall not have disposed by testament of his share in the community property, the surviving spouse shall have a legal usufruct over so much of that share as may be inherited by the descendants. This usufruct terminates when the surviving spouse contracts another marriage, unless confirmed by testament for life or for a shorter period.
>
> ....
>
> A usufruct authorized by this article is to be treated as a legal usufruct and is not an impingement upon legitime.
>
> If the usufruct authorized by this article affects the rights of heirs other than children of the marriage between the deceased and the surviving spouse or affects separate property, security may be required by the naked owner.

La.C.C. art. 890.

The parties have not cited us to any cases which resolve the issues raised in this appeal. Every case cited by the parties is clearly distinguishable in one way or another. Nevertheless, a review of some of the cited jurisprudence is appropriate.

In *T.L. James & Co., Inc. v. Montgomery*, 332 So.2d 834 (La.1975), on rehearing (1976) (cited by the trial judge) the court dealt with the status of employee retirement and profit sharing plans. The decedent/employee named as his beneficiary his son from his first marriage. The decedent was still married to his second wife, by whom he had another son, and was still employed at the time of his suicide. The court noted that life insurance proceeds, when there is a beneficiary named, form no part of a decedent's estate; but it also noted that life insurance is sui generis and had previously "refused to extend the rationale of the cases dealing with life insurance to other problems where the conflict is between the urge to bring about freedom of disposition and the fundamental and elementary principles of forced heirship and the community property system...." At 845. With regard to the retirement and profit-sharing plans, the Court found them to be property belonging to the community established by the decedent and his widow.

> However, the forced heirs of the decedent and his first wife are entitled to an accounting to support any claim that some value of these benefits existed prior to the second marriage. In the event such a contention is supported, the claims of the forced heirs and the first wife that this value is attributable to the first community must be given effect.

At 846. Having initially ruled that a designation of beneficiary was invalid since it was not in testamentary form, the Court reconsidered that issue on rehearing. It reiterated

> This contractual agreement [the designation of beneficiary], as we have held, cannot (in the absence of legislation so authorizing) prejudice the rights of forced heirs or the community ownership of spouses of the wage earner, essentially, because rights of forced heirship and of spouses in community acquisitions are fundamental concepts of our legal system.

At 853. The Court concluded

> [S]o long as the constractual [sic] devolution of the decedent's interest to the beneficiary does not infringe upon the legitime of a complaining forced heir nor upon the community ownership of a complaining spouse, no prohibition of law prevents the courts from recognizing the contractual rights of the beneficiary to the ownership of the proceeds (so acquired by reason of the contract between the deceased employee, his employer, and the respective plans).

At 854. Finally, the Court awarded to the first son as beneficiary the proceeds of the retirement and profit-sharing plans, subject to the legitime, if it had been invaded, of the second son and the community property claims of the widow. The claims of the first wife were dismissed, since she had pleaded community contributions only in the alternative should her son's claims as beneficiary not be recognized.

The Supreme Court considered in *Sims v. Sims*, 358 So.2d 919 (La.1978), the interest of a spouse in her husband's retirement and held such retirement benefits to be an asset of the community. That case, however, arose out of partition litigation between husband and wife; and there were no other parties involved.

The case of *Tucker v. District Atty.'s Retirement System*, 445 So.2d 514 (La.App. 3rd Cir.1984) writ den. 447 So.2d 1080 (La.1984) dealt with an unpartitioned community existing from the decedent's first marriage. While his second wife was the beneficiary of his retirement benefits, contributions to those benefits were made during the first marriage. The court permitted a supplemental partition of these benefits.

An unmarried decedent, with illegitimate children and surviving parents, designated the defendant as beneficiary of his retirement benefits in *Parish of East Baton Rouge v. Burrell*, 429 So.2d 226 (La.App. 1st Cir.1983). The court held the illegitimate children were forced heirs and remanded the case for an evidentiary hearing on whether there were sufficient other assets to satisfy their legitime.

In *Matter of Succession of Sims*, 464 So.2d 991 (La.App. 1st Cir.1985), writ den. 467 So.2d 532 (La.1985), the court dealt with federal retirement benefits to which the decedent contributed during both his first and second marriages. His first wife litigated her entitlement to retirement benefits years earlier, resulting in a recognition of her interest in future retirement benefits. *Sims v. Sims*, supra. At the time of decedent's death he had not yet retired; and his widow, the second wife, was receiving a "survivor's annuity" and not "retirement benefits." The court held that federal law preempted our community property laws and that the first wife was barred from getting any portion of the annuity.

The district court, in the case at Bar, held the succession of Winston H. Sims indebted to Marcella Sims in the amount of $7,223.48, plus interest from date of judgment, representing one-half of the total contributions made during the community existing between Winston and Marcella Sims. The court reasoned, in pertinent part, that:

> "the survivor annuity ... [being paid Elizabeth] is not subject to any claim and since no retirement benefits are available, the value of the interest of Mrs. Marcella Sims can only be the value of one-half of the community contributions to the system or nothing at all. The language of Sims is sufficiently clear to indicate that the action analogized to a partition in kind included at a minimum the reimbursement of Mrs. Marcella Sims' contributions". (Brackets ours).

At 1002.

The State paid to the decedent's widow and child the contributions he had made to the retirement system prior to his death, but his first wife was his named beneficiary. The court in *Jackson v. State, Tchrs.' Retire. System*, 407 So.2d 416 (La.App. 1st Cir.1981), held that the widow and children had to reimburse the retirement system so that it could in turn pay the beneficiary.

> The surviving partner in community (surviving spouse) may be entitled to an accounting of community contributions to the retirement system from the decedent's estate or his heirs ... but not from the beneficiary or the retirement system. Thus, we reject the contention that, as surviving spouse, she is entitled to be recognized as owner of one-half of the benefits attributable to contributions made during the existence of the community between her and the decedent.

At 418 (citations omitted) (emphasis added).

In *Bendler v. Marshall*, 513 So.2d 369 (La.App. 4th Cir.1987), writ den. 514 So.2d 1180 (1987), the decedent's federal retirement benefits were not considered in the partition with his first wife. After death, his second wife received a widow's annuity; and his first wife sued for the share attributable to the contributions made during her marriage to decedent. Reversing the trial court, which had awarded reimbursement to the first wife, and citing *Matter of Succession of Sims*, supra, the court held that the first wife was not entitled to a pro-rata share of the survivor's annuity and she was not entitled to any reimbursement from the widow. "While plaintiff is entitled to make a claim for reimbursement, she is not entitled to make that claim against the defendant, who is the decedent's surviving spouse and designated survivor for purposes of the decedent's annuity plan." At 371.

Our circuit, in dealing with the issues of military retirement pay and military insurance, held that the retirement was community property but the policy, acquired prior to the marriage, was separate property. *Inzinna v. Inzinna*, 456 So.2d 691 (La.App.1984), writ den. 461 So.2d 317 (La.1984). The court recognized that the proceeds of the insurance policy were not subject to community claims but passed directly to the named beneficiary; however, the wife was entitled to one-half any increase in the policy's cash value attributable to community contributions. In this case, there were no claims other than those of the former husband and wife and neither party had died.

The issue in *Flanner v. Succession of Flanner*, 338 So.2d 355 (La.App. 3rd Cir.1977), writ den. 340 So.2d 999 (La.1977), was the characterization of U.S. savings bonds in the names of decedent and his widow. The decedent's children from his first marriage sought to re-open the succession, which they had previously renounced in favor of their stepmother, so as to assert a right to these bonds. The court held that transfer of decedent's property interest in the bonds to his widow was valid, subject to any claims of forced heirs whose legitime was prejudiced.

The Third Circuit has considered the effect of an I.R.A. beneficiary designation, although neither party has cited Succession of *McVay v. McVay*, 476 So.2d 1070 (La.App.1985). The court was called upon to characterize, among other assets, an I.R.A. account payable to the decedent's widow as beneficiary. Children from decedent's prior marriage challenged the widow's claim that the I.R.A. should be excluded from the descriptive list of the succession's assets. The court held that the widow's position was the correct one, citing 26 U.S.C. Section 408(g) that "[t]his section shall be applied without regard to any community property laws." We agree with this conclusion.

The court went on, however, to analogize I.R.A. accounts to U.S. savings bonds, resulting in a further holding that the community of acquets and gains should be deemed to have included an amount equal to the I.R.A. amount, citing *Fontenot v. Fontenot*, 339 So.2d 897 (La.App. 3rd Cir.1976), writ den. 342 So.2d 217 (La.1977). We do not agree, believing that I.R.A. accounts are more like the retirement plans in *T.L. James & Co., Inc. v. Montgomery*, supra. There is no reason to treat I.R.A.'s differently from other retirement plans.

"When no rule for a particular situation can be derived from legislation or custom, the court is bound to proceed according to equity. To decide equitably, resort is made to justice, reason, and prevailing usages." La.C.C. art. 4.

We do not know whether or not the community existing between Egan and his first wife was fully partitioned or even if such a community existed. We also do not know whether the legitime of Egan's children has been satisfied by assets other than the I.R.A.'s at issue, although that has been urged in brief. We do know the following facts by stipulation: (1) Ilsa is the sole owner of one-half the contributions made to the I.R.A.'s during her marriage to Egan; (2) Egan's interest in these I.R.A.'s, both separate and community, totals $7,747.00; and (3) Egan's children have received cash of $18,253.00, a house and lot, stock, household furnishings, and employee retirement benefits from the succession.

Absent a showing that community property rights of Egan's first wife, who is not a party, or forced heirship rights have been infringed, we see no justification for requiring Egan's widow and beneficiary to reimburse her stepchildren. No such showing has been made; and we therefore reverse the judgment of the trial court insofar as it requires reimbursement from Ilsa Tatum Egan to Donna Egan Pechon, Dawn M. Egan, and Earl E. Egan, III. Donna Egan Pechon, Dawn M. Egan, and Earl E. Egan, III must pay the costs of this appeal.

REVERSED.

H. *Succession of Kathryn Lambert*

12 So. 3d 415 (La. App. 3d Cir. 2009)

GREMILLION, Judge.

Julie Lambert Boudreaux, daughter of the deceased Kathryn Lucille Andrews Lambert, appeals the trial court's judgment in favor of her father, Jerry Lambert, finding that Julie was not entitled to receive a 1/4 share of retirement funds upon Jerry's remarriage. For the following reasons, we affirm.

FACTUAL AND PROCEDURAL BACKGROUND

Kathryn died May 1, 1994, leaving behind a Last Will and Testament which provided:

> At my death, I leave all of the property I die possessed of to my two children, Julie Ann Boudreaux and Michael Glenn Lambert, in the proportions of an undivided one-half (½) interest to each, subject to the statutory usufruct which I hereby confirm in favor of my husband, Jerry Glenn Lambert, to last until his death or remarriage.

Since her death, litigation concerning Jerry's IRA, which was community property, has been ongoing. A judgment of possession recognized Julie and her brother as naked owners of their mother's one-half interest in the IRA account. Following Jerry's remarriage in 1997, his children demanded their one-half interest in the account. Jerry responded by seeking to have the IRA account removed from the list of community assets. The trial court found that the IRA account was community property and that La.R.S. 9:1426 applied to it to create a continuing usufruct in favor of Jerry.

I

n an unpublished opinion rendered in November 2007, we affirmed the finding of the trial court that the IRA account was community property, but remanded the case for a determination of whether the IRA was in pay status at the time of Kathryn's death. We stated, "the legal usufruct created by La.R.S. 9:1426 would unquestionably exist if a recurring payment was being made from the Main Stay IRA at the time of Kathryn's death." Following a hearing in April 2008, the trial court found that the IRA was in a pay status prior to Kathryn's death and that the legal usufruct provided by La.R.S. 9:1426 applied to the IRA and "to all funds and proceeds from that account."

Julie now appeals and asserts as error the trial court's failure to address the applicability of La.R.S. 9:1426 to "lump sum payments" or "mandatory withdrawals" as required by federal law.

DISCUSSION

Appellate review of a question of law is simply a decision as to whether the trial court's decision is legally correct or incorrect. *Jim Walter Homes, Inc. v. Jessen*, 98–1685 (La.App. 3 Cir. 3/31/99), 732 So.2d 699. If the trial court's decision was based on its erroneous application of law, its decision is not entitled to deference by the reviewing court. *Kem Search, Inc. v. Sheffield*, 434 So.2d 1067 (La.1983). When an appellate court finds that a reversible error of law was made in the lower court, it must redetermine the facts de novo from the entire record and render a judgment on the merits. *Lasha v. Olin Corp.*, 625 So.2d 1002 (La.1993).

***

The issues in this case are whether La.R.S. 9:1426 applies to a "lump sum periodic payment" or to a "mandatory withdrawal" as required by federal law. Julie argues that the usufruct attaches to "the periodic payments but not to the principle." Julie goes on to state:

> There is nothing in this statutory provision which allows [Jerry] to withdraw either voluntarily or by any mandatory provision of federal tax law without having to pay over to [Julie] her 25% share of the principle of the retirement funds.

> It is respectfully submitted that the judgment of the trial court be modified to require [Jerry] to pay over to [Julie] 25% of the principle of any periodic or mandatory withdrawals from retirement funds required by federal law.

This issue appears to be res novo in Louisiana law and one that is not addressed by La.R.S. 9:1426. However, in examining the purpose behind La.R.S. 9:1426, we find that the legislature intended to protect the surviving spouse's usufruct of community retirement funds until his death in priority over the claims of naked ownership of the heirs' portion of the funds. The article does not distinguish between types of payments, only calling them "recurring payments." It does not distinguish between recurring payments comprised of principle versus interest, or a combination of both, although we note that the usufruct applies to any portion of the continuing "recurring payments." The overall policy of protecting a surviving spouse's ability to provide for himself during retirement appears to outweigh the heirs' right to the community portion. Spaht and Moreno, 16 La.Civ. L. Treatise, Matrimonial Regimes § 3.44 (3 ed.) recently addressed some of the issues surrounding IRA accounts in relation to La.R.S. 9:1426 (emphasis added) (footnotes omitted):

> A narrow Louisiana statute adopted in 1990 protects the covered spouse who is collecting IRA or other pension benefits when the other spouse dies. It was originally added to the Louisiana Civil Code as Article 890, redesignated as La.Civ.Code art. 890.1 and provided that the covered spouse will continue to receive the cash flow coming from the IRA until death even if the heirs of the deceased spouse might have claims to part of the asset under community property principles. In 1997, Article 890.1 was redesignated as La.R.S. 9:1426.
>
> R.S. 9:1426 applies to "a public or private pension or retirement plan, an annuity policy or plan, an individual retirement account, a Keogh plan, simplified employee plan, or any other similar retirement plan." If a spouse dies while the surviving spouse is receiving "a recurring payment" from the plan, the survivor enjoys a legal usufruct over the continuing recurring payment which was the deceased spouse's share of their community if the source of the benefit is traced to payments made by or on behalf of the survivor. The usufruct is mandatory and applies even if a testament provides otherwise.
>
> Although R.S. 9:1426 calls this a "legal usufruct," it is not provided that the usufruct terminates upon remarriage, as Civil Code Article 890 provides with respect to the regular legal usufruct of the surviving spouse. As a legal usufruct, it would be free of the normal requirements of security, but R.S. 9:1426 goes further and so specifies in the third paragraph. It also provides that such a usufruct is not an impingement on the legitime of forced heirs.

> The basic policy behind R.S. 9:1426—protecting the rights of the living spouse to a retirement benefit at the expense of the heirs of the deceased spouse—would seem to apply also in the case of a death of the other spouse before regular distributions are begun. However, R.S. 9:1426 strictly construed seems to apply if the "recurring payment is being made ... and one spouse dies." As suggested in the next section, the underlying policy seems broader, and the provision might well be construed to apply more broadly by analogy.
>
> Since the right of the living spouse is a usufruct of money that would otherwise go to the heirs, the usufructuary has the right to spend those funds. In so doing, the usufructuary incurs the obligation to compensate the naked owners for those sums at the termination of the usufruct, which would normally be upon the death of the usufructuary.

Spaht and Moreno go on to discuss the case where recurring payments have not yet begun when the spouse dies. In addressing the issue of principle versus interest and forcing a surviving spouse to distribute a "lump sum" amount to the naked owners upon the death of a spouse, these authors note the unresolved complexities created by the statute, but suggest that public policy in favor of the surviving spouse outweighs the naked owners' rights (emphasis added):

> This apparent conclusion under the general law and R.S. 9:1426 is obviously a messy, complicated one. For example, the continuing IRA payment could be partly return of principal and partly investment income. The latter would presumably be a fruit owned by the usufructuary and the former would have to be accounted for to the naked owners at the termination of the usufruct over the recurring benefit.
>
> In any event, the IRA fund could well be considered as any other community asset in the absence of special rules, and there appear to be no special state law rules to govern the situation other than Article 890 by its terms and R.S. 9:1426 by analogy. Perhaps the trust law might be invoked, with the result that the heir's interest is not in the underlying IRA assets but in the beneficial rights under the trust. And, like life insurance ownership by the non-covered spouse, it is a right that is virtually worthless. Also, it could be a disastrous tax situation if a state court in such a situation would order half the account paid to the heirs. This would probably be a distribution of the IRA subject to taxation and penalty, to be paid by the initial contracting spouse.
>
> Despite its complexity, however, this approach does balance the rights of the parties so as to give substantial protection to the surviving spouse's interests and does fulfill the policy of providing retirement income to spouses no longer able to work, rather than benefitting what would normally be the next generation.

....

> It would diminish [the surviving spouse's] interests to give half of [his IRA fund] up to the heirs of the deceased. Even under state policies, where a statutory usufruct would allow the survivor to enjoy the benefits of the fund until death or remarriage, there is a similar policy which may militate against recognition of the heirs' claims.

Id.

Spaht & Moreno suggest that the public policy in favor of the surviving spouse is so strong, that a fortiori, La.R.S. 9:1426 would probably apply even if recurring payments had not yet begun. Thus, any mandatory federal withdrawals are "recurring payments" within the meaning of the statute. The law provides us with nothing to restrict a broad reading of La.R.S. 9:1426. Accordingly, we find that federally mandated withdrawals fall within its ambit. Accordingly, we affirm the trial court's finding that any mandatory federal withdrawals of principle and/or interest are "recurring payments" subject to Jerry's usufruct.

The situation of voluntary lump sum withdrawals presents a more difficult issue. Although it is clear that the policy is to protect the retirement funds of the surviving spouse, one can envision a situation in which the surviving spouse withdraws a large portion of the funds pursuant to his legal usufruct and disposes of all of the money leaving nothing to reimburse the naked owner at his death. However, there is no present issue regarding lump sum withdrawals and this court does not issue advisory opinions. Accordingly, we leave this issue for another day.

CONCLUSION

The judgment of the trial court finding that Jerry's IRA account was in pay status, and that his usufruct applies to recurring payments from his IRA account, is affirmed. Additionally, we find that federally mandated withdrawals are "recurring payments" within the meaning of La.R.S. 9:1426. All costs of this appeal are assessed against Julie Lambert Boudreaux.

AFFIRMED.

I. Questions

1. When H and W divorce, one of the assets to be divided is H's interest in a defined benefit plan provided by his employer—the State of Louisiana. In order to begin collecting benefits, H must work for 30 years. 10 of those 30 years occurred during to H's marriage to W. The remainder occurred either before or after marriage. H's annual benefit is expected to be $90,000. How will the plan be treated at divorce? What, if anything, will W be entitled to?

2. Assume that in (1), the benefits do not commence until H retires and they cease entirely at H's death. After determining the respective interests of each spouse in the defined benefit plan, what methods can the court use to divide the asset? If you represented one of the spouses, which method would you advocate?

3. How would your answers to (1) and (2) change if H was employed by a private corporation rather than the state? Are the changes substantive or procedural?

4. How would your answers to (1) and (2) change if H's retirement plan was a defined contribution plan rather than a defined benefit plan?

5. H and W are married. W has a child from a prior marriage, C. W has a defined contribution plan through her employer, the State of Louisiana, that she has acquired entirely during her marriage to H. W names C as the beneficiary of the plan. The plan provides that upon W's death, any accumulated but unpaid proceeds will be paid to the named beneficiary. W dies. How will the proceeds be distributed? What rights might H have?

6. Would your answer to (5) be different if W worked for a private corporation rather than the State of Louisiana?

7. When H and W divorce, H is nearing retirement. Although he has not yet begun to collect Social Security benefits, which the court determines are worth $100,000. All of H's right to Social Security benefits was acquired during his marriage to W. How will the Social Security benefits be treated?

8. Same facts as #7. Suppose that in addition to H's future Social Security benefits, the only other asset for division is a community home worth $100,000. How will the community property be divided? What, if anything, can the court do to ensure H and W are treated fairly?

4.13 ADDITIONAL ISSUES OF FEDERAL LAW: UNITED STATES SAVINGS BONDS

A. Introduction

United States Savings Bonds can be registered in several different ways. Bonds registered as sole owner bonds designate one individual as the owner. Only the owner can redeem the bond for cash or engage in other transactions. If the owner still owns the bond at death, then the bond becomes part of the owner's estate and is distributed in accordance with his will or state intestacy laws. Co-owner bonds, in contrast, list two people as the owners. Upon the death of the first owner the survivor becomes the full owner of the bond. This form of registration is similar to a joint tenancy with right of survivorship. The ability of the two owners to make transactions with a co-owner bond depends on whether the bond is an electronic bond or a paper bond. Either owner, without the knowledge or consent of the other owner, can engage in transactions with paper bonds. Paper bonds have not been sold since January 2012. Electronic co-owner bonds designate one owner as the primary owner and the other owner as the secondary owner. The primary owner can engage in transactions and can authorize the secondary owner to do so as well. Finally, bonds may be registered as beneficiary bonds. Beneficiary bonds are payable to the named owner of the bond during the owner's lifetime. If the owner does not present the bond for payment during life then the designated beneficiary automatically becomes the owner of the bond.

Questions have arisen with respect to the interplay between the various registration options and community property laws.

B. *J.W. Free v. James F. Bland*

369 U.S. 663 (1962)

Mr. Chief Justice WARREN delivered the opinion of the Court.

We are called upon to determine whether the Treasury Regulations creating a right of survivorship in United States Savings Bonds pre-empt any inconsistent Texas community property law by virtue of the Supremacy Clause, Article VI, Clause 2, of the Constitution.

The petitioner is the widower of Mrs. Mary Ida Free, and the respondent is her son by a previous marriage. Mr. and Mrs. Free were domiciled in Texas. That State follows the community property system; except in certain instances not here material, all property acquired by either spouse during marriage belongs to the community of the husband and wife. Property purchased with community property retains a community character...During the years 1941 to 1945, petitioner Free, using community property, purchased several United States Savings Bonds, series 'E' and 'F'. The bonds were all issued to 'Mr. or Mrs.' Free. Under the Treasury Regulations promulgated under 31 U.S.C. s 757c(a), 31 U.S.C.A. s 757c(a) which govern bonds issued in that form, when either co-owner dies, 'the survivor will be recognized as the sole and absolute owner.' 31 CFR s 315.61. After Mrs. Free passed away in 1958, this controversy arose between the husband, who claimed exclusive ownership by operation of the Treasury Regulations, and the son, who, as the principal beneficiary under his mother's will, claimed an interest in the bonds by virtue of the state community property laws. Respondent son demanded either one-half of the bonds or reimbursement for the loss of Mrs. Free's community half interest in the bonds which was converted into petitioner's separate property by operation of the federal regulations.

***

The Supreme Court of Texas' interpretation of the Supremacy Clause is not in accord with controlling doctrine. The relative importance to the State of its own law is not material when there is a conflict with a valid federal law, for the Framers of our Constitution provided that the federal law must prevail. Article VI, Clause 2. This principle was made clear by Chief Justice Marshall when he stated for the Court that any state law, however clearly within a State's acknowledged power, which interferes with or is contrary to federal law, must yield. *Gibbons v. Ogden*, 9 Wheat. 1, 210—211, 6 L.Ed. 23. See *Franklin National Bank v. New York*, 347 U.S. 373, 74 S.Ct. 550, 98 L.Ed. 767; *Wissner v. Wissner*, 338 U.S. 655, 70 S.Ct. 398, 94 L.Ed. 424; *Sola Electric Co. v. Jefferson Electric Co.*, 317 U.S. 173, 63 S.Ct. 172, 87 L.Ed. 165. Thus our inquiry is directed toward whether there is a valid federal law, and if so, whether there is a conflict with state law.

Article I, Section 8, Clause 2 of the Constitution delegates to the Federal Government the power '(t)o borrow Money on the credit of the United States.' Pursuant to this grant of power, the Congress authorized the Secretary of the Treasury, with the approval of the President, to issue savings bonds in such form and under such conditions as he may from time to time prescribe, subject to certain limitations not here material. 31 U.S.C. s 757c(a), 31 U.S.C.A. s 757c(a). Cf. *United States v. Sacks*, 257 U.S. 37, 42 S.Ct. 38, 66 L.Ed. 118. Exercising that authority, the Secretary of the Treasury issued savings bonds under regulations which provided, inter alia, that the co-owner of a savings bond issued in the 'or' form who survives the other co-owner 'will be recognized as the sole and absolute owner' of the bond, 31 CFR s 315.61,5 and that '(n)o judicial determination will be recognized which would * * * defeat or impair the rights of survivorship conferred by these regulations,' 31 CFR s 315.20.6 The Treasury has consistently maintained that the purpose of these regulations is to establish the right of survivorship regardless of local state law, and a majority of the States which have considered the problem have recognized this right. The respondent, however, contends that the purpose of the regulations is simply to provide a convenient method of payment. This argument depends primarily on the distinction between stating that the surviving co-owner will 'be recognized as' the sole owner and stating that the surviving co-owner will 'be' the sole owner. This distinction is insubstantial. The clear purpose of the regulations is to confer the right of survivorship on the surviving co-owner. Thus, the survivorship provision is a federal law which must prevail if it conflicts with state law. See *Wissner v. Wissner*, 338 U.S. 655, 70 S.Ct. 398, 94 L.Ed. 424.

The success of the management of the national debt depends to a significant measure upon the success of the sales of the savings bonds. The Treasury is authorized to make the bonds attractive to savers and investors. One of the inducements selected by the Treasury is the survivorship provision, a convenient method of avoiding complicated probate proceedings. Notwithstanding this provision, the State awarded full title to the co-owner but required him to account for half of the value of the bonds to the decedent's estate. Viewed realistically, the State has rendered the award of title meaningless. Making the bonds security for the payment confirms the accuracy of this view. If the State can frustrate the parties' attempt to use the bonds' survivorship provision through the simple expedient of requiring the survivor to reimburse the estate of the deceased co-owner as a matter of law, the State has interfered directly with a legitimate exercise of the power of the Federal Government to borrow money.

***

We hold, therefore, that the state law which prohibits a married couple from taking advantage of the survivorship provisions of United States Savings Bonds merely because the purchase price is paid out of community property must fall under the Supremacy Clause.

***

C. *Gust Yiatchos v. Pearle W. Yiatchos*

376 U.S. 306 (1964)

Mr. Justice WHITE delivered the opinion of the Court.

Two Terms ago in *Free v. Bland*, 369 U.S. 663, 82 S.Ct. 1089, 8 L.Ed.2d 180, where federal savings bonds purchased with community funds were registered in a co-ownership form and the registered co-owners were husband and wife, the survivor was held entitled to the proceeds of the bonds without liability to account in any amount to the beneficiaries of the deceased co-owner, despite conflicting state law purporting to forbid a married couple to make survivorship arrangements with respect to community property and requiring such property to pass as part of the estate of the deceased in accordance with his will or the state intestacy laws. The success of the management of the national debt was deemed to depend upon the successful sale of the savings bonds, one of the inducements to purchasers being survivorship provisions which afforded 'a convenient method of avoiding complicated probate proceedings.' 369 U.S., at 669, 82 S.Ct., at 1093. State law interfered with a legitimate exercise of federal power and was required to give way under the Supremacy Clause of the Constitution.

The Court nevertheless recognized that the federal law was not to be used as a shield for fraud or to prevent relief 'where the circumstances manifest fraud or a breach of trust tantamount thereto on the part of a husband while acting in his capacity as manager of the general community property.' 369 U.S., at 670, 82 S.Ct., at 1094. The scope and application of the exception to the regulatory imperative—'the doctrine of fraud applicable under federal law in such a case,' 369 U.S., at 670—671, 82 S.Ct., at 1094—were left to decision in other cases.

This is one of those cases. Petitioner is the brother of Angel Yiatchos who died in 1958 and who in 1950—1951 purchased with community funds belonging to himself and his wife United States Savings Bonds in the face amount of $15,075. The deceased was the registered owner of the bonds and they were made payable on his death to his brother, the petitioner. The deceased left a will made in 1954, naming his wife as executrix and bequeathing all cash and bonds owned by him at the time of his death to his brother, four sisters and a nephew. Petitioner brought suit in the appropriate court in the State of Washington to establish his ownership of the bonds, relying upon the federal regulations providing for registration of the savings bonds in the beneficiary form and providing that in the case of the death of the registered owner 'the beneficiary will be recognized as the sole and absolute owner, and payment or reissue will be made as though the bond were registered in his name alone.' 31 CFR s 315.66. The trial court, on stipulated facts, sustained the claims of the wife and the other beneficiaries under the will who insisted that since the bonds were purchased with community funds and were community property at the death of the deceased they must be divided into two equal parts, one-half to go to the wife and the other half to be distributed in accordance with the will. The Supreme Court of Washington affirmed, holding that the deceased's 'purchase with community funds of bonds payable to him alone or, after his death, payable exclusively to his brother was in fraud of the rights of the respondent wife' and 'a void endeavor to divest the wife of any interest in her own property.' The deceased having been under a fiduciary duty to manage the community funds for the benefit of the community, '(a) breach of this duty (was) a constructive fraud.' Petitioner's claim to any part of the bonds as beneficiary named therein was rejected since '(r)espondent widow had a vested one-half interest in the bond proceeds' and since '(t)he descent of decedent's interest is controlled by RCW 11.04.050, and, therefore, must be distributed according to the terms of the will.' *In re Yiatchos' Estate*, 60 Wash.2d 179, 182, 373 P.2d 125, 127. We granted certiorari to consider an asserted conflict with *Free v. Bland*, supra, which was decided while this case was on appeal in the Washington Supreme Court and which that court considered in rendering its own judgment.

Under the federal regulations petitioner is entitled to the bonds unless his deceased brother committed fraud or breach of trust tantamount to fraud. Since the construction and application of a federal regulation having the force of law, *Public Utilities Comm'n of California v. United States*, 355 U.S. 534, 542—545, 78 S.Ct. 446, 451—453, 2 L.Ed.2d 470; *Standard Oil Co. of California v. Johnson,* 316 U.S. 481, 484, 62 S.Ct. 1168, 1169, 86 L.Ed. 1611, are involved, whether or not there is fraud which will bar the named beneficiary in a particular case must be determined as a matter of federal law, *Free v. Bland*, supra; *Clearfield Trust Co. v. United States*, 318 U.S. 363, 63 S.Ct. 573, 87 L.Ed. 838. But in applying the federal standard we shall be guided by state law insofar as the property interests of the widow created by state law are concerned. It would seem obvious that the bonds may not be used as a device to deprive the widow of property rights which she enjoys under Washington law and which would not be transferable by her husband but for the survivorship provisions of the federal bonds.

Proceeding on these premises, we note that under Washington law spouses may agree to change the status of community property either by an agreement to become effective on the death of either spouse, Rev.Code Wash. s 26.16.120; *In re Yiatchos' Estate*, 60 Wash.2d 179, 182, 373 P.2d 125, 127, or by gift during lifetime; *Hanley v. Most*, 9 Wash.2d 429, 458, 115 P.2d 933, 944. Thus the widow in this case could have consented to a gift of community property to her husband's brother or to the inclusion of the bonds in that portion of the estate which belonged to her husband and which he could dispose of at the time of his death. If she gave such consent, or if she ratified the purchase and registration of the bonds, the conduct of the husband was not, for federal purposes, fraud or breach of trust sufficient to avoid the command of the regulations, and petitioner would be entitled to all of the bonds

.

So far petitioner apparently agrees, but he denies the need for further inquiry, claiming all of the bonds because the record is silent about the knowledge or consent of the wife, she having made no claim of fraud and produced no facts negativing her consent or knowledge. But we think the course suggested by the United States in its amicus curiae brief is preferable. The factual record was made by the stipulation of the parties prior to decision of *Free v. Bland,* supra. Before precluding the widow because of her own conduct, she should have an opportunity upon remand to prove the actual facts concerning her knowledge or participation in the purchase and registration of the bonds.

Petitioner, however, also objects to a remand because further inquiry into consent or acquiescence rests upon the erroneous assumption that the wife could object to the husband's transfer of the bonds after his death. Since the present value of the bonds, or even their face value, is less than one-half the community property, the deceased, says petitioner, was not attempting to give away property belonging to his wife but was only making use of a simple device provided by federal law to dispose of what he could give by will under the Washington law. The validity of this contentention turns on a question of state law about which we are not entirely clear and which may be resolved upon remand. According to the court below, the widow had a 'vested one-half interest' in the bonds, which may mean that under Washington law the wife before and after death has a half interest in each item of the community estate, including the particular bonds involved in this case and cannot be forced to take cash or something else of equal value upon a division of the community property between herself and those entitled to take her husband's half. Under such circumstances, since we cannot say that this property right, if it exists, is insubstantial, to allow all of the bonds to pass to the designated beneficiary would effect an involuntary and impermissible conversion of the widow's assets.

On the other hand, Rev. Code Wash. s 26.16.030 provides that 'The husband shall have the management and control of community personal property, with a like power of disposition as he has of his separate personal property, except he shall not devise by will more than one-half thereof.' If under Washington law, the widow, after her husband's death, has no interest in specific assets owned by the community and her half of the community estate may be satisfied from property or money other than the bonds, petitioner is entitled to all of the bonds for then there is no fraud or breach of trust in derogation of the widow's property rights under state law. Upon dissolution of the community one-half of the community property belonged to Angel Yiatchos, who was free, as of the time of dissolution, to dispose of this half as he pleased. He might have left it to his brother by will. Instead he elected to effect the same result by utilizing federal savings bonds with their convenient feature of permitting ownership spanning two lives. On the assumption, then, that the wife is entitled to half of the estate, but not half of each particular item of property, the bonds have not been used as an instrument of fraud; and the survivorship provisions of the federal regulations must control, preempting, if necessary, inconsistent state law which interferes with the legitimate exercise of the Federal Government's power to borrow money. *Free v. Bland*, supra.

Petitioner is therefore entitled to all of the bonds if the widow consented to making him the beneficiary or if under Washington law the surviving spouse does not have a one-half interest in each community asset. But even if the wife is not barred by her own consent or by the nature of her interest from claiming a half interest in the bonds, petitioner is entitled to the other half, the half which belonged to the deceased and could be disposed of by him to the beneficiaries of his choice. The Washington court deemed the transaction void ab initio and required the deceased's half to pass by his will rather than by virtue of the bonds and the force of the regulation. But the petitioner was entitled to the proceeds only on the death of the husband, and then only if the bonds had not matured or been cashed. During the husband's life he was the registered owner of the bonds, and was therefore entitled at any time to convert them into cash upon presentation and surrender 'as though no beneficiary had been named in the registration.' 31 CFR s 315.65. Aside from possible consequences of the wife's consent or ratification, as long as Angel Yiatchos was alive the bonds were community property, and could be used by him—the manager of the community and the registered owner of the bonds—for community purposes just as the assets used to purchase them could have been so used. Thus, the holding of the court below, which requires that the bonds be disposed of by will or by state intestacy provisions, is nothing more than a state prohibition against utilizing savings bonds to transmit property at death, and is, for reasons stated above, forbidden by *Free v. Bland*, supra.

We add but one caveat to our holding that petitioner is entitled to at least one-half the bonds. The bonds, it would appear, are less than one-half the gross estate, but the record does not compare the value of the bonds with one-half the net estate after payment of debts. It is our understanding that the deceased's interest in the community property is chargeable with his separate debts and with one-half the community debts. *Ryan v. Ferguson*, 3 Wash. 356, 28 P. 910. It would not contravene federal law as expressed in the applicable regulations to require the bonds to bear the same share of the debts that they would have borne if they had been passed to petitioner as a specific legacy under the will rather than by the survivorship provisions of the bonds.

The judgment of the Washington court is reversed insofar as it relates to one-half of the bonds, subject to the above remarks concerning the portion of the debts which may be allocable thereto. As to the other half the judgment is vacated and the case remanded for further proceedings not inconsistent with this opinion. It is so ordered.

Judgment reversed in part and vacated in part and case remanded.

4.14 ADDITIONAL ISSUES OF FEDERAL LAW: INTELLECTUAL PROPERTY RIGHTS

A. *George G. Rodrigue, Jr. v. Veronica Hidalgo Rodrigue*

218 F. 3d 432 (5th Cir. 2000)

WIENER, Circuit Judge:

Our task in this appeal, before us under Federal Rule of Civil Procedure 54(b), is to sort out and reconcile the respective rights and obligations of authors under federal copyright law and their spouses under Louisiana community property law when those two legal regimes intersect. Defendant–Appellant Veronica Hidalgo Rodrigue ("Veronica") asks us to reverse the district court's ruling that, by virtue of copyright law, her ex-husband, Plaintiff–Appellee George Godfrey Rodrigue, Jr. ("George"), holds all ownership rights in intellectual property that he created during the parties' marriage, to the exclusion of any rights she might otherwise have in those creations by virtue of community property law. Agreeing with Veronica, we reverse and remand with instructions.

I.
Facts and Proceedings

George and Veronica were married in Louisiana in 1967 and were divorced there in 1993. In the absence of an election by them to have any other marital property regime apply, the Rodrigues' Louisiana marriage effected the "legal regime" of matrimonial property, establishing between them a community of acquets and gains, commonly referred to simply as the community.

During the marriage, George became a widely acclaimed, highly successful, and very prolific painter. He created numerous paintings both during the existence of the community and after its termination, a number of which depicted a stylized and easily recognizable image of a blue dog. Modeled after the family pet, Tiffany, the first blue dog painting was created in 1984. George obtained certificates of copyright for some but not all of his paintings.

Divorce terminated the community that had existed between Veronica and George throughout their marriage. As a general proposition, the Louisiana Civil Code provides that, on termination of the community, the property formerly belonging to it becomes subject to the provisions governing co-ownership: "Each spouse owns an undivided one-half interest in former community property and its fruits and products" until partition.

Following the dissolution of his marriage with Veronica, George and co-Plaintiff-Appellee Richard Steiner, George's former business associate, filed this action in federal court seeking a declaration that George is the sole owner of intellectual property rights in all the paintings, particularly the blue dog image. They also sought to enjoin Veronica from (1) seeking a declaration of her co-ownership of those works, (2) making image transfers, and (3) suing for copyright infringement. Veronica filed a counterclaim in an effort to obtain a declaration that she owns an undivided one-half interest in (1) all intellectual property rights (including, but not limited to, the blue dog) generated during the existence of the community and (2) all post-community artworks that are "derivative" of that intellectual property. Veronica also sought an accounting for her half-interest in the proceeds of post-community use of those copyrights and derivatives.

After the parties filed cross-motions for summary judgment, the district court granted George's, grounding its decision in federal copyright preemption of state community property law. Veronica filed a motion for reconsideration which the court did not address, entering instead an order dismissing all of her claims. Veronica filed a second motion for reconsideration which the court granted to the extent that the previous order purported to resolve all claims of all parties. The court certified the preemption issue for immediate appeal pursuant to Rule 54(b) and stayed the remaining issues.

In a scholarly and thorough analysis, the district court concluded that, as a matter of conflict preemption, subjecting copyrights on works of the author-spouse to Louisiana community property law would damage federal interests in national uniformity and efficient exchange of copyrights. The court held that, as a result of this conflict, the state marital property law is preempted and cannot appertain. The court also considered 17 U.S.C. § 301, the express preemption provision of the federal Copyright Act of 1976 ("the Copyright Act" or "the Act") but concluded that it did not apply because Louisiana's community property law does not purport to provide rights "equivalent" to those specified by the Act. And the court rejected Veronica's "transfer" argument that, even though § 201(a) of the Copyright Act specifies that a copyright "vests initially" in the author at the time of creation of the work, it is transferred to the community by operation of law immediately following such initial vesting.

In concluding that federal law preempts state law in this instance, the district court voiced particular concern about the practicability of copyright co-management by spouses. Still, in describing problems associated with co-management, the court flagged a possible solution: The author-spouse could retain and exercise sole management and control of the copyright without depriving the non author-spouse of the "more tangible benefits." Instead of so holding, however, the court demurred to Congress to decide whether to adopt that approach.

We are convinced that the district court visualized the correct method for reconciling the apparent conflict, but we disagree about the need for a congressional fix. We therefore adopt the approach considered but rejected by that court, and we reverse.

II.
Analysis

We review the grant of summary judgment de novo, applying the same standards as the district court.

George contends that provisions of both the Copyright Act and the U.S. Constitution preempt state community property law, preventing his copyrighted artistic works from ever having become property of the community that was created by his marriage to Veronica and thereby exempting his copyrights from division and partition of the community after divorce. Section 201(a) of the Act specifies that a "[c]opyright in a work protected under this title vests initially in the author or authors of the work." In facial contrast, Louisiana Civil Code article 2338 declares that "property acquired during the existence of the legal regime through the effort, skill, or industry of either spouse" is community property. George insists that federal law, which specifies that the copyrights in the blue dog and other images "vest [ ] initially" in him as the "author," cannot be harmonized with state law, which would hold those self-same copyrights to have been community property and to belong now to the two former spouses in indivision. He argues that, because, under the Supremacy Clause, state law is preempted to the extent that it conflicts with federal law, his copyrights are immune from Louisiana community property law.

We do not disagree with George's general premise; we do disagree, though, with his expansive view of the scope of the conflict between copyright law and community property law, and thus with the extent of the preemptive effect of such conflict. We are satisfied that the conclusion we reach today—that an author-spouse in whom a copyright vests maintains exclusive managerial control of the copyright but that the economic benefits of the copyrighted work belong to the community while it exists and to the former spouses in indivision thereafter—is consistent with both federal copyright law and Louisiana community property law and is reconcilable under both.

We begin by delineating the precise scope of the language of § 201(a)10 on which George bases his sweeping preemption theory. This subsection pertains only to "copyright," which, by the Act's own definition at § 106, is a finite bundle of but five fundamental rights, being the exclusive rights of reproduction, adaptation, publication, performance, and display. Notably, none of these rights either expressly or implicitly include the exclusive right to enjoy income or any of the other economic benefits produced by or derived from copyrights.

Section 201(a) specifies that the copyright "vests" in the author. Except in its title, this subsection never uses the words "own" or "ownership," and the Act does not speak of ownership per se or globally, but only in the sense of the five exclusive attributes listed in § 106. "To vest" means to give an immediate, fixed right of present or future enjoyment; to accrue to; to be fixed; to take effect. " 'To own' means to have a good legal title; to hold as property; to have a legal or rightful title to; to have; to possess." When analyzed in the framework of the Act's inclusion of only five express attributes of ownership while omitting, inter alia, the attribute of enjoyment of economic benefits, Congress's reference to immediate vesting of the copyright, and not to vesting of ownership, supports the more limited construction advocated by Veronica. We agree with her insistence that, in and of itself, "vesting" of the copyright and its five (and five only) statutorily delineated attributes in one spouse does not preclude classification of other attributes of ownership of a copyright as community property. Moreover, by its very title, § 201(a) addresses only initial—not permanent—vesting of the copyright in the author. And, even though the author's copyright arises at the moment of creation of the work, the Act explicitly allows for subsequent vesting in non-authors, either jointly with the author or subsequent to him by virtue of transfer of all or lesser portions of the copyright.

True, the copyright "vests initially" in the "author," and the "author" is the "originator," the "maker," the person to whom a work "owes its origin." We do not question that George is the sole "author" of the copyrights here at issue. Neither do we mean to suggest that Veronica's co-ownership interests arise from co-authorship. We do conclude, though, that the language of § 201(a), providing that a bundle of but five specific rights, those listed in § 106, "vests initially" in the author, does not ineluctably conflict with any provision of Louisiana matrimonial property law that would recognize that Veronica does have an economic interest in George's copyrights.

As a useful framework for understanding the Louisiana Civil Code provisions on which our holding ultimately rests, we begin with general concepts of Louisiana property law. In the Civil Law, the bundle of rights that together constitutes full ownership18 of property comprises three separate sub-bundles: (1) usus—the right to use or possess, i.e., hold, occupy, and utilize the property; (2) abusus—the right to abuse or alienate, i.e., transfer, lease, and encumber the property, and (3) fructus—the right to the fruits, i.e., to receive and enjoy the earnings, profits, rents, and revenues produced by or derived from the property. In Louisiana, those three facets of ownership may be allocated in various combinations among different persons, with each having less than full ownership. For example, the owner of a legal usufruct ("usufructuary") has the right to use the property burdened with the usufruct (usus) and to enjoy the fruits of that property (fructus), but does not have the right to alienate the property (abusus); that right belongs to the naked owner, albeit subject to the usufruct.

When the property in question is a copyright, allocation of these attributes of ownership within the community property framework, according to the rule we announce today, produces a division similar to usufruct but different in combination: The author-spouse alone holds the elements of usus and abusus—a combination that comprises the exclusive rights to possess, use, transfer, alienate, and encumber the copyright as he sees fit—free of any management, consent, or participation of the non-author spouse. Obviously, § 106's "five fundamental rights" of reproduction, adaptation, publication, performance, and display are includable harmoniously in the conjointment of usus and abusus in the author-spouse. But the community during its existence (and the former spouses or other successors after its termination) holds the element of fructus, i.e., the right to receive and enjoy the economic benefits produced by or derived from the copyright. The exclusive right of the author-spouse to the abusus of the copyright, like that of the naked owner of property burdened by a usufruct, is nevertheless subject to the continuing fructus rights of the community so long as the copyright remains vested in the author-spouse, unless partition should modify the situation.

With those general Civil Law property concepts in mind, we turn next to the Civil Code's articles on marital property. In broadest form, the Code embodies the concept of "equal management" of property belonging to the community: Each spouse, acting alone, has the right to manage, control, or dispose of community property. If this general principle were to be applied across the board to copyrights created by one spouse in community, however, an irreconcilable conflict with the author-spouse's five exclusive § 106 rights of reproduction, adaptation, publication, performance, and display would result. In apparent recognition that such conflicts would likely occur in connection with "movables issued or registered in" the name of one of the spouses, the Civil Code specifies, as an exception to equal management, that such spouse alone has exclusive management rights (the combination of usus and abusus) but preserves for the spouses jointly the right to enjoy the benefits (the fructus) of such property. We conclude that copyrights come within the category of exceptional movables contemplated by such provisions.

Numerous examples of exclusive management of community property and shared enjoyment of those assets exist: A paycheck issued by the employer in the name of the employee-spouse alone can be cashed, deposited, or otherwise negotiated only by that spouse; yet, the proceeds of the paycheck, representing earnings of one spouse in community, belong to the community. Likewise, a motor vehicle purchased with community funds but titled in the name of one spouse alone can be sold, leased, or encumbered only by the named spouse; yet the proceeds of any such disposition belong to the community. And when, during the existence of the community, one spouse joins an existing partnership or joins in the formation of a new one, the partner-spouse has the exclusive right to participate in the partnership and to manage, alienate, or encumber that interest; yet the economic benefits—and liabilities—flowing from the partnership belong to the community.

In concluding that copyrights should be treated the same as paychecks, cars, and partnership interests, we rely initially on Louisiana Civil Code article 2351 which proclaims that "[a] spouse has the exclusive right to manage, alienate, encumber, or lease movables issued or registered in his name as provided by law." This right of exclusive management of those kinds of movables is not coterminous with the community but continues as long as the copyright is vested in the author-spouse, even after partition of the property formerly belonging to the community is complete.29 Under Louisiana law a copyright is a "movable," and under federal law a copyright is issued or registered in the name of the author-spouse. In compatible combination, these two systems of law provide for the author-spouse's exclusive management of copyrights created during the existence of the community and thereafter until completion of the partition of the property of the former community, while at the same time ensuring that the non author-spouse is not deprived of his or her right to one-half of the economic benefits of the copyright.

The economic benefits that flow from particular types of one-spouse assets, including but not limited to cars, paychecks, partnership interests—and copyrights—can inure to the benefit of the community without doing violence to the legal results intended by the Louisiana Legislature or Congress in providing for vesting of title in one spouse only, results designed with third parties in mind, not spouses or other co-owners. In the context of these clearly established concepts and principles, we conclude that federal copyright law does not conflict with, and therefore does not preempt, Louisiana community property law to the extent of denying the entitlement of the non-author spouse (Veronica) to an undivided one-half interest in the economic benefits of the copyrighted works created by the author (George) during the existence of the community, and of the derivatives of such works following its termination.

In confirmation of this conclusion, we look first to the express preemption provision in the Act itself. When we do so we reach the same initial conclusion as did the district court, that the Act does not mandate the monolithic preemption of Louisiana community property law in toto. Section 301(a) of the Act states that "all legal or equitable rights that are equivalent to any of the exclusive rights within the general scope of copyright ... are governed exclusively by this title." For openers, "the general scope of copyright" is not broad enough to cover the entire body of marital property law; that is, copyright law does not occupy the entire "field" and thereby totally eclipse all state marital property law. We do not understand George to quarrel with this basic premise.

Indeed, the Copyright Act, in defining the scope of its own preemptive effect, expressly acknowledges that state law continues to operate unless there is a direct and irreconcilable clash between a state law right and an exclusive right under the Act with which such state law right is equivalent. Section 301(b) expresses that "[n]othing in [§ 301(a) of the Copyright Act] annuls or limits any rights or remedies under the common law or statutes of any State with respect to ... activities violating legal or equitable rights that are not equivalent to any of the exclusive rights within the general scope of copyright as specified by section 106." To repeat, the only ownership rights that the Act grants exclusively to the author are the rights to (1) reproduce, (2) prepare derivative works, (3) distribute copies, (4) perform, and (5) display the work. Among the entire "bundle" of rights comprising full ownership of property generally, the preemptive effect of federal copyright law extends only to this explicitly-enumerated, lesser-included quintet. As those five exclusive rights of the author conflict with Louisiana's general principle of equal management of community property, that principle cannot operate. Instead Civil Code article 2351's special exception for exclusive management by one spouse applies.

Notably absent from the Copyright Act's exclusive sub-bundle of five rights is the right to enjoy the earnings and profits of the copyright. Nothing in the copyright law purports to prevent non-preempted rights from being enjoyed by the community during its existence or thereafter by the former spouses in community as co-owners of equal, undivided interests.

The § 301 preemption provision of the Copyright Act was intended to accomplish a "fundamental and significant change" in the existing state of the law, under which published works were governed by federal copyright law and unpublished works were governed by the common law of copyright. The new statute substituted a single, uniform system in place of the existing anachronistic and highly complicated dual system. That goal was accomplished in part by specifying a limited preemption which trumps only those common law or state law rights that are equivalent to federal copyright, such as state laws that purport to grant copyright protection to particular works. We discern nothing in the Act's plain wording or legislative history to indicate that Congress—fully aware of the existence of community property laws in a number of states—had any intention of preempting that entire body of non-federal law as well. Our conclusion is buttressed by the explicit clarification in § 301(b)(3), noted above, that the preemptive effect does not extend beyond the subject matter of the Act.

George nevertheless insists in the alternative that, even if § 301 preemption does not apply, "conflict preemption" does because designating copyrights as community property would do substantial damage to important federal interests. In this argument, George fails (or refuses) to recognize the jurisprudential corollary that "[s]tate family and family-property law must do 'major damage' to 'clear and substantial' federal interests before the Supremacy Clause will demand that state law be overridden." He attempts to bolster his conflict preemption argument by demonizing the Louisiana Civil Code doctrine of equal management: If copyrights were to be deemed community property, George contends, both he and Veronica would have the right, acting alone, to control, encumber, or dispose of the copyrights, which in turn would impair federal interests in uniformity and efficient exchange of rights to ensure predictability, and in providing incentives to authors to create. George argues that (1) copyrights will not be amenable to efficient or predictable exchange if spouses have equal rights to impair or dispose of such rights, possibly in conflicting manners, (2) predictability and uniformity will not be served if varying state laws are applied to copyright management issues, and (3) authors will have less incentive to create if they must share the fruits of their creative works. His reliance on these three arguments is misplaced.

George's first contention is negated by our ready recognition today that the author-spouse has the exclusive right to manage and control the copyright, i.e., to deal with it in any manner that is not inconsistent with federal copyright law. This conclusion is supported by our acknowledgment that the general rule of equal management is pre-empted vis à vis copyrights and by Louisiana Civil Code article 2351's provision for the exclusive management of movables registered or issued in the name of one spouse. As equal management does not apply to copyrights, federal interests in predictability and efficiency are not impaired by it. A potential purchaser or licensee will still be able to obtain good "title" from the author-spouse alone free of interference from the other spouse.

George's second contention does not persuade us that allowing differing state laws—in particular, community property laws that differ from state to state among the eight that presently have some version of such marital property regimes—to apply just to the economic benefit derived from copyrights will somehow damage the federal interests in predictability and uniformity. Indeed, the Act itself subjects copyrights to varying state laws for other purposes. For example, copyrights are expressly transferrable by conveyance, and such conventional transfers are governed by individual, non-uniform state contract laws; yet no significant obstruction of federal interests has occurred to prompt preemption. In like manner, copyrights are expressly transferable by testamentary disposition or in intestacy, either of which is likely to produce co-ownership of undivided interests in the copyright among the author's heirs or legatees. State law governs such death-related transfers and the resulting co-ownerships they produce, and does so routinely without impairing federal interests. The litigation and management issues arising from contractual conveyance and post-mortem devolution of copyrights has not resulted in obstruction of federal interests leading to preemption of state law, and we discern no reason why the community property result we decree today should fare differently.

As for George's third contention—that community entitlement to the "fruits" of copyrights would lessen the author's incentive to create or exploit his works, thereby conflicting with the federal interest in encouraging authorship—we decline to assume globally that the commercial and economic interests of spouses during marriage are so at odds that one spouse would be disinclined to create copyrightable works merely because the economic benefits of his endeavors would inure to the benefit of their community rather than to his separate estate. As for a former spouse's lack of incentive following divorce, we perceive the presence of the proverbial stick and carrot. To mix metaphors, the carrot is the half-a-loaf incentive of the author to exploit pre-divorce copyrights to the best of his ability rather than shelve them and receive no benefit whatsoever; the stick is exemplified by the provision of the Louisiana Civil Code that specifies an affirmative duty "to manage prudently" former community property that remains under one spouse's exclusive control. Indeed, that article imposes a higher duty on a spouse managing former community property than the Code otherwise imposes on that same spouse during the marriage or on a third party co-owner who is not a former spouse. "The reason for imposing a higher standard of care in managing former community property is that, after termination of the community property regime, the law no longer assumes that a spouse who has former community property under his control will act in the best interest of both spouses in managing it." Although we need not and therefore do not reach the question of specific management duties, we observe that this affirmative duty imposed by Louisiana law refutes George's argument regarding a former spouse's disincentive to exploit fully a copyright simply because the economic benefits are subject to community property laws. We are convinced that the duty imposed by Louisiana is consistent with—not contrary to—the federal interest in encouraging authorship and exploitation of copyrights, just as we are convinced that most if not all authors will continue to exploit their copyrights after termination of the community rather than cutting off their noses to spite their faces by letting copyrighted works languish.

III.
Conclusion

In the end, we disagree with the district court only to the extent that it held the conflict between Louisiana community property law and federal copyright law irreconcilable absent congressional intercession. We therefore reverse the court's grant of summary judgment declaring George alone to be the owner of the blue dog and other copyrights created during his marriage to Veronica. Accordingly, we remand this case, appealed pursuant to Rule 54(b), for entry of an appropriate ruling regarding Veronica's rights with respect to the copyrights and for consistent disposition of all remaining issues still pending before that court.

Specifically, we instruct the district court to determine on remand which copyrights are subject to the rules of community property law that we announce today, either directly as works created during the existence of the community of acquets and gains or derivatively as works created after the termination of the community but based on pre-divorce works. Even though the parties briefed the issue of derivative works in the instant appeal, the district court has not yet ruled on it so that issue is not ripe for our consideration and disposition. In holding that George alone is the owner of all copyrights in the artistic works, the district court denied Veronica's cross-motion for a summary judgment declaring her economic interests in the copyrights, including determination of which post-divorce works were derivative of the artwork created during the marriage. That ruling, however, was not certified to be a final judgment ready for appeal under Rule 54(b). As we now hold that Veronica does have economic rights with respect to the copyrights at issue, the district court must determine on remand which works are derivative as well.

We further instruct the district court, following such determinations, to enter judgment recognizing Veronica's entitlement to an undivided one-half interest in the net economic benefits generated by or resulting from copyrighted works created by George during the existence of the community and from any derivatives thereof. Such judgment also must recognize George's continued entitlement to the exclusive control and management of the five rights in such intellectual property specified in § 106, albeit subject to any duty that he might ultimately be held to owe Veronica to "manage prudently" all such copyrights and derivatives thereof under his control.

We acknowledge that it is for the state court that has jurisdiction over judicial partition and settlement of the Rodrigue community to determine both the proper method for establishing the value of Veronica's share of these net economic benefits and the proper procedure for delivery of that share to her, whether that be, for example, by (1) an accounting based on the present value of the appraised fair market value of the fully exploited copyrights and derivatives during their expected lifetimes, (2) periodic accountings and payments to Veronica as the copyrights and derivatives are exploited and proceeds are derived from them, or (3) some other altogether different procedure. It follows, of course, that Veronica may continue to pursue judicial partition of former community property in that forum.

Finally, in the interest of judicial economy, we reserve to this panel limited appellate jurisdiction over this case with respect to future appeals—if any—from judgments rendered by the district court on remand in implementation of our instructions.

REVERSED and REMANDED WITH INSTRUCTIONS.

B. Note

Other community property jurisdictions have considered whether patents are subject to federal preemption. At least two reported decisions in Texas have held that the federal law governing patents does not preempt the application of state community property laws. *See Sheshtawy v. Sheshtawy*, 150 S.W. 3d 772 (Tex. App. Ct. 2004); *Alsenz v. Alsenz*, 101 S.W. 3d 648 (Tex. App. Ct. 2003).

4.15 ADDITIONAL ISSUES OF FEDERAL LAW: FEDERAL AND MILITARY PENSIONS

A. Introduction

The United States Supreme Court was not receptive to community property policies in deciding that federal retirement plans would be the separate property of the covered employee. Congress, however, reversed those decisions and provided for the application of state community property laws in significant areas.

In *Hisquierdo v. Hisquierdo*, 439 U.S. 572 (1979), the court reasoned that the Railroad Retirement Act pre-empted state law. It held that benefits under the act were not to be considered community property subject to division under California law upon divorce of the covered spouse. More significant, at least in terms of numbers affected was *McCarty v. McCarty*, 453 U.S. 210 (1981) holding that military retirement benefits were not subject to division upon divorce as community property.

Shortly afterwards, Congress enacted 10 U.S.C.§ 1408 to allow state courts to apply community property law to members whose "residence other than because of military assignment" or whose "domicile" is in the territorial jurisdiction of the court. In such a case, the court "may treat disposable retired or retainer pay payable to a member for pay periods beginning after June 25, 1981, either as property solely of the member or as property of the member and his spouse in accordance with the law of the jurisdiction of such court." By its terms, the statute affects pension payments for pay periods beginning after June 25, 1981, the day before the decision in *McCarty* was announced. In a state like Louisiana, which treated military retirement benefits as community property prior to *McCarty*, the effect of the statute is to retroactively erase the small time period in which the benefits would have been considered separate property.

The court construed 10 U.S.C. §1408(c)(1) literally in *Mansell v. Mansell*, 490 U.S. 581 (1989), stating that the provision grants the states power to treat retirement pay as community, but not that portion treated as disability benefits.

U.S.C.A. § 10:1408. Payment of retired pay in compliance with court orders

(c) Authority for court to treat retired pay as property of the member and spouse.--(1) Subject to the limitations of this section, a court may treat disposable retired pay payable to a member for pay periods beginning after June 25, 1981, either as property solely of the member or as property of the member and his spouse in accordance with the law of the jurisdiction of such court. A court may not treat retired pay as property in any proceeding to divide or partition any amount of retired pay of a member as the property of the member and the member's spouse or former spouse if a final decree of divorce, dissolution, annulment, or legal separation (including a court ordered, ratified, or approved property settlement incident to such decree) affecting the member and the member's spouse or former spouse

(A) was issued before June 25, 1981, and

(B) did not treat (or reserve jurisdiction to treat) any amount of retired pay of the member as property of the member and the member's spouse or former spouse.

B. *Lillian Slay Russell v. Gerald L. Russell*

520 So. 2d 435 (La. App. 3d Cir. 1987)

DOMENGEAUX., Judge.

Plaintiff, Lillian Slay Russell filed suit against her former husband, defendant, Gerald L. Russell, seeking a community property interest in certain military disability retirement benefits being paid to defendant. From a final judgment holding these benefits to be defendant's separate property, and in addition, reducing plaintiff's alimony amount, plaintiff has appealed.

FACTS

On January 31, 1955, defendant, Gerald Russell entered the U.S. Army. He married plaintiff, Lillian Slay Russell on October 5, 1958. On September 21, 1972, defendant retired from the Army after being credited with serving 19 years, 11 months and 5 days. Mr. Russell would have been eligible to retire after completing twenty years, but instead, he chose to retire under 10 U.S.C. § 1201 because he had been determined to be 30 % permanently disabled. Payments entitled "military retirement disability benefits" commenced on January 1, 1977.

After nineteen years of marriage, plaintiff and defendant were divorced on June 1, 1978. For fourteen of these years defendant had been in the Army and had accrued time towards retirement benefits. A community property agreement signed by both parties after the divorce made no reference to the military disability retirement benefits.

In 1983, Mrs. Russell sued Mr. Russell for her community interest in these payments. Initially, she claimed that military disability retirement benefits are community property just like other retirement benefits and therefore, subject to community partition. Alternatively, she argued that even if military disability retirement benefits are not community property, the payments defendant is receiving are not, in fact, disability benefits but instead, are a combination of both disability and retirement benefits, the latter of which are community assets. Defendant contested plaintiff's claim by arguing that these payments were disability benefits and, by law, were his separate property.

Defendant moved for summary judgment which was granted. In ruling for the defendant, the trial court held that the benefits defendant was receiving were solely for disability and, by law, could not be subject to community property partition.

Earlier in these proceedings, we reviewed the correctness of the summary judgment granted by the trial court. See Russell v. Russell, 465 So.2d 181 (La. App. 3rd Cir.

1985). In that opinion we discussed other Circuit Court decisions which involved military disability retirement benefits, including Inzinna v. Inzinna, 456 So.2d 691 (La. App. 5th Cir.), *writ denied*, 461 So.2d 317 (La. 1984). We concluded that "disability retirement pay, although nominally a disability pension, can be a community asset if and to the extent that some amount thereof reflects non-disability retirement credible service." at 465 So.2d 183. We then set aside the judgment and remanded the case for a further determination of exactly what type of pension defendant was receiving; specifically, whether or not it represented a calculable combination of both disability and non-disability benefits.

After a trial on the merits, the trial court again concluded that the payments were solely disability benefits and therefore, constituted defendant's separate property. The Court also ruled that there was a significant enough change in circumstances to warrant lowering plaintiff's alimony from $ 200.00 to $100.00 a month because the plaintiff was now gainfully employed. Plaintiff has appealed the correctness of both rulings by the trial court.

In McCarty v. McCarty, 453 U.S. 210, 101 S. Ct. 2728, 69 L.Ed.2d 589 (1981), the United States Supreme Court held that federal law preempted the application of state law in the area of military retirement benefits. The Court further ruled that military retirement benefits were the separate property of the retiring spouse.

The following year Congress enacted the "Uniformed Services Former Spouses Protection Act", which legislatively overruled McCarty, supra. Subsequently codified in Title 10 of the United States Code, the key provision removing federal preemption in the area of military retirement benefits can be found in 10 U.S.C. § 1408(c)(1) which provides that:

"Subject to the limitations of this section, a court may treat disposable retired or retainer pay payable to a member for pay periods beginning after June 25, 1981 [the decision date of McCarty, supra], either as property solely of the member or as property of the member and his spouse in accordance with the law of the jurisdiction of such court."

Thus, military retirement benefits, termed "disposable retired or retainer pay" in 10 U.S.C. 1408(c)(1) were again subject to the application of state community property laws.

However, the original definition of "disposable retired or retainer pay" in 10 U.S.C. § 1408(a)(4) read as follows:

"The total monthly retired or retainer pay to which a member is entitled (other than the retired pay of a member retired for disability under Chapter 61 of this title [10 U.S.C. §§ 1201 et seq.]) . . . " (emphasis added).

The apparent exclusion of disability retirement pay from the definition of "disposable retired or retainer pay" led to conflicting interpretations by our Circuit Courts on whether or not state courts were free to apply state laws to military disability retirement benefits.

In Campbell v. Campbell, 474 So.2d 1339 (La. App. 2nd Cir.) *writ denied*, 478 So.2d 148 (La. 1985), the Second Circuit concluded that federal law does not preempt state law in the area of Veterans Administration disability retirement benefits. This holding was based on the Court's interpretation that it was Congress' intent, through the use of such specific language, to only overrule the holding of McCarty. Since McCarty addressed only non-disability retirement benefits, the Court concluded that the language used in 10 U.S.C. § 1408(a)(4) was aimed only to overrule McCarty, and did not intend to create an area of federal preemption in regard to military disability retirement benefits.

In Inzinna, supra, and in our prior opinion in this case, both the Fifth Circuit and this Circuit concluded that the language in 10 U.S.C. § 1408(a)(4) does create an area of federal preemption regarding military disability retirement benefits. Consequently, payments that compensate a retiring member for a disability are the member's separate property. We remanded this case for a further determination of what percentage of Mr. Russell's payments are for his disability and what percentage, if any, are for his retirement, only the latter of which is subject to community division.

In 1986, Congress amended 10 U.S.C. § 1408(a)(4) to read as follows:

"Disposable retired or retainer pay" means the total monthly retired or retainer pay to which a member is entitled less amounts which (E) in the case of a member entitled to retired pay under chapter 61 of this title [10 USC §§ 1201 et seq.], are equal to the amount of retired pay of the member under that chapter computed using the percentage of the member's disability on the date when the member was retired (or the date on which the member's name was placed on the temporary disability retired list);

(As amended Nov. 14, 1986, P. L. 99-661, Div. A, Title VI, Part D, § 644(a), 100 Stat. 3887.) (emphasis added).

The new definition of disposable retired or retainer pay clearly indicates that Congress intended to exclude from disposable retired or retainer pay those benefits that are paid as compensation for a member's disability. Therefore, we hold that all past, present and future benefits paid to Mr. Russell that are compensation for his disability are his separate property and are not subject to community division. However, any amounts paid in excess of his disability compensation would be part of the disposable retired or retainer pay. Thus, this excess amount would be subject to a community property claim by Mrs. Russell for the fourteen years she and defendant were married while defendant was enlisted in the Army.

Thus, it is necessary to again remand this case for determination of exactly how the Army calculated defendant's retirement disability benefits. Specifically, it is necessary to learn whether defendant is receiving 50% or 30% of his final basic pay. If defendant is receiving 50% of his final basic pay, Mrs. Russell has a community interest in that portion which exceeds 30% of defendant's final basic pay. Because a 50% rate of retirement pay would be calculated on defendant's 20 years of service, Mrs. Russell's community interest in the excess amount would be limited to the fourteen years that she and defendant were married while he was in the service. If defendant is receiving only 30% of his final basic pay, this is his separate property and not susceptible to a claim by Mrs. Russell. Inasmuch as the record is devoid of the Army's method of calculation of defendant's retirement disability benefits, we are unable to determine what benefits defendant is receiving. We must therefore again remand this case for further evidence concerning the method of calculation.

CHAPTER 5: MANAGEMENT OF ASSETS

5.1 IN GENERAL

A. J. Thomas Oldham, *Management of the Community Estate During an Intact Marriage*, 56 L. & CONTEMP. PROBS. 99 (1993)

I

INTRODUCTION

The states of this country accept one of two very different marital property regimes. The common law system is based upon title; neither spouse has an interest in the property of the other, unless property is jointly owned. In contrast, community property systems accept the concept that spouses each have an equal, vested interest in all property accumulated, by either's effort, during marriage. The significance of these distinctions at dissolution has ebbed, however: All common law states now permit some type of property adjustment at dissolution, whether the dissolution is by divorce or death. The economic ramifications of divorce certainly are becoming more similar, regardless whether the marriage is dissolved in a common law or marital property state.

In contrast, the two marital property systems operate quite differently in an intact marriage. In common law states, as long as no divorce action has been filed, property is managed by the owner. Under such a system, one spouse could have no power to manage any property accumulated during marriage, even if the property was acquired during marriage by the other spouse's effort. If the acquiring spouse is the record owner, that spouse can sell the property, or even give it away without the other's consent. In contrast, spouses in community property states are equal owners of all property acquired during marriage due to either's effort, regardless of title. Community property states have accepted for quite some time that the equal ownership principle imposes some limitations during marriage upon the management powers of one spouse.

Rules regarding the management of community property are only now being fully developed, in part because the rule of male management prevailed until the 1970s. Although the community property systems of that period accepted that both spouses had a vested, equal interest in community property accumulations as soon as they were acquired, the husband was considered the best "trustee" of the marital estate. No such gender-specific notions persist. This change, while undoubtedly increasing the power of women during marriage, has greatly complicated rules regarding management of the community estate. Should both spouses jointly manage all of the community, or should one spouse have the power to manage specific assets? If the latter, how will the identity of the managing spouse be determined and communicated to third parties? Also, if only one spouse is permitted to manage the community, must that spouse satisfy a standard of care when acting on behalf of the community?

***

B. Some Implemented Management Systems

Separate property is managed by the spouse who owns it. This is without question the best rule for management of separate property, as long as the separate property is not the homestead.

Turning to community property, after the demise of male management, three different systems have been utilized to allocate management power. One system requires spouses to act jointly regarding community property, and is customarily referred to as joint management. Another system, known as sole management, gives one spouse the sole power to manage particular community assets. The third system, called equal management, gives either spouse, acting alone, the power to manage the community.

Each system has its drawbacks. Joint management ensures that both owners will have the opportunity to participate in management of the community, but this requirement could place a substantial burden upon commerce, particularly if it were applied to all transactions involving any amount of community property. Furthermore, some spouses might not want to manage; the joint management system would burden them, unless some way of opting-out were created. Also, what should occur under such a system if only one spouse purports to transfer community property? There are possibilities other than that it is void ab initio.

The sole management system clearly specifies who will have management power over each item of community property. However, if each spouse does not accumulate (or in some states have record ownership of) the same amount of property during marriage, this system would grant one spouse power over more than half of the community estate, even though both spouses possess a present, vested fifty percent interest. If one spouse works outside the home and the other does not, in many instances the spouse working in the home would manage little or no community property.

The equal management system, like the joint management system, reflects a general notion of equality; it does present a problem, however, if the spouses disagree, and especially if they give contradictory instructions to a third party. In addition, even though either spouse in theory may exercise management power, one might argue that the system facilitates the usurpation of management of the community by the dominant spouse. Also, equal and sole management both permit one spouse to affect the property interests of the other without giving that spouse notice.

No state has accepted one of these management systems for all transactions involving community property. Each has adopted a combination of management rules, in which some transactions are governed by one set of rules, and others by another set. The next few sections discuss in more detail how each system works in practice, as well as the various problems that have been encountered in their implementation.

1. Joint Management. Joint management provides maximum protection to one spouse that his or her property rights will not be jeopardized without notice and consent. The concomitant cost of the system is its increased burden upon commercial transactions involving married people. This burden is of two types: first, logistical problems are created by requiring the approval of both spouses before a transaction can be completed; second, the system leaves open to challenge transactions that have been completed by one spouse where the other party did not know he was dealing with a married person, or where the party believed the married person was dealing with separate property (or sole or equal management community property). In light of these burdens, in most states joint management is applied only to significant transactions whose structure would not be unduly burdened by the joint management requirement.

Each state's joint management rule is somewhat different; some differ quite markedly. Wisconsin's joint management system pertains only to gifts of more than a "reasonable" amount of the community property, as well as transactions affecting the "homestead." In contrast, the California joint management system covers gifts of any community personal property, the sale or encumbrance of all community property realty and of the furnishings, furniture, and other personal property used in the family home. Three states require spouses to act jointly in connection with either a purchase or a sale of community property real estate. Three states require joint management for the sale of a community property business. Two states appear to require the consent of both spouses for the sale of any asset of the community property business if both spouses participate in the management of the business.

***

A much greater impediment on commerce would be imposed if every transaction involving community property, not just some transactions such as sales of community realty and sales of a community business, required joint action. For example, imagine what would occur if both spouses were required to go together to make every purchase. Similarly, many investment decisions, such as stock market sales, are quickly made; a requirement of joint consent could burden these transactions. For this reason, no state has accepted a general rule of joint management. States have attempted to carve out a set of transactions that generally involve substantial amounts of money (such as sales of community real estate or a community property business) or important items (such as household furnishings or clothing). In most instances, joint management has been applied only to these transactions.

Unfortunately, some states have deviated from this sensible general approach. In Texas, property acquired in any way other than those set forth in section 5.22(a) of the Texas Family Code is joint management property, as is property consisting of commingled accumulations by both spouses. There is no need to extend joint management to all such transactions. The Texas situation is undesirable in two respects. First, joint management is extended to some transactions where its protection is not needed. Second, joint management protection is not extended to transactions where it would be helpful, such as in sales of community realty (other than the homestead) or sales of a community business. The Texas Legislature should reconsider the rules regarding the scope of joint management.

In addition to the Texas deviations mentioned above, a number of other states require all gifts of community property to be made jointly, regardless of the value of the gift. As discussed below, although it is apparent that gifts present different concerns than commercial transactions, it is unnecessary to extend joint management to gifts of a small amount of community property.

When evaluating the importance of joint management rules, it would be useful to know how often spouses would--in the absence of a legal requirement--attempt to complete important transactions involving community property without informing the other spouse. Unfortunately, there are no studies on this point. A number of cases have been reported under joint management regimes where one spouse has unilaterally attempted to convey the community interest in realty, suggesting the problem is not uncommon.

If joint management were applied to all transactions involving community property, both spouses would receive prior notice of transactions affecting the community and could decide whether to consent. However, such a regime would impose many costs upon commercial transactions involving married people. These costs should be imposed only when a significant community concern is involved.

If the goal of the joint management system is to apply joint management to transactions that frequently involve a substantial amount of money, one could question whether the currently articulated scope of joint management is sensible. In many instances, a substantial portion of family wealth is in the form of personalty. Current joint management legislation does not encompass personalty, except for gifts and transactions involving community property businesses or home furnishings. Still, transactions involving the conveyance of real estate or the sale of a business usually are not effected quickly, and therefore are not substantially burdened by the joint consent requirement. If joint management were extended to cover more transactions involving personalty, these transactions could be significantly burdened. This concern probably explains the California legislature's 1973 decision not to enact a bill requiring joint management for every transaction involving $1000 or more of community funds.

"Joint management" connotes that both spouses consent to the transaction. This consent could be established in a number of ways. Oral consent could be considered adequate. A requirement for written consent would be more burdensome, but would provide clearer evidence of consent. A number of states impose different rules for satisfying the joint consent requirement, depending upon what type of transaction is involved. In connection with the sale or encumbrance of community property, many states, including California, require both spouses to sign "any instrument" by which real estate is sold or encumbered. In contrast, a California spouse managing a community (personal) property business, may unilaterally sell the business, but must give prior written notice to the other spouse before the sale. Nevada and Washington statutes require that if only one spouse participates in management of a community property business, that spouse unilaterally may sell assets of the business in the ordinary course of business. These statutes imply that the other spouse's consent is required for sales not in the ordinary course of business, but do not specify what is required to satisfy that requirement. Arizona and Louisiana have a different approach: the same standard is applied to all joint management transactions. Arizona requires the "joinder" of both spouses. Louisiana requires the "concurrence" of both.

Even if a transaction is considered sufficiently important to require joint management, it does not follow that both spouses must sign all documents relating to the transaction. It would suffice if both spouses are informed of the material terms of the transaction and approve of these terms. Indeed, that would seem to be the goal of joint management. No policy would be advanced by requiring spouses to sign all documents relating to the transaction. Also, both spouses should not have to approve nonmaterial changes in the terms of the agreement. Joint management rules should be fashioned so that both spouses are given the opportunity to review and approve the material terms of the transaction, while not establishing needless additional burdens upon commercial transactions involving married people.

***

2. Sole Management. Sole management arises in different ways in different states. In Texas, a spouse has sole management power over certain types of acquisitions enumerated in the Family Code--most importantly, his or her earnings--as long as that spouse does not mix these acquisitions with acquisitions of the other spouse. In addition, a Texas spouse has the presumptive power to manage property if the spouse has record title, or if the spouse has possession and there is no title document.

In Wisconsin, if title is in the name of one spouse, that spouse has the exclusive power to manage. This rule applies to personalty and realty, other than the homestead. New Mexico and Louisiana have adopted a similar system for personalty where one spouse has title.

California, Louisiana, Nevada, and Washington have established sole management for community property businesses in some instances. In California, if one spouse "is operating or managing" a community property business, that spouse has sole management power. A "sole manager" of a Louisiana community property business has sole management power. In Nevada and Washington, where only one spouse "participates" in management of a community property business, that spouse has sole management power for transactions in the ordinary course of business...

The sole management system facilitates transactions for the family, in that one spouse can act for the community. Merchants and others do not have to worry about determining whether someone is married and, if so, about obtaining the consent of each spouse before completing a transaction. Also, if one believes that the law affects how couples behave, the system may minimize spousal disputes by specifying which spouse has the power to deal with various types of property.

Critics of sole management would object, however, that this system deprives the nonmanaging spouse of control over the vested fifty percent interest he or she has in each item of the community. Feminist critics would note that under systems such as that in Texas, the nonmanager is normally the housewife, and that the system thereby reinforces a patriarchal power system in marriage. From this perspective, the equal management system is perceived to be more consistent with the philosophy of the community property system. This probably explains why the equal management system has been accepted by all community property states except Texas as the system that generally governs transactions not subject to joint management.

3. Equal Management. Under an equal management system, either spouse is entitled to manage community property. This system, like the sole management system, facilitates transactions involving married people. It also is consistent with the community property concept that each spouse is an owner of each item of the community as soon as it is acquired.

The equal management system is not free of problems, however. Because both spouses concurrently possess management power, this approach can create marital discord. It might encourage a spouse to act preemptively. For example, if one spouse wants to sell an item of community property and the other does not, the spouse wishing to sell cannot be stopped, unless the other is willing and able to hide the item.

Upon reflection, the potential for disputes should not be damning criticism of the equal management system. Disputes certainly could still arise regarding the use of community funds under the sole management system, even if, in theory, the law gives the nonmanager no "right" to manage. Indeed, disputes between spouses could arise under any management system. Equal management is more consistent with the joint ownership rights of the spouses than is sole management, however. Also, if one spouse is to be designated the sole manager, how would this spouse be selected? The Texas system, which permits the spouse who earns the property to be the manager, is inconsistent with contemporary notions of gender equality and partnership marriage. Equal management therefore seems preferable to sole management, at least in those situations where joint management does not apply.

One might challenge whether any real difference exists between the sole management system and the equal management system. As long as joint action is not required, the significance of the legal rules regarding the mechanics of management by one spouse is not clear. Will the spouses learn of these rules, and if they do, will their behavior be affected? If the rule has some effect (and it seems likely that it does), a preference for equal management over sole management seems inevitably to flow from the conceptual underpinnings of the community property system.

Third parties might be a bit nervous about an equal management system. For example, assume a spouse uses community property to purchase stock held by a broker. What should occur if one spouse calls the broker and orders the stock sold, and the other calls and orders the stock not sold? This problem must explain the enactment in some states of an exception to equal management for personalty titled in one spouse's name. However, this exception could be utilized by one spouse to undercut equal management significantly, particularly if there is no "add-a-name" remedy.

***

B. Louisiana Approach

Louisiana was the last community property jurisdiction to overhaul its management regime. Change was long overdue. Before 1979, each spouse retained an undivided one-half ownership interest in the community property, but the husband alone was empowered to manage nearly all of the community property. Under the "head and master scheme," wife held ownership rights, but was virtually powerless to manage that which she owned in community.

The management powers of the spouses under the head and master scheme are described in the following excerpt:

Legislative Symposium: Management
39 La. L. Rev. 149 (1979)

Head and Master

Presently, the husband is the "head and master" of the community of gains under Civil Code article 2404. This designation is considered to be one of the provisions of the legal community which cannot be contractually altered; thus, the wife cannot be made head of the community, nor can a contract stipulate a joint or equal management scheme (although there are some transactions involving certain community property which a husband cannot enter without his wife's consent.) The basis of this restriction is Civil Code article 2327, which prohibits a marital contract which would derogate from the "rights resulting from the power of the husband . . . which belong to the husband as head of the family." Consequently, the husband is the sole manager of the community property, and the wife has no management powers except through him-- *i.e.*, through an express or implied mandate. The courts generally presume that the husband has authorized his wife to contract in his name for ordinary family expenses and for the education of the children.

Limitation on Husband's Power

The husband's managerial powers are not totally unrestricted. Since 1825, article 2404 has prohibited the inter vivos donation of community immovables or of a whole or a quota of movables except for the "establishment of the children of the marriage." More recently, his power to enter onerous transactions with respect to certain community property has been limited. The first restriction of this sort made it possible to record a declaration designating certain property as the family home. After recordation, the husband cannot sell, lease, or mortgage the home without the wife's written consent. The wife may make this recordation if the husband fails to do so, although until recently she had to wait until his inaction had lasted for six months after acquisition of the property. In 1962, Civil Code article 2334 was amended to require the wife's written consent to the sale, lease, or mortgage of any community property registered in her name alone. She could likewise require her written consent for the sale, encumbrance, or lease of all community immovables registered in the name of both spouses by recording in the parish of situs an authentic act declaring that her authority or consent was required. The husband continued to have unrestricted powers with respect to onerous transactions affecting community property registered in his name alone-- a significant loophole in the protective measures since he alone has the power to acquire community property and he can thus determine in whose name it will be held.

In 1977, the burden of inaction was shifted with respect to community immovables in the name of both spouses; presently, the wife's consent is required in the sale, encumbrance, or lease of such immovables, unless she has recorded in the parish of situs an authentic declaration that her authority or consent is not required. The declaration may specify certain property or encompass all property in the parish; it may even apply generally to property acquired in the future, although, in that case, the wife can later file a contrary declaration withdrawing her authority or consent. The latter amendment also now requires the wife's consent to the alienation, encumbrance, or lease of the family home standing in the husband's name alone, unless a declaration as described above has been recorded.

Thus, while the wife presently has no independent management powers, she may exercise a veto over transactions affecting property in her name and property deemed of particular importance to the family, *i.e.*, the family home and immovable property held in both spouses' names. However, the protection this veto power affords is far from complete; it basically leaves intact the loophole for community property in the husband's name and likewise leaves all community movables not in the wife's name alone subject to his unrestricted powers of onerous alienation. Such movables may constitute a significant part of the family wealth, since the category of movables includes such things as stock shares, bank certificates, valuable paintings or antiques, and actions for damages. Furthermore, while these statutory changes have afforded some protection to the wife and family, they have also served to protect the head and master management scheme when it has been subjected to constitutional challenges. Recently, a four- man majority of the state supreme court was able to avoid reaching an equal- protection- based constitutional challenge to the present management provisions, principally by noting that the complaining wife could have prevented her husband's mortgage of the family home had she followed the statutorily prescribed method.

The 1979 comprehensive revision of Louisiana's community property regime abolished the head and master scheme and adopted a system of equal management. Each spouse acting on his or her own authority can now dispose of community property, unless otherwise provided by law. Husband and wife are equal managers in this regard, and not mandataries or agents of each other. Equality was achieved by also giving the wife the powers of disposition the husband had formerly exercised exclusively. When the wife is using those powers, she is not an agent, but one of two principals exercising a statutory power. Neither spouse needs the authorization of the other to act. Indeed, since the community is not a juridical person or separate entity, the spouses are not acting as agents for it. The community concept is at base a special relationship between the spouses, and the analogy to corporations or partnerships is not apt, for the latter are separate entities. While the failure to make the community a separate entity poses some problems, especially at termination, the policy choice was clear. Civil Code Article 2336 specifies that each spouse owns a half interest in the "community property". The community does not own anything.

C. Katherine S. Spaht & Cynthia Samuel, *Equal Management Revisited: The 1979 Legislative Modifications of the 1978 Matrimonial Regimes Law*, 40 LA. L. REV. 116 (1980).

***

MANAGEMENT OF COMMUNITY PROPERTY

The most controversial issue in the lengthy course of the matrimonial regimes law revision and, indeed, the issue that originally prompted the revision, was that of management of the community property. By enacting Act 627 of 1978, the legislature finally chose equal management of the community property by the spouses as the general rule of management. As part of the new scheme of management, the legislature also required concurrence of the spouses for certain enumerated transactions and gave exclusive management of other transactions to one spouse. Desiring that the version of equal management ultimately to take effect be more refined than that in Act 627, but not wishing to rekindle debate on the new management scheme, the legislature ordained an interim study of Act 627 by the Law Institute, limited to improving the expression and furthering the implementation of the policy already determined and enunciated in the Act. The Law Institute complied by making its revisions to Act 627 consistent with Act 627's equal management scheme, although disclaiming all responsibility for any chaos, corruption, or calamity that equal management might occasion. Consequently, Act 709 contains no major changes in the management scheme of Act 627.

Several variations between the two acts are, however, more than semantical. One such variation occurs in the enumeration of acts requiring concurrence of the spouses. Whereas Act 627 required concurrence for the alienation, encumbrance, or lease of community furniture or furnishings in use in the family home, Act 709 requires concurrence in these transactions involving "furniture or furnishings while located in the family home." Under Act 627, if the wife removed the family television set from the family home where it was being used and sold it to a good faith purchaser, the sale would have been voidable by the husband. During the debate on Act 627, concern was expressed as to how a prospective purchaser of furniture typically used in a home would know whether the furniture was actually used in the home of the seller- spouse. The legislature decided to place the risk of dealing with one spouse alone, where home furniture is concerned, on the third party, in the interest of insuring the other spouse's participation in the disposal or encumbrance of these essential family assets.

The Law Institute felt that this result was inconsistent with the general rule which the institute intended to recommend to the 1979 legislature for the transfer of ownership of corporeal movables by a possessor. This rule, subsequently enacted, provides: "A transferee in good faith for fair value acquires the ownership of a corporeal movable, if the transferor, though not owner, has possession with the consent of the owner, as pledgee, lessee, depositary or other person of similar standing." The Law Institute apparently thought that in the example of the television set, the new provision on the transfer of ownership would mean that the sale could not be annulled by the husband. It is not clear, because of the difficulty in applying the provision on transfer of ownership to a community movable, whether this result would have followed. Who is "the owner" of a community movable when each spouse owns a present undivided one- half interest in the community property? Is the transferor- spouse by virtue of the legal regime automatically a person of similar standing to a pledgee, lessee, or depositary of the non-transferor spouse? The applicability of the transfer of ownership provision to community movables should have been discussed rather than assumed; if the provision was inapplicable, then there was no reason to alter the language of Act 627's concurrence requirement for transactions involving furniture and furnishings in use in the family home. Nevertheless, to protect the good faith transferee for value of a corporeal movable, as the provision attempts to do, the Law Institute recommended total deletion of transactions involving family home furniture and furnishings from the list of transactions requiring concurrence of the spouses. The Joint Legislative Subcommittee was unwilling to abandon entirely the concurrence requirement where family furniture was concerned and reached a compromise in the language ultimately enacted in Act 709. Under Act 709, in the example of the television set, the sale would be voidable by the husband only if the television set was sold in place while located in the family home. Once removed from the family home, furniture is subject to the power of either spouse acting alone to dispose of or encumber it. The compromise concurrence requirement at least prevents one spouse from secretly placing a chattel mortgage on furniture located in the home without the consent of the other spouse, an act which could have been accomplished under the Law Institute recommendation.

Article 2348 of Act 709 restates more clearly than did Act 627 that a spouse whose concurrence would be required for an act may, with respect to particular community property, renounce in advance the right to concur. The new wording, plus the explanatory comment, makes it clear that the renouncing spouse does not, merely by renouncing the right to concur, become a party to the transaction for which concurrence would have been required. The second sentence in article 2348 is new and states that a spouse may also renounce the right to participate in the management of a community enterprise, This relates to the "business exception" to the general rule of equal management whereby "the spouse who is sole manager of a community enterprise has the exclusive right to alienate, encumber, or lease its movables . . . ." The exclusive management for which the business exception provides does not arise when both spouses are participating in the management of the business. In that case each spouse could equally manage the untitled movable assets of the business. Act 627 did not explicitly recognize a spouse's right to participate in the management of a community business run by the other spouse; however, that right was implicit in the spouses' relationship as co- owners and equal managers generally of the community property. The business exception was intended to apply only if one spouse voluntarily refrained from participating in the management of the business; it did not mean that a spouse could be involuntarily and completely excluded from such participation. The second sentence of article 2348 of Act 709 indirectly acknowledges the right to participate in the management of a community business. A spouse who has not renounced the right to participate cannot be excluded from the business.

When the right to participate has been renounced, the question may arise as to whether the renunciation will be effective against third parties who have no notice of it. There is no requirement in Act 709 for recordation of the renunciation and, since only movables are involved, the general law does not require recordation. The spouse who has renounced, and who thereafter attempts to participate in the business in order to sell a movable asset of the business to a third party, can hardly be expected to produce the renunciation. Therefore, how will the third party know if a spouse has disabled himself by renunciation from acting as an equal manager of the community business? If the renunciation affects third parties, then the result is contrary to the legislative intent of article 2330, which, for the protection of third parties, does not allow a spouse by matrimonial agreement to restrict his powers as an equal manager. The second sentence of article 2348 would inconsistently permit a spouse unilaterally to restrict his equal management power with respect to a community business. Thus, in order to avoid violating the objectives of article 2330, the renunciation should not be regarded as affecting third parties.

Another variation between the two acts is the remedy for an unauthorized alienation, encumbrance, or lease of community property. Both acts allow damages for fraud or bad faith management of the community property as a remedy between the spouses, but they differ slightly as to the remedy against third parties. Act 627 made any unauthorized act concerning community property voidable at the instance of the other spouse. Article 2353 of Act 709 dictates this result with respect to acts done by a spouse in violation of the concurrence requirement and with respect to the "business exception," but does not dictate relative nullity for an act done in violation of the management rules governing movables registered in one spouse's name or partnership interests. The omission does not signify legislative intent to make the management rules governing movables registered in one spouse's name or governing partnership interests effective only between the spouses. Rather, the legislature intended that the general law be consulted to determine if the transaction can be avoided in the unlikely event that a spouse sells or encumbers a movable registered in the name of the other spouse or an interest in a partnership in which the other spouse was a partner. Unfortunately, the general law offers no clear answer because of the ownership and management rules that are peculiar to community property. For example, Civil Code article 2452, declaring that the sale of a thing belonging to another is null, does not precisely fit the situation in which a spouse disposes of a community car registered in the name of the spouse, since the "thing" belongs equally to the seller and his spouse. Likewise, analogy to an agent exceeding his authority is problematic since the spouses are not co- mandataries with respect to community property transactions. Nor can the answer be that the seller- spouse has conveyed his undivided one- half interest in the property, since article 2337 prohibits a spouse from disposing of his undivided interest in a particular community thing prior to termination of the regime. With respect to *registered* corporeal movables, new article 520, whereby a person in possession of a corporeal movable can, with consent of the owner, transfer title to a good faith transferee for value, is explicitly made inapplicable. The various registration laws for movables may not offer solutions. In the case of vehicle title registration laws, the jurisprudence has held that the transfer of ownership of a vehicle is governed by the Civil Code despite noncompliance with the Vehicle Certificate of Title Law. Similar jurisprudence can be found under the old Uniform Stock Transfer Act. Title laws for movables are intended to protect the transferee of the person whose name is on the title by declaring the transfer unassailable and by giving the transferee an action for breach of contract if a properly endorsed certificate cannot be delivered. These title laws are not addressed to the situation where the transferee, having dealt with the spouse of the person whose name appears on the certificate, wishes to complete the transfer. Common sense and the negative implication of the title laws indicate that any transfer by someone whose name does not appear on the certificate is assailable by the person whose name does appear thereon. But the grounds for the assault and its extent (i.e., whether the transfer is an absolute or relative nullity) must be sought in the general law. For the sake of thoroughness, the legislature should amend article 2353 to provide, as did Act 627, that a transaction in violation of any of the management rules, including those involving registered movables and partnership interests, is relatively null.

During the interim study the Advisory Committee had recommended a prescription of three years from the day the transaction is discovered for an action by a spouse to annul an unauthorized transaction by the other spouse. The legislature, however, did not enact a specific prescription for this action, thus necessitating a search of the general law for the appropriate prescription. Article 2221, which provides a ten- year prescription for nullity or rescission of an agreement in cases of certain vices of consent and incapacities, is the provision most clearly applicable to this situation, since it gave as an example of its application an unauthorized act executed by a married woman. The deletion of that example by other legislation in 1979 should not be taken as relevant to the use of article 2221's prescription in the situation described; the deletion was simply part of a comprehensive act removing, among other things, all references in the Civil Code to the incapacities of married women. If article 2221 does not provide the appropriate prescription, then article 3542, providing a five- year prescription for the nullity or rescission of contracts, may arguably be applicable. It is to be hoped that in the next session the legislature will adopt the preferable, shorter three- year prescriptive period. This period is of sufficient length to allow a spouse a fair opportunity to annul an unauthorized transaction, yet its brevity provides security of transactions to third parties.

5.2 EQUAL MANAGEMENT, GENERALLY

A. Introduction

Louisiana's general management rule is one of equal management. Civil Code article 2346 provides that: "Each spouse acting alone may manage, control, or dispose of community property unless otherwise provided by law." Numerous transactions fall within the scope of the "unless otherwise provided by law" language of the article and will be examined in subsequent sections.

B. *Ronnie Magnon v. Albert Leger*

539 So. 2d 1305 (La. App. 3d Cir. 1989)

YELVERTON, J.

We reverse this summary judgment and remand for further proceedings because there is a factual issue still unresolved.

Plaintiff's petition alleges that Albert and Barbara Leger, although not living together, were husband and wife. She lived in the family home. It was damaged by a hurricane. She engaged Ronnie Magnon to make necessary repairs. The repairs came to $7,500. When he finished, she paid him in part by giving him a bill of sale to a community owned tractor, and Magnon took possession of the tractor.

The petition further alleges that defendant Albert Leger seized the tractor claiming that Magnon acquired no interest therein by virtue of the transaction between him and

Barbara.

Magnon then filed suit against Albert Leger for possession of the tractor or in the alternative, damages. In response, Leger filed a motion for summary judgment which the district court granted. This is the judgment appealed.

The summary judgment evidence included the bill of sale from Barbara Leger to Magnon given in consideration of $7,500 worth of repairs to the house. Barbara's affidavit was also filed. It declared that the family home had been damaged in 1985 by a hurricane, that in order to preserve the residence, repairs were required, and that in 1986 Ronnie Magnon made the necessary repairs to the house. The affidavit further declared that Barbara was not receiving any alimony or child support, that she had no money to pay for the repairs to the residence, and that in partial payment for labor and materials needed for that community obligation, she transferred ownership of the tractor to Ronnie Magnon and provided him a bill of sale to evidence that transfer.

The summary judgment evidence also included interrogatories and answers, which Mr. Leger offered to support the argument that Magnon only claimed an undivided interest in the tractor. Interrogatory No. 1 asked, "Under what authority do you claim an interest in the tractor involved in this lawsuit?" Magnon's answer was, "Petitioner claims an interest in the tractor involved in this lawsuit pursuant to a bill of sale obtained March 17, 1986." Based on this answer, Leger argued the application of Civil Code Article 2337, which states:

> A spouse may not alienate, encumber, or lease to a third person his undivided interest in the community or in particular things of the community prior to the termination of the regime."

Arguing that the result of the attempted sale of Barbara's undivided interest in the tractor was the absolute nullity of the purported sale, Mr. Leger asked for and obtained a summary judgment in his favor.

In our opinion summary judgment was inappropriate. Obligations incurred during the existence of the community for the common interest of the spouses are community obligations. La. C.C. art. 2360 and La. C.C. art. 2361. Patin v. Patin, 462 So.2d 1356 (La. App. 3rd Cir. 1985), *writ denied* 466 So.2d 470 (La. 1985). Further, one spouse may dispose of movable community property acting alone to satisfy a community obligation. La. C.C. arts. 2345 and 2346. Patin v. Patin, *supra.*

The conclusion that the first interrogatory and its response established as an undisputed fact that the sale was an attempted sale of only Barbara's undivided one- half interest is not a sound summary judgment factual conclusion. This evidence is, at the very least, equivocal. The word interest could mean the whole interest, or something less than the whole interest. Moreover, in interrogatory No. 2, the appellant was asked, "If you purchased the tractor, give the date of the purchase, the name and address of the seller, the total purchase price paid and state whether or not you have a bill of sale for the tractor." The appellant answered this interrogatory in the affirmative that he owned the tractor. In interrogatory No. 3 the appellant was asked, "If you claim that you purchased an interest in the tractor, give the bank or other financial institution an account number out of which the funds came for you to pay the purchase price for the tractor." The appellant answered, "No funds were transferred for payment. Rather, the balance owed by Barbara Leger and Albert Leger for materials and labor provided by petitioner for repairs to the home at Rt. 1, Box 441F, Scott, Louisiana, was reduced by that amount." Additionally, the bill of sale suggested that complete ownership of the tractor was being conveyed, as did the pleadings.

There is in the summary judgment evidence of considerable doubt as to what interest in the tractor was being conveyed, and a summary judgment may not be granted where a material fact is in doubt. Sanders v. Hercules Sheet Metal, Inc., 385 So.2d 772 (La. 1980).

The summary judgment is reversed and the case is remanded to the trial court for further proceedings consistent with this opinion, including ultimately all facets of the merits of this case. Albert Leger will pay the costs of this appeal.

REVERSED AND REMANDED.

C. Note

In *Succession of Caraway*, 639 So.2d 415 (La. App. 2d Cir. 1994), the aged husband granted a power of attorney to his daughter which included power to sell and transfer property. "Thus, his daughter could deal with his assets, community or separate, and engage in other financial activities, to the same extent as her father." That power included spending community funds, in this case, interest paid on certificates of deposit.

5.3 EXCLUSIVE MANAGEMENT BY ONE SPOUSE

A. Introduction

Louisiana Civil Code articles 2350-2352 contain a number of exceptions to the general rule of equal management. These articles afford one of the spouses the exclusive management rights of certain assets. Article 2350 provides that "[t]he spouse who is the sole manager of a community enterprise has the exclusive right to alienate, encumber, or lease its movables unless the movables are issued in the name of the other spouse or the concurrence of the other spouse is required by law." Article 2351 gives a spouse "the exclusive right to manage, alienate, encumber, or lease movables issued or registered in his name as provided by law." This article applies to most registered movables including automobiles, boats, and shares of stock. Article 2352 is similar. It affords a spouse who is a partner in a partnership or a member in a limited liability company the exclusive right to manage, alienate, encumber, or lease his interest in the company. Articles 2350-2352 apply automatically, by operation of law. In contrast, Civil Code article 2348 allows a spouse to voluntarily renounce his right to participate in a transaction that would ordinarily require his concurrence. The effect of a renunciation is to vest exclusive management power in the other spouse.

Another exception to equal management that vests management rights in one spouse exclusively is clear from the jurisprudence and is demonstrated in the materials that follow: privity of contract. This exception, which is not express in the Civil Code, applies to a wide array of transactions.

B. Janis Lynn Kile, Comment, *Management of Community Assets: Incorporeal Movables*, 42 LA. L. REV. 770 (1981)

***

The other limitation on the actions of the managing spouse arises from the concept of privity of contract. This limitation, referred to in a comment to article 2346, suggests that a spouse may not interfere with a contract entered into by the other spouse and a third party. The comment seems to indicate that the legislature intended that conflicts between equal management and privity of contract should be resolved in favor of privity of contract. The resolution of this conflict is important because of its effect on the management of contractual rights.

Contractual rights are included in community property, for the community of acquets and gains is a "patrimonial mass, that is, a universality of assets and liabilities." Property in the matrimonial regimes articles thus means patrimony in the broadest sense, including contractual rights. The contractual right, however, is to be distinguished from the property which is acquired by the contract. This distinction is evident in the comment to article 2346:

> A spouse acting alone may manage, control, and dispose of community property acquired by virtue of a contract made by the other spouse, unless this is property that the acquiring spouse has the exclusive right to manage or property that requires joint management. Nevertheless, he may not affect the legal relations and responsibilities of the spouse who incurred the obligation and the other party or parties to that contract, because, in principle, contracts produce effects as between the parties only.

If one spouse contracts on behalf of the community for the purchase of movable or immovable property, article 2346 seemingly would subject this contractual right to equal management, because contractual rights are not listed in any of the exceptions to equal management. Equal management of the contractual right is consistent with the public policy the revision sought to achieve. Equal management encourages sharing in the decision- making process and participation by both spouses in the management of community property. However, equal management of a contractual right conflicts with the basic concept of privity of contract. If indeed the legislature did intend to adopt privity of contract, it effectively created another exception to equal management, an exception which is not contained in the articles regulating joint and exclusive management.

Although privity of contract is a common law phrase, the principle is contained in Civil Code article 1780: "Those only are parties to a contract, who have given their consent to it, either expressly or by implication." Privity is also expressed in article 1889: "No one can, by a contract in his own name, bind anyone but himself or his representatives. Louisiana jurisprudence has held that "a third person not a party to a contract cannot sue for damages for its breach or to recover contractual benefits. These principles of privity of contract might apply to the management of community property, thereby requiring that only the spouse who is a party to the contract can cancel the contract, extend the time for performance, enforce the contract, or recover damages for its breach. The application of privity to the management of contractual rights is consistent with the policy interest of protecting third parties. Third parties should not be at the mercy of a spouse with whom they did not contract.

The application of these principles to the management of community property is seen in the following example. If the wife orders a car from a dealer, and the husband cancels the order, his action would affect the legal relation between the wife and the car dealer. The dealer should not abide by the husband's cancellation. If the dealer does comply with the husband's request, the wife can sue the dealer for breach of contract. If, after the wife receives the car, payments are not made, the wife is the "proper defendant in an action to enforce the obligation." If the equal management principle were applied, the husband could cancel the wife's contract and sue for performance or damages. Although the management articles apparently subject contractual rights to equal management, the principle of privity of contract should prevent the spouse who is not a party to the contract from affecting the legal relations and responsibilities of the contracting spouse.

If, in another example, both the husband and wife are freelance photographers, and the husband contracts with a third person to take pictures at a wedding, the wife cannot appear at the scheduled time and claim the right to take the pictures. The husband's obligation to take the pictures is personal; he has a legal duty to perform this obligation.

With contracts involving personal obligations, the argument is even stronger that privity of contract will prevent the non- contracting spouse from performing the personal obligation of the other spouse. Although the contractual right apparently is subject to equal management by the management articles, since it does not fall into one of the recognized exceptions, the wife may not perform the obligation, for to do so would affect the legal relations and responsibilities of her husband. When the third person refuses to let the wife take the pictures, she will have no remedy against him.

Management of Incorporeal Movables

Community assets which are incorporeal movables are managed according to the framework provided in the management articles. Incorporeal movables which are issued or registered in someone's name will be subject to either equal, joint, or exclusive management, depending on how the movable is registered. Nonregistered incorporeal movables are not included in either of the exceptions to equal management, so they are subject to equal management. Contractual rights and the community property portion of a spouse's personal injury claim are incorporeal movables which are not registered.

Contractual Rights

In addition to the contractual rights discussed in the previous section, other contractual rights that might form part of the community property are pledges, promissory notes payable to bearer, subscription rights, accounts receivable, interests in pension plans, and partnership interests. While partnership interests and community enterprises are governed by specific provisions, the other contractual rights are not subject to joint or exclusive management, so they will be governed by equal management. In each case, however, the spouse who did not incur the obligation should not be able to affect the legal relations and responsibilities of the spouse who did incur the obligation.

If magazine subscriptions, "book of the month" clubs, and offers to purchase season tickets are issued in the name of one spouse, these subscription rights arguably might be subject to the exclusive management of that spouse. However, because no provision of the law provides that the subscription right be "issued or registered" in someone's name (although it is customary to do so), exclusive management under article 2351 does not apply. While the basic principle of equal management could be invoked to govern such agreements, since arguably these rights are not issued or registered in one name as provided by a law covering such rights, the principle of privity of contract ought to cover the situation to allow only the person who is a party to the contract to manage the rights under that contract. Once the magazine and tickets have been received, however, they are things that form part of the community, and are subject to equal management.

Another contractual right that the husband and wife might own is a partnership interest, as when one spouse is a partner with a third person. Article 2352 provides for exclusive management of the partnership interest by the spouse who is a partner. Without the exception contained in article 2352, the interest that one spouse has in a partnership might otherwise fall under the presumption of equal management. The partnership *interest* is a right separate from the partnership *assets*; the latter will be managed according to the partnership agreement.

The contractual rights (and other assets) which are part of a business owned by the spouses will be managed according to the Civil Code articles governing "community enterprises." The community enterprise articles apply only to businesses which are not legal entities. Thus, if the husband and wife form a corporation, management of this corporation will be according to the articles of incorporation. Likewise, if the husband and wife form a partnership, the partnership agreement will regulate the partnership.

Community enterprises may undertake such activities as ordering merchandise and supplies, borrowing money, and selling nonnegotiable accounts receivable. If the community enterprise desires to sell or pledge nonnegotiable accounts receivable in an effort to avoid bankruptcy, the ability of one spouse to sell the accounts depends on how the business is managed. If one spouse is the "sole manager" of the community enterprise or if the other spouse has renounced his right to concur in the management of the community enterprise, exclusive management applies and only the managing spouse may exercise control over the accounts. However, joint management applies and consent of the other spouse is necessary if the transaction involves "all or substantially all" of the assets of the community enterprise. If both the husband and wife participate in the management of the community enterprise, then equal management applies.

Article 2353 renders the sale of the accounts to a third party voidable if the "non-managing" spouse exercises control or if consent of the other spouse is not secured when concurrence is required by law. Therefore, third parties dealing with a business owned by a husband and wife should exercise caution when they cannot easily "identify at least one spouse who unquestionably participates in management [of the community enterprise]." Perhaps the articles regulating the management of the community enterprise should be amended to clarify the meaning of "sole manager." This phrase is presently undefined. An alternative solution is to amend the articles so that third parties may assume that the enterprise is subject to equal management unless one spouse has expressly renounced the right to participate in the management. Under this arrangement third parties would not want to deal with only one spouse unless shown the express renunciation of the other spouse.

C. *Isabelle Canale v. Gus Mayer, Co., Limited*

481 So. 2d 170 (La. App. 4 Cir. 1985)

WARD, Judge.

Isabelle Canale sued Gus Mayer Company, Ltd., a New Orleans department store, for breach of a contract of deposit. She alleged that Gus Mayer failed to return five articles of clothing which she had deposited for safekeeping with the store's fur storage department. Without giving reasons for his decision, the Trial Judge ruled in favor of Gus Mayer. Mrs. Canale appeals. We reverse the Trial Court and render judgment in favor of Mrs. Canale.

The following facts in the case are undisputed. Mrs. Canale took her furs to Gus Mayer's store in the spring of 1978. In keeping with Gus Mayer's usual practice, Mrs. Canale was issued temporary receipt tickets for the articles. Gus Mayer later mailed permanent receipts to Mrs. Canale. Those five permanent receipts issued to "Mrs. I. Canale" and captioned "Customer's Receipt and Storage Contract" are in the record and list the following articles of clothing with values assigned by Mrs. Canale at the time she placed the articles in storage:

Azurene Glacial Mink/Grey Leather Stroller	$700.00
A.H. Jacket	400.00
Leopard Jacket	200.00
Sheared Beaver/A.H. Mink Collar Short Jacket	500.00
Glacial Mink Hat	150.00

The following statement is printed on each receipt:

This Receipt must be returned to us when the articles are taken out of storage. In case the Receipt is lost, it is necessary that we be notified at once.

The conditions on the reverse of the receipts state that the value declared by the depositor is agreed to be the value of the deposited article. None of the other conditions are asserted by either party. Mrs. Canale had the receipts in her possession at all times and gave no one authority to claim the furs from Gus Mayer.

In December of 1979 when Mrs. Canale attempted to claim the furs, the Gus Mayer personnel could not find them. Mrs. Canale was ultimately told, and an employee of Gus Mayer's fur department testified, that Mrs. Canale's husband had telephoned the store and asked that the furs be sent to a suburban store where someone would pick them up. An unidentified woman attempted to claim the furs at the downtown store shortly after Mrs. Canale's husband's telephone call, but Gus Mayer had no record of when or to whom the furs were released from the suburban store. The Gus Mayer representative testified that the store had found it "very difficult" to require the receipts from customers before releasing furs from storage. If the person claiming a garment did not have the receipt however, it was store policy to require some personal identification along with a description of the garment being claimed.

Much evidence was presented by Gus Mayer regarding Mrs. Canale's marital situation and related problems during the period when the furs were stored at Gus Mayer. These circumstances included mysterious disappearances of virtually all of Mrs. Canale's property from her home, grand jury and FBI investigations of her husband's activities, and Mrs. Canale's frequent changes of residence during the period. Despite the inferences which Gus Mayer would have us draw from Mrs. Canale's unfortunate domestic situation, we find manifest error in the Trial Court judgment absolving Gus Mayer of liability.

Our jurisprudence has established that a depositary has a contractual obligation to its depositors and must act as a prudent administrator. Brown & Blackwood v. Ricou- Brewster Building Co., 239 La. 1037, 121 So.2d 70 (1960). The duty of a compensated depositary is to be rigorously enforced. La.C.C. art. 2938. When a depositor proves the existence of a deposit contract and that the deposited articles were not returned, a presumption arises that the depositary has breached the contract. Federal Insurance Co. v. C & W Transfer and Storage Co., 282 So.2d 563 (La.App. 4th Cir.1973); Comment, *Bailment and Deposit in Louisiana*, 35 La. L. Rev. 825 (1975).

We believe the undisputed facts of this case give rise to the presumption that Gus Mayer breached its contract with Mrs. Canale, and we are not convinced by Gus Mayer's defense that it acted prudently in releasing the furs to an agent of Mrs. Canale's husband. Civil Code Article 2949 states:

The depositary must restore the thing deposited only to him who delivered it, or *in whose name the deposit was made*, or who was pointed out to receive it (emphasis added).

Gus Mayer contends that because the costs of the fur storage were charged on a store account in the name of Mrs. Canale's husband, he was the person "in whose name the deposit was made." This contention is flatly contradicted by the receipts issued to "Mrs. I. Canale." Moreover, the strong terms of the deposit contract evidenced by those receipts clearly assured Mrs. Canale that the furs were safe with Gus Mayer until she presented the receipts and claimed the furs.

Hence, we hold Gus Mayer liable for failure to return the furs to Mrs. Canale.

D. *Wade Joseph Schexnayder v. Yolande Schexnayder & Son, Inc.*

119 So. 3d 624 (La. App. 5 Cir. 2013)

MARC E. JOHNSON, Judge.

Defendant, Melissa Schexnayder, appeals the trial court's granting of a writ quo warranto in favor of plaintiff, Wade Schexnayder, in which the trial court determined that Ms. Schexnayder did not carry her burden of proving she had authority to hold the office of president of Yolande Schexnayder & Son, Inc. ("YSS"), and that Mr. Schexnayder continues to have the voting rights of 7,500 shares of stock that were the subject of an Act of Donation to Ms. Schexnayder in 2008. For the reasons that follow, we affirm.

FACTS & PROCEDURAL HISTORY

YSS, which is in the business of selling clay and dirt material, is a closely held corporation that was incorporated in September 1989 by plaintiff's grandfather, Yolande Schexnayder, and Yolande's son, Carroll Schexnayder. At the time of incorporation, YSS issued 5,000 shares of stock to Yolande and his wife Beatrice, and 5,000 shares of stock to Carroll and his wife Sharleen. In 1992, both Yolande and Carroll donated 2,500 shares of their YSS stock to Mr. Schexnayder for a total of 5,000 shares. Later, in 2007, Yolande made a second donation of 2,500 shares of stock to Mr. Schexnayder, giving him a total of 7,500 shares in YSS.

On September 22, 2008, Mr. Schexnayder executed an Act of Donation donating all of his separate property, including his interest in YSS, to Ms. Schexnayder with the stipulation that the donated property "form part of the community existing between the Donor and the Donee." Thereafter, in 2009, Mr. Schexnayder purchased an additional 5,833.34 shares of YSS stock from relatives who had inherited the shares from their parents. And, in 2010, both Mr. and Mrs. Schexnayder purchased 1,666.68 shares of YSS stock from various relatives.

Between February 2008 and January 2012, Mr. Schexnayder was the president of YSS and ran the day-to-day operations of the business. At the same time Mr. Schexnayder became president, he used his shares to vote Ms. Schexnayder to the board of directors.

On December 22, 2011, Ms. Schexnayder, as Secretary/Treasurer of YSS, issued a Notice of Meeting of the Shareholders and Board of Directors of YSS set for January 5, 2012. At the shareholders' meeting, YSS's corporate attorney advised that upon review of several documents, including the 2008 Act of Donation by Mr. Schexnayder to Ms. Schexnayder, he determined that Ms. Schexnayder was the owner of 11,250, or 75%, shares of YSS stock, and Mr. Schexnayder was the owner of 3,750 shares, or 25%, shares of YSS stock. According to Mr. Schexnayder, he objected to this determination but his objection was not noted in the minutes of the meeting. Thereafter, a new board of directors was elected, which included Mr. Schexnayder, Ms. Schexnayder and Matt Milazzo, who was present through a proxy and was elected to the board solely through Ms. Schexnayder's votes.

Immediately after the shareholders meeting, a meeting of the board of directors was held. During the meeting, Mr. Schexnayder was removed as President of YSS, and Ms. Schexnayder was elected president through her votes and those of Mr. Milazzo by proxy. Ms. Schexnayder also used her votes and those of Mr. Milazzo by proxy to elect herself as Treasurer of YSS.

On February 7, 2012, Mr. Schexnayder filed a Petition for Mandamus and Quo Warranto, for Temporary Restraining Order and for Injunctive Relief claiming, among other things, that Ms. Schexnayder wrongfully usurped control of YSS. He sought issuance of a writ of quo warranto be issued to force Ms. Schexnayder to explain by what authority she acted in removing him as president of YSS and voting herself in as president and her brother-in-law, Matt Milazzo, in as a director. Mr. Schexnayder further sought to enjoin Ms. Schexnayder from further acting as a YSS officer.

A show cause hearing was held on May 21, 2012. At the conclusion of the hearing, the trial court determined that Ms. Schexnayder had not carried her burden of proving that she had the right to vote the 7,500 shares of stock that were donated to her in 2008, and thus had not shown she had the right to vote herself as President and Treasurer of YSS. The trial court noted that the 2008 donation clearly stated the stocks were to be community property and made no reference to voting rights. It further noted the stock certificates for the 7,500 shares were still in Mr. Schexnayder's name, and there had been no request to transfer the stock certificates to Ms. Schexnayder's name, despite the passage of more than three years from the act of donation to the January 2012 meeting. As such, the trial court granted the writ quo warranto in favor of Mr. Schexnayder and found he continues to have the voting rights to the 7,500 shares of stock he donated to Ms. Schexnayder.

ISSUE

On appeal, Ms. Schexnayder challenges the trial court's determination that the Act of Donation did not transfer the voting rights of the 7,500 shares of stock. She maintains that the voting rights were included in the donation of the stock and that Mr. Schexnayder would have had to have made a specific reservation in the donation in order to retain those voting rights, which he did not do. She also contends the trial court erred in relying on parole evidence, specifically the conduct of the parties after the act of donation, to determine the intent of the parties regarding the voting rights of the donated shares.

LAW & ANALYSIS

***

Ms. Schexnayder claimed she validly held the office of president by virtue of an election by the board of directors in which she held the majority of voting shares through the voting rights of 7,500 shares of stock that were donated to her by Mr. Schexnayder in 2008. The 2008 Act of Donation states, in pertinent part:

> WADE J. SCHEXNAYDER, SR., a person of the full age of majority, domiciled in the Parish of St. James, State of Louisiana ["Donor"], who declared that, in consideration of the love and affection which he bears to his spouse, Melissa D. Schexnayder, he does, by these presents, make a gift and donation inter vivos, UNTO said:
>
> MELISSA D. SCHEXNAYDER ["Donee"], hereby appearing for the purpose of accepting the same of the following:
>
> All of Donor's separate property, including, but not limited to, bank accounts, brokerage accounts, publicly traded securities, annuities, life insurance, all of Donor's interests in the Successions of Yolande and Beatrice Schexnayder, the Succession of Carroll Schexnayder, Sr., and all of Donor's right, title and interest in and to the following entities: Yolande Schexnayder & Son, Inc., Schexnayder Industrial Services, Inc., Schexnayder Holdings, L.L.C., Belle Vue Estates and Acadia Development Corporation.
>
> TO HAVE AND TO HOLD unto the said Donee, her heirs and assigns, forever, SUBJECT, HOWEVER, TO THE FOLLOWING STIPULATION: The donated property shall form part of the community existing between the Donor and the Donee.

[Emphasis in original.]

No one disputes that this Act of Donation included the 7,500 shares of YSS stock that Mr. Schexnayder owned as his separate property. However, the parties dispute the effect of this donation. Ms. Schexnayder argues that this Act of Donation gave her the exclusive right to vote all 7,500 shares. Conversely, Mr. Schexnayder contends the Act of Donation only gave Ms. Schexnayder an undivided one-half interest in the 7,500 shares of stock and not any real rights, such as voting rights.

Under La. R.S. 12:601, the person in whose name a stock certificate is issued is the legal owner, and a corporation and its officers are bound to recognize as legal owner only the person in whose name a stock certificate is issued. While a stock certificate is prima facie evidence of ownership, actual ownership may be determined from the facts and circumstances of a case. *Ackel v. Ackel*, 595 So.2d 739, 741 (La.App. 5th Cir.1992). Only shareholders of record on the books of the corporation are entitled to vote at meetings, unless otherwise provided in the articles of incorporation. La. R.S. 12:75; *Pollock v. Pollock Engineering Co., Inc.*, 365 So.2d 1186, 1189 (La.App. 3rd Cir.1978).

In this case, Mr. Schexnayder's name appears on a 1992 stock certificate for 5,000 shares. Additionally, the evidence shows a valid donation of 2,500 shares of stock from Yolande to Mr. Schexnayder in 2007 with reference to a 1989 stock certificate, which was admitted into evidence. Although Mr. Schexnayder's name does not appear on the 1989 stock certificate for the 2,500 shares, the record shows a valid transfer of the stock ownership to Mr. Schexnayder. *See In re Interdiction of Vicknair*, 01–902 (La.App. 1 Cir. 6/21/02); 822 So.2d 46, 51. The record shows that Ms. Schexnayder's name does not appear on either of the stock certificates relating to these 7,500 shares. Thus, we must determine the effect the 2008 Act of Donation had on the stock ownership.

Under La. C.C. art. 2343.1, "[t]he transfer by a spouse to the other spouse of a thing forming part of his separate property, with the stipulation that it shall be part of the community, transforms the thing into community property." [Emphasis added.] Comment (b) of this Article explains that, "[i]n effect, the transferor conveys to the other spouse one-half of what he owns and retains the other half as co-owner under the regime of acquets and gains." Under the general principles of community property, "[e]ach spouse owns a present undivided one-half interest in the community property." La. C.C. art. 2336.

Contrary to Ms. Schexnayder's position that the Act of Donation gave her the 7,500 shares of YSS stock unencumbered as her separate property, we find that the clear and unambiguous language of the 2008 Act of Donation, indisputably made the 7,500 shares of stock a part of the community. As such, Ms. Schexnayder owned an undivided one-half interest in the shares.

Generally, either spouse acting alone may manage, control, or dispose of community property unless otherwise provided by law. La. C.C. art. 2346. Under La. C.C. art. 2351, each spouse has the exclusive right to manage, alienate or encumber moveables issued or registered in his name. Shares of stock are incorporeal movables, and shares of stock issued in the name of a spouse are subject to management by that spouse exclusively. La. C.C. art. 473; *Champagne v. Champagne*, 07–1078 (La.App. 1 Cir. 6/27/08); 992

So.2d 1072, 1075; *Rao v. Rao*, 05–0059 (La.App. 1 Cir. 11/4/05); 927 So.2d 356, 366, *writ denied*, 05–2453 (La.3/24/06); 925 So.2d 1232.

In *Pollock*, supra, a wife filed a writ of mandamus after her divorce claiming she was the owner of one-half of the 80 shares of stock of the defendant corporation. The wife sought an order to force the corporation to cancel the stock certificates in the name of her ex-husband and to issue a new stock certificate showing her as owner of half of the shares, or 40 shares. The trial court found the 80 shares of stock were community property and refused to order the corporation to issue a new certificate for 40 shares in the wife's name because there had been no partition of the community. However, the trial court ordered the corporation to recognize the wife as the owner in indivision with her husband and to afford her all rights accompanying such ownership, including the right to vote at shareholder meetings.

The appellate court found the trial court correctly determined that upon dissolution of the community by divorce, Mr. and Mrs. Pollock became owners in indivision of an undivided one-half interest in the 80 shares of stock. However, the appellate court found the trial court erred in ordering the corporation to afford the wife all the rights and privileges of a stockholder. Citing La. R.S. 12:601 and 12:75, the court explained that the wife, as co-owner in indivision of the stock, was not entitled to any of the rights of a shareholder. The court noted that the wife's remedy was to have the community partitioned.

In the present case, as previously stated, Ms. Schexnayder owned the 7,500 shares of stock in indivision with Mr. Schexnayder by virtue of the donation of the stock to the community. However, like Pollock, her ownership interest in the stock did not give her autonomous control over the stock. *See also In re Succession of Moss*, 00–62 (La.App. 3 Cir. 6/21/00); 769 So.2d 614, 621, *writ denied*, 00–2834 (La.12/8/00); 776 So.2d 462. Rather, Mr. Schexnayder, in whose name the stock certificates are issued and to whom the shares were transferred, retains exclusive management rights relating to the 7,500 shares, as well as the right to vote the shares under La. R.S. 12:75. As explained in Pollock, Ms. Schexnayder's undivided one-half ownership interest in the shares by mere virtue of the shares having been donated to the community does not give her all the rights afforded to a shareholder, including the right to vote the shares.

Accordingly, we find the district court correctly determined Ms. Schexnayder did not properly hold the office of President of YSS because she did not have the right to vote the 7,500 shares that were in Mr. Schexnayder's name. As such, Ms. Schexnayder's vote, using the 7,500 shares to vote herself in as president, was invalid.

DECREE

For these reasons, we find the district court did not err in granting the writ quo warranto in favor of plaintiff, Wade Schexnayder, and determining that Mr. Schexnayder retained the right to vote the 7,500 shares of YSS stock. Accordingly, the trial court's June 5, 2012 judgment is affirmed. Defendant, Melissa Schexnayder, is to bear the costs of this appeal.

AFFIRMED

E. Note

One of the more controversial questions relating to the sole and exclusive management scheme relates to when a spouse will be considered sole manager of a community enterprise, such that the equal management scheme is trumped by sole and exclusive management powers. Very few Louisiana cases delve into the subject. One case that does appear to speak to the issue is *Doughty v. Insured Lloyds Ins. Co.*, 576 So.2d 461 (La. 1991). But that case is best explained by tort law and its special policies rather than under the matrimonial regimes legislation. In *Doughty*, husband alone appeared to manage an unincorporated lumber business that was community property. The spouses' son was killed by a defective planer in the lumber mill. The spouses sued their insurer, asserting a survival action and a wrongful death claim, based on strict liability principles of Civil Code Article 2317, which makes one responsible for damages caused by "things which we have in our custody." The court of appeal denied the spouses recovery on the basis that they were responsible for the damages, as they had custody of the planer.

The Louisiana Supreme Court granted writs on the wife's claim and ultimately held she was entitled to recover. Although she was an owner (in community) of the planer, liability is based on *custody* or *garde*, which is a factual matter. The court concluded that because of wife's lack of involvement in the business and the fact that the benefit she received from the use of the planer was "not substantial", she did not have *garde* and, therefore, was not precluded from recovering.

The court went further in dictum that should be kept in context. (1) The court stated that the husband was the sole manager of the community enterprise and had the exclusive right to alienate, encumber or lease its movables. However, there is no indication in the opinion as to how such an exclusive right was obtained. He may have been the de facto manager, but there is no indication that the wife waived her right to manage the property. In such a case, his sole management authority is questionable. (2) The court stated that wife had no authority or control over "the operation of her husband's business." But earlier in the opinion, the court noted that all assets of the business were community. The business was not organized as a corporation or partnership. As such, wife owned one-half of the business, or, more properly, of all the community assets devoted to the business. (3) The court described wife's ownership interest in the defective planer as "remote" and noted that she only had the "contingent right to claim half ownership" when the community was dissolved. That language is inconsistent with the plain language of Civil Code Article 2336: "Each spouse owns a present undivided one-half interest in the community property." (4) The court noted that wife could not partition property during the community. That is correct, but all the more reason to conclude that she is an owner of the property.

The court is on safer grounds when it returns to a torts policy analysis and states, "Although she was an owner by virtue of the community property laws, she was not in a better position than an innocent victim to detect, evaluate or take steps to eliminate an unreasonable risk of harm arising in the defective planer."

F. Questions

1. During marriage, W operates a snowball stand. W does not bother to incorporate the business, but rather operates it as a sole proprietor. H and W have agreed that W will be in charge of running the snowball stand because H is too busy with his alligator hunting business to get involved. W wants to sell the old icemaker and buy a newer one. Can she do that acting alone? Why or why not?

a. Suppose W likes the old icemaker, but H is convinced that a newer one would make the business more profitable. Can H sell the icemaker? Why or why not?

b. Suppose H decides that what the business really needs is to do some advertising. H wants to run some ads for the snowball stand in the local paper. Can he do that? Why or why not?

2. During marriage W acquires a whole-life life insurance policy insuring her own life. She uses community funds to purchase the policy. W initially names H as the beneficiary of the policy but later decides she wants to change the beneficiary designation to name her sister. Does W need H's consent? *See e.g. Talbot v. Talbot*, 864 So. 2d 590 (La. 2003); *Allianze Life Ins. Co. v. Oates*, 756 So. 2d 667 (La. App. 2 Cir. 2000).

5.4 CONCURRENCE OF BOTH SPOUSES

A. Introduction

Louisiana Civil Code article 2347 contains a number of exceptions to the general rule of equal management. The article requires that both spouses concur in certain transactions that are likely to be particularly significant to the well being of the family and the spouses.

Art. 2347. Alienation of community property; concurrence of other spouse

> A. The concurrence of both spouses is required for the alienation, encumbrance, or lease of community immovables, standing, cut, or fallen timber, furniture or furnishings while located in the family home, all or substantially all of the assets of a community enterprise, and movables issued or registered as provided by law in the names of the spouses jointly.
>
> B. The concurrence of both spouses is required to harvest community timber.

Concurrence is also required for certain gratuitous transfers of community property.

Art. 2349. Donation of community property; concurrence of other spouse

> The donation of community property to a third person requires the concurrence of the spouses, but a spouse acting alone may make a usual or customary gift of a value commensurate with the economic position of the spouses at the time of the donation.

B. *South Central Bell v. John and Evelyn Eisman*

430 So. 2d 256 (La. App. 5th Cir. 1983)

GAUDIN, Judge.

This is an appeal by South Central Bell Telephone Company from a judgment ordering it to pay $28,566.00 in trespass damages to Mr. and Mrs. John Eisman because the telephone company installed an underground conduit and manhole on the Eismans' property without obtaining full permission.

South Central Bell did negotiate with Mr. Eisman and he executed a servitude contract authorizing the work, but appellant did not secure Mrs. Eisman's signature.

The trial judge held that the agreement was relatively null and that it became absolutely null when Mrs. Eisman did not ratify it. We affirm this legal determination," and we affirm' the awards of $1,500.00 for the right- of- way servitude and $2,066.00 for resodding of the lawn. However, we reduce the award for general damages from $25,000.00 to $5,000.00, and we award this sum to Mrs. Eisman and not to the Eismans' jointly.

BACKGROUND

In March and April, 1980, an agent for South Central Bell, Larry Brasseaux, had contacts with Mr. Eisman and obtained his signature on a servitude agreement for a consideration of $214. 00. The check was delivered to Mr. Eisman on April 23, 1980, and work on the underground conduit proceeded to its conclusion. In August, 1980, South Central Bell alleges, Mr. and Mrs. Eisman began to park their car in such a manner as to interfere with the company's access to the underground conduit's manhole. On November 10, 1980, South Central Bell filed a petition in the 29th Judicial District Court seeking declaratory and injunctive relief.

Mr. and Mrs. Eisman answered and reconvened, asserting that the servitude was invalid and that South Central Bell had trespassed.

Following trial, the district judge denied South Central Bell's request for declaratory and injunctive relief, awarded damages to Mr. and Mrs. Eisman and ordered the telephone company to pay all costs.

The judgment also contained this clause:

> "Alternatively, should the plaintiff decide to remove the conduit and manhole from the defendant's property, they must restore the property to its previous condition and reimburse the defendants for all court costs and attorney's fees in connection with this proceeding."

SPECIFICATION OF ERRORS

From this adverse judgment, South Central Bell contends on appeal that the trial judge erred:

(1) In not concluding that Mrs. Eisman's actions constituted ratification of the servitude agreement executed by her husband;
(2) In not finding that South Central Bell had a valid servitude;
(3) In refusing to apply LSA-- R.S. 19:14;
(4) In deciding that South Central Bell had trespassed and that it was liable for

trespass damages; and
(5) In awarding excessive damages.

DID MRS. EISMAN CONSENT?

Since January 1, 1980, when Articles 2337, 2347 and 2353 became effective, the assent of *both* husband and wife is required on certain agreements. These articles read:

Article 2337

"A spouse may not alienate, encumber or lease to a third person his undivided interest in the community or in particular things of the community prior to the termination of the regime."

Article 2347

"The concurrence of both spouses is required for the alienation, encumbrance, or lease of community immovables, furniture or furnishings while located in the family home, all or substantially all of the assets of a community enterprise and movables issued or registered as provided by law in the names of the spouses jointly."

Article 2353

"When the concurrence of the spouses is required by law, the alienation, encumbrance or lease of community property by a spouse is relatively null unless the other spouse has renounced the right to concur . . ."

These provisions are relatively new, and there are no reported cases on the relationship between them and servitude contracts. However, the unmistakable thrust of these articles, insofar as servitude agreements are concerned, is that contracts signed by only one spouse are *relatively* null and that the agreements become *absolutely* void and of no effect unless confirmed by the other spouse.

A relatively null act *can* be validated by subsequent ratification, and it is South Central Bell's contention that Mrs. Eisman *did* acknowledge and recognize the contract signed by her husband.

Appellant's agent (Brasseaux) testified that he was unaware that the law had been changed and that the servitude contract needed the signatures of both Mr. and Mrs. Eisman. Appellees suggest that this admission is odd in that Mr. Brasseaux earns his livelihood as a right-of-way agent and the changes in Louisiana community property laws which became effective on January 1, 1980, were substantial and were well publicized while under legislative consideration and, thereafter.

Regardless, the record does contain testimony by telephone company representatives indicating that Mrs. Eisman' condoned the conduit installation and that she sanctioned the servitude agreement signed by her husband. The trial judge, however, obviously placed more credence in Mrs. Eisman's contrary declarations.

In his "Reasons for Judgment," the judge said:

"The fact remains that Mrs. Eisman never signed the agreement and according to her testimony, continued to object to the location of the manhole on her property; although, testimony seems to indicate that Mrs. Eisman discussed with construction officials various operations on her property. She testified she objected throughout and even contacted the telephone company officials in Birmingham, Alabama, concerning the problems and trespass on her property."

The trial judge found that South Central Bell ". . . proceeded without a valid servitude from Mrs. Eisman . . ."and". . . acted with impropriety . . ." Further, the trial judge said that South Central Bell ". . . could not enter on defendant's property in good faith and that it violated the property rights of . . . Mrs. Eisman."

There is a, reasonable basis in the record for these findings, and we cannot say that they are manifestly erroneous. See Canter v. Koehring Co., 283 so.2d 716 (La.1973), and Arceneaux v. Domingue, 365 50.2:1 1330 (La.1978).

South Central Bell did produce more witnesses than the Eismans, but, as Judge L. Julian Samuel wrote in U.S. Fidelity and Guaranty Co. v. Fiffie, 211 So.2d 690 (La. App. 4th Cir.1968):

> "Witnesses are weighed and not counted. A fundamental function of the trier of fact, be, it judge or jury, is to determine the facts and this is not done by counting noses."

We cannot, therefore, find that Mrs. Eisman either gave her consent or that her actions comprised a ratification. The trial judge did not make either determination, nor can we.

DAMAGES

As there was no binding servitude contract, trespass damages are due.

The award of $28,566.00 to Mr. and Mrs. Eisman jointly was itemized as follows:

(1) $25,000.00 for improper entry and trespass;
(2) 1,500.00 for right-of-way servitude; and
(3) 2,066.00 for resodding of lawn.

We find no fault with the award to the Eismans of items(2) and (3). With regard to the first item, however, it is difficult to associate general damages with Mr. Eisman as he had authorized the construction and anticipated it.

Mrs. Eisman, however, is entitled to an award for mental pain, and anguish, and we set this amount at $5,000.00. The award of $25,000.00 in general damages, which included mental pain and anguish, was beyond the range of the district court's discretion, considering, the evidence and testimony adduced at the trial.

CONCLUSION

The award of $25,000.00 in general trespass damages is reduced to $5,000.00, with this amount awarded to Mrs. Eisman personally. In all other respects, the judgment of the district court is affirmed.

AFFIRMED IN PART, AMENDED IN PART AND RENDERED.

C. Note

In *Kee v. Frances Camel Construction*, 532 So.2d 378 (La. App. 3d Cir. 1988), wife was held to have ratified a servitude agreement executed by her husband as grantor where she did not object to his signing and "she signed the agreement in the capacity of a witness."

D. *Cajun Capital, Inc. v. Joseph Bourque*

532 So. 2d 272 (La. App. 3d Cir. 1988)

YELVERTON, Judge.

In July 1986 Joseph Bourque signed a listing agreement giving Cajun Capital, Inc. (Cajun) the exclusive right to sell the community property enterprise known as "Mary Lou's Flowers & Gifts" in New Iberia, Louisiana. The Mary Lou of this enterprise was his wife. The agreement was for a period of six months. The listing agreement declared that if the business was sold at any time during its duration, the seller would pay Cajun a brokerage commission of 12% of the gross sales price or $ 5,000, whichever was larger.

Less than a month later a representative of Cajun showed the business to Angie Boudreaux who, on July 25, 1986, signed a confidentiality agreement.

A few days after that, in early August 1986, a Cajun representative and Angie Boudreaux met and Angie Boudreaux deposited $100 as good faith money which was to be returned to her at closing. One week later Joseph Bourque and his wife, Mary Lou Bourque, conveyed the community property enterprise to Angie Boudreaux and her husband, Artie James Boudreaux, for the sum of $19,000. Cajun apparently did not participate in this act of sale.

The above events were recited by the trial judge as being the facts upon which the reasons for his decision rested.

As a result of the above transactions, Cajun demanded a brokerage commission of $5,000, along with all costs of enforcing the agreement, and attorney's fees. When the Bourques refused to pay, Cajun filed suit.

The Bourques resisted the suit contending that the listing agreement was a nullity, because Mary Lou never signed it and it constituted an encumbrance of community property which required the consent of both spouses in accordance with La. C.C. art. 2347. The trial court agreed, declaring the listing agreement an absolute nullity and unenforceable, and dismissed Cajun's suit.

Cajun filed this appeal. For reasons which follow, we reverse and remand.

Until January 1, 1980, when the new matrimonial regimes enactments were incorporated into the Civil Code, C.C. art. 2404 characterized the husband as "head and master" of the community of acquets and gains, giving him sole authority to administer community effects and to alienate immovable property belonging to the community without his wife's participation or consent. The new provisions which went into effect in 1980, dealing with management of community property, establish the principle of equal management by means of C.C. art. 2346, which declares:

Mary Lou's Flowers & Gifts is apparently a community enterprise and, if so, the alienation, encumbrance, or lease of the whole enterprise would require concurrence of the spouses.

Mary Lou joined in the act of sale to Artie James and Angie Boudreaux, but she did not sign the exclusive listing agreement.

The precise question before us, therefore, is whether the requirement of concurrence applies to an exclusive listing agreement for the sale of all or substantially all of the assets of a community enterprise.

In our opinion, the provisions of C.C. art. 2347 do not apply to a listing agreement because a listing agreement is not an alienation, encumbrance, or lease. The obligation to pay a commission which Joseph Bourque undertook when he signed the listing agreement was not a real obligation, defined by C.C. art. 1763 as a duty correlative and incidental to a real right. A real obligation attaches to a thing, either movable or immovable. C.C. art. 1764. If the obligation which Bourque undertook when he signed the listing agreement had been an encumbrance on the assets of the community enterprise, the obligation would have attached to the business and become the obligation of the acquirers, the Boudreauxs, when they bought that enterprise. Of course that did not happen. The Bourques recognized this when in their conveyance to the Boudreauxs:

"Appearer, [sic] JOSEPH E. BOURQUE and MARY LOU BOURQUE, being duly sworn, declared that there is no outstanding indebtedness on the above described movable property and on the inventory, declaring that all previous outstanding indebtedness on said items having been fully paid and liquidated and knows [sic] of no liens or encumbrances on any of said property" (emphasis supplied).

An encumbrance creates real obligations. Since the listing agreement did not create a real obligation, it was not an encumbrance.

Since we are dealing here with the management act of one spouse that did not operate as an encumbrance of all or substantially all of the assets of the community enterprise, C.C. art. 2347 does not apply. The trial court was accordingly in error in concluding that the listing agreement was null solely for want of the concurrence of Mrs. Bourque.

E. Note

Dictum in the per curiam opinion in *Lupo v. Lupo*, 475 So.2d 402 (La. App. 1st Cir. 1985) suggested that a contract of suretyship required the concurrence of both spouses. Suretyship, however, does not involve encumbrance of any property; it is simply a contractual undertaking "by which a person binds himself to a creditor to fulfill the obligation of another upon the failure of the latter to do so." LA. CIV. CODE art. 3035. The questionable dictum was disregarded in *Rayne State Bank v. Fruge*, 546 So.2d 637 (La. App. 3d Cir. 1989), which held that a wife's continuing guaranty for her son's obligation was valid and could be enforced against community property.

F. *Stockmon v. Van Alstyne*

976 So. 2d 336 (La. App. 2d Cir. 2008)

CARAWAY, J.

Plaintiff, Sandra Blankenship Stockmon ("Stockmon"), was employed by defendant, Forrest Franklin Van Alstyne II ("Van Alstyne"), in his insurance business in 1992. At that time, Stockmon was nineteen years old. She was employed as a secretary. Van Alstyne described Stockmon as a very good employee throughout the time of her employment from 1992 until 2004, when Van Alstyne sold his agency. In 2004, Van Alstyne was 62 years old and had experienced health problems which led to his sale of the business.

This dispute concerns a contractual agreement between the parties reached in January 1996 following Stockmon's decision to leave employment with Van Alstyne for a better paying job. In an effort to prevent Stockmon's leaving, Van Alstyne made certain proposals which were listed on a one-page contract, as follows:

ONE YEAR CONTRACT
01-16-96
AGREEMENT BETWEEN SANDRA D. BLANKENSHIP AND F.F. VAN ALSTYNE

1. Raise effective 01-15-98-will be $323.00 per week less deductions.
2. Review every six (6) months with *annual* raise of $100.00 per month.
3. Christmas bonus according to company profit.
4. Five hundred dollar ($500.00) bonus to be paid 02-10-96.
5. Write health insurance on Sandra within the next seven (7) working days.

She will pay $75.00 per month toward her health insurance; we will deduct this weekly from her payroll ($17.31/week). This will go toward her disability, maternity and major medical. She can add husband and child at any time with her paying the cost.

6. Retirement plan will be started within seven (7) working days of this agreement with five (5) year provision from vesting.
7. Ownership of company will begin 01-01-96 in the amount of one (1) percent each year until Frank retires. Sandra will have the first option to buy the business from Frank at his retirement.
8. Sandra will have five (5) sick days per year and one (1) week paid vacation along with the usual paid holidays. After five (5) years of continued service Sandra will have two (2) weeks paid vacation.
9. Frank will pay for continuing education classes required to renew insurance license.

Both parties signed the agreement. While provision number 7 concerning Stockmon's ownership of the company is the subject of this suit, most of the other listed benefits were provided to Stockmon throughout the remainder of her employment. One exception was the promise of a retirement plan. Van Alstyne provided Stockmon instead with a life insurance policy in which her husband was named the beneficiary. She indicated at trial that she did not question Van Alstyne about the matter, trusting at the time that the policy with its cash value was what he intended to provide her as the "retirement plan."

In April 2004, Van Alstyne sold the agency for $500,000. Stockmon testified that she was made aware of the sale of the business after it had been transacted. She continued in the employment of the purchaser. Nevertheless, because of the "company" ownership rights she received in the 1996 agreement, she eventually brought this suit against Van Alstyne and his wife, Barbara Gail Van Alstyne (hereinafter "Gail"), for an accounting of Stockmon's interest in the agency. According to Stockmon, after the execution of the 1996 agreement, she and Van Alstyne never again discussed provision number 7 of the contract or the accrual of any profits from the business to which she might be entitled. According to Van Alstyne, later in 1996 he mentioned the matter to her with the idea of incorporating his business and making her a minority shareholder. However, Van Alstyne testified that at that time Stockmon rejected any arrangements to formalize her ownership interest.

Following a bench trial, the trial court ruled in favor of Stockmon, enforcing her ownership provision of the agreement. She was recognized as an 8% owner of the business-one percent for each year between 1996 and 2003. She was awarded 8% of the sale price of the business ($40,000) plus her share of profits for certain profitable years less her share of the loss experienced by the business in the first four months of 2004. Van Alstyne appeals the judgment award of $56,595.85.

Discussion

***

The next assignments of error by the appellants concern Van Alstyne's wife, Gail. They argue that since the contract involved an interest in the community-owned business, it required Gail's concurrence under Civil Code Article 2347. They also argue alternatively that because of the lack of her concurrence in the contract, the judgment holding her liable for the debt was in error.

Significantly, after the filing of Stockman's initial petition in this matter, Van Alstyne filed a peremptory exception of nonjoinder, alleging the insurance agency was a community business enterprise by virtue of his twenty-eight year marriage to Gail, making her an indispensable party to the proceeding. A hearing on the exception never occurred. Instead, plaintiff amended her petition to add Gail as a party defendant.

Each spouse acting alone may manage, control or dispose of community property unless otherwise provided by law. La. C.C. art. 2346. The concurrence of both spouses is required for the alienation, encumbrance, or lease of ... all or substantially all of the assets of a community enterprise. La. C.C. art. 2347. According to Comment (b) to Article 2347, the community enterprise contemplated in this article is a business that is not a legal entity. The transfer of a partnership interest is the exclusive right of the spouse who is a partner. La. C.C. art. 2352.

An obligation incurred by a spouse during the existence of a community property regime for the common interest of the spouses or for the interest of the other spouse is a community obligation. La. C.C. art. 2360. During the marriage, either spouse acting alone may incur a community obligation. *Sciortino v. Bank of Louisiana,* 97-1420 (La.App. 4th Cir.1/28/98), 705 So.2d 813, *writ denied,* 98-721 (La.5/15/98), 719 So.2d 463. Except for separate obligations specified under Civil Code Article 2363, all obligations incurred by a spouse during the existence of a community property regime are presumed to be community obligations. La. C.C. art. 2361. *McConathy v. McConathy,* 25,542 (La.App. 2d Cir.2/23/94), 632 So.2d 1200, *writ denied,* 94-750 (La.5/6/94), 637 So.2d 1052.

Civil Code Article 2345 provides that "[A] separate or community obligation may be satisfied during the community property regime from community property and from the separate property of the spouse who incurred the obligation."

The Van Alstyne agency was a community enterprise exclusively under his management in 1996. Under La. C.C. art. 2347, we do not find that Van Alstyne's undertaking to provide Stockmon with a portion of the ownership of the business amounted to alienation of "all or substantially all" of the business. Therefore, no concurrence was necessary on the part of Gail for validity of this contract.

Likewise, the contract benefited the community enterprise by retaining the services of an able employee. Therefore, the contract gave rise to a community obligation for which Gail's continued ownership in the community may be held liable in accordance with Civil Code Article 2345.

We find no merit in these assignments of error.

Conclusion

For the reasons expressed herein, we find no merit in the appellants' assignments of error and the trial court's judgment is affirmed. Costs of appeal are assessed to appellants.

AFFIRMED.

G. *Succession of Louis F. Wagner; Succession of Leila Mae Cornay Wagner*

993 So. 2d 709 (La. App. 1st Cir. 2008)

GUIDRY, J.

These consolidated appeals arise from the successions of a husband and wife who died approximately nine months apart. The first appellant asserts the trial court erred in annulling a donation of gold coins from the husband to his son and in finding certain funds were donated to the couple's daughter to construct a guest house on her property. The second appellant complains the trial court erred in denying a reimbursement claim for certain community stocks sold by the son and in ordering the wife's estate to pay interest to the husband's estate on community assets in her possession at the time of her death. For the following reasons, we affirm in part, vacate in part, and remand.

FACTS AND PROCEDURAL HISTORY

Louis and Leila Wagner (the Wagners) were married on April 23, 1937, and had two children, Warren and Faye Wagner. Following Louis Wagner's death on May 22, 2001, Warren filed a petition for probate of his father's last will and testament, which named him as universal legatee and executor of his father's estate. While that succession was still under administration, Leila Wagner died on March 3, 2002. Except for a $100,000.00 bequest to a grandson, Leila left her entire estate to Faye. Subsequently, Faye opened her mother's succession with a petition for probate and was appointed as executrix thereof. The two successions were later consolidated, although the consolidation order specifically provided they would continue to be administered separately. Several issues arose in the proceedings regarding the classification of certain properties as being either community or separate in nature and as to the validity of certain donations made by Louis and Leila to one or the other of their children.

Following a hearing on various petitions and motions, the trial court rendered judgment, dated July 12, 2004, declaring a 1999 donation of gold coins by Louis Wagner to Warren to be a nullity based on the court's findings that the coins were community in nature and Leila Wagner did not consent to the donation. Leila Wagner was recognized as the owner of and sent into possession of one-half of the coins. The trial court also denied Warren's claim that his father's succession owned an interest in a guest house constructed on Faye's property, where the Wagners resided for several years before their deaths. The court concluded the funds used to construct the house were donated to Faye by her parents, and further denied Warren's claim for reimbursement for one-half of the money. Warren appealed this judgment, but the appeal was dismissed by this court as being taken from a partial judgment not certified as final...

***

GOLD COINS

By authentic act dated August 27, 1999, Louis Wagner donated to his son, Warren, certain gold coins having a value at that time of approximately $450,000.00. The coins were purchased by Louis Wagner, at Warren's suggestion, in 1997 and 1998. According to Warren's testimony, his father told him he purchased the coins with his separate funds. Nevertheless, he concealed the donation from his wife and asked Warren to do the same. Warren admitted that he complied with his father's request.

Louisiana Civil Code article 2349 provides that, except for usual and customary gifts, "[t]he donation of community property to a third person requires the concurrence of the spouses ...." Additionally, La. C.C. art. 2353 provides that, when the concurrence of a spouse is required by law, as in the case of true donations, the alienation of community property by one spouse without the consent of the other is relatively null, unless the other spouse has renounced his right to concur. See *Wilkerson v. Wilkerson*, 42,324, pp. 13-14 (La.App. 2d Cir.8/15/07), 962 So.2d 1137, 1145; *Ackel v. Ackel*, 595 So.2d 739, 743 (La.App. 5th Cir.1992); 16 Louisiana Civil Law Treatise, Matrimonial Regimes, § 5.15, 404 (3d ed.2007). In this case, it is undisputed that Leila Wagner did not consent to the donation of the gold coins. Nor was there any evidence that she had renounced her right to concur in transactions alienating community property.

At the time of Louis Wagner's death in May 2001, Leila Wagner was neither aware of the donation of the gold coins to Warren, nor had consented to it. Thereafter, on July 18, 2001, she filed a petition in the Succession of Louis F. Wagner captioned "Petition for Partition, For Return of Community Assets, and For Other Relief." She made the following allegations in Paragraph V of this petition:

> Upon information and belief, petitioner represents that prior to the death of Louis Frank Wagner, the decedent was persuaded by his son and now succession representative herein, Warren Wagner, to transfer ownership of community assets, without the knowledge or consent of petitioner. Petitioner represents that certain community assets were transferred to an improperly formed limited liability company, as well as to Warren Wagner individually, to the great detriment of petitioner. (Emphasis added.)

Subsequently, on October 3, 2001, after learning through discovery proceedings of the donation of the gold coins, she filed an amended petition designated "Petition for Possession, For Return of Community Assets, And for Other Relief." In the amended petition, she specifically asserted the gold coins were community property and requested that cause be shown why she should not be sent into immediate possession of one-half of the community assets, including the gold coins.

A hearing was held on this matter in April 2004. Warren admitted therein that both he and his father concealed the donation of the coins from his mother. However, he indicated that although he knew the coins were purchased during his parents' marriage, his father told him they were purchased with his separate funds. He noted that he knew his father had separate funds derived from an earlier inheritance from his brother. He further pointed out that in the gift tax return his father filed in connection with the donation, his father indicated the coins were separate property. However, when questioned by opposing counsel, Warren conceded that at least one of the checks used to pay for the coins may have been written on a community checking account, although he continued to maintain his father put the funds into that account. On his father's instructions, Warren personally wrote the check drawn on that account, which was listed in the name of "Mr. Or Mrs. Louis F. Wagner."

Following the hearing, the trial court rendered judgment declaring the donation of the coins to be a nullity. In reaching its decision, the trial court concluded the coins were purchased with community funds and were, therefore, community in nature. The court noted that while Warren claimed his father's separate funds were used to purchase the coins, no evidence was presented establishing this claim. Accordingly, the donation of these community assets without the consent of Leila Wagner was declared null, and the Estate of Leila Wagner was recognized as owner of one-half of the coins. The trial court also rejected Warren's claim that he had acquired ownership of the coins by acquisitive prescription,

On appeal, Warren does not challenge the classification of the coins as community property....

***

In the alternative, Warren argues that despite the fact that his mother did not consent to the donation of the coins, the donation was nonetheless valid under the usual or customary gift exception provided by La. C.C. art. 2349. As previously noted, article 2349 provides that a true donation of community property to a third party generally requires the consent of both spouses. However, the article further provides that one spouse acting alone can make a "usual or customary gift of a value commensurate with the economic position of the spouses at the time of the donation." La. C.C. art. 2349. Under those circumstances, a donation of community property may be valid, even without the concurrence of both spouses. See La. C.C. art. 2349; 16 Louisiana Civil Law Treatise, Matrimonial Regimes, § 5.14, 401 (3d ed.2007).

Warren asserts that should this court uphold the donation of the construction funds to Faye, the size of this donation would establish it was usual and customary for the Wagners to make large donations to their children. He further contends the donation of the coins was commensurate with the Wagners' economic positions at the time of the donation, since the detailed descriptive list indicated they had over four million dollars in community assets, even without including the coins. Accordingly, he argues the donation of the coins falls within the usual and customary gift exception provided by article 2349.

We find this argument lacks merit. Even though the record reflects the Wagners did in fact regularly give large monetary gifts to their children and grandchildren, those gifts were more typically in the range of $10,000.00 to $20,000.00. While the record does establish several gifts that were substantially larger, none of them even approach the approximately $450,000.00 value of the gold coins. Other than the donation of the coins, the largest gift either parent acting alone gave to one of the children was a $100,000.00 certificate of deposit that Leila Wagner gave to Faye. However, Leila Wagner admitted in her amended petition that the certificate of deposit was a community asset for which she must account to Louis Wagner's estate. In effect, she conceded her gift to Faye was not a valid donation of her husband's interest in this community asset, suggesting such large gifts by the Wagners were not usual and customary.

With respect to the donation of the construction funds, we first note that unlike the donation of the gold coins, it was not a purely gratuitous donation. A purely gratuitous donation is one "made without condition and merely from liberality...." La. C.C. art. 1523. In this case, the Wagners donated the money to Faye with the understanding that she would use it to construct a guest house on her property where they could live the rest of their lives. Moreover, the Wagners did live in the house for several years prior to their deaths.

Secondly, even if the donation of $165,000.00 to Faye for the construction of the guest house had been purely gratuitous, it still does not support Warren's position. The donation of the construction funds was agreed to by both parents, so that it actually constituted a donation of only $82,500.00 from each parent. In contrast, the gold coins were worth approximately $450,000.00, and were donated to Warren by his father acting alone. Thus, the record does not support Warren's contention that a donation of this size was a usual and customary gift.

H. *Alice Rooney Schindler v. Charles V. Schindler*

131 So. 3d 439 (La. App. 5 Cir. 2013)

JUDE G. GRAVOIS, Judge.

The succession of plaintiff, Alice Rooney Schindler, appeals a trial court judgment finding that certain donations inter vivos made by Mrs. Schindler's late husband, Charles

V. Schindler, allegedly from their community property, were remunerative in nature, thus denying her request to nullify the donations. For the reasons that follow, we affirm.

PROCEDURAL BACKGROUND

In 2003, before her death, Alice Rooney Schindler filed suit against her husband, Charles V. Schindler, for separation of property in order to stop him from spending their community funds without her consent and to separate the remainder of their property. She later amended her suit to include as defendants several persons to whom Mr. Schindler gave money. Mr. Schindler died in 2004 during the pendency of the suit. Mrs. Schindler died in 2007; her succession was thereupon substituted as party-plaintiff. The defendants who went to trial were Cindy Moore and Trudy Davis. After a two-day bench trial, the trial court rendered judgment in favor of Ms. Moore and Ms. Davis, dismissing plaintiff's claims against them with prejudice at plaintiff's costs. Following the denial of plaintiff's motion for a new trial, plaintiff appealed the judgment only as to Ms. Moore.

***

FACTS

The record and the briefs show that Mr. and Mrs. Schindler were married in 1951. They had seven sons together and lived in New Orleans. Sometime around 1964, they began living separate and apart, though they never sought a formal legal separation, divorce, or separation of property until Mrs. Schindler's suit in 2003.

As found by the trial court, the record reflects that the parties were relatively wealthy. Mr. Schindler received a large personal injury settlement in the 1970s, which he invested in stocks that apparently performed very well. Mrs. Schindler testified in her deposition that the stock was ultimately converted to municipal bonds in the 2000s, with two $500,000 bonds being placed in Mrs. Schindler's name alone, and with three $500,000 bonds being placed in Mr. Schindler's name alone. The parties also owned several other income-producing rental properties, as well as acreage (which included a "camp") near Meadville, Mississippi. A CPA's report entered into evidence shows that at the time of Mr. Schindler's death, the community was valued at between $3.8 and $4.8 million. Evidence and testimony showed that Mr. and Mrs. Schindler were very generous with their wealth, making donations to various family members and friends. As noted by the trial court in its reasons for judgment:

> The Schindlers appear to have been very generous with their wealth. They bought houses for their son Jon, Anna Schindler (ex-daughter-in-law), and Cindy Moore (Charles' god-daughter).... They purchased a car for their son Michael, and gave him the down payment for his home.... They helped their son Jon pay child support, and paid all of his expenses.... They paid tuition for two

> of their grandchildren, and helped Anna Schindler with tuition at Tulane University.... They donated a municipal bond in the amount of $500,000.00 to Anna Schindler, and gave $250,000.00 to Kip Briggs (Anna Schindler's boyfriend).

Mrs. Schindler testified in her deposition that she "kept the books" for both herself and Mr. Schindler, although if he wanted money, he would just "write himself a check." She agreed that they each had money that they could spend without the other's permission, although she testified that when she bought a house for Anna Schindler, her ex-daughter-in-law with whom she lived and who provided her with physical care for an extended period of time, including after she suffered two strokes, she told Mr. Schindler about that purchase.

Mr. Schindler in his later years suffered serious health problems as well, including cancer of the stomach or esophagus. Because none of his children apparently desired or was able to provide care for him, he sought the services of defendants Trudy Davis and Cindy Moore, among others, as caregivers. After being introduced to each other in late 1999, Ms. Davis began taking care of Mr. Schindler around January of 2000 until approximately June of 2003, according to her testimony. Mrs. Schindler alleged that Mr. Schindler gave Ms. Davis two checks totaling $9,000, plus an additional $102,000 for the purchase of a house, from their community property and to which she did not consent, although she admitted that he did tell her of his intent to fund Ms. Davis' house purchase beforehand.

***

FOURTH ASSIGNMENT OF ERROR

Were the funds donated a usual and customary amount?

Lastly, Mrs. Schindler argues that the amount of funds donated to Ms. Davis was not a usual and customary amount. However, she argues merely that the amount was such, over $100,000, that no spouse should be able to give that amount away without the other spouse's consent.

As noted above, the trial court included in its reasons for judgment a short recitation of some of the various donations made by the Schindlers, jointly or separately. The amount of those donations, as noted above by the trial court, makes it clear that the donations totaling $111,000 made by Mr. Schindler to Ms. Davis were quite in line with, and were in fact less than, the very generous donations that the Schindlers made to others who were or were not their family members, and/or who provided or did not provide care to them. Under the particular facts and circumstances of this case, we agree with the trial court's finding that the amount of funds donated by Mr. Schindler to Ms. Davis was a usual and customary amount relative to the Schindlers. Accordingly, this assignment of error is without merit.

***

I. UNIFORM MARITAL PROPERTY ACT: GIFTS OF MARITAL PROPERTY

Gifts of Marital Property to Third Persons

(a) A spouse acting alone may give to a third person marital property that the spouse has the right to manage and control only if the value of the marital property given to the third person does not aggregate more than [$500] in a calendar year, or a larger amount if, when made, the gift is reasonable in amount considering the economic position of the spouses. Any other gift of marital property to a third person is subject to subsection (b) unless both spouses act together in making the gift.

(b) If a gift of marital property by a spouse does not comply with subsection (a), the other spouse may bring an action to recover the property or a compensatory judgment in place of the property, to the extent of the noncompliance. The other spouse may bring the action against the donating spouse, the recipient of the gift, or both. The action must be commenced within the earlier of one year after the other spouses has notice of the gift or 3 years after the gift. If the recovery occurs during marriage, it is marital property. If the recovery occurs after a dissolution or the death of either spouse, it is limited to one-half of the value of the gift and is individual property.

J. Questions

1. W is tired of H interfering with her snowball business, an unincorporated sole proprietorship. W thinks that putting the business into an LLC, of which W is the sole member and manager would improve things. In order to do this, W needs to form an LLC and then sell or transfer all of the assets of the business into the LLC. Can W go through with this transaction on her own?

2. H incorporates his alligator hunting business and the corporation's stock registry shows that H is the sole shareholder. The corporation owns the boats, vehicles, and other equipment required for alligator hunting. The corporation also acquires a parcel of immovable property on which to hunt alligators. The stock in the corporation is community property. H, who is also the president of the company, decides to lease the boats and vehicles during the off-season. Does he need W's consent?

5.5 ALTERNATIVES TO CONCURRENCE

A. Introduction

The Civil Code contemplates several alternatives to obtaining a spouse's concurrence. Civil Code article 2348 allows a spouse to preemptively renounce his right to concur in transactions otherwise requiring his concurrence. When a spouse simply refuses to concur in a transaction or is unable to concur due to physical incapacity, mental incompetence, commitment, imprisonment, or absence, Article 2355 allows the other spouse to seek court authority to proceed without the spouse's concurrence. Article 2355.1 allows a spouse to seek court approval to engage in transactions otherwise falling within the exclusive management rights of the other spouse where the other spouse is an absent person.

B. *Roger D. Allen v. Rita Amisson Allen*

611 So. 2d 790 (La. App. 4 Cir. 1992)

PLOTKIN, Judge.

FACTS:

Roger Allen, who has filed suit for divorce against Rita Allen, seeks a court order requiring Mrs. Allen to sign a promissory note guaranteeing a loan of $35,000. The loan will be used to pay income tax liabilities of $40,673, incurred by the couple in 1991. The $5,673 difference will be made up by Roger Allen. The loan is to be repaid over six years with quarterly payments in excess of $2,000. Each party is to pay one-half of the quarterly payments.

The loan will be secured by a $75,000 retirement account funded through Roger Allen's employment. Because the retirement account is community property both spouses must sign the loan documents and promissory note. The retirement account trustee refuses to grant the loan unless both parties sign the appropriate documents. Rita Allen has refused to sign the documents.

Roger Allen argues that if the loan is not made he will be forced to liquidate a portion of the retirement account to pay the tax liability, thus, the community will have to pay an additional $17,200 in penalties and taxes. These expenses will result from two sources: (1) money taken out of the retirement account is treated as normal income and is therefore subject to taxation and (2) money taken out of the retirement account prematurely is subject to a ten percent penalty.

However, Rita Allen argues that she is unable to afford her share of the quarterly payments, which will exceed $1,000. She works for a printing company and earns approximately $22,000 a year.

LOUISIANA CIVIL CODE ARTICLE 2355-

The trial judge ordered Rita Allen to sign the promissory note. Although much of the discussion took place off the record, apparently the trial judge felt that Roger Allen's proposal would benefit the community by $17,200 and Rita Allen's "arbitrary" refusal to sign was the only obstacle to the loan's implementation.

Although no written reasons were issued, the judge clearly relied on La.C.C. art. 2355 as authority for requiring her to sign the agreement. Article 2355 provides:

> A spouse, in a summary proceeding, may be authorized by the court to act without the concurrence of the other spouse upon showing that such action is in the best interest of the family and that the other spouse arbitrarily refuses to concur or that concurrence may not be obtained due to the physical incapacity, mental incompetence, commitment, imprisonment, temporary absence of the other spouse, or because the other spouse is an absent person.

This article is a deviation from the normal requirement that a concurrence between spouses is required to alienate or encumber community property. See La.C.C. art. 2347, 2349, 2350, 2353. The article was designed to dissolve irreconcilable disputes between spouses which, if allowed to continue, would harm the family as a whole.

In order to grant exclusive power to manage the community property to one spouse, the court must find that the other spouse's dissent is arbitrary or that his consent may not be obtained for one of the enumerated reasons. Then the court must be convinced that the action sought to be taken is in the best interest of the family. The word "family" as used in La.C.C. art. 2355 refers to the immediate family; the father, mother and children. See Official Revision Comment (1979); La.C.C. art. 3506(12).

By the clear language of the article, the court is empowered to authorize one spouse to manage the community exclusively. This power means that the agreements entered into by one spouse will not be relatively null due to the lack of concurrence of the other spouse. La.C.C. art. 2353. Additionally, the agreement entered into will be considered a community, not a separate, obligation. La.C.C. art. 2360.

In the instant case, La.C.C. art. 2355 empowers the court to authorize Roger Allen to manage the community property in such a way as to pay the tax liability. Roger Allen has chosen to encumber the retirement account by taking a loan against it. Thus, La.C.C.

art. 2355, via a court order, grants Roger Allen the legal authority to encumber this portion of community property without his wife's concurrence.

However, even though Roger Allen may be granted the legal authority to encumber the retirement account, the account trustee will not allow him to do so because the trustee requires both spouses' signatures prior to granting the loan. Facing this dilemma, the trial court decided to go one step further in applying La.C.C. art. 2355. The court, rather than empowering Roger Allen to act alone, which is pointless in this case, ordered Rita Allen to concur with the proposal by signing the promissory note. Nothing in this article permits the court to order the dissenting spouse to agree and comply with the management decisions being undertaken by the other spouse. The fact that the trustee of the account will not grant the loan without both signatures is beyond the ambit of La.C.C. art. 2355. The trial judge, pursuant to art. 2355, cannot order the dissenting spouse to execute the promissory note.

Accordingly, the trial court's order requiring Rita Allen to sign the promissory note guaranteeing the loan of $35,000 is reversed.

WRIT GRANTED.

5.6 EFFECT OF LACK OF CONCURRENCE

A. Introduction

Where the concurrence of a spouse is required by law but is not obtained, the transaction typically results in a null or void transaction. The majority of the community property states hold that such a transaction is merely voidable (a relative nullity) and that only the non-joining spouse has the right to seek to void the transaction. Louisiana follows this approach. *See* La. Civ. Code art. 2353.

B. *Claudio Hemb v. Michelle Toca wife of/and Wallace J. Landry, III*

731 So. 2d 1031 (La. App. 4 Cir. 1999)

BYRNES, Judge.

The trial court rendered summary judgment in favor of defendants-appellees, Michelle Toca, wife of, and Wallace J. Landry, III, individually and Landry Properties 7051, Inc., dismissing the claim of the plaintiff- appellant, Claudio Hemb, against them.

The judgment also held against Claudio Hemb "as to liability only for the improper filing of a Notice of Lis Pendens." The amount of liability is not fixed in the judgment. In support of the judgment the trial court issued the following written reasons:

The immovable property at issue is community property. Michelle Toca Landry never signed an Agreement to Purchase. The contract is a nullity. Summary judgment is appropriate.

No other reasons were given. Claudio Hemb appealed. We vacate and remand.

Claudio Hemb executed a purchase agreement dated March 24, 1997, in which he agreed to purchase the property located at 7051 Argonne Blvd. from the Landrys. Mr. Landry signed the agreement, but Mrs. Landry did not. Subsequently, Mr. Landry tendered Hemb a document entitled, "As Is Waiver of Redhibition Addendum to Purchase Agreement."

Hemb would not agree to the redhibition waiver and the closing scheduled for April 21, 1997 never took place. The Landrys then sold the property in "as is" condition to Landry Properties 7051, Inc., a corporation they formed for this purpose. The Landrys then scheduled a second closing at which they tendered title from the corporation without the waiver of redhibition clause and the "as is" condition language.

Hemb refused to go through with the sale, concluding that the unrestricted title conveyed by the corporation would be only as good as the corporation, which in turn was only as good as the property, apparently, the only asset of the corporation. In other words, the Landrys having transferred the property to the corporation with the waiver of redhibition clause, Hemb would have no right to pursue them personally for any redhibition claim. Hemb felt that his purchase agreement entitled him to this right.

Hemb then filed this suit and a Notice of Lis Pendens against the Landrys' and their corporation based on the original contract and purchased another home. Hemb's petition prays for specific performance and/or damages. He also alleged quasi contractual claims. The Landrys reconvened for damages caused by the filing of the Lis Pendens.

It is undisputed that the immovable property at issue is community property and that neither Michelle Toca Landry nor Landry Properties 7051, Inc. executed a purchase agreement with Hemb. The trial court granted summary judgment in favor of the Landrys for the reasons quoted near the beginning of this opinion, i.e., the nullity of the purchase agreement in the absence of Mrs. Landry's signature. Hemb does not dispute the fact that Mrs. Landry's concurrence to the agreement to sell the community family home is necessary. See La. C.C. art. 2347. However, Hemb argues that the nullity was relative only and the agreement was susceptible of ratification after the fact by Mrs. Landry, and that Mrs. Landry in fact ratified the agreement.

The Landrys contend that as a matter of law the purchase agreement is an absolute nullity insusceptible of ratification by Mrs. Landry. None of the cases cited by the Landrys support the position that the failure of the spouse to sign may not be cured by ratification, if ratification can be proved. However, LSA- C.C. art. 2353 states in pertinent part:

When the concurrence of the spouses is required by law, the alienation, encumbrance, or lease of community property by a spouse is relatively null unless the other spouse has renounced the right to concur. [Emphasis added.]

Comment "(b)" under this Article states:

An act entered into by a spouse without the concurrence of the other spouse when such concurrence is required by law is a relative nullity.

LSA- C.C. art. 2031 provides that: "A contract that is relatively null may be confirmed."

Hemb argues that the ratification may be inferred from the following: (1) Mrs. Landry listed the property for sale; (2) Mrs. Landry concurred in her husband's execution of the Purchase Agreement; (3) Mrs. Landry signed a special power of attorney on the date of the first closing for her husband to sign for her; (4) Mrs. Landry was involved in the formation of Landry Properties 7051, Inc.; (5) Mrs. Landry signed the act of sale transferring the property to the corporation; (6) Mrs. Landry as president of the corporation signed a resolution authorizing the resale of the property to Mr. Hemb.

Mrs. Landry in her deposition acknowledged that she signed a special power of attorney authorizing her husband to act on her behalf and that that power of attorney contains no "as is" or waiver of redhibition clause. Defendants do not dispute the fact that the power of attorney contains language authorizing the sale to be made with full warranty. This would normally be sufficient to ratify the original purchase agreement. Had Mrs. Landry wished or intended to limit the warranty to an "as is" sale she could and should have expressed such a limitation in the language of the power of attorney. The power of attorney speaks for itself. At the very least the power of attorney raises a genuine issue of material fact precluding summary judgment in favor of the defendants at this stage of the proceedings. Accordingly, it was error for the trial court to grant summary judgment in favor of the defendants.

For the foregoing reasons, we vacate the judgment of the trial court and remand this case for further proceedings consistent with this opinion.

JUDGMENT VACATED; CASE REMANDED.

C. *Anthony J. Zeller, Sr. and Hope P. Zeller v. Lionel Webre and Nunnie Webre*

17 So. 3d 55 (La. App. 5 Cir. 2009)

MARION F. EDWARDS, Judge.

Defendants/Appellants, Lionel and Nunnie Webre, appeal a judgment of the district court in favor of plaintiffs/appellees, Anthony and Hope Zeller, ordering the Webres to convey the rights, title, and interest in certain immovable property upon payment of all sums due.

In June 2007, Anthony and Hope Zeller filed a Petition for Damages and Enforcement of Contract, averring that they entered into a contract with Lionel and Nunnie Webre to purchase a home at 702 Kinler Street in Luling, Louisiana. The contract price was $30,000, of which $29,000 was financed by the owners. The Zellers urged that they had paid 120 payments of $300 per month and that the Webres were refusing to follow the terms of the contract. They requested specific performance, or, in the alternative, return of monies paid, and damages.

The Webres filed an Answer and Reconventional Demand, stating that Nunnie Webre did not sign nor did she have knowledge of the agreement. Further, it was alleged the Zellers lived on the property as lessees. The Webres averred that the Zellers signed rental agreements on the property on September 9, 1993; April 17, 2004; March 2, 2006; and March 18, 2007, and that they have repeatedly failed to timely pay the rent due. They demanded $47,884 in late payment fees.

Following trial, the court granted judgment in favor of the Zellers, finding that it was the intent of the parties to have a lease/purchase agreement, that the monthly rentals would be applied toward payment of the principle and interest, and that the Webres were entitled to reimbursement of all insurance premiums. The court ordered that, upon payment of all sums due to the Webres, they were to convey the property to the Zellers.

All other requests were denied and dismissed.

The Webres appeal.

The document at issue is handwritten and reads:

> Anthony & Hope Zeller agree to buy from Lionel and Nunnie Webre a wood frame house located at 702 Kinler St. Luling.

Price $30,000

Owners will finance $29,000 Balance. After a $1000 down payment is made by the Buyers. a[sic] interest rated of 8% over 180 months (15years)

Seller will pay insurance premiums from an amount that will be added to monthly payment from Buyer. This will be set up just as a commercial financial institution would do it.

Both Parties agree that paperwork regarding the sale of said property is to be paid by Buyer. The period prior to the Sales transaction specifically Sept 1 until final paper work is done will be handeled [sic] as a lease with intentions to buy. This monthly Rate will be $300 per month.

The purpose of this hand written paper is so all parties involved will have a full understanding of the transactions that follow and will lead to the final Act of Sale.

This document will contain conditions of interest to both parties (buyers and sellers) any special concerns should be listed here so they can be included in the final draft of Act of Sale.

The document is signed by Lionel Webre, Hope P. Zeller, and Anthony Zeller and is dated September 21, 1993. On June 4, 2007, it was filed in the Clerk of Court's Office for the Twenty–Ninth Judicial District.

At trial, Mrs. Zeller testified that the payments made by them were "rent to own. We were going to pay $300 a month for 15 years and then we were going to own the house." Both the Webres knew the Zellers were buying the house. An amount of $500 was initially paid on the down payment at the time of the agreement. They tried to complete the down payment a couple of times but were told by the Webres that they did not want to do the paperwork at that time. Finally, on April 7, 2007, Mrs. Zeller left the payment with Mrs. Webre. That check was cashed. Mr. Zeller testified to the same effect and further stated that he did upkeep on the house because there was an agreement to buy it. Mr. Zeller understood that, at the end of the fifteen-year period, papers would be drawn up, and "I would have my house after paying him $300.00 a month." No formal act of sale took place.

Mr. Webre testified that, in 1993, the Zellers expressed an interest in buying the house, and he was interested in selling it. He stated that the paper at issue was an agreement by him to sell. The document stated that the Zellers agreed to buy the house, and he intended that, when he received the entire down payment, the paperwork would be done. Since the final paperwork had never been done, he considered the property as being leased. Although the monthly payments were not always timely, the entire monthly amount has been paid. The sale documents were not prepared because the Zellers had not completed their down payment. Mr. Webre told his wife that he drafted the agreement.

Mrs. Webre, a former real estate agent, testified that she did not know about the agreement to sell prior to the execution of the document, and she was angry when she was shown the paper about a week later. She did not want to sell the property and had not intended to do so, but she never put anything in writing. She never refused any payments offered by the Zellers. The second part of the deposit was received on April 7, 2007, but, according to Mrs. Webre, the Zellers never attempted to complete payment before that time. A number of receipts admitted into evidence were signed by Mrs. Webre on many of which she had scratched out the notation "rent." Mrs. Webre did not offer an explanation.

Entered into evidence were a number of invoices and receipts for improvements on the property. Further, a document meant for the zoning board, written and signed by Mr. Webre in connection with a home business application on behalf of Zeller, was introduced. That paper stated that Webre was the property owner and that "Anthony [Zeller] is renting with an option to purchase this property."

On appeal, the Webres urge the contract was null because it involves alienation of community property without spousal consent and because it fails to satisfy the formal requirements for a sale of immovable property.

Initially, we note that it is undisputed that Mr. Webre wrote and provided all of the language in the agreement. Accordingly, any ambiguous language is to be interpreted against him and in favor of the Zellers.

It is undisputed that the Kinler Street property is community property. The Webres cite La. C.C. art. 2337, which holds that a spouse may not alienate, encumber, or lease to a third person his undivided interest in the community or in particular things of the community prior to the termination of the regime. The Official Comments to that article state that this provision does not prevent the alienation, encumbrance, or lease to a third person of a portion of the community or things of the community in full ownership, but is aimed simply at preventing a third party from owning an undivided interest in the community or in particular things of the community. In the present case, it is not argued that Mr. Webre was attempting to sell only his own undivided interest in the property.

According to La. C.C. art. 2347, the concurrence of both spouses is required for the alienation, encumbrance, or lease of community immovables. When the concurrence of the spouses is required by law, the alienation, encumbrance, or lease of community property by a spouse is relatively null unless the other spouse has renounced the right to concur. La. C.C. art. 2353. A contract is relatively null when it violates a rule intended for the protection of private parties, as when a party lacked capacity or did not give free consent at the time the contract was made. A contract that is only relatively null may be confirmed. La. C.C. art. 2031. Confirmation of a contract, as referred to in Article 2031, involves making the contract valid by formal assent. La. C.C. art. 1843 states that ratification is a declaration whereby a person gives his consent to an obligation incurred on his behalf by another without authority. Tacit ratification results when a person, with knowledge of an obligation incurred on his behalf by another, accepts the benefit of that obligation.

> [A]ssent can be evidenced through the typical actions signifying ratification of a defective contract.... While no clear definition exists in the statutes or case law as to what confirmation acts validate a relatively null contract, jurisprudence makes it clear that acts sufficient to ratify a contract will act as confirmation of the contract. Confirmation and ratification are used almost interchangeably, or as non-exclusive actions. When a contract is ratified through the subsequent actions of the parties, that contract is confirmed by that ratification....

There is no indication in the record that Mrs. Webre has specifically renounced her right to concur. However, it appears that the Webres have incorrectly equated the concurrence required by Article 2347 with the initial consent and/or lack of Mrs. Webre's signature on the agreement.

A tacit confirmation may result from voluntary performance of the obligation. La. C.C. art. 1842. In the present case, Mrs. Webre acknowledged that she became aware of the agreement about one week after it was confected. On approximately thirty-eight receipts, which she signed herself, she scratched out the notation of the payment as "rent." There is no evidence in the record that she did not do so voluntarily or that she undertook any action to indicate or demonstrate that she did not intend to honor the contract. While Mrs. Webre obviously understood the import of the act, she offered no explanation for her failure to take any steps to oppose it. Additionally, we note the answer filed by the Webres stated that "[t]he defendants agree to sell the property to the plaintiffs as per the purchase agreement signed on September 21, 1993."

A number of Louisiana cases support the proposition that the non-signing spouse may subsequently ratify an unsigned agreement affecting community property, including immovable property. In *South Central Bell Tel. Co. v. Eisman*, the trial court gave credence to the wife's testimony that she called the company officials to object and complain about trespass on her property. In *Kee v. Camel Const.*, ratification by the wife was found to have occurred to cure the relative nullity in a grant of a right-of-way executed only by the husband. The project for which the right-of-way was granted lasted over eighteen months. Mrs. Kee was obviously aware of the project, voiced no objection to her husband signing the right-of-way agreement, and was obviously aware of the agreement as she signed the agreement in the capacity of a witness. In *First Fed. Sav.*

and Loan of Warner Robins, the appellate court found the trial court correctly determined that the wife ratified a subordination on a mortgage by signing her joint tax returns, taking advantage of substantial tax benefits attributable to the subordination.

In the present case, we find that the conduct of Mrs. Webre, a person experienced in real estate transactions, operated as a tacit confirmation sufficient to cure the relatively null agreement. Although Mrs. Webre did not sign nor subsequently wish to sell the property, the pleadings, evidence, and testimony supports a finding that her actions and/or inaction confirmed the contract.

The Webres cite a case from this Court, *Holland v. Barrios*, for the proposition that La. C.C. art. 2347 is strictly enforced. In that case, the husband executed an agreement to sell a community immovable to a third party; his wife signed as a witness, then the couple subsequently donated the immovable to their children. The third party sought specific performance of the agreement to sell and the nullity of the donation. The Barrios' children asserted that the agreement to sell was a nullity because the wife did not sign the agreement as an owner, but only as a witness. We concluded that, since the wife "did not sign the document as a party, but merely as a witness, ... the agreement is unenforceable because it purports to alienate, encumber or lease community property based on Mr. Barrios' signature alone." We do not find that opinion controlling here. *Holland v. Barrios* involved a summary judgment in which the court made its determination based on the face of the agreement, without testimony or other evidence other than the third party's affidavit. Further, that court did not directly address the issue of confirmation or ratification of a relatively null contract.

As to the form of the agreement, La. C.C. art. 2620 defines an option to buy or sell as a contract whereby a party gives to another the right to accept an offer to sell, or to buy, a thing within a stipulated time. Such option must set forth the thing and the price, and meet the formal requirements of the sale it contemplates. A sale or promise of sale of an immovable must be made by authentic act or by act under private signature. La. C.C. art. 2440. An act that fails to be authentic because of the lack of competence or capacity of the notary public, or because of a defect of form, may still be valid as an act under private signature. La. C.C. art. 1834. The Civil Code further requires that an act under private signature need not be written by the parties, but must be signed by them. La. C.C. art. 1837. However, the Official Comments under this Article, Section (b) states in pertinent part: "This article is not intended to change the jurisprudential rule that an Act under private signature is valid even though signed by one party alone...."

***

Thus, the courts of this state have repeatedly declined to find an agreement to purchase or sell invalid simply because one party failed to sign the instrument but some point later that same party exhibited some outward manifestation of acceptance beyond oral assent.

Just as Mrs. Webre's actions and/or inaction indicate that she confirmed the agreement, so also do they serve to indicate as an outward manifestation, or ratification of her acceptance of such. The existence of the subsequent "leases" does not invalidate the prior agreement which designates that the rent would be applied to the purchase price.

For these reasons, we affirm the judgment of the trial court. Because of our findings above, we find it unnecessary to address the Webres remaining assignments of error.

AFFIRMED.

D. *Artie M. Webb v. Pioneer Bank and Trust Company*

530 So. 2d 115 (La. App. 2d Cir. 1988)

JONES, Fred W., Judge

Alleging that her signature on a note and mortgage had been forged by her husband, plaintiff sued to annul the note, cancel the mortgage, and for damages from the former husband, the bank employee who notarized the mortgage, and the creditor bank. From a judgment ordering cancellation of the mortgage but rejecting the demand for damages, plaintiff appealed.

James Webb and Artie Webb were married in 1941 and in the ensuing years had four children. Mrs. Webb left the management of family finances to her husband, turning her paycheck over to him even after she became the sole wage earner in 1981. Webb did most of the writing of checks and Mrs. Webb never reviewed bank statements. The family banking was done at Pioneer Bank and Trust Company in Shreveport, from which Webb secured several loans over the years.

The Webbs were judicially separated in 1985 and subsequently divorced. Following the separation Mrs. Webb discovered a past due loan notice from Pioneer Bank. Upon inquiry, she was informed that the bank held a note and mortgage, purportedly signed by Mrs. Webb along with her husband on January 28, 1981, for some $40,000. Mrs. Webb informed the bank official that the signatures were not hers, but made the $225.50 monthly payments for several months before filing this suit in August 1985.

At the trial the 61 year old plaintiff testified that she had been the primary financial support of the family for some years prior to the separation and was making $5.17 per hour. Webb, who had a drinking problem, was not employed when the loan in question was made. Mrs. Webb admitted signing the credit application for the loan, but stated that she did not realize its import at the time. Before this loan her house payments were $78 per month. This loan increased those payments to $310 per month. Plaintiff denied signing the note and mortgage in question. There was testimony that, since learning of the forged signature on the instruments, plaintiff had been extremely upset, frequently wept, and suffered physical difficulties.

Robert Foley, an expert in the examination of Forensic Documents, stated he had compared plaintiff's acknowledged signature on canceled checks and her purported signature on the note and mortgage. It was his opinion that the person who signed the checks was not the same person as the one who signed the note and mortgage.

Gary Parker, who notarized the mortgage, testified that he was formerly employed by Pioneer Bank as a Vice- President and loan officer. He said that Webb was a regular bank customer to whom several loans had been made. In 1979 a $7500 mortgage loan was made to Webb for home improvements, with a portion of the proceeds used to repay a prior loan. Parker knew that Webb was married but never met Mrs. Webb.

When Webb approached Parker for another loan in 1981, Parker provided him with a loan application for the couple to sign and informed Webb that his wife would have to sign the note and mortgage. At the time, the bank's policy was not to lend more than $2,000 without collateral and without the spouse's signature. Parker could not recall whether Mrs. Webb's signature to the note and mortgage was affixed in his presence, although he was the notary.

The note and the mortgage were for $40,600.30, but Webb only received $15,000. Of this, $7448 was used to pay off the prior loan and interest payments (included in the note and mortgage) amounted to $24,475.80. Later, $3,000 was used to buy a bank money order for one of the Webb daughters.

Webb did not testify.

In a written opinion, the trial judge found that plaintiff had proved her signature on the note and mortgage was forged and ordered cancellation of the mortgage as null and void. On the other hand, he concluded that the loaned proceeds of $15,000 had benefitted the community. Therefore, the note was deemed a community obligation which was not voided by plaintiff's forged signature. Further, plaintiff's claim for damages was rejected because the trial judge found no evidence the existence of the mortgage caused her any more harm or mental anguish than the knowledge of the existing community obligation alone.

Plaintiff argued, on appeal, that the trial judge erred in finding the forged note created a community obligation because loan proceeds obtained fraudulently by one spouse cannot benefit the community. She also contended that Parker clearly violated the duties imposed upon notaries by La. R.S. 35:1- 17 and is liable, as well as his bank employer, for damages.

1) Did the promissory note, containing plaintiff's forged signature, represent a community obligation?

La. C.C. Article 2346 establishes the principle of equal management of community property. It provides that "each spouse acting alone may manage, control, or dispose of community property unless otherwise provided by law." Consequently, the consent or concurrence of both spouses is required only in those instances specified by law. See comment (a) to the article.

La. C.C. Article 2347 mandates the concurrence of both spouses for the alienation, encumbrance or lease of community property. An unauthorized encumbrance of community property is a relative nullity. La. C.C. Article 2353. Also see Coburn v. Commercial National Bank, 453 So.2d 597 (La. App. 2d Cir. 1984), *writ denied*, 457 So.2d 681 (La. 1984). Here, the trial judge correctly found the mortgage to be null. The question is whether the underlying obligation secured by the mortgage, represented by the promissory note in favor of Pioneer Bank, is a community obligation or is an obligation of Webb's separate estate.

A community obligation is defined as one ". . . incurred by a spouse during the existence of a community property regime for the common interest of the spouses or for the interest of the other spouse." La. C.C. Article 2360. Plaintiff argues that this loan was the result of an "intentional wrong not perpetrated for the benefit of the community" (La. C.C. Article 2363) and was thus a separate obligation of Webb.

In order to determine whether this money benefited the community, or was used for the "common interest of the spouses", it is necessary to examine the uses to which it was put. Bank records received in evidence revealed that about half of the proceeds was used to repay a community obligation. An officer of the bank testified that, according to its records, Webb also used a substantial amount to purchase a money order for one of the children of the marriage.

The fact that this loan was obtained without plaintiff's knowledge or consent does not affect its validity as a community obligation, since plaintiff's consent was not required by the law. La. C.C. Article 2346. Evidence in the record supports the finding of the trial judge that the loan was incurred for the common interest of the spouses and benefited the community. Therefore, the loan obtained and the promissory note executed by plaintiff's former husband, even if fraudulently, was properly characterized as a community obligation. See Ledet v. Ledet, 496 So.2d 381 (La. App. 4th Cir. 1986); First Security Bank & Trust Co. v. Dooley, 480 So.2d 842 (La. App. 2d Cir. 1985).

2) Although the note represented a community obligation, was plaintiff entitled to

damages because of the forgery of her name to the note and the mortgage?

As pointed out, Article 2347 requires the signature of both spouses for the encumbrance of community property. Further, Pioneer Bank would not have made this loan without Mrs. Webb's signature on the note and the mortgage. In the Coburn case, supra, we held that a bank was at fault for not releasing a mortgage when the bank had actual or constructive knowledge that the plaintiff wife, who had not signed the mortgage, was sole owner of the premises affected by the mortgage.

Here, since the loan would not have been made without a note and mortgage signed by plaintiff, she would have had a decisive voice in determining whether a note for some $40,000 should be signed to liquidate a community obligation of about $7500. Of course, as the primary wage earner of the family who would be burdened with payment of the obligation over a period of many years, plaintiff had a direct interest in the transaction. She was not consulted. Her signature was forged to critical instruments, and she was obviously damaged.

There is no question concerning the fault of Webb, who forged the plaintiff's signature on the note and the mortgage. As the notary, Parker was negligent in failing to exercise ordinary care in ascertaining the genuineness of the signature allegedly affixed in his presence. See La. R.S. 35:2,198; Levy v Western Casualty & Surety Co., 43 So.2d 291 (La. App. 2d Cir. 1949). As the employer of Parker, the bank is liable to plaintiff for his negligent action.

In calculating damages, we again note that $15,000 received for execution of the $40,000 plus note and mortgage was used for the benefit of the community. Plaintiff would have expected to pay interest on this. Consequently, consistent with the reasoning in the Coburn case, we find that plaintiff was damaged in the amount of $20,000 by the forgery of Webb and the negligence of Parker, for which the bank was liable. In addition, plaintiff is entitled to the sum of $2500 for her mental anguish and distress.

For these reasons, insofar as it rejects plaintiff's demand for damages, the judgment of the trial court is REVERSED and there is judgment in favor of plaintiff, Mrs. Artie Webb, and against the defendants, James Webb, Gary Parker and Pioneer Bank & Trust Company, in solido, for the sum of $22,500, with legal interest from date of judgment until paid.

All court costs, both in the trial court and on appeal, are assessed to defendants-appellees.

E. Note

The matrimonial regimes section of the Civil Code contains no special rules regarding prescription of actions to annul a transfer of community property on grounds of failure to obtain the concurrence required by law. In the absence of any special regulation, Louisiana Civil Code articles 2032 and 2033, governing the prescription of actions for relative nullity and the effects of relative null contracts in general apply. The analogy is sometimes a strained one, as the contractual nullity provisions do not translate perfectly in the community property concurrence context.

5.7 FRAUD OR BAD FAITH MANAGEMENT

A. J. Thomas Oldham, *Management of the Community Estate During an Intact Marriage*, 56 L. & CONTEMP. PROBS. 99 (1993)

***

IV

DUTIES OF A MANAGING SPOUSE

A. Should a Manager Be Considered a Trustee?

If both spouses join in a transaction, no breach of duty claim usually arises, at least where both have participated and neither relied on the other to look out for the community's interest. Questions involving duty of care frequently arise in connection with unilateral management transactions or when one spouse refuses to agree to a reasonable joint-management transaction proposed by the other. When one spouse acts on behalf of the community, such actions obviously can affect the community interest of the other spouse in the property. These situations present the issue of what standard of care is applicable to the managing spouse. Courts, legislators, and commentators frequently make utterances such as "spouses are fiduciaries" or "spouses are held to the duties of those in a confidential relationship." However, it is not clear what these statements should or do mean in the context of a spouse's decisions regarding the management of community property. These purported rules have been further complicated by other statements by courts and legislatures to the effect that spouses need only act "in good faith."

***

Most courts have reached the sensible conclusion that a spouse must satisfy only a duty to act in good faith when managing the community estate. This seems to mean merely that the spouse must not intentionally deplete the estate. For example, in *Andrews v. Andrews*, a Texas case where the wife claimed that her husband had violated his management duties to the community by making unsuccessful investments in real estate that caused the community to lose money, the court concluded that a spouse will not be liable for an "unwise" investment made in good faith.

Most investments are made in good faith. For example, *Hauge v. Hauge* involved a divorce where the wife challenged the husband's investments of community property in horses. Although the community estate lost $200,000, the court found that these investments were made in good faith. The court emphasized that the husband received professional investment advice and that the investment was "not like Las Vegas gambling." The court cannot mean that a spouse must consult an investment adviser before making an investment decision. The court implies that a manager must satisfy a duty of care, and that if the spouse consulted an investment adviser this would be relevant to that determination.

The new California provision states that the relationship of the spouses is a "fiduciary relationship subject to the same rights and duties of nonmarital business partners . . . . " Some cases have held that, among other things, in a commercial partnership, a partner is liable for damages caused by his negligence, without regard to good faith.

During an intact marriage, it would be undesirable to impose liability for mere negligence upon a manager spouse. The good faith standard is sufficient. The spouse has a fifty percent interest in the property and has a strong incentive not to dissipate it. Even if a spouse is negligent and the community suffers a loss, this risk is a cost that should be borne by the community. If a spouse does something brilliant, the other shares in any financial reward. Losses due to a spouse's negligence are also appropriately charged to the community. In other contexts, no one contends that a spouse should reimburse the community for losses suffered due to that spouse's negligence. For example, if one spouse negligently causes a car accident driving to work or commits professional malpractice, the tortfeasor is not liable to the community for any losses.

If a spouse acts in bad faith, of course, liability should result. For example, a spouse who knows that an investment is a poor business decision, but invests to help a friend or lover, is acting in bad faith. Similarly, intentional destruction of community property by the spouse is considered bad faith. To satisfy the duty of good faith, a spouse must act with the primary goal of benefitting the community.

The claims in cases such as *Andrews* and *Hauge*, however, are very different. In these cases, the nonmanager is arguing that liability to the community should result because the manager made a bad investment decision. All would agree such decisions occur. Indeed, spouses appearing in divorce court frequently have made more than their share of such decisions; the ramifications of these decisions may be one of the principal reasons the parties are divorcing. In what situations of this type, if any, should the manager be liable?

Bad financial decisions can cause great burdens on a marriage. However, the wisdom or fairness of holding a manager spouse liable for bad investment decisions is questionable, even if he or she might be considered negligent. Spouses fairly frequently make unilateral decisions regarding risky investments. Some are successful; some are not. Some investments undoubtedly are made after little reflection or investigation and are later regretted. Still, the benefit of successful investments rashly made accrues to the community, so it does not seem unfair to charge the community for those that are unsuccessful. In addition to the decisions in *Andrews* and *Hauge*, a number of courts have agreed with the contention that a spouse should not be liable for negligent management.

***

B. Consumption Decisions

1. In General. A spouse traditionally has not been liable to the community for unilateral consumption decisions. This rule undoubtedly stems from a sensible judicial unwillingness to resolve, at divorce or at any other time, disagreements between spouses about spending marital funds.

Unilateral decisions regarding consumption expenditures present different policy concerns from those arising relating to unilateral investment decisions. It was noted above that the spouses have similar interests regarding investments; each spouse wants to maximize the value of the community estate. In contrast, there is no congruence of interests regarding consumption decisions (unless one would say that each spouse is "interested" in seeing the other happy). One spouse might want to spend community funds on one thing, and the other might prefer another use of the funds. Also, consumption choices could benefit one spouse disproportionately, thus presenting the possibility that one spouse might try to usurp more than his or her share of the community. This suggests that some mechanism is needed to deter this from occurring.

***

A spouse who objects to the other's consumption decisions does have some available remedies. If the spouse is having difficulty exercising equal management rights over the community estate, in Wisconsin, California, and possibly other states, the objecting spouse could bring an "add-a-name" action. Alternatively, the unhappy spouses may wish to have the community estate partitioned into two separate estates. Finally, mediation may also be a useful remedy in these situations.

2. Gambling, Drinking, and Drug Use. If a spouse gambles with community funds and loses, the loss creates a management issue. In *Hauge v. Hauge*, as noted above, the Wisconsin court justified its refusal of a remedy to the objecting spouse by noting that, among other things, the other spouse's equine investment was not like Las Vegas

gambling. It is interesting to consider why this is significant. Presumably all but the most neurotic gamblers try to win. Is not the risky investment a use of community funds intended "in good faith" to enhance the community? Indeed, it may be difficult to state any meaningful distinction between gambling and a risky stock market investment.

Few cases discuss whether a spouse breaches a duty to the other spouse if community funds are "dissipated" on drugs or alcohol. This expenditure is not an "investment" of community funds, but a consumption decision. Courts rarely have held a consumption decision during an intact marriage to be a breach of duty, even if one spouse spends community funds on things that do not benefit the other spouse. Still, the amounts that could conceivably be spent on drugs could be very high, higher than most other types of consumption expenditures. Therefore, courts might be inclined to find this type of consumption to be a bad faith expenditure if the amount spent was sufficiently great. Alternatively, drug addiction and alcoholism could be treated as diseases for which the spouse should not be penalized.

**

Marriage of Stitt involved a divorce of a couple where one of the spouses had been convicted of embezzlement during the marriage. In its decision, the court concluded that the community should not be liable for the spouse's legal fees in connection with the embezzlement. The court emphasized the criminal nature of the wrongdoing.

In *Bergman v. State*, the husband was convicted of arson. The state attempted to collect court costs awarded the state in the prosecution from the spouses' community property, but the court held that the community was not liable. The court emphasized the criminality of the husband's behavior and decided that it was not done in furtherance of any community benefit.

In Louisiana, a spouse usually need not reimburse the community for any loss suffered due to that spouse's torts. However, if the community suffers a loss due to a spouse's intentional tort, and the tort is unrelated to the community, the community can obtain reimbursement from the tortfeasor. This liability for intentional torts unrelated to the community could be analogized to losses due to criminal activities.

C. The Duty to Account for Missing Community Property

At dissolution, courts do not require a spouse to account for all community money handled during the marriage. However, if a valuable asset disappears on the eve of a filing of a divorce action, a different policy is appropriate. If only one spouse had access to the property, courts will place the burden upon that spouse to verify that the property was used for appropriate purposes, such as family living expenses. A spouse who cannot do so is properly charged for the value of the asset. This treatment of assets that have disappeared when the marriage breaks down stems from the common-sense concern that a spouse might be tempted to hide, or possibly dissipate, community assets before the assets are divided.

D. Is a Unilateral Action in Violation of Joint Management Rules a Breach of Duty?

All states require some community property transactions to be made jointly. Despite these rules, a spouse may try to conduct such transactions unilaterally, sometimes incurring significant damage to the community. If the objecting spouse challenges the transaction before the closing of the deal, the transaction will not be completed and the spouses may need only to reimburse a third party for out-of-pocket costs. However, if the objecting spouse does not learn of the transaction until after the closing, the cost to the community could be much greater.

Should a unilateral action by a spouse in violation of joint management be a violation of a spouse's duty to the other, creating a right to recover damages? One factor that gives pause is that a spouse might not be aware of the joint management rules. However, in some cases it is clear that the spouse has notice of the rules. When this is established, in cases involving failure to obtain the consent of one spouse, it does seem reasonable to hold the involved spouse liable for any damage to the community. In *Webb v. Pioneer Bank & Trust Co.*, one spouse refinanced a loan on community realty by forging the other's signature. The objecting spouse obtained a judgment against the signing spouse for the amount of the loan not used to pay off the prior loan, and also recovered damages for mental anguish.

E. The Suit To Recover for a Breach of Duty

The UMPA and Wisconsin both provide that a spouse can recover for a breach of duty by the other spouse whenever the objecting spouse's property interest has been harmed. California initially required "substantial" damage. The revised California provision deleted this requirement; an objecting spouse may now recover whenever there has been or will be an "impairment to" or "detrimental impact" on the objecting spouse's property interest. The original California limit presumably was added to ensure that court calendars would be burdened only by disputes pertaining to a substantial amount of money. Drafters of the current revisions must have convinced the legislators either that the initial limit was unfair, or that the proposed change would not significantly increase the number of cases filed.

Under the Wisconsin provision, a spouse must bring suit within six years after he receives notice of the facts relating to the breach. In California, the action must be brought within three years after the spouse learns the facts; however, the claim may be brought later in connection with the economic resolution of the dissolution of marriage.

The recent California revisions made other changes to the provisions regarding remedies for a breach of a spouse's fiduciary duty. The law already permitted spouses to challenge at divorce any breach of duty, regardless of when it occurred or when the complaining spouse learned of it. Now, upon a showing of a breach of duty, the recent revisions seem to permit an objecting spouse to recover a minimum of fifty percent of the value of the property involved, plus attorneys' fees and costs, regardless of whether the objecting spouse suffered a financial loss. It is unclear why the drafters felt a need to award an objecting spouse more than the financial loss suffered, plus attorneys' fees. Another section seems to authorize punitive damages on a showing of fraud. In all other cases, however, an amount equal to the financial loss suffered, plus attorneys' fees, is all that should be awarded to the objecting spouse.

F. Is There Such a Thing as a Community Opportunity?

If a spouse owns separate property, she frequently chooses whether to use community property or separate property when an investment is made. Some have questioned whether a spouse has a duty to make investments during marriage with community funds. This problem is fueled by statements that spouses are "partners." Similarly, the new California provision states that "in transactions between themselves," spouses shall be "subject to the same rights and duties of nonmarital business partners, as provided in [s] ections . . . 15021 . . . of the Corporations Code . . . . " Section 15021 of the California Corporations Code (section 21 of the Uniform Partnership Act), among other things, incorporates the notion of partnership opportunity.

A partner may not usurp a "partnership opportunity." In a commercial partnership, a partnership opportunity is one that relates to the partnership business. Many courts agree that an opportunity is only a partnership opportunity if the partnership has the financial wherewithal to take advantage of it. If a potential investment is a partnership opportunity and a partner attempts to appropriate it for his own account, he must share the profit with the other partners.

It is difficult to understand how the notion of partnership opportunity could be useful to community property analysis. A potential investment is a partnership opportunity only if the agent learned of the opportunity while performing work on behalf of the principal. The business opportunity is, therefore, derived from the agency. The partner does not have to share profits from any other investments or opportunities, as long as the investment is not similar to those engaged in by the partnership. No analogous distinction exists for spouses; the scope of the community's "investment business" is limitless. From this perspective, every investment opportunity discovered or selected by a spouse during marriage would be a community opportunity, as long as there was sufficient community property (or credit) available at the time to fund the investment.

***

B. Louisiana Approach

Unlike some other community property jurisdictions, the Louisiana Civil Code does not affirmatively impose a fiduciary duty or a duty to act in good faith on the spouses. Rather the Code speaks in terms of fraud and bad faith:

Art. 2354. Liability for fraud or bad faith

A spouse is liable for any loss or damage caused by fraud or bad faith in the management of the community property.

When a spouse is found liable for fraud or bad faith under 2354, it is somewhat unclear what remedies are available. The cases show that money damages are appropriate sometimes. Some jurisdictions expressly authorize the "add-a-name" remedy, which permits a court to add the aggrieved spouse's name to the title of property. California Family Code §1101(c), for example, allows the court to "order that the name of a spouse shall be added to community property held in the name of the other spouse alone or that the title of community property held in some other title form shall be reformed to reflect its community character…" It is somewhat unclear whether this remedy is allowed in Louisiana. *Thigpen*, below, indicates that the add-a-name remedy may not be available in Louisiana. However, *Thigpen* was decided under pre-revision matrimonial regimes laws and its continued impact has not been considered in much depth. *Auger*, below, distinguishes *Thigpen* and suggests that annulment of a transaction may be appropriate in some circumstances. *Auger* is also decided under prior law and falls short of addressing the availability of the add-a-name remedy.

C. *Carol J. Aymond, Jr. v. Donna D. Aymond*

758 So. 2d 886 (La. App. 3d Cir. 2000)

THIBODEAUX, Judge.

Carol J. Aymond, Jr. and Donna D. Aymond appeal a judgment of the trial court which partitioned the community of acquets and gains which existed between them. Both parties assert several assignments of error. We amend and affirm the trial court's judgment and remand for a supplemental partition, if necessary, of community income received by Mr. Aymond in 1998.

I.

ISSUES

Carol Aymond asks that we consider:

Whether the trial court erred in failing to reimburse him for penalties in the amount of $18,892.70 which were incurred by the community for Mrs. Aymond's early withdrawal of certificates of deposit.

II.

FACTS

Carol J. Aymond, Jr. and Donna Aymond were married in 1967 and lived together until about April 17, 1996, when Donna Aymond left their matrimonial domicile in Avoyelles Parish. Two children, Jaimie and Chantel, who have attained the age of majority, were born to this marriage. Throughout the marriage, Mrs. Aymond was a housewife and Mr. Aymond was and continues to be an attorney and a farmer.

The Aymonds accumulated a vast amount of community property which consisted of real estate, certificates of deposit, cattle, coins and other movable items. On June 26, 1996, Mrs. Aymond secured a judgment for alimony pendente lite in the amount of $4,500.00 per month, cash payment, continuation and payment of a hospitalization policy, and the payment of car insurance on her automobile, as well as the use of a 1996 Lincoln. On September 15, 1996, Mrs. Aymond filed a Petition for Partition of Community Property. Each party filed Detailed Descriptive Lists of Property and each party traversed the list of the other. Experts were appointed by the court to appraise certain described items of community property. Mr. Aymond claimed that upon Mrs. Aymond's departure from the matrimonial domicile, she prematurely cashed in community certificates of deposit (CD's) in the name of both parties in an amount of over a half million dollars. Mr. Aymond filed for a Separation of Property on November 22, 1996, claiming mismanagement and fraud by Mrs. Aymond. The court granted the Separation of Property Judgment which terminated the community of acquets and gains effective April 19, 1996. On January 27, 1999, a trial on the merits of the Partition was held and judgment was rendered.

Carol J. Aymond, Jr. and Donna D. Aymond both appeal the trial court's judgment.

III.

LAW AND DISCUSSION
Standard of Review

A court of appeal may not set aside a trial court's factual findings unless clearly wrong or manifestly erroneous. *Rosell v. ESCO*, 549 So.2d 840 (La. 1989). The following two- tier test exists for appellate review of facts: 1) whether there is a reasonable factual basis in the record for the finding of the trial court, and 2) whether the record establishes that the finding is not manifestly erroneous. *Mart v. Hill*, 505 So.2d 1120, 1127 (La. 1987). If a reasonable factual basis exists, an appellate court may set aside a trial court's factual finding only if after reviewing the record in its entirety, it determines the trial court's finding was clearly wrong. *Stobart v. State, Through Dep't of Transp.*, 617 So.2d 880, 882 (La. 1993).

Penalties for Early Withdrawal of Certificates of Deposit (CD's)

Mr. Aymond argues that the trial court erred in failing to reimburse him for penalties in the amount of $18,892.70 which were incurred by the community for Mrs. Aymond's early withdrawal of numerous CD's. Mr. Aymond alleges Mrs. Aymond committed fraud and was in bad faith in so doing.

La. Civ. Code art.1953 defines fraud as, "a misrepresentation or a suppression of the truth made with the intention either to obtain an unjust advantage for one party or to cause a loss of convenience to the other. Fraud may also result from silence or inaction." Based on this forthright definition and the evidence produced from the record, we do not find that Mrs. Aymond defrauded the community.

Although Mrs. Aymond's actions were somewhat ill- advised, we do not find they were fraudulent. Mrs. Aymond was a housewife of several years who had no gainful employment to generate income. We agree with the trial court that Mrs. Aymond was simply attempting to maintain various funds for her support. Penalties were incurred; however, they are not recoverable absent a showing of fraud. La.Civ.Code art. 2354 maintains that, "[a] spouse is liable for any loss or damage caused by fraud or bad faith in the management of the community property." The trial court found neither fraud nor bad faith in this case. This finding is reasonable. Therefore, Mr. Aymond was appropriately denied reimbursement for penalties on early withdrawal of the certificates of deposit.

AMENDED AND, AS AMENDED, AFFIRMED. REMANDED FOR A DETERMINATION OF 1998 COMMUNITY INCOME, IF NECESSARY.

D. Note

In *Cabral v. Cabral*, 543 So.2d 952 (La.App. 5th Cir. 1989), *writ denied*, 548 So.2d 328, a real estate investment produced substantial losses and large community debts. The wife argued that the losses resulted from the husband's fraud or bad faith. The court disagreed: "Although he admitted that he might have been more attentive in managing the project, the trial judge correctly noted that Mr. Cabral also invested during the marriage substantial separate funds to reduce the extreme difficulty into which the community had fallen because of the high interest rates prevailing at the time. We further agree with the trial judge's conclusion that there was simply no evidence to show that Mr. Cabral continued to impoverish the community or to take advantage of it in any way."

In *Pellerin v. Pellerin*, 550 So.2d 1250 (La. App. 4th Cir.1989), the wife claimed that her husband caused the corporation he controlled to unreasonably withhold dividends on common stock which would have been community. The court disagreed, concluding that it was typical for such small family corporations not to pay dividends on common shares. Also, the company retained liquid assets because of exposure to two lawsuits. The wife "failed to show that [the company's refusal to pay dividends] was capricious or retained to deprive the community."

In *Landry v. Landry*, 610 So.2d 1045 (La. App. 3d Cir. 1992), a husband received 110,000 shares of stock as compensation for his work for a small corporation. Apparently after some shares had been issued, but before others were, the employer proposed and the husband signed a restrictive agreement that provided that if the employee separated from his wife or left the company, the company could repurchase all the stock for ten cents per share for each year of employment with the company. "When presented with the agreement, defendant took it home and discussed it with plaintiff. She was fully aware of the terms of the agreement and only requested that defendant try to get an unrelated provision changed ... before he signed it. Defendant had the provision changed and then signed the document."

There was no suggestion that the changes in the restrictions were proposed by the husband or for his benefit. Presumably it was a device for the company to insulate itself from the domestic problems of its employees and to encourage the employees to stay with the company. There was no showing that the husband, upon the company exercising its rights, unfairly benefitted. The money produced by the repurchase was a community asset subject to partition. The court was implicitly concluding that execution of such agreements, at least with the spouse's knowledge and apparent failure to object, was not sufficient to constitute fraud or bad faith management.

Indeed, though not discussed, there was no indication of any damage suffered by the wife. She claimed to be damaged to the extent of the difference in the amount received and the market value of the stock. But it would be difficult to prove the value of stock subject to such restrictive transfer agreements. Perhaps fraud or bad faith could be involved if it could be shown that such agreements triggered by divorces would be used to harm the interest of the nonemployee while granting the employee some other, perhaps disguised, increased benefits.

In *Landry*, marital difficulties resulted in the husband not being in possession of the stock certificates and he was apparently unable to obtain them from plaintiff. The corporation then canceled those certificates in the husband's name and reissued them. At that point, the husband turned in those new certificates and received $88,000. The proceeds were invested by the husband in a certificate of deposit in the names of both parties. However, he did not tell the wife of the repurchase or the existence of the CD. The court found that it was not fraud or bad faith for the husband to fail to tell her about the events. "Failure to disclose this transaction to plaintiff simply does not amount to fraud or bad faith by the defendant."

E. *Frances Page Thigpen v. Pooler B. Thigpen, Sr.*

91 So. 2d 12 (La. 1956)

McCALEB, Justice.

This case involves a settlement of the community of acquets and gains formerly existing between plaintiff, Mrs. Frances Page Thigpen, and her husband, Pooler B. Thigpen, Sr., one of the defendants, the community having been dissolved as of May 7, 1952, by a decree of separation from bed and board.

The principal issue in the case concerns a transfer from defendant to his son, Pooler B. Thigpen, Jr., of all the real property owned by the community which existed between plaintiff and defendant, along with the attendant crops, cattle and farm equipment. This transfer, made by authentic act on June 27, 1951, was for a recited consideration of $31,000 of which $1,000 was paid in cash and the balance represented by 15 promissory notes, each for the sum of $2,000, payable over a period of 15 years. The purported sale was made subject to a balance of $8,004.31 owing on a chattel mortgage on the cattle granted by defendant in favor of the Tallulah Production Credit Association in the principal amount of $10,000.

Plaintiff seeks to have the sale set aside as a simulation or, in the alternative, that she be decreed the owner of one-half of said property, alleging that the transfer was made in fraud of her vested rights in the community. The trial judge held for defendant on this issue, finding the sale to be neither a simulation nor in fraud of plaintiff's rights.

Before addressing ourselves to the legal problems presented it is necessary to delve somewhat into the backgrounds of the parties involved up to June 27, 1951, the date of the alleged sale.

Defendant was first married to Delia Lancaster, which marriage was terminated by the latter's death. Two children were born of this marriage, one of whom, Pooler B. Thigpen, Jr., is a co-defendant in the instant suit, being the vendee in the purported sale of June 27, 1951.

In 1938, after the death of his first wife, defendant married plaintiff and three children were born of this union. It was during this marriage that defendant purchased three tracts of land in Madison Parish, Louisiana, totaling some 494 acres, that were purportedly sold to his son on June 27, 1951. The largest of these tracts, known as Enoka Plantation, was purchased in 1942 and the parties established the matrimonial domicile on this property, where it remained until their separation.

There is evidence that the relationship between plaintiff and defendant was deteriorating rapidly in the early part of 1951 and, on November 14, 1951, plaintiff filed suit against her husband praying for a separation from bed and board, the custody of their children, $400 per month for maintenance and for an inventory and appraisement of the property and a writ of sequestration. Since both parties in their pleadings in the separation suit made various allegations of misconduct which, if testified to, would have been a source of great humiliation to all concerned, the parties agreed, upon the suggestion of the court, that defendant would secure the separation on the ground of abandonment. His answer was amended accordingly and, on May 7, 1952, judgment was rendered against Mrs. Thigpen decreeing a separation from bed and board.

The record leaves no doubt that the sale under attack was inspired by the hostility between defendant and his wife and we also think that the circumstances surrounding the transaction make the conclusion inescapable that it was his deliberate intent to injure his wife at a time when dissolution of the community estate was imminent. Let us examine these circumstances.

At the time of the sale, defendant's son was an employee of the State Highway Commission and had not theretofore engaged to any great extent in the business of farming. It is evident also that the son had not the financial resources to make such a sizeable purchase, it being shown that his bank account carried only small sums prior to the sale (his largest balance in May, 1951 being $255.65 and in June, $107.59), yet his uncorroborated testimony is that the $1,000 which he gave his father as a cash payment on the purchase price had been kept by him at his residence. After the sale defendant remained in full possession of the homestead and the only change resulting from the transfer was that the son came on the property each day and apparently took over the management of the farming operations. However, defendant continued to exercise some control of these operations, selling, either for his own account or that of his son or for their joint account, an undetermined number of cattle and paying the proceeds from these sales, amounting to approximately $6,000, to Tallulah Production Credit Association, the holder of the chattel mortgage.

Although the sale was by authentic act and timely registered, the wife had no actual notice thereof. Indeed, defendant concealed from plaintiff the fact of the sale for, when she asked him to explain the presence of his son on the plantation, he informed her that he had engaged him "to work for me".

While the foregoing factors stamp the transaction with the badge of fraud and also create a presumption of simulation under Article 2480 of the Civil Code, see Succession of Combre, 217 La. 955, 47 So.2d 734 and Stipe v. Simon, 223 La. 542, 66 So.2d 330, we are unable to sustain plaintiff's primary demand to set aside the sale as defendants have successfully rebutted the presumption of simulation by written and oral evidence revealing a valuable consideration passing to defendant from his son. The sale was by authentic act and one of the witnesses thereto testified that he distinctly remembered the payment of the stated cash consideration of $1,000. In addition, the son gave his father promissory notes in the amount of $30,000 secured by a vendor's lien and special mortgage on the property.

Counsel for plaintiff vigorously assail the reality of the $1,000 cash payment by the son, claiming that defendant actually furnished the money. Whereas the circumstantial evidence tends to support this claim (it being shown that the father made several large withdrawals from the community bank account shortly before the alleged sale and it appearing that the son had not a sufficient amount in his own bank account to supply the $1,000 cash payment), the sale cannot be considered as simulated under the jurisprudence since the son has obligated himself to pay $30,000 in addition, evidenced by promissory notes secured by vendor's lien and special mortgage on the property. Brown v. Brown, 30 La.Ann. 966; Renshaw v. Dowty, 39 La.Ann. 608, 2 So. 58, Peyton v. Roth, 149 La. 147, 88 So. 773; Harman v. Defatta, 182 La. 463, 162 So. 44; Citizens' Bank & Trust Co. v. Willis, 183 La. 127, 162 So. 822 and Succession of Nelson, 224 La. 731, 70 So.2d 665. The notes are presently assets of the community and we feel bound to give recognition to the obligation created by them as real consideration for the transfer.

On the other hand, as we have above indicated, we think it clear that the sale was conceived in fraud by the defendant and deliberately confected for the purpose of injuring plaintiff's interest in the community estate.

In her alternative claim based on fraud, plaintiff asks that we recognize her as owner of an undivided interest in the property in indivision with defendant's son. This we cannot do as the law does not give to a wife, who has sustained injury by a conveyance of community property in fraud of her rights, a right of action for rescission of the transaction--such as the revocatory action available to creditors for the purpose of setting aside the fraudulent conveyances of their debtors.

The only article of our Code granting to a wife a remedy for the injury sustained as the result of a transfer of the community property, such as the one presented here, is Article 2404 which primarily recognizes the right of the husband, as head and master of the community, to administer its effects, dispose of its revenues and alienate them by onerous title without the consent and permission of his wife. It provides, however, that he may not give away the immovables nor even the whole or a quota of the movables except for the establishment of the children of the marriage. The fourth paragraph of the Article reads:

> But if it should be proved that the husband has sold the common property, or otherwise disposed of the same by fraud, to injure his wife, she may have her action against the heirs of her husband, in support of her claim in one-half of the property, on her satisfactorily proving the fraud.

Imprimis, counsel for defendant contend that this provision affords the wife an action against the heirs of the husband only and not against the husband himself.

This contention is without merit. Article 2404 of the present Civil Code can be traced to Article 66 of the Civil Code of 1808, which provided:

> The husband is the head and master of the partnership or community of gains; he administers said effects; disposes of the revenues which they produce, and may sell and even give away the same without the consent and permission of his wife, *because she has no sort of right in them until her husband be dead.*
>
> But if it should be proved that the husband has sold said estate or otherwise disposed of the same by fraud to injure his wife, she may have her action against the heirs of her husband, in support of her claim of one half of said estate, on her satisfactorily proving the fraud" (emphasis supplied).

It is readily seen that this article, the last paragraph of which is virtually identical to the last paragraph of Article 2404 of the present Civil Code (reproduced earlier in this opinion), contemplates the wife having no rights in the community until the death of her husband. However, it has long since been established that the wife has a vested interest in community property at the time it is acquired and is entitled to one-half of the assets of the community at its dissolution, whether it be by death, divorce or judicial separation. Consequently, the only logical view to be accorded Article 2404 is that it gives to the defrauded wife an action against her husband in the event the community is dissolved by divorce or judicial separation. This right was specifically recognized in Oliphint v. Oliphint, 219 La. 781, 54 So.2d 18.

In the case at bar, there is not the slightest doubt of the defendant's intent to injure plaintiff's community interest by selling the land to his son at a time when a dissolution of the community by suit for separation or divorce was imminent. Hence, it remains only to determine whether she has suffered a loss by reason of the sale, that is, whether the consideration given by defendant's son was less than the market value of the property conveyed.

The act of sale specifies the real estate conveyed therein to be valued at $17,290. This means that the herd of cattle and the farm equipment were valued at $31,000 less $17,290, or $13,710.

Plaintiff alleges and testifies that the 99 head of cattle included in the sale had a market value of $16,000 at the time of the transfer. However, this valuation is unsubstantiated and conflicts with an appraisement made in May, 1953, pursuant to a court order, which put a value of $11,730 on 175 head of cattle. Plaintiff asserts that this Court should take judicial cognizance of the fact that the bottom fell out of the cattle market in July of 1952. This, of course, we will not do and, since plaintiff has offered no real proof as to the market value of the cattle or the farm equipment conveyed on June 27, 1951, we are constrained to hold that $13,710 was a fair price for same.

Conversely, we do not feel that $17,290 was an equitable price for the land conveyed.

Enoka Plantation contains 420 acres of black land or buckshot soil, suitable for row crops and pasture. The plantation includes a residence, a large barn and several tenant houses. The value put on Enoka in the appraisement of May, 1953, was $29,400, or $70 per acre.

The three witnesses called by plaintiff to testify as to the market value of Enoka as of June, 1951, gave the following estimates: $28,000, $29,400 and $38,610. Two of these witnesses are to be regarded as experts, having been engaged in the real estate business for many years in the Louisiana- Arkansas-Mississippi River Delta country.

Defendant called three witnesses (two farmers and a banker living in the vicinity) who placed a much lower value on the property. One witness thought it was worth $25 per acre, another estimated $22.50 per acre and the third merely stated that he would not pay as much as $35 per acre for it. Their testimony indicates that the figures given by them were not so much what the market value of this land was in June of 1951 but, rather, what they would pay for it.

After considering the conflicting testimony we are convinced that the market value of Enoka Plantation at the time of the sale was $29,400, the value placed upon it less than two years after the sale by the appraisers appointed in these proceedings, it being our view that the property's value had not appreciably changed since 1951.

As to the other two tracts conveyed, totaling some 74 acres, we are for the same reasons inclined to value it at the figure given by the appraisers. This was $50 per acre, or a total of $3,700.

Accordingly, we find the market value of the property at the time of the conveyance to be $13,710 for the cattle and equipment; $29,400 for Enoka Plantation and $3,700 for the other two tracts, or a total of $46,810. Deduction from this the sum of $31,000 received by defendant leaves a deficiency below market value of $15,810, thus, resulting in a loss to plaintiff of $7,905, which she is entitled to recover from defendant.

F. *Billie Ruth Dykes Auger v. Kenneth Donald Auger*

381 So. 2d 879 (La. App. 2d Cir. 1980)

PRICE, Judge.

Billie Ruth Dykes Auger brought this action against her former husband, Kenneth Donald Auger, seeking to annul the conveyances made by defendant of an undivided interest in several tracts of land which plaintiff contends were made by him prior to their separation with the intent to defraud plaintiff of her community interest in the properties. Pursuant to the sustaining of an exception of no cause or right of action, plaintiff by amended pleadings abandoned her request to annul the sales and sought to recover judgment against defendant for the amount which she contends she was damaged by the alleged fraudulent transfers.

The trial court found defendant executed the conveyances to his father and brother with the intent to reduce plaintiff's community interest and in fraud of her rights. The court awarded her judgment for $13,302.25 which was calculated as being one- half the amount by which the market value of the husband's interest in the several tracts exceeded the consideration recited in the subject conveyances.

Plaintiff appealed and assigned as error the trial court's failure to award her damages based on the full market value of the properties since it was shown no consideration had been paid. By supplemental brief filed after oral argument, plaintiff also questioned the correctness of the trial court's sustaining of the exception of no cause or right of action. The exception was based on the premise that the wife has no right of action to rescind or annul the conveyances by the husband of community property, but must seek redress under La. C.C. Art. 2404 as interpreted by the Supreme Court in Thigpen v. Thigpen, 231 La. 206, 91 So.2d 12 (1956). Thigpen holds that Art. 2404 "vests in the wife by necessary implication a right of action to hold her husband responsible, in an action for settlement of the community property following its dissolution by a judgment of separation from bed and board or divorce; for the losses resulting to her by reason of the husband's sales of the community property during the marriage, disposed of by fraud and with intent to injure her."

Thigpen also holds that ". . . the law does not give to a wife, who has sustained injury by a conveyance of community property in fraud of her rights, a right of action for rescission of the transaction- -such as the revocatory action available to creditors for the purpose of setting aside the fraudulent conveyances of their debtors."

Thigpen does not hold, however, that an action cannot be maintained by the wife to annul a simulated sale where there was no intent to actually divest title and the transaction is a mere sham. A simulated contract has no substance at all and may be declared null at any time at the demand of any person in interest. Spiers v. Davidson, 233 La. 239, 96 So.2d 502 (1957); Williams v. Smith, 340 So.2d 401 (La.App. 2d Cir. 1976).

While the trial court may have misinterpreted Thigpen in sustaining the exception of no cause or right of action, plaintiff nevertheless acquiesced in the ruling of the court and proceeded to try the case under the theory of the Thigpen construction of Art. 2404. We also note that the vendees in the disputed conveyances were not made defendants which would preclude rendition of a valid judgment annulling the transfers in the present posture of the case. Furthermore, the application of Art. 2404 as expanded by Thigpen would appear to afford plaintiff an adequate remedy under the circumstances which have developed in this litigation.

We find no error in the trial court's conclusion that the sales were made in fraud of plaintiff's community rights, but find the calculation of damages by the court to be in error and amend the judgment to increase the award to plaintiff and affirm.

The parties married in June 1963 and physically separated about April 12, 1971. Prior to the plaintiff filing suit for a legal separation on May 5, 1971, defendant conveyed his interest by authentic act in seven tracts of land which had been acquired in indivision with his father, J. A. Auger, and his brother, Don Juan Auger, during the marriage with plaintiff. Six of the conveyances were made to J. A. Auger and Don Juan Auger jointly for recited cash considerations of between $500 and $5,000 which in all total $11,500. The seventh conveyance was to Don Juan Auger for the stated cash consideration of $11,000 and assumption of the balance due on the purchase price of the property transferred.

The plaintiff and defendant were reconciled in January 1972. However, they separated again in September 1972 and plaintiff secured a judgment of separation on January 3, 1973, and ultimately the parties were divorced.

Plaintiff testified that following her reconciliation with defendant in January 1972, he admitted to her that the transactions in question were invalid and were effected for the sole purpose of preventing plaintiff from "getting her part of the property." However, she testified he assured her that since they had resumed their marital relation, title to the properties would be reconveyed to the community. This testimony was substantiated by the testimony of Mrs. Janelle Auger, divorced wife of Don Juan Auger, who stated that defendant divulged to her his plan to place title in his young niece so that plaintiff would be prevented from claiming ownership in these tracts.

Although defendant admits that at the time he executed the transfers he was aware that his marriage was failing, he contends that his sole motive for these conveyances was to simply liquidate part of his indebtedness to his father before the properties became entangled with legal obstacles due to his domestic troubles. His explanation of this indebtedness involves a complicated business relationship existing among defendant, his brother, and father. The three engaged in the purchase and sale of timber and operated a corporation known as "J. A. Auger and Sons." All three were required to co- sign notes of indebtedness on loans from the several banks furnishing operating capital. Prior to the disputed conveyances defendant engaged in several large timber purchases separate and apart from his father and brother. He contends he sustained substantial losses on these ventures and that his father co- signed loans made by him at the Farmerville Bank to cover these losses.

The trial court found that the evidence established a prima facie case that the defendant had deliberately transferred the properties with the intent to reduce his wife's community interest. The court based its conclusion on the following factors: that the parties had experienced marital difficulties and physically separated a few days prior to the dates of the transfers; the filing of a suit for legal separation was imminent; the vendees in the deeds were defendant's closest relatives and business associates; the cash consideration recited in the deeds was admittedly never paid to defendant; no attempt was made to reduce to writing any understanding among the parties as to what specific indebtedness was to be credited with the amounts shown in the deeds; it appeared that arbitrary "round figures" were placed in the deeds as the expressed consideration; and the single most valuable property interest was conveyed to Don Juan Auger alone, who never testified concerning the manner in which the recited cash consideration of $11,000 was to be paid.

We find the evidence amply supports the trial court's conclusion that the transfers were made with deliberate intent to reduce plaintiff's community interest and therefore no manifest error was committed in this regard.

The trial court found the expert testimony to establish a total market value of $52,104.50 for all of the subject properties. Plaintiff does not take issue with this finding on appeal. However, she contends the trial court should have awarded her one- half that value without deducting from that sum the cash consideration recited in the seven deeds as there is no evidence to corroborate J. A. Auger's testimony that he gave defendant credit for these specific amounts on the indebtedness owed to him by defendant. We are constrained to agree with plaintiff's position. Since defendant admits the recited cash considerations were not paid in any of the transactions, the burden is upon him to prove with some degree of certainty the actual consideration on which he relies to support the conveyances.

The record is unclear as to any specific indebtedness which defendant or the community owed to J. A. Auger at the time of the conveyances. The evidence at best shows there was a probability of substantial liability resulting from J. A. Auger being either a co- maker or endorser of loans for defendant. It is not clearly shown that any of the loans were in default at the time of the transfers.

We therefore conclude the trial court erred in deducting the recited amount of cash consideration from the established market value in fixing the amount plaintiff was damaged.

The parties did not bring an action for an accounting and liquidation of the community in this proceeding and when such an action is instituted, defendant will then have an opportunity to establish the full amount of any indebtedness the community actually owes to his father and may make proper claim for an offsetting credit in that proceeding.

The judgment appealed is amended to increase the amount awarded to the sum of $26,052.25 and as amended is affirmed. Costs of this appeal are assessed to defendant.

5.8 ESTOPPEL AND THE PUBLIC RECORDS DOCTRINE

A. Introduction

The doctrine of estoppel and the public records doctrine attempt to strike a balance between the competing concerns of aggrieved spouses and innocent third parties. Louisiana Civil Code article 2342 provides, in part, that:

> A. A declaration in an act of acquisition that things are acquired with separate funds as the separate property of a spouse may be controverted by the other spouse unless he concurred in the act. It may also be controverted by the

forced heirs and the creditors of the spouses, despite the concurrence by the other spouse.

B. Nevertheless, when there has been such a declaration, an alienation, encumbrance, or lease of the thing by onerous title, during the community regime or thereafter, may not be set aside on the ground of the falsity of the declaration.

This article provides a limited estoppel rule that precludes a spouse from later challenging an act of sale or other acquisition that states that the property is to be the separate property of the other spouse. The article only applies where the aggrieved spouse concurred in the transaction. It does not apply, therefore, to a unilateral self-serving declaration by a spouse that he or she is using separate funds and is acquiring property as his or her separate property. Paragraph B offers protection to third parties who acquire an interest in the property by onerous title. It essentially allows a third party to rely on a self-serving unilateral declaration made in the act of acquisition.

Louisiana Revised Statute §35:11 furthers the protection afforded to innocent third parties by providing an exception to the public records doctrine. The public records doctrine usually operates in the negative. Section 35:11, however, allows a third party to rely on statements regarding marital status in some instances.

La. Rev. Stat. § 35:11. Marital status of parties to be given

A. Whenever notaries pass any acts they shall give the marital status of all parties to the act, viz: If either or any party or parties are men, they shall be described as single, married, or widower. If married or widower the christian and family name of wife shall be given. If either or any party or parties are women, they shall be described as single, married or widow. If married or widow, their christian and family name shall be given, adding that she is the wife of or widow of . . . the husband's name.

B. A declaration as to one's marital status in an acquisition of immovable property by the person acquiring the property creates a presumption that the marital status as declared in the act of acquisition is correct and, except as provided in Subsection C of this Section, any subsequent alienation, encumbrance, or lease of the immovable by onerous title shall not be attacked on the ground that the marital status was not as stated in the declaration.

C. Any person may file an action to attack the subsequent alienation, encumbrance, or lease on the ground that the marital status of the party as stated in the initial act of acquisition is false and incorrect; however, such action to attack the alienation, encumbrance, or lease shall not affect any right or rights acquired by a third person acting in good faith.

D. The presumption provided in Subsection B of this Section is hereby declared to be remedial and made retroactive to any alienation, encumbrance, or lease made prior to September 1, 1987. Any person who has a right as provided in Subsection C of this Section, which right has not prescribed or otherwise been extinguished or barred upon September 1, 1987 and who is adversely affected by the provisions of Subsection C of this Section shall have six months from September 1, 1987 to initiate an action to attack the transaction or otherwise be forever barred from exercising his right or cause of action.

B. *Beverly Williams McElwee v. William Tandy McElwee*

255 So. 2d 883 (La. App. 2d Cir. 1972)

PRICE, Judge

The trial court held that a 180 acre tract of land in Section 19, Township 21 North, Range 4 West, Claiborne Parish, Louisiana, was correctly excluded from the inventory of community effects and was properly listed on the schedule of property belonging to the separate estate of Beverly McElwee. This property was originally a part of a 240 acre tract belonging to Beverly McElwee's mother, Mrs. Alice Meadows. Upon being emancipated by marriage, Beverly McElwee, in 1938, filed suit against her mother for a final accounting as natural tutrix. Pursuant to a monetary judgment against Mrs. Meadows, a writ of seizure and sale was issued directing the sale of the 240 acre tract to satisfy the amount owing under the judgment. The property was purchased at the sheriff's sale by John T. Swann, who transferred the property by cash deed dated March 23, 1939, to Beverly McElwee and her two attorneys in the proportion of an undivided three- fourths to Beverly McElwee and one eighth to each attorney. A partition deed was executed on March 30, 1959, wherein the property was divided in kind with 180 acres being conveyed to Beverly W. McElwee and her husband, William Tandy McElwee, Jr. In support of her position that this property was acquired with separate and paraphernal funds for her separate estate, Beverly McElwee presented a certified copy of an instrument bearing the signature of William Tandy McElwee, Jr., in which it is declared by Tandy McElwee that the tract acquired from Swann and subsequently partitioned between Beverly McElwee and her attorneys, was purchased with funds inherited by Beverly McElwee for her separate estate, and that he appeared in the partition deed for convenience only. Tandy McElwee further declared the community had no interest in the property. Although the instrument was prepared for execution before a notary and two witnesses, the authentication was never completed. The first paragraph suggests it was prepared in April, 1959, and the evidence reveals the document was not recorded until after the parties separated.

Tandy McElwee contends the 180 acre tract is presumed to be community property under La.Civ.Code Article 2402 because it was acquired during the marriage. Fortier v. Barry, 111 La. 776, 35 So. 900 (1904); Houghton v. Hall, 177 La. 237, 148 So. 37 (1933); Montgomery v. Bouanchaud, 179 La. 312, 154 So. 8 (1934); Betz v. Riviere, 211 La. 43, 29 So.2d 465 (1947).

This presumption may be rebutted by the wife upon establishing proof of the paraphernality of the funds used for purchase under her separate administration and control, and that the purchase was made for the benefit of her separate estate. The husband is estopped to deny the paraphernal nature of the property where the deed of acquisition recites the property is purchased by the wife for her separate estate, with separate funds under her own administration and control, and the husband executes the instrument acknowledging these facts to be true. Succession of Barr, 219 So.2d 817 (La. App. 2d Cir. 1969).

We think the same rule should extend to an acknowledgment made in a separate instrument executed for this purpose. The Third Circuit Court has so held in the case of Airhart v. Airhart, 153 So.2d 140 (La. App. 3d cir. 1963). It is immaterial that the instrument is not a notarial act insofar as the parties to the immediate transaction are concerned. See Morgan v. Hathaway, 77 So.2d 169 (La. App. 1st Cir. 1954), in which a counter letter was held sufficient on which to base estoppel. We think the evidence is sufficient to establish the genunineness of Tandy McElwee's signature on the instrument. There is no doubt from the evidence that Tandy McElwee understood the significance of the transaction and he does not claim to have executed same through error or as the result of misrepresentation. In fact, in his testimony Tandy McElwee admitted he would have made no claim against this property had Beverly McElwee not claimed an interest in the 740 acre tract in which he contends his ownership therein is his separate property. We find no error in the finding of the trial judge that this property was correctly included on the schedule of separate property belonging to Beverly McElwee.

C. *Succession of C.V. Norwood v. Margaret Cox Curtis Norwood,*

519 So.2d 338 (La. App. 2d Cir. 1988)

SEXTON, Judge.

***

Having concluded that the funds deposited into the separate account were community, it therefore follows that any property purchased with these community funds was community unless Mrs. Norwood can demonstrate otherwise. Although Mr. and Mrs. Norwood specifically declared in the acts of purchase of the various properties that Mrs. Norwood was purchasing them with her separate funds, the heirs are not bound thereby and may controvert such a declaration. LSA-C.C. Art. 2342.

In conclusion, we are of the view that the record does not demonstrate that the trial court was manifestly erroneous in determining that Mrs. Norwood failed to carry the heavy burden required to rebut the presumption that the funds in her "separate checking account" and the property acquired with funds therefrom during the marriage was part of the community estate. We therefore affirm the judgment at appellant's cost.

D. *Elizabeth Langley Camel v. Ellen H. Waller*

526 So. 2d 1086 (La. 1988)

CALOGERO, Justice.

This is a suit for partition by licitation brought by a divorced wife against parties whose chain of title derives from her former husband. She claims to be an owner in indivision of two pieces of immovable property. The properties were purchased by her ex- husband during the marriage and during the existence of a community of acquets and gains. They were sold by him after the community was terminated by judgment of separation from bed and board. In both acquisitions and in the subsequent acts of sale of the two properties the husband declared that he was judicially separated from plaintiff. In fact he and plaintiff were not judicially separated at the time the property was acquired, although they were judicially separated by the time the property was sold.

The immediate parties to the suit (the plaintiff- wife and the current record owners of the property) agreed by stipulation on the issue to be decided in this case:

Does the original plaintiff, Elizabeth Langley Camel, have any ownership interest in either unit number 1 or unit number 4 of the French Quarter Court Condominiums and - - if so - - in what percentage for each unit?

We granted this writ to decide whether the courts below were correct in dismissing plaintiff's suit for partition by licitation of these two pieces of property.

Elizabeth Langley Camel and Patrick Camel were married in East Baton Rouge Parish on June 16, 1962. The couple voluntarily separated on August 16, 1975. On December 29, 1975, Patrick Camel purchased Condominium Unit Number 4 in French Quarter Court located in the City of Baton Rouge from JDA Investment Properties, Inc. for the sum of $25,000.00. In the act of sale he declared that he had been "married but once and then to Elizabeth Langley Camel, born Langley, from whom he is judicially separated", when in truth the couple were still married at the time. On that same day, Patrick Camel and one Ellen H. Waller purchased Condominium Unit Number 1 of French Quarter Court Condominiums for the sum of $26,000.00. In that act of sale,

Patrick Camel similarly declared that he had been "married but once and then to Elizabeth Langley Camel, born Langley, from whom he is judicially separated."

On January 12, 1977, a little over a year after the purchases, Elizabeth Camel filed a petition for separation from bed and board on the grounds of living separate and apart. She asked that a temporary restraining order be granted prohibiting Patrick Camel from alienating, encumbering or disposing of any and all community property. The temporary restraining order was granted on January 25, 1977. A preliminary injunction to the same effect was issued on February 3, 1977. On August 22, 1977, the judgment of separation was granted by default. Neither the temporary restraining order, the preliminary injunction, nor the judgment of separation were ever recorded.

On March 20, 1978, some eight months after the judgment of separation had been granted, Patrick Camel and Ellen Waller sold Unit #1 to William Walker Swyres for $43,000.00. In the act of sale, Patrick Camel accurately declared that he was then judicially separated from Elizabeth Camel.

On March 23, 1978, just three days after the sale of Unit #1 to Squyres, Patrick Camel sold Unit #4 to Ellen Waller for $33,088.82. In this act of sale, Patrick Camel again accurately declared that he was judicially separated from Elizabeth Camel. Ellen Waller remains as owner of Unit #4.

On December 15, 1978 Elizabeth Camel was granted a judgment of divorce. That judgment was recorded on that same date in the Parish of East Baton Rouge.

Some eight months after the judgment of divorce was rendered, William Swyres sold Unit #1 to Karen Jayne Barber and Vaughn Barber on August 23, 1979 for the sum of $56,000.

To date no judicial partition of the community which existed between Patrick and Elizabeth Camel has been effected, nor do the parties contend that there has been a voluntary partition which has settled the couple's rights in these two condominium units.

On December 7, 1983, Elizabeth Camel filed in East Baton Rouge Parish the lawsuit which is the subject of the district court judgment below and this review, a petition for partition by licitation. She alleged that she was the owner of an undivided one fourth interest in Unit #1, in common with the record owners, Karen and Vaughn Barber. She also alleged that she was an undivided one half owner of Unit #4, in common with the record owner, Ellen Waller.

Plaintiff filed a second amended and supplemental petition in which she alleged the bad faith of defendant Ellen Waller in that "she knew or should have known his (Patrick

Camel's) interest in the property was formerly community property . . ." and that plaintiff "owned an undivided interest in the units." These allegations of bad faith were later withdrawn by plaintiff in an additional stipulation of facts.

In the course of this proceeding Ellen Waller moved for summary judgment, as did Karen and Vaughn Barber. Both motions for summary judgment were denied by the trial judge.

The trial judge rendered judgment in response to the stipulated issue, finding that Elizabeth Camel "has no interest whatsoever in either Unit No. 1 or Unit No. 4 of the French Quarter Court Condominiums." Plaintiff's suit was dismissed with prejudice. On appeal the First Circuit Court of Appeal affirmed the trial court's judgment.

A married person's rights in property purchased by the other spouse during the existence of a community vest in that person by operation of law at the time of the acquisition of the property. Thigpen v. Thigpen, 231 La. 206, 91 So. 2d 12 (1957); Phillips v. Phillips, 160 La. 813, 107 So. 584 (1926). Thus, plaintiff, although not a named vendee in her husband's acquisition, acquired an interest in the two condominiums not apparent on the public records at or after the time her husband purchased them.

On the other hand, defendants purchased property on the strength of a public record which was silent regarding plaintiff's interest. The record showed that at the time of the acquisition of the two units Patrick Camel was the vendee and he was judicially separated from Elizabeth Langley Camel. When Patrick Camel and Ellen Waller sold Unit # 1 to William Squyres (who later sold it to defendants Karen and Vaughn Barber) and when Patrick Camel sold Unit # 4 to defendant Ellen Waller, the record reflected the same state of affairs existing then.

Thus, this case pits a plaintiff relying on longstanding legal principles favoring rights in community property against defendants relying on the public records doctrine. The competition between these conflicting legal principles has been noted in various law review articles and cases.

The outset legal question posed by the parties is whether defendant purchasers may rely, to defeat plaintiff's community property rights and relative to the public records doctrine, upon the marital description given by Patrick Camel in the acts by which he acquired the property in dispute. As noted, he had stated that he was judicially separated.

The answer, of course, is that such purchaser cannot rely on that declaration of marital status so as to validate the purchaser's acquisition in preference to the interest of the ex- wife. Succession of James, 147 La. 944, 86 So. 403 (1920); Redmann, 39 Tul. L. Rev. at 500. See also, Gulf Union Mortgage Corp. v. Michael & Barber Construction

Co., 251 So. 2d 459 (La. App. lst Cir. 1971) ("The fact that an instrument is recorded does not have the effect of making all recitals contained therein true." Id. at 462).

The present statutes establishing the public records doctrine are Civil Code article 1839 and La. Rev. Stat. §§ 9:2721 and 2756.

Art. 1839, entitled Transfer of immovable property provides:

A transfer of immovable property must be made by authentic act or act under private signature . . .

An instrument involving immovable property shall have effect against third persons only from the time it is filed for registry in the parish where the property is located.

La. Civ. Code Ann. art. 1839 (West 1987)

La. R.S. 9:2721 provides:

No sale, contract, counter letter, lien, mortgage, judgment, surface lease, oil, gas or mineral lease or other instrument of writing relating to or affecting immovable property shall be binding on or affect third persons or third parties unless and until filed for registry in the office of the parish recorder of the parish where the land or immovable is situated; and neither secret claims or equities nor other matters outside the public records shall be binding on or affect such third parties.

La. Rev. Stat. Ann. § 9:2721 (West 1965).

La. R.S. 9:2756 provides:
All sales, contracts and judgments affecting immovable property, which shall not be so recorded, shall be utterly null and void, except between the parties thereto. The recording may be made at any time, but shall only affect third persons from the time of the recording.

The recording shall have effect from the time when the act is deposited in the proper office, and indorsed by the proper officer.

La. Rev. Stat. Ann. § 9:2756 (West Supp. 1988).

These three statutes, operating in tandem comprise the public records doctrine as it applies here. See also, La. Rev. Stat. Ann. §§ 9:2721- 2733, 2741- 2759 (on Registry) (West 1965 & Supp. 1988).

The public records doctrine is "founded upon our public policy and social purpose of assuring stability of land titles . . . . " Blevins v. Manufacturers Record Publishing Co., 235 La. 708, 772, 105 So. 2d 392, 414 (1958) (Tate, J. on rehearing). But as Justice Lemmon notes, that doctrine does not "create rights in a positive sense, but rather has the negative effect of denying the effectiveness of certain rights unless they are recorded." Phillips v. Parker, 483 So. 2d 972 (La. 1986) (Lemmon, J.) Also, as Judge Redmann has so aptly pointed out, it is an essentially negative doctrine. Third persons are not allowed to rely on what is contained in the public records but can instead "rely . . . on the absence from the public record of those interests that are required to be recorded." Redmann, The Louisiana Law of Recordation: Some Principles and Some Problems, 39 Tul. L. Rev. 491 (1965). Thus, a third party is not protected by reliance on a recitation of marital status in the public records, Succession of James, supra at 944, 86 So. at 403, but can rely on the absence of a claim from the records. State ex rel. Hebert v. Recorder of Mortgages, 175 La. 94, 143 So. 15 (1932); Westwego Canal & Terminal Co. v. Pizanie, 174 La. 1068, 142 So. 691 (1932). "[T]he primary concern of the public records doctrine is the protection of third persons against unrecorded interests." Phillips, 483 So. 2d at 976. "[N]o right of any nature in immovable property can have any effect against third parties unless it is registered in the conveyance records or recorded in the mortgage records for the parish in which the property is situated . . . ." Sarpy, Form in Louisiana Contracts Involving Rights in Property, 14 Tul. L. Rev. 16, 25(1939).

Thus, the public records doctrine in its operative effect in a case of this sort, does not protect a third party purchaser by permitting him to rely upon a prior purchaser's misstated marital status in the latter's acquisition. But as will be recited in the reasons stated hereinafter, that doctrine does serve to protect these third party purchasers in a case like the one under consideration here.

The landmark decision of McDuffie v. Walker established the principle that a third person can acquire valid title from the owner of record even where the record owner is not the true owner since an act of sale of immovable property not recorded is null as to third parties. McDuffie v. Walker, 125 La. 152, 51 So. 100 (1909).

This system of registry, designed to protect the security of title to real estate, stands in stark contrast to La. Civ. Code art. 2452's declaration that "the sale of a thing belonging to another is null". La. Civ. Code Ann. art. 2452 (West 1952).

The right to ownership of property is embedded in our law. La. Const. of 1974, art. 1, § 4; La. Const. of 1921, art. 1, § 2. Yet the public records doctrine has been given effect to the prejudice of the acquiring party where there is an absence of recordation. One type of acquiring party who has drawn special attention in the jurisprudence is the spouse in community. Courts favoring the acquiring spouse who does not appear in a recorded deed have often alluded to the long statutory and jurisprudential legal history that has evolved to ensure the protection of the community property system, e.g.,

Succession of James, 147 La. 944, 86 So. 403 (1920), a system designed to promote the stabilization and economic protection of the family. T.L. James & Co., Inc. v. Montgomery, 332 So. 2d 834, 842 (La. 1975); Daggett, Policy Questions on Marital Property Law in Louisiana, 14 La. L. Rev. 528 (1954).

Also of significant note for the purpose of this opinion is the fact that until the 1979 revision of Book III, Title VI of the Louisiana Civil Code (Matrimonial Regimes) accomplished by 1979 La. Acts, No. 709 (effective Jan. 1, 1980), the marital property law of this state characterized the husband as "head and master" of the community of acquets and gains. Under this scheme, the husband had sole authority to administer community effects and could alienate immovable property belonging to the community without his wife's participation or consent. La. Civ. Code Ann. art. 2404, repealed by 1979 La. Acts, No. 709, § 1 (effective Jan. 1, 1980); Pitre v. Pitre, 247 La. 594, 172 So. 2d 693 (1965); Humphreys v. Royal, 215 La. 567, 41 So. 2d 220 (1949).

In spite of her husband's false declaration in the act of acquisition that he was judicially separated at the time of the purchase (in effect, claiming that the property was his separate property), the property here in dispute is presumed to be community property since it was acquired during the existence of the community and since the act did not contain the required double declaration that he purchased the property with his separate funds and for his separate estate. Smith v. Smith, 230 La. 509, 89 So. 2d 55 (1956); Slaton v. King, 214 La. 89, 36 So.2d 648 (1948); Succession of Bell, 194 La. 274, 193 So. 645 (1940). But even where the presumption of community applies, as here, the husband as head and master of the community was at liberty to sell community property standing in his name alone without his wife's consent. Azar v. Azar, 239 La. 941, 120 So.2d 485 (1960); Provost v. Harrison, 205 La. 21, 16 So. 2d 892 (1944); Demarets v. Demarets, 144 La. 173, 80 So. 240 (1918); Op. Att'y Gen. 1942- 44, p. 472.

It was inevitable that the tenets concerning the matrimonial regime of community property and the public records doctrine, both deeply embedded in this state's legal history, would collide. And of course they did. In Succession of James, 147 La. at 944, 86 So. at 403, this court rejected the argument that the public records doctrine protects the third party mortgagee from the undisclosed interest of a spouse in community, a husband in that case, where the acquiring, and later mortgaging spouse (a wife) declared in both instruments that she was single.

In the interim between the decision in James and the later decision of this Court in Humphreys v. Royal, the James case was cited as authority only rarely and then never in the context of a contest between community property law and the public records doctrine. Johnson v. Johnson, 213 La. 1092, 36 So. 2d 396 (1948); Mathews v. D'Asaro, 14 La. App. 328, 126 So. 246 (1930); Bench and Bar: Trends in Louisiana Law of the Family, 9 La. L. Rev. 89, 100 (1934). However, other decisions reflected the continuing struggle between the two concepts in cases where a claimant's interest in land arose by operation of law on the termination of the community either by dissolution or by the death of one spouse. See, for example, Thompson v. Thompson, 211 La. 468, 30 So. 2d 321 (1947); Stone v. Jefferson, 196 La. 1057, 200 So. 461 (1940); Bell v. Canal Bank & Trust Co., 193 La. 142, 190 So. 359 (1939); Chachere v. Superior Oil Co., 192 La. 193, 187 So. 321 (1939); Porterfield v. Parker, 189 La. 720, 180 So. 498 (1938); Long v. Chailan, 187 La. 507, 175 So. 42 (1937), after remand, 196 La. 380, 199 So. 222 (1940); Beard v. Nunn, 172 La. 155, 133 So. 429 (1931); Otis v. Texas Co., 153 La. 384, 96 So. 1 (1922) (reversed on rehearing).

Then came this court's decision in Humphreys v. Royal, 215 La. 567, 41 So. 2d 220 (1949). The relevant facts were different from those in James. There a husband acquired property during a marriage, declaring in the act of purchase that he was a single man. He then sold, following an unrecorded divorce. But the equities were also different. In Humphreys, it was not the divorced wife who was championing the cause of a wife's rights in community property, but a land speculator who had purchased his interest in the property from the wife.

The majority in Humphreys did not denigrate the wife's legally operative acquisition, but rather distinguished the James decision by stating that a judgment affecting immovable property had not been rendered in James (the James' community terminated upon the death of the vendee- mortgagor, Mrs. James) while a judgment of divorce had been rendered in Humphreys. The Humphreys majority held, without fuller explanation, that an "unrecorded divorce judgment affecting the immovable property in controversy is utterly null and void as to the defendant here, a third party". Id. at 573, 41 So. 2d 222.

That opinion drew a dissent which complained that the settled law until then had resolved the conflict "in favor of the community owner rather than in favor of the one relying on the registry", and that the majority had permitted "the husband in this case, by his false and untrue statements made in the deeds that he was a single man, to take away from the wife her vested interest in the property." The dissenter, alluding also to James, opined that "it is the duty of a person who deals with a purchaser of immovable property to find out whether he or she was married or single at the date of such purchase." Id. at 575- 77, 41 So. 2d at 223 (Hawthorne, J., dissenting).

Humphreys and its legal analysis did not meet with consistent acclaim among the law review writers who discussed the case. See 39 Tul. L. Rev. at 502- 04; 32 Tul. L. Rev. at 677; 24 Tul. L. Rev. at 375; Note, Sales - Effect of Recordation on Community Rights, 11 La. L. Rev. 389 (1951). But cf., 22 La. L. Rev. at 433- 34; 12 La. L. Rev. at 513. But Humphreys was not wrong in its result, as will be seen hereinafter.

The debate on the interplay of community property rights and the public records doctrine continued following the Humphreys pronouncement. Head v. Bradley & Braud, Inc., 368 So. 2d 723 (La. 1979) (Tate, J., dissenting from denial of writs); Hodgeson v. McDaniel, 233 La. 180, 96 So. 2d 481 (1957); Bishop v. Copeland, 222 La. 284, 62 So. 2d 486 (1952); Gregory v. Womack, 300 So. 2d 213 (La. App. 2d Cir.), writ denied, 302 So. 2d 622 (1974) (wife had "ample protection of her rights in the property had she complied with the Louisiana laws relating to registry." Id. at 215.); Speights v. Nance, 142 So. 2d 418 (La. App. 2d Cir. 1962); Shapiro v. Bryan, 132 So. 2d 97 (1961) (wife under duty to record notice of her suit for separation to prevent husband's sale of community property).

The results in these cases indicate that the law in this area is by no means settled. Furthermore, a recent statutory change in the law may affect the outcome of future similar cases. La. R.S. 35:11. We need not consider in this case whether the 1987 amendments to La. R.S. 35:11 are to be afforded retroactive application because plaintiff brought her action well before the six month grace period following the effective date of the statute, in fact, some several years before its enactment.

Compare the action taken by the Legislature here with the proposed resolution in § 9 of the Uniform Marital Property Act. Unif. Marital Property Act, 9A U.L.A. 120 (1987). See also, Wellman, Third Party Interests Under the Uniform Marital Property Act, 21 Houston L. Rev. 717 (1984).]

We perceive Humphreys and the case at bar to be distinguishable from Succession of James, but for reasons different from those stated by the majority in Humphreys. Furthermore, in the context here involved (prior to the 1980 Revision of Civil Code provisions on matrimonial regimes, and unaffected by 1987 statutory amendments to La. R.S. 35:11, we apply the public records doctrine here favorably to the third party purchaser and contrary to the plaintiff, former wife in community.

While the purchaser may not rely on the misstated marital status in Patrick Camel's acquisition (that he was judicially separated and thus acquiring for his separate estate), nonetheless, a third party purchaser we hold, can rely upon the absence from the public record of the instrument which would have signaled that Patrick Camel was no longer in singular control of property which he might have acquired. That instrument was the judgment which terminated the community. Until such instrument was recorded the purchaser could have assumed that Mr. Camel was judicially separated, as he had declared upon acquisition, or single, in which event he could later sell the property without the participation of a wife or ex- wife, or that he was not judicially separated or single but rather married and living in community, and thus had not lost his right as head and master of the community to dispose of community property alone.

Unlike Isiah Payne, the husband in Humphreys, Mary James, the acquiring and later mortgaging "femme sole" in Succession of James, had no power to encumber or alienate community property as wife, for under the prevailing law the wife was not head and master of the community.

"This case (Humphreys v. Royal) is not contrary to the Succession of James. Whereas the wife in the James case had no power to defeat her spouse's vested interest in the community property, the husband in the Humphreys case did have such power, and as far as third parties were concerned recordation of the judgment of divorce, like recordation of a prior sale, was necessary to destroy that power. Article 2266 of the Louisiana Civil Code requires recordation for final judgments as it does for contracts affecting immovable property."

12 La. L. Rev. at 513.

In the case under consideration, Elizabeth Camel acquired an undivided interest, albeit unrecorded, in the two properties. Yet so long as the marriage existed, her interest was subject to being defeated simply by her husband's act of conveying the community interest. Elizabeth Camel could have alerted third party purchasers to the newly acquired right of joint control attending her undivided co- ownership interest by recording her judgment of separation, if not her injunctions, in the parish "where the land or immovable is situated" (in this case the parish of matrimonial domicile - East Baton Rouge Parish). She did not do so. Consequently, "the judgment affecting immovables", that is, a judgment changing the husband's right to convey alone, to a right of joint control, is not "binding on" and does not "affect third persons". La. Rev. Stat. Ann. § 9:2721 (West 1965). In this context Elizabeth Camel's "claim", the right to enjoy joint control of property owned in indivision, which is "outside the public records" "shall [not] be binding on or affect third persons", La. R.S. 9:2721, and indeed, it is "utterly null and void, except between the parties . . . . " La. Rev. Stat. Ann.§ 9:2756 (West Supp. 1988).

Consequently, the absence of the judgment terminating the community, a judgment which created in plaintiff the right to exercise control over formerly community property, permitted third party purchasers to acquire free and clear of her claims the property which her husband as head and master of the community was at liberty to convey alone, absent recorded notice to the contrary.

We hold, in this context, that plaintiff's interest, which could have been cemented by recordation, is defeated because the public records doctrine prevails.

The law is well settled that a third person can acquire a good title to immovable property from the owner of record, even though he has been apprised of the equities or rights of others in the property that did not appear of record, in accordance with the law of registry.

Bell v. Canal Bank & Trust Co. 193 La. 142, 190 So. 359 (1939) (citing, inter alia, Mc Duffie v. Walker, 125 La. 152, 51 So. 100 (1909) (other citations omitted)).

One more noteworthy comment in this case is that recordation of the judgment of divorce after transfer of Unit #1 (Camel and Waller to Squyres) but before the transfer from Squyres to the Barbers does not require a different result regarding plaintiff's claim against the Barbers. Since Squyres was free to rely on the absence of any recorded instrument evidencing Elizabeth Camel's right of control in the property, he acquired the property in preference to plaintiff's interest and was thereafter at liberty to transfer to the Barbers all the rights in the property which he had acquired.

DIXON, C.J., respectfully dissents with reasons.
DENNIS, J., concurs with reasons.
LEMMON, J., concurs.

NOTE

The 1987 Revisions to LA. REV. STAT. §35:11 that were too new to be applied in *Camel v. Waller* further entrench the likelihood that an innocent third party purchaser will prevail in a contest with an innocent spouse. The 1987 revisions added Subsections B, C, and D.

But see McAlister v. Federal Land Bank, 566 So.2d 173 (La. App. 2d Cir. 1990), involved a wife's unilateral declaration in an act of acquisition that the property was her separate asset. The court suggested that this declaration could not be contested by a third person who acquired the property by an onerous title. The case is weak, since it appears the property was probably the wife's separate property in any event.

Compare LA. REV. STAT. ANN. §35:11 to the UMPA's provision on balancing spousal rights with those of third parties:

UNIFORM MARITAL PROPERTY ACT: PROTECTION OF BONA FIDE PURCHASERS

Protection of Bona Fide Purchasers Dealing with Spouses

(a) In this section:

(1) "Bona fide purchaser" means a purchaser of property for value who:

(i) has not knowingly been a party to fraud or illegality affecting the interest of the spouses or other parties to the transaction;

(ii) does not have notice of an adverse claim by a spouse; and

(iii) has acted in the transaction in good faith.

(2) "Purchase" means to acquire property by sale, lease, discount, negotiation, mortgage, pledge, or lien or otherwise to deal with property in a voluntary transaction other than a gift.

(3) A purchaser gives "value" for property acquired:

(i) in return for a binding commitment to extend credit;

(ii) as security for or in total or partial satisfaction of a pre-existing claim;

(iii) by accepting delivery pursuant to a pre-existing contract for purchase; or

(iv) generally, in return for any other consideration sufficient to support a simple contract.

(b) Notice of the existence of a marital property agreement, a marriage, or the termination of a marriage does not affect the status of a purchaser as a bona fide purchaser.

(c) Marital property purchased by a bona fide purchaser from a spouse having the right to manage and control the property under Section 5 is acquired free of any claim of the other spouse. The effect of this subsection may not be varied by a marital property agreement.

CHAPTER 6: DEBTS OF THE SPOUSES

6.1 INTRODUCTION

A. Introduction

Today, the community property jurisdictions take one of two approaches in determining a creditor's ability to seize community property in satisfaction of a debt. Under the community debt system, the property available for seizure by a creditor depends on the classification of the debt. Community debts and obligations may be satisfied from community property. There is some variation among the states applying this system with respect to what property is available to a creditor of a separate debt. Arizona, Washington, New Mexico, and Wisconsin use this approach. Under the managerial system, the property that a spouse manages is obligated for his debts regardless of the purpose of his debts. In an equal management jurisdiction, like Louisiana, this means that all of a spouse's separate property and all of the community property is liable for his debts. The rationale behind the managerial system is that any property that the debtor-spouse could have used voluntarily to hay his debt should be subject to seizure by the creditor. Louisiana, Texas, California, Idaho, and Nevada have all adopted some variation of the managerial system.

B. Pre-1980 Regime in Louisiana

Before 1980, the only statutory provision which directly governed debts provided that debts contracted during the existence of a community regime must be "acquitted out of the common fund" and those contracted after termination of the regime from the separate property of the incurring spouse. No distinction was made in the article as to whether the debt was contracted by the husband or the wife. However, the Civil Code designated the husband as head and master of the community, with the power to administer its effects and dispose of the revenues and assets by onerous title, without the consent of his wife. By virtue of the power invested in the husband under the head and master scheme, the jurisprudence accepted the proposition that community property fell within the husband's patrimony. Thus, if the husband incurred a debt, his creditors could seek satisfaction from the community property and his separate property. The wife, on the other hand, had a patrimony which consisted of her separate property and, as of 1975, her earnings (community property). Thus, a creditor of the wife could seize only her separate property and her earnings in satisfaction of his debt.

Because a creditor of the wife was restricted in the seizure of community assets, the jurisprudence, relying on general principles of law, recognized that in some cases the wife who incurred an obligation bound her husband and his patrimony. Under Civil Code Article 131, if the wife were a "public merchant", defined as carrying on a separate trade, she could obligate herself in anything relating to her trade "and in such case, her husband is bound also, if there exists a community of property between them." Later jurisprudence held the husband responsible even if he did not consent to the wife's acting as a public merchant, because the earnings of the wife constituted community property. This provision was the only statute imposing liability upon the husband for a debt incurred by the wife on the basis of living under a regime of community property.

Louisiana courts, in the mid-twentieth century, developed doctrines to expand the wife's ability to manage community assets and incur debts on behalf of her husband. This was a reflection of the common practices of married couples as wives became more active in running the household as well as in being an income earner. Indeed, it was suggested that modern practices in which the wife was more often than not the shopper and the check writer may have established a custom which granted her greater powers. Informal tolerance of the wife contracting debts, the use of joint checking and credit card accounts, the practice of paying debts incurred by the wife, and similar actions were construed to be sufficient grounds from which third persons could infer that the husband had authorized the wife to act for him.

First, if the wife were acting as her husband's mandatary, by virtue of an express or implied mandate, her husband as principal would be bound. The wife, on the other hand, as mandatary was only bound if she indicated an intention to be bound. Secondly, the jurisprudence recognized a customary mandate between the husband and the wife such that she could contract for necessaries and bind him if he failed to provide them. Some authors offered the opinion that the customary mandate, arguably a version of inherent authority, was legally supported not by pure consential mandate principles but in fact by principles of negotiorum gestio. Thus, the husband's "affair" to be managed by the gestor, was his legal obligation to support his wife. The wife or a third person might act as gestor in instances where the intervention was appropriate. Thirdly, the jurisprudence recognized that if the husband knew of the wife's transactions and did nothing to repudiate them, he was deemed to have ratified her acts. Although the last instance in which liability was imposed upon the husband adopted mandate principles of ratification, the jurisprudence never required proof of mandate, other than the relationship of husband and wife, nor required proof that the obligation had been contracted in the name of the husband-principal.

The course of decisions was not linear, of course, and there are problematic references in some cases to the wife being empowered to bind the community, a legal impossibility since the community did not have (and still does not have) a legal personality. More properly, the wife bound the husband who was manager of the community, and as such, his separate property was also bound. Indeed, the agency and mandate principles involved are not unique to the community property regime. The same principles apply to spouses under a separate property regime and to unmarried persons who authorize others to act for them or ratify the actions of others. Another anomaly in the cases was the tendency to bind the husband even if the wife did not purport to act in his name but to act for herself.

As to liability for offenses and quasi-offenses, the jurisprudence developed the "community mission" doctrine to hold the husband responsible for torts committed by his wife. If the husband expressly or impliedly authorized the act by the wife which ultimately caused the damage, the husband was liable to the victim if the wife was on a "community mission." "Community mission" was defined as "the *legitimate* pursuits of the wife, whether for wholesale recreation and pleasure or for other purposes consonant with the intangible and imponderable obligations of the marital relationship. . ." The closest parallel under principles of vicarious tort liability is the responsibility of the employer or master for torts committed by his employee or servant in the course and scope of his employment. Since the wife's patrimony consisted almost exclusively of her separate property, failure to articulate with precision the basis of the "community mission" doctrine under general tort principles was excusable. The victim of a tortious act committed by a married woman was assured recovery from all community property, not just her earnings.

Though the 1980 Revision does not expressly repudiate these expanded agency and mandate doctrines, it implicitly repudiates them. The new principles of asset management adopted under the revision make the former doctrines unnecessary and provide a more direct solution to the problem. Comment (b) to Civil Code Article 2346 states directly, "This provision does not make each spouse mandatary of the other. A spouse who contracts with a third person. . .does not obligate the separate property of the other spouse." It appears that the better view is that the expansion of the implied authorization and implied ratification concepts should be restricted and not carried over into the new law.

In any event, the scope of the inquiry as to the spouses' powers under the new legislation is more precise than under the old. The key is no longer the factually-centered inquiry of making inferences about the authority of the wife based on the husband's conduct. The inquiry is the legal issue of determining what powers are granted by the code to the spouses. One can perhaps argue that once a spouse is disabled from acting in a particular transaction, as when the other is the exclusive manager, it might be appropriate to determine if the manager authorized the other spouse to act as an agent. But here again, the old cases expanding the concept of authorization to act should not be readily followed under the new scheme with new policy concerns and a new focus.

C. Post-1980 Regime in Louisiana

Under the new (post-1980) debt legislation, the nearly exclusive focus of the inquiry should be directed at the identity of the incurring spouse. Regardless of whether an obligation is separate or community, Louisiana Civil Code articles 2345 and 2357 allow creditors access to the entirety of the community property and to the separate property of the incurring spouse. Article 2345 explains that "[a] separate or community obligation may be satisfied during the community property regimes from community property and from the separate property of the spouse who incurred the obligation." Article 2357 imposes a similar rule following the termination of the community property regime: "An obligation incurred by a spouse before or during the community property regime may be satisfied after termination of the regime from the property of the former community and from the separate property of the spouse who incurred the obligation." Generally, the only property that is exempt from seizure under the Revision is the separate property of the non-incurring spouse.

Louisiana courts, however, have had a difficult time adjusting to these changes in the law, as evidenced by the following series of cases. Some of this confusion probably stems from inconsistencies between the substantive laws of Articles 2345 and 2357 and the procedural rules contained in Articles 686 and 735 of the Louisiana Code of Civil Procedure.

6.2 CONTRACTUAL OBLIGATIONS

A. *First Security Bank and Trust Company v. Bobbie K. Dooley*

480 So.2d 842 (La. App. 2d Cir. 1985)

NORRIS, Judge

This is a suit for default on two promissory notes. The plaintiff, First Security Bank & Trust Company, sued the maker of the notes, Bobbie, K. Dooley and her husband, Vol Dooley. The trial court awarded judgment for the plaintiff against Bobbie K. Dooley individually and against Bobbie K. Dooley and Vol Dooley, in their capacity as owners, co-partners and managers of the community in existence at the time the obligations were incurred. Defendant, Vol Dooley, appeals asserting he should not be held individually liable for debts incurred solely by his wife without his knowledge, consent, or authority.

FACTS

Defendant, Bobbie K. Dooley, borrowed money on two occasions from First

Security Bank & Trust Company and executed two unsecured promissory notes to evidence the debts. The first note was executed on August 22, 1983 for the principal sum of $7,828.14. The second note was executed on September 15, 1983 for the principal sum of $2,083.97. The parties have stipulated that the Dooleys were married and living together at the time the notes were executed. However, the parties physically separated in late October of 1983. Mrs. Dooley filed a suit for legal separation against her husband on January 9, 1984. The instant collection action was filed on June 15, 1984 and consolidated for trial with the separation suit. Bobbie K. Dooley, filed a third party demand against her husband claiming that if she was held liable on the notes, then he should be held responsible for one- half of the judgment since the notes were a community obligation. Vol Dooley filed an exception of no right and/or no cause of action to his wife's third party demand claiming that the obligations sued on were not community obligations and alternatively, he claimed that she had no cause or, right of action under Louisiana law to seek a judgment against him.

The trial court found the two notes were signed by Bobbie K. Dooley without the knowledge, consent or authority of her husband. However, the trial court ultimately found the debts were incurred for the common interest of the community and were, therefore, a community obligation. Accordingly, the lower court awarded judgment against Bobbie K. Dooley individually, and against Bobbie K. Dooley and Vol Dooley as co- owners of the community in existence at the time the obligations evidenced by the notes were incurred.

DISCUSSION

Vol S. Dooley appeals the trial court's ruling asserting that he should not be held individually liable on the two notes. He initially argues that the notes are not community obligations under LSA- C.C. art. 2360. Alternatively, he argues that if the notes are community obligations, there should be no individual or personal liability on his part.

Appellant's initial argument that the notes are not community obligations rests upon two separate theories. First, Mr. Dooley contends that since the loans were made without his permission, authority, or knowledge they are not community obligations. We disagree. Under LSA art. 2346, either spouse, acting alone may manage, control, or dispose of community property unless otherwise provided by law. Comment (a) to article 2346 states:

> This provision establishes the principle of equal management of community property. Each spouse has the right to manage community property *without the consent or concurrence of the other spouse* unless otherwise provided by law (emphasis added)

The exceptions specifically provided by law are then set forth in the following article, LSA- C.C. art. 2347, none of which apply to the instant case. Thus, by law, Bobbie K. Dooley had the managerial authority to incur a community obligation, notwithstanding the lack of her husband's consent or concurrence.

Secondly, Mr. Dooley contends that the notes do not represent a community obligation because they were incurred neither for the common interest of the spouses nor solely for his interest alone. As noted above, the trial court found the loans were incurred for the common interest of the spouses. This being a factual determination it will not be disturbed on appeal in the absence of manifest error. Arceneaux v. Domingue, 365 So.2d 1330 (La. 1978).

The weight of the evidence presented in the instant case indicates that the loans were incurred for the common interest of the spouses. Mrs. Dooley testified that the proceeds of the loans were spent on home improvements. The fact that the Dooley home was extensively renovated before the parties physically separated was clearly established by testimony and photographs. Mr. Dooley himself admitted that considerable sums were spent on home improvement. Both parties obviously benefitted by the improvements which cost between $12,000 and $16,000. Mr. Dooley was aware of these improvements, participated in the selection of certain items, lived in the home after the improvements were made, and particularly enjoyed the new jacuzzi his wife had installed. Based upon the evidence presented, we do not find the trial court was manifestly erroneous in finding that the loans were incurred for the common interest of the spouses, and thus were community obligations.

We recognize that the trial court found that a part of the proceeds was spent on a major son's education. However, this expenditure, standing alone, does not affect the status of the loans as community obligations. LSA- C.C. art. 2361 creates the presumption that all obligations incurred during the existence of the community are community obligations, except as provided by LSA- C.C. art. 2363. Article 2363 provides in pertinent part:

> A separate obligation of a spouse is one incurred by that spouse prior to the establishment or after termination of a community property regime, *or one incurred during the existence of a community regime though not for the common interest of the spouses or for the interest of the other spouse* (emphasis added).

The community character of the instant loan obligations is not affected by the expenditure for the major son because according to the evidence this expenditure was for the common interest of the spouses. Mr. Dooley testified that he would "have no complaint" about his wife doing anything for their children. Even if Mr. Dooley was unaware of his wife actually providing financial assistance to their children, he did not oppose such assistance. Thus, he had a common interest in such expenditures. His wife's action in utilizing a portion of the loan proceeds for this purpose merely relieved him of the need to act.

Secondly, even assuming arguendo that obligations incurred to aid major children are not for the common interest of the spouses, we conclude that Mr. Dooley failed to overcome the presumption of community indebtedness. LSA- C.C. art. 2361. While part of the loan proceeds in the instant case may have been spent on a major son, there is no indication of how much was spent for this purpose. On the contrary, the weight of the evidence suggests that most of the loan money was spent for the intended purpose, home improvements. Thus, in the absence of any showing that a specific amount was used to aid the major child, we find the lower court did not err in concluding that Mr. Dooley failed to overcome the article 2361 presumption.

Since we have concluded the trial court did not err in finding the two notes to be community obligations, we now address the extent of Mr. Dooley's liability.

The trial court held Mrs. Dooley individually liable and both Mr. and Mrs. Dooley liable as co- owners of the community property regime in existence at the time the debts were incurred. In reaching this result the trial court utilized LSA- C.C. art 2345, which provides for satisfaction of obligations during community. We do not find the trial court was in error in its application of the law. However, if there is a final judgment in the consolidated separation suit before the subject notes are satisfied, then the governing authority will be LSA- C.C. art. 2357, which provides for satisfaction of obligations after termination of the community. Under either article the result in the instant case remains the same. Mrs. Dooley is liable both individually and as a co- partner and/or owner of the community, since she is the spouse who incurred the obligations. The debts may be satisfied from her separate property or from her interest in the community. Mr. Dooley, on the other hand, is only liable up to the "value" of his interest in the former "community. See Spaht and Samuels, Equal Management Revisited, 40 La.L.Rev:, 83, 126 (1979); and Bridgeman & Conway v. Korner Realty Co., 405 So.2d 344 (La.App. 4th Cir.1981).

Finally, Mr. Dooley claims that the trial court overruled his exception of no right and/or cause of action and requests that we reverse that ruling. It does not appear, however, that the lower court overruled Mr. Dooley's exception. In fact, the judgment below is silent with regard to Mrs. Dooley's third party demand. This silence constitutes a rejection of that demand in the absence of a special reservation. Guaranty Bank & Trust Co. v. Carter, 394 So.2d 701 (La.App. 3d Cir.1981); Marshall v. Greater New Orleans Expressway, 372 So.2d 724 (La.App. 4th Cir. 1979), and cases cited therein. There being no express reservation in the judgment, Mrs. Dooley's third party demand is considered as having been rejected by the trial court. This rejection has the same effect as sustaining Mr. Dooley's exception. Mrs. Dooley has not appealed. Therefore, the judgment dismissing her third party demand is final and not before this court. *Guaranty Bank*, supra 394 So.2d at 702.

For the reasons hereinabove expressed, paragraphs 3 and 4 of the lower court's judgment are amended to clarify the extent of appellant's liability as follows:

IT IS THEREFORE ORDERED, ADJUDGED AND DECREED that there be judgment herein in favor of plaintiff, First Security Bank and Trust Company, and against Bobbie K. Dooley, individually and against Bobbie K. Dooley and Vol S. Dooley in their capacity as owners, co- partners and managers of the community of acquets and gains that was in existence between them at the time the obligations were incurred, with Vol S. Dooley's liability being limited to the extent of his interest in the community property pursuant to LSA- C.C. art. 2357, on note one in the full and true sum of $8,479.62, together with judicial interest from date of judicial demand until paid for all costs of this proceeding.

B. *R. Hunter Bridges, III v. Milton Osborne*

525 So.2d 337 (La. App. 1st Cir. 1988)

LANIER, Judge.

This action commenced as a sui for collection of the open account balance due on an oral contract to paint and repair one- half of a duplex apartment house and for the attorney fee authorized by La.R.S. 9:2781. The defendant husband filed an answer in which he denied owing the debt and reconvened against the plaintiffs asserting a tort claim for damages for malicious prosecution. On the day of trial, the defendant wife filed a single pleading containing a dilatory exception raising the objections of vagueness and prematurity and an answer. The trial court rendered judgment from the bench in favor of the plaintiffs and against the husband and wife for $1,178.40, with legal interest thereon from date of judicial demand until paid, an attorney fee of 25 % of the principal and interest due, and all costs, subject to a credit of $200 paid after suit was filed. This suspensive appeal was taken by the husband.

FACTS

In October of 1985, TradeMasters Maintenance and Repair Service (TradeMasters) was hired by the owner (a Mrs. Willis) of one- half of a duplex located at 1416 Sharlo Avenue in Baton Rouge, Louisiana, to paint her half of the building. TradeMasters is a trade name used by R. Hunter Bridges, III and his wife, Kandi O. Bridges. Hunter Bridges contacted Mrs. Yvonne Osborne about painting the other one- half of the duplex. Mrs. Yvonne Osborne is married to Milton Osborne, Jr. TradeMasters subsequently was hired to paint the Osborne one- half of the duplex. During the painting, some repairs were done, and the total cost of painting and repair of the Osborne one- half of the duplex was $1,478.40. The work on the Osborne one- half was completed on October 27, 1985, and a billing for this work was sent out on October 28, 1985, payable by November 4, 1985.

When this bill was not timely paid, Kandi Bridges called Yvonne Osborne to discuss payment. Mrs. Osborne advised she could not pay the bill in full. Mrs. Bridges and Mrs. Osborne agreed that one- half of the bill would be paid in November of 1985 and the other one- half would be paid in December of 1985. Mrs. Bridges sent out a second billing dated November 14, 1985, which stated the following: "If you wish to pay 2 of bill, then please pay $739.20 no later than Nov. 27. A balance of $739.20 will be due no later than Dec. 11."

On December 4, 1985, TradeMasters received $300 along with a copy of the November 14, 1985 billing which had the following written on it:

$300 Enclosed

Will send balance ASAP

Thank you

Yvonne Osborne

On December 6, 1985, TradeMasters sent out a third billing which gave credit for the $300 payment and stated "[b]alance due no later than December 14, 1985."

No payment was made by December 14, 1985. On December 18, 1985, the attorney for TradeMasters made demand by certified mail for payment within fifteen days. This suit was filed on January 16, 1986. TradeMasters received a $200 payment on January 30, 1986.

Only Mr. Osborne appealed the judgment of the trial court. Mrs. Osborne did not appeal, and the judgments of the trial court against her are final, definitive and executory. Mr. Osborne individually has no standing to complain on appeal about judgments adverse to Mrs. Osborne.

LIABILITY OF HUSBAND (OR WIFE) FOR COST OF PAINTING AND REPAIR OF HIS (OR HER) SPOUSE'S SEPARATELY OWNED IMMOVABLE RENTAL PROPERTY

Mr. Osborne contends the trial court committed error by finding him liable for the cost of the painting and repair work performed by TradeMasters. Mr. Osborne cites

La.C.C. arts. 2363 and 2360 and asserts the following:

At the outset it should be noted that there is not a scintilla of evidence in the record to show that Appellants were married at the time the obligation involved herein was incurred. Furthermore, even if the Court was justified in implicitly finding that Appellants were married at the time of the obligation, there was no evidence to prove that the obligation was incurred for the common interest of Appellants or for the interest of Appellant MILTON OSBORNE.

For an obligation to be a community obligation it must have been incurred during the existence of a community property regime pursuant to Article 2360. In this case, there was no evidence of there being a community property regime at the time the obligation was incurred. Moreover, there was no evidence that the obligation was for Appellants, common interest or for the interest of Appellant MILTON OSBORNE. Therefore, the Court erred in finding MILTON OSBORNE liable for the debt involved herein.

Mr. Osborne testified he was married to Mrs. Osborne in 1981. On cross- examination, Mr. Osborne admitted he was married to Yvonne Osborne at the time of trial (October 20, 1986). Mr. Osborne was not questioned about the status of this marriage at the time the obligation to repair and paint the duplex was incurred in October of 1985. However, Mr. Bridges gave the following testimony:

Q. Okay . . . when did - - what was the arrangement, if any, that you came up with with Mrs. Osborne?

A. Okay, I called Mrs. Osborne. I told them I needed - - I was going to paint the duplex.

Q. Whose duplex?

A. Mrs. Willis' duplex.

Q. Okay.

A. But I couldn't see having a half painted duplex so I called Mrs. Osborne and said, "Look," I said, "I'm going to paint Mrs. Willis' duplex." I said, "Do you want your half painted?" She said, "Wait just a minute. I'll get back with you. I'm going to talk to my husband."

Q. Okay.

A. That's the very words that she said. She called me back and said, "Yes, go ahead." I stated a price.

Q. Did she tell you who her husband was?

A.No, she didn't.

Q. So again you did not talk to Mr. Osborne not one time, right? Had no dealing whatsoever with him; is that correct?

> A. No.
>
> Q. Okay.
>
> A. But I must point out that she did get - - try - - she did point out and say that she has to get back - - that she'll get back with me, she'll talk to her husband.
>
> Q. Was there any reason for suing Mr. Osborne? Why did you sue Mr. Osborne?
>
> A. Joint ownership.
>
> Q. Do you have any proof of that being a joint ownership?
>
> A. No. What - - how - - what proof should I have? The only proof I've got is what she said: "I'll have to speak to my husband first and then I'll get back with you."

We believe it reasonably can be inferred from these facts that Mr. and Mrs. Osborne were married in October of 1985 and were not separated or divorced.

Nature of Ownership of One - Half Interest in Duplex

As previously indicated, Mr. Bridges testified he assumed the duplex was jointly owned because Mr. and Mrs. Osborne were husband and wife. The plaintiffs introduced no documentary evidence to show the property was community property. Mr. Osborne testified Mrs. Osborne acquired her interest in the property in 1974 or 1975, that he and Mrs. Osborne were married in 1981 and that the duplex was Mrs. Osborne's separate property. Mr. Osborne introduced no documentary evidence to show the duplex was separate property. Mrs. Osborne did not appear or testify.

The trial court found the duplex was community property with the following rationale:

> Also, this morning while your testimony indicated that it's her separate property, I have no evidence whatsoever to establish that ownership or to prove that it was not community property, or that you did not receive any benefits from the revenues from this property or in any way.

The property of married persons is either community or separate. La.C.C. art. 2335. Generally, community property comprises property acquired during the existence of the marriage, and includes, among other things, rents received from separate property. La.C.C. arts. 2338 and 2339. Separate property comprises, among other things, property acquired by a spouse prior to the establishment of a community property regime. La.C.C. art. 2341. Property in the possession of a spouse during the existence of a regime of community of acquets and gains is presumed to be community, but either spouse may prove that it is separate property. La.C.C. art. 2340. Comment (c) for La.C.C. art. 2340 provides as follows:

The presumption of community under this provision is rebuttable. For example the presumption is rebutted *as to property acquired prior to marriage by evidence establishing the date of acquisition* and as to property inherited during marriage by the judgment of possession.

The presumption of community may be rebutted by parol evidence. Levraea v. Franchina, 499 So.2d 264 (La. App. 1st Cir. 1986); cf. Succession of Erbelding, 509 So.2d 568 (La. App. 3rd Cir. 1987).

Mr. Osborne specifically testified that Mrs. Osborne acquired her interest in the duplex prior to the Osborne marriage. This evidence rebuts the presumption of community by showing a date of acquisition prior to the marriage. We are unable to tell from the trial court's reasons for judgment whether Mr. Osborne's testimony was rejected on credibility grounds or the evidence submitted was considered insufficient because no documentary evidence was submitted. If the basis of the ruling was the former, the ruling is manifestly erroneous because there is nothing in the record or the reasons for judgment to justify rejecting the testimony. If the basis of the ruling was the latter, it is legally wrong. In either situation, this portion of the assignment of error has merit.

Nature of the Obligation to Paint and Repair Mrs. Osborne's Separate Property Duplex

An obligation incurred by a spouse may be either a community obligation or a separate obligation. La.C.C. art. 2359. An obligation incurred by a spouse during the existence of a community property regime for the common interest of the spouses or for the interest of the other spouse is a community obligation. La.C.C. art. 2360. Except as provided in La.C.C. art. 2363, all obligations incurred by a spouse during the existence of a community property regime are presumed to be community obligations. La.C.C. art. 2361. La.C.C. art. 2363 provides as follows: [omitted]

Comment (c) for La.C.C. art. 2363 explains the last clause of the last sentence thereof as follows:

An obligation incurred by a spouse for his separate property is a separate obligation to the extent that it does not benefit the community, the family, or the other spouse. Thus, an obligation incurred for the separate property of a spouse may be in part a community obligation and in part a separate obligation of the spouse who incurred it.

Thus, the plaintiffs may have a claim against Mr. Osborne to the extent that the painting and repairing of Mrs. Osborne's half of the duplex benefitted the community. La.C.C. arts. 2345 and 2363.

The evidence shows that Mrs. Osborne rented her separate property interest in the duplex. Rent is community property. La.C.C. arts. 2338 and 2339. Ordinary expenditures required in the production of community property profits (rents) from the separate property of a spouse (Mrs. Osborne's duplex) are community obligations. Succession of Ratcliff, 209 La. 224, 24 So.2d 456 (1945).

The costs of the painting and repairs performed by the plaintiffs on Mrs. Osborne's duplex are ordinary expenditures necessary to maintain the property in a condition to make it attractive, safe and livable for renters. As such, these expenditures are a community obligation for which both Mr. and Mrs. Osborne are responsible. See La. C.C. art. 2345.

The result reached by the trial court in its judgment is correct.

AFFIRMED.

C. *Wynell S. Lawson v. Rodney B. Lawson*

535 So.2d 851 (La. App. 2d Cir. 1988)

MARVIN, Judge.

In this action on two promissory notes executed by her son while he was married, plaintiff appeals a judgment that rejected her demands against her ex-daughter-in-law. Plaintiff contends her son's ex-wife is personally liable for the debt up to the value of the ex- wife's interest in the property formerly comprising the community estate which terminated when the son and daughter-in-law were separated before plaintiff brought her action. Only plaintiff's son signed the notes. The trial court found the obligation on the notes was not a community obligation but a separate obligation of plaintiff's son. Plaintiff does not contest this finding.

The ex- wife concedes that the property of the former community may be seized and sold to satisfy the debt, but contends she is not *personally* liable for the debt. At this juncture under this record, the ex- wife has not moved to partition the former community estate or to assert claims for reimbursement against her ex-husband.

We affirm the judgment which cast only the son for the $50,000 due on the notes, with interest, and attorney fees. CC Arts. 2345, 2357.

NON- DEBTOR SPOUSE'S LIABILITY

CC Arts. 2345 and 2357 identify the property available to a creditor for satisfaction of obligations incurred before or during the debtor's marriage, if the spouses live under a community property regime.

These articles were part of the extensive community property law revisions enacted in Act 709 of 1979, effective January 1, 1980. Recent cases and law review commentaries discuss and explain the import and meaning of these articles. We have omitted footnotes from all law review excerpts quoted in this opinion.

Under Art. 2345 and the first paragraph of Art. 2357, the creditor of a spouse has the same property available to satisfy the debt after the community regime has ended as he had during its existence: all assets of the community, including the interest of the non- debtor spouse, as well as the separate property of the spouse who incurred the debt. Note, *Termination of the Community*, 42 La. L. Rev. 789 (1982), at 789- 791, 793. The creditor cannot seize the non- debtor spouse's separate property to satisfy the other spouse's obligation unless the non- debtor spouse disposes of property of the former community for a purpose other than the satisfaction of community obligations, or assumes in writing responsibility for half of each community obligation incurred by the other spouse. Riley, *Analysis of the 1980 Revision of the Matrimonial Regimes Law of Louisiana*, 26 Loy. L. Rev. 453 (1980), at 509- 510.

The above analysis criticizes the legislature's decision to make one spouse's interest in community property available to satisfy the other spouse's separate debt:

> Article 2357 . . . permits the separate creditor of one spouse to seize all the assets of the former community whether or not they are still in the possession of his debtor. The creditor can thus demand payment of one spouse's separate debt out of property that belongs to the other spouse--the half interest in the former community property now owned exclusively by the non-debtor spouse. Nothing in the article limits such a creditor's right to the not-yet-partitioned property; therefore, he can apparently follow it even after partition. This gives separate debtor spouses and their creditors far greater rights than those enjoyed by husbands and their separate creditors prior to the 1980 revision; the result is at once bad law and bad economics. . . . .
>
> Before 1980, a husband who ceased to be head and master of the former community property upon dissolution of the regime had no right to use more than his own one- half interest in the former community property to pay his separate obligations; *nor had his creditor any right against his wife's interest*. 26 Loy. L. Rev. at 507- 508 (our emphasis).

The legislature's intent to protect creditors in the second paragraph of Art. 2357 is suggested in 42 La. L. Rev., *Termination of the Community, supra*, at 793- 794:

> *Article 2357 reflects a creditor- oriented scheme*, an orientation which pervades

the entire scope of the revisions. Evidence of the concern for creditors' rights is found in the second paragraph of article 2357, under which *a spouse who disposes of property of the former community for a purpose other than the satisfaction of a community obligation becomes liable for all obligations incurred by the other spouse up to the value of the disposed property* (our emphasis).

Professor Riley's *Analysis, supra*, describes the second paragraph of Art. 2357 as "a valiant attempt to preserve for all creditors the entire assets of the former community, by imposing upon the spouse who disposes of them for other purposes a *penalty in the form of personal liability* for all obligations, separate and community, incurred by the other spouse, up to the value of the property thus disposed." 26 Loy. L. Rev. at 512, with our emphasis.

When the first two paragraphs of Art. 2357 are read together, it is apparent that the non- debtor spouse is *not* personally liable for separate or community debts incurred by the other spouse *unless* the non- debtor spouse has disposed of former community property, which would have been available to satisfy all pre- termination obligations incurred by either spouse, and has done so for a purpose other than the satisfaction of community obligations. If personal liability attaches, it extends to the value of the former community property which is no longer available to the creditor, and not to the value of the non-debtor spouse's interest in the entire community estate, as plaintiff argues.

By the community property law revisions the legislature protects creditors, as noted above, but some limitations are placed on the creditor's recourse against the non- debtor spouse, according to several members of the advisory committee of the joint legislative subcommittee that recommended to the legislature Act 709 of 1979 and its predecessor, Act 627 of 1978:

> [U]nder the 1978 enactment, improvident credit transactions of either the husband or the wife can cause the loss of accumulated community assets and result in the garnishment of the salaries of both. . . . Act 627, however, limits the extent of possible injury for *it does not personally obligate the spouse who was not a party to the transaction.* Bilbe, "Management" of Community Assets Under Act 627, 39 La. L. Rev. 409 (1979), at 411, 413 (our emphasis).
>
> A proposal to impose responsibility equally on spouses at dissolution for one- half of the community obligations, regardless of who contracted them, was rejected by the legislature. Spaht and Samuel, *Equal Management Revisited: 1979 Legislative Modifications of the 1978 Matrimonial Regimes Law*, 40 La. L. Rev. 83 (1979), at 122.

Considering the legislature's rejection of the proposal to make the non- debtor spouse personally liable for half of the *community* obligations incurred by the other spouse, we cannot conclude the legislature intended to impose personal liability for the other spouse's *separate* obligations. We conclude the legislature imposed *personal* liability on the non- debtor spouse in only two circumstances:

> - - for *separate or community obligations* incurred by the other spouse if the non- debtor spouse disposes of former community property other than for the satisfaction of community obligations (second paragraph of Art. 2357); or
>
> - - for *half of each community obligation* incurred by the other spouse if the non- debtor spouse assumes this liability in writing (third paragraph of Art. 2357).

Even should we assume the debt was a community obligation, we have no evidence that the wife assumed responsibility for half of it. We have no evidence that the wife disposed of any property of the former community. On this record, she cannot be cast in judgment on the notes although, as she concedes, her interest in the former community property may be seized to satisfy the judgment against the husband.

In Shel- Boze, Inc. v. Melton, 509 So.2d 106 (La. App. 1st Cir. 1987), the husband's creditor sued and obtained a judgment against the husband and his corporation. The wife was not named in the suit or in the judgment. The creditor executed on the judgment by garnishing the wife's wages. After the garnishment, the spouses were legally separated. The creditor was allowed to keep the funds garnished before the legal separation because those earnings were community property. It was held that after the legal separation, the wife's earnings became her separate property and were not available to satisfy the husband's debt.

The seizure of community assets to satisfy a judgment against one spouse may raise due process problems if the other spouse is not notified of the initial action or of the seizure. *See* Hargrave, *Developments in the Law, 1985-1986 - Louisiana Constitutional Law*, 47 La. L. Rev. 333 (1986). Such a challenge was raised, but was rejected, in Shel- Boze, Inc., *supra*. We do not have the problem in this appeal.

Professor Hargrave's article makes these observations about Art. 2357:

> The basic policy is simply that community assets are available to satisfy the debts of each spouse.
>
> It would be hard to defend a scheme making spouses *personally* liable for the debts of the other, but the Louisiana scheme does not do this. It only makes the existing community assets available to the creditor. 47 La. L. Rev. at 335 (emphasis in original).

Compare the effect of Art. 2357 on the administration of a deceased spouse's succession discussed in Cavanaugh, *Problems in the Law of Successions: Succession Representatives, Surviving Spouses, and Usufructuaries*, 47 La. L. Rev. 21 (1986), at 37- 38, fn. 51. *See* First Guaranty Bank v. Alford, 366 So.2d 1299 (La. 1978), and Gentilly Ornamental Iron Works, Inc. *v. Hawkins*, 273 So.2d 634 (La. App. 4th Cir. 1973).

Promissory notes signed by only one spouse were involved in Fowler v. Dunshee, 511 So.2d 1323 (La. App.5th Cir. 1987), and First Sec. Bank and Trust Co. v. Dooley, 480 So.2d 842 (La. App.2d Cir. 1985). In Fowler, the husband signed the note but the creditor sued only the wife. The trial court found the wife was personally liable for the community debt. On appeal, the judgment was amended to limit the wife's liability "to the extent of her interest in the property of the former community[.]" The court summarized the law:

> [T]he spouse who has not incurred the obligation becomes personally liable only by disposing of assets of the former community for a purpose other than payment of community obligations. Therefore, whether the obligation incurred by Mr. Dunshee is deemed a separate or a community obligation is immaterial. The assets of the former community - not Ms. Dunshee's separate property nor Ms. Dunshee personally - are liable for the debt. 511 So.2d at 1325 (citations omitted).

The plaintiff in *Dooley, supra*, sued both spouses on notes signed only by the wife. Judgment was rendered against the wife "individually" and against the husband and wife "in their capacity as owners, co- partners and managers of the community in existence at the time the obligations were incurred." This court amended the judgment to limit the husband's liability "to the extent of his interest in the community property" for these reasons:

> Mrs. Dooley is liable both individually and as co- partner and/or owner of the community, since she is the spouse who incurred the obligations. The debts may be satisfied from her separate property or from her interest in the community. Mr. Dooley, *on the other hand, is only liable up to the "value" of his interest in the former community. See* Spaht and Samuels, *Equal Management Revisited*, 40 La. L. Rev. 83, 126 (1979); and Bridgeman & Conway v. Korner Realty Co., 405 So.2d 344 (La. App. 4th Cir. 1981). 480 So.2d at 845 (emphasis added).

The cited portion of the law review article discusses personal liability of the non-debtor spouse who has disposed of former community property other than to pay community debts. We did not mention in *Dooley* any factual basis for applying this provision of Art. 2357. If Mr. Dooley disposed of community property other than to pay community debts, his personal liability would correspond to the value of the property he disposed of, not to the value of his entire interest in the former community.

Bridgeman, cited in Dooley, considered whether a separation of property agreement effective January 1, 1980, precluded the husband's judgment creditor from garnishing the wife's wages after that date under a garnishment order rendered in 1979. The court interpreted Art. 2357, which also took effect on January 1, 1980, to mean that the non- debtor spouse's separate property could not be seized to satisfy obligations incurred by the other spouse. The court found the creditor had no vested right to the wife's unearned wages and discontinued the garnishment after her earnings became her separate property. Bridgeman does not otherwise address the issue of the non- debtor spouse's liability for the other spouse's obligations.

Dooley should not be construed to support plaintiff's argument that the non-debtor spouse *who has not disposed of community assets* after the community regime ends is personally liable in an amount of money not exceeding his or her interest in the *entire* former community.

CONCLUSION

Earnings or other assets acquired by a spouse after the community regime ends are classified as separate property. A money judgment against the ex- wife would subject her separate property to the risk of seizure to satisfy the husband's separate debt, contrary to Art. 2357. The rejection of plaintiff's demands against the ex-wife in the judgment was correct and does not preclude plaintiff from seizing the interest of the ex- wife in former community property to satisfy the judgment against plaintiff's son. *See* Bridgeman & Conway, *supra*, and Shel-Boze. Inc., *supra*.

At plaintiff's cost, the judgment is AFFIRMED.

D. *Ford Motor Credit Company v. Barbara P. Epps*

708 So. 2d 825 (La. App. 3d Cir. 1988)

DOUCET, Chief Judge.

This is an appeal from a deficiency judgment in favor of petitioner- appellee, Ford Motor Credit Company, and against the defendants-appellants, Nathaniel Epps, Sr. and Barbara Epps, in the amount of $8,463.25.

FACTS

Barbara Epps bought a vehicle from appellee, Ford Motor Credit Corporation (FMCC), signed an installment contract with her signature and forged her husband's signature. After default, appellee seized and sold the vehicle pursuant to executory process and proceeded against both Barbara and Nathaniel Epps, Sr. praying for a deficiency judgment in the amount of $8,463.25.

At trial, the court agreed with appellants' contention that, due to the forgery, Nathaniel was not a party to the installment contract. However, the trial court disagreed with appellants' allegation that because the document supporting the petition for executory process was not executed in authentic form the petition for deficiency judgment must fall. The trial court found that the executory proceeding resulting in the sale and seizure of the vehicle was valid as to Barbara Epps. Nevertheless, the trial court found that both Barbara and Nathaniel were liable for the deficiency judgment insofar as the debt was a community debt. Defendants now appeal. We find no error in the ruling of the trial court and affirm.

ASSIGNMENT OF ERROR

Appellants contend that the trial court was clearly wrong in ruling that the community of acquits and gains existing between Mr. and Mrs. Epps was liable for a deficiency judgment which was rendered pursuant to an executory process based upon fraud.

DISCUSSION

The trial court found the following in its written reasons for judgment, which state, in part: This Court finds that there was in fact a vice of fraud in the contract between Ford Motor Credit Company and Nathaniel Epps, Sr., however, I do not find such a vice exist between the Petitioners and Barbara Epps. This Courts finds that Barbara Epps signed her name and forged her husband's signature, Nathaniel Epps, Sr., through her own admission in testimony. The effect was that she signed her name twice once as Barbara Epps and secondly as Nathaniel Epps, Sr., both having a binding effect on her as a valid signature. The contract as to Nathaniel Epps is rescinded as the vice of fraud requires it.

Be it as it may, it is the ruling and finding of this Court that the defendant Barbara Epps is liable for a deficiency judgment in this matter and that Nathaniel Epps, Sr. is released as a party to this initial contract, however, under the laws of matrimonial regime, he is liable in solido with his wife for any and all community debts.

The defect in the underlying security agreement relied upon by appellants is the signature of Nathaniel, which Barbara forged. There is no doubt that Barbara Epps signed the contract and is personally liable on the contract. Therefore, we find that the trial court was correct in finding that Barbara is estopped from claiming her own fraud as a defense to liability on the contract.

In determining whether the trial court was correct in determining that Nathaniel was also liable for the deficiency judgment as a member of the community of acquits [sic]and gains, we note that FMCC did not plead either in the original petition for executory process or in the supplemental petition for deficiency that Nathaniel was the husband of Barbara or that he is liable as a member of the community. FMCC merely alleges that Nathaniel signed the contract and that the vehicle was seized and sold in an executory proceeding. The answer to the original petition for executory process denies these allegations and further alleges that Nathaniel Epps, Sr., did not sign the contract.

However, the defendants-appellants, in their answer to the supplemental petition for a deficiency judgment, allege that "the name of Nathaniel Epps, Sr. was signed by his wife without his knowledge or authority." Additionally, at the trial, Barbara Epps testified that she is married to Nathaniel Epps, Sr. and that they are presently living together in community and were living together in community when she signed his name to the plaintiff's installment contract. Additionally, she testified that she and her husband did not have a separate property agreement. Nathaniel also testified and did not dispute that Barbara was his wife or the fact that they did not have a separate property agreement.

Therefore, insofar as evidence was introduced at the trial as to the defendants' marital relationship without objection, we consider the pleadings expanded to include an allegation that the parties are married and that Nathaniel is a member of the community of acquets and gains. See La. Code Civ. P. art.1154.

Finally, the parties make no argument that the automobile at issue was not community property.

La. Civ. Code arts. 2338 and 2340 define community property. La. Civ. Code art. 2338 states:

> The community property comprises: property acquired during the existence of the legal regime through the effort, skill, or industry of either spouse; property acquired with community things or with community and separate things, unless classified as separate property under Article 2341...; and all other property not classified by law as separate property.

La. Civ. Code art. 2340 states that "[t]hings in the possession of a spouse during the existence of a regime of community of acquets and gains are presumed to be community, but either spouse may prove that they are separate property."

Additionally, La. Civ. Code arts. 2360 and 2361, discussed community obligations. La. Civ. Code art. 2360 states that "[a]n obligation incurred by a spouse during the existence of a community property regime for the common interest of the spouses or for the interest of the other spouse is a community obligation."

La. Civ. Code art. 2361 states "[e]xcept as provided in Article 2363, all obligations incurred by a spouse during the existence of a community property regime are presumed to be community obligations."

The Civil Code, as set forth above, states that the community is liable for the debts of both the husband or wife unless it is shown that the debt was not incurred for the benefit of the community. Therefore, it is presumed that the automobile purchased by Barbara Epps was purchased for the benefit of the community unless proved otherwise.

La. Civ. Code art. 1850 states that "[a] party whose interest is favored by a presumption established by law need not offer other proof."

In this case, Nathaniel has not attempted to carry his burden of rebutting the presumption that the obligation at issue is a community debt. Thus, it is presumed that the automobile purchased by Barbara was of benefit to the community. A creditor is free to pursue either member of the community of acquets and gains or both. As stated in La. Code Civ. P. art. 735, "[e]ither spouse is the proper defendant, during the existence of the marital community, in an action to enforce an obligation against community property . . ."

Therefore, Nathaniel is a proper defendant to be held in judgment in an action to enforce an obligation against community property.

CONCLUSION

The trial court was correct in finding Barbara liable as a party to the contract between herself and FMCC and both Barbara and Nathaniel liable for Barbara's debt as members of the community of acquets and gains.

Based upon the foregoing, we find no error in the judgment of the trial court. Costs of these proceedings to be paid by defendants-appellants, Nathaniel Epps, Sr. and Barbara Epps.

AFFIRMED.

6.3 DELICTUAL OBLIGATIONS

A. *Feddrick Thomas, Jr. v. Inez E. Champagne*

638 So. 2d 1151 (La. App. 1st Cir. 1994)

SHORTESS, Judge.

Feddrick Thomas, Jr. (plaintiff) sued Inez E. Champagne (Mrs. Champagne) and State Farm Mutual Automobile Insurance Company (State Farm) for damages arising out of an automobile accident on June 6, 1991. Mrs. Champagne and her husband, August Champagne (Mr. Champagne), were en route to a district business meeting in Lafayette for Lawson Products, Inc. (Lawson), which employed Mr. Champagne as a salesman. Mrs. Champagne had volunteered to drive while her husband assembled his notes for the meeting the following day. Mrs. Champagne was accompanying her husband to join him for dinner with other salespersons and their spouses, but was not attending or participating in the business meeting. Mr. Champagne stated that about four miles after entering Highway 90, plaintiff, a state trooper, put on his blue flashing lights and came to a "controlled stop but an unexpected stop" in front of a tree branch which partially obstructed the roadway. Unable to stop in time, Mrs. Champagne struck plaintiff's vehicle from behind.

State Farm, Mrs. Champagne's insurer, deposited its policy limits in the registry of the court. Plaintiff thereafter dismissed State Farm and the Champagnes from the suit, reserving rights against Lawson. On the same day these defendants were dismissed, plaintiff amended his petition to add Lawson as a defendant based on a theory of respondeat superior. Lawson filed a motion for summary judgment, arguing there was no legal basis on which it could be held responsible. The trial court granted the motion.

Plaintiff does not contend, nor do any facts suggest, that the accident was caused in any way by the negligence of Mr. Champagne. Thus, Lawson cannot be held liable for Mrs. Champagne's negligence unless her negligence can be imputed to Mr. Champagne, and thereafter to Lawson. Unless one can be held responsible as a matter of law for the torts of a person whose negligence is sought to be charged to him, the doctrine of imputed negligence cannot be applied. Gaspard v. LeMaire, 245 La. 239, 158 So.2d 149 (1963).

The depositions and affidavits show there was no direct relationship between Lawson and Mrs. Champagne. She was not a Lawson agent or employee. Furthermore, Mr. Champagne had no authority to appoint an agent on Lawson's behalf for any reason. Plaintiff does not contest these facts. Rather, he argues Mrs. Champagne's negligence may be imputed to Mr. Champagne under a "community mission," or, alternatively, a "joint venture or mission" theory. Plaintiff seeks to have Mrs. Champagne's negligence imputed to her husband, then seeks to hold Lawson responsible under the respondeat superior theory that an employer is liable for the torts of its employee while acting in the course and scope of his employment.

Plaintiff concedes that the fault of one spouse cannot be imputed to the other merely because of the marital relationship. Lewis v. Till, 395 So.2d 737 (La.1981). However, plaintiff suggests Mr. Champagne is liable as head and master of the community for his wife's torts if she was expressly or impliedly authorized by her husband and was attending to a community mission or affair. In support of this proposition, plaintiff cites Tandy v. Simoneaux, 344 So.2d 406 (La.App. 1st Cir.1977), and Aisole v. Dean, 560 So.2d 647 (La.App. 4th Cir.1990), rev'd in part on other grounds, 574 So.2d 1248 (La.1991). While we agree that Tandy states this proposition, we decline to follow it because it is a pre-Till case and because the head-and- master regime was found to be unconstitutional in 1979 and was legislatively repealed in 1980. The Aisole case deals with whether an obligation is a community or separate obligation and expressly recognizes that fault is not imputed merely because of the marital relationship. Aisole, 560 So.2d at 652. While Aisole may suggest that if the Champagnes were on a community mission, plaintiff's damages might be a community obligation, it does not suggest Mrs. Champagne's fault can be imputed to Mr. Champagne.

Plaintiff also argues that when the passenger is the owner of the vehicle and the driver is on a mission for the owner, the passenger may be held liable.

To constitute a joint venture in the operation of a vehicle, there must be a joint interest in the object and purpose of the mission and an equal right, express or implied, on the part of each of the parties to direct or control the conduct of the other in the operation of the vehicle. Barnett v. Globe Indem. Co., 557 So.2d 300 (La. App. 4th Cir.1990). The existence of a joint venture is a question of fact. Cajun Electric Power Co-Op., Inc. v. McNamara, 452 So.2d 212 (La. App. 1st Cir.), writ denied, 458 So.2d 123 (La.1984).

The trial court found from the deposition testimony that "there can be no conclusion but that Mr. Champagne exercised no control over the manner in which his wife operated the vehicle. Therefore, the Court must conclude that there is no basis for imposing liability to Mr. Champagne through the joint venture theory." We agree. Mrs. Champagne voluntarily assumed the role as driver and neither Mr. nor Mrs. Champagne claimed Mr. Champagne ever had any control over her actions. Furthermore, plaintiff cites no facts to support his contention that Mrs. Champagne was on a mission for Mr. Champagne. Therefore, this argument has no merit.

We agree with the trial court that there is no legal basis for imposing Mrs. Champagne's negligence upon her husband. Lawson has shown that no material issues of fact exist in this case and that it is entitled to summary judgment as a matter of law. Therefore, the judgment of the trial court is affirmed at plaintiff's costs.

AFFIRMED.

B. Note

A number of cases have recognized the principle that one is not vicariously liable for the torts of his spouse. It should follow that a plaintiff passenger should be able to recover against a third-party tortfeasor without having the driver spouse's negligence imputed to the passenger. *See Geraci v. Louisiana DOTD*, 589 So.2d 1215 (La. App. 4th Cir. 1991) (affirming the wife-guest passenger's damage award against the state (90%) and her husband-driver (10%) and refusing to lower plaintiff's damage award for husband's fault); *Mayo v. Nissan Motor Corp.*, 639 So.2d 773 (La. App. 3d Cir. 1994) (court refused to impute the husband-boat operator's negligence to the wife-passenger: "However, our jurisprudence has held that unless a plaintiff could be held responsible, as a matter of law, for the torts of the person whose negligence is sought to be charged to him, the doctrine of imputed negligence cannot be applied; *Osbon v. National Union Fire Ins. Co.,* 632 So.2d 1158 (La. 1994) (refusing to impute husband's arson to insured wife for the purpose of denying coverage: "specifically, we do not believe that the legislature intended to impute the incendiary actions of an insured to the innocent co-insured who has no control over the unauthorized conduct. Nor do we think that the legislature intended to penalize an innocent insured, here, a victim of arson, with the perpetrator of a wrongful act."). These cases have departed from dictum otherwise in *Bienvenu v. State Farm Mut. Auto. Ins. Co.*, 545 So.2d 581 (La. App. 5th Cir. 1989).

6.4 DUE PROCESS CONCERNS

A. Introduction

As illustrated by the following articles, the Louisiana Code of Civil Procedure does not expressly require that a non-debtor spouse receive any notice that his or her interest in community property is being seized in connection with a debt incurred by the other spouse.

La. Code Civ. Proc. art. 686. Marital community.

Either spouse is the proper plaintiff, during the existence of the marital community, to sue to enforce a community right; however, if one spouse is the managing spouse with respect to the community right sought to be enforced, then that spouse is the proper plaintiff to bring an action to enforce the right.

When doubt exists whether the right sought to be enforced is a community right or is the separate right of the plaintiff spouse, that spouse may sue in the alternative to enforce the right.

When only one spouse sues to enforce a community right, the other spouse is a necessary party. Where the failure to join the other spouse may result in an injustice to that spouse, the trial court may order the joinder of that spouse on its own motion.

La. Code Civ. Proc. art. 735. Marital community.

Either spouse is the proper defendant, during the existence of the marital community, in an action to enforce an obligation against community property; however, if one spouse is the managing spouse with respect to the obligation sought to be enforced against the community property, then that spouse is the proper defendant in an action to enforce the obligation.

When doubt exists whether the obligation sought to be enforced is a community obligation or the separate obligation of the defendant spouse, that spouse may be sued in the alternative.

When only one spouse is sued to enforce an obligation against community property, the other spouse is a necessary party. Where the failure to join the other spouse may result in an injustice to that spouse, the trial court may order the joinder of that spouse on its own motion.

As explained by the following cases, due process concerns impose additional notice requirements than those expressed in the Louisiana Code of Civil Procedure.

B. *Altonette Jackson v. Raoul Galan*

631 F. Supp. 409 (E.D. La. 1986)

SEAR, Judge.

The plaintiff, Altonette Jackson, brought this civil rights action pursuant to 42 U.S.C. § 1983 against Charles E. Spahr, Distributor, described in the pleadings simply as a Louisiana partnership; Raoul Galan, in his official capacity as Clerk of Court for Jefferson Parish, Louisiana; and Harry Lee, in his official capacity as Sheriff of Jefferson Parish. Thereafter, plaintiff filed a motion for partial summary judgment seeking declaratory and permanent injunctive relief against all defendants. Plaintiff prays for judgment declaring that the actions taken by the defendants garnishing her wages without notice and hearing constitute state action and action under color of state law, depriving her of her due process rights under the Fourteenth Amendment and within the meaning of 42 U.S.C. § 1983. Plaintiff seeks determination of only the issue of liability of the private defendant, Charles E. Spahr, Distributer (hereafter "Spahr"), at this time, reserving her right to litigate the issue of quantum at a later date.

The defendants have filed opposition memoranda as well as motions for summary judgment. All defendants contend that the plaintiff has failed to state a claim upon which relief can be granted and that, in any event, the claim has prescribed. The defendants also raise the defense of good faith. Defendants Spahr and Galan claim that the plaintiff has failed to exhaust state remedies. Defendant Galan asserts that he is an improper party to this action because the facts giving rise to plaintiff's claim occurred prior to the commencement of his term in office. Finally, defendant Lee maintains that the court lacks subject matter jurisdiction over the plaintiff's claim for attorney's fees.

I. Factual and Procedural Background

The facts giving rise to this litigation are not in dispute. Accordingly, I find:

(1) On September 3, 1981, Spahr filed suit on a promissory note in the Twenty-Fourth Judicial District Court for the Parish of Jefferson, Louisiana, naming as defendants Jackson Truck Service, Inc., Bernice Jackson and Charles Jackson. At the time the suit was filed and at all pertinent times thereafter, plaintiff Altonette Jackson was the wife of Charles Jackson.

(2) Jackson Truck Service, Inc. was at all pertinent times a corporation owned by Bernice Jackson, plaintiff's mother-in- law, and Charles Jackson.

(3) On or about October 28, 1980, Bernice and Charles Jackson, individually and on behalf of Jackson Truck Service, Inc., executed a bearer promissory note in the sum of $5,000 and negotiated the note to Spahr. Plaintiff did not sign the note.

(4) Plaintiff was not named as a party-defendant in the state court proceeding, nor was she served with either pre- or post-judgment process; and plaintiff made no appearance in the state court action.

(5) On November 11, 1981, a default judgment for $5,000 plus interest, costs and attorney's fees was entered in the state proceeding in favor of Spahr and against Jackson Truck Service, Inc., Bernice Jackson and Charles Jackson. Plaintiff was not named as a judgment debtor.

Service of the judgment upon the plaintiff was neither requested nor attempted.

(6) On or about May 1, 1982, Spahr filed a garnishment petition against Sears Roebuck and Co., the plaintiff's employer. Plaintiff was not served with a copy of the garnishment petition.

(7) More than a year later, on or about July 7, 1983, Spahr obtained a judgment against Sears Roebuck and Co. ordering the garnishment of plaintiff's wages in satisfaction of the November 11, 1981 judgment. Plaintiff was not served with a copy of the garnishment judgment.

(8) Between September 27, 1983 and July 25, 1985, plaintiff's wages, in an amount totaling $5,737.90, were seized by the Sheriff of Jefferson Parish pursuant to a writ of fieri facias processed and issued by the Clerk of Court for Jefferson Parish. Between those dates, the sum of $5,383.57 was forwarded by the Sheriff to Spahr pursuant to the judgment of garnishment. The sum of $354.33 was retained by the Sheriff for his commission.

On November 13, 1984, plaintiff filed a complaint in this Court and moved for a preliminary injunction seeking to enjoin further garnishment of her wages. A hearing was held on November 27, 1984 and, after considering the law, evidence and arguments of counsel, I granted plaintiff's motion on December 6, 1984.

II. Law

The plaintiff does not challenge the constitutionality of Louisiana's community property laws. Rather, she challenges the procedure allowed by those laws of taking property with neither notice nor hearing.

Louisiana Code of Civil Procedure article 735 provides in pertinent part:

> Either spouse is the proper defendant, during the existence of the marital community, in an action to enforce an obligation against community property . . . When only one spouse is sued to enforce an obligation against community property, the other spouse is a necessary party. . .

Louisiana Code of Civil Procedure article 926(8) establishes the dilatory exception of nonjoinder of a necessary party and article 928 dictates that dilatory exceptions must be pleaded prior to answer or judgment by default. If they are not, they are considered waived.

Taken singly, these articles are apparently harmless and, in fact, have the salutary effect of enhancing creditors' rights and "greasing the wheels" of litigation procedure. However, as the plaintiff has unfortunately discovered, the combination of these articles can result in a blatant invasion of due process rights. If, for instance, the spouse who is sued on a community obligation fails to raise the dilatory exception of nonjoinder of a necessary party, the other spouse is placed in the inauspicious position of having his or her property placed at peril of seizure with neither notice nor hearing. Of course, it is axiomatic that at a minimum the Due Process Clause of the Fourteenth Amendment requires that "deprivation of life, liberty or property by adjudication be preceded by notice and opportunity for hearing appropriate to the nature of the case." Mullane v. Central Hanover Bank & Trust Co., 339 U.S. 306, 70 S.Ct. 652, 656-57, 94 L.Ed. 865 (1950).

A. Failure to State a Claim

Defendants rely, in large part, upon the case of Lugar v. Edmundson Oil Co., 457 U.S. 922, 102 S.Ct. 2744, 73 L.Ed.2d 482 (1982) for the proposition that the plaintiff has failed to state a claim upon which relief can be granted. In *Lugar* the plaintiff brought a civil rights action under 42 U.S.C. § 1983 against his creditor/lessor after the latter had affected a prejudgment attachment of the plaintiff's property. The attachment was accomplished through a Virginia statute which required only that Edmundson allege, in an *ex parte* petition, a belief that Lugar was disposing of or might dispose of his property to the prejudice of his creditors. The clerk of the state court thereafter issued a writ of attachment which was in turn executed by the county sheriff.

Although the Lugar court was mainly concerned with the state action requirement of plaintiff's § 1983 cause of action an issue germane to the instant motion defendants here cite language which, they contend, supports their motions for summary judgment. That language reads:

> Petitioner did present a valid cause of action under § 1983 insofar as he challenged the constitutionality of the Virginia statute; he did not insofar as he alleged only misuse or abuse of the statute.

102 S.Ct. at 2756 [footnote omitted].

The above quoted language was, in fact, addressed to the state action issue in Lugar. This much is clear from a reading of a previous portion of the Supreme Court's opinion:

> Count two alleged that the deprivation of property resulted from respondents' "malicious, wanton, willful, oppressive [*sic*], [and] unlawful acts." By "unlawful," petitioner apparently meant "unlawful under state law." To say this, however, is to say that the conduct of which petitioner complained could not be ascribed to any

governmental decision; rather, respondents were acting contrary to the relevant policy articulated by the State . . . That respondents invoked the statute without the grounds to do so could in no way be attributed to a state rule or a state decision. Count two, therefore, does not state a cause of action under § 1983 but challenges only private action.

Id. at 2755.

The more pertinent portion of the court's opinion, however, fully supports the conclusion that Ms. Jackson's claims fall squarely within the ambit of 42 U.S.C. § 1983. As the Lugar majority explained:

Count one is a different matter. That count describes the procedures followed by respondents in obtaining the prejudgment attachment . . . Although it is not clear whether petitioner is referring to the state-created procedure or the misuse of that procedure by respondents, we agree with the lower courts that the better reading of the complaint is that petitioner challenges the state statute as procedurally defective under the Fourteenth Amendment.

While private misuse of a state statute does not describe conduct that can be attributed to the State, the procedural scheme created by the statute obviously is the product of state action. This is subject to constitutional restraints and properly may be addressed in a § 1983 action, if the second element of the state-action requirement is met as well.

Id. at 275-56 [emphasis supplied] [footnote omitted].

This is precisely Ms. Jackson's complaint. She does not allege abuse or misuse of the Louisiana codal scheme. Instead, she avers that the state procedure, fully complied with by the defendants, has resulted in an unconstitutional deprivation of her property in violation of the Fourteenth Amendment. That complaint is perfectly suited to a § 1983 cause of action.

Furthermore, there is no doubt that defendant Spahr is a "state actor" within the meaning of 42 U.S.C. § 1983. In United States v. Price, 383 U.S. 78, 86 S.Ct. 1152, 16 L.Ed.2d 267 (1966), the United States Supreme Court held that:

Private persons, jointly engaged with state officials in the prohibited action, are acting "under color" of law for purposes of the statute. To act "under color" of law does not require that the accused be an officer of the State. It is enough that he is a willful participant in joint activity with the State or its agents.

86 S.Ct. at 1157 [footnote omitted]. That holding is reinforced by numerous subsequent Supreme Court cases, including Lugar, *supra.*

Of course the Sheriff of Jefferson Parish and the Clerk of Court were also acting under color of state law in processing, issuing and executing the writ of fieri facias authorizing the garnishment of plaintiff's wages. Fuentes v Shevin, 407 U.S. 67, 92 S.Ct. 1983, 32 L.Ed.2d 556 (1972); Norton v. Liddel, 620 F.2d 1375 (10th Cir.1980); United States v. Wiseman, 445 F.2d 792 (2d Cir.1971), *cert. denied*, 404 U.S. 967, 92 S.Ct. 346, 30 L.Ed.2d 287 (1971).

III. Remedies

A. Declaratory Relief

Considering the foregoing, plaintiff is entitled to judgment declaring the following:

(1) Charles E. Spahr, Distributor's use of Louisiana's garnishment procedures against plaintiff constitutes state action and action under color of state law within the meaning of the Fourteenth Amendment to the United States Constitution and 42 U.S.C. § 1983.

(2) The Clerk of Court for Jefferson Parish's actions in processing and issuing the writ of fieri facias authorizing the garnishment of plaintiff's wages constitute state action and action under color of state law within the meaning of the Fourteenth Amendment to the United States Constitution and 42 U.S.C. § 1983.

(3) The Sheriff of Jefferson Parish's actions in executing the writ of fieri facias and taking into his possession plaintiff's wages constitute state action and action under color of state law within the meaning of the Fourteenth Amendment to the United States Constitution and 42 U.S.C. § 1983.

(4) The seizure by garnishment of plaintiff's wages based upon a judgment arising out of an action in which she was neither named as a party defendant nor served with process of any kind deprived plaintiff of her property without due process of law in violation of the Fourteenth Amendment to the United States Constitution.

B. Injunctive Relief

Plaintiff also seeks injunctive relief against all defendants in this proceeding. Plaintiff can be fully compensated monetarily by proceeding in an action for damages against defendant Spahr. That action, of course, would arise under 42 U.S.C. § 1983 and, if successful, would provide the plaintiff with the legal remedies provided by that statute. *See* Wright & Miller, Federal Practice and Procedure: Civil §§ 2944 at 392-402. Accordingly, plaintiff's application for an injunction is DENIED.

The plaintiff further prays for determination of the liability of defendant Spahr and the return of her withheld wages. Because I have found that (1) Spahr is a state actor for purposes of the Fourteenth Amendment and 42 U.S.C. § 1983; (2) Spahr is not entitled to a good faith defense; and (3) plaintiff's wages were seized in violation of her due process rights, the liability of defendant Spahr has been determined. Since the amount of wages seized in violation of plaintiff's constitutional rights is an element of damages, I do not reach that issue in this proceeding. That issue is properly for consideration at the trial of the merits of plaintiff's claim.

C. *Doris Lancaster Magee v. Honorable J. Al Amiss*

502 So. 2d 568 (La. 1987)

WATSON, Justice.

A separated wife, Doris Lancaster Magee, seeks recognition of or recompense for her undivided one-half interest in a community home, which was sold at a sheriff's sale, without notice to her, because of a $1,856 judgment in satisfaction of a roofing lien.

FACTS

On September 1, 1970, lot forty-three, East Broadmoor Subdivision, Parish of East Baton Rouge, was purchased by Archibald Carter Magee, Sr., for $33,500 from Mary B. and John D. Sutheriand. The Act of Sale recites that the purchaser was "married to and living with Doris L. Magee, born Lancaster, domiciled in the Parish of East Baton Rouge." Subsequently, on July 9, 1971, Doris Lancaster Magee received a judgment of separation in East Baton Rouge Parish, and the parties were enjoined against alienating any property pending a settlement of the community. The judgment of separation was not recorded in the mortgage records until April 30, 1980, after the sheriff's sale. No notice of lis pendens, judgment of divorce, or community property settlement was ever recorded.

On September 14, 1979, Reynolds Roofing Company, Inc., received a $1,856 judgment to satisfy a lien on the Magee property; a writ of fieri facias issued; and lot forty-three of East Broadmoor Subdivision was seized. Archibald Magee was appointed custodian of the property. When first offered for sale with appraisal, there were no bids on the property. On April 2, 1980, it sold at public auction to H. Mitchell Stockmann for $49,000. After the first mortgage balance of $14,381.18, the Reynolds' judgment and expenses were paid, the sheriff transferred the net proceeds of $30,646.76 to Dr. Magee.

The recorded proces-verbal of the sheriff's sale recites that the certificate of mortgages recorded against the property included none in the names of Archibald C. Magee, *Doris L. Magee*, John D. Sutherland, and Mary B. Sutherland, except those relating to the Magee purchase and the Reynolds' lien.

On October 16, 1980, lot forty-three was sold by Stockmann and his wife to Don Alan and Connie Summers Iglehart for $85,000, and the Igleharts mortgaged the property to River City Federal Savings and Loan Corporation for $68,000.

Doris Magee filed suit, naming as defendants: Sheriff Amiss of East Baton Rouge Parish; Don Alan and Connie Summers Iglehart; River City Federal Savings and Loan Corporation; and Archibald Magee, alleged to be a nonresident. She asked that the sheriff's sale be declared a nullity insofar as it purported to convey her undivided one-half interest in the property to Stockmann and that the Stockmanns' sale to the Igleharts also be annulled. Alternatively, she asked judgment against Archibald C. Magee for one-half of the proceeds from the sheriff's sale. Cited as garnishee was the American Bank & Trust Company at Baton Rouge, which allegedly holds assets belonging to Archibald Magee.

The Igleharts filed a third party demand against Sheriff Amiss, the Stockmanns, and Reynolds. In answer, the Stockmanns alleged the existence of a counter letter nullifying their liability as vendors; contended that the sale to the Igleharts was "substantially" below the property's appraised or market value because of "potential litigation," and pleaded discussion against the Igleharts' title insurer and examiner. The Stockmanns third partied Archibald Magee and Reynolds.

Rejecting Doris Magee's claim that she had been denied due process under the state and federal constitutions, the trial court granted summary judgment and dismissed Doris Magee's suit against the sheriff. The summary judgment in favor of the sheriff is now final. Summary judgment was also granted in favor of defendant, River City, and third party defendants, Reynolds and the Stockmanns.

The court of appeal found that Reynolds had properly filed suit against Archibald Magee as head and master of the community under LSA-C.C.P. art. 735 which then provided that the husband is the proper defendant in an action to enforce an obligation against the community; that the sheriff correctly sold the property to satisfy the judicial mortgage created by the Reynolds' judgment; and that the unrecorded judgment of separation had no effect as to Reynolds, the Stockmanns, the Igleharts, and River City, who were third parties protected by the public records doctrine. The court of appeal affirmed the summary judgment in favor of River City, the Stockmanns, and Reynolds and remanded for further proceedings as to Doris Magee's claim against Archibald Magee. A writ was granted to review the judgment of the court of appeal.

LEGAL ANALYSIS

LSA-C.C. art. 2404 formerly allowed the husband, as head and master of the community, to alienate its assets by an onerous title without his wife's consent. Article 2404 was repealed. As of January 1, 1980, LSA-C.C. art. 2347 requires the concurrence of both spouses for the alienation, encumbrance or lease of community immovables. Although a lien would appear to be an encumbrance, the Comments under Article 2347 note, in pertinent part:

> "(a) Encumbrances imposed by law are not subject to the requirement of concurrence by the spouses. Thus, a transaction by one of the spouses acting alone may give rise to a vendor's privilege, or a mechanic's or materialman's lien on community property. Likewise, the recordation of a judgment against a spouse gives rise to a judicial mortgage on community property situated in the parish in which recordation takes place...."

LSA-C.C. art. 2404 was declared unconstitutional as a denial of equal protection under the Fourteenth Amendment in Kirchberg v. Feenstra, 609 F.2d 727 (5 Cir., 1979), affirmed on March 23, 1981, at 450 U.S. 455, 101 S.Ct. 1195, 67 L.Ed.2d 428 (1981). The Fifth Circuit opinion was not retroactive, but it was rendered on December 12, 1979, prior to the sheriff's sale. However, Kirchberg involved a conventional mortgage, not a judicial mortgage. Kirchberg recognized a cause of action against the State of Louisiana by a plaintiff wife.

In distributing the proceeds of this sale, the sheriff acted according to LSA-C.C.P. art. 2373 by paying debtor Magee the surplus. However, the property had been acquired by Archibald Carter Magee, Sr., while married to and living with Doris Lancaster Magee, from John D. and Mary B. Sutherland. The certificate of mortgages incorporated in the sheriff's recorded processes-verbal noted no mortgages against the property in the names of Archibald C. Magee, Doris L. Magee, John D. Sutherland or Mary B. Sutherland. The certificate of mortgages and the recorded deed revealed Doris L. Magee's interest in the seized property. Compare Long v. Chailan, 196 La. 380, 199 So. 222 (1941), where the husband's marital status was not apparent in his deed to the land. Here, the public records did not show that Doris Magee's interest had been alienated. The judgment of separation had not been recorded, and no divorce or property settlement of the community had been recorded. As to third parties, the community remained intact.

However, the provisions of Civil Code Article 2347, effective January 1, 1980, specifically prohibited alienation of Mrs. Magee's interest without her concurrence.

Since the judicial sale, an alienation, took place after Article 2347 was effective, she was entitled at a minimum to notice; the failure to notify voided the sale as to her interest.

One with a legally protected property interest, such as Doris Magee, is entitled to notice of the property's pending sale. "Notice by mail or other means as certain to ensure actual notice is a minimum constitutional precondition to a proceeding which will adversely affect the liberty or property interests of *any* party, . . .if its name and address are reasonably ascertainable." Mennonite Bd. of Missions v. Adams, 462 U.S. 791 at 800, 103 S.Ct. 2706 at 2712, 77 L.Ed.2d 180 at 188 (1983). Mennonite involved lack of notice, except by publication, to a mortgagee. As a result, Mennonite held that the purchaser of the property could not quiet his title.

The legal regime of community property between the Magees terminated with their separation from bed and board. The debt to Reynolds Roofing was a separate obligation incurred after termination of the community property regime. While the house was still owned in indivision by the Magees, Dr. Magee apparently had sole use and occupancy of the residence from 1971 until he had it reroofed in 1978. When this debt to Reynolds was incurred, a community debt would have been unlawful under LSA-C.C. art. 150, which provided:

> "From the day on which the action of separation shall be brought, it shall not be lawful for the husband to contract any debt on account of the community, nor to dispose of the immovables belonging to the same, and any alienation by him made after that time, shall be null, if it be proved that such alienation was made with the fraudulent view of injuring the rights of the wife."

In Otis v. Texas Co., 153 La. 384, 96 So. 1 (1923) it was held that plaintiffs were on notice of facts sufficient to elicit inquiry as to their vendor's title. Therefore, plaintiffs were not innocent third persons purchasing in good faith and acquired only that title owned by their vendor. Breaux-Renoudet Cypress-Lumber Co. v. Shadel, 52 La.Ann. 2094, 28 So. 292 (1900) and Succession of Rogge, 49 La.Ann. 37, 21 So. 170 (1897).

LSA-C.C. art. 2620, "Rights acquired at execution sale" states:

> "This sale on execution transfers the property of the thing to the purchaser as completely as if the owner had sold it himself; but it transfers only the rights of the debtor such as they are."

CONCLUSION

Since the judgment of separation had not been recorded, Reynolds acted legally in filing suit only against Archibald Magee. The record does not reveal why Dr. Magee would allow a valuable piece of community property to be sold in satisfaction of a small separate debt; the facts suggest that he was attempting to liquidate his and his former wife's interests in the property without her sharing in the proceeds. See LSA-C.C. art. 150, supra.

On April 21, 1980, when lot forty-three was sold at sheriff's sale, the interest of Doris Magee in the property seized and sold at auction was apparent on the face of the public records, appearing in the recorded deed to which attention was directed by the certificate of mortgages. Alienation of the property without her consent required some notice to her apart from mere publication and advertisement of the sale. LSA-C.C. art. 2347. Her due process rights were violated by the lack of notice. A co-owner like Doris Magee would be entitled to at least the minimum protection recognized in Mennonite. The purchaser here could not acquire good title to her interest in the property.

Both sets of purchasers, the Stockmanns and the Igleharts, were aware from the certificate of mortgages that Doris Magee had an undivided one-half interest in the property. For this reason, the Stockmanns acquired the property for only $49,000. As the Stockmanns judicially admitted in their pleadings, even the subsequent sale to the Igleharts for $85,000 represented "substantially" less than the property's appraised or market value. The Stockmanns also judicially admitted that the property they purchased was prone to "potential litigation".

The issue is whether the Stockmanns and the Igleharts acquired the entire property under these circumstances.

The Stockmanns were not good faith purchasers and acquired only the undivided one-half interest in the property owned by Archibald Magee. LSA-C.C. art. 2620; Otis v. Texas Co., supra. When the Igleharts acquired the property from the Stockmanns on October 16, 1980, the Igleharts had further notice that their title was defective because the Magee judgment of separation had been recorded in East Baton Rouge Parish on April 30, 1980. Under these circumstances, neither the Stockmanns nor the Igleharts can claim to be good faith purchasers of the entire property. What they acquired was what was owned by the judgment debtor, Archibald Magee, an undivided one-half interest in lot forty-three. LSA-C.C. art. 2620.

Neither the Stockmanns nor their successors were good faith purchasers of the entire property and they acquired only Archibald Magee's undivided one-half interest. Doris Magee, therefore, retains an undivided one-half interest in lot forty-three of East Broadmoor Subdivision in the Parish of East Baton Rouge.

The summary judgment in favor of Reynolds Roofing Company, Inc., is affirmed. The summary judgment in favor of River City Federal Savings and Loan Corporation, H. Mitchell Stockmann and Linda Rushing Stockmann is reversed, and the matter is remanded for trial of the demands against the Igleharts, River City and Archibald Magee, as well as the third party demands involving the Stockmanns, the Igleharts, Archibald Magee, and the Igleharts' title insurer and examiner.

AFFIRMED IN PART; REVERSED IN PART

LEMMON concurs.

DENNIS, Justice, concurring.

Even though the judgment of separation was never recorded, and the community remained intact as to third parties, the deed made it clear that the wife had an ownership interest in the property as a co-partner in community with Mr. Magee. She was thus entitled to receive notice of the judicial sale. Mennonite Board of Missions v. Adams, 462 U.S. 791, 103 S.Ct. 2706, 77 L.Ed.2d 180 (1983) and Bonner v. B-W Utilities, 452 F.Supp. 1295 W.D. La. 1978). The lack of notice invalidated the sale at least as to the wife's interest. The good or bad faith of the purchasers at the judicial sale was irrelevant.

D. *Colonial Bank v. Rosita T. Perkins*

528 So. 2d 172 (La. App. 4 Cir. 1987)

LOBRANO, Judge.

The only issue before this court is whether the trial court was correct in dismissing relator's motion because of improper use of summary proceedings.

Relator obtained a money judgment against Mr. Perkins. That judgment was recorded and thus acts as a judicial mortgage. Relator seeks a writ of seizure and sale pursuant to that judgment against assets belonging to the community existing between Mr. Perkins and his former wife, respondent. In order to meet due process requirements prior to seizing the property, relator filed a rule against respondent "to show cause why the seizure should not issue."

Respondent objected that this was an improper use of summary proceedings. We disagree.

La. Code of Civil Procedure Article 2592 provides in part:

> "Summary proceedings may be used for trial or disposition of the following matters only: (1) an incidental question arising in the course of litigation . . . "

The question raised by relator's rule to show cause is whether the judgment against the husband only can be used as a basis for a writ of seizure against community property of the husband and wife, now divorced. The trial court did not reach the merits of this issue.

We are of the opinion that this issue is incidental to the principal action against the husband. It affords the wife the opportunity to object to the seizure of her interest in the community property prior to it actually being seized. We hold that summary procedure is proper under these circumstances.

We therefore grant this writ and remand to the trial court for further proceedings.

E. Note

See Hargrave, *Developments in the Law, Louisiana Constitutional Law*, 47 LA. L. REV. 333 (1986) (describing the tension between the substantive law regarding what property of the non-incurring spouse may be seized and the procedural rules regarding appropriate notice of seizure); Rubin & Carter, *Notice of Seizure in Mortgage Foreclosures and Tax Sale Proceedings: The Ramifications of Mennonite*, 48 LA. L. REV. 535 (1988) (exploring the constitutional notice requirements under *Mennonite*).

F. *French Market Homestead v. Helene Marie Ulrich Hudleston wife of Albert J. Huddleston*

579 So. 2d 1079 (La. App. 5 Cir. 1991)

KLIEBERT, Judge.

French Market Homestead, FSA, plaintiff sued Albert Huddleston and his wife, Helene, via ordinaria on a promissory note, signed by both, in the amount of $1,750,000 plus interest, late charges, costs, and attorney fees. The note was alleged to be delinquent and secured by a mortgage on several condo units of the Chateau Village Retail Office Condominium.

When the Huddlestons failed to answer the petition, plaintiff, on January 21, 1988, confirmed a default judgment against both of them in the amount of One Million Seven Hundred Sixteen Thousand Five Hundred Fifty Two and 61/100 ($1,716,552.61) Dollars plus interest thereon at the rate of Six Hundred Thirty Four Dollars and 89/100 ($634.89) Dollars per day from April 1, 1987, until paid, plus accrued late charges as of October 31, 1987, in the amount of Eight Thousand Five Hundred Seventy-Nine Dollars and 28/100 ($8,579.23) Dollars, plus ten (10%) percent attorneys' fees on all said principal and interest plus all costs of the proceedings. The judgment further recognized and maintained the mortgage on immovable property granted by the Huddlestons.

After judgment was rendered plaintiff sought to execute on it by requesting the issuance of a writ of fieri facias and seizure thereunder of the mortgaged immovable property. Thereafter, both of the Huddlestons petitioned the court to nullify the judgment of January 21, 1988 and requested an injunction to arrest the seizure and sale of the mortgaged immovable property under the writ of fieri facias. Following hearings, the trial court found Mrs. Huddleston was not properly served with the underlying lawsuit and therefore enjoined the seizure and sale of her undivided one-half interest in the immovable property. Further, it dismissed Mr. Huddleston's request for preliminary injunction, thus allowing the seizure and sale to proceed against his undivided one-half interest in the immovable property. Mr. Huddleston has neither appealed nor answered the appeal, thus, the denial of his request for a preliminary injunction is final.

On appeal, plaintiff contends the trial court erred in enjoining the seizure and sale of Mrs. Huddleston's undivided one-half interest in the community property because the judgment on which the writ of fieri facias was based was rendered in a via ordinaria proceeding against the husband on a community obligation, hence, service on him was sufficient to justify the judgment against the community and the seizure of a community asset for its satisfaction. Defendant argues her interest in the property cannot be seized and sold because that portion of the underlying judgment against her on which the sale is based is null for lack of service. Additionally, she argues that since she personally executed the promissory note and is record owner of the property in indivision with her husband, her concurrence is required to sell the property.

Thus, the issue on appeal is whether a judgment creditor can seize and sell immovable community property to satisfy a community obligation incurred by both when only one spouse has been sued and cast in judgment on the community obligation.

LSA-Civil Code Article 2345 provides as follows:

> "A separate or community obligation may be satisfied during the community property regime from community property and from the separate property of the spouse who incurred the obligation."

LSA-Code of Civil Procedure Article 735 provides in pertinent part as follows: "[E]ither spouse is the proper defendant, during the existence of the marital community, in an action to enforce an obligation against community property; ..."

It is undisputed that the Huddlestons' community has not been terminated; the encumbrance is a community obligation executed by both, Mr. and Mrs. Huddleston; and, the property securing the obligation and subject to the seizure and sale is community. Therefore, in our view plaintiff has the right to proceed against either spouse, Code of Civil Procedure Article 735, and seize *community* property to satisfy the *community* obligation. C.C. Article 2345. Rayne State Bank and Trust Co. v. Fruge, 546 So.2d 637 (3rd Cir. 1989); Shel-Boze, Inc. v. Melton, 509 So.2d 106 (1st Cir. 1987). Because Mrs. Huddleston was also an obligor on the note, in order for her *separate* property to be available to satisfy the obligation plaintiff must proceed to judgment against her. See Lawson v. Lawson, 535 So.2d 851 (2nd Cir. 1988); Rayne State Bank and Trust Co., *supra.*

Mrs. Huddleston argues however that since she is the record owner of the community immovable, in indivision with her husband, her concurrence is required to sell the property, pursuant to LSA-Civil Code Articles 2336, 2337, 2347 and 2353. We disagree.

By executing the mortgage on the community immovable, Mrs. Huddleston concurred in the encumbrance of the property. A natural consequence of that encumbrance, after default on the promissory note, is the seizure and sale of the community immovable to satisfy the defaulted community obligation. At that point, a creditor, plaintiff herein, could seize and sell the community immovable to satisfy the community obligation.

A judicial mortgage is an encumbrance imposed by law, thus not subject to the concurrence of a spouse. LSA-Civil Code Article 2347, comment (a); Rayne State Bank and Trust Co., *supra;* Magee v. Amiss, 502 So.2d 568 (La. 1987).

Magee v. Amiss is a case similar to, but distinguishable from the one before us. In Magee, a separated husband incurred a separate obligation which caused a lien to be filed on a community immovable. The public records did not reflect the Magees were separated (community terminated). The lienholder caused the community immovable to be seized and sold to satisfy the separate debt ($1,856) of Mr. Magee. Mrs. Magee sued to protect her interest in the property sold by the sheriff.

In voiding the sale of her interest in the property, the Supreme Court found Mr. Magee acted unlawfully under LSA-Civil Code Article 150, since repealed, in that the facts suggested he was attempting to liquidate his and his wife's interests in the property without her sharing in the proceeds. Further, as the lien on the community immovable was perfected due to the separate obligation of Mr. Magee, Mrs. Magee did not concur in the encumbrance as required by LSA-Civil Code Article 2347. Because the public records reflected her ownership interest in the property, due process required she be entitled to at least the minimum notice requirement recognized in Mennonite Bd. of Missions v. Adams, 462 U.S. 791, 103 S.Ct. 2706, 77 L.Ed.2d 180 (1983), i.e., "Notice by mail or other means as certain to ensure actual notice is a minimum constitutional precondition to a proceeding which will adversely affect the liberty or property interest of any party ..."

In the case at bar, Mrs. Huddleston concurred in the encumbrance (a mortgage) on the property; therefore, there is no violation of Article 2347. A judgment was obtained against one spouse (C.C.P. Article 735) recognizing the community mortgage; thus allowing the community immovable to be seized and sold to satisfy the community obligation. LSA-C.C. Article 2345. Although she was record owner of the property, there was no due process violation because she clearly had notice prior to the sale as evidenced by the fact she sued to and did enjoin the sale before it proceeded. However, this does not mean the sale could not proceed. Under Civil Code Article 2345 and Code of Civil Procedure Article 735, the creditor has the right to satisfy a community obligation out of community property in a suit in which one spouse is named. Rayne State Bank and Trust Co., *supra*; Shel-Boze, Inc. *supra*.

For the foregoing reasons, the trial court judgment enjoining the sale of Mrs. Huddleston's interest in the community immovable property is set aside and vacated, and the case remanded to the trial court for further proceedings.

All costs of this appeal are to be borne by Mrs. Huddleston.

GAUDIN, Judge, dissenting.

I respectfully dissent.

This is an appeal from the granting of a preliminary injunction by a district judge who was concerned about (1) the undisputed fact that Mrs. Helen M. Huddleston did not receive service of process of the original petition and (2) the distinct possibility that her interest in the subject property was illegally seized.

It is also undisputed that Mrs. Huddleston is a record part owner of the property and that she was required to sign the promissory note and act of mortgage on which this litigation is based; yet, there was no attempt to serve her. These concerns, I believe, justify the issuance of the preliminary injunction.

The Court's foregoing opinion makes it appear that the merits of the nullity petition have already been heard in district court. By setting aside the preliminary injunction and remanding for further proceedings, this Court is sending the case back for a hearing on the merits while at the same time allowing Mrs. Huddleston's community property interest to be sold.

G. Note

In *Gewalt v. Stevens*, 757 So.2d 705 (La. App. 1st Cir. 1999) the defendant raised on appeal the failure of the plaintiffs to join defendant's wife in a petitory action involving alleged community property. The defendant urged that under the Code of Civil Procedure his spouse was a party needed for just adjudication. The court expressed the view "that both spouses *should* be made parties to any suit to enforce an obligation against community property, if at all possible" *id.* at 708; however, defendant's wife is not a party needed for just adjudication "in view of the fact that her husband has been able to adequately protect their joint interest in the action and in view of the fact that complete relief can be accorded in her absence." *Id.* Furthermore, citing its own opinion in *Shel-Boze, infra*, the court concluded that "where, as here, the spouses reside together at the time, service of prior notice on one spouse alone does not offend the due process rights of the other with respect to the enforcement of an obligation against community property." *Id. See Shel-Boze, Inc. v. Melton*, 509 So.2d 106 (La. App. 1st Cir. 1987) and *Kerico v. Doran Chevrolet, Inc.*, 572 So.2d 103 (La. App. 1st Cir. 1990).

H. *Rayne State Bank and Trust Company v. Flossie Martin Fruge*

546 So. 2d 637(La. App. 3d Cir. 1989)

KNOLL, Judge.

This appeal concerns the seizing of community funds to satisfy a judgment against the wife.

Mark Rufus Fruge appeals the trial court's dismissal on a peremptory exception of no cause of action of his petition for a preliminary injunction and a petition to annul a $350,000 default judgment rendered against his wife, Flossie Martin Fruge. The trial court ruled that Rayne State Bank and Trust Company (Rayne State) was permitted to execute its judgment against all the community property owned by the Fruges.

Mr. Fruge, who was not a party to Rayne State's suit against Mrs. Fruge, contends that the trial court erred: (1) in sustaining Rayne State's exception of no cause of action; and, (2) in declaring the default judgment against Mrs. Fruge enforceable against their community property.

FACTS

Between September 30, 1985, and October 2, 1986, Mrs. Fruge executed three continuing guaranty agreements for her son's company, Apple Service, Inc., in favor of Rayne State. Apple Service eventually defaulted on its loans.

On April 27, 1987, Rayne State filed suit against Mrs. Fruge on the continuing guaranties she executed. The record reflects that she was personally served on April 28, 1987. After Mrs. Fruge failed to answer the lawsuit, a judgment by default was entered against her on May 21, 1987, and the default was confirmed on May 28, 1987.

Mrs. Fruge did not tell her husband that she signed the continuing guaranties or that she was sued. He had no knowledge of Mrs. Fruge's activity in this regard. In his brief, he states that he had always managed the financial affairs of the community.

On July 31, 1987, Rayne State filed a rule to show cause against Mr. Fruge, seeking a declaration that its judgment against Mrs. Fruge was enforceable against certain community funds in Mr. Fruge's name which were deposited in Rayne State. Subsequently, Rayne State amended its rule, asking for a judicial declaration that its judgment could be executed against all community property of Mr. and Mrs. Fruge.

Mr. Fruge, alleging fraud and ill practices, filed a petition to annul the default judgment, and sought the issuance of a preliminary injunction, restraining Rayne State from enforcing its judgment against the community property. Rayne State interposed peremptory exceptions of no cause of action and no right of action to Mr. Fruge's petition.

Mr. Fruge's petition and Rayne State's exceptions were consolidated for hearing. The matter was submitted on the record. The trial court maintained Rayne State's exception of no cause of action and recognized Rayne State's right to enforce its judgment against the Fruges' entire community.

NO CAUSE OF ACTION

Mr. Fruge contends that he was a party interested in opposing the effect of the judgment against Mrs. Fruge and that the trial court erred in dismissing his petition for nullity because of the failure to state a cause of action.

An exception of no cause of action is tried solely on the petition and attached documents. In ruling on a peremptory exception of no cause of action, the trial court must accept all well pleaded facts in the petition and attached documents as true, and must resolve any doubt in favor of the sufficiency of the pleadings to state a cause of action. Meldean's, Inc. v. Rivers, 410 So.2d 837 (La.App. 3rd Cir.1982), *writ denied,* 414 So.2d 376 (La.1982).

The cause of action in the case sub judice is an action for nullity. Defendant urged the trial court to annul the judgment against Mrs. Fruge under two broad categories:

one, involving Rayne State's failure to include him as a party defendant; and that Rayne State's judgment was acquired by fraud and ill practices.

LSA-C.C.P. Art. 2002 provides in pertinent part: "A final judgment shall be annulled if it is rendered:

(2) Against a defendant who has not been served with process as required by law and who has not entered a general appearance, or against whom a valid judgment by default has not been taken; or

Except as otherwise provided in Article 2003, an action to annul a judgment on these grounds may be brought at any time."

Mr. Fruge contends he was an indispensable party to Rayne State's suit against Mrs. Fruge. In the alternative, Mr. Fruge argues that the failure to make him a defendant in the action against Mrs. Fruge violated the due process clause of the United States Constitution.

We note from the outset that Rayne State's action against Mrs. Fruge was not an action to enforce a claim against the community, but rather to determine her liability to the bank with regard to the continuing guaranties she signed.

Each spouse acting alone may manage, control, or dispose of community property unless otherwise provided by law. LSA-C.C. Art. 2346. The concurrence of both spouses is required for the alienation, encumbrance, or lease of community immovables, furniture or furnishings while located in the family home, and all or substantially all of the assets of a community enterprise. LSA-C.C. Art. 2347.

Using C.C. Art. 2347, Mr. Fruge contends that one spouse cannot incur an obligation that, when reduced to judgment, will encumber the community. We disagree.

Comment (a) to LSA-C.C. Art. 2347, quoted with approval in Magee v. Amiss, 502 So.2d 568 (La.1987), explains the word, encumbrance, as follows: "(a) Encumbrances imposed by law are not subject to the requirement of concurrence by the spouses. Thus, a transaction by one of the spouses acting alone may give rise to a vendor's privilege, or a mechanic's or materialman's lien on community property. Likewise, the recordation of a judgment against a spouse gives rise to a judicial mortgage on community property situated in the parish in which recordation takes place."

A continuing guaranty, treated jurisprudentially as a contract of suretyship, King Musical Instruments, Inc. v. Arceneaux Music, 441 So.2d 786 (La.App. 3rd Cir.1983), is an accessory contract by which a person binds himself to a creditor to fulfill the obligation of another upon the failure of the latter to do so. LSA-C.C. Art. 3035.

Considering the foregoing, it is clear that Mrs. Fruge's guaranty did not encumber the community. Accordingly, the concurrence of Mr. Fruge was not required.

Moreover, once Rayne State obtained its judgment against Mrs. Fruge, the judgment could be satisfied during the community property regime from community property and from Mrs. Fruge's separate property. LSA-C.C. Art. 2345.

Furthermore, Rayne State was not required to join Mr. Fruge because under LSA-C.C.P. Art. 735 "[e]ither spouse is the proper defendant, during the existence of the marital community, in an action to enforce an obligation against community property; ... When only one spouse is sued ..., the other spouse is a necessary party...." In the present case, Rayne State sued Mrs. Fruge to determine her liability to it for the guaranties she signed. As noted above, since these guaranties did not alienate, encumber or lease community property as delineated in LSA-C.C. Art. 2347, Mr. Fruge's concurrence was not required. Thus, Rayne State was not required to join Mr. Fruge as a defendant to its action involving the guaranties Mrs. Fruge signed. Shel-Boze, Inc. v. Melton, 509 So.2d 106 (La.App. 1st Cir.1987).

Therefore, we find no merit to Mr. Fruge's contentions that his signature was required on the guaranties, and that he should have been made a defendant in the action against Mrs. Fruge.

DUE PROCESS

Mr. Fruge contends that if Rayne State can execute its judgment against all of the Fruges' community property that such action constitutes the unlawful taking of his property without due process.

Although we have decided that Mr. Fruge's concurrence was not required on the guaranties and he was not an indispensable party to the action against Mrs. Fruge, Mr. Fruge, as the owner of a legally protected property interest in the community property was entitled to notice prior to the execution of judgment by Rayne State against community property. Magee, *supra* at page 571.

In Mennonite Bd. of Missions v. Adams, 462 U.S. 791, 103 S.Ct. 2706, 2712, 77 L.Ed.2d 180 (1983), the United States Supreme Court stated: "Notice by mail or other means as certain to ensure actual notice is a minimum constitutional precondition to a proceeding which will adversely affect the liberty or property interests of any party, whether unlettered or well versed in commercial practice, if its name and address are reasonably ascertainable."

In the case sub judice, after the suspensive appeal period lapsed, Rayne State filed a summary proceeding against Mr. Fruge, asking him to show cause why the judgment against Mrs. Fruge should not be executed against community property in which he had an interest. Mr. Fruge was served with this rule, and filed the responsive pleadings which form the basis of this appeal. We find the rule served as adequate notice to Mr. Fruge, therefore, there was no violation of due process.

For the foregoing reasons, the judgment of the trial court is affirmed. Costs of this appeal are assessed to Mr. Fruge.

AFFIRMED.

6.5 LOUISIANA'S DEBT COLLECTION RULES IN COMPARATIVE CONTEXT

A. Andrea B. Carroll, *The Superior Position of the Creditor in the Community Property Regime: Has the Community Become a Mere Creditor Collection Device*, 47 SANTA CLARA L. REV. 1 (2007)

***

II. The Exceptional Creditor Bent of the Community Property Regime

Modern creditors in community property regimes have access to a mass of spousal property almost inconceivable in non-community property states. Of course, they may access their debtor's property. But much more may be available as well.

A. Preventing the "$2 Bankruptcy": Creditor Rights to Community Property for Premarital Debts

One not well-versed in the intricacies of the community property regime will likely find the protection afforded antenuptial creditors of the spouses among its most shocking features. It is axiomatic in non-community property states-- sometimes referred to as "common law states"--that a creditor's collection efforts must be directed solely toward his debtor's property. When a debtor in a common law state marries, the creditor's ability to collect remains unaffected. The mere fact of marriage neither hurts nor helps a third-party creditor, who may continue to seize any property owned by the debtor spouse. But this is not so in the community property regime. A great windfall comes to the creditor whose struggling debtor marries an employed person in a community property state. That creditor's rights are substantially expanded by the marriage alone.

While some states now limit creditor access to community property for the antenuptial debts of the spouses, several still provide surprisingly expansive creditor protection. Louisiana's community property regime is by far the most creditor-friendly on this front. It allows the premarital creditor of a spouse for all manner of debts access to the *5 entirety of the community property, including the community property interests of the debtor and non-debtor spouses alike. Other American community property jurisdictions go almost as far. Idaho has at least suggested that seizure of any and all community property is appropriate for the satisfaction of a premarital debt and California has legislatively recognized an antenuptial creditor's ability to seize the entirety of the spouses' community property, save any earnings of the non-debtor spouse that are isolated in a distinct account.

The history behind Louisiana's move toward full community liability for premarital debts is indeed interesting. The Louisiana Supreme Court first provided for this unprecedented access to all community property for premarital debts at a time when state legislation arguably prohibited such access.

The Louisiana Civil Code, from its inception in the year 1808, provided in article 2403 that "the debts of both husband and wife, anterior to the marriage, must be acquitted out of their own personal and individual effects." Article 2403 was drawn from Spanish sources, including legislation providing that "each spouse has the obligation to satisfy from his separate assets his own (or non-community) debts which he contracted before marriage." The plain language of both the Louisiana enactment and its Spanish source provision certainly seemed to indicate that only the separate property of each spouse could be seized by a creditor for a debt pre-dating the debtor's marriage. Such a result appears logical and just, insofar as premarital debts necessarily have no connection to the community. The satisfaction of these debts, under the Louisiana and Spanish statutes, appeared to be limited to property with which the debts were connected--namely, the separate property of the debtor spouse--leaving the spouses' community property free for seizure by community creditors.

***

...The new "equivalent" to article 2403 is Louisiana Civil Code article 2345, which has remained unchanged since 1979 and provides that "[a] separate or community obligation may be satisfied during the community property regime from community property and from the separate property of the spouse who incurred the obligation." Although the new legislation does not expressly address premarital debts, the Louisiana jurisprudence has consistently held that the rule applies to allow seizure of 100% of the community property for both ante- and post-nuptial debts.

Historical materials surrounding the enactment of Louisiana Civil Code article 2345 reveal little about the purpose or motives of the legislature in approving the result in Creech and continuing to allow creditors full access to community property for premarital debts. But other community property states' struggles with the same problem provide some insight. Most state laws allowing access to all or some community property for a spouse's premarital debts are a direct reaction to the so-called "marital bankruptcy."

Early in the history of the American community property regime, following the Spanish model, most states rejected the liability of any community property whatsoever for premarital debts. As the United States economy became more creditor-focused, though, concern grew over the idea that the debtor's marriage often frustrated the separate creditor's attempt to collect a debt. If community property could not be seized for premarital debts, and virtually all property acquired after marriage, including the earnings of both spouses, became community property, the creditor's ability to rely on his debtor's earning stream to satisfy the debt would all but evaporate. A debtor marrying into a community property regime under these old rules of creditor collection basically limited his creditor to attempting to collect from the property the debtor took into the marriage. The debtor spouse's future earnings would be immune from the day of the marriage forward. The problem was dubbed the "marital bankruptcy" or the "$2 bankruptcy," as debtors were said to be able to effectively shield themselves from liability to their creditors merely by obtaining a $2 marriage license.

It is the possibility of this inequitable marital bankruptcy, and the Hobson's choice between it and a windfall to the creditor arising solely from his debtor's marriage, that likely led states such as Idaho, Louisiana, and California to begin allowing the seizure of some community property for premarital debts. The question now, however, is whether those legislatures have overcorrected. If Louisiana's rule allowing full access to community property, for instance, is an attempt to prevent the "$2 bankruptcy," has it gone too far? The potential prejudice to a creditor caused by his debtor's marriage could be eliminated in any number of ways that do not involve allowing a creditor to seize all of the spouses' community property and that are likewise more protective of the community. It is, perhaps, a function of the modern legislative process--in which creditors' lobbies abound--that the most creditor-friendly of all solutions was chosen.

***

B. UMPA

A comparison to other debt collection rules demonstrates just how creditor friendly the Louisiana rules are.

Uniform Marital Property Act § 8. Obligations of Spouses.

(a) An obligation incurred by a spouse during marriage, including one attributable to an act or omission during marriage, is presumed to be incurred in the interest of the marriage or the family.

(b) After the determination date:

(i) a spouse's obligation to satisfy a duty of support owed to the other spouse or to a child of the marriage may be satisfied only from all marital property and all other property of the obligated spouse that is not marital property;

(ii) an obligation incurred by a spouse in the interest of the marriage or the family may be satisfied only from all marital property and all other property of that spouse that is not marital property;

(iii) an obligation incurred by a spouse before or during marriage that is attributable to an obligation arising before marriage or to an act or omission occurring before marriage may be satisfied only from property of that spouse that is not marital property and that part of marital property which would have been the property of that spouse, but for the marriage; and

(iv) any other obligation incurred by a spouse during marriage, including one attributable to an act or omission during marriage, may be satisfied only from property of that spouse that is not marital property and that spouse's interest in marital property and in that order.

(c) This [Act] does not alter the relationship between spouses and their creditors with respect to any property or obligation in existence on the determination date.

(d) Provisions of a written consent signed by a creditor which diminish the rights of the creditor provided in this section are binding on the creditor.

(e) No provision of a marital property agreement adversely affects the interest of a creditor unless the creditor had actual knowledge of that provision when the obligation to that creditor was incurred. The effect of this subsection may not be varied by a marital property agreement.

(f) This [Act] does not affect the exemption of any property of spouses under other law.

CHAPTER 7: TERMINATION

7.1 INTRODUCTION

This chapter examines both the causes and effects of the termination of the community property regime. Louisiana Civil Code article 2356 contemplates six causes of termination (1) death of a spouse; (2) judgment of declaration of death of a spouse; (3) declaration of nullity of the marriage; (4) judgment of divorce; (5) judgment of separation of property; and (6) matrimonial agreement that terminates the community. Matrimonial agreements are considered in more detail in Chapter 8.

The first two causes for termination rarely give rise to much litigation. The death of a spouse automatically terminates the community property regime on the date of death and there is rarely any question with respect to the timing of that date. In some circumstances the date of death, or even the fact of death, may be uncertain. In those instances, Louisiana Civil Code articles 54, *et seq.* allow the court to enter a judgment fixing the date of death.

The third cause of termination is by far the most complex. As illustrated in the materials that follow, Louisiana recognizes the putative spouse doctrine. This doctrine allows the civil effects of marriage, including the community property regime, to flow in favor of one or both spouses even though the marriage itself is either an absolute or relative nullity. Reported decisions involving the putative spouse doctrine are surprisingly common.

The fourth and fifth causes—judgments of divorce and judgments of separation—are also considered. They give rise to some timing issues and often present interesting questions of management of the former community property as well as liability for debts.

The effects of termination are also considered in this chapter. Civil Code article 2358 explains that termination gives rise to claims for reimbursement. Reimbursement claims hinge on questions of valuation, timing, and classification of assets and liabilities as either community or separate. Termination often occurs before a partition of the community property. In this case the spouses, or former spouses, become co-owners of the former community property. A special set of management and accounting rules applies to co-ownership in this context.

Finally, this chapter considers some aspects relating to partition of former community property.

7.2 CAUSES OF TERMINATION: DEATH & DIVORCE

A. *Succession of William J. Moss*

769 So. 2d 614 (La. App. 3d Cir. 2000)

THIBODEAUX, Judge.

We again consider the effect of transfer restrictions on the Moss estate's shares of Coury Moss, Inc. stock. The trial court awarded Sharon K. Coury Moss, the surviving spouse of the deceased shareholder, William J. Moss, and administratrix of his estate, ownership of one-half of the stock presently held by the Succession of William J. Moss, but found that she had no right to stock not yet in the succession. The appellant, A. Sam Coury, also a shareholder in the corporation, argues that the trial court erred in concluding that Mrs. Moss owns one-half of Mr. Moss' stock and petitions this Court to determine the nature of the ownership of that stock. We amend and affirm in part the trial court's judgment and reverse in part.

I.

ISSUE

We shall determine the nature of the surviving spouse's interest in Coury Moss, Inc. stock owned by and owed to her deceased husband.

II.

FACTS

In 1979, William J. Moss and A. Sam Coury agreed to form a corporation, Coury Moss, Inc., for the purpose of operating an automobile dealership. On June 28, 1979, they executed a Shareholders' Agreement which provided that at the corporation's inception, one thousand shares of stock would be issued of which Mr. Coury would own seventy-five percent and Mr. Moss would own twenty-five percent. The Agreement further provided that Mr. Moss would buy two-thirds of Mr. Coury's stock in the corporation over a period of five years, from December 1980-1984 at book value. The Agreement identified the corporation as a "closed corporation" and required that upon the death or disability of any shareholder, his stock must be offered for sale to the remaining shareholder for book value.

On July 3, 1979, the shareholders executed Articles of Incorporation. The Articles mandated, inter alia, that they applied to the shareholders and their transferees or heirs, and placed certain restrictions on the sale or transfer of the corporation's stock.

Specifically, Article X mandated that any shareholder wishing to sell his stock must first offer it to the corporation for book value. Article XI required that upon the death or disability of any shareholder, his heirs or representatives must transfer his stock, except twenty-five percent of the corporation's stock, to the corporation at book value.

Pursuant to the Shareholders' Agreement, Mr. Coury transferred one hundred shares of stock per year to Mr. Moss from 1980-1982, for a total of three hundred shares. In 1983, he refused to transfer additional shares due to Mr. Moss' alleged breaches of the Agreement. Mr. Moss brought suit against Mr. Coury in November 1985 to compel the transfer of the remaining two hundred shares. Mr. Coury answered the petition and reconvened seeking a cancellation of the Agreement and return of the three hundred shares transferred thereunder. Mr. Moss died in 1989 and his succession representative and surviving spouse, Sharon Moss, were substituted as plaintiffs. After a myriad of trials and appeals, this Court held in Moss v. Coury, 97-640 (La.App. 3 Cir. 12/10/97); 704 So.2d 1248, writ denied, 98-783 (La.5/29/98); 720 So.2d 340, that Mr. Moss had not breached any prerequisites to the stock transfer; Mr. Coury breached the Agreement by not making the transfer; and, the Succession of William J. Moss was entitled to specific performance under the Agreement. The Court ordered Mr. Coury to transfer the remaining two hundred shares owed under the Agreement to the Succession of William J. Moss at the agreed price, opining that Mr. Coury's right to repurchase the stock under the Articles of Incorporation was contingent upon the initial transfer.

Mrs. Moss petitioned the trial court to declare that under Louisiana community property law, she is entitled to ownership of one-half of the stock currently held by and owed to her husband's succession. She asked that court to find that her stock ownership was not subject to the transfer upon death restrictions in the Articles of Incorporation.

The trial court partially granted the motion for the declaratory judgment, decreeing that "Sharon K. Moss is the rightful owner of 275 shares or one-half (1/2) of those 550 shares of Coury Moss, Inc. stock currently held and voted by the Succession of William J. Moss." The trial court denied that part of the motion in which Mrs. Moss sought to be declared owner of one-half of the two hundred shares Mr. Coury owes to the succession under the Shareholders' Agreement based on its finding that the claim was premature because those shares had not yet been transferred to the succession. Mr. Coury brought this appeal.

Community Property

Unless they validly contract otherwise, spouses domiciled in Louisiana are under the legal regime of community acquets and gains. La. Civ. Code arts. 2328 and 2334. The property of married persons is either community or separate. La. Civ. Code art. 2335. Community property includes all property acquired during the existence of the legal regime through the effort, skill, or industry of either spouse. La. Civ. Code art. 2338. The community is a patrimonial mass that includes both assets and liabilities.

La. Civ. Code art. 2336 cmt. (c). Each spouse owns a present undivided one- half interest in the community property. La. Civ. Code art. 2336.

Obligations incurred by a spouse during the existence of a community property regime are presumed to be community obligations with few exceptions. La. Civ. Code art. 2361; Bridges v. Bridges, 96-1191 (La. App. 3d Cir. 3/12/97); 692 So.2d 1186. This presumption is rebuttable upon proof by clear and convincing evidence that the debt was not incurred for the benefit of the community. La. Civ. Code art. 2363; Keene v. Reggie, 96-740 (La. App. 3d Cir. 10/22/97); 701 So.2d 720. We find no such evidence in the record.

A debt owed to a corporation as a result of a conventional obligation executed by a spouse during the existence of the community is a community liability. Krielow v. Krielow, 93-2539 (La. 4/11/94); 635 So.2d 180. As a community obligation, the debt is subject to equal division during the partition of the community. Both rights and obligations arising from contracts are heritable. La. Civ. Code art.1984. Obligations incurred by a spouse during the community regime may be satisfied after termination of the regime from the property of the former community and from the separate property of the spouse who incurred the obligation. La. Civ. Code art. 2357.

Death of one of the spouses terminates the legal regime of community property. La. Civ. Code art. 2356. Neither the community nor things of the community may be judicially partitioned prior to the termination of the regime. La. Civ. Code art. 2336. The surviving spouse continues to be a co- owner of an undivided one-half interest in community assets until they are partitioned. Cf. Hare v. Hodgins, 586 So.2d 118 (La. 1991).

When partitioning community property, the court may divide particular assets or liabilities equally or unequally, taking into consideration the nature and source of the asset or liability, the economic condition of the spouses, and any other relevant circumstances. La. R.S. 9:2801(4)(c). "The court is required to divide the community assets and liabilities so that each spouse receives property of an equal net value." Hare, 586 So.2d at 123 (citing La. R.S. 9:2801(4)(b)).

Because the patrimonial mass of community property includes both assets and liabilities, it is clear that Mrs. Moss owns an undivided one-half interest in the shares of Coury-Moss, Inc. stock currently held by the Succession of William J. Moss. This fact is not in dispute. Mrs. Moss asserts that she is also entitled to one-half of the remaining two hundred shares owed by Mr. Coury after the succession pays the purchase price. The trial court erroneously concluded that it could not partition this property. We will do so now. We find that Mrs. Moss is also entitled to one-half of the two hundred shares owed to the Succession of William J. Moss. Likewise, she is responsible for paying one-half of the purchase price for these shares in her individual capacity and not as testamentary executrix.

Having resolved the ownership of the community property, we shall now ascertain the nature of that ownership.

Effect of the Stock Transfer Restrictions

The trial court did not resolve whether Mrs. Moss' stock ownership was subject to the transfer restrictions. We shall now decide this issue.

Mrs. Moss asserts that she is the owner of one-half of the stock to which her husband was entitled under the Shareholders' Agreement but that her ownership is not subject to any restrictions. Basically, she seeks to enforce the express terms of the Shareholders' Agreement while simultaneously avoiding the terms of the Articles of Incorporation. When her argument is considered in light of these contracts, we understand her position to be that each spouse enjoys the contractual freedom to acquire community property but is precluded from contractually regulating that acquisition.

In support of her argument, Mrs. Moss cites Messersmith v. Messersmith, 229 La. 495, 86 So.2d 169 (1956) and Mestayer v. Williams, 569 So.2d 1102 (La. App. 3d Cir. 1990). Her contention is that under Messersmith, restrictive provisions in a corporation's charter cannot negate a spouse's interest as co-owner in community and, thus, she is entitled to exclusive management and control of her vested interest in one-half of her husband's stock. She cites Mestayer to show that this Court recently followed the Messersmith holding.

Mr. Coury argues that Messersmith, 229 La. 495, 86 So.2d 169, and Mestayer, 569 So.2d 1102, do not invalidate the effect of the Articles of Incorporation on a surviving spouse's one-half interest in corporate stock. His position is that those cases are distinguishable because: they concerned the division of community property after divorce; neither the husbands nor wives in those cases were parties to the restrictive contracts; and those transfer restrictions applied to the sale of stock (requiring that the stock first be offered to the corporation) and not to transfer upon death. He concludes that those courts did not invalidate the stock restrictions and that those wives would be bound by the transfer restrictions if they attempted to sell the stock.

These cases guide our determination that a surviving spouse owns a one-half interest in stock her deceased husband acquired during their marriage. The cases do not reach the paramount issue in this case concerning the nature of the spouse's ownership.

Although generally either spouse acting alone may manage, control or dispose of community property, La. Civ. Code art. 2346, the Civil Code tempers this right with regard to certain property. Each spouse has the exclusive right to manage or encumber movables issued or registered in his or her name as provided by law. La. Civ. Code art.

2351 (emphasis added). Shares of stock are incorporeal movables. La. Civ. Code art. 473. Stock issued in the name of a spouse is subject to management by that spouse exclusively. La. Civ. Code art. 2351 cmt. (a); Ackel v. Ackel, 595 So.2d 739 (La. App. 5 Cir. 1992). Applying these principles to the facts here, it is clear that Mr. Moss had the right to execute the Articles of Incorporation thereby making stock issued in his name subject to transfer restrictions in the event of his death.

Transfer restrictions placed on the mortis causa sale of stock are valid. Louisiana Weekly Pub. Co., Inc. v. First Nat'l. Bank of Commerce, 483 So.2d 929 (La. 1986). Although restrictions on a shareholder's right to transfer his shares are strictly construed, they are enforced according to their express provisions. Id. Courts are constrained to implement a stock transfer agreement which is unambiguous, clearly sets forth the terms of the agreement, and was executed by capable parties. See Barras & Breaux v. Champeaux, 526 So.2d 1231 (La. App. 3d Cir.1988).

By their express terms, the Articles of Incorporation "bind and obligate" not only the two incorporating shareholders, but also "such other persons who may hereafter join or become associated with them or their successors." Since this restrictive contract was executed during the existence of the community and affected community property, the obligation it created is a community obligation. La. Civ. Code art. 2361; Cutting v. Cutting, 625 So.2d 1112 (La. App. 3d Cir. 1993), writ denied, 93-2770 (La. 1/7/94); 631 So.2d 453. Mrs. Moss' ownership interest in the stock does not give her autonomous control over the stock; rather, her interest is subject to the transfer at death restrictions in the Articles of Incorporation. See Doughty v. Insured Lloyds Ins. Co., 576 So.2d 461 (La. 1991).

Community Property Partition

We now partition the five hundred fifty shares of Coury Moss, Inc. stock currently held by the Succession of William J. Moss and divide the stock equally between the succession and Mrs. Moss individually. We also equally divide the two hundred shares owed by Mr. Coury to the succession pursuant to the Shareholders' Agreement. The amount owed to Mr. Coury for the remaining two hundred shares is to be paid by both the succession and Mrs. Moss in her individual capacity, one-half of the sum by each. After this payment is made, Mr. Coury must transfer the remaining two hundred shares he owes, one hundred shares to Mrs. Moss and one hundred shares to the succession. The seven hundred fifty shares will be divided evenly, with Mrs. Moss holding three hundred seventy-five shares and the succession holding three hundred seventy- five shares.

The transfer upon death provisions in the Articles of Incorporation apply to all of the Coury Moss, Inc. stock held by both Mrs. Moss and the succession. These restrictions have been triggered by Mr. Moss' death and are now applicable. The restrictions require the heirs and representatives of a deceased shareholder to transfer the shareholder's stock to the corporation for book value, reserving up to twenty-five percent of the corporation's stock for themselves.

Of the seven hundred fifty shares at issue here, the succession and Mrs. Moss may retain a total of twenty-five percent of the corporation's stock, two hundred fifty shares, and must transfer five hundred shares to Coury Moss, Inc. Consistent with Louisiana community property law, we hereby divide this obligation equally. Mrs. Moss is entitled to keep one hundred twenty-five shares of Coury Moss, Inc. stock and must transfer two hundred fifty of her shares to the corporation for book value. Similarly, the succession may keep one hundred twenty-five shares of Coury Moss, Inc. stock and must transfer two hundred fifty shares to the corporation for book value. The shares they retain will continue to be subject to the Shareholders' Agreement and the Articles of Incorporation.

III.

CONCLUSION

Therefore, we affirm that portion of the trial court judgment declaring Mrs. Moss the owner of her one-half interest in the stock; we reverse that part of the judgment which declined to assign the stock owed under the Shareholders' Agreement; we partition the stock equally between Mrs. Moss and the Succession of William J. Moss; and we find that the stock held by both is subject to the transfer restrictions in the Shareholders' Agreement and the Articles of Incorporation.

AMENDED IN PART AND, AS AMENDED, AFFIRMED IN PART; REVERSED IN PART; AND RENDERED.

B. Note

In 1995, the legislature implicitly confirmed the approach of the jurisprudence in treating death as a cause of termination of the community differently from other causes. By reenacting Louisiana Civil Code article 2369.1 to provide special rules in the articles that follow for the management of former community property in addition to ordinary rules of co-ownership, the legislature expressly excluded the new rules' application to a termination by "death or judgment of declaration of a death of a spouse." Comment (b) does caution, however, that until there is an administration of the succession initiated by petition the ordinary rules of co-ownership apply to former community property: "When the community regime terminates because of the death or judgment of declaration of death of a spouse, the general rules of co-ownership, under the first paragraph of this Article apply to former community property."

C. Divorce: Timing of Dissolution

Civil Code article 159 provides:

> A judgment of divorce terminates a community property regime retroactively to the date of filing of the petition in the action in which the judgment of divorce is rendered. The retroactive termination of the community shall be without prejudice to rights of third parties validly acquired in the interim between the filing of the petition and recordation of the judgment.

Both the first and second sentences have given rise to litigation on occasion. In *Lambert v. Lambert*, 480 So. 2d 748 (La. App. 3d Cir. 1985) the court explained that where both spouses have filed petitions for divorce, it is the petition upon which the divorce is actually granted that is relevant for determining the retroactive date of termination, regardless of which petition was actually filed first.

In *Certified Sec. Systems, Inc. v. Ward*, 559 So.2d 497 (La. App. 4th Cir. 1990), *writ denied,* 565 So.2d 446, the trial court dismissed a suit filed by plaintiff against both the husband and wife on a contract for installation of a security system. The wife had contacted a security company after she filed suit for separation from bed and board, and the representative of the company was informed that the couple was separated. He also knew that the husband no longer resided in the house, but he permitted the husband alone to sign the contract even though it had been prepared for the wife's signature only. After the company failed to receive payment for installation, it filed suit against both the husband and wife. The company argued on appeal that the obligation was a community obligation incurred for the benefit of both spouses during the interim between filing of suit and the judgment of separation. Relying on the equivalent of current Louisiana Civil Code article 159, the company contended that the retroactive effect of the judgment of separation could not prejudice the rights of the company validly acquired in the interim. The court of appeal concluded that the company was not prejudiced because it had been put on notice that the parties were separated and contemplating divorce. Therefore, the obligation was to be treated as a post-termination obligation and only husband's share of the community assets and his separate property could be seized in satisfaction of the debt.

For spouses divorcing after a covenant marriage, LA. REV. STAT. ANN. §9:309 sets out the effect of a judgment of separation from bed and board on community property:

LA. R.S. 9:309. Separation from bed and board in a covenant marriage; effects

A. (1) Separation from bed and board in a covenant marriage does not dissolve the bond of matrimony, since the separated husband and wife are not at liberty to marry again; but it puts an end to their conjugal cohabitation, and to the common concerns, which existed between them.

(2) Spouses who are judicially separated from bed and board in a covenant marriage shall retain that status until either reconciliation or divorce.

B. (1) The judgment of separation from bed and board carries with it the separation of goods and effects and is retroactive to the date on which the original petition was filed in the action in which the judgment is rendered, but such retroactive effect shall be without prejudice to the liability of the community for the attorney fees and costs incurred by the spouses in the action in which the judgment is rendered, or to rights validly acquired in the interim between commencement of the action and recordation of the judgment.

(2) Upon reconciliation of the spouses, the community shall be reestablished between the spouses, as of the date of filing of the original petition in the action in which the judgment was rendered, unless the spouses execute prior to the reconciliation a matrimonial agreement that the community shall not be reestablished upon reconciliation. This matrimonial agreement shall not require court approval.

(3) Reestablishment of the community under the provisions of this Section shall be effective toward third persons only upon filing notice of the reestablishment for registry in accordance with the provisions of Civil Code Article 2332. The reestablishment of the community shall not prejudice the rights of third persons validly acquired prior to filing notice of the reestablishment nor shall it affect a prior community property partition between the spouses.

7.3 CAUSES OF TERMINATION: NULLITY

A. Christopher L. Blakesley, *The Putative Marriage Doctrine*, 60 TUL. L. REV. 1 (1985)

I. INTRODUCTION: HISTORY, CONCEPTUALIZATION AND DEFINITION

The classic putative marriage doctrine is substantive, ameliorative or corrective; it is designed to allow all the civil effects—rights, privileges, and benefits—which obtain in a legal marriage to flow to parties to a null marriage who had a good faith belief that their 'marriage' was legal and valid. Most jurisdictions in the United States have developed equitable analogues to the putative spouse doctrine that provide all or part of the relief afforded by the classic doctrine.

If a marriage is declared to be null or void, that declaration is retroactive to the day that the null marriage was contracted. It could be said that the action in nullity does not produce a null marriage, but merely declares that the marriage has never existed. However, many jurisdictions only apply the relation-back doctrine when it will substantially fulfill justice and equity. Thus, generally, a marriage declared null produces no effects of marriage whatsoever. Unless some protective or corrective measure intercedes, the normal civil effects of marriage simply do not flow from a marriage which is null. Thus, for example, if the results are consistent with the concept of nullity, a minor party to the null marriage would not be emancipated; nor marital property regime would ever exist; all donations in contemplation of marriage should be null, as well as all donations in or since the marriage contract that were made to the party as spouse; children of the couple born during the null marriage would be illegitimate; children of the couple who would have been legitimated by the marriage have not been legitimated; neither 'spouse' has a right to workers' compensation or a wrongful death action through the other; and neither spouse would have a right to the marital portion of the other's estate.

The putative marriage doctrine is a device developed to ameliorate or correct the injustice which would occur if civil effects were not allowed to flow to a party to a null marriage who believes in good faith that he or she is validly married. A putative marriage, therefore, is a marriage which is in reality null, but which allows the civil effects of a valid marriage to flow to the party or parties who contracted it in good faith. It is a marriage which has been solemnized in proper form and celebrated in good faith by one or both parties, but which, by reason of some legal infirmity, is either void or voidable. The doctrine developed as a canon law palliative to protect those persons who went through a marriage ceremony in the good faith belief that the marriage was valid and proper, when it was actually null due to some impediment. It provides that, notwithstanding its nullity, the civil effects of a legal marriage flow to the parties who, in good faith, contract an invalid marriage.

The French scholar and jurist Marcel Planiol thus defined the putative marriage doctrine and described its purpose:

> [It is] recognized that the null marriage, contracted in good faith, produces its effects, as if it had been valid until the judicial sentence declares it to be null. The sentence terminates the marriage, as would a divorce. The marriage henceforth produces no effect. But those it had produced subsist. . . . In other words, on account of the good faith of the parties, the nullity takes place without retroactivity. Such a marriage is called a putative marriage (putativus, deemed to be what it is not).

In 1978, a federal district court in Louisiana similarly defined the doctrine and expressed its purpose and underlying rationale:

> A marriage contracted when one spouse is a party to a previously undissolved marriage is absolutely null; however, equity demands that innocent persons not be injured through an innocent relationship. Natural law and reason will protect innocent persons so long as they deserve or need the protection of the law. Once the need or the reason for a protection ceases to exist, natural law no longer should extend its shield.

The classic putative marriage doctrine derives from canon law and has no Roman source. It is generally considered to have developed solely in so-called 'civilian' or civil code jurisdictions (France and Spain, for example). However, in reality, the doctrine existed, at least with regard to the issue of legitimacy, in early English family law as well. There is therefore an historical basis for its adoption in common-law jurisdictions. During the twelfth, thirteenth, and fourteenth centuries, canon law and the law of the land in England held that some civil effects of a marriage obtained, even though a marriage was null due to impediments such as consanguinity or a preexistent valid marriage. If the parents of a child had entered into a marital union which was null for some reason, although solemnized with the rites of the church, and if, at the time of the child's conception, one or both of the parents had a good faith belief that there was no impediment to the marriage, the child was considered legitimate. Even though there was no legally valid marriage, at least that civil effect of a valid marriage flowed to the good faith party or parties and their children. Pollock and Maitland report Bracton's knowledge of this principle:

> [He] wrote it down as an indubitable part of English law. In a passage which he borrowed from the canonist Tancred, he holds that there can be a putative marriage and legitimate off-spring even when the union is invalid owing to the existence of a previous marriage. 'If a woman in good faith marries a man who is already married, believing him to be unmarried, and has children by him, such children will be adjudged legitimate and capable of inheriting.'

This is precisely what the classic putative marriage theory provides. Unfortunately, this ameliorative doctrine was lost in later English history.

Generally today, and historically in Spanish, French, and English canon law, the putative marriage doctrine only applies if some sort of attempt at a proper ceremony is undertaken by the parties and one or both 'spouses' has a good faith belief that there is no impediment to the marriage. The putative marriage doctrine has been part of the family law of Louisiana from the beginning of western occupation and has been codified in the Louisiana Civil Code since 1808. Articles 117 and 118 of the Louisiana Civil Code have provided since that time:

> Art. 117. The marriage, which has been declared null, produces nevertheless its civil effects as it relates to the parties and their children, if it has been contracted in good faith.
>
> Art. 118. If only one of the parties acted in good faith, the marriage produces its civil effects only in his or her favor, and in favor of the children born of the marriage.

The French Civil Code more articulately presents the policy which motivates the application of the classic putative spouse doctrine and the equitable analogues which have been developed by states that have not formally adopted the doctrine. Articles 201 and 202 of the French Civil Code provide:

> Article 201. The marriage which has been declared null nonetheless produces its effects in relation to the spouses when it has been contracted in good faith. If good faith exists only on the part of one of the spouses, the marriage only produces its effects in relation to this spouse.
>
> Article 202. The marriage also produces its effects in relation to the children despite the fact that neither spouse was in good faith. Questions of their custody are ruled upon as in matters of divorce.

From as early as 1820, the Louisiana courts, in keeping with the codal requirement, have held that a woman who has had a good faith belief that she was legally married to her 'spouse,' although in reality she was not, is entitled to the 'civil effects' of that marriage. The civil effects were deemed to include all the advantages and benefits allowed by law to a lawful wife.

The Spanish civil-law rule governing putative marriage also had an impact on Louisiana judicial interpretation of code articles, as well as on the law in other jurisdictions, including Texas and California. In Louisiana, the impact of Spanish doctrine is seen, for example, in relation to termination of the civil effects of a putative marriage. Louisiana jurisprudence provides that the civil effects cease when good faith ends, in accordance with Spanish doctrine, rather than at the time the marriage is declared null, as adherence to French doctrine would require.

Although the Texas legislature abolished Spanish civil law in 1840, and although family law (including the putative marriage doctrine) in Texas had been based upon Spanish-Mexican law up to that time, Texas cases after 1840 have continued to recognize the putative marriage doctrine. The decisions, however, have not been consistent in their rationale. Although there has never been any doubt that Texas law provides relief for the good faith putative spouse, some decisions suggest a continuation of the classic Spanish doctrine while others reject the classic doctrine and adopt an equitable equivalent. Prior to 1840, and in several later decisions, Texas courts recognized the putative spouse doctrine as fundamental law born of the Spanish Siete Partidas, which applied throughout Spanish America. These courts, applying the classic putative marriage doctrine, held that the putative spouse is entitled to all the incidents and privileges pertaining to a lawful marriage. Certainly, Las Siete Partidas provided that the putative spouse is so entitled. Three decisions made subsequent to the Act of 1840, held that the putative spouse doctrine of Las Siete Partidas was the applicable law. These decisions, however, related to marriages which had occurred prior to 1840, when Texas abolished the Spanish-Mexican law. The Act of January 20, 1840, which adopted the common law for Texas, stated that the rights of parties married in Texas prior to its passage 'shall be regulated by the law as it aforetime was.' Thus, although the Spanish-Mexican law was the appropriate law to apply in those cases, the decisions do not answer the question of whether the complete classic putative spouse doctrine should apply to null marriages contracted after 1840. Some subsequent Texas decisions held that, after 1840, equity was necessary to provide the putative spouse with the incidents of marriage; the putative spouse doctrine was no longer a matter of substantive law, but a remedy in equity. Furthermore, the courts reasoned that since the putative marriage doctrine was now an equitable matter, all of the civil effects of marriage no longer automatically flow, but the courts can equitably pick and choose. However, the syllabus to a 1905 decision of the Texas Supreme Court states:

> Under the act of January 20, 1840, entitled 'An act to adopt the common law of England, to repeal certain Mexican laws, and to regulate the marital rights of parties,' the body of which is, with reference to married persons, inconsistent with the rules of common law, and conformable in the main to the Spanish law, the common-law rule declaring void the marriage of a woman to a man who is under the impediment of a prior existing marriage does not apply to a woman who contracts the marriage in good faith and without knowledge of the impediment, but so long as she continues to act innocently she has as to property aquired during that time, the rights of a lawful wife, and the corresponding obligations, and power to convey, with the consent of her supposed husband, and notwithstanding her infancy, her separate property.

Finally, in 1975, the Texas Supreme Court definitively ruled that a putative spouse has the right to all the incidents of a legal marriage, at least insofar as property division is concerned. Thus, although the Act of 1840 abolished Spanish law in Texas to follow the common law of England, it may not have abrogated the doctrine of putative marriage, which continued in the Spanish civil-law tradition. Nevertheless, certain benefits, such as workers' compensation benefits, do not flow to the putative spouse in Texas.

In California, putative marriage has also been preserved in the law, although the cases refer to equity and fundamental fairness as their foundation, rather than to California's Spanish legal heritage. While not acknowledging the impact of California's Spanish heritage on the doctrine, the decisions which establish the effects of putative marriage clearly reflect Spanish influence. The California Civil Code has recognized the doctrine since 1969. Code sections 4452 and 4800 provide for equal division of property, and California case law allows all the other incidents of marriage available under the Spanish putative marriage rule.

II. RECOGNITION OF THE DOCTRINE OF PUTATIVE MARRIAGE OR AN ANALOGUE

Historically, the courts of many states in the United States have recognized the putative marriage doctrine or an analogue thereof. Several other states have explicitly adopted all or part of the doctrine by statute.

The approach and rationale in adopting the putative spouse doctrine has usually been similar to that taken by the State of Washington. In the early twentieth century, the Supreme Court of Washington stated:

> Where a woman in good faith enters into a marriage contract with a man, and they assume and enter into the marriage state pursuant to any ceremony or agreement recognized by the law of the place, which marriage would be legal except for the incompetency of the man which he conceals from the woman, a status is created which will justify a court in rendering a decree of annulment . . . and . . . awarding to the innocent, injured woman such proportion of the property as, under all the circumstances, would be just and equitable.

Subsequent cases further defined this doctrine to allow the innocent party to retain one-half the property acquired through the joint efforts of the parties during the invalid marriage. The Washington courts supported these holdings by applying a partnership theory to property acquired during a putative marriage. The 'partnership—joint effort' theory, however, was not expanded to include all community property, so Washington has not adopted the 'pure' or 'classic' putative spouse doctrine which would divide the property and provide other civil effects of marriage in precisely the same manner as a legal marriage. The Washington Supreme Court has specifically stated that 'property acquired by a man and a woman not married to each other, but living together as husband and wife, is not community property, and, in the absence of some trust relation, belongs to the one in whose name the legal title to the property stands.' However, in the same case the court recognized in dictum an equitable 'joint-effort' theory which would allow an innocent good faith spouse to recover certain property acquired during the 'marriage.' Indeed, subsequent cases have recognized a broad range of equitable principles available to provide equitable distribution of property.

Oklahoma, a non-community property state, provides another example of an analogue to the putative spouse doctrine established through case law. In 1920, the Supreme Court of Oklahoma stated that where a 'marriage' entered by a party who had a good faith belief that it was valid was found to be void, the court had the power to make an equitable division of the property jointly accumulated by the parties while they lived together as supposed husband and wife. A more recent Oklahoma decision awarded a good faith spouse in a void marriage a one-half interest in property acquired, partially with her own funds, during the course of the 'marriage.'

Recently, several states have adopted the notion of putative marriage by statute. Perhaps the most striking example is section 305 of the Illinois Marriage and Dissolution of Marriage Act, which provides:

> Any person, having gone through a marriage ceremony, who has cohabited with another to whom he is not legally married in the good faith belief that he was married to that person is a putative spouse until knowledge of the fact that he is not legally married terminates his status and prevents acquisition of further rights. A putative spouse acquires the rights conferred upon a legal spouse, including the right to maintenance following termination of his status, whether or not the marriage is prohibited, under Section 212, or declared invalid, under Section 301. If there is a legal spouse or other putative spouse, rights acquired by a putative spouse do not supersede the rights of the legal spouse or those acquired by other putative spouses, but the court shall apportion property, maintenance and support rights among the claimants as appropriate in the circumstances and in the interests of justice. This Section shall not apply to common law marriages contracted in the State after June 30, 1905.

The Illinois act is derived from the Uniform Marriage and Divorce Act section 209, which adopts, and in its comments enthusiastically recommends, adoption of the putative marriage doctrine. Illinois' adoption of the putative spouse doctrine abrogated prior Illinois case law which conferred no rights of marriage on any parties to a null marriage, even if they were in good faith. The Illinois act has been upheld against the charge that it is unconstitutionally vague.

Similarly, Colorado, Minnesota, and Montana are among the states which have recently adopted the putative marriage doctrine by legislation. The Minnesota statute reads:

> Any person who has cohabited with another to whom he is not legally married in the good faith belief that he was married to that person is a putative

> spouse until knowledge of the fact that he is not legally married terminates his status and prevents acquisition of further rights. A putative spouse acquires the rights conferred upon a legal spouse, including the right to maintenance following termination of his status, whether or not the marriage is prohibited or declared a nullity. If there is a legal spouse or other putative spouses, rights acquired by a putative spouse do not supersede the rights of the legal spouse or those acquired by other putative spouses, but the court shall apportion property, maintenance, and support rights among the claimants as appropriate in the circumstances and in the interest of justice.

This statute reversed the long-established case-law rule in Minnesota. The Montana statute is essentially identical to that of Minnesota.

These adoptions of the putative marriage doctrine apparently concur with the ancient canon law ethic, repeated by the European civil codes, by old English family law, by the Louisiana Civil Code, and recently by the Uniform Marriage and Divorce Act, that fairness and equity require that a good faith putative spouse receive the same rights, benefits and prerogatives as a legal spouse. Specifically, the commissioners' note to the Uniform Act supports the recommendation to adopt the doctrine with a list of purposes and advantages afforded to the adopting state. Some of the benefits noted are:

> (1) to provide legislative foundation for achieving the obviously just results provided by the putative spouse doctrine; (2) to spell out specifically the rights conferred upon a putative spouse; (3) to state specifically when the status of putative spouse terminates; (4) to eliminate any distinction which some courts might attempt between prohibited marriages and those which merely are subject to declaration of invalidity; (5) to provide specifically for equitable apportionment, . . . either where there are a legal spouse and a putative spouse, or where there are several putative spouses.

The primary purpose of the putative spouse doctrine and its analogues is to aid those persons who have a good faith belief that they are married, and who, in the absence of a putative spouse statute, may be denied both the economic and status-related incidents of marriage.

***

V. CIVIL EFFECTS

A null marriage produces no civil effects. It is as if no marriage at all has taken place. In contrast, a good faith putative marriage or equitable analogue produces, depending on the law of the state involved, all or some of the civil effects of a legal marriage.

Louisiana Civil Code articles 117 and 118 are an example of the classic civil-law putative marriage doctrine. These articles provide that a marriage which has been declared null nevertheless produces its civil effects for the good faith party or parties and for their children.

In 1973, the Louisiana Supreme Court listed civil effects which flow from a classic civil code putative marriage:

> The jurisprudence has declared the following to be civil effects which flow from putative marriage: the legitimacy of the children. . .; the right of the putative wife to claim workmen's compensation from her husband's employer. . .; the right of the putative wife to her proportionate share of the community property . . .; the right of the putative wife to inherit as a wife in the succession of the husband . . .; the right of the putative wife to be considered as the 'widow' under her husband's insurance policy. . .; the right of the putative wife to the marital portion, when she is otherwise qualified.

This section will consider these civil effects and how they apply in the various jurisdictions of the United States.

A. Legitimacy of Children

Virtually all jurisdictions that recognize the putative spouse doctrine or an analogue to it provide that children of the putative marriage are legitimate. Some states, due to the constitutionally questionable nature of discrimination against illegitimate children, have eliminated the status of illegitimacy or provided that civil effects such as support and right to inherit flow from the parent-child relationship, whether or not the child is legitimate.

B. Division of Property Acquired During the 'Marriage'

The overwhelming weight of authority in the United States provides that a party who believed in good faith that his null marriage was valid has a right to some portion of the property accumulated during the relationship. This is generally an equal share or an undivided one-half interest, although those states which apply an equitable remedy reserve the right to change the formula when equity requires.

One might expect that the classic putative marriage doctrine would apply in states that, due to their civil-law antecedents, are community property jurisdictions. In reality, Louisiana is the only state that applies the pure or classic putative marriage doctrine, that is, it establishes the same community property regime that exists in a valid marriage rather than an equivalent or analogue. Details of the community property regime vary from state to state. Generally, however, one may say that it provides that all marital property, the acquets and gains acquired during the marriage by the husband and wife and not the separate property of either, is owned in community by both of them. The spouses each have a right to an undivided one-half interest in this community of acquets and gains.

In the classic system, a putative spouse is entitled to the same rights in the community of acquets and gains as a legal spouse; an actual community property regime, not some equivalent or analogue, exists for the putative spouse. Thus, Louisiana law provides that a putative spouse is a party to the community property regime, just as a legal spouse is. Other community property jurisdictions in the United States which have a very strong Spanish legal heritage, including California and Texas, use equitable notions to divide property after the 'dissolution' of a putative marriage. Louisiana, California, and Texas provide a laboratory for study of the confluence of civil and common law. The approach in those states to the division of property provides interesting and practical material for consideration by practicing attorneys, scholars, and legislators faced with the problem in any jurisdiction.

***

B. Applicable Louisiana Statutes

The Louisiana Civil Code contemplates both relatively null marriages and absolutely null marriages. Article 94 provides that "[a] marriage is absolutely null when contracted without a marriage ceremony, by procuration, or in violation of an impediment." The legal impediments to marriage are discussed in Articles 88-90. They include (1) an existing marriage; (2) spouses having the same gender (although the Constitutionality of this impediment is suspect, at best); and (3) spouses who are related to each other. In the case of any of these impediments, the marriage is an absolute nullity and "[a] declaration of nullity is not required, but an action to recognize the nullity may be brought by any interested persons." La. Civ. Code art. 94. As will be seen, a judgment of nullity may be needed in order to terminate the civil effects afforded to a spouse in an absolutely null marriage under the putative spouse doctrine.

Article 95 provides that "[a] marriage is relatively null when the consent of one of the parties to marry is not freely given." Typically, a relatively null marriage will be confirmed or ratified and the marriage will become a legal marriage. Prior to confirmation, however, Article 95 provides that a relatively null marriage "may be declared null upon application of the party whose consent was not free."

Articles 96 and 97 are the Louisiana codification of the putative spouse doctrine:

Art. 96. Civil effects of absolutely null marriage; putative marriage

An absolutely null marriage nevertheless produces civil effects in favor of a party who contracted it in good faith for as long as that party remains in good faith.

When the cause of the nullity is one party's prior undissolved marriage, the civil effects continue in favor of the other party, regardless of whether the latter remains in good faith, until the marriage is pronounced null or the latter party contracts a valid marriage.

A marriage contracted by a party in good faith produces civil effects in favor of a child of the parties.

A purported marriage between parties of the same sex does not produce any civil effects.

Art. 97. Civil effects of relatively null marriage

A relatively null marriage produces civil effects until it is declared null.

Under Article 96, the civil effects of a putative marriage depend on two factors: (1) the good or bad faith of each spouse; and (2) whether the cause of nullity is an undissolved prior marriage. The *Thomason* case, below, illustrates the first possibility: one spouse is in good faith, one spouse is in bad faith, cause of nullity is not an undissolved prior marriage. The *Prince* case, below, illustrates the second possibility: both spouses in good faith, cause of nullity is undissolved prior marriage. The *Patton* case, which is discussed in *Prince*, below, illustrates a third possibility: one spouse in good faith, one spouse in bad faith, cause of nullity is prior undissolved marriage. A fourth possibility exists as well: both spouses in good faith, no prior undissolved marriage.

C. *Barbara Ann Hughes Thomason v. Roger Randolph Thomason Sr.*

776 So. 2d 553 (La. App. 3d Cir. 2000)

DOUCET, Chief Judge.

The Defendant, Roger Randolph Thomason, appeals the trial court's determination that, although the marriage was invalid, Barbara Ann Hughes Thomason was in good faith and entitled to the civil effects of marriage as a putative spouse.

Barbara Thomason filed for a divorce in December 1998. In his answer to the petition for divorce, Mr. Thomason stated that no marriage had taken place. A hearing was held on December 6, 1999, at which the following facts were brought to light. The parties met in a sanitarium where both were being treated for tuberculosis. After being released they continued to see each other and on April 5, 1958, Roger asked Barbara to go to Mississippi with him to get married. They went to the courthouse in Port Gibson, Mississippi and obtained a marriage license. At this point the parties' version of events diverge. Barbara testified that they then went to a house and spoke to a man. Although no ceremony was held, she thought this was the justice of the peace and that she was married to Roger. They left the house and checked into a hotel together. She testified that Roger gave her a wedding ring. The next day they returned to Louisiana.

Roger disagreed with this account. At the hearing, he testified that after getting the license they were unable to find a justice of the peace; that they never went to anyone's house but simply checked into a hotel. He testified that he knew no marriage had taken place. It is undisputed that from that time until Barbara left the matrimonial domicile, the two held themselves out as married.

On December 6, 1999, the court held a hearing to determine the issues of marriage and putative spouse status. After hearing the evidence of both parties. The trial court made the following findings:

From the testimony of both parties, the Court has determined that even though Barbara Hughes Thomason "believed" that they were married on April 5, 1958, in reality, they were not. It is this Court's opinion that Roger Randolph Thomason took advantage of Barbara's ignorance about marriage and deliberately did not say that they were not married after leaving the home of the justice of the peace and never told Barbara. Although Roger testified that one time during the marriage, he told Barbara that they were not legally married, this Court does not find his testimony to be credible.

This Court has determined that Barbara Ann Hughes Thomason did not know during all the years she was together with Roger that her marriage was defective in the eyes of the law. This does not mean that she is to blame for the marriage not being valid, only that she trusted and loved someone so completely that she never thought they would be deceitful to her.

The court rendered judgment finding that the two were never validly married but that Barbara was in good faith until Roger filed his answer to her petition for divorce and was, therefore, "entitled to the civil effects of the marriage as a putative spouse." Roger appeals.

GOOD FAITH

Roger's first two assignments of error address the existence of good faith on the part of Barbara and the date on which her good faith, if any, ended. "Good faith" is defined as an honest and reasonable belief that the marriage was valid and that no legal impediment to it existed. Saacks v. Saacks, 96- 736 (La.App. 5 Cir. 1/28/97), 688 So.2d

673. "Good faith" consists of being ignorant of the cause which prevents the formation of the marriage, or being ignorant of the defects in the celebration which caused the nullity. Saacks v. Saacks, supra; Rebouche v. Anderson, 505 So.2d 808 (La.App. 2 Cir.1987), writ denied, 507 So.2d 228 (La.1987). The question of whether a party is in good faith is subjective, and depends on all the circumstances present in a given case. Saacks v. Saacks, supra; In Re Succession of Gordon, 461 So.2d 357 (La.App. 2 Cir.1984), writ denied, 464 So.2d 319 (La.1985). Although the good faith analysis test incorporates the objective elements of reasonableness, the inquiry is essentially a subjective one. Saacks v. Saacks, supra; Rebouche v. Anderson, supra. Alfonso v. Alfonso, 99-261, p. 5 (La.App. 5 Cir. 7/27/99); 739 So.2d 946, 948-49.

Roger testified that because they never found a justice of the peace and never went through a marriage ceremony, Barbara had to know that they were not married. Barbara testified that she thought they were married when they signed the license and saw the man she thought was a justice of the peace. Roger further argues that any good faith belief Barbara had in the validity of the marriage ended when he told her they were not really married shortly before their first child was born. He testified that he told her because he thought they should get married to legitimate the child, but that she did not want to hear it. Barbara testified that the validity of the marriage was never brought into question until Roger filed his answer to the petition.

The determination of whether good faith is present is a factual question and the finding of the trial judge is entitled to great weight on appeal. That factual determination will not be overturned unless it is shown to be clearly wrong. Any doubt as to the existence of good faith is to be resolved in favor of a finding of good faith.

Id. at p. 5; 739 So.2d at 949.

In this case, the trial court apparently based its determination on a credibility evaluation, accepting Barbara's testimony over that of Roger.

In this case, it was not Barbara's testimony which was inconsistent, but Roger's. Throughout his testimony instances of obvious inconsistencies with his deposition testimony were pointed out. Under the circumstances, his credibility is far more questionable than that of Barbara. Therefore, we find no error in the trial court's decision to credit Barbara's testimony. We further find no manifest error in his decision to find that Barbara was in good faith and entitled to the civil benefits of marriage as a putative spouse.

END DATE OF THE COMMUNITY REGIME

Roger further contends that even if Barbara was in good faith until he filed his answer, the trial judge erred in ordering that the community regime be ended retroactive to the date the Defendant filed his answer, that is the date the trial court found that good faith ended. Roger argues that the law requires that the community regime be terminated retroactive to the date of filing the petition for divorce.

La.Civ.Code art. 159 provides that:

> A judgment of divorce terminates a community property regime retroactively to the date of filing of the petition in the action in which the judgment of divorce is rendered. The retroactive termination of the community shall be without prejudice to rights of third parties validly acquired in the interim between the filing of the petition and recordation of the judgment.

However, in this case there will be no judgment of divorce since there was no marriage. The petition for divorce is moot. La.Civ.Code art. 96 provides in pertinent part that: "An absolutely null marriage nevertheless produces civil effects in favor of a party who contracted it in good faith for as long as that party remains in good faith." We agree with the trial court that Barbara remained in good faith until Roger filed his answer to her petition on April 20, 1999. Therefore, the court correctly found that Barbara continued to be entitled to the civil effects of marriage until that date.

CONCLUSION

For these reasons, the judgment of the trial court is affirmed. Costs of this appeal are to be paid by Roger Thomason.

AFFIRMED.

D. *Clementine Prince v. Irita B. Hopson and Victoria H. Albert*

89 So. 2d 128 (La. 1956)

HAWTHORNE, Justice.

Plaintiff-appellee, Clementine Prince, instituted this proceeding seeking to be declared the owner of a lot of ground purchased by her during the existence of her marriage with James Brough, deceased. The defendants are Victoria H. Albert, surviving legal wife of James Brough, and Irita B. Hopson, sole issue of the marriage between Brough and Victoria H. Albert and the only living child of Brough. The defendants claim the ownership of, or an interest in, this property.

The facts giving rise to this litigation are as follows: James Brough, the deceased, married Victoria H. Albert on December 31, 1907, and of this marriage one child was born, Irita Elizabeth Brought, now wife of Willie Ray Hopson. In January, 1919, James Brough filed a suit against his wife for an absolute divorce on the ground of seven years' separation. A preliminary default was entered in that case, but final judgment was never rendered. Clementine Prince, relying upon the statement of James Brough that he was divorced from his first wife, was by a minister of the gospel married to Brough on May 19, 1919, after a marriage license to perform said ceremony had been duly obtained. After this marriage Clementine Prince and James Brough lived together as man and wife until his death on May 18, 1940, for a period of approximately 21 years, and in fact Clementine Prince did not know that Brough had not been divorced until she attempted to borrow money on the property here involved in 1955, some 15 years after his death. Moreover, his first wife, Victoria Albert, believed that she and the deceased were divorced, and she had contracted a marriage with Elijah Albert.

The property here involved, which is a lot of ground in the City of New Orleans, was sold according to the deed by Elizabeth McCluskey to Clementine Brough on March 4, 1939, during the time she and James Brough were living together as husband and wife. Although this deed names the vendee as Clementine Prince, wife of James Brough, it contains no recitation of paraphernality. The consideration named is $215 in cash.

After trial on the merits the district judge concluded that the marriage of James Brough and Clementine Prince was an absolute nullity, and that James Brough was in bad faith, and rendered judgment recognizing Clementine Prince Brough to be the owner of the property in question. From this judgment defendants have appealed.

There is no doubt that Clementine Prince contracted her marriage with James Brough in good faith; in fact, this is not even an issue in the case and is conceded by all parties. Moreover, in spite of the trial judge's ruling to the contrary, there is no allegation, no evidence, and no contention that James Brough himself was in bad faith in contracting the second marriage with Clementine Prince. Victoria Albert in her answer states that both she and James Brough believed that they had been legally divorced, and there is no evidence to the contrary. The law is well settled in this state that where a man and a woman marry and live together as husband and wife, as James Brough and Clementine Prince did for 21 years, there is a presumption that they have been validly married, and that the marriage though null was nevertheless contracted in good faith. Succession of Braud, 170 La. 411, 127 So. 885; Succession of Chavis, 211 La. 313, 29 So.2d 860; Succession of Verrett, 224 La. 461, 70 So.2d 89, citing Succession of Fields, 222 La. 310, 62 So.2d 495.

Under these circumstances there is only one conclusion that can be reached, and that is that both Clementine Prince and James Brough were is good faith at the time their marriage was contracted, although this marriage was a nullity.

Since the marriage of Clementine Prince and James Brough was contracted in good faith, under Article 117 of the Civil Code this marriage produced its civil effects, and the existence of a community of acquets and gains between them is such a civil effect.

It is well settled in this state that property purchased in the name of either spouse during the existence of the community of acquets and gains is presumed to be community property....

***

Since Clementine Prince and James Brough both contracted their null marriage in good faith, the question then arises: How should we divide this property acquired during the coexistence of both the first and the second marriage, or during the existence of the putative community? The claimants are Victoria H. Albert, the legal wife; Irita B. Hopson, legitimate child of the first marriage, and Clementine Prince, putative wife of James Brough.

In Waterhouse v. Star Land Co., Ltd., 139 La. 177, 71 So. 358, 360, this court said:

> 'It is a fixed rule of property in the state of Louisiana that property which has been earned during the existence of a putative marriage belongs one half to the legal wife and the other half to the reputed wife. The children of the respective marriages have therefore no interest in it. * * *'

In support of this statement the court relied on the cases of Patton v. Cities of Philadelphia and New Orleans, 1 La.Ann. 98; Hubbell v. Inkstein, 7 La.Ann. 252; Succession of Navarro, 24 La.Ann. 298, and Jermann v. Tenneas, 39 La.Ann. 1021, 3 So. 229, Id., 44 La.Ann. 620, 11 So. 80. To these cases we might add Abston v. Abston, 15 La.Ann. 137, and the later cases of Ray v. Knox, 164 La. 193, 113 So. 814, and Succession of Fields, 222 La. 310, 62 So.2d 495, 499.

In Succession of Fields, supra, this court quoted with approval from Ray v. Knox, supra, as follows:

> "And the rule was correctly laid down in Patton v. [Cities of] Philadelphia [and New Orleans], 1 La.Ann. 98, an has since been followed, that where a man marries, and afterwards contracts a second marriage without the first having been dissolved, the community property acquired during the coexistence of said two marriages belongs exclusively and in equal shares to said two wives as long as the second wife is in good faith, i. e., as long as she has no certain knowledge of the existence of the first marriage, and the bigamous husband has no share whatever in said property. Cf. [LSA] R.C.C. Art. 117 supra."

The famous case of Patton v. Cities of Philadelphia and New Orleans, supra, is the source from which this rule of property springs. In that case Abraham Morehouse was married to Abigail Young, by whom he had children and whom he abandoned in the

State of New York. He came to Louisiana and here in bad faith as clearly shown by the facts contracted a second marriage with Eleonore Hook, untruthfully representing himself as a widower. Children were also born of this putative marriage. In disposing of the property left by Morehouse at his death, this court applied the Spanish law, and concluded that the property should go one-half to the legal wife and one-half to the putative wife, the forced heirs getting nothing, on the theory that Morehouse had wronged the second wife by creating a bigamous marriage and for his wrong the second wife had a claim in damages against the husband equal to his share in the community. The court applied the Spanish law because Morehouse's death in 1813 gave rise to the cause of action before the incorporation in our Civil Code of Articles 117 and 118 (Articles 119 and 120 of the Code of 1825). Articles 117 and 118 read as follows:

> 'Art. 117. The marriage, which has been declared null, produced nevertheless its civil effects as it relates to the parties and their children, if it has been contracted in good faith.
>
> 'Art. 118. If only one of the parties acted in good faith, the marriage produces its civil effects only in his or her favor, and in favor of the children born of the marriage.'

The holding in the Patton case has been followed ever since by this court, even though, as pointed out in Hubbell v. Inkstein, supra, decided in 1852, the decision in the Patton case was under the former laws of the country (Spanish) which had been repealed at the time of the decision of this court in the Hubbell case. The court in the Hubbell case deduced that the reasoning of the Patton case had equal force under both the Spanish law and the system of law existing at the time of that decision. We note, however, that in the Hubbell case the court did not mention Articles 119 and 120 of the Code of 1825 (now Articles 117 and 118).

Be that as it may, in none of the cases cited above which rely on the Patton case and apply the rule of law there announced, was the good faith of both parties to the second marriage considered or discussed in connection with Article 117 of the Civil Code. Moreover, in these cases the good faith of both parties to the second marriage was not a factor. Again, where the property acquired during the putative marriage was divided between the two wives, the facts in most of those cases clearly show that the husband in contracting a second marriage was in bad faith. Such is not a fact in the case which we now have under consideration, as both parties to the second marriage here were in good faith, and the rule of law announced in the Patton case cannot be reconciled with the express provisions of Article 117 of our Civil Code in regard to a situation where both parties are in good faith. To follow the Patton rule in the instant case and to give to the putative wife the husband's one-half of the property acquired during the existence of the putative community would be to deny to him and his heirs the civil effects of the second marriage, in the teeth of the provisions of Article 117.

James Brough being in good faith in his second marriage, this marriage also produced its civil effects as to him, and accordingly he became the owner of an undivided one-half of all property acquired during the existence of the putative community, for under the provisions of Article 2402 of the Code community property consists, among other things, of the estate which the parties to the marriage may acquire during such marriage by purchase, even though the purchase be only in the name of one of the spouses and not of both. Thus, although the property in the instant case was purchased in the name of the second wife, it fell into the putative community. Accordingly when James Brough died one-half of this property belonged to his succession. He was survived by one child, Irita B. Hopson, who therefore inherited his share of the community property under Article 915 of the Civil Code which provides: '* * * In the event the deceased leave descendants, his or her share in the community estate shall be inherited by such descendants in the manner provided by law.'

We have disposed of James Brough's one-half of the community property acquired during the putative marriage, but the serious question remains: What division shall we make of the remaining one-half of this property?

As we have heretofore pointed out, James Brough's second wife, Clementine Prince, was also in good faith when the marriage was contracted and remained in good faith until after his death. Under the provisions of Article 117 she would therefore be entitled to one-half of all property acquired during the existence of the putative community although the marriage was a nullity. However, during this entire time the legal community was also in existence, and it likewise was not dissolved until James Brough's death, and during the coexistence of both these communities the property was acquired. Under Article 2406 of the Civil Code the effects which compose the community of acquets and gains are divided into two equal portions between the husband and the wife or between their heirs at the dissolution of the marriage. Consequently under the provisions of this article Victoria Albert, the legal wife, is also entitled to the remaining one-half of such property. The provisions of our law which give to each of these wives one-half of the property are of equal dignity and rank. However, it is impossible to give to each wife under these laws one-half of the entire property, as there remains to be divided between them only one-half of the property because James Brough's one-half is inherited by his daughter. The question then presented is: How should the remaining one-half of the property be divided between the legal wife and the putative wife?

Articles 117 and 118 of the Louisiana Civil Code are literal translations of Articles 201 and 202 of the French Civil Code, and, as heretofore pointed out, their provisions first appeared in our Code as Articles 119 and 120 of the Code of 1825. For a solution of this problem, then, we think it is proper to look to the French commentators who have had occasion to discuss it.

Under the views of Aubry and Rau; Baudry-Lacantinerie; Colin and Capitant; and Ripert and Boulanger, where both parties to a putative marriage are in good faith the husband is entitled to his share of all property acquired during the existence of both the legal and the putative marriage under Article 201 of the French Code, and accordingly he or his heirs take as civil effects one-half of the entire property acquired from the date of the legal marriage to its dissolution. See Colin et Capitant, 1 Traité de droit civil (1953) 375, no 623; Ripert et Boulanger, 1 Traité él<

Under the view which these commentators deem to be the most equitable, in the instant case the legal wife, Victoria H. Albert, and the putative wife, Clementine Prince, would each be entitled to an undivided one-fourth interest in the property in question.

The French commentators also allow the children to inherit community property from a father who contracted a second marriage in bad faith, which seems to us to be correct under Article 118 of our Code. See Colin et Capitant, 1 Traité de droit civil (1953) 376, no 624; Comment, The Civil Effects of a Putative Marriage, 1 Loy.L.Rev. 54, 67 (1941). Of course we are not here called upon to, nor do we think we should, go that far because of our decision in Patton v. Philadelphia and the cases which followed the ruling announced there-holding, in effect, as we have pointed out above, that children do not inherit community property acquired by their father during a second marriage contracted in bad faith. However, we see no reason why we should not accept such a solution where both parties to the marriage are shown to be in good faith, and by adopting this solution we certainly are following the provisions of Article 117 by allowing to the husband who is in good faith the civil effects of his second marriage, and we are also following the provisions of the article as to the putative wife's share as far as we can possibly do so by recognizing her to be entitled to the civil effects of her marriage, which she also contracted in good faith.

Although the lot here in question was purchased for $215, the record shows that after it was bought certain improvements were built on it, and it was stipulated during the trial that the total amount spent for these purposes was approximately $4,800, the greater portion of which was spent by Clementine Prince after her husband's death. Consequently there is reserved to her the right to claim from these two defendants in a proper proceeding the proportionate share of the enhanced value of the property resulting from improvements placed upon it after the death of James Brough.

For the reasons assigned the judgment of the district court is annulled and set aside, and it is now ordered, adjudged, and decreed that there be judgment declaring the property here involved together with the improvements thereon to be owned in indivision in the proportion of one-half to Irita B. Hopson, one-fourth to Victoria H. Albert, and one-fourth to Clementine Prince, said property being more particularly described as 'Lot 19, in Square 578, bounded by N. Villere, Andry, Flood and N. Robertson Streets, and measures 32 feet front on N. Villere Street, by a depth between parrallel lines of 170 feet, 9 inches and 6 lines, and starts at a distance of 120 feet from the corner of N. Villere and Andry Streets'. There is reserved to plaintiff, Clementine Prince, the right to claim from the defendants the proportionate share of the enhanced value of the property resulting from the improvements placed upon it after the death of James Brough. All costs in these proceedings are to be paid by the litigants in the proportion of one-fourth by plaintiff-appellee and three-fourths by defendants-appellants.

FOURNET, C. J., absent.

7.4 CAUSES OF TERMINATION: JUDGMENT OF SEPARATION OF PROPERTY

A. Introduction

A judgment of separation of property terminates the community property regime. Louisiana Civil Code article 2374 allows a spouse to seek a judgment terminating the community property regime during marriage for any one of four grounds.

First, a spouse may seek a judgment of separation of property "[w]hen interest of a spouse in a community property regime is threatened to be diminished by the fraud, fault, neglect, or incompetence of the other spouse, or by the disorder of the affairs of the other spouse..." This grounds for a judgment of separation is considered in *Pan American Import Co.*, below.

Second, "[w]hen a spouse is an absent person, the other spouse is entitled to a judgment decreeing separation of property. Civil Code article 47 explains that "[a]n absent person is one who has no representative in this state and whose whereabouts are not known and cannot be ascertained be diligent effort." After a spouse has been an absent person for five years, Article 54 allows a court to declare them dead, which would also terminate the community property regime.

Third, Article 2374 allows a judgment of separation of property upon the motion of either spouse if (1) a petition for divorce has already been filed; and (2) there is "proof that the spouses have lived separate and apart without reconciliation for at least thirty days from the date of, or prior to, the filing of the petition for divorce." This provision allows spouses who are divorcing to go ahead and terminate the community property regime proactively. Motions for judgments of separation of property are routinely filed in connection with Article 102 divorces and are often granted on the basis of proof submitted by affidavit.

Fourth, Article 2374 allows a judgment of separation of property when the spouses have simply lived separate and apart continuously for a period of six months. This option is helpful for spouses who no longer live together as spouses, but who, for whatever reason, do not wish to actually obtain a divorce.

The effects of a judgment of separation—and the timing of its effectiveness—depends on the grounds upon which it is granted. Article 2375 contains detailed rules:

Art. 2375. Effect of judgment

A. Except as provided in Paragraph C of this Article, a judgment decreeing separation of property terminates the regime of community property retroactively to the day of the filing of the petition or motion therefor, without prejudice to rights validly acquired in the interim between filing of the petition or motion and rendition of judgment.

B. If a judgment has been rendered on the ground that the spouses have lived separate and apart either after the filing of a petition for divorce without having reconciled or for six months, a reconciliation reestablishes the regime of community property between the spouses retroactively to the day of the filing of the motion or petition therefor, unless prior to the reconciliation the spouses execute a matrimonial agreement to the contrary. This agreement need not be approved by the court and is effective toward third persons when filed for registry in the manner provided by Article 2332. The reestablishment of the community is effective toward third persons when a notice thereof is filed for registry in the same manner.

C. If a judgment is rendered on the ground that the spouses were living separate and apart without having reconciled for at least thirty days from the date of, or prior to, the filing of the petition for divorce, the judgment shall be effective retroactively to the date the petition for divorce was filed, without prejudice to rights validly acquired in the interim. All subsequent pleadings or motions involving matters incidental to the divorce shall be filed in the first filed suit.

The *Brar* case, below, considers some of these timing issues.

Finally, Article 2376 allows creditors to intervene in a proceeding for a judgment of separation of property or to annul such a judgment in some cases:

Art. 2376. Rights of creditors

The creditors of a spouse, by intervention in the proceeding, may object to the separation of property or modification of their matrimonial regime as being

> in fraud of their rights. They also may sue to annul a judgment of separation of property within one year from the date of the rendition of the final judgment. After execution of the judgment, they may assert nullity only to the extent that they have been prejudiced.

The *Pan American Import Co.* case, below, also illustrates the operation of this statute.

B. Pan American Import Company v. Janet Buck

452 So. 2d 1167 (La. 1984)

MARCUS, Justice.

Pan American Import Co., Inc. (Pan Am) employed Janet Buck from June 1976 until August 1977 when she was fired for embezzling $61,374.62 from the company. Pan Am was reimbursed $25,000 from its bonding company and recovered $7,681.68 from customers. To recover the balance of $28,692.94, Pan Am filed suit in June 1978 against Janet Buck and her live-in boyfriend Jerry Verrette. Janet and Jerry were subsequently married on November 16, 1978. In March 1981, the trial judge granted Pan Am's motion for summary judgment against Janet Verrette for $26,142.94. Janet Verrette did not appeal the summary judgment and it became executory in May 1981. Pan Am immediately instituted garnishment proceedings against Jerry Verrette's salary to collect on the judgment. Jerry Verrette filed a petition to enjoin the garnishment and to recover damages for wrongful garnishment. The trial judge refused to grant injunctive relief, but did order the garnished funds placed in escrow until the suit between Pan Am and Jerry Verrette was resolved.

In July 1981, Jerry Verrette petitioned the court for a judicial separation of property pursuant to La. Civ. Code art. 2374, alleging that his interest in the community regime between Janet and him was threatened to be diminished due to the fault, neglect and/or incompetence of Janet and by the disorder of Janet's affairs. Pursuant to La. Civ. Code art. 2376, Pan Am intervened in the suit, objecting to the separation of property on the ground that the separation would be in fraud of its rights. This case was consolidated for trial with the earlier suit by Pan Am still pending against Jerry Verrette.

After a trial on the merits, the trial judge dismissed Pan Am's suit against Jerry Verrette for recovery of the money Janet embezzled from the company. In the second case, the judge rendered judgment in favor of Jerry Verrette granting him a separation of property retroactive to July 10, 1981, the date of filing. He held that "[t]here is nothing fraudulent about Verrett [sic] trying to shield his income from a pre-nuptial creditor of his wife. There is utterly no deceit involved. He is attempting to exercise a right conferred by the Code which inevitably is prejudicial to the creditors of the spendthrift spouse." The trial judge, however, denied Verrette any damages for wrongful garnishment because the seizure of his income as community property to satisfy a separate debt of his wife was valid when it was executed.

Pan Am appealed both judgments of the trial court. The court of appeal affirmed the trial judge's dismissal of Pan Am's suit against Jerry Verrette seeking to hold him liable in solido with Janet for the amount she embezzled from Pan Am. However, the court of appeal reversed the trial judge's grant of a separation of the community regime between Jerry and Janet Verrette. The court found, under La. Civ. Code art. 2376, that the separation of property was "in fraud" of Pan Am's rights as a creditor because the separation terminated Pan Am's rights to garnish Jerry Verrette's salary. The court defined fraud as used in article 2376 as "synonymous with 'bad faith'" and held that "when the sole purpose of a petition to separate community property is admittedly to avoid payment of a preexisting debt, we believe that the petitioners are in bad faith and that separation of the community will unfairly deprive creditors of their rights."

On the application of Jerry and Janet Verrette, we granted certiorari solely to consider the issue of whether Jerry Verrette should have been granted a separation of property in this case.

The question presented for our consideration is whether Jerry Verrette's separation of property under La. Civ. Code art. 2374 is "in fraud of" Pan Am's rights as a creditor, thereby enabling Pan Am to prevent the separation under La. Civ. Code art. 2376.

Articles 2374 and 2376 were added to the Code as part of the community property revision of 1979 and have never before been considered by this court. Although the articles are new, they have the effect of extending to both spouses and to their creditors rights that were previously only afforded to the wife as protection of her dowry and to the husband's creditors. Article 2374 enables a spouse to obtain a judicial separation of property when his or her interest in the community "is threatened to be diminished by the fraud, fault, neglect, or incompetence of the other spouse, or by the disorder of the affairs of the other spouse." However, article 2376 permits the creditors of either spouse to intervene in the proceeding and object to the separation if it is "in fraud of their rights."

In this case, Jerry Verrette's interest in the community regime was clearly being threatened by Janet's fiscal mismanagement; thus, the requirements of article 2374 were met. Yet, the question remains whether his termination of the community regime, thereby removing from Pan Am's reach Jerry's salary under garnishment to satisfy Janet's debt, was "in fraud of" Pan Am's rights.

We cannot look to prior jurisprudence interpreting the phrase "in fraud of their rights" because no case had ever before considered the matter. However, we can consult the revocatory action articles in pari materia and by analogy consider the interpretation given fraud under those articles. The right of a creditor under article 2376 to object to a separation of property is akin to a revocatory action because the creditor in both actions is avoiding a transaction or proceeding made in fraud of his rights. Article 1969 expresses the general purpose behind the revocatory action: "every act done by a debtor with the intent of depriving his creditor of the eventual right he has upon the property of such debtor, is illegal, and ought, as respects such creditor, to be avoided." Thus the law establishes the revocatory action, which is "an action to annul any contract made in fraud of [creditors'] rights." La. Civ. Code art. 1970. The meaning of "fraud" as used in that article is illustrated by article 1978, which provides that:

> No contract shall be avoided by this action but such as are made in fraud of creditors, and such as, if carried into execution, would have the effect of defrauding them. If made in good faith, it cannot be annulled, although it prove injurious to the creditors; and although made in bad faith, it cannot be rescinded, unless it operate to their injury.

Hence, the two elements of fraud in the context of a revocatory action are bad faith and injury to the creditor. Further, it has been held that the creditor must suffer a present injury; a future injury will not suffice. The court in Feist v. Willer & Gamm, Inc., 16 La. App. 618, 133 So. 797 (1931), quoted with approval in Martin Lebreton Insurance Agency v. Phillips, 364 So. 2d 1032 (La. 1978), stated:

> However, we are of the opinion that the injury which it is essential that plaintiff in a revocatory action, should show, relates to a present injury and not a future injury which might occur, if and when the insolvent debtor obtains some property.
>
> The revocatory action, we think, is given to individual creditors in contemplation that they have or will proceed under their judgments against the property of the debtor, and that when the action sought to be revoked is merely a preference, such preference must relate to property which is subject to execution under their judgments and not to property which may become subject to execution in the near or distant future. [Citations omitted.]

In conformity with the interpretation given fraud under the revocatory action articles, we will also interpret fraud as used in article 2376 to require bad faith and present injury to the complaining creditor. We find that, in the instant case, Pan Am did not suffer a present injury by being deprived of the right to garnish Jerry's salary because that salary constituted future property against which Pan Am had no present right of execution. Thus we hold that, under La. Civ. Code art. 2376, Pan Am has no right to object to Jerry's separation of property because it was not made "in fraud of" Pan Am's rights. This conclusion pretermits the need to decide whether Jerry was in bad faith.

Such an interpretation of fraud in article 2376 puts a spouse who chooses to go separate in property under article 2374 in the same position, relative to a creditor seeking to garnish the non-debtor spouse's salary, as a spouse who obtains a separation of property by getting a judicial separation of marriage or a divorce. However, article 2374 enables the spouse to terminate the community regime without having to end the marriage, thereby protecting the sanctity of the family unit, evidently one of the goals of the legislature in enacting article 2374. Such an interpretation of fraud in article 2376 also promotes consistency within the Code because it equalizes the position of the spouse who goes separate in property under article 2374 with that of the spouse who obtains a separation of property via a matrimonial agreement before or during marriage or by a judicial separation of the marriage or divorce.

Therefore, we reverse the judgment of the court of appeal . . . and reinstate the district court's grant of the separation of property.

C. *Ravinderjit S. Brar v. Luckwinder Gill Brar*

796 So. 2d 810 (La. App. 3d 2001)

AMY, Judge.

The appellant/husband appeals the trial court's judgment ordering him to pay interim spousal support and granting his wife use and occupancy of the family home. For the following reasons, we affirm the judgments as amended.

Factual and Procedural Background

On March 25, 1998, Dr. Ravinderjit S. Brar and Luckwinder Gill Brar were married in Gaddandob, India. At that time, Dr. Brar was residing in Marksville, Louisiana, working as an emergency room doctor at Avoyelles Parish Hospital and practicing internal medicine. On returning to the United States the couple established their matrimonial domicile in Alexandria, Louisiana.

On July 14, 2000, Dr. Brar filed a petition for divorce, pursuant to La. Civ. Code art. 103(1), claiming that he and Mrs. Brar had physically separated on or about January 15, 2000. On July 24, 2000, Mrs. Brar filed an answer, reconventional demand, and rule to show cause wherein she requested, among other things, interim spousal support and use of the family home. The rule on the incidental matters was heard September 11, 2000. Thereafter, the trial court ordered that Dr. Brar pay $4,500.00 per month in interim spousal support and awarded Mrs. Brar occupancy and use of the family home.

On September 8, 2000, Dr. Brar filed a rule to show cause for separation of property in accordance with the provisions of La. Civ. Code art. 2374(C), which allows either spouse to request a judgment decreeing a separation of property upon proof that the couple has lived separate and apart, without reconciliation, for more than thirty days after the filing of a petition for divorce. A judgment on the rule was signed October 23, 2000, ordering the separation of property and decreeing the parties to be living under a separate property regime retroactively to September 8, 2000, the date Dr. Brar filed the rule.

Dr. Brar appealed from both judgments, alleging:

> (1) The court erred as a matter of law when it made the judgment granting a separation of property, based upon the parties living separate and apart without reconciliation for thirty (30) days after the filing of the petition for divorce, effective retroactive to the date the rule for separation of property was filed rather than to the date the original petition for divorce was filed.
>
> (2) The court abused its discretion in granting defendant interim spousal support in the amount of $4,500.00 per month.
>
> (3) The court erred by not considering the plaintiff-appellant's request for rental value set forth in his answer to reconventional demand.

Discussion of the Merits

Judgment of Separation

In his first assignment of error, Dr. Brar alleges that the judgment of separation of property is legally erroneous because it declares that the separate property regime is to be effective retro-actively to September 8, 2000, the date Dr. Brar filed the rule to show cause, rather than July 14, 2000, the date he filed his divorce petition, which he claims is contradictory to the law controlling such judgments.

La. Civ. Code art. 2375, which governs the effect of a judgment of separation of property, states in pertinent part:

> A. Except as provided in Paragraph C of this Article, a judgment decreeing separation of property terminates the regime of community property retroactively to the day of the filing of the petition or motion therefor,....
>
> C. If a judgment is rendered on the ground that the spouses were living separate and apart after the filing of a petition for divorce without having reconciled, the judgment shall be effective retroactively to the date the original petition for divorce was filed, without prejudice to rights validly acquired in the interim between filing of the petition or motion and rendition of judgment.

In her brief to this court, Mrs. Brar argues that Dr. Brar is estopped from claiming an error in the judgment since his attorney prepared and submitted the judgment to the trial court and, by doing so, acquiesced in the judgment and the effective date stated therein. Alternatively, she alleges that it would have been error for the trial court to order the judgment retroactive to the date of filing the divorce petition because the petition itself is invalid in that it incorrectly states that the couple had been separated for six months prior to its filing, which was expressly denied by Mrs. Brar in her answer.

After review, we find no merit in Mrs. Brar's first contention that Dr. Brar has "judicially confessed" or voluntarily acquiesced in the date the separation of property judgment would become effective and therefore, should now be estopped from challenging this issue on appeal. There is no proof in the record which indicates that the parties expressly agreed or stipulated as to which date would serve as the effective date of the judgment. Thus, we find the issue is properly before us on appeal. Moreover, we reject Mrs. Brar's assertion that the original divorce petition cannot serve as the effective date of the separation of property judgment because she believes that the statements made by Dr. Brar in his petition were false, rendering the petition invalid. The express provisions of La. Civ. Code art. 2375(C) only require that a petition for divorce be filed, it does not require that the petitioner ultimately prevail in the divorce proceeding in order for the separation of property judgment to be effective retroactively to the filing date of the divorce petition.

An examination of the written judgment reveals that while it states the separate property regime shall be effective retroactively to the date the rule was filed, it also cites La. Civ. Code art. 2375(C), which requires that the judgment be effective retroactively to the date of the original petition for divorce was filed. Due to this internal contradiction in the judgment, and in light of the clear mandate of La. Civ. Code art. 2375(C), we find that this judgment contains a legal error regarding the date the judgment shall become effective. Accordingly, we order that it be amended to reflect that the separation of property regime shall be applicable retroactive to July 14, 2000, the date the original divorce petition was filed.

DECREE

For the foregoing reasons, we amend the trial court's judgment of separation of property signed October 23, 2000, to decree that the parties are living under a regime of separation of property regime retroactive to July 14, 2000. In all other respects that judgment and the judgment signed September 26, 2000, are affirmed. All costs of this appeal are assessed against the plaintiff/appellant, Dr. Ravinderjit S. Brar.

AFFIRMED AS AMENDED.

D. Note

Consider the impact of a spousal reconciliation after the award of a judgment of separation of property. Louisiana Civil Code article 2375(B) is designed to address this. In particular, read *in pari materia*, paragraphs C and D of article 2374 with paragraphs B and C of article 2375. Do they make any sense?

7.5 PROHIBITION OF ACTS OF DISPOSITION AND OTHER PROVISIONAL RELIEF

A. Applicable Statutes

LA. REV. STAT. § 9:371. Injunction against alienation or encumbrance; spouse's right to demand

In a proceeding for divorce, a spouse may obtain an injunction restraining or prohibiting the disposition or encumbrance of community property until further order of the court.

LA. CODE CIV. PROC. art. 3601. Injunction, grounds for issuance; preliminary injunction; temporary restraining order

A. An injunction shall be issued in cases where irreparable injury, loss, or damage may otherwise result to the applicant, or in other cases specifically provided by law; provided, however, that no court shall have jurisdiction to issue, or cause to be issued, any temporary restraining order, preliminary injunction, or permanent injunction against any state department, board or agency, or any officer, administrator or head thereof, or any officer of the State of Louisiana in any suit involving the expenditure of public funds under any statute or law of this state to compel the expenditure of state funds when the director of such department, board or agency, or the governor shall certify that the expenditure of such funds would have the effect of creating a deficit in the funds of said agency or be in violation of the requirements placed upon the expenditure of such funds by the legislature.

* * *

C. During the pendency of an action for an injunction the court may issue a temporary restraining order, a preliminary injunction, or both, except in cases where prohibited, in accordance with the provisions of this Chapter.

D. Except as otherwise provided by law, an application for injunctive relief shall be by petition.

LA. CODE CIV. PROC. art. 3604. Form, contents, and duration of restraining order

A. A temporary restraining order shall be endorsed with the date and hour of issuance; shall be filed in the clerk's office and entered of record; shall state why the order was granted without notice and hearing; and shall expire by it terms within such time after entry, not to exceed ten days, as the court prescribes. A restraining order, for good cause shown, and at any time before its expiration, may be extended by the court for one or more periods not exceeding ten days each. The party against whom the order is directed may consent that it be extended for a longer period. The reasons for each extension shall be entered of record.

B. Nevertheless, a temporary restraining order issued in conjunction with a rule to show cause for a preliminary injunction prohibiting a spouse from:

(1) Disposing of or encumbering community property;

(2) Harming the other spouse or a child; or

(3) Removing a child from the jurisdiction of the court, in a suit for divorce shall remain in force until a hearing is held on the rule for the preliminary injunction.

* * *

LA. CODE. CIV. PROC. art. 3944. Injunctive relief in divorce actions; bond not required in certain cases

Either party to an action for divorce may obtain injunctive relief as provided in Part V of Chapter 1 of Code Title V of Code Book I of Title 9 (R.S. 9:371 et seq.) of the Revised Statutes without bond.

LA. REV. STAT. § 9:374. Possession and use of family residence or community movables or immovables.

A. When the family residence is the separate property of either spouse, after the filing of a petition for divorce or in conjunction therewith, the spouse who has physical custody or has been awarded temporary custody of the minor children of the marriage may petition for, and a court may award to that spouse, after a contradictory hearing, the use and occupancy of the family residence pending the partition of the community property or one hundred eighty days after termination of the marriage, whichever occurs first. In these cases, the court shall inquire into the relative economic status of the spouses, including both community and separate property, and the needs of the children, and shall award the use and occupancy of the family residence to the spouse in accordance with the best interest of the family.

The court shall consider the granting of the occupancy of the family residence in awarding spousal support.

B. When the family residence is community property or is owned by the spouses in indivision, or the spouses own community movables or immovables, after or in conjunction with the filing of a petition for divorce or for separation of property in accordance with Civil Code Article 2374, either spouse may petition for, and a court may award to one of the spouses, after a contradictory hearing, the use and occupancy of the family residence and use of community movables or immovables pending partition of the property or further order of the court, whichever occurs first. In these cases, the court shall inquire into the relative economic status of the spouses, including both community and separate property, and the needs of the children, if any, and shall award the use and occupancy of the family residence and the use of any community movables or immovables to the spouse in accordance with the best interest of the family. If applicable, the court shall consider the granting of the occupancy of the family residence and the use of community movables or immovables in awarding spousal support.

C. A spouse who, in accordance with the provisions of Subsection A or B of this Section, uses and occupies or is awarded by the court the use and occupancy of the family residence, a community immovable occupied as a residence, or a community manufactured home as defined in R.S. 9:1149.2 and occupied as a residence, regardless of whether it has been immobilized, shall not be liable to the other spouse for rental for the use and occupancy, except as hereafter provided. If the court awards use and occupancy to a spouse, it shall at that time determine whether to award rental for the use and occupancy and, if so, the amount of the rent. The parties may agree to defer the rental issue for decision in the partition proceedings. If the parties agreed at the time of the award of use and occupancy to defer the rental issue, the court may make an award of rental retroactive to the date of the award of use and occupancy.

D. The court may determine whether a residence is separate or community property, or owned in indivision, in the contradictory hearing authorized under the provisions of this Section.

E. (1) In a proceeding for divorce or thereafter, a summary proceeding shall be undertaken by the court upon request of either party to allocate the use of community property, including monetary assets, bank accounts, savings plans, and other divisible movable property pending partition.

(2) The court shall determine allocation of community property after considering:

(a) The custody of the children and exclusive use and occupancy of the family residence.

(b) The total community property.

(c) The need of a spouse for funds to maintain a household prior to partition.

(d) The need of a spouse to receive legal representation during the course of the proceedings.

(3) Upon court order, each spouse shall provide the other a complete accounting of all allocated community property to demonstrate compliance with Civil Code Article 2369.3.

LA. REV. STAT. § 9:308. Separation from bed and board in covenant marriage; suit against spouse; jurisdiction, procedure, and incidental relief.

***

D. In a proceeding for a separation from bed and board in a covenant marriage or thereafter, a court may award a spouse all incidental relief afforded in a proceeding for divorce, including but not limited to spousal support, claims for contributions to education, child custody, visitation rights, child support, injunctive relief and possession and use of a family residence or community movables or immovables.

B. *USAA Life Ins. Co v. Krake*

7 So.3d 78 (La. App. 5th Cir. 2009)

FREDERICKA HOMBERG WICKER, Judge.

Appellant Terri A. Krake appeals a grant of summary judgment in favor of appellee Amie Accardo Krake. We affirm.

FACTS AND PROCEDURAL HISTORY

The relevant facts are these. On February 29, 2008, USAA Life Insurance Company ("USAA Life") filed a Petition for Concursus, Injunctive Relief, and Declaratory Judgment alleging that Amie Accardo Krake ("Mrs. Krake"), Terri Krake, and the estate of Dr. Patrick R. Krake ("Dr. Krake") had competing claims to the proceeds of two USAA insurance policies. USAA deposited the policy proceeds in the registry of the court and was dismissed from the case with prejudice.

Mrs. Krake married Dr. Krake in LaPlace, Louisiana on August 9, 1991. Mrs. Krake and Dr. Krake did not execute a matrimonial agreement prior to marriage and have been

Louisiana domiciliaries since 1991. Four children were born of the marriage. On May 23, 2004, Dr. Krake purchased a twenty year term life insurance policy from the USAA Life Insurance Company with proceed benefits in the amount of $1,000,000 ("the USAA policy"). Mrs. Krake was **3 named as the primary beneficiary in the USAA policy. No contingent beneficiary was named.

On July 14, 2005, Dr. Krake purchased an additional twenty year term life insurance policy with proceed benefits in the amount of $1,000,000. Again, Mrs. Krake was named as the primary beneficiary in the policy. Again, no contingent beneficiary was named.

On January 2, 2007, Mrs. Krake filed for a no-fault divorce pursuant to article 102 of the Louisiana Civil Code. Amie Accardo Krake v. Patrick Raymond Krake, 640–272, Twenty–Fourth J.D.C. (2/2/07). On January 8, 2007, the trial court signed a temporary restraining order prohibiting Dr. Krake "from transferring, moving, disposing of, alienating, visiting any safety deposit boxes or otherwise encumbering any of the assets of the community of acquets and gains ... including, but not limited to, negotiating or liquidating ... life insurance without the direct written consent" of Mrs. Krake. On March 28, 2007, Dr. Krake and Mrs. Krake stipulated that "the temporary restraining orders should be made (mutual) preliminary injunctions against the parties." The parties also stipulated that they would refrain from "alienating, encumbering, concealing, or disposing of the community property previously existing between the parties." Both stipulations were made the judgment of the court on March 28, 2007.

On August 27, 2007, Dr. Krake and Mrs. Krake were scheduled to meet with the trial judge for the purpose of determining Dr. Krake's child support and spousal support obligations. Dr. Krake allegedly became upset at the meeting and threatened to purposefully refuse to see his children. Later that day, Dr. Krake changed the beneficiary on the USAA policy. Specifically, he removed Mrs. Krake from her status as primary beneficiary and inserted his sister Terri A. Krake as primary beneficiary. On a hard copy of the electronic form filed with USAA to accomplish this task, Dr. Krake prominently wrote "Give Amie Nothing." Dr. Krake died on the night of December 31, 2007. On February 12, 2008, Terri Krake filed a Claimant's Statement with USAA wherein she alleged that she was entitled to the proceeds of the USAA policy.

USAA filed a Petition for Concursus, Injunctive Relief, and Declaratory Judgment on February 29, 2008. USAA admitted that the proceeds of the life insurance policy were due but averred that there "is ... a controversy with respect to the identity of the claimants to the benefits, whether all claimants are proper, and which of the claimants are entitled to payment of the benefits of the Policy under Louisiana law." On April 25, 2008, Mrs. Krake filed a Motion for Summary Judgment. In the memorandum accompanying Mrs. Krake's Motion, Mrs. Krake alleged that she was entitled to the proceeds of the USAA policy because Dr. Krake's execution of the change of beneficiary form was in derogation of the trial court's March 28, 2007 preliminary injunction. Terri Krake filed a Cross Motion for Summary Judgment on June 17, 2008. In the memorandum accompanying Terri Krake's Cross Motion, Terri Krake alleged that Dr. Krake was free to change the beneficiary of the USAA policy despite the existence of the trial court's preliminary injunction.

The motions were scheduled for hearing on July 11, 2008. After the hearing, the trial court granted Mrs. Krake's motion and denied Terri Krake's motion. This timely appeal followed.

Terri Krake assigns two errors to the proceedings below. First, she alleges that the trial court erred in applying Louisiana's community property laws to the USAA policy. Second, she alleges that the trial court erred in finding that the March 28, 2007 preliminary injunction prohibited Dr. Krake from changing the beneficiary designation.

***

SECOND ASSIGNMENT OF ERROR

In her second assignment of error, Terri Krake alleges that the trial court erred in finding that the March 28, 2007 preliminary injunction prohibited Dr. Krake from changing the beneficiary of the USAA policy. More specifically, she argues that the preliminary injunction did not apply to the USAA policy because the injunction made no specific reference to insurance policies. In the alternative, she argues that the language of the injunction did not prevent Dr. Krake from changing the beneficiary.

Terri Krake's assertion that the injunction did not apply to the USAA policy because the injunction did not specifically make reference to insurance policies is wholly without merit. As aforementioned, the temporary restraining order prohibited Dr. Krake from "transferring, moving, disposing of, alienating ... or otherwise encumbering any of the assets of the community ... including, but not limited to ... life insurance." On March 28, 2007, the terms of the temporary restraining order were "made (mutual) preliminary injunctions against the parties." Thus, the terms of the March 28 injunction expressly prohibited Dr. Krake from transferring, moving, disposing of, alienating, or otherwise encumbering life insurance policies.

In the alternative, Terri Krake alleges that "neither the language in the temporary restraining order issued January 7, 2007, [nor] the interim stipulated order dated March 27, 2007, operated to enjoin Dr. Krake from management of the policy issued by USAA, including but not limited to his right to change the beneficiary." She argues that the order and injunction only "enjoined both parties from alienating, encumbering, or concealing community property." Thus, the argument follows, Dr. Krake was free to change the beneficiary of the USAA policy because he did not alienate, encumber, or conceal community property. As we discussed above, the insurance policy is community property.

La. C.C.P. art. 3611 provides:

> Disobedience of or resistance to a temporary restraining order or preliminary or final injunction is punishable as a contempt of court. The court may cause to be undone or destroyed whatever may be done in violation of an injunction, and the person aggrieved thereby may recover the damages sustained as a result of the violation

In the instant case, the trial court held Dr. Krake in contempt and invalidated the beneficiary change under La. C.C.P. art. 3611. The trial judge noted that "[t]here was no doubt in [his] mind that the changing of the beneficiary on the part of [Dr. Krake] was not an accident" and that by doing so, Dr. Krake was "messing with the community until an ultimate fair and equitable distribution was implemented."

No reported Louisiana case has addressed the issue of whether a temporary restraining order prohibiting spouses from transferring or otherwise disposing of their marital assets while a divorce is pending prevents a spouse from changing the beneficiary of a life insurance policy. Other courts in other states have dealt with similar factual situations. For example, in Gleed v. Noon, 415 Mass. 498, 614 N.E.2d 676 (1993), a wife filed for divorce from her husband on November 3, 1989. On November 6 and November 15, 1989, the probate court signed temporary restraining orders preventing the spouses from "withdrawing, transferring, conveying, assigning, spending, encumbering, pledging, bequeathing or otherwise divesting themselves of any assets in which they have acquired an interest during their marriage to each other and which are subject to division by [the probate court]." Gleed, 614 N.E.2d at 677. In January of 1990, the husband changed the beneficiary on his life insurance policy from his wife to his daughter. The policy had been acquired during the marriage. Id. After the husband died on June 27, 1990, his will was admitted to probate, and his former wife sought a judgment declaring that the husband had violated the terms of the restraining order by changing the beneficiary on his life insurance policy. The probate court entered the declaratory judgment, but the Supreme Judicial Court of Massachusetts reversed, noting that:

> [i]n this case the order did not specifically prohibit, restrain, or prevent the decedent from changing the beneficiary on any of his policies or accounts and the decedent could not have been guilty of contempt for doing so if he had survived. Absent a specific court order preventing or prohibiting the beneficiary change, the decedent had the right to change the beneficiary designation on the pension plan, IRA, and life insurance policy while retaining ownership in compliance with the injunction

Id. at 678.

A different result was reached in Candler v. Donaldson, 272 F.2d 374 (6th Cir.1959), a case cited by Mrs. Krake. In Candler, during divorce proceedings, an injunction was entered against a husband preventing him from "from selling, assigning, encumbering, hypothecating, mortgaging, concealing, giving away, or in any manner disposing of any of the properties and assets of either or both of the parties hereto." Candler, 272 F.2d at 376. Approximately four months later, the husband changed the beneficiary on a life insurance policy from his wife to his mother. The husband died six weeks after the change. Id. The insurer admitted that proceeds were due and filed an interpleader action in the federal Eastern District of Michigan. The trial court found that the mother was entitled to the proceeds, but the United States Court of Appeals for the Sixth Circuit reversed. The court reasoned:

> It is true that neither the order nor the injunction expressly directed the insured not to change the beneficiary. But the order directed the insured to continue in force 'all life insurance policies ... during the pendency of this suit and until a final adjudication of this cause shall be made' and restrained the insured from 'assigning ... or otherwise disposing of the property hereinbefore mentioned, as well as any other property he may own, possess or have interest in until a final adjudication of the interests of these parties in said property may properly be made by this Honorable Court.' This was a temporary order preliminary to a later final order adjudicating the property rights of the parties ... Giving due consideration to the other provisions of the order, we think it was the purpose of the order to preserve the status quo between the parties until the final adjudication of property rights between the parties could be made. Under the circumstances, the word 'dispose' is broad enough to cover any material change by the husband in his existing property rights until a final adjudication of the cause.

Id. at 377.

This Court agrees with the sentiment of the Sixth Circuit in Candler. As was the case in Candler, the temporary restraining order and injunction in the instant case did not explicitly prohibit the decedent from changing the beneficiary on the insurance policy. However, the purpose of the injunction in the instant case was obviously to maintain the status quo until remaining community property issues could be resolved. This is reflected in the language of the order and the trial court's comments. Dr. Krake stipulated that he would refrain from "disposing of the community property previously existing between the parties." We agree with the Candler court that, under the circumstances, the word "dispose" should be interpreted broadly so as to include a beneficiary change on a life insurance policy. Further, we note that the "trial court is vested with great discretion in determining whether a party should be held in contempt for disobeying a court order, and the court's decision should be reversed only when the appellate court discerns an abuse of that discretion," Boudreaux v. Vankerkhove, 2007–2555 (La.App. 1 Cir. 8/11/08), 993 So.2d 725, 733; Fink v. Bryant, 2001–0987, p. 7

(La.11/28/01), 801 So.2d 346, 350. Here, we cannot say that the trial court abused its discretion in interpreting the language of the injunction and in finding that Dr. Krake had violated it.

Accordingly, this assignment of error has no merit.

CONCLUSION AND DECREE

For the foregoing reasons, the judgment of the trial court is affirmed. Costs to be paid by appellant. AFFIRMED.

C. *Margaret McCarroll v. Donald McCarroll*

701 So. 2d 1280 (La. 1997)

KNOLL, Justice.

Even though lesion in an extrajudicial partition is the setting for this community property litigation, the central issue before us concerns the assessment of fair rental value for a spouse's use of the family residence. La.R.S. 9:374(C).1 Plaintiff, Margarette McCarroll, seeks to rescind an extrajudicial partition of community property on account of lesion under La.Civ.Code art. 814.2 The lower courts found the partition was not lesionary because plaintiff had received the exclusive use of the community home for the years leading up to and following the partition, and that the rental value of the family home should be counted as consideration received by plaintiff in the partition. McCarroll v. McCarroll, 95-1972 (La.App. 1 Cir. 6/28/96), 680 So.2d 681. There is a split among the circuits over the assessment of fair rental value of the family residence pending termination of the marriage or partition of the community property. We granted writs to determine whether the rental value of the family home should have been assessed against Mrs. McCarroll for purposes of determining whether the partition was lesionary. McCarroll v. McCarroll, 96-2700 (La.1/24/97), 686 So.2d 852.

Our treatment of this issue will resolve the conflict among the circuits.

Finding that the fair rental value should not have been assessed against Mrs. McCarroll to the extent employed, we reverse the rulings of the lower courts, find that the partition was lesionary under La.Civ.Code art. 814, and remand for a judicial partition of the community assets.

FACTS

Margarette McCarroll and Donald McCarroll were married on July 25, 1958. The McCarrolls were legally separated on November 16, 1976, and after a period of reconciliation in 1977, a judgment of divorce was entered in favor of Mrs. McCarroll on January 28, 1980. At the time of their divorce, one of their children was over the age of eighteen and two were still minors, living at home. Partition of the community property was discussed by the parties, and Mr. McCarroll attempted to have a written settlement executed on several occasions. However, the community property regime which existed between the parties during their eighteen-year marriage was not partitioned until March 3, 1990, when the parties entered into a community property settlement. The settlement, which was in the form of an authentic act, stated:

> COMMUNITY PROPERTY SETTLEMENT BETWEEN DONALD McCARROLL AND MARGUERITE MARTIN McCARROLL
>
> BEFORE ME, the undersigned authority, personally came and appeared DONALD McCARROLL and MARGUERITE MARTIN McCARROLL, who being first sworn, deposed and said they were formerly married, and said marriage ended in divorce in the Twenty First Judicial District Court for the Parish of Tangipahoa, State of Louisiana, on the 28th day of January, 1980, and that they do by these presents enter into the following settlement of the community of acquets and gains which formerly existed between the parties.
>
> DONALD McCARROLL takes as his part, and MARGUERITE MARTIN McCARROLL does hereby transfer to DONALD McCARROLL, all of her right, title and interest in and to:
>
> 1. A lot 218 feet on the North side of Highway 190 by a depth of 131 feet in Section 23, Township 6 South, Range 6 East, being the property purchased from Holland heirs in COB 182, Page 332 of the Livingston Parish Clerk and Recorder's Office.
>
> 2. Any and all movable property in the name of DONALD McCARROLL or in his possession that was acquired during the community of acquets and gains.
>
> MARGUERITE MARTIN McCARROLL further acknowledges that she has received the sum of $5,000.00 in cash.
>
> MARGUERITE MARTIN McCARROLL takes as her part, and DONALD McCARROLL does hereby transfer to MARGUERITE MARTIN McCARROLL, in addition to the $5,000 previously mentioned, all right, title and interest in and to Any and all movable property in the name of MARGUERITE MARTIN McCARROLL or in her possession.

The remaining property belonging to the parties shall be held in indivision.

Three months after this agreement was signed, on July 31, 1990, Donald McCarroll retired from his job at Chevron after nearly 35 years. Upon his retirement, he received a substantial retirement package and profit-sharing/stock benefit plan, having a combined value in excess of $300,000. The record reflects that Mrs. McCarroll did not know the value of the retirement package at the time she signed the settlement agreement. She later discovered this information after Mr. McCarroll's Paine Weber statement was mistakenly mailed to her home.

On June 10, 1992, Mrs. McCarroll filed a petition to partition the community property, including the family home and the community portion of Donald McCarroll's retirement benefits. Donald McCarroll answered the petition, asserting that the retirement benefits had already been partitioned pursuant to the March 3, 1990, settlement executed by the parties. Donald argued that since the retirement benefits were "movable property in his name and possession," they were partitioned in the settlement agreement. Mrs. McCarroll amended her petition, seeking to rescind the March 3, 1990 settlement based on lesion.

The trial court bifurcated the issue of lesion from the actual partition of the community property. Initially the trial court noted that the March 3, 1990, settlement was ambiguous as to whether the parties intended to include the Chevron retirement package in the settlement. A hearing was held to determine the intent of the parties as to Mr. McCarroll's retirement.

At the hearing, Mr. McCarroll's brother, Wendall McCarroll, and his sister, Joan Perilloux, testified that they each had loaned Mr. McCarroll $2,500 in 1979 so that Mr. McCarroll could settle the community property. Mrs. Perilloux testified that she met Mr. McCarroll and Mrs. McCarroll at her mother's house in 1979, and that in a verbal agreement, Mrs. McCarroll exchanged her rights to the Chevron retirement in exchange for $5,000, the furniture in the house, for the use of the family residence until the children were grown. Wendall McCarroll acknowledged being at the house when the agreement was made, but stated that he did not know the terms of the agreement. Although Margarette McCarroll denied that this 1979 transaction took place, shortly thereafter Mr. McCarroll moved out of and Mrs. McCarroll moved into the family home with two of the children.

Hobart Pardue, the attorney who prepared the March 3, 1990, settlement agreement, testified that he had explained to both parties that the settlement would include "monies, claims, or anything they might have," but that he was not informed of the existence of the retirement benefits. Mr. Pardue also testified that it was his understanding that Mrs. McCarroll would have use of the family home.

The trial court concluded that the parties intended to partition all community property save and except the family home, and that the Chevron retirement benefits had been included in the March 3, 1990 settlement.4 The trial court further concluded that pursuant to the verbal agreement between the parties, Mrs. McCarroll was to receive the exclusive use and possession of the family home.

A second hearing was held on the issue of lesion of the settlement agreement. Evidence was adduced as to the value of the community property described in the settlement, including the building in Livingston Parish and the family furniture. Professor Dian Tooley Arruebarrena testified as an expert witness in the area of community property, specifically with respect to the valuation of the community portion of the retirement and benefit plans. Several real estate appraisals of the family home were introduced, and an appraiser for Donald McCarroll testified as to the fair rental value of the family home.

After taking the case under advisement, the trial court issued a judgment on March 13, 1995. In its written reasons, the trial court held that the March 3, 1990, agreement was not lesionary and dismissed Mrs. McCarroll's motion to rescind, stating:

> This court finds that the defendant has established by a preponderance of the evidence that the fair rental value of the home was $425.00 per month.

* * * * * *

> This court further found that plaintiff, through parole evidence allowed by both parties as additional consideration for the agreement, had actual exclusive use and possession of the family home.

* * * * * *

> Assuming arguendo that the figures submitted in her "Lesion Analysis" are correct, the figures themselves dispense with plaintiff's argument. Plaintiff states that "[i]f she received less than [$44,028], it's lesionary." (See plaintiff's Lesion Analysis). Plaintiff states that she received $7,000 in cash and furniture, but makes no mention of the in-kind value she received regarding the exclusive use of the family home pursuant to the March 3, 1990 agreement.
>
> The defendant in this matter has established by a preponderance of evidence that the fair rental value of the home is $425.00 per month. Reducing this amount by one-half, this court finds that the plaintiff, over the 190 months of her exclusive use and possession of the home, received a total of $40,375 in rental value. In total, plaintiff received $47,375, which is above the $47,028 lesionary threshold figure cited by plaintiff.

The court of appeal affirmed the judgment of the trial court, and found no manifest error in the trial court's ruling that under the verbal agreement in 1979, Mr. McCarroll's benefits were included in the settlement, and that as additional consideration, Mrs. McCarroll received use and possession of the family home. McCarroll, 680 So.2d 681.

The court of appeal cited the jurisprudence of its own circuit, holding that "when there is no evidence of court ordered rent or an agreement between the parties, the occupying spouse is not liable for rent." McElwee v. McElwee, 93-1010 (La.App. 1 Cir. 8/17/94), 649 So.2d 975; Wochomurka v. Wochomurka, 552 So.2d 405 (La.App. 1 Cir.1989). Nevertheless, it distinguished the case sub judice from prior rental payment cases. The court of appeal held that La.R.S. 9:374(C) did not prevent the assessment of rental value in determining the issue of lesion, since the use of the family home was Mrs. McCarroll's additional consideration for the subsequent written property settlement rather than an asset to be partitioned. The court stated:

> The present case is distinguishable from McElwee and Wochomurka. In those cases, there was no evidence that the occupying spouse gave any consideration for the use and occupancy of the community home. Herein, the record reflects that at the time she began occupying the home, Mrs. McCarroll verbally agreed that in exchange for the retirement and profit sharing benefits, she would receive exclusive use of the community home. We note that because La.R.S. 9:374(C) does not require that rental agreements between the spouses be in writing, a verbal agreement can support a trial court's award of rental payments. The record in this case contains evidence of a verbal agreement between the parties wherein they contemplated an exchange of the benefits for the use of the community home. Accordingly, we find that the trial judge did not err in including rental payments as part of Mrs. McCarroll's consideration for the subsequent written community property partition agreement which divided the retirement and profit sharing benefits.

McCarroll, 680 So.2d at 688-89.

Although it noted that Mrs. McCarroll had occupied the family home for only 121 months on the date the written settlement was executed, and for only 182 months when judgment was rendered, the court held that the trial court did not err in selecting a term of 190 months for Mrs. McCarroll's occupancy. The court of appeal reasoned that the settlement agreement "contemplated ALL future use of the community home by Mrs. McCarroll." McCarroll, 680 So.2d at 688. The court of appeal held that the **9 inclusion of eight additional months of occupancy following the issuance of judgment reflected the reasonable time limitation for partitioning the family home. Finally, the court conducted the following lesion analysis:

The record establishes the following values for the partitioned community property:

1. Albany property-one-half owned by the McCarroll's	30,000
2. Chevron retirement	42,437
3. Chevron profit sharing	42,972
4. Movables in Mrs. McCarroll's possession	2,000
5. $5,000 cash	5,000

Total Community Property Contained in Partition 122,409

> If Mrs. McCarroll did not receive three-fourths of her one-half of the divided community property, the partition agreement is lesionary. La.Civ.Code art. 814. One-half of the divided community property is $61,205.00. Three-fourths of this amount is $45,903.00. Mrs. McCarroll received $7,000.00 in cash and movables. As additional consideration for the agreement, she received exclusive use of the family home for 190 months. If the fair rental value of $425.00 per month is reduced by one-half, Mrs. McCarroll received, as additional consideration, $40,375.00 in rental value. In total, Mrs. McCarroll received $47,375.00, which is over the three-fourths lesionary figure.
>
> Accordingly, we find no error in the trial judge's conclusion that the partition agreement was not lesionary.

McCarroll, 680 So.2d at 689. (Footnotes omitted).

Mrs. McCarroll assigns and briefs the following errors: 1) The court of appeal erred in assessing the rental value for Margarette McCarroll's use of the family home; 2) The court of appeal erred in its lesion analysis; 3) The court of appeal erred in failing to partition all the community property.

***

La.R.S. 9:374(C)

La.R.S. 9:374(C) provides for the award of rental payments for a spouse's occupancy of the family residence pending partition of the community:

> A spouse who uses and occupies or is awarded by the court the use and occupancy of the family residence pending either the termination of the marriage or the partition of the community property in accordance with the provision of R.S. 9:374(A) or (B) shall not be liable to the other spouse for rental for the use and occupancy, unless otherwise agreed by the spouses or ordered by the court.

The circuit courts of appeal of this state have differing views on the issue of whether an assessment of rent may be made retroactively for a spouse's occupation of the family home pending partition of the community property. In interpreting the above statute, the First and Second Circuit Courts of Appeal have relied upon principles of co-ownership in holding that a spouse who has exclusive use of the matrimonial domicile is not liable to the other spouse for rental payments unless ordered to pay rental by the trial court or agreed by the parties at the time of occupancy. Wochomurka, 552 So.2d 405, disallowed a retroactive award of rent to a co-owning spouse. The court stated:

> [T]he Louisiana legislature intended that a spouse who is awarded the use and occupancy of the marital home pending the judicial partition, shall not be liable to the other spouse for rental payments on the home unless ordered to pay by the trial court at the time of the award of use and occupancy.
>
> * * * * * *
>
> The general rule of law that a co-owner has the right to use the common property without the payment of rent is controlling in this case.
>
> Wochomurka, 552 So.2d at 406. See also, McElwee v. McElwee, 93-1010 (La.App. 1 Cir. 8/17/94), 649 So.2d 975; Bolden v. Bolden, 524 So.2d 10 (La.App. 1 Cir.1988); Williams v. Williams, 509 So.2d 77 (La.App. 1 Cir.1987).

The Second Circuit Court of Appeal, in McConathy v. McConathy, 25,542 (La.App. 2 Cir. 2/23/94), 632 So.2d 1200, amplified the holding in Wochomurka, stating:

> Once the community of acquets and gains has been dissolved by separation, the spouses become co-owners, or owners in indivision of the marital home. As such, the spouses are entitled to the use, enjoyment, and disposition of the property. LSA-C.C. Arts. 477 and 480. A corollary right permits the use and occupancy of the property by the co-owner without the payment of rent.

Pursuant to LSA-R.S. 9:374, the trial court may order rental payments on the family home. However, the order must also be made at the time of the award of use and occupancy. This court reasoned in the Jones case that:

> We do not believe the legislature intended to give a trial court blanket discretion to order rental payments at the time of partition, which might be years after the use and occupancy award.

McConathy, 632 So.2d at 1207-08, (citations omitted), citing Jones v. Jones, 605 So.2d 689, 693 (La.App. 2 Cir.1992), writ den'd, 607 So.2d 571 (La.1992).

The Third and Fourth and Fifth Circuit Courts of Appeal interpret La.R.S. 9:374(C) as an authorization for the trial courts to award rental value at any time, including retroactively. In Nichols v. Nichols, 95-1290 (La.App. 3 Cir. 3/20/96), 671 So.2d 1069, the Third Circuit Court of Appeal affirmed the retroactive assessment of 112 months rent, stating:

> Consistently this court has ruled that, under La.R.S. 9:374(C), the decision to award rent to a non-occupant spouse rests soundly within the trial court's discretion. Rozier v. Rozier, 583 So.2d 87 (La.App. 3 Cir.1991); LeBlanc v. LeBlanc, 490 So.2d 763 (La.App. 3 Cir.), writ denied, 494 So.2d 332 (La.1986).

> Moreover, where the facts so warrant, the trial court enjoys vast discretion to devise rental assessments under La.R.S. 9:374(C).

Nichols, 671 So.2d at 1072.

This Court previously addressed this issue in a per curiam opinion, Bodenheimer v. Freitag, 94-2573 (La.1/6/95), 651 So.2d 251, but failed to resolve the split in the circuits.9 Finding the issue now squarely before us, we hold that rental payments may not be retroactively assessed under La.R.S. 9:374(C) unless otherwise agreed by the spouses or ordered by the court.

After carefully scrutinizing the appellate court decisions, we find that the First and Second Circuits were correct in their application of principles of co-ownership in making their determination. La.Civ.Code art. 2369.1 provides, in pertinent part:

> After termination of the community property regime, the provisions governing co-ownership apply to former community property, unless otherwise provided by law or by juridical act.

The use and management of a thing held in indivision is determined by agreement of all the co-owners. La.Civ.Code art. 801. A co-owner is entitled to use the thing held in indivision according to its destination, but he cannot prevent another co-owner from making such use of it. La.Civ.Code art. 802. Nevertheless, it is well established that a co-owner need not pay rent to another co-owner for his exclusive use of the co-owned property. In Juneau v. Laborde, 228 La. 410, 82 So.2d 693 (La.1955), this Court stated:

> This claim cannot be sanctioned, for defendant was a co-owner of the property and was entitled, as such, to occupy it without becoming liable to plaintiffs for rent. Becnel v. Becnel, 23 La.Ann. 150; Balfour's Heirs v. Balfour, 33 La.Ann. 297; Toler v. Bunch, 34 La.Ann. 997 and Perez v. Guitard, 14 Orleans App. 191. In determining the amount due and recoverable by a co-owner out of possession from his co-owner in possession, a clear distinction should be drawn between the personal occupancy, use and enjoyment of property by the possessor and the rents and revenues derived by him therefrom, either from a lease or by his own industry or exploitation. As to the latter, he must account to his co-owner for all rents and revenues he has received because, in obtaining these fruits, he acts not only for himself but also as the agent of his co-owner for the latter's just proportion.

On the other hand, the co-owner who takes possession of the common property does not have to account to his coproprietor, because the right of occupancy is vested in him by virtue of his ownership. Article 494, Civil Code. This right of co-owners to possession of the property being equal and coextensive, neither becomes indebted to the other for his personal occupancy and enjoyment, save, probably, that a co-owner, who has been deprived of the right of possession by reason of his co-owner's exclusive occupancy, may claim damages from the date upon which he has demanded occupancy and has been refused by the possessor. But, even in these instances, the co-owner in possession cannot be enjoined from occupying the property or cultivating it. The remedy of the co-owner out of possession is, as stated in Moreira v. Schwan, 113 La. 643, 37 So. 542, 543, '...by suit for a partition and settlement of accounts, or for a division of profits, if any.'

Juneau, 82 So.2d at 695-96. (Footnotes omitted).

Under the principles enunciated in Juneau, a co-owner in exclusive possession may be liable for rent, but only beginning on the date another co-owner has demanded occupancy and has been refused. This underlying principle amply supports the requirement that for the assessment of rent under La.R.S. 9:374(C), there must be an agreement between the spouses or a court order for rent contemporaneous with the award of occupancy.

If the parties cannot reach an agreement, either spouse may petition the court for the occupancy of the family home under La.Civ.Code art. 105, and the determination of occupancy and rent is governed by La.R.S. 9:374. At the time occupancy is awarded under La.R.S. 9:374(B), the trial court has the opportunity to weigh the arguments of both spouses on the rent issue at a contradictory hearing.10 La.R.S. 9:374(B) provides that the trial court shall consider the relative economic status of the parties, the needs of the children, and the effect of the award of the occupancy on alimony and child support. La.R.S. 9:374, when read as a whole, contemplates that any award of rent shall be made in conjunction with the determination of occupancy and in light of the factors in La.R.S. 9:374(B).

Public policy also weighs heavily against the retroactive award of rent under La.R.S. 9:374(C). As is plainly illustrated by the case sub judice, when the community is not partitioned for many years, the retroactive assessment of rent is extremely prejudicial to the occupying spouse. Such retroactive assessment deprives the occupying spouse of the ability to make an informed and meaningful decision regarding his or her finances and housing budget. There is no corollary prejudice to the non-occupying spouse under this interpretation of the statute, since that spouse has the ability to invoke a court proceeding to determine occupancy and rent at any time. La.Civ.Code art. 105.

In addressing the propriety of the trial court's ruling, the court of appeal noted that under the jurisprudence of its own circuit, where there is no prior agreement between the parties, the occupying spouse cannot be retroactively assessed rent for the occupancy of the family home. Nevertheless, the court of appeal distinguished the instant case from the prior cases since it found that the record reflected that there was a prior agreement between the parties with respect to rent. The court of appeal found that Mrs. McCarroll's agreement to waive her rights to the community portion of the retirement benefits constituted a verbal agreement between the parties that justified the trial court's award of retroactive rent under La.R.S. 9:374(C). It therefore affirmed the trial court's determination that the rental value should be included in the lesion analysis. We agree, but as found herein above, the agreement among the parties regarding Mrs. McCarroll's exclusive use of the family residence did not extend beyond 1984. Thus, finding that there was an agreement between the parties whereby Mrs. McCarroll waived her rights to the benefits, and Mr. McCarroll agreed to her occupancy of the family home until the children were eighteen years of age, we find that agreement could have been properly considered as in-kind value for purposes of determining whether the March 3, 1990, agreement was lesionary.

CONCLUSION

Utilizing the figures accepted by the appellate court and reducing Mrs. McCarroll's exclusive use of the family residence to approximately seventy months as opposed to the 190 found by the trial court), there is no question that the March 3, 1990, community property settlement was lesionary. Mrs. McCarroll received only $5,000 cash, movables in her possession valued at $2,000, and rental value for approximately 70 month's use of the family residence. We therefore reverse the findings of the lower courts that the settlement agreement was not lesionary. However, because of our inability to specifically ascertain the date that the last McCarroll child reached the age of eighteen and because the trial court made no definite findings of fact with the respect to the value of some elements of the community, we therefore remand this case to the district court to judicially partition the community property.

DECREE

For the foregoing reasons, we reverse the judgment of the lower courts. The March 3, 1990, community property settlement executed by Donald McCarroll and Margarette McCarroll was lesionary. We therefore grant Margarette McCarroll's amended petition, and rescind the March 3, 1990, settlement. This case is remanded to the district court for further proceedings consistent with the foregoing opinion.

7.6 Effect of Termination on Pre-Termination Creditors

A. Applicable Statute

LA. CIV. CODE art. 2357. Satisfaction of obligation after termination of regime

An obligation incurred by a spouse before or during the community property regime may be satisfied after termination of the regime from the property of the former community and from the separate property of the spouse who incurred the obligation. The same rule applies to an obligation for attorney's fees and costs in an action for divorce incurred by a spouse between the date the petition for divorce was filed and the date of the judgment of divorce that terminates the community regime.

If a spouse disposes of property of the former community for a purpose other than the satisfaction of community obligations, he is liable for all obligations incurred by the other spouse up to the value of that community property.

A spouse may by written act assume responsibility for one-half of each community obligation incurred by the other spouse. In such case, the assuming spouse may dispose of community property without incurring further responsibility for the obligations incurred by the other spouse.

B. *TICOS, L.L.C., as Assignee of First USA Bank, v. Rachel K. Hartman*

4 So.3d 973 (La. App. 2d Cir. 2009)

BROWN, Chief Judge.

Appellant, Kasey Robert Hartman, the ex-spouse of a judgment debtor, appeals from an order authorizing the seizure/garnishment of his salary in favor of appellee, Ticos, L.L.C. ("Ticos"). For the following reasons, the order of the trial court, dated April 28, 2008, is vacated.

Facts and Procedural Background

Rachel K. Hartman and Kasey Robert Hartman were married on April 28, 2001. They did not have a separate property agreement. On December 5, 2007, Ticos filed suit against Rachel seeking to make a judgment from the Shreveport City Court, dated October 6, 2007, executory in the First Judicial District Court. The district court made the judgment executory on December 6, 2007. The original debt sued upon in Shreveport City Court involved a revolving credit account in the name of Rachel Hartman. Kasey Robert Hartman was neither named as a defendant nor served with process in the city court proceedings.

On December 20, 2007, Ticos filed a motion to enforce the judgment against the community property of the Hartmans, wherein Kasey was made a defendant in rule. This motion was not heard until April 28, 2008. In the meantime, on January 10, 2008, Rachel filed for divorce, alleging that the parties had lived separate and apart in excess of one year. Judgment was rendered on February 11, 2008, granting the parties' divorce retroactive to the filing date.

On April 28, 2008, the trial court granted Ticos' motion to enforce its judgment against the community property and authorized the seizure/garnishment of Kasey's salary.

Discussion

The legal regime of community property is terminated by, among other things, a judgment of divorce. La. C.C. art. 2356. An obligation incurred by a spouse before or during the community property regime may be satisfied after termination of the regime from the property of the former community and from the separate property of the spouse who incurred the obligation. La. C.C. art. 2357.

Clearly, the community property regime existing between Rachel and Kasey Hartman was terminated by the divorce retroactive to the date of filing, January 10, 2008. The trial court's order authorizing the seizure/garnishment of Kasey's salary occurred after the community regime had ended. At that time Kasey's salary was his separate property. Accordingly, we find that since Kasey did not incur the obligation at issue, his separate property cannot be seized to satisfy that obligation.

Conclusion

For the reasons stated above, the judgment of the trial court authorizing the seizure/garnishment of Kasey Robert Hartman's salary is hereby vacated. Costs are assessed to Ticos, L.L.C., as Assignee of First USA Bank.

C. *Stewart Title Guaranty Co. v. John B. Kiefer*

1997 WL 625491 (E.D. La. 1997)

ORDER AND REASONS

FALLON, District J.

Before the Court is a motion for summary judgment filed by plaintiff, Security Title Guarantee Corporation of Baltimore. For the reasons that follow, the motion is GRANTED IN PART and DENIED IN PART.

BACKGROUND

The plaintiffs in these consolidated actions, Stewart Title Guaranty Company ("Stewart") and Security Title Guarantee Corporation of Baltimore ("Security"), are both title insurers. Each of them had an underwriting agency agreement with Charter

Title, Ltd. ("Charter"), who was authorized to execute title insurance commitments and title insurance on behalf of Security, Stewart, and other title insurers. In addition, Charter's closing attorneys provided virtually all services necessary to close real estate transactions, including title examinations, and receipt and disbursement of sales proceeds, loan proceeds, and escrow funds. Premiums and other closing-funds were to be kept in escrow accounts. Charter filed a bankruptcy petition on January 17, 1995, on which date deficiencies in Charter's escrow accounts amounted to more than $1 million.

Stewart and Security have each sued various employees and attorneys of Charter to recover unpaid premiums as well as losses resulting from the escrow shortages. Security Title has amicably resolved all of its tort claims, reserving only its contract claim for unpaid premiums against J.B. Kiefer and Ann Kiefer. The motion before the Court is for summary judgment on these claims.

Security's Claim against J.B. Kiefer

The only remaining claim of Security against J.B. Kiefer is for failure to pay premiums due Security pursuant to the agency agreement, dated August 1, 1985, entered into between Security and Charter (the "Agency Agreement"), signed by J.B. Kiefer in both his personal and representative capacities. See Security's Exhibit 1. In addition to signing the Agency Agreement in his personal capacity, J.B. Kiefer executed an addendum to the Agency Agreement, dated August 1, 1985, in which J.B. Kiefer did "guarantee compliance by [Charter] with all terms and conditions of the [Agency Agreement] and did "[a]ssume personal liability to Security for any default or breach of agency agreement by [Charter]" (the "Guaranty"). See Security's Exhibit 1 to Exhibit B. According to the affidavit of Robert H. Schapiro, general counsel and senior vice president of Security Title, Charter has breached the Agency Agreement by failing to remit to Security its contractual share of premiums. See Security's Exhibit B. Also according to Schapiro's affidavit, the amount of premiums that remains due and owing under the Agency Agreement is $101,426.95.

J.B. Kiefer does not dispute the validity of the Agency Agreement or the Guaranty. Nor does he contend that premiums do not remain owing. Instead, Kiefer argues that the amount owed is in dispute and that his obligations have been extinguished.

Accordingly, the Court finds that no genuine issue of material fact exists and that Security is entitled to judgment as a matter of law against J.B. Kiefer in the amount of $93,426.95.

Security's Claim against Anne Kiefer

Security's claim against Ann Kiefer is based upon the community of acquets and gains that she had with J.B. Kiefer at the time the debt was incurred. In addition, Security alleges that Ann Kiefer received $100,000 of community funds and placed them into her separate Legg Mason account. Accordingly, Security claims that Ann Kiefer is liable to Security under Civil Code article 2357 to the extent that she is in possession of property of the former community and personally liable to the extent she has disposed of any assets of the former community.

Article 2357 reads:

> An obligation incurred by a spouse before or during the community property regime may be satisfied after termination of the regime from the property of the former community and from the separate property of the spouse who incurred the obligation....
>
> If a spouse disposes of property of the former community for a purpose other than the satisfaction of community obligations, he is liable for all obligations incurred by the other spouse up to the value of that community property.

La Civ.Code Ann. art 2357 (West Supp. 1997). The revision comment following article 2357 states that the article "contemplates satisfaction of both personal and community obligations after termination of a community property regime." La. Civ. Code Ann. art. 2357, 1979 revision comment (West 1985). Thus, "[c]reditors may seize property of the former community in the hands of either spouse." Id.; see also Lawson v. Lawson, 535 So.2d 851, 852 (La. App. 2d Cir. 1988).

Ms. Kiefer does not dispute that the obligation in question arose during the existence of the community. She argues, however, that a genuine issue of fact exists as to whether it is a community obligation because Security has not shown that the obligation was incurred for the common interest of the spouses. See Civ. Code art. 2360, 2361, 2363 (West 1985 & Supp. 1997).

Ms. Kiefer's efforts are misplaced. Under article 2357, "'whether the obligation incurred by Mr. [Kiefer] is deemed a separate or community obligation is immaterial." Lawson, supra, 535 So.2d at 854 (quoting Fowler v. Dunshee, 511 So.2d 1323, 1325 (La. App. 5th Cir. 1987)). Regardless of the debt's classification, as a debt incurred during the existence of the community, the assets of the former community are liable for the debt without regard to which spouse has possession of them. Id. And, regardless of whether the debt is separate or community, she is not personally liable for the obligation and it may not be satisfied out of her separate property unless she has disposed of property of the former community for a purpose other than the satisfaction of community obligations, in which case, she is liable to the extent of the property of the former community that "is no longer available to the creditor." Lawson, 535 So.2d at 853.

Security argues that Anne Kiefer is personally liable for the amount of the Legg Mason transfer, made on the date that the community regime was terminated, moving $100,000 from a joint Legg Mason account (# 3586054) held by J.B. Kiefer and Anne Kiefer to a new Legg Mason account (# 7644545) in Anne Kiefer's name only. Ann Kiefer argues that summary judgment is precluded because Security has not proved that the $100,000 was used "for a purpose other than the satisfaction of community obligations." La. Civ. Code Ann. art. 2357 (West Supp. 1997). The Court disagrees.

Security has demonstrated that Anne Kiefer diverted $100,000 from a community bank account to her separate bank account. Ms. Kiefer offers no evidence tending to dispute that these funds were property of the former community. Thus, to the extent that the $100,000 has remained intact and Anne Kiefer has not disposed of it, Kiefer's obligation to Security may be satisfied out of it pursuant to the first paragraph of article 2357. Nor does Ms. Kiefer offer any facts tending to show that, after diverting the funds to her separate account, she later used them to satisfy community debts. Thus, to the extent that Anne Kiefer has disposed of the $100,000, she is personally liable up to the value of the amount that is no longer available to satisfy debts incurred during the existence of the community.

If Security were seeking only a declaratory judgment, the lack of precise evidence regarding the cash flows out of the separate Leg. Mason account would not preclude summary judgment. However, for purposes of a money judgment against Anne Kiefer personally, it is necessary to determine precisely how much of the $100,000 was depleted, for she is personally liable under article 2357 only to that extent. The affidavit of Special Agent Cox indicates merely that as of September 21, 1995 the balance in the account was "at least $40,760.00." Security's Exhibit D. Security offers no evidence indicating whether the balance was revealed to equal this estimated amount--conceivably, it could have been much lower or significantly higher. More importantly, Security submits nothing to demonstrate the current balance. For this reason, with respect to Security's claim against Anne Kiefer personally, the Court finds that genuine issues exists which preclude summary judgment.

With respect to Security's alternative claim pursuant to Civil Code article 2036, the Court finds that it was timely brought but finds that genuine issues of fact remain. For example, while this Court does not doubt that Security can prove at trial that J.B. Kiefer was insolvent at the time of or was rendered insolvent by the $100,000 transfer, Security has offered no evidence to satisfy this element of the revocatory action.

Therefore, for the foregoing reasons, IT IS ORDERED that Security Title's motion for summary judgment is HEREBY GRANTED IN PART, in that it is granted with respect to Security's claims against J.B. Kiefer, and DENIED IN PART, in that it is denied with respect Security's claims against Anne Kiefer, except that Security is entitled without further need of trial to a declaratory judgment stating that its judgment against J.B. Kiefer may be satisfied from the property of the former community property regime that existed between Anne Kiefer and J.B. Kiefer, including such property as may be in the possession of Anne Kiefer.

7.7 VOLUNTARY PARTITION

A. Introduction

After the termination of the community property regime, the spouses (or former spouses) are co-owners of all of the former community property. For obvious reasons, continued co-ownership of property by former spouses is often undesirable. The former community property may be partitioned in two ways: judicially or extra judicially. In an extra judicial partition the spouses voluntarily agree to the appropriate division of the former community property. An extra-judicial partition (often referred to as a "community property settlement") is essentially a type of contract or compromise. As a result, an extra-judicial partition can be attacked due to fraud, duress, or error. Civil Code article 814 provides that lesion is an additional grounds for challenge:

Art. 814. Rescission of partition for lesion

> An extrajudicial partition may be rescinded on account of lesion if the value of the part received by a co-owner is less by more than one-fourth of the fair market value of the portion he should have received.

If, however, the extra-judicial partition is more appropriately described as a contract of compromise then it cannot be challenged on the grounds of lesion or error of law. Civil Code article 3082 provides that a contract of compromise "may be rescinded for error, fraud, and other grounds for the annulment of contracts." That Article also provides, however, that "a compromise cannot be rescinded on the grounds of error of law or lesion."

B. *Robert Dean Hoover v. Anne Marie Olivier Hoover*

813 So. 2d 329 (La. 2002)

CALOGERO, Chief Justice.

We granted this writ to consider whether the community property settlement of former spouses Robert Dean Hoover and Anne Marie Olivier Hoover is a transaction or compromise, or an extra judicial partition and whether the lower courts erred in dismissing Anne Hoover's claim of lesion. Upon review of the facts and the applicable law, we find that the agreement is an extra judicial partition for which lesion remains a viable remedy.

FACTS

Robert Dean Hoover (Robert) and Anne Marie Olivier Hoover (Anne) were married on August 30, 1980. On November 16, 1994, Robert filed a petition for divorce under La. Civ. Code art. 102. On June 5, 1995, Robert filed a new divorce petition pursuant to La. Civ. Code art. 103. A judgment of divorce was rendered on July 18, 1995. That judgment resolved issues of child and spousal support but did not address division of the former spouses' property. The parties instead signed a "community property settlement." The document was executed by the parties but never made a judgment of the court. At the time that the "community property settlement" was executed, Robert represented Robert Lynn Mizell (Mizell) in a tort suit, and had a contingency fee contract. The value of that contract was not specifically included in the "community property settlement." On September 4, 1998, Anne filed a "Motion to Partition Discovered Community Asset or in the Alternative to Set Aside Community Property Partition Based on Fraud and/or Lesion." The motion alleged that the value of the Mizell contract should have, but was not, included in the property partition. The motion requested that the Mizell contract be deemed "an un-partitioned asset" and that the value be divided between the parties. In the alternative, Anne requested that the partition agreement be rescinded on the basis of fraud. In the second alternative, Anne alleged that the community property partition was lesionary.

After answering the petition, Robert moved for summary judgment alleging that there is no genuine issue of material fact regarding certain claims asserted in Anne's petition. Robert also filed Exceptions of prescription and no cause of action. After a hearing, the trial court granted Robert's motion for summary judgment and dismissed Anne's claim. The court did not reach Robert's exceptions.

Anne appealed, alleging the trial court erred in dismissing her claims of fraud and lesion. The First Circuit affirmed the trial court's rulings. The court first addressed the dismissal of Anne's fraud claim. The court noted that in support of his motion for summary judgment, Robert attached his own affidavit as well as the affidavit of Nancy Sue Gregorie, the attorney who represented Anne in connection with the community property settlement. Both affidavits show that prior to the parties' execution of the partition agreement, Robert informed Anne that other contingency fee cases existed which were not part of the partition agreement; Robert refused to provide Anne with detailed information on these other matters unless Anne propounded formal discovery; and Anne, being aware of Robert's position, chose to sign the partition agreement without conducting further discovery. The court of appeal found that through the affidavits, Robert demonstrated an absence of factual support for Anne's claim that Robert fraudulently concealed the Mizell case. The appellate court then noted that Anne then failed to demonstrate that she would be able to meet her evidentiary burden of proof on the allegation of fraud at trial, and hence summary judgment was proper under La. Code Civ. Proc. art. 966.

The court next turned to Anne's lesion claim and found that the trial court properly disposed of that allegation as well. The court found that while Louisiana Civil Code article 814 allows an extrajudicial partition to be rescinded on account of lesion, the property agreement between Robert and Anne was a transaction or compromise. The court noted that the parties were fully aware of the consequences of their actions and Anne chose to accept the settlement as written despite knowledge that Robert had contingency fee cases pending. The court of appeal held that because La. Civ. Code art 3078 disallows a lesionary attack on a transaction or compromise, the trial court properly denied the claim.

Two court of appeal judges, writing separately, concurred in part and dissented in part. Both judges agreed that the trial court properly dismissed Anne's fraud-based claim, but both dissented on the majority's treatment of Anne's claim for lesion. The dissenting court of appeal judges believed a conflict existed between La. Civ. Code arts. 814 and 3078. The dissenters noted that while La. Civ. Code art. 814 permits an attack on an extrajudicial partition on the basis of lesion, La. Civ. Code art. 3078 disallows lesionary attacks on a transaction or compromise. The dissenting judges believed that in this instance, the partition agreement was an extrajudicial partition subject to a lesionary attack. The dissenters noted that *Williamson v. Amilton,* 13 La. Ann. 387, 388 (1858) provides support for the determination that extrajudicial partitions, even if they have qualities of a transaction or compromise, are nonetheless subject to claims for lesion.

LAW AND ANALYSIS

Relator, Anne Hoover, argues that the lower courts erred in dismissing her claim for lesion by granting Robert's motion for summary judgment. Anne claims that the lower courts were in error in finding that the partition agreement constituted a transaction and compromise for which lesion is unavailable under La. Civ. Code art. 3078. Anne contends that the agreement was, instead, an extrajudicial partition which is subject to a claim for lesion pursuant to La. Civ. Code art. 814. We agree.

Transaction or Compromise v. Extrajudicial Partition

Louisiana Civil Code articles 3078 and 814 are indeed, seemingly at odds. La. Civ. Code art. 814 allows an extrajudicial partition to be attacked for lesion, but La. Civ. Code art. 3078 disallows lesionary challenges of a transaction or compromise. Oftentimes, however, as is the case here, extrajudical partitions have qualities of a transaction or compromise and the question becomes which codal article applies. We find that the case of *Williamson v. Amilton,* 13 La. Ann. 387, 388 (1858) provides a well-reasoned analysis for resolving the conflict.

Williamson involved facts strikingly similar to those presently before the court. In *Williamson,* a husband and wife, after divorce, entered into a voluntary partition of the community property. The wife subsequently filed a claim for rescission of the petition on the basis of lesion. The husband opposed the wife's claim, contending that the voluntary partition was a transaction or compromise which was not assailable for lesion. The law at that time, like now, disallowed an attack on a transaction or compromise on the basis of lesion, but allowed lesionary attacks on certain partitions.

The *Williamson* court recognized the apparent conflict in the law, but reconciled the provisions in holding that "a partition, even when it takes upon itself the aspect and qualities of a compromise, may be attacked for lesion beyond one-fourth; but the partition once made, if disputes grow out of it, and the parties compromise on those disputes, this compromise is unassailable for lesion."

We find that the *Williamson* rationale, made under laws similar to those in the civil code today, applies to the situation currently before us. The rationale is in accordance with concepts of fundamental equity and fairness which form the basis for the lesion remedy. The law of lesion serves to ensure that one party does not benefit to the detriment of another and ensures that manipulation and deception do not become routine elements of property division. Parties who enter into extrajudicial partitions do so without benefit of prior court approval, and hence, the law provides protection in the event that one party receives less by more than one-fourth of the fair market value of the portion he should have received. *See* La. Civ. Code art. 814.

Here, the parties entered into a community property partition agreement which, by its very nature, had some aspects or qualities of a transaction or compromise. The parties distributed the assets and debts of the community through mutual consent, agreeing on which assets would be assigned to which spouse and who would be responsible for certain community debts. But, as stated in *Williamson,* the fact that the partition agreement has some aspects and qualities of a transaction or compromise does not make the agreement unassailable for lesion. Here, the agreement was an extrajudicial partition, and La. Civ.Code art. 814 allows Anne to attack the partition for lesion. The lower courts erred in finding otherwise.

Robert, however, is not contending that lesion is unavailable because the partition agreement is a transaction or compromise. In fact, Robert's counsel conceded at oral argument that the agreement was an extrajudicial partition. It is Robert's position that Anne's claim for lesion should be dismissed, not because it arises out of a transaction or compromise, but because Anne failed to produce factual support for that claim in response to Robert's motion for summary judgment.

Dismissal of Lesion Pursuant to Summary Judgment

According to Robert, the law of summary judgment mandates that Anne's lesionary claim be dismissed. He argues that after Anne filed her petition, he filed a motion for summary judgment pointing out lack of factual support for all of Anne's claims. At that point, Robert contends, the burden of proof shifted to Anne who failed to produce factual support sufficient to establish that she would be able to satisfy her evidentiary burden of proof at trial. Therefore, Robert argues, summary judgment was properly granted.

The law of summary judgment is set forth in Louisiana Code of Civil Procedure article 966. Subsection C(2) of that statute addresses the burden of proof and reads as follows:

> The burden of proof remains with the movant. However, *if the movant will not bear the burden of proof at trial on the matter that is before the court on the motion for summary judgment,* the movant's burden on the motion does not require him to negate all essential elements of the adverse party's claim, action, or defense, but rather to point out to the court that there is an absence of factual support for one or more elements essential to the adverse party's claim, action, or defense. Thereafter, if the adverse party fails to produce factual support sufficient to establish that he will be able to satisfy his evidentiary burden of proof at trial, there is no genuine issue of material fact. (Emphasis provided).

Under Louisiana Code of Civil Procedure article 966, Robert is correct. The burden of proving lesion rests with Anne. Thus, Robert, in his motion for summary judgment needed only to point out to the court that there was an absence of factual support for one or more elements of Anne's claim for lesion. Thereafter, the burden would have shifted to Anne to produce factual support sufficient to establish that she will be able to satisfy her evidentiary burden of proof as to the lesion claim at trial. A careful reading of the trial court pleadings, however, reveals that Robert never moved for summary judgment on the lesion claim in the trial court.

Robert's motion for summary judgment alleges that "there is no genuine issue of fact material to the claims or causes of action alleged in the motion/petition filed by Anne Marie Olivier Hoover." The memorandum in support of the motion, however, requests judgment as a matter of law on only three issues: (1) "plaintiff's main demand" which is Anne's allegation that the Mizell fee was an unpartitioned community asset; (2) the "disclosure/fraud" issue which is Anne's alternative argument that Robert fraudulently concealed the Mizell fee; and (3) Robert's "affirmative defenses" wherein Robert asserts that the doctrines of estoppel and transaction/compromise.

Neither the summary judgment motion nor the memorandum attacks Anne's claim of lesion. The overarching language in the motion which states that Robert is challenging "the causes of action alleged in the motion/petition" coupled with a memorandum that briefs only the "main demand", "disclosure/fraud" issue and Robert's "affirmative defenses" is insufficient to place Anne on notice that Robert was moving for summary judgment on the issue of lesion. Robert, as movant, failed to adequately place the lesion issue before the court and hence, the trial judge erred in dismissing the claim. The court cannot render a motion for summary judgment dismissing a claim which has not been challenged by the pleading. Because the summary judgment dismissing the lesion claim was in error, the court of appeal also erred in affirming that decision. Anne's remedy of lesion claim remains a viable remedy at this stage of the proceedings and the matter will be remanded to the district court.

In conclusion, we find that the lower courts erred in finding that the partition agreement between Anne and Robert Hoover was a transaction or compromise. While the agreement may have had some aspects and qualities of a compromise, it was nonetheless, an extrajudicial partition for which lesion is a remedy under Louisiana Civil Code article 814. Furthermore, Anne's claim for lesion was improperly dismissed on a motion for summary judgment as Robert Hoover's motion did not request disposition of that particular issue. Because the trial court was without authority to dismiss Anne's alternative claim for lesion, it remains a viable remedy at this stage of the proceedings and we remand the matter to the trial court for further proceedings.

REVERSED AND REMANDED.

C. *Marie Elaine D'Amico Ransome v. Al Jerome Ransome*

834 So. 2d 1223 (La. App. 1st Cir. 2002)

CARTER, C. J.

Al Ransome appeals a Family Court judgment which, among other things, denied his reconventional demand on the basis that an agreement between him and his former spouse was a transaction or compromise not subject to claims for lesion.

FACTS AND PROCEDURAL HISTORY

Marie Ransome and Al Ransome were divorced January 27, 1993. That same date, they executed an agreement styled "Agreement to Partition Community Property" (the agreement), which was not made a judgment of the court. Ms. Ransome subsequently filed a petition to recover damages for Mr. Ransome's alleged breach of the agreement and to enforce certain provisions of the agreement. Mr. Ransome then filed a reconventional demand asserting that the agreement should be set aside for lesion.

After a trial, the Family Court determined that the agreement constitutes a transaction or compromise that cannot be attacked on the basis of lesion, and denied Mr. Ransome's reconventional demand. The Family Court then rendered judgment in favor of Ms. Ransome in the amount of $4,588,284.50, plus interest and attorneys fees, and ordered Mr. Ransome to pledge certain stock to Ms. Ransome, as well as indemnify and hold Ms. Ransome harmless from certain debts and from any and all liability for any indebtedness secured by certain property. Mr. Ransome appeals.

RECONVENTIONAL DEMAND

On appeal, Mr. Ransome contends the Family Court erred in denying his reconventional demand because, he argues, the agreement is not a transaction or compromise. In support of his argument, Mr. Ransome relies on the recent supremecourt case of *Hoover v. Hoover,* 2001-2200 (La. 4/3/02), 813 So.2d 329. In *Hoover*, the court reconciled an apparent conflict between LSA-C.C. arts. 814 and 3078, and determined that an extrajudicial community property partition, although having some aspects and qualities of a transaction or compromise, was subject to claims for lesion. 813 So.2d at 333. Based on *Hoover*, Mr. Ransome argues, the agreement at issue herein is subject to claims for lesion. Ms. Ransome disagrees, arguing that the agreement between Mr. Ransome and her constitutes a transaction or compromise because it resolves child support and alimony issues, in addition to partitioning the community property.

In this case, the agreement was not attached to or made a part of a judgment of the court. Rather, the agreement was entered without any manner of court approval. Thus, the agreement is extrajudicial as opposed to judicial in nature. *See, e.g., Lapeyrouse v. Lapeyrouse,* 98-0271, p. 3 (La. App. 1st Cir. 2/19/99), 729 So.2d 682, 684; *Junca v. Junca,* 98-1723, p. 6 (La. App. 1st Cir. 12/28/99), 747 So.2d 767, 770, *writ denied,* 2000-1120 (La. 6/2/00), 763 So.2d 601. Under *Hoover*, if this extrajudicial agreement were strictly a community property partition, it would be subject to claims of lesion. The issue in this case is whether an extrajudicial partition becomes a transaction or compromise when the parties include in it the resolution of incidental matters. Based on the particular facts of this case, we find that it does not.

In this case, the parties considered and resolved incidental matters between them in dividing the community property. Thus, the agreement has some aspects and qualities of a transaction or compromise. However, the agreement is primarily a community property partition and was entered into voluntarily, without benefit of court approval and without being made a part of a judgment. In such cases, the law provides protection in the event that the partition is lesionary, i.e., one party receives less by more than one-fourth of the fair market value of the portion he should have received. *Hoover,* 813 So.2d at 333. The fact that a partition agreement has some aspects and qualities of a transaction or compromise does not make the agreement unassailable for lesion. *Hoover,* 813 So.2d at 333.

The agreement at issue was extrajudicial and, although having some aspects and qualities of a transaction or compromise, is subject to Mr. Ransome's claims for lesion. This determination is in accordance with concepts of fundamental equity and fairness that, the supreme court noted, form the basis for the lesion remedy. *See Hoover,* 813 So.2d at 333.

The Family Court erred in denying Mr. Ransome's reconventional demand on the basis that the agreement is unassailable for lesion. Therefore, we reverse the judgment of the Family Court in its entirety. We pretermit discussion of the remaining issues relating to the Family Court's judgment.

* * *

CONCLUSION

For the reasons set forth herein, the judgment of the Family Court is reversed. Judgment is hereby rendered, vacating for lack of subject matter jurisdiction the July 6, 1998 ruling of the Nineteenth Judicial District Court on Mr. Ransome's motion to compel. This matter is remanded to the Family Court for further proceedings in accordance with the views expressed herein. Costs of this appeal are assessed to Marie Elaine D'Amico Ransome.

REVERSED, RENDERED, AND REMANDED.

D. *Archie Millet v. Althea Mae Bergeron Millet*

888 So.2d 291 (La.App. 5th Cir. 2004)

THOMAS F. DALEY, Judge.

In this civil suit, the defendant, Althea Mae Bergeron Millet (hereinafter referred to as Althea Millet), argues that the Consent Judgment based on the community property partition should have been set aside because of lesion, fraud, mistake, or failure of consideration. The trial court denied all of Althea Millet's, motions except for the Motion to Rescind because of lesion. The plaintiff/appellee, Archie Millet, filed a Peremptory Exception of Res Judicata to the claim of lesion, which the trial court granted.

In her sole Assignment of Error, Althea Millet argues that the trial court erred in failing to annul the judgment because of fraud, mistake, or failure of consideration.

The parties were married on May 17, 1995. On February 18, 2003, the parties were divorced and on the same day signed a Consent Judgment, in which Archie Millet agreed to pay $5,400.00 in spousal support in $300.00 per month increments for eighteen months. In addition, the community property was partitioned awarding Althea Millet the Cocodrie camp, the trailer, the vehicle, and movable property, including the furniture in her possession and previous sums of cash paid to her by Archie Millet. Archie Millet was awarded the movable property in his possession, his personal items from the Cocodrie camp, the 401(k) from his employment, and "all other work benefits." Archie Millet's award of all other work benefits was made part of the Consent Judgment in a handwritten amendment. On February 26, 2003, Althea Millet filed a Motion for New Trial, Alternatively Motion to Rescind Community Property Settlement on Account of Lesion, Alternatively Motion to Annul Judgment on Account of Fraud, Mistake or Failure of Consideration. Althea Millet argued that the Consent Judgment, based on the community property partition, should be set aside because of fraud, mistake, or failure of consideration. She alleged that she did not receive her fair share of the community property, because the Cocodrie camp was destroyed by a hurricane between the time the parties agreed to the partition and the signing of the final judgment. Althea Millet claimed that Archie Millet did not insure the camp and she was unable to insure the camp and protect her interests, because Archie Millet never signed the lease over to her until after the camp was destroyed by the hurricane. Therefore, the lease of the camp awarded to her in the partition was worthless. The trial court stated at the hearing on Althea Millet's motions that it would only consider rescinding the property settlement and dividing the property judicially, if there was lesion beyond moiety.

A Consent Judgment is a transaction or compromise between parties who prevent or put an end to a lawsuit by adjusting their differences by mutual consent balancing the hope of gain against the fear of loss. Randall v. Martin, 03-1311 (La. App. 5th Cir. 2/23/04), 868 So.2d 913, 915; LSA-C.C. art. 3071. Courts are guided by the general principle "that the contract must be construed as a whole and in light of attending events and circumstances," when applying the rule of construction set forth in LSA-C.C. art. 3073. Robinson v. Robinson, 99-3097 (La. 11), 778 So.2d 1105, 1122; LSA-C.C. art.2050. The meaning and intent of the parties is ordinarily determined from the four corners of the instrument. Robinson v. Robinson, supra; Randall v. Martin, supra. The intent of the parties making the compromise is controlled by the words of the compromise instrument in light of the surrounding circumstances at the time of its execution. Id. Since public policy favors these compromise agreements and the finality of the settlements, the party seeking rescission of a settlement agreement bears the burden of proving its invalidity. Randall v. Martin, supra. Consent of the parties may only be vitiated by error, fraud, or duress. LSA-C.C. art.1948. Therefore, the only circumstances under which the settlement can be set aside are when there was error as to the person or matter in dispute, fraud, or violence in the execution of the agreement, or where the agreement is against public policy. Rumore v. Wamstad, 99-557, p. 4 (La. App. 5th Cir. 2/8/00), 751 So.2d 452, 455; LSA-C.C. art.1968, 3079.

An error only vitiates consent when it concerns a cause without which a party would not have incurred the obligation and that cause was known or should have been known by the other party. LSA-C.C. art. 1949. When there exists a dispute regarding the scope of the compromise and there is substantiating evidence of mistaken intent, parties are permitted to raise factual issues regarding the unequivocal language of the instrument. Randall v. Martin, supra. The substantiating evidence must establish that the releasor was mistaken as to what he or she was signing, even though fraud was not present; or that the releasor did not fully understand the nature of the rights being released or that the releasor did not intend to release certain aspects of his or her claim. Id.

Fraud is a misrepresentation or a suppression of the truth made with the intent to obtain an unjust advantage for one party or to cause loss or inconvenience for the other party. Fraud may result from silence or inaction. LSA-C.C. art. 1953. Fraud does not vitiate consent when the party against whom the fraud was directed could have ascertained the truth without difficulty, inconvenience, or special skill." LSA-C.C. art.1954.

In this case, the Consent Judgment was signed and made the judgment of the court on February 18, 2003. The handwritten amendment on the Consent Judgment was initialed by the parties and their respective counsel. In fact, in her Motion for New Trial, Althea Millet states that under the terms of the settlement Archie Millet was to receive his employment benefits, including 401(k) and pension at his place of employment." During the hearing on the Exception of Res Judicata, Althea Millet testified that both she and Archie Millet initialed the consent agreement above the date where the handwritten amendment is located. She did not allege that Archie Millet and his attorney committed fraud or made a mistake, but rather that her counsel added the amendment to the Consent Judgment without her knowledge or approval after she signed it. Althea Millet wanted the community assets divided, allowing her to retain a half share of Archie Millet's retirement funds. Althea Millet testified that her attorney admitted to misunderstanding her desire. Althea Millet claims that her attorney told her on the date that the Consent Judgment was signed that they would not be dividing community assets. Archie Millet's counsel reminded the Court during the February 18, 2003 hearing on the partition of community property that the Consent Judgment was read into the record and court questioned the parties making sure that they understood exactly what they signed.

The Consent Judgment clearly states that it is an agreement between the parties to partition the community property. The handwritten notation is initialed by both the parties and their respective counsel. Despite her assertions to the contrary, there would have been no need for Althea Millet to initial above the date, if there had not been a handwritten amendment. In its Reasons for Judgment on granting defendant's Exception of Res Judicata, the trial court found that the Consent Judgment provided in relevant part that: ...Archie Millet is hereby awarded the 401(k) at his place of employment and all other work benefits at his place of employment." It appears that the trial court relied on the February 18, 2003 hearing at which the trial judge allegedly questioned the parties about the Consent Judgment. During that hearing, the trial court may have determined by its questioning of the parties that Archie Millet was to receive all other work benefits. Unfortunately, the trial transcript of that hearing is not in the record. When the record lacks a transcript that is pertinent to an issue raised on appeal, the inadequacy of the record is attributable to the appellant." Kennedy v. Kennedy, 36,974 (La. App. 2d Cir. 3/5/03), 840 So.2d 679, 684. The trial judge who questioned the parties about the Consent Judgment was in the best position to interpret their intent. We find nothing in the record before us to indicate that the trial court erred in concluding that the consent agreement awarded Archie Millet his 401(k) and all other work benefits at his place of employment.

While there appears to have been some miscommunication between Althea Millet and her attorney, Althea Millet has failed to prove that Archie Millet was aware or should have been aware of any error or mistake in the confection or execution of the Consent Judgment, or that he committed fraud about which she could not have ascertained the truth without difficulty, inconvenience, or special skill.

Likewise, Althea Millet has not proven failure of consideration in regards to her share of the community property. The purpose of a transaction or compromise partitioning the community property by mutual consent is a division of the property by the parties in hopes of each retaining those items they desire the most out of fear of losing them. In this case, Althea Millet chose to retain the Cocodrie Camp leased during their marriage with all of the inherent problems associated with property in that area. She now argues that a portion of her share of the community, specifically the Cocodrie camp, is worthless, because in the time between when they agreed to the partition and the signing of the Consent Judgment the camp was destroyed by a hurricane. The failure of a party to the transaction to anticipate the value of the property will not render void a complete contract. Pioneer Valley Hosp., Inc. v. Elmwood Partners, L.L.C., 01-453, p. 6 (La. App. 5th Cir. 10/17/01), 800 So.2d 932, 937. Neither of the parties in this case could have anticipated the future value of the Cocodrie camp lease. But, since the Cocodrie Camp was used by the Millets during their marriage, Althea Millet had to have been aware that the Cocodrie area, like most of Louisiana, was subject to hurricanes, and that, therefore, the possibility existed that the camp might be destroyed by a hurricane at any time, when she voluntarily agreed to the partition of the community property. Yet, the record contains no evidence that their lease on the camp was ever insured during the Millets' marriage; that Althea Millet attempted, but was unable to obtain insurance; or that as a condition of the agreement Althea Millet insisted that the lease on camp be insured during the interim period before she took possession. In fact, neither party could have anticipated the future value of any of the property that was partitioned by this agreement. The value of any item over time is subject to an increase or decrease in value or perceived value. That may be one reason why public policy favors the finality of settlements. In addition, the record contains no objective indication of the condition or value of the camp before or after the hurricane. Indeed, while the record does not allude to it, Archie Millet may have lost all of his personal items that were stored at the Cocodrie camp, and thereby their value, during the same hurricane. Regardless, Archie Millet cannot be penalized for failing to anticipate during the partition of the community property that the camp would be damaged by a hurricane, thereby possibly reducing its value. The alleged change in the value of the lease of the Cocodrie camp does not void the completed compromise mutually agreed to by the Millets.

For the foregoing reasons, the judgment of the trial court is affirmed.

AFFIRMED.

E. *William R. Adams v. Lilly J. Adams*

503 So.2d 1052 (La. App. 2d Cir. 1987)

LINDSAY, Judge.

William and Lilly Adams were separated by a judgment of separation from bed and board which was rendered on September 19, 1985. Thereafter, the parties entered into a community property settlement contract on September 24, 1985. However, the parties failed to attach to the community property settlement contract an exhibit which described the immovable property belonging to the community. The immovable property described on the exhibit was to be conveyed to Mr. Adams. He was to assume all community debts. William Adams brought suit on October 14, 1985, seeking to force Lilly Adams to sign an amendment to the community property settlement contract which would include the required property descriptions. The suit was later amended to include the description of the "Gin lot," a parcel of land which neither William Adams nor Lilly Adams realized they owned until after the community property settlement contract was negotiated and signed. In her answer to William R. Adam's petition, Lilly Adams requested that the contract be set aside in its entirety due to failure of consent. She also sought alimony pendente lite, despite a provision in the community property settlement contract wherein she purportedly waived her rights to alimony of any kind. The trial judge found the community property settlement contract to be valid and ordered it amended to add the requested immovable property descriptions, including a description of the "Gin Lot," and ordered that Lilly Adams receive $600 per month as alimony pendente lite. For the reasons discussed below, the judgment of the trial court is affirmed in part and reversed in part.

BACKGROUND FACTS

William and Lilly Adams were married on June 25, 1972 and lived together as husband and wife until their legal separation. Once William and Lilly Adams decided to separate they went to the office of Calvin Adams, attorney and brother of William Adams, to seek advice. It was determined that a separation would be obtained by Mrs. Adams based upon the grounds of abandonment and that a community property settlement would be entered into as quickly as possible. A judgment of separation from bed and board was obtained on September 19, 1985.

Calvin Adams, and numerous other people, advised Lilly Adams to obtain her own attorney. However, Mrs. Adams testified that she trusted Calvin Adams and she felt that he would be fair to her. Additionally, Mrs. Adams was worried about the expense of obtaining her own attorney. She was also concerned about William Adams' threat of declaring bankruptcy and leaving her with one-half of the large and numerous community debts which totaled $349,678.99. Hence, Mrs. Adams relied upon the advice of Calvin Adams.

Immediately after obtaining their separation, William and Lilly Adams inventoried the household items together, with William Adams assigning a value to the items. Together, the parties decided that certain movable property would go to Mrs. Adams and others to Mr. Adams. Moreover, Mrs. Adams was to receive $10,000 in cash and a new automobile, plus automobile and hospitalization insurance for one year. Mr. Adams was to receive the community immovable property described on "Exhibit B" of the contract and he was to assume all the community debts.

Mrs. Adams testified that Mr. Adams consistently told her that she must take the property as offered and agree not to seek alimony. If she refused, he would have to file bankruptcy. Moreover, Mrs. Adams stated that Mr. William Adams cursed her and although he never hit her, he did shake her several times.

Mrs. Adams obtained a copy of the proposed community property settlement contract on September 23, 1985. Attached to the proposed contract was the exhibits, one of which was Exhibit B. Exhibit B contained the property description of the immovable property, with the exception of the description of the "Gin Lot." Cliff Adams, father of William, testified that he saw Mrs. Adams at her home on the night of September 23, 1985. The community property settlement contract was laid out on a kitchen cabinet. She stated to him that she basically understood the contract, but did not understand a portion of the contract that was typed single spaced. He explained to her that these were descriptions of the various tracts of immovable property owned by the community.

Mrs. Adams testified that she spoke to two different attorneys about the community property settlement contract before she signed it. The first attorney told her that she (the attorney) could not tell Mrs. Adams anything until she investigated the Adams' financial situation and had a chance to look at the proposed community property settlement. Likewise, the second attorney consulted by Mrs. Adams stated that, even though he had a copy of the proposed community property settlement contract, he could not tell her if the division of property was fair until he investigated the community's financial standing. On September 24, 1985, Mrs. Adams proceeded to sign the contract which purported to settle the community.

As required by the contract, William Adams attempted to obtain releases for Mrs. Adams from debts due on the real estate which was conveyed to him in the community property settlement contract. In so doing, it was discovered that the attachment to the contract which described the various tracts of immovable property had been inadvertently omitted from the contract which was actually signed and filed in the conveyance records of Madison Parish. Thus, pursuant to a provision in the community settlement contract, Mr. Adams requested that Mrs. Adams sign an amendment adding these various property descriptions. Mrs. Adams spoke with her attorney about signing the amendments and was advised not to sign. Because of her refusal to sign, William Adams filed this suit.

ACTION BY THE TRIAL COURT

The trial court found the community property settlement contract to be valid, despite Mrs. Adams' contention that it was void for lack of consent. Further, the court ordered that the contract be amended to include "Exhibit B" as originally written, and that "Exhibit B" be amended to include a description of the "Gin Lot." Last, the trial court awarded Mrs. Adams the sum of $600 per month as alimony pendent lite.

ISSUES

Mrs. Adams appeals, assigning as error the trial court's determination that the contract is valid, that "Exhibit B" be incorporated into the contract and that the "Gin Lot" also be included.

* * *

I. FAILURE OF CONSENT

Mrs. Adams contends that the community property settlement contract should be voided in its entirety because of the failure of her consent. A contract is formed by the consent of the parties established through offer and acceptance. LSA-C.C. Art. 1927. Consent may be vitiated by error, fraud, or duress. LSA- C.C. Art. 1948. Mrs. Adams contends that the consent given by her to the contract was induced through error, fraud and duress.

A. Error

The cause which prompted Lilly Adams and William Adams to enter into the subject contract was the equitable division of all assets which formerly comprised the community which existed between them. The error complained of lies in the omission from the subject contract of their interest in certain immovable property (the "Gin Lot") owned by them. The cause of the error was the ignorance of both Lilly Adams and William Adams at the time the contract was entered into of any ownership interest in that property. Apparently, William Adams' father had donated a share of ownership in this property to them while they were out of the state. Lilly Adams contends that the omission of the Gin Lot is sufficient error to cause the entire contract to be declared null and void.

Error may concern a cause when it bears on the nature of the contract, or the thing that is the contractual object or a substantial quality of that thing, or the person or the qualities of the other party, or the law, or any other circumstance that the parties regarded, or should have regarded, as a cause of the obligation. LSA-C.C. Art. 1950. In the instant case, the error does not concern a cause of the contract since the contractual object is the division of the community property listed in the contract. Neither party knew of their interest in the "Gin Lot" and therefore, neither could have intended to maintain or relinquish their interest in that lot. While it is probable that the parties believed they had divided the entirety of the community property owned by them, (see discussion of intent, infra) the contract reflects an intent to change the ownership interest of the parties only as to the listed assets. Therefore, the error in omitting from the contract an asset which neither party knew they owned is not one which can cause the contract to be declared null. Hence, this portion of the assignment of error lacks merit.

B. Fraud

Article 1953 of the Louisiana Civil Code defines fraud as the misrepresentation or suppression of the truth made with the intention either to obtain an unjust advantage for one party or to cause a loss or inconvenience to the other. Fraud may also result from silence or inaction. However, fraud does not vitiate consent when the party against whom the fraud was directed could have ascertained the truth without difficulty, inconvenience, or special skill. This exception does not apply when a relation of confidence has reasonably induced a party to rely on the other's assertions or representations. LSA-C.C. Art. 1954. Unlike the vice of error, which vitiates consent only when it concerns a cause without which the obligation would not have been incurred, the error induced by fraud need not concern the cause of the obligation to vitiate consent, but it must concern a circumstance which has substantially influenced that consent. LSA-C.C. Art. 1955. Last, fraud may be established by a preponderance of the evidence and may be established by circumstantial evidence. LSA-C.C. Art. 1957.

Mrs. Adams contends that fraud is established by two facts. The first is the trust she placed in Calvin Adams. The second is the statements made by Calvin and William Adams' [sic] that unless Mrs. Adams accepted the community property settlement as proposed, Mr. Adams would be forced to declare bankruptcy and Mrs. Adams would have to take responsibility for her share of the community debts. Mrs. Adams placed emphasis on the trust that she placed in attorney Calvin Adams to fairly represent her, as well as her husband. However, the essential concept from which fraud evolved is not the relationship of trust, but the misrepresentation or suppression of the truth.

If the truth were misrepresented or suppressed herein, it would be in the claims of impending bankruptcy and the sharing of community debts. William Adams' sole source of income is from farming. The community property settlement contract establishes the value of the community assets at $400,277.33. These values were not contested at trial. Likewise, the community property settlement contract establishes the community debt at $349,678.89. Mr. Adams testified that his farming operation was faltering. Under these circumstances we cannot say that bankruptcy would not be a serious consideration at the time the contract was confected. Moreover, Mrs. Adams would continue to be liable for community obligations. See: LSA-C.C. Art. 2367.

For the reasons given above, and because the burden of proof was on Mrs. Adams, we conclude that she had not proved a misrepresentation or a suppression of the truth. Therefore, this assignment of error is without merit.

C. Duress

Mrs. Adams also contends that she was under great duress during this time. In addition to the emotional and psychological strain of going through a separation, Mrs. Adams testified that she was placed in a situation in which she felt she was expected to make a quick decision as to the community property settlement contract. Moreover, if she failed to agree to the property settlement she would be faced with huge debts and no way of paying them. Additionally, Mrs. Adams testified that although William never hit her, he did shake her at times. Also, the parties cursed each other on occasion.

Consent is vitiated when it has been obtained by duress of such a nature as to cause a reasonable fear of unjust and considerable injury to a party's person, property, or reputation. Age, health, disposition, and other personal circumstances of a party must be taken into account in determining reasonableness of the fear. LSA-C.C. Art. 1959.

Most of the violence or threats of which Mrs. Adams complained surround the claims by Mr. Adams to declare bankruptcy and statements made to Mrs. Adams concerning her obligation to pay her portion of the community debts. However, a threat of doing a lawful act or a threat of exercising a right does not constitute duress. LSA-C.C. Art. 1962.

Another aspect of the duress claimed by Mrs. Adams is the emotional and mental strain caused by going through a separation and division of property. However, the conflicting emotions caused by the strain of going through a critical period in one's life is not the type of strain constituting legal duress. Compare: Allen v. Volunteers of America, 378 So.2d 1030 (La. App. 2d Cir.1979).

Last, Mrs. Adams failed to prove a reasonable fear of unjust or considerable injury to her person. There is some testimony that Mr. Adams had physically shaken her prior to the separation. However, if any violence occurred by Mr. Adams, there is no testimony establishing it was in any way associated with the community property settlement contract. For the foregoing reasons, this portion of the assignment of error also lacks merit.

In light of the above, we conclude that the trial judge did not err in holding that the community property settlement contract was valid and binding.

CONCLUSION

Therefore, we uphold the ruling of the trial court in all respects, except in the awarding to Mrs. Adams of alimony pendente lite and the inclusion of the "Gin lot" in the community property settlement contract. Insofar as the trial court judgment awards alimony pendente lite to Mrs. Adams and amends the subject contract to include the "Gin lot", the judgment is reversed and set aside.

Accordingly:

IT IS ORDERED, ADJUDGED, AND DECREED, that the "Community Property Settlement With Lump Sum Payment in Lieu of Alimony Pendente Lite and Permanent Alimony," recorded in COB "68" at page 1, bearing register no. 71009 of the conveyance records of Madison Parish, Louisiana, is a valid and binding partition agreement between the parties and that lesion is not applicable here.

IT IS FURTHER ORDERED, ADJUDGED, AND DECREED, that there be judgment herein in favor of plaintiff, William R. Adams, recognizing his ownership of the community immovable property described on "Exhibit B" referred to hereafter and amending the "Community Property Settlement With Lump Sum Payment in Lieu of Alimony Pendente Lite and Permanent Alimony", referred to above, to include and recognize his ownership of the immovable property previously owned by the community previously existing between William R. Adams and Lilly J. Adams, consisting of that property described on "Exhibit B", pages 2 through 7, attached to and made a part of the trial court judgment, with the exception of the immovable property referred to in these proceedings as the "Gin Lot", which is fully described hereafter.

IT IS FURTHER ORDERED, ADJUDGED, AND DECREED, that the following described immovable property, referred to in these proceedings as the "Gin Lot", forms a part of the community of acquets and gains formerly existing between William R. Adams and Lilly J. Adams and was not partitioned by the above mentioned contract and remains owned in indivision by the parties, the property being described in Exhibit B of the trial court's judgment, page 7.

IT IS FURTHER ORDERED, ADJUDGED, AND DECREED, that the judgment in favor of Lilly J. Adams awarding her the sum of $600.00 per month alimony pendente lite effective from November 22, 1985 is reversed and set aside.

IT IS FURTHER ORDERED, ADJUDGED, AND DECREED, that the damages sought by William R. Adams against Lilly J. Adams are denied.

IT IS FURTHER ORDERED, ADJUDGED, AND DECREED, that the costs of these proceedings in the trial court and in this Court are apportioned equally between the parties.

AFFIRMED IN PART, REVERSED IN PART, AND RENDERED.

F. *Claudine Mason McCoy Delaney v. Mack Allen McCoy*

93 So. 3d 845 (La. App. 2d Cir. 2012)

Before BROWN, GASKINS and MOORE, JJ.

GASKINS, J.

The plaintiff, Claudine Mason McCoy Delaney, appeals from a trial court judgment granting an exception of res judicata in favor of the defendant, Mack Allen McCoy, Sr., finding that their prior community property settlement disposed of any claims Ms. Delaney had to Mr. McCoy's retirement benefits. For the following reasons, we reverse and remand the matter to the trial court for further proceedings.

FACTS

The parties were married on November 16, 1973. On June 27, 1979, Mr. McCoy filed a petition for separation. On July 10, 1979, a judgment of separation was entered terminating the community property regime between the parties. On September 19, 1979, Ms. Delaney filed a petition for settlement of the parties' community property. Mr. McCoy worked for the Shreveport Fire Department. During the course of the proceedings, Ms. Delaney propounded interrogatories to Mr. McCoy regarding the existence of a retirement plan, profit sharing, or stock purchase plan. He answered, "the parties have no vested interest in any retirement plan."

Trial was held on the matter and on December 14, 1979, a judgment was entered, ordering that the community property be partitioned and setting forth which items of the former community were to be partitioned in kind and which were to be partitioned by licitation. The judgment did not mention retirement benefits. On January 16, 1980, the parties entered into an extrajudicial agreement partitioning the community property in kind. The agreement was not filed into the suit record. No mention was made in the agreement of retirement benefits. On January 29, 1980, on joint motion of the parties, the trial court signed a judgment dismissing the case with prejudice.

In December 2007, Mr. McCoy retired from the fire department. In 2008, Ms. Delaney filed a supplemental petition for partition of community property, alleging that Mr. McCoy's retirement benefits accruing during the marriage had been omitted from the prior community property partition. She alleged that the parties were married for 2,050 days and she requested her proportionate share of Mr. McCoy's retirement benefits as well as her share of his retirement benefits deposited during Mr. McCoy's participation in the deferred retirement option program (DROP).

Mr. McCoy filed exceptions of *res judicata* and no right and no cause of action. The trial court denied the exceptions. Mr. McCoy filed a motion for rehearing in the trial court, alleging the discovery of the prior extrajudicial community property settlement agreement. He claimed that the document contained language of transaction and compromise. The trial court granted the rehearing and granted the exception of *res judicata.* In reasons for judgment, the trial court stated:

> As the record reflects this matter was before the Court in 1979 on a partition suit and the judgment of the trial court in 1979 case [was] that the Court at that time found that Mr. McCoy had no retirement benefits that were accrued during the community. As a matter of fact, the Court in 1979 found that Mr. McCoy had no retirement benefits which were community property, and as a matter of fact, were not listed in the list of assets recognized as community property in the judgment. Subsequent to the judgment rendered in 1979 the parties entered into a voluntary transaction and compromise, entitled "Community Property Settlement" and in this community property settlement it indicates that there was a settlement of all claims that either party have or may have against the community of acquets and gains formerly existing. The jurisprudence is clear that compromise and transaction has the authority of a thing adjudged and forms the basis of Res Judicata.

Ms. Delaney appealed the trial court decision granting the exception of *res judicata.* See *Delaney v. McCoy,* 46,103 (La.App.2d Cir.4/13/11), 63 So.3d 327. She argued that the trial court incorrectly found that the issue of retirement benefits had been previously adjudicated based on the omission of those benefits from the list of community assets in the prior community property settlement. This court noted that the trial court mentioned the record of the prior proceedings in granting the exception of *res judicata,* but the record of the prior lawsuit, the judgment, and the extrajudicial community property settlement were not introduced into evidence. We found that it was incumbent upon Mr. McCoy, as the party pleading the exception of *res judicata,* to introduce into evidence in the trial court the suit record in the prior case, the prior judgment, and the community property settlement. By failing to introduce these documents into evidence, we found that Mr. McCoy did not meet his burden of proof. This court denied Mr. McCoy's motion to supplement the record with the absent documents because they were not introduced into evidence in the trial court. We reversed the trial court judgment and remanded for further proceedings.

On remand, a hearing was held in the trial court in June 2011. All pertinent suit records regarding the partition were filed into evidence along with the extrajudicial community property settlement. On August 17, 2011, the trial court signed a judgment again granting the exception of *res judicata* and denying the exceptions of no right and no cause of action. The trial court incorporated the reasons for judgment given for the prior judgment. Ms. Delaney again appealed.

RES JUDICATA

In the present appeal, Ms. Delaney urges that the trial court erred in finding that consideration of partition of the retirement benefits was barred by *res judicata.* She argues that the trial court erred in granting the exception of *res judicata* based upon the reasoning that no retirement benefits were contained in the detailed descriptive list in the community property partition, and therefore, the trial court, in 1979, made a finding that the retirement benefits were not community property. This argument has merit.

Discussion

The law on community property partitions has changed since the original proceedings in this matter. In 1979–1980, during the prior community property partition, the "item theory" of partition in kind applied. Under that theory, it was necessary that each particular community effect be capable of division between the spouses. Normally, community property consists of different assets not capable of "item by item" division in kind. If property could not be partitioned in kind, it was partitioned by licitation. In 1982, La. R.S. 9:2801 was enacted which adopts the "aggregate theory" of partition whereby different assets of equal value are allotted to each spouse, provided that the property each ultimately receives is of equal net value. See Katherine S. Spaht and Richard D. Moreno, Matrimonial Regimes § 7.26, in 16 Louisiana Civil Law Treatise (3d ed. 2007).

The parties agree that the law on *res judicata* has changed since 1979 and 1980 when the hearing on the partition was held and the settlement agreement was entered, that those changes were substantive, and that the prior law is applicable to this matter. The exception of *res judicata* is currently governed by La. R.S. 13:4231. This statute became effective on January 1, 1991, and applies to all civil actions filed on or after that date. The preclusive authority of a judgment rendered in an action filed before January 1, 1991, shall be determined by the law in effect prior to that date. Acts 1990, No. 521, § 5. See also *Thurston v. Thurston,* 31,895 (La.App.2d Cir.8/20/99), 740 So.2d 268. Thus, the law of *res judicata* applicable to the present case is set forth in former La. C.C. art. 2286:

> The authority of the thing adjudged takes place only with respect to what was the object of the judgment. The thing demanded must be the same; the demand must be founded on the same cause of action; the demand must be between the same parties, and formed by them against each other in the same quality.

Under this provision, for *res judicata* to apply, there must be: 1) an identity of the parties; 2) an identity of "cause"; and 3) an identity of the thing demanded. The words "cause of action" as used in the statute are interpreted to mean "cause." The civilian concept of cause is the juridical or material fact which is the basis of the right claimed, or the defense pleaded. The "thing demanded" has been defined as the "kind of relief sought." *Thurston v. Thurston, supra; Gautney v. Gautney,* 35,398 (La.App.2d Cir.4/3/02), 814 So.2d 717.

The doctrine of *res judicata* is strictly construed. Any doubt regarding compliance with its requirements is to be resolved in favor of maintaining the plaintiff's action. *Thurston v. Thurston, supra.* The party urging the exception of *res judicata* has the burden of proving each essential element by a preponderance of the evidence. The absence of any of these requisite elements is fatal to a plea of *res judicata. Thurston v. Thurston, supra.* See *Blalock v. Blalock,* 312 So.2d 366 (La.App.2d Cir.1975).

Numerous cases have dealt with facts similar to those in the present case where retirement benefits were not included in a community property partition or settlement. One spouse's retirement benefits are community property in the proportion set forth in *Sims v. Sims,* 358 So.2d 919 (La.1978). Community property which is not disposed of by the community property settlement agreement remains owned in indivision by the parties. *Rollison v. Rollison,* 541 So.2d 375 (La.App.2d Cir.1989); *Mire v. Mire,* 2006–511 (La.App.3d Cir.9/27/06), 962 So.2d 1. All persons who hold property in common may seek a partition. La. C.C. art. 1308; *Rollison v. Rollison, supra.*

Under the section of the Civil Code dealing with the rescission of partition of succession properties, the mere omission of a thing belonging to the succession is not ground for rescission, but simply for a supplementary partition. La. C.C. art. 1401. By analogy, this principle applies to the partition of the community. When co-owned property is omitted from the spouse's partition, the jurisprudence holds that each spouse continues as co-owner and is entitled to a supplemental partition. *Sullivan v. Sullivan,* 42,923 (La.App.2d Cir.2/13/08), 976 So.2d 329, *writ denied,* 2008–0816 (La.6/6/08), 983 So.2d 921; *Rollison v. Rollison, supra.* Even when an original partition explicitly purports to be a full and final property settlement between the spouses, the courts have allowed supplemental partitions of omitted assets when the facts and intent of the parties warrant it. *Sullivan v. Sullivan, supra; Mire v. Mire, supra; Goodwyne v. Goodwyne,* 94–0079 (La.App.4th Cir.6/30/94), 639 So.2d 1210, *writ denied,* 94–2035 (La.11/4/94), 645 So.2d 211; *Moreau v. Moreau,* 457 So.2d 1285 (La.App.3d Cir.1984).

When neither party mentions retirement pay during negotiations and settlement, the failure to include the retirement pay in the settlement agreement is a "mere omission" which can be amended by a supplemental partition. La. C.C. art. 1401; *Rollison v. Rollison, supra; Succession of Tucker,* 445 So.2d 510 (La.App.3d Cir.1984), *writ denied,* 447 So.2d 1077 (La.1984).

The issue of whether a pension was considered in property settlement discussions is a question of fact, with the factfinder afforded much discretion. *Faucheux v. Faucheux,* 97–1369 (La.App.4th Cir.1/28/98), 706 So.2d 654, *writ denied,* 98–0482 (La.4/9/98), 717 So.2d 1146. Where one spouse knows of pension rights, but there is no clear showing that there was a discussion and waiver of those rights, the claiming spouse retains the right to seek a supplemental partition of the pension benefits. See *Faucheux v. Faucheux, supra.*

The record shows that in the proceedings held in 1979 and 1980, the only mention of retirement benefits was one interrogatory propounded by Ms. Delaney to Mr. McCoy. Mr. McCoy answered that there was no "vested interest" in retirement benefits. There was no further discussion of retirement benefits. Retirement benefits were not mentioned in the trial to partition the community. Following that hearing, in oral reasons for judgment, the trial court meticulously set forth the disputed items of property considered at that hearing, and announced its decision as to the classification of each item as separate or community property. The trial court found that the proceeds from the sale of timber and cattle were Mr. McCoy's separate property. A certificate of deposit in the original amount of $3,000, purchased by Mr. McCoy, was found to be community because funds had been comingled. However, the trial court found that Mr. McCoy was entitled to the original $3,000. The mobile home that parties had lived in was found to be Mr. McCoy's separate property. A note for $5,000 executed a few days after the marriage to facilitate the purchase of the mobile home was found to be a community debt for which no reimbursement was due. There was then some discussion off the record concerning division of motor vehicles owned by the parties. There was no discussion or decision regarding retirement benefits.

A written judgment was signed and filed on January 18, 1980, partitioning the community. The trial court ordered that the community owed the separate estate of Mr. McCoy $26,943.84. The mobile home was decreed to be Mr. McCoy's separate property. Each party was found to be in possession of approximately $9,651 of former community funds which they were allowed to retain. The trial court listed several items of movable property and immovable property of approximately three acres that was not subject to being partitioned in kind. The trial court directed a partition by licitation of those items and ordered a sale, with the proceeds to be divided between the parties. There was no mention in the judgment of retirement benefits. The partition by licitation was avoided when the parties entered into an extrajudicial community property settlement, dividing the items in kind. The record fails to show that retirement benefits were considered in that agreement.

In the present matter, there is an identity of the parties and an identity of cause. However, the thing demanded is not the same. Mr. McCoy argues that the thing demanded in the 1979 partition was all assets and liabilities of the community estate. The record shows that even though all assets were demanded, there was no consideration of the existence of and entitlement to a pro rata share of Mr. McCoy's retirement benefits in the prior partition proceedings. There was no express waiver by Ms. Delaney of her pro rata share of any retirement benefits she might be entitled to. See and compare *Gautney v. Gautney, supra; Thurston v. Thurston, supra.* The record is clear that retirement benefits were not divided or waived in prior proceedings. The trial court's statement in this case that the trial court in 1979 found that Mr. McCoy had no retirement benefits is erroneous and is not supported by the record. According to the jurisprudence, if any retirement benefits accrued during the marriage of the parties, then Ms. Delaney is entitled to a pro rata share that has not been divided, is still co-owned by the parties in indivision, and is now properly subject to a supplemental partition. Because the thing demanded in the present suit is not the same as that demanded in the prior proceedings, Ms. Delaney's claim is not barred by *res judicata.* See *Rollison v. Rollison, supra; Blalock v. Blalock, supra.* See and compare *Sullivan v. Sullivan, supra.* The trial court's judgment in this matter, granting Mr. McCoy's exception of *res judicata,* was erroneous and is reversed.

TRANSACTION AND COMPROMISE

Ms. Delaney contends that the trial court erred in finding that the matter is *res judicata* by reasoning that the language within the parties' extrajudicial settlement agreement had the effect of a transaction and compromise barring supplemental partition of retirement benefits accrued during the parties' marriage. This argument has merit.

Discussion

At the time of the prior proceedings in 1979 and 1980, La. C.C. art. 3071 provided:

> A *transaction or compromise* is an agreement between two or more persons, who, for preventing or putting an end to a lawsuit, adjust their differences by mutual consent, in the manner which they agree on, and which every one of them prefers to the hope of gaining, balanced by the danger of losing.
>
> This contract must be either reduced into writing or recited in open court and capable of being transcribed from the record of the proceeding. The agreement recited in open court confers upon each of them the right of judicially enforcing its performance, although its substance may thereafter be written in a more convenient form.

At that time, La. C.C. art. 3073 stated:

> Transactions regulate only the differences which appear clearly to be comprehended in them by the intention of the parties, whether it be explained in a general or particular manner, unless it be the necessary consequence of what is expressed; and they do not extend to differences which the parties never intended to include in them.
>
> The renunciation, which is made to all rights, claims, and pretensions, extends only to what relates to the differences on which the transaction arises.

Former La. C.C. art. 3078 stated:

> Transactions have, between the interested parties, a force equal to the authority of things adjudged. They can not be attacked on account of any error in law or any lesion. But an error in calculation may always be corrected.

In the present case, the extrajudicial community property settlement entered into by the parties in 1980 stated:

> It is further understood and agreed that this settlement includes the settlement of all claims which Mack Allen McCoy and Claudine Mason McCoy, or either of them, have or may have against the community of acquets and gains formerly existing between Mack Allen McCoy and Claudine Mason McCoy in favor of either of their separate estates.
>
> Each party acknowledges that he and she received in said partition, property equal in value to that conveyed herein and the agreement of each party being entered into herein for the consideration of settling the dispute existing between the parties hereto with reference to the partition and liquidation with reference thereto.

The trial court found that this language constituted a transaction and compromise which barred Ms. Delaney from now claiming entitlement to retirement benefits that were omitted from the prior partition. The jurisprudence does not support the trial court's decision.

In *Robinson v. Robinson,* 1999–3097 (La.1/17/01), 778 So.2d 1105, the Louisiana Supreme Court considered the issue of whether boilerplate language in a community property agreement precluded the former wife from later seeking her portion of the former husband's retirement benefits. That language stated:

> Husband and Wife further agree that they have hereby accomplished a complete liquidation of the community of acquets and gains formerly existing between them, and they do accordingly hereby mutually release and forever discharge each other from any and all further claims and demands and any and all further accounting between them. It is the intention of the parties that henceforth there shall be, as between them, only such right and obligations as are specifically provided for in this Agreement, and the parties acknowledge that the allocation made to them has resulted in each party's receiving an equal share of the community property.
>
> ....
>
> The Wife, for herself, her heirs, executors, administrators, and assigns, hereby releases and relinquishes unto the Husband, his heirs, executors, administrators, and assigns, all right of future support, all right of dower, inheritance, descent, and distribution, and right to dissent from his will, and any and all other rights arising out of their marriage relationship, and to any and all property or interest in property, real,

> personal, and mixed, now owned or hereafter acquired by Husband, and hereby agrees that Husband henceforth may acquire, hold, manage, alienate, lease, and convey his property without her knowledge, further consent, or joinder, in accordance with the provisions of law, the same as if she never had been married to him, and further does hereby release, relinquish, and renounce any and all right to administer upon his estate.
>
> ....
>
> Husband and Wife have accomplished a complete liquidation and division of their property in full settlement of all of their property rights, ... under the community of acquets and gains laws in the State of Louisiana, or any other provision of the law of any other jurisdiction, statutory or otherwise, and hereby ratify the division of such property, and agree that the same amounts to an equitable division of their property.

The supreme court found that this language did not transfer the former wife's interests in the former husband's pension plan to him. According to the supreme court, Louisiana jurisprudence is clear; general divestiture language does not necessarily divest the non-employee spouse of his or her right in the employee spouse's pension. When the agreement does not expressly address the employee spouse's pension, the issue of whether the agreement divests the non-employee spouse of any community property rights in the pension depends upon the intent of the parties. See also *Gautney v. Gautney, supra.* In *Robinson,* the pension plan was not listed in the parties' agreement nor was it discussed as part of the settlement. Therefore, the supreme court found that the pension was not partitioned. Both parties were co-owners in indivision of the pension benefits and the former wife could seek to partition this asset.

In the case of *Sherrill v. Sherrill,* 25,889 (La.App.2d Cir.6/22/94), 639 So.2d 794, this court addressed a similar argument where the husband claimed that a community property settlement contained a residual disposition clause which barred the wife from seeking a supplemental partition of retirement benefits. In *Sherrill,* the clause stated:

> As a result hereof, the parties hereto discharge each other from any further accounting to the community formerly existing between them, or to each other, the same being fully liquidated as set forth above.

The former husband argued that this language barred the former wife's later claim for her share of his retirement benefits. This court rejected that argument, finding that, because there was nothing in the settlement specifically addressing retirement benefits, the former wife's rights were preserved. We also found that none of the provisions contained in the community property settlement transferred ownership of the former wife's interest in retirement benefits to her former husband.

This court's reasoning was based in part on *Moreau v. Moreau, supra,* where the parties' community property settlement did not mention Mr. Moreau's retirement benefits. Mrs. Moreau later sought her share of those benefits. Mr. Moreau claimed that the following clause barred Mrs. Moreau from receiving the retirement benefits:

> As a result of the transfers and agreements made herein, the parties hereby mutually discharge each other from any further accountings of the community which formerly existed between them, the same being fully liquidated as above set forth.

The court in *Moreau* found that this provision did not constitute a waiver of the former wife's rights to her share of the former husband's retirement benefits. See also *Succession of Tucker, supra.*

Similarly, in *Lamartiniere v. Lamartiniere,* 520 So.2d 828 (La.App.3d Cir.1987), the parties executed a community property settlement agreement entitled, "Act of Compromise, Partition, and Community Property Settlement." The agreement did not include partition of retirement benefits, but the former husband claimed that it was intended to be a final and complete settlement of all differences the parties had in reference to the divorce.

The court found that even though the agreement contained language that usually is employed in a compromise transaction, such agreements regulate only the differences which appear clearly to be comprehended in them by the intention of the parties, citing former La. C.C. art. 3073, set forth above. The court observed that the agreement disclosed that the parties went to great lengths to set out all of the differences they intended to settle and partitioned the assets they had under consideration "down to the last tea-cup." According to the court, it was inconceivable that so substantial an asset as the husband's retirement rights would have been omitted from the listed assets partitioned, if the parties intended to include them in the partition. The court concluded that the retirement rights of the former husband were not intended to be included in the partition, and the agreement entered into by the parties did not bar the former wife from pursuing her community interest therein. *Lamartiniere v. Lamartiniere, supra.*

In *Gautney v. Gautney, supra,* the principles set forth in *Robinson v. Robinson, supra,* dealing with contractual community property partitions were extended to partition judgments. This court stated that, "Although *Robinson* dealt with a contractual partition and compromise and not a partition judgment as in this case, the preclusive effect rejected by *Robinson* likewise does not apply in this case."

In this case, there is no showing that the parties considered Mr. McCoy's retirement benefits in the litigation and judgment dividing community assets, or in the extrajudicial community property settlement. The jurisprudence is clear that, without a showing that Ms. Delaney expressly waived her rights to retirement benefits, or that the value of the retirement benefits was used to calculate the division of the property, residual disposition language did not constitute a transaction and compromise. Ms. Delaney is not barred from asserting her alleged right to her pro rata share of Mr. McCoy's retirement benefits. We reverse the trial court judgment granting Mr. McCoy's exception of *res judicata* and remand for further proceedings.

CONCLUSION

For the reasons set forth above, we reverse the trial court judgment granting an exception of *res judicata* in favor of the defendant, Mack Allen McCoy, Sr. We remand this matter to the trial court for further proceedings. Costs in this court are assessed to Mr. McCoy.

REVERSED AND REMANDED.

G. Note

It is important to remember that an extrajudicial partition is a contract, and is therefore subject to the rules regulating conventional obligations, except to the extent that special provisions of the contract of partition modify or depart from those rules. The partition may be annulled for error, fraud or duress, the vices of consent referred to in Louisiana Civil Code article 1948.

In *Tarver v. Tarver,* 441 So.2d 451 (La. App. 2d Cir. 1983), *writ denied,* 445 So.2d 1232 (1984), the husband sought to annul a community property settlement for error of law. The settlement agreement had been incorporated into a judgment of divorce. The error of law alleged by the husband was that he thought in 1974 that his military pension rights were community property, but in *McCarty v. McCarty* the United States Supreme Court determined that such rights were the separate property of the husband. The Second Circuit Court of Appeal concluded that a judgment could only be annulled for reasons specified in the Code of Civil Procedure, not for error of law. However, the court added that the underlying agreement was "...a contract made for the purpose of avoiding litigation of the issue of the community nature of military retirement...." and a compromise may not be rescinded for error of law.

Characterization of the underlying community property settlement in the *Tarver* case was unnecessary to the holding and inconsistent with prior decisions to the contrary. Even if the agreement is properly characterized as a partition, it may be rescinded for vices such as error, fraud or duress.

Doctrinal writers suggest that error of law is not a ground for annulment of a partition because the law provides other remedies for error of law. For example, if property is excluded from the partition because the parties believe it to be separate property, the spouse aggrieved is entitled to seek a supplemental partition. However, if separate property is included in the partition under the mistaken assumption that it is community property, as in the *Tarver* case, the remedy to be asserted will be reformation of the partition on the grounds of mutual error.

H. *Elise Chance Taylor v. Richard David Taylor*

772 So.2d 891 (La. App. 2d Cir. 2000)

NORRIS, Chief Judge.

Former husband asserted a claim of lesion against a voluntary community property settlement which included an obligation of contractual spousal support; the district court rejected this claim and ordered him to comply with the terms of the agreement. Finding the agreement lesionary, we reverse.

Factual Background

On February 7, 1998 Richard and Elise Taylor were married. Approximately eight months later, on October 24, 1998, Elise left the matrimonial domicile; she filed her original petition for divorce on November 4, 1998. On November 12, 1998, the parties signed an "Act of Partition and Community Property Settlement" which, among other things, granted Elise spousal support of $2,000.00 a month for life, and half of any future proceeds from certain oil and gas leases held by Sandstone Exploration, LLC, Richard's company. Although the document was never filed into the divorce suit record, it was filed into the conveyance records of Bienville Parish.

Subsequently, in the first week of December, 1998, Richard announced his intention not to abide by the terms of the agreement, claiming that misrepresentations were made by Elise during negotiations and that the agreement was lesionary. Accordingly, he filed a Petition for Rescission on December 29, 1998; Elise answered and reconvened, claiming that Richard breached the contract and also seeking attorney fees. The parties were ultimately divorced on June 3, 1999, with the former community regime being terminated retroactive to November 4, 1998. Trial on the Petition for Rescission was held on September 23-24, 1999. In a judgment dated October 18, 1999, the district court granted Elise's motion for involuntary dismissal, dismissing Richard's Petition for Rescission and ruling in favor of Elise on her reconventional demand, ordering Richard to comply with the terms of the original agreement and pay accrued spousal support. Attorney fees of $3,000.00 were also awarded to Elise. This appeal followed.

Law and Analysis

An extrajudicial partition may be rescinded on account of lesion if the value of the part received by a co-owner is less by more than one-fourth of the fair market value of the portion he should have received. La.C.C. art. 814. Lesion cannot be waived. Harmon v. Harmon, 508 So.2d 616, 620-21 (La. App. 2d Cir.), writ denied, 513 So.2d 1210 (La. 1987); Picard v. Picard, 97-1258 (La. App. 3d Cir. 4/1/98), 708 So.2d 1292, 1295.

The proper method of establishing lesion beyond one-fourth is twofold: (1) the community property's true value (net value) must be ascertained; and (2) it must then be determined from the property acquired whether a party received value less than 3/4 of 1/2 share of the true value of the property partitioned. McCarroll v. McCarroll, 96-2700 (La. 10/21/97), 701 So.2d 1280, 1285; Cowling v. Cowling, 486 So.2d 1060 (La. App. 2d Cir. 1986); La. C.C. art. 2590; La. C.C. art. 814 comment (b). The party claiming this remedy has the burden of proving lesion beyond one-fourth and must establish the claim by clear and convincing evidence. King v. King, 493 So.2d 679, 681 (La. App. 2d Cir. 1986); Ozane v. Ozane, 392 So.2d 774, 777 (La. App. 3d Cir. 1980).

From the record, we note that the community had a gross value of $46,380.51 and a net value of $40,542.68. According to the agreement, $ 42, 452.13 of the community assets were conveyed to Elise and $3,928.38 to Richard, with Richard assuming the $5,837.83 in outstanding community debts. As such, even disregarding the oil and gas leases, the agreement is lesionary, for Richard should have, at a minimum, received $15,203.51 of the community's value. In addition, Richard also agreed to pay the community's 1998 state and federal tax liability, to maintain a $100,000.00 life insurance policy on himself but payable to Elise, to pay Elise's health insurance policy until she was covered by another policy, to contribute $2,000.00 yearly into Elise's I.R.A. account for 11 years, and to pay $2,000.000 per month contractual alimony, "regardless of remarriage, until his or her death, whichever comes first."

In brief, Elise contends that the agreement is not lesionary because it is in reality a "transaction and compromise" from which Richard has reduced his potential exposure to future alimony payments and litigation, and that parties are free to contract accordingly. This argument has no merit, for even if a partition has the qualities of a transaction and comprise, it may nevertheless be attacked for lesion. Harmon, supra.

While it is true that the value of a provision in a community property settlement which reduces a future obligation or exposure can be added as consideration to the value of other assets received for the purpose of considering whether the agreement is lesionary, see, e.g., King v. King, 493 So.2d 679, 682 (La. App. 2d Cir. 1986), we fail to see the value in the present case and Elise has provided no evidence to controvert Richard's strong showing that he did not receive his legally-mandated minimum share of the community. Cowling v. Cowling, 486 So.2d 1060 (La. App. 2d Cir. 1986); see also, Ozane v. Ozane, 392 So.2d 774, 777 (La. App. 3d Cir. 1980) (unsupported or speculative values are not to be included in lesion calculations). In fact, under the present agreement, Richard received nothing and actually incurred a substantial liability by assuming the community's debts and 1998 tax debt; any value associated with avoiding future spousal support adjustments would therefore have to be substantial, but Elise made no showing in this regard other than her speculation that the present settlement might reduce Richard's future spousal support obligation. Moreover, in the present agreement, Richard waived his statutory future right to reduce, terminate, or contest for fault his spousal support obligation-tangible benefits accruing in favor of Elise--which, at a minimum, offsets the purely speculative benefit gained by locking his spousal support payments in a particular level. Accordingly, based on the record before us, we conclude that the agreement was a partition subject to lesion and should be rescinded.

Decree

For the foregoing reasons, we reverse the judgment of the lower court. The November 12, 1998 "Act of Partition and Community Property Settlement" executed by Richard and Elise Taylor was lesionary. The portion of the agreement pertaining to spousal support is not severable from the remainder of the agreement, and is likewise null. We therefore grant David Taylor's petition and rescind the November 2, 1998 settlement. Costs are assessed to Elise Chance Taylor.

REVERSED.

I. *Lynn Musso Junca v. Harold J. Junca, Jr.*

747 So.2d 767 (La. App. 1st Cir. 1999)

PARRO, J.

From a judgment sustaining his ex-wife's peremptory exception raising the objection of res judicata in his action for damages and for reformation of a community property settlement, the ex-husband appeals. For the following reasons, we affirm the judgment of the trial court.

Facts and Procedural History

At a January 30, 1997 hearing on Lynn's rule to set permanent alimony, increase child support, assess rent, and receive housing expenses and on her motion for contempt, the parties entered various stipulations into the record to settle the entire case, including the community property issues. The trial court informed the parties that the stipulations would be the law of the case and encouraged them to voice any objections to the agreement. No objections were entered. On May 22, 1997, the court signed a consent judgment, prepared and approved as to form and content by the parties and by their counsel, which incorporated these stipulations. The consent judgment provided, in pertinent part:

> The Court considering the pleadings filed herein and the consent of the parties hereto renders judgment as follows:
>
> IT IS FURTHER ORDERED, ADJUDGED AND DECREED that the Court adopts the community property settlement which is attached hereto as Exhibit "A" as a judgment of this Court and shall have all the effect as if it had been rendered by this Court.

The community property settlement was attached to the judgment and, by the terms of the judgment, made a part thereof. The agreement specifically recited that by the settlement, the parties intended to settle all their disputes and settle and release all causes of action arising during the existence of the community of acquets and gains.

In response to Harold's petition, Lynn filed a peremptory exception raising the objection of res judicata and a dilatory exception raising the objections of want of amicable demand and vagueness. She asserted that the settlement constituted a transaction or compromise under Louisiana Civil Code article 3071, and therefore was not subject to attack on the grounds of lesion.

After a hearing on this matter, the trial court ruled that the consent judgment was a transaction or compromise under Article 3071 and was not susceptible to an attack on the grounds of lesion. Accordingly, the trial court granted Lynn's exception raising the objection of res judicata, which mooted the remaining objections raised by Lynn, and dismissed Harold's petition for damages and reformation of the settlement agreement. Harold's subsequent motion for new trial on the issue of res judicata was denied by the trial court. Harold appeals, contending the trial court erred in granting the exception raising the objection of res judicata based on a finding that the settlement constituted a transaction or compromise.

Discussion

A contract may be annulled on grounds of lesion only in those cases provided by law. LSA-C.C. art. 1965. By 1990 La. Acts No. 991, § 1, the legislature enacted Louisiana Civil Code article 2369.1 concerning the applicability of the general provisions governing co-ownership contained in Articles 797 through 818 after termination of the community property regime. Article 2369.1 provides that after termination of the community property regime, the general provisions governing co-ownership apply to former community property unless otherwise provided by law or by juridical act.

By 1995 La. Acts No. 433, § 1, the legislature amended Article 2369.1, added a second paragraph to this article, and enacted Louisiana Civil Code articles 2369.2 through 2369.8. Section 3 of Act 433 made the act applicable to former community property that was co-owned by spouses or former spouses on or after January 1, 1996, regardless of when the community regime terminated. Generally, when the community terminates for a cause other than death or judgment of declaration of death of a spouse, such as by judgment of divorce or separation of property, Articles 2369.2 through 2369.8 apply to the former community property that is still co-owned by the spouses. LSA-C.C. art. 2369.1. The comments following Article 2369.1 make it clear that the general provisions governing co-ownership apply to former community property unless otherwise provided by law or juridical act. LSA-C.C. art. 2369.1, comments-1995 (a). Articles 2369.2 through 2369.8 are instances in which the law provides otherwise. Therefore when the community property regime terminates by declaration of the nullity of the marriage, judgment of divorce or separation of property, or matrimonial agreement that terminates the community, the provisions of those articles, rather than the general provisions governing co-ownership, would apply to former community property. See LSA-C.C. art. 2369.1, comments -1995(b); see also LSA-C.C. art. 2356.

Although the parties were divorced by judgment rendered on February 18, 1994, and an action for judicial partition was filed on March 17, 1994, community property issues were not heard by the court until January 30, 1997. In May 1997, the parties signed a community property settlement which was incorporated into the May 22, 1997 consent judgment of the trial court that (among other things) partitioned the former community property. Accordingly, as of January 1, 1996, the former community property was still co-owned by Lynn and Harold, and the provisions of 1995 La. Acts No. 433, § 1, apply in this case. Because their community property regime was terminated by something other than the death of a spouse or declaration of death of a spouse, Articles 2369.2 through 2369.8 apply, rather than the general provisions governing co-ownership.

In this case, Harold sought a partition of the former community property pursuant to Louisiana Revised Statutes 9:2801; therefore, this matter was the subject of litigation. As with other issues raised in the proceedings between these parties, several issues concerning the partition were disputed. Although the partition claim had not proceeded to trial, the parties agreed to submit stipulations regarding the partition of the former community property to the court in conjunction with other incidental matters that were scheduled for hearing on January 30, 1997. Following the stipulations by the parties, the actual partition was adopted and made the judgment of the court. Once this was accomplished, the partition became a judicial partition not subject to being set aside on account of lesion under Louisiana Civil Code article 814. Our conclusion on this point finds support in this court's decision in Lapeyrouse v. Lapeyrouse, 98-0271 (La. App. 1st Cir. 2/19/99), 729 So.2d 682, where this court summarized the situation as follows:

> [A]ll issues were hotly disputed and litigation was progressing under the provisions of LSA-R.S. 9:2801. In the instant case, a judgment of partial partition was rendered after trial. The remainder of the property was partitioned after the court ordered descriptive lists and traversals, conducted a pre-trial conference, and set a trial date. The actual partition was adopted and made a part of the judgment of the court. Once this was accomplished, the partition became a judicial partition not subject to being set aside by lesion under article 814 of the Louisiana Civil Code.

Lapeyrouse, 729 So.2d at 684 (footnotes omitted).

Furthermore, an agreement entered into by the parties for the explicit purpose of settling their community property partition suit is a transaction or compromise and cannot be attacked on the basis of lesion. Dornier v. Live Oak Arabians, Inc., 602 So.2d 743, 747-748 (La. App. 1st Cir.), writ denied, 608 So.2d 177 (La. 1992). Like Dornier and Lapeyrouse, the settlement in this case was entered into for the purpose of settling the partition suit, as well as other matters in litigation, and was attached to and made the judgment of the court. Therefore, the partition settlement also constituted a compromise within the meaning of Article 3071, which cannot be attacked on the basis of any lesion and has a force equal to the authority of things adjudged. See LSA-C.C. art. 3078. The trial court correctly recognized the res judicata effect of the settlement.

Harold would have this court distinguish this case from the facts presented in Dornier and Lapeyrouse in light of the following language contained in the settlement:

> [T]he parties acknowledge the existence of an action for lesion in partitions in the Louisiana Civil Code, and do hereby expressly waive and renounce the benefit of said action for lesion to the extent that such would allow the rescission of this agreement; further, should either party claim and prove such lesion, the aggrieved party is restricted to the recovery of damages from the other party in an amount necessary to make the partition equal, but such aggrieved party shall not in any event enjoy the right to rescind this agreement.

As a transaction or compromise, Harold asserts that any interpretation of the settlement must be under the general rules pertaining to contracts. We agree that a contract between two parties is the law between them. LSA-C.C. art. 1983. Courts are bound to give legal effect to all written contracts according to the true intent of the parties, and this intent is to be determined by the words of the contract when they are clear, explicit, and lead to no absurd consequences. See LSA-C.C. arts. 2045 and 2046. The meaning and intent of the parties to the written contract must be sought within the four corners of the instrument and cannot be explained or contradicted by parol evidence. See LSA-C.C. art. 2046.

By including the paragraph quoted previously, the parties simply acknowledged their understanding that certain rights may exist and attempted to restrict any such rights with respect to lesionary action by waiving and renouncing rescission of the settlement. The parties agreed their only remedy for such a claim would be monetary damages. Based on the language used by the parties, this court concludes that by using the phrase "should either party claim and prove such lesion" (emphasis added), the action contemplated by the parties is the type of action for lesion in partitions described in the Louisiana Civil Code. Although the parties may have thought such a cause or right of action existed and, therefore, sought to limit its effects, this presumption was incorrect. Because under the facts of this case, the Louisiana Civil Code does not afford Harold a right or cause of action for lesion, the paragraph in question is inapplicable to the facts of this case.

Decree

For the foregoing reasons, the judgment of the trial court sustaining Lynn Musso Junca's peremptory exception raising the objection of res judicata and dismissing Harold Junca, Jr.'s suit is affirmed. Costs of this appeal are assessed to Harold Junca, Jr.

AFFIRMED.

7.8 JUDICIAL PARTITION

A. Introduction

When parties cannot agree on an extrajudicial partition of community property, they must partition their property judicially. LOUISIANA REVISED STATUTES §9:2801 governs the process by which Louisiana courts are to partition community property:

LA. REV. STAT. § 9:2801. Partition of community property and settlement of claims arising from matrimonial regimes and co-ownership of former community property

A. When the spouses are unable to agree on a partition of community property or on the settlement of the claims between the spouses arising either from the matrimonial regime, or from the co-ownership of former community property following termination of the matrimonial regime, either spouse, as an incident of the action that would result in a termination of the matrimonial regime or upon termination of the matrimonial regime or thereafter, may institute a proceeding, which shall be conducted in accordance with the following rules:

> (1)(a) Within forty-five days of service of a motion by either party, each party shall file a sworn detailed descriptive list of all community property, the fair market value and location of each asset, and all community liabilities. For good cause shown, the court may extend the time period for filing a detailed descriptive list. If a party fails to file a sworn detailed descriptive list timely, the other party may file a rule to show cause why its sworn detailed descriptive list should not be deemed to constitute a judicial determination of the community assets and liabilities. At the hearing of the rule to show cause, the court may either grant the request or, for good cause shown, extend the time period for filing a sworn detailed descriptive list. If the court grants the request, no traversal shall be allowed.
>
> (b) Each party shall affirm under oath that the detailed descriptive list filed by that party contains all of the community assets and liabilities then known to that party. Amendments to the descriptive lists shall be permitted. No inventory shall be required.

(2) Within sixty days of the date of service of the last filed detailed descriptive list, each party shall either traverse or concur in the inclusion or exclusion of each asset and liability and the valuations contained in the detailed descriptive list of the other party. For good cause shown, the court may extend the time period for a party to traverse or concur in the detailed descriptive list of the other party. The trial of the traverses may be by summary procedure. At the trial of the traverses, the court shall determine the community assets and liabilities; the valuation of assets shall be determined at the trial on the merits. The court, in its discretion, may by ordinary procedure try and determine at one hearing all issues, including those raised in the traverses.

(3) The court may appoint such experts pursuant to Articles 192 and 373 of the Louisiana Code of Civil Procedure as it deems proper to assist the court in the settlement of the community and partition of community property, including the classification of assets as community or separate, the appraisal of community assets, the settlement of the claims of the parties, and the allocation of assets and liabilities to the parties.

(4) The court shall then partition the community in accordance with the following rules:

(a) The court shall value the assets as of the time of trial on the merits, determine the liabilities, and adjudicate the claims of the parties.

(b) The court shall divide the community assets and liabilities so that each spouse receives property of an equal net value.

(c) The court shall allocate or assign to the respective spouses all of the community assets and liabilities. In allocating assets and liabilities, the court may divide a particular asset or liability equally or unequally or may allocate it in its entirety to one of the spouses. The court shall consider the nature and source of the asset or liability, the economic condition of each spouse, and any other circumstances that the court deems relevant. As between the spouses, the allocation of a liability to a spouse obligates that spouse to extinguish that liability. The allocation in no way affects the rights of creditors.

(d) In the event that the allocation of assets and liabilities results in an unequal net distribution, the court shall order the payment of an equalizing sum of money, either cash or deferred, secured or unsecured, upon such terms and conditions as the court shall direct. The court may order the execution of notes, mortgages, or other documents as it deems necessary, or may impose a mortgage or lien on either community or separate property, movable or immovable, as security.

(e) In the event that the allocation of an asset, in whole or in part, would be inequitable to a party, the court may order the parties to draw lots for the asset or may order the private sale of the asset on such terms and conditions as the court deems proper, including the minimum price, the terms of sale, the execution of realtor listing agreements, and the period of time during which the asset shall be offered for private sale.

(f) Only in the event that an asset cannot be allocated to a party, assigned by the drawing of lots, or sold at private sale, shall the court order a partition thereof by licitation. The court may fix the minimum bids and other terms and conditions upon which the property is offered at public sale. In the event of a partition by licitation, the court shall expressly state the reasons why the asset cannot be allocated, assigned by the drawing of lots, or sold at private sale.

B. Those provisions of a domestic relations order or other judgment which partitions retirement or other deferred work benefits between former spouses shall be considered interlocutory until the domestic relations order has been granted "qualified" status from the plan administrator and/or until the judgment has been approved by the appropriate federal or state authority as being in compliance with applicable laws. Amendments to this interlocutory judgment to conform to the provisions of the plan shall be made with the consent of the parties or following a contradictory hearing by the court which granted the interlocutory judgment. The court issuing the domestic relations order or judgment shall maintain continuing jurisdiction over the subject matter and the parties until final resolution.

C. In the absence of an agreement between the parties for an extension of time or the granting by the court of an extension for good cause, if a party fails to comply with any time limit provided in this Section, upon motion of the other party or upon its own motion, the court may award reasonable attorney fees and court costs to the other party for the filing of or the response to the motion. If the court rules, pursuant to Subparagraph (A)(1)(a) of this Section, that the other party's sworn detailed descriptive list be deemed to constitute the assets and liabilities of the community, then the court shall not award attorney fees and court costs to the other party.

The Local Rules adopted by some judicial districts provides more insight into the actual methodology the busy courts use to divide assets between former spouses who are unable or unwilling to reach an agreement on their own. For example, Local Rule 37.6 for the Family Court of the Parish of East Baton Rouge provides, in part, as follows:

> **Section 7. Alternatives for Resolution of Disposition of Assets.** The parties may choose, or the court on its own motion, may order one or more of the following four alternatives:
>
> A. Auction to be conducted using the bid list form: (See Form K).
>
> B. Alternative Selection: The compiled lists, (See Form H) as described above shall be divided by placing each item on a separate slip of paper with each grouped according to category. The first party shall draw blind, a slip containing the name/description of an item from the first category. That party shall then set a price for the item drawn. Said category and price shall be within the parameters of the two values given the to the other party who has the option to buy or refuse the item at that price. If the party refuses, then the party who drew the item and set the price, must purchase the property at that price. The parties then alternate drawing from the category until the disposition of all items in that category. The parties shall continue in this process for all categories.
>
> ...

B. *Lucius Joseph Pitre v. Judith Maria Boren Pitre*

501 So. 2d 344 (La. App. 3d Cir. 1987)

KNOLL, Judge.

Lucius Joseph Pitre appeals the judicial partition of community property owned by him and his Wife, Judith Marie Borne Pitre. The parties were divorced in 1981 but were unable to agree on a community property settlement. Pursuant to LSA-R.S. 9:2801 each party submitted a version of the community's assets and liabilities through sworn descriptive lists.

Trial on the merits was conducted on November 26, 1984, in which evidence was adduced establishing the various assets and liabilities of the community. A disparity existed between the wife and husband's valuation on several items; particularly disputed was the amount Mr. Pitre owed Eula M. Savoie, the owner of a meat products company, for meat products he distributed through Pitre Distributors, a community enterprise operated during the existence of his marriage to Mrs. Pitre. The trial court did an admirable job sifting through the conflicting values presented. In its written reasons for judgment, the trial court explained: "[T]he suit culminating in divorce was filed August 7, 1981. The community terminated retroactively as of that date. (See Article 159 of the Civil Code.) We must determine the amount due Mrs. Savoie [the owner of the meat company for whom Pitre distributes meat products] as of that date."

Mr. Pitre appeals contending the trial court's ruling is contrary to the law and evidence in that it values the assets and liabilities of the community enterprise as of the date of filing for the divorce as opposed to the time of the trial on the merits of the partition suit as directed by LSA--R.S. 9:2801(4)(a), which provides in pertinent part as follows:

> *"(4) The court shall then partition the community in accordance with the following rules:*
>
> *(a) The court shall value the assets as of the time of trial on the merits, determine the liabilities, and adjudicate the claims of the parties."*

The record shows that both Pitre Distributors and Savoie's Sausage and Meat Products, Inc. had loosely structured accounting systems. Mr. Pitre used the community enterprise's checkbook to pay personal debts including alimony and debts of his second family. Savoie's system of accounting allowed jobbers to carry a debt. Pitre Distributors' debt as of the date of the trial on the merits totaled $28,194 and, based on the record, accrued after the filing for divorce but prior to the trial to partition the community. Mr. Pitre asserts that the majority of the debt had been accruing over the years, but that Savoie's changed their accounting system by moving the standing debt into a new account and having current Pitre payments or credits imputed to the standing debt. After carefully reviewing the record, we are in agreement with the trial judge that the debt of Pitre Distributors as of the termination of the community, August 7, 1981, was $9,059. This figure was arrived at by reviewing Savoie's records as of that date noting that the amount included the standing debt which was removed from Savoie's accounting records.

We arrive at this determination only after carefully reviewing R.S. 9:2801 and applicable jurisprudence. R.S. 9:2801 contemplates assets and liabilities existing at the termination of the community of acquets and gains. The statute requires the valuation of community assets as of the time of trial because those assets can appreciate or depreciate in value. See Queenan v. Queenan, 492 So.2d 902 (La. App. 3rd Cir.1986), *writ denied*, 496 So.2d 1045 (La.1986); and Patin v. Patin, 462 So.2d 1356 (La.App. 3rd Cir.1985), *writ denied*, 466 So.2d 470 (La.1985). Liabilities existing at the time of termination, such as the debt owed to Savoie, do not appreciate or depreciate and, therefore, are fixed at the time of termination of the community. Accordingly, the trial court was correct in its determination that any liability incurred by Mr. Pitre, through Pitre Distributors, after the termination of the community on August 7, 1981, was not attributable to Mrs. Pitre.

THE DISTRIBUTION OF ASSETS AND LIABILITIES

Having found that the trial court properly determined the $9,059 debt, we now consider the equity of the partition. Under R.S. 9:2801 the trial judge has broad discretion, when the parties cannot agree, to divide the assets and liabilities of the former community between the parties so that each receives property of net equal value.

The parties do not challenge the trial court's valuation of community assets, except for the disagreement over the date the assets and liabilities of the community enterprise are to be valued, which are as follows:

1	Home	$59,500
2	Furniture	1,510
3	1975 Trailer	13,000
4	Horses	2,500
5	Business Assets	48,073
		$124,583

Items (1) and (2) were in possession of and allocated to Mrs. Pitre. Items (3)-(5) were in possession of and allocated to Mr. Pitre.

Community liabilities yet to be paid were correctly listed in the judgment. However, certain separate liabilities of Mr. Pitre were also included in the liabilities to be paid by him and will be removed from this calculation. The trial court's calculations are as follows:

Current principal balance on home mortgage indebtedness	$35,959
Reimbursement for ½ of the home mortgage payments paid by Mr. Pine while Mrs. Pitre was occupying the home	7,346
Trailer note	16,338
Business Debts:	
Eula Savoie	9,059
Buck Exxon	107
King's	243
Liabilities on 3 business vehicles	23,851
TOTAL	$83,949

Mrs. Pitre assumed the home mortgage of $35,959 leaving her solvent in the amount of $25,051. Mr. Pitre assumed the remaining community debts listed in (2)-(4) totaling $47,990 leaving him solvent in the amount of $15,583. Thus, Mr. Pitre appears to be entitled to a credit in the amount of $4,734.

In its reasons for judgment, the trial court stated that "there remains less than $3,000 of required equalization payment. With the intangible value in the business going to the husband, their [sic] need be no equalization. It is noted that most of the changes in assets and liabilities in the business subsequent to termination would be offsetting."

The record shows that Pitre Distributors did not have intangible value, therefore, the trial court was probably placing a monetary value on the business' goodwill. This court has recently held that goodwill of a medical corporation was not a distinct community asset susceptible of partition, McCarron v. McCarron, 498 So.2d 1139 (La.App. 3rd Cir.1986). For a discussion on intangible assets see Boyle v. Boyle, 459 So.2d 735 (La.App. 4th Cir.1984), *writ denied*, 462 So.2d 651 (La.1985). Thus we conclude that Pitre Distributors had no intangible value. However, all of the assets used in Pitre Distributors were community property for which Mr. Pitre paid no rent. The rental value of the assets of the business is sufficient not to require an equalization payment by Mrs. Pitre. Therefore, we find the partition judgment is an equitable distribution of community assets and liabilities.

For the above and foregoing reasons, the judgment of the trial court is affirmed. All costs of this appeal are assessed to Lucius Joseph Pitre.

AFFIRMED.

LABORDE, J., dissents for written reasons assigned.

LABORDE, Judge, dissenting.

Justice would be better served if this case were reversed and remanded; therefore, I respectfully dissent.

As the majority correctly points out, the trial court determined *one liability* as of the time of termination, *i.e.,* the $9,059 debt to Eula Savoie. What is not pointed out is that the complement of the liabilities were determined as of the time of trial. Why were not *all* liabilities determined as of the same time?

LSA--R.S. 9:2801(4)(a) mandates that the trial court "value the community assets as of the time of trial on the merits, determine the liabilities, and adjudicate the claims of the parties." The majority correctly holds that assets must be valued at the time of trial on the merits. It interprets the comma between "merits" and "determine" as a time warp signal to mean that liabilities may be determined at any point between the petition for separation and the trial on the merits. I cannot accept this interpretation. The statute was designed to facilitate the trial court's job of valuation by fixing the time of valuation. The liabilities and assets should be determined as of the same time--the time of trial on the merits.

Apart from the internal inconsistency of the majority's opinion (and assuming arguendo that liabilities are to be fixed at the time of termination), I feel that the evidence in the record is so incomplete that this court is unable to reach a decision as to the amount of liabilities burdening Pitre Distributor at the time of termination. La. C.C.P. art 2146; Cheramie v. Bone, 444 So.2d 200 (La. App. 1st Cir. 1983); Bodin v. Bodin, 392 So.2d 759 (La. App. 3d Cir. 1980).

As I felt that this case should be reversed and remanded for the reasons stated above, I dissent.

C. *Noushin Razzaghe-Ashrafi v. Mohammad A. Razzaghe-Ashrafl*

558 So. 2d 1368 (La. App. 2d Cir. 1990)

DOMENGEAUX, Chief Judge.

These two consolidated appeals concern the validity of a judicial partition of community property and the steps taken after its rendition to enforce it as a money judgment. Although we address both appeals in one opinion, we will render a separate decree in each case. *See* Noushin Razzaghe-Ashrafi v. Mohammad Ali Razzaghe-Ashrafi, 558 So.2d 1374 (La. App. 3d Cir. 1990), also rendered today, bearing our docket No. 88-1368.

Plaintiff, Mrs. Noushin Razzaghe-Ashrafi, and defendant Dr. Mohammad Ali Razzaghe-Ashrafi, were married in Tehran, Iran, in 1962. The couple moved to New York in 1972, where they remained until 1978, when they established their matrimonial domicile in Louisiana. On April 21, 1986, the parties were divorced on the grounds of living separate and apart for one year. The termination date of the community was established as January 31, 1986.

On July 24, 1986, Mrs. Ashrafi filed this suit for judicial partition of the community of acquets and gains formerly existing between her and Dr. Ashrafi. After a trial on January 20, 1988, the district judge determined the net value of the community totaled $424,281.00. He rendered judgment in favor of Mrs. Ashrafi for her half of the community, $212,140.50, plus interest at seven percent per annum, subject to a credit for the cash and other community assets allocated to her.

Dr. Ashrafi appealed devolutively from this judgment (#88-1167). Mrs. Ashrafi then began enforcement of the judgment by ruling her husband into court for a judgment debtor examination pursuant to La.C.C.P. art. 2451. The trial judge dismissed the examination after concluding the partition judgment was not a money judgment. Mrs. Ashrafi appeals from this ruling (#88-1368).

Dr. Ashrafi also argues the trial court erred in qualifying the court-appointed expert, Mr. Bill Ford, as an appraiser for all purposes, particularly in the valuation of such movable property as jewelry and carpets. The trial judge did not place Mr. Ford's qualifications in the record. However, statements by the trial judge indicated the court had often accepted Mr. Ford as an expert in the past. Furthermore, the trial judge declared all jewelry appraised by Mr. Ford to be the separate property of Mrs. Ashrafi; hence, Ford's evaluation of these items was not added into the community. As to the Persian carpets, the Ashrafis possessed ten carpets of various sizes, four of which the trial judge declared to be the separate property of Mrs. Ashrafi. The court then allocated the remaining carpets so that each party received an equal number of carpets in each size. We find the trial court did not err in accepting Ford as an expert appraiser.

In his final assignment of error, Dr. Ashrafi argues the trial judge erred in valuing his medical corporation as of the termination date of the community, rather than at the time of trial, as required by La. R.S. 9:2801(4)(a). Dr. Ashrafi faults the court for making "no effort to value the interests in the parties in the medical corporation as of the trial," yet at trial, he produced no evidence of the corporation's value on that date. As shown by numerous motions to compel discovery Dr. Ashrafi has attempted to thwart these proceedings at every turn, with his uncooperative attitude creating undue delay.

As we recognized in Queenan v. Queenan, 492 So.2d 902 (La. App. 3d Cir. 1986), *writ denied*, 496 So.2d 1045 (La. 1986), a trial judge is given broad discretion in adjudicating the community regime. We further stated in Queenan, regarding the time of valuation:

> The purpose of all this [9:2801(4)(a)] is to provide an occasion for the court to get a handle on the situation. It does not mean that the court is frozen by any statutory time level or particular valuation at any particular time or for any particular purpose, but simply to place values on the assets for the purpose of accounting, allocation, and adjudication in accordance with the further provisions of R.S. 9:2801(4) (b, c, d and e).
>
> 492 So.2d 902, at 941.

Given the source of the delay in this matter and the limited evidence produced by Dr. Ashrafi, we find no error in the trial court's valuation of the medical corporation.

We now turn to Mrs. Ashrafi's appeal regarding the trial judge's dismissal of the judgment debtor examination. The trial judge considered the partition judgment to be a recognition of Mrs. Ashrafi's interest in the total assets of the community, rather than a judgment for the payment of money. We disagree.

The authority to render a money judgment in a community property partition is found in La. R.S. 9:2801(4)(c), which provides in pertinent part:

> The court shall allocate or assign to the respective spouses all of the community assets and liabilities. In allocating the assets and liabilities, the court may divide a particular asset or liability equally or unequally or may allocate it in its entirety to one of the spouses. . . .
>
> In the event that the allocation of assets and liabilities results in an unequal net distribution, *the court shall order the payment of an equalizing sum of money*, either cash or deferred, secured or unsecured, upon such terms and conditions as the court shall direct. . . .

From a community with a net value of $413,298.38, Mrs. Ashrafi was allocated assets totaling only $50,556.57. Assets allocated to Dr. Ashrafi totaled $362,741.81. For practical reasons, the trial judge allocated entirely to Dr. Ashrafi the community's two most valuable assets: the family home and Dr. Ashrafi's medical corporation. As a nonphysician, Mrs. Ashrafi cannot acquire stock in a medical corporation. La. R.S. 12:905(B). Pearce v. Pearce, 482 So.2d 108 (La.App. 4th Cir.1986). At the time of trial

Dr. Ashrafi was occupying the family home, and Mrs. Ashrafi had established her residence in Texas.

Under La.R.S. 9:2801(4)(c), Mrs. Ashrafi is entitled to a sum of money to correct this unequal net distribution. The trial court apparently intended this result because the judgment states Dr. Ashrafi is to receive full title to the medical corporation "after the payment of the sums mentioned hereinabove to plaintiff, Noushin Razzaghe-Ashrafi." However, nowhere in the judgment does the trial court calculate this amount of money. Based upon the allocation of assets in the trial court judgment and the net value of the community, which we have adjusted to reflect the accounting error discussed above, we determine this amount to be $156,092.62. We reach this figure as follows:

Net value of community	$413,298.38
Mrs. Ashrafi's one-half interest	$206,649.19
Less assets allocated to her:	
Certificate of Deposit	$37,265.57
1981 Toyota automobile	$3,200.00
Household items (listed in judgment)	$10,091.00
	- 50,556.57
	$156,092.62

We therefore amend the trial court judgment rendered in our docket #88-1167, as follows: As provided in the trial court judgment, Dr. Ashrafi is to receive full title to the home, the medical corporation, the Buick LeSabre, all household items in his possession and all bank accounts in his name. Dr. Ashrafi is ordered to deliver to Mrs. Ashrafi the six Persian carpets and title to the Toyota automobile, also as provided in the judgment. Mrs. Ashrafi is entitled to the sum of $156,092.62, plus legal interest thereon from date of judicial demand until paid, which sum represents her interest in the community, less those assets allocated to her by the trial judge. In all other respects, the trial court judgment is affirmed. For clarification, we attach a copy of the trial court judgment as "Appendix A".

D. Note

An obligation incurred as a result of an intentional wrong may be a community obligation if incurred for the benefit of the community. *See* Article 2363 and SPAHT & HARGRAVE, 16 LOUISIANA CIVIL LAW TREATISE--MATRIMONIAL REGIMES § 7.12. In Succession of LeBlanc, 577 So.2d 105 (La. App. 4th Cir. 1991), the husband owed a debt to the Social Security Administration as the result of a fraud he committed. The court classified the obligation as a community debt since there is a presumption that an obligation incurred during the existence of the community regime is a community obligation and no evidence was introduced to rebut the presumption. *See* Article 2360.

Although the wife alleged she had no knowledge of the husband's fraud, she did admit to cashing the checks for him.

7.9 ACCOUNTING

A. Applicable Statute

LA. CIV. CODE art. 2369. Accounting between spouses; prescription

A spouse owes an accounting to the other spouse for community property under his control at the termination of the community property regime.

The obligation to account prescribes in three years from the date of termination of the community property regime.

B. *Kathleen G. Roberts v. William V. Roberts*

542 So.2d 517 (La. App. 5th Cir. 1989)

CHEHARDY, Judge.

Kathleen Griffin Roberts appeals from a judgment judicially partitioning community property. Both parties further appeal from a permanent alimony judgment rendered at the same time.

On appeal Kathleen Roberts asserts the trial judge erred in his classification and valuation of certain community assets and liabilities; in the amount awarded to William Roberts for his reimbursement claim; and in omitting community rental income from the partition judgment. . . .

Mr. Roberts answered the appeal filed by Mrs. Roberts. . . .

In the next issue, Mrs. Roberts asserts that testimony during the trial gave rise to a suspicion there existed one or more bank accounts not accounted for by Mr. Roberts. She contends Mr. Roberts mentioned a Greater New Orleans Homestead account which may have had a balance of $48,000 at the time the separation was filed and the community terminated in October 1983. She further asserts it was proven he had a balance of $42,143 in a Gulf Federal Savings and Loan account in December 1982, the month prior to the physical separation. In addition. Mrs. Roberts claims Mr. Roberts' testimony indicated there may have been two other unreported accounts in Security Homestead and First National Bank.

After reviewing the record, we agree there exists some confusion regarding the various accounts, both joint and those which were obtained after the judicial separation became effective on October 11, 1983. And in fact, Mr. Roberts admitted that as to the Gulf Federal account a balance remained in December 1982 but he could not state with certainty what happened to the money. However, it appears that the funds in the Gulf Federal account disappeared during the existence of the community, which would preclude a requirement for accounting unless there was evidence of fraud or bad faith. (See LSA-C.C. arts. 2354 and 2369.) At any rate, the testimony shows Mr. Roberts was adequately cross-examined on the question of the accounts, and a remand would serve no other purpose than to give Mrs. Roberts an improper retrial of the issue.

Next, Mr. Roberts contends the judgment should be amended in respect to the following 12 items:

...

The partition to Mrs. Roberts of $56,000 used by her prior to the termination of the community, (First National Bank of Commerce Money Market Account No. 78-44-533);

....

The omission of community rental income from the judgment;

...

The first item Mrs. Roberts requests amendment of is the termination date of the community. The trial judge stated in his reasons for judgment that he was adjusting Mr. Roberts' claim for reimbursement to conform with the community termination on January 4, 1984. Mrs. Roberts asserts, and we agree, that the community terminated on October 11, 1983, the date the separation petition was filed.

The January date reflects the date the separation was granted but once the separation was granted. The community ended retroactively to the date the petition was filed. LSA-C.C. art. 155.

***

The fifth item complained of is the partition to Mrs. Roberts of the FNBC Money Market Account valued at $56,000. Mrs. Roberts asserts these funds were withdrawn by her to live on prior to filing suit. Furthermore, since the funds were withdrawn during the existence of the community, she contends she need not account for them.

The trial judge determined Mrs. Roberts was accountable for the funds and stated she could not use them for her expenses in the absence of a court-ordered judgment of support. Presumably he based his conclusion on LSA-C.C. art. 2369, which provides for an accounting between spouses for community assets under a spouse's control at the termination of the community. However, the article by its language applies to assets in existence when the community ends, it does not apply to assets used while the regime of acquets and gains is still operating. To remedy the loss of an asset caused by a spouse during the community property regime, the complaining spouse must look to LSA-C.C. art. 2354.

That article provides that a spouse is liable for fraud or bad faith in the management of the community. Otherwise, unless specifically provided for, either spouse is entitled to manage community assets regardless of whether they are physically separated or not. Only judicial separation or divorce terminates the rights and obligations imposed by the community property regime. Consequently, the $56,000 FNBC Money Market account will be deleted from the partition judgment.

***

The ninth item requiring our attention involves the community rental income, which was apparently inadvertently omitted from the judgment. Mrs. Roberts contends this item should be partitioned to Mr. Roberts with a value of $157,912, representing the monies Mr. Roberts received from the rentals from October 1983 to date of trial.

The parties received income from the rental of three pieces of property, one on David Drive and two on L & A Road. Mr. Roberts testified he received the rentals as follows:

October 1, 1983-December 31, 1983	$17,682.00
January 1, 1984-December 31, 1985	69,388.00
January 1, 1986-July 31, 1986	33,978.00
August 1, 1986-April, 1987	36,864.00
	$157,912.00

Of that amount he stated he paid Mrs. Roberts $30,120 as part of an alimony judgment. He calculated the total as follows:

November, 1984 (date of alimony judgment) to November, 1985: 12 months times $1,200 (representing rental monthly)	=	$14,400
December, 1985 to July, 1986: 8 months times $1,200	=	$9,600
August, 1986 to April, 1987: 9 months times $680	=	$6,120

Mr. Roberts testified he reduced Mrs. Roberts share of the rentals ordered by the alimony judgment due to the loss of the tenant at the David Drive property as represented by the final nine months of payments. Subtracting her $30,120 and an equal amount for his share, the amount left to be accounted for is $97,672, not $157,912. Consequently, we will amend the judgment in this respect by partitioning $97,672 to Mr. Roberts for rental property income. The judgment will further reflect the division in kind of $60,240.

AFFIRMED IN PART, AMENDED IN PART AND RENDERED AS AMENDED.

C. Note

A claim for reimbursement for the use of community funds to improve separate property (the construction of a house with community funds upon separate property) is not a claim for an accounting under Article 2369 and therefore is not subject to a three prescriptive period. *Bordelon v. Cobb*, 596 So.2d 268 (La. App. 3d Cir. 1992).

Art. 2369.3, comment (c)

(c) The provisions of this Article overlap to some extent those of Civil Code Article 2369 (rev. 1979). Article 2369, however, focuses on a moment in time at which a spouse may have control over community property. That moment is the date of termination of the community. As to former community property over which the spouse had control at that moment, a duty is imposed upon that spouse "to account", *i.e.*, to explain what happened to the property that was then under his control. To invoke that duty a spouse need prove only that the other spouse had control of former community property at the moment of termination of the regime. Then the burden shifts to the other spouse to prove what disposition was made of the property. This obligation is subject to a very short prescriptive period of three years from the date of termination of the community regime. *See* C.C. Art. 2369 (rev. 1979).

7.10 CO-OWNERSHIP OF FORMER COMMUNITY PROPERTY

LA. CIV. CODE art. 2369.1. Application of co-ownership provisions

After termination of the community property regime, the provisions governing co-ownership apply to former community property, unless otherwise provided by law or by juridical act.

When the community property regime terminates for a cause other than death or judgment of declaration of death of a spouse, the following Articles of this Subsection also apply to former community property until a partition, or the death or judgment of declaration of death of a spouse.

LA. CIV. CODE art. 2369.2. Ownership interest.

Each spouse owns an undivided one-half interest in former community property and its fruits and products.

LA. CIV. CODE art. 2369.3. Duty to preserve; standard of care

A spouse has a duty to preserve and to manage prudently former community property under his control, including a former community enterprise, in a manner consistent with the mode of use of that property immediately prior to termination of the community regime. He is answerable for any damage caused by his fault, default, or neglect.

A community enterprise is a business that is not a legal entity.

LA. CIV. CODE art. 2369.4. Alienation, encumbrance, or lease prohibited

A spouse may not alienate, encumber, or lease former community property or his undivided community interest in that property without the concurrence of the other spouse, except as provided in the following Articles. In the absence of such concurrence, the alienation, encumbrance, or lease is a relative nullity.

LA. CIV. CODE art. 2369.5. Alienation of registered movables

A spouse may alienate, encumber, or lease a movable issued or registered in his name as provided by law.

LA. CIV. CODE art. 2369.6. Alienation; encumbrance, or lease of movable assets of former community enterprise

The spouse who is the sole manager of a former community enterprise may alienate, encumber, or lease its movables in the regular course of business.

LA. CIV. CODE art. 2369.7. Court authorization to act alone

A spouse may be authorized by the court in a summary proceeding to act without the concurrence of the other spouse, upon showing all of the following:

(1) The action is necessary.

(2) The action is in the best interest of the petitioning spouse and not detrimental to the interest of the nonconcurring spouse.

(3) The other spouse is an absent person or arbitrarily refuses to concur, or is unable to concur due to physical incapacity, mental incompetence, commitment, imprisonment, or temporary absence.

LA. CIV. CODE art. 2369.8. Right to partition; no exclusion by agreement; judicial partition

A spouse has the right to demand partition of former community property at any time. A contrary agreement is absolutely null.

If the spouses are unable to agree on the partition, either spouse may demand judicial partition which shall be conducted in accordance with R.S. 9:2801.

7.11 REIMBURSEMENT CLAIMS

A. Applicable Statutes

LA. CIV. CODE art. 2359. Obligations; community or separate.

An obligation incurred by a spouse may be either a community obligation or a separate obligation.

LA. CIV. CODE art. 2360. Community obligation.

An obligation incurred by a spouse during the existence of a community property regime for the common interest of the spouses or for the interest of the other spouse is a community obligation.

LA. CIV. CODE art. 2361. Obligations incurred during marriage; presumption.

Except as provided in Article 2363, all obligations incurred by a spouse during the existence of a community property regime are presumed to be community obligations.

LA. CIV. CODE art. 2362. Alimentary obligation

An alimentary obligation imposed by law on a spouse is deemed to be a community obligation.

LA. CIV. CODE art. 2362.1. Obligation incurred in an action for divorce

An obligation incurred before the date of a judgment of divorce for attorney fees and costs in an action for divorce and in incidental actions is deemed to be a community obligation.

LA. CIV. CODE art. 2363. Separate obligation

A separate obligation of a spouse is one incurred by that spouse prior to the establishment of a community property regime, or one incurred during the existence of a community property regime though not for the common interest of the spouses or for the interest of the other spouse.

An obligation resulting from an intentional wrong or an obligation incurred for the separate property of a spouse is likewise a separate obligation to the extent that it does not benefit both spouses, the family, or the other spouse.

LA. CIV. CODE art. 2358. Claims for reimbursement between spouses

A spouse may have a claim against the other spouse for reimbursement in accordance with the following Articles.

A claim for reimbursement may be asserted only after termination of the community property regime, unless otherwise provided by law.

LA. CIV. CODE art. 2358.1. Source of reimbursement

Reimbursement shall be made from the patrimony of the spouse who owes reimbursement.

LA. CIV. CODE art. 2364. Satisfaction of separate obligation with community property or former community property

If community property has been used during the existence of the community property regime or former community property has been used thereafter to satisfy a separate obligation of a spouse, the other spouse is entitled to reimbursement for one-half of the amount or value that the property had at the time it was used.

LA. CIV. CODE art. 2365. Satisfaction of community obligation with separate property

If separate property of a spouse has been used either during the existence of the community property regime or thereafter to satisfy a community obligation, that spouse is entitled to reimbursement for one-half of the amount or value that the property had at the time it was used.

If the community obligation was incurred to acquire ownership or use of a community corporeal movable required by law to be registered, and separate property of a spouse has been used after termination to satisfy that obligation, the reimbursement claim shall be reduced in proportion to the value of the claimant's use after termination of the community property regime. The value of that use and the amount of the claim for reimbursement accrued during the use are presumed to be equal.

The liability of a spouse who owes reimbursement is limited to the value of his share of all community property after deduction of all community obligations. Nevertheless, if the community obligation was incurred for the ordinary and customary expenses of the marriage, or for the support, maintenance, or education of children of either spouse in keeping with the economic condition of the spouses, the spouse is entitled to reimbursement from the other spouse regardless of the value of that spouse's share of all community property.

LA. CIV. CODE art. 2366. Use of community property or former community property for the benefit of separate property

If community property has been used during the existence of the community property regime or former community property has been used thereafter for the acquisition, use, improvement, or benefit of the separate property of a spouse, the other spouse is entitled to reimbursement for one-half of the amount or value that the community property had at the time it was used.

Buildings, other constructions permanently attached to the ground, and plantings made on the separate property of a spouse with community property belong to the owner of the ground. The other spouse is entitled to reimbursement for one-half of the amount or value that the community property had at the time it was used.

LA. CIV. CODE art. 2367. Use of separate property for the benefit of community property

If separate property of a spouse has been used during the existence of the community property regime for the acquisition, use, improvement, or benefit of community property, that spouse is entitled to reimbursement for one-half of the amount or value that the property had at the time it was used. The liability of the spouse who owes reimbursement is limited to the value of his share of all community property after deduction of all community obligations.

Buildings, other constructions permanently attached to the ground, and plantings made on community property with separate property of a spouse during the existence of the community property regime are community property. The spouse whose separate property was used is entitled to reimbursement for one-half of the amount or value that the separate property had at the time it was used. The liability of the spouse who owes reimbursement is limited to the value of his share in all community property after deduction of all community obligations.

LA. CIV. CODE art. 2367.1. Use of separate property for the benefit of separate property

If separate property of a spouse has been used during the existence of the community property regime for the acquisition, use, improvement, or benefit of the other spouse's separate property, the spouse whose property was used is entitled to reimbursement for the amount or value that the property had at the time it was used.

Buildings, other constructions permanently attached to the ground, and plantings made on the land of a spouse with the separate property of the other spouse belong to the owner of the ground. The spouse whose property was used is entitled to reimbursement for the amount or value that the property had at the time it was used.

LA. CIV. CODE art. 2367.2. Component parts of separate property

When a spouse with his own separate property incorporates in or attaches to a separate immovable of the other spouse things that become component parts under Articles 465 and 466, Article 2367.1 applies.

LA. CIV. CODE art. 2367.3. Satisfaction of separate obligation with separate property

If a spouse uses separate property during the existence of the community property regime to satisfy the separate obligation of the other spouse, the spouse whose property was used is entitled to reimbursement for the amount or value the property had at the time it was used.

LA. CIV. CODE art. 2368. Increase of the value of separate property

If the separate property of a spouse has increased in value as a result of the uncompensated common labor or industry of the spouses, the other spouse is entitled to be reimbursed from the spouse whose property has increased in value one-half of the increase attributed to the common labor.

B. *Bert F. Allbritton v. Linda T. Allbritton*

561 So. 2d 125 (La. App. 3d Cir. 1990)

KING, Judge.

The issues presented by this appeal are whether gifts of money and furnishings made during the marriage are separate property or community property and whether an attorney's fee incurred during the marriage, in connection with a DWI, is a separate or community debt.

Bert Fowler Allbritton (hereinafter plaintiff) filed a petition against his wife, Linda Tannehill Allbritton (hereinafter defendant), from whom he was legally separated, for a partition of the community property. After trial on the merits, the trial court classified certain gifts made during the marriage, by defendant's grandmother and defendant's father, as defendant's separate property and accordingly awarded her the property and reimbursement from the matrimonial regime for her separate funds she spent for the benefit of the community. The trial judge also classified plaintiff's attorney's fees, incurred during the marriage as a result of a DWI, as his separate debt. On the basis of this classification of the gifts and debt the trial court ordered a partition of the community. Plaintiff appeals. We affirm in part, reverse in part, amend in part; and render judgment.

Plaintiff's Attorney's Fee

Plaintiff contends that the trial court erred when it classified an attorney's fee incurred during the existence of the community, as a result of a DWI charge against plaintiff, as his separate debt. Debts acquired during the community property regime are presumed to be community obligations. La. C.C. Art. 2361. Whether or not the DWI charge can be classified as an "intentional wrong" not for the benefit of the community, under La. C.C. Art. 2363, would depend on whether or not plaintiff was on a community mission at the time he was charged. Defendant did not present any evidence to rebut the presumption that the attorney's fee was a community debt or to prove that plaintiff was not on a community mission at the time he was charged with DWI.

Furthermore, though the plaintiff's obligation from the DWI charge may have been a personal responsibility insofar as the criminal consequences, it does not necessarily follow that the fee incurred defending the criminal charge are also his personal responsibility. The attorney's fee may have actually benefitted the community, for example, by keeping plaintiff out of jail to support defendant and pay community debts. Regardless, we find that defendant has not carried her burden of proving the debt for the attorney's fee incurred during the existence of the community was the separate debt of plaintiff.

For these reasons, we find that the trial court was clearly wrong and erred in finding plaintiff's attorney's fee, incurred during the existence of the community, were his separate debt. Therefore, plaintiff is entitled to reimbursement from the community for his attorney's fee in the amount of $750.00.

Partition of Assets and Debts

AFFIRMED IN PART; REVERSED IN PART; AMENDED IN PART; AND, AS AMENDED, RENDERED.

DISSENT: KNOLL, Judge, concurring in part and dissenting in part.

I agree with the majority that the donations by the wife's father were gifts only to the wife and not to the community.

For reasons which follow, I respectfully disagree with the majority reversing the trial court on a factual determination that the grandmother's gifts were the separate property of the wife, and that the attorney's fees were a community obligation.

Finally, the majority concludes that the husband's attorney's fees for the defense of a DWI prosecution were a community obligation because the wife failed to rebut the presumption found in LSA-C.C. Art. 2361 that it was a community debt. The majority interprets LSA-C.C. Art. 2363: "would depend on whether or not plaintiff was on a community mission at the time he was charged." I disagree.

LSA-C.C. Art. 2363 provides exceptions to the general rule that it is presumed that an obligation of the community. LSA-C.C. Art. 2363 provides in pertinent part:

"A separate obligation of a spouse is . . . one incurred during the existence of a community property regime though not for the common interest of the spouses or for the interest of the other spouse. *An obligation resulting from an intentional wrong not perpetrated for the benefit of the community,* or an obligation incurred for the separate property of a spouse to the extent that it does not benefit the community, the family, or the other spouse, is likewise a separate obligation." (Emphasis added.)

Moreover, Comment (b) to LSA-C.C. Art. 2363 states:

"An obligation incurred during the existence of a community property regime though not for the common interest of the spouses or for the interest of the other spouse is a separate obligation."

The obligation to pay attorney's fees resulted from the husband's commission of a criminal act. In my view, the obligation of attorney's fees for a criminal offense, in this case a DWI, was not perpetrated for the benefit of the community, nor for the common interest of the spouses or for the interest of the other spouse. The determination of whether the attorney's fees are a community obligation or a separate obligation does not turn upon whether the husband was on a community mission. It should be analyzed under Article 2363, *i.e.*, committing an intentional wrong not for the benefit of the community. I fail to see how a DWI offense can benefit the community. The obligation, the attorney's fees, was as a result of the husband's DWI; therefore, I would classify this as his separate obligation. Accordingly, I find that the presumption of community established in LSA-C.C. Art. 2361 is not applicable, and the trial court properly found that this was the husband's separate obligation by virtue of LSA-C.C. Art. 2363.

C. *Nancy Dill Carroll v. Mark Francis Carroll*

753 So. 2d 395 (La. App. 1st Cir. 2000)

FOIL, Judge.

In this appeal from a community property partition judgment, the former husband challenges two aspects of the trial court's decree. For the following reasons, we affirm.

FACTS AND PROCEDURAL BACKGROUND

Mark Francis Carroll and Nancy Dill Carroll were married on September 17, 1983. On February 26, 1997, after filing suit for divorce, Nancy petitioned for the partition of the community property. A hearing of the matter was held on January 14, 1998, at which time the issues of reimbursement and payment of attorney's fees were taken under advisement. Of relevance in this appeal are two aspects of the court's subsequent decree. In written reasons for judgment issued on January 20, 1998, the trial court ruled that Nancy's attorney's fees in the amount of $6,159.37 are chargeable as a community debt. It further awarded Nancy full ownership of the former marital domicile. Judgment was later signed in conformity with the court's reasons on May 6, 1998. This appeal by Mark followed.

ATTORNEY'S FEES

In his first assignment of error, Mark claims that the trial court committed reversible **error when it found that** attorney's fees incurred by Nancy in connection with her petition for divorce, petition for protective orders, and petition for partition of community property following the termination date of the community property regime were a community obligation under La. Civ.Code art. 2362.1. That articles provides that "[a]n obligation for attorney's fees and costs in action for divorce incurred before the date of the judgment of divorce that terminates the community property regime is a community obligation of that regime." Mark argues that attorney's fees incurred in connection with community property partition proceedings or protective order proceedings should not be included in the category of attorney's fees incurred "in an action for divorce."

In its reasons for judgment, the trial court found that the terminology "in an action for divorce" contemplates such incidental matters as community property partition proceedings and proceedings under La. R.S. 46:2131 et seq. (Domestic Abuse Assistance). We agree with the trial court's interpretation of the article and find no error in its ruling made on that basis. Accordingly, this assignment of error has no merit.

* * *

For the above reasons, the judgment appealed from is affirmed at appellant's cost.

AFFIRMED.

D. *Ellis R. McGee v. Patricia Ann Gabriel McGee*

905 So. 2d 300 (La. App. 1st Cir. 2005)

McCLENDON, Judge.

On appeal in this action to partition a community, the husband challenges the trial court's designation of an obligation incurred jointly by both spouses during the existence of the community as his separate debt and the trial court's computation of his wife's claim for reimbursement. For the following reasons, we reserve in part and amend in part the judgment of the trial court.

Ellis R. McGee and Patricia Ann Gabriel McGee married in 1976. During their marriage and the existence of their matrimonial regime, the McGees secured a loan evidenced by a promissory note in favor of Premier Mortgage Company/Homestead Lending, Inc. (now Centrust). The loan was secured by a mortgage on a tract of immovable property that was obtained by Mr. McGee prior to his marriage to Mrs. McGee. The couple used the proceeds of the loan to construct a house on that property.

The McGees divorced in 2002. Subsequently, Ms. McGee filed a petition for the judicial partition of the community property. On October 1, 2003, the trial judge rendered judgment partitioning the community. Therein, among other things, the judge declared the tract of immovable property and all appurtenances located thereon to be the separate property of Mr. McGee and the loan to be the separate obligation of Mr. McGee. With respect to the above-mentioned loan, the court further awarded Ms. McGee reimbursement in the sum of $15,540.86, "one-half of all community funds paid toward the principal, excluding payments on interest" during the existence of the matrimonial regime of the parties. Mr. McGee appeals that judgment.

The trial judge's reasons for judgment reflect that she applied Civil Code articles 2359, 2360, 2361, and 2363 to the facts herein in classifying the loan as the separate obligation of Mr. McGee. LSA-C.C. art. 2359 provides that "[a]n obligation incurred by a spouse may be either a community obligation or a separate obligation." Furthermore, "[a]n obligation incurred by a spouse during the existence of a community property regime for the common interest of the spouses or for the interest of the other spouse is a community obligation." LSA- C.C. art. 2360. "Except as provided in Article 2363, all obligations incurred by a spouse during the existence of a community property regime are presumed to be community obligations." LSA-C.C. art. 2361. In this regard, LSA-C.C. art. 2363 specifically provides as follows:

> A separate obligation of a spouse is one incurred by that spouse prior to the establishment of a community property regime, or one incurred during the existence of a community property regime though not for the common interest of the spouses or for the interest of the other spouse. An obligation incurred after termination of a community property regime, except an obligation incurred for attorney's fees and costs under Article 2362.1, is a separate obligation.
>
> An obligation resulting from an intentional wrong not perpetrated for the benefit of the community, or an obligation incurred for the separate property of a spouse to the extent that it does not benefit the community, the family, or the other spouse, is likewise a separate obligation.

Initially, on appeal, Mr. McGee asserts that the trial court erred in applying these codal articles to the facts of this case. Mr. McGee avers that said articles are inapplicable herein because each uses the language "obligation of *a spouse* " (emphasis added), thereby limiting their application to debts incurred by one spouse rather than, as is the case herein, a debt incurred jointly by both spouses. Mr. McGee asserts that the proper analysis is simply that, because the obligation was incurred by both spouses during the existence of their matrimonial regime it is a community debt.

Recognizing the difficulty in applying Civil Code articles 2359-2361 and 2363 to certain factual scenarios, we, too, question the applicability of these articles to obligations incurred jointly by both spouses. However, we need not reach that issue herein as applying either legal analysis to the facts of this case yields the same result--that is, that this debt is a community obligation.

It is undisputed that the loan in question was executed by both spouses during the existence of the parties' matrimonial regime. Therefore, applying the foregoing codal articles, there is a presumption that it is a community debt. LSA-C.C. art. 2361. This presumption can be rebutted if the debt is not incurred for "the common interest of the spouses." LSA-C.C. art. 2363. However, it is undisputed that this debt was incurred to construct a home in which the McGees resided during their marriage. Thus, the debt was incurred for the common interest of the spouses. Therefore, applying the foregoing articles, the debt would be a community obligation. Similarly, if the foregoing articles are inapplicable, because the debt was incurred during the marriage by both spouses, it would also constitute a community obligation. Therefore, we conclude that the loan clearly constitutes a community obligation, and the trial judge erred in classifying it as the separate obligation of Mr. McGee. We will reverse the portion of the trial court's judgment that classified the debt as the separate obligation of Mr. McGee and declare the debt to be a community obligation.

Mr. McGee further asserts that the trial court erred in ordering him to reimburse Ms. McGee the sum of $15,540.86, one-half of all community funds paid during the existence of the matrimonial regime toward the principal debt owed to Premier Mortgage.

Louisiana Civil Code article 2366 provides that "[u]pon termination of the community, the other spouse is entitled to one-half of the amount or value that the community assets had at the time they were used" for the benefit of the separate property. *See McKey v. McKey,* 449 So.2d 564, 567 (La. App. 1st Cir. 1984). Therefore, Mr. McGee must reimburse Ms. McGee for the community funds used to build the house on his separate property. *See Brehm v. Brehm,* 00-0201, p. 4 (La. App. 5th Cir. 6/27/00), 762 So.2d 1259, 1263, *writ denied,* 00-2286 (La. 10/27/00), 772 So.2d 657. The proper measure of the reimbursement is "one-half of the amount or value that the community assets had at the time they were used," not the sums applied to the mortgage over the years. LSA-C.C. art. 2366; *see Dupre v. Dupre,* 522 So.2d 694, 695 (La. App. 5th Cir.), *writ denied,* 523 So.2d 1341 (La.1988). Mr. McGee listed the amount of community funds used in building the house as $69,000.00. Therefore, one-half of the actual value of the community funds used is $34,500.00. It is undisputed that the balance of the loan at the time of the filing of the detailed descriptive lists was $44,082.81. Therefore, as a community obligation, Ms. McGee owed Mr. McGee one-half of the balance of the loan at the time of the partition, or $22,041.40.

After offsetting the amount of Ms. McGee's reimbursement by the amount of her loan obligation, we find that Mr. McGee owes Ms. McGee $12,458.60 for the use of community funds associated with the construction of a house on his separate property. Therefore, we will amend the judgment of the trial court to reduce the reimbursement award from $15,540.86 to $12,458.60.

For the foregoing reasons, we reverse the judgment of the trial court to the extent that it classifies the Premier Mortgage Company/Homestead Lending, Inc. (now Centrust) loan as the separate obligation of Ellis McGee and declare the loan to be a community obligation. We further amend the judgment to award Ms. McGee the sum of $12,458.60 for the reimbursement of principal paid on the loan, and affirm the judgment, as amended. Costs are to be shared equally by Patricia Ann Gabriel McGee and Ellis R. McGee.

REVERSED IN PART; AFFIRMED IN PART, AS AMENDED.

E. *Richard Warren Palmer v. Kathy Ann Peek Palmer*

693 So. 2d 1226 (La. App. 2d Cir. 1997)

CARAWAY, Judge.

Kathy Ann Peek Palmer Worley was awarded by the trial court legal interest on her share of certain mineral revenues calculated from the time of receipt of those funds by her former husband, Richard Warren Palmer, during the pendency of this partition proceeding. Mr. Palmer appeals, alleging that legal interest on the funds is due only from the date of judgment. We affirm.

Factual and Procedural History

The Louisiana community property regime that existed between Kathy Peek Palmer Worley ("Ms. Palmer") and Richard Warren Palmer ("Mr. Palmer") was dissolved on August 10, 1988 by legal separation. On January 6, 1989, Ms. Palmer filed a Petition for Partition of Community Property. An amended petition was filed on July 20, 1989 in which Ms. Palmer filed a detailed descriptive list and requested that the court order Mr. Palmer to do the same. Mr. Palmer filed a descriptive list on August 23, 1989. Among the items on the list were mineral interests in the state of Mississippi listed as the separate property of Mr. Palmer.

In August, 1990, Mr. Palmer filed a declaratory judgment action in Mississippi regarding the separate property status of the Mississippi property holdings which were acquired during the marriage in his name. While the action was pending, the parties reached a partial settlement in this Louisiana proceeding for the partition of most of their community assets. Expressly excluded from the settlement was the Mississippi mineral interests which the parties agreed would be owned in accordance with the final ruling in the Mississippi declaratory judgment action. In the settlement agreement, Mr. Palmer paid Ms. Palmer for his possession and expenditures of certain community funds since the termination of the community. However, the settlement expressly provided that it did not include any additional accountings which might be due by Mr. Palmer for the Mississippi mineral interests.

Reversing both the trial court and intermediate appellate court, the Mississippi Supreme Court held on February 9, 1995 that the disputed mineral interests were jointly owned by Mr. and Ms. Palmer. Pursuant to the judgment and in accordance with the prior settlement agreement, the appropriate assignments of the mineral interests were made to Ms. Palmer for her one-half interest in the disputed property and Ms. Palmer thereafter began directly receiving royalties or other payments.

Ms. Palmer then filed, in this partition action, a rule for an accounting of all sums due her and arising from her co-ownership of the Mississippi mineral interests and legal interest on all sums due her as provided by law. The parties subsequently agreed by stipulation that the net revenues derived from the Mississippi property from the date of termination of the community through January 31, 1995 totaled $453,411.00. As a result of the agreement, Mr. Palmer had paid Ms. Palmer $226,705.50, which is one-half the net revenues derived from the Mississippi properties from the date of the termination of the community regime through January 31, 1995. Based on those stipulations, the parties presented to the trial court only the issue of when legal interest on the mineral revenues received by Mr. Palmer would accrue.

The sole issue presented in this appeal is whether the trial court erred in finding that Ms. Palmer is entitled to interest on the sums received by her former husband during the pendency of this partition proceeding, from the time of the receipt of each payment by Mr. Palmer until his payment to Ms. Palmer in 1995 of her share. Likewise, as to certain accrued revenues received after the termination of the community and prior to this suit, Mr. Palmer disputes the award of interest on those revenues from the date of judicial demand.

Discussion

Mr. Palmer argues that the provisions governing co-ownership apply to the property in question citing La. Civil Code arts. 2369.1 and 480. Under these provisions, it is asserted that Mr. Palmer, as a co-owner of the property, was entitled to use the co-owned revenues, without the payment of rent to the other co-owner, Ms. Palmer. Therefore, because "interest" is "rent" on money, Mr. Palmer asserts he owes no interest on the co-owned sums he received.

The underlying disputed assets of this partition action were the Mississippi mineral interests which the parties agreed in their partial settlement to divide based on the outcome of the Mississippi declaratory judgment action. From the underlying assets, the royalties or other mineral revenues which Mr. Palmer received were the "products" derived from those mineral interests as that term is defined in La. C.C. art. 488. Under La. C.C. art. 798, the products of the mineral interests are shared by the co-owners in proportion to their ownership. Under the second paragraph of that article, a co-owner who produces the product must account to the other co-owner after the costs of the product are deducted. In view of Ms. Palmer's demands in this action, Mr. Palmer, as the single recipient of the mineral revenues, owed the obligation to account to his co-owner upon his receipt of each monthly accrual.

Mr. Palmer's argument that he could "use" Ms. Palmer's share of the products of the co-owned property during the pendency of this action is misplaced. On the one hand, "use" of revenues or money as that concept is considered under La. C.C. art. 536

would mean that Mr. Palmer could expend or consume Ms. Palmer's share of the revenues. Given Mr. Palmer's duty to account for products under Article 798 and his further duties under Civil Code articles 799 and 800 to preserve co-owned property, Mr. Palmer's use of Ms. Palmer's mineral revenues as a consumable fund would be clearly a breach of these duties. On the other hand, if the "use" for which Mr. Palmer argues concerns the investment of Ms. Palmer's share of revenues, any interest earned on such investment would be a civil fruit for which the obligation to Ms. Palmer under Article 798 would also apply. See La. C.C. art. 551.

The issue of interest which these mineral revenues could have earned is properly viewed as Ms. Palmer's damages under La. C.C. art. 2000 for the delay which she suffered for Mr. Palmer's refusal to recognize her ownership in the mineral interests and to pay her for the revenues derived therefrom. The critical fact is that Mr. Palmer received the co- owned revenues or "products" during the pendency of an action in which he ultimately did not prevail. Although he may not have been obligated to employ the revenues to earn interest and there being no evidence presented at the trial of the rule to show that he did, in fact, earn interest, Ms. Palmer was damaged. Upon Mr. Palmer's receipt of the revenues, the co-owned product came into existence in the form of money, which by its unique nature allows for the immediate and separate use by co-owners. Mr. Palmer's action in this suit prevented the other co-owner's use of money in violation of the principles reflected in La. C.C. arts. 798 and 802 for which damages in the form of legal interest may be assessed.

Conclusion

For these reasons, the judgment of the trial court awarding legal interest on the mineral revenues received by Mr. Palmer is affirmed. Costs of this appeal are assessed to appellant.

AFFIRMED.

F. *Diana Roque v. Raymond Tate*

631 So. 2d 1385 (La. App. 5 Cir. 1994)

GOTHARD, Judge.

This is an appeal of a trial court decision, ordering plaintiff/appellant to reimburse defendant/appellee one-half of the sum paid by appellee on the community home after termination of the community. Appellant also appeals the trial court's denial of her motion for new trial. For the following reasons, we amend, and as amended, affirm.

On May 13, 1985, a judgment of divorce was granted in favor of appellee, Raymond Tate and against appellant, Diana Roque (formerly Diana Roque Tate). Ms. Roque was awarded custody of the two minor children and Mr. Tate was ordered to pay child support of $86.15 weekly, the house note on the family home where Ms. Roque was permitted to live, medical insurance and school tuition. The community property was not partitioned. On August 16, 1985, possession of the former family home, which was purchased during the existence of the community of acquets and gains, was granted to Mr. Tate after Ms. Roque moved with their two minor children to Guatemala.

On June 17, 1986, Ms. Roque filed a petition for partition of the community property. On August 8, 1991, a trial on the merits of the community property partition was held. On June 16, 1992, the trial court rendered judgment, granting to Mr. Tate reimbursement from the community the sum of $11,158.00, which represented half of his separate funds paid towards the mortgage indebtedness on the community home after the divorce was granted.

Ms. Roque filed a motion for new trial, alleging that the judgment was contrary to the law and evidence and that a letter Mr. Tate sent to the trial judge after the trial on the merits constituted newly discovered evidence, which improperly tainted the trial. By judgment dated December 22, 1992, Ms. Roque's motion was denied. This appeal followed.

REIMBURSEMENT

On appeal, Ms. Roque argues that while a spouse is entitled to reimbursement for separate funds used to pay a community obligation after the community has terminated (LSA-C.C. art. 2365), after termination, the laws of co-ownership apply (LSA-C.C. art. 2369.1). Her argument continues that, pursuant to LSA-C.C. art. 806, Mr. Tate's reimbursement for the mortgage payments should be reduced in proportion to the value of his enjoyment (*i.e.*, he lived in the home "rent-free" while she paid rent elsewhere). Appellant's reliance on C.C. art. 806 is misplaced. Article 806, which addresses a co-owner's right to reimbursement for expenses paid on the co-owned property, provides:

A co-owner who on account of the thing held in indivision has incurred necessary expenses, expenses for ordinary maintenance and repairs, or necessary management expenses paid to a third person, is entitled to reimbursement from the other co-owners in proportion to their shares.

If the co-owner who incurred the expense had the enjoyment of the thing held in indivision, his reimbursement shall be reduced in proportion to the value of the enjoyment.

Under the provisions of this article, Ms. Roque argues that she should have been given an offset for the value of Mr. Tate's enjoyment of the property since he occupied it to her exclusion during the time in question. She contends the trial court erred in not giving her that offset. However, the heading of art. 806 is: "Expenses of maintenance and management." Under 806, a co-owner who has incurred necessary expenses or maintenance and management expenses is entitled to reimbursement from the other co-owners; except that if he who incurred these expenses had the enjoyment of the thing, the reimbursement is to be reduced in proportion to the value of his enjoyment. A mortgage is not such an expense, it is "a nonpossessory right created over property to secure the performance of an obligation." LSA-C.C. art. 2378. Moreover, the Tate mortgage was not incurred by Mr. Tate, it was an obligation which attached against Mr. Tate and Ms. Roque (the community) at the moment of sale.

Ms. Roque argues that since Mr. Tate was able to live in the community home while she paid rent elsewhere, Mr. Tate enjoyed a windfall by also not having to pay rent. However, "rent" cannot be awarded to Ms. Roque in this instance. LSA-R.S. 9:374(C) provides:

A spouse who uses and occupies or is awarded by the court the use and occupancy of the family residence pending either the termination of the marriage or the partition of the community property in accordance with the provisions of R.S. 9:374(A) or (B) shall not be liable to the other spouse for rental for the use and occupancy, unless otherwise agreed by the spouses or ordered by the court.

While there has been some conflict in our appellate circuits on whether a trial court is precluded under R.S. 9:374(C) from awarding rent for use of the community home pending the partition where no such rent was awarded at the time the use was designated, in the matter before us, no rent was ordered by the trial court at any time, nor was any rental agreement between the spouses made. LSA-R.S. 9:374(C) (formerly LSA-R.S. 9:308(C), which was amended by Act 678 of the 1986 Louisiana Legislative Session) applies retroactively. *Allen v. Allen*, 602 So.2d 759, 761- 62 (La.App. 3rd Cir.1992). Accordingly, Ms. Roque is not entitled to rental payments as an offset to any reimbursement owed Mr. Tate.

The controlling law in this situation is LSA-C.C. art. 2365, which provides in pertinent part:

> If separate property of a spouse has been used to satisfy a community obligation, that spouse, upon termination of the community property regime, is entitled to reimbursement for one-half of the amount or value that the property had at the time it was used. The liability of a spouse who owes reimbursement is limited to the value of his share in the community after deduction of all community obligations.

Read together with C.C. art. 2358 (making the claim for reimbursement a personal right asserted by one spouse against the other), Mr. Tate is entitled to reimbursement from Ms. Roque for one-half of his separate property which he used to satisfy the community obligation pending the partition of the community property. Williams v. Williams, 590 So.2d 649 (La.App. 3d Cir.1991); Oliver v. Oliver, 561 So.2d 908, 911-14 (La.App. 2nd Cir.1990). At the trial on August 8, 1991, Mr. Tate's uncontroverted testimony was that he paid a total of $22,216.00 in separate funds towards the community obligation. The June 16, 1992 judgment awarded Mr. Tate $11,158.00. Insofar as the amount of judgment is in error, we hereby amend the judgment to award Mr. Tate $11,108.00 as reimbursement for one-half of his separate property paid toward the community obligation. Pursuant to the second sentence of art. 2365 above, this claim is to be satisfied from Ms. Roque's share of the net value of the community.

AMENDED, AND AS AMENDED, AFFIRMED.

CANNELLA, J., dissents.

CANNELLA, Judge, dissenting.

I respectfully dissent from the majority opinion because I believe that the trial court erred in ordering plaintiff to reimburse defendant for one-half of the mortgage payments he made, after termination of the marriage, on the family home which he occupied. I reach this conclusion for several reasons.

First, we have a line of cases in this circuit which clearly holds that the husband, who pays the mortgage on the family home with his separate property when ordered to do so as part of his child support obligation, as here, is only entitled to reimbursement of one-half of the principal portion of those payments and not one-half of the whole mortgage payment. *Halverson v. Halverson*, 589 So.2d 1153 (La. App. 5th Cir. 1991), writs denied, 600 So.2d 655 (La. 1991); *Guttuso v. Guttuso*, 540 So.2d 1293 (La. App. 5th Cir. 1989); *Lowe v. Lowe*, 463 So.2d 755 (La. App. 1985). Based on this line of cases and the record before us, the trial court erred in awarding defendant reimbursement for the mortgage payments in excess of one-half of the principal amount.

Furthermore, in my view, even if the mortgage payments were not ordered as part of the child support obligation, nothing more than one-half of the principal payments should be awarded. The result should be the same in this case as in the reverse situation where community property is used to pay the mortgage note on one spouse's separate property, which is used as the family home. *Parker v. Parker*, 517 So.2d 264 (La. App. 1st Cir. 1987); *Longo v. Longo*, 474 So.2d 500 (La. App. 4th Cir. 1985); *Cook v. Cook*, 457 So.2d 235 (La. App. 4th Cir. 1984); *Hurta v. Hurta*, 260 So.2d 324 (La. App. 4th Cir. 1972). The rational [sic] behind those cases is that the use of the separate asset by the community was an enjoyment of the natural and civil fruits of the separate property for which the community must bear the cost. In other words, the interest costs paid by the community on the separate property of one spouse that is being occupied by the community are not reimbursed because they are considered a business cost of maintaining and using the natural and civil fruits of the property. Likewise, in this case, defendant should not be allowed reimbursement of the interest costs he paid while having the exclusive separate use and occupancy of the community property. As in the reverse situation described above, those costs should be borne by defendant as part of his maintenance and use of the natural and civil fruits of the community property by his separate estate.

Every other result causes defendant to be unjustly enriched. Plaintiff was required to pay rent to house herself and the minor children. If defendant is reimbursed as he requests, the effect is to allow him to live rent-free during that six-year period. This is precisely the kind of unjust result that the Legislature sought to remedy in enacting La. R.S. 9:374(C). It's purpose is to enable the courts to allow an offset as rental for the use and occupancy of the family home, when, as here, the circumstances warrant it and it has not been previously precluded by earlier agreement or judgment. Thus, I respectfully disagree with the majority that La. R.S. 9:374(C) precludes diminution of defendant's reimbursement award by a rental set-off.

I also disagree with the majority that La. R.S. 9:374(C) can be applied retroactively, as interpreted in this case. The majority interprets the provision to preclude a rental award unless it was made at the time use of the home was granted. It then applies the provision to a situation where the use was granted before the statute was enacted. In the case relied on by the majority to support retroactive application, *Allen*, *supra*, the court did not interpret the statute to preclude rent, but interpreted it to afford the trial court a discretionary remedy to apply in equitably partitioning the community. As a discretionary tool to promote equity, the court was correct that it could be applied retroactively. *See*, *Burrell v. Burrell*, 518 So.2d 569 (La. App. 4th Cir. 1987). The majority here chooses to interpret the statute restrictively, to preclude a rental award absent a prior award of use in the judgment. I feel that it cannot be applied retroactively to a case where the judgment of use was rendered before the statute was enacted.

I believe that the majority misconstrues the case as one where plaintiff has sought an award rather than defendant. The issue before the court is not whether plaintiff is entitled to rent, but whether defendant is entitled to reimbursement against plaintiff of $11,108 of separate funds that he voluntarily spent, pursuant to a judgment, in favor of the community. It is his burden to prove that he is entitled to that award. In this case, where defendant enjoyed the exclusive use of the property in question, disobeyed a court order to pay the "house note" as part of his child support obligation and was unjustly enriched by living rent-free, he has not, in my view, met his required burden.

Accordingly, I dissent from the majority opinion.

In accord, Roger v. Roger, 751 So.2d 354 (La. App. 5th Cir. 2000).

G. *Karen J. Gibson v. Delbert Wayde Gibson*

692 So. 2d 708 (La. App. 3d Cir. 1997)

GREMILLION, Judge.

The only issue arising from this appeal is whether the trial court was correct in finding that Delbert Gibson acted prudently in withdrawing community funds from a retirement fund thereby incurring tax liability on his behalf and on behalf of his ex-wife, Karen Gibson.

FACTS

The following can be gleaned from the written and oral joint stipulations of the parties. During their marriage, Delbert was employed by Oryx Energy Company. While so employed, he deposited community funds into a capital accumulation plan and a retirement plan. Subsequent to their divorce, Delbert either terminated or was terminated from his employment with Oryx. Sometime thereafter, he withdrew all the funds from the capital accumulation plan and the retirement plan. These withdrawals were done without the knowledge or consent of Karen. When the funds were withdrawn, Oryx deducted approximately 20% of the funds for taxes. The remaining funds were divided equally between Delbert and Karen. As a result, she received $32,310.72 with $8,321.40 being withheld by Oryx for taxes.

Karen filed a motion to traverse the detailed descriptive list of community property, claiming that Delbert should reimburse her for the taxes paid out of her portion because he did not administer the funds in a prudent manner. The trial court found that while Delbert was not entitled to substantially alter or alienate the accounts without Karen's consent under La.Civ.Code art. 797, there was no evidence that he acted in bad faith. The trial court held that when a former spouse undertakes the management of co-owned property, he has the duty to act as a prudent administrator. As such, the trial court found that she failed to show that Delbert acted imprudently because she would have had to pay taxes on the funds at some time in the future even if she had rolled the funds over into an individual retirement account.

DISCUSSION

In its decision, the trial court relied on La. Civ. Code arts. 797 et seq., the code articles dealing with co-ownership of property, in making its decision. After reviewing the record and the relevant law, we find that the trial court committed an error of law by applying those articles instead of La. Civ. Code arts. 2369.2 and 2369.3, and we now reverse.

"Each spouse owns an undivided one-half interest in former community property and its fruits and products." La. Civ. Code art. 2369.2. "A spouse has a duty to preserve and to manage prudently former community property under his control ... in a manner consistent with the mode of use of that property immediately prior to termination of the community regime. He is answerable for any damage caused by his fault, default, or neglect." La. Civ. Code art. 2369.3. Comment (a) to Art. 2369.3 provides the following insight:

This Article changes the law. First, it imposes on a spouse who has control of former community property an affirmative duty "to preserve and to manage" such property. In contrast, Civil Code Article 800 (rev. 1990), applicable to ordinary co-owners, provides for a right but not a duty to act for the preservation of the property. Such a duty arises only if the co-owner undertakes to act as a negotiorum gestor or he is appointed as administrator. *See* Symeonides & Martin, The New Law of Co-ownership: A Kommentar, 68 Tul. L. Rev. 701, 746 (1993). Similarly, the co-ownership articles of the Civil Code do not impose on one co-owner an affirmative duty to manage the co-owned thing unless that owner assumed the qualities of a gestor or was appointed as an administrator. *See* C.C. Arts. 801, 803 (rev.1990); Symeonides & Martin, *supra* at 738-748. Second, this Article imposes a higher standard of care than that provided by Civil Code Article 799 (rev. 1990) for ordinary co-owners.

This Article also imposes a higher standard of care in managing and maintaining such former community property than the standard imposed during the marriage for managing community property. *See* C.C. Art. 2354 (rev.1979). The reason for imposing a higher standard of care in managing former community property is that, after termination of the community property regime, the law no longer assumes that a spouse who has former community property under his control will act in the best interest of both spouses in managing it.

In the case sub judice, Delbert simply withdrew all the funds in the retirement account without advising Karen of his intentions. As a result, she suffered a 20% loss of the corpus of the account. Further, Karen verified through a Certified Public Accountant, that had she been consulted she could have rolled the funds from the two accounts over into an individual retirement account in her name, avoided tax and/or penalty consequences, and continued to earn interest on a tax-free basis. At the very least, she could have decided how and when to withdraw the funds that belonged to her. Therefore, Delbert failed to preserve the former community property "in a manner consistent with the mode of use of that property immediately prior to termination of the community regime." La. Civ. Code art. 2369.3. Surely, it seems that if one purpose of the accounts in question is to avoid tax liability, any act that incurs such liability would be imprudent. Furthermore, bad faith is not required under Article 2369.3 because the spouse is "answerable for any damage caused by his fault, default, or neglect." *Id.* (emphasis added). As such, Delbert is liable to Karen for her share of the tax liability, $8,321.40, together with legal interest from the date of judicial demand.

CONCLUSION

The judgment of the trial court is reversed and set aside, and it is ordered, adjudged, and decreed that judgment be rendered in favor of Karen Gibson and against Delbert Gibson in the amount of $8,321.40, together with legal interest from the date of judicial demand and for all costs of these proceedings.

REVERSED AND RENDERED.

H. *Roger E. Reinhardt v. Linda Kay Anderson Reinhardt*

728 So. 2d 503 (La. App. 2d Cir. 1999)

PEATROSS, J.

Plaintiff, Roger Reinhardt, and Defendant, Linda Kay Anderson Reinhardt, both appeal various aspects of this complex community property case. For the reasons expressed, we reverse in part, amend in part and, as amended, affirm.

Facts and Procedure

Linda Kay Anderson Reinhardt (Kay) and Roger Reinhardt (Roger) were married on June 16, 1962. Together, they raised three children. Roger's father died in 1977 and his mother died in 1981, leaving Roger and his sister as their sole heirs.

Roger also had an aunt, Lillian Reinhardt, who died in 1991. Before her death, Roger and Kay moved his Aunt Lillian to the Monroe area to care for her. Aunt Lillian granted Roger a power of attorney and made substantial donations before her death; including $20,000 to pay a mortgage owed by the Reinhardts; approximately $74,400 in checks made out to Roger or Kay or one of the children; and New York Life Insurance policies on the three children which Roger transferred to his own name through the power of attorney. On Aunt Lillian's death, Roger and his sister were left as her sole heirs.

Kay's parents died within months of each other, in 1986 and 1987. Kay and her brother, Wayne, were their sole heirs. Part of Kay's and Wayne's inheritance included immovable property. Kay and Roger borrowed some money and bought Wayne's interest in the land and the loan was repaid with money Kay inherited from her parents.

On September 12, 1994, Roger filed for divorce and the judgment of divorce was signed on March 27, 1996. On June 29, 1995, Kay filed a petition to partition the community property and for reimbursement of separate funds used to pay community debts. Both parties filed detailed descriptive lists. On March 21 and 22, 1996, at a trial on the merits, classification of property, allocation of property and reimbursement issues were decided and a judgment was rendered. Roger was ordered to pay Kay $22,974.41 in equalizing payments. Finding an error in calculation, the trial court increased Roger's equalizing payment to $111,100.06. Roger and Kay both appeal parts of the judgment, raising classification, allocation, reimbursement and valuation issues. Roger additionally contests the date interest should begin to accrue on the equalizing payment.

Expenses paid from Kay's separate funds

After the termination of the community property regime, the provisions governing co-ownership apply to former community property. La. C.C. art. 2369.1. A co-owner who has incurred necessary expenses, expenses for ordinary maintenance and repairs or necessary management expenses paid to a third person, concerning the co-owned, former community property, is entitled to reimbursement from the other co-owner. La. C.C. art. 806. If the co-owner who incurred the expenses had the enjoyment of the thing, his reimbursement shall be reduced in proportion to the value of the enjoyment. La. C.C. art. 806. In addition, co-owners share the fruits of the thing held in indivision. La. C.C. art. 798.

Kay appeals the trial court's denial of her claim for reimbursement of one-half of expenses she incurred relative to a community home at 100 N. Inglewood. Those expenses totaled $816.86. The trial court found that Kay had been allowed to use community funds to improve the house to suit her needs and taste. Part of the expenses for which Kay is seeking reimbursement is the refund of $450 to renters when she decided to move into and enjoy the house which she co-owned with Roger. It is not manifestly erroneous for the trial court to deny Kay reimbursement of expenses when Kay had the enjoyment of the thing which she and Roger co-owned.

Kay appeals the trial court's refusal to award her one-half the rental income from a community-owned mobile home. Kay alleges that the mobile home was rented for $175 per month for 18 months, yielding a total rental income of $1,575. The renter was Roger's nephew who, according to Roger, paid Kay rent for two months until she evicted him. Roger subsequently moved the mobile home and collected five months' rent from his nephew. Since this was a co-owned mobile home, the co-owners are each entitled to one-half of the fruits. As such, it was manifestly erroneous for the trial court not to award one-half of the total rent revenue to each co-owner. Kay received two months' rent, or $350; Roger received five months' rent, or $875; the total revenue was $1,225. Each co-owner should receive $612.50. Since Kay has already received $350, Roger owes her an additional $262.50 in rental income.

Decree

The judgment is therefore amended in accordance with the summary given above. It is ordered, adjudged and decreed that Plaintiff, ROGER REINHARDT, pay unto Defendant, LINDA KAY ANDERSON REINHARDT, an equalizing payment of Fifty-eight thousand, one hundred seventy-seven & 85/100 ($58,177.85) dollars, together with legal interest thereon from date of judicial demand until paid.

Costs are assessed equally to the parties.

REVERSED IN PART, AMENDED IN PART AND, AS AMENDED, AFFIRMED.

I. *Dora Ellen Kline v. Kenneth Michael Kline*

741 So. 2d 670 (La. App. 3d Cir. 1999)

SAUNDERS, Judge.

This matter arises from a 1985 separation and, finally, a 1987 divorce of Dora Ellen Kline (hereinafter "Dora") and Kenneth Michael Kline (hereinafter "Mike"). Dora occupied their home after the separation, as awarded by the trial court, but abandoned it in 1987, after the divorce was final. Mike, pursuant to only a verbal understanding between he and Dora, and in the absence of a court order, occupied the home until 1997. Mike rented the home out for the first half of 1997 and then finally sold it for $119,000.00 on August 14, 1997. At trial, Mike sought reimbursement for one- half of his expenditures, for one-half of the mortgage payments he made with his separate property, and for one-half the enhancement value of the property. Dora sought rental reimbursements from Mike for the nine years he occupied the home. The lower court ruled in favor of Mike, granting reimbursements for his expenditures, enhancements, and his mortgage payments, and denying rental payments to Dora. The trial court did, however, deny Mike's claim of reimbursement for real estate taxes and insurance expenses, and found a $5,000.00 loan in the couple's favor prescribed. We affirm and remand.

FACTS

Dora and Mike were married on March 14, 1977. Mike had a small home building business and financed the construction of their family home through Mike's mother, Glyn Ann Kline (Ann). On March 11, 1982, they signed a mortgage in favor of Ann for $41,542.00. On the same date, Dora and Mike also signed a promissory note in the amount of $6,542.00 and a promissory note in the amount of $41,542.00. Ann transferred money into the couple's account as money was needed. Dora and Mike ultimately borrowed an additional unsecured $5,000.00 from Ann to make the house habitable.

In November 1985, Dora filed a petition for separation at which time she was awarded the exclusive occupancy of the home and Mike was ordered to pay the mortgage and insurance on the home as part of his support obligation. At the time of the separation, the house was still very much unfinished. A Judgment of Divorce was rendered on October 8, 1987; Mike was subsequently ordered to pay child support and permanent alimony.

When Dora gained occupancy of the home, she charged the purchase and installation of carpeting at Sears. Mike was ordered by the court to pay this bill. She continued to live in the former marital domicile, located at 1329 Lawton Drive, in Sulphur, Louisiana, until November 1987 when she abandoned the property. Upon her abandonment, no formal agreement was reached between the parties regarding the house. However, pursuant to a verbal agreement between the parties, Mike moved back into the home and resided there for the next nine years until August 16, 1996. During Mike's occupancy, he made extensive repairs made necessary due to Dora's neglect; he essentially finished the home, adding a pool, concrete driveway, new sewer system, a new heat pump, landscaping, and much more as indicated by the record. Mike rented the home from January 1997 through July of that same year and finally sold the home on August 14, 1997, for $119,000.00.

A Petition for Partition and Accounting and a Sworn Descriptive List was filed by Dora on November 8, 1988. Mike filed his initial descriptive list in November of 1995 and later filed two supplemental and amending lists. He also raised a claim for reimbursement to his separate estate for expenses on the former community residence and later, through an amending pleading, added additional costs for repair of the home. In response, Dora filed a Rule to Determine Rental Reimbursement pursuant to La.R.S. 9:374.

At trial, Mike sought reimbursement for one-half of his separate property expenditures servicing the community construction loan and reimbursement for one-half of expenses he incurred improving the home. The lower court found that Dora owed Mike reimbursement for one-half of his separate property that Mike paid on the mortgage and that he was entitled to reimbursement for one- half of the enhanced value of the property attributable to improvements that he made. The trial court also found that the $5,000.00 portion of the construction loan not secured by the mortgage had prescribed and denied Mike's reimbursement claims for real estate taxes and insurance.

ASSIGNMENT OF ERROR NO. 1

Reimbursement for Repairs/Maintenance

Regarding Mike's claim for reimbursement, he must prove that the work was necessary and that such work enhanced the value of the property. Jones v. Jones, 605 So.2d 689 (La. App. 2d Cir.), writ denied, 607 So.2d 571 (La. 1992). Once the community of acquets and gains is dissolved by separation, the spouses become co-owners in indivision of the marital home. Bolden v. Bolden, 524 So.2d 10 (La. App. 1st Cir. 1988). We find that the trial court had sufficient evidentiary support to reimburse Mike's expenses. La.Civ.Code. art. 2369.3 states, in pertinent part:

> A spouse has a duty to preserve and to manage prudently former community property under his control, including a former community enterprise, in a manner consistent with the mode of use of that property immediately prior to termination of the community regime. He is answerable for any damage caused by his fault, default, or neglect.

The comments to Article 2369.3 explain that unlike ordinary co-owners, this article imposes a higher and affirmative duty of care for the management of former community property since the presumption that a spouse will act in the best interest of the community no longer exists. Additionally, Comment (f) recognizes the entitlement that La.Civ.Code art. 806 grants, to-wit: "[a] spouse who incurs expenses in compliance with the obligation imposed by this Article is entitled reimbursement for one-half the costs in accordance with general principles of the law of co-ownership." Article 806 provides, in pertinent part, the following:

> A co-owner who on account of the thing held in indivision has incurred necessary expenses, expenses for ordinary maintenance and repairs, or necessary management expenses paid to a third person, is entitled to reimbursement from the other co-owners in proportion to their shares.

When Dora occupied the home, this affirmative duty was imposed upon her. The record provides ample evidence, including photos and testimony from which reasonable factfinders could agree, that Dora failed to properly discharge her duty of care. Dora must answer for all damages done to the property due to her fault, default or neglect. La. Civ. Code art. 2369.3.

When Mike moved back into the home, he found that Dora had left it in a state of severe disrepair. The septic pond, which requires regular maintenance, had been neglected and was overgrown with vegetation. He found rotten wood on the exterior of the house. The lock on the front door was destroyed due to a key broken off in the lock. The door to the storeroom and the stairway to the attic had been damaged. Garage walls and cabinets had been sprayed with spray paint in different colors. Dora's dogs and cats, which were kept in the house, damaged door trims and soiled new carpet to the point that it had to be replaced. The fireplace doors were inoperable. The fireplace mantel, mini blinds, curtains, several electrical outlet cover plates and switch covers, bathroom mirrors, prismatic panels on fluorescent lights, and shelves and closet rods were missing. The door to one of the bedrooms had a hole in it and in another bedroom closet, the ceiling had a hole in it. Both the dishwasher and the oven in the kitchen were broken. Dora had also removed the air conditioner condensing unit.

Through documentation and testimony, Mike provided evidence upon which a factfinder could reasonably find that during his occupancy of the home, he repaired and replaced all items that were either damaged or removed during Dora's occupancy. He completed all unfinished construction and made extensive improvements to the home. Mike replaced the carpeting which had been destroyed by Dora's pets. He replaced the exterior lock rendered inoperable by the broken key; repainted the garage walls defaced with spray paint; replaced door trim; installed new fireplace doors; replaced the missing fireplace mantel, prismatic panels, closet rods and shelves, electrical outlet and switch cover plates, bathroom mirrors, mini blinds, and curtains, and central air conditioning condensing unit; cleaned the septic oxidation pond; replaced the rotten wood; repaired the sheetrock in the ceiling; and installed a new dishwasher and oven.

We find, after a review of the record, ample evidence upon which a factfinder might determine that Mike's extensive work not only maintained, but also prudently repaired those damages left by Dora's neglect. In addition, his further construction reasonably enhanced the value of the home as supported by the sale on August 14, 1997, for $119,000.00.

The Mortgage

Dora argues that under McCarroll and co-ownership principles, Mike's enjoyment of the house for nine years should reduce his claims for mortgage reimbursements. We do not read McCarroll to deny Mike's claim for payments that he made on the community obligation--the mortgage. The very same argument that Dora asserts was attempted in Roque v. Tate, 631 So.2d 1385 (La. App. 1st Cir. 1994). There, while the claimant acknowledged that her ex-husband was entitled to reimbursements for separate funds used to pay a community obligation, she argued, as Dora argues now, that under Article 806, his reimbursement for mortgage payments should be reduced in proportion to his enjoyment of the home. The Roque court held, and we agree, that the mortgage was a community obligation under La. Civ. Code art. 2365 and, as such, entitled the husband to one-half his separate property used to satisfy the community obligation. Contrary to what Dora asserts, the rationale of McCarroll does not alter the principles applied in Roque nor offer any new construction which would demand a different result. McCarroll used co- ownership principles to explain only why co-owners and now occupants of community property do not have to pay rent, that is in sum, that the equal and co-extensive right of possession of co-owners precludes any obligation of rent between co-owners where one is not deprived the right of occupancy from the other. The holding of the McCarroll decision does not reach the issue of community obligations as Dora would have this court believe.

CONCLUSION

A review of the record reveals no manifest errors of the factual findings, nor errors of law, made by the lower court. We affirm Mike's award of reimbursement for his mortgage payments and for one-half the enhancement value of the property attributable to improvements he made. We affirm the trial court's finding that the $5,000.00 loan prescribed, the denial of rental reimbursements to Dora, and the denial of Mike's reimbursement claims for taxes and insurance. We remand for recalculation of the payoff amount.

DECREE

In light of the foregoing, we affirm the trial court's judgment, remanding only for recalculation of the amortization schedule. Costs to be paid by appellant.

AFFIRMED AND REMANDED.

J. *John H. Norman v. Mary Kathryn Kite Norman*

775 So. 2d 18 (La. App. 4 Cir 2000)

JONES, Judge.

Plaintiff/Appellant, John H. Norman seeks review of the trial court's judgment regarding calculations of certain assets, liabilities, and reimbursement claims of former community property owned by him and his former wife.

FACTS

Mary Kathryn Kite Norman and John H. Norman were married on September 6, 1969. Mr. Norman filed a petition for separation and divorce on November 7, 1990, and a judgment of separation was entered on August 15, 1991. The termination date for the community of acquits and gains is established as November 7, 1990.

Ms. Norman was given custody of the two minor children, Hudson and Caroline, and occupancy of the family home at 3625 Red Oak Court. Mr. Norman assumed control of two rental properties that the couple owned. The first property, located at 833-835 Opelousas Street, in the Algiers section of the City of New Orleans, was purchased in 1979 for $53,000. It was appraised in June 1979 for $85,000 and re-appraised in April 1981 for $127,000. The second rental property, located at 616-618 Belleville Street, Algiers also in the section of the city, was purchased in the early eighties for $55,000. Shortly after purchase, this property was appraised for $100,000. Throughout the eighties the properties were adequately maintained and managed and consistently rented, but were never profitable.

In 1990, when Mr. Norman assumed control of the two rental properties, his Statement of Income and Expenses which he filed in the trial court that December, stated that the monthly rental payments for the two properties totaled $1,379 or $16,548 per year. Subsequently, the rental income dramatically declined and the properties deteriorated. By 1993, the properties were uninhabitable and Mr. Norman had allowed the insurance on the rental properties to lapse and the mortgages to become delinquent.

Furthermore, in 1989, the couple had been forced to borrow $10,000 from their son's trust fund to pay off an obligation at Pelican Homestead.

The community partition trial was heard on February 26, 1999 and February 27, 1999. The court took the matter under advisement and ordered the parties to submit post-trial memoranda. On May 25, 1999, the trial court rendered judgment and reasons for judgment. The parties stipulated to many of the community's assets, liabilities, and reimbursement claims. After reconsidering extensive testimony, documentary evidence concerning issues surrounding the rental properties and the family home and the post-hearing memoranda, the trial court, entered an amended judgment on June 2, 1999 on the following issues:

(1) The trial court found that Mr. Norman mismanaged the two rental properties of which he assumed control in 1990. The court found that evidence revealed a dramatic drop in the collection of rent, a failure to list vacant apartments through rental agencies or newspaper ads, a failure to make minimal repairs and replace movables such as washers, dryers and air conditioners which were stolen from the properties, delinquent

mortgage payments resulting in foreclosure of the Belleville property, and the lapsing of insurance on the rental properties.

As a result of the mismanagement of the rental properties the trial court determined that the community sustained a loss of rental income. The court awarded Ms. Norman one half of the rental payments received by Mr. Norman after the termination of the community and one half of the loss of future rent which Mr. Norman would have received if the rentals had continued under the same terms from the termination of the community until the date of the partition trial. The trial court found that the average rental income from 1991 to 1998 was $16,500 per year and that the total rental value lost to the community is $132,000.

The court further ordered reimbursement to Mr. Norman for expenses incurred on the properties located at Opelousas and Belleville, including the mortgages paid on the properties and maintenance expenses. However, the court excluded the following expenses due to Mr. Norman's mismanagement of the rental properties: (1) legal fees and cost of bringing the Belleville property out of foreclosure, (2) time Mr. Norman spent maintaining and managing the rental property, and (3) Mr. Norman's separate labors in caring for and maintaining the rental properties.

Finally, the trial court assigned a value to the property located at 616-618 Belleville Street at $105,000 and the property located at 833-835 Opelousas Avenue at $125,000. The court stated that it was not assigning a loss of value on the rental properties.

It is from these findings that the plaintiff/appellant, John H. Norman appeals.

DISCUSSION

In his appeal, Mr. Norman asserts eleven assignments of error. These are consolidated as follows:

1. Whether the trial court's findings regarding Mr. Norman's duties and credits toward the two rental properties were erroneous.

2. Whether the trial court erred in reimbursing Ms. Norman for expenses incurred and in denying Mr. Norman rent during her occupancy of the former matrimonial domicile at 3625 Red Oak Court.

3. Whether the trial court disregarded several of the parties' stipulations and made clerical errors.

We amend the trial court's findings and affirm as amended.

RENTAL PROPERTIES:
833-835OPELOUSAS AVENUE and 616-618 BELLEVILLE STREET

CALCULATION OF THE LOST RENTAL INCOME

In this assignment of error, Mr. Norman claims that the trial court used gross rental income figures instead of net rental income figures to calculate the lost rental income. He argues that the proper method of determining the lost rental income is to calculate the average gross rent received between 1982 and 1989 ($15,760), and subtract from that figure the average gross rent received between 1991 and 1998 ($2,606), to reach the average lost gross rent per year ($13,154). These figures are taken from the parties' income tax returns. Mr. Norman also asserts that the trial court did not subtract his expenses in its calculations, and failed to note that he reduced the debt at the end of the period he managed the properties.

Ms. Norman argues that the trial court determined the lost rental income correctly, but conservatively, by failing to consider the possible rise in rental rates in Algiers during the period Mr. Norman managed the properties. According to Mr. Norman's Statement of Income and Expenses filed with the court in December 1990, the rental units were producing $1,379 per month or $16,558 per year. The trial court rounded the yearly figure to $16,500 and multiplied it by eight to reach $132,000 in total lost rental income for the years Mr. Norman had control of the property. Ms. Norman also asserts that Mr. Norman was reimbursed $127,383 for expenses and mortgages on the properties, therefore resulting in lost net rental income.

The record indicates that the trial court was well within its vast discretion in determining future rental loss. The court cited Kyson v. Kyson, 596 So.2d 1308, 1319-1323 (La. App. 2d Cir. 1991), where in the Court of Appeals for the Second Circuit held that a wife was entitled to one-half of lost net future rents until the partition trial, when the husband breached his duty of prudent administration by terminating a profitable community lease without the other spouse's knowledge or agreement. Kyson v. Kyson, 596 So.2d 1308, 1319-1323 (La. App. 2d Cir. 1991). Furthermore, Louisiana Civil Code Article 2369.3, comment (d) states, "The phrase 'in a manner consistent with the mode of use of that property immediately prior to termination of the community regime' is intended to particularize the standard against which to judge the acts of a spouse undertaken to preserve and especially to manage the former community property."

In the present case, the trial court found that Mr. Norman breached his duty of prudent administration by failing to properly manage the properties and allowing them to deteriorate. Therefore, the trial court made its calculations based on what the rental income would have been had Mr. Norman maintained the status quo. When Mr. Norman assumed control of the properties, the rental income was approximately

$16,500 per year according to Mr. Norman's Statement of Income and Expenses in December 1990. If Mr. Norman had maintained that level of rental income, rental income would have equaled $132,000 for the eight year period he had control. The trial court did not attempt to consider the rise in rental rates, for this would have been merely speculative. Therefore, the ruling of the trial court is not clearly wrong.

JOHN H. NORMAN'S DUTIES AND CREDITS REGARDING THE RENTAL PROPERTIES

In his fourth, fifth and sixth assignments of error, Mr. Norman argues that the trial court erroneously expected him to use separate funds to pay community debts; the trial court erred in not reimbursing him for attorney's fees and court costs associated with foreclosure proceedings against one of the rental properties; and the trial court erred in not reimbursing him for his time and management of the rental properties.

Mr. Norman argues that there is no legal requirement to use separate property to satisfy a community debt. He cites Cooper v. Cooper, 619 So.2d 1210 (La. App. 1st Cir. 1993), where a spouse was seeking reimbursement for community funds used to satisfy a community debt. The court denied reimbursement, stating that a spouse is not obligated to pay a community debt with separate funds.

In the present case, Mr. Norman asserts that when community funds are unavailable or non-existent, he should not have to use separate funds to satisfy the debt. The Louisiana Civil Code is silent as to whether separate funds **shall** be used to satisfy a community debt. However, Article 2369.3 imposes a duty to preserve and maintain prudently former community property under a spouse's control. Comment (a) states that this duty is higher than the standard of care imposed on a co-owner and higher than the standard imposed during the marriage. Comment (f), in reference to Article 806, provides for reimbursement of separate funds if used in compliance with this article. Therefore, it seems the intent of Article 2369.3 is that in the absence of community funds a spouse may be forced to use reimbursable separate funds to satisfy a community debt.

Next, Mr. Norman argues that he should be reimbursed for one-half the attorney's fees and court costs associated with foreclosure proceedings against the Belleville street property. He claims that in 1991, he did not have the means in separate or community funds to pay the mortgage and fell behind in his payments, therefore litigation ensued. Ms. Norman refutes this argument and asserts that Mr. Norman found $15,000 "somewhere" to bring the mortgage current and $3,400 in attorney's fees. This was prior to his parents' death and inheritance.

The trial court found that the attorney's fees and court costs associated with foreclosing proceedings were an unnecessary expense that resulted from Mr. Norman's mismanagement of the property. The court stated in its reasons for judgment that Mr. Norman's actions of allowing these properties to fall into disrepair and the mortgages to become delinquent were troubling. Furthermore, the court was not convinced that Mr. Norman lacked the financial strength to adequately maintain the properties. We find the trial court was not manifestly erroneous or clearly wrong in this finding of fact.

Finally, Mr. Norman asserts that he should be reimbursed for his time in managing and maintaining the properties. He presents no legal basis for this assertion. Conversely, Louisiana Civil Code Article 2369.1 states that after the termination of the community regime, the provisions governing co-ownership govern former community property. Co-ownership Article 806, comment (c) states, "A co-owner is not allowed to receive anything for his own management of the thing that is held in indivision unless he is entitled to such a recovery under a management plan adopted by agreement of all the co- owners, by judgment, or under the law of unjust enrichment." There is no evidence in the record of a management plan. Therefore, the ruling of the trial court is not clearly wrong.

REIMBURSEMENTS REGARDING THE FAMILY DOMICILE AT 3625 RED OAK COURT

In his seventh, eighth and ninth assignments of error, Mr. Norman argues that the trial court erroneously reimbursed Ms. Norman for monthly neighborhood association fees and an alarm system; the trial court erroneously failed to reduce Ms. Norman's reimbursements by ten percent for her use of one room of the family home for business purposes; and the trial court erred in failing to award Mr. Norman rent for Ms. Norman's occupancy of the family domicile.

Mr. Norman contends that the monthly fees for the homeowner's association and expenses associated with the alarm system are items of routine maintenance and do not confer a substantial economic benefit to the property. Ms. Norman argues that the homeowner's association fee is mandatory for all homeowners in the subdivision and a failure to pay the fee would result in a lien on the property. The alarm system has been in place since the couple purchased the house and was necessary for their protection. Ms. Norman asserts that the failure to pay these expenses would have made her vulnerable to a claim for mismanagement.

Expenses incurred between the termination of the community and partition of the community are awarded only when the party claiming reimbursement can prove that the work was necessary and value of the property was enhanced. Jones v. Jones, 605 So.2d 689, 693 (La. App. 2d Cir. 1992). Items of maintenance occasioned by the use of the dwelling are not reimbursable. Jurgelsky v. Pinac, 614 So.2d 1331, 1336 (La. App. 3d Cir. 1993).

The trial court found that these claims were necessary and conferred an economic benefit to the community. They existed prior to the termination of the community and are reasonable in accordance with the duty to preserve and maintain the property in the manner in which it was always kept. Reimbursements are factual determinations and absent an abuse of discretion the trial court's decision should not be disturbed on appeal. Rosell v. ESCO, 549 So.2d 840 (La.1989). Therefore, we find no error by the trial court.

DECREE

For the foregoing reasons, we affirm the judgment of the trial court regarding: the calculation of net lost rental income to Ms. Norman, the denial of reimbursements to Mr. Norman for attorney's fees and time spent managing the rental property, the reimbursements to Ms. Norman for expenses incurred at the Red Oak Court home, the denial of a ten percent reimbursement to Mr. Norman for Ms. Norman's use of one room in the family home for business purposes, the denial of rent to Mr. Norman for Ms. Norman's occupancy of the family home, and Mr. Norman's purchase of an automobile as satisfaction of a debt owed to the son. However, we amend the trial court's judgment as to the valuations of the two rental properties and the calculations of community assets and reimbursements. As herein indicated, the judgment of the trial court is affirm as amended. Mr. Norman is to pay all costs of this appeal.

AMENDED AND AFFIRMED AS AMENDED.

K. *Randall D. Ostarly v. Lori A. Serpas Ostarly*

988 So. 2d 276 (La. App. 4 Cir. 2008)

EDWIN A. LOMBARD, Judge.

The defendant/appellant, Lori A. Serpas Ostarly, appeals from the judgment of community property partition issued by the trial court on September 29, 2004. After review of the record in light of the arguments of the parties and the applicable law, we affirm the judgment of the trial court.

Relevant Facts and Procedural History

The appellant and the defendant/appellee, Randall D. Ostarly, were married on June 28, 1997. Mr. Ostarly filed a petition for divorce on December 16, 1999. The petition was granted and the judgment of divorce was signed on October 13, 2000. The appellant filed a petition to partition community property, rule for return of separate property, and for injunctive relief on April 19, 2001. After the filing of descriptive lists and amended descriptive lists, the matter was tried on September 2, 2004. The trial judge signed the judgment on September 29, 2004, but did not provide written reasons for judgment.

Pursuant to a motion for new trial, the trial court issued an amended judgment on December 17, 2004, awarding judicial interest but ordering that all other provisions of the judgment signed on September 29, 2004, remain in full force and effect.

On appeal, the appellant raises two assignments of error, arguing that the trial court erred in (1) failing to award her damages for the conversion of her household furnishings, and (2) determining that she owes the appellee $2556.76 in reimbursement for loan payments on the 1999 Harley Davidson that, while a community asset during the matrimonial regime, remained solely in the appellee's sole possession.

***

Assignment of Error No. 2

Next, citing Davezac v. Davezac, 483 So.2d 1197 (La.App. 4th Cir.1986), the appellant argues that the trial court erred in granting the appellee $2556.75 in reimbursements or loan payments on the 1999 Harley Davidson motorcycle because it remained in the sole possession of the appellee.

Pursuant to La. Civ.Code art. 2358, upon termination of a community property regime, a spouse may have a claim for reimbursement against the other spouse. Further, in accordance with La. Civ.Code art. 2365, if the separate property of a spouse has been used to satisfy a community obligation, upon termination of the community property regime the spouse is entitled to reimbursement for one-half of the amount or value that the property had at the time it was used. In Davezac, this court created an exception wherein a party who had possession and use of the family automobile was not reimbursed for the payment on the loan note because of the rapid depreciation of the value of an automobile is directly related to its use.

In this case, the record indicates that, in addition to the motorcycle at issue, the community assets initially included two family automobiles, a 1997 Jeep and a 1997 BMW. After the couple separated, the appellant kept the BMW, leaving the appellee with the Jeep and his motorcycle. The BMW was apparently damaged while in the appellant's possession and subsequently repossessed. Community debts included notes on both the BMW and motorcycle. In the partition of the community assets, the appellee became full owner of the Jeep (valued at $2000.00) and the motorcycle (stipulated value of $12,070.00). The appellant was ordered to reimburse the appellee for half of the payments he made on the BMW note after December 16, 1999, until its repossession (totaling $7802.10), as well as for one-half of the community debt for the motorcycle after December 16, 1999, less $5000.00 for the appellee's use of the vehicle. The community debt on the motorcycle note paid by the appellee was $10,113.53.2 In light of the appellee's use of the motorcycle, however, the trial court reduced this amount by $5000.00 before apportioning the community debt between the parties. Accordingly, the appellant was ordered to reimburse $2,556.75 of the community debt on the motorcycle note.

The appellant argues, in effect, that Davezac is applicable to all movable vehicles. However, La. Civ.Code art. 2365 does not distinguish between movable and immovable property and we decline to extend Davezac to cover all movable property. In this case, the trial court took into account the appellee's use of the motorcycle and, accordingly, we do not find that the trial court abused its discretion in ordering the appellant to reimburse the appellee for the remaining portion of the community debt on the motorcycle.

Conclusion

The judgment of the trial court is affirmed.

L. *Troy Benoit v. Tammy Williams Benoit*

91 So. 3d 1015 (La. App. 1st Cir. 2012)

GUIDRY, J.

This appeal arises from a trial court judgment partitioning the community of acquets and gains formerly existing between Troy Benoit and Tammy Williams Benoit. For the reasons that follow, we vacate the judgment of the trial court.

FACTS AND PROCEDURAL HISTORY

Troy and Tammy Benoit were married on December 31, 2000. This was Troy and Tammy's second marriage to one another. On March 8, 2006, Troy filed a petition for La. C.C. art. 102 divorce. In his petition, Troy sought, among other things, partition of the community of acquets and gains in accordance with La. R.S. 9:2801. Tammy filed an answer and reconventional demand also seeking partition of community property. A final judgment of divorce was subsequently rendered on December 15, 2006.

On January 14, 2008, Tammy filed a detailed descriptive list of assets and liabilities of the community. Troy filed a sworn detailed descriptive list on April 14, 2008 and filed an amended detailed descriptive list on August 6, 2008. Thereafter, Troy and Tammy filed a combined detailed descriptive list on October 28, 2009.

A trial of the community property partition was held on January 5, 2010. Prior to the presentation of evidence, Troy and Tammy stipulated as to the classification, allocation, and/or valuation of certain assets, liabilities, and claims for reimbursement. Following a trial on the remaining contested issues, the trial court issued reasons for judgment on February 8, 2010, and signed a judgment on April 8, 2010, partitioning the community of acquets and gains. Tammy and Troy both filed motions for new trial, which were denied. Tammy and Troy now separately appeal from the trial court's April 8, 2010 judgment.

DISCUSSION

Legal Principles and Standard of Review

The provisions of La. R.S. 9:2801 set forth the procedure by which community property is to be partitioned when the spouses are unable to agree on a partition of community property. La. R.S. 9:2801 A; Hoover v. Hoover, 10–1245, p. 3 (La.App. 1st Cir.3/17/11), 62 So.3d 765, 767. ...

***

Allocation of Property Located at 1181 Clipper Drive

Tammy asserts that the trial court erred in allocating the family home located at 1181 Clipper Drive, Slidell, Louisiana, to Troy pursuant to the provisions of La. R.S. 9:2801, because the home was not community property, but was co-owned property, having been acquired by the parties prior to their marriage.

Though originally listed on the parties' combined detailed descriptive list as a community asset, the documentary evidence and testimony admitted at the partition proceeding demonstrates that the property was actually purchased by Troy and Tammy ten days prior to their second marriage. The parties do not dispute that based on this evidence, the home is not community property, but rather, is co-owned by the parties in indivision. Accordingly, the partition of this piece of property is governed by the articles of the Civil Code concerning ownership of property in indivision, La. C.C. arts. 707–818, not by La. R.S. 9:2801.

Louisiana Civil Code article 797 provides "[o]wnership of the same thing by two or more persons is ownership in indivision. In the absence of other provisions of law or juridical act, the shares of all co-owners are presumed to be equal." Any co-owner has a right to demand partition of a thing held in indivision. La. C.C. art. 807. The mode of partition may be determined by agreement of all the co-owners, in the absence of which a co-owner may demand judicial partition. La. C.C. art. 809. Louisiana Civil Code article 810 requires the court to partition in kind when the thing held in indivision is susceptible to division into as many lots of nearly equal value as there are shares and the aggregate value of all lots is not significantly lower than the value of the property in the state of indivision. La. C.C. art. 810. When the thing held in indivision is not susceptible to partition in kind, the court shall decree a partition by licitation or by private sale, and the proceeds shall be distributed to the co-owners in proportion to their shares. La. C.C. art. 811.

Therefore, because the family home located at 1181 Clipper Drive is not susceptible to division into lots, the home has to be sold, and the proceeds distributed equally between Troy and Tammy.

Value of Homeowner's Insurance Proceeds

Tammy next asserts that the trial court erred in valuing the amount of homeowner's insurance proceeds received by Troy for damage to the family home as a result of Hurricane Katrina.1 Prior to the presentation of evidence at the community property partition proceeding, the parties stipulated that the value of the insurance proceeds was $170,577.62. Both Troy and Tammy testified that two insurance payments, one for $25,000.00 and one for $55,100.00, had already been divided between them. Accordingly, the trial court, in valuing this asset, deducted these amounts from the total amount stipulated to between the parties. Because Troy failed to provide an accounting of the insurance proceeds prior to trial, and because the evidence does not conclusively establish that these two payments were excluded in arriving at the stipulated value of the insurance proceeds, we find the trial court's valuation of this community asset to be reasonably supported by the record and does not constitute an abuse of discretion. See Rao v. Rao, 05–0059, p. 6 (La.App. 1st Cir.11/4/05), 927 So.2d 356, 360–361, writ denied, 05–2453 (La.3/24/06), 925 So.2d 1232.

Reimbursement Claims in Favor of Troy

Tammy asserts that Troy is not entitled to reimbursement for his payment of several community obligations during the existence of the community, including the first and second mortgages on the family home, property taxes, income taxes, and a truck note, because these obligations were paid with community, and not his separate funds. Louisiana Civil Code article 2365 provides, in part:

> If separate property of a spouse has been used either during the existence of the community property regime or thereafter to satisfy a community obligation, that spouse is entitled to reimbursement for one-half of the amount or value that the property had at the time is was used.

Property of married persons is generally characterized as either separate or community. La. C.C. art. 2335. Louisiana Civil Code article 2338 provides:

> [C]ommunity property comprises: property acquired during the existence of the legal regime through effort, skill, or industry of either spouse; property acquired with community things or with community and separate things, unless classified as separate property under Article 2341; property donated to the spouses jointly; natural and civil fruits of community property; damages

> awarded for loss or injury to a thing belonging to the community; and all other property not classified by law as separate property.

Regarding the classification of property as separate, La. C.C. art. 2341 provides, in part, that a spouse's separate estate "comprises ... property acquired by a spouse prior to the establishment of a community property regime [and] property acquired by a spouse with separate things or with separate and community things when the value of the community thing is inconsequential in comparison with the value of the separate things used."

Property in the possession of a spouse during the existence of the community property regime is presumed to be community, but either spouse may rebut the presumption. La. C.C. art. 2340. The spouse seeking to rebut the presumption bears the burden of proving by a preponderance of the evidence that property is separate in nature. Hoover, 10–1245 at p. 7, 62 So.3d at 770. A trial court's finding regarding the nature of property as being either community or separate is a factual determination subject to the manifest error/clearly wrong standard of review. Corkern v. Corkern, 05–2297, p. 6 (La.App. 1st Cir.11/3/06), 950 So.2d 780, 785, writ denied, 06–2844 (La.2/2/07), 948 So.2d 1083.

At the partition hearing, the parties testified that subsequent to their first marriage, but prior to their second marriage, Troy received settlement funds as a result of a motorcycle accident he had during the first marriage, which had rendered him a paraplegic. Troy deposited these funds into an investment account with Merrill–Lynch, and subsequently with Smith–Barney and Raymond James. These accounts generated interest and dividends, which were placed into a joint checking account bearing Troy's and Tammy's names, which was attached to Troy's investment accounts. The parties stipulated that the interest and dividends generated from these separate investment accounts during the existence of the community totaled $119,859.00. Bank records admitted into evidence at the hearing reflect that expenses of the parties, including community obligations, were paid out of the joint checking account.

From our review of the record, it is evident that the community obligations exceeded the value of the interest and dividends placed into the joint checking account. The stipulated amounts paid during the second marriage for the first mortgage, homeowner's insurance, income taxes, and property taxes totaled $113,364.00. Additionally, during the marriage $1,049.00 was paid on the second mortgage and $1,986.00 was paid on the note for Troy's truck. These community obligations, alone, total $116,399.00. Further, the parties do not dispute that additional community obligations were paid from the checking account, including the Capital One line of credit, credit cards, and expenses for the management of the investment accounts, which generated the interest and dividends.

Additionally, Troy's testimony and the testimony of Kurt Arcement, manager of Troy's investment accounts for over ten years, indicated that additional funds necessary to cover expenditures of the parties were automatically transferred into the joint checking account from the separate investment accounts. For the years 2002–2005, between $49,296.00 and $63,017.00 in separate funds were deposited annually into the joint checking account to cover additional expenditures.

Tammy asserts because separate funds were commingled with community funds, all funds in the joint checking account became community. However, in the instant case, the separate funds were not mixed with community funds such that they are no longer capable of identification, and the amount of separate funds deposited into the account far exceeds the amount of interest and dividends deposited into the account. See Granger v. Granger, 98–429, p. 6 (La.App. 3rd Cir.12/9/98), 722 So.2d 107, 111; see also La. C.C. art. 2341. Further, looking at the figures stipulated to or admitted into evidence regarding the community obligations paid out of the joint checking account, the amount of interest and dividends was insufficient to cover those expenditures. Accordingly, we cannot say that the trial court erred in finding that separate funds were used during the community to pay the first and second mortgages on the family home, homeowner's insurance, income taxes, property taxes, and Troy's truck note, and in awarding Troy reimbursement for one-half of those payments.

Allocation of Interest and Dividends to Troy

Tammy asserts that the trial court erred in allocating to Troy the interest and dividends generated on Troy's separate investment accounts during the community, offset by the amount paid to Mr. Arcement for management of the separate and community property in the accounts, because these were not an asset or an obligation of the community in existence at the time of trial.

In her reasons for judgment, the trial court found that the value of the Smith Barney checking account was $119,859.00, less the management fees of $41,666.00 charged by Mr. Arcement. However, we find that the trial court's factual finding is not reasonably supported by the record. The parties stipulated prior to the hearing that the amount of interest and dividends generated during the existence of the community on Troy's separate property totaled $119,859.00. The parties did not, however, stipulate that this was the value of that account, nor is there any evidence in the record to support that this was the value of this asset at the time of trial. See La. R.S. 9:2801 A(4)(a).

According to the evidence introduced at the hearing, the interest and dividends deposited into the checking account were depleted during the community such that additional separate funds had to be deposited into the account to cover expenditures. Additionally, the fees charged by Mr. Arcement for management of Troy's accounts were paid each quarter, and were not shown to be a debt owed by the community at the time of trial. Therefore, from our review of the record, the trial court erred in finding that the amount of interest and dividends generated during the community was an existing asset of the community at the time of trial, and likewise erred in finding that the management fees charged by Mr. Arcement were a debt owed by the community at the time of trial. Accordingly, the trial court abused its discretion in allocating the amount of interest and dividends generated during the community, less an amount for management fees charged by Mr. Arcement, to Troy.

Allocation and Valuation of Capital One Line of Credit

Tammy next argues that the trial court erroneously allocated an obligation in the amount of $31,161.99 to her, representing an amount allegedly due on a Capital One line of credit obtained on behalf of TAT, Real Estate, L.L.C., and guaranteed by Troy and Joseph Lamy.

During the marriage, Troy and Tammy formed TAT Real Estate, L.L.C. The original members were Troy, Tammy, and Tammy's brother. However, Joseph "Bubby" Lamy, Troy's good friend and Tammy's current husband, was substituted for Tammy's brother as a member of the LLC. In April 2005, TAT Real Estate purchased real property at 792 Pine Tree Street, Slidell, Louisiana, which was financed by a second mortgage on the Clipper Drive property. TAT Real Estate bought the Pine Tree property with the intention of making repairs to the home and "flip[ping] it." Thereafter, Troy and Mr. Lamy made repairs to the home, which were financed by a line of credit with Capital One. After the Pine Tree property was fully repaired, it sustained significant damage from Hurricane Katrina. Because there was no insurance on this property, Troy made draws on the line of credit to make needed repairs.

The parties do not dispute that the line of credit was originally obtained during the existence of the community. Rather, Tammy asserts that the trial court erred in allocating to her an obligation in the amount of $31,161.99, which represented amounts drawn on the line of credit subsequent to the termination of the community.

An obligation incurred by a spouse during the existence of a community property regime for the common interest of the spouses is a community obligation. La. C.C. art. 2360. However, an obligation incurred by a spouse prior to the establishment or after termination of a community property regime is a separate obligation. See La. C.C. art. 2363 and 1979 Revision Comment (a).

Troy admitted that he made draws on the line of credit subsequent to the termination of the community in order to make repairs to the Pine Tree property following Hurricane Katrina. Troy, nevertheless, argues that the additional indebtedness is attributable to the community, because he had a duty to preserve and prudently manage former community property under his control.

Louisiana Civil Code article 2369.3 provides, in part, that a "spouse has a duty to preserve and to manage prudently former community property under his control ... in a manner consistent with the mode of use of that property immediately prior to termination of the community regime." Article 2369.3, however, is usually addressed when a former spouse asserts a claim for compensation due to the breach of this article concerning management of a community business, or when a former spouse asserts a claim for reimbursement for one-half of the expenses incurred in compliance with the obligation imposed by this article. See La. C.C. art. 2369.3, 1995 Comment (f); see also Knighten v. Knighten, 00–1662, pp. 3–5 (La.App. 1st Cir.9/28/01), 809 So.2d 324, 328–329, writ denied, 01–2846 (La.1/4/02), 805 So.2d 207; Clemons, 42,129 at p. 6, 960 So.2d at 1073. Contrary to Troy's argument on appeal, we do not find that this article applies to the classification of an obligation as community or separate or to the valuation of that asset or liability. Rather, those determinations are controlled by La. C.C. arts. 2359–2363 and La. R.S. 9:2801 A(4).

Therefore, because Troy admitted that he made draws on the line of credit subsequent to the termination of the community, the trial court erred in finding that the amount of the community obligation for the Capital One line of credit was $31,161.99. Rather, the evidence in the record establishes that at the time of the termination of the community, the Capital One line of credit had a balance of $3,836.10. Accordingly, that is the amount on the Capital One line of credit for which the community is liable. Furthermore, because of the nature of this debt, we find that the obligation should be allocated to Troy. See La. R.S. 9:2801 A(4)(c).

Reimbursement for Payments Made on Capital One Line of Credit

Tammy also contends that the trial court erred in recognizing a reimbursement claim in favor of Troy and against her in the amount of $6,161.50, representing one-half of the alleged payments made by Troy on the Capital One line of credit after the termination of the community. As stated above, the majority of the outstanding debt obligation on the Capital One line of credit was incurred by Troy subsequent to the termination of the community. As of the termination date of the community, the balance on the line of credit was $3,836.10. Because Troy is only entitled to reimbursement for one-half of his separate property that was used to satisfy the community obligation, he is only entitled to reimbursement for one-half of the balance owed on the line of credit as of the date of termination of the community, or $1,918.05.6 See La. C.C. art. 2365.

Reimbursement Funds Used to Purchase Nissan Maxima

Tammy asserts that the trial court erred in recognizing a claim for reimbursement made by Troy for one-half of separate funds allegedly used to purchase a Nissan Maxima. In its reasons for judgment, the trial court stated that "[i]t is undisputed that the Maxima was purchased during the marriage with [h]usband's separate funds." However, according to the record, both Troy and Tammy testified that Troy purchased the Maxima with funds he received from his personal injury settlement prior to their second marriage, though the Maxima was titled in both of their names. Accordingly, because the vehicle is not community property, but is co-owned property or separate property acquired prior to the marriage, Troy is not entitled to reimbursement for separate funds used to purchase the vehicle. See La. C.C. arts. 2365 and 2367.

Reimbursement for Credit Card Expenditures

The trial court awarded Troy $10,524.00 in reimbursement, representing one-half of expenditures made by Tammy on Discover, Chase Visa, and Citi Dividend Platinum credit cards during the existence of the community. Tammy does not dispute that she used these credit cards during the existence of the community for the benefit of the community. However, she asserts that the funds used to pay the credit card charges were community funds, and therefore, Troy is not entitled to reimbursement for payment of the community obligation with community funds. See La. C.C. art. 2365.

This argument is identical to the argument raised with regard to the reimbursement awarded to Troy for payment of the first and second mortgages on the family home, income taxes, property taxes, and truck note. For the reasons previously discussed, we find no error in the trial court's determination that the credit card debt is a community obligation that was paid with separate funds, for which Troy is entitled to reimbursement.

Recognition and/or Value of Community Obligation to Capital One Visa

The trial court found that a community obligation in the amount of $4,168.85 was owed to Capital One Visa for the account ending in 237. However, from our review of the record, we find no evidence to support this conclusion. Exhibit 20 offered into evidence by Troy at the partition proceeding contains statements from May 2006, which is two months after the termination of the community of acquets and gains, through the date of trial. Further, the May 2006 statement indicates that the previous balance on the account was $0. Therefore, because the record is devoid of evidence that an obligation to Capital One Visa existed during the community property regime, the trial court erred in allocating this obligation, in the amount of $4,168.85, to Troy.

Reimbursement for Post–Termination Payments to CLECO

Tammy asserts that the trial court erred in recognizing a reimbursement claim in favor of Troy for one-half of the amounts paid to CLECO for service provided to the Pine Tree property after the termination of the community. Troy argues that the CLECO bills are a community obligation, which he paid with separate funds, and therefore, he is entitled to reimbursement under La. C.C. art. 2365. However, Troy admits that the charges for which he seeks reimbursement were not incurred during the community, but were incurred after the termination of the community. Accordingly, this indebtedness is a separate obligation, paid with separate funds. See La. C.C. art. 2363 and 1979 Revision Comment (a). For the reasons previously stated with regard to the allocation and valuation of the Capital One line of credit and reimbursement awarded to Troy for payments made on the line of credit, we find that the trial court erred in awarding Troy reimbursement for one-half of the amounts paid to CLECO after the termination of the community.

Reimbursement for Post–Termination Payments on Community Automobile

Troy asserts that the trial court erred in denying his claim for reimbursement for payments made on a community automobile following the termination of the community with separate funds.

Louisiana Civil Code article 2365 currently provides, in pertinent part:

> If separate property of a spouse has been used either during the existence of the community property regime or thereafter to satisfy a community obligation, that spouse is entitled to reimbursement for one-half of the amount or value that the property had at the time it was used.
>
> If the community obligation was incurred to acquire ownership or use of a community corporeal movable required by law to be registered, and separate property of a spouse has been used after termination to satisfy that obligation, the reimbursement claim shall be reduced in proportion to the value of the claimant's use after termination of the community property regime. The value of that use and the amount of the claim for reimbursement accrued during the use are presumed to be equal.

Article 2365 was amended by Acts 2009, No. 204, § 1, which added the second paragraph regarding registered community corporeal movables. Prior to the 2009 amendment, Article 2365 provided, in pertinent part:

> If separate property of a spouse has been used to satisfy a community obligation, that spouse, upon termination of the community property regime, is entitled to reimbursement for one-half of the amount or value that the property had at the time it was used. The liability of a spouse who owes reimbursement is limited to the value of his share in the community after deduction of all community obligations.

Troy asserts that the amended version of La. C.C. art. 2365 was not in effect during the period for which he seeks reimbursement, i.e. March 2006 through 2009; and during that period, the jurisprudence in this circuit allowed these types of reimbursement claims. See Williams v. Williams, 509 So.2d 77 (La.App. 1st Cir.1987). Further, Troy asserts because the 2009 amendment to La. C.C. art. 2365 represents a substantive change in the law, it can be applied prospectively only. See La. C.C. art. 6.

In determining whether a newly-enacted provision is to be applied prospectively only, or may also be applied retroactively, La. C.C. art. 6 requires a two-fold inquiry. First, the court must determine whether the amendment to the statute expresses the legislative intent regarding retroactive or prospective application. Keith v. U.S. Fidelity and Guaranty Co., 96–2075, p. 6 (La.5/9/97), 694 So.2d 180, 183. If no such intent is expressed, the enactment must be classified as either substantive, procedural, or interpretative. Keith, 96–2075 at p. 6, 694 So.2d at 183.

In enacting the amended version of Article 2365, the legislature did not express its intent regarding retroactive or prospective application. Therefore, we must determine whether the 2009 amendment was substantive or interpretive.

Substantive laws either establish new rules, rights, and duties or change existing ones. Interpretive laws, on the other hand, do not create new rules, but merely establish the meaning that the interpreted statute had from the time of its initial enactment. It is the original statute, not the interpretive one, that establishes the rights and duties. St. Paul Fire & Marine Insurance Co. v. Smith, 609 So.2d 809, 817 (La.1992). When an existing law is not clear, a subsequent statute clarifying or explaining the law may be regarded as interpretive, and the interpretive statute may be given retroactive effect because it does not change, but merely clarifies, pre-existing law. St. Paul Fire & Marine Insurance Co., 609 So.2d at 817.

As noted by the Louisiana Supreme Court, the suggested distinction between interpretive legislation "clarifying," and substantive legislation "amending" or "changing," existing law is an obscure one. There is no bright line between substantive laws, which change existing standards, and interpretive laws, which change existing standards by re-defining and returning to their ostensible "original" meaning. St. Paul Fire & Marine Insurance Co., 609 So.2d at 819.

The revision comments to Article 2365 state that the second paragraph of this Article is new and incorporates the substantial volume of Louisiana jurisprudence that has limited a spouse's right to reimbursement for the use of separate funds after termination of the community property regime to satisfy a community note obligation for an automobile of which the claimant spouse has the exclusive use. La. C.C. art. 2365, 2009 Revision Comment (b). The First Circuit, however, did not follow the other four circuits in so limiting a spouse's right to reimbursement, finding that the plain language of then Article 2365 did not provide a basis for treating reimbursement claims differently depending on the nature of the property for which the debt was paid. See Williams, 509 So.2d at 80. Additionally, 2009 Revision Comment (c) notes that the jurisprudence has previously reduced a spouse's right to reimbursement without any authority in the Civil Code.

Because the original codal article did not distinguish reimbursement claims based on the nature of the property subject to the obligation, and it was not until the 2009 amendment that a claimant spouse's right to reimbursement was reduced, or effectively eliminated, based on the nature of the property, we find that the 2009 amendment is substantive, in that it represents a distinct change in the rights of the parties. Under La. C.C. art. 6, a substantive change in the law cannot be applied retroactively.

Therefore, because Article 2365, as enacted prior to the 2009 amendment, did not limit a claimant spouse's right to reimbursement for one-half of the payments made on a community vehicle after termination of the community, and this court applied the plain language of the statute as written, we find that the trial court erred in failing to award Troy reimbursement for one-half of the monthly notes paid on the community automobile from the time of the termination of the community until the effective date of the 2009 amendment, August 15, 2009. Accordingly, we reverse the trial court judgment on this issue and award Troy $6,796.50 in reimbursement for one-half of the truck note payments.

Reimbursement of Funds to Repair Clipper Drive Residence

Troy asserts that the trial court erred in denying his claim for reimbursement for separate funds used to repair the Clipper Drive home after Hurricane Katrina. In denying Troy's reimbursement claim, the trial court found that Troy's failure to timely file an accounting of the homeowner's insurance proceeds, as required by two previous consent judgments, precluded him from introducing evidence accounting for funds used to make repairs to the residence.

First, we reiterate that the Clipper Drive home is not community property but is co-owned by Troy and Tammy in indivision. Accordingly, the Civil Code articles regarding co-ownership apply. Louisiana Civil Code article 806 provides:

> A co-owner who on account of the thing held in indivision has incurred necessary expenses, expenses for ordinary maintenance and repairs, or necessary management expenses paid to a third person, is entitled to reimbursement from the other co-owners in proportion to their shares.

Though Troy was precluded from introducing evidence at the community property partition proceeding of the repairs made to the Clipper Drive home following Hurricane Katrina, he did proffer receipts and pictures of the repairs. However, even considering the proffered evidence, we find that Troy failed to put forth sufficient evidence to establish a claim for reimbursement.

Troy testified that he made repairs to the Clipper Drive home, but he did not provide details as to the total repairs made, nor did he quantify the amount of funds used to make such repairs. Additionally, though the proffered evidence consists of photos of the repairs and numerous receipts, Troy admitted in his testimony that the proffered receipts were for repairs made to the Clipper Drive residence and the Pine Tree property. Troy, however, did not offer any testimony or evidence separating the expenses paid for repairs to the Clipper Drive home from those made to the Pine Tree Street property. Finally, when combined with the fact that Troy failed to provide a complete and detailed accounting of the homeowner's insurance proceeds he received as required by two previous consent judgments, it is impossible for us to determine from the record before us what expenses were incurred in making the repairs to the Clipper Drive home or the amount thereof. Therefore, we find no error in the trial court's denial of this reimbursement claim.

Reimbursement to Troy for Mortgage Payments on Clipper Drive Residence

Troy asserts that the trial court erred in valuing his claim for reimbursement for payments made on the mortgage on 1181 Clipper Drive. Specifically, Troy contends that the trial court erred in reducing reimbursement for one-half of the mortgage payments based on the value of Troy's enjoyment of the property under the Civil Code articles regarding co-ownership.

In accordance with La. C.C. art. 806, a co-owner who has incurred necessary expenses or maintenance and management expenses is entitled to reimbursement from the other co-owners, except that if he who incurred the expenses had the enjoyment of the thing, the reimbursement is to be reduced in proportion to the value of his enjoyment. A mortgage, however, is not such an expense. It is a nonpossessory right created over property to secure the *1029 performance of an obligation. Lupberger v. Lupberger, 00–2571, p. 11 (La.App. 4th Cir.12/5/01), 805 So.2d 264, 271, writ denied, 02–0653 (La.5/24/02), 816 So.2d 308; Roque v. Tate, 93–389, p. 3 (La.App. 5th Cir.2/9/94), 631 So.2d 1385, 1386, writ not considered, 94–0625 (La.4/29/94), 637 So.2d 457; see also La. C.C. art. 3278.

Furthermore, though the property itself was co-owned by the parties in indivision, the mortgage at issue was incurred by the spouses during the existence of the community and as such, it is presumed to be a community obligation. See La. C.C. arts. 2360 and 2361. Troy and Tammy do not dispute that the mortgage on the Clipper Drive home is a community obligation. Therefore, the controlling law is not the Civil Code articles relating to co-ownership of property, but La. C.C. art. 2365, regarding reimbursement for satisfaction of a community obligation with separate property. See Lupberger, 00–2571 at p. 11, 805 So.2d at 271. Accordingly, the trial court erred in applying La. C.C. art. 806 to reduce Troy's reimbursement claim.

Tammy, however, asserts that even if the trial court erred in reducing Troy's mortgage reimbursement claim based on the value of Troy's enjoyment of the property under La. C.C. art. 806, which the trial court determined to be the rental value of the property, it was still correct in deducting the rental value of the property under La. R.S. 9:374.

Louisiana Revised Statute 9:374 provided, in part:

> B. When the family residence is community property or the spouses own community movables or immovables, after or in conjunction with the filing of a petition for divorce or for separation of property in accordance with Civil Code Article 2374, either spouse may petition for, and a court may award to one of the spouses, after a contradictory hearing, the use and occupancy of the family residence and use of community movables or immovables to either of the spouses pending further order of the court. In these cases, the court shall inquire into the relative economic status of the spouses, including both community and separate property, and the needs of the children, if any, and shall award the use and occupancy of the family residence and the use of any community movables or immovables to the spouse in accordance with the best interest of the family. If applicable, the court shall consider the granting of the occupancy of the family home and the use of community movables or immovables in awarding spousal support.
>
> C. A spouse who uses and occupies or is awarded by the court the use and occupancy of the family residence pending either the termination of the marriage or the partition of the community property in accordance with the provisions of La. R.S. 9:374(A) or (B) shall not be liable to the other spouse for rental for the use and occupancy, except as hereafter provided. If the court awards use and occupancy to a spouse, it shall at that time determine whether or not to award rental for the use and occupancy and, if so, the amount of the rent. The parties may agree to defer the rental issue for decision in the partition proceedings. If the parties agreed at the time of the award of use and occupancy to defer the rental issue, the court may make an award of rental retroactive to the date of the award of use and occupancy. [Emphasis added.]

Assuming, arguendo, that Tammy has a claim for rental reimbursement for Troy's use and occupancy of the family residence that was co-owned, and not community property, we find that she failed to preserve this claim under the provisions of La. R.S. 9:374(C).8

In her answer and reconventional demand to the petition for 102 divorce filed by Troy, Tammy sought use and occupancy of the family home, and alternatively, requested the assessment of a rental value for Troy's exclusive use of the home. By consent judgment dated August 17, 2006, the trial court ordered:

[T]hat the motions filed on behalf of Troy Benoit and Tammy Williams Benoit for exclusive use and occupancy of the family home shall be continued indefinitely. Tammy Williams Benoit's rule for rental value assessment against Troy Benoit should the Court award exclusive use and occupancy of the family home to Troy Benoit shall be reserved to her and to be determined at the time of the partition of the community property. [Emphasis added.]

However, the exclusive use and occupancy of the family home was never awarded to Troy by the court. Rather, Tammy testified at the hearing that she did not pursue her claim for exclusive use and occupancy of the family home, because following Hurricane Katrina, Troy had nowhere else to go and she did not want to "put Troy on the street." Further, though Tammy stated that there was an agreement to allow Troy to remain in the family home, because she had other living arrangements, this agreement was never reduced to judgment, nor is there evidence that at the time the parties allegedly made an agreement regarding use and occupancy of the family home they also agreed to defer the rental issue.

From our review of the record, and based on the clear language of the August 17, 2006 consent judgment, we do not find that the parties contemporaneously agreed at the time of the award of use and occupancy of the family home to defer the rental issue as required by La. R.S. 9:374(C). As such, Troy is not liable to Tammy for rental for his use and occupancy under La. R.S. 9:374.

Therefore, based on the foregoing, we find that the trial court abused its discretion in offsetting the amount of reimbursement owed to Troy for payments made on the mortgage on 1181 Clipper Drive by the rental value of the property. Accordingly, we find that Troy is entitled to reimbursement for one-half of the total mortgage payments made during the community and up to the time of trial in the amount of $67,802.50.

Deferral and Security of Equalization Payment

Finally, Troy asserts that the trial court erred in permitting Tammy eighteen months to make the equalizing cash payment without proper security. According to La. R.S. 9:2801 A(4)(d), in the event that the allocation of assets and liabilities results in an unequal net distribution, the court shall order the payment of an equalizing sum of money, either cash or deferred, secured or unsecured, upon such terms and conditions as the court may direct. Further, the court may order the execution of notes, mortgages, or other documents as it deems necessary, or may impose a mortgage or lien on either community or separate property, movable or immovable, as security. La. R.S. 9:2801 A(4)(d). Accordingly, a trial court is only required to order the payment of an equalizing sum of money. The determinations of whether that sum should be cash or deferred, secured or unsecured and what terms and conditions, if any, should be applied to the payment are left to the discretion of the trial court. See Trahan v. Trahan, 10–0109, p. 7 (La.App. 1st Cir.6/11/10), 43 So.3d 218, 224, writ denied, 10–2014 (La.11/12/10), 49 So.3d 889.

In its judgment, the trial court ordered that "Tammy Williams Benoit shall pay to Troy Benoit an equalizing cash payment of $21,993.18, which equalizing cash payment shall act as a mortgage on 792 Pine Street, Slidell, Louisiana until paid. The equalizing cash payment shall accrue legal interest until paid. Tammy Williams Benoit shall have eighteen (18) months to remit the equalizing payment to Troy Benoit." However, based on the findings of this court, Tammy's equalizing cash payment has drastically increased. Therefore, given the circumstances, this matter should be remanded to the trial court for reconsideration.

CONCLUSION

For the above and foregoing reasons, we vacate the trial court's judgment of partition and remand this matter to the trial court to enter a new judgment in conformity with the findings of this court and to fashion a repayment plan under such terms and conditions as the trial court deems appropriate.

JUDGMENT VACATED AND REMANDED WITH INSTRUCTIONS.

M. *Lisa Womack Gill v. Craig Gerard Gill*

895 So. 2d 801 (La. App. 2d Cir. 2005)

CARAWAY, J.

In this case, the trial court divided the community property acquired during the parties' marriage and awarded certain reimbursement claims. Both parties have appealed, raising numerous issues regarding the valuation and division of the property. We amend the judgment in part, and as amended, affirm the partition of the community property.

Facts

Lisa and Craig Gill were married on September 19, 1999. The couple began their marriage residing in the home of Lisa and her previous husband, who had died of cancer in 1998. Lisa had two sons. One of the boys resided with Lisa when she married Craig.

In June of 2000, Lisa and Craig purchased a new house and fifteen acres of land for the sum of $170,000. Lisa used $113,697 of her separate property for the purchase of the home, closing costs and improvements to the house. The remaining value of the house and property was financed through Winnsboro State Bank.

* * *

At the time of the marriage, Craig worked as a funeral director with Riser Funeral Home in Winnsboro. These earnings were placed into their joint account at Progressive State Bank. On June 8, 2001, Craig and Lisa purchased the Riser Funeral Home for the price of $375,000. Lisa utilized $45,000 of her separate funds as a down payment. The transaction for the acquisition of the business actually placed title to the immovable property in Craig and Lisa. The price listed in the deed for the land and building for the funeral home was the entire $375,000 purchase price for the business.

By January of 2002, Craig moved out of the family home and began residing in the funeral home. Lisa filed for divorce on February 20, 2002, and the parties were granted a judgment of divorce on February 6, 2003. When the parties could not amicably settle the community, trial for the partition of property occurred in June and December 2003. In relevant part, the trial court valued the subject properties and classified as community property the house and fifteen acres, the land and building for Gill First National Funeral Home, Gill LLC, Lisa's CPA practice, the 2000 Ford vehicle, and the parties' checking accounts. Community debt consisted of the loans relating to the purchase of the funeral home, the house and land and the 2000 Ford vehicle.

In partitioning the assets, the trial court awarded Lisa the house and fifteen acres, the 2000 Ford vehicle, some house furniture and certain bank accounts with balances totaling $7,911.81. Craig was allocated the land and building for the funeral home, Gill LLC and two trailers. The court assessed Craig with $115,102.02 and Lisa with $46,122.25 in reimbursements and, after partition of the assets, ordered Craig to pay Lisa an equalizing payment in the amount of $20,167.05 (including the $3,915 contained in Craig's Franklin State Bank checking account). Both parties appeal the court's valuation of Gill LLC and Lisa's CPA practice and certain reimbursements.

Discussion

* * *

Another of Lisa's reimbursement claims under Article 2365 concerns her payments on the family home mortgage. Lisa continued to live in the home after the marriage without agreement between the spouses or court order governing the occupancy of the home. The partition placed full ownership of the home in her name. The record indicates that the parties stipulated that Lisa paid $20,401 on the home mortgage debt from February 2, 2002 until December of 2003.

Interpreting Article 2365 for community automobile debt, the courts have held that a spouse who has the exclusive use of an automobile following the termination of the community is not entitled to credit for notes she paid on the vehicle. See, Bergeron v. Bergeron, 96-1586 (La. App. 3d Cir. 4/9/97), 693 So.2d 199; Preis v. Preis, 94-442 (La. App. 3d Cir.11/2/94), 649 So.2d 593,writs denied, 94-2939, 94-2942 (La. 1/27/95), 649 So.2d 392. Davezac v. Davezac, 483 So.2d 1197 (La. App. 4th Cir. 1986), explained that this occurs because an automobile rapidly depreciates so that its use is directly related to its depreciation. We agree with this reasoning. The car note payments by the spouse using the vehicle are considered as payment for the depreciation caused by such use. Therefore, the trial court's rejection of this reimbursement claim is affirmed.

Regarding the family home, however, reimbursement under Article 2365 is viewed differently. The rapid depreciation concept is not present for a home, the value of which more typically appreciates. Also, the use of the family home after the termination of the community is the subject of the special statutory provision, La. R.S. 9:374(C), which allows for the possibility of an adjudication and award of rent for the use of the home in favor of the non-occupying spouse. When the non-occupying spouse seeks no court ruling under the statute or reaches no agreement with the other spouse for the payment of rent, the general rule of the law of co-ownership applies and "neither [spouse] becomes indebted to the other for his personal occupancy." McCarroll v. McCarroll, 96-2700 (La. 10/21/97), 701 So.2d 1280, 1290; La. C.C. arts. 2369.1 and 802. Thus, under the ruling in McCarroll interpreting these principles, the non-occupying spouse is barred from receiving a retroactive assessment of rent to a spouse whose occupancy was not the result of a court order imposing rent or an agreement for including rent.

In the absence of receiving rent, which would serve to offset all or a portion of an Article 2365 reimbursement claim against him, the non-occupying spouse is required to reimburse the occupying spouse for her payments on the mortgage indebtedness on the family home. Ball v. Ball, 32,851 (La. App. 2d Cir. 3/1/00), 757 So.2d 824. From this authority, the trial court erred in this case in not awarding Lisa her reimbursement claim for her payments on the community indebtedness after the termination of the community. That portion of the trial court's ruling is reversed.

Note

Gill v. Gill allows reimbursement for post-termination, pre-partition expenditures, a result also sanctioned by the First, Fourth, and Fifth Circuits. *See Moody v. Moody*, 622 So. 2d 1381 (La. App. 1st Cir. 1983); *Davezac v. Davezac*, 483 So. 2d 1197 (La. App. 4th Cir. 1986); *Gachez v. Gachez*, 451 So. 2d 608 (La. App. 5th Cir. 1984). The Third Circuit, in *Bordelon v. Bordelon*, 942 So. 2d 708 (La. App. 3d Cir. 2006), held that the Civil Code;s reimbursement scheme contemplates recoupment of monies paid out only during the existence of the community property regime.

Four Louisiana Circuits have denied a spouse's reimbursement claims for payments made on automobile indebtedness, for the reasons described in *Gill. See also Mason v. Mason*, 927 So. 2d 1235 (La. App. 2d Cir. 2006); *Sheridon v. Sheridon*, 867 So. 2d 38 (La. App. 3d Cir. 2004); *Davezac v. Davezac*, 483 So. 2d 1197 (La. App. 4th Cir. 1986); *Gachez v. Gachez*, 451 So. 2d 608 (La. App. 5th Cir. 1984). The First Circuit is the only one to allow reimbursement for all types of property, noting that the Civil Code makes no distinctions based on type of property. *See Williams, infra.*

N. *James E. Oliver v. Joe Ann Cotton Oliver*

561 So. 2d 908 (La. App. 2d Cir. 1990)

LINDSAY, Judge.

This appeal arises from a judgment rendered in a suit for judicial partition of the community between James E. Oliver and Joe Ann Cotton Oliver. Mr. Oliver appealed, citing several alleged errors by the trial court. Mrs. Oliver answered the appeal.

FACTS

The parties were married June 3, 1959. Of this marriage two children were born, both of whom have now achieved majority. The parties physically separated in July of 1982. Mrs. Oliver moved to Lafayette, Louisiana, where she obtained employment. Mr. Oliver remained at the matrimonial domicile in Shreveport.

On September 23, 1982, Mr. Oliver filed a petition for separation. Mrs. Oliver did not contest these proceedings, and a judgment of legal separation was signed October 27, 1982. At this point, the community was dissolved, retroactive to the filing of the separation suit on September 23, 1982.

On April 29, 1983, Mr. Oliver filed a petition for divorce. The divorce was granted by judgment signed on June 1, 1983.

On June 15, 1987, Mrs. Oliver filed a petition for judicial partition of the community property. After lengthy discovery proceedings, trial on the merits was held on February 10, 1989. On the same day, in response to Mrs. Oliver's claims for an accounting for community funds allegedly withdrawn by Mr. Oliver, Mr. Oliver filed an exception of prescription based on LSA-C.C.Art. 2369. This article provides that the obligation to account prescribes in three years from the date of the termination of the community property regime.

At trial, the parties entered into a joint stipulation which established a number of the community assets and their values, as well as outstanding community debts and some reimbursement claims. The stipulation set forth a formula for computing the value of Mrs. Oliver's interest in her husband's Riley-Beaird retirement plan.

The stipulation further outlined disputed community assets and values as well as disputed reimbursement claims asserted by the parties. The stipulation pointed out that disputed issues at the time of trial included the interest and/or rent claim by Mrs. Oliver against Mr. Oliver for his use and possession of the community home following the separation of the parties; Mr. Oliver's claim for interest payments in the amount of \$3,766.17 made to CNB on a loan; Mr. Oliver's salary from March of 1982 until the termination of the community; and the formula to be used to compute the parties' reimbursement claims.

Next, the trial court considered the one remaining dispute as to classification of debts as community or separate. The trial court specifically found that Mr. Oliver was entitled to reimbursement as provided by law for interest payments he made in the amount of \$3,766.17 on a CNB loan originally taken out by Mrs. Oliver to pay community debts prior to their physical separation. The original loan from CNB was a community obligation, which Mr. Oliver refinanced in November of 1982.

The trial court also addressed the formula by which the parties' various reimbursement claims were to be computed. Both parties claimed that they had expended their separate funds to pay community debts. These claims included the parties' stipulated claims against each other (\$29,903 for Mr. Oliver and \$2,339.25 for Mrs. Oliver), as well as Mr. Oliver's claim for reimbursement of his separate funds in the amount of \$3,766.17, representing interest payments on the loan at CNB. Based upon this court's rationale in Nash v. Nash, 486 So.2d 1011 (La. App. 2d Cir. 1986), the trial court found that each spouse was entitled to be reimbursed in the amount of one-half of each claim from the mass of the community estate instead of full reimbursement.

Mr. Oliver appealed suspensively. He assigned as error the following: (1) the trial court erred in (a), ordering reimbursement to Mr. Oliver from the community of acquets and gains, and (b) in limiting his reimbursement to only one-half of the separate funds he used to satisfy community obligations; (2) the trial court erred in overruling his exception of prescription as to the \$5,000 withdrawal he made on September 20, 1982; and (3) the trial court erred in awarding Mrs. Oliver legal interest on her undivided interest in the community from the date the community terminated on September 23, 1982, until paid.

Mrs. Oliver answered the appeal. She assigned as error the following: (1) the trial court's failure to require Mr. Oliver to account for all of his withdrawals of community funds; (2) Mr. Oliver's failure to account for his salary of $13,500; and (3) the trial court's classification of $3,766.17 in interest payments on the CNB loan as a community debt. In brief, Mrs. Oliver refers to her first two assignments of error only in her response to the prescription issue.

REIMBURSEMENT

Mr. Oliver argues that the trial court erred when it ordered that he receive reimbursement from the community, rather than from Mrs. Oliver, of one-half of the separate funds he used to satisfy community debts, which consisted primarily of mortgage payments on the family home. In so ordering, the trial court observed that it was bound by this court's decision in Nash v. Nash, *supra*. In Nash, this court adopted the rationale in Gachez v. Gachez, 451 So.2d 608 (La. App. 5th Cir. 1984), *writ denied*, 456 So.2d 166 (La. 1984). Mr. Oliver argues that Gachez improperly applied L.C.C. Art. 2365. We agree.

The applicable articles are LSA-C.C. Art. 2336, 2358 and 2365 which provide as follows:

In Gachez, *supra*, the Fifth Circuit ignored Art. 2358. The court simply held that under Art. 2365 a spouse was entitled to reimbursement from the community assets of one-half of the amount of separate funds expended on mortgage payments on the family home, a community debt. The court acknowledged that the spouse seeking full reimbursement, rather than one-half, had cited several cases in support of his argument. However, the court found that those cases arose "prior to the enactment of C.C. art. 2365 and codification of the law relating to one-half reimbursement."

Interpretation of the Civil Code articles governing reimbursement between spouses upon termination of the community has been addressed by various law review commentators. The rationale in Gachez in particular has invited scrutiny by legal scholars. See Spaht, "Developments in the Law, 1984-1985 - Matrimonial Regimes", 46 L.L.R. 559, 565-566 (1986).

A recently published commentary discussed reimbursement calculations as follows:

> "By the allocation of assets and liabilities and necessary adjustments, each spouse is to receive one-half of the net value of the community. For purposes of reimbursement, it is *after* that calculation that reimbursement claims can be asserted. It is improper to deduct a reimbursement claim from the total net value of the community assets. The claim for reimbursement is a personal right *asserted by one spouse against the other, not against an entity called the community*. Secondly, the amount of reimbursement is one-half of the amount expended, rather than the total amount. The limitation [provided in the last

> paragraph of Art. 2365] imposed upon the claim for reimbursement was not intended to permit the claim to be asserted against the total net community. It was intended to permit reimbursement only if the spouse from whom it was claimed had a share of former community property that was sufficient to satisfy the claim." (emphasis supplied)

K. Spaht and L. Hargrave, Matrimonial Regimes § 7.14, p. 285 in 16 Louisiana Civil Law Treatise, (1989).

The various courts of appeal have differed in their application of Gachez. It has been cited with approval by this circuit in Gilley v. Ketchens, 478 So.2d 638 (La. App. 2d Cir. 1985); *Nash, supra*; and *Kaplan v. Kaplan*, 522 So.2d 1344 (La. App. 2d Cir. 1988). Its rationale was also applied in *Freeman v. Freeman*, 552 So.2d 636 (La. App. 2d Cir. 1989). However, those cases simply relied upon Gachez and a literal reading of Arts. 2365 or 2367 (a companion reimbursement article concerning the use of separate property to acquire or benefit community property) with no analysis of the reasons for the rule or its application in conjunction with C.C. Art. 2358 and prior jurisprudence.

However, in Davezac v. Davezac, 483 So.2d 1197 (La. App. 4th Cir. 1986), the Fourth Circuit specifically declined to follow Gachez because of its erroneous interpretation of Art. 2365. The court discussed Art. 2365 and a line of cases in the jurisprudence which included Kennedy and Lentz, *supra*:

> "Although this article, a part of the 1979 revision of our law on matrimonial regimes, was not in existence when the cited cases arose, we do not consider them to be inconsistent with the article. As we read it appellant is entitled to be reimbursed one-half of the payments he made out of appellee's share of the community. The article would seem to prevent reimbursement in this case if there were no community assets but it does not purport to direct reimbursement to appellant from the mass of the community. To adopt appellee's interpretation would lead to the inequitable result of appellant being "reimbursed" for one-half of the amounts he paid from funds of which he owns half. The net result would be that he would pay seventy-five percent of the payments to maintain a community asset from which the wife would eventually derive one-half of the proceeds.

We agree with appellee that the Gachez case supports her position. However, for the reasons stated we have concluded that Gachez is incorrect in its interpretation of Art. 2365 and we decline to follow the case. Therefore, this portion of the trial court's judgment is to be amended to provide that reimbursement to appellant for one-half of the mortgage payments shall be made from appellee's share of the assets of the former community."

In Sellers v. Landry, 489 So.2d 440 (La. App. 3rd Cir. 1986), the Third Circuit agreed with the conclusion reached in Davezec. It held that the spouse seeking reimbursement was entitled to full reimbursement from the gross community assets or one-half of the value of the expended separate property from the other spouse's one-half of the divided community assets. The court noted that the result would be the same in either case.

In *Williams v. Williams*, 509 So.2d 77 (La. App. 1st Cir. 1987), the First Circuit adopted the holding in Sellers, supra. It found that, while Art. 2365 stated that a spouse was entitled to reimbursement of one-half of the separate funds used to pay community debts, Art. 2365 "does not purport to direct reimbursement to appellant from the mass of the community." As in Sellers, *supra*, the court approved full reimbursement from the gross community funds or one-half reimbursement from the other spouse's one-half of the gross community assets following their division between the spouses.

We further note that the Fifth Circuit, which handed down Gachez, recently cited Williams, *supra*, with approval in Cabral v. Cabral, 543 So.2d 952 (La. App. 5th Cir. 1989), writs denied, 548 So.2d 328, 332. In a discussion of Arts. 2365 and 2367, the court noted: "It has further been held that the reimbursement of one-half of the separate property used for community purposes is to be made from the other spouse's one-half interest in the community, rather than from the total mass of community property, *Williams v. Williams* [citation omitted]." The Second Circuit has also cited the Williams and Davezac cases with approval in Dilley v. Dilley, No. 21,401-CA, also rendered this day.

Articles 2336, 2358, and 2365, as laws in pari materia, must be construed and read together. Art. 2336 provides that the community of acquets and gains is not a legal entity, but a patrimonial mass. The patrimony of each spouse includes only an undivided one-half of the mass of the community property during the existence of the regime. Furthermore, Art. 2358 provides that the reimbursement claims are made between the spouses, not against "the community." In Art. 2365 it is established that a spouse is entitled to reimbursement of one-half. We find that the correct interpretation of these articles mandates recovery from Mrs. Oliver, to the extent of community assets, of one-half of Mr. Oliver's separate property which was used to pay community debts of $29,903.00. We hereby acknowledge that Nash, supra, and its progeny, to the extent that they adopted Gachez's erroneous interpretation of the reimbursement articles, contain error which we can no longer follow.

Furthermore, in the interest of justice, we apply the corrected reimbursement formula to both parties. Thus, Mrs. Oliver is entitled to reimbursement of one-half of the stipulated amount of $2,339.25 from Mr. Oliver's half of the community. LSA-C.C.P.Art. 2164.

LOAN INTEREST PAYMENTS

Mrs. Oliver argues that the trial court erred in recognizing as a community debt the interest payments of $3,766.17 paid by Mr. Oliver on the renegotiated CNB loan. The evidence demonstrated that the CNB loan was taken out by Mrs. Oliver on February 5, 1982, to pay off community debts. In November of 1982, (after the termination of the community), the bank gave Mr. Oliver the option of either renewing the note in his own name or paying off the loan. He chose to renew it. Mr. Oliver paid $3,766.17 in interest payments. The note was stamped "paid" on September 6, 1988. The trial court found that this sum paid by Mr. Oliver was a community obligation and that he was entitled to a reimbursement claim.

We agree with the trial court. Although Mr. Oliver did not consult Mrs. Oliver prior to renewing the note, his actions were obviously in the best interest of the community. The evidence fails to demonstrate that Mr. Oliver intended to create a new separate obligation. To the contrary, he was merely maintaining the status quo on payment of an already existing community debt. To find otherwise would be to ignore the financial reality facing a solidary obligor in Mr. Oliver's position. Also, see *Michel v. Michel*, 484 So.2d 829, 832 (La. App. 1st Cir. 1986).

We find no merit in this assignment of error.

CONCLUSION

Accordingly, we amend and affirm as amended. The judgment is hereby amended to provide that reimbursement to each spouse shall be made from the other spouse's one-half share of the community and that legal interest is awarded to Mrs. Oliver on her one-half of $6,000 from the date of judicial demand, June 15, 1987, until the date of this opinion. . . .

O. *Susan Munson v. Lawrence Munson*

772 So. 2d 141 (La. App. 3d Cir. 2000)

WOODARD, Judge.

In this community property partition litigation, Mr. Lawrence Munson appeals a trial court's decision, awarding Ms. Susan Munson full ownership of their former family home on Thirteenth Street in Lake Charles, Louisiana (the 13th Street home), a Dodge mini-van, a boat and trailer, the Whitney National Bank account's balance, along with a $25,637.53 judgment.

Furthermore, Mr. Munson maintains that the trial court erred when it awarded Ms. Munson one-half of the total amount which the community remitted on a separate property mortgage. We find inapposite the well-established jurisprudential exception that community may only be reimbursed for that part of the payment accruing to the mortgage's principal but not to interests. We find such an exception applicable when the mortgaged separate property benefitted the community. Finding no error in the trial court's decision that Mr. Munson's separate property did not benefit the community, we affirm.

Ms. and Mr. Munson, both had children from prior unions when they married on February 24, 1984. They did not have any children together. Apparently, they separated in August of 1993, and on June 27, 1994, Ms. Munson petitioned for divorce. On July 27, 1994, upon the Munsons' stipulation, the trial court signed a judgment, awarding the use and occupancy of their 13th Street family home to Ms. Munson. They also agreed that their community property was to be deemed terminated. The trial court entered a divorce judgment on August 25, 1994.

On February 29, 1996, Mr. Munson filed a petition to partition their former community property. In a judgment entered on December 3, 1999, the trial court awarded the 13th Street home's full ownership to Ms. Munson, as well as a Dodge mini-van, a boat and trailer, the Whitney National Bank account's balance, along with $25,637.53. Mr. Munson appeals.

MR. MUNSON'S SEPARATE MORTGAGE PAYMENTS

During their marriage, the community paid a total of $57,820.00 on Mr. Munson's separate property mortgage payments. Ms. Munson sought, and the trial court awarded her, one-half of the payment, namely, $28,910.00. Mr. Munson appeals, arguing that the trial court's decision amounts to a legal error.

Relying on Major v. Major and Longo v. Longo, Mr. Munson insists that the trial court erred when including in its award, the community assets repaying the mortgage interest.

La.Civ.Code art. 2364 provides that "[i]f community property has been used to satisfy a separate obligation of a spouse, the other spouse is entitled to reimbursement upon termination of the community property regime **for one-half of the *amount or value* that the property had at the time it was used**" (emphases added). Article 2364 clearly and unambiguously provides for the actual value of the used community property to serve as a restitution measure.

The Longo-Major courts, along with others, departed from Article 2364's and its predecessors' precepts, in the specific situation where the community property receives benefits from the separate property upon which the mortgage attaches. The Major-Longo jurisprudence read Article 2364 in pari materia with La.Civ.Code art. 2339, which provides, in relevant part, that "[t]he natural and civil fruits of the separate property of a spouse ... are community property." The Major-Longo courts found an interest payment to be no more than the cost of maintaining such natural and civil fruits which arise out of a spouse's separate property but ultimately accrue to the community's use or benefit.

In the case sub judice, our thorough review of the record reveals that Mr. Munson's separate property at issue did not benefit the community in the way described in the Major-Longo jurisprudence. His property neither generated any rent, to which the community property would be entitled, nor was it used as the Munson's family home. Ms. Munson testified that she did not possess a key to the property and that she never went to it after the first year of their marriage. Accordingly, we find the Major-Longo jurisprudence to be inapposite to the case sub judice and affirm the trial court's decision.

CONCLUSION

For the aforementioned reasons, we affirm the trial court's decision and cast all costs against Mr. Munson.

AFFIRMED.

P. *Carmela C. Brehm v. Milton L. Brehm, Jr.*

762 So. 2d 1259 (La. App. 5 Cir. 2000)

McMANUS, Judge.

Plaintiff, Carmella C. Brehm, and defendant, Milton C. Brehm, Jr., appeal from a district court judgment partitioning the community. For the following reasons, we affirm in part, reverse in part and render.

On appeal, Mr. Brehm assigns these trial court errors:

The trial court erred as a matter of law in holding that the matrimonial domicile on the separate estate of Mr. Brehm became community property through the use of community funds to construct improvements.

Ms. Brehm assigned these trial court errors:

In the event that this Court finds that the matrimonial domicile is Mr. Brehm's separate property, the trial court erred in failing to find that Ms. Brehm is entitled to the increased value of the property attributable to common labor of the spouses.

FACTS

The parties, Mr. Brehm and Ms. Brehm, were married for approximately thirty years, and had four daughters. The record reflects that Ms. Brehm left the matrimonial domicile in August of 1993. On January 13, 1994, the parties were granted a judgment of divorce.

On May 17, 1994, Ms. Brehm filed a petition of community property. On March 16, 1998, the parties entered into a consent judgment which reflected those issues on which the parties agreed. On March 27, 1998, the court rendered a judgment in open court. On September 9, 1999, the court signed a written judgment in accordance with the court's oral judgment. In its judgment, the trial court ruled that the marital domicile, valued at $140,000, is community property, and that the money inherited by both Mr. and Ms. Brehm is community property because it was commingled. The trial court further ruled that Ms. Brehm owes reimbursement to the community for cashing the Lincoln National Life Insurance policies in the amount of $15,856.68, subject to a credit of all fees. The trial court further ruled that Ms. Brehm owes reimbursement to Mr. Brehm for permanent periodic alimony, and health insurance and automobile insurance premiums. The trial court further ruled that Mr. Brehm is entitled to reimbursement for paying the homeowners' insurance premiums to Liberty Mutual Insurance Company (Liberty Mutual) and Prudential Property and Casualty Insurance Company (Prudential), flood insurance, property and casualty insurance, and termite and pest control costs. The trial court further ruled that the lot adjacent to 1721 High Street is Mr. Brehm's separate property. Finally, the trial court ordered that both parties be responsible for the tax consequences of the rendered judgment.

VALUATION OF MATRIMONIAL DOMICILE

Mr. Brehm argues that the matrimonial domicile did not become community property by the use of community funds to construct the house and subsequent improvements. Ms. Brehm responds that the matrimonial domicile became community property through the uncompensated labor of the spouses. She further responds that the couple re-financed the matrimonial domicile for $10,000 on August 6, 1969, and that the sale and re-sale was an act of donation which gave her an undivided half interest in the house.

The matrimonial domicile of the parties is located at 1721 High Avenue in Metairie, Louisiana. There were two adjoining, vacant lots before the parties were married. After the parties were married, they spent $23,588.93 of community funds to build a home on one of the vacant lots. There is no dispute on appeal as to the separate nature of the lots that belong to Mr. Brehm.

LSA-C.C. art. 2366 provides, in pertinent part:

Buildings, other constructions permanently attached to the ground, and plantings made on the separate property of a spouse with community assets belong to the owner of the ground. Upon termination of the community, the other spouse is entitled to one-half of the amount or value that the community assets had at the time they were used.

Since the matrimonial domicile was built with community funds on Mr. Brehm's separate property, Ms. Brehm is entitled to a claim for reimbursement for one half of the funds used to build the home. See Barr v. Barr, 613 So.2d 1159, 1164 (La. App. 5th Cir. 1993); McDonald v. McDonald, 607 So.2d 984, 987 (La. App. 3d Cir. 1992); Bordelon v. Cobb, 596 So.2d 268, 270 (La. App. 3d Cir. 1992).

Ms. Brehm argues that she is entitled to the increased value of the property from the spouses' uncompensated labor. We disagree.

LSA-C.C. art. 2368 states:

If the separate property of a spouse has increased in value as a result of the uncompensated common labor or industry of the spouses, the other spouse is entitled to be reimbursed from the spouse whose property has increased in value one-half of the increase attributed to the common labor.

A claimant spouse under LSA-C.C. art. 2368 has the burden of proving: (1) the property is separate, (2) the property increased in value, and (3) the increase in value was based on the uncompensated or undercompensated labor of the other spouse; the burden then shifts to the other spouse to prove that the increase in value was due to factors other than the uncompensated or undercompensated labor. Salley v. Salley, 95-0387 (La. 10/16/95), 661 So.2d 437, 438; Krielow v. Krielow, 93-2539 (La. 4/11/94), 635 So.2d 180, 183.

In Stubbs v. Stubbs, 610 So.2d 892 (La. App. 1st Cir. 1992),writ denied, 612 So.2d 62 (La.1993), the First Circuit found that the increase in value of the home, which was separate property, was attributable to common labor of the parties. In Stubbs, the testimony of the parties established that during the marriage, the parties shared the labor required to expand the roof of the house, add a porch, add a living room and add a garage to the house. Id. at 897. The parties also placed paneling in the house and installed new carpeting. Id.

In this case, the marital domicile was built with community funds during Mr. and Ms. Brehm's marriage. The cost of building the house was $23,588.93. Both Mr. and Ms. Brehm testified that improvements were made to the house. The record reflects that Ms. Brehm painted, installed new wallpaper, and performed other routine repairs and improvements while Mr. Brehm added a new roof and a new patio to the house. While the Brehms did perform routine maintenance during the marriage, the record indicates that the substantial part of the significant work was performed by hired contractors. Therefore, Ms. Brehm is not entitled to the increased value of the house.

Ms. Brehm also argues that the sale and resale of the house to Citizens Homestead Association constituted an act of donation effecting a change in ownership which provided her with one half interest in the house. We disagree. In 1969, the Brehms sold the property for $10,000.00 to Citizens Homestead Association and simultaneously Citizens Homestead Association resold the property to the Brehms. The sale and resale of the property effected no change in the ownership of the matrimonial domicile because the transaction was entered into for the purpose of providing the homestead with a vendor's lien and first mortgage. Succession of Tucker v. Poche, 449 So.2d 1020, 1022 (La.1984).

Therefore, Ms. Brehm is only entitled to $11,794.47, which is half of the initial construction costs of building the house. Since we find that the matrimonial domicile is Mr. Brehm's separate property, Mr. Brehm is not entitled to a claim of reimbursement for paying the homeowner's insurance, flood insurance, property and casualty insurance, and termite and pest control costs.

REIMBURSEMENT FOR ALIMONY, HEALTH INSURANCE, AND CAR INSURANCE

Subsequent to this Court's reversing the trial court's award of permanent alimony to Ms. Brehm in Brehm v. Brehm, 685 So.2d 377 (La. App. 5th Cir. 11/26/96), writ denied, 688 So.2d 505 (La. 2/7/97), Mr. Brehm requested reimbursement for the permanent periodic alimony, and health and automobile insurance premiums that he paid during the time period that the issue of permanent alimony remained unresolved. Ms. Brehm argues that Mr. Brehm is not entitled to reimbursement for the total amount paid to Ms. Brehm for alimony, and health insurance and automobile insurance premiums. Ms. Brehm further argues that the trial court erred in granting Mr. Brehm reimbursement for this claim because he received tax benefits.

The legal regime of community property is terminated by the judgment of divorce. LSAC.C. art. 2356. An obligation incurred during the existence of the community for the common interest of the spouses or for the interest of the other spouse is a community obligation. LSAC.C. art. 2360. An obligation is separate when incurred prior to marriage, or during the community, though not for the common interest of the spouses or for the interest of the other spouse, or when incurred after termination of a community property regime. LSAC.C. art. 2363. If community property has been used to satisfy a separate obligation of an individual, the other individual is entitled to reimbursement upon the termination of the community, for one-half of the amount the property had at the time it was used. LSAC.C. art 2364.

The termination of the community occurred on January 13, 1994 and Mr. Brehm paid Ms. Brehm's health and automobile insurance premiums until the issue of permanent alimony was resolved. Since Ms. Brehm was not awarded permanent alimony, Mr. Brehm is entitled to reimbursement for the permanent periodic alimony, and health and automobile insurance premiums that he paid.

For the foregoing reasons, we reverse the trial court's judgment finding that the matrimonial domicile is community property, and we reverse the trial court's judgment granting Mr. Brehm reimbursement for the homeowner's insurance premiums, flood insurance, and termite and pest control costs. We further reverse the trial court's judgment ruling that all of the funds which Mr. Brehm received from his mother is community property and we find that Mr. Brehm is entitled to a reimbursement claim for $17,771.15. We affirm all other portions of the trial court judgment.

REVERSED IN PART; AFFIRMED IN PART, AND RENDERED.

Q. *Carl J. Krielow v. Lynn N. Krielow*

635 So. 2d 180 (La. 1994)

In this action to partition community property, we granted writs to determine whether the lower courts applied the wrong burden of proof on a spouse who sought to show that uncompensated or undercompensated community labor performed by the other spouse on his separate property during the course of the marriage enhanced, or increased the value of, his separate property.

We reverse and remand. C.C. Art. 2368; Abraham v. Abraham, 87 So.2d 735 (La. 1956); Deliberto v. Deliberto, 400 So.2d 1096 (La. App. 1st Cir. 1981).

We also address the correctness of the other rulings of which the applicant spouse, hereafter Lynn Krielow, complains. A debt assumed by the respondent spouse, hereafter Carl Krielow, to facilitate his brother's investment in a computer venture, was properly classified as a community obligation.

The record indicates that Lynn Krielow paid some community expenses with her separate funds. The lower courts disagreed on the amount she should be reimbursed because those courts found the community bordered on insolvency. We direct the trial court to determine on remand which of the debts it finds that were paid by Lynn were for the "ordinary and customary expenses of the marriage" and which of the debts she paid were for "community obligations," that were other than "ordinary and customary expenses of the marriage." This distinction in C.C. Art. 2365, which the trial court did not address, is critical to whether the separate property of the obligor spouse is liable for the reimbursement to the obligee spouse. Comment (a), Art. 2365.

FACTUAL SUMMARY

Lynn Naebers and Carl Krielow married on June 20, 1980, about six years after he and his brothers created a family owned corporation, Krielow Brothers, Inc., hereafter KBI. The community terminated in November of 1988 with the filing of a motion for a legal separation. A judgment of divorce was rendered a year later. Carl Krielow filed a petition for partition of the community property on August 1, 1989. The judgment partitioning the community property was signed on March 18, 1992.

Carl Krielow and his two brothers each owned one-third of the corporate stock of KBI, 1980 to 1984. In 1984, the mother of the three acquired 90 percent of the KBI stock, who, in turn, granted KBI an irrevocable option to repurchase the shares. By action of its board of directors, including Carl Krielow, before the community was terminated in 1988, KBI exercised its option, acquiring the mother's shares as treasury stock and thereafter sold some of the shares to Carl, increasing his stock to his original one-third of the shares. The appellate court noted in its opinion that Carl's one-third shares in KBI "increased from $32,000 [in 1984] to $320,000 [in 1988]," but attributed the increase to the mother's "causing the corporation to repurchase [her] stock. 622 So.2d 732." The record does not allow the conclusion that the mother "caused" this to occur, but compels the contrary conclusion because her share ownership was subject to the irrevocable option of KBI to repurchase her shares, which KBI exercised.

BURDEN OF PROOF

If the separate property of a spouse has increased in value as a result of the uncompensated common labor or industry of the spouses, the other spouse is entitled to be reimbursed from the spouse whose property has increased in value one-half of the increase attributed to the common labor. C.C. Art. 2368.

After finding that the stock increased in value during the marriage, the trial court concluded that Lynn failed to prove by "a preponderance of the evidence that the increase in value was a result of Carl's labor and industry, and not as a result of other factors." Our emphasis. The trial court stated: Probably the most tell-tale evidence came from Mr. Ellis, Lynn's CPA and expert witness who candidly admitted on cross-examination that he did not know what caused the increase in value. Certainly, after analyzing the corporation and, in particular, with his expertise, he would be in a better position than the court to conclude that the increase in value was as a result of Carl's labor and industry, and not as a result of other factors, if this were the case. However, even after his analysis, he could not so conclude and neither can this court. The appellate court said: [T]he trial court applied the proper standard: Lynn, the claimant spouse, has the initial burden of proving that the increase in value of Carl's separate property is the result of the uncompensated common labor and industry of the spouses; then, if Lynn meets her burden of proof, the burden shifts to Carl to prove that any increase in the value of his separate property is due to the ordinary course of things, rise in value, or chances of trade.

The trial court did not impose the "proper" burden, but misapplied Art. 2368 by declaring that Mrs. Krielow was required to show that the increase in value of Carl's stock was "not a result of other factors."

The claimant spouse must first prove that common or community labor of the spouses was expended on separate property. A spouse should not be permitted to deprive the community of a spouse's earnings that would be community property when that community labor enhances or increases the value of the laboring spouse's separately owned property. If a claim exists because the laboring spouse was either uncompensated or undercompensated, the measure of reimbursement is one-half of the increase attributable proportionately to the uncompensated labor of the spouse. Katherine S. Spaht and W. Lee Hargrave, in Matrimonial Regimes, s 7.17, 16 Louisiana Civil Law Treatise (1989), carefully explain and discuss the controlling authorities derived from Abraham v. Abraham, 230 La. 78, 87 So.2d 735 (La.1956).

Under former Art. 2408, the jurisprudence required proof of 1) the condition of the property at the time of the marriage; 2) the value of the property at dissolution in the state it was at the time of the marriage; 3) the real value of said property with all of the improvements in the condition it was at the time of dissolution of the community; and 4) the difference between the two estimates. The present Art. 2368 does not impose a greater burden. Spaht and Hargrave, supra, citing Babin v. Nolan, 6 Rob 508, 514 (1844); McKey v. McKey, 449 So.2d 564 (La.App. 1st Cir.1984); and Deliberto v. Deliberto, 400 So.2d 1096 (La.App. 1st Cir.1981).

Regarding former Art. 2408, this court has stated: [W]hen it is shown that community labor, expenses or industry has provided an increase to the separate property, the burden shifts to the owner of the separate property to rebut this proof and affirmatively establish that the increase is due only to the ordinary course of things, rise in values or chances of trade. Abraham v. Abraham, 87 So.2d at 739. Compare Guarisco v. Guarisco, 526 So.2d 1126 (La. App. 1st Cir. 1988); Fontenot v. Fontenot, 339 So.2d

897 (La. App. 3d Cir. 1976), *writ denied*, 342 So.2d 217 (1977); and Mohr v. Mohr, 374 So.2d 203 (La. App. 4th Cir. 1979), which failed to adhere to the Abraham standard and required the claimant to show that the enhancement did not result in the ordinary course of events.

Hartfield v. Hartfield, 602 So.2d 179 (La. App. 3d Cir. 1992); Deliberto v. Deliberto, *supra*; and Downs v. Downs, 410 So.2d 793 (La. App. 3d Cir.), *writ denied*, 414 So.2d 375 (1982), rejected Fontenot as inconsistent with Abraham because it placed the burden of persuasion on the claimant to prove that the increase was not due to the ordinary course of things.

Regarding the appellate jurisprudential inconsistency, Spaht and Hargrave commented: If it is proved that separate property has increased in value due to the uncompensated labor of a spouse, then arguably there is proof that the property did not increase due to the ordinary course of things. Furthermore, shifting the burden of persuasion to the spouse whose separate property has increased in value to prove that the increase was due to the ordinary course of things seems eminently fair. Many times the separate property alleged to have increased in value is a separate partnership interest or separate stock in a closely held corporation. Under such circumstances the spouse in a position to know whether an increase in value is the result of a rise in property values or inflation is the spouse whose separate property has benefitted. Spaht and Hargrave, supra, at 311.

By enacting Art. 2368, the legislature did not intend to overrule the jurisprudence interpreting Art. 2408. We shall continue to follow the standard pronounced by this court in Abraham, supra.

Mrs. Krielow established a prima facie case that her husband's separately owned stock increased in value during the marriage. Carl Krielow contends that Lynn failed in her burden because her CPA, Ellis, could not distinctly fix the value of KBI, the separately owned corporation, on the date of marriage in 1980 or on the date the community terminated in 1988.

The trial court found that the value of the separate property increased during the marriage. The court of appeal did not refute or upset this finding. We make no specific finding about value, but note that the testimony indicates that KBI may have been worth \$12,000 at the time of the marriage in 1980, \$0 in 1984, and at \$960,000 in 1988 when the community was terminated. In 1988, Carl Krielow owned one-third of the shares of KBI.

The trial court did not reach the question of whether Carl was uncompensated or undercompensated. The court of appeal stated: We find that Mr. Ellis' testimony and other record evidence is not sufficient to meet Lynn's burden of proving that the value of Carl's separate property was increased by his uncompensated labor. 622 So.2d at 735.

While Carl Krielow concedes that the appellate court erroneously stated that the trial court applied the "proper" standard, he asserts the appellate court found the trial court properly followed the jurisprudence and placed the initial burden of proof upon his ex-wife. Carl Krielow contends that notwithstanding the trial court's applying the wrong standard, the record demonstrates that Lynn Krielow failed to meet her burden of proof even under the correct standard.

Carl Krielow claims that Lynn Krielow failed to prove that he was undercompensated for the work he performed for KBI. Citing Pellerin v. Pellerin, 550 So.2d 1250 (La. App. 4th Cir. 1989); and Phillips v. Wagner, 470 So.2d 262 (La. App. 5th Cir.), writ denied, he argues that Lynn may satisfy this burden by proving that the amount of compensation received by him from KBI was less than that which he could have received in the open market. Carl asserts that CPA Ellis was unable to testify as to the amount of compensation that he could have obtained in the open market. Noting that the growth of the corporation occurred when he owned only 3.33 percent of the shares, Carl asserts that he had no practical power to fix his own compensation. CPA Ellis explained that competent people, officers and management make a business entity such as KBI grow and increase in value.

Noting his ex-wife's contention that the corporation only paid or allowed him to "draw" money that was absolutely necessary for the subsistence of the community, Carl Krielow asserts that the record is not only devoid of such evidence, but establishes otherwise. Carl points to testimony showing that KBI provided him and Lynn with a full-time house-keeper/sitter, the unrestricted use of a new Volvo automobile equipped with a cellular phone, and the funds sufficient to make political contributions.

The record shows that Carl Krielow began working full-time for KBI in mid-1984, bidding and overseeing KBI jobs in various locations. He worked without any salary his first year, and thereafter remained active as an employee and director of KBI. Lynn Krielow emphasizes a KBI promotional brochure showing Carl Krielow as vice-president, director, and one of the two operating officers of KBI. Prior to Carl Krielow's being solely employed by KBI, KBI had no revenue, no income, and no increase in assets. During the community, Carl was not paid a salary by KBI, but was paid or allowed " draws" from corporate accounts, which income he reported on a Federal Tax 1099 form rather than the usual W-2 forms used by salaried employees.

Carl and his brother, Bill Krielow, ran and managed KBI. The other brother- stockholder, Chris, had no interest in the day-to-day operations of KBI. Carl Krielow, on the other hand, worked solely for and devoted all of his time to KBI. We must conclude through Carl's competency, KBI flourished. Carl has been a director and an employee of KBI since it was first formed in 1974. Regardless of his ownership percent, Carl Krielow and his brother, Bill, are, and have been, the primary managerial officers of KBI.

Carl's draws were relatively low, according to this record. KBI also paid Carl's telephone and utility bills and furnished him with vehicles. The CPA, Ellis, concluded that the community should have received an additional $177,332 between 1984 and 1988, and that Carl Krielow's low income from KBI was not the result of lack of profitability. We must conclude on this record that Carl Krielow was undercompensated to some degree which the trial court shall determine on remand.

Because Lynn Krielow has established on this record that Carl's undercompensated community labor for KBI enhanced or increased Carl's separately owned stock, the burden shifts to Carl, as the owner of the separate property, to prove that some or all of the enhancement occurred because of other factors. It is Carl who has failed to meet his burden of proof.

Once a claimant has established that the increase in separate property of the other spouse is entirely or partially due to the under or uncompensated community labor of the other spouse, the claimant is entitled to one-half of the enhanced value of the separate property. Even if that value exceeds the value of the uncompensated labor, the claimant is nevertheless entitled to recover the greater amount. Art. 2368 does not impose a limitation on the amount recoverable. See Deliberto, *supra*, at 1103.

We shall reverse the judgment in this respect and remand to the trial court to allow the proper measure of reimbursement to be determined and judgment entered in favor of Lynn Krielow consistent with this opinion. Because we remand, we discuss the other issues.

OTHER ISSUES

The trial court did not resolve whether the increase in value of the separate property was attributable to Carl Krielow's mother, Maxine, rather than to Carl. The appellate court stated, "Mr. Ellis admitted that Carl's stock increased from $32,000 to $320,000 during this time solely as a result of Maxine's action as majority [90 percent] shareholder in causing the corporation to repurchase treasury stock." Our emphasis. We conclude the appellate court was clearly wrong about the cause of the increase for the following reasons:

The mother, Maxine Krielow, did not exercise any authority during the time she owned 90 percent of KBI's stock, 1984-1988, according to this record. She was not a director and was never actively involved KBI's operations. She was only a stockholder, subject to KBI's exercise of the irrevocable option mentioned. The Board of Directors chose to exercise the option and repurchase Maxine Krielow's stock. She had nothing to do with the board's decision. CPA Ellis found Carl Krielow's stock increased in value because he purchased the treasury stock derived from the corporation's exercise of the option to buy back the stock from Maxine Krielow. This increased his stock value perhaps from $32,000 to $320,000, as the appellate court noted.

Although Maxine Krielow held 90 percent of the stock for about four years, her three sons, the 10 percent owners, had more capital at risk. Originally, each brother's stock was valued at $1,000, but two months before the sale to Maxine, each brother loaned the corporation $10,000. The next year, each brother agreed to convert or recharacterize his loan as his contribution to capital surplus. No additional stock was issued the brothers, however. The purpose of the sale to Maxine Krielow was to protect one brother's interest from a seizure and to facilitate KBI's attempts to be awarded public contracts in a new venture by having a female as its majority shareholder.

Carl's temporary decrease in percentage of stock ownership did not decrease his efforts for KBI. As the corporate business increased, the amount of his "draw" did not. Even though Carl Krielow asserts that he did not perform any labor or industry that caused the increase in value of the stock, the record belies his contention.

The efforts or labor of Carl and Bill Krielow are responsible for whatever increase KBI enjoyed. Maxine Krielow was not responsible for the growth.

Lynn Krielow also contends that the court of appeal applied the incorrect standard of proof as to the valuation of property, and consequently erred in concluding that she failed to establish the value of Carl's separate property at the inception of the community. In concluding that the evidence was not sufficient to meet her burden of proving that the value of Carl's separate property was increased by his uncompensated labor, the appellate court stated that Ellis had been unable to establish the value of the stock at the inception of the community in 1980.

The appellate court erred in requiring Lynn to prove the exact value of the separate property at the inception of the community. Estimates, not exact figures, are sufficient in some circumstances under Art. 2368. [A]n estimate should be placed on the value of the separate property if it were unimproved at the time of marriage or that an estimate should be made of the value at the time of dissolution, but if possible, as the property stood at the time of marriage (i.e., with or without improvements). Deliberto, *supra,* at 1099, citing Babin v. Nolan, 4 Rob. 278 (1843). Our Emphasis.

We find that a claiming spouse is not required to prove an exact value on a date during which time KBI did not keep a record of value.

Lynn Krielow further contends that the court of appeal erred in denying her reimbursement for the payment of community expenses with her separate funds. She asserts that because she paid community debts for the ordinary and customary expenses of the marriage, amounting to $4,791.31, she is entitled to reimbursement regardless of the solvency of the community. La.C.C. Art. 2365. If separate property of a spouse has been used to satisfy a community obligation, that spouse upon termination of the community property regime, is entitled to reimbursement for one-half of the amount or value that the property had at the time it was used. The liability of a spouse who owes reimbursement is limited to the value of his share in the community after deduction of all community obligations. Nevertheless, if the community obligation was incurred for the ordinary and customary expenses of the marriage, or for the support, maintenance, and education of children of either spouse in keeping with the economic condition of the community, the spouse is entitled to reimbursement from the other spouse regardless of the value of that spouse's share of the community. La.C.C. Art. 2365. Our Emphasis. [I]f the community obligation discharged with separate property is one incurred for the ordinary and customary expenses of the marriage, or for the support, maintenance, and education of the children, in keeping with the economic condition of the community, there is an obligation for reimbursement even if there are no sufficient community assets. In such a case, reimbursement may be made from the separate property of the other spouse. La.C.C. Art. 2365, Comment (a).

The trial court initially upheld Lynn's claim for reimbursement of $4,791.31 for community debts she paid with her separate funds, but in Supplemental Reasons for Judgment the court found no reimbursement was due because the community was insolvent. The trial court did not consider whether the community debts Lynn paid were for the "ordinary and customary expenses of the marriage." C.C. Art. 2365.

Determining the community to be solvent by $658.86, the appellate court granted Lynn reimbursement for one half of that amount, mentioning that she failed to prove that the debts were incurred for the ordinary and customary expenses of the marriage because the copies of invoices and checks she presented were not self-explanatory.

Lynn Krielow maintains that her listing of community debts established that the debts she paid were for ordinary and customary expenses of the marriage. Her documentary evidence consists of invoices which she contends are self- explanatory and sufficient to show payment for debts incurred for the ordinary and customary expenses of the marriage. Lynn's descriptive list included the following alleged debts and liabilities of the community:

Broussard's Men Shop	12.77
Visa	987.15
State Farm	55.83
State Farm	109.25

Sears	163.35
Lord & Taylor	75.23
Porter Stevens	368.50
Hayes Cleaner	22.55
Maison Blanc	573.34
D.H. Holmes	76.95
Bell South Mobility (use of car phone)	122.51
Bell South Mobility (phone)	977.84
Brown Appliance & T.V. Co. of Welch (dryer repair)	30.21
Dr. Lee J. Monlezun, Jr.	45.00
Jennings American Legion Hospital	11.73
Dr. Donald McSpadden	225.00
AAA Body & Paint	1047.28

The burden of proof is on the party claiming reimbursement to show by a preponderance of the evidence the nature of the indebtedness, whether the community obligation(s) were incurred for the ordinary and customary expenses of the marriage. House payments, taxes, and insurance premiums are ordinary and customary expenses of the marriage. Moody v. Moody, 622 So.2d 1381 (La.App. 1st Cir.1993); Williams v. Williams, 590 So.2d 649 (La.App. 3d Cir.1991).

On remand the trial court shall distinguish which of the debts were for the ordinary and customary expenses of the marriage and which were not and, in each instance, determine whether Carl Krielow's liability for reimbursement is or is not "limited to the value of his share in the community." Art. 2365.

DECREE

The judgment of the court of appeal is reversed and the case is remanded to the trial court to resolve, in accord with this opinion, the issues remaining.

WATSON, J., dissents, believing that the trial court and the Court of Appeal were correct.

ON REHEARING

PER CURIAM

Having considered the application for rehearing filed by Carl Krielow, we agree with his assertion regarding the shares of KBI stock held by his mother, Maxine Krielow, 1984-88, that were subject to the option of KBI to repurchase, only in these respects:

When KBI exercised its option and repurchased Mrs. Krielow's shares, those shares, representing 90 percent of the outstanding stock of KBI, became treasury shares, causing the share interest held by each of the Krielow brothers to increase from 3.33 percent to 33.33 percent of the outstanding stock of the corporation. This percentage increase resulted solely because Mrs. Krielow's shares became treasury shares after the option to repurchase her shares was exercised by KBI through its board of directors. We incorrectly stated in our original opinion that Carl Krielow thereafter purchased some of the treasury shares to increase his share interest to 33.33 percent.

Before, after and during the four years that Mrs. Krielow held the KBI shares that were subject to the option, the three Krielow brothers continued to control the management and operations of KBI as its directors and officers, each owning one-third of the shares of KBI that were not subject to becoming treasury shares of KBI at the option of the corporation. As our original opinion notes, Mrs. Krielow exercised no authority over KBI's affairs or operations while she held the shares that were subject to the option.

Consequently and because one-third of the "control" of the corporation was at all times owned or exercised by Carl Krielow as director, officer and stockholder, we decline Carl Krielow's suggestion in his rehearing application that we should limit, on remand, the claim of reimbursement to the community as if he owned only 3.3 percent of the KBI stock as his separate property. Compare Abraham v. Abraham, 87 So.2d 735 and discussion of the case law in Deliberto v. Deliberto, 400 So.2d 1096, cited in the original opinion. Abraham squarely holds that if undercompensated community labor "substantially contributes" to the enhancement in value of one spouse's separate property, the spouse who does not own the separate property is entitled to one-half of the enhancement. The important circumstance is that the [substantial] contribution to enhancement result from community labor, industry or expense. Abraham, 87 So.2d 738-39. Neither case suggested "limiting" the nonowner spouse's recovery by the percentage that the community laborer was "undercompensated." Deliberto suggested that cases allowing the limitation of reimbursement in some circumstances have been overruled sub silentio or have been ignored.

As we noted in our original opinion, Carl Krielow was "undercompensated to some degree which the trial court shall determine on remand." We refrained from making a "specific finding about [the] value" that Carl Krielow's stock may have been enhanced by undercompensated community labor, whether the undercompensation "substantially" enhanced his separate property. The trial court on remand shall determine whether Krielow's undercompensated community labor substantially enhanced the value of his separately owned KBI stock.

La.Civ.Code art. 2368 effectively codifies the principle of former art. 2408 and Abraham: If the separate property of one spouse has increased in value substantially as a result of [under or un-]compensated common labor, the other spouse is entitled to be reimbursed from the spouse [owner of separate property] ... one-half of the increase attributed to the common labor.

On the current record in this appeal we shall not decide, in the abstract, issues arising when the value of the undercompensated community labor is grossly disproportionate, below or above, the value of the enhancement of a spouse's separate property.

With these clarifications, we deny Carl Krielow's application for a rehearing.

WATSON, J., would grant rehearing.

R. *Sheila Salley v. Richard Salley*

661 So. 2d 437 (La. 1995)

KIMBALL, Justice.

Sheila Salley ("Sheila"), plaintiff/appellant, and Richard Salley ("Richard"), defendant/ appellee, were married on November 24, 1973. The couple separated on May 17, 1991, and filed for divorce on May 21, 1991. A judgment of divorce was rendered on January 6, 1992. On January 11, 1993, Sheila instituted this action to partition community property, alleging proceeds from the redemption of stock owned by Richard were community property. The trial court ruled in favor of Richard, and the third circuit court of appeal affirmed. Salley v. Salley, No. 94-418 (La. App. 3d Cir. 11/23/94), 647 So.2d 1164. We granted writs to determine the proper allocation of the burden of proof under *Krielow v. Krielow*, 93-2539 (La. 4/11/94), 635 So.2d 180, to proceeds of a stock redemption in a closely held family corporation. *Salley v. Salley*, No. 95-0387 (La. 4/7/95), 652 So.2d 1339.

FACTS

Richard began work with James Salley, Inc., a family-owned chain of food stores, in 1972 as a stockboy. He later worked as a cashier, as a clerk in the produce department and in the meat department, and as a manager of a store. Richard eventually became president of James Salley, Inc.

Richard's parents, James W. Salley, Sr. and Mildred Salley, owned and operated James Salley, Inc. At various times from December 1972 to 1982, James and Mildred Salley donated to Richard a total of 370 shares in the corporation. These shares were valued at $37,000.00.

In June of 1986, Richard and his father redeemed their James Salley, Inc. stock to the corporation. As a result of the redemption of his shares, Richard received $814,000.00. Richard made several purchases with the funds earned in the redemption, including immovable property and a variety of securities.

In this suit to partition community property, Sheila alleges that the increase in the value of the stock from $37,000.00 to $814,000.00 is community property. The trial court held that Sheila failed to prove the stock increased in value and, therefore, the proceeds of the stock redemption were Richard's separate property. The third circuit affirmed, holding that although Sheila did prove that the stock increased in value, she had failed to prove that the increase in the value of the stock was due to the uncompensated or undercompensated labor of either spouse as required by La.Civ.Code art. 2368 and *Krielow v. Krielow, supra*. We granted Sheila's writ application because she alleged the court of appeal improperly allocated the burden of proof and improperly required her to prove the community endured hardship, inequities, or sacrifices in order for her to satisfy her burden. Because we find the court of appeal neither improperly allocated the burden of proof nor placed an inappropriate burden on Sheila, we affirm.

LAW

Louisiana Civil Code article 2368 states:

If the separate property of a spouse has increased in value as a result of the uncompensated common labor or industry of the spouses, the other spouse is entitled to be reimbursed from the spouse whose property has increased in value one-half of the increase attributed to the common labor.

In *Krielow v. Krielow*, 93-2539 (La. 4/11/94), 635 So.2d 180, this court addressed the burden of proof under Civil Code article 2368. Lynn Krielow, in a suit against Carl Krielow to partition community property, alleged that stock which was the separate property of Carl had increased in value during the marriage, and the increase was community property. At trial Lynn proved the stock increased in value during the marriage as a result of Carl's undercompensated labor. The district court and the court of appeal held under Article 2368 that the increase was not community property because Lynn failed to prove the increase was not a result of factors other than the uncompensated or undercompensated labor of the other spouse. *Krielow v. Krielow*, 622 So.2d 732 (La. App. 3d Cir. 1993). We reversed, holding that a claimant spouse under Article 2368 has the burden of proving: (1) the property is separate, (2) the property increased in value, and (3) the increase in value was based on the uncompensated or undercompensated labor of the other spouse; the burden then shifts to the other spouse to prove that the increase in value was due to factors other than the uncompensated or undercompensated labor. *Krielow, supra*, 93-C-2539 at p. 8, 635 So.2d at 185.

Thus, after a claimant spouse has proven the property is separate, he or she must then prove that the property increased in value during the existence of the matrimonial regime. *Krielow* established that in order for a plaintiff to show increase in value he or she must prove: (1) the condition of the property at the time of the marriage, (2) the value of the property at dissolution in the state it was at the time of the marriage, (3) the real value of said property with all of the improvements in the condition it was at the time of dissolution of the community, and (4) the difference between the two estimates. *Krielow, supra*, 93-C-2539 at p. 4, 635 So.2d at 183.

Once the claimant spouse has proven the property is separate and it increased in value, in order to prevail under Article 2368 he or she must then prove common or community labor of the spouses was expended on the separate property. *Krielow, supra*, 93-C-2539 at p. 4, 635 So.2d at 183. It is not necessary, however, for the claimant spouse to show that his or her labor was expended on the separate property; it is enough to show the labor of either spouse was so expended. In *Abraham v. Abraham*, 87 So.2d 735 (La. 1956), this court examined Article 2408, the predecessor to Article 2368. In *Abraham*, we held "common labor or industry of the spouses" means the labor of either spouse during the existence of the marriage. Thus, the word "common," as used in the article, is synonymous with "community." *Abraham, supra*, 87 So.2d at 738.

Further, a claimant spouse must show the common labor expended on the separate property was uncompensated or undercompensated. *Krielow, supra*, 93-C-2539 at p. 8, 635 So.2d at 185; *see also* Katherine S. Spaht and W. Lee Hargrave, Matrimonial Regimes, § 7.18, 16 Louisiana Civil Law Treatise (1989). Once the claimant spouse proves that uncompensated or undercompensated community labor was expended on the separate property and caused it to increase in value, the burden then shifts to the owner of the separate property to prove that some or all of the enhancement in value of the separate property occurred because of factors other than the uncompensated or undercompensated community labor. *Krielow, supra*, 93-C-2539 at p. 8, 635 So.2d at 185.

Article 2368 is based on the following policy, as we enunciated in *Krielow*:

A spouse should not be permitted to deprive the community of a spouse's earning that would be community property when that community labor enhances or increases the value of the laboring spouse's separately owned property. If a claim exists because the laboring spouse was either uncompensated or undercompensated, the measure of reimbursement is one-half of the increase attributable proportionately to the uncompensated labor of the spouse.

Krielow, *supra*, 93-C-2539 at p. 4, 635 So.2d at 183 (emphasis added). The salary and wages of a spouse are community property. La.Civ.Code art. 2338. Therefore, because a spouse's compensation in return for his labor or industry is community property, La.Civ.Code art. 2338, to the extent that the spouse's uncompensated or undercompensated labor increases the value of his separate property, the community has a claim against him.

ANALYSIS

In her first three assignments of error Sheila asserts the court of appeal misapplied *Krielow* in allocating to her, rather than to Richard, the burden of proving the capital gain on the stock was a result of the uncompensated or undercompensated labor of either spouse.

Applying *Krielow* to the instant case, the initial determination to be made is whether the stock and the money received upon its redemption were Richard's separate property. Since Richard's parents donated the stock to him individually, the shares of stock were Richard's separate property. La.Civ.Code art. 2341. Thus, the money received when Richard sold the stock back to James Salley, Inc. is also Richard's separate property as it is "property acquired with separate things" under La.Civ.Code art. 2341.

Changing the form of separate property from stock to cash through a sale of stock in exchange for cash does not change the nature of the property from separate to community.

Sheila alleges, however, that the proceeds of the redemption became community property because the increase in value of the separate property was the result of uncompensated or undercompensated community labor.

In *Stobart v. State Through DOTD*, 617 So.2d 880 (La. 1993), this court held that "[a] court of appeal may not set aside a trial court's or jury's finding of fact in the absence of 'manifest error' or unless it is 'clearly wrong.'" *Id.* at 882. A review of the record reveals contradictory evidence presented by each party which involved the trial judge's determination of witness credibility to resolve. After a thorough review of the record we cannot say that the trial court's finding was manifestly erroneous.

The trial court held Sheila failed to prove the stock increased in value, while the court of appeal determined that "Sheila Salley arguably established that her former husband's stock in Salley's Food Store, Inc., increased in value during the existence of the community property regime." *Salley*, *supra*, No. 94-418 at p. 7, 647 So.2d at 1167. We agree with the court of appeal's finding that Sheila Salley satisfied her burden of proving the stock increased in value. The evidence shows, and the parties do not dispute, that Richard's 370 shares of stock were originally valued at $37,000.00 and were redeemed during the marriage for $814,000.00; thus, the value of the stock increased by $777,000.00 during the existence of the matrimonial regime.

Because the separate property of Richard was found to have increased in value during the marriage, we must next determine whether Sheila proved the increase in value was a result of Richard's uncompensated or undercompensated labor.[i] Addressing this issue, the third circuit stated:

> We find nothing in the record, however, that even remotely suggests that the increase in the value of the stock was due to Richard's uncompensated or undercompensated labor.
> *Salley, supra*, No. 94-418 at p. 7, 647 So.2d at 1167.

During the fourteen years Richard was employed by James Salley, Inc. he received over $750,000.00 in salary and wages. Sheila made no allegations in the trial court and presented no evidence, expert or otherwise, that the salary and wages paid to Richard were below the market level for the various positions in which he was employed. As stated in Krielow, supra, 93-C-2539 at p. 8, 635 So.2d at 185, the burden is on Sheila to prove that Richard was uncompensated or undercompensated. There is no evidence in this record to suggest Richard's salary was below market value for the services he performed for James Salley, Inc. or that he was in any way undercompensated for his labor.

Under *Krielow*, the claimant spouse is not required to prove that he or she contributed to the increase in the value of the separate property nor that the community endured any hardship, inequities, or sacrifices that contributed to the increased value of the separate property. However, the language in the court of appeal's opinion to that effect is dictum and of no consequence because Sheila failed to prove that Richard was uncompensated or undercompensated in the first place.

Sheila also argues the lower courts erred in finding Richard was not undercompensated based on the fact that James Salley, Inc. never paid dividends on its stock, even though the stock increased in value by $777,000.00. Harry G. Henn and John R. Alexander, in Laws of Corporations state:

> [T]he distribution of dividends, even on shares with a dividend preference, is usually discretionary, within the business judgment rule of the board of directors.

Only when abuse of discretion is shown will courts substitute their own judgment and order a distribution of dividends. Abuse of discretion is found only if there is evidence of fraud or bad faith or a clear case of unreasonableness.

Harry G. Henn and John R. Alexander, § 327 Laws of Corporations 913-14 (1983). Given that the distribution of dividends falls under the discretion of the board of directors and that Sheila has neither alleged nor presented evidence of any fraud, bad faith, or unreasonableness in James Salley, Inc.'s failure to pay dividends, we find Sheila has failed to prove Richard was undercompensated because he did not receive dividends on the stock he owned.

We also find that, in this case the corporation's failure to pay dividends is irrelevant. Sheila's burden under Article 2368 is to prove Richard's labor was undercompensated. As stated earlier, Sheila put on no evidence to show Richard's salary was below market level for the various positions he held, and, in fact, the salaries appear to be more than adequate. Additionally, Sheila has not alleged that James Salley, Inc., as part of its employment contract with Richard, promised to pay him dividends on any James Salley, Inc. stock he owned. Therefore, in this case, we see no connection between the failure of James Salley, Inc. to pay dividends to its stockholders and the issue of whether Richard was undercompensated as an employee of that company.

Because Sheila failed to carry her burden of proving Richard was undercompensated, the burden did not shift to Richard to prove the enhancement in value resulted from other factors.

CONCLUSION

Sheila failed to prove the increase in the value of Richard's James Salley, Inc. stock was a result of the uncompensated or undercompensated labor of Richard as required by La.Civ.Code art. 2368 and *Krielow v. Krielow, supra.* Therefore, we affirm the judgment of the court of appeal.

Sheila also assigns as error the trial court's rulings that a certificate of deposit and an undivided one-half interest in a twenty acre tract of land are Richard's separate property. We find no manifest error in the trial court's rulings.

AFFIRMED.

JOHNSON, J., dissents.

CHAPTER 8: MATRIMONIAL AGREEMENTS

8.1 MATRIMONIAL AGREEMENTS GENERALLY

Louisiana enjoys a unique historical acceptance of marriage contracts. As a result of Louisiana's French and Spanish legal heritage, marriage contracts have been recognized and widely accepted since the 1700's. Both the 1808 and 1870 codifications expressly allowed marriage contracts and regulated their form and content. Louisiana law continues to expressly approve of a variety of marriage contracts. In contrast, common law jurisdictions traditionally viewed marriage contracts less favorably. Many common law jurisdictions accepted and enforced marriage contracts regulating the distribution of property upon the death of a spouse—and particularly contracts that waived one spouse's rights in the estate of the other spouse. In the case of second marriages, for example, these contracts presumably facilitated marital harmony by "allow[ing] the marriage to occur without disturbing third-party rights."[11] However, common law jurisdictions treated marriage contracts regulating the relationship between the spouses or division of property at divorce with overt hostility. Unlike Louisiana, most states lacked statutes specifically addressing marriage contracts that were effective at some time earlier than the death of a spouse. Moreover, many courts believed these types of marriage contracts violated public policy by encouraging divorce. Divorce-focused agreements were "antithetical to the marriage contract" and any "contracts which tend to induce a separation of husband and wife [were] utterly void and of no force or effect."[12] As views of marriage, divorce, and family changed, marriage contracts gained greater acceptance in common law jurisdictions.

Responding to these changes and concerns of lack of uniformity of state treatment of marriage contracts, the Uniform Law Commission drafted the Uniform Premarital Agreement Act (UPAA) in 1983. As of 2012, twenty-two states and the District of Columbia had enacted some version of the UPAA. The UPAA grants spouses broad freedom to contract regarding the economic consequences of marriage. However, many substantive requirements and evidentiary burdens of the UPAA are more onerous than the laws in Louisiana. On the whole, the UPAA continues to treat marriage contracts with a greater degree of suspicion than Louisiana law.

---

[11] William F. Fraatz, Comment: *Enforcing Antenuptial Contracts in Minnesota: A Practice in Search of a Policy Basis in the Wake of McKee-Johnson v. Johnson*, 77 MINN. L. REV. 441 (1996).
[12] *Id.*

8.2 MATRIMONIAL AGREEMENTS, FORM AND TIMING REQUIREMENTS

A. Introduction

Louisiana Civil Code article 2331 requires that matrimonial agreements be executed in the form of an authentic act or an act under private signature duly acknowledged. If a matrimonial agreement gratuitously re-characterizes separate property as community property, then it most likely must be in the form of an authentic act. La. Civ. Code art. 2343.1. Consistent with Louisiana's public records doctrine, Louisiana Civil Code article 2332 provides that a matrimonial agreement is not effective with respect to third parties until it is filed for recordation in the appropriate conveyance records. Unfortunately, no state-wide registration is available and spouses owning property in multiple parishes may have to record their matrimonial agreement in multiple locations. Article 2332 explains that the agreement is "effective toward third persons as to immovable property, when filed for registry in the conveyance records of the parish in which the property is situated and as to movables when filed for registry in the parish or parishes in which the spouses are domiciled."

Louisiana allows spouses to enter into a matrimonial agreement either before or after marriage. Regardless of the timing, the form requirements of Article 2331 apply. Spouses entering into a post-nuptial agreement, however, face an additional burden. Article 2329 requires court approval for post-nuptial agreements that modify or terminate the legal regime of community property. Article 2329 requires a "joint petition and a finding by the court that this serves their best interests and that they understand the governing principles and rules." Spouses are free to enter into a post-nuptial agreement that opts-in to the default matrimonial regime without the necessity of court approval. Article 2329 also contains an exception for married couples who move into Louisiana from another state: "During the first year after moving into and acquiring a domicile in this state, spouses may enter into a matrimonial agreement without court approval."

Article 2333 imposes an additional requirement in the case of minors: "Unless fully emancipated, a minor may not enter into a matrimonial agreement without the written concurrence of his father and mother or of the parent having his legal custody, or of the tutor of his person."

B. *Randall C. Rush v. Lynn Peuschold Rush*

115 So. 3d 508 (La. App. 1st Cir. 2013)

KUHN, J.

This appeal was taken by appellant, Lynn E. Peuschold, from a judgment declaring a purported matrimonial agreement to be valid as to form. For the following reasons, we convert this appeal into a supervisory writ, reverse the trial court judgment, and render declaratory judgment in favor of appellant.

PROCEDURAL BACKGROUND

On January 30, 1993, Ms. Peuschold, and appellee, Randall C. Rush, signed a matrimonial agreement purporting to establish a separation of property regime between them during their contemplated marriage. The document was executed before a notary, but was not signed by witnesses. Thereafter, the parties were married on February 18, 1993, and two children were born of the marriage.

On August 31, 2011, Mr. Rush filed a petition for divorce in which he alleged that the parties were separate in property due to the prenuptial matrimonial agreement they executed. On September 30, 2011, over eighteen years after the parties married, Mr. Rush executed an acknowledgement by authentic act of his signature on the 1993 matrimonial agreement. In response to Mr. Rush's request for admission of facts, Ms. Peuschold admitted that she signed the matrimonial agreement, but stated that her response was not "deemed an acknowledgement of any nature or kind under oath."

In her answer to the divorce petition, Ms. Peuschold denied that a separate property regime existed, and she filed a reconventional demand asserting that the matrimonial agreement was invalid as to form. Additionally, on January 13, 2012, she filed a petition for declaratory judgment seeking a declaration that the matrimonial agreement was invalid and that a community of acquets and gains existed between the parties. Ms. Peuschold asserted that the agreement was invalid as to form because it was neither an authentic act due to the lack of witnesses, nor was it an act under private signature duly acknowledged by both spouses. She further alleged that the agreement was invalid due to vices of consent.

At a hearing limited to the issue of the alleged vices of form, the trial court considered the dispositive issue to be whether Ms. Peuschold's admission that she signed the matrimonial agreement operated as an acknowledgement of the agreement under La. C.C. art. 1836, which sets forth the manner in which private acts may be acknowledged. Concluding that it did, the trial court rendered judgment that the matrimonial agreement was valid as to form. Without reasons, the trial court designated the judgment as a final judgment pursuant to La. C.C.P. art. 1915(B)(1). Ms. Peuschold now appeals, alleging in three assignments of error that the trial court erred in finding the matrimonial agreement valid as to form.

***

VALIDITY OF THE MATRIMONIAL AGREEMENT

Ms. Peuschold argues that, in finding the matrimonial agreement valid as to form, the trial court ignored the requirements of La. C.C. art. 2329. Specifically, she argues that La. C.C. art. 2331, which sets forth the form requirements for matrimonial agreements, must be read in conjunction with the temporal requirement of Article 2329 that spouses who wish to enter into a matrimonial agreement during marriage modifying or terminating a matrimonial regime must obtain court approval. Since the matrimonial agreement at issue was not acknowledged until over eighteen years after the parties' marriage and no court approval was obtained, she asserts it was invalid as to form. We agree.

Under Articles 2329 and 2331, parties may enter into a matrimonial agreement either before or during marriage concerning all matters not prohibited by public policy. Article 2331 requires that such matrimonial agreements be "made by authentic act or by an act under private signature duly acknowledged by the spouses." Additionally, although Article 2331 does not impose a temporal requirement for the spousal acknowledgements, Article 2329 requires that, in order for spouses to enter into a matrimonial agreement that modifies or terminates a matrimonial regime during marriage, the spouses must file a joint petition and obtain court approval for the agreement.

Since both Articles 2329 and 2331 deal with the execution of matrimonial agreements, they must be read in pari materia. See La. C.C. art. 13. When two statutes can be reconciled by a fair and reasonable interpretation, the court must read the statutes so as to give effect to each. *In re First Columbia Life Insurance Company*, 97–1083 (La.App. 1st Cir.9/29/98), 724 So.2d 790, 794, *writ not considered*, 98–2789 (La.1/8/99), 734 So.2d 1222. Further, due to the strong legislative policy against spouses giving up their community rights during marriage without judicial supervision, the formalities of Article 2329 must be construed stricti juris. *Poirier v. Poirier*, 626 So.2d 868, 870 (La.App. 3d Cir.1993), *writ denied*, 94–0161 (La.3/11/94), 634 So.2d 389.

In the instant case, it is undisputed that the matrimonial agreement is not in authentic form due to the absence of witnesses. *See* La. C.C. art. 1833. Nevertheless, the trial court accepted Mr. Rush's argument that the 1993 matrimonial agreement was valid as to form under Article 2331 because it was an act under private signature duly acknowledged by both spouses, Mr. Rush's acknowledgement being an authentic act executed on

September 30, 2011, and Ms. Peuschold's acknowledgement consisting of her admission during discovery that she signed the agreement. The trial court erred in doing so.

Regardless of whether Ms. Peuschold's admission that she signed the matrimonial agreement operated as an acknowledgement, that admission occurred during the existence of the marriage, as did Mr. Rush's own acknowledgement. Thus, even though the parties executed the matrimonial agreement by private act prior to their marriage, they did not perfect all of the elements of form required by Article 2331 prior to their marriage. Therefore, no valid matrimonial agreement existed at the time that the parties entered into marriage, and a community of acquets and gains was created by operation of law. *See* La. C.C. arts. 2327 & 2334. Nor could the mere acknowledgement of the private act during the marriage validate the matrimonial agreement, since Article 2329, which must be strictly construed, mandates that spouses can only modify or terminate a matrimonial regime during marriage by filing a joint petition and obtaining court approval. No such joint petition was filed or court approval obtained in the instant case. Accordingly, we find that the 1993 matrimonial agreement was invalid as to form due to the failure of the parties to comply with the requirements of Articles 2329 and 2331.

CONCLUSION

For the reasons assigned, we grant this writ and reverse the judgment of the trial court. Additionally, we hereby render judgment in favor of Lynn E. Peuschold, and against Randall C. Rush, declaring that a community of acquets and gains existed between the parties during their marriage because the January 30, 1993 matrimonial agreement they executed is invalid due to lack of proper form. All costs of this appeal are assessed to Mr. Rush.

WRIT GRANTED; REVERSED AND RENDERED.

C. *Amy Strong Muller v. Carl Muller, Jr.*

72 So. 3d 364 (La. App. 5 Cir. 2011)

SUSAN M. CHEHARDY, Judge.

Plaintiff/appellant, Amy Strong Muller ("Mrs. Muller"), appeals a judgment of the district court denying her petition to have a premarital matrimonial agreement declared null and void ab initio. Mrs. Muller alleged in her petition that she and her then fiance', Carl Muller Jr. ("Mr. Muller"), entered into the agreement on April 7, 1995 in St. John the Baptist Parish, and the agreement was duly recorded on that same day. The couple was married on the following day, April 8, 1995. The record indicates that the marriage broke down at some point, although their marital status at the time of the hearing indicates the couple was not yet divorced.

Mrs. Muller's original petition indicated that the agreement was "executed before a notary", but was not in authentic form or duly acknowledged by the parties, in accordance with La. C.C. art. 2331. Specifically, she urged that although the agreement bore the signature of a notary, there were no witnesses to the party's signatures, and as a result the agreement should be set aside for lack of proper form. Mrs. Muller filed a Motion for Summary Judgment, which was converted to an ordinary proceeding, and the matter went to trial on the merits on November 19, 2009. Following the trial that took place in November 2009, the trial court orally granted judgment in favor of Mrs. Muller, but the judgment was not reduced to writing.

Although the date is unclear from the record, at some point before the judgment was reduced to writing the trial court decided to reconsider its earlier ruling, granted a new trial on its own motion, and reheard the matter on January 13, 2010.1 Following that hearing, the trial court, in a judgment dated April 6, 2010, denied Mrs. Muller's petition finding the agreement to be valid. Mrs. Muller appeals.

At the hearing in January 2010 that forms the basis of this appeal, Mr. Muller testified that he could not recall who presented whom with the actual premarital matrimonial agreement, that he did not recall if he or Mrs. Muller prepared it, whether he obtained the form from an attorney, or if he downloaded it from a computer. He remembered taking the document to a notary, but admitted that there were no witnesses present when he executed the document. He denied Mrs. Muller's allegation that the agreement was signed by her at home prior to the time he brought it to the notary. He did not remember who had the agreement recorded. Mr. Muller could not recall whether or not he worked for several years following the marriage, although he did "cash jobs" sometimes "as long as I stayed under the federal limit." He did not recall if he had gone back to work in 1997, or exactly where he worked from 1997 till the parties moved their matrimonial domicile to Mississippi in 1999.

Mrs. Muller testified that the primary reason for the premarital matrimonial agreement was Mr. Muller's concern that her income would be used to calculate an increase in child support for Mr. Muller's child from a previous marriage. Mrs. Muller testified that Mr. Muller downloaded the form from the computer in their home, and presented it to her for her signature the day before their planned nuptials. She testified that she believed he would not marry her if she did not sign it. She testified that there was no one present at their home when she signed the document and, after she executed the agreement, Mr. Muller took the document to a notary with whom he was familiar, who notarized it. However, no witnesses signed the agreement. She did not testify as to how the document came to be recorded. Mrs. Muller testified that, once they were married, Mr. Muller never mentioned the premarital matrimonial agreement again.

According to the testimony of both parties, while they did observe certain formalities of a separate property regime, such as separate bank accounts and separate tax returns, they both testified that they acquired several pieces of real estate during the marriage, and that none of the acts of sale referenced or mentioned the premarital matrimonial agreement. Mrs. Muller also testified that she utilized a substantial portion of her income, and a separate property inheritance from her uncle, to pay expenses on renovation and upkeep of their joint properties, and to pay loans and other obligations that directly benefited Mr. Muller.

Following the second trial in this matter, the trial court entered judgment with written reasons dated April 6, 2010. While the trial court determined that the agreement had not been signed before a notary or two witnesses, and, as such, the premarital agreement was invalid as an authentic act, the trial court found that the agreement was valid as an act under private signature, duly acknowledged. The court reasoned that, the act was duly acknowledged because, in open court, Mrs. Muller twice admitted the signature as her own before numerous witnesses. The trial court went on to state that *Ritz v. Ritz*, a case from this Court,

> arbitrarily assumes that because all elements of an authentic act must be met *before* the marriage, then the same must be applied to all elements of an act under private signature duly acknowledged.... Pertinent statutory law is devoid of any reference to such requirement.... The 5th Circuit in *Ritz* combined two ideas that should not be combined and created a requirement that simply does not exist. (Emphasis in original).

The trial court further held, "The agreement benefitted both parties and was executed prior to the marriage. Therefore, the policy concern that necessitates court approval for agreements made during the marriage does not apply in this case."

La. C.C. art. 2331 states, "A matrimonial agreement may be executed by the spouses before or during marriage. It shall be made by authentic act or by an act under private signature duly acknowledged by the spouses." La. C.C. art. 2329 states, in pertinent part,

> Spouses may enter into a matrimonial agreement that modifies or terminates a matrimonial regime during marriage *only* upon joint petition and a finding by the court that this serves their best interests, and that they understand the governing principles and rules. They may, however, subject themselves to the legal regime by a matrimonial agreement at any time without court approval. (Emphasis added.)

In the case before us, the trial court incorrectly concludes, as a matter of law, that La. C.C. art. 2329 is inapplicable to this matter. The dictates of La. C.C. art. 2329 are not mere policy concerns, but a mandate made part of a statutory enactment that casts a suspicious eye on the establishment of a separation of property regime effected during the marriage. The codal requirement that any party entering into an agreement that modifies or terminates the matrimonial regime after marriage must do so by joint petition and a finding by a court that the modification is in the best interest of both parties, is without exception. The factual circumstances of this or any other case cannot act to vitiate its requirements. See *Lauga v. Lauga*, 537 So.2d 758 (La.App. 4th Cir.1989).

In *Ritz v. Ritz*, supra, this Court was faced with a factual situation similar to the matter now before us. Mr. and Mrs. Ritz entered into a premarital matrimonial contract that evidence showed failed as an authentic act. In considering whether or not the document sufficed as an act under private signature, we stated in Ritz:

> Mr. Ritz avers that because Mrs. Ritz admitted in court, as well as in her deposition, that she signed the document, the contract has been duly *acknowledged* and thus qualifies as an act under private signature. However, there is *nothing* in the record to indicate that *any* acknowledgment took place prior to or even during the marriage. We note that La. C.C. art. 2331, *supra*, has made *acknowledgment* a *requisite* to the validity of a matrimonial contract under private signature. Except for the exception stated in [La. C.C.] art. 2329, *supra*, just as all requirements of a pre-marital authentic act *must* be met *prior* to the marriage, so too, must all elements of an act under private signature *duly acknowledged* be done *prior*, or antecedent, to the marriage.

Ritz, supra at 1185 (Emphasis in original).

We find that the trial court's abrogation of the Ritz case was in error. The case before us presents no single fact that deviates from Ritz, and its premise remains sound. Both Mr. and Mrs. Muller testified that the document in question was executed prior to their marriage. Yet, even the trial court found that Mrs. Muller's signature was not properly witnessed by the notary and, as such, the document is not in authentic form.

Further, the record does not indicate that Mr. or Mrs. Muller duly acknowledged the matrimonial agreement before the marriage.

The issue is whether a party can duly acknowledge a signature on a premarital matrimonial agreement after the marriage. Here, Mrs. Muller did admit that her signature was on the premarital matrimonial document. However, as in *Ritz*, we note that "all elements of an act under private signature duly acknowledged be done prior, or antecedent, to the marriage." *Id.* We hold that a post-nuptial acknowledgement cannot vitiate the mandate of La. C.C. art. 2329 that any matrimonial agreement entered into during the marriage to modify or terminate a matrimonial regime must be by joint petition, and after a finding by the court that the agreement serves the best interests of the parties. For these reasons, the ruling of the trial court is reversed, and the premarital matrimonial agreement between these parties is declared to be null and void ab initio. Costs of these proceedings are assessed against the appellee, Mr. Muller.

REVERSED
EDWARDS, J., dissents.

McMANUS, J., dissents for the reasons assigned by Judge EDWARDS, C.J.

CRAIN, J., P.T., dissents for the reasons assigned by Judge EDWARDS, C.J.

EDWARDS, C.J., dissents.

I dissent from the majority opinion reversing the judgment in the present case. In my opinion, insofar as it determined that acknowledgement of a matrimonial agreement executed before the marriage must also be acknowledged as an act under private signature prior to the marriage, *Ritz v. Ritz* was incorrect. La. C.C. art. 2331 does not specify the time period in which an act under private signature must be acknowledged. In addition, La. C.C. art. 1836, in pertinent part, states:

> An act under private signature is regarded prima facie as the true and genuine act of a party executing it when his signature has been acknowledged, and the act shall be admitted in evidence without further proof.
>
> An act under private signature may be acknowledged by a party to that act by recognizing the signature as his own before a court, or before a notary public, or other officer authorized to perform that function, in the presence of two witnesses. An act under private signature may be acknowledged also in any other manner authorized by law.

There is nothing in either Louisiana Civil Code Article 2331 or Civil Code Article 1836 requiring that authentication must occur within a certain time, or before the marriage. La. C.C. art. 2331 does not specify the time period in which an act under private signature must be acknowledged. The general rules of authentication of private acts, La. C.C. arts. 1836 et seq., do not provide any express time period for acknowledgment. Our ruling in Ritz provided neither statutory nor jurisprudential authority for a determination that acknowledgment of a matrimonial agreement executed before the marriage must be acknowledged as an act under private signature prior to the marriage. Indeed, there is no such authority. Rather, the policy behind the requirement of acknowledgment of an act under private signature is, rather than cautionary (as with an authentic act), simply an evidentiary one, adding to the reliability of the written agreement as to what was actually executed by the parties.

For these reasons, I respectfully dissent, and would have reversed *Ritz v. Ritz* en banc, affirming the judgment of the trial court.

D. *Pattie Gilbert Shaw v. Gregory Stephen Shaw*

87 So. 3d 235 (La. App. 2d Cir. 2012)

BROWN, Chief Judge.

Questions concerning community or co-owned property and the retroactive application of a final child support judgment are at issue in this appeal. We affirm in part and reverse in part.

Facts and Procedural Background

After three years of living together, appellant, Gregory Stephen Shaw, and appellee, Pattie Gilbert Shaw, married on February 2, 2001. One child was born during this marriage. On February 19, 2009, Ms. Shaw filed a petition for divorce, custody, and permanent child support.

The Shaws executed a post-nuptial agreement on July 11, 2001, whereby they acknowledged a partition of their community property and established a separate property regime. A judgment approving the Shaws' petition was signed on July 13, 2001.1 Prior thereto, on May 31, 2001, Pattie Shaw formed Lancer Link Express, Inc. At the time of the post-nuptial execution, Lancer Link Express had not begun business operations or acquired any assets.

The Shaws worked together out of their home as freight brokers for Lancer Link Express. Upon the breakdown of their marriage, Mr. Shaw left the employ of the business. While the record is light on specifics, it is known that Mr. Shaw was unemployed for an extended period, during which he allegedly survived monetarily on unemployment benefits, raiding his retirement accounts, selling his baseball cards and gambling (the child support worksheet filed in the record shows that he earned $1,300 monthly shooting pool at Fast Eddies). Mr. Shaw attempted to start a competing freight brokerage firm until Ms. Shaw enjoined him from contacting Lancer Link Express clients. Ultimately, Mr. Shaw obtained full-time employment with Ashley Ann Energy. We also note that, on the date of judicial demand, February 19, 2009, the petition filed by Ms. Shaw sets forth her belief that Mr. Shaw was "living from his vehicle and/or residing at American Best Value Inn, Bossier City, Louisiana."

***

Community property

Mr. Shaw contends that the trial court erred in ruling that the parties' post-nuptial agreement terminated the existence of the community property regime as to property acquired before its execution. Specifically, Mr. Shaw contends that the trial court erred in ruling that all outstanding stock in Lancer Link Express was the separate property of Ms. Shaw.

The legal regime of married persons is the community of acquets and gains. La. C.C. art. 2327. Spouses may enter into a matrimonial agreement during marriage to modify or terminate the matrimonial regime only upon a joint petition and a finding by the court that it serves the parties' best interests. La. C.C. art. 2329. A matrimonial agreement is a contract establishing a regime of separation of property or modifying or terminating the legal regime. Spouses are free to establish by matrimonial agreement a regime of separation of property or modify the legal regime as provided by law. The provisions of the legal regime that have not been excluded or modified by agreement retain their force and effect. La. C.C. art. 2328.

As noted infra, the Shaws executed a post-nuptial agreement on July 11, 2001, whereby they acknowledged a partition of their community property and established a separate property regime. This agreement was approved by a judgment signed on July 13, 2001. Lancer Link Express was formed by Ms. Shaw on May 31, 2001. At the time of the parties' post-nuptial agreement, Lancer Link Express had not begun business operations or acquired any assets.

Mr. Shaw contends that since the company was formed prior to the establishment of the parties' separate party regime, it remains community property held in indivision by the parties since no partition of the property of their "community" has ever been effected. The trial court found, however, that the post-nuptial agreement clearly terminated the community of acquets and gains relating to all property acquired during the parties' marriage, including ownership of Lancer Link Express. We agree.

Relevant portions of the Shaws' post-nuptial agreement state:

> Paragraph II: During the marriage the parties have not acquired property, which was classified as community property under their previous regime. The parties hereby settle all claims, rights, and obligations resulting from their community property regime and enter into a separation of property regime.
>
> Paragraph VI: IN CONNECTION BOTH PARTIES DO ASSERT AND AFFIRM THAT THEY HAVE READ THIS AGREEMENT AND FULLY UNDERSTAND IT AND THAT THEY HAVE RECEIVED

> SUBSTANTIALLY EQUAL PROPERTY IN THIS PARTITION AGREEMENT ...
>
> Paragraph VIII: Each party agrees and stipulates that this agreement is a compromise of the disputes existing between them and has entered into for the purpose of partitioning the community of gains previously existing between them ... (Emphasis added).

It is clear that the parties intended to terminate the community property regime, and that they did in fact partition all existing community property prior to the establishment of their separate property regime. Mr. Shaw's claim to the contrary is not supported by the executed agreement.

***

E. *In re Dudley J. Boyer, Jr. and Pamela Donnell Boyer*

616 So. 2d 730 (La. App. 1st Cir. 1993)

EDWARDS, Judge.

The issue in this suit to have a matrimonial agreement terminating the legal regime declared null is whether the failure of the trial court to hold a hearing with the parties and the signing of the agreement before it was approved by the court rendered the agreement an absolute nullity. We find that, under the circumstances here, the failure to hold a hearing and the pre-approval signing of the document did not nullify the agreement. We reverse the summary judgment granted by the trial court declaring the matrimonial agreement and a partition null and remand for further proceedings.

Both parties to the matrimonial agreement, Pamela Donnell Boyer and her husband, Dudley J. Boyer, Jr., were represented by independent counsel. The matrimonial agreement terminating the community of acquets and gains that existed between the parties was executed before a notary and two witnesses, in compliance with Civil Code article 2331, on April 12, 1985; as was a partition of the community property owned at that time. Mrs. Boyer's attorney acted as notary on both of these documents. The parties, through their attorneys, submitted to the court a joint petition for establishment of a separate property regime and an affidavit executed by Mr. Boyer and Mrs. Boyer, and notarized by Mrs. Boyer's attorney, stating that they had sought legal counsel, they had read the petition and the agreement, they understood the rules and principles involved, and that the agreement was in their best interest. Neither party requested a hearing or appeared before the court. The trial court reviewed the agreement and submitted documents and found that the parties understood the governing rules and principles and that the agreement was in the best interests of the parties. Court approval of the matrimonial agreement was obtained on April 19, 1985. That judgment was not appealed, and is definitive. The matrimonial agreement and the partition agreement were filed in the parish conveyance records on April 24, 1985.

On September 24, 1990, Mrs. Boyer filed a suit for declaratory judgment seeking to have the matrimonial agreement and the contemporaneously executed partition declared null and void. The petition alleged that the agreement was an absolute nullity because: (1) she had signed only under duress, and (2) the procedure followed to obtain court approval was defective.

Mrs. Boyer filed a motion for summary judgment praying that the agreement and the partition be declared null. As a basis for the summary judgment, she argued that the agreement was defective because: (1) the agreement was signed before court approval was given for the document to be signed, (2) a hearing, as contemplated by LSA-C.C. article 2329, was not held, (3) the trial court that granted approval was misled into believing that the agreement had not been signed on April 12, and (4) the agreement was not in authentic form. It was also argued that, if the agreement was null and without legal effect, the partition, which was entered into only because of the contemplated termination of the matrimonial regime, must also be declared null.

The trial court granted the motion for summary judgment and found that the agreement and the partition were null and without legal effect because the procedures followed to obtain court approval for the agreement were insufficient to validate the agreement. Specifically, the trial court found that no hearing was conducted and the agreement was signed before court approval was obtained. Because the agreement was invalid, the cause for the partition of the community property failed. Defendant, Mr. Boyer appealed.

Louisiana Civil Code article 2329 provides:

> Spouses may enter into a matrimonial agreement before or during marriage as to all matters that are not prohibited by public policy.
>
> Spouses may enter into a matrimonial agreement that modifies or terminates a matrimonial regime during marriage only upon joint petition and a finding by the court that this serves their best interests and that they understand the governing principles and rules. They may, however, subject themselves to the legal regime by a matrimonial agreement at any time without court approval.
>
> During the first year after moving into and acquiring a domicile in this state, spouses may enter into a matrimonial agreement without court approval.

Clearly, article 2329 imposes certain procedural limitations on the spouse's ability to implement a contract for the termination of the legal regime during their marriage.

The trial court must be satisfied that the spouses both agree to the change, that the spouses understand the rules and principles underlying a change in the matrimonial regime, and that the agreement appears to serve the best interest of the spouses.

The probable goal of the limitations appears to be the legislature's attempt to protect the less worldly spouse and to prevent that spouse from entering into disadvantageous agreements that the spouse did not fully understand. See Spaht and Samuel, Equal Management Revisited: 1979 Legislative Modifications of the 1978 Matrimonial Regimes Law, 40 La.L.Rev. 83, 90-91 (1979). However, the best interest requirement, under traditional Civil Code analysis, does not dictate perfect symmetry in the agreement concerning assets or opportunities, if both spouses freely consented to the agreement. Neither should the agreement be judged based on a hindsight view of the success of various assets or opportunities. See id. at 95-97.

Signing the agreement in the form required by Civil Code article 2331 is one of the necessary steps in achieving a valid agreement modifying or terminating the matrimonial regime. Obviously, the clearest route to a valid agreement would be to sign the submitted agreement after the court has approved the document. However, we find no language in article 2329 that requires a specific time sequence.

The parties were seeking the court's approval of the agreement to terminate the matrimonial regime, not the court's permission to sign or to contract. Under Civil Code article 2328, the parties are free to contract a separate property regime or to modify the legal regime, subject to certain procedural limitations. To complete the process, article 2329 requires a joint petition and court approval of the submitted contract or matrimonial agreement before the parties can enter into or, in other words, implement or participate in the agreement. To be able to submit an agreement to the trial court for approval, an agreement between the parties must be negotiated and finalized, at the very least, in spirit, if not by signing.

The spouses here each sought and obtained independent legal counsel and the petition to establish a separate property regime was submitted jointly. Mrs. Boyer does not claim that she did not join in the petition or that she did not sign or understand the matrimonial agreement. Rather she alleges that the document is defective because it was signed by the parties before court approval was granted.

We fail to see how the pre-approval signing of the document, under the facts here, defeats the goal of the legislature or the requirements of article 2329. Mrs. Boyer was represented by her own counsel. The agreement and the joint petition are very clear on the purpose of the documents; the purpose being to terminate the matrimonial regime. After court approval was obtained, the agreement between the spouses met the requirements of law and became a valid matrimonial agreement terminating the matrimonial regime. Of course, if the court had disapproved the agreement between the parties, the process could not be completed and the matrimonial agreement would have no validity and could not be implemented.

We find no requirement in article 2329 for a hearing before the court can grant approval. Certain statutory laws in Louisiana do require a full hearing before a trial court can make a decision, but article 2329 is not one of them. Of course, it is within the discretion of the trial court to order a hearing and the parties may ask for a hearing. Neither was not done in this case.

The trial court did not base its grant of summary judgment on Mrs. Boyer's arguments that the trial court was misled or that the agreement was not in authentic form, nor do we find these arguments to have merit. Although the matrimonial agreement submitted to the trial court exhibited no signatures, it clearly stated, in the closing paragraph, that the document had been signed in the presence of the undersigned notary and two witnesses on April 12, 1985. The agreement filed in the public record contained the required signatures and met the requirements of Civil Code article 1833. Mr. Boyer disputes the allegation that the court was misled and the record reveals no evidence that any attempt was made to mislead the court or to purposefully conceal the fact that the agreement had been signed on April 12.

Even assuming, for the sake of Mrs. Boyer's nullity argument, that the pre-approval signing created, at best, a relative nullity, the agreement was ratified by the parties after the approval was granted and the parties filed the documents in the public record. See Clay v. Clay, 358 So.2d 649, 651 (La.App. 1st Cir.1978). Mrs. Boyer makes no claim in the record that she did not agree to the filing or that the matrimonial agreement and partition of property was not followed.

For these reasons, we reverse the grant of summary judgment and remand for further proceedings consistent with this opinion. The costs of the appeal are assessed to appellee, Mrs. Boyer.

REVERSED AND REMANDED.

SHORTESS, J., agrees with the majority. Summary judgment was not the appropriate way to decide this dispute.

F. *Iona Senora Wells Williams v. Michael David Williams*

760 So. 2d 469 (La. App. 3d Cir. 2000)

GREMILLION, Judge.

In this case, the defendant, Michael David Williams, husband of the plaintiff, Iona Senora Wells Williams, appeals the judgment of the trial court which upheld a post-nuptial agreement entered into by the couple. Michael appealed. For the following reasons, we reverse and render.

FACTUAL AND PROCEDURAL BACKGROUND

Iona and Michael were married on July 12, 1996, after having dated and lived together for many years. Agreements affecting the matrimonial regime and spousal support were subsequently confected and are at issue in this suit. Following an original handwritten agreement allegedly signed by the parties in January 1997, the parties signed an agreement on July 2, 1997, before a notary and two witnesses. The face of the document indicates that the couple agreed to terminate the community property regime and, further, provided, that in the event of separation or divorce, Michael would provide the following support for Iona: $2,500.00 per month, medical, and health insurance coverage for the remainder of her life, and medical/health expenses not covered by insurance. The agreement also provided that Michael would maintain a life insurance policy on himself and designate Iona as the beneficiary.

In a Joint Petition for Modification of Matrimonial Regime, filed on July 7, 1997, the parties presented the agreement and represented to the trial court that they were subject to the "legal regime of community property under the laws of the State of Louisiana," that they wished to terminate the community property regime, and that they had reached an agreement as to the division of community property they believed to be fair and equitable. By this joint petition, they asked "that they be allowed to terminate the legal regime of community property presently existing between them and to establish and enter into a regime of separation of property, as allowed by Civil Code Article 2329."

On July 9, 1997, the trial court signed the following order: "IT IS ORDERED that Michael David Williams and Iona Senora Wells Williams be and are hereby allowed to terminate the legal regime of community property as allowed by Civil Code Article 2329." The order and the agreement were filed with the Clerk of Court for Beauregard Parish on July 14, 1997.

The instant matter was instituted on June 15, 1998, when Iona filed a Petition for Divorce alleging that she was entitled to divorce, pursuant to La.Civ.Code art. 102, after she and Michael had lived separate and apart in excess of 180 days. She further asked for a hearing on a motion to show cause why Michael should not provide the support described in the above agreement. An order to show cause was subsequently signed by the trial court. In a separate action, Iona filed a Petition for Breach of Contract and Enforcement of Contract to Terminate Matrimonial Regime, wherein she alleged entitlement to enforcement of the provisions of the marital agreement. Following Michael's filing of a rule to show cause, a Judgment of Divorce was signed and filed on January 21, 1999. As the issues remaining in each of the actions filed by Iona dealt with enforcement of the marital agreement, the two matters were consolidated.

Following the filing of additional motions regarding the agreement and alimony by Iona, a hearing was held on the matter on March 4, 1999. During the hearing, Iona sought enforcement of the terms of the agreement, while Michael contended, chiefly, that he entered into the agreement out of duress and that the contract should not be enforced either due to a failure of cause or because the terms are against public policy. The trial court heard witness testimony, including that of the parties, and also reviewed exhibits, including the petition to terminate the marital regime, the order doing so, and the signed agreement. The court found in favor of Iona, giving the following reasons for enforcement:

> We have two documents in evidence here, P–1, which is dated January 10, 1997; and the court record in C–97–614, which basically is a contract styled "Termination of Matrimonial Regime Between Michael David Williams and Iona Senora Wells Williams" and the petition, which asks for permission to terminate. Both of those documents were signed by Michael David Williams, the P–1, there having been some notations made on by him in addition to his signature. The termination document was executed nearly seven months later, on July 2, 1997, prepared by an attorney which both Mr. Williams and Ms. Williams state was their attorney. The Court finds no reason why the provisions of the termination of matrimonial regime document, including the paragraph B which refers to payment of alimony pendente lite or permanent alimony, why these should not be enforced. My primary reason that I do not think that there is any reason why they should not be enforced is I do not see that there was any duress which would have continued from January 10 up to July 2, 1997. There may have been some duress that may have arisen from some other things; but, generally speaking, I believe that this was a document that Mr. Williams was quite willing to execute of his own free will, although it may have been that he was doing so because he thought it would make things better at home.
>
> In any event, I think it's extremely significant that this couple had been together for a period of 19 years and lived together for a period of ten years. And, quite frankly, I think when [counsel for Michael] asked Ms. Williams—or Ms. Wells—why Mr. Williams would want to execute an agreement that

> provided for this, I think it pretty well summed it up that he felt responsible, that they had been together all this time, that she had done a lot of things for him during that time. In short, that he felt it was his moral responsibility.

Therefore, it is the holding of the Court that there is no need for a fault hearing in this matter; that the parties have contractually agreed to the payment of interim spousal support—which was previously called alimony pendente lite and permanent alimony—in the amount of $2,500 per month. And that is the Court's ruling.

Michael appeals, assigning several errors, primarily arguing that the agreement was not statutorily sufficient, no lawful cause existed for the obligation, and, alternatively, that the agreement was entered into as a result of duress. Iona has answered the appeal alleging that Michael's appeal is frivolous and requesting attorney's fees and expenses associated with the appeal.

DISCUSSION

Validity of Matrimonial Agreement

In his first assignment of error, Michael contends that the trial court erred in not finding that the agreement was invalid due to statutory deficiencies. He contends that the agreement did not comply with La.Civ.Code art. 2329, in that no judicial determination was made that the agreement was in the best interest of the parties and that the parties understood the governing principles and rules.

***

We begin our review by observing that this is not a case where the parties entered into the agreement within the first year of moving into and acquiring domicile in the state, a situation which would not have required court approval according to the third paragraph of Article 2329. Rather, the agreement at issue was entered into during the marriage and required judicial approval as described in the second paragraph of Article 2329. Thus, the trial court was required to make a twofold determination: 1) that the joint petition to terminate the matrimonial regime serves the parties' best interests and; 2) that the parties understand the governing principles and rules.

Despite the necessity for the trial court's consideration of the matrimonial agreement before it was signed, there is no indication that any procedure was followed in this case other than the submission of a joint petition with the attached agreement, which was followed by an order by the trial court. According to Article 2329, this procedure, as a matter of law, was insufficient to terminate the matrimonial regime and, therefore, we find error in the trial court's failure to recognize the lack of compliance with the codal requirement. See Poirier v. Poirier, 626 So.2d 868 (La.App. 3 Cir.), writ denied, 634 So.2d 389 (La.1994); Lauga v. Lauga, 537 So.2d 758 (La.App. 4 Cir.1989). Because the matrimonial agreement does not meet the formal requirements found in Article

2329, we find that it is null and void insofar as it modifies or terminates the matrimonial regime of the parties.

***

8.3 CAPACITY AND CONSENT TO CONTRACT, CONSCIONABILITY

A. Introduction

No special capacity rules exist for matrimonial agreements in Louisiana. Revision Comment (b) to Civil Code article 2328 explains that the general obligations rules applicable to other contracts apply to matrimonial agreements. Spouses are presumed to have capacity to execute matrimonial agreements and the validity of an agreement depends on the free consent of both spouses. Error, fraud, and duress are the only grounds available for challenging consent. Unlike many other jurisdictions, validity of the prenuptial agreement is unaffected by failure of the parties to obtain separate legal representation. However, lack of separate representation is often an important factor in determining whether a party's consent was vitiated by fraud, error, or duress.

In some respects, Louisiana's approach to capacity and consent is more lenient than the approach taken under the UPAA and the adopting jurisdictions. The UPAA addresses capacity by explaining when an agreement is not enforceable. Specifically, Section 6 of the UPAA provides that "a premarital agreement is not enforceable if a party against whom enforcement is sought" is able to prove that "the party did not execute the agreement voluntarily." Voluntariness is similar to the requirement of free consent and can generally be challenged on the grounds of fraud, duress, or mistake. In adopting the UPAA, some states added additional requirements. California Family Code §1615, for example, provides premarital agreements are deemed involuntary unless the court makes certain findings of fact. The court must find that the parties were represented by independent counsel (or gave an informed waiver and met other requirements) and the parties must have had at least seven days between being presented with the agreement and signing the agreement. Louisiana has no corresponding waiting period or requirement for independent representation, as is amply illustrated in the following cases.

Section 6 of the UPAA also provides that an agreement may be unenforceable if it was "unconscionable when it was executed." Unconscionability is a question of law to be decided by the court. The Comment to Section 6 explains that this standard "includes protection against onesidedness, oppression, or unfair surprise." Furthermore, "in the context of negotiations between spouses as to the financial incidents of their marriage, the standard includes protection against overreaching, concealment of assets, and sharp dealing not consistent with the obligations of marital partners to deal fairly with each other." Unconscionability alone will not invalidate the prenuptial agreement. Rather, the party challenging the agreement must prove "the agreement was unconscionable when it was executed and, before execution of the agreement the party:"

> (i) was not provided a fair and reasonable disclosure of the property or financial obligations of the other party;
> (ii) did not voluntarily and expressly waive, in writing, any right to disclosure of the property or financial obligations of the other party beyond the disclosure provided; and
> (iii) did not have, or reasonably could not have had, an adequate knowledge of the property or financial obligations of the other party.

UPAA §6.

The practical effect of Section 6 is to require a full disclosure of the assets and liabilities of both spouses at the time the agreement is executed or a waiver of that disclosure. Louisiana has no comparable requirement. However, many Louisiana prenuptial agreements include waiver language nonetheless.

B. *Rosemary Brumfield v. H. Alva Brumfield, III*

477 So. 2d 1161 (La. App. 1st Cir.)

EDWARDS, Judge.

This is a suit by Rosemary Meyers Brumfield (Rosemary) against her former husband, H. Alva "Beau" Brumfield III (Beau), in which she sought to have declared null and void a marriage contract executed by them on December 19, 1968, the day before they were married. Mrs. Brumfield also prayed for other relief in her petition, resulting in a decision by this court reported in 415 So.2d 520 (La.App. 1st Cir.1982). The case presently before us concerns only the validity of the pre-nuptial agreement, other contentions between the parties having been disposed of elsewhere.

The facts and events surrounding the execution of the contract are in dispute. Beau Brumfield, an attorney, testified that the agreement was signed by Rosemary and himself on the day before their wedding, at his law office, in the presence of a notary and two witnesses. Rosemary, on the other hand, denied that it happened that way at all. She said she was ill that entire day and stayed at home, at her parents' house, in the company of family and friends. She testified that Beau and his secretary, Linda Nugent, brought the contract over for her to sign.

By Rosemary's account, Beau first presented her with the document in the living room. She asked to read it but he said no, that it was legal and she would not understand it. At that point she was "really in kind of a huff" and went to her bedroom.

Beau followed her there and they continued their conversation. Beau said the document was very important and had to be signed before they were married the next day. Rosemary again asked to read it but Beau refused, again telling her it was a legal paper and that she would not understand it. She said she would not sign, whereupon Beau said he would not marry her. At that point she angrily told him to leave the house. "... Then he started begging me to sign it. He said it was very important, that it had to be signed, that it protected our community property."

She went on to testify that Beau never referred to the paper as a marriage contract or as a contract of any sort. He said it was based on inside information that he and his father, also an attorney, had concerning the legal future of community property in Louisiana. The Supreme Court, Beau told her, was going to "knock down" the community property laws of the state, but this document had been drawn in such a way as to protect the community between the two of them regardless what the Supreme Court did. He made no further explanation. Finally, she signed the contract without reading it.

Her testimony continued to the effect that she put the incident completely out of her mind, saying nothing about it to her family or friends. Then, about seven or eight years later, she had occasion to speak with Beau's legal secretary at that time, Betty Wilkinson, about Betty's marriage contract. Betty said she had signed such a paper without knowing what it was, and had defeated it in court.

"... In listening to her conversation," Rosemary testified, "I remember telling her that I signed some kind of paper but that mine protected community property ... "I remember she either said that you are crazy if that is what you think it is, or something like that.... From what she said, I got the idea that it probably wasn't what I thought it was."

By now, Rosemary testified, she was sufficiently awakened to get a draft copy of the contract she had signed and to confront Beau with it.

> ... I read it and the second paragraph is the one that I was concerned about. I faced Beau with it that night and said you know, this is not what you told me it was, and I understand this second paragraph clearly, and it does not say it protects our community property. He told me at that time that I still did not understand it, then he had told me that I would not understand the legal jargon or whatever, and that I would misunderstand it, and that was why he had not let me read it originally and that I still misunderstood it. The next night he came in with legal sheets of properties that were ours.

They talked about the list of properties, Beau persuading her that there was a community and that these holdings were part of it. He repeated that she had misunderstood the agreement. "We never really talked about it again, but I was really confused," she testified. "I wasn't ever—I didn't really know whether to believe him or not."

Beau finally revealed the truth to her, she said, on the day they separated in January of 1981.

The Saturday that he told me he was moving out, at the end—he had a long discussion and at the end he said, 'By the way, that contract you signed says you own nothing, absolutely nothing. I have lied about it all these years and you don't so much as own the clothes on your back, so get your kids and get a job and get out of this house,' is what he said.

Rosemary's testimony concluded with this exchange:

Q. I want to know why you signed this contract without reading it.

> A. I loved him and I trusted him and he was an attorney and I knew nothing about legal matters. I guess the main reason was that I loved him very much and I trusted him.

The contract in question was introduced into evidence by both sides. Defendant produced a greatly enlarged photocopy measuring three (3) feet across and two and one-half (2½) feet in length. It was placed upon a stand facing the jury and remained there through three days of testimony. Many of the witnesses referred to it as they answered questions.

The second paragraph, which Rosemary testified had troubled her, was clear and direct, totally free of ambiguity:

> ... [S]aid intended husband and wife shall be separate in property. Accordingly, they hereby formally renounce those provisions of the Revised Civil Code which establish a community of acquets and gains between husband and wife.

It was signed by R.C. Meyers III and by John Jeffries as witnesses; H. Alva Brumfield III and Rosemary Meyers; and by Sylvia Roberts, notary public.

The witnesses to the contract split their testimony, one testifying for each side. John Jeffries, an attorney who had known Beau for many years, said he signed with Rosemary and Beau at Beau's law office. Richard Meyers III, Rosemary's brother, said he signed the paper in blank, at his parents' house, with no one present other than himself and Beau Brumfield.

Sylvia Roberts, an attorney who shared space in the Brumfield law office, served as the notary public. She testified that everything had been done properly, with all parties in her presence as recited in the agreement. She testified further that she had great reverence for the duties and responsibilities of a notary and that she had never notarized anything unless the persons involved were present, signing before she did.

Rosemary testified about other matters besides the signing of the contract. She said she was sick with a fever that day and did not leave the house until evening, when she attended the wedding rehearsal and dinner afterward. She did not attend a wedding party after the dinner, however, because she was still not feeling well. Rosemary said that her illness was the result of a smallpox vaccination she had received several days before. This was in preparation for a honeymoon trip to Europe, a last-minute gift from Beau.

Corroborating testimony came from her mother and sister who said that, between them, they were at the house with Rosemary all day; from Denise Whittington, who said she greeted Beau Brumfield at the door when he arrived to bring Rosemary the contract; and from Rosemary's co-workers at her job, who verified that she had been unwell all that week.

Beau Brumfield testified that he did not go to the Meyers residence at all on the day in question. He said that he met Rosemary and her brother at the law office, by pre-arranged appointment, to sign the contract. He said Rosemary had read the contract, knew what it said and what it meant, and that she desired the protection it would offer her. He spoke at length about his own vulnerability to suit and judgment, and how the agreement would keep Rosemary safe in the event that a judgment were obtained against him which might exceed his ability to pay.

Beau said Rosemary was not sick at all that day. He said she attended the wedding rehearsal, was happy and outgoing, and drank champagne with the guests. His counsel introduced a series of photographs taken at the rehearsal dinner showing Rosemary holding a wine glass and having it refilled. Beau admitted that she did not attend the party after the dinner, but said she was full of life and that he could hardly keep up with her two days later in New York.

There was rebuttal testimony in which Rosemary said she had done no drinking at the rehearsal dinner but had stood around with a glass, posing for pictures and trying to be sociable. In addition, there was rebuttal testimony showing that in the Brumfield law practice it was not unusual for documents to be signed in blank at the office or elsewhere, and to be notarized later.

This case was tried before a jury in January, 1984. The testimony was totally irreconcilable. The jury found for the plaintiff. The court entered judgment for Rosemary, declaring the purported marriage contract null and void, thus restoring her right to community property. Defendant brought this suspensive appeal specifying eight assignments of error.

***

JURY'S FINDING OF FRAUD

Defendant contends in this third assignment of error that the trial court should have granted a motion for judgment notwithstanding the verdict, on the ground that the jury's finding of fraud is contrary to the law and the evidence.

LSA–C.C. art. 1847 defines the kind of fraud sufficient to nullify a contract.

> Fraud, as applied to contract, is the cause of an error bearing on a material part of the contract, created or continued by artifice, with design to obtain some unjust advantage to the one party, or to cause an inconvenience or loss to the other.

A charge of fraud is most serious and grave. Fraud is never to be imputed to anyone except upon legal evidence which must be strong and convincing, not merely probable or of a suspicious nature. Packwood v. Johnson, 264 So.2d 663 (La.App. 1st Cir.1972). Although Article 1847 is found in that portion of the Civil Code dealing with nullity of contracts resulting from defects of consent, including error, it is clear that to constitute fraud the error must be caused by fraudulent misrepresentation. Buston v. McKendrick, 64 So.2d 844, 223 La. 62 (1953); Broussard v. Fidelity Standard Life Insurance Co., 146 So.2d 292 (La.App. 3rd Cir.1962).

In the case before us, defendant contends that a review of the entire record cannot support a finding of fraud by strong and convincing evidence. This contention is not correct. Testimony is evidence. The record contains sufficient testimony for conclusive proof of fraud, assuming the testimony can be believed.

Rosemary's evidence, stated in one paragraph, is that defendant went to her home and, through persuasion and deception, obtained her signature on a contract which he did not allow her to read; that he persuaded Richard Meyers III to sign the agreement in blank, as a witness; that, in spite of his denials, he and his secretary, Linda Nugent, were seen at the Meyers home that day by Denise Whittington; that several years later he compounded his deception by showing Rosemary a list of holdings purported to be property held in community by the two of them; and that when the marriage ended in separation in 1981, he confessed that he had lied to her about the nature of the contract from the beginning.

This tapestry of deception, assuming again that it can be believed, proves fraud beyond any doubt and beyond the requirements of law. All doubts are removed and all legal standards of proof are met when a party asserts the triumph of his own duplicity. The question before us, then, is not only a matter of law and evidence, but of believability.

By its very nature, fraud has as many different styles and disguises as those who engage in it. Some kinds of fraud are more easily proved than others. In the case of commercial or industrial fraud, for instance, a team of auditors can often go in and examine books, records and inventories, and in a few hours produce tangible proof of deception. It is much different in the case of intimate fraud between lovers. Usually no one is present except the two parties, and records are quite often not kept. Yet there is no doctrine that intimate fraud cannot be successfully proved.

Since there is sufficient evidence to prove plaintiff's case, the question is whether it can be believed. There is an ancient principle in our law that it is the peculiar province of a jury to pass on the credibility of witnesses. A verdict will not be disturbed on questions of fact involving the credibility of witnesses unless that verdict is manifestly erroneous. Selser v. Revol, 152 La. 447, 93 So. 675 (1922); Continental Bank & Trust Co. v. Sacks, 152 La. 97, 92 So. 747 (1922); Moret v. New Orleans Rys. Co., 112 La. 863, 36 So. 759 (1904).

In Hardie v. Allen, 50 So.2d 74 (Orleans App.1951), the court said at page 76:

> The law requires exceptionally strong proof to sustain a charge of fraud.... But upon questions of fraud in fact, an appellate court will be reluctant to interfere with the verdict of the jury, and it seems that more deference will be paid to verdicts on questions of fraud than to verdicts on other questions of fact. (citations omitted)

This principle has endured because it is based on the jury's advantage in hearing and seeing the testimony firsthand. They observe the demeanor of witnesses and hear the nuances of voice. These things must be respected on appeal since they cannot be shown in a written record.

Was the jury's verdict manifestly erroneous? A finding that the defendant went to the Meyers residence on the day in question is certainly not unreasonable. There is testimony by Rosemary and two witnesses placing him there. Although there were no witnesses to the private conversation regarding the contract, evidence of Beau's presence there, at all, is most damaging to his case. A major part of his defense was that he did not go to the Meyers home for any reason that day. His counsel produced testimony tending to show that he was elsewhere at the hour in question. Thus a finding that he visited Rosemary is also a finding that he went there to obtain her signature. Although thoughtful people may differ with this line of reasoning, it is supported by the evidence and it cannot be called "manifestly erroneous."

The legal standard to be applied when reviewing a jury's findings is set out in Gardner v. Allstate Insurance Company, 422 So.2d 1380 (La.App. 1st Cir.1982):

> The record of the proceeding must reveal a reasonable factual basis for the finding of the trial court, and a further determination that the finding is not clearly wrong.

The jury's verdict in the case at bar meets this test in spite of conflicting testimony. Defense counsel writes extensively in his brief concerning the irreconcilability of the testimony, urging that the jury's verdict is unsupported. It is true that the two sides had conflicting versions of the facts, but this does not mean the verdict is legally flawed.

Even though appellant has shown conflicting testimony as to each of these findings, it is not proper to substitute our judgment ... when there is a reasonable factual basis in the record supporting such a finding and the finding is not clearly wrong. As was stated in Martin v. Feiber, 357 So.2d 5 (La.App. 1st Cir.1977), "[A]ppellate courts must accord great weight to the factual findings of the trier of fact. When testimony is in conflict, reasonable evaluations of credibility and reasonable inferences of fact drawn by the trier of fact should not be disturbed on appeal...." The valuations of credibility in this case are supported by reasonable evidence. Dundy v. Louisiana State University, 394 So.2d 650 (La.App. 1st Cir.1980).

We conclude that plaintiff successfully carried the burden of proof required for a case of fraud and that the jury's verdict is supported by the evidence. Defendant's third assignment of error is without merit.

***

C. *John Haas Weinstein v. Linda Allen Weinstein*

62 So. 3d 878 (La. App. 3d Cir. 2011)

PAINTER, Judge.

Defendant, Linda Allen Weinstein, appeals the trial court's judgment regarding the existence of a community regime between her and her former husband, John Haas Weinstein, and the amount of child support to be paid for their minor child. For the following reasons, we affirm in part and reverse in part.

FACTS AND PROCEDURAL HISTORY

John and Linda were married on August 8, 1986. On August 7, 1986, the day before the wedding, they signed a separation of property agreement. Two children were born of the marriage, only one of whom was a minor at the time of the ruling from the child support hearing appealed herein. On August 7, 1997, they filed a joint petition to affirm an agreement establishing a community property regime. On that same day, an order was signed recognizing the agreement establishing a community property regime. They separated in March 2004, and a judgment of divorce was signed on April 1, 2005.

On January 21, 2010, after a lengthy hearing, the trial court rendered a partial final judgment finding that the prenuptial agreement was effective in creating a separation of property regime between the parties. The judgment also granted a motion for involuntary dismissal as to the claims that the trial court order established a community regime in August 1997. Linda appeals.

DISCUSSION

***

Prenuptial Agreement

Linda next asserts that the trial court erred in finding the prenuptial agreement to be valid and in granting the motion for involuntary dismissal in that regard. She argues that she signed the contract as a result of fraud on the part of John and that John was in violation of the rules of professional conduct in that he was her lawyer at the time they entered into the contract and was prohibited from contracting with her where they had differing interests in the contract.

> Consent, which is necessary for the formation of a valid contract, may be vitiated by error, fraud, or duress. La. C.C. art. 1948. In order to establish that a party's consent to a contract has been vitiated due to error, the error must concern a cause without which the obligation would not have been incurred and that cause was known or should have been known to the other party. La. C.C. art. 1949. Cause is defined as the reason why a party obligates himself. La. C.C. art. 1967.
>
> Error may concern a cause when it bears on the nature of the contract, or the thing that is the contractual object or a substantial quality of that thing, or the person or the qualities of the other party, or the law, or any other circumstance that the parties regarded, or should in good faith have regarded, as a cause of the obligation.

La. C.C. art. 1950. However, in order to establish that a party's consent has been vitiated due to fraud, the error need not concern the cause of the obligation, but it must concern a circumstance that has substantially influenced the party's consent. La. C.C. art. 1955.

Greenland v. Greenland, 08–2568, pp. 4–5 (La.App. 1 Cir. 12/9/09), 29 So.3d 647, 651, writ denied, 10–0004 (La.3/5/10), 28 So.3d 1011.

Louisiana Civil Code Article 1953 defines fraud as "a misrepresentation or a suppression of the truth made with the intention either to obtain an unjust advantage for one party or to cause a loss or inconvenience to the other." Further, "[f]raud need only be proved by a preponderance of the evidence and may be established by circumstantial evidence." La.Civ.Code art. 1957. *See Alvis v. CIT Group/Equip. Fin., Inc.*, 05–0563 (La.App. 3 Cir. 12/30/05), 918 So.2d 1177, writ denied, 06–0226 (La.4/24/06), 926 So.2d 552. In support of her allegations of fraud, Linda introduced into evidence a diary entry by John written approximately ten years after his marriage in which he examined his feelings about his marriage and ways in which he felt he could or could have improved his relationship with his wife and his failures in so doing. The trial court did not feel that this document was evidence of fraud, and we cannot say that it rises to the level of indicating "a misrepresentation or a suppression of the truth made with the intention either to obtain an unjust advantage for one party or to cause a loss or inconvenience to the other" at the time the marriage agreement was entered.

Linda further asserts that John violated the rules of professional conduct by entering into a marriage contract with her while he was acting as her attorney. As John notes, there is no positive law prohibiting an attorney from entering a prenuptial agreement with a client. However, John argues that his representation of her in connection with her prior divorce did not encompass representation as to the prenuptial contract. We agree that to assert a conflict in this regard, Linda had the burden of showing that John's representation extended to the prenuptial contract.

The relationship between an attorney and his client is purely contractual in nature and results only from a clear and express agreement between the parties. *Keller v. LeBlanc*, 368 So.2d 193 (La.App. 1 Cir.1979). Establishment of an attorney-client relationship is adequately proven when it is shown that the advice and assistance are sought and received in matters pertinent to his profession or when the agreement of representation has been made under conditions acceptable to both parties. *State v. Green,* 493 So.2d 1178 (La.1986); *Lirette v. Roe*, 93–0441 (La.App. 4 Cir. 1/13/94) 631 So.2d 503. *Spicer v. Gambel*, 00–1995 (La.App. 4 Cir. 6/20/01), 789 So.2d 741, 744.

While it is well established that the existence of an attorney-client relationship depends to a great degree on the client's subjective belief that it exists, the belief must be reasonable. *St. Paul Fire and Marine Ins. Co. v. GAB Robins N. Am., Inc.*, 08–331

(La.App. 4 Cir. 11/19/08), 999 So.2d 72. Additionally, "[a]greement of an attorney to represent a client as to a particular matter does not create an agency relationship as regards other business affairs of the client." *Massey v. Cunningham*, 420 So.2d 1036, 1038 (La.App. 5 Cir.1982), quoting *Tullier v. Tanson Enterprises, Inc.*, 359 So.2d 654 (La.App. 1st Cir.1978).

It is uncontested that John, as well as several other attorneys, represented Linda in connection with a prior divorce. However, our examination of the record does not reveal enough proof to show that the scope of that representation extended to the prenuptial agreement. The record does not contain any testimony from Linda as to her subjective belief in this regard, nor did she introduce a contract evidencing an attorney-client relationship in connection with the prenuptial agreement.

Additionally, the record shows that Linda received advice to seek separate legal representation with regard to the prenuptial agreement and chose not to follow that advice. Counsel for Linda called Anthony Fazzio, an attorney practicing in Lafayette, Louisiana, to testify at the hearing on the marital regime. In response to questioning by counsel for Linda, Fazzio testified as follows: John was a friend since law school, and he had occasionally been co-counsel on cases with John. He enrolled as counsel on Linda's prior divorce at John's request. John and Linda showed up at his office without an appointment, and Linda asked to speak to him in private and told him that John wanted her to sign a prenuptial agreement. He asked her if she understood that he was a friend of John's. He further instructed her that she should get someone to read the document and prepare it from her point of view. He told her that while it would protect her if anyone sued John, it would also keep her from sharing in his successes, and she responded by saying that she was not interested in John's money. A short time later, John and Linda came back, and the agreement was signed and notarized in front of witnesses.

In light of the evidence of record, we find no error in the trial court's ruling with regard to the validity of the prenuptial agreement and in granting the motion for involuntary dismissal in that regard.

Attorney–Client Privilege

Linda next asserts that the trial court erred in finding that there was no attorney-client privilege between Linda and attorneys Shepton Hunter, John Haas Weinstein, Anthony Fazzio, and David L. Carriere as to the prenuptial agreement. However, we find no error in this finding. We have already found that Linda failed to carry her burden of showing that John was acting as her legal representative in connection with the prenuptial agreement. Further, there is no evidence that David Carriere ever acted as Linda's legal representative. With regard to the attorney-client privilege, if any, arising out of an attorney-client relationship between Linda and either Fazzio or Hunter, we find that Linda waived any such privilege by calling them as witnesses and questioning them concerning potentially privileged matters. La.Code. Evid. art. 502 provides that the holder of a privilege may waive it by disclosing the privileged information or by consenting to its disclosure. Linda consented to the disclosure of any information testified to by Fazzio and Hunter at her behest.

***

8.4 TERMINATION OF AGREEMENTS

A. Introduction

Spouses are free to terminate an existing matrimonial agreement during marriage. Louisiana Civil Code article 2329 provides that spouses may "subject themselves to the legal regime by a matrimonial agreement at any time without court approval." The cases that follow examine the intent and form requirement needed to terminate an existing matrimonial agreement.

B. *Ned Martello v. Laurie B. Martello*

960 So. 2d 186 (La. App. 1st Cir. 2007)

PARRO, J.

This is an appeal from a judgment in connection with a hearing on matters incidental to a divorce. For the reasons that follow, we amend in part and affirm as amended. We also vacate in part and remand with instructions.

Factual and Procedural Background

On September 1, 1995, Ned Martello (Ned) and Laurie Bales (Laurie) entered into a prenuptial agreement; they were married on September 9, 1995. Of their marriage, two children were born: Nicholas on February 29, 1996, and Ned "Jacob" on August 30, 1999. Jacob was born with disabilities and is a special needs child.

On December 16, 2004, Ned filed a petition for divorce and incidental relief. On December 30, 2004, the parties executed a letter agreement purportedly canceling the prenuptial agreement. Subsequently, Laurie filed an answer and a reconventional demand. In response to her filing, Ned filed an answer, a first supplemental and amending petition, and a rule to set the incidental matters for a hearing.

***

Cancellation of the Prenuptial Agreement

A matrimonial regime is a system of principles and rules governing the ownership and management of the property of married persons as between themselves and toward third persons. LSA–C.C. art. 2325. The matrimonial regime may be legal, contractual, or partly legal and partly contractual. LSA–C.C. art. 2326. The legal regime is the community of acquets and gains. LSA–C.C. art. 2327. A matrimonial agreement is a contract establishing a regime of separation of property or modifying or terminating the legal regime. Spouses are free to establish by matrimonial agreement a regime of separation of property or modify the legal regime as provided by law. The provisions of the legal regime that have not been excluded or modified by agreement retain their force and effect. LSA–C.C. art. 2328.

Spouses may enter into a matrimonial agreement before or during marriage as to all matters that are not prohibited by public policy. Spouses may enter into a matrimonial agreement that modifies or terminates a matrimonial regime during marriage only upon joint petition and a finding by the court that this serves their best interests and that they understand the governing principles and rules. They may, however, subject themselves to the legal regime by a matrimonial agreement at any time without court approval. LSA–C.C. art. 2329.

A matrimonial agreement shall be made by authentic act or by an act under private signature duly acknowledged by the spouses. LSA–C.C. art. 2331. Louisiana Civil Code article 1833 defines an authentic act, in pertinent part, as follows:

> An authentic act is a writing executed before a notary public or other officer authorized to perform that function, in the presence of two witnesses, and signed by each party who executed it, by each witness, and by each notary public before whom it was executed.
>
> To be an authentic act, the writing need not be executed at one time or place, or before the same notary public or in the presence of the same witnesses, provided that each party who executes it does so before a notary public or other officer authorized to perform that function, and in the presence of two witnesses and each party, each witness, and each notary public signs it.

A matrimonial agreement, or a judgment establishing a regime of separation of property, is effective toward third persons as to immovable property, when filed for registry in the conveyance records of the parish in which the property is situated and as to movables when filed for registry in the parish or parishes in which the spouses are domiciled. LSA–C.C. art. 2332.

Prior to their marriage, Laurie and Ned entered into a prenuptial agreement establishing a regime of separation of property. This document was recorded in the conveyance records of Livingston Parish to serve as notice to third persons. On December 30, 2004, the parties entered into a letter agreement addressed to the clerk of court of the "21st District Court of Louisiana" referred to as a "Cancellation of Prenuptial Agreement" that provided:

> After some discussion, together, we, Ned Joseph Martello and Laurie Lynn Bales, Allen, Martello have agreed to have canceled the prenuptial agreement that we had file[d] with this court on or around September 8, 1995 prior to our marriage together in the Parish of Tangipahoa on September 9, 1995. Please enter into record with this court our wish to have said agreement canceled as of this date, December 30, 2004.

This letter agreement was signed by Ned and Laurie before a notary and in the presence of two witnesses. Although addressed to the clerk of court, the content of this notarized document evidenced more than merely a request for cancellation of the recordation of the agreement. It evidences an agreement by the spouses to terminate their contractual matrimonial regime, which was a regime of separation of property. Pursuant to their December 30, 2004 agreement, the parties subjected themselves to the legal regime; thus, court approval was not necessary. See LSA–C.C. arts. 2328, 2329.

Ned challenged the trial court's finding that the cancellation of the prenuptial agreement was valid and enforceable. This document was executed after Ned filed his petition for a divorce. He explained that he drafted the document in an effort to make his marriage work. Ned further explained that he was in desperate need of refinancing the family home, which was subject to an adjustable rate mortgage of 11 ½ percent, and that Laurie's signature was needed for refinancing. According to Ned, she would only agree to sign the refinancing document if he cancelled the prenuptial agreement. Laurie testified that they had argued about the prenuptial agreement for 10 years. The fact that Ned's gesture did not work in repairing his marriage or was motivated by immediate financial considerations does not mean that there was no meeting of the minds as to the parties' desire to cancel the prenuptial agreement. It is undisputed that Ned was not forced to sign the cancellation agreement, which was done in the presence of a notary and two witnesses. Lacking any evidence that the consent of either party was vitiated by error, fraud, or duress, we find no error in the trial court's recognition of the validity of the December 30, 2004 agreement. See LSA–C.C. art. 1948.

On appeal, Ned further urged that the trial court erred in failing to determine the * effect of the cancellation agreement. However, he did not brief this assignment of error. Therefore, this matter is considered abandoned for purposes of this appeal in accordance with the Uniform Rules, Courts of Appeal, Rule 2–12.4.21.

***

C. Jenkins v. Marietta W. Leonard and James Richard Wilson, III

87 So. 3d 230 (La. App. 2d Cir. 2012)

BROWN, Chief Judge.

This appeal is from the trial court's judgment rendered in an action for declaratory judgment filed by the Succession of Willie Jenkins to have six properties located in Jackson Parish removed from the judgment of possession rendered in the Succession of Thelma Atkins Jenkins.

On January 10, 1975, Willie Jenkins and Thelma Atkins Wilson Jenkins were married. Each spouse had been married previously, and each had children from his/her prior union. Three days before their marriage, on January 7, 1975, Willie and Thelma entered into a Marriage Contract wherein they renounced the community property regime in favor of a separate property regime. This premarital agreement was signed, witnessed and notarized, then filed for registry in the conveyance records of Jackson Parish, Louisiana.

During the marriage, ten properties were acquired. Four of these (tracts described in deeds introduced into evidence as Exhibits # 2, 4, 5 and 111) are co-owned property; they are not at issue in the instant appeal. Two other properties (described in deeds introduced into evidence as Exhibits # 9 and 10) were determined by the trial court to be the separate property of Willie Jenkins; these properties are also not at issue in this appeal. What is at issue in this appeal are the remaining four properties: three were held to be co-owned and thus one-half of each was found to be duly included in the Succession of Thelma Jenkins (properties described in deeds introduced into evidence as Exhibits # 1, 3 and 82); and one which the trial court failed to address in its judgment (property described in deed introduced into evidence as Exhibit # 7).

Willie predeceased his wife Thelma. His succession was opened, and an executrix was appointed. Thereafter, Thelma died. Her succession was opened, and a judgment of possession was rendered, placing defendants, Marietta W. Leonard and James Richard Wilson, III, into possession of certain described properties, which included full ownership of the ten tracts referred to above.

The executrix of the Succession of Willie Jenkins asked the heirs of Thelma Jenkins to amend the judgment of possession to reflect the “true ownership” of the ten tracts. The heirs refused, and the instant action for declaratory judgment was instituted by plaintiff. On behalf of the Succession of Willie Jenkins, the executrix sought judgment declaring that at the time of her death, Thelma Jenkins owned an undivided one-half interest in four tracts (those described in Exhibits # 2, 4, 5 and 11) and had no interest in the other six tracts.

The matter was tried solely on the basis of documentary exhibits submitted by plaintiff, which included the marriage license and marriage contract of Willie and Thelma Jenkins; the judgment of possession in Thelma Jenkins' succession; and ten deeds numbered # 1–5, 7–11.3 The trial court found two of the tracts to be the separate property of Willie Jenkins # 9 and 10) and therefore improperly included in the judgment of possession of the Succession of Thelma Jenkins. The court then found seven of the tracts to be co-owned property, and declared that only one-half of each was to be included in the judgment of possession in the Succession of Thelma Jenkins. As noted above, one tract (# 7) was omitted from the judgment.

Plaintiff, the Succession of Willie Jenkins, has appealed from the trial court's judgment, urging error in the court's determination of the ownership of the properties described in Exhibits # 1, 3 and 8, and in its failure to determine the ownership of the property described in Exhibit # 7. For the reasons set forth below, we reverse in part and render judgment in accordance with reasons set forth herein.

Discussion

The law in effect when Willie and Thelma Jenkins were married (prior to 1980) provided that the regime for married persons was the community of acquets and gains, which exists by operation of law in all cases where there is no stipulation to the contrary. As provided by the legislature in the matrimonial regimes revision, Acts 1979, No. 709, § 1, effective January 1, 1980, spouses living under a separate property regime prior to the Act would continue to do so subject to its provisions. The parties could modify or limit the legal regime and could agree that it would not even exist between them. La. C.C. art. 2332 (1870); *McAlpine v. McAlpine*, 94–1594 (La.09/05/96), 679 So.2d 85. A matrimonial agreement had to be made by an act before a notary and two witnesses and had to be entered into prior to the marriage. La. C.C. arts. 2328, 2329 (1870); *Succession of Ventre*, 96–559 (La.App. 3d Cir.11/06/96), 682 So.2d 988. The authentic act constituted full proof of the agreement it contained, and was valid as to third persons from the date of its recordation. La. C.C. art. 2332.

Any provision in a marriage contract that is not violative of law or public policy is binding on the contracting parties as long as the contract lasts. *Desobry v. Schlater*, 25 La.Ann. 425 (1873). There is no public policy against a marriage contract abrogating the existence of a community of acquets and gains. *Sarpy v. Sarpy*, 323 So.2d 851 (La.App. 4th Cir.1975). The court in *Clay v. United States*, 161 F.2d 607 (5th Cir.1947), pointed out that the terms in a duly executed prenuptial agreement override any tacit understanding or conduct of the parties during the existence of the marriage.

***

In a marriage contract duly executed by authentic act and recorded three days before their wedding, Willie and Thelma Jenkins established a separate property regime. In this agreement, the soon-to-be spouses provided that:

> [S]aid intended husband and wife each shall be separate in property. Accordingly, they and each of them does hereby formally renounce those provisions of the Revised Civil Code which establish a community of acquets and gains between husband and wife.
>
> All property and effects of the said husband and wife, whether owned by him or by her at the time of the celebration of said intended marriage, or acquired by him or by her during said marriage, are hereby declared to be separate property, and that of the wife, separate and paraphernal property, and they and each of them does hereby expressly reserve to themselves individually the entire administration of their respective particular movable and immovable property, and the respective free enjoyment of each of the fruits and revenues of each.
>
> Each of them did further declare that each individually shall, after the marriage, be responsible for the individual obligations which each has before the marriage, and which each incurs individually after the marriage.

The heirs of Thelma Jenkins, defendants-appellees, argue that one phrase in one sentence in the marriage contract makes "very little sense." The one-sentence paragraph must be read as a whole. The sentence clearly states that "each of them does hereby expressly reserve to themselves individually the entire administration of their respective particular movable and immovable property, and the respective free enjoyment of each of the fruits and revenues of each."

There is no evidence that the Jenkinses executed or recorded anything thereafter or otherwise indicated an intent to formally terminate their separate property regime and/or to establish a community property regime. Furthermore, in addition to the contractual regime they established in their marriage agreement, in which they clearly renounced the legal regime of a community of acquets and gains and chose instead a separate property regime for their marriage, the couple renounced the provisions in the Louisiana Civil Code which establish a community property regime between a husband and a wife.

Therefore, the presumption of community afforded by La. C.C. art. 2340, which provides that things in the possession of a spouse during the existence of a regime of community of acquets and gains are presumed to be community, is inapplicable. See K. Spaht & L. Hargrave, Matrimonial Regimes § 8.2, in 16 Louisiana Civil Law Treatise (West, 2d ed.1997). See *Lee v. Lee*, 03–1483 (La.App. 3d Cir.03/17/04), 868 So.2d 316; *Toups v. Toups*, 97–393 (La.App. 3d Cir.10/08/97), 702 So.2d 822.

Although living under a contractual regime of separate property, Willie and Thelma Jenkins apparently occasionally opted to acquire and treat certain assets as co-owned property, such as the four tracts that are not at issue in this case. We note that in these four deeds, the vendee or purchaser is clearly and specifically described as "Willie Jenkins and Thelma A. Jenkins, married to and living with each other...."

There was no evidence whatsoever that Willie and Thelma Jenkins altered the separate property regime they established in their marriage contract. The couple's purchase of several assets together did not manifest an intent to abolish the marital regime they established by contract nor did it somehow convert their marital regime from separate to one of acquets and gains. The trial court erred in concluding otherwise and in applying La. C.C. art. 2340's presumption of community to the assets at issue in this case.

As noted infra, there was no testimony whatsoever in this case and the only documentary evidence considered by the trial court on classification of the properties at issue was the marriage license and marriage contract of Willie and Thelma Jenkins; the Judgment of Possession in Thelma Jenkins' succession; and the ten property deeds, seven of which were not signed by Willie Jenkins. We note that he did sign the other three deeds; however, Thelma's signature appears on none of the deeds. In two of the deeds the purchaser is described as Willie Jenkins. In four of the deeds, the purchaser is listed as Willie Jenkins, and there is varying descriptive language indicating his marriage to Thelma. The only four deeds which describe the vendees/purchasers in the plural and not the singular sense are those which the parties have agreed are co-owned property.

One deed describes the purchaser as "Willie Jenkins, husband of Thelma Jenkins, with who he is living and residing in community." Another deed describes the purchaser as "Willie Jenkins, married twice, first to Celestine Jenkins (nee Bradford) from whom he is legally divorced and then to Thelma Wilson Jenkins (nee Atkins) with who [sic] he is now living in full community ..."

When a couple has clearly chosen to be separate in property and has followed the legal prerequisites to accomplish their intent, the mere inclusion of the name of a spouse and one's marital status in a deed does not, standing alone, constitute evidence of an intent to make an asset community rather than separate. A commonsense reading of the vendee/purchaser language in the deeds in Exhibits 1, 3, 7 and 8 leads to the inescapable conclusion that Willie Jenkins was the purchaser and therefore, without any other evidence to the contrary, these tracts are his separate property and were therefore improperly included in the Succession of Thelma Jenkins.

Having found no reasonable basis for the trial court's factual findings in this case, and further that the court was clearly wrong in classifying the properties described in

Exhibits # 1, 3, and 8 as community rather than separate, we reverse that portion of the trial court's judgment related to these three tracts. We also find that the property described in Exhibit # 7 is the separate property of Willie Jenkins and therefore improperly included in the Succession of Thelma Jenkins.

***

8.5 SUBSTANCE OF AGREEMENTS: POSSIBILITIES AND LIMITS

A. Introduction

Louisiana Civil Code article 2329 allows spouses to enter into matrimonial agreements "as to all matters that are not prohibited by public policy." Civil Code article 2330 and the comments following it provide some guidance:

La. Civ. Code art. 2330. Limits of contractual freedom

> Spouses may not by agreement before or during marriage, renounce or alter the marital portion or the established order of succession. Nor may the spouses limit with respect to third persons the right that one spouse alone has under the legal regime to obligate the community or to alienate, encumber, or lease community property.

REVISION COMMENTS—1979

> (a) Spouses may not by matrimonial agreement renounce or alter the marital portion or the established order of succession prior to the death of a spouse. After the death of a spouse, the survivor may, of course, renounce the marital portion. The rules establishing the marital portion and the order of succession are rules of public order that may not be derogated from by agreement. C.C. Art. 11 (1870).
>
> (b) A matrimonial agreement is a contract. An antenuptial matrimonial agreement may contain testamentary provisions. See C.C. Arts. 1734-1755 (1870) and C.C. art. 1976 (Rev.1984).
>
> (c) Spouses may not limit, with respect to third persons, the right that a spouse has under the law to obligate the community or to dispose of community property. A limitation on this right produces effects as between the spouses only. Thus, third persons may rely on Articles 2345, 2346, 2360, and 2363, infra,

under which a spouse may obligate the community or dispose of community property without the concurrence of the other spouse.

(d) Article 2330 excludes contractual freedom as to certain matters in the light of strong public policy. However, this provision does not deprive the spouses of flexibility in determining the ownership and management of their property. For example, the spouses may by matrimonial agreement provide for contribution to the expenses of the marriage, for apportionment of community property according to fixed shares, or for the reservation of fruits as separate property. The spouses may, further, determine that their existing or future property shall be subject to the matrimonial regime. In such a case, a matrimonial agreement may in fact be a donation governed by the rules of substance and form applicable to donations.

Jurisprudence has also established that reciprocal duties of spouses (fidelity, support, and assistance) that are codified in the Civil Code article 98 are another public policy limitation. As illustrated by the cases that follow, the bulk of the litigation concerns the duty of support and the ability of spouses to modify or waive rights to spousal support.

B. *Clifford Favrot, Jr. v. Katherine Boulet Barnes*

332 So. 2d 873 (La App. 4 Cir. 1976)

REDMANN, Judge.

An ex-husband appeals from an alimony award as unwarranted and, alternatively, excessive. Because this court en banc has today decided that an ex-wife must show circumstances which make her unable to support herself by working before she can obtain post-divorce alimony, Ward v. Ward, La.App.1976, 332 So.2d 868, we remand to allow the parties to present evidence on this point.

Entitlement

This prospective husband and wife, in middle age, had each been married before. They executed a pre-marital agreement stipulating separateness of property. We first reject the husband's argument that the agreement's waiver by each of every 'claim to the property' of the other in case of divorce or death is a waiver of alimony. If public policy were to allow such a waiver, this agreement does not constitute one. Alimony to a divorced wife is not a 'claim to the property' of the husband; it is a claim against the husband, limited by his 'income', C.C. 160.

The spouses had other pre-marital discussions in which, at the husband's instance, they agreed to limit sexual intercourse to about once a week. The husband asserts, as divorce-causing fault, that the wife did not keep this agreement but sought coitus thrice daily. The wife testifies she kept their agreement despite her frustration at not being 'permitted' at other times even to touch her husband.

We reject the view that a premarital understanding can repeal or amend the nature of marital obligations as declared by C.C. 119: 'The husband and wife owe to each other mutually, fidelity, support and assistance.' Marriage obliges the spouses to fulfill 'the reasonable and normal sex desires of each other.' Mudd v. Mudd, 1944, 206 La. 1055, 20 So.2d 311. It is this abiding sexual relationship which characterizes a contract as marriage, Phillpott v. Phillpott, La.App.1973, 285 So.2d 570, writ refused La.App., 288 So.2d 643, rather than, e.g., domestic employer-employee, or landlord-tenant. Persons may indeed agree to live in the same building in some relationship other than marriage. But that is not what our litigants did. They married.

The law does not authorize contractual modification of the 'conjugal association' except '(i)n relation to property,' C.C. 2325 . C.C. 2327 prohibits alteration of marriage like that agreed to here which the wife allegedly breached: 'Neither can husband and wife derogate by their matrimonial agreement from the rights resulting from the power of the husband over the person of his wife . . ..' Nor—because the rights over the person are largely mutual, C.C. 119 and La.Const. art. 1 s 3—can their matrimonial agreement derogate from the power of the wife over the person of her husband.

The fault here alleged by the husband is not, in law, any fault.

***

C. *Michael L. McAlpine v. Jonnie Fox McAlpine*

679 So. 2d 85 (La. 1996)

ON REHEARING

VICTORY, Justice.

We granted rehearing in this case to reconsider the correctness of our original opinion in which we held that antenuptial agreements waiving permanent alimony are null and void as against public policy. After further review, we reverse our original opinion and hold that such antenuptial agreements are enforceable, but are subject to the same grounds for rescission as other contracts. Further, we agree with the trial court's determination in this case that Mrs. McAlpine entered into the antenuptial agreement freely and voluntarily and not under undue duress. Lastly, consistent with our original opinion, we agree with the trial court's holding that the Mercedes Benz was not a gift to Mrs. McAlpine.

FACTS AND PROCEDURAL HISTORY

About a week prior to their marriage in 1989, Michael McAlpine and Jonnie Fox signed an antenuptial agreement which provided for a separate property regime and for a waiver of alimony pendente lite and permanent alimony. The agreement provided, inter alia, that Jonnie Fox would receive $25,000 at divorce if the parties were married less than six years and $50,000 if they were married six years or more, regardless of fault or need on the part of Jonnie Fox. The parties were divorced on May 18, 1992. On October 5, 1992, Jonnie Fox McAlpine filed a rule to show cause why she (1) should not be awarded permanent alimony pursuant to article 112 of the Louisiana Civil Code, and (2) should not have a Mercedes Benz automobile returned to her, claiming it to be a gift to her from Mr. McAlpine.

The trial court held the antenuptial agreement to be enforceable, held that the Mercedes Benz was not a gift, and dismissed Mrs. McAlpine's rule. The Fourth Circuit Court of Appeal reversed the trial court's ruling in part, holding the antenuptial agreement void as against public policy, but affirmed the trial court with regard to the automobile, and remanded the case for further proceedings. McAlpine v. McAlpine, 93-2467 (La.App. 4th Cir. 5/17/94), 637 So.2d 1163. Mr. McAlpine's writ of certiorari was granted, 94-1594 (La.9/30/94), 642 So.2d 860, and on original hearing, with Justice Kimball dissenting, this Court affirmed, concluding that LSA-C.C. art. 112 was enacted to protect the public interest by preventing needy former spouses from having to seek public assistance and that any act in derogation of article 112 is void under LSA-C.C. art. 7. 94-1594 (La.2/9/95). LSA-C.C. art. 7 provides that "[p]ersons may not by their juridical acts derogate from laws enacted for the protection of the public interest. Any act in derogation of such laws is an absolute nullity." LSA-C.C. art. 7.

We now conclude that permanent alimony was not enacted to protect the public interest, but for the benefit of individuals. Further, we conclude that if protection of the public interest was ever a proper consideration for permanent alimony, that day has long since passed.

DISCUSSION

Article 6 of the Code Napoleon, the original source of LSA-C.C. art. 7, provides "one may not by private conventions derogate from the force of laws which concern public order and good morals." Planiol explains that this test gives a necessary sanction to a great number of legal provisions which do not specifically define their degree of authority. The law very often sets forth a rule without saying whether or not it permits derogations from its provisions. 1 Planiol, Civil Law Treatise, No. 290 (La. State Law Institute Translation 1959). Planiol's fourth category of private laws affecting public order is the protection of contracting parties. He explains:

> (4) Protection of the Contracting Parties. A new conception of public order here presents itself. The modern law-maker, considering that the two parties to a certain juridical act are not equally able to defend their interests, prohibits them from departing from certain rules which he has laid down for their protection. It is for this reason that almost all provisions relating to contracts of labor are of public order because the law-maker desires to protect the laborer or the employee against the master. And likewise in contracts for transportation by land all clauses providing for irresponsibility are prohibited (Art. 103, Commercial Code, amended by the law of March 17, 1905). This is done because the law-maker thinks that the traveler or shipper is constrained to submit to the will of the carrier. And again, in contracts of insurance, the law of July 13, 1930 was made imperative, because the insured could not discuss upon a plane of equality with the insurer.

Id., No. 292, p. 201.

Nowhere in Planiol do we find a reference to permanent alimony as enacted for the public interest or order. Rather, Planiol states:

> Divorce having destroyed the marriage, no effects of it should continue. Upon what idea is founded persistence of the obligation of support between two persons who have nothing in common? Its basis is found in a principle already mentioned more than once. Whatever act of man causes damage to another obliges him by whose fault it happened to repair it, says Art. 1382. As long as the marriage lasted it gave each of the spouses an acquired position upon which each could count. The community of life permitted the spouse without means to share the welfare of the other. Suddenly through no fault of the spouse in question, he or she find himself or herself devoid of resources and plunged into poverty. It is manifestly in such a case as this that the guilty party should be made to bear the consequences of his wrongful acts.
>
> It is thus seen that the responsibility for alimony is based upon a concept entirely foreign to Art. 212.3 It is no longer a duty due by a spouse to a spouse because there are no longer any spouses. The duty is to make pecuniary amends for the consequences of an illicit act. This obligation subsisting after divorce partakes, in the highest degree, of the nature of an indemnity. It is intended to restore to the spouse without means something of the resources of which he or she is thenceforth deprived through the other's fault.
>
> This indemnity nevertheless merely counterbalances the privation of the right of support which was vested in the spouse. It becomes transformed into alimony. This is why alimony follows the general rules applicable to alimentary pensions.

Id., No. 1259, pp. 696-697 (cites omitted throughout).

Prior to 1855, a wife, after obtaining divorce, was not entitled to alimony in Louisiana. See Player v. Player, 162 La. 229, 110 So. 332 (1926). In 1855, article 160 was adopted, granting alimony only to "the wife who had obtained the divorce out of the property of her husband, not to exceed one-third of her husband's income." 110 So. at 332. Thus, the husband would have been proven to be "at fault" under then article 138 of the Civil Code because our law then allowed divorce only based on fault and did not allow a divorce for merely living separate and apart prior to 1916. When no-fault divorce was first recognized by Act 269 of 1916, allowing either party to obtain a divorce, there was no provision in LSA-C.C. art. 160 allowing alimony to a not-at-fault wife where the husband obtained the divorce based on seven years of living separate and apart. Thus, in 1928, article 160 was amended to allow alimony to the wife who proves she has not been at fault, where the husband obtained the "no-fault" divorce based on seven years of living separate and apart. This eliminated the required "fault" of the husband in granting alimony to the wife. In 1934, article 160 was amended to substitute the phrase "seven years or more" to "for a certain period of time" in light of the fact that the Legislature had reduced the seven year requirement to four years, and would later reduce it to two years, in 1938. The period is now 180 days from the service of a filed petition for divorce or six months. LSA-C.C. arts. 102 and 103. In 1979, article 160 was amended to allow alimony to the "spouse" who has not been at fault. Present article 112 is article 160 of the Louisiana Civil Code of 1870, as amended by Acts 1986, No. 229, Sec. 1. LSA-C.C. art. 112, Editor's note. Thus, we see from the beginning of alimony in Louisiana that "fault" played an extremely important role, as Planiol said it did in French law.

In Player, we characterized alimony after divorce as a "pension," stating as follows:

> As the marriage is forever dissolved, there is no obligation arising from it. The law accords, not alimony in such a case, but a pension, to the unfortunate spouse who has obtained the divorce. This pension becomes revocable in case it should become unnecessary, and in case the wife should contract a second marriage.

Player, supra at 333 (citing State v. Judge, 114 La. 44, 38 So. 14 (1905); 3 Laurent, p. 403; Act 247 of 1916). Player was cited by this Court in 1940 for the proposition that alimony after divorce "is in the nature of a pension accorded by law to the wife without fault against whom a judgment of divorce has been rendered." Fortier v. Gelpi, 195 La. 449, 197 So. 138, 140 (1940) (citing Player, supra); see also Ward v. Ward, 339 So.2d 839 (La.1976) (legislatively overruled on other grounds by Act 72 of 1979, amending LSA-C.C. art. 160.) The Court in Fortier went even further and called this alimony a "pure gratuity" to be granted "in the discretion of the court." Id.

In Hays v. Hays, 240 La. 708, 124 So.2d 917 (1960), the husband argued that, since divorce dissolved the bonds of matrimony and thus his obligation to support his wife, and since permanent alimony was "a mere gratuity," an award of permanent alimony constituted a taking of his property for private purposes in violation of the federal and state constitutions. 124 So.2d at 918. We disagreed and explained our definition of "gratuity" in the context of permanent alimony:

> By this statement this court meant that after divorce there no longer exists an obligation under the marriage contract for the husband to support and maintain his wife, as this contract has been dissolved. In other words, the court had in mind that the wife after divorce no longer has the absolute right to demand of her divorced husband support and assistance since the dissolution of the marriage contract relieved him of that obligation; that consequently the right of the wife to be awarded alimony under Article 160 does not flow from the marriage contract, and that insofar as this contract is concerned, the alimony is a gratuity in the nature of a pension. However, the court's statement cannot be construed to mean that there is no obligation on the divorced husband to pay alimony under certain circumstances.
>
> Divorce is not one of the inalienable rights granted by the federal or the state Constitution, and the lawmakers of the state may make laws regulating divorce and impose conditions under which a citizen of this state may obtain a divorce. Alimony is incidental and related to divorce, and its imposition is within the power which the lawmakers have to regulate and impose conditions for a divorce. Consequently, when the Legislature enacted Article 160 of the Civil Code, it was simply saying to a citizen of this state, as it had a constitutional right to do, that if cause exists for a divorce, it may be had subject to the condition that the court may in certain specified circumstances require the husband to pay alimony. By paying this alimony the husband is discharging an obligation imposed upon him by the court under authority of law, and his property is in no sense being unconstitutionally taken. (Emphasis added).

Id.

The first time in the jurisprudence that we find permanent alimony described as a means to keep women off public assistance is Justice Barham's dissent in Montz v. Montz, 253 La. 897, 221 So.2d 40 (1969). There, Justice Barham characterized permanent alimony as "socio-economic legislation ... intended to assign responsibility for the dependency of such divorced women so as to relieve them from destitution and the State from their care." 221 So.2d at 44 (dissenting opinion of Justice Barham). Likewise, relying on this statement, courts and commentators began to characterize permanent alimony as a means to keep divorced women from becoming wards of the state. See Loyacano v. Loyacano, 358 So.2d 304 (La.1978), vacated on rehearing, 358

So.2d 304 (La.1978), vacated and remanded, 440 U.S. 952, 99 S.Ct. 1488, 59 L.Ed.2d 766 (1979)5 ("[t]he general policy consideration and practical reason which appear to have induced the legislature to provide alimony after divorce was to prevent divorced women without sufficient means from becoming wards of the state." 358 So.2d at 308-309, n. 12 (relying on Barham dissent in Montz)); Teasdel v. Teasdel, 493 So.2d 1165, 1168 (La.1986) ("[p]ermanent alimony is a pension which is designed to prevent a former spouse from becoming a public charge." (no citation)); Spaht, Katherine Shaw, Developments in the Law, 1979-1980, Persons, Rehabilitative Alimony, 41 La.L.Rev. 372 (1981) (the reason for alimony after divorce is to provide support for those who need it with a minimal amount of social dislocation "by extracting it from those who have provided similar maintenance in the past." (citing Montz dissent and Loyacano, 358 So.2d at 309, n. 12)); Pugh, Nina Nichols, The Evolving Role of Women in the Louisiana Law: Recent Legislative and Judicial Changes, 42 La.L.Rev. 1571 (1982) ("[a]lthough the awarding of alimony after divorce was based originally upon a delictual principle in that the spouse from whom it was sought had breached his or her marital obligation of mutual support, such alimony came to represent a societal response to the needy who would otherwise become charges of the state." 42 La.L.Rev. at 1589 (citing Loyacano and later Montz dissent for same proposition)). Thus, commentators and courts, and in fact this Court on original hearing, base the proposition that permanent alimony was enacted to keep divorced spouses from becoming wards of the state on statements that were not law: Loyacano, which was vacated on rehearing and by the United States Supreme Court, and the dissenting opinion in Montz.

In light of the history of article 160, and courts' and commentators' interpretation of article 160, we must consider whether alimony after divorce is a "law enacted for the public interest" such that any waiver would be an absolute nullity. While other laws governing marriage and children are often enacted for the public interest and non-waivable, an examination and comparison of the laws in this area that have, and have not, been declared non-waivable provides valuable insight.

In Holliday v. Holliday, 358 So.2d 618, 620 (La.1978), we held prenuptial waivers of alimony pendente lite void as contrary to the public policy of this State, expressed in LSA-C.C. arts. 119, 120 and 148, that a husband should support and assist his wife during the existence of the marriage. We held that this legal obligation of support, as well as the fact that the conditions affecting entitlement to alimony pendente lite could not be foreseen at the time antenuptial agreements are entered, overrides the premarital anticipatory waiver of alimony. Id. at 620. We noted that we expressed no opinion on the antenuptial waiver of permanent alimony, reserving it for another day. Id., n. 6.

Thus, alimony pendente lite is based on the statutorily imposed duty of the spouses to support each other during marriage. See LSA-C.C. art. 98 ("Married persons owe each other fidelity, support, and assistance.") We have historically noted the difference between alimony pendente lite and permanent alimony. Player v. Player, supra.

Comment (e) to LSA-C.C. art. 98 states that "[t]he spouses' duties under this Article, as a general rule are matters of public order from which they may not derogate by contract." On the other hand, there is no corresponding statutory duty of support mandating permanent alimony between former spouses.

While we have held that alimony pendente lite is a law enacted for the public interest, the reasoning behind Justice Calogero's argument in the Holliday dissent, that alimony pendente lite is not a law of public order, is really applicable to permanent alimony. Justice Calogero dissented, stating as follows:

> Neither am I persuaded by relator's contention and the majority's inference that alimony pendente lite is, in the public interest, essential to avoid a wife's becoming a social burden and/or ward of the state. This attitude is a demeaning one which is inconsistent with the realities of the day. It is simply not correct to assume that all, or most, women are incapable of financial independence but must, instead, be wholly dependent upon either their husbands or the state.

Furthermore, in this case, as in almost all marriages where the spouses have entered into an antenuptial agreement, there is no community of acquets and gains. The wife thus has the same control over her property between separation and divorce as she had prior to separation and prior to marriage. An antenuptial waiver by the wife of alimony pendente lite would make the wife no more of a burden on the state than she was prior to marriage. I therefore view alimony pendente lite as a right which is provided for the benefit of the individual and not for the protection of public order and good morals.

Id. at 622 (Calogero dissent). In today's world, more women than ever are in the workforce and are capable of financial independence. Further, a waiver of permanent alimony would make the spouse incapable of financial independence no more of a burden than he or she was before marriage.

The Civil Code limits spouses' rights, before and during marriage, to renounce or alter the marital portion or the established order of succession. LSA-C.C. art. 2330. The legislature determined that these rules were rules of public order that may not be derogated by agreement. LSA-C.C. art. 2330, comment (a). We believe that had the legislature intended to limit spouses' rights to waive post-divorce alimony in the same way, it would have made this clear. Instead, the Civil Code contains no prohibition against the waiver of post-divorce alimony.

Further, the Civil Code limits individuals' rights in other areas where a derogation of such rights would result in the individual becoming a public burden. An individual is forbidden from divesting himself of all his property by a donation inter vivos. LSA-C.C. art. 1497. Also, the right to contract not to compete is limited. LSA-R.S. 23:921. "Both of these situations demonstrate the underlying state concern that a person cannot by convention deprive himself of the ability to support himself." Note, Louisiana's

Forbidden Antenuptial Waiver of Alimony Pendente Lite, 39 La.L.Rev. 1161, 1168 (1979). But, as stated in the above case note, alimony is distinguishable:

> To assume that a wife's waiver of alimony automatically occasions the danger that she will become a ward of the state is to assume that the only revenue which married women have is the salary earned by their husbands. Such an assumption is unrealistic in light of modern social trends....
>
> Because waiver of alimony presents a severely limited likelihood that a spouse will become a ward of the state, this public interest should not be considered a public policy unlawfully contravened by the antenuptial waiver of alimony after divorce.

Id. at 1168, 1169, 1171. Clearly, a waiver of permanent alimony does not deprive a spouse of his or her ability to support herself.

In other situations involving spouses, waivers in certain areas are clearly allowed. The Civil Code gives spouses, before or during marriage, the right to enter into a matrimonial agreement as to all matters that are not prohibited by public policy. LSA-C.C. art. 2329. A "matrimonial agreement" is defined as "a contract establishing a regime of separation of property or modifying or terminating the legal regime." LSA-C.C. art. 2328. Thus, parties, before or during marriage, can waive their right to the legal regime. As with permanent alimony, this deprives a spouse of the other's earnings and property acquired during marriage that would otherwise become community property, and potentially involves greater consequences on the part of the non-earning spouse than would a waiver of permanent alimony, which is limited to one-third of the other spouse's income and is only to provide sufficient means for support.

We have also allowed a waiver of a court-ordered child support payment between divorced spouses where the agreement met the requirements for a conventional obligation and fostered the continued support and upbringing of the child. Dubroc v. Dubroc, 388 So.2d 377 (La.1980). Further, we have held that "where a consent decree providing for alimony or child support is to be rendered, the parties may reserve the right to an initial judicial determination of a proper alimony or child support award and waive any requirements to prove a change of circumstances." Aldredge v. Aldredge, 477 So.2d 73, 74 (La.1985). We held that such a waiver is not prohibited by the Civil Code and is not violative of public policy, partly because of the permissive nature of the right to seek a reduction or discharge in child support payments. Id.

Another situation where waiver is allowed is post-separation waivers of alimony. In Nelson v. Walker, 250 La. 545, 197 So.2d 619 (1967), we characterized, in dictum, the post-separation waiver of alimony pendente lite and permanent alimony as a relative nullity caused by the then incapacity of spouses to contract with each other. 197 So.2d at 625. We stated that this nullity was susceptible of ratification once the incapacity ceased, i.e., upon divorce. Id.; see also Ward v. Ward, supra and Russo v. Russo, 205 La. 852, 18 So.2d 318 (La.1944). Former LSA-C.C. art. 1790 was amended in 1978, removing the incapacities of husband and wife to contract.

Subsequently, courts have allowed post-separation waivers of permanent alimony and alimony pendente lite. Klein v. Klein, 485 So.2d 970 (La.App. 5th Cir.), writ denied, 489 So.2d 921 (La.1986); deMontluzin v. deMontluzin, 464 So.2d 948 (La.App. 4th Cir.1985); Jones v. Jones, 459 So.2d 1200 (La.App. 5th Cir.1984), writ denied, 462 So.2d 649 (La.1985) (post-separation waiver of permanent alimony valid); Braning v. Braning, 449 So.2d 670 (La.App. 4th Cir.1984); Cunningham v. Cunningham, 448 So.2d 910 (La.App. 3d Cir.1984) ("[a]limony after divorce can be made the subject of a contract and is considered a consent decree."); Beringer v. Beringer, 415 So.2d 429 (La.App. 1st Cir.1982); King v. King, 390 So.2d 250 (La.App. 3d Cir.1980), writ denied, 396 So.2d 884 (La.1981); Monk v. Monk, 376 So.2d 552 (La.App. 3d Cir.1979). Allowing a waiver of permanent alimony in return for a lump sum and treating it as a consent decree is in accordance with the provision of LSA-C.C. art. 112(B) that allows the court to award permanent alimony in a lump sum with the parties' consent.

To allow post-separation waivers of permanent alimony and not prenuptial waivers, as violative of the public order, would be incongruous. Either permanent alimony is a law established for the protection of the public interest, and, as such, a waiver of such is an absolute nullity under article 7, or it is not. On original hearing, "[w]e distinguish[ed] without overruling" most of the above cases allowing waivers of permanent alimony in post-separation agreements because there, "unlike in an antenuptial agreement, the conditions which affect entitlement to alimony after divorce can be foreseen at the time of the contract." McAlpine v. McAlpine, 95-1594, p. 6 La.2/9/95). "Thus, the spouse who may be placed in necessitous circumstances by the agreement is in a much better position to protect him or herself and the risk that the spouse may become a ward of the state is significantly reduced." Id. at 6-7. However, on reconsideration, we find that such a distinction is not justified under article 7 of the Civil Code, which decrees any act in derogation of a law enacted for the protection of the public interest is an absolute nullity. The concept of foreseeability is generally not a requirement for valid contracts.

Finally, to hold that antenuptial waivers of permanent alimony are invalid as a matter of public policy would be illogical because permanent alimony is granted only to spouses not-at-fault. Surely the grant of permanent alimony to "innocent" spouses and not "guilty" spouses cannot be a law enacted for the public interest under LSA-C.C. art. 7. Is it really arguable that the state has an interest in keeping not-at-fault divorced spouses off state support but has no such interest in keeping at-fault divorced spouses off the public dole? It is much more probable that the legislature in originally providing for permanent alimony did it not to keep needy ex-wives off public support, but to attempt to rectify the loss suffered by an innocent wife at the hands of an at-fault husband. If preventing divorced spouses from becoming a public burden was really a law enacted for the public interest it probably would have applied to all wives (now spouses), innocent or not.

Our holding today is in accordance with the majority of states that now hold that antenuptial waivers of permanent alimony are not per se invalid as against public policy. As stated by two family law commentators, since 1970, with the advent of no-fault divorce and the changes in society that such laws represent, public policy has changed and the traditional rule that prenuptial waivers of permanent alimony were void ab initio has given way to the more realistic view that such agreements are valid and enforceable under certain conditions. Freed & Walker, Family Law in the Fifty States: An Overview (1985-1986), 19 Fam.Law Q. 331, 438. Rather than encouraging divorce, these agreements provide couples with the opportunity to plan for the future and safeguard their financial interests.9 Without this option, potential spouses may choose to live together informally without the benefit of marriage. Thus, these agreements may actually encourage marriage in some instances.

CONCLUSION

We conclude that permanent alimony is not a law enacted for the public interest. Rather, it was enacted to protect individuals, i.e., not-at-fault divorced spouses in need. Thus, the prohibition found in article 7 of the Civil Code does not apply.

Article 2031 of the Civil Code establishes that "[a] contract is relatively null when it violates a rule intended for the protection of private parties, as when a party lacked capacity or did not give free consent at the time the contract was made." LSA-C.C. art. 2031. The rules applicable to the validity of premarital agreements waiving permanent alimony are the same as for other contracts, namely, the Civil Code articles dealing with capacity, consent, error, fraud, and duress. The trial court in this case found that the antenuptial agreement was not the result of fraud, error or duress and, after careful review of the record, we agree with the court of appeal that these findings were not manifestly erroneous. In addition, the trial court was not manifestly erroneous in finding that the Mercedes Benz was not a gift to Mrs. McAlpine.

DECREE

For the reasons stated herein, the judgment of the court of appeal, reversing the trial court's dismissal of Mrs. McAlpine's claim for permanent alimony, is reversed and the trial court's judgment of March 24, 1993 is reinstated. The judgment of the trial court holding that the Mercedes Benz was not a gift to Mrs. McAlpine is affirmed.

REVERSED IN PART; AFFIRMED IN PART.

CALOGERO, C.J., additionally assigns concurring reasons.

WATSON, J., dissented and would hold that the contract between the lawyer and his wife invalid for duress.

JOHNSON, J., concurring in part, dissenting in part and assigns reasons.

CALOGERO, Chief Justice, additionally, assigns concurring reasons.
I respectfully concur in the judgment reversing the court of appeal's decision and reinstating the trial court's decision. I believe the majority is correct in its conclusion that C.C. art. 112 was not enacted for either the preservation of public order or good morals. Thus, C.C. art. 7 is not implicated in the waiver of permanent alimony by antenuptial agreement. I write separately to emphasize that in the absence of a provision enacted to protect the public interest, freedom of contract is the rule. "[F]reedom of parties to contract ... is essential to both our society and system of government." Holliday v. Holliday, 358 So.2d 618, 622 (La.1978) (Calogero, C.J., dissenting). Furthermore, this case presents a more compelling case than the Holliday case, as the former concerns a waiver of permanent alimony, whereas the latter concerned only a waiver of alimony pendente lite.

JOHNSON, Justice, concurring in part/dissenting in part.

I join the majority in concluding that antenuptial agreements waiving permanent alimony are enforceable, but dissent from the majority opinion that this agreement was entered into voluntarily.

This was not the typical arms-length negotiated contract. In fact, Mrs. McAlpine was presented with this pre-nuptial agreement one week prior to the wedding, and after the wedding invitations had been mailed. Neither Mr. McAlpine who is an attorney, or his attorney who drafted the document suggested to Mrs. McAlpine that she obtain legal counsel. All of the facts suggest coercion or overreaching to me, and I would set aside the antenuptial agreement.

For the foregoing reasons, I respectfully concur in part; and dissent in part.

D. Kent W. Hall, Sr. v. Tina Williams Hall

4 So. 3d 254 (La. App. 5 Cir. 2009)

WALTER J. ROTHSCHILD, Judge.

Plaintiff, Kent Hall, Sr., appeals from the August 28, 2007 trial court judgment on the issues of interim spousal support1 and calculation of child support. For the following reasons, we affirm.

Kent Hall, Sr. ("Kent") and Tina Williams Hall ("Tina") were married on May 18, 1997. Prior to the parties' marriage, on April 23, 1997, Kent and Tina executed a matrimonial agreement that provided for a separate property regime and contained a waiver of interim and final spousal support, among other things. On May 29, 2000, the parties' son, Kyle Hall, was born. No other children were born of this marriage. On September 28, 2005, Kent filed a Petition for Divorce, and a Judgment of Divorce was rendered on May 3, 2006.

***

LAW AND DISCUSSION

On appeal, in his first assignment of error, Kent asserts that the trial court erred in awarding interim spousal support to Tina, notwithstanding the waiver of interim spousal support in the matrimonial agreement. He cites LSA-C.C. art. 2329, which provides that spouses may enter into a matrimonial agreement as to all matters that are not prohibited by public policy, but he asserts that there is no statutory codification of the matters currently prohibited by public policy. He argues that although the Louisiana Supreme Court in Holliday v. Holliday, 358 So.2d 618 (La.1978) found a prenuptial waiver of interim spousal support, or alimony pendente lite, was void as being contrary to public policy, in that case the Court cited former Louisiana Civil Code articles that were gender-based and would be constitutionally infirm today.

The trial judge ordered Kent to pay Tina $5,800 per month for interim spousal support from November 2005 to November 2006. LSA-C.C. art. 98 provides that married persons owe each other fidelity, support, and assistance. A spouse's right to claim interim spousal support is based on this statutorily-imposed duty of spouses to support each other during marriage. LSA-C.C. art. 98; McAlpine v. McAlpine, 94-1594 (La.9/5/96), 679 So.2d 85, 90. Comment (e) to LSA-C.C. art. 98 explains that the spouses' duties under this article, as a general rule, are matters of public order from which they may not derogate by contract.

Interim spousal support is designed to assist the claimant in sustaining the same style or standard of living that he or she enjoyed while residing with the other spouse, pending the litigation of the divorce. Speight v. Speight, 03-1152, p. 2 (La.App. 3 Cir. 2/4/04),

866 So.2d 344, 346. The purpose of interim spousal support is to maintain the status quo without unnecessary economic dislocation until a final determination of support can be made and until a period of time for adjustment elapses that does not exceed, as a general rule, 180 days after the judgment of divorce. Id. The court may award an interim spousal support allowance to a spouse based on the needs of that spouse, the ability of the other spouse to pay, and the standard of living of the spouses during the marriage. LSA-C.C. arts. 111 and 113; Loftice v. Loftice, 07-1741, p. 4 (La.App. 1 Cir. 3/26/08), 985 So.2d 204, 207.

In Holliday v. Holliday, 358 So.2d 618, 620 (La.1978), the Louisiana Supreme Court held that prenuptial waivers of alimony pendente lite are void as contrary to public policy. Although the former Louisiana Civil Code articles cited by the Holliday Court referred only to a husband's duty to support his wife, the current law providing that each spouse has a duty to support the other spouse does **5 not conflict with or invalidate the holding of the Holliday case. Rather, the current law simply extends the benefits of interim spousal support to either spouse.

See Loftice v. Loftice, 07-1741 at 11, 985 So.2d at 211, in which the First Circuit discussed the Holliday case and the current law regarding interim spousal support, and it found that a waiver of interim spousal support in a prenuptial agreement would be void as against public policy. See also McAlpine v. McAlpine, in which the Louisiana Supreme Court discussed the Holliday case and the public policy considerations involved in waivers of alimony pendente lite versus permanent alimony.

Based on the applicable statutory law and the jurisprudence, we agree with the trial court that the waiver of interim spousal support in the matrimonial agreement executed by Kent and Tina is invalid as against public policy. Accordingly, this assignment of error is without merit.

In his second assignment of error, Kent argues that, in the alternative, the trial court erred in awarding an amount of interim spousal support greater than the amount stipulated in the matrimonial agreement. The parties' matrimonial agreement provides in pertinent part:

> Should this waiver of alimony pendente lite be deemed invalid for any reason whatever, then the parties stipulate and agree that Kent W. Hall shall pay to Tina Marie Williams the sum of $1,000.00 per month as alimony pendente lite ....

As stated in the previous assignment of error, interim spousal support is designed to assist the claimant in sustaining the same style or standard of living that he or she enjoyed while residing with the other spouse, pending the litigation of the divorce. Interim support preserves parity in the levels of maintenance and support and avoids unnecessary financial dislocation until a final determination of support can be made.

Loftice, 07-1741 at 4, 985 So.2d at 207; Lambert v. Lambert, 06-2399, p. 10 (La.App. 1 Cir. 3/23/07), 960 So.2d 921, 928. The trial court is vested with much discretion in determining an award of interim spousal support, and such a determination will not be disturbed absent a clear abuse of discretion. Kirkpatrick v. Kirkpatrick, 41,851, p. 4 (La.App. 2 Cir. 1/24/07), 948 So.2d 390, 393.

We find that the same public policy considerations that prohibit waivers of interim spousal support in prenuptial agreements also prohibit the parties from setting an amount of interim spousal support that is insufficient, based on the needs of that spouse, the ability of the other spouse to pay, and the standard of living of the spouses during the marriage. Therefore, we find no error in the trial court's award of interim spousal support greater than the amount set forth in the matrimonial agreement. This assignment of error is without merit.

***

E. Harold J. Barber v. Deborah Barber

38 So. 3d 1046 (La. App. 1st Cir. 2010)

McCLENDON, J.

This is an appeal of a trial court judgment granting a former spouse the right to seek permanent spousal support and reimbursement based on a matrimonial agreement signed by the parties prior to their marriage. For the following reasons, we amend in part, reverse in part, and render.

FACTS AND PROCEDURAL HISTORY

Harold J. Barber and Deborah Carpenter Barber were married on November 14, 1999, and established their matrimonial domicile in Washington Parish. No children were born of the marriage. The parties separated on November 4, 2006, and on November 14, 2006, Mr. Barber filed a petition for divorce. Mr. Barber alleged that the parties entered into a separate property agreement on November 12, 1999. He further desired exclusive use of the family home in Franklinton, asserting that it was his separate property. An amending and supplemental petition was filed on May 15, 2007, in which Mr. Barber sought a divorce based on the parties living separate and apart for more than six months.

On June 11, 2007, Mrs. Barber filed a rule for interim periodic spousal support and rental assessment, in which she asserted she was in necessitous circumstances and suffering from multiple sclerosis. She also asserted that although she had no objection to Mr. Barber's exclusive use and occupancy of the family home, she requested that Mr. Barber be assessed a rental value for his use of the former matrimonial domicile.

Also, on June 11, 2007, Mrs. Barber filed an answer and reconventional demand. In her reconventional demand, Mrs. Barber asserted that the matrimonial agreement signed on November 12, 1999 was invalid and unenforceable as it was improperly perfected, signed under duress, and signed through misrepresentation and fraud. She further contended that she was not allowed legal representation nor given the opportunity to have the agreement reviewed by anyone. As such, Mrs. Barber requested a declaration that all property acquired during the marriage be deemed community property, entitling her to interim spousal support, permanent and final support, medical insurance coverage, reimbursement and credit of funds paid for obligations and debts during the marriage, and all fruits, revenues and increases of property belonging to the community.

Mr. Barber was granted a judgment of divorce on June 14, 2007.

On August 5, 2008, Mr. Barber filed a motion for declaratory judgment seeking a judgment declaring the prenuptial agreement valid. A trial on the motion was held on August 20, 2008. The trial court determined that the stresses and time limitations that Mrs. Barber underwent did not amount to vices of duress or error. The trial court also determined that the contract was an authentic act. The trial court then stated:

> An examination of the contract reveals that the references to spousal support are contained in paragraph six of the otherwise lawful agreement. In the same sentence of that paragraph, the parties agree to waive interim and final spousal support. As was previously noted, the waiver of interim spousal support has been unlawful for thirty years, and was unlawful at the time this agreement was written. The court finds the provisions of paragraph six of the agreement to be inextricably bound, and strikes the entire paragraph. In all other regards, the contract is found to be lawful.

Judgment was signed on December 10, 2008, allowing Mrs. Barber the right to seek interim and permanent spousal support from Mr. Barber. The judgment also added the following: "That Deborah Barber is reserved the right to seek reimbursement of contribution to the estate of Harold Barber, as per law."

Mr. Barber appealed, alleging that the trial court erred in ruling that the waiver of temporary and permanent support were so "inextricably bound" so as to render the waiver of permanent support unenforceable. He also asserts that the trial court erred in ruling that Mrs. Barber had not waived her right to seek reimbursement.

DISCUSSION

When parties are bound by a valid contract and material facts are not in conflict, the contract's application to the case is a matter of law. An appellate review that is not founded upon any factual findings made at the trial court level, but is based upon an independent review and analysis of the contract within the four corners of the document, is not subject to the manifest error rule of law. In such cases, appellate review is simply whether the trial court was legally correct. *Boh Bros. Const. Co., L.L.C. v. State ex rel. Dept. of Transp. and Development*, 08–1793, p. 3 (La.App. 1 Cir. 3/27/09), 9 So.3d 982, 984, writ denied, 09–0856 (La.6/5/09), 9 So.3d 870; *Claitor v. Delahoussaye*, 02–1632, p. 11 (La.App. 1 Cir. 5/28/03), 858 So.2d 469, 478, *writ denied*, 03–1820 (La.10/17/03), 855 So.2d 764.

Generally, legal agreements have the effect of law upon the parties, and, as they bind themselves, they shall be held to a full performance of the obligations flowing therefrom. In other words, a contract between the parties is the law between them, and the courts are obligated to give legal effect to such contracts according to the true intent of the parties. LSA–C.C. 2045; *Boh Bros. Const. Co., L.L.C*, 08–1793 at p. 4, 9 So.3d at 984.

The Louisiana Civil Code gives spouses, before or during marriage, the right to enter into a matrimonial agreement as to all matters that are not prohibited by public policy. LSA–C.C. art. 2329; *Loftice v. Loftice*, 07–1741, p. 11 (La.App. 1 Cir. 3/26/08), 985 So.2d 204, 211. However, the supreme court in *Holliday v. Holliday*, 358 So.2d 618, 620 (La.1978), held that prenuptial agreements in which a spouse waives his or her right to alimony pendente lite in the event of separation are null and void as against public policy. The public policy the court referred to was that a husband should support and assist his wife during the existence of the marriage. The court determined that this legal obligation of support, as well as the fact that the conditions affecting entitlement to alimony pendente lite could not be foreseen at the time prenuptial agreements are entered into, overrides the premarital anticipatory waiver of alimony. *Holliday*, 358 So.2d at 620; *Loftice*, 07–1741 at p. 11, 985 So.2d at 211.

Thus, alimony pendente lite, or what is now known as interim spousal support, is based on the statutorily imposed duty of the spouses to support each other during marriage. LSA–C.C. art. 984; *Loftice*, 07–1741 at p. 11, 985 So.2d at 211. See also *McAlpine v. McAlpine*, 94–1594, p. 9 (La.9/5/96), 679 So.2d 85, 90. However, there is no corresponding statutory duty of support mandating permanent spousal support between former spouses. See *McAlpine*, 94–1594 at p. 9, 679 So.2d at 90. The court in *McAlpine* determined that permanent spousal support, unlike interim support, is not a law enacted for the public interest, but rather was enacted to protect individuals. Therefore, there is no prohibition against the waiver of post-divorce permanent spousal support. *McAlpine*, 94–1594 at p. 16, 679 So.2d at 93.

Relative to the nullity of a provision of an agreement, LSA–C.C. art. 2034 provides:

> Nullity of a provision does not render the whole contract null unless, from the nature of the provision or the intention of the parties, it can be presumed that the contract would not have been made without the null provision.

According to the 1984 Revision Comments, the above article "directs the court to consider the totality of the parties' intentions before annulling the agreement when only a portion of it is null." LSA–C.C. art. 2034, 1984 Revision Comment. Accordingly, like other questions of contract interpretation, whether an agreement is severable is controlled generally by the intent of the parties as expressed by the contract terms and/or language. *Hudson v. City of Bossier City*, 05–0351, p. 20 (La.4/17/06), 930 So.2d 881, 894. See also *Lebouef v. Liner*, 396 So.2d 376, 378 (La.App. 1 Cir.1981).

In its judgment, the trial court found the provisions of Paragraph 6 concerning interim and permanent spousal support "inextricably bound" and struck the entire paragraph. The judgment also included the reservation of Mrs. Barber's right to seek reimbursement. Except for these exclusions, the matrimonial agreement was held to be valid and enforceable as an authentic act.

While we agree with the trial court that the waiver of interim spousal support is against public policy and must be stricken from the agreement, we cannot say that the entire paragraph must be stricken. Paragraph 6 of the matrimonial agreement specifically provides:

> The appearers do further hereby expressly waive one from the other any and all entitlement to interim spousal support, final spousal support, or any support payments of whatsoever kind, character or nature, each of said appearers declaring that they are not and would not be entitled to any such alimony or support in the event of a dissolution of the marriage.

Although the agreement regarding interim spousal support and final spousal support are in the same sentence, they are two distinct provisions with different interests and different requirements. It does not appear that the portion of the sentence regarding interim support is so entangled or tied up with the rest of the sentence that it cannot be deleted without striking the entire paragraph. Accordingly, despite the difficult circumstances presented, we must reverse in part the judgment of the trial court insofar as it struck the entire paragraph regarding spousal support, and we amend the judgment to strike only that portion of Paragraph 6 as it concerns interim spousal support.

Mr. Barber also argues that the trial court erred in ruling that Ms. Barber had not waived her right to seek reimbursement. He asserts that Paragraph 4 of the matrimonial agreement contains a mutual waiver of the parties' respective rights of reimbursement. Thus, according to Mr. Barber, the inclusion of the reservation in the judgment that contradicted the trial court's written reasons, finding all provisions of the agreement valid except the waiver of support, was error.

Paragraph 4 of the matrimonial agreement provides:

> Any increase or improvement of separate property of either appearer, as separate property as set forth in this agreement, arising or made during the marriage, as the result of common labor, expense or industry of the appearers, shall not create any right to a reward in favor of that appearer or the legal representative of that appearer to whom the property, which has been increased or improved, does not belong.

As previously stated, a contract between the parties is the law between them, and the courts are obligated to give legal effect to such contracts according to the true intent of the parties. LSA–C.C. art. 2045; *Boh Bros. Const. Co., L.L.C.*, 08–1793 at p. 4, 9 So.3d at 984. Thus, when the words of a contract are clear and explicit and lead to no absurd consequences, no further interpretation may be made in search of the parties' intent. LSA–C.C. art. 2046. Also, to determine the meaning of words used in a contract, a court should give them their "generally prevailing meaning." LSA–C.C. art. 2047.

By the plain and clear words of Paragraph 4 of the matrimonial agreement, Mrs. Barber waived her right to reimbursement. Thus, it was error for the trial court to reserve to her those rights.

CONCLUSION

For the above reasons, we reverse in part the December 10, 2008 judgment of the trial court, insofar as it strikes the entire Paragraph 6 of the matrimonial agreement, and amend the judgment to only strike that portion regarding the waiver of any interim spousal support. Further, we reverse that portion of the judgment reserving to Ms. Barber the right to seek reimbursement of contribution to the estate of Mr. Barber, as per law. All costs of this appeal are assessed to Deborah Barber.

REVERSED IN PART, AMENDED IN PART, AND RENDERED.

F. Succession of Alfred Jay Moran

545 So. 2d 369 (La. 1988)

WATSON, Justice.

Plaintiff, Mrs. Murray Hurley, has intervened in the Succession of Alfred Jay Moran,2 claiming rights under a marriage contract with the decedent signed shortly before their marriage on February 1, 1980.

FACTS

According to the trial court's reasons for judgment, plaintiff and Moran separated on October 12, 1981. Decedent, Alfred Jay Moran, filed suit for divorce on February 2, 1982, and received a judgment on February 3, 1983. The basis for the judgment is not in the record, but counsel for plaintiff submits that both parties were decreed free from fault.

At issue is Paragraph IX of the marriage contract which reads as follows:

> "Husband hereby binds and obligates himself to make a will in which he will leave to Wife the entire disposable portion of his estate, as well as a usufruct to her for her lifetime on the remainder of both his separate and community property, and agrees not to alter or amend such provision by any codicil or will and shall incorporate the agreement contained in this paragraph in any new will or wills subsequently made by him."

Moran apparently never carried out the marriage contract by making a will in favor of his wife. Prior to the marriage, he had made a last will and testament dated December 14, 1979. Subsequently, he executed codicils on August 26, 1980; May 11, 1984; May 14, 1984; and May 17, 1984, none of which mentioned plaintiff. After Moran's death on June 8, 1984, the testament and codicils were probated. Plaintiff's action to annul the probate was dismissed, and the dismissal was affirmed.

Subsequently, plaintiff filed this petition to assert a claim as a creditor of the succession. The trial court maintained exceptions of no right and no cause of action and dismissed plaintiff's suit.

The court of appeal reversed and remanded for trial, relying on LSA-C.C. art. 1888 which stated in 1980 when the antenuptial contract was confected that:

"A future succession may become the object of an antenuptial agreement."

The court of appeal held that Moran's promise not to change his will was against public policy but his promise to leave the disposable portion of his estate was valid. A writ was granted to review the judgment of the court of appeal. 525 So.2d 1049 (La.1988).

LAW

A marriage contract is only valid as to matters not prohibited by public policy. LSA-C.C. art. 2329.7 Since a testator cannot renounce the right to revoke a will, a testamentary gratuity to a spouse is always precarious, being revocable at will.

Spouses are bound to the terms of their marriage contract only for the duration of the marriage, and testaments made after dissolution of the marriage are not affected. After a divorce, a marriage contract is void and has no future effect.

In general, an inter vivos donation comprehends only the present property of the donor. An inter vivos donation of future property is null. However, the prohibition against an inter vivos donation of future property does not apply to antenuptial marriage contracts. "To give and yet to retain is not valid outside of marriage." Potestative donative conditions are also allowed in marriage contracts. LSA-C.C. art. 1529; LSA-C.C. art. 1532.

The succession of a living person may not be the object of a contract other than an antenuptial agreement. LSA-C.C. art. 1976.17 The only exception to the general prohibition against contracts about successions of living persons is the right to donate a future succession interest in an antenuptial marriage contract. A donation by marriage contract can include property to be left on the day of decease. LSA-C.C. art. 1735; LSA-C.C. art. 1745.20 However, an inter vivos donation by an antenuptial marriage contract, stipulated to take effect at the donor's death, is irrevocable only to a limited extent. The donor cannot thereafter dispose of the donation by a gratuitous act. LSA-C.C. art. 1736. Compare LSA-C.C. art. 1468.24

LSA-C.C. art. 156, in conjunction with LSA-C.C. art. 159, deals with the loss of advantages or donations conferred by a marriage contract after a separation or divorce. According to these articles, the party against whom a separation or divorce is pronounced loses the advantages or donations conferred by the marriage contract.

The effect of C.C. art. 156, which is adopted by reference in C.C. art. 159, is discussed in Vaughn v. Coco, 409 So.2d 282 (La.App. 1 Cir.1981). In Vaughn, Judge Cole noted that Article 156, which corresponds to Article 299 in the Code Napoleon, has been treated as self-operative in accord with Planiol's interpretation of the French article. However, Vaughn dealt with a "guilty" spouse. Articles 156 and 159 preceded the concepts of no fault or mutual fault divorces first introduced by Act 269 of 1916.

In Parquin v. Finch, 1 Mart.N.S. 465 (1823) the marriage contract stipulated that, absent issue of the marriage, the survivor would inherit the community. The provision was decreed valid, allowing the surviving husband to inherit.

Succession of McCloskey, 29 La.Ann. 237 (1877) decided that an inter vivos donation of future property in a marriage contract made the surviving wife a creditor of the estate. McCloskey distinguished a donation to take effect on the death of the donor from a testamentary disposition. The donee was held to be a creditor of the estate rather than a legatee.

Succession of Cunningham, 142 La. 701, 77 So. 506 (1918) held that a judgment of divorce in favor of a wife did not revoke a testamentary disposition to "my Dear Wife," when the testament had not been revoked.

In Riddell v. Riddell, 146 La. 37, 83 So. 369 (1919), the marriage contract stipulated that the wife would inherit one-half of the husband's estate if the parties remained married at the husband's death. The widow was allowed to annul a subsequent donation to her husband's son insofar as it impinged on the prior "irrevocable" donation. Riddell relied on LSA-C.C. art. 1736. Since the donation to the son was gratuitous, the widow was allowed to enforce the conditional donation to her in the marriage contract.

Thigpen v. Thigpen, 231 La. 206, 91 So.2d 12 (1956) allowed a husband who had secured a divorce on the ground of abandonment to revoke the donation of a diamond ring to his wife because she had lost that advantage of marriage by the divorce decree against her. Since the ring had been donated during the marriage, it was held to be community property.

Robinson v. Robinson, 524 So.2d 218 (La.App. 3 Cir.1988) writ denied 531 So.2d 480 (La.1988) concluded that, where there is mutual fault, all donations or advantages conferred by the marriage are revoked by operation of law, because a party must be free from fault to retain any advantage from a marriage.

CONCLUSION

When Alfred Jay Moran received a judgment of divorce, the bonds of matrimony between the parties were dissolved and they were placed "in the same situation with respect to each other as if no marriage had ever been contracted between them". Under Articles 156 and 159, the party against whom the divorce was pronounced lost all the advantages "conferred by the marriage contract." Even if those articles apply in a no fault divorce, the advantages and donations referred to would be those conferred prior to the divorce, those in effect when the marriage was dissolved.

Moran's promise not to revoke or amend a will in his wife's favor was a potestative condition, which he could alter by his unilateral act.

Strong public policy considerations militate against contracting with regard to the succession of a living person and in favor of a testator having the power to revoke his will. The sole exception to both rules has been an inter vivos donation of future succession rights to a prospective spouse by an antenuptial marriage contract. The importance of marriage and the family unit justify this narrow exception, but it cannot be extended to the present situation.

In Parquin, the community was intact because the parties had remained married, and the disposition by marriage contract was valid and enforceable.

McCloskey points out the crucial distinction between an inter vivos conditional donation of future property and a testamentary legacy. Moran did not make a donation in this marriage contract; he agreed to make a will in his wife's favor. Such a potestative promise, only tolerated in a marriage contract, was subject to revocation at his option.

This case differs from Succession of Cunningham, supra. The Moran marriage contract did not contain an inter vivos donation to take effect at the donor's death. Instead, Alfred Jay Moran promised to make a will in favor of his future wife, but the provision in the marriage contract that he would not revoke that will is unenforceable under LSA-C.C. art. 1690.

In Cunningham, the testamentary disposition had not been revoked, and the fault-free spouse was entitled to inherit. Here, Moran never wrote a will pursuant to the marriage contract.

Riddell, supra, involved a donation in the marriage contract itself and not a promise of future performance. The distinction is between a present gift of future property to take effect at the donor's death and a promise to leave property by will.

The marriage contract of the Morans was no longer in effect after their divorce. It could not govern their future affairs. At dissolution of the marriage, plaintiff was entitled to the benefits which had been conferred by the marriage contract, but those benefits did not include an inter vivos donation of succession rights. Moran's potestative promise to make an irrevocable will in his wife's favor has no legal effect.

***

G. Elizabeth H. Fielding v. George H. Van Geffen

473 So. 2d 317 (La. App. 1st Cir. 1985)

CARTER, Judge.

This is an appeal in a suit to enforce a marriage contract.

FACTS

On August 22, 1979, prior to the celebration of their marriage, Elizabeth H. Fielding and George H. Van Geffen entered into a marriage contract. By the terms of the contract, both Fielding and Van Geffen renounced the provisions of the law which establish a community of acquets and gains and elected to remain separate in property. Van Geffen also promised to pay Fielding $200,000.00, payable at the rate of $1,500.00 per month.

On August 24, 1979, Fielding and Van Geffen were married. Shortly after their wedding, on September 7, 1979, Van Geffen opened a savings account for his wife with Pelican Homestead and Savings Association in New Orleans, Louisiana. On that same day, Van Geffen made an initial deposit of $1,500.00. Thereafter, Van Geffen made four similar deposits, for a total of $7,500.00. No subsequent payments were made.

In March of 1980, Fielding and Van Geffen separated. A judgment of divorce was subsequently rendered on August 20, 1982.

On December 2, 1982, Fielding filed suit against Van Geffen for $192,500.00, the amount due under the marriage contract. The trial court judgment was rendered on December 14, 1983, and signed on February 15, 1984, in favor of defendant and dismissed, with prejudice, plaintiff's suit. From this adverse judgment, plaintiff appeals.

ARGUMENT

A contract between two parties is the law between them. LSA-C.C. art. 1901; Oncale v. Aetna Cas. and Sur. Co., 417 So.2d 471 (La.App. 1st Cir.1982). Courts are bound to give legal effect to all written contracts according to the true intent of the parties, and this intent is to be determined by the words of the contract when they are clear, explicit, and lead to no absurd consequences. LSA-C.C. art. 1945; Leenerts Farms, Inc. v. Rogers, 421 So.2d 216 (La.1982); Bonfanti Marine, Inc. v. Clement, 439 So.2d 537 (La.App. 1st Cir.1983). The meaning and intent of the parties to the written contract must be sought within the four corners of the instrument and cannot be explained or contradicted by parol evidence. LSA-C.C. art. 2276; Smith v. Leger, 439 So.2d 1203 (La.App. 1st Cir.1983); Carter's Ins. Agency, Inc. v. Franklin, 428 So.2d 808 (La.App. 1st Cir.1983); Tauzin v. Claitor, 417 So.2d 1304 (La.App. 1st Cir.1982), writ denied 422 So.2d 423 (La.1982).

The pertinent portions of the marriage contract provide, as follows:

ARTICLE II

> All property and effects of the said intended husband, whether owned by him at the time of the celebration of the said intended marriage or acquired during the said marriage, are hereby declared to be his separate and paraphernal property.

ARTICLE III

> All property and effects of the said intended wife, whether owned by her at the time of the celebration of the said intended marriage or acquired during said marriage, are hereby declared to be her separate and paraphernal property, and she does hereby expressly reserve to herself the entire administration of her movable and immovable property, and the free enjoyment of her revenues.

ARTICLE IV

> The said intended husband does hereby agree to pay to the said intended wife the sum of $200,000.00, payable at the rate of $1,500.00 per month. This obligation and promise shall cease upon the death of the said intended wife, but shall not cease upon the death of the said intended husband.

The marriage contract, signed by both Fielding and Van Geffen, clearly indicates an intention by both parties to renounce the legal provisions establishing a community of acquets and gains and to remain separate in property. Additionally, in exchange for the renunciation of the community and election to remain separate in property, Van Geffen agreed to pay Fielding $200,000.00, payable in monthly installments of $1,500.00. The contract contained no provisions limiting the obligation in the event of separation and divorce. In fact, the only qualifications on the obligation was that upon the death of Fielding, the obligation to pay the monthly installments would cease.

The trial court erred in holding that the agreement of Van Geffen to pay Fielding $200,000.00 was an onerous donation included within a commutative (marriage) contract with the revocation of the marriage revoking the donation.

The entire marriage contract is a valid commutative contract based on valid consideration with each party giving up certain benefits and in return obtaining other benefits. Further there is no ambiguity in the terms of the agreement, and Article IV thereof is clear and enforceable.

Since Van Geffen has paid only $7,500.00 toward this obligation, Fielding is entitled to the remaining $192,500.00 due and owing under the marriage contract as per the terms of said contract.

Accordingly, the judgment of the trial court dismissing plaintiff's claim is reversed. Judgment is hereby rendered in favor of plaintiff, Elizabeth H. Fielding, and against defendant, George H. Van Geffen, for the sum of $1,500.00 per month from February

7, 1980, until the obligation is extinguished as per the terms of the marriage contract, together with legal interest on each installment from its due date until paid.

Costs of this appeal are to be assessed against defendant.

REVERSED AND RENDERED.

8.6 MARRIAGE REQUIREMENT: COHABITATION AND PALIMONY AGREEMENTS

A. Marsha Garrison, *Nonmarital Cohabitation: Social Revolution and Legal Regulation*, 42 FAM. L. Q. 309 (2008)

***

II. The Cohabitation Revolution

In 1958, members of the American Bar Association's new Section of Family Law were not expecting their membership dues to provide them with new opportunities to master the law of cohabitation—there was no law of cohabitation. Prostitution was regulated by the criminal code. Common-law marriage was regulated by marriage law, and at this time about a third of the states recognized a cohabiting couple as a married couple if they had held themselves out as married and the evidence showed that promises to be married had been exchanged.

In between these two extremes, legal regulation of cohabitation was sparse. Indeed, it could be boiled down to two sentences: Cohabitation created no rights or obligations. Cohabitants could not agree to create rights or obligations based on their intimate relationship.

The bar on relationship-based contracts between cohabitants did not bar other sorts of deals, however; cohabitants in most states could enter into any arrangement that was open to noncohabitants. Thus, one cohabitant might enter into a valid and binding business partnership with the other. Cohabitants could also enter into legally binding contracts for non-sexual services severable from their relationship.

In addition to these contract alternatives, a disappointed cohabitant could often rely on one or another equitable doctrine for relief. The purchase money resulting trust frequently protected the cohabitant who had paid money toward the purchase of property when title was taken in the name of his or her partner. Quantum meruit provided a means of obtaining payment for services rendered for which the expected payment had not been made. Constructive trust provided "a flexible remedy imposed in a wide variety of situations to prevent unjust enrichment." These various forms of equitable relief ensured that, in many cases, one cohabitant who had been cheated by the other could obtain recovery for some or all of his losses.

Although family law sanctioned business contracts and provided equitable remedies for cohabitants, it did not provide for relationship-based relief. The principle that cohabitation in itself—a "meretricious relationship" as the courts put it during this time period—created no legal rights or obligations flowed from several different public-policy concerns. First, courts viewed nonmarital cohabitation as socially undesirable, and they wanted to discourage such arrangements. Second, relational contracts between cohabitants were widely viewed as thinly veiled prostitution contracts. Third, because the parties' arrangement was private and litigation occurred only when their relationship had broken down, solid evidence of their understanding was often lacking. Finally, open cohabitation was rare, and those who engaged in the practice were generally very poor, very bohemian, or both; existing equitable remedies seemed adequate to handle the legal problems such cohabitants brought to court.

The last point deserves special emphasis. In 1958, cohabitation outside of marriage was widely viewed as shameful, and middle-class Americans thus cohabited very rarely. It is likely that the vast majority of the new Family Law Section members literally did not know anyone who did cohabit or had cohabited outside of marriage. The movies and television offered no glimpses of such relational possibilities, and the Census Bureau did not even bother counting cohabiting couples. What almost no one foresaw in 1958 was the rapidity with which the stigma traditionally attached to nonmarital cohabitation would vanish. The culturally cataclysmic 1960s were about to begin and, by the time the decade ended, youthful attitudes toward cohabitation had already shifted dramatically.

Among the remarkable cultural shifts of the 1960s was a new attitude toward premarital sex. To be more precise, the 1960s witnessed a profound shift in attitudes toward female premarital sex. Before the 1960s, a young man could "sow a few wild oats" without fear of serious social censure. Of course, he risked venereal disease if he patronized a prostitute. And he risked a shotgun wedding if he impregnated a girl from a respectable family. But if the young man got away with it—whatever the "it" might be—he typically suffered no reputational harm. For young women, on the other hand, premarital sex posed extraordinary risks. The first and largest of these risks was pregnancy. The best outcome that pregnancy could produce was a shotgun wedding. A furtive stay at a home for unwed mothers or an illegal, and perhaps dangerous, abortion represented the only alternatives to that wedding. Even if pregnancy was averted, the young woman who engaged in premarital sex risked serious reputational loss. "Nice" girls did not; "fast" girls who did faced gossip, snickers, and damaged marriage prospects.

During the 1960s, technology and social change combined to change these traditional norms. The new birth control pill offered young women, for the first time, near certain protection from pregnancy that was both within their own control and divorced from the sexual act itself; in order to obtain the safety that the pill offered, a young woman did not even have to admit, to herself or her partner, that she had planned to engage in intercourse. The women's movement offered this same young woman the chance to imagine gaining what had always been male prerogatives, including the possibility of premarital sex without reputational loss. And the social upheaval that accompanied the civil rights movement and Vietnam War produced a new world in which the vision of sex without reputational harm became a reality. In 1958, nice girls did not engage in premarital sex. In 1968, many young women, particularly college-age women, no longer wanted to be nice girls. And by 1978, the divide between nice and naughty girls had simply disappeared.

With premarital sex came open premarital cohabitation. What began as a countercultural innovation associated with hippies and antiwar activists became, with remarkable rapidity, an accepted part of youth culture. The new norms for the young also rapidly spread into older age cohorts; by 1988, the parents of young cohabitants were often choosing to cohabit themselves.

The numbers tell the story here. Between 1970 and 2000, the number of U.S. unmarried-cohabitant households rose almost ten-fold, from 523,000 to 4,880,0000. The number of individuals who have ever cohabited has also risen sharply; among women born between 1950 and 1954, women who came of age in the late 1960s and early 1970s, 24% cohabited before marriage; among women born between 1965 and 1969, 55% cohabited before marriage. Nor is there any sign that the trend in favor of premarital cohabitation has yet abated.

In recent years, the ranks of cohabitants have been further swelled by older couples who have already been married. Some of these older cohabitants have already been divorced and thus feel hesitant about a new marital commitment; some, making use of cohabitation's new respectability, have chosen cohabitation over marriage for more pragmatic reasons.

The net result is that cohabitation is now a multifaceted and multi-generational phenomenon. It includes young men and women who are sharing living space with a dating partner in order to save money, more committed couples who are testing the strength of their relationship, engaged couples who are planning to marry, committed couples who view their relationship as marital but have chosen to avoid marriage for practical reasons such as the potential loss of alimony or a surviving-spouse entitlement, and many couples whose motives are mixed or who disagree about the nature of their relationship.

The extraordinary rise of cohabitation is not unique to the United States. Equivalent developments have taken place in all common-law countries and across the civil-law nations of northern and central Europe. With cohabitation has come an enormous increase in nonmarital birth. In 1940, 3.8% of U.S. births were nonmarital; in 2002, 33.8% of U.S. births were. In some Scandinavian nations, nonmarital births now outweigh marital births.

III. The Legal Response: A Bang or a Whimper?

A. Marvin and Its Reception

Once cohabitation moved from the fringes to the center of society, it was less obvious that law should play the same role in regulating cohabitational relationships. Thus, in the watershed Marvin case, the California Supreme Court urged that "the prevalence of nonmarital relationships in modern society and the social acceptance of them" required courts to forgo the application of traditional legal standards "based on alleged moral considerations that have apparently been so widely abandoned by so many":

> [T]he nonenforceability of agreements expressly providing for meretricious conduct rested upon the fact that such conduct, as the word suggests, pertained to and encompassed prostitution. To equate the nonmarital relationship of today to such a subject matter is to do violence to an accepted and wholly different practice ....
>
> We conclude that the judicial barriers that may stand in the way of a policy based upon the fulfillment of the reasonable expectations of the parties to a nonmarital relationship should be removed.

Relying on the new social acceptability of cohabitation, the Marvin majority not only approved the enforcement of explicit relational contracts between cohabitants, but also authorized trial courts to "inquire into the conduct of the parties to determine whether that conduct demonstrates an implied contract or implied agreement of partnership or joint venture, or some other tacit understanding between the parties." In addition to recovery based on express and implied contracts, the court also approved continued reliance on equitable remedies—quantum meruit, constructive trust, resulting trust—that had provided relief to cohabitants in the pre-Marvin era, and it left open the possibility of "additional equitable remedies to protect the expectations of the parties to a nonmarital relationship in cases in which existing remedies prove inadequate...." In sum, Marvin promised to dramatically expand the range of rights and remedies available to cohabiting couples. The decision also suggested that a major shift in the legal status of cohabitation was underway.

The extended national press coverage and academic commentary that the Marvin case received, both before and after the California Supreme Court's decision, furthered the impression that Marvin had ushered in a new era for cohabitants. And Marvin has undeniably assumed the stature of a path-breaking opinion.

Marvin has been cited in approximately 200 other court decisions, about half of which came from the California courts, and approximately 300 law review articles. It is still a fixture of family law classes, appearing as a principal case in each of the eleven casebooks currently on the market. The term "palimony" has entered general usage, particularly in the context of entertainers, sports figures, and wealthy entrepreneurs.

There is no question that Marvin altered the way both courts and the public think about cohabitant rights and remedies.

B. The Aftermath of Marvin

Today, Marvin represents, at least in the United States, the dominant approach to cohabitant claims. Appellate courts in at least twenty-six states and the District of Columbia have now approved some relational contract claims between cohabitants, although a few of these jurisdictions have disapproved recovery based on an implied contract. Only five states have disapproved of all forms of relief based on a cohabiting relationship. Perhaps surprisingly, however, Marvin's bold language has not produced results markedly different from those permissible under pre-Marvin case law. As Professor Ann Lacquer Estin put it, "[w]ith all its celebrity, the Marvin decision stands more as a cultural icon than as a legal watershed."

Consider the aftermath of the Marvin decision itself. On remand, the trial court held a three-month trial, at the end of which it found that "no express contract was negotiated between the parties" and that "the conduct of the parties ... does not reveal any implementation of any contract nor ... give rise to an implied contract." The court went on to conclude that there was no "mutual effort" that might support a recovery and that, "in good conscience," no equitable remedies—resulting trust, constructive trust, or quantum meruit—were applicable. In the court's view, the plaintiff's relationship with wealthy, successful Lee Marvin had been helpful to her, not hurtful. Despite its finding that there was unjust enrichment and no contract, express or implied, the court nonetheless awarded the plaintiff $104,000 in alimony "so that she may have the economic means to reeducate herself and to learn new, employable skills or to refurbish those utilized, for example, during her most recent employment and so that she may return from her status as companion of a motion picture star to a separate, independent but perhaps more prosaic existence." But this award—one that was not sanctioned by the contract approach outlined in Marvin—was promptly struck down on appeal. Michele Triola "Marvin" walked away from the landmark decision that she had won in the California Supreme Court with nothing.

Cohabitants who followed Michele Marvin into California courtrooms learned that her failure to turn what looked like a favorable decision into a solid cash recovery was not entirely due to the specifics of Michele's case. While we have no solid evidence of how many Marvin plaintiffs have won in the courtroom or accepted a favorable settlement, California appellate decisions show that the Marvin requirements have been strictly construed and that an award is by no means easy to obtain. Nor did the California courts use Marvin as a springboard for fashioning new cohabitant rights and obligations.

Indeed, since Marvin, the California Supreme Court has revisited the legal problems posed by cohabitation only rarely. I could find only two decisions in which a supreme court majority cited Marvin for a proposition related to its substantive holding: in Foley v. Interactive Data Corp., the court held that the claims of a discharged employee for breach of an implied-contract promise to discharge only for good cause survived the statute of frauds, and in Koebke v. Bernardo Heights Country Club, the court held that California's civil rights act barred discrimination against registered domestic partners by denying them benefits or services extended to spouses. Dissenting members of the court have cited Marvin in decisions denying cohabitants the right to maintain a claim for loss of consortium, finding that cohabitants are not protected against housing discrimination by California's Fair Employment and Housing Act, and holding that a cohabitant who quit her job to follow her boyfriend did not have good cause and thus was not entitled to unemployment insurance when she had not shown an imminent marriage or a marriage-related obligation.

California appellate courts have cited Marvin more frequently, but they too have only rarely expanded on Marvin's central holding. In Cochran v. Cochran, the appellate court held that a viable Marvin claim does not require full-time cohabitation. But in Taylor v. Fields and Bergen v. Wood, appellate courts disallowed Marvin claims when there had been no cohabitation. California courts have held that a post-mortem Marvin action does not violate a no-contest clause in the decedent cohabitant's will, at least as long as the will does not specifically disallow such an action. But they have also held that when title to real property is at issue, the Marvin plaintiff must establish her claim to the property by clear and convincing evidence. They have held that Marvin claims are civil actions based on contract law and dismissed Marvin lawsuits that violate the statute of limitations for contract claims. They have disallowed the award of temporary alimony to a Marvin plaintiff and declined to permit cohabitants not registered under California's Domestic Partnership Law to make use of its dissolution procedures or rely on the putative spouse doctrine. They have held that the marital communication privilege is inapplicable to cohabitants.

California courts have also been fairly cautious in interpreting Marvin's continued ban on prostitution agreements. They have disallowed contracts that clearly involved the exchange of valuable consideration for sex. Although they have concluded that agreements to have a child together and to perform services as a bodyguard, secretary, and real estate counselor did not represent impermissible sex-for-pay contracts, they have found that an agreement to be a lover, companion, homemaker, traveling companion, and cook was an invalid sex-for-hire contract.

Finally, like the Marvin trial court, California courts have treated the evidentiary requirements implied in Marvin very seriously. Although there are reported appellate decisions upholding judgments in favor of Marvin plaintiffs, there are more decisions affirming judgments against Marvin plaintiffs where the trial court found insufficient evidence of a cohabitation agreement or unjust enrichment. There are also cases in which the appellate court overturned a trial court judgment based on insufficient evidence of a cohabitation agreement or unjust enrichment.

Courts outside of California have also tended to take a cautious approach to claims based on cohabitation. Although the majority of U.S. jurisdictions have followed Marvin, only one high court, in Washington, has gone beyond Marvin's contract model to permit recovery based on the fact of cohabitation, without any showing of unjust enrichment or an agreement. Courts in other states have also been wary of expanding the legal status of cohabitants: they have almost invariably followed the California Supreme Court in declining to extend to cohabitants rights available to married couples; virtually none, for example, have extended the right to obtain loss of consortium damages to cohabitants when a partner is injured or authorized cohabitants to obtain other public benefits available to married couples.

***

B. *Mary Ann Schwegmann v. John G. Schwegmann*

441 So. 2d 316 (La. App. 5 Cir. 1983)

KLIEBERT, Judge.

This is a devolutive appeal by Ms. Mary Ann Blackledge, plaintiff, from a judgment dismissing, on a motion for summary judgment, all of the causes of action alleged in her petition against Mr. John G. Schwegmann, Jr. (hereafter Mr. Schwegmann), et al, defendants, except the cause to recover in quantum meruit for the value of uncompensated services performed separate and apart from the relationship of concubinage.

Ms. Blackledge asserts that the allegations of her petition raise six causes of action against the defendants: (1) Specific performance and/or damages based on breach of contract; (2) Recognition of constructive trust or damages based on implied contract; (3) Declaratory relief; (4) Quasi Contract and/or Quantum Meruit; (5) Interference with contract rights; and (6) Declaration of simulation and/or revocatory action. Additionally, though not an itemized cause, she asserts the existence of a partnership and prays for its dissolution and/or distribution of its assets.

Notwithstanding Rule 2-12-4 of the Uniform Rules for the Courts of Appeal, Ms. Blackledge's brief did not particularize errors in the trial court judgment or specify issues on appeal. Rather, she argues that there are issues of fact and as a matter of law, her petition contains valid causes of action; hence, the granting of the motion to summarily dismiss her claims was error. We disagree and affirm the judgment of the trial court.

The petition alleged a contract entered into by Ms. Blackledge and Mr. Schwegmann in May, 1966, whereby they agreed to live together and, while doing so, combine their skills, efforts, labor and earnings and to share equally any and all assets and property acquired and accumulated as a result of their joint skills, efforts, labor and earnings. The horns of the legal dilemma upon which the petition places her is apparent from her testimony given by deposition. As facts are elicited to show the confection of an agreement, the nature of the services or their value, the same facts establish that the alleged agreement, if in fact proven, is meretricious and, therefore, void.

Ms. Blackledge claims she and Mr. Schwegmann lived together, without marriage, for twelve years pursuant to an oral agreement. The agreement, according to her, was confected in 1966 when Mr. Schwegmann told her he wanted to "share everything" with her and she said "okay". At the time of this conversation, Mr. Schwegmann was a twice divorced, middle age male who owned a chain of supermarkets and other assets, and Ms. Blackledge was a 24 year old unmarried female who had no property or other financial assets. The claimed contractual agreement was never reduced to writing and there was no witness to the alleged conversation in which it was confected.

Following the confection of the alleged contractual agreement, Ms. Blackledge and Mr. Schwegmann lived together continuously from May 1966 to May 1978. In this time frame, Ms. Blackledge contends she rendered services as a companion, housekeeper and cook, as well as a mother to Mr. Schwegmann's children, and as a business advisor, political assistant and confidante to him and his controlled corporations.

Throughout the time they lived together, Ms. Blackledge and Mr. Schwegmann had sexual relations on a regular basis. Ms. Blackledge's living expenses, dental and medical bills, clothing costs, entertainment and traveling expenses were paid for by Mr. Schwegmann. He also provided her with a monthly allowance check during their cohabitation and continued the checks after they ceased living together until the time this suit was filed. The sexual relationship also continued during visits after the cohabitation had terminated.

In the absence of specific assignments of error or issues, we will discuss each of the asserted causes of action (itemized above as [1] thru [6]) under the captions indicated below.

BREACH OF CONTRACT

Since the issue arises on a motion for summary judgment, we did not need to and made no determination as to whether the so-called contract alleged in the petition and testified to by Ms. Blackledge was in fact proven. Rather, for the purpose of this motion, we consider the facts alleged in the petition, as expanded on and amplified in the depositions as true.

Counsel for Ms. Blackledge prays for specific performance of the alleged oral contract or alternatively damages for breach of the contract. The defendants contend no valid contract could be confected because (1) the alleged "contractual agreement " is a universal partnership and consequently invalid because it is not in writing; (2) the object of the alleged contract was not certain, hence, it violates the requirements of La.C.C. Articles 1779(3) and 1886; consequently no contract was confected; (3) the alleged contract is not supported by adequate consideration; and (4) the alleged contract is void because it is meretricious. The trial judge ruled on only the first and last of defendants' contentions, thus negating the necessity of his considering the others.

A universal partnership is defined by La.C.C. Article 28293 as follows:

"Universal partnership is a contract by which the parties agree to make a common stock of all the property they respectively possess; they may extend it to all property real or personal, or restrict it to personal only; they may, as in other partnerships, agree that the property itself shall be common stock or that the fruits only shall be such; but property which may accrue to one of the parties, after entering into the partnership, by donation, succession or legacy, does not become common stock, and any stipulation to that effect, previous to the obtaining the property aforesaid, is void."
and expanded on in the two subsequent articles as follows:

> Art. 2830. A universal partnership of profits include all the gains that may be made from whatever source, whether from property or industry, with the restriction contained in the last article, and subject to all legal stipulations to be made by the parties.
>
> Art. 2831. If nothing more is agreed between the parties, than that there shall be a universal partnership, it shall extend only to the profits of the property each shall possess, and of their credit and industry.

As found by the trial judge, the contractual agreement alleged in the petition "fits exactly the codal definition of universal partnership". Ms. Blackledge testified she and Mr. Schwegmann were going to pool all of their assets and share the fruits of their labor, thus clearly asserting an intention to confect a partnership. Indeed, among others, the plaintiff's petition asks the court to consider the conduct and agreement of the parties as a partnership and prays for its dissolution and the distribution of its assets to the partners.

Under the provisions of La.C.C. Article 2834, a universal partnership cannot be created "... without a writing signed by the parties ..." Hence, Louisiana does not recognize as a valid universal partnership an oral agreement between a man and a woman who live together and agree to split certain properties standing in the name of one of them. Heatwole v. Stansbury, 212 La. 685, 33 So.2d 196 (1947); Foshee v. Simkin, 174 So.2d 915 (1st Cir.1965); Chambers v. Crawford, 150 So.2d 61 (2nd Cir.1963); Gadlin v. Deggs, 23 So.2d 704 (4th Cir.1945).

Ms. Blackledge testified her alleged understanding or agreement was not reduced to writing. Therefore, under the jurisprudence above cited, the trial court held the oral contract alleged by the plaintiff, even if proven, would be a universal partnership and, as such, invalid because not made in writing.

In her brief on appeal, counsel for Ms. Blackledge states "historically concubinage cases have couched the agreement as a universal partnership "; but then argues "there is no statutory reason why the courts began to apply partnership law to any oral contract". Consequently, "there is no explanation [why] within the body of concubinage law except that the goals of the parties were joint and the state is a community property state". We suggest the explanation is found in the fact that the community of acquets and gains created by the marriage is legally considered a partnership between the partners in the marriage.

In most concubinage cases, as is the case here, the goal of the plaintiff is to obtain for the concubine the civil benefits which would flow to the wife as a marital partner. In the absence of the marriage, some relationship, other than a sexual one, must exist between the parties for the civil benefits to flow to the person acting as the pseudo wife. Consequently, it is logical for the concubine's counsel to urge a partnership akin to the community of acquets and gains which applies to marital partners and for the court to apply partnership law in denying it.

As argued by counsel for Ms. Blackledge, it was theoretically and legally possible for the parties to establish a commercial or some partnership other than a universal partnership. However, the facts are that under the allegations of the petition and the testimony of Ms. Blackledge the relationship created was that of a universal partnership, not some other type. Additionally, this court cannot lose track of reality. Although it was theoretically and legally possible for the parties to marry and thus create a legal partnership based on a sexual relationship, the facts here are that the parties did not marry. Hence, as subsequently pointed out in this opinion-however the relationship is categorized-under the law the alleged agreement is a meretricious one and therefore void. For the same reason, applying the present partnership articles of the Civil Code (which do not require the partnership to be in writing) would not produce the results desired by the plaintiff.

Accordingly, we uphold the trial judge's ruling that the alleged oral agreement asserted by Ms. Blackledge would be a universal partnership and thus be invalid because not made in writing. Further, even if the alleged agreement was not required to be in writing, it would be unenforceable because it is a meretricious one. Hence, except as we hereafter expand on the concept of a meretricious agreement under the caption Quantum Meruit, it is unnecessary for us to consider the other grounds urged by the defendants as defense to the plaintiff's claim for breach of an alleged contract.

RECOGNITION OF CONSTRUCTIVE TRUST OR DAMAGES BASED ON IMPLIED CONTRACT

Ms. Blackledge contends the fact she and Mr. Schwegmann lived together as man and wife for twelve years caused a contract to be implied between them. On the basis of this implied contract she asserts the creation of a constructive trust for her benefit over the joint assets held by Mr. Schwegmann or alternatively the right to recover damages based on his breach of the "implied contract". She argues the constructive trust is imposed as an equitable remedy to protect her interest in the joint properties because she had a "reasonable expectation and belief" she and Mr. Schwegmann had an agreement and she had the greatest confidence and trust he would carry out the agreement.

The legal concept for a constructive trust is to impose an equitable lien on property because of a fiduciary relationship between the parties. The heart and soul of the equitable lien is a fiduciary relationship. Neither in the pleadings nor in the deposition of Ms. Blackledge is there established the requisite fiduciary relationship. Further, it is clear the Louisiana Civil Code prohibits the imposition of a constructive trust on property. Succession of Onorato, 219 La. 1, 51 So.2d 804 (1951); In re Liquidation of Canal Bank & Trust Co., 181 La. 856, 160 So. 609, 616 (1935); see also Mansfield Hardwood Lumber Company v. Johnson, 268 F.2d 317 (5th Cir.1959); In re Hagin, 21 F.2d 434, 437 (E.D.La.1927), aff'd sub nom. Phoenix Bldg. & Homestead Ass'n v. E.A. Carrere's Sons, 33 F.2d 563 (5th Cir.1929); Bankhead v. Maryland Casualty Company, 197 F.Supp. 879 (E.D.La.1961).

Her theory for recovery under an implied contract requires the characterization of her relationship with Mr. Schwegmann as a marriage, when in fact they were never married and neither of them ever believed they were married to each other. As a matter of fact, Ms. Blackledge testified she knew Mr. Schwegmann had a marriage contract (against formation of a community of acquets and gains) with his second wife because, as she stated, "he wanted the property protected in the event of a divorce".

In oral arguments and in appellant's briefs, counsel for plaintiff strenuously urges the novelty of the relationship and importance of her case in a changing society. The trial judge rejected the argument and gave excellent legal written reasons for doing so. Therefore, we adopt his reasons which follow as our own:

> "Claims like the plaintiff's are not foreign to Louisiana courts. Louisiana law has defined a person in Miss Blackledge's position as a concubine, a woman who 'occupies the position, performs the duties, and assumes the responsibilities of a wife, without the title and privileges flowing from a legal marriage.' Purvis v. Purvis, 162 So. 239, 240 (La.App. 2d Cir.1935). Louisiana terminology for the man with whom a concubine lives is 'paramour'.

A great body of jurisprudence has grown up confirming that concubines and paramours have no rights in each other's property. Jackson v. Hampton, 134 So.2d 114 (La.App. 2d Cir.1961); Rochelle v. Hezeau, 15 La.Ann. 306 (1860). See also Mintz & Mintz, Inc. v. Color, 250 So.2d 816 (La.App. 4th Cir.1971) (where no garnishment of a woman's wages could be had for the debt of her paramour) and Sims v. Matassa, 200 So. 666 (La.App. 1st Cir.1941) (where no seizure of a woman's property could be accomplished to satisfy her paramour's debt).

The Fourth Circuit Court of Appeal recently refused to recognize a concubine as a surviving spouse in community and succinctly described Louisiana law: 'The law could scarce be plainer: a sharing of bed and table, for a night or for a lifetime, does not by itself constitute marriage.' Succ. of Donohue, 389 So.2d 879, 880 (La.App. 4th Cir.1980). See also Sesostris Youchican v. Texas & P.R. Co., 147 La. 1080, 86 So. 551 (1920); Foshee v. Simkin, supra."

A substantial portion of the plaintiff counsel's brief is devoted to a historical analysis of the Louisiana Law on concubinage to show that its development was predicated on public policy construed by the judiciary. She then argues that changes in the mores of society as regards cohabitation have changed so radically, we should not impose on a man and woman who cohabitate without marriage a standard based on moral considerations merely to protect Victorian values which have been abandoned by so many in our society. Therefore, she urges it is time for the courts of Louisiana to develop a legal vehicle to protect the property rights obtained during cohabitation by a male and female in a sexual relationship without benefit of marriage. In support of the contentions, she urges a constitutionally protected right against discrimination between wives and concubines. She compares the discrimination she sees to that formerly existing between legitimate and illegitimate children and says concubinage discriminates against black heritage and culture but more particularly against women.

We neither agree with her appreciation of the sociological changes nor the necessity for a change in legal philosophy as to concubinage nor do we see the violation of a constitutionally protected right against discrimination. The State has valid reason to discourage relationships which serve to erode the cornerstone of society, i.e., the family. In every known civilized society, replacement of its members is performed within the context of the family. Although it is conceivably possible that sexual relations and child rearing could be deregulated or governed by norms that do not entail the encouragement, support and protection of family institutions, past experiments in that direction have failed. (See "The Attempt to Abolish the Family in Russia" in The Great Retreat by Nicholas S. Timasheff, Copyright 1946 by E.P. Dutton & Co., Inc. Further, in the case of the children, legitimate or illegitimate, they were not the cause of their status, but here the status of concubine was a voluntary and desired one, for the parties neither married, wanted to marry, nor believed they were married.

Under present Louisiana law, unmarried cohabitation does not give rise to property rights analogous to or similar to those of married couples. Concubines have no implied contract or equitable liens that afford them any rights in the property of their paramours. Moreover, in our view, although Victorian, the values sought to be protected by the formulation of those legal concepts are imperative if we are to maintain our civilized society.

QUASI CONTRACT AND QUANTUM MERUIT

The plaintiff asserts a right to recover compensation for the services rendered to Mr. Schwegmann under a quasi contract or quantum meruit theory. Under our law, when one benefits or is unjustly enriched from the labor of another, the law implies a promise to pay a reasonable amount for the labor, even in the absence of a specific contract. La.C.C. Article 1965. Bordelon Motors, Inc. v. Thompson, 176 So.2d 836 (3rd Cir.1965).

Here Ms. Blackledge testified that she rendered domestic services and business services and here claims compensation for both. Since the trial court and we reached conclusions based on the nature of the services, we consider each category of services separately.

Domestic Services

Ms. Blackledge stated in her deposition that she performed domestic services including cooking, cleaning, chauffering, taking care of Mr. Schwegmann's daughter, and acting as a nurse to him after his stroke. She also stated that she and Mr. Schwegmann had sexual relations: (1) on their first date in October or November of 1958; (2) throughout the time they dated before living together; (3) while they lived together in his house; and (4) when she visited after she left his house, and that this was one of the reasons Mr. Schwegmann paid her money. In describing her alleged agreement with Mr. Schwegmann, she testified that part of her promise was to "be a wife to him " and that "John and I made all the commitments and agreements to each other that anyone would take when they got married ". She understood a condition of the agreement to be that while they lived together neither of them would have sexual relations with anyone else.

Clearly from her testimony, the domestic services of child care, nursing, cooking, etc., were inextricably interwoven with sexual services in a concubinage relationship. Louisiana law clearly disallows claims in quantum meruit by concubines for domestic services when the services are interwoven with the sexual relationship.

From early in Louisiana law, where parties to a contract cohabit in a sexual relationship and their agreement to cohabit is part of the basis for the agreement between them, the agreement is unenforceable because it is an unlawful contract for meretricious services. Delamour v. Roger, 7 La.Ann. 152 (1852). See also La.C.C. Article 1892; Sparrow v. Sparrow, 231 La. 966, 93 So.2d 232 (1957); and Foshee v. Simkin, 174 So.2d 915 (1st Cir.1965) for more recent cases.

More recently, the First Circuit Court of Appeal in Guerin v. Bonaventure, 212 So.2d 459 (1st Cir.1968) at pages 464-65 denied the claims of a concubine in quantum meruit in the following language:

> "In view of the parties living together as man and wife, it was only natural that plaintiff lend some assistance to the paramour who furnished full subsistence and a home for plaintiff and her child as if they were his lawful wife and offspring. In this manner plaintiff received full remuneration for services rendered to defendant Bonaventure in performing the duties of mistress of his household and some measure of assistance in his various business enterprises.
>
> All of the circumstances considered, the services rendered by plaintiff are so completely intertwined with her illegal cohabitation with Bonaventure as to be utterly indistinguishable therefrom. In such circumstances, the remuneration received in the form of support and subsistence over the years is in law deemed full remuneration therefor. Consequently she has failed to establish her right to legal remedy or redress."

Clearly, the plaintiff here has no valid cause of action to recover in quantum meruit for the domestic services she claims to have rendered for by her own testimony the domestic services were inextricably interwoven with the sexual relationship.

Business Services

Plaintiff testified she performed business services for Mr. Schwegmann and his corporations by (1) helping him write editorials for Schwegmann's newspaper advertisements; (2) rendering investment advice; (3) assisting and rendering advice as to Mr. Schwegmann's political career; and (4) keeping him informed of things she saw in the stores which could have an adverse effect on the business. Under our law, the plaintiff may be entitled to compensation for the rendition of the services if the services were in fact rendered and do meet the prerequisites of the equitable principles formulated by the jurisprudence for recovery. In the Bonaventure case, supra, the Third Circuit clearly stated the equitable principles upon which recovery can be had:

> "Our jurisprudence appears settled to the effect that predicated upon equitable principles, the claims of a paramour and concubine will be recognized and enforced with respect to joint or mutual commercial ventures, provided such enterprises arose independently of the illicit relationship. Heatwole v. Stansbury, 212 La. 685, 33 So.2d 196; Sparrow v. Sparrow, 231 La. 966, 93 So.2d 232; Foshee v. Simkin, La.App., 174 So.2d 915.
>
> The rationale of the rule pronounced in the Heatwole, Sparrow and Foshee cases, supra (and the numerous authorities therein cited) is that where the concubinage is merely incidental to the business arrangement, the equitable rights of both parties will be recognized and enforced provided they be established by strict and conclusive proof. Stated otherwise, the rule is that if the commercial enterprise is independent of the illegal cohabitation, each party may assert his rights in the common endeavor."

Since the issue arose on a motion for summary judgment the trial judge concluded and we agree the plaintiff must be given every benefit of the doubt. Conceivably given the opportunity to do so, she could establish real and substantial business services performed for the defendants, including Mr. Schwegmann, that have not been previously compensated and which were separate and distinct from the concubinage relationship. Accordingly, we agree with the trial judge's ruling excepting her claim of compensation for business services from the summary dismissal of her claims.

OTHER ASSERTED CAUSES OF ACTION

In addition to those discussed above, the plaintiff in her petition asserted that (1) she was entitled to declaratory relief because an actual controversy has arisen between her and the defendants relative to her legal rights; (2) the defendants other than Mr. Schwegmann have interfered with the contractual rights she obtained through her agreement with Mr. Schwegmann, and (3) she is a creditor of the defendant Mr. Schwegmann and his purported sale of the stock of his controlled corporations to his son was a simulation or in fraud of her rights as a creditor and consequently should be revoked. The trial judge rejected her contentions on the grounds the request for declaratory relief and the claim for interference with her contractual rights are collaries to her claim for breach of contract or implied contract and falls for the same reasons those asserted claims fell. Additionally, he rejected the claims in simulation or revocation because the plaintiff was not a creditor of Mr. Schwegmann. Counsel for the plaintiff makes little or no direct comment relative to these rulings in her brief. In our view, the trial judge's ruling was proper.

CONCLUSION

After a careful review of the record, the arguments of counsel, and the trial judge's ruling, we cannot say the trial judge erred in his findings, his rulings or in his determination and application of the laws of Louisiana to the record before us. Paramount in the review of the petition is the recognition it was molded in conformity with the distinctions drawn by the Supreme Court of the State of California in Marvin v. Marvin, 18 Cal.3d 660, 134 Cal.Rptr. 815, 557 P.2d 106 (1976). But also paramount in the review of the plaintiff's deposition is the recognition that her testimony does not produce a factual setting consistent with the allegations of the petition. Furthermore, we do not believe the prevalence and social acceptance of non-marital sexual relationship at this time is justifiable grounds to abandon the Louisiana concept of the unlawfulness of a concubinage relationship.

To equate the non-marital relationship of concubinage to a marital relationship is to do violence to the very structure of our civilized society. Without the family, the State cannot exist and without marriage the family cannot exist. Thus, aside from religious or moralistic values, the State is justified in encouraging the legitimate (marriage) over the illegitimate (concubinage), for to do otherwise is to spread the seeds of destruction of the civilized society.

Unwed cohabitors involved in concubinage relationships have voluntarily chosen not to marry and they should not expect to receive the civil effects flowing by virtue of a marital state. In the absence of ceremonial marriage, in order to discourage the relationship, the State has not established, for a male and female who cohabit, statutory obligations of fidelity, support and assistance, nor a statutory recognition of a right to support or to assistance upon termination of the relationship. As the Louisiana courts have previously stated, discouraging the establishment of a sexual relationship without ceremonial marriage is in the interest of protecting the moral fabric of society and its preservation against those who flaunt its standards and values. See Succession of Battiste, 145 So.2d 668 (4th Cir.1962) and Texada v. Spence, 166 La. 1020, 118 So. 120 (1928).

Accordingly, the judgment of the trial court is affirmed and the case remanded to the trial court to proceed on the merits of the plaintiff's claim for compensation for business services. All costs of the appeal to be borne by the plaintiff.

AFFIRMED AND REMANDED.

---

www.ingramcontent.com/pod-product-compliance
Lightning Source LLC
LaVergne TN
LVHW062242200926
848484LV00006B/1590
* 9 7 8 1 6 0 0 4 2 2 0 7 2 *